The Economics of Uncertainty
Volume I

The International Library of Critical Writings in Economics

Series Editor: Mark Blaug

Professor Emeritus, University of London
Professor Emeritus, University of Buckingham
Visiting Professor, University of Exeter

This series is an essential reference source for students, researchers and lecturers in economics. It presents by theme an authoritative selection of the most important articles across the entire spectrum of economics. Each volume has been prepared by a leading specialist who has written an authoritative introduction to the literature included.

A full list of published and future titles in this series is printed at the end of this volume.

The Economics of Uncertainty Volume I

Risk

Edited by

John D. Hey

Professor of Economics and Statistics
University of York, UK

THE INTERNATIONAL LIBRARY OF CRITICAL WRITINGS IN ECONOMICS

An Elgar Reference Collection
Cheltenham, UK • Brookfield, US

338.5
E195
VOL. 1

Published by
Edward Elgar Publishing Limited
8 Lansdown Place
Cheltenham
Glos GL50 2HU
UK

Edward Elgar Publishing Company
Old Post Road
Brookfield
Vermont 05036
US

A catalogue record for this book is available from the British Library

Library of Congress Cataloging in Publication Data
The economics of uncertainty / edited by John D. Hey.
    (International library of critical writings in
  economics) (An Elgar reference collection)
    Includes bibliographical references and index.
    Contents: v. 1. Risk — 2. Uncertainty and dynamics.
    1. Uncertainty. 2. Risk. I. Hey, John Denis. II. Series.
    III. Series: An Elgar reference collection.
  HB615.E34 1997
  338.5—dc20   96-28857
                                                          CIP

ISBN 1 85898 277 4 (2 volume set)

Printed in Great Britain by Galliard (Printers) Ltd, Great Yarmouth

Contents

Acknowledgements

The editor and publishers wish to thank the authors and the following publishers who have kindly given permission for the use of copyright material.

Academic Press Inc. for articles: Eddie Dekel (1986), 'An Axiomatic Characterization of Preferences Under Uncertainty: Weakening the Independence Axiom', *Journal of Economic Theory*, **40** (2), 304–18; Graham Loomes and Robert Sugden (1987), 'Some Implications of a More General Form of Regret Theory', *Journal of Economic Theory*, **41** (2), April, 270–87; S.H. Chew and L.G. Epstein (1989), 'A Unifying Approach to Axiomatic Non-Expected Utility Theories', *Journal of Economic Theory*, **49** (2), 207–40.

American Economic Association for article: Mark J. Machina (1987), 'Choice Under Uncertainty: Problems Solved and Unsolved', *Journal of Economic Perspectives*, **1** (1), Summer, 121–54.

Blackwell Publishers Ltd for articles: Graham Loomes and Robert Sugden (1982), 'Regret Theory: An Alternative Theory of Rational Choice Under Uncertainty', *Economic Journal*, **92** (368), December, 805–24; Mark J. Machina (1985), 'Stochastic Choice Functions Generated from Deterministic Preferences Over Lotteries', *Economic Journal*, **95**, September, 575–94.

Cambridge University Press for article: Isaac Levi (1986), 'The Paradoxes of Allais and Ellsberg', *Economics and Philosophy*, **2** (1), 23–53.

Econometric Society for articles: Daniel Kahneman and Amos Tversky (1979), 'Prospect Theory: An Analysis of Decision Under Risk', *Econometrica*, **47** (2), March, 263–91; Mark J. Machina (1982), '"Expected Utility" Analysis without the Independence Axiom', *Econometrica*, **50** (2), March, 277–323; Chew Soo Hong (1983), 'A Generalization of the Quasilinear Mean with Applications to the Measurement of Income Inequality and Decision Theory Resolving the Allais Paradox', *Econometrica*, **51** (4), July, 1065–92; Menahem E. Yaari (1987), 'The Dual Theory of Choice Under Risk', *Econometrica*, **55** (1), January, 95–115; S.H. Chew, L.G. Epstein and U. Segal (1991), 'Mixture Symmetry and Quadratic Utility', *Econometrica*, **59** (1), January, 139–63; Faruk Gul (1991), 'A Theory of Disappointment Aversion', *Econometrica*, **59** (3), May, 667–86; David W. Harless and Colin F. Camerer (1994), 'The Predictive Utility of Generalized Expected Utility Theories', *Econometrica*, **62** (6), November, 1251–89; John D. Hey and Chris Orme (1994), 'Investigating Generalizations of Expected Utility Theory Using Experimental Data', *Econometrica*, **62** (6), November, 1291–326.

Elsevier Science B.V. for article: John Quiggin (1982), 'A Theory of Anticipated Utility', *Journal of Economic Behavior and Organization*, **3** (2–3), June/September, 323–43.

Helbing & Lichtenhahn Verlag AG, Basle and Frankfurt/M. for article: John D. Hey (1984), 'The Economics of Optimism and Pessimism: A Definition and Some Applications', *Kyklos*, **37** (Fasc. 2), 181–205.

Institute for Operations Research and the Management Sciences for article: Joao L. Becker and Rakesh K. Sarin (1987), 'Lottery Dependent Utility', *Management Science*, **33** (11), November, 1367–82.

Kluwer Academic Publishers for articles: W. Kip Viscusi (1989), 'Prospective Reference Theory: Toward an Explanation of the Paradoxes', *Journal of Risk and Uncertainty*, **2**, 235–63; Peter Wakker (1990), 'Under Stochastic Dominance Choquet-Expected Utility and Anticipated Utility are Identical', *Theory and Decision*, **29** (2), September, 119–32; Amos Tversky and Daniel Kahneman (1992), 'Advances in Prospect Theory: Cumulative Representation of Uncertainty', *Journal of Risk and Uncertainty*, **5** (4), October, 297–323.

Review of Economic Studies Ltd for article: Graham Loomes and Robert Sugden (1986), 'Disappointment and Dynamic Consistency in Choice Under Uncertainty', *Review of Economic Studies*, **LIII** (2, No. 173), April, 271–82.

Springer Verlag GmbH & Co. for article: M. Weber and C. Camerer (1987), 'Recent Developments in Modelling Preferences Under Risk', *OR Spektrum*, **9**, 129–51.

Every effort has been made to trace all the copyright holders but if any have been inadvertently overlooked the publishers will be pleased to make the necessary arrangement at the first opportunity.

In addition the publishers wish to thank the Library of the London School of Economics and Political Science and the Marshall Library, Cambridge University, for their assistance in obtaining these articles.

Introduction

John D. Hey

The past two decades have seen enormous theoretical advances in the understanding of the process of economic decision making under risk and uncertainty. This two-volume set of readings contains virtually all of these theoretical advances. It is organized in three parts: the first two dealing with *static* situations and the third with *dynamic* situations. Volume I comprises the first part and deals with situations of *risk*, that is when probability distributions can be used to describe the lack of certainty involved in the decision process; Part I of Volume II deals with situations of *uncertainty*, that is when probability distributions are not *ab initio* associated with uncertain outcomes.

A little history may help to put the volumes into perspective. My interpretation of the historical facts is the identification of three phases of theoretical work each followed by experimental investigations of that theoretical work. These volumes deal almost exclusively with the *third* phase of theoretical work – which started in the early 1950s and is still ongoing. But let me first talk about the first two phases – I shall concentrate mainly on the theoretical work, though mention will have to be made of the experimental work, which provided the motivation for the respective subsequent phases of theoretical work.

The first phase relates to *Expected Value Maximization* as the theoretical decision rule; the publication of Bernoulli (1738) could be regarded as where the 'theoretical' phase ended and the 'experimental' phase began – this latter ending with the publication of von Neumann and Morgenstern (1947) and later Savage (1954) and Anscombe and Aumann (1963; Chapter 2, Volume II). These three publications define the beginning of the second phase of theoretical work, that relating to *(Subjective) Expected Utility Maximization* as the theoretical decision rule, and the consequent clarification of the treatment of both *risk* and *uncertainty*. The second phase of experimental work was primarily motivated by Allais (1952) and Ellsberg (Chapter 1, Volume II), related to the theories of decision making under *risk* and under *uncertainty* respectively. The third phase of theoretical work began with a trickle (Allais 1952 and Kahneman and Tversky, Chapter 1, Volume I) which later (in the 1980s) turned into a torrent, a subset of which forms the material for these volumes, which might be captured under the (rather misleading) title of *Generalized Expected Utility Maximization*. There has also been a third phase of experimental work, investigating this third phase of theoretical work, but this is only partly the concern of these volumes (more detail[1] can be found in Hey 1996). First I must briefly set the scene by describing the earlier phases.

The First Phase: Expected Value Maximization

The start of this phase is lost in historical mists, though Samuelson (1977, p. 38) remarks that 'Pascal [1623–1662] can be taken as a convenient name for those mathematicians who seem to base behaviour decisions on the "expected value of money (wealth or income)"'. The end of this phase can be marked by Bernoulli's (1738) discussion of the 'thought experiment', now known as the St Petersburg paradox. Essentially the experiment asks the maximum buying price for a given risky gamble (one which yields £2^i with probability 1/2, for $i = 1, 2, \ldots$), and the generally accepted response is that most (all?) individuals would specify a finite rather than an infinite (which is the expected value of the risky gamble) amount of money as their maximum. This would appear to spell the death-knell of expected value maximization. Indeed, in Bernoulli (1738) it spelt also the onset of the labour pains preceding the formal birth of (subjective) Expected Utility theory.

The Second Theory Phase: (Subjective) Expected Utility Maximization

Eventually twins were born, their final arrival separated by several years. First on the scene was (von Neumann-Morgenstern) Expected Utility theory, for decision problems under risk, followed a few years later by (Savage/Anscombe-Aumann) Subjective Expected Utility theory, for decision problems under uncertainty.

Expected Utility Theory: Decision Under Risk

I now need some notation. Consider a one-off decision problem in which the decision-maker is to choose from a set of risky choices, characterized as follows. The generic choice C will lead (after Nature has chosen) to *one* of the final outcomes or consequences $x_1, x_2, \ldots x_n$. The actual final outcome will be determined stochastically, with x_i being the final outcome with probability p_i ($i = 1, 2, \ldots, n$). The x's are complete descriptions of all aspects of the final outcomes relevant to the decision-maker, and, of course, $\Sigma^n_{i=1} p_i = 1$. I will write:

$$C \equiv [x_1, p_1; x_2, p_2; \ldots ; x_n, p_n] \tag{1}$$

This decision problem is described as one *under risk* since it is presumed that the probabilities are known and given and understood as such by the decision-maker. Expected utility theory characterizes the solution to the decision problem as the choice of C which maximizes $U(C)$, given by:

$$U(C) = \sum_{i=1}^{i=n} p_i u(x_i) \tag{2}$$

where $u(.)$ is the individual's (von Neumann-Morgenstern) utility function (unique up to a linear transformation). If we number the n outcomes so that x_n is the individual's most preferred outcome and x_1 the least preferred, and if we normalize the utility function so that $u(x_n) = 1$ and $u(x_1) = 0$, then intermediate values of $u(.)$ are determined by ascertaining from our individual the values of the probabilities u_i for which our individual is indifferent between $[x_i, 1]$ and $[x_1, (1 - u_i); x_n, u_i]$. Clearly, from (2), $u(x_i) = u_i$. One key axiom of this theory is that such a (unique) u_i exists for all x_i.

A further crucial axiom of expected utility theory is the *Independence Axiom* (IA):

$$C_1 \sim C_2 \rightarrow [C_1, p; C_3, (1 - p)] \sim [C_2, p; C_3, (1 - p)] \text{ for all } p \text{ and } C_3.$$

Here $\sim$ denotes indifference. What this axiom asserts is that if an individual is indifferent between two risky choices C_1 and C_2, then that individual should also be indifferent between two mixtures: one that leads to C_1 with probability p and some third choice C_3 with probability $1 - p$, and another which leads to C_2 with probability p and the same alternative C_3 with probability $1 - p$.

This axiom allows us to argue that the individual is indifferent between C (as described in (1)) and the (compound) lottery:

$$[[x_1, (1 - u_1); x_n, u_1], p_1; [x_1, (1 - u_2); x_n, u_2], p_2; \ldots ; [x_1, (1 - u_n); x_n, u_n]; p_n]$$

and, in turn, the individual is indifferent (using the Reduction of Compound Lotteries Axiom, RCLA) between this and the equivalent single stage lottery:

$$[x_1, \{p_1(1 - u_1) + p_2(1 - u_2) + \ldots + p_n(1 - u_n)\}; x_n, \{p_1 u_1 + p_2 u_2 + \ldots + p_n u_n\}]$$

the attractiveness of which amongst all such gambles involving just the worst and best outcomes is determined by the probability of gaining the best outcome:

$$p_1 u_1 + p_2 u_2 + \ldots + p_n u_n \equiv p_1 u(x_1) + p_2 u(x_2) + \ldots + p_n u(x_n)$$

Hence the theory.

Subjective Expected Utility Theory: Decision Under Uncertainty

Now consider a decision problem in which probabilities are *not* given. Instead, suppose that outcome x_i results when 'state of the world' S_i occurs ($i = 1, 2, \ldots, n$). Suppose further that the description of the final outcomes (the x's) are complete in themselves and are *not* conditional on which state of the world occurs. If we continue to assume (as we have implicitly done so far) that our decision-maker has a complete transitive preference ordering over all such uncertain choices, which I now denote by:

$$C \equiv [x_1, S_1; x_2, S_2; \ldots ; x_n, S_n] \tag{3}$$

then, by adding to our set of axioms, we can infer not only the existence of a (subjective) utility function $u(.)$ over the x's, but also the existence of a subjective probability measure $p(.)$ over the S's. Denote by $p_i \equiv p(S_i)$ the subjective probability implicitly attached by our decision-maker to state of the world S_i.

In essence (see Anscombe and Aumann, Chapter 2, Volume II, p. 33) p_i is such that

$$[u^{-1}(p_i), 1] \sim [u^{-1}(1), S_i; u^{-1}(0), S_i^c] \tag{4}$$

where S_i^c denotes the complement of S_i (that is, if S_i^c happens, S_i does not, and vice versa). In (4) the left-hand choice leads to an outcome which yields utility p_i with certainty, whilst the right-hand choice is our uncertain choice which leads to an outcome which yields utility 1 if state of the world S_i occurs and to an outcome which yields utility 0 if S_i does *not* occur. Applying (1) to (4) (Anscombe and Aumann extend the axiom set so that one can) immediately gives $p_i = p(S_i)$. Representation (2) continues to specify preference over the set of all C.

Intuitively the crucial axioms are those that lead to a unique (up to a linear transformation) specification of the utility function $u(.)$ over outcomes, *independent of the states of the world*, and the unique specification of the probability measure $p(.)$ over states of the world, *independent of the outcomes*. If such 'independence axioms' are violated then (subjective) expected utility theory breaks down, as indeed it does if the other axioms are violated.

The Second Experimental Phase: The Allais and Ellsberg Paradoxes

Fairly soon after the respective births of the new conventional wisdom, experimental investigations of that wisdom began to appear – motivated by two paradoxes: that of Allais (for decision under risk); and that of Ellsberg (for decision under uncertainty).

The Allais Paradox and Subsequent Experimental Work

This relates to Expected Utility theory for decision under risk. A simple expositional device – the Marschak-Machina triangle – which is used in many of the articles reprinted in these volumes, will prove useful in explaining how certain tests were constructed and why. Consider choice problems involving just ($n =$) 3 final outcomes: x_1, x_2 and x_3, where outcomes are numbered, as before, so that x_1 is the worst outcome (the least preferred by our decision-maker), x_2 is in-between in terms of preferences, and x_3 is the best outcome (the most preferred by our decision maker). Risky choices yielding one or other of these three outcomes can be completely described by the respective probabilities p_1, p_2 and p_3; or indeed, since these three must sum to unity, by any two of them. Take p_1 and p_3; then the set of all possible risky choices (over x_1, x_2 and x_3) can be represented by the triangle drawn in Figure 1: each point in this triangle represents some such risky choice. (For example, the point A represents a 50:50 gamble between x_2 and x_3.) An individual's preferences over these risky choices can be represented by his or her indifference map in the triangle. Consider the case when the individual obeys the axioms of Expected Utility theory; preferences are represented by (1), and hence indifference curves are given by:

$$p_1 u_1 + p_2 u_2 + p_3 u_3 = \text{constant}$$

where $u_i \equiv u(x_i)$. Since $p_1 + p_2 + p_3 = 1$ we can eliminate p_2 from this expression, and hence, after some manipulation, derive the following expressions for an Expected Utility (EU) indifference curve:

$$p_3 = constant + \frac{(u_2 - u_1)}{(u_3 - u_2)} p_1 \tag{5}$$

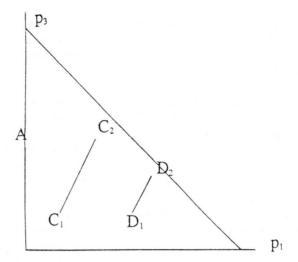

Figure 1   The Marschak-Machina Triangle

Three things are immediate from this: first EU indifference curves are *upward sloping* (since $u_3 > u_2 > u_1$ since x_3 is preferred to x_2 which is preferred to x_1); second EU indifference curves are *straight lines*, since (5) is linear in the p's; third, EU indifference curves are *parallel* straight lines, since the slope[2] $(u_2 - u_1)/(u_3 - u_2)$ is constant (recall that the x's – and hence the u's – are given and fixed). The last two of these are the implication of the Independence Axiom, though the second can be derived from a weaker axiom, the *Betweenness Axiom* (BA):

$$C_1 \sim C_2 \rightarrow C_1 \sim C_2 \sim [C_1, p; C_2, (1 - p)] \text{ for all } p.$$

Note that the Independence Axiom implies, but is not implied by, the Betweenness Axiom. In words, the Betweenness Axiom states that if an individual does not mind which of two risky choices he or she gets, then equally well the individual does not mind if some random device chooses for him or her.

The importance property that EU indifference curves are parallel straight lines formed the basis for most of the early tests of Expected Utility theory. Consider Figure 1: choose any two points C_1 and C_2 (such that the line $C_1 C_2$ is upward sloping;[3] then choose any other two points D_1 and D_2 such that the line $D_1 D_2$ is *parallel* to the line $C_1 C_2$, (and where D_1 is lower than D_2 – as C_1 is lower than C_2). Now ask our individual whether he or she prefers C_1 or C_2; and then whether he or she prefers D_1 or D_2. If our individual behaves in accordance with Expected Utility theory then either (1) he or she strictly prefers C_1 to C_2 *and* D_1 to D_2; or (2) he or she is indifferent between C_1 and C_2 *and* between D_1 and D_2; or (3) he or she strictly prefers C_2 to C_1 *and* D_2 to D_1.

Most of the early tests took a stated preference of C_1 over C_2 combined with a preference for D_2 over D_1 (or of C_2 over C_1 and of D_1 over D_2) as being inconsistent with (the implications of) EU. In many experiments, with large numbers of subjects asked the same two pairwise choice questions, the usual finding was that $C_1 D_2$ (when configured as in

Figure 1) was observed significantly more often than $C_2 D_1$. The inference drawn from these results was that indifference curves were not parallel, but instead *fanned out* across the triangle. This became known as the *fanning-out hypothesis* – and motivated many of the subsequent generalizations of EU.

An alternative approach to that of experimentally *testing* (the axioms of) EU theory is that of *estimation*. Two routes have been followed – one valid and one, at least to me, invalid. The latter was followed by Allais and involved the elicitation/estimation of the (allegedly von Neumann-Morgenstern) utility function by two different procedures – and then demonstrating that these two functions were different. The first of these two procedures was the genuine procedure described above; the second was not. Let me be specific and let me restrict attention to the case where we wish to elicit the function over monetary outcomes in the range £0 to £1000. Fix $u(£0) = 0$ and $u(£1000) = 1$. The genuine procedure for finding the x such that our individual has $u(£x) = 0.5$ is to find the x such that our individual is indifferent between £x for sure and a 50:50 gamble between £0 and £1000.

The apparently invalid procedure for finding the x such that $u(£x) = 0.5$ is by asking the individual to specify the value of x such that increasing his or her payment from £0 to £x increases his or her happiness by exactly the same amount as increasing it from £x to £1000. I personally find this question meaningless (and certainly impossible to motivate correctly).

An alternative but valid way of eliciting two (potentially different) utility functions is to use different end-points or to use different chaining procedures; for example to elicit the x with a utility of 0.25 one can either elicit indifference between [£x, 1] and [£0, 0.75; £1000, 0.25] or elicit indifference between [£x, 1] and [£0, 0.5; £y, 0.5] where y such that $u(£y) = 0.5$ has already been elicited. A number of studies (see Camerer 1995) have suggested that differently elicited functions are different – which casts doubt on the assumptions of EU which imply that utilities exist *independent of the context*.

The Ellsberg Paradox and Subsequential Experimental Work

This was virtually all to do with *testing* (the axioms of) *Subjective* Expected Utility (SEU) theory – particularly those concerned with the existence of a well-defined probability measure over the various states of the world – and was largely motivated by Ellsberg's (1961) Paradox (Chapter 1, Volume II), of which there were two versions: the 2-colour and the 3-colour versions. Consider the former: in this the subject is confronted with two urns. Urn 1 contains 50 black and 50 white balls; urn 2 contains 100 balls each of which is either black or white, though the numbers of each are not known. A choice is defined by an urn and a colour; a choice is played out by picking one ball at random from the specified urn; if it is of the specified colour the subject gets outcome x_2; if it is not, the subject gets outcome x_1; as before x_1 and x_2 are picked by the experimenter so that x_2 is preferred by the subject to x_1. In financially motivated experiments x_2 is usually some money prize while x_1 is a consolation prize.

Ellsberg's conjecture was that many people would be indifferent between 1W and 1B, be indifferent between 2W and 2B, but *strictly* prefer either of 1W and 1B to either of 2W and 2B. He did not actually carry out any experimental tests of this conjecture (though others subsequently have) so he did not indicate how such preferences could accurately be elicited, but his conjecture has commanded widespread approval (and was indeed confirmed by the subsequent experiments). It is rather damaging for Subjective Expected Utility theory since it denies the existence of subjective probabilities (which sum to one) for urn 2.

The Third Theory Phase: Generalized Expected Utility Maximization

This proceeded on two fronts: one responding to the Allais Paradox and subsequent experiments; the second responding to the Ellsberg Paradox and subsequent experiments. The first of these is the subject matter of Volume I, the second the subject matter of Part I of Volume II. However, in some respects, these developments have overlapped and partially converged since many of the responses to the Ellsberg Paradox adopted a modelling stance in which uncertainty was characterized through risk. This is all rather oud – though perhaps the inevitable response to the practical problems involved with the experimental implementation of the Ellsberg Paradox.

On Risk

This is the subject matter of Volume I. All chapters listed below refer to Volume I.

The set of theories of decision making under risk provoked by the experimental evidence arising out of the Allais Paradox is large: a partial list, in alphabetical order, includes: Allais' 1952 theory (Allais 1952) [see also Allais (1953)]; Anticipated Utility theory (Quiggin, Chapter 4); Cumulative Prospect theory (Tversky and Kahneman, Chapter 21); Disappointment theory (Lommes and Sugden, Chapter 10, and Bell 1985); Disappointment Aversion theory (Gul, Chapter 20); Implicit Expected (or linear) Utility theory (Dekel, Chapter 8); Implicit Rank Linear Utility theory – see also Chew and Epstein, Chapter 16; Implicit Weighted Utility theory – see also Chew and Epstein Chapter 16; Lottery Dependent EU theory (Becker and Sarin, Chapter 11); Machina's Generalized EU theory (Machina, Chapter 3); Perspective theory (Ford, 1987); Prospect theory (Kahneman and Tversky, Chapter 1); Prospective Reference theory (Viscusi, Chapter 17); Quadratic Utility theory (Chew, Epstein and Segal, Chapter 19); Rank Dependent Expected (or Linear) Utility theory (Chew, Karni and Safra, 1987); Regret theory (Loomes and Sugden, Chapters 2 and 12); SSB theory (Fishburn, 1984); Weighted EU theory (Chew, Chapter 5, and Dekel, Chapter 8); Yaari's Dual theory (Yaari, Chapter 15). Some are special cases of others; most are generalizations of EU theory. Some (including others not mentioned here) are now forgotten – consigned to the wastepaper basket of academia; others have yet to become known. Some were specifically designed to explain observed behaviours; others seem to have been merely designed for intellectual amusement; all display the great ingenuity of the economist's mind.

Let me begin with a subset of these theories, indeed a subset of the theories included in these volumes, a subset I am tempted to call the *useful* theories among those listed. All try to explain the Allais Paradox and associated empirical evidence; some try to explain it as *parsimoniously* as possible – though what precisely this might mean is not clear; others try and explain it as reasonably as possible – perhaps using some psychological theory; others try and explain it as elegantly as possible.

Let me give some illustrations. I begin with axiomatically based theories, and with the apparent observation that the Independence Axiom is violated (since the experimental evidence does not seem consistent with parallel straight line indifference curves). An obvious response is either to weaken the Independence Axiom or to drop it entirely. If one follows the latter route, one gets Implicit Expected (or Linear) Utility theory (Chapter 8) in which only betweenness (in addition to completeness and transitivity) holds. In this theory, all that one can say is that the indifference curves in the Marschak-Machina triangles are straight lines; the only testable implication, therefore, is that of betweenness (linearity). Somewhat stronger predictions are given by theories which weaken the Independence Axiom somewhat but do not completely drop it. Different weakenings are provided by Weighted EU theory (Chapters 5 and 8) and by Disappointment Aversion theory (Chapter 20); in the former, the indifference curves in the Marschak-Machina triangle fan out linearly from a point to the south-west of the origin of the triangle; in the latter, they fan out in the bottom right of the triangle and fan in in the upper left of the triangle. However, this description omits cross-triangle restrictions, which, in these cases, make substantial differences: Weighted EU requires $(n - 2)$ extra parameters (where n is the number of outcomes) whereas Disappointment Aversion requires just one extra parameter. On the criterion of the number of extra parameters needed, one could say that Disappointment Aversion theory is much more parsimonious than Weighted EU theory.

An equally parsimonious generalization of EU theory is that provided by Prospective Reference theory (Chapter 17): this specifies that choice is determined by the maximization of a weighted average of the expected utility using the correct probability weights and the expected utility using equal probability weights for the non-null outcomes. The extra parameter is the weight parameter. The implication of this theory is that indifference curves in the triangle are linear *within the triangle*, but display discontinuities at the boundaries (where at least one of the outcomes becomes null).

A subset of theories start from an attempt at a psychological explanation of Allais Paradox phenomena; one of the earliest was Prospect Theory (Chapter 1), which has been partially superseded by Cumulative Prospect theory (Chapter 21). Two somewhat more parsimonious psychologically-based theories are Regret theory (Chapters 2 and 12) and Disappointment theory (Chapter 10 – a precursor of, and generalization of, Disappointment Aversion theory, Chapter 20) – both out of the same stables. Both incorporate *ex ante* consideration of *ex post* psychological feelings: of regret, or rejoicing, concerning what has happened compared to what would have happened if the individual had chosen differently, in Regret theory; and of disappointment, or delight, concerning what has happened compared with what the individual expected to happen, in Disappointment theory. While Disappointment theory is like all the other theories listed above (except SSB theory) in that it is a *holistic* theory, Regret theory (and SSB theory) is *not*, in that it is a theory of choice from a pair. It therefore does not necessarily lead to transitive choice patterns; nor indeed to the existence of indifference curves in the triangle (though they do exist when choices are played out independently – moreover, in this case, they look the same as in Weighted EU theory, though the cross-triangle restrictions are not the same).

One very elegant theory which starts neither from axioms nor from psychological considerations is Machina's Generalized EU theory (Chapter 7). This simply starts from the assumption that there exists a complete transitive preference ordering $V(.)$ over the set of all C which is *differentiable* in a particular sense. (Whether differentiability is a desirable *economic* property is another issue.) Moreover, to add testability to the theory, that is to impose some structure on the indifference map in the Marschak-Machina triangle, the following restrictions on $V(.)$ are imposed: first, that stochastically dominating choices are preferred to stochastically dominated choices; second, that the individual behaves in a more risk averse fashion with respect to stochastically dominating choices than with respect to stochastically dominated gambles. The first of these restrictions implies that indifference curves in the triangle slope up; the second that they *fan out* (not necessarily linearly) across the triangle. There is an obvious testable implication here: indifference curves should get steeper as one moves to better parts of the triangle. Note, however, that it does not appear to be particularly strong (though Machina might claim otherwise).

One final very important class of theories comes under the heading of Rank Dependent EU theory (with generalization to Implicit Rank Linear theory) of which special cases are Anticipated Utility (Chapter 4) and Yaari's Dual Model (Chapter 15). This class of theories builds on an interpretation of the experimental evidence (perhaps first proposed by Kahnemann and Tversky in Chapter 1) that subjects misperceive (or manipulate or transform in some way) supposedly objective probabilities. Early work in this area (including that of Kahnemann and Tversky (Chapter 1) and Handa, 1977) presumed that the raw probabilities themselves were transformed. It was soon pointed out that, in this case, violations of dominance should be observed – or, at least, observed much more frequently than appeared to be the case. This observation led to the new class of theories in which de-cumulative probabilities were transformed. Consider again (2) and re-write it[4] as

$$U(C) = \sum_{i=1}^{i=n} \left(\sum_{j=i}^{j=n} p_j \right) [u(x_i) - u(x_{i-1})] \qquad (6)$$

Recall that x_1 is the worst outcome, x_2 the second worst, and so on. Equation (6) expresses expected utility as $u(x_1)$, plus $[u(x_2) - u(x_1)]$ times the probability of getting at least x_2, plus $[u(x_3) - u(x_2)]$ times the probability of getting at least x_3, ... , plus $[u(x_n) - u(x_{n-1})]$ times the probability of getting (at least) x_n.

Now suppose the individuals distort the decumulative probabilities – the $\sum_{j=i}^{n} p_j$ – the probability of getting at least x_i. Instead of using the 'correct' probabilities $\sum_{j=i}^{n} p_j$, they use $w (\sum_{j=i}^{n} p_j)$ where $w(.)$ is some *weighting function*. Impose the 'natural restrictions': $w(0) = 0$, $w(1) = 1$ and $w(.)$ increasing, perhaps strictly, and we get Rank Dependent EU theory.

$$U(C) = \sum_{i=1}^{i=n} w \left(\sum_{j=i}^{j=n} p_j \right) [u(x_i) - u(x_{i-1})] \qquad (7)$$

The immediate implication of this class of theories is that indifference curves in the triangle are no longer linear – since (7) is not linear in the p_i – and that their precise shape depends upon the properties of $w(.)$. We can, however, show that in general, the indifference curves are parallel along the hypotenuse ($p_2 = 0$), and get flatter as one moves *up* the vertical axis ($p_1 = 0$) and as one moves *rightwards* along the horizontal axis ($p_3 = 0$).

This brief overview omits some of the papers reprinted in Volume I. Let me briefly comment on those I have not yet described. I would have liked to have included Allais's influential 1953 paper, since, in many ways, it was the stimulus for all the others – frequently quoted and often debated – but this turned out not to be possible. While the specific theory advanced in it (and perhaps more fully in Allais (1952) – in which preferences depend not just on Expected Utility but also on the variance – and perhaps even the skewness and kurtosis – of utility) perhaps does not get the attention its author thinks it deserves, it is a seminal piece in many ways.

I have – perhaps rather arrogantly – included Hey (Chapter 6) as it, like Quiggin (Chapter 4), was a precursor of the now-popular Rank Dependent Expected Utility theory; also it explains perhaps more intuitively where the 'bending' of the probabilities comes from: in my story from optimism (which is the over-weighting of the probabilities associated with relatively good outcomes) and from pessimism (the over-weighting of the probabilities associated with relatively bad outcomes). Machina (Chapter 7) is in a rather different category, as it is a theory of stochastic choice built on top of a theory of deterministic preferences. Rather an odd combination, at a first glance, but understandable when one realizes that the theory supposes convex indifference curves in the Marschak-Machina Triangle – which implies that deliberate randomization is an optimal strategy. Levi (Chapter 9) is also in a different category, but for a different reason: here is a contribution from a philosopher seeking a wider perspective and a less precisely defined decision context. Perhaps for that reason, it may not find much favour amongst economists – though there is much to be learned from it. Becker and Sarin (Chapter 11) has links to Rank Dependent Expected Utility theory and to Disappointment and Regret theories, in that utility depends upon the context and not just the outcome.

Machina (Chapter 13) and Weber and Camerer (Chapter 14) are included because they are both summaries of the theoretical literature up to the date of publication; whilst they necessarily ignore literature after that date, they both show insight and help to put the theoretical developments into perspective. Chapter 16 by Chew and Epstein in a sense also tries to do this, by building an integrated theoretical structure into which many, though not all, of the theories can be fitted – thus showing the relationship of the theories one to each other. Wakker (Chapter 18) links together some of the literature on the *risk* side with some of the literature on the *uncertainty* side.

Finally I have included two papers of a rather different *genre* – Harless and Camerer (Chapter 22) and Hey and Orme (Chapter 23). These are *empirical* (experimental) pieces which try to answer the questions: which of these various new theories are the 'better' ones; and which are 'better' than Expected Utility theory? As will be seen, these questions are not easy to answer (and, indeed, not easy to formulate) but trying to do so does raise important issues about the whole exercise. There are some interesting methodological issues here!

On Uncertainty

A fuller overview of recent work in this area can be found in Camerer and Weber (1992). The key papers are reprinted in Part I of Volume II. What is particularly revealing is how recent theorizing has been informed by earlier experiments. One key branch starts from the experimental observation that subjective probabilities which are *additive* (in particular, adding to one over the entire set of states of the world) cannot exist. This branch responds by building a theory of expected utility behaviour (called Choquet EU) which uses *non-additive probabilities* – Gilboa (Chapter 5) and Schmeidler (Chapter 9) are in this category. This may seem perverse,[5] but becomes understandable when the expected utility formula (for a situation of risk) is written as in (6) above. Based on this our rule for decision under uncertainty is written as:

$$U(C) = \sum_{i=1}^{i=n} w(\bigcup_{j=i}^{j=n} S_j) \, [u(x_i) - u(x_{i-1})] \tag{8}$$

where $w(S)$ is the 'weight' or 'non-additive probability' attached to state of the world S. It is clear from (8) that there is no presumption that $\sum_{i=1}^{n} w(S_i) = 1$; moreover, since

$$w(\bigcup_{j=i}^{j=n} S_j) = 1$$

must be the case, it is immediate from (8) that if $C = [x, S_1; x, S_2; ...; x, S_n]$ then

$$U(C) = u(x)$$

as one would hope. (That is, the utility of an 'uncertain' choice which always leads to outcome x is simply the utility of x itself.)

A second branch of the theoretical literature responding to the Ellsberg Paradox begins with considerations of the actual implementation of the Ellsberg experiment: in particular, the practical construction of urn 2 (the urn of unknown composition). Suppose one were to try and carry out the Ellsberg experiment, and suppose you wanted your subjects to be fully informed as to the task they faced. Suppose further one subject were to ask you: 'how was the composition of urn 2 determined?', or 'how will the composition of urn 2 be determined?'. How would you answer? Obviously there are a number of possible responses, but the most natural, and perhaps apparently fairest, would be to use some kind of randomizing device – for example to pick a number at random from a discrete uniform distribution over the range 0 to 100, and use that to determine the composition.

Such considerations lead naturally to the characterization of urn 2 in terms of a *second order probability distribution* (to use Camerer and Weber's 1992 phrase), and indeed many of the new 'explanations' of the Ellsberg Paradox use such a characterization – which is, in a sense, odd, as it tries to characterize uncertainty through risk. Of course, if subjects are EU, this characterization does *not* lead to an explanation. More specifically, if subjects obey the RCLA (the Reduction of Compound Lotteries Axiom) again we do not get an explanation. We need an alternative view as to how subjects process multi-stage lotteries: one such view is Segal's *Certainty Equivalent* story (Chapter 21). This, combined with some non-EU story at the single-stages, provides an explanation. In brief, it works as follows: consider how an individual processes (and hence compares) several different *multi-stage* risky choices. One way to process a multi-stage gamble is simply to reduce to the equivalent single-stage gamble – and use one of the theories of decision making under risk to evaluate it. An alternative is to apply a form of backward induction: consider the final stage – of which there will be a number of alternatives depending on the resolution of the earlier stages. Take each of the various possible final stage gambles and reduce each to a *certainty equivalent* – by using the appropriate decision rule. Then replace each of the final stage gambles by the respective certainty equivalent and carry out the same procedure on the penultimate stage – and continue working backwards until one reaches the first stage. Evaluate this in the same fashion. This gives a certainty equivalent for the entire multi-stage gamble. Of course, if the 'appropriate decision rule' is EU, then the certainty equivalent of the multi-stage gamble obtained in this fashion will be *precisely the same* as the certainty equivalent of the single stage gamble obtained by the usual rules of reduction from the multi-stage gamble. But if the decision rule is *not* EU, then these two certainty equivalents will (in general) *not* be the same – in which case we will get (in general) different decisions when gambles are presented in a multi-stage format rather than in their equivalent single-stage formulations.[6] This is the essence of Segal's explanation of the Ellsberg Paradox.

There are other formulations which also start from the presumption that individuals, when confronted with the Ellsberg Urn problem, think of it as a multi-stage gamble: at the first stage the proportion p of white balls is determined from some distribution of possible p values; at the second stage a ball is drawn from an urn in which a proportion p are white. Different theories differ in their description of the first-stage distribution of p and in the way that these two-stage gambles are evaluated and processed: for example, there is the maxmin theory of Gilboa and Schmeidler (Chapter 8) which evaluates the two-stage gamble on the basis of the *least favourable* value of p and which ignores all the other possible values. Gilboa (Chapter 7) proposes something similar. I do not intend to go into detail here – what is really crucial for my argument is that these theories recast the 'uncertain' world of the Ellsberg Urn problem in a risky (albeit two-stage) world. After this recasting has been done, the previously discussed theories of decision under risk (as well as other theories) come into play. The 'uncertainty' implicit in the Ellsberg Urn problem has been theorized away.

The following papers are also included in Part I of Volume II. Anscombe and Aumann (Chapter 2) is included as it is very much a seminal paper which is quoted and used by much of the subsequent literature. It, along with the book by Savage (1954), laid the theoretical foundation for the modelling of decision-taking based on subjective probabilities. Gärdenfors and Sahlin is a rather early attempt to explain how individuals – unsure about so-called 'objective' probabilities – might bend them in the light of the context. Dobbs (Chapter 10) has an interesting story which involves *ex ante* anticipation of the *ex post* updating of subjective probabilities using Bayes theorem. Machina and Schmeidler (Chapter 11) do for the probability component of Subjective Expected Utility theory what Machina (Chapter 3, Volume I) did for the utility component of Expected Utility theory.

Finally, Sarin and Winkler (Chapter 12) propose an approach in which the utility gained by the decision-maker is not independent of the context but depends upon the ambiguity or uncertainty present in the decision context; whilst Fishburn (Chapter 13) almost brings us back full circle to Allais (1952) with a story where preferences in an uncertain world depend not only upon Expected Utility but also on the variance of Utility: if Allais were dead, he would be smiling in his grave!

Theories of Dynamic Decision Making

One of the great joys of Expected Utility theory is that it is not only a theory of static –
one-off – decision making, but it can also be used to describe dynamic – multi-stage –
decision making. This is not the place to go into technical detail, but the rough outline
can be explained briefly. Take a dynamic decision-making problem – one in which there
is an interleaved sequence of chance nodes and choice nodes. Suppose, for simplicity of
the exposition, that there is also a final stage – in which the decision-maker gets his or
her final payoff, or outcome. Any sequence of choices along this dynamic tree can be
described in terms of a *strategy* – and the set of all possible sequences of choices can be
translated into a set of all possible strategies. Each strategy has associated with it a set
of possible outcomes – each with a corresponding probability (in a risky world). So by
this device, one can convert a multi-stage dynamic decision problem into a one-off choice
problem – that of the choice of a *strategy*. One can then solve it by some appropriate
decision rule. Take Expected Utility theory – if this is the relevant decision rule, then the
decision-maker chooses that strategy which yields the highest expected utility. However,
and this is the crucial point, one can show that an alternative way of arriving at the same
best strategy is to use *backward induction*, as follows. One first imagines that one is at
one of the final decision nodes. As this is just a one-off problem, one can find the best
choice at that node by using Expected Utility. Having done that, one can eliminate at the
various final stages the choices that are not the best – thus eliminating choice at the final
stage. One then works back to the penultimate stage and repeats the argument. One
continues backwards in a similar fashion until one reaches the first decision node – and
the problem is solved. Moreover, *if one is using Expected Utility theory as the decision
rule then this procedure leads to exactly the same decisions as the strategy procedure
described above.*

Unfortunately, if the decision rule is *not* Expected Utility theory, then this procedure
does *not* work – an alternative story of dynamic decision theory is needed. This is the
concern of the papers in Part II of Volume II. Moreover, additional problems may arise –
for example, concerning whether early or late resolution of uncertainty is preferred. This
is particularly the concern of the earlier papers in Part II – those by Spence and Zeckhauser
(Chapter 14), Selden (Chapter 15) and Epstein (Chapter 17). In Chapter 16 Kreps and
Porteus look at the preferences induced by Expected Utility theory and explores the
consequences. Hammond (Chapter 18) and Machina (Chapter 20) are concerned with more
philosophical issues, particularly whether people with non-Expected-Utility preferences are
necessarily time inconsistent in the sense that they set out planning to do something at some
point in the future but when they get there they do something different. Epstein and Zin
(Chapter 19) and Segal (Chapter 21) are more practically orientated, examining how people
may tackle multi-stage decision problems even though they are not Expected Utility
maximizers. Essentially their solution is the Certainty Equivalent method, described above.
Epstein and Zin show how this approach can be used to solve the problem of optimal
consumption in a dynamic context. Finally, Epstein and LeBreton (Chapter 22) and Gilboa
and Schmeidler (Chapter 23) examine how beliefs might be updated through time; the first
showing that Bayesian updating 'must' be used if beliefs are in some sense dynamically
consistent; the second exploring how beliefs might be updated when they are represented

by a non-additive probability measure – one of the key concerns of Part I of Volume II. All these papers are demanding – either technically or philosophically.

Conclusions

These volumes contain many key papers in an important area of economics – that of decision making, in both static and dynamic worlds, under risk and uncertainty. In various ways (for example, philosophically and technically), the material gets more and more difficult as the volumes proceed. At the same time, economists' understanding of the key issues gets less and less rigorous as the volumes proceed: whilst static risk is fairly well understood, static uncertainty is somewhat less so, whilst dynamic decision making is hardly understood at all. I suspect that the coming decade will see changes and greater understanding, particularly of the processes involved in dynamic decision making. I would like to think that the publication of this book might contribute to that greater understanding.

Notes

1. Indeed some parts of this Introduction have been adapted from Hey (1996).
2. Note that the more concave is the utility function – that is, the more risk-averse is our individual, the steeper are the parallel indifference lines.
3. Tests of the upward-slopingness of EU indifference curves were generally not carried out – it being considered self-evident.
4. Where, by convention, $u(x_0) = 0$.
5. The initial stumbling block – the apparent paradox that, if probabilities did not sum to 1, then the expected value of a constant was less than that constant – was avoided by the Choquet formulation, described below.
6. A further discussion of multi-stage gambles can be found in Machina (Chapter 20, Volume II).

References

Abdellaoui, M. and Munier, B. (1995), 'On the Fundamental Risk-Structure Dependence of Individual Preferences Under Risk', GRID Working paper.

Allais, M. (1952), 'Fondemonts d'une Theórie Positive des Choix Comportant un Risque et Critique des Postulats et Axioms de L'Ecole Americaine', *Econometrie*, **15**, 257–332. (English translation in Allais and Hagen 1979.)

Allais, M. (1953), 'Le Comportment de l'Homme Rationnel devant le Risque: Critique des Postulats et Axiomes de l'Ecole Americaine', *Econometrica*, **21** (4), 503–46.

Allais, M. and Hagen, O. (1979), *Expected Utility Hypothesis and the Allais Paradox*, Reidel.

Bell, D. (1985), 'Disappointment in Decision Making Under Uncertainty', *Operations Research*, **33**, 1–27.

Bernoulli, D. (1738), 'Specimen Theoriae Novae de Mensura Sortis' in *Commentarii Academiae Scientarum Imperialis Petropolitane*, Vol. **7**. (English translation by L. Sommer, 'Exposition of a New Theory on the Measurement of Risk', *Econometrica*, 1954, **22**, 23–36.)

Camerer, C.F. (1995), 'Individual Decision Making' in J.H. Kagel and A.E. Roth (eds), *Handbook of Experimental Economics*, Princeton University Press.

Camerer, C.F. and Weber, M. (1992), 'Recent Developments in Modeling Preferences: Uncertainty and Ambiguity', *Journal of Risk and Uncertainty*, **5**, 325–70.

Chew, S.H., Karni, E. and Safra, Z. (1987), 'Risk Aversion in the Theory of Expected Utility with Rank Dependent Probabilities', *Journal of Economic Theory*, **42**, 370–81.

Einhorn, H.J. and Hogarth, R.M. (1986), 'Decision Making under Ambiguity', *Journal of Business*, **59**, S225–S250.

Fishburn, P. (1984), 'SSB Utility Theory: An Economic Perspective', *Mathematical Social Science*, **8**, 63–94.

Ford, J.L. (1987), *Economic Choice under Uncertainty: A Perspective Theory Approach*, Edward Elgar.

Handa, J. (1977), 'Risk, Probabilities and a New Theory of Cardinal Utility', *Journal of Political Economy*, **85**, 97–122.

Hey, J.D. (1996), 'Experiments and the Economics of Individual Decision Making under Risk and Uncertainty', in D.M. Kreps and K.F. Wallis (eds), *Advances in Economics and Econometrics: Theory and Applications*, Cambridge: Cambridge University Press, forthcoming.

Kagel, J.H. and Roth, A.E. (eds) (1995), *Handbook of Experimental Economics*, Princeton University Press.

Samuelson, P.A. (1977), 'St. Petersburg Paradoxes: Defanged, Dissected, and Historically Described', *Journal of Economic Literature*, **15**, 24–55.

Savage, L.J. (1954), *The Foundations of Statistics*, NY: Wiley.

Von Neumann, John and Morgenstern, Oskar (1947), *Theory of Games and Economic Behaviour*, 2nd edition, Princeton University Press.

ECONOMETRICA

VOLUME 47   MARCH, 1979   NUMBER 2

PROSPECT THEORY: AN ANALYSIS OF DECISION UNDER RISK

BY DANIEL KAHNEMAN AND AMOS TVERSKY[1]

This paper presents a critique of expected utility theory as a descriptive model of decision making under risk, and develops an alternative model, called prospect theory. Choices among risky prospects exhibit several pervasive effects that are inconsistent with the basic tenets of utility theory. In particular, people underweight outcomes that are merely probable in comparison with outcomes that are obtained with certainty. This tendency, called the certainty effect, contributes to risk aversion in choices involving sure gains and to risk seeking in choices involving sure losses. In addition, people generally discard components that are shared by all prospects under consideration. This tendency, called the isolation effect, leads to inconsistent preferences when the same choice is presented in different forms. An alternative theory of choice is developed, in which value is assigned to gains and losses rather than to final assets and in which probabilities are replaced by decision weights. The value function is normally concave for gains, commonly convex for losses, and is generally steeper for losses than for gains. Decision weights are generally lower than the corresponding probabilities, except in the range of low probabilities. Overweighting of low probabilities may contribute to the attractiveness of both insurance and gambling.

1. INTRODUCTION

EXPECTED UTILITY THEORY has dominated the analysis of decision making under risk. It has been generally accepted as a normative model of rational choice [24], and widely applied as a descriptive model of economic behavior, e.g. [15, 4]. Thus, it is assumed that all reasonable people would wish to obey the axioms of the theory [47, 36], and that most people actually do, most of the time.

The present paper describes several classes of choice problems in which preferences systematically violate the axioms of expected utility theory. In the light of these observations we argue that utility theory, as it is commonly interpreted and applied, is not an adequate descriptive model and we propose an alternative account of choice under risk.

2. CRITIQUE

Decision making under risk can be viewed as a choice between prospects or gambles. A prospect $(x_1, p_1; \ldots; x_n, p_n)$ is a contract that yields outcome x_i with probability p_i, where $p_1 + p_2 + \ldots + p_n = 1$. To simplify notation, we omit null outcomes and use (x, p) to denote the prospect $(x, p; 0, 1-p)$ that yields x with probability p and 0 with probability $1-p$. The (riskless) prospect that yields x with certainty is denoted by (x). The present discussion is restricted to prospects with so-called objective or standard probabilities.

The application of expected utility theory to choices between prospects is based on the following three tenets.

(i) Expectation: $U(x_1, p_1; \ldots; x_n, p_n) = p_1 u(x_1) + \ldots + p_n u(x_n)$.

[1] This work was supported in part by grants from the Harry F. Guggenheim Foundation and from the Advanced Research Projects Agency of the Department of Defense and was monitored by Office of Naval Research under Contract N00014-78-C-0100 (ARPA Order No. 3469) under Subcontract 78-072-0722 from Decisions and Designs, Inc. to Perceptronics, Inc. We also thank the Center for Advanced Study in the Behavioral Sciences at Stanford for its support.

That is, the overall utility of a prospect, denoted by U, is the expected utility of its outcomes.

(ii) Asset Integration: $(x_1, p_1; \ldots; x_n, p_n)$ is acceptable at asset position w iff $U(w + x_1, p_1; \ldots; w + x_n, p_n) > u(w)$.

That is, a prospect is acceptable if the utility resulting from integrating the prospect with one's assets exceeds the utility of those assets alone. Thus, the domain of the utility function is final states (which include one's asset position) rather than gains or losses.

Although the domain of the utility function is not limited to any particular class of consequences, most applications of the theory have been concerned with monetary outcomes. Furthermore, most economic applications introduce the following additional assumption.

(iii) Risk Aversion: u is concave ($u'' < 0$).

A person is risk averse if he prefers the certain prospect (x) to any risky prospect with expected value x. In expected utility theory, risk aversion is equivalent to the concavity of the utility function. The prevalence of risk aversion is perhaps the best known generalization regarding risky choices. It led the early decision theorists of the eighteenth century to propose that utility is a concave function of money, and this idea has been retained in modern treatments (Pratt [33], Arrow [4]).

In the following sections we demonstrate several phenomena which violate these tenets of expected utility theory. The demonstrations are based on the responses of students and university faculty to hypothetical choice problems. The respondents were presented with problems of the type illustrated below.

Which of the following would you prefer?

> A: 50% chance to win 1,000,   B: 450 for sure.
>
>   50% chance to win nothing;

The outcomes refer to Israeli currency. To appreciate the significance of the amounts involved, note that the median net monthly income for a family is about 3,000 Israeli pounds. The respondents were asked to imagine that they were actually faced with the choice described in the problem, and to indicate the decision they would have made in such a case. The responses were anonymous, and the instructions specified that there was no 'correct' answer to such problems, and that the aim of the study was to find out how people choose among risky prospects. The problems were presented in questionnaire form, with at most a dozen problems per booklet. Several forms of each questionnaire were constructed so that subjects were exposed to the problems in different orders. In addition, two versions of each problem were used in which the left-right position of the prospects was reversed.

The problems described in this paper are selected illustrations of a series of effects. Every effect has been observed in several problems with different outcomes and probabilities. Some of the problems have also been presented to groups of students and faculty at the University of Stockholm and at the

University of Michigan. The pattern of results was essentially identical to the results obtained from Israeli subjects.

The reliance on hypothetical choices raises obvious questions regarding the validity of the method and the generalizability of the results. We are keenly aware of these problems. However, all other methods that have been used to test utility theory also suffer from severe drawbacks. Real choices can be investigated either in the field, by naturalistic or statistical observations of economic behavior, or in the laboratory. Field studies can only provide for rather crude tests of qualitative predictions, because probabilities and utilities cannot be adequately measured in such contexts. Laboratory experiments have been designed to obtain precise measures of utility and probability from actual choices, but these experimental studies typically involve contrived gambles for small stakes, and a large number of repetitions of very similar problems. These features of laboratory gambling complicate the interpretation of the results and restrict their generality.

By default, the method of hypothetical choices emerges as the simplest procedure by which a large number of theoretical questions can be investigated. The use of the method relies on the assumption that people often know how they would behave in actual situations of choice, and on the further assumption that the subjects have no special reason to disguise their true preferences. If people are reasonably accurate in predicting their choices, the presence of common and systematic violations of expected utility theory in hypothetical problems provides presumptive evidence against that theory.

Certainty, Probability, and Possibility

In expected utility theory, the utilities of outcomes are weighted by their probabilities. The present section describes a series of choice problems in which people's preferences systematically violate this principle. We first show that people overweight outcomes that are considered certain, relative to outcomes which are merely probable—a phenomenon which we label the *certainty effect*.

The best known counter-example to expected utility theory which exploits the certainty effect was introduced by the French economist Maurice Allais in 1953 [2]. Allais' example has been discussed from both normative and descriptive standpoints by many authors [28, 38]. The following pair of choice problems is a variation of Allais' example, which differs from the original in that it refers to moderate rather than to extremely large gains. The number of respondents who answered each problem is denoted by N, and the percentage who choose each option is given in brackets.

PROBLEM 1: Choose between

    A: 2,500 with probability .33,   B: 2,400 with certainty.

         2,400 with probability .66,

         0 with probability   .01;

    N = 72   [18]   [82]*

PROBLEM 2: Choose between

    C: 2,500 with probability .33,   D: 2,400 with probability .34,

       0 with probability   .67;   0 with probability   .66.

    $N = 72$ [83]*   [17]

The data show that 82 per cent of the subjects chose B in Problem 1, and 83 per cent of the subjects chose C in Problem 2. Each of these preferences is significant at the .01 level, as denoted by the asterisk. Moreover, the analysis of individual patterns of choice indicates that a majority of respondents (61 per cent) made the modal choice in both problems. This pattern of preferences violates expected utility theory in the manner originally described by Allais. According to that theory, with $u(0) = 0$, the first preference implies

$$u(2,400) > .33u(2,500) + .66u(2,400) \text{ or } .34u(2,400) > .33u(2,500)$$

while the second preference implies the reverse inequality. Note that Problem 2 is obtained from Problem 1 by eliminating a .66 chance of winning 2400 from both prospects under consideration. Evidently, this change produces a greater reduction in desirability when it alters the character of the prospect from a sure gain to a probable one, than when both the original and the reduced prospects are uncertain.

A simpler demonstration of the same phenomenon, involving only two-outcome gambles is given below. This example is also based on Allais [2].

PROBLEM 3:

    A: (4,000,.80),   or   B: (3,000).

    $N = 95$ [20]   [80]*

PROBLEM 4:

    C: (4,000,.20),   or   D: (3,000,.25).

    $N = 95$ [65]*   [35]

In this pair of problems as well as in all other problem-pairs in this section, over half the respondents violated expected utility theory. To show that the modal pattern of preferences in Problems 3 and 4 is not compatible with the theory, set $u(0) = 0$, and recall that the choice of B implies $u(3,000)/u(4,000) > 4/5$, whereas the choice of C implies the reverse inequality. Note that the prospect $C = (4,000, .20)$ can be expressed as $(A, .25)$, while the prospect $D = (3,000, .25)$ can be rewritten as $(B,.25)$. The substitution axiom of utility theory asserts that if B is preferred to A, then any (probability) mixture (B, p) must be preferred to the mixture (A, p). Our subjects did not obey this axiom. Apparently, reducing the probability of winning from 1.0 to .25 has a greater effect than the reduction from

.8 to .2. The following pair of choice problems illustrates the certainty effect with non-monetary outcomes.

PROBLEM 5:

A: 50% chance to win a three-week tour of England, France, and Italy;

B: A one-week tour of England, with certainty.

$N = 72$ [22]

[78]*

PROBLEM 6:

C: 5% chance to win a three-week tour of England, France, and Italy;

D: 10% chance to win a one-week tour of England.

$N = 72$ [67]*

[33]

The certainty effect is not the only type of violation of the substitution axiom. Another situation in which this axiom fails is illustrated by the following problems.

PROBLEM 7:

A: (6,000, .45),   B: (3,000, .90).

$N = 66$ [14]   [86]*

PROBLEM 8:

C: (6,000, .001),   D: (3,000, .002).

$N = 66$ [73]*   [27]

Note that in Problem 7 the probabilities of winning are substantial (.90 and .45), and most people choose the prospect where winning is more probable. In Problem 8, there is a *possibility* of winning, although the probabilities of winning are minuscule (.002 and .001) in both prospects. In this situation where winning is possible but not probable, most people choose the prospect that offers the larger gain. Similar results have been reported by MacCrimmon and Larsson [28].

The above problems illustrate common attitudes toward risk or chance that cannot be captured by the expected utility model. The results suggest the following empirical generalization concerning the manner in which the substitution axiom is violated. If (y, pq) is equivalent to (x, p), then (y, pqr) is preferred to (x, pr), $0 < p, q, r < 1$. This property is incorporated into an alternative theory, developed in the second part of the paper.

268   D. KAHNEMAN AND A. TVERSKY

The Reflection Effect

The previous section discussed preferences between positive prospects, i.e., prospects that involve no losses. What happens when the signs of the outcomes are reversed so that gains are replaced by losses? The left-hand column of Table I displays four of the choice problems that were discussed in the previous section, and the right-hand column displays choice problems in which the signs of the outcomes are reversed. We use $-x$ to denote the loss of x, and $>$ to denote the prevalent preference, i.e., the choice made by the majority of subjects.

TABLE I

PREFERENCES BETWEEN POSITIVE AND NEGATIVE PROSPECTS

Positive prospects			Negative prospects		
Problem 3:	(4,000, .80) <	(3,000).	Problem 3':	(−4,000, .80) >	(−3,000).
N = 95	[20]	[80]*	N = 95	[92]*	[8]
Problem 4:	(4,000, .20) >	(3,000, .25).	Problem 4':	(−4,000, .20) <	(−3,000, .25).
N = 95	[65]*	[35]	N = 95	[42]	[58]
Problem 7:	(3,000, .90) >	(6,000, .45).	Problem 7':	(−3,000, .90) <	(−6,000, .45).
N = 66	[86]*	[14]	N = 66	[8]	[92]*
Problem 8:	(3,000, .002) <	(6,000, .001).	Problem 8':	(−3,000, .002) >	(−6,000, .001).
N = 66	[27]	[73]*	N = 66	[70]*	[30]

In each of the four problems in Table I the preference between negative prospects is the mirror image of the preference between positive prospects. Thus, the reflection of prospects around 0 reverses the preference order. We label this pattern the *reflection effect*.

Let us turn now to the implications of these data. First, note that the reflection effect implies that risk aversion in the positive domain is accompanied by risk seeking in the negative domain. In Problem 3', for example, the majority of subjects were willing to accept a risk of .80 to lose 4,000, in preference to a sure loss of 3,000, although the gamble has a lower expected value. The occurrence of risk seeking in choices between negative prospects was noted early by Markowitz [29]. Williams [48] reported data where a translation of outcomes produces a dramatic shift from risk aversion to risk seeking. For example, his subjects were indifferent between (100, .65; −100, .35) and (0), indicating risk aversion. They were also indifferent between (−200, .80) and (−100), indicating risk seeking. A recent review by Fishburn and Kochenberger [14] documents the prevalence of risk seeking in choices between negative prospects.

Second, recall that the preferences between the positive prospects in Table I are inconsistent with expected utility theory. The preferences between the corresponding negative prospects also violate the expectation principle in the same manner. For example, Problems 3' and 4', like Problems 3 and 4, demonstrate that outcomes which are obtained with certainty are overweighted relative to uncertain outcomes. In the positive domain, the certainty effect contributes to a risk averse preference for a sure gain over a larger gain that is merely probable. In the negative domain, the same effect leads to a risk seeking preference for a loss that is merely probable over a smaller loss that is certain. The same psychological principle—the overweighting of certainty—favors risk aversion in the domain of gains and risk seeking in the domain of losses.

Third, the reflection effect eliminates aversion for uncertainty or variability as an explanation of the certainty effect. Consider, for example, the prevalent preferences for (3,000) over (4,000, .80) and for (4,000, .20) over (3,000, .25). To resolve this apparent inconsistency one could invoke the assumption that people prefer prospects that have high expected value and small variance (see, e.g., Allais [2]; Markowitz [30]; Tobin [41]). Since (3,000) has no variance while (4,000, .80) has large variance, the former prospect could be chosen despite its lower expected value. When the prospects are reduced, however, the difference in variance between (3,000, .25) and (4,000, .20) may be insufficient to overcome the difference in expected value. Because (−3,000) has both higher expected value and lower variance than (−4,000, .80), this account entails that the sure loss should be preferred, contrary to the data. Thus, our data are incompatible with the notion that certainty is generally desirable. Rather, it appears that certainty increases the aversiveness of losses as well as the desirability of gains.

Probabilistic Insurance

The prevalence of the purchase of insurance against both large and small losses has been regarded by many as strong evidence for the concavity of the utility function for money. Why otherwise would people spend so much money to purchase insurance policies at a price that exceeds the expected actuarial cost? However, an examination of the relative attractiveness of various forms of insurance does not support the notion that the utility function for money is concave everywhere. For example, people often prefer insurance programs that offer limited coverage with low or zero deductible over comparable policies that offer higher maximal coverage with higher deductibles—contrary to risk aversion (see, e.g., Fuchs [16]). Another type of insurance problem in which people's responses are inconsistent with the concavity hypothesis may be called probabilistic insurance. To illustrate this concept, consider the following problem, which was presented to 95 Stanford University students.

PROBLEM 9: Suppose you consider the possibility of insuring some property against damage, e.g., fire or theft. After examining the risks and the premium you find that you have no clear preference between the options of purchasing insurance or leaving the property uninsured.

It is then called to your attention that the insurance company offers a new program called *probabilistic insurance.* In this program you pay half of the regular premium. In case of damage, there is a 50 per cent chance that you pay the other half of the premium and the insurance company covers all the losses; and there is a 50 per cent chance that you get back your insurance payment and suffer all the losses. For example, if an accident occurs on an odd day of the month, you pay the other half of the regular premium and your losses are covered; but if the accident occurs on an even day of the month, your insurance payment is refunded and your losses are not covered.

Recall that the premium for full coverage is such that you find this insurance barely worth its cost.

Under these circumstances, would you purchase probabilistic insurance:

	Yes,	No.
$N = 95$	[20]	[80]*

Although Problem 9 may appear contrived, it is worth noting that probabilistic insurance represents many forms of protective action where one pays a certain cost to reduce the probability of an undesirable event—without eliminating it altogether. The installation of a burglar alarm, the replacement of old tires, and the decision to stop smoking can all be viewed as probabilistic insurance.

The responses to Problem 9 and to several other variants of the same question indicate that probabilistic insurance is generally unattractive. Apparently, reducing the probability of a loss from p to $p/2$ is less valuable than reducing the probability of that loss from $p/2$ to 0.

In contrast to these data, expected utility theory (with a concave u) implies that probabilistic insurance is superior to regular insurance. That is, if at asset position w one is just willing to pay a premium y to insure against a probability p of losing x, then one should definitely be willing to pay a smaller premium ry to reduce the probability of losing x from p to $(1-r)p, 0 < r < 1$. Formally, if one is indifferent between $(w - x, p; w, 1 - p)$ and $(w - y)$, then one should prefer probabilistic insurance $(w - x, (1 - r)p; w - y, rp; w - ry, 1 - p)$ over regular insurance $(w - y)$.

To prove this proposition, we show that

$$pu(w - x) + (1 - p)u(w) = u(w - y)$$

implies

$$(1 - r)pu(w - x) + rpu(w - y) + (1 - p)u(w - ry) > u(w - y).$$

Without loss of generality, we can set $u(w - x) = 0$ and $u(w) = 1$. Hence, $u(w - y) = 1 - p$, and we wish to show that

$$rp(1 - p) + (1 - p)u(w - ry) > 1 - p \qquad \text{or} \qquad u(w - ry) > 1 - rp$$

which holds if and only if u is concave.

This is a rather puzzling consequence of the risk aversion hypothesis of utility theory, because probabilistic insurance appears intuitively riskier than regular insurance, which entirely eliminates the element of risk. Evidently, the intuitive notion of risk is not adequately captured by the assumed concavity of the utility function for wealth.

The aversion for probabilistic insurance is particularly intriguing because all insurance is, in a sense, probabilistic. The most avid buyer of insurance remains vulnerable to many financial and other risks which his policies do not cover. There appears to be a significant difference between probabilistic insurance and what may be called contingent insurance, which provides the certainty of coverage for a specified type of risk. Compare, for example, probabilistic insurance against all forms of loss or damage to the contents of your home and contingent insurance that eliminates all risk of loss from theft, say, but does not cover other risks, e.g., fire. We conjecture that contingent insurance will be generally more attractive than probabilistic insurance when the probabilities of unprotected loss are equated. Thus, two prospects that are equivalent in probabilities and outcomes could have different values depending on their formulation. Several demonstrations of this general phenomenon are described in the next section.

The Isolation Effect

In order to simplify the choice between alternatives, people often disregard components that the alternatives share, and focus on the components that distinguish them (Tversky [44]). This approach to choice problems may produce inconsistent preferences, because a pair of prospects can be decomposed into common and distinctive components in more than one way, and different decompositions sometimes lead to different preferences. We refer to this phenomenon as the *isolation effect*.

PROBLEM 10: Consider the following two-stage game. In the first stage, there is a probability of .75 to end the game without winning anything, and a probability of .25 to move into the second stage. If you reach the second stage you have a choice between

        (4,000, .80)   and   (3,000).

Your choice must be made before the game starts, i.e., before the outcome of the first stage is known.

Note that in this game, one has a choice between $.25 \times .80 = .20$ chance to win 4,000, and a $.25 \times 1.0 = .25$ chance to win 3,000. Thus, in terms of final outcomes and probabilities one faces a choice between (4,000, .20) and (3,000, .25), as in Problem 4 above. However, the dominant preferences are different in the two problems. Of 141 subjects who answered Problem 10, 78 per cent chose the latter prospect, contrary to the modal preference in Problem 4. Evidently, people ignored the first stage of the game, whose outcomes are shared by both prospects, and considered Problem 10 as a choice between (3,000) and (4,000, .80), as in Problem 3 above.

The standard and the sequential formulations of Problem 4 are represented as decision trees in Figures 1 and 2, respectively. Following the usual convention, squares denote decision nodes and circles denote chance nodes. The essential difference between the two representations is in the location of the decision node. In the standard form (Figure 1), the decision maker faces a choice between two risky prospects, whereas in the sequential form (Figure 2) he faces a choice between a risky and a riskless prospect. This is accomplished by introducing a dependency between the prospects without changing either probabilities or

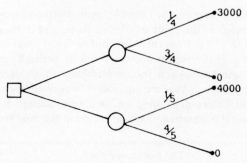

FIGURE 1.—The representation of Problem 4 as a decision tree (standard formulation).

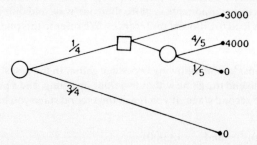

FIGURE 2.—The representation of Problem 10 as a decision tree (sequential formulation).

outcomes. Specifically, the event 'not winning 3,000' is included in the event 'not winning 4,000' in the sequential formulation, while the two events are independent in the standard formulation. Thus, the outcome of winning 3,000 has a certainty advantage in the sequential formulation, which it does not have in the standard formulation.

The reversal of preferences due to the dependency among events is particularly significant because it violates the basic supposition of a decision-theoretical analysis, that choices between prospects are determined solely by the probabilities of final states.

It is easy to think of decision problems that are most naturally represented in one of the forms above rather than in the other. For example, the choice between two different risky ventures is likely to be viewed in the standard form. On the other hand, the following problem is most likely to be represented in the sequential form. One may invest money in a venture with some probability of losing one's capital if the venture fails, and with a choice between a fixed agreed return and a percentage of earnings if it succeeds. The isolation effect implies that the contingent certainty of the fixed return enhances the attractiveness of this option, relative to a risky venture with the same probabilities and outcomes.

PROSPECT THEORY 273

The preceding problem illustrated how preferences may be altered by different representations of probabilities. We now show how choices may be altered by varying the representation of outcomes.

Consider the following problems, which were presented to two different groups of subjects.

PROBLEM 11: In addition to whatever you own, you have been given 1,000. You are now asked to choose between

      A: (1,000, .50),   and   B: (500).

      $N = 70$ [16]   [84]*

PROBLEM 12: In addition to whatever you own, you have been given 2,000. You are now asked to choose between

      C: (−1,000, .50),   and   D: (−500).

      $N = 68$ [69*]   [31]

The majority of subjects chose B in the first problem and C in the second. These preferences conform to the reflection effect observed in Table I, which exhibits risk aversion for positive prospects and risk seeking for negative ones. Note, however, that when viewed in terms of final states, the two choice problems are identical. Specifically,

      A = (2,000, .50; 1,000, .50) = C,   and   B = (1,500) = D.

In fact, Problem 12 is obtained from Problem 11 by adding 1,000 to the initial bonus, and subtracting 1,000 from all outcomes. Evidently, the subjects did not integrate the bonus with the prospects. The bonus did not enter into the comparison of prospects because it was common to both options in each problem.

The pattern of results observed in Problems 11 and 12 is clearly inconsistent with utility theory. In that theory, for example, the same utility is assigned to a wealth of $100, 000, regardless of whether it was reached from a prior wealth of $95,000 or $105,000. Consequently, the choice between a total wealth of $100,000 and even chances to own $95,000 or $105,000 should be independent of whether one currently owns the smaller or the larger of these two amounts. With the added assumption of risk aversion, the theory entails that the certainty of owning $100,000 should always be preferred to the gamble. However, the responses to Problem 12 and to several of the previous questions suggest that this pattern will be obtained if the individual owns the smaller amount, but not if he owns the larger amount.

The apparent neglect of a bonus that was common to both options in Problems 11 and 12 implies that the carriers of value or utility are changes of wealth, rather than final asset positions that include current wealth. This conclusion is the cornerstone of an alternative theory of risky choice, which is described in the following sections.

3. THEORY

The preceding discussion reviewed several empirical effects which appear to invalidate expected utility theory as a descriptive model. The remainder of the paper presents an alternative account of individual decision making under risk, called prospect theory. The theory is developed for simple prospects with monetary outcomes and stated probabilities, but it can be extended to more involved choices. Prospect theory distinguishes two phases in the choice process: an early phase of editing and a subsequent phase of evaluation. The editing phase consists of a preliminary analysis of the offered prospects, which often yields a simpler representation of these prospects. In the second phase, the edited prospects are evaluated and the prospect of highest value is chosen. We next outline the editing phase, and develop a formal model of the evaluation phase.

The function of the editing phase is to organize and reformulate the options so as to simplify subsequent evaluation and choice. Editing consists of the application of several operations that transform the outcomes and probabilities associated with the offered prospects. The major operations of the editing phase are described below.

Coding. The evidence discussed in the previous section shows that people normally perceive outcomes as gains and losses, rather than as final states of wealth or welfare. Gains and losses, of course, are defined relative to some neutral reference point. The reference point usually corresponds to the current asset position, in which case gains and losses coincide with the actual amounts that are received or paid. However, the location of the reference point, and the consequent coding of outcomes as gains or losses, can be affected by the formulation of the offered prospects, and by the expectations of the decision maker.

Combination. Prospects can sometimes be simplified by combining the probabilities associated with identical outcomes. For example, the prospect (200, .25; 200, .25) will be reduced to (200, .50). and evaluated in this form.

Segregation. Some prospects contain a riskless component that is segregated from the risky component in the editing phase. For example, the prospect (300, .80; 200, .20) is naturally decomposed into a sure gain of 200 and the risky prospect (100, .80). Similarly, the prospect (−400, .40; −100, .60) is readily seen to consist of a sure loss of 100 and of the prospect (−300, .40).

The preceding operations are applied to each prospect separately. The following operation is applied to a set of two or more prospects.

Cancellation. The essence of the isolation effects described earlier is the discarding of components that are shared by the offered prospects. Thus, our respondents apparently ignored the first stage of the sequential game presented in Problem 10, because this stage was common to both options, and they evaluated the prospects with respect to the results of the second stage (see Figure 2). Similarly, they neglected the common bonus that was added to the prospects in Problems 11 and 12. Another type of cancellation involves the discarding of common constituents, i.e., outcome-probability pairs. For example, the choice between (200, .20; 100, .50; −50, .30) and (200, .20; 150, .50; −100, .30) can be reduced by cancellation to a choice between (100, .50; −50, .30) and (150, .50; −100, .30).

Two additional operations that should be mentioned are simplification and the detection of dominance. The first refers to the simplification of prospects by rounding probabilities or outcomes. For example, the prospect (101, .49) is likely to be recoded as an even chance to win 100. A particularly important form of simplification involves the discarding of extremely unlikely outcomes. The second operation involves the scanning of offered prospects to detect dominated alternatives, which are rejected without further evaluation.

Because the editing operations facilitate the task of decision, it is assumed that they are performed whenever possible. However, some editing operations either permit or prevent the application of others. For example, (500, .20; 101, .49) will appear to dominate (500, .15; 99, .51) if the second constituents of both prospects are simplified to (100, .50). The final edited prospects could, therefore, depend on the sequence of editing operations, which is likely to vary with the structure of the offered set and with the format of the display. A detailed study of this problem is beyond the scope of the present treatment. In this paper we discuss choice problems where it is reasonable to assume either that the original formulation of the prospects leaves no room for further editing, or that the edited prospects can be specified without ambiguity.

Many anomalies of preference result from the editing of prospects. For example, the inconsistencies associated with the isolation effect result from the cancellation of common components. Some intransitivities of choice are explained by a simplification that eliminates small differences between prospects (see Tversky [43]). More generally, the preference order between prospects need not be invariant across contexts, because the same offered prospect could be edited in different ways depending on the context in which it appears.

Following the editing phase, the decision maker is assumed to evaluate each of the edited prospects, and to choose the prospect of highest value. The overall value of an edited prospect, denoted V, is expressed in terms of two scales, π and v.

The first scale, π, associates with each probability p a decision weight $\pi(p)$, which reflects the impact of p on the over-all value of the prospect. However, π is not a probability measure, and it will be shown later that $\pi(p) + \pi(1-p)$ is typically less than unity. The second scale, v, assigns to each outcome x a number $v(x)$, which reflects the subjective value of that outcome. Recall that outcomes are defined relative to a reference point, which serves as the zero point of the value scale. Hence, v measures the value of deviations from that reference point, i.e., gains and losses.

The present formulation is concerned with simple prospects of the form $(x, p; y, q)$, which have at most two non-zero outcomes. In such a prospect, one receives x with probability p, y with probability q, and nothing with probability $1 - p - q$, where $p + q \leq 1$. An offered prospect is strictly positive if its outcomes are all positive, i.e., if $x, y > 0$ and $p + q = 1$; it is strictly negative if its outcomes are all negative. A prospect is regular if it is neither strictly positive nor strictly negative.

The basic equation of the theory describes the manner in which π and v are combined to determine the over-all value of regular prospects.

If $(x, p; y, q)$ is a regular prospect (i.e., either $p + q < 1$, or $x \geq 0 \geq y$, or $x \leq 0 \leq y$), then

(1) $\qquad V(x, p; y, q) = \pi(p)v(x) + \pi(q)v(y)$

where $v(0) = 0$, $\pi(0) = 0$, and $\pi(1) = 1$. As in utility theory, V is defined on prospects, while v is defined on outcomes. The two scales coincide for sure prospects, where $V(x, 1.0) = V(x) = v(x)$.

Equation (1) generalizes expected utility theory by relaxing the expectation principle. An axiomatic analysis of this representation is sketched in the Appendix, which describes conditions that ensure the existence of a unique π and a ratio-scale v satisfying equation (1).

The evaluation of strictly positive and strictly negative prospects follows a different rule. In the editing phase such prospects are segregated into two components: (i) the riskless component, i.e., the minimum gain or loss which is certain to be obtained or paid; (ii) the risky component, i.e., the additional gain or loss which is actually at stake. The evaluation of such prospects is described in the next equation.

If $p + q = 1$ and either $x > y > 0$ or $x < y < 0$, then

(2) $\qquad V(x, p; y, q) = v(y) + \pi(p)[v(x) - v(y)]$.

That is, the value of a strictly positive or strictly negative prospect equals the value of the riskless component plus the value-difference between the outcomes, multiplied by the weight associated with the more extreme outcome. For example, $V(400, .25; 100, .75) = v(100) + \pi(.25)[v(400) - v(100)]$. The essential feature of equation (2) is that a decision weight is applied to the value-difference $v(x) - v(y)$, which represents the risky component of the prospect, but not to $v(y)$, which represents the riskless component. Note that the right-hand side of equation (2) equals $\pi(p)v(x) + [1 - \pi(p)]v(y)$. Hence, equation (2) reduces to equation (1) if $\pi(p) + \pi(1 - p) = 1$. As will be shown later, this condition is not generally satisfied.

Many elements of the evaluation model have appeared in previous attempts to modify expected utility theory. Markowitz [29] was the first to propose that utility be defined on gains and losses rather than on final asset positions, an assumption which has been implicitly accepted in most experimental measurements of utility (see, e.g., [7, 32]). Markowitz also noted the presence of risk seeking in preferences among positive as well as among negative prospects, and he proposed a utility function which has convex and concave regions in both the positive and the negative domains. His treatment, however, retains the expectation principle; hence it cannot account for the many violations of this principle; see, e.g., Table I.

The replacement of probabilities by more general weights was proposed by Edwards [9], and this model was investigated in several empirical studies (e.g.,

[**3**, **42**]). Similar models were developed by Fellner [**12**], who introduced the concept of decision weight to explain aversion for ambiguity, and by van Dam [**46**] who attempted to scale decision weights. For other critical analyses of expected utility theory and alternative choice models, see Allais [**2**], Coombs [**6**], Fishburn [**13**], and Hansson [**22**].

The equations of prospect theory retain the general bilinear form that underlies expected utility theory. However, in order to accomodate the effects described in the first part of the paper, we are compelled to assume that values are attached to changes rather than to final states, and that decision weights do not coincide with stated probabilities. These departures from expected utility theory must lead to normatively unacceptable consequences, such as inconsistencies, intransitivities, and violations of dominance. Such anomalies of preference are normally corrected by the decision maker when he realizes that his preferences are inconsistent, intransitive, or inadmissible. In many situations, however, the decision maker does not have the opportunity to discover that his preferences could violate decision rules that he wishes to obey. In these circumstances the anomalies implied by prospect theory are expected to occur.

The Value Function

An essential feature of the present theory is that the carriers of value are changes in wealth or welfare, rather than final states. This assumption is compatible with basic principles of perception and judgment. Our perceptual apparatus is attuned to the evaluation of changes or differences rather than to the evaluation of absolute magnitudes. When we respond to attributes such as brightness, loudness, or temperature, the past and present context of experience defines an adaptation level, or reference point, and stimuli are perceived in relation to this reference point [**23**]. Thus, an object at a given temperature may be experienced as hot or cold to the touch depending on the temperature to which one has adapted. The same principle applies to non-sensory attributes such as health, prestige, and wealth. The same level of wealth, for example, may imply abject poverty for one person and great riches for another—depending on their current assets.

The emphasis on changes as the carriers of value should not be taken to imply that the value of a particular change is independent of initial position. Strictly speaking, value should be treated as a function in two arguments: the asset position that serves as reference point, and the magnitude of the change (positive or negative) from that reference point. An individual's attitude to money, say, could be described by a book, where each page presents the value function for changes at a particular asset position. Clearly, the value functions described on different pages are not identical: they are likely to become more linear with increases in assets. However, the preference order of prospects is not greatly altered by small or even moderate variations in asset position. The certainty equivalent of the prospect (1,000, .50), for example, lies between 300 and 400 for most people, in a wide range of asset positions. Consequently, the representation

278   D. KAHNEMAN AND A. TVERSKY

of value as a function in one argument generally provides a satisfactory approximation.

Many sensory and perceptual dimensions share the property that the psychological response is a concave function of the magnitude of physical change. For example, it is easier to discriminate between a change of 3° and a change of 6° in room temperature, than it is to discriminate between a change of 13° and a change of 16°. We propose that this principle applies in particular to the evaluation of monetary changes. Thus, the difference in value between a gain of 100 and a gain of 200 appears to be greater than the difference between a gain of 1,100 and a gain of 1,200. Similarly, the difference between a loss of 100 and a loss of 200 appears greater than the difference between a loss of 1,100 and a loss of 1,200, unless the larger loss is intolerable. Thus, we hypothesize that the value function for changes of wealth is normally concave above the reference point ($v''(x) < 0$, for $x > 0$) and often convex below it ($v''(x) > 0$, for $x < 0$). That is, the marginal value of both gains and losses generally decreases with their magnitude. Some support for this hypothesis has been reported by Galanter and Pliner [17], who scaled the perceived magnitude of monetary and non-monetary gains and losses.

The above hypothesis regarding the shape of the value function was based on responses to gains and losses in a riskless context. We propose that the value function which is derived from risky choices shares the same characteristics, as illustrated in the following problems.

PROBLEM 13:

$$(6,000, .25), \quad \text{or} \quad (4,000, .25; 2,000, .25).$$

$N = 68 \quad [18] \qquad\qquad\qquad [82]^*$

PROBLEM 13':

$$(-6,000, .25), \quad \text{or} \quad (-4,000, .25; -2,000, .25).$$

$N = 64 \quad [70]^* \qquad\qquad\qquad [30]$

Applying equation 1 to the modal preference in these problems yields

$$\pi(.25)v(6,000) < \pi(.25)[v(4,000) + v(2,000)] \qquad \text{and}$$

$$\pi(.25)v(-6,000) > \pi(.25)[v(-4,000) + v(-2,000)].$$

Hence, $v(6,000) < v(4,000) + v(2,000)$ and $v(-6,000) > v(-4,000) + v(-2,000)$. These preferences are in accord with the hypothesis that the value function is concave for gains and convex for losses.

Any discussion of the utility function for money must leave room for the effect of special circumstances on preferences. For example, the utility function of an individual who needs $60,000 to purchase a house may reveal an exceptionally steep rise near the critical value. Similarly, an individual's aversion to losses may increase sharply near the loss that would compel him to sell his house and move to a less desirable neighborhood. Hence, the derived value (utility) function of an individual does not always reflect "pure" attitudes to money, since it could be affected by additional consequences associated with specific amounts. Such perturbations can readily produce convex regions in the value function for gains and concave regions in the value function for losses. The latter case may be more common since large losses often necessitate changes in life style.

A salient characteristic of attitudes to changes in welfare is that losses loom larger than gains. The aggravation that one experiences in losing a sum of money appears to be greater than the pleasure associated with gaining the same amount [17]. Indeed, most people find symmetric bets of the form $(x, .50; -x, .50)$ distinctly unattractive. Moreover, the aversiveness of symmetric fair bets generally increases with the size of the stake. That is, if $x > y \geq 0$, then $(y, .50; -y, .50)$ is preferred to $(x, .50; -x, .50)$. According to equation (1), therefore,

$$v(y) + v(-y) > v(x) + v(-x) \qquad \text{and} \qquad v(-y) - v(-x) > v(x) - v(y).$$

Setting $y = 0$ yields $v(x) < -v(-x)$, and letting y approach x yields $v'(x) < v'(-x)$, provided v', the derivative of v, exists. Thus, the value function for losses is steeper than the value function for gains.

In summary, we have proposed that the value function is (i) defined on deviations from the reference point; (ii) generally concave for gains and commonly convex for losses; (iii) steeper for losses than for gains. A value function which satisfies these properties is displayed in Figure 3. Note that the proposed S-shaped value function is steepest at the reference point, in marked contrast to the utility function postulated by Markowitz [29] which is relatively shallow in that region.

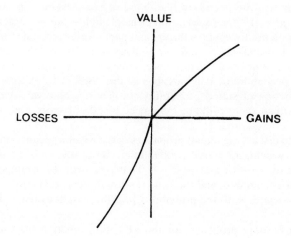

FIGURE 3.—A hypothetical value function.

280   D. KAHNEMAN AND A. TVERSKY

Although the present theory can be applied to derive the value function from preferences between prospects, the actual scaling is considerably more complicated than in utility theory, because of the introduction of decision weights. For example, decision weights could produce risk aversion and risk seeking even with a linear value function. Nevertheless, it is of interest that the main properties ascribed to the value function have been observed in a detailed analysis of von Neumann–Morgenstern utility functions for changes of wealth (Fishburn and Kochenberger [14]). The functions had been obtained from thirty decision makers in various fields of business, in five independent studies [5, 18, 19, 21, 40]. Most utility functions for gains were concave, most functions for losses were convex, and only three individuals exhibited risk aversion for both gains and losses. With a single exception, utility functions were considerably steeper for losses than for gains.

The Weighting Function

In prospect theory, the value of each outcome is multiplied by a decision weight. Decision weights are inferred from choices between prospects much as subjective probabilities are inferred from preferences in the Ramsey-Savage approach. However, decision weights are not probabilities: they do not obey the probability axioms and they should not be interpreted as measures of degree or belief.

Consider a gamble in which one can win 1,000 or nothing, depending on the toss of a fair coin. For any reasonable person, the probability of winning is .50 in this situation. This can be verified in a variety of ways, e.g., by showing that the subject is indifferent between betting on heads or tails, or by his verbal report that he considers the two events equiprobable. As will be shown below, however, the decision weight $\pi(.50)$ which is derived from choices is likely to be smaller than .50. Decision weights measure the impact of events on the desirability of prospects, and not merely the perceived likelihood of these events. The two scales coincide (i.e., $\pi(p) = p$) if the expectation principle holds, but not otherwise.

The choice problems discussed in the present paper were formulated in terms of explicit numerical probabilities, and our analysis assumes that the respondents adopted the stated values of p. Furthermore, since the events were identified only by their stated probabilities, it is possible in this context to express decision weights as a function of stated probability. In general, however, the decision weight attached to an event could be influenced by other factors, e.g., ambiguity [10, 11].

We turn now to discuss the salient properties of the weighting function π, which relates decision weights to stated probabilities. Naturally, π is an increasing function of p, with $\pi(0) = 0$ and $\pi(1) = 1$. That is, outcomes contingent on an impossible event are ignored, and the scale is normalized so that $\pi(p)$ is the ratio of the weight associated with the probability p to the weight associated with the certain event.

We first discuss some properties of the weighting function for small probabilities. The preferences in Problems 8 and 8' suggest that for small values of p, π

is a subadditive function of p, i.e., $\pi(rp) > r\pi(p)$ for $0 < r < 1$. Recall that in Problem 8, (6,000, .001) is preferred to (3,000, .002). Hence

$$\frac{\pi(.001)}{\pi(.002)} > \frac{v(3,000)}{v(6,000)} > \frac{1}{2} \qquad \text{by the concavity of } v.$$

The reflected preferences in Problem 8' yield the same conclusion. The pattern of preferences in Problems 7 and 7', however, suggests that subadditivity need not hold for large values of p.

Furthermore, we propose that very low probabilities are generally over-weighted, that is, $\pi(p) > p$ for small p. Consider the following choice problems.

PROBLEM 14:

$$(5,000, .001), \qquad \text{or} \qquad (5).$$
$$N = 72 \quad [72]^* \qquad\qquad\qquad [28]$$

PROBLEM 14':

$$(-5,000, .001), \qquad \text{or} \qquad (-5).$$
$$N = 72 \quad [17] \qquad\qquad\qquad [83]^*$$

Note that in Problem 14, people prefer what is in effect a lottery ticket over the expected value of that ticket. In Problem 14', on the other hand, they prefer a small loss, which can be viewed as the payment of an insurance premium, over a small probability of a large loss. Similar observations have been reported by Markowitz [29]. In the present theory, the preference for the lottery in Problem 14 implies $\pi(.001)v(5,000) > v(5)$, hence $\pi(.001) > v(5)/v(5,000) > .001$, assuming the value function for gains is concave. The readiness to pay for insurance in Problem 14' implies the same conclusion, assuming the value function for losses is convex.

It is important to distinguish overweighting, which refers to a property of decision weights, from the overestimation that is commonly found in the assessment of the probability of rare events. Note that the issue of overestimation does not arise in the present context, where the subject is assumed to adopt the stated value of p. In many real-life situations, overestimation and overweighting may both operate to increase the impact of rare events.

Although $\pi(p) > p$ for low probabilities, there is evidence to suggest that, for all $0 < p < 1$, $\pi(p) + \pi(1-p) < 1$. We label this property subcertainty. It is readily seen that the typical preferences in any version of Allias' example (see, e.g., Problems 1 and 2) imply subcertainty for the relevant value of p. Applying equation (1) to the prevalent preferences in Problems 1 and 2 yields, respectively,

$$v(2,400) > \pi(.66)v(2,400) + \pi(.33)v(2,500), \qquad \text{i.e.,}$$

$$[1 - \pi(.66]v(2,400) > \pi(.33)v(2,500) \qquad \text{and}$$

$$\pi(.33)v(2,500) > \pi(.34)v(2,400); \qquad \text{hence,}$$

$$1 - \pi(.66) > \pi(.34), \qquad \text{or} \qquad \pi(.66) + \pi(.34) < 1.$$

Applying the same analysis to Allais' original example yields $\pi(.89) + \pi(.11) < 1$, and some data reported by MacCrimmon and Larsson [28] imply subcertainty for additional values of p.

The slope of π in the interval $(0, 1)$ can be viewed as a measure of the sensitivity of preferences to changes in probability. Subcertainty entails that π is regressive with respect to p, i.e., that preferences are generally less sensitive to variations of probability than the expectation principle would dictate. Thus, subcertainty captures an essential element of people's attitudes to uncertain events, namely that the sum of the weights associated with complementary events is typically less than the weight associated with the certain event.

Recall that the violations of the substitution axiom discussed earlier in this paper conform to the following rule: If (x, p) is equivalent to (y, pq) then (x, pr) is not preferred to (y, pqr), $0 < p, q, r \leq 1$. By equation (1),

$$\pi(p)v(x) = \pi(pq)v(y) \qquad \text{implies} \qquad \pi(pr)v(x) \leq \pi(pqr)v(y); \qquad \text{hence,}$$

$$\frac{\pi(pq)}{\pi(p)} \leq \frac{\pi(pqr)}{\pi(pr)}.$$

Thus, for a fixed ratio of probabilities, the ratio of the corresponding decision weights is closer to unity when the probabilities are low than when they are high. This property of π, called subproportionality, imposes considerable constraints on the shape of π: it holds if and only if log π is a convex function of log p.

It is of interest to note that subproportionality together with the overweighting of small probabilities imply that π is subadditive over that range. Formally, it can be shown that if $\pi(p) > p$ and subproportionality holds, then $\pi(rp) > r\pi(p)$, $0 < r < 1$, provided π is monotone and continuous over $(0, 1)$.

Figure 4 presents a hypothetical weighting function which satisfies overweighting and subadditivity for small values of p, as well as subcertainty and subproportionality. These properties entail that π is relatively shallow in the open interval and changes abruptly near the end-points where $\pi(0) = 0$ and $\pi(1) = 1$. The sharp drops or apparent discontinuities of π at the endpoints are consistent with the notion that there is a limit to how small a decision weight can be attached to an event, if it is given any weight at all. A similar quantum of doubt could impose an upper limit on any decision weight that is less than unity. This quantal effect may reflect the categorical distinction between certainty and uncertainty. On the other hand, the simplification of prospects in the editing phase can lead the individual to discard events of extremely low probability and to treat events of extremely high probability as if they were certain. Because people are limited in their ability to comprehend and evaluate extreme probabilities, highly unlikely events are either ignored or overweighted, and the difference between high probability and certainty is either neglected or exaggerated. Consequently, π is not well-behaved near the end-points.

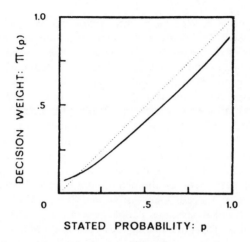

FIGURE 4.—A hypothetical weighting function.

The following example, due to Zeckhauser, illustrates the hypothesized nonlinearity of π. Suppose you are compelled to play Russian roulette, but are given the opportunity to purchase the removal of one bullet from the loaded gun. Would you pay as much to reduce the number of bullets from four to three as you would to reduce the number of bullets from one to zero? Most people feel that they would be willing to pay much more for a reduction of the probability of death from 1/6 to zero than for a reduction from 4/6 to 3/6. Economic considerations would lead one to pay more in the latter case, where the value of money is presumably reduced by the considerable probability that one will not live to enjoy it.

An obvious objection to the assumption that $\pi(p) \neq p$ involves comparisons between prospects of the form $(x, p; x, q)$ and $(x, p'; x, q')$, where $p + q = p' + q' < 1$. Since any individual will surely be indifferent between the two prospects, it could be argued that this observation entails $\pi(p) + \pi(q) = \pi(p') + \pi(q')$, which in turn implies that π is the identity function. This argument is invalid in the present theory, which assumes that the probabilities of identical outcomes are combined in the editing of prospects. A more serious objection to the nonlinearity of π involves potential violations of dominance. Suppose $x > y > 0$, $p > p'$, and $p + q = p' + q' < 1$; hence, $(x, p; y, q)$ dominates $(x, p'; y, q')$. If preference obeys

284   D. KAHNEMAN AND A. TVERSKY

dominance, then

$$\pi(p)v(x) + \pi(q)v(y) > \pi(p')v(x) + \pi(q')v(y),$$

or

$$\frac{\pi(p) - \pi(p')}{\pi(q') - \pi(q)} > \frac{v(y)}{v(x)}.$$

Hence, as y approaches x, $\pi(p) - \pi(p')$ approaches $\pi(q') - \pi(q)$. Since $p - p' = q' - q$, π must be essentially linear, or else dominance must be violated.

Direct violations of dominance are prevented, in the present theory, by the assumption that dominated alternatives are detected and eliminated prior to the evaluation of prospects. However, the theory permits indirect violations of dominance, e.g., triples of prospects so that A is preferred to B, B is preferred to C, and C dominates A. For an example, see Raiffa [34, p. 75].

Finally, it should be noted that the present treatment concerns the simplest decision task in which a person chooses between two available prospects. We have not treated in detail the more complicated production task (e.g., bidding) where the decision maker generates an alternative that is equal in value to a given prospect. The asymmetry between the two options in this situation could introduce systematic biases. Indeed, Lichtenstein and Slovic [27] have constructed pairs of prospects A and B, such that people generally prefer A over B, but bid more for B than for A. This phenomenon has been confirmed in several studies, with both hypothetical and real gambles, e.g., Grether and Plott [20]. Thus, it cannot be generally assumed that the preference order of prospects can be recovered by a bidding procedure.

Because prospect theory has been proposed as a model of choice, the inconsistency of bids and choices implies that the measurement of values and decision weights should be based on choices between specified prospects rather than on bids or other production tasks. This restriction makes the assessment of v and π more difficult because production tasks are more convenient for scaling than pair comparisons.

4. DISCUSSION

In the final section we show how prospect theory accounts for observed attitudes toward risk, discuss alternative representations of choice problems induced by shifts of reference point, and sketch several extensions of the present treatment.

Risk Attitudes

The dominant pattern of preferences observed in Allais' example (Problems 1 and 2) follows from the present theory iff

$$\frac{\pi(.33)}{\pi(.34)} > \frac{v(2,400)}{v(2,500)} > \frac{\pi(.33)}{1 - \pi(.66)}.$$

Hence, the violation of the independence axiom is attributed in this case to subcertainty, and more specifically to the inequality $\pi(.34) < 1 - \pi(.66)$. This analysis shows that an Allais-type violation will occur whenever the v-ratio of the two non-zero outcomes is bounded by the corresponding π-ratios.

Problems 3 through 8 share the same structure, hence it suffices to consider one pair, say Problems 7 and 8. The observed choices in these problems are implied by the theory iff

$$\frac{\pi(.001)}{\pi(.002)} > \frac{v(3,000)}{v(6,000)} > \frac{\pi(.45)}{\pi(.90)}.$$

The violation of the substitution axiom is attributed in this case to the sub-proportionality of π. Expected utility theory is violated in the above manner, therefore, whenever the v-ratio of the two outcomes is bounded by the respective π-ratios. The same analysis applies to other violations of the substitution axiom, both in the positive and in the negative domain.

We next prove that the preference for regular insurance over probabilistic insurance, observed in Problem 9, follows from prospect theory—provided the probability of loss is overweighted. That is, if $(-x, p)$ is indifferent to $(-y)$, then $(-y)$ is preferred to $(-x, p/2; -y, p/2; -y/2, 1-p)$. For simplicity, we define for $x \geqslant 0$, $f(x) = -v(-x)$. Since the value function for losses is convex, f is a concave function of x. Applying prospect theory, with the natural extension of equation 2, we wish to show that

$$\pi(p)f(x) = f(y) \qquad \text{implies}$$

$$f(y) \leqslant f(y/2) + \pi(p/2)[f(y) - f(y/2)] + \pi(p/2)[f(x) - f(y/2)]$$

$$= \pi(p/2)f(x) + \pi(p/2)f(y) + [1 - 2\pi(p/2)]f(y/2).$$

Substituting for $f(x)$ and using the concavity of f, it suffices to show that

$$f(y) \leqslant \frac{\pi(p/2)}{\pi(p)} f(y) + \pi(p/2)f(y) + f(y)/2 - \pi(p/2)f(y)$$

or

$$\pi(p)/2 \leqslant \pi(p/2), \qquad \text{which follows from the subadditivity of } \pi.$$

According to the present theory, attitudes toward risk are determined jointly by v and π, and not solely by the utility function. It is therefore instructive to examine the conditions under which risk aversion or risk seeking are expected to occur. Consider the choice between the gamble (x, p) and its expected value (px). If $x > 0$, risk seeking is implied whenever $\pi(p) > v(px)/v(x)$, which is greater than p if the value function for gains is concave. Hence, overweighting $(\pi(p) > p)$ is necessary but not sufficient for risk seeking in the domain of gains. Precisely the same condition is necessary but not sufficient for risk aversion when $x < 0$. This analysis restricts risk seeking in the domain of gains and risk aversion in the domain of losses to small probabilities, where overweighting is expected to hold.

Indeed these are the typical conditions under which lottery tickets and insurance policies are sold. In prospect theory, the overweighting of small probabilities favors both gambling and insurance, while the S-shaped value function tends to inhibit both behaviors.

Although prospect theory predicts both insurance and gambling for small probabilities, we feel that the present analysis falls far short of a fully adequate account of these complex phenomena. Indeed, there is evidence from both experimental studies [37], survey research [26], and observations of economic behavior, e.g., service and medical insurance, that the purchase of insurance often extends to the medium range of probabilities, and that small probabilities of disaster are sometimes entirely ignored. Furthermore, the evidence suggests that minor changes in the formulation of the decision problem can have marked effects on the attractiveness of insurance [37]. A comprehensive theory of insurance behavior should consider, in addition to pure attitudes toward uncertainty and money, such factors as the value of security, social norms of prudence, the aversiveness of a large number of small payments spread over time, information and misinformation regarding probabilities and outcomes, and many others. Some effects of these variables could be described within the present framework, e.g., as changes of reference point, transformations of the value function, or manipulations of probabilities or decision weights. Other effects may require the introduction of variables or concepts which have not been considered in this treatment.

Shifts of Reference

So far in this paper, gains and losses were defined by the amounts of money that are obtained or paid when a prospect is played, and the reference point was taken to be the status quo, or one's current assets. Although this is probably true for most choice problems, there are situations in which gains and losses are coded relative to an expectation or aspiration level that differs from the status quo. For example, an unexpected tax withdrawal from a monthly pay check is experienced as a loss, not as a reduced gain. Similarly, an entrepreneur who is weathering a slump with greater success than his competitors may interpret a small loss as a gain, relative to the larger loss he had reason to expect.

The reference point in the preceding examples corresponded to an asset position that one had expected to attain. A discrepancy between the reference point and the current asset position may also arise because of recent changes in wealth to which one has not yet adapted [29]. Imagine a person who is involved in a business venture, has already lost 2,000 and is now facing a choice between a sure gain of 1,000 and an even chance to win 2,000 or nothing. If he has not yet adapted to his losses, he is likely to code the problem as a choice between $(-2,000, .50)$ and $(-1,000)$ rather than as a choice between $(2,000, .50)$ and $(1,000)$. As we have seen, the former representation induces more adventurous choices than the latter.

A change of reference point alters the preference order for prospects. In particular, the present theory implies that a negative translation of a choice problem, such as arises from incomplete adaptation to recent losses, increases risk seeking in some situations. Specifically, if a risky prospect $(x, p; -y, 1-p)$ is just acceptable, then $(x-z, p; -y-z, 1-p)$ is preferred over $(-z)$ for $x, y, z > 0$, with $x > z$.

To prove this proposition, note that

$$V(x, p; y, 1-p) = 0 \quad \text{iff} \quad \pi(p)v(x) = -\pi(1-p)v(-y).$$

Furthermore,

$$V(x-z, p; -y-z, 1-p)$$

$$= \pi(p)v(x-z) + \pi(1-p)v(-y-z)$$

$$> \pi(p)v(x) - \pi(p)v(z) + \pi(1-p)v(-y)$$

$$\quad + \pi(1-p)v(-z) \qquad \text{by the properties of } v,$$

$$= -\pi(1-p)v(-y) - \pi(p)v(z) + \pi(1-p)v(-y)$$

$$\quad + \pi(1-p)v(-z) \qquad \text{by substitution,}$$

$$= -\pi(p)v(z) + \pi(1-p)v(-z)$$

$$> v(-z)[\pi(p) + \pi(1-p)] \qquad \text{since } v(-z) < -v(z),$$

$$> v(-z) \qquad \text{by subcertainty.}$$

This analysis suggests that a person who has not made peace with his losses is likely to accept gambles that would be unacceptable to him otherwise. The well known observation [31] that the tendency to bet on long shots increases in the course of the betting day provides some support for the hypothesis that a failure to adapt to losses or to attain an expected gain induces risk seeking. For another example, consider an individual who expects to purchase insurance, perhaps because he has owned it in the past or because his friends do. This individual may code the decision to pay a premium y to protect against a loss x as a choice between $(-x + y, p; y, 1-p)$ and (0) rather than as a choice between $(-x, p)$ and $(-y)$. The preceding argument entails that insurance is likely to be more attractive in the former representation than in the latter.

Another important case of a shift of reference point arises when a person formulates his decision problem in terms of final assets, as advocated in decision analysis, rather than in terms of gains and losses, as people usually do. In this case, the reference point is set to zero on the scale of wealth and the value function is likely to be concave everywhere [39]. According to the present analysis, this formulation essentially eliminates risk seeking, except for gambling with low probabilities. The explicit formulation of decision problems in terms of final assets is perhaps the most effective procedure for eliminating risk seeking in the domain of losses.

Many economic decisions involve transactions in which one pays money in exchange for a desirable prospect. Current decision theories analyze such problems as comparisons between the status quo and an alternative state which includes the acquired prospect minus its cost. For example, the decision whether to pay 10 for the gamble (1,000, .01) is treated as a choice between (990, .01; −10, .99) and (0). In this analysis, readiness to purchase the positive prospect is equated to willingness to accept the corresponding mixed prospect.

The prevalent failure to integrate riskless and risky prospects, dramatized in the isolation effect, suggests that people are unlikely to perform the operation of subtracting the cost from the outcomes in deciding whether to buy a gamble. Instead, we suggest that people usually evaluate the gamble and its cost separately, and decide to purchase the gamble if the combined value is positive. Thus, the gamble (1,000, .01) will be purchased for a price of 10 if π $(.01)v(1,000) + v(−10) > 0$.

If this hypothesis is correct, the decision to pay 10 for (1,000, .01), for example, is no longer equivalent to the decision to accept the gamble (990, .01; −10, .99). Furthermore, prospect theory implies that if one is indifferent between $(x(1 − p), p; −px, 1 − p)$ and (0) then one will not pay px to purchase the prospect (x, p). Thus, people are expected to exhibit more risk seeking in deciding whether to accept a fair gamble than in deciding whether to purchase a gamble for a fair price. The location of the reference point, and the manner in which choice problems are coded and edited emerge as critical factors in the analysis of decisions.

Extensions

In order to encompass a wider range of decision problems, prospect theory should be extended in several directions. Some generalizations are immediate; others require further development. The extension of equations (1) and (2) to prospects with any number of outcomes is straightforward. When the number of outcomes is large, however, additional editing operations may be invoked to simplify evaluation. The manner in which complex options, e.g., compound prospects, are reduced to simpler ones is yet to be investigated.

Although the present paper has been concerned mainly with monetary outcomes, the theory is readily applicable to choices involving other attributes, e.g., quality of life or the number of lives that could be lost or saved as a consequence of a policy decision. The main properties of the proposed value function for money should apply to other attributes as well. In particular, we expect outcomes to be coded as gains or losses relative to a neutral reference point, and losses to loom larger than gains.

The theory can also be extended to the typical situation of choice, where the probabilities of outcomes are not explicitly given. In such situations, decision weights must be attached to particular events rather than to stated probabilities, but they are expected to exhibit the essential properties that were ascribed to the weighting function. For example, if A and B are complementary events and neither is certain, $\pi(A) + \pi(B)$ should be less than unity—a natural analogue to subcertainty.

The decision weight associated with an event will depend primarily on the perceived likelihood of that event, which could be subject to major biases [45]. In addition, decision weights may be affected by other considerations, such as ambiguity or vagueness. Indeed, the work of Ellsberg [10] and Fellner [12] implies that vagueness reduces decision weights. Consequently, subcertainty should be more pronounced for vague than for clear probabilities.

The present analysis of preference between risky options has developed two themes. The first theme concerns editing operations that determine how prospects are perceived. The second theme involves the judgmental principles that govern the evaluation of gains and losses and the weighting of uncertain outcomes. Although both themes should be developed further, they appear to provide a useful framework for the descriptive analysis of choice under risk.

The University of British Columbia
and
Stanford University

Manuscript received November, 1977; final revision received March, 1978.

APPENDIX[2]

In this appendix we sketch an axiomatic analysis of prospect theory. Since a complete self-contained treatment is long and tedious, we merely outline the essential steps and exhibit the key ordinal properties needed to establish the bilinear representation of equation (1). Similar methods could be extended to axiomatize equation (2).

Consider the set of all regular prospects of the form $(x, p; y, q)$ with $p + q < 1$. The extension to regular prospects with $p + q = 1$ is straightforward. Let $\geq$ denote the relation of preference between prospects that is assumed to be connected, symmetric and transitive, and let $\simeq$ denote the associated relation of indifference. Naturally, $(x, p; y, q) \simeq (y, q; x, p)$. We also assume, as is implicit in our notation, that $(x, p; 0, q) \simeq (x, p; 0, r)$, and $(x, p; y, 0) \simeq (x, p; z, 0)$. That is, the null outcome and the impossible event have the property of a multiplicative zero.

Note that the desired representation (equation (1)) is additive in the probability-outcome pairs. Hence, the theory of additive conjoint measurement can be applied to obtain a scale V which preserves the preference order, and interval scales f and g in two arguments such that

$$V(x, p; y, q) = f(x, p) + g(y, q).$$

The key axioms used to derive this representation are:
Independence: $(x, p; y, q) \geq (x, p; y'q')$ iff $(x', p'; y, q) \geq (x', p'; y', q')$.
Cancellation: If $(x, p; y'q') \geq (x', p'; y, q)$ and $(x', p'; y'', q'') \geq (x'', p''; y', q')$, then $(x, p; y'', q'') \geq (x'', p''; y, q)$.
Solvability: If $(x, p; y, q) \geq (z, r) \geq (x, p; y' q')$ for some outcome z and probability r, then there exist y'', q'' such that

$$(x, p; y''q'') \simeq (z, r).$$

It has been shown that these conditions are sufficient to construct the desired additive representation, provided the preference order is Archimedean [8, 25]. Furthermore, since $(x, p; y, q) \simeq (y, q; x, p)$, $f(x, p) + g(y, q) = f(y, q) + g(x, p)$, and letting $q = 0$ yields $f = g$.

Next, consider the set of all prospects of the form (x, p) with a single non-zero outcome. In this case, the bilinear model reduces to $V(x, p) = \pi(p)v(x)$. This is the multiplicative model, investigated in [35] and [25]. To construct the multiplicative representation we assume that the ordering of the probability-outcome pairs satisfies independence, cancellation, solvability, and the Archimedean axiom. In addition, we assume sign dependence [25] to ensure the proper multiplication of signs. It should be noted that the solvability axiom used in [35] and [25] must be weakened because the probability factor permits only bounded solvability.

[2] We are indebted to David H. Krantz for his help in the formulation of this section.

290   D. KAHNEMAN AND A. TVERSKY

Combining the additive and the multiplicative representations yields

$$V(x, p; y, q) = f[\pi(p)v(x)] + f[\pi(q)v(y)].$$

Finally, we impose a new distributivity axiom:

$$(x, p; y, p) \simeq (z, p) \quad \text{iff} \quad (x, q; y, q) \simeq (z, q).$$

Applying this axiom to the above representation, we obtain

$$f[\pi(p)v(x)] + f[\pi(p)v(y)] = f[\pi(p)v(z)]$$

implies

$$f[\pi(q)v(x)] + f[\pi(q)v(y)] = f[\pi(q)v(z)].$$

Assuming, with no loss of generality, that $\pi(q) < \pi(p)$, and letting $\alpha = \pi(p)v(x)$, $\beta = \pi(p)v(y)$, $\gamma = \pi(p)v(z)$, and $\theta = \pi(q)/\pi(p)$, yields $f(\alpha) + f(\beta) = f(\gamma)$ implies $f(\theta\alpha) + f(\theta\beta) = f(\theta\gamma)$ for all $0 < \theta < 1$.

Because f is strictly monotonic we can set $\gamma = f^{-1}[f(\alpha) + f(\beta)]$. Hence, $\theta\gamma = \theta f^{-1}[f(\alpha) + f(\beta)] = f^{-1}[f(\theta\alpha) + f(\theta\beta)]$.

The solution to this functional equation is $f(\alpha) = k\alpha^c$ [1]. Hence, $V(x, p; y, q) = k[\pi(p)v(x)]^c + k[\pi(q)v(y)]^c$, for some $k, c > 0$. The desired bilinear form is obtained by redefining the scales π, v, and V so as to absorb the constants k and c.

REFERENCES

[1] ACZÉL, J.: *Lectures on Functional Equations and Their Applications.* New York: Academic Press, 1966.

[2] ALLAIS, M.: "Le Comportement de l'Homme Rationnel devant le Risque, Critique des Postulats et Axiomes de l'Ecole Americaine," *Econometrica*, 21 (1953), 503–546.

[3] ANDERSON, N. H., AND J. C. SHANTEAU: "Information Integration in Risky Decision Making," *Journal of Experimental Psychology*, 84 (1970), 441–451.

[4] ARROW, K. J.: *Essays in the Theory of Risk-Bearing.* Chicago: Markham, 1971.

[5] BARNES, J. D., AND J. E. REINMUTH: "Comparing Imputed and Actual Utility Functions in a Competitive Bidding Setting," *Decision Sciences*, 7 (1976), 801–812.

[6] COOMBS, C. H.: "Portfolio Theory and the Measurement of Risk," in *Human Judgment and Decision Processes*, ed. by M. F. Kaplan and S. Schwartz. New York: Academic Press, 1975, pp. 63–85.

[7] DAVIDSON, D., P. SUPPES, AND S. SIEGEL: *Decision-making: An Experimental Approach.* Stanford: Stanford University Press, 1957.

[8] DEBREU, G.: "Topological Methods in Cardinal Utility Theory," *Mathematical Methods in the Social Sciences*, ed. by K. J. Arrow, S. Karlin, and P. Suppes. Stanford: Stanford University Press, 1960, pp. 16–26.

[9] EDWARDS, W.: "Subjective Probabilities Inferred from Decisions," *Psychological Review*, 69 (1962), 109–135.

[10] ELLSBERG, D.: "Risk, Ambiguity and the Savage Axioms," *Quarterly Journal of Economics*, 75 (1961), 643–669.

[11] FELLNER, W.: "Distortion of Subjective Probabilities as a Reaction to Uncertainty," *Quarterly Journal of Economics*, 75 (1961), 670–690.

[12] ————: *Probability and Profit—A Study of Economic Behavior Along Bayesian Lines.* Homewood, Illinois: Richard D. Irwin, 1965.

[13] FISHBURN, P. C.: "Mean-Risk Analysis with Risk Associated with Below-Target Returns," *American Economic Review*, 67 (1977), 116–126.

[14] FISHBURN, P. C., AND G. A. KOCHENBERGER: "Two-Piece von Neumann-Morgenstern Utility Functions," forthcoming.

[15] FRIEDMAN, M., AND L. J. SAVAGE: "The Utility Analysis of Choices Involving Risks," *Journal of Political Economy*, 56 (1948), 279–304.

[16] FUCHS, V. R.: "From Bismark to Woodcock: The "Irrational" Pursuit of National Health Insurance," *Journal of Law and Economics*, 19 (1976), 347–359.

[17] GALANTER, E., AND P. PLINER: "Cross-Modality Matching of Money Against Other Continua," in *Sensation and Measurement*, ed. by H. R. Moskowitz et al. Dordrecht, Holland: Reidel, 1974, pp. 65–76.

PROSPECT THEORY   291

[18] GRAYSON, C. J.: *Decisions under Uncertainty: Drilling Decisions by Oil and Gas Operators.* Cambridge, Massachusetts: Graduate School of Business, Harvard University, 1960.

[19] GREEN, P. E.: "Risk Attitudes and Chemical Investment Decisions," *Chemical Engineering Progress,* 59 (1963), 35–40.

[20] GRETHER, D. M., AND C. R. PLOTT: "Economic Theory of Choice and the Preference Reversal Phenomenon," *American Economic Review,* forthcoming.

[21] HALTER, A. N., AND G. W. DEAN: *Decisions under Uncertainty.* Cincinnati: South Western Publishing Co., 1971.

[22] HANSSON, B.: "The Appropriateness of the Expected Utility Model," *Erkenntnis,* 9 (1975), 175–194.

[23] HELSON, H.: *Adaptation-Level Theory.* New York: Harper, 1964.

[24] KEENEY, R. L., AND H. RAIFFA: *Decisions with Multiple Objectives: Preferences and Value Tradeoffs.* New York: Wiley, 1976.

[25] KRANTZ, D. H., D. R. LUCE, P. SUPPES, AND A. TVERSKY: *Foundations of Measurement.* New York: Academic Press, 1971.

[26] KUNREUTHER, H., R. GINSBERG, L. MILLER, P. SAGI, P. SLOVIC, B. BORKAN, AND N. KATZ: *Disaster Insurance Protection: Public Policy Lessons.* New York: Wiley, 1978.

[27] LICHTENSTEIN, S, AND P. SLOVIC: "Reversal of Preference Between Bids and Choices in Gambling Decisions," *Journal of Experimental Psychology,* 89 (1971), 46–55.

[28] MACCRIMMON, K. R., AND S. LARSSON: "Utility Theory: Axioms versus Paradoxes," in *Expected Utility Hypothesis and the Allais Paradox,* ed. by M. Allais and O. Hagen, forthcoming in *Theory and Decision.*

[29] MARKOWITZ, H.: "The Utility of Wealth," *Journal of Political Economy,* 60 (1952), 151–158.

[30] ———: *Portfolio Selection.* New York: Wiley, 1959.

[31] MCGLOTHLIN, W. H.: "Stability of Choices among Uncertain Alternatives," *American Journal of Psychology,* 69 (1956), 604–615.

[32] MOSTELLER, F., AND P. NOGEE: "An Experimental Measurement of Utility," *Journal of Political Economy,* 59 (1951), 371–404.

[33] PRATT, J. W.: "Risk Aversion in the Small and in the Large," *Econometrica,* 32 (1964), 122–136.

[34] RAIFFA H.: *Decision Analysis: Introductory Lectures on Choices Under Uncertainty.* Reading, Massachusetts: Addison-Wesley, 1968.

[35] ROSKIES, R.: "A Measurement Axiomatization for an Essentially Multiplicative Representation of Two Factors," *Journal of Mathematical Psychology,* 2 (1965), 266–276.

[36] SAVAGE, L. J.: *The Foundations of Statistics.* New York: Wiley, 1954.

[37] SLOVIC, P., B. FISCHHOFF, S. LICHTENSTEIN, B. CORRIGAN, AND B. COOMBS: "Preference for Insuring Against Probable Small Losses: Insurance Implications," *Journal of Risk and Insurance,* 44 (1977), 237–258.

[38] SLOVIC, P., AND A. TVERSKY: "Who Accepts Savage's Axiom?," *Behavioral Science,* 19 (1974), 368–373.

[39] SPETZLER, C. S.: "The Development of Corporate Risk Policy for Capital Investment Decisions," *IEEE Transactions on Systems Science and Cybernetics,* SSC-4 (1968), 279–300.

[40] SWALM, R. O.: "Utility Theory—Insights into Risk Taking," *Harvard Business Review,* 44 (1966), 123–136.

[41] TOBIN, J.: "Liquidity Preferences as Behavior Towards Risk," *Review of Economic Studies,* 26 (1958), 65–86.

[42] TVERSKY, A.: "Additivity, Utility, and Subjective Probability," *Journal of Mathematical Psychology,* 4 (1967), 175–201.

[43] ———: "Intransitivity of Preferences," *Psychological Review,* 76 (1969), 31–48.

[44] ———: "Elimination by Aspects: A Theory of Choice," *Psychological Review,* 79 (1972), 281–299.

[45] TVERSKY, A., AND D. KAHNEMAN: "Judgment under Uncertainty: Heuristics and Biases," *Science,* 185 (1974), 1124–1131.

[46] VAN DAM, C.: "Another Look at Inconsistency in Financial Decision-Making," presented at the Seminar on Recent Research in Finance and Monetary Economics, Cergy-Pontoise, March, 1975.

[47] VON NEUMANN, J., AND O. MORGENSTERN, *Theory of Games and Economic Behavior,* Princeton: Princeton University Press, 1944.

[48] WILLIAMS, A. C.: "Attitudes toward Speculative Risks as an Indicator of Attitudes toward Pure Risks," *Journal of Risk and Insurance,* 33 (1966), 577–586.

[2]

The Economic Journal, **92** (December 1982), 805-824
Printed in Great Britain

REGRET THEORY: AN ALTERNATIVE THEORY OF RATIONAL CHOICE UNDER UNCERTAINTY*

Graham Loomes and Robert Sugden

The main body of current economic analysis of choice under uncertainty is built upon a small number of basic axioms, formulated in slightly different ways by von Neumann and Morgenstern (1947), Savage (1954) and others. These axioms are widely believed to represent the essence of rational behaviour under uncertainty. However, it is well known that many people behave in ways that systematically violate these axioms.[1]

We shall initially focus upon a paper by Kahneman and Tversky (1979) which presents extensive evidence of such behaviour. Kahneman and Tversky offer a theory, which they call 'prospect theory', to explain their observations. We shall offer an alternative theory which is much simpler than prospect theory and which, we believe, has greater appeal to intuition.

The following notation will be used throughout. The ith *prospect* is written as X_i. If it offers increments or decrements of wealth $x_1, ..., x_n$ with probabilities $p_1, ..., p_n$ (where $p_1 + ... + p_n = 1$) it may be denoted as $(x_1, p_1; ...; x_n, p_n)$. Null consequences are omitted so that the prospect $(x, p; 0, 1-p)$ is written simply as (x, p). Complex prospects, i.e. those which offer other prospects as consequences, may be denoted as $(X_i, p_i; ...; X_n, p_n)$. We shall use the conventional notation $\succ$, $\succcurlyeq$ and $\sim$ to represent the relations of strict preference, weak preference and indifference. We shall take it that for all prospects X_i and X_k, $X_i \succcurlyeq X_k$ or $X_i \preccurlyeq X_k$; but we shall not in general require that the relation $\succcurlyeq$ is transitive.

I. KAHNEMAN AND TVERSKY'S EVIDENCE

Kahneman and Tversky's experiments offered hypothetical choices between pairs of prospects to groups of university faculty and students. Table 1 lists a selection of their results, which reveal three main types of violation of conventional expected utility theory:

(a) The 'certainty effect' or 'common ratio effect', e.g. the conjunction of $X_5 \prec X_6$ and $X_9 \succ X_{10}$ and the conjunction $X_{13} \prec X_{14}$ and $X_{15} \succ X_{16}$. There is also a 'reverse common ratio effect', e.g. the conjunction of $X_7 \succ X_8$ and $X_{11} \prec X_{12}$.

(b) The original 'Allais Paradox' or 'common consequences effect', e.g. the conjunction of $X_1 \prec X_2$ and $X_3 \succ X_4$.

(c) The 'isolation effect' in two-stage gambles, e.g. the conjunction of $X_9 \succ X_{10}$ and $X_{17} \prec X_{18}$.

---

* We particularly wish to thank Michael Jones-Lee, Mark Machina and two anonymous referees for many helpful suggestions and criticisms.

[1] For a survey and discussion of much of the evidence, see Allais and Hagen (1979) and Schoemaker (1980, 1982).

Table 1 also reveals a 'reflection effect' where a change of sign on the consequences is associated with a reversal of the modal preference and the risk attitude that characterises it, e.g. $X_5 < X_6$ and $X_7 > X_8$. One instance of the reflection effect, revealed in Problems 14 and 14', may be interpreted as an

Table 1

Kahneman and Tversky problem no.	Prospects offered†	Modal preference	Percentage of subjects with modal preference	Characterisation of modal preference
1	$X_1 = (2,500, 0\cdot33;$ $\quad 2,400, 0\cdot66)$ $X_2 = (2,400, 1\cdot00)$	$X_1 < X_2$	82*	Risk averse
2	$X_3 = (2,500, 0\cdot33)$ $X_4 = (2,400, 0\cdot34)$	$X_3 > X_4$	83*	Not clear
3	$X_5 = (4,000, 0\cdot80)$ $X_6 = (3,000, 1\cdot00)$	$X_5 < X_6$	80*	Risk averse
3'	$X_7 = (-4,000, 0\cdot80)$ $X_8 = (-3,000, 1\cdot00)$	$X_7 > X_8$	92*	Risk loving
4	$X_9 = (4,000, 0\cdot20)$ $X_{10} = (3,000, 0\cdot25)$	$X_9 > X_{10}$	65*	Not clear
4'	$X_{11} = (-4,000, 0\cdot20)$ $X_{12} = (-3,000, 0\cdot25)$	$X_{11} < X_{12}$	58	Not clear
7	$X_{13} = (6,000, 0\cdot45)$ $X_{14} = (3,000, 0\cdot90)$	$X_{13} < X_{14}$	86*	Risk averse
8	$X_{15} = (6,000, 0\cdot001)$ $X_{16} = (3,000, 0\cdot002)$	$X_{15} > X_{16}$	73*	Risk loving
10	$X_{17} = (X_5, 0\cdot25)$ $X_{18} = (X_6, 0\cdot25)$	$X_{17} < X_{18}$	78*	Risk averse
14	$X_{19} = (5,000, 0\cdot001)$ $X_{20} = (5, 1\cdot000)$	$X_{19} > X_{20}$	72*	Risk loving
14'	$X_{21} = (-5,000, 0\cdot001)$ $X_{22} = (-5, 1\cdot000)$	$X_{21} < X_{22}$	83*	Risk averse

* Statistically significant at the 0·01 level.
† Consequences are increments or decrements of wealth, measured in Israeli pounds.

example of simultaneous gambling and insurance, since $X_{19} > X_{20}$ indicates a willingness to enter an actuarially fair lottery offering a small probability of a large prize, while $X_{21} < X_{22}$ signifies a willingness to take out actuarially fair insurance against a small probability of a large loss. We also note an interesting mixture of risk attitudes. Sometimes risk aversion is associated with problems involving increments of wealth, e.g. $X_{13} < X_{14}$, and sometimes with problems involving decrements, e.g. $X_{21} < X_{22}$. Likewise, risk loving is sometimes associated with problems involving increments, e.g. $X_{15} > X_{16}$, and sometimes with problems involving decrements, e.g. $X_7 > X_8$.

Simultaneous gambling and insurance, the reflection effect, and the mixture of risk attitudes may all be accommodated by conventional expected utility theory, though only at the cost of certain fairly arbitrary assumptions and some rather unsatisfactory implications.[1] But no accommodation is possible for the effects listed in (a), (b) and (c) above – the observations here simply violate one or more of the conventional axioms.

[1] See Friedman and Savage (1948), Markowitz (1952) and Hirschleifer (1966).

However, in the next section we shall outline the framework of an alternative theory which not only explains the reflection effect and simultaneous gambling and insurance, but also predicts the behaviour described in (*a*), (*b*) and (*c*). We shall then argue that, besides being predictable, such behaviour can be defended as rational, and that our model therefore provides the basis for an alternative theory of rational choice under uncertainty.

II. THE FRAMEWORK OF AN ALTERNATIVE THEORY

We consider an individual in a situation where there is a finite number, n, of alternative *states of the world*, any one of which might occur. Each state j has a probability p_j where $0 < p_j \leqslant 1$ and $p_1 + \ldots + p_n = 1$. These probabilities may be interpreted either as objective probabilities known to the individual or, in the absence of firm knowledge of this kind, as subjective probabilities which represent the individual's degree of belief or confidence in the occurrence of the corresponding states. The individual's problem is to choose between *actions*. Each action is an n-tuple of *consequences*, one consequence for each state of the world. We shall write the consequence of the ith action in the event that the jth state occurs as x_{ij}. Consequences need not take the form of changes in wealth, although in our applications of our theory, we shall interpret x_{ij} as an increment or decrement of wealth, measured relative to some arbitrary level (which need not be the individual's current wealth). Notice that actions, unlike prospects, associate consequences with particular states of the world. Thus a number of different actions might correspond with the same prospect. We shall recognise this difference by using the symbol A for actions, reserving X for prospects. Thus far, our theory has a close resemblance to Savage's, except in that we take probabilities as given, just as von Neumann and Morgenstern do.

A choice problem may involve any number of available actions, but we shall begin by analysing problems where there is only a pair of actions to choose between. All of Kahneman and Tversky's evidence concerns the behaviour of people choosing between pairs of prospects. Choices between three or more actions raise some additional issues, which we shall discuss in Section IV.

Our first assumption is that for any given individual there is a *choiceless utility function* $C(.)$, unique up to an increasing linear transformation, which assigns a real-valued utility index to every conceivable consequence. The significance of the word 'choiceless' is that $C(x)$ is the utility that the individual would derive from the consequence x if he experienced it *without having chosen it*. For example, he might have been compelled to have x by natural forces, or x might have been imposed on him by a dictatorial government. Thus – in contrast to the von Neumann–Morgenstern concept of utility – our concept of choiceless utility is defined independently of choice. Our approach is utilitarian in the classical sense. What we understand by 'choiceless utility' is essentially what Bernoulli and Marshall understood by 'utility' – the psychological experience of pleasure that is associated with the satisfaction of desire. We believe that it is possible to introspect about utility, so defined, and that it is therefore meaningful to talk about utility being experienced in choiceless situations.

Now suppose that an individual experiences a particular consequence as the result of an act of choice. Suppose that he has to choose between actions A_1 and A_2 in a situation of uncertainty. He chooses A_1 and then the jth state of the world occurs. He therefore experiences the consequence x_{1j}. He now knows that, had he chosen A_2 instead, he would be experiencing x_{2j}. Our'introspection suggests to us that the psychological experience of pleasure associated with having the consequence x_{1j} in these circumstances will depend not only on the nature of x_{1j} but also on the nature of x_{2j}. If x_{2j} is a more desirable consequence than x_{1j}, the individual may experience *regret*: he may reflect on how much better his position would have been, had he chosen differently, and this reflection may reduce the pleasure that he derives from x_{1j}. Conversely, if x_{1j} is the more desirable consequence, he may experience what we shall call *rejoicing*. the extra pleasure associated with knowing that, as matters have turned out, he has taken the best decision.

We guess that many readers will recognise these experiences. For example, compare the sensation of losing £100 as the result of an increase in income tax rates, which you could have done nothing to prevent, with the sensation of losing £100 on a bet on a horse race. Our guess is that most people would find the latter experience more painful, because it would inspire regret. Conversely, compare the experience of gaining £100 from an income tax reduction with that of winning £100 on a bet. Now we should guess that most people would find the latter experience more pleasurable. This concept of regret resembles Savage's (1951) notion in some ways, but it will emerge that our theory is very different from his minimax regret criterion.

We shall incorporate the concepts of regret and rejoicing into our theory by means of a *modified utility function*. Suppose that an individual chooses action A_i in preference to action A_k, and that the jth state of the world occurs. The actual consequence is x_{ij} while, had he chosen differently, x_{kj} would have occurred. We shall write $C(x_{ij})$ as c_{ij} and we shall then say that the individual experiences the *modified utility* m^k_{ij} where:

$$m^k_{ij} = M(c_{ij}, c_{kj}). \tag{1}$$

The function $M(.)$ assigns a real-valued index to every ordered pair of choiceless utility indices. The difference between m^k_{ij} and c_{ij} may be interpreted as an increment or decrement of utility corresponding with the sensations of rejoicing or regret. To formulate regret and rejoicing in this way is to assume that the degree to which a person experiences these sensations depends only on the choiceless utility associated with the two consequences in question – 'what is' and 'what might have been' – and is independent of any other characteristics of these consequences. Given this assumption, it is natural to assume in addition that if $c_{ij} = c_{kj}$ then $m^k_{ij} = c_{ij}$: if what occurs is exactly as pleasurable as what might have occurred, there is neither regret nor rejoicing. It is equally natural to assume that $\partial m^k_{ij}/\partial c_{kj} \leqslant 0$: the more pleasurable the consequence that might have been, the more regret – or less rejoicing – is experienced. (We include as a limiting case the possibility that a person might not experience regret or rejoicing at all.) We also make the uncontroversial assumption that $\partial m^k_{ij}/\partial c_{ij} > 0$: that, other things being equal, modified utility increases with choiceless utility.

Our theory is that the individual chooses between actions so as to maximise the mathematical expectation of modified utility. We may define the *expected modified utility* E_i^k of action A_i, evaluated with respect to action A_k, by:

$$E_i^k = \sum_{j=1}^{n} p_j m_{ij}^k. \qquad (2)$$

Faced with a choice between A_i and A_k, the individual will prefer A_i, prefer A_k or be indifferent between them according to whether E_i^k is greater than, less than or equal to E_k^i.

Why, it may be asked, do we assume that people maximise the mathematical expectation of modified utility? Principally because this is a simple assumption which yields implications consistent with empirical evidence. We do not claim that maximising expected modified utility is the only objective that is consistent with a person being rational. However – and we shall say more about this in Section V – we believe that this is not *irrational*, and that, given the utilitarian premises of our approach, there is at least a presumption that people who experience regret and rejoicing will seek to maximise expected modified utility. Notice that, in our theory, someone who does not feel regret or rejoicing at all will simply maximise expected choiceless utility. This special case of our theory corresponds with expected utility theory in its traditional or Bernoullian form, in which utility is interpreted as a psychological experience. To assume that people maximise expected modified utility is to generalise Bernoulli's theory in a very natural way, since the individual who *does* experience rejoicing and regret can be expected to try to anticipate those feelings and take them into account when making a decision under uncertainty.

We shall now show that all of the experimental evidence described in Section I is consistent with regret theory. We shall do this by taking a restricted form of our general theory and by showing that the experimental evidence is consistent with this restricted form.

The particular restriction involves a simplifying assumption about the function $M(.)$. We shall assume that the degree of regret or rejoicing that a person experiences depends only on the difference between the choiceless utility of 'what is' and the choiceless utility of 'what might have been'. This allows us to define a *regret–rejoice function* $R(.)$ which assigns a real-valued index to every possible increment or decrement of choiceless utility, and then to write:

$$m_{ij}^k = c_{ij} + R(c_{ij} - c_{kj}). \qquad (3)$$

It follows from the assumptions we have made about $M(.)$ that $R(0) = 0$ and that $R(.)$ is non-decreasing. In the limiting case in which $R(\xi) = 0$ for all ξ, regret theory would yield exactly the same predictions as expected utility theory. Since we wish to emphasise the differences between the two theories we shall assume that $R(.)$ is strictly increasing and three times differentiable.

Now suppose, as before, that an individual has to choose between the actions A_i and A_k. The individual will have the weak preference $A_i \geqslant A_k$ if and only if:

$$\sum_{j=1}^{n} p_j [c_{ij} - c_{kj} + R(c_{ij} - c_{kj}) - R(c_{kj} - c_{ij})] \geqslant 0. \qquad (4)$$

It is convenient to define a function $Q(.)$ such that for all ξ,

$$Q(\xi) = \xi + R(\xi) - R(-\xi). \tag{5}$$

Thus $A_i \geqslant A_k$ if and only if:

$$\sum_{j=1}^{n} p_j[Q(c_{ij} - c_{kj})] \geqslant 0. \tag{6}$$

$Q(.)$ is an increasing function which has the following property of symmetry: for all ξ, $Q(\xi) = -Q(-\xi)$. Thus to know the value of $Q(\xi)$ for all $\xi \geqslant 0$ is to know the value of $Q(\xi)$ for all ξ.

Three alternative simplifying assumptions about $Q(.)$ can be distinguished:

Assumption 1. $Q(.)$ is linear or equivalently, for all ξ, $R''(\xi) = R''(-\xi)$. It follows immediately from (6) that in this case the individual will behave exactly as if he were maximising expected choiceless utility. Thus regret theory would yield the same predictions as expected utility theory and choiceless utility indices would be operationally indistinguishable from von Neumann–Morgenstern utility indices.

Assumption 2. $Q(.)$ is concave for all positive values of ξ or equivalently, for all $\xi > 0$, $R''(\xi) < R''(-\xi)$.

Assumption 3. $Q(.)$ is convex for all positive values of ξ or equivalently, for all $\xi > 0$, $R''(\xi) > R''(-\xi)$.

On the face of it, there seems to be no *a priori* reason for preferring any one of these assumptions to the others. They are simply alternative assumptions about human psychology and a choice between them should be made mainly on the basis of empirical evidence.[1] We shall therefore show that all the evidence listed in Table 1 is consistent with the restricted form of our theory under Assumption 3. In contrast, Assumption 1 would predict no violations of expected utility theory, while Assumption 2 would predict violations, but in the opposite direction to those generally observed.

III. SOME IMPLICATIONS OF REGRET THEORY

We shall now derive some implications of our theory concerning choices between pairs of *statistically independent* prospects. In our theory, a choice problem cannot be analysed unless a matrix of state-contingent consequences can be specified, and a given pair of prospects (i.e. probability distributions of consequences) may

---

[1] We say 'mainly' because there may be some theoretical reasons for expecting Assumption 3 to be true more often than either of the other two assumptions. Notice that it is a sufficient (but not a necessary) condition for Assumption 1 to hold that, for all ξ, $R'''(\xi) = 0$. Similarly it is sufficient for Assumption 2 to hold that, for all ξ, $R'''(\xi) < 0$; and it is sufficient for Assumption 3 to hold that, for all ξ, $R'''(\xi) > 0$. Consider the following three alternative cases: that $R(.)$ is linear, that it is everywhere convex, and that it is everywhere concave. Linearity entails that for all ξ, $R''(\xi) = 0$ and so entails Assumption 1. Convexity entails that for all ξ, $R'(\xi) > 0$ and $R''(\xi) > 0$. Since, given these two conditions, $R'''(\xi) \leqslant 0$ cannot hold for all ξ, the simplest assumption to make is that for all ξ, $R'''(\xi) > 0$. This in turn entails Assumption 3. Concavity entails that for all ξ, $R'(\xi) > 0$ and $R''(\xi) < 0$. Since $R'''(\xi) \leqslant 0$ cannot hold for all ξ, the simplest assumption to make is again that for all ξ, $R'''(\xi) > 0$. So Assumption 3 fits with both convexity and concavity, while Assumption 1 is appropriate only for linearity – which is only one point on a continuous spectrum which ranges from extreme convexity to extreme concavity.

be capable of being represented by many different matrices. However, the assumption of statistical independence ensures that there is a unique matrix for each pair of prospects. In most of Kahneman and Tversky's experiments, subjects were simply asked to choose between pairs of prospects. In such cases, we suggest, the most natural assumption for subjects to make is that the prospects are independent. Given this assumption, we can show that the evidence of Table 1 is entirely consistent with regret theory. As before, we shall use x_1 and x_2 to represent consequences. We shall use c_1 and c_2 to represent the choiceless utility indices $C(x_1)$ and $C(x_2)$. For simplicity, we choose a transformation of $C(.)$ such that $C(o) = o$; and we assume that $C(.)$ is an increasing function.

(a) The 'common ratio effect', and its reverse

Our theory yields the following prediction, which violates expected utility theory:

Let $X_i = (x_1, \lambda p)$ and $X_k = (x_2, p)$ be independent prospects, where $1 \geqslant p > 0$ and $1 > \lambda > 0$. If there exists some probability $\bar{p}$ such that $X_i \sim X_k$ when $p = \bar{p}$, then (i) (the common ratio effect) if $x_1 > x_2 > 0$, then $p < \bar{p} \Rightarrow X_i \succ X_k$ and $p > \bar{p} \Rightarrow X_i \prec X_k$ and (ii) (the reverse common ratio effect) if $0 > x_2 > x_1$, then $p < \bar{p} \Rightarrow X_i \prec X_k$ and $p > \bar{p} \Rightarrow X_i \succ X_k$.

In proving this result, it is convenient to begin by stating a general property of our theory. Let $X' = (x_1, p_1)$ and $X'' = (x_2, p_2)$ be any two independent prospects. The choice between these prospects may be represented by the matrix given in

Table 2

Action corresponding with prospect	$p_1 p_2$	$p_1(1-p_2)$	$(1-p_2)p_2$	$(1-p_1)(1-p_2)$
X'	x_1	x_1	0	0
X''	x_2	0	x_2	0

Table 2, where each column represents a different state of the world, and the probability that each state will occur is given at the top of its column. Applying Expression (6) to Table 2, we find: that

$$X' \gtrless X'' \text{ iff } p_1 Q(c_1) - p_2 Q(c_2) - p_1 p_2 [Q(c_1) - Q(c_1 - c_2) - Q(c_2)] \gtrless o. \quad (7)$$

Thus in the case where $X_i = (x_1, \lambda p)$ and $X_k = (x_2, p)$,

$$X_i \gtrless X_k \text{ iff } p\{\lambda Q(c_1) - Q(c_2) - \lambda p[Q(c_1) - Q(c_1 - c_2) - Q(c_2)]\} \gtrless o. \quad (8)$$

By assumption, $Q(c)$ is convex for all $c > 0$ so that when $c_1 > c_2 > 0$, $[Q(c_1) - Q(c_1 - c_2) - Q(c_2)] > 0$. Given this inequality, the common ratio effect follows straightforwardly from Expression (8). Conversely, when $0 > c_2 > c_1$, $[Q(c_1) - Q(c_1 - c_2) - Q(c_2)] < 0$; and this implies the reverse common ratio effect.

The evidence of Problems 3 and 4 is consistent with the existence of the common ratio effect. Let $x_1 = 4,000$, $x_2 = 3,000$ and $\lambda = 0.8$. Then if $p = 1.0$, X_5

$= (x_1, \lambda p)$ and $X_6 = (x_2, p)$. If $p = 0.25$, $X_9 = (x_1, \lambda p)$ and $X_{10} = (x_2, p)$. The conjunction of preferences $X_5 \prec X_6$ and $X_9 \succ X_{10}$ violates expected utility theory but is consistent with regret theory (corresponding with the case $1.0 > \bar{p} > 0.25$). Over half of Kahneman and Tversky's subjects had this conjunction of preferences. Further evidence of the common ratio effect is provided by Problems 7 and 8, while Problems 3' and 4' reveal the reverse common ratio effect.

(b) The 'common consequences effect' or Allais paradox

Our theory yields a further prediction, which also violates expected utility theory:

Let $X_i = (x_1, p_1; x_2, \alpha)$ and $X_k = (x_2, p_2 + \alpha)$ be independent prospects where $1 \geqslant p_2 > p_1 > 0$ and $(1 - p_2) \geqslant \alpha \geqslant 0$. If there exists some probability $\bar{\alpha}$ such that $X_i \sim X_k$ when $\alpha = \bar{\alpha}$, then (i) (the common consequences effect) if $x_1 > x_2 > 0$, then $\alpha < \bar{\alpha} \Rightarrow X_i \succ X_k$ and $\alpha > \bar{\alpha} \Rightarrow X_i \prec X_k$ and (ii) (the reverse common consequences effect) if $0 > x_2 > x_1$, then $\alpha < \bar{\alpha} \Rightarrow X_i \prec X_k$ and $\alpha > \bar{\alpha} \Rightarrow X_i \succ X_k$.

According to regret theory,

$$X_i \gtrless X_k \text{ iff } p_1 Q(c_1) - p_2 Q(c_2) - p_1(p_2 + \alpha)[Q(c_1) - Q(c_1 - c_2) - Q(c_2)] \gtreqless 0. \quad (9)$$

Because $Q(c)$ is assumed to be convex for all $c > 0$, $[Q(c_1) - Q(c_1 - c_2) - Q(c_2)]$ is positive if $x_1 > x_2 > 0$ and negative if $0 > x_2 > x_1$. Given these two propositions, Expression (9) entails both the common consequences effect and the reverse common consequences effect.

The evidence of Problems 1 and 2 is consistent with the existence of the common consequences effect. Let $x_1 = 2,500$, $x_2 = 2,400$, $p_1 = 0.33$ and $p_2 = 0.34$. Then if $\alpha = (1 - p_2)$, $X_1 = (x_1, p_1; x_2, \alpha)$ and $X_2 = (x_2, p_2 + \alpha)$. If $\alpha = 0, X_3 = (x_1, p_1; x_2, \alpha)$ and $X_4 = (x_2, p_2 + \alpha)$. The conjunction of preferences $X_1 \prec X_2$ and $X_3 \succ X_4$ violates expected utility theory but is consistent with regret theory (corresponding with the case $0.66 > \bar{\alpha} > 0$). At least 65% of Kahneman and Tversky's subjects had this conjunction of preferences. Kahneman and Tversky did not publish any results relevant to our prediction of a reverse common consequences effect.

(c) The 'isolation effect' in the two-stage gambles

In Kahneman and Tversky's Problem 10, their respondents were offered a two-stage gamble. In the first stage there was a 0.75 probability of the gamble ending with a null consequence and a 0.25 probability of going through to the second stage. Before embarking on the first stage, respondents were asked to choose which of X_5 or X_6 they would prefer if they got through to the second stage.

According to the compound probability axiom of expected utility theory, $X_{17} = (X_5, 0.25)$ is equivalent to $(4,000, 0.20)$ which is simply prospect X_9; and $X_{18} = (X_6, 0.25)$ is equivalent to $(3,000, 0.25)$ which is prospect X_{10}. Thus expected utility theory makes no distinction between Problem 10 and Problem 4.

However, regret theory does make a distinction. The simple prospects X_9 and X_{10} are regarded as statistically independent, and Problem 4 is therefore represented by the matrix of state-contingent consequences shown in Table 3a. By contrast, prospects X_{17} and X_{18} are not statistically independent: the first stage of the gamble is common to both, and if the state occurs under which the gamble comes to an end, the individual receives the same null consequence whichever prospect was chosen. Hence Problem 10 is represented by the matrix of state-contingent consequences shown in Table $3b$. Since Tables $3a$ and $3b$ are

Table $3a$

Action corresponding with prospect	0·60	0·20	0·15	0·05
X_9	0	0	4,000	4,000
X_{10}	0	3,000	0	3,000

Table $3b$

Action corresponding with prospect	0·75	0·20	0·05
X_{17}	0	4,000	0
X_{18}	0	3,000	3,000

different, our theory provides no reason to suppose that an individual will have the same preferences between X_{17} and X_{18} as between X_9 and X_{10}.

Before analysing this example further, we present a result which holds for regret theory in its most general form, and which we shall call the *separability principle*.

Let $S_1, ..., S_n$ be mutually exclusive events (i.e. non-intersecting sets of states of the world) with the non-zero probabilities $p_1, ..., p_n$ where $p_1 + ... + p_n = 1$. Let $S'_1, ..., S'_{n+1}$ be mutually exclusive events with the probabilities $\mu p_1, ..., \mu p_n$, $1 - \mu$, where $0 < \mu < 1$. Let $A_i = (x_{11}, ..., x_{1n})$ and $A_k = (x_{21}, ..., x_{2n})$ be any two actions defined in relation to the events $S_1, ..., S_n$. Let Let A_a and A_b be actions defined in relation to the events $S'_1, ..., S'_{n+1}$, such that $A_a = (x_{11}, ..., x_{1n}, y)$ and $A_b = (x_{21}, ..., x_{2n}, y)$, y being any consequence common to both actions. Then $A_a \geqslant A_b$ if and only if $A_i \geqslant A_k$.

The proof is straightforward. If E_i^k and E_k^i are the expected modified utilities of A_i and A_k, evaluated in relation to one another, then $E_a^b = \mu E_i^k + (1 - \mu) C(y)$ and $E_b^a = \mu E_k^i + (1 - \mu) C(y)$. Hence $E_i^k \geqslant E_k^i \Leftrightarrow E_a^b \geqslant E_b^a$, which entails $A_i \geqslant A_k \Leftrightarrow A_a \geqslant A_b$. The separability principle entails Savage's sure-thing principle as a special case. Let μ remain constant, and let us construct two new actions, A_c and A_d, which are the same as A_a and A_b except that the common consequence y is replaced by the common consequence z. It is clear that $A_i \geqslant A_k \Leftrightarrow A_c \geqslant A_d$, and hence it follows that $A_a \geqslant A_b \Leftrightarrow A_c \geqslant A_d$, which is Savage's sure-thing principle.

Returning to Kahneman and Tversky's evidence, let A_5 and A_6 be the actions corresponding to the independent prospects X_5 and X_6, and let A_{17} and A_{18} be the actions corresponding to X_{17} and X_{18} in Table 3b. Since $E_{17}^{18} = \mu E_5^6 + (1-\mu)C(0)$ and $E_{18}^{17} = \mu E_6^5 + (1-\mu)C(0)$, it follows that $X_5 < X_6 \Leftrightarrow X_{17} < X_{18}$. We have already seen in (a) above that the conjunction $X_5 < X_6$ and $X_9 > X_{10}$ is consistent with our theory. Thus it follows that the conjunction $X_9 > X_{10}$ and $X_{17} < X_{18}$, which violates conventional expected utility, is also consistent with regret theory.

(d) The 'reflection effect'

The results in (a), (b) and (c) above were derived without making any assumption about $C(.)$ other than that it is monotonically increasing. We shall derive our results in (d) and (e) by making the additional assumption that $C(.)$ is linear; and, for convenience, we shall choose a transformation of that linear function such that for all x, $C(x) = x$.

Consider two independent prospects, $X_i = (x_1, p_1)$ and $X_k = (x_2, p_2)$. Their 'reflections' are denoted $X_i' = (-x_1, p_1)$ and $X_k' = (-x_2, p_2)$. From Expression (7) we know that $X_i \geqslant X_k$ if and only if:

$$p_1 Q(x_1) - p_2 Q(x_2) - p_1 p_2 [Q(x_1) - Q(x_1 - x_2) - Q(x_2)] \geqslant 0. \qquad (10)$$

Now exactly the same inequality is necessary and sufficient for $X_i' \leqslant X_k'$. Hence $X_i \geqslant X_k \Leftrightarrow X_i' \leqslant X_k'$. Thus if $C(.)$ is linear, the reflection effect is always observed.

Our intuition is that $C(.)$ is not linear but concave. If this is correct, the reflection effect will not always be observed, and in particular, individuals will reject actuarially fair 50–50 gambles, rather than being indifferent towards them. This point is discussed further in Section V.

(e) Mixed risk attitudes; simultaneous gambling and insurance

Consider two independent prospects which offer an actuarially fair gamble: $X_i = (0, 1)$ and $X_k = (x, p; -px/(1-p), 1-p)$, where $0 < p < 1$ and $x > 0$. Maintaining our previous assumption about $C(.)$ we can apply Expression (7) and rearrange to give:

$$X_i \gtrless X_k \text{ iff } Q\left(\frac{px}{1-p}\right) - \frac{p}{1-p} Q(x) \gtrless 0. \qquad (11)$$

From the assumption that $Q(x)$ is convex for all $x > 0$, it follows that $X_i \gtrless X_k$ as $p \gtrless 0.5$. So the individual will accept small-stake large-prize fair gambles ($p < 0.5$) but reject large-stake small-prize fair gambles ($p > 0.5$). Insurance typically involves paying a small premium to avoid a small probability of a large loss; thus in terms of our theory – which does not use the concept of a 'reference point' – to buy actuarially fair insurance is to reject a large-stake small-prize fair gamble, and thus it is consistent with our theory that an individual may simultaneously insure and accept small-stake large-prize gambles. Moreover, we can construct both small-stake large-prize fair gambles, and large-stake small-prize fair gambles either with all consequences positive or with all consequences negative. Thus a mixture of risk attitudes in both the positive and the negative domain is also consistent with our theory.

These conclusions would require some modification if $C(.)$ were assumed to be concave rather than linear. In this case it can be shown that $X_i > X_k$ if $p \geqslant 0.5$, but it is no longer possible to make a firm prediction when $p < 0.5$. However, if an individual is more strongly influenced by the shape of $Q(.)$ than by the non-linearity of $C(.)$, simultaneous gambling and insurance is still consistent with our theory.

IV. TRANSITIVITY OF PREFERENCES AND MULTI-ACTION PROBLEMS

One controversial property of our theory is that $\geqslant$, the relation of weak preference, is not necessarily transitive. Consider the three actions shown in Table 4 in relation to an individual for whom $C(.)$ is linear. Relative to A_1, A_2 is a large-stake small-prize fair gamble, so that the individual would have the preference $A_1 \succ A_2$ if he had to choose between these two actions. If, as our theory entails, the individual acts according to the separability principle outlined in Section III (c), state S_1 can be ignored in a comparison between A_2 and A_3. Thus, relative to A_2, A_3 is also a large-stake small-prize fair gamble, and so $A_2 \succ A_3$. However, relative to A_1, A_3 is a small-stake large-prize fair gamble, so that $A_3 \succ A_1$. This is not to say that our theory specifically predicts non-transitive pairwise choices (since the $C(.)$ function need not be linear); but such choices can be consistent with the theory.

Table 4

Action	S_1 0·4	S_2 0·2	S_3 0·4
A_1	6	6	6
A_2	0	10	10
A_3	0	0	15

The example shows that an individual will necessarily make non-transitive choices if (i) he acts according to the separability principle (or according to the sure-thing principle), (ii) he always accepts small-stake large-prize fair gambles and (iii) he always rejects large-stake small-prize fair gambles. In the light of the evidence that many people simultaneously gamble and insure one might well argue that a satisfactory theory of choice under uncertainty should encompass the case of the individual who acts according to (ii) and (iii). To say this is to say that either the sure-thing principle or the axiom of transitivity must be dropped. Our theory differs from many of its rivals by dropping transitivity rather than the sure-thing principle.

This raises two questions. One is whether a theory that allows non-transitive pairwise choices can be regarded as a theory of rational behaviour; this issue is discussed in Section V. The other question is how to extend our theory to deal with multi-action choice problems: since in our theory the relation $\geqslant$ is not necessarily transitive, we cannot deal with choices from sets of three or more actions simply by invoking the idea of a preference ordering. We shall argue that the logic of regret and rejoicing points towards a different way of generalising a theory of pairwise choice.

Consider the problem of choosing one action from a set S. The logic of our approach requires that the individual should evaluate each action in turn by asking himself what sensations of regret or rejoicing he would experience in each state of the world, were he to choose that action. Since to choose one action is to reject all of the others, the individual could experience regret or rejoicing in contemplating any of the rejected actions. This idea might be formulated in the following way. As before, we use E_i^k to represent the expected modified utility of choosing action A_i in a situation where the only alternative is action A_k. Now let E_i^S represent the expected modified utility of choosing A_i from the set of actions S. It seems natural to make E_i^S a weighted average of the values of E_i^k for each of the actions A_k in S (other than A_i itself). One way of building this idea into our theory would be to assign *action weights* a_k^S to each action A_k in S, normalised so that these weights sum to unity. Then E_i^S could be defined as:

$$E_i^S = \sum_{k \in S} \frac{a_k^S}{1 - a_i^S} E_i^k \quad (k \neq i). \tag{12}$$

The individual's decision rule, as in the case of pairwise choice, would be to maximise expected modified utility. We hope in the future to formulate a theory of action weights, but in the example which follows we shall just make the simplest assumption – that each action has the same weight.

Table 5

Action	1/3	1/3	1/3
A_1	1	1	1
A_2	0	0	3
A_3	0	3	0

This illustrative example refers to the choice problem shown in Table 5. As before, we shall assume that $C(x) = x$, and we shall make a particular assumption about the regret–rejoice function, that over the relevant range, $R(\xi) = 1 - 0.8^\xi$. In this case, and for these three actions, the relation $\geqslant$ happens to be transitive; $A_2 \succ A_1$, $A_3 \succ A_1$, $A_2 \sim A_3$. It is tempting (but, we suggest, wrong) to conclude from this that A_1 will not be chosen from the set $\{A_1, A_2, A_3\}$. If the action weights are equal to one another then $E_1^S = 0.946$, $E_2^S = 0.899$ and $E_3^S = 0.899$, so that, according to the decision rule, A_1 *will* be chosen. Whether or not such behaviour can be defended as rational will be discussed in Section V.

V. THE POSITIVE AND NORMATIVE STATUS OF REGRET THEORY

The experimental results published by Kahneman and Tversky, wide-ranging though they are, form only a small fraction of the evidence accumulated in the past 30 years to show consistent and repeated violations of certain axioms of expected utility theory. Regret theory is one of a number of alternative theories that have been proposed in the light of this evidence; other theories have been presented by, for example, Allais (1953), Kahneman and Tversky (1979), Fishburn (1981) and Machina (1982). We shall shortly compare our theory with these others, but first let us discuss a possible argument against regret theory.

It might be objected that regret theory is limited to cases where probabilities are known, and that it rests on assumptions about non-observable functions, whereas expected utility theory is built on clear behavioural axioms which make it possible, in principle, to construct a series of choice problems which will reveal the individual's von Neumann–Morgenstern utility function.

While we do not share the methodological position that the only satisfactory theories are those formulated entirely in terms of empirical propositions, we would point out that if an individual behaves according to our model, it is possible in principle to infer from observations of his choices: his subjective probabilities; his $C(.)$ function (unique up to a positive linear transformation); and his $Q(.)$ function (which, for any given transformation of $C(.)$, will be unique up to a positive linear transformation with a fixed point at the origin). Thus each of the assumptions about $C(.)$ and $Q(.)$ required to generate our predictions is in principle capable of empirical refutation. (For an outline of the procedures involved, see the Appendix.)

The other criteria that are commonly used to evaluate positive theories are predictive power, simplicity and generality. Regret theory yields a wide range of firm predictions that are supported by experimental evidence, and it does so on the basis of a remarkably simple structure. Only the two functions $C(.)$ and $Q(.)$ are required. As far as $C(.)$ is concerned, some of the most important predictions of our model – the common ratio effect, the common consequences effect, their reverses, and the isolation effect – require only that this function is monotonically increasing; the additional assumption of linearity yields clear predictions concerning the reflection effect and simultaneous gambling and insurance. In generating all these predictions, the other crucial assumption is simply that $Q(\xi)$ is convex for all $\xi > 0$.

Thus in comparison with Kahneman and Tversky's 'prospect theory' – which is also consistent with all the evidence in Table 1 – regret theory is very simple indeed. Kahneman and Tversky's theory superimposes on expected utility theory a theory of systematic violations. Among their many assumptions are: (i) the rounding of probabilities up or down, and the complete editing out of 'small' probabilities; (ii) a 'decision weight function' which overweights small probabilities, underweights large probabilities, involves 'subcertainty', 'sub-proportionality' and 'subadditivity', and which is discontinuous at both ends, thus implying certain 'quantal effects'; and (iii) a 'value function' (essentially a utility function) which *must* have at least one point of inflection (at the individual's 'reference point' – which may or may not move around) but which can, if required, have no less than five points of inflection. We believe that against the complex and somewhat ad hoc array of assumptions required by prospect theory the principle of Occam's Razor strongly favours the straightforwardness of regret theory.

Allais's and Machina's theories are considerably simpler than prospect theory, but they cannot explain all of the evidence in Table 1. Both of these theories assume that the individual has a preference ordering over prospects. Thus two of the fundamental principles of expected utility theory are retained: that pair-wise choices are transitive and that courses of action associated with identical probability distributions of consequences are equivalent to one another. (We shall call this latter principle the *equivalence axiom*.) Allais and Machina break away from expected utility theory by dropping the independence axiom; given that the equivalence axiom is retained, this amounts to abandoning the sure-thing principle. Our strategy is radically different: we retain the sure-thing principle while jettisoning both the equivalence axiom and the transitivity axiom. As a result we are able to predict the isolation effect in two-stage gambles, a form of observed behaviour that contravenes the equivalence axiom and therefore cannot be explained by either Allais or Machina. We are also able to predict the systematic occurrence of the reflection effect. Although Allais's and Machina's theories are not contradicted by the reflection effect, they do not predict it.

Fishburn's model is more like regret theory (although he does not mention any notion of regret) in that he also drops the transitivity axiom. However, his model is presented in terms of prospects rather than actions, and therefore does not accommodate the isolation effect. On the other hand, if we restrict ourselves to statistically independent prospects (and Fishburn does so – see his p. 9), then our theory and his basic axioms are compatible, and provide an interesting example of how an axiomatic treatment and a more introspective psychologically-based approach may complement each other.[1]

However, having indicated that our theory provides certain predictions and explanations that the other theories mentioned do not, we should make it clear that we are not claiming that regret theory can explain *all* of the behavioural regularities revealed by experimental research into choice under uncertainty. So far we have focused on a number of patterns of behaviour observed by Kahneman and Tversky; but we have not dealt with every one of their observations, still less with the vast amount of evidence accumulated by other researchers.

Some of the experimental findings do not appear to be completely consistent. In relation to this paper, the most significant case concerns the reflection effect. Hershey and Schoemaker (1980*a*) and Payne *et al.* (1980) have published results that show this effect to be not nearly as strong or as general as Kahneman and Tversky's evidence suggests. However, this may not present any great difficulties for regret theory since, as we noted in Section III (*d*), the *general* prediction of the reflection effect requires $C(.)$ to be linear. Instances in which the reflection effect is weak or absent may well be explicable if $C(.)$ is assumed to be concave.

There are nevertheless certain observations that simply cannot be accounted for by regret theory in the form presented here. One example is the 'framing' effect discussed by Tversky and Kahneman (1981) and the very similar 'context' effect observed by Hershey and Schoemaker (1980*b*). In these cases exactly the

---

[1] At a late stage, we have received a copy of a Working Paper by David E. Bell (1981) which is of great interest. Quite independently he has developed a model which also explicitly incorporates a notion of regret, using multi-attribute utility theory along the lines suggested by Keeney and Raiffa (1976). We note that when both models are applied to the same phenomena – the original Allais paradox, simultaneous insuring and gambling, and the reflection effect – the conclusions are strikingly similar.

same choice problem – that is, exactly the same when formulated in terms of a matrix of state-contingent consequences – receives markedly different responses, depending on the way the choice is presented. Another example is the 'translation' effect observed by Payne *et al.* (1980). This effect occurs when an individual prefers one prospect to another, but reverses his preference when the same sum of money is deducted from every consequence of both prospects. The observed pattern of reversal is not predicted by regret theory. Finally, systematic violations of the sure-thing principle have been observed (cf. Moskowitz (1974); Slovic and Tversky (1974)). And although there is some evidence that individuals violate the sure-thing principle much less often than they violate some other axioms (Tversky and Kahneman (1981, footnote 15)), as it stands our theory does not explain that behaviour.

On the other hand, there is some additional evidence that gives further support to regret theory. A particular instance is the form of 'preference reversal' observed by Lindman (1971) and Lichtenstein and Slovic (1971, 1973) and subsequently confirmed, after rigorous testing, by Grether and Plott (1979). This preference reversal occurs when an individual, faced with a pairwise choice between gambles A and B, chooses A; but when asked to consider the two gambles separately, places a higher certainty equivalent value on B. We have shown elsewhere (Loomes and Sugden (1982)) that the most commonly observed reversal pattern is predicted by regret theory even in its restricted form.

Of course, we acknowledge that there is no simple theory that gives a unified explanation of all the experimental evidence, and regret theory is no exception in this respect. But we have tried to construct a theory that explains as much of the evidence as possible on the basis of very few assumptions. We do not believe that choiceless utility and regret are the only factors that influence behaviour under uncertainty, but just that these two factors seem to be particularly significant. Indeed, we have become increasingly convinced by evidence of framing, context and translation effects that the notion of reference points deserves further consideration, although we have not tried to deal with that issue in this paper.

In constructing our theory we have avoided any assumptions of misperceptions or miscalculations by individuals. We do not doubt that in reality misperceptions and miscalculations occur, and sometimes in systematic rather than random ways. Nonetheless, our inclination as economists is to explain as much human behaviour as we can in terms of assumptions about rational and undeceived individuals. Thus we believe that regret theory does more than predict certain systematic violations of conventional expected utility theory: it indicates that such behaviour is not, in any meaningful sense of the word, irrational.

In claiming this we are breaking the terms of a truce that many theorists (with the notable exception of Allais) have tacitly accepted. Proponents of expected utility theory often concede that their theory has serious limitations as a predictive device but insist that its axioms have strong normative appeal as principles of rational choice. Thus Morgenstern (1979, p. 180) argues for expected utility theory on the grounds that 'if people deviate from the theory, an explanation of the theory and of their deviation will cause them to re-adjust their behaviour'. Similarly, Savage (1954, pp. 102–3) admits that when confronted with a pair of

28

choice problems rather like Problems 1 and 2, he behaved in accordance with the common consequences effect and in violation of his own axioms. But, he says, he was able to convince himself that this behaviour was mistaken (though even after realising his 'mistake' he continued to feel an 'intuitive attraction' to that behaviour). At the other side of the truce, proponents of alternative theories have often been willing to accept these claims. Kahneman and Tversky (1979, p. 277) maintain that the departures from expected utility theory that prospect theory describes 'must lead to normatively unacceptable consequences' which a decision-maker would, if he realised the error of his ways, wish to correct. Similarly, Machina (1982, p. 277) notes the 'normative appeal' of the axioms of expected utility theory before going on to propose a positive theory that dispenses with one of these axioms.

However, we shall challenge the idea that the conventional axioms constitute the only acceptable basis for rational choice under uncertainty. We shall argue that it is no less rational to act in accordance with regret theory, and that conventional expected utility theory therefore represents an unnecessarily restrictive notion of rationality.

Regret theory rests on two fundamental assumptions: first, that many people experience the sensations we call regret and rejoicing; and second, that in making decisions under uncertainty, they try to anticipate and take account of those sensations.

In relation to the first assumption, it seems to us that psychological experiences of regret and rejoicing cannot properly be described in terms of the concept of rationality: a choice may be rational or irrational, but an experience is just an experience. As far as the second assumption is concerned, if an individual does experience such feelings, we cannot see how he can be deemed irrational for consistently taking those feelings into account.

We do not claim that acting according to our theory is the *only* rational way to behave. Nor do we suggest that all individuals who act according to our theory must violate the conventional axioms. Some individuals may experience no regret or rejoicing at all, while some others may have linear $Q(.)$ functions: in these special cases of our theory, we would predict that the individual's behaviour would conform with all the conventional axioms.

On the other hand, individuals with non-linear $Q(.)$ functions of the kind described in this paper may consistently and knowingly violate the axioms of transitivity and equivalence without ever accepting, even after the most careful reflection, that they have made a mistake. So these axioms do not necessarily have the self-evident or overwhelming normative appeal that many theorists suppose. We shall now try to show why we do not accept the idea that the transitivity and equivalence axioms are necessary conditions for rational choice under uncertainty.

Underlying those two axioms is a common idea: that the value placed on any action A_i depends only on the interaction between, on the one hand, the probability-weighted consequences offered by A_i and, on the other hand, the individual's pattern of tastes, including his attitude to risk.

That is what is symbolised when, for any individual, an expected utility number is assigned to an action, that expected utility number being quite independent of the range and nature of the available alternative actions. From this idea, that there is some value in 'having A_i' which is quite independent of the value of 'having A_k', and that if 'having A_i' gives more value than 'having A_k' then $A_i \succ A_k$, it follows that there must exist a complete and transitive preference ordering over all actions.

It also follows that the particular state pattern of consequences is of no special significance: if each action is evaluated independently, it does not matter how the consequence of that action under any state of the world compares with the consequence(s) of any other action(s) under the same state. Thus only the probability distribution of consequences matters, and all actions, simple or complex, which share the same probability distribution will be assigned the same expected utility number and must be regarded as equivalent for the purposes of choice decisions.

But if people experience regret and rejoicing, these arguments are illegitimate. In regret theory the proposition $A_i \succcurlyeq A_k$ cannot be read as 'having A_i is at least as preferred as having A_k'; it should rather be read as 'choosing A_i and simultaneously rejecting A_k is at least as preferred as choosing A_k and simultaneously rejecting A_i'. Thus the transitivity of the relation 'is at least as preferred as' (which we do not dispute) does not entail the transitivity of our relation $\succcurlyeq$; and so non-transitive choices do not indicate any logical inconsistency on the part of the decision-maker.

The idea that non-transitive choices are irrational is sometimes argued as follows. Suppose (as in the example discussed in connection with Table 4 in Section IV) that there are three actions A_1, A_2, A_3, such that $A_1 \succ A_2$, $A_2 \succ A_3$, and $A_3 \succ A_1$. Then, it is said, no choice can be made from the set $\{A_1, A_2, A_3\}$ without there being an inconsistency with one of the original preference statements: whichever action is chosen, another is preferred to it (cf. MacKay (1980, p. 90)). The principle that is being invoked here is Chernoff's axiom: if A_i is chosen from some set S, and if S' is a subset of S that contains A_i, then A_i must be chosen from S'. But we suggest the appeal of this axiom derives from the supposition that the value of choosing an action is independent of the nature and combination of the actions simultaneously rejected; and regret theory does not accept this supposition. Since $A_1 \succ A_2$ means only that choosing A_1 from the set $\{A_1, A_2\}$ is preferred to choosing A_2 from the set $\{A_1, A_2\}$ there is no implication that choosing A_1 from the set $\{A_1, A_2, A_3\}$ is preferred to choosing A_2 from the set $\{A_1, A_2, A_3\}$. A similar argument applies to the example discussed in connection with Table 5 in Section IV, where (despite the fact that the relation $\succcurlyeq$ happens to be transitive) there is another violation of Chernoff's axiom.

A second common objection to non-transitivity runs like this. If someone prefers A_1 to A_2, A_2 to A_3, and A_3 to A_1, every one of the actions is less preferred than another; so might he not get locked into an endless chain of choice in which he can never settle on any one action? Worse, might not a skilful bookmaker capture all his wealth by confronting him with a suitably constructed sequence of pairwise choices? But these objections rest on a fallacy. To suppose that the individual can get locked into a cycle of choices, it is necessary to suppose that all three actions are feasible. But if this is indeed the case, then propositions about pairwise choices – about how choices are made when there are only two feasible actions – are not relevant. The bookmaker can bankrupt his client only if he can successively persuade him to believe in each of a long chain of mutually inconsistent propositions about the feasible set.

Finally, there is no reason why the equivalence axiom should be regarded as a necessary condition for rational choice, even when the choice is between two simple actions with identical probability distributions of consequences. Consider

Table 6

Action	0·25	0·25	0·25	0·25
A_i	3	2	1	0
A_k	0	3	2	1

A_i and A_k in Table 6. If each action were evaluated independently, there would be no grounds for preferring 'having A_i' to 'having A_k', or vice versa. But in our model the decision is between 'choosing A_i and simultaneously rejecting A_k' and 'choosing A_k and simultaneously rejecting A_i'. These two alternatives are associated with different probability mixes of regret and rejoicing. (In terms of our theory, to choose A_i and reject A_k is to incur a 0·25 probability of $R(+3)$ and a 0·75 probability of $R(-1)$, while to choose A_k and reject A_i is to incur a 0·25 probability of $R(-3)$ and a 0·75 probability of $R(+1)$.) So for an individual who experiences regret and rejoicing, the two courses of action cannot be regarded as identical. It would therefore not be unreasonable for such an individual to prefer one to the other.

VI. CONCLUSION

The evidence presented by Kahneman and Tversky and many others points to a number of cases where commonly observed patterns of choice violate conventional expected utility axioms. The fact that these violations are neither small-scale nor randomly distributed may indicate that there are some important factors affecting many people's choices which have been overlooked or misspecified by conventional theory.

We suggest that one significant factor is an individual's capacity to anticipate feelings of regret and rejoicing. We therefore offer an alternative model which takes those feelings into consideration. This model yields a range of predictions consistent with the behaviour listed in Table 1 and provides an account of these and other choice phenomena which conventional theory has so far failed to explain.

That is the positive side of regret theory. But we believe that our approach also has strong normative implications. We have argued that our theory describes a form of behaviour which, although contravening the axioms of expected utility theory, is rational. Thus, while we do not suggest that behaving according to those conventional axioms is irrational, we *do* suggest that those axioms constitute an excessively restrictive definition of rational behaviour.

University of Newcastle
Date of receipt of final typescript: April 1982

Appendix: *Inferring subjective probabilities and $C(.)$ and $Q(.)$ functions from choices*

The following procedure will reveal, for any individual, which of two events has the higher subjective probability. Let S_1 and S_2 be any two non-intersecting and non-empty events (i.e. sets of states of the world). Let S_3 be the event that comprises all those states of the world not in S_1 or S_2. Let x, y, z be any three consequences such that the person in question prefers x to y (under certainty). Consider the two actions $A_i = (x, y, z)$ and $A_k = (y, x, z)$, which are defined in relation to the events S_1, S_2, S_3. It then follows from the separability principle (see Section III) that A_i is preferred to, indifferent to, or less preferred than A_k as the subjective probability of S_1 is greater than, equal to, or less than that of S_2. This procedure is broadly similar to the one proposed by Savage (1954) for inferring subjective probabilities for individuals who behave according to his postulates.

The restricted form of our theory (see Section III) uses two functions for the analysis of modified utility: $C(.)$ and $Q(.)$. $C(.)$ can be identified, up to a positive linear transformation, by confronting the individual with choices involving 50–50 gambles. Consider any two prospects of the form $X_i = (x_1, 1)$, $X_k = (x_2, 0.5; x_3, 0.5)$ where $x_3 > x_1 > x_2$, so that the corresponding choiceless utility indices are $c_3 > c_1 > c_2$. Then:

$$X_i \lessgtr X_k \text{ iff } 0.5\, Q(c_1 - c_2) - 0.5\, Q(c_3 - c_1) \gtrless 0.$$

But since $Q(.)$ is increasing, it follows that:

$$X_i \lessgtr X_k \text{ iff } 0.5\,(c_1 - c_2) - 0.5\,(c_3 - c_1) \gtrless 0.$$

Thus in this case, the individual chooses *as though* maximising expected *choiceless* utility. So $C(.)$ can be identified from experiments in much the same way as von Neumann–Morgenstern utility functions are identified.

If $C(.)$ is known, and if a particular transformation has been chosen, it is possible to define consequences in terms of their choiceless utilities. Let x_1 and x_2 be consequences such that $c_1 = 0$ and $c_2 = -1$. Let x_3 be any consequence such that $c_3 = \xi$ where $\xi > 0$ and $\xi \neq 1$. Consider the two prospects $X_i = (x_1, 1)$ and $X_h = (x_2, p; x_3, 1-p)$. Then:

$$X_i \lessgtr X_h \text{ iff } \frac{Q(\xi)}{Q(1)} \gtrless \frac{p}{1-p}.$$

Thus if one can find a value of p such that the individual is indifferent between X_i and X_h it is possible to infer the value of $Q(\xi)/Q(1)$. So if $Q(1)$ is set equal to any arbitrary positive value, the value of $Q(\xi)$ can then be determined by experiment for all $\xi > 0$; hence the concavity, convexity or linearity of $Q(.)$ over any interval can be established.

REFERENCES

Allais, M. (1953). 'Le comportement de l'homme rationnel devant le risque; critique des postulats et axiomes de l'ecole Americaine.' *Econometrica*, vol. 21, pp. 503-46.
—— and Hagen, O. (1979). *Expected Utility Hypothesis and the Allais Paradox*. Dordrecht: Reidel.
Bell, D. E. (1981). 'Regret in decision-making under uncertainty.' *Harvard Business School Working Paper* 82-15.
Fishburn, P. C. (1981). 'Nontransitive measurable utility.' *Bell Laboratories Economics Discussion Paper* 209.
Friedman, M. and Savage, L. J. (1948). 'The utility analysis of choices involving risks.' *Journal of Political Economy*, vol. 56, pp. 279-304.
Grether, D. M. and Plott, C. R. (1979). 'Economic theory of choice and the preference reversal phenomenon.' *American Economic Review*, vol. 69, pp. 623-38.
Hershey, J. C. and Schoemaker, P. J. H. (1980a). 'Prospect theory's reflection hypothesis: a critical examination.' *Organizational Behavior and Human Performance*, vol. 25, pp. 395-418.
—— and —— (1980b). 'Risk taking and problem context in the domain of losses: an expected utility analysis.' *Journal of Risk and Insurance*, vol. 47, pp. 111-32.
Hirschleifer, J. (1966). 'Investment decisions under uncertainty: applications of the state preference approach.' *Quarterly Journal of Economics*, vol. 80, pp. 252-77.
Kahneman, D. and Tversky, A. (1979). 'Prospect Theory: an analysis of decision under risk.' *Econometrica*, vol. 47, pp. 263-91.
Keeney, R. L. and Raiffa, H. (1976). *Decisions with multiple objectives*. New York: Wiley.
Lichtenstein, S. and Slovic, P. (1971). 'Reversals of preference between bids and choices in gambling decisions.' *Journal of Experimental Psychology*, vol. 89, pp. 46-55.
—— and —— (1973). 'Response-induced reversals of preference in gambling: an extended replication in Las Vegas.' *Journal of Experimental Psychology*, vol. 101, pp. 16-20.
Lindman, H. R. (1971). 'Inconsistent preferences among gambles.' *Journal of Experimental Psychology*, vol. 89, pp. 390-7.
Loomes, G. and Sugden, R. (1982). 'A rationale for preference reversal.' *Newcastle Discussion Papers in Economics* No. 63.
Machina, M. J. (1982). '"Expected utility" analysis without the independence axiom.' *Econometrica*, vol. 50, pp. 277-323.
MacKay, A. F. (1980). *Arrow's Theorem: the Paradox of Social Choice*. New Haven, Conn.: Yale University Press.
Markowitz, H. M. (1952). 'The utility of wealth.' *Journal of Political Economy*, vol. 60, pp. 151-8.
Morgenstern, O. (1979), 'Some reflections on utility.' In *Expected Utility Hypotheses and the Allais Paradox*. (Ed. M. Allais and O. Hagen). Dordrecht: Reidel.
Moskowitz, H. (1974). 'Effects of problem presentation and feedback on rational behavior in Allais and Morlat type problems.' *Decision Sciences*, vol. 5, pp. 225-42.
Payne, J. W., Laughhunn, D. J. and Crum, R. L. (1980). 'Translation of gambles and aspiration level effects in risky choice behavior.' *Management Science*, vol. 26, pp. 1039-60.
Savage, L. J. (1951). 'The theory of statistical decision.' *Journal of the American Statistical Association*, vol. 46, pp. 55-67.
—— (1954). *The Foundations of Statistics*. New York: Wiley.
Schoemaker, P. J. H. (1980). *Experiments on Decisions under Risk: the Expected Utility Hypothesis*. Boston: Martinus Nijhoff.
—— (1982). 'The expected utility model: its variants, purposes, evidence and limitations.' *Journal of Economic Literature*, forthcoming.
Slovic, P. and Tversky, A. (1974). 'Who accepts Savage's axiom?' *Behavioral Science*, vol. 19, pp. 368-73.
Tversky, A. and Kahneman, D. (1981). 'The framing of decisions and the psychology of choice.' *Science*, vol. 211, pp. 453-8.
von Neumann, J. and Morgenstern, O. (1947). *Theory of Games and Economic Behaviour*. (2nd edition). Princeton: Princeton University Press.

[3]
ECONOMETRICA

VOLUME 50   MARCH, 1982   NUMBER 2

"EXPECTED UTILITY" ANALYSIS WITHOUT THE INDEPENDENCE AXIOM[1]

By Mark J. Machina[2]

Experimental studies have shown that the key behavioral assumption of expected utility theory, the so-called "independence axiom," tends to be *systematically* violated in practice. Such findings would lead us to question the empirical relevance of the large body of literature on the behavior of economic agents under uncertainty which uses expected utility analysis. The first purpose of this paper is to demonstrate that the basic concepts, tools, and results of expected utility analysis do not depend on the independence axiom, but may be derived from the much weaker assumption of smoothness of preferences over alternative probability distributions. The second purpose of the paper is to show that this approach may be used to construct a simple model of preferences which ties together a wide body of observed behavior toward risk, including the Friedman-Savage and Markowitz observations, and both the Allais and St. Petersburg Paradoxes.

1. INTRODUCTION

As an approach to the theory of individual behavior toward risk, the expected utility model is characterized by the simplicity and normative appeal of its axioms, the familiarity of the notions it employs (utility functions and mathematical expectation), the elegance of its characterizations of various types of behavior in terms of properties of the utility function (risk aversion by concavity, the degree of risk aversion by the Arrow-Pratt measure, etc.), and the large number of results it has produced. It is thus not surprising that most current theoretical research in the economics of uncertainty, as well as virtually all applied work in the field (e.g. optimal trade, investment, or search under uncertainty)[3] is undertaken in the expected utility framework.[4]

Nevertheless, the expected utility hypothesis is still a particular hypothesis concerning individual preferences over alternative probability distributions over wealth. In the years following its revival by von Neumann and Morgenstern in the *Theory of Games and Economic Behavior* [99], it became generally recognized that expected utility theory depended crucially on the empirical validity of the

[1] An earlier version of this paper was presented to the 1979 North American Summer Meetings of the Econometric Society, Montreal, June, 1979.

[2] I would like to thank Vince Crawford, Peter Diamond, Mark Durst, Ted Groves, Frank Hahn, Klaus Heiss, Walt Heller, David Kreps, Andreu Mas-Colell, Eric Maskin, Jim Mirrlees, David Newbery, Mike Rothschild, anonymous referees, the Editor, and especially Franklin Fisher for helpful comments on this material. They are, of course, not responsible for errors. I am also grateful to the National Science Foundation and the Social Science Research Council for financial support.

[3] See, for example, Helpman and Razin [42] and Levhari and Srinivasan [51].

[4] The one significant exception to this statement is the "state preference" approach to behavior toward risk (see, for example, Debreu [18, Ch. 7] or Hirshleifer [44]). However, since this approach works with distributions of payoffs over states rather than with distributions of probability mass over payoffs, many of the issues discussed in the present paper do not bear directly on this approach.

so-called "independence axiom."[5] One of several equivalent versions of this axiom reads "a risky prospect A is weakly preferred (i.e. preferred or indifferent) to a risky prospect B if and only if a $p:(1-p)$ chance of A or C respectively is weakly preferred to a $p:(1-p)$ chance of B or C, for arbitrary positive probability p and risky prospects A, B, and C." In particular, the role of the other axioms of the theory, which essentially amount to the assumptions of completeness and continuity of preferences, is essentially to establish the *existence* of a continuous preference function over probability distributions, in much the same way as is done in standard consumer theory.[6] It is the independence axiom which gives the theory its empirical content by imposing a restriction on the *functional form* of the preference function. It implies that the preference function may be represented as the expectation with respect to the given distribution of a fixed utility function defined over the set of possible outcomes (i.e. ultimate wealth levels). In other words, the preference function is constrained to be a linear functional over the set of distribution functions, or, as commonly phrased, "linear in the probabilities."

The high normative appeal of the independence axiom has been widely (although not universally)[7] acknowledged. However, the evidence concerning its *descriptive* validity is not quite as favorable. The example of its systematic violation in practice which is perhaps best known to economists is the famous "Allais Paradox." This example (described below) consists of asking individuals to choose a most preferred prospect out of each of two specific pairs of risky prospects. Researchers have found that the particular choices made by the great majority of subjects in this situation violate the independence axiom, and hence are inconsistent with the hypothesis of expected utility maximization.

In addition, a large amount of research on the validity of the expected utility model has appeared in the psychology literature, where experimenters have similarly discovered that preferences are in general *not* linear in the probabilities. Edwards, in one of his reviews of this literature, asserted of expected utility maximization that "in 1954 it was already clear that it too [i.e. as well as expected value maximization] does not fit the facts" [26, p. 474].

Although these findings have led some researchers, both psychologists and economists, to propose alternative theories of behavior toward risk,[8] expected utility theory continues to be the dominant framework of analysis in the economics literature. Since it is likely to remain so in the future, it would seem crucial that we have some idea of the descriptive realism of the theory in light of the apparent invalidity of its key behavioral assumption. In other words, "*how*

---

[5] Although this axiom did not appear explicitly in the original von Neumann-Morgenstern axiom system, Malinvaud [59] has shown it to have been implicitly assumed in their pre-axiomatic formulation. Two important early formulations of the axiom are those of Marschak [61] and Samuelson [80], each of whom refer to similar work by other authors.

[6] See, for example, Debreu [18, Ch. 4].

[7] See the debate between Wold, Schackle, Savage, Manne, Charnes, and Samuelson on the *a priori* plausibility of the independence axiom in the October, 1952 issue of this journal, as well as the remarks in Allais [3, pp. 99-103].

[8] See, for example, the set of models discussed in Section 2.5 below.

robust are the concepts, tools, and results of expected utility theory to failures of the independence axiom?"

The first purpose of this paper is to demonstrate that expected utility analysis is in fact quite robust to failures of the independence axiom. Specifically, it is shown that, far from depending on the independence axiom (i.e. linearity of the preference functional), the basic concepts, tools, and results of expected utility analysis may be derived by merely assuming smoothness of preferences (i.e. that the preference functional is differentiable in the appropriate sense). This implies that while the independence axiom, and hence the expected utility hypothesis, may not be empirically valid, the implications and predictions of theoretical studies which use expected utility analysis typically *will* be valid, provided preferences are smooth. Several such results, including the Arrow-Pratt theorem, are formally proven for the general case of smooth preferences.

The second purpose of this paper is to demonstrate that this general analytic approach, termed "generalized expected utility analysis," may be used to construct a simple, yet evidently quite powerful model of individual behavior toward risk. Specifically, it is shown that two simple hypotheses concerning the shape of a fixed nonlinear preference functional over probability distributions serve to generate predictions consistent with (i) the typical behavior exhibited in the Allais Paradox, (ii) other experimental evidence regarding systematic violations of the independence axiom, (iii) the general observations on insurance and lotteries made by Friedman and Savage in their classic article on the expected utility hypothesis, (iv) the subsequent observation by Markowitz and others that preferences over alternative gambles are relatively independent of the level of current wealth (and hence that utility functions apparently shift when wealth changes), and (v) the typical behavior exhibited in the St. Petersburg Paradox and its generalizations. Thus, a number of seemingly unrelated aspects of behavior toward risk are seen to be jointly consistent with the hypothesis that the individual is maximizing a fixed preference functional defined over distributions, which in addition is particularly simple in shape.

Section 2 of this paper offers a historical overview of the expected utility model as a descriptive model, treating each of the above five behavioral observations, and discussing the various, and often ad hoc, modifications of the model which have been made to account for some of them. The applications of the tools and theorems of expected utility theory to the analysis of general nonlinear preference functionals is developed in Section 3. In Section 4 this approach is used to construct a simple model of preferences which is consistent with (and in some cases predicts) each of the above five aspects of behavior. Among other things, it is argued that this model offers (i) a simple characterization of the exact nature of observed violations of the independence axiom, (ii) a reconciliation of the relative independence of gambling behavior to current wealth with the hypothesis of a fixed preference ranking of probability distributions over ultimate wealth, and (iii) a resolution of the debate in the expected utility literature concerning the boundedness of the utility function. The paper concludes (Section 5) with some brief remarks on the topics of testing the model and applications of the analysis to the study of social welfare functionals.

2. EXPECTED UTILITY MAXIMIZATION AS A DESCRIPTIVE MODEL

In this section we consider several classes of observations concerning individual preferences over risky prospects, and give an account of how the expected utility model has been used, and in some cases adapted and modified, to account for these various types of behavior.

2.1. *Insurance, Lotteries, Skewness Preference, and the Friedman-Savage Hypothesis*

The primary motivation for the classic article by Friedman and Savage [33] came from their observations that "the empirical evidence for the willingness of persons of all income classes to buy insurance is extensive" [33, p. 285, or 91, p. 66], that "the empirical evidence for the willingness of individuals to purchase lottery tickets, or engage in similar forms of gambling, is also extensive" [33, p. 286, or 91, p. 67], and their belief that a large number of individuals purchase both.[9] They offer as a von Neumann-Morgenstern utility function which explains these particular observations one which has the form shown in Figure 1. The key aspect of such a utility function is that it is concave, and hence locally risk averse, about low outcome levels (i.e. low levels of ultimate wealth), linear (to a second order approximation) and hence locally risk neutral at the inflection point, and convex (locally risk loving) for high outcome values.[10]

In addition to its well known implications concerning the purchase of insurance and lottery tickets, another implication of the utility function of Figure 1, noted by Markowitz [60, p. 156], is that an individual with such a utility function will tend to prefer positively skewed distributions (ones with large right tails) over negatively skewed ones (ones with large left tails). The purchase of a lottery ticket, for example, induces a positively skewed distribution if initial wealth was certain, and insuring against a small probability-low outcome event transforms a negatively skewed distribution into a symmetric (certain) one. Since a mean preserving increase in risk (see [74]) which is "centered" in the upper tail of a symmetric distribution induces positive skewness, and one which is centered in the lower tail induces negative skewness, a preference for positive over negative skewness suggests that the individual will tend to prefer increases in risk in the upper tail of a given initial distribution of wealth over equivalent risk increases in the lower tail. Such a tendency is clearly an implication of the utility function of Figure 1.

The notion of a relative preference for (equivalently, a lower aversion to) risk increases in the upper rather than the lower tail of an initial distribution may be formalized by adopting the following definition:

---

[9] See also the comments of Adam Smith and Alfred Marshall in this regard quoted in [33, p. 284 or 91, p. 65], as well as the reference to a distant relative of the author [33, p. 280 or 91, p. 58].

[10] Mention should be made of the various attempts (e.g. Flemming [32], Hakansson [39], Kim [47], and Kwang [50]) to reconcile the simultaneous purchase of insurance and lottery tickets with the assumption of general risk aversion via such assumptions as indivisibility of expenditure, imperfect capital markets, etc.

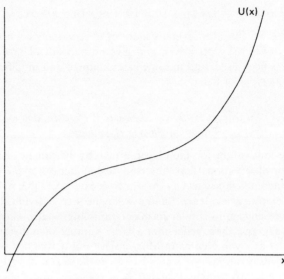

FIGURE 1

DEFINITION: If $F(\cdot)$ and $F^*(\cdot)$ are two cumulative distribution functions over a wealth interval $[0, M]$, then F^* is said to differ from F by a *simple compensated spread* if the individual is indifferent between F and F^*, and if $[0, M]$ may be partitioned into disjoint intervals I_L and I_R (with I_L to the left of I_R) such that $F^*(x) \geqq F(x)$ for all x in I_L and $F^*(x) \leqq F(x)$ for all x in I_R.[11]

A relative preference for risk increases in the upper rather than the lower tail of an initial distribution then implies that, if a given set of changes in the probabilities of the elements of the set $A \subset [0, M]$ can be represented as a sequence of simple compensated spreads, then the same respective changes in the probabilities of the set $A + c = \{x + c \mid x \in A\}$ are weakly preferred if the constant c is positive, and weakly not preferred if it is negative.[12]

[11] This definition is motivated by the "single crossing property" of Diamond and Stiglitz [19], and it is clear that when the individual is an expected utility maximizer, sequences of simple compensated spreads are equivalent to mean utility preserving increases in risk [19, pp. 341–345].

[12] It is important to distinguish between this behavioral principle and the Kahneman and Tversky "reflection effect" [46, pp. 268–269], which states that the preference ranking over a pair of prospects (defined in terms of gains and losses) reverses when all the outcome values are reversed in sign. Since such an effect concerns the relative rankings within two *distinct* pairs of prospects, and since any spread of probability mass relating the initial pair of prospects is itself "reflected," it is quite distinct from the present principle, which concerns the ranking of a *single* pair of prospects, each of which is obtained from a given initial distribution by a spread which, though horizontally translated, is not reflected. Note that while Kahneman and Tversky's associated hypothesis of "risk aversion in the positive domain [i.e. among prospects involving gains] . . . accompanied by risk seeking in the negative domain" [46, p. 268] is supported by their examples 7, 7', 10, 11, 12, 13, and 13', preferences in problems 1, 3, and 3' may be explained by positive skewness preference, and in problems 2, 4, and 4' by the differences in the expected values of the prospects. Examples 8, 8', 14, and 14', on the other hand, actually contradict their hypothesis.

There is evidence to suggest that positive skewness preference and a relative preference for risk increases in the upper rather than the lower tails of distributions are also exhibited by an important class of individuals not characterized by the utility function of Figure 1, namely global risk averters. Tsaing [**94**, pp. 359–360] and Hirshleifer [**45**, pp. 282–283] have argued that positive skewness preference is evidently prevalent among risk averse investors, the former pointing to a number of financial devices which allow investors to increase the positive skewness of their returns. Indeed, such preferences were espoused as long ago as the eighteenth century by Condorcet (see [**82**, pp. 44–45]). Evidence of a relative preference for risk increases in the upper as opposed to the lower tail of an initial distribution has also been uncovered by Mosteller and Nogee. At one point in their experiment [**66**, pp. 386–389], subjects were asked to leave written instructions to an "agent" who would be faced with a sequence of gambling opportunities in their absence. Although these instructions were predominantly risk averse, they frequently suggested that the agent play more liberally when doing well. In other words, there were some gambles the agent was instructed always to take, and some, never to take. Such a policy would result in some particular distribution of winnings. The designation of additional gambles which should be taken only if cumulative winnings have been high enough indicates that there are some further increases in risk which would be preferred if they occurred in the upper tail of this distribution, but not preferred if they occurred in the lower tail.[13]

2.2. *The St. Petersburg Paradox, the Structure of Lotteries, and the Boundedness of Utility*

At a later point in their article [**33**, pp. 296–297, or **91**, pp. 84–85], Friedman and Savage point out that an individual with a utility function as in Figure 1 and with initial wealth near the inflection point would always pay more for a lottery ticket offering a probability p of $\$Z$ than for a ticket with two such chances (i.e. probability $2p$) of winning $\$Z/2$. On this basis, they reject the shape in Figure 1 as inconsistent with their final observation, namely that (lottery designers are presumably profit maximizers, and) "lotteries typically have more than one prize" [**33**, p. 294, or **91**, p. 80]. Writers from Cournot (see [**90**, n. 127]) through Menger [**63**, p. 226] and Markowitz [**60**, pp. 153–154] have made essentially this same point, namely that the amount the individual would pay for a $1/n$ chance of winning $\$nZ$, though possibly increasing at first, is an eventually declining function of n. In light of this, Friedman and Savage modified their original proposed shape so as to include a terminal concave section, as in Figure 2.[14,15]

---

[13] Markowitz [**60**, pp. 155–156] has noted that such instructions also imply what has been seen to be a related behavior, namely positive skewness preference.

[14] Strictly speaking, the terminal segment must be *sufficiently* concave (see [**33**, n. 34]).

[15] Markowitz [**60**] subsequently modified the theory further by adding a third inflection point to the left of the first one, since "the individual generally will prefer one chance in ten of owing $10,000,000 rather than owing $1,000,000 for sure" [**60**, p. 154]. Thus, the amount the individual would pay to avoid a $1/n$ chance of losing $\$nZ$ may similarly eventually decline in n. An alternative explanation is that the individual views the actual consequences of owing either amount as identical (i.e. total bankruptcy) and simply acts to minimize the probability of this common outcome.

"EXPECTED UTILITY" ANALYSIS   283

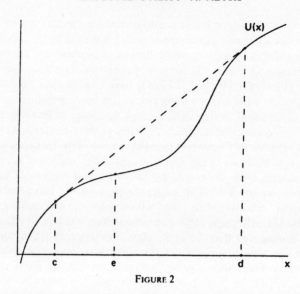

FIGURE 2

A second objection to the utility function of Figure 1 comes from the typical response to the famous "St. Petersburg Paradox" and its generalizations.[16] The original form of this paradox was the observation that an individual typically would never forgo a significant amount of wealth to engage in the gamble which offered a payoff of $\$2^{i-1}$ with probability 2^{-i} for $i = 1, 2, \ldots$, even though the expected winnings from this gamble are infinite. Since an individual with a Figure 1 utility function clearly *would* forgo any finite sure level of wealth to take this gamble, such a utility function must be abandoned as unrealistic. In his classic article, Menger [63] generalized the paradox by showing that whenever the utility function was unbounded, similar gambles could be constructed which also had infinite certainty equivalents,[17] so that the utility function of Figure 2 must be further modified so as to be bounded for all outcome levels. More recently, Arrow [6, pp. 63–69] (see also Samuelson [82, pp. 35–36 and footnote 14]) has shown that an individual with unbounded utility must violate either the completeness or the continuity axiom of expected utility theory.[18]

A common objection to the "evidence" posed by the St. Petersburg Paradox and to the extent of the problems posed by unbounded utility has been that no person, or for that matter, no society, could ever offer such a gamble to the individual, and therefore it is meaningless to ask how much such a gamble would be worth. However, as has been shown (see Aumann [9, p. 444] and Samuelson [82, pp. 32–34]), the incompatibility of unbounded utility with "reasonable"

---

[16]See Samuelson [82] for a historical and critical overview of the literature surrounding the paradox, and Shapely [86, 87] and Aumann [9] for more recent comments.

[17]Let $x_i = U^{-1}(2^i)$ and consider the gamble which offers $\$x_i$ with probability 2^{-i} for $i = 1, 2, 3, \ldots$.

[18]See also Ryan [79], Arrow [7], Shapley [86, 87], Aumann [9], Fishburn [29], and Russell and Seo [78] on this issue.

behavior may be demonstrated even if only distributions with finite numbers of outcomes are considered. The simplest such instance is the implication that, if utility is unbounded, for any arbitrarily large amount C and arbitrarily small positive probability p, there will always be some amount Z such that the individual will prefer a p chance of winning Z to a certain gain of C.

The evidence thus suggests that the utility function of Figure 1 must be replaced by one as in Figure 2, that $U(\cdot)$ must be bounded, and furthermore that the second inflection point must occur at an empirically relevant outcome level.[19] Although such restrictions are necessary to make the expected utility model consistent with the observations considered above, they reduce the elegance with which the observations of Section 2.1 were modelled by the utility function of Figure 1. In particular, the degree of risk aversion is no longer monotonic in the outcome level. Thus, for example, a Mosteller-Nogee subject with a Figure 2 utility function would instruct an agent to play more liberally when doing well, *provided winnings have not been too high*, and, if playing conservatively at this high wealth level results in sufficient losses, more liberal gambles ought once again to be taken.

2.3. *The Relative Invariance of Gambling Behavior to Initial Wealth and the Markowitz Hypothesis*

The next objection to (and modification of) the original Friedman-Savage utility function concerned not so much the typical shape of the utility function, but rather the more fundamental issue of the stability of preferences. Recall that the independence axiom, in conjunction with the other axioms of expected utility theory (see, for example, Herstein and Milnor [43]) implies that the preference ranking corresponds to the expectation of a fixed utility function defined over final consequences, or in other words, ultimate levels of wealth. Indeed, Friedman and Savage, in their discussion of the standard method of estimating the utility function by fixing its values at two arbitrary wealth levels, pointed out that the expected utility hypothesis would be violated if the use of another pair of wealth levels as reference points "yielded a utility function differing in more than origin and unit of measure from the one initially obtained" [33, p. 292, or 91, pp. 77–78]. Thus, when faced with alternative gambles, that is, prospects expressed in terms of *deviations* from current wealth, the individual will choose that gamble whose implied distribution over ultimate wealth levels has the highest expected utility.[20] This procedure of "integrating" (i.e. convoluting) alternative gambles with initial wealth before ranking is referred to by Kahneman and Tversky as "asset integration" [46, p. 264].

---

[19]Stiglitz [92] has argued that the requirement of boundedness does not rule out the case of $U(x)$ being convex for all x less than a trillion dollars. If such were the case, however, we would not observe lotteries offering multiple prizes of values less than this amount, nor would the individual's valuation of a $1/n$ chance of n start declining until n were at least one trillion.

[20]Hence Edwards' statement that "the fundamental idea of a utility scale is such that the whole structure of a subject's choices [over such gambles] should be altered as a result of [the change in initial wealth due to] each previous choice (if the choices are real ones involving money gains or losses)" [24, p. 395].

"EXPECTED UTILITY" ANALYSIS   285

However, as noted by Markowitz [60], the assumption that the utility function of Figure 2 is defined over ultimate wealth levels is *not* consistent with the observed tendency of individuals of all wealth levels to purchase insurance and lottery tickets.[21] Individuals with wealth levels less than c ("poor") or greater than d ("well to do") would never accept any fair bets, for example, yet "even poor people, apparently as much as others, buy sweepstakes tickets, play the horses, and participate in other forms of gambling. Rich people play roulette and the stock market" [60, p. 153]. Similarly, an individual with wealth just below d would be willing to take an expected loss for the privilege of *underwriting* insurance against large losses. In addition, individuals with wealth near $(c + d)$ /2 would prefer all symmetric and other fair bets of up to at least $(d - c)/2$, even though "generally people avoid symmetric bets" [60, p. 154]. Noting that individuals of all wealth levels tend to behave as if their initial wealth was near the left inflection point e in Figure 2, Markowitz hypothesized that changes in wealth caused the utility function to shift horizontally so as to keep this inflection point at or near the current or "customary" level of wealth.[22]

The experimental evidence similarly suggests that individual gambling behavior at different initial wealth levels is more indicative of a shifting utility function than of movements along a fixed utility function. In reestimating the "utility curves" of subjects after periods of a few days to several weeks (during which their wealth must surely have changed by amounts greater than those involved in the experiment), Davidson, Suppes, and Siegel found that seven of their eight subjects "gave responses which were substantially consistent with the original results" and that three of them "performed the rather astonishing feat of exactly duplicating their first choices (they were given no hint as to what their earlier choices had been)" [17, pp. 68–69, 81]. Since Mosteller and Nogee also failed to account for wealth changes between sessions, their conclusion that "on the basis of empirical curves [constructed from data obtained over several sessions] it is possible to estimate future behavior in comparable but more complicated risk-taking situations" [66, p. 403] also supports this conclusion.[23] In a somewhat different context, Edwards [23] observed preferences over pairs of prospects involving fixed probabilities and a common (though variable) expected value and noted that "if the utility curve is non-linear . . . then a markedly different set of choices should be made at each different EV-level (since at each different EV-level different amounts of money, falling at different places on the utility curve, are involved in the bets)" [23, p. 87]. Finding that the observed choices generally did not depend on the expected value level, he was led to reject the existence of "one utility curve consistent with all these sets of choices" [23, p. 87].

[21] This implication was also noted by Friedman and Savage [33, pp. 300–301 or 91, pp. 90–91] (see also Hirshleifer [44, pp. 259–261]).

[22] Markowitz suggested that the utility function might also undergo a horizontal expansion as it shifts to the right, so that the distance between the inflection points might be an increasing function of initial wealth [60, p. 155].

[23] Note that neither Davidson, Suppes, and Siegel nor Mosteller and Nogee found that individuals typically exhibited constant absolute risk aversion, which would also have served to explain their observations.

Presumably as a result of their survey data, Kahneman and Tversky have also concluded that "the preference order of prospects [defined in terms of gains and losses] is not greatly altered by small or even moderate variations in asset position" [46, p. 277]. Most recently, Binswanger [12] has used experimentally obtained data on the risk preferences of rural Indian villagers to conduct an explicit test of the asset integration hypothesis, which was formally rejected in favor of the alternative of a shifting utility function.[24]

The Markowitz hypothesis of a shifting utility function implies that changes in initial wealth essentially cause the individual to go back and *rerank* the entire "consumption set" of distributions over ultimate wealth levels. Such a hypothesis, asserting that preferences cannot be defined independently of the current consumption point is, in the words of Eden, "disturbing to economists who use the assumption of 'constant tastes' quite heavily . . . it is hard to see how positive economics can do without this assumption and it is almost impossible to think of welfare economics without it" [20, p. 125]. While the phenomenon of a relative invariance of gambling behavior to initial wealth, and in particular a simultaneous propensity to insure, buy lottery tickets, and avoid symmetric bets at all wealth levels may well contradict the joint hypothesis of constant tastes *and expected utility maximization*, such behavior (including the insurance-lotteries-symmetric bets observation) is not incompatible with the existence of *any* fixed preference ranking over ultimate wealth distributions, as will be shown in Sections 4.4 and 4.5 below. Thus, before dropping the assumption of constant tastes in order to save the assumption that the individual is maximizing the expectation of some utility function at each initial wealth level, it is crucial that we examine the extent to which this latter assumption is in fact warranted by the data.[25]

[24]The evidence on the effect of changes in wealth *within* sessions, however, is less conclusive. In an analysis of some of the subjects of their pilot study, Mosteller and Nogee found at least some evidence that the greater the amount of money "on hand," the greater the propensity to gamble [66, pp. 399–402], although that portion of the evidence which they present seems inconclusive, and Edwards has in fact interpreted them as concluding that "the amount of money possessed by the subjects did not seriously influence their choices" [24, pp. 395]. Mosteller and Nogee's analysis of the original Preston and Baratta data, on the other hand, "did *not* reveal . . . any evidence of differential bidding for gambles at the beginning and end of the game [i.e. session]" [66, p. 398]. Similarly, while McGlothlin found a tendency for bettors at pari-mutuel horse races to increase both the size of their wagers and the proportion of long-shot bets during the course of the racing day (i.e. "session"), he also found that, with the exception of the seventh ("feature") race of the day and the final eighth race (where "bettors apparently refrain from making bets which would not recoup their losses if successful" [62, p. 614]), "the first six races all yield E-vs.-odds patterns that do not differ from the pattern for the total sample by more than the sampling error" [62, p. 610]. Since intra-session wealth changes are due solely to gambling gains and losses, differences in the short and long run effects of such changes might be related to Davidson, Suppes, and Siegel's observations that "winning or losing several times in a row made subjects sanguine or pessimistic and tended to produce altered responses to the same offers" and "if the same syllable [on a random die] came up three times in succession, for example, the subjective probability would temporarily decrease for most subjects" [17, pp. 53, 54].

[25]See Section 4.4, however, for references to some experimentally observed choice behavior (under both certainty and uncertainty) of a different nature which apparently *does* contradict the assumption of constant tastes.

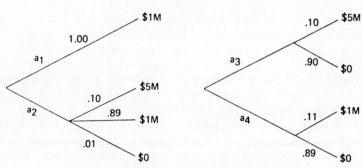

FIGURE 3.—The Allais Paradox ($1M = $1,000,000).

2.4. *Systematic Violation of the Independence Axiom: The Allais Paradox*

In this section and the next we consider the evidence that, even at a fixed initial asset position, individual rankings over alternative risky prospects tend to *systematically* violate the independence axiom, and hence are inconsistent with the hypothesis of expected utility maximization.

The most widely discussed of such examples is the famous "Allais Paradox" (see, for example, Allais [2,3,4], Allais and Hagen [5], Raiffa [70, pp. 80–86], or Morrison [64]), where the individual is asked to rank a particular pair of risky prospects a_1 and a_2, and then asked to rank the pair a_3 and a_4, where the payoffs and their corresponding probabilities are given in Figure 3. Since the shifts in probability mass in moving from prospect a_1 to a_2 and from a_4 to a_3 both consist of lowering the probability of winning $1M$ by .11 and raising the probabilities of winning $5M$ and $0 by .10 and .01 respectively, an expected utility maximizer would either prefer a_2 to a_1 and a_3 to a_4 (i.e. prefer the common shift) if the sign of $[.01 U(w) - .11 U(w + 1M) + .10 U(w + 5M)]$ is positive, or else prefer a_1 to a_2 and a_4 to a_3 (i.e. not prefer the shift) if the sign is negative, where w is initial wealth.

Allais and others (e.g. Raiffa [70, p. 80], Morrison [64]), however, have found that the majority of subjects questioned prefer a_1 in the first pair and a_3 in the second, a pair of choices which violates the independence axiom. Morrison, for example, reported that when presented to a class of first year MBA students who had not been exposed to expected utility theory, 80 per cent made the above choices, and that even when presented to a similar class which had been exposed to the theory, the percentage of such "inconsistent" choices was still 50 per cent. Indeed, Savage himself made these choices when presented with the example, although he later changed his preferences to conform with the independence axiom [83, pp. 101–103].[26] The fact that the *same* pair of choices are made by so high a percentage of subjects makes the Allais Paradox a key example of the systematic violation of the independence axiom. Finally, it should be noted that

---

[26]Note that the version of the paradox presented in [83] differs from Figure 3 in that the labeling of prospects 3 and 4 is reversed and all payoffs are scaled down by $\frac{1}{2}$.

this example is not an isolated case: individuals faced with similar choice situations have tended to violate the axiom in what will be shown to be the same systematic fashion (see, for example, the evidence reported in Kahneman and Tversky [46, Problems 1 & 2 and Table 1], Hagen [38, pp. 285–296], and MacCrimmon and Larsson [57, pp. 350–369], most of which involves more moderate payoff levels than in the Allais Paradox).

One characterization of how such behavior systematically violates the independence axiom involves comparing the class of utility functions which rank a_1 over a_2 with the class of functions which rank a_3 over a_4. Note that the prospects a_1 and a_2 respectively stochastically dominate[27] a_4 and a_3, and recall that a utility function $U(\cdot)$ ranks a_1 over a_2 (a_3 over a_4) if and only if $[.01 U(w) - .11 U(w + 1M) + .10 U(w + 5M)]$ is negative (positive), or equivalently, if and only if receiving \$1M with certainty is preferred (not preferred) to a 10/11 chance of \$5M. Thus, in evaluating the change from a_1 to a_2, the typical individual acts as if using a utility function which is more risk averse than the one "used" to evaluate the change from a_4 to a_3. An analysis of the above cited evidence of Kahneman and Tversky, Hagen, and MacCrimmon and Larsson similarly reveals a tendency for individuals to violate the independence axiom by ranking the stochastically dominating pair of prospects "according to" a utility function which is more risk averse than the one "used" to rank the stochastically dominated pair.[28]

An alternative characterization of such behavior, in a form more directly comparable to the independence axiom, involves the notion of the "conditional certainty equivalent" of a prospect. Returning to Figure 3, define the prospect a^* as a 1/11:10/11 chance of winning \$0 or \$5M respectively, and let E be an event with probability .11. Then the prospects a_1, a_2, a_3, and a_4 have the same distributions as the compound prospects which respectively yield \$1M, a^*, a^*, and \$1M if E occurs, and \$1M, \$1M, \$0, and \$0 if $\sim E$ occurs. It is clear that the independence axiom requires that the conditional certainty equivalent of a^* in E, that is, the amount which the individual would, *ex ante*, just be willing to substitute for a^* if E occurs, be independent of what would ensue if $\sim E$ were to occur. However, the typical preference for a_1 over a_2 and a_3 over a_4 implies that the conditional certainty equivalent of a^* in E is less than \$1M when $\sim E$ yields \$1M with certainty and greater than \$1M when $\sim E$ yields \$0. A similar analysis of Kahneman and Tversky [46, Problems 1 & 2] and MacCrimmon and Larsson [57, pp. 360–369] (i.e. that portion of the above cited evidence which can be formulated in this framework) also reveals the general property that, for a given event E and prospect a^*, stochastically dominating shifts in the conditional distribution of wealth in $\sim E$ will lower the conditional certainty equivalent of a^*

---

[27] Throughout this paper, "stochastic dominance" refers to first order stochastic dominance (see Hadar and Russell [37]).

[28] Note that in some of these examples the vectors of changes in the probabilities of the payoffs between each pair are not identical (as in the Allais Paradox) but rather scalar multiples of each other, a fact which has no bearing on the applicability of the above type of calculation.

in E. Thus, contrary to the precepts of the independence axiom, the more that individuals stand to lose if the event E occurs (that is, the better off they would be in $\sim E$), the more risk averse they become in evaluating a given risky prospect a^* in E. Equivalently, individuals are less risk averse toward a given prospect a^* in E if E is the "preferred event" (i.e. when $\sim E$ involves low outcome values) than when E is not the preferred event (i.e. when $\sim E$ involves high outcome values).[29]

A possible objection to the validity of this (and the following) evidence against the independence axiom is that individuals, when shown how their choices violated the axiom, would, like Savage, change their preferences to conform with it (see the discussions in Savage [83, pp. 102–103], Raiffa [70, pp. 80–86], and MacCrimmon [56, pp. 9–11]). While this phenomenon would clearly be a testimony to the *normative* appeal of the axiom, it is irrelevant to the positive theory of behavior toward risk (would an insurance company base its estimate of the pedestrian fatality rate on the widely held belief that the individual, *if reminded*, would always choose to look both ways before crossing a street?). Finally, there is evidence that the ability of experimenters to talk subjects out of preferences which violate the independence axiom may not be due to its "intuitive appeal" so much as the subject's desire to conform with the explicit or implicit beliefs of the experimenter. MacCrimmon [56, pp. 9–11] and Slovic and Tversky [88] reported that, when presented with opposing written arguments, subjects whose initial choices conformed to the axiom were about as likely to change their preferences as subjects who initially violated it.[30]

2.5. *Systematic Violation of the Independence Axiom:* *Oversensitivity to Changes in Small Probabilities and the* *Subjective Expected Utility Hypothesis*

The third important characterization of how the independence axiom is systematically violated, namely that, relative to expected utility maximization, individuals are oversensitive to changes in the probabilities of small probability-outlying events, may also be illustrated by the Allais Paradox. Note that the

---

[29] It is important to distinguish this type of behavior from that discussed in Section 2.1. Roughly speaking, the current aspect is that the individual's aversion to the riskiness of a^* in E grows with a general rise in the payoff levels in $\sim E$, whereas the earlier aspect was that it drops if there is a uniform rise in the payoffs in E (i.e. a uniform rise in the payoff levels of a^* itself).

[30] Although in a similar study Moskowitz found that presenting subjects with opposing written arguments and allowing them to discuss these among themselves led to a net decrease in the proportion of violations of the axiom, nevertheless 73 percent of the initial "Allais type" preference rankings expressed by subjects remained unchanged after the discussions [65, pp. 232–237, Table 6]. (When the written arguments were presented but no discussion was allowed, he found no net change in the degree of conformity with the axiom and a "persistency rate" of Allais type choices of 93 percent [65, p. 234, Tables 4 & 6].) Moskowitz also found that, of the three alternative forms of representing the choice problem he presented, that form which was judged the "clearest representation" by the majority of subjects (the "tree" diagram) led to the lowest degree of conformity with the axiom, the highest proportion of Allais type violations, and the highest persistency rate of these violations [65, pp. 234, 237–238].

common shift from a_1 to a_2 and from a_4 to a_3 may be thought of as moving .10 units of probability mass from the outcome $w + 1M$ to the outcome $w + 5M$ and moving .01 units of mass from $w + 1M$ to w. When the initial prospect is a_1, the upward movement of the .10 mass is not enough to compensate for the downward movement of the .01 mass, and the shift is not preferred. However, when the initial prospect is a_4, the outcome w is no longer such an "outlying event" of the initial distribution, since (relative to a_1) its probability has increased from 0 to .89. As a result, the individual is no longer as sensitive to the .01 rise in the probability of this event (at the expense of the preferred event $w + 1M$) and this downward movement of mass is now more than compensated by the upward movement of the .10 mass, so the shift (to a_3) is preferred.

Alternatively (and as will be seen below, equivalently), changing the initial prospect from a_1 to a_4 may be viewed as making the outcome $w + 5M$ "more outlying" relative to w and $w + 1M$, since, although the probability of this outcome hasn't changed, in moving from a_1 to a_4 a probability mass of .89 has moved *farther away* from the outcome level $w + 5M$. Thus, with the outcome $w + 5M$ more of an outlying event in the distribution a_4 than in a_1, the individual is now more sensitive to changes in its probability, and the upward movement of mass from $w + 1M$ to $w + 5M$ is now more than enough to compensate for the downward movement from $w + 1M$ to w, so the shift becomes preferred. A similar analysis of the evidence of Kahneman and Tversky, Hagen, and MacCrimmon and Larsson cited in the previous section also reveals this general tendency for individuals to be "oversensitive" to changes in the probabilities of low probability-outlying events.

A second source of evidence that individuals violate the independence axiom via a systematic oversensitivity to the probabilities of low-probability events are the empirical fittings by both psychologists and economists of the so-called "subjective expected utility" models.[31] Such models assume that the individual transforms the known set of objective probabilities $\{p_i\}$ of a risky prospect into their corresponding "subjective probabilities" $\{\pi(p_i)\}$ (called "decision weights" by Kahneman and Tversky [46]) and then maximizes the value of $\sum_i x_i \cdot \pi(p_i)$ ("subjective expected value" or SEV) or the value of $\sum_i U(x_i) \cdot \pi(p_i)$ ("subjective expected utility" or SEU), where p_i is the probability of the outcome value x_i. Since the independence axiom requires that $\pi(p_i)$ be linear, empirical estimates of the $\pi(p_i)$ function would yield information regarding the nature of any systematic violation of the axiom.

Such studies have on the whole found that, relative to linearity, individuals overemphasize small probabilities and underemphasize large probabilities. Applications of the SEV model to a wide range of both experimentally and nonexperimentally generated data have consistently yielded estimated $\pi(p)$ functions which are proportionately greater from small values of p than for large ones (see

---

[31] A systematic presentation and discussion of this class of models is given in Edwards [25, 27] (see also Wallsten [100] and the references cited there, as well as the surveys of Edwards [24, 26] and Luce and Suppes [54]). Modified versions of these models have recently been introduced into the economics literature by Handa [40] (see also Fishburn [30]) and Kahneman and Tversky [46].

for example Preston and Baratta [69], Griffith [36], Sprowls [89], Nogee and Lieberman [67], and Ali [1]). Although Ali [1] and others have argued that an estimated $\pi(p)$ function which overweights small probabilities is exactly what we would expect if the SEV model (which constrains the outcome values x_i to enter in linearly) were (mis)applied to choice data generated by an expected utility maximizer with terminally convex utility, Edwards has shown in another context that observed nonlinear "probability preferences" cannot be completely accounted for by utility considerations alone (Edwards [21; 22, p. 66; 23, pp. 84–95; 25, pp. 211–212]). Experiments by Edwards [25] and Tversky [95, 96] designed to overcome this problem by obtaining joint estimates of $\pi(p_i)$ and $U(x_i)$ in the SEU model continued to reveal a preponderant tendency towards overemphasizing small probabilities relative to larger ones.[32] Finally, in a somewhat different type of experiment designed to distinguish between behavior due to the curvature of the utility function and that due to exaggeration of small probabilities, Yaari [101] found that "acceptance sets" for bets were generally convex, which ruled out the possibility of convexities in the utility function, and implied that the risk loving behavior exhibited by seven of his seventeen subjects can only be explained (in the SEU framework, at least) by an exaggeration of the small probabilities of the favorable outcomes in these gambles. Although Rosett [71, 72] has subsequently argued that the experimental design in [101] was not sufficient to rule out the existence of convex portions of the utility function, he noted that his objection did not apply to Yaari's conclusion regarding the exaggeration of small probabilities [71, p. 535; 72, pp. 77–82], and indeed has also obtained evidence of such exaggeration in a subsequent experiment of his own [73, pp. 489, 492].

Since $\pi(0)$ must necessarily equal zero, a tendency for individuals to deviate from a linear $\pi(p)$ function in the direction of a relative overemphasis of small probabilities implies that, at least for values of p below a certain level, $\pi(p)$ must be a concave function of p. Since the sensitivity to a change in the probability of an outcome value x_i in the SEU model is given by $U(x_i) \cdot \pi'(p_i)$, this evidence reaffirms the principle that the individual is more sensitive to changes in the probabilities of events when their initial probabilities are low than when they are high.[33]

Although the SEU model allows for a relatively straightforward estimation of the individual's relative sensitivity to changes in low versus high probabilities, it

---

[32] In other experimental applications of the SEU model, Wallsten obtained mixed evidence on whether $\pi(p)$ differed from p by more than a scale factor [100, p. 39] and, though they conducted no formal estimation, Lichtenstein [52, p. 168] and Kahneman and Tversky [46, p. 281] similarly concluded that individuals overweight small probabilities.

[33] Some researchers (e.g. Preston and Baratta [69, p. 188]) have found that the slope of $\pi(p)$ may start rising again for values of p near unity. This would reflect the fact that, as the probability of the outcome value x_i approaches one, the probabilities of all other outcomes must go to zero, and as a result, the individual becomes increasingly sensitive to shifts which increase the probability of x_i at the expense of these other outcome values. In other words, the effect of a given shift of probability mass from x_j to x_i (which equals $U(x_i)\pi'(p_i) - U(x_j)\pi'(p_j)$) is large in magnitude when either $p_i \simeq 1$ and $p_j \simeq 0$ or when $p_i \simeq 0$ and $p_j \simeq 1$.

MARK J. MACHINA

exhibits many undesirable properties. Once $\pi(p)$ is nonlinear, for example, behavior is no longer characterized by the shape of $U(\cdot)$ alone, and the main results of expected utility theory (such as the characterization of risk aversion by the concavity of $U(\cdot)$) no longer apply. More important, however, is the fact that, except in the case when it reduces to expected utility, the SEU model is incapable of incorporating the property of monotonicity (i.e. a preference for stochastically dominating distributions) in the sense that any individual maximizing $\sum_i U(x_i) \cdot \pi(p_i)$ with a nonlinear $\pi(p)$ function will *necessarily* prefer some distributions to ones which stochastically dominate them.[34] Similarly, unless $\pi(p)$ is linear, no subjective expected utility maximizer can exhibit general risk aversion (i.e. aversion to all mean preserving increases in risk), even over restricted ranges of possible outcomes.[35] In the author's view, this *intrinsic* incompatibility of the SEU model with the plausible behavioral properties of risk aversion, and especially general monotonicity, makes it unacceptable as a descriptive model of behavior toward risk.

It is useful to keep in mind the distinction between an oversensitivity to changes in the probabilities of small probability events and any tendency, under conditions of uncertainty rather than risk, to *overestimate* the probabilities of rare events. Since in this section and the preceding one we have treated behavior in situations where the individuals are told the relevant probabilities, this latter tendency, while it may exist, is irrelevant to the behavior considered here. Similarly, note that the principle of oversensitivity to changes in the probabilities of small probability-outlying events is not contradicted by the fact that individuals often tend to neglect altogether (i.e. treat as impossible) events of very low probability (see the references cited in Arrow [6, p. 14] and Samuelson [82, pp. 39–40]). The neglect (for all practical purposes) on an increase in the probability of disaster from 0 to .0000001 would only violate this principle if the same absolute increase in the probability of disaster was *not* neglected when the initial probability was .5000000.[36]

---

[34] As a result of their proof of this, Kahneman and Tversky [46, pp. 283–284] modify their model to require that the stochastically dominated distributions be eliminated from the choice set before the rest of the alternatives are ranked by their modified SEU function. However, they point out that this process permits what they call "indirect violations of dominance" ([46, p. 284]) and may result in intransitive choices.

[35] To see this, note that a mean preserving spread of probability mass from the outcome x_2 to the outcomes $x_1 = x_2 - t$ and $x_3 = x_2 + t$ will not be preferred if and only if $[U(x_1) \cdot \pi'(p_1) - 2U(x_2) \cdot \pi'(p_2) + U(x_3) \cdot \pi'(p_3)]$ is nonpositive, which will be true for all p_1, p_2, p_3, and small t if and only if $\pi'(p)$ is constant and $U(\cdot)$ is concave. It is straightforward to verify that this incompatibility with general risk aversion (as well as with general monotonicity) extends to all "additive" models with a maximand of the form $\sum_i f(x_i, p_i)$ where $f(\cdot, \cdot)$ is smooth and not identically equal to $U(x_i) \cdot p_i$ for some $U(\cdot)$.

[36] Note finally that the violations of expected utility discussed in this section and the preceding one cannot be explained by merely observing that individual rankings are often stochastic. Such "random" preferences over risky prospects were noted by Mosteller and Nogee [66] and have been explicitly incorporated into the expected utility model by Fishburn [28, 31] (see also Luce and Raiffa [53, pp. 371–384] and the references mentioned there). While randomness clearly characterizes real life choice, stochastic *expected utility* models cannot account for the systematic violations of the independence axiom which have been considered, since such models would predict that, in the Allais Paradox for example, either a_1 and a_4 are chosen most of the time, or else a_2 and a_3 are.

3. THE ANALYSIS OF GENERAL NONLINEAR PREFERENCE FUNCTIONALS

In this section we demonstrate the robustness of expected utility analysis to violations of the independence axiom by showing how the fundamental concepts, tools, and results of expected utility theory may be applied to the general case of an individual possessing a "smooth" preference ranking over alternative probability distributions over ultimate wealth.

3.1. *Smooth Preferences and the "Local Utility Function"*

We take as our choice set the set $D[0, M]$ of all probability distribution functions $F(\cdot)$ over the interval $[0, M]$ and assume that the individual's preference ranking over this set is complete, transitive, and representable by a real-valued preference functional $V(\cdot)$ on $D[0, M]$.[37] Throughout this paper, all integrals will be taken over the interval $[0, M]$ unless otherwise specified.

For the purpose of defining continuity of preferences, the most appropriate topology to place on $D[0, M]$ is the topology of weak convergence, which defines a sequence $\{F_n(\cdot)\} \subset D[0, M]$ as converging to $F(\cdot)$ if and only if $F_n(x) \rightarrow F(x)$ at each continuity point x of $F(\cdot)$.[38] This topology renders as convergent the following sequences, each of which economic agents are likely to "think of" as convergent: (i) pointwise convergence of the density functions of a sequence of continuous distributions, (ii) the "collapse" of a sequence of distributions to the degenerate distribution $G_c(\cdot)$, which from now on will be used to denote the distribution which assigns unit mass to the point c, and (iii) the convergence of the sequence $\{G_{c_n}(\cdot)\}$ to $G_c(\cdot)$, where $c_n \rightarrow c$. Finally, since it may be shown that a sequence $\{F_n(\cdot)\}$ converges to the distribution $F(\cdot)$ in this topology if and only if $\int g(x)dF_n(x) \rightarrow \int g(x)dF(x)$ for all continuous $g(\cdot)$ on $[0, M]$, the weak convergence topology is the weakest (i.e. coarsest) topology on $D[0, M]$ for which the expected utility functional $\int U(x)dF(x)$ is continuous for all continuous $U(\cdot)$ on $[0, M]$.

The condition of differentiability of $V(\cdot)$ requires in addition the existence of a norm on the space $\Delta D[0, M] = \{\lambda(F^* - F) \mid F, F^* \in D[0, M], \lambda \in R^1\}$. Lemma 1 in the Appendix shows that the weak convergence topology on $D[0, M]$ is in fact induced by the L^1 metric $d(F, F^*) \equiv \int |F^*(x) - F(x)| dx$, which induces the norm $\|\lambda(F^* - F)\| \equiv |\lambda| \cdot d(F, F^*)$ on $\Delta D[0, M]$.[39]

Adopting this norm, our differentiability or "smoothness" condition will be that the preference functional $V(\cdot)$ be *Fréchet differentiable on the space* $D[0, M]$ *with respect to the norm* $\| \cdot \|$. Fréchet differentiability is the natural notion of differentiability on spaces such as $D[0, M]$ (i.e. subsets of Banach spaces),[40] and the function $V(\cdot)$ is said to be Fréchet differentiable at the point F in $D[0, M]$ if

---

[37] We assume throughout this section that the outcome space $[0, M]$ is bounded. In particular, note that the metric we shall define on $D[0, M]$ is only applicable if this is the case.

[38] See, for example, Billingsley [10, 11].

[39] This follows since $\Delta D[0, M]$ is a linear subspace of $L^1[0, M]$ and $\| \cdot \|$ is just the L^1 norm restricted to this subspace.

[40] See, for example, Rudin [77, p. 248] or Luenberger [55, pp. 172–177].

294   MARK J. MACHINA

there exists a continuous linear functional $\psi(\,\cdot\,;F)$ defined on $\Delta D[0,M]$ such that

(1) $$\lim_{\|F^*-F\|\to 0}\frac{|V(F^*)-V(F)-\psi(F^*-F;F)|}{\|F^*-F\|}=0.$$

In particular note that convergence here is required to be uniform in $\|F^*-F\|$.[41]
    An equivalent method of representing this notion is to write

(2) $$V(F^*)-V(F)=\psi(F^*-F;F)+o(\|F^*-F\|),$$

where $o(\,\cdot\,)$ denotes a function which is zero at zero and of a higher order than its argument. By footnote 39 and the Hahn-Banach theorem, there exists a continuous linear extension of $\psi(\,\cdot\,;F)$ to $L^1[0,M]$. Thus, by the Riesz representation theorem on $L^1[0,M]$,[42] we have that for any $F^*\in D[0,M]$,

(3) $$\psi(F^*-F;F)=\int(F^*(x)-F(x))h(x;F)\,dx$$

$$=-\int(F^*(x)-F(x))\,dU(x;F),$$

where $h(\,\cdot\,;F)\in L^\infty[0,M]$ and

(4) $$U(x;F)\equiv-\int_0^x h(s;F)\,ds,$$

from which it follows that $U(\,\cdot\,;F)$ is absolutely continuous and hence differentiable almost everywhere on $[0,M]$ (see Klambauer [48, p. 122]).
    Substituting (3) into (2) and integrating by parts (see Lemma 2 in the Appendix) yields

(5) $$V(F^*)-V(F)=\int U(x;F)(dF^*(x)-dF(x))+o(\|F^*-F\|).$$

From (5) we see that a differential movement from the distribution $F(\,\cdot\,)$ to a distribution $F^*(\,\cdot\,)$ changes the value of the preference functional $V(\,\cdot\,)$ by $\int U(x;F)(dF^*(x)-dF(x))$, that is, by the difference in the expected value of $U(x;F)$ with respect to the distributions $F^*(\,\cdot\,)$ and $F(\,\cdot\,)$. In other words, in ranking differential shifts from an initial distribution $F(\,\cdot\,)$, the individual acts *precisely as would an expected utility maximizer*, with "local utility function" $U(x;F)$.[43] Intuitively, the fact that any Fréchet differentiable preference function

[41] Note that this is a stronger requirement than just that the directional derivative exist for all directions F^*-F and be linear in the direction. This latter condition, known as Gateaux differentiability (see Luenberger [55, pp. 171-172]), is not even sufficient to ensure continuity.
[42] See, for example, Klambauer [48, p. 172] or Royden [76, p. 103].
[43] Note that the local utility function at a distribution $F(\,\cdot\,)$ displays the usual affine invariance properties of a von Neumann-Morgenstern utility function, since from (5) it is clear that neither an additive nor a multiplicative transformation of $U(\,\cdot\,;F)$ will alter the ranking of differential shifts from $F(\,\cdot\,)$. Note that by analogy with standard indifference curve analysis, however, the local utility functions $U(\,\cdot\,;F)$ and $U(\,\cdot\,;F^*)$ of the indifferent distributions $F(\,\cdot\,)$ and $F^*(\,\cdot\,)$ can only be used to compare respective differential shifts from these distributions if the functions $U(\,\cdot\,;F)$ and $U(\,\cdot\,;F^*)$ are not subjected to different multiplicative transformations.

may be thought of as "locally expected utility maximizing" follows from the fact that differentiable functions are "locally linear," and that for preference functionals over probability distributions, linearity is equivalent to expected utility maximization.[44]

The simplest example of such a nonlinear preference functional is the specification

(6) $$\tilde{V}(F) \equiv \int R(x)\,dF(x) + \frac{1}{2}\left[\int S(x)\,dF(x)\right]^2$$

$$= E_F[R(x)] + \frac{1}{2}\left[E_F[S(x)]\right]^2,$$

which may be termed "quadratic in the probabilities,"[45] and with local utility function

(7) $$\tilde{U}(x;F) = R(x) + S(x)\left[\int S(z)\,dF(z)\right] = R(x) + S(x)E_F[S(z)],$$

where $E_F[\cdot]$ denotes expectation with respect to the probability distribution $F(\cdot)$.[46] Thus, an individual with such a preference function would prefer a differential shift from the distribution $F(\cdot)$ to a distribution $F^*(\cdot)$ if and only if the sign of $[E_{F^*}[\tilde{U}(x;F)] - E_F[\tilde{U}(x;F)]]$ is positive.

3.2. *The Mathematical Characterization of Behavior*

While the function $U(\cdot;F)$ may be used to rank differential shifts from an initial distribution $F(\cdot)$, in general there will be no neighborhood of $F(\cdot)$ in $D[0,M]$, however small, over which the ranking induced by the local utility function corresponds exactly to the ranking induced by the preference functional itself. Nevertheless, the present extension of expected utility analysis may similarly be applied to nondifferential (i.e. global) situations in much the same manner in which standard multivariate calculus may be used to show that a nonlinear but differentiable function will exhibit certain global properties (such as monotonicity) throughout a region provided its linear approximations at every point in the region exhibit the property in question, even though the linear approximations at different points in the region will in general be different linear functions. In other words, in a large body of cases, if the appropriate qualitative property (e.g. concavity) holds for every local utility function throughout a region, then the preference functional will display the corresponding behavioral

---

[44] An earlier special case of this result, proven in Samuelson [81, pp. 34–37] and discovered by the author in the course of writing this paper, is that an individual with "smooth" preferences will rank alternative differential deviations of the payoff levels from an initially certain distribution according to expected *value* maximization. This follows from the present result coupled with the fact that expected utility maximizers with differentiable utility functions will rank such differential changes in the payoffs according to expected value.

[45] This functional form can be shown to be a special case of the most general quadratic form $\frac{1}{2}\iint T(x,z)\,dF(x)\,dF(z)$ where without loss of generality we may assume $T(x,z) \equiv T(z,x)$, and with local utility function $\int T(x,z)\,dF(z)$.

[46] We assume $R(\cdot)$ and $S(\cdot)$ to be absolutely continuous with $R'(\cdot), S'(\cdot) \in L^\infty[0,M]$.

property (e.g. risk aversion) throughout the region, *even though the local utility functions are not the same throughout the region* (i.e. even though the individual is not an expected utility maximizer).

The general method by which such results can be proven is the use of path integrals in the space $D[0, M]$. Specifically, if the path $\{F(\cdot;\alpha)|\alpha \in [0,1]\}$ is smooth enough so that the term $\|F(\cdot;\alpha) - F(\cdot;\alpha^*)\|$ is differentiable in α at $\alpha = \alpha^*$, then from equation (5) we have

$$(8) \qquad \frac{d}{d\alpha}(V(F(\cdot;\alpha)))\Big|_{\alpha^*} = \frac{d}{d\alpha}\left(\int U(x; F(\cdot;\alpha^*))\, dF(x;\alpha)\right)\Big|_{\alpha^*}$$

$$+ \frac{d}{d\alpha}\left(o(\|F(\cdot;\alpha) - F(\cdot;\alpha^*)\|)\right)\Big|_{\alpha^*}$$

$$= \frac{d}{d\alpha}\left(\int U(x; F(\cdot;\alpha^*))\, dF(x;\alpha)\right)\Big|_{\alpha^*},$$

since the derivative of the higher order term $o(\cdot)$ will be zero at zero. Combining (8) and the Fundamental Theorem of Integral Calculus yields that

$$(9) \qquad V(F(\cdot;1)) - V(F(\cdot;0)) = \int_0^1 \left[\frac{d}{d\alpha}\left(\int U(x; F(\cdot;\alpha^*))\, dF(x;\alpha)\right)\Big|_{\alpha^*}\right] d\alpha^*,$$

which illustrates how the individual's reaction to the shift from $F(\cdot;0)$ to $F(\cdot;1)$ will depend on the characteristics of the local utility function at each point (i.e. distribution) along the path $\{F(\cdot;\alpha)|\alpha \in [0,1]\}$. As a first application of this method, we have the following theorem.

THEOREM 1: *Let $V(\cdot)$ be a Fréchet differentiable preference function on $D[0, M]$. Then $V(F^*) \geq V(F)$ whenever $F^*(\cdot)$ stochastically dominates $F(\cdot)$ if and only if $U(x; F)$ is nondecreasing in x for all $F(\cdot) \in D[0, M]$. (Proof in Appendix.)*

To ensure strict monotonicity (i.e. strict preference for stochastic dominance) we shall assume from now on that $U(x; F)$ is strictly increasing in x for all $F(\cdot)$ in $D[0, M]$. This would be true in the quadratic example of equations (6) and (7), for example, if $R(x)$ was strictly increasing and $S(x)$ either nonnegative and nondecreasing or else nonpositive and nonincreasing. Consider now Theorem 2.

THEOREM 2: *Let $V(\cdot)$ be a Fréchet differentiable preference function on $D[0, M]$. Then $V(F^*) \leq V(F)$ whenever $F^*(\cdot)$ differs from $F(\cdot)$ by a mean preserving increase in risk if and only if $U(x; F)$ is a concave function of x for all $F(\cdot) \in D[0, M]$. (Proof in Appendix.)*

Thus, a sufficient condition for the quadratic preference functional $\tilde{V}(\cdot)$ of equation (6) to exhibit global risk aversion is that $R(x)$ be concave and $S(x)$ either everywhere concave and nonnegative or else everywhere convex and nonpositive.

Theorem 2 has two important implications for the generality of expected utility theory, which follow from the "if" and "only if" parts of the theorem, respectively. The first is that researchers, who in order to study the behavior of risk averters in various situations have modelled them as expected utility maximizers with concave utility functions, are likely to have proven results which are also valid in the more general case of smooth preferences. The second is that concavity of a cardinal function of wealth is a *complete characterization* of risk aversion, in the sense that *any* risk averter must possess concave local utility functions, whether or not he or she is an expected utility maximizer. Thus, the researcher who would like to drop the expected utility hypothesis and study the nature of general risk aversion can apparently work completely within the framework of expected utility analysis.

3.3. *Behavioral Equivalencies*

Besides its elegant characterizations of types of behavior in terms of mathematical properties of the utility function, another of the useful aspects of expected utility theory is the behavioral equivalencies it implies. Indeed, it is *only* those theorems which relate various types of behavior which are ultimately meaningful, and the only reason one studies the behavior implied by, say, a concave utility function in some situation is because of the behavior it implies or to which it is equivalent in other situations.

It is in this respect, however, that the independence axiom would seem to be instrumental in deriving results in expected utility theory. For the independence axiom is essentially a global restriction on preferences, as it implies that the local utility functions at all distributions $F(\cdot)$ in $D[0, M]$ are identical. Thus, for example, knowing that an individual is averse to small mean preserving spreads about all certain (i.e. degenerate) distributions implies that the common local utility function is concave, which by Theorem 2 implies that the individual is averse to increases in risk about all initial distributions. Clearly, however, such a result no longer holds when the independence axiom is replaced by the *local* assumption of smoothness of preferences.

Nevertheless, it is possible to prove various behavioral equivalencies in the general case of smooth preferences and, as with Theorems 1 and 2, although these results do not require the independence axiom, they do follow the basic structures of the corresponding expected utility results. As a first example, consider again the expected utility result that aversion to all mean preserving increases in risk is implied by the local condition of aversion to all mean preserving spreads about certain (degenerate) distributions and the global restriction imposed by the independence axiom, which requires that if $F^*(\cdot)$ is weakly preferred to $F(\cdot)$, then the distribution $(1 - p)F^{**}(\cdot) + pF^*(\cdot)$ will be weakly preferred to $(1 - p)F^{**}(\cdot) + pF(\cdot)$, for arbitrary p, F, F^*, and F^{**}. Together these conditions imply (but are *not* implied by) the condition that for arbitrary p, F, and F^{**}, the distribution $(1 - p)F^{**}(\cdot) + pG_{\mu_F}(\cdot)$ is weakly preferred to $(1 - p)F^{**}(\cdot) + pF(\cdot)$ (where μ_F is the mean of F), i.e. in any compound lottery, the individual would always prefer to substitute (ex ante) the mean of any of the possible risky prizes for the risky prize itself. Note that this last condition requires merely that the conditional certainty equivalent (see Section 2.4) of the distribution F always be no greater than its mean, and not that it necessarily be some constant value independent of p and F^{**}, as does the independence axiom. The following theorem shows that in the case of behavioral equivalencies as well, the expected utility result provides the complete structure of the corresponding more general result, but that the sort of global equality condition imposed by the independence axiom may be replaced by the weaker requirement that the appropriate qualitative condition (i.e condition (i) of the theorem) hold throughout.

THEOREM 3: *The following properties of a Fréchet differentiable preference function $V(\cdot)$ on $D[0, M]$ are equivalent*: (i) *for arbitrary distributions $F(\cdot), F^{**}(\cdot) \in D[0, M]$ and arbitrary probability p, $V((1 - p)F^{**} + pG_{\mu_F}) \geqq V((1 - p)F^{**} + pF)$, where μ_F is the mean of F*; (ii) *$U(x; F)$ is concave in x for all $F \in D[0, M]$; and* (iii) *if $F^{*}(\cdot)$ differs from $F(\cdot)$ by a mean preserving increase in risk, then $V(F^{*}) \leqq V(F)$. (Proof in Appendix.)*

As a final example, we consider the Arrow-Pratt theorem of expected utility theory, which, as extended by Diamond and Stiglitz [19, Theorem 3], relates the mathematical condition of different levels of the Arrow-Pratt measure of absolute risk aversion to the behavioral conditions of differing certainty equivalents of risky prospects, effects of compensated increases in risk, and demands for a risky asset. Once again, the independence axiom (i.e. the requirement of constant conditional certainty equivalents) may be replaced by the requirement that the conditional certainty equivalents of one individual are always no greater than the corresponding conditional certainty equivalents of the other individual, regardless of whether the conditional certainty equivalents of either individual are constant (i.e. independent of p and F^{**}).

Proceeding similarly, we define the "conditional demand for a risky asset" as the value of α which yields the most preferred distribution in the set $\{(1 - p) F^{**} + pF_{(1-\alpha)r+\alpha\tilde{z}} | \alpha \in R^1\}$,[47] where r is a positive constant and $\tilde{z}$ a nonnegative random variable with mean greater than r, i.e. as the optimal proportion of a portfolio to place in the risky asset when there is some probability $(1 - p)$ that for exogenous reasons (such as bankruptcy) the distribution of wealth will be $F^{**}(\cdot)$ regardless of the composition of the portfolio. While the independence axiom requires that such conditional demands be a constant independent of p or F^{**}, we require merely that the conditional demands for one individual always be no greater than the corresponding ones of the other individual, regardless of whether these conditional demands vary with p or F^{**}.

---

[47]Where $F_{(1-\alpha)r+\alpha\tilde{z}}(\cdot)$ stands for the distribution function of $(1 - \alpha)r + \alpha\tilde{z}$, etc.

In order to confine our study of asset demand to the case of "regular" optima, we adopt the following condition—a generalization of the condition that indifference curves in the (σ, μ) plane be upward sloping and bowed downward—which serves to rule out both risk lovers and "plungers" as in the classic study of Tobin [93, pp. 77–78].

DEFINITION: A risk averse individual is said to be a *diversifier* if, for all distributions $F^{**}(\cdot)$, positive probabilities p, positive constants r, and nondegenerate nonnegative random variables $\tilde{z}$, the individual's preferences over the set of distributions $\{(1 - p)F^{**} + pF_{(1-\alpha)r+\alpha\tilde{z}} | \alpha \in R^1\}$ are strictly quasiconcave in α.[48]

THEOREM 4: *The following conditions on a pair of Fréchet differentiable preference functionals $V(\cdot)$ and $V^*(\cdot)$ on $D[0, M]$ with respective local utility functions $U(x; F)$ and $U^*(x; F)$ are equivalent:*

(i) *For arbitrary distributions $F(\cdot)$, $F^{**}(\cdot) \in D[0, M]$ and positive probability p, if c and c^* respectively solve $V((1 - p)F^{**} + pF) = V((1 - p)F^{**} + pG_c)$ and $V^*((1 - p)F^{**} + pF) = V^*((1 - p)F^{**} + pG_{c^*})$, then $c \leq c^*$, (i.e. the conditional certainty equivalents for $V(\cdot)$ are never greater than the corresponding ones for $V^*(\cdot)$).*

(ii) *For all $F(\cdot) \in D[0, M]$, $U(x; F)$ is at least as concave a function of x as $U^*(x; F)$ (i.e. for all F, $U(x; F)$ is a concave transform of $U^*(x; F)$), so that if these functions are twice differentiable in x, then $- U_{11}(x; F)/U_1(x; F) \geq - U_{11}^*(x; F)/U_1^*(x; F)$ for all x, where subscripts denote partial derivatives with respect to x.*

(iii) *If the distribution $F^*(\cdot)$ differs from $F(\cdot)$ by a simple compensated spread from the point of view of $V^*(\cdot)$ (see Section 2.1) so that $V^*(F^*) = V^*(F)$, then $V(F^*) \leq V(F)$.*

If both individuals are diversifiers and have differentiable local utility functions, then the above conditions are equivalent to:

(iv) *For any distribution $F^{**}(\cdot) \in D[0, M]$, positive probability p, positive constant r, and nonnegative random variable $\tilde{z}$ with $E[\tilde{z}] > r$, if α and α^* yield the most preferred distributions of the form $(1 - p)F^{**} + pF_{(1-\alpha)r+\alpha\tilde{z}}$ for $V(\cdot)$ and $V^*(\cdot)$ respectively, then $\alpha \leq \alpha^*$ (i.e. the conditional demands for risky assets are never greater for $V(\cdot)$ than for $V^*(\cdot)$).[49]*

(*Proof in Appendix.*)

Thus the Arrow-Pratt measure of risk aversion, when applied to the local utility functions, yields a necessary and sufficient condition for one individual to

---

[48] This condition ensures that preferences are either (i) strictly monotonic in α or (ii) admit of a unique optimum value of α and are monotonically increasing in α below this optimum value and monotonically decreasing in α above it.

[49] Note that special cases of conditions (i) and (iv) are that the unconditional certainty equivalents are higher for $V(\cdot)$ and that the unconditional demands for the risky asset are higher for $V^*(\cdot)$, respectively.

be more risk averse than another, so that in particular, expected utility results involving the Arrow-Pratt measure as a measure of comparative risk aversion will typically apply to any pair of individuals with smooth preferences. Similarly, the Arrow-Pratt measure is evidently a sufficient tool for the analysis of comparative risk aversion in the general case. The results of this section suggest that much of the rest of expected utility analysis may be similarly generalized.[50]

4. THE SHAPE OF THE INDIVIDUAL PREFERENCE FUNCTIONAL

In this section we present a pair of hypotheses concerning the shape of the individual preference functional and show that these hypotheses are consistent with, and in many cases actually imply, each of the aspects of behavior discussed in Section 2.

4.1. *The Hypotheses*

The following hypotheses describe (I) the typical shape of a local utility function about a given initial distribution and (II) how the local utility function changes when evaluated at different initial distributions, that is, how $U(x; F)$ varies with x and F, respectively. Although they have other equivalent formulations, each is most conveniently expressed in terms of the "Arrow-Pratt" term $-U_{11}(x; F)/U_1(x; F)$ used in Theorem 4.

HYPOTHESIS I: *For any distribution $F(\cdot) \in D[0, M]$, $-U_{11}(x; F)/U_1(x; F)$ is a nonincreasing function of x over $[0, M]$.*

HYPOTHESIS II: *For any $x \in [0, M]$ and distributions $F(\cdot), F^*(\cdot) \in D[0, M]$, if $F^*(\cdot)$ stochastically dominates $F(\cdot)$, then $-U_{11}(x; F^*)/U_1(x; F^*) \geq -U_{11}(x; F) /U_1(x; F)$. (That is, with respect to the partial order on $D[0, M]$ induced by the relation of stochastic dominance, $-U_{11}(x; F)/U_1(x; F)$ is "nondecreasing in F.")*

Thus, the assumptions that $R(\cdot)$ and $S(\cdot)$ are positive, increasing, exhibit declining absolute risk aversion in the Arrow-Pratt sense, and that $S(\cdot)$ is at least as concave as $R(\cdot)$, are sufficient (though not necessary) for the quadratic preference functional $\tilde{V}(\cdot)$ of equation (6) to satisfy both hypotheses.

It is important to note that Hypothesis I does not imply "decreasing absolute risk aversion in wealth" as it would if the individual were an expected utility maximizer. The willingness of an individual to insure against small risks about a certain wealth level c, for example, is given by $-U_{11}(c; G_c)/U_1(c; G_c)$, so that the effect of a wealth increase on this willingness to insure also depends on how this term is affected by changes in its second argument $G_c(\cdot)$ (see Machina [58]).

---

[50] In particular, note that the general approach and many of the specific results of this section may be extended to Fréchet differentiable preference functionals over multivariate (e.g. multi-commodity or intertemporal) distributions.

"EXPECTED UTILITY" ANALYSIS   301

4.2. *Insurance, Lotteries, and Skewness Preference*

The types of behavior discussed in Section 2.1 all pertain to the individual's ranking of alternative shifts from an initial probability distribution over ultimate wealth. In this section we show that, when the alternative shifts are small enough, each of these types of behavior is consistent with or implied by Hypothesis I. Although Hypothesis I only suggests and is not strong enough to imply that such behavior extends to "large" shifts, the less the preference functional deviates from linearity (i.e. the less the shape of $U(\cdot\,; F)$ depends on F) the more this will tend to be the case as well.

As seen in Figure 4, Hypothesis I is consistent both with general risk aversion in the neighborhood of the initial distribution (Figure 4a) or with aversion to increases in risk involving low outcome values coupled with a preference for increases in risk involving high outcome values (Figure 4b).[51] Thus, since the purchase of an insurance policy against a low outcome-small probability event and the purchase of a lottery ticket yielding a small chance of a large outcome both induce small changes in the initial distribution of wealth, an individual with a local utility function as in Figure 4b would tend to purchase both, while another individual (or the same individual at another initial distribution) with local utility function as in Figure 4a would be among the class of people who purchase insurance but not lottery tickets.[52]

To determine the implications of Hypothesis I with regard to skewness preference, note that, just as in expected utility theory, Hypothesis I implies that $U_{111}(x; F)$ is positive. If $U(x; F)$ is an analytic function of x over $[0, M]$, we may

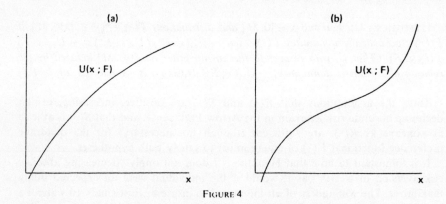

FIGURE 4

---

[51] There is of course a third case which satisfies Hypothesis I, namely a local utility function which is everywhere convex and has a nonincreasing Arrow-Pratt term. Since such a case implies that the individual prefers all small increases in risk, we shall not consider it further. The discussion in Section 4.4 below, however, will apply to this case as well.

[52] Note that this would be true even if the initial distribution of wealth were nondegenerate, provided that the outcome of the lottery and the event to be insured against were independent of the initial distribution of wealth.

302   MARK J. MACHINA

write

(10) $E_{F^*}\left[U(x;F)\right] = U(\mu_{F^*};F) + \sum_{n=2}^{\infty}\left(\frac{1}{n!}\right)c_n^{F^*}\cdot U_{(n)}(\mu_{F^*};F)$

$$\equiv g(\mu_{F^*}, c_2^{F^*}, c_3^{F^*}, \dots),$$

where c_n^F is the nth central moment of the distribution $F(\cdot)$ and $U_{(n)}(x;F)$ $= d^n U(x;F)/dx^n$. When $F^*(\cdot)$ is close to $F(\cdot)$, the first order Taylor expansion of g about the moments of $F(\cdot)$ gives

(11) $V(F^*) - V(F) \simeq E_{F^*}\left[U(x;F)\right] - E_F\left[U(x;F)\right]$

$$= \left[U_1(\mu_F;F) + \sum_{n=2}^{\infty}\left(\frac{1}{n!}\right)c_n^F\cdot U_{(n+1)}(\mu_F;F)\right]$$

$$\times(\mu_{F^*} - \mu_F) + \sum_{n=2}^{\infty}\left(\frac{1}{n!}\right)U_{(n)}(\mu_F;F)(c_n^{F^*} - c_n^F).$$

Thus, that component of the change from $F(\cdot)$ to $F^*(\cdot)$ which is commonly taken to represent the increase in skewness, namely $c_3^{F^*} - c_3^F$, is multiplied by the positive coefficient $U_{(3)}(\mu_F;F)/3! = U_{111}(\mu_F;F)/3!$.[53]

Finally, Hypothesis I implies that the individual will have a relative preference for (equivalently, a lower aversion to) small increases in risk in the upper rather than the lower tail of an initial wealth distribution, in the sense described in Section 2.1. To see this, let $F^*(\cdot)$ differ from $F(\cdot)$ by a differential simple compensated spread. Starting from $F(\cdot)$ again and applying this same differential increase in risk to outcome values which are all uniformly greater by the (positive or negative) constant c yields the distribution $F^{**}(\cdot)$ defined by $F^{**}(x) - F(x)$ $\equiv F^*(x - c) - F(x - c)$. Since $E_{F^*}[U(x;F)] - E_F[U(x;F)] = 0$ by assumption and $E_{F^{**}}[U(x;F)] - E_F[U(x;F)]$ equals $E_{F^*}[U(x + c;F)] - E_F[U(x + c;F)]$ by construction of $F^{**}(\cdot)$, we have that if c is positive (negative), then $F^{**}(\cdot)$ will be weakly preferred (weakly not preferred) to $F(\cdot)$, since by Hypothesis I $U(x + c; F)$ will be no less concave (at least as concave) a function of x as $U(x;F)$.

4.3. *Violations of the Independence Axiom*

In this section we offer formal characterizations of the various types of systematic violations of the independence axiom discussed in Sections 2.4 and 2.5 and demonstrate their equivalence to Hypothesis II.

The first type of behavior, mentioned in Section 2.4, was that if the two pairs of distributions (F_1, F_2) and (F_3, F_4) differ by the same "shift" (i.e. changes in the probabilities) or by scalar multiples of the same shift, so that $F_4(x) - F_3(x) \equiv \lambda \cdot$

---

[53] Mention should be made of Hanson and Menezes' [41] objections to the use of the third derivative of utility as a measure of skewness preference, which will apply to the present case as well.

$(F_2(x) - F_1(x))$ for some $\lambda > 0$, and if (F_3, F_4) respectively stochastically dominate (F_1, F_2), then the individual will rank F_3 and F_4 as if using a von
Neumann-Morgenstern utility function which is no less risk averse than the one
"used" to rank F_1 and F_2. Thus, if F_2 differs from F_1 by a simple compensated
spread, then F_3 will be weakly preferred to F_4. On the other hand, if F_4 differs
from F_3 by a simple compensated spread, then F_2 will be weakly preferred to F_1.

The second type of behavior discussed in Section 2.4 concerns the "nonindependence" of the conditional certainty equivalent of a risky prospect $F(\cdot)$ in
an event E with respect to the conditional distribution of wealth in $\sim E$. In
particular, it was observed that stochastically dominating shifts in this latter
distribution tended to lower the conditional certainty equivalent of F in E.

The third characterization of how individuals systematically violate the independence axiom, discussed in Section 2.5, was that, relative to expected utility
maximization, individuals are oversensitive to changes in the probabilities of low
probability-outlying events. Recall from Section 2.5 that if $x_1 < x_2 < x_3$ are three
outcome levels in $[0, M]$, then any rightward shift of the probability mass of the
initial distribution within the interval $[x_2, x_3]$ may be said to change the initial
distribution so as to make the event x_3 "less outlying relative to the events x_1 and
x_2." Similarly, any shift of mass from the interval $[x_2, x_3]$ to the interval $[x_3, M]$
may also be said to make the outcome x_3 less outlying to x_1 and x_2, since, for
example, if the bulk of the initial distribution of wealth were near the level
\$10,000, moving probability mass from near this level to the outcome level
\$5,000,001 would make both this event *as well as the event of winning five million
exactly* less outlying relative to events closer to the bulk of the distribution.
Finally, a further rightward shift of mass within the interval $[x_3, M]$ may also be
said to make x_3 less outlying relative to x_1 and x_2, since it changes the initial
distribution in a way which makes x_3 less of a "large outcome" relative to the
new initial distribution (or alternatively, it results in x_3 becoming closer to the
"center" of the new distribution, and farther from the "right edge"). We thus
adopt the following definition.

DEFINITION: If $x_1 < x_2 < x_3$ are three outcome levels in $[0, M]$, then any
rightward (leftward) shift of the probability mass of the initial distribution within
the interval $[x_2, M]$ is said to change the initial distribution so as to make x_3 *less*
(*more*) *outlying relative to the outcome levels* x_1 *and* x_2. Similarly, any leftward
(rightward) shift of mass within the interval $[0, x_2]$ is said to make the event x_1
less (*more*) *outlying relative to* x_2 *and* x_3.

Our definition of the individual's sensitivity to changes in the probabilities of
events is also motivated by the discussion of Section 2.5. If $x_1 < x_2 < x_3$, define
the "marginal rate of substitution between a shift of probability mass from x_2 to
x_1 and a shift of probability mass from x_2 to x_3" (abbreviated MRS$(x_2 \to x_1, x_2
\to x_3)$) as the amount of mass which must be shifted from x_2 to x_1 per unit
amount shifted from x_2 to x_3 in order to keep the individual indifferent, when the

304   MARK J. MACHINA

amounts shifted are infinitesimally small. From equation (5), this marginal rate of substitution is seen to equal $(U(x_3; F) - U(x_2; F))/(U(x_2; F) - U(x_1; F))$ where F is the initial distribution.[54] Marginal rates of substitution between other pairs of shifts of mass between the three outcome levels may be defined similarly.

It is clear that for an expected utility maximizer these marginal rates of substitution will not depend on the initial distribution $F(\cdot)$. We thus say that a given change in the initial distribution makes the individual "more (less) sensitive to changes in the probability of x_3 relative to changes in the probabilities of x_1 and x_2," if the change raises (lowers) both MRS($x_2 \to x_1, x_2 \to x_3$) and MRS($x_2 \to x_1, x_1 \to x_3$), that is, if a shift of mass from either x_1 or x_2 up to x_3 now requires a larger (smaller) shift from x_2 to x_1 to leave the individual indifferent. Note that since these last two marginal rates of substitution will always differ by unity, we may define this effect in terms of its effect on MRS($x_2 \to x_1, x_2 \to x_3$) alone. Similarly, a change in the initial distribution makes the individual more (less) sensitive to changes in the probability of x_1 relative to changes in the probabilities of x_2 and x_3 if it raises (lowers) MRS($x_2 \to x_3, x_2 \to x_1$) (and hence MRS($x_2 \to x_3, x_3 \to x_1$)), so that a shift of mass from either x_2 or x_3 down to x_1 now requires a greater (lesser) compensating shift from x_2 up to x_3. Since MRS($x_2 \to x_3, x_2 \to x_1$) $= 1/$MRS($x_2 \to x_1, x_2 \to x_3$), we may combine these notions and adopt the following definition.

DEFINITION: If $x_1 < x_2 < x_3$, a given change in the initial distribution is said to both make the individual *weakly more (weakly less) sensitive to changes in the probability of x_3 relative to changes in the probabilities of x_1 and x_2* and make the individual *weakly less (weakly more) sensitive to changes in the probability of x_1 relative to changes in the probabilities of x_2 and x_3* if it preserves or raises (preserves or lowers) the value of MRS($x_2 \to x_1, x_2 \to x_3$).[55]

A final characterization of how the independence axiom is systematically violated in the special case of preferences over two-outcome distributions has been termed the "certainty effect" by Kahneman and Tversky [46] and the "common ratio" effect by MacCrimmon and Larsson [57] (see also Allais [3, pp. 90–92], Tversky [98], and Hagen [38][56]). This states that if an individual with initial wealth w is indifferent between a p chance of winning an (additional) amount x and a pq chance of winning y, then a pqr chance of winning y will be (weakly) preferred to a pr chance of winning x, for p, q, and $r \in [0, 1]$.[57] The

---

[54] Note that MRS($x_2 \to x_1, x_2 \to x_3$) is mathematically well defined even though x_2 may not lie in the support of $F(\cdot)$. In this case its behavioral interpretation may be seen to be the ratio of the amounts of probability mass which must be respectively shifted to x_1 and to x_3 from some outcome value which *is* in the support in order to leave the individual as well off as if the same total amount of mass had been shifted to x_2.

[55] Note that from the previous footnote this definition does not require that x_2 lie in the support of the initial distribution.

[56] Note that the "Bergen Paradox" in Hagen [38, pp. 278–279, 290–292] is a special case of this effect as well.

[57] Note that this condition differs from the version in Kahneman and Tversky [46] in that all strict inequalities have been made weak.

"EXPECTED UTILITY" ANALYSIS   305

following theorem demonstrates that this effect is implied by each of the three types of behavior discussed in this section, which are in turn all equivalent to Hypothesis II.

THEOREM 5: *The following properties of a Fréchet differentiable preference function $V(\cdot)$ on $D[0,M]$ with twice differentiable local utility functions are equivalent:*

(i) *Hypothesis II.*

(ii) *Let $F_1(\cdot), F_2(\cdot), F_3(\cdot)$, and $F_4(\cdot) \in D[0,M]$ be such that F_3 and F_4 respectively stochastically dominate F_1 and F_2 and $F_4(x) - F_3(x) \equiv \lambda \cdot (F_2(x) - F_1(x))$ for some $\lambda > 0$. Then, if F_2 differs from F_1 by a simple compensated spread, $V(F_4) \leqq V(F_3)$. Similarly, if F_4 differs from F_3 by a simple compensated spread, then $V(F_2) \geqq V(F_1)$.*

(iii) *Given an event E with probability $p > 0$ and $F(\cdot), F^*(\cdot), F^{**}(\cdot) \in D[0,M]$ such that F^{**} stochastically dominates F^*, if c^* and c^{**} are the conditional certainty equivalents of F in E when the distribution of wealth in $\sim E$ is F^* and F^{**} respectively (i.e. if $V((1-p)F^* + pG_{c^*}) = V((1-p)F^* + pF)$ and $V((1-p) F^{**} + pG_{c^{**}}) = V((1-p)F^{**} + pF))$, then $c^* \geqq c^{**}$.*

(iv) *If x, y, and z are three outcome levels in $[0,M]$, then any change in the initial distribution of wealth which makes x more outlying relative to y and z makes the individual weakly more sensitive to changes in the probability of x relative to changes in the probabilities of y and z.*

In addition, each of these properties imply:

(v) *(The "Certainty Effect" or "Common Ratio" Effect) If, for some w, x, and $y \geqq 0$ and p,q, and $r \in [0,1]$ $V((1-p)G_w + pG_{w+x}) = V((1-pq)G_w + pqG_{w+y})$, then $V((1-pr)G_w + prG_{w+x}) \leqq V((1-pqr)G_w + pqrG_{w+y})$.*

(Proof in Appendix.)

Note that, unlike the examples in Section 4.2, Theorem 5 is "global" in that it applies to both small and large shifts in the distribution of wealth.

When choice is restricted to alternative distributions of the form F_{p_1,p_3}

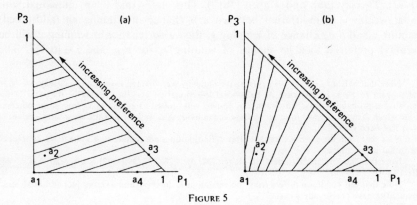

FIGURE 5

$= p_1 G_{x_1} + (1 - p_1 - p_3)G_{x_2} + p_3 G_{x_3}$, over the fixed outcomes $x_1 < x_2 < x_3$, Hypothesis II possesses a straightforward graphical interpretation in terms of indifference curves in the (p_1, p_3) plane, as in Figures 5a and 5b. It is clear that the slopes of these indifference curves, which indicate the individual's relative sensitivity to changes in p_1 versus changes in p_3, are given by $\mathrm{MRS}(x_2 \to x_3, x_2 \to x_1) = (U(x_2; F_{p_1,p_3}) - U(x_1; F_{p_1,p_3}))/(U(x_3; F_{p_1,p_3}) - U(x_2; F_{p_1,p_3}))$. Thus if the individual is an expected utility maximizer the slope will be a constant, as in Figure 5a, with a steeper slope indicating a higher level of risk aversion. However, if the individual satisfies Hypothesis II, stochastically dominating shifts in F_{p_1,p_3}, represented by upward or leftward movements in the (p_1, p_3) plane, will make the local utility function more risk averse and thus raise the slope of the indifference curves, so that the indifference curves will appear "fanned out," as in Figure 5b. The relatively steeper slopes in the region near the vertical axis than in the region near the horizontal axis illustrates the individual's greater sensitivity to changes in p_1 relative to p_3 when p_1 is small relative to p_3, and vice versa.[58]

If $x_1 = \$0$, $x_2 = \$1$ million, and $x_3 = \$5$ million, then the points corresponding to the four prospects of the Allais Paradox (Figure 3) form a parallelogram, as in Figures 5a and 5b. This illustrates why an expected utility maximizer must prefer either a_2 and a_3 if the common slope of the indifference curve is relatively flat (as in Figure 5a) or else a_1 and a_4 if it is relatively steep. Figure 5b illustrates how an individual satisfying Hypothesis II might violate the independence axiom by making the typical choices of a_1 and a_3.

4.4. *The Relative Invariance of Gambling Preferences to Initial Wealth*

In this section we demonstrate that a *fixed* preference functional $V(\cdot)$ satisfying Hypotheses I and II will tend to rank alternative gambles (expressed in terms of deviations from present wealth) relatively independently of the level of current wealth so that, unlike in the case of the expected utility model, there is no need to drop the assumption of stable preferences over $D[0, M]$ in order to accommodate the types of behavior discussed in Section 2.3.

To see this, recall that any cardinal (von Neumann-Morgenstern or local) utility function is completely characterized by its Arrow-Pratt function $-U_{11}/U_1$. Figure 6 illustrates the two alternative shapes of the local utility function of an individual with nonstochastic initial wealth level c (i.e. initial distribution $G_c(\cdot)$) together with their respective Arrow-Pratt functions, which by Hypothesis I are downward sloping. By Hypothesis II, if initial wealth increases to c^* (i.e. $G_c(\cdot)$ shifts to $G_{c^*}(\cdot)$), the Arrow-Pratt functions will shift upward, or alternatively, since they are downward sloping, shift rightward. This implies that the local utility functions will similarly shift rightward, as illustrated by the relative locations of the functions $U(\cdot; G_c)$ and $U(\cdot; G_{c^*})$ in Figure 6.

---

[58] This diagram clearly also applies to choices over distributions of the form $(1 - p)F + p_1 G_{x_1} + (p - p_1 - p_3)G_{x_2} + p_3 G_{x_3}$ for fixed $x_1 < x_2 < x_3$, p, and $F(\cdot)$, that is, over alternative ways of distributing a probability mass of p over $x_1, x_2,$ and x_3.

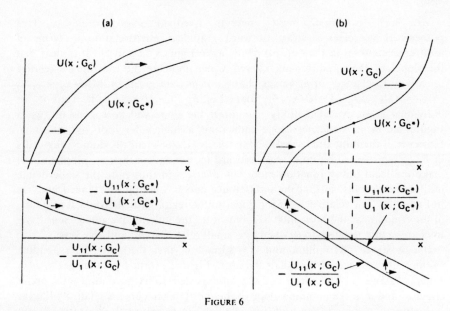

FIGURE 6

It is clear the Hypotheses I and II are not strong enough to ensure that the rightward shift in the local utility function induced by the change in initial wealth will be parallel and by the exact distance of $c^* - c$. To the extent that this happens, however, the individual's ranking of alternative gambles about initial wealth will be exactly preserved. In any event, the two hypotheses interact to ensure that preferences over gambles are less dependent upon the level of initial wealth than in the case of either of the fixed Friedman-Savage utility functions of Figures 1 and 2. In particular, it is quite possible for an individual with a fixed preference functional satisfying Hypotheses I and II to purchase insurance, purchase lottery tickets, and avoid small fair bets about all nonstochastic wealth levels. This would be the case whenever the local utility function in Figure 4b shifted so as to always keep the inflection point somewhat to the right of initial wealth (an example of such a preference functional is given in Section 4.5 below). Thus, for the purposes of explaining the behavior discussed in Section 2.3, the Markowitz assumption that shifts in initial wealth cause the entire linear preference functional to change may be replaced by the assumption that such shifts cause the *linear approximation* of a fixed nonlinear preference functional to change in the same qualitative manner. Finally, note that the two hypotheses imply that arbitrary stochastically dominating shifts in arbitrary nondegenerate initial wealth distributions will similarly cause the local utility function to shift rightward.

Besides the behavioral phenomenon of a relative invariance of gambling behavior to initial wealth, another potentially important set of behavioral observations which *cannot* be explained by Hypotheses I and II are the findings by some experimenters that individuals' expressed preferences over certain pairs of gambles can apparently be systematically reversed by increasing initial wealth by some amount and lowering each of the possible payoffs of the gambles (including zero) by the same amount, even though the two situations represent a choice over the same pair of distributions over ultimate wealth levels (see Kahneman and Tversky [46, p. 273]). Note that while this phenomenon is conceptually distinct from the "relative invariance . . . " phenomenon (which concerns the case when initial wealth, but not the gambles, is changed), the two are not mutually inconsistent, since an individual with an instantaneously shifting Markowitz utility function exhibits both.[59] It is, however, clearly incompatible with the existence of any fixed preference ranking over $D[0, M]$, and to the extent that it and similar observations of preference reversals and intransitivities in choice under certainty and uncertainty[60] are found to be systematic and pervasive, the behavioral model presented here must be either generalized or replaced. The point of the present section, however, is that the more extensively documented "*relative invariance* . . . " phenomenon does *not* contradict the assumption of stable preferences over $D[0, M]$, and in fact is implied by a preference ranking satisfying Hypotheses I and II.

4.5. The St. Petersburg Paradox, Lottery Prize Structures, and the Boundedness of Utility

In Section 2.2 it was seen that an individual with a Friedman-Savage utility function as in Figure 1 must necessarily violate each of the following "reasonable," and more to the point, commonly observed, types of behavior: (i) the amount that an individual with even minimal wealth would pay for a $1/n$ chance of winning $\$nZ$ eventually declines in n (so that lotteries will tend to have more than one prize), (ii) the individual would not forgo *any* finite sure gain to take the St. Petersburg gamble, and more generally, will assign a finite certainty equivalent to any probability distribution over nonnegative wealth levels, and (iii) there will exist a low enough positive probability p and a high enough payoff $\$C$ such that the individual will prefer a sure gain of $\$C$ to a p chance of winning any arbitrarily large prize $\$Z$.

Recall that in order to make the Friedman-Savage model compatible with these observations it was necessary to replace the terminal convex segment of the utility function with a bounded terminal concave segment.[61] In this section we

---

[59] It is interesting to note that although Markowitz observed that his model implied that such a change in initial wealth and the payoffs could yield an immediate preference reversal, he felt that it was "plausible to expect the chooser to act in the same manner in both situations" and sought to "resolve this dilemma" by introducing a lag between wealth changes and the shifting of the utility function [60, p. 155].

[60] See, for example, Kahneman and Tversky [46, pp. 271–273], Tversky [97, 98], Grether [34], Grether and Plott [35], and the references cited in these articles.

[61] Note that this adjustment is necessary regardless of whether it is assumed that the utility function shifts when initial wealth changes.

"EXPECTED UTILITY" ANALYSIS   309

demonstrate that, not only are these types of behavior completely consistent with Hypotheses I and II, but they are also consistent with the individual's local utility functions all possessing the terminally convex, unbounded "Friedman-Savage" shape of Figure 4b.

We demonstrate this by means of a specific example. Since each of the above types of behavior assumes that the potential outcome space is unbounded, we define the following preference functional over the space $D[0, \infty)$ of all probability distributions over the nonnegative reals:

$$(12) \qquad \bar{V}(F) \equiv E_F\big[x/(1+x)\big] - .1 \cdot \exp\big(-E_F[\exp(x)]\big),$$

where $\exp(\cdot)$ is the exponential function. It is clear that for any M, the restriction of $\bar{V}(\cdot)$ to $D[0, M]$ is Fréchet differentiable with local utility function

$$(13) \qquad \bar{U}(x; F) = x/(1+x) + .1 \cdot \exp\big(-E_F[\exp(z)]\big) \cdot \exp(x),$$

and with Arrow-Pratt term

$$(14) \qquad -\bar{U}_{11}(x; F)/\bar{U}_1(x; F)$$

$$= -1 + (3+x)\Big/\Big[(1+x)\big(1 + .1 \cdot (1+x)^2$$

$$\times \exp(x - E_F[\exp(z)])\big)\Big].$$

It is not difficult to show that for any $F(\cdot)$, $-\bar{U}_{11}(x; F)/\bar{U}_1(x; F)$ is positive for low values of x, strictly decreasing in x, and eventually negative as x gets large. Thus $\bar{V}(\cdot)$ satisfies Hypothesis I over any $D[0, M]$ and (fixing F and letting M grow large enough) has local utility functions all of the shape of Figure 4b. Similarly, stochastically dominating shifts in F will raise $-\bar{U}_{11}(x; F)/\bar{U}_1(x; F)$, so that Hypothesis II is also satisfied. Since the following theorem demonstrates that $\bar{V}(\cdot)$ will prefer a certain wealth w to any other distribution in $D[0, 2w]$ with the same mean, we have that an individual with this preference functional will purchase insurance, engage in lotteries, and avoid all symmetric and other small fair bets about all nonstochastic initial wealth levels. The following theorem also demonstrates that such an individual will exhibit each of the types of behavior listed at the beginning of this section.

THEOREM 6: *The preference functional* $\bar{V}(F) \equiv E_F[x/(1+x)] - .1 \cdot \exp(-E_F[\exp(x)])$ *defined over* $D[0, \infty)$ *exhibits each of the following properties*:
   (i) *If* $\pi(n, w, Z)$ *is the amount that an individual with initial wealth* $\$w$ *would pay for a* $1/n$ *chance of winning an additional* $\$nZ$, *then for any* $w > \$.04$, $\pi(n, w, Z)$ *is an eventually declining function of* n.
   (ii) *For each* $F(\cdot) \in D[0, \infty)$, *there will exist a finite value* w *such that* $\bar{V}(F) < \bar{V}(G_w)$.

310   MARK J. MACHINA

(iii) *For any certain initial wealth level w and probability $p < 1$, there exists a finite C such that* $\overline{V}(G_{w+C}) > \overline{V}((1 - p)G_w + pG_{w+Z})$ *for all nonnegative* Z.[62]

(iv) *If $F^*(\cdot)$ is any nondegenerate distribution in $D[0, 2w]$ with mean w, then $\overline{V}(F^*) < \overline{V}(G_w)$, so that in particular, $\overline{V}(\cdot)$ will prefer $G_w(\cdot)$ to all other symmetric distributions in $D[0, \infty)$ with mean w.*

(*Proof in Appendix.*)

Thus, generalized expected utility analysis allows us to model a willingness to purchase lottery tickets at all wealth levels (as well as other aspects of behavior) yet avoid the adverse behavioral implications of unbounded von Neumann-Morgenstern utility functions discussed in Section 2.2. The essence of this resolution of the "boundedness of utility" debate is that the assumption of terminally convex local utility functions merely implies that the *linear approximations* to the preference functional are unbounded linear functionals, whereas the assignment of infinite certainty equivalents by an expected utility maximizer with unbounded utility, i.e. the property that $\int U(x) dF(x) = \infty = \lim_{w \to \infty} U(w)$ for some $F(\cdot)$'s in $D[0, \infty)$, follows from the fact that for such an individual the *preference functional itself* is an unbounded linear functional. Once we drop the assumption of linearity of the preference functional (i.e. the independence axiom), however, these two conditions are seen to be quite distinct, for although $\overline{V}(\cdot)$ has unbounded local utility functions, $\overline{V}(F) < 1 = \lim_{w \to \infty} \overline{V}(G_w)$ for all $F(\cdot)$ in $D[0, \infty)$.

5. CONCLUSION

5.1 Testing Hypotheses on Preferences

It is clear that conditions (ii), (iii), and (iv) of Theorem 5 offer three (equivalent) ways of generating further refutable implications of Hypothesis II. It is straightforward to verify, for example, that the hypothesis implies that any individual preferring a_1 to a_2 or a_4 to a_3 in the Allais Paradox (Figure 3) must prefer the prospect (a_5) of a .89:.11 chance of winning $5 million or $1 million respectively to the prospect (a_6) of a .99:.01 chance of winning $5 million or $0.[63] More generally, Hypothesis II would be violated by any triple of preferred prospects out of the pairs (a_1, a_2), (a_3, a_4), and (a_5, a_6) other than (a_1, a_3, a_5), (a_1, a_4, a_5), (a_2, a_3, a_5), or (a_2, a_3, a_6).

A more general approach to testing hypotheses on preferences is to parametrize $V(\cdot)$ and estimate it directly. Thus, for example, for the quadratic

---

[62] Note that this particular condition is slightly stronger than the corresponding condition (iii) listed at the beginning of this section.

[63] This is true since the shift from a_5 to a_6 is the same as from a_1 to a_2 and from a_4 to a_3, and since a_5 stochastically dominates a_1 and a_4.

preference functional $\tilde{V}(\cdot)$ of equation (6), we have from equation (7) that

$$(15) \quad -\frac{\tilde{U}_{11}(x;F)}{\tilde{U}_1(x;F)} = \left[\frac{R'(x)}{R'(x) + E_F[S(z)] \cdot S'(x)}\right]\left[-\frac{R''(x)}{R'(x)}\right]$$

$$+ \left[\frac{E_F[S(z)] \cdot S'(x)}{R'(x) + E_F[S(z)] \cdot S'(x)}\right]\left[-\frac{S''(x)}{S'(x)}\right].$$

Equations (7) and (15) show how the properties of the preference functional depend on the properties of $R(\cdot)$ and $S(\cdot)$. Thus, if $R(\cdot)$ and $S(\cdot)$ are both positive, increasing, and concave, $\tilde{U}(\cdot;F)$ will be as well, and if, in addition, $S(\cdot)$ is more concave than $R(\cdot)$, then a stochastically dominating shift in F will, by raising $E_F[S(z)]$, raise $-\tilde{U}_{11}(x;F)/\tilde{U}_1(x;F)$. A particularly flexible four parameter functional form for $\tilde{V}(\cdot)$ can be obtained by adopting the parametrizations

$$(16) \quad \hat{R}(x) \equiv \int_0^x \exp\left(-az - \tfrac{1}{2}bz^2\right)dz \quad \text{and}$$

$$\hat{S}(x) \equiv \int_0^x \exp\left(-cz - \tfrac{1}{2}d \cdot z^2\right)dz,$$

which give $-\hat{R}''(x)/\hat{R}'(x) = a + bx$ and $-\hat{S}''(x)/\hat{S}'(x) = c + d \cdot x$. Thus, depending on the values of a, b, c, and d, $\hat{R}(\cdot)$ and $\hat{S}(\cdot)$ could be concave, convex, or have inflection points, and possess increasing, decreasing, or constant Arrow-Pratt terms, thus allowing for a wide range of behavior. Estimation of these parameters, say by a least squares fitting of predicted versus actual reported or observed certainty equivalents of alternative distributions, would allow for a direct test of Hypotheses I and II, as well as other hypotheses concerning the shape of $V(\cdot)$. (In this particular parametrization, Hypothesis I is valid when b and d are nonpositive, Hypothesis II is valid when $a + bx \leq c + d \cdot x$ for all $x \in [0, M]$, and the independence axiom is equivalent to the condition that $a = c$ and $b = d$.)

Finally, while the joint consistency of Hypotheses I and II with the existence of a preference functional was demonstrated directly by the example (12), it would be useful to know whether other additional or alternative hypotheses on how $U(x;F)$ varies with x and F are similarly consistent with the existence of some $V(\cdot)$. Expressing the local utility function in "normalized form" so that $U(0;F) = 0$ for all F,[64] and defining

$$(17) \quad Q(\alpha, \beta) \equiv V((1 - \alpha - \beta)F + \alpha G_{z_\bullet} + \beta G_{x_\bullet})$$

$$- V((1 - \alpha - \beta)F + \alpha G_0 + \beta G_{x_\bullet})$$

$$- V((1 - \alpha - \beta)F + \alpha G_{z_\bullet} + \beta G_0)$$

$$+ V((1 - \alpha - \beta)F + \alpha G_0 + \beta G_0),$$

---

[64] From the discussion in footnote 43, it is clear that we may replace $U(x;F)$ by $U(x;F) - U(0; F)$ to obtain this normalized form.

312   MARK J. MACHINA

we obtain

(18) $\dfrac{d}{d\alpha}\left(U(x^*;(1-\alpha)F+\alpha G_{z\cdot})-U(x^*;(1-\alpha)F+\alpha G_0)\right)\Big|_{\alpha=0}$

$=\dfrac{d^2}{d\alpha d\beta}\left(Q(\alpha,\beta)\right)\Big|_{\alpha=\beta=0}$

$=\dfrac{d}{d\beta}\left(U(z^*;(1-\beta)F+\beta G_{x\cdot})-U(z^*;(1-\beta)F+\beta G_0)\right)\Big|_{\beta=0}.$

In other words, (for $U(x;F)$ in normalized form), starting from any initial distribution $F(\cdot)$, an infinitesimal shift of probability mass from z^* to 0 will have the same effect on $U(x^*;F)$ as an equal shift of mass from x^* to 0 has on $U(z^*;F)$. While the question of sufficiency is beyond the scope of this paper, we thus have that a necessary condition for a hypothesis on how $U(x;F)$ varies with x and F to be consistent with the existence of some $V(\cdot)$ function is that it satisfy the symmetry or "integrability" condition (18).

5.2. *"Locally Utilitarian" Social Welfare Functionals*

Much of the analysis of Sections 3 and 4 admits of a straightforward interpretation in terms of the properties of an anonymous social welfare functional (SWF) $V(\cdot)$ defined over cumulative wealth distribution functions $F(\cdot)$ over a fixed population or measure space of agents. Because of the direct nature of the extensions, we offer neither proofs nor formal statements of theorems, but rather merely outline the types of results which may be obtained.

An important special case of such a SWF is the "utilitarian" (i.e. additively separable) functional $\int U(x)dF(x)$, where $U(x)$ is the social utility of an individual possessing wealth level x. It follows from Section 3.1, therefore, that if an arbitrary *nonutilitarian* SWF is "smooth enough," there will exist at each wealth distribution $F(\cdot)$ a cardinal "local social utility of wealth function" $U(\cdot;F)$ such that a small change from $F(\cdot)$ to a new wealth distribution $F^*(\cdot)$ will improve social welfare (i.e. raise $V(\cdot)$) if and only if it raises aggregate local social utility, that is, if $\int U(x;F)dF^*(x)\geq\int U(x;F)dF(x)$. It is clear from Theorem 1 that $V(\cdot)$ will satisfy the Pareto criterion (i.e. prefer an increase in any individual's wealth) if and only if all its local social utility functions are increasing in x. By Theorem 2 and the work of Atkinson [8], $V(\cdot)$ satisfies the Pigou-Dalton condition (i.e. is increased by costless transfers of wealth from the rich to the poor)[65] if and only if $U(x;F)$ is always concave in x. Similarly, Theorem 4 implies that the following conditions on a pair of SWF's $V(\cdot)$ and $V^*(\cdot)$ are equivalent: (i) costly (i.e. aggregate wealth lowering) transfers from richer to poorer individuals which preserve the value of $V^*(\cdot)$ will preserve or raise $V(\cdot)$;

---

[65] Other equivalent versions of this condition for utilitarian and nonutilitarian SWF's are discussed in Dasgupta, Sen, and Starrett [16] and Rothschild and Stiglitz [75].

(ii) the maximum acceptable cost of effecting a complete redistribution of wealth among any subgroup of society is no lower for $V(\cdot)$ than for $V^*(\cdot)$;[66] and (iii) the local social utility of wealth functions of $V(\cdot)$ are at least as concave as the corresponding ones of $V^*(\cdot)$. These equivalencies provide a natural extension of the relation "more inequality averse" to arbitrary (i.e. not necessarily utilitarian) SWF's.

Hypotheses I and II similarly admit of straightforward normative interpretations. It follows from equation (5) that the maximum acceptable proportionate deadweight loss in transferring a small amount of wealth from an individual with wealth x_b to one with wealth $x_a < x_b$ (where this loss is taken from the transferred wealth) is given by

(19) $1 - (U_1(x_b; F) / U_1(x_a; F))$

$$= 1 - \exp\left(- \int_{x_a}^{x_b} (- U_{11}(x; F) / U_1(x; F)) \, dx\right).$$

Hypothesis I thus implies that this maximum acceptable loss will be preserved or increased if x_a and x_b are lowered by a common amount, so that (in this sense, at least) society is at least as willing to expend resources in redistributing wealth among the poor than among the rich. Hypothesis II implies that, for fixed x_a and x_b, society's willingness to redistribute wealth between these two individuals will be preserved or increased by an improvement in the absolute wealth levels of (any or all) *other* members of society, in contrast to the utilitarian case where this willingness is independent of the wealth levels of others.[67] Together, as in Section 4.4, the two hypotheses imply that, compared with the utilitarian case of a fixed $U(\cdot)$ function, society's notions of inequality or poverty are "relative" in the sense that the local social utility function will shift rightward in response to a general increase in wealth levels.

5.3. Related Work

Besides the work of Kahneman and Tversky [46], recent years have seen a revival of interest in non-expected utility maximizing behavior. Although none of the following take the approach developed here, the reader is referred to Allais [4], Chew and MacCrimmon [14, 15], Hagen [38], Kreps and Porteus [49], MacCrimmon and Larsson [57], and Selden [84].

University of California, San Diego

Manuscript received April, 1980; final revision received July, 1981.

---

[66] In both this and the previous condition, the cost of the transfer is assumed to be taken out of the transferred wealth, and not born by any other member of society.

[67] See Rothschild and Stiglitz [75], Sen [85, pp. 39–41], and the references cited there for a general discussion of the implications of additive separability in this context.

314   MARK J. MACHINA

APPENDIX

LEMMA 1: *The topology of weak convergence on $D[0, M]$ is induced by the L^1 metric $d(F^*, F)$ $\equiv \int |F^*(x) - F(x)| dx$ on $D[0, M]$.*

PROOF: Assume $F_n(x) \to F(x)$ at all continuity points x of $F(\cdot)$. Since $F(\cdot)$ is a cumulative distribution function this implies $|F_n(x) - F(x)| \to 0$ almost everywhere on $[0, M]$. Since $|F_n(x) - F(x)|$ is bounded by unity, by the Bounded Convergence Theorem (see Klambauer [48, pp. 59–60]) we have $d(F_n, F) = \int |F_n(x) - F(x)| dx \to 0$.

Conversely, let $g(\cdot)$ be an arbitrary continuous function on $[0, M]$ and ϵ an arbitrary positive number. By the Weierstrass Approximation Theorem, there exists a polynomial $\tilde{g}(\cdot)$ on $[0, M]$ such that $|\tilde{g}(x) - g(x)| < \epsilon/4$ for all $x \in [0, M]$. Also, since $\tilde{g}(\cdot)$ is a polynomial its derivative $\tilde{g}'(\cdot)$ is bounded on $[0, M]$ by some finite L. Thus, for any n, $|\int g(x)(dF_n(x) - dF(x))| < (\epsilon/2) + |\int \tilde{g}(x)(dF_n(x) - dF(x))|$, which by Lemma 2 equals $(\epsilon/2) + |\int (F_n(x) - F(x))\tilde{g}'(x) dx| \le (\epsilon/2) + L \cdot d(F_n, F)$ which, if $d(F_n, F) \to 0$, becomes less than ϵ as $n \to \infty$.   *Q.E.D.*

LEMMA 2: *If $F(\cdot)$ is a cumulative distribution function on $[0, M]$ and $g(\cdot)$ is absolutely continuous over $[0, M]$, then $\int g(x) dF(x) = g(M) - \int F(x) dg(x)$.*

PROOF: Let $\{x_i\}_{i=1}^{n+1}$ be a grid on $[0, M]$ (i.e. $0 = x_1 < \cdots < x_{n+1} = M$) with norm defined as $\max_i(x_{i+1} - x_i)$. Then $g(M) = g(M) \cdot F(M) = \sum_{i=1}^n (F(x_{i+1})g(x_{i+1}) - F(x_i)g(x_i)) + F(0)g(0)$ $= [F(0)g(0) + \sum_{i=1}^n (F(x_{i+1}) - F(x_i))g(x_i)] + [\sum_{i=1}^n (F(x_{i+1}) - F(x_i))(g(x_{i+1}) - g(x_i))] + [\sum_{i=1}^n F(x_i)(g(x_{i+1}) - g(x_i))]$. As the norm of the grid goes to zero, the first and third bracketed terms go to $\int g(x) dF(x)$ and $\int F(x) dg(x)$ respectively. By uniform continuity of $g(\cdot)$, there will exist for each positive ϵ a positive δ such that if the norm of the grid is less than δ, then $|g(x_{i+1}) - g(x_i)|$ $< \epsilon$ for all i, so that the absolute value of the second bracketed term is less than $\epsilon \cdot \sum_{i=1}^n (F(x_{i+1}) - F(x_i)) \le \epsilon$, so that as the norm of the grid goes to zero, we obtain the desired result.   *Q.E.D.*

PROOF OF THEOREM 1: Assume $F^*(\cdot)$ stochastically dominates $F(\cdot)$, and define $F(x; \alpha) \equiv \alpha F^*(x) + (1 - \alpha)F(x)$ for all $(x, \alpha) \in [0, M] \times [0, 1]$. From (9) we have

$$V(F^*) - V(F) = V(F(\cdot; 1)) - V(F(\cdot; 0))$$

$$= \int_0^1 \left[\frac{d}{d\alpha} \left(\int U(x; F(\cdot; \alpha^*)) dF(x; \alpha) \right) \Big|_{\alpha^*} \right] d\alpha^*$$

$$= \int_0^1 \left[\int U(x; F(\cdot; \alpha^*))(dF^*(x) - dF(x)) \right] d\alpha^*.$$

However, if $U(x; F(\cdot; \alpha^*))$ is nondecreasing in x for all $F(\cdot; \alpha^*)$, then it follows from expected utility theory that the last bracketed expression will be nonnegative for all α^*, so that $V(F^*) \ge V(F)$.

Conversely, assume that for some $\tilde{F}(\cdot) \in D[0, M]$ and $0 \le x^* < x^{**} \le M$ we have $U(x^*; \tilde{F})$ $> U(x^{**}; \tilde{F})$. Defining $F^*(x; \alpha) \equiv \alpha G_{x^*}(x) + (1 - \alpha)\tilde{F}(x)$ and $F^{**}(x; \alpha) \equiv \alpha G_{x^{**}}(x) + (1 - \alpha)\tilde{F}(x)$, so that $F^*(\cdot; 0) = F^{**}(\cdot; 0)$, we have from equation (8) that

$$\frac{d}{d\alpha} (V(F^*(\cdot; \alpha)) - V(F^{**}(\cdot; \alpha))) \Big|_{\alpha = 0}$$

$$= \frac{d}{d\alpha} \left[\int U(x; \tilde{F})(\alpha dG_{x^*}(x) + (1 - \alpha) d\tilde{F}(x)) \right.$$

$$\left. - \int U(x; \tilde{F})(\alpha dG_{x^{**}}(x) + (1 - \alpha) d\tilde{F}(x)) \right] \Big|_{\alpha = 0}$$

$$= U(x^*; \tilde{F}) - U(x^{**}; \tilde{F}) > 0,$$

so that for some small positive α^* we have $V(F^*(\cdot; \alpha^*)) > V(F^{**}(\cdot; \alpha^*))$, even though $F^{**}(\cdot; \alpha^*)$ stochastically dominates $F^*(\cdot; \alpha^*)$.   *Q.E.D.*

PROOFS OF THEOREMS 2 AND 3: Theorems 2 and 3 follow directly from the equivalence of conditions (i), (ii), and (iii) of Theorem 4 when $V^*(F)$ is defined to identically equal $\int x \cdot dF(x)$ (so that $U^*(x; F) \equiv x$).   *Q.E.D.*

"EXPECTED UTILITY" ANALYSIS   315

PROOF OF THEOREM 4: (i)→(ii): Assume that for some $F^{**}(\cdot) \in D[0, M]$, $U(\cdot; F^{**})$ was not at least as concave as $U^*(\cdot; F^{**})$, so that for some q and $0 \leq x_1 < x_2 < x_3 \leq M$,

$$0 < (U(x_2; F^{**}) - U(x_1; F^{**}))/(U(x_3; F^{**}) - U(x_1; F^{**})) < q$$

$$< (U^*(x_2; F^{**}) - U^*(x_1; F^{**}))/(U^*(x_3; F^{**}) - U^*(x_1; F^{**})) < 1.$$

Let $F(\cdot) \equiv qG_{x_3}(\cdot) + (1 - q)G_{x_1}(\cdot)$. Applying equation (8) and simplifying yields

$$\frac{d}{dp}\left(V((1 - p)F^{**} + pF) - V((1 - p)F^{**} + pG_{x_2}))\right)\bigg|_{p=0}$$

$$= \int U(x; F^{**})(dF(x) - dG_{x_2}(x))$$

$$= qU(x_3; F^{**}) + (1 - q)U(x_1; F^{**}) - U(x_2; F^{**}) > 0,$$

and similarly that

$$\frac{d}{dp}\left(V^*((1 - p)F^{**} + pF) - V^*((1 - p)F^{**} + pG_{x_2}))\right)\bigg|_{p=0} < 0.$$

This implies that, for some small positive p, $V((1 - p)F^{**} + pF) > V((1 - p)F^{**} + pG_{x_2})$ and $V^*((1 - p)F^{**} + pF) < V^*((1 - p)F^{**} + pG_{x_2})$, which respectively imply $c > x_2$ and $c^* < x_2$, contradicting (i).

(ii)→(iii): Let $F^*(\cdot)$ differ from $F(\cdot)$ by a simple compensated spread from the point of view of $V^*(\cdot)$, with I_L and I_R the intervals referred to in the definition of simple compensated spread (Section 2.1). Define $\phi^+(x) = \max[F^*(x) - F(x), 0]$, $\phi^-(x) = \min[F^*(x) - F(x), 0]$, and $F(x; \alpha, \beta) = F(x) + \alpha\phi^+(x) + \beta\phi^-(x)$ for all x in $[0, M]$. For $\alpha \in [0, 1]$, define $\beta(\alpha)$ as the solution to $V^*(F(\cdot; \alpha, \beta(\alpha))) = V^*(F) = V^*(F^*)$. Smoothness and strict monotonicity of $V^*(\cdot)$ ensure that $\beta(\alpha)$ is unique, increasing, differentiable, and that $\beta(0) = 0$ and $\beta(1) = 1$, so that for any α^* in $[0, 1]$,

(A.1) $$0 = \frac{d}{d\alpha}\left(V^*(F(\cdot; \alpha, \beta(\alpha)))\right)\bigg|_{\alpha^*}$$

$$= \frac{d}{d\alpha}\left(\int U^*(x; F(\cdot; \alpha^*, \beta(\alpha^*))) dF(x; \alpha, \beta(\alpha))\right)\bigg|_{\alpha^*}$$

$$= \int U^*(x; F(\cdot; \alpha^*, \beta(\alpha^*)))[d\phi^+(x) + \beta'(\alpha^*) \cdot d\phi^-(x)].$$

Proceeding similarly with the preference functional $V(\cdot)$ yields

(A.2) $$V(F^*) - V(F) = V(F(\cdot; 1, 1)) - V(F(\cdot; 0, 0))$$

$$= V(F(\cdot; 1, \beta(1))) - V(F(\cdot; 0, \beta(0)))$$

$$= \int_0^1 \left[\frac{d}{d\alpha}(V(F(\cdot; \alpha, \beta(\alpha))))\bigg|_{\alpha^*}\right] d\alpha^*.$$

where, as in (A.1), the last bracketed term is seen to equal

(A.3) $$\int U(x; F(\cdot; \alpha^*, \beta(\alpha^*)))[d\phi^+(x) + \beta'(\alpha^*) \cdot d\phi^-(x)].$$

From (A.1) and the definitions of ϕ^+ and ϕ^- it is seen that the shift $\phi^+(\cdot) + \beta'(\alpha^*) \cdot \phi^-(\cdot) \in \Delta D[0, M]$ is a mean utility preserving increase in risk with respect to the utility function $U^*(\cdot; F(\cdot; \alpha^*, \beta(\alpha^*)))$ (see Diamond and Stiglitz [19, pp. 341–345]). Thus, by Condition (ii) of the present theorem and Theorem 3 of Diamond and Stiglitz [19], the term (A.3) is nonpositive for all α^* in $[0, 1]$, which from (A.2) implies that $V(F^*) \leq V(F)$.

(iii)→(i): Since $(1 - p)F^{**} + pF$ differs from $(1 - p)F^{**} + pG_{c^*}$ by a simple compensated spread

MARK J. MACHINA

with respect to $V^*(\cdot)$ (where $I_L = [0, c^*)$), we have $V((1-p)F^{**} + pG_{c^*}) \geq V((1-p)F^{**} + pF)$ $= V((1-p)F^{**} + pG_c)$, so that by monotonicity, $c^* \geq c$.

(ii) → (iv): If for some $F^{**}(\cdot)$, p, r, and $\tilde{z}$ we have $\alpha^* < \alpha$ there would exist some $\bar{\alpha} \in (\alpha^*, \alpha)$ such that

$$\frac{d}{d\alpha}\left(V^*((1-p)F^{**} + pF_{(1-\alpha)r+\alpha\tilde{z}})\right)\Big|_{\bar{\alpha}} < 0 < \frac{d}{d\alpha}\left(V((1-p)F^{**} + pF_{(1-\alpha)r+\alpha\tilde{z}})\right)\Big|_{\bar{\alpha}}.$$

Let $F_{\tilde{z}}(\cdot)$ be the distribution of $\tilde{z}$ and

$$\bar{F}(\cdot) = (1-p)F^{**}(\cdot) + pF_{(1-\bar{\alpha})r+\alpha\tilde{z}}(\cdot).$$

From (ii) and Pratt [68], we have that $x_1 < x_2$ implies $U_1(x_2; F)/U_1(x_1; F) \leq U_1^*(x_2; F)/U_1^*(x_1; F)$ for all F in $D[0, M]$. Thus

$$0 < \frac{d}{d\alpha}\left(V((1-p)F^{**} + pF_{(1-\alpha)r+\alpha\tilde{z}})\right)\Big|_{\bar{\alpha}}$$

$$= \frac{d}{d\alpha}\left(\int U(x; \bar{F})((1-p)dF^{**}(x) + p\,dF_{(1-\alpha)r+\alpha\tilde{z}}(x))\right)\Big|_{\bar{\alpha}}$$

$$= p\frac{d}{d\alpha}\left(\int U((1-\alpha)r + \alpha z; \bar{F})\,dF_{\tilde{z}}(z)\right)\Big|_{\bar{\alpha}}$$

$$= pU_1(r; \bar{F})\left[\int_0^r (z-r)\left(U_1((1-\bar{\alpha})r + \bar{\alpha}z; \bar{F})/U_1(r; \bar{F})\right)dF_{\tilde{z}}(z)\right.$$

$$\left. + \int_r^M (z-r)\left(U_1((1-\bar{\alpha})r + \bar{\alpha}z; \bar{F})/U_1(r; \bar{F})\right)dF_{\tilde{z}}(z)\right]$$

$$\leq pU_1(r; \bar{F})\left[\int_0^r (z-r)\left(U_1^*((1-\bar{\alpha})r + \bar{\alpha}z; \bar{F})/U_1^*(r; \bar{F})\right)dF_{\tilde{z}}(z)\right.$$

$$\left. + \int_r^M (z-r)\left(U_1^*((1-\bar{\alpha})r + \bar{\alpha}z; \bar{F})/U_1^*(r; \bar{F})\right)dF_{\tilde{z}}(z)\right].$$

since monotonicity of $V^*(\cdot)$ and the fact that the mean of z is greater than r imply that α^* and therefore $\bar{\alpha}$ is positive, which in turn implies that $(1-\bar{\alpha})r + \bar{\alpha}z$ will be greater than (less than) r if and only if z is greater than (less than) r. However, the positivity of the last bracketed term implies that

$$\frac{d}{d\alpha}\left(V^*((1-p)F^{**} + pF_{(1-\alpha)r+\alpha\tilde{z}})\right)\Big|_{\bar{\alpha}} > 0,$$

which is a contradiction.

(iv) → (ii): If for some $\tilde{F} \in D[0, M]$ $U(\cdot; \tilde{F})$ is not at least as concave as $U^*(\cdot; \tilde{F})$, from Pratt [68] there will exist $x_1 < x_2$ and $\beta \in (0, 1)$ such that

$$U_1(x_2; \tilde{F})/U_1(x_1; \tilde{F}) > \beta > U_1^*(x_2; \tilde{F})/U_1^*(x_1; \tilde{F}),$$

so that for some small positive δ,

$$\frac{U(x_2 + \delta; \tilde{F}) - U(x_2; \tilde{F})}{U(x_1; \tilde{F}) - U(x_1 - \beta\delta; \tilde{F})} > 1 > \frac{U^*(x_2; \tilde{F}) - U^*(x_2 - \delta; \tilde{F})}{U^*(x_1 + \beta\delta; \tilde{F}) - U^*(x_1; \tilde{F})}.$$

This implies that for some positive probability p, $V(F_b) < V(F_c)$ and $V^*(F_a) > V^*(F_b)$, where

$$F_a(\cdot) = (1-p)\tilde{F}(\cdot) + \frac{p}{2}G_{x_1+\beta\delta}(\cdot) + \frac{p}{2}G_{x_2-\delta}(\cdot),$$

$$F_b(\cdot) = (1-p)\tilde{F}(\cdot) + \frac{p}{2}G_{x_1}(\cdot) + \frac{p}{2}G_{x_2}(\cdot), \quad \text{and}$$

$$F_c(\cdot) = (1-p)\tilde{F}(\cdot) + \frac{p}{2}G_{x_1-\beta\delta}(\cdot) + \frac{p}{2}G_{x_2+\delta}(\cdot).$$

Letting

$$\alpha_a = 1 - \delta(1 + \beta)/(x_2 - x_1) < \alpha_b = 1 < \alpha_c = 1 + \delta(1 + \beta)/(x_2 - x_1).$$

$r = (x_1 + \beta x_2)/(1 + \beta)$, and $\tilde{z}$ the random variable with distribution $F_{\tilde{z}}(\cdot) = \frac{1}{2} G_{x_1}(\cdot) + \frac{1}{2} G_{x_2}(\cdot)$, tedious algebra yields that

$$F_a = (1 - p)\tilde{F} + pF_{(1 - \alpha_a)r + \alpha_a \tilde{z}},$$

$$F_b = (1 - p)\tilde{F} + pF_{(1 - \alpha_b)r + \alpha_b \tilde{z}},$$

and

$$F_c = (1 - p)\tilde{F} + pF_{(1 - \alpha_c)r + \alpha_c \tilde{z}}$$

which, since both individuals are diversifiers, implies that the optimal value of α for $V(\cdot)$ is greater than α_b and that the optimal value of α for $V^*(\cdot)$ is less than α_b, contradicting (iv).   Q.E.D.

PROOF OF THEOREM 5: (i) → (iv): Assume $x < y < z$. Then, by definition, any shift in the initial distribution which serves to make x more outlying relative to y and z must be a stochastically dominating shift, which by Hypothesis II preserves or raises the value of $- U_{11}(\xi; F)/U_1(\xi; F)$ for all ξ. From Pratt [68], this will preserve or lower the value of $(U(z; F) - U(y; F))/(U(y; F) - U(x; F))$ = MRS($y \to x, y \to z$), which by definition makes the individual weakly more sensitive to changes in the probability of x relative to changes in the probabilities of y and z. A similar argument applies when x is greater than y and z.

(iv) → (i): Assume $F^*(\cdot)$ stochastically dominates $F(\cdot)$, and let $x_1 < x_2 < x_3$ be arbitrary elements of $[0, M]$. Then the shift from F to F^* may be decomposed into a leftward shift of mass within the interval $[0, x_2]$ and a subsequent rightward shift within $[x_2, M]$ (where any mass that is ultimately shifted across x_2 is first shifted to it, then rightward from it). Since the first component of the shift makes x_1 more outlying relative to x_2 and x_3, it makes the individual weakly more sensitive to changes in the probability of x_1 relative to changes in the probabilities of x_2 and x_3, and hence preserves or lowers MRS($x_2 \to x_1, x_2 \to x_3$). Similarly, the second component of the shift makes x_3 less outlying relative to x_1 and x_2, and hence also preserves or lowers MRS($x_2 \to x_1, x_2 \to x_3$). Thus for the entire shift we have

$$(U(x_3; F^*) - U(x_2; F^*))/(U(x_2; F^*) - U(x_1; F^*))$$

$$\leq (U(x_3; F) - U(x_2; F))/(U(x_2; F) - U(x_1; F)).$$

From Pratt [68], we know that if this inequality holds for arbitrary $x_1 < x_2 < x_3$, then for all x, $- U_{11}(x; F^*)/U_1(x; F^*) \geq - U_{11}(x; F)/U_1(x; F)$.

(i) → (ii): Assume F_2 differs from F_1 by a simple compensated spread. Identifying F_2 with F^*, F_1 with F, and V with V^*, define I_L, I_R, $\phi^+(\cdot)$, $\phi^-(\cdot)$, $F(\cdot; \alpha, \beta)$, and $\beta(\cdot)$ as in the proof of the implication (ii) → (iii) in Theorem 4. Then, as in equation (A.1) we have

$$0 = \frac{d}{d\alpha} \left(V(F(\cdot; \alpha, \beta(\alpha))) \right)\Big|_{\alpha^*} = \int U(x; F(\cdot; \alpha^*, \beta(\alpha^*)))[d\phi^+(x) + \beta'(\alpha^*) \cdot d\phi^-(x)],$$

so that the shift $\phi^+(\cdot) + \beta'(\alpha^*) \cdot \phi^-(\cdot)$ is seen to be a mean utility preserving increase in risk with respect to the utility function $U(\cdot; F(\cdot; \alpha^*, \beta(\alpha^*)))$.

Similarly, since $F_4(\cdot) = F_3(\cdot) + \lambda \cdot (\phi^+(\cdot) + \phi^-(\cdot)) = F_3(\cdot) + \lambda \cdot \phi^+(\cdot) + \lambda \cdot \beta(1) \cdot \phi^-(\cdot)$, we have

$$V(F_4) - V(F_3) = \int_0^1 \left[\frac{d}{d\alpha} \left(V(F_3 + \alpha \cdot \lambda \cdot \phi^+ + \beta(\alpha) \cdot \lambda \cdot \phi^-) \right)\Big|_{\alpha^*} \right] d\alpha^*$$

$$= \lambda \cdot \int_0^1 \left[\int U(x; F_3 + \alpha^*\lambda\phi^+ + \beta(\alpha^*)\lambda\phi^-) \right.$$

$$\left. \times (d\phi^+(x) + \beta'(\alpha^*) d\phi^-(x)) \right] d\alpha^*.$$

318   MARK J. MACHINA

Thus, by Hypothesis II and the argument in the proof of the implication (ii) → (iii) in Theorem 4, to prove that the above bracketed term is nonpositive for all α^* it suffices to demonstrate that the distribution $F_3 + \alpha^*\lambda\phi^+ + \beta(\alpha^*)\lambda\phi^-$ stochastically dominates $F(\cdot; \alpha^*, \beta(\alpha^*))$ for all α^*.

Now, since $F_4(x) - F_2(x) = F_3(x) - F_1(x) + (\lambda - 1)\phi^+(x) + (\lambda - 1)\phi^-(x)$ is nonpositive for all x in $[0, M]$ as is $F_3(x) - F_1(x)$, and since α^* and $\beta(\alpha^*)$ both lie in the unit interval, we have that for all x in I_L,

$$F_3(x) + \alpha^*\lambda\phi^+(x) + \beta(\alpha^*)\lambda\phi^-(x) - F_1(x) - \alpha^*\phi^+(x) - \beta(\alpha^*)\phi^-(x)$$

$$= F_3(x) - F_1(x) + \alpha^*(\lambda - 1)\phi^+(x)$$

(since $\phi^-(x) = 0$ on I_L), which will be nonpositive regardless of the sign of $(\lambda - 1)$. A similar argument for the case of x in I_R establishes the required stochastic dominance result.

A similar argument applies in the case when F_4 differs from F_3 by a simple compensated spread.

(ii) → (iii): Condition (iii) follows from monotonicity and Condition (ii) by defining

$$F_1 = (1 - p)F^* + pG_{\cdot\cdot}, \qquad F_2 = (1 - p)F^* + pF, \qquad F_3 = (1 - p)F^{**} + pG_{\cdot\cdot}, \qquad \text{and}$$

$$F_4 = (1 - p)F^{**} + pF.$$

(iii) → (i): The proof of this implication corresponds almost directly to the proof of the implication (i) → (ii) in Theorem 4 and is omitted.

(ii) → (v): Condition (v) is seen to be a special case of Condition (ii) when F_3, F_4, F_1, and F_2 are defined to equal the four respective arguments of $V(\cdot)$ in Condition (v), with $\lambda = 1/r$ (the case when $r = 0$ is trivial).   Q.E.D.

PROOF OF THEOREM 6:(i): Define

$$F(\cdot; n, w, Z) \equiv \left(1 - \frac{1}{n}\right)G_w(\cdot) + \frac{1}{n}G_{w+nZ}(\cdot).$$

Then from (8),

$$\frac{d}{dn}\left(\bar{V}(F(\cdot; n, w, Z))\right) = Z \cdot \bar{U}_1(w + nZ; F(\cdot; n, w, Z))/n$$

$$- \left(\bar{U}(w + nZ; F(\cdot; n, w, Z)) - \bar{U}(w; F(\cdot; n, w, Z))\right)/n^2.$$

Substituting from (13) and rearranging gives

(A.4) $$\frac{d}{dn}\left(\bar{V}(F(\cdot; n, w, Z))\right) = \left\{-Z^2/((1 + w + nZ)^2(1 + w))\right\}$$

$$+ \left\{.1 \cdot \left(Z - \frac{1}{n}\right)\exp\left(w + nZ - E_{F(\cdot; n, w, Z)}[\exp(z)]\right)/n\right\}$$

$$+ \left\{.1 \cdot \exp\left(w - E_{F(\cdot; n, w, Z)}[\exp(z)]\right)/n^2\right\}.$$

Since

$$E_{F(\cdot; n, w, Z)}[\exp(z)] = \left(1 - \frac{1}{n}\right)\exp(w) + \frac{1}{n}\exp(w + nZ),$$

we have that the first of the three terms on the right hand side of (A.4) goes to zero at rate $1/n^2$, and the second and third terms go to zero at a faster rate, so that for fixed w and Z, as n grows large enough, $d(\bar{V}(F(\cdot; n, w, Z)))/dn$ eventually becomes negative. It is also clear that for given w and Z there will exist a finite $n(w, Z)$ such that $n > n(w, Z)$ implies that $d(\bar{V}(F(\cdot; n, \bar{w}, Z)))/dn < 0$ for all $\bar{w} \in [0, w]$.

By definition, $\pi(n, w, Z)$ is the solution to $\bar{V}(F(\cdot; n, w - \pi(n, w, Z), Z)) = \bar{V}(G_w)$ or, if $\bar{V}(F(\cdot; n, 0, Z)) \geq \bar{V}(G_w)$, then $\pi(n, w, Z) = w$. Since $\bar{V}(F(\cdot; n, 0, Z)) \to 0$ as $n \to \infty$, and $\bar{V}(G_{.04}) > 0$, provided

"EXPECTED UTILITY" ANALYSIS   319

$w \geqq \$.04$, $\pi(n, w, Z) < w$ for large enough n. Thus for given $w^* \geqq \$.04$ and Z, we have that for large enough n^*.

$$\frac{d}{dn}(\pi(n, w^*, Z))\Big|_{n^*} = \cdot \frac{\left[(d/dn)(\bar{V}(F(\cdot; n, w^* - \pi(n^*, w^*, Z), Z)))|_{n^*}\right]}{\left[(d/dw)(\bar{V}(F(\cdot; n^*, w - \pi(n^*, w^*, Z), Z)))|_{w^*}\right]}.$$

Since the denominator in the above expression is always positive, and for $n^* \geqq n(w^*, Z)$, the numerator is always negative, we have that for fixed $w \geqq \$.04$ and Z, $d(\pi(n, w, Z))/dn$ is eventually negative for large enough n.

(ii): It is clear that for any $F(\cdot) \in D[0, \infty)$, $\bar{V}(F) < 1$, and since $\lim_{w \to \infty} \bar{V}(G_w) = 1$, for any $F(\cdot) \in D[0, \infty)$, there will exist some finite w such that $\bar{V}(F) < \bar{V}(G_w)$.

(iii): By definition,

$$\bar{V}((1-p)G_w + pG_{w+Z}) = (w + w^2 + (p + w)Z)/((1+w)(1+w+Z))$$

$$- .1 \cdot \exp(-(1-p)\exp(w) - p \cdot \exp(w + Z)),$$

which is always strictly less than unity and approaches $(p + w)/(1 + w) < 1$ as $Z \to \infty$. Thus, since $\lim_{w \to \infty} \bar{V}(G_w) = 1$, there will exist some finite C such that $\bar{V}(G_{w+C}) > \bar{V}((1-p)G_w + pG_{w+Z})$ for all finite Z.

(iv): Defining $F(x; \alpha) \equiv \alpha F^*(x) + (1 - \alpha)G_w(x)$, we have from equation (9) that

$$\bar{V}(F^*) - \bar{V}(G_w) = \int_0^1 \left[\int_0^{2w} \bar{U}(x; F(\cdot; \alpha))(dF^*(x) - dG_w(x))\right] d\alpha.$$

Since the mean of F^* is w, and since from (13) or (14) it is clear that a mean preserving spread in F will increase the concavity of $\bar{U}(\cdot; F)$, to show that the inner integral in the above equation is always negative it suffices to show that $\bar{U}_{11}(x; G_w) < 0$ for all $x \in [0, 2w]$, or, since $\bar{U}_{111}(x; G_w)$ is easily shown to be positive, that $\bar{U}_{11}(2w; G_w) = -2/(1 + 2w)^3 + .1 \cdot \exp(2w - \exp(w)) < 0$ for all nonnegative w.

The last inequality is equivalent to $g(w) \equiv \exp(w) - 2w - 3 \cdot \ln(1 + 2w) + \ln(20) > 0$ for all $w \geqq 0$. Since $g(\cdot)$ is strictly convex and $g'(0) < 0$ and $g'(1.3) > 0$, $g(\cdot)$ will attain its minimum at $w^* \in (0, 1.3)$ where $g'(w^*) = \exp(w^*) - 2 - 6/(1 + 2w^*) = 0$. At this point, $g(w^*) = g(w^*) - g'(w^*) = -2w^* - 3 \cdot \ln(1 + 2w^*) + 6/(1 + 2w^*) + \ln(20) + 2 > 0$.   Q.E.D.

REFERENCES

[1] ALI, M. M.: "Probability and Utility Estimates for Racetrack Bettors," *Journal of Political Economy*, 85(1977), 803–815.

[2] ALLAIS, M.: "Le Comportement de l'Homme Rationnel devant le Risque, Critique des Postulats et Axiomes de l'Ecole Americaine," *Econometrica*, 21(1953), 503–546. (Summarized version of [3].)

[3] ———: "The Foundations of a Positive Theory of Choice Involving Risk and a Criticism of the Postulates and Axioms of the American School," Part II of [5], *Expected Utility Hypotheses and the Allais Paradox*, ed. by M. Allais and O. Hagen. Dordrecht, Holland: D. Reidel Publishing Co., 1979. (Translated from *Econometrie*, Colloques Internationaux du Centre National de la Recherche Scientifique, Vol. XL, Paris, 1953, pp. 257–332.)

[4] ———: "The So-Called Allais Paradox and Rational Decisions Under Uncertainty," Part V of [5], *Expected Utility Hypotheses and the Allais Paradox*, ed. by M. Allais and O. Hagen. Dordrecht, Holland: D. Reidel Publishing Company, 1979.

[5] ALLAIS, M., AND O. HAGEN, EDS.: *Expected Utility Hypotheses and the Allais Paradox*. Dordrecht, Holland: D. Reidel Publishing Company, 1979.

[6] ARROW, K. J.: *Essays in the Theory of Risk Bearing*. Amsterdam: North Holland, 1974.

[7] ———: "The Use of Unbounded Utility Functions in Expected-Utility Maximization: Response." *Quarterly Journal of Economics*, 88(1974), 136–138.

[8] ATKINSON, A. B.: "On the Measurement of Inequality," *Journal of Economic Theory*, 2(1970), 244–263.

320   MARK J. MACHINA

[9] AUMANN, R. J.: "The St. Petersburg Paradox: A Discussion of Some Recent Comments," *Journal of Economic Theory*, 14(1977), 443–445.

[10] BILLINGSLEY, P.: *Convergence of Probability Measures*. New York: John Wiley & Sons, 1968.

[11] ———: *Weak Convergence of Measures: Applications in Probability*. Philadelphia: Society for Industrial and Applied Mathematics, 1971.

[12] BINSWANGER, H. P.: "Attitudes Toward Risk: Theoretical Implications of an Experiment in Rural India," *Economic Journal*, forthcoming.

[13] BORCH, K., AND J. MOSSIN, EDS.: *Risk and Uncertainty: Proceedings of a Conference Held by the International Economic Association*. London: Macmillan and Co., 1968.

[14] CHEW, S. H., AND K. R. MACCRIMMON: "Alpha-Nu Choice Theory: A Generalization of Expected Utility Theory," University of British Columbia Faculty of Commerce and Business Administration Working Paper No. 669, July, 1979.

[15] ———: "Alpha Utility Theory, Lottery Composition and the Allais Paradox," University of British Columbia Faculty of Commerce and Business Administration Working Paper No. 686, September, 1979.

[16] DASGUPTA, P., A. SEN, AND D. STARRETT: "Notes on the Measurement of Inequality," *Journal of Economic Theory*, 6(1973), 180–187.

[17] DAVIDSON, D., P. SUPPES, AND S. SIEGEL: *Decision Making: An Experimental Approach*. Stanford, California: Stanford University Press, 1957.

[18] DEBREU, G.: *Theory of Value: An Axiomatic Analysis of General Equilibrium*. New Haven: Yale University Press, 1959.

[19] DIAMOND, P., AND J. E. STIGLITZ: "Increases in Risk and in Risk Aversion," *Journal of Economic Theory*, 8(1974), 337–360.

[20] EDEN, B.: "On Aversion to Positive Risks and Preference for Negative Risks," *Economics Letters*, 4(1979). 125–129.

[21] EDWARDS, W.: "Probability-Preferences in Gambling," *American Journal of Psychology*, 66(1953), 349–364.

[22] ———: "Probability-Preferences Among Bets With Differing Expected Values," *American Journal of Psychology*, 67(1954), 56–67.

[23] ———: "The Reliability of Probability-Preferences," *American Journal of Psychology*, 67(1954), 68–95.

[24] ———: "The Theory of Decision Making," *Psychological Bulletin*, 51(1954), 380–417.

[25] ———: "The Prediction of Decisions Among Bets," *Journal of Experimental Psychology*, 50(1955), 201–214.

[26] ———: "Behavioral Decision Theory," in *Annual Review of Psychology*, ed. by P. Farnsworth, O. McNemar, and Q. McNemar. Palo Alto: Annual Reviews, Inc., 1961.

[27] ———: "Subjective Probabilities Inferred from Decisions," *Psychological Review*, 69(1962), 109–135.

[28] FISHBURN, P.: "Binary Choice Probabilities between Gambles: Interlocking Expected Utility Models," *Journal of Mathematical Psychology*, 14(1976), 99–122.

[29] ———: "Unbounded Utility Functions in Expected Utility Theory," *Quarterly Journal of Economics*, 90(1976), 163–168.

[30] ———: "On Handa's 'New Theory of Cardinal Utility' and the Maximization of Expected Return," *Journal of Political Economy*, 86(1978), 321–324.

[31] ———: "A Probabilistic Expected Utility Theory of Risky Binary Choices," *International Economic Review*, 19(1978), 633–646.

[32] FLEMMING, J. S.: "The Utility of Wealth and the Utility of Windfalls," *Review of Economic Studies*, 36(1969), 55–66.

[33] FRIEDMAN, M., AND L. J. SAVAGE: "The Utility Analysis of Choices Involving Risk," *Journal of Political Economy*, 56(1948), 279–304. Reprinted in [91] *Readings in Price Theory*, ed. by G. Stigler and K. Boulding, Chicago: Richard D. Irwin, Inc., 1952. (See especially the correction in [91, p. 71].)

[34] GRETHER, D. M.: "Recent Psychological Studies of Behavior under Uncertainty," *American Economic Review, Papers and Proceedings*, 68(1978), 70–74.

[35] GRETHER, D. M., AND C. R. PLOTT: "Economic Theory of Choice and the Preference Reversal Phenomenon," *American Economic Review*, 69(1979), 623–638.

[36] GRIFFITH, R. M.: "Odds Adjustment by American Horse-Race Bettors," *American Journal of Psychology*, 62(1949), 290–294.

[37] HADAR, J., AND W. RUSSELL: "Rules for Ordering Uncertain Prospects," *American Economic Review*, 59(1969), 25–34.

[38] HAGEN, O.: "Towards a Positive Theory of Preferences Under Risk," in [5], *Expected Utility Hypotheses and the Allais Paradox*, ed. by M. Allais and O. Hagen. Dordrecht, Holland: D. Reidel Publishing Company, 1979, pp. 271–302.

[39] HAKANSSON, N. H.: "Friedman-Savage Utility Functions Consistent with Risk Aversion," *Quarterly Journal of Economics*, 84(1970), 472–487.

[40] HANDA, J.: "Risk, Probabilities, and a New Theory of Cardinal Utility," *Journal of Political Economy*, 85(1977), 97–122.

[41] HANSON, D. L., AND C. F. MENEZES: "On a Neglected Aspect of the Theory of Risk Aversion," *Western Economic Journal*, 9(1971), 211–217.

[42] HELPMAN, E., AND A. RAZIN: *A Theory of International Trade Under Uncertainty*. New York: Academic Press, 1978.

[43] HERSTEIN, I. N., AND J. MILNOR: "An Axiomatic Approach to Measurable Utility," *Econometrica*, 21(1953), 291–297.

[44] HIRSHLEIFER, J.: "Investment Decision Under Uncertainty: Applications of the State-Preference Approach," *Quarterly Journal of Economics*, 80(1966), 252–277.

[45] ———: *Investment, Interest, and Capital*. Englewood Cliffs, New Jersey: Prentice-Hall, Inc., 1970.

[46] KAHNEMAN, D., AND A. TVERSKY: "Prospect Theory: An Analysis of Decision under Risk," *Econometrica*, 47(1979), 263–291.

[47] KIM, Y. C.: "Choice in the Lottery-Insurance Situation: Augmented Income Approach," *Quarterly Journal of Economics*, 87(1973), 148–156.

[48] KLAMBAUER, G.: *Real Analysis*. New York: American Elsevier, 1973.

[49] KREPS, D., AND E. PORTEUS: "Temporal von Neumann-Morgenstern and Induced Preferences," *Journal of Economic Theory*, 20(1979), 81–109.

[50] KWANG, N. Y.: "Why Do People Buy Lottery Tickets? Choices Involving Risk and the Indivisibility of Expenditure," *Journal of Political Economy*, 73(1965), 530–535.

[51] LEVHARI, D., AND T. N. SRINIVASAN: "Optimal Savings Under Uncertainty," *Review of Economic Studies*, 36(1969), 153–163.

[52] LICHTENSTEIN, S.: "Bases for Preferences Among Three-Outcome Bets," *Journal of Experimental Psychology*, 69(1965), 162–169.

[53] LUCE, R., AND H. RAIFFA: *Games and Decisions: Introduction and Critical Survey*. New York: John Wiley & Sons, 1957.

[54] LUCE, R., AND P. SUPPES: "Preference, Utility, and Subjective Probability," in *Handbook of Mathematical Psychology, Volume III*, ed. by R. Luce, R. Bush, and E. Galanter. New York: John Wiley & Sons, 1965.

[55] LUENBERGER, D. G.: *Optimization by Vector Space Methods*. New York: John Wiley & Sons, 1969.

[56] MacCRIMMON, K. R.: "Descriptive and Normative Implications of the Decision-Theory Postulates," in [13], *Risk and Uncertainty: Proceedings of a Conference Held by the International Economic Association*. London: Macmillan and Co., 1968.

[57] MacCRIMMON, K. R., AND S. LARSSON: "Utility Theory: Axioms versus 'Paradoxes'," in [5], *Expected Utility Hypotheses and the Allais Paradox*, ed. by M. Allais and O. Hagen. Dordrecht, Holland: D. Reidel Publishing Company, 1979.

[58] MACHINA, M. J.: "A Stronger Characterization of Declining Risk Aversion," *Econometrica*, forthcoming.

[59] MALINVAUD, E.: "Note on von Neumann-Morgenstern's Strong Independence Axiom," *Econometrica*, 20(1952), 679.

[60] MARKOWITZ, H.: "The Utility of Wealth," *Journal of Political Economy*, 60(1952), 151–158.

[61] MARSCHAK, J.: "Rational Behavior, Uncertain Prospects, and Measurable Utility," *Econometrica*, 18(1950), 111–141. ("Errata," *Econometrica*, 18(1950), 312.)

[62] McGLOTHLIN, W. H.: "Stability of Choices Among Uncertain Alternatives," *American Journal of Psychology*, 69(1956), 604–615.

[63] MENGER, K.: "The Role of Uncertainty in Economics," in *Essays in Mathematical Economics in Honor of Oskar Morgenstern*, ed. by M. Shubik. Princeton: Princeton University Press, 1967. (Translated from *Zeitschrift für Nationaloekonomie*, Band V, Heft 4, 1934, pp. 459–485.)

[64] MORRISON, D. G.: "On the Consistency of Preferences in Allais' Paradox," *Behavioral Science*, 12(1967), 373–383.

[65] MOSKOWITZ, H.: "Effects of Problem Representation and Feedback on Rational Behavior in Allais and Morlat-Type Problems," *Decision Sciences*, 5(1974), 225–242.

[66] MOSTELLER, F., AND P. NOGEE: "An Experimental Measurement of Utility," *Journal of Political Economy*, 59(1951), 371–404.
[67] NOGEE, P., AND B. LIEBERMAN: "The Auction Value of Certain Risky Situations," *Journal of Psychology*, 49(1960), 167–179.
[68] PRATT, J. W.: "Risk Aversion in the Small and in the Large," *Econometrica*, 32(1964), 122–136.
[69] PRESTON, M. G., AND P. BARATTA: "An Experimental Study of the Auction-Value of an Uncertain Outcome," *American Journal of Psychology*, 61(1948), 183–193.
[70] RAIFFA, H.: *Decision Analysis: Introductory Lectures on Choice Under Uncertainty*. Reading, Mass.: Addison-Wesley, 1968.
[71] ROSETT, R. N.: "The Friedman-Savage Hypothesis and Convex Acceptance Sets: A Reconciliation," *Quarterly Journal of Economics*, 81(1967), 534–535.
[72] ———: "Measuring the Perception of Risk," in [13], *Risk and Uncertainty: Proceedings of a Conference Held by the International Economic Association*. London: Macmillan and Company, 1968.
[73] ———: "Weak Experimental Verification of the Expected Utility Hypothesis," *Review of Economic Studies*, 38(1971), 481–492.
[74] ROTHSCHILD, M., AND J. STIGLITZ: "Increasing Risk: I. A Definition," *Journal of Economic Theory*, 2(1970), 225–243. ("Addendum," *Journal of Economic Theory*, 5(1972), 306.)
[75] ———: "Some Further Results on the Measurement of Inequality," *Journal of Economic Theory*, 6(1973), 188–204.
[76] ROYDEN, H.: *Real Analysis*. New York: Macmillan, 1963.
[77] RUDIN, W.: *Functional Analysis*. New York: McGraw-Hill, 1973.
[78] RUSSELL, W. R., AND T. K. SEO: "Admissible Sets of Utility Functions in Expected Utility Maximization," *Econometrica*, 46(1978), 181–184.
[79] RYAN, T. M.: "The Use of Unbounded Utility Functions in Expected Utility Maximization: Comment," *Quarterly Journal of Economics*, 88(1974), 133–135.
[80] SAMUELSON, P. A.: "Utility, Preference, and Probability," abstract of a paper given before the conference on "Les Fondements et Applications de la Théorie du Risque en Econométrie," Paris, May, 1952. Reprinted as Chapter 13 in *Collected Scientific Papers of Paul A. Samuelson*, Volume 1, ed. by J. Stiglitz. Cambridge, Mass.: MIT Press, 1966.
[81] ———: "The St. Petersburg Paradox as a Divergent Double Limit," *International Economic Review*, 1(1960), 31–37.
[82] ———: "St. Petersburg Paradoxes: Defanged, Dissected, and Historically Described," *Journal of Economic Literature*, 15(1977), 24–55.
[83] SAVAGE, L. J.: *The Foundations of Statistics*. New York: Dover Publications, 1972. (Revised and enlarged version of the work originally published by John Wiley & Sons, New York, in 1954.)
[84] SELDEN, L.: "A New Representation of Preferences over 'Certain × Uncertain' Consumption Pairs: The 'Ordinal Certainty Equivalent' Hypothesis," *Econometrica*, 46(1978), 1045–1060.
[85] SEN, A.: *On Economic Inequality*. Oxford: Oxford University Press, 1973.
[86] SHAPLEY, L. S.: "The St. Petersburg Paradox: A Con Game?" *Journal of Economic Theory*, 14(1977), 439–442.
[87] ———: "Lotteries and Menus: A Comment on Unbounded Utilities," *Journal of Economic Theory*, 14(1977), 446–453.
[88] SLOVIC, P., AND A. TVERSKY: "Who Accepts Savage's Axiom?" *Behavioral Science*, 19(1974), 368–373.
[89] SPROWLS, R. C.: "Psychological-Mathematical Probability in Relationships of Lottery Gambles," *American Journal of Psychology*, 66(1953), 126–130.
[90] STIGLER, G.: "The Development of Utility Theory," Chapter 5 in *Essays in the History of Economics* by G. Stigler. Chicago: University of Chicago Press, 1965. (Reprinted from *Journal of Political Economy*, 58(1950), 307–327, 373–396.)
[91] STIGLER, G., AND K. BOULDING, EDS.: *Readings in Price Theory*. Chicago: Richard D. Irwin, Inc., 1952.
[92] STIGLITZ, J. E.: "Review of *Aspects of the Theory of Risk Bearing—Yrjö Jahnsson Lectures*, by K. J. Arrow," *Econometrica*, 37(1969), 742–743.
[93] TOBIN, J.: "Liquidity Preference as Behavior Toward Risk," *Review of Economic Studies*, 25(1957–1958), 65–86.
[94] TSAING, S. C.: "The Rationale of the Mean-Standard Deviation Analysis, Skewness Preference, and the Demand for Money," *American Economic Review*, 62(1972), 354–371.
[95] TVERSKY, A.: "Utility Theory and Additivity Analysis of Risky Choices," *Journal of Experimental Psychology*, 75(1967), 27–36.

"EXPECTED UTILITY" ANALYSIS   323

[96] ———: "Additivity, Utility, and Subjective Probability," *Journal of Mathematical Psychology*, 4(1967), 175–201.

[97] ———: "Intransitivity of Preferences," *Psychological Review*, 76(1969), 31–48.

[98] ———: "A Critique of Expected Utility Theory: Descriptive and Normative Considerations," *Erkenntnis*, 9(1975), 163–173.

[99] VON NEUMANN, J., AND O. MORGENSTERN: *Theory of Games and Economic Behavior*. Princeton: Princeton University Press, 1944. Second Edition, 1947. Third Edition, 1953.

[100] WALLSTEN, T. S.: "Subjectively Expected Utility Theory and Subject's Probability Estimates: Use of Measurement-Free Techniques," *Journal of Experimental Psychology*, 88(1971), 31–40.

[101] YAARI, M.: "Convexity in the Theory of Choice Under Risk," *Quarterly Journal of Economics*, 79(1965), 278–290.

[4]

Journal of Economic Behavior and Organization 3 (1982) 323–343. North-Holland

A THEORY OF ANTICIPATED UTILITY

John QUIGGIN*

Australian Bureau of Agricultural Economics, Canberra City, ACT 2601, Australia

Received July 1980, final version received December 1982

A new theory of cardinal utility, with an associated set of axioms, is presented. It is a generalization of the von Neumann–Morgenstern expected utility theory, which permits the analysis of phenomena associated with the distortion of subjective probability.

1. Introduction

The expected utility theory of von Neumann and Morgenstern (1944) (hereafter NM) is a powerful tool for the analysis of decisions under risk. However, people in both experimental and real-life situations frequently do not conform to the NM axioms. A number of decision problems have been designed for which most people make choices violating the NM axioms. The most celebrated of these is the Allais paradox [Allais (1953)]. Similar problems, which do not involve the extremely large amounts of money used in Allais' problem, have been constructed by MacCrimmon (1968), Kahneman and Tversky (1979), Schoemaker and Kunreuther (1979), and Slovic et al. (1977). Kunreuther et al. (1978) examined the insurance behaviour of home owners in flood-prone and earthquake-prone areas, and found results inconsistent with the NM theory.

These observations are clearly related to the well-known fact that many people who are normally risk-averse are willing to engage in gambles at long odds. Friedman and Savage (1948) offer an ingenious explanation using an S-shaped utility curve, but this raises as many problems as it solves. For example, what about people whose present wealth does not lie in the convex segment of the curve?

One explanation which is intuitively appealing, is that individuals tend to substitute 'decision weights' for probabilities. This has been argued by Fellner (1961) and Edwards (1962). It has also been recognised by practical users of expected utility theory. Thus, Officer and Halter (1968) and

*I would like to thank Ted Sieper, Jock Anderson and two referees for their helpful comments and criticism.

Anderson, Dillon and Hardaker (1977, pp. 69–70) suggest that questionnaires used in eliciting risk preferences should use only 50–50 choices, i.e., gambles with two outcomes each occurring with equal probability.

Unfortunately, it has proved difficult to construct a theory which embodies this insight. Handa (1977) attempted this, but his theory was shown by Fishburn (1978) to imply maximisation of expected returns when violations of dominance were excluded. Karmarkar (1978, 1979) refined Handa's theory with his Subjectively Weighted Utility model, but this reduces to the NM theory when violations of dominance are excluded (see below). The 'prospect theory' of Kahneman and Tversky is more complex and realistic, but it admits 'indirect violations of dominance' and thus intransitivity in pairwise choices.

In this paper, an axiomatic approach to the problem is adopted. It has been observed that the most intractable difficulties with the practical application of NM theory are related to the axiom of irrelevance of independent alternatives. In MacCrimmon's experiments, subjects were given the opportunity to reconsider choices which violated the NM axioms. In most cases, e.g., violations of transitivity, they readily agreed that their original choices had been erroneous, but they were unwilling to alter choices which violated the independence axiom. When arguments based upon this axiom were put to them, their answers indicated that they did not accept the validity of the axiom. A substantial proportion of subjects continued to reject the axiom even after an individual discussion with the experimenter. These results were largely replicated by Slovic and Tversky (1974).

In this paper, a new theory is derived, based on a set of axioms weaker than those of NM, and in particular a weaker form of the independence axiom. Because it is based on a weighted sum of utilities formed using 'decision weights', rather than a mathematical expectation it is termed 'anticipated utility' (AU) theory.

Like expected utility theory, it maintains transitivity in pairwise choices and does not admit violations of dominance.

Two basic criticisms of this approach could be made. First, it could be argued that NM theory is sufficient for all practical purposes. This would be the case if violations of NM theory were merely random erroneous judgements, which were avoided in making important decisions or if, because of self-selection, most important economic decisions will be made by individuals conforming to the NM axioms. (It is worth noting that this latter argument may be used to justify the use of expected wealth maximization rather than expected utility maximization.) However, these arguments are based on the premise that, on consideration, all 'rational' people will accept the NM axioms and seek to make decisions in conformity with them. As McCrimmon's experiments showed, this is not the case, at least for business executives.

Alternatively AU theory could be criticised for not being general enough. McCrimmon's experiments showed a number of violations of axioms shared by AU and NM theory, such as intransitivities [also examined by Tversky (1969)] and violations of dominance [Coombs (1975)]. Other behavioural violations of AU theory, such as context effects, have been examined by Hershey and Schoemaker (1980), and Kahneman and Tversky (1979).

There are a number of answers to this second objection. First, in contrast to the NM independence axiom, transitivity and dominance rules command virtually unanimous assent even from those who sometimes violate them in practice. (Some of Tversky's subjects refused to believe that they could have made such errors.)

Second, at least in the case of transitivity violations, these problems appear to arise mostly in unfamiliar situations. In such situations, decision rules which normally produce rational choices may break down.

Third, transitivity and dominance rules are essential to almost all economic theories of decisions under certainty. Thus, if a theory of decision under uncertainty is to be consistent with any of the large body of economic theory which has already been developed (much of which has substantial empirical support), it must satisfy these rules.

There are, however, a number of generalisations of AU theory which could be considered without violating these rules. Indeed, the anticipated utility function developed here is one of a number of possibilities considered (but not developed or axiomatized) by Allais (1952).

The principal difference between AU theory, and previous analyses of 'decision weights', such as that of Handa, lies in the fact that these approaches sought to derive weights as a function of individual probabilities. This created immediate difficulties with probabilities of the form $1/n$. Severe violations of dominance are generated unless the weight, $w(1/n)$ is set equal to $1/n$. If, say, the weight is less than $1/n$, we may consider an initial situation in which a sum of money, X, is received with certainty, and compare it with the situation where this sum is augmented by a small but positive random variable x, $0 < x \leqq \varepsilon$, where x takes n different values x_i each with probability $1/n$. For sufficiently small ε it is apparent that

$$U(X) > \sum_{i=1}^{n} w(1/n)U(X + x_i). \tag{1*}$$

That is, the certain event is preferred, even though the random variable has a superior outcome with probability 1.

If this anomaly is to be avoided, a similar argument will establish the requirement that $w(k/n) = k/n$, for $1 \leqq k \leqq n$. Consider the choice between a fixed sum X received with probability k/n (with nothing received otherwise), and k sums of the form $X + x_i$ (or $X - x_i$), each with probability $1/n$. Thus, if violations of dominance are to be avoided, a decision weighting function of this type must be an identity function, and the resulting theory is identical to that of NM. A formal proof of this is given by Fishburn (1978).

AU theory avoids these difficulties, because probability weights are derived from the entire probability distribution, rather than from individual probabilities. Typically, events at extremes of the range of outcomes are likely to be 'overweighted'. In such cases, at least some 'intermediate' outcomes, perhaps with the same objective probability, must be underweighted.

This may be illustrated by the following example. Suppose an individual's normal wage income is uniformly distributed over a range from $20 000 to $21 000. There is also a 1/100,000 chance that s/he will win a contest for which the prize is a job paying $1 000 000 a year. This probability is, in fact, precisely equal to that of receiving any specified income in the relevant range, e.g., $21 439.72. Nevertheless, we would not expected the two events to be treated in the same way. The factors which might lead someone to overweight the probability of winning the contest, would not be likely to have the same effect on an 'intermediate' outcome, even with the same objective probability. Because two events with the same objective probability need not have the same weight, the problems described above do not apply to AU theory. While this point is fairly easy to grasp intuitively, formalizing it presents some difficulties. These are addressed in the following section.

2. An outline of the theory

The theory deals with individual preferences over a set X of outcomes, and an associated set Y of prospects.[1] The set X of outcomes provides a partition of the possible states of the world into mutually exclusive events. Each prospect $y \in Y$ consists of a pair of vectors $\{(x_1, x_2, \ldots, x_n); (p_1, \ldots, p_n)\}$, such that $x_1, x_2, \ldots, x_n \in X$ and $\sum_i p_i = 1$. If the prospect y is selected, the individual will receive outcome x_i with probability p_i. The number of distinct possible outcomes, n, will not, in general, be the same for different prospects.[2] In particular, prospects of the form $\{(x);(1)\}$ in which an outcome is received with certainty, will play an important role. For simplicity, such prospects will not be distinguished from the corresponding elements $x \in X$, and X will be treated as a subset of Y.

Individual preferences are denoted by a relationship P which is assumed to be complete, reflexive and transitive, and by the associated indifference relationship I. If an outcome $c \in X$ is indifferent to a risky prospect $y \in Y$, it

[1] My use of the term 'prospect' differs from that of Kahneman and Tversky who use it to denote a change from some initial position.
[2] Thus, if $X = R$, Y is a subspace of the space of finite-dimensional simplices over R. See Dugundji (1966, ch. 15).

will be called the certainty equivalent of y, denoted $c = CE(y)$. If two outcomes are indifferent they will not be distinguished.

The object of a utility theory is the construction of a function V on Y such that $V(y) \geq V(y')$ if, and only if, yPy'. The NM theory involves constructing a function U on X and setting $V(y) = \sum_i p_i U(x_i)$. Handa offers the seemingly symmetrical proposal $V(y) = \sum_i w(p_i)x_i$, where the x_i are assumed to represent some quantity of a given good and w is a real-valued function on the unit interval such that $w(0) = 0$. Kahneman and Tversky combine the two, setting $V(y) = \sum_i w(p_i)U(x_i)$, where the x_i are assumed to represent changes from some initial situation. Karmarkar suggests setting

$$V(y) = \sum_i w(p_i)U(x_i) \Big/ \sum_i w(p_i), \quad \text{where}$$

$$w(p) = p^\alpha / [p^\alpha + (1-p)^\alpha], \qquad 0 < \alpha \leq 1. \tag{1}$$

Each of these alternatives to NM theory encounter the problems mentioned above. Kahneman and Tversky themselves point to the difficulties which arise with their approach (and *a fortiori* that of Handa) when w is non-linear. Further discussion is given by Karmarkar (1979).

In general, if w is non-linear it is possible to find an 'overweighted' pair of probabilities p and $1-p$ such that

$$w(p) + w(1-p) > 1. \tag{2}$$

If x_1 and x_2 are chosen so that x_1 is very slightly preferred to x_2, then

$$U(x_1) < w(p)u(x_1) + w(1-p)U(x_2). \tag{3}$$

Yet the prospect x_1 clearly dominates $\{(x_1, x_2); (p, 1-p)\}$ in the strong sense that its outcome will be preferred (or at least indifferent) with probability 1. Kahneman and Tversky avoid this implication by assuming that dominated prospects are 'edited out' but this leads to the undesirable result that pairwise choices are intransitive. Note again that, if w is linear, so that $w(p) + w(1-p) = w(1)$ the theory reduces to that of NM.

A more complex example shows that the problem of dominance applies to Karmarkar's theory. Suppose that, for some p, $w(p) < 2w(p/2)$. Then we can find $x_1 P x_2 P x_3$ such that

$$(w(p)U(x_1) + w(1-p)U(x_3))/(w(p) + w(1-p))$$

$$< (w(p/2)U(x_1) + w(p/2)U(x_2) + w(1-p)U(x_3))/(2w(p/2) + w(1-p)). \tag{4}$$

All that is required is that $U(x_2)$ should be very close to $U(x_1)$ and substantially greater than $U(x_3)$. However, $\{(x_1, x_3); (p, 1-p)\}$ dominates $\{(x_1, x_2, x_3); (p/2, p/2, 1-p)\}$. (Note that this dominance result does not require the NM axiom of independence of irrelevant alternatives. See section 3.) Since a similar result applies if $w(p) > 2w(p/2)$, preservation of dominance implies

$$w(p_i) \Big/ \sum_i w(p_i) = p_i \quad \text{for all} \quad p = (p_1, p_2, \ldots, p_n). \tag{5}$$

In this case, Karmarkar's approach is identical to that of NM.

All of these counter-examples require some assumptions on the 'richness' of the set X of outcomes, such as those made by Fishburn (1978). However, they will always apply if X is an interval on the real line, and any viable theory must be able to cover this case.

As was stated above, the fundamental problem in these theories is that any two outcomes with the same probability must have the same decision weight. This fails to take account of the fact that, while individuals may distort the probability of an extreme outcome in some way, they need not treat 'intermediate' outcomes with the same probability in the same fashion.

In order to formalize this observation, it is necessary to order the possible outcomes x_i, and the corresponding probabilities, p_i, in each prospect. We assume that the outcomes are ordered from worst to best, i.e., $x = (x_1, x_2, \ldots, x_n)$, where $x_n P x_{n-1} P, \ldots, P x_2 P x_1$ and $p = (p_1, p_2, \ldots, p_n)$, where p_i is the probability of outcome x_i.

The anticipated utility function is defined to be

$$V = h(p) \cdot U(x) = \sum_i h_i(p) U(x_i), \tag{6}$$

where U is a utility function with properties similar to that of NM, while $h(p)$ is a vector of decision weights satisfying $\sum_i h_i(p) = 1$. In general, $h_i(p)$ depends on all the p_js and not just on p_i. Thus, for example, the fact that $p_j = p_k$ would not imply that $h_j(p) = h_k(p)$. It is obviously necessary to require that if $p_i = 0$, then $h_i = 0$. For simplicity of scaling, it will be assumed that $h(1) = 1$.

More significantly, it will be assumed that $h(\frac{1}{2}, \frac{1}{2}) = (\frac{1}{2}, \frac{1}{2})$. The claim that the probabilities of 50–50 bets will not be subjectively distorted seems reasonable, and, as stated above, has proved a satisfactory basis for practical work [Anderson, Dillon and Hardaker (1977)]. The experiments discussed by Handa yielded crossover points such that $h_1(p) = (p_1$ for values of p_1 less than $\frac{1}{2}$ but they did not take risk aversion into account. As discussed below, risk aversion can easily be confused with pessimism [roughly, setting $h_i(p) < p_i$ for the more favourable outcomes].

J. Quiggin, A theory of anticipated utility 329

The description of the function h would at first sight appear to be an infinite task since no bound has been imposed on the number of different outcomes, n, in a given prospect, y. However, it can be shown that a knowledge of $h(p, 1-p)$ for each $p \in [0,1]$ is sufficient to determine $h(p)$ for any probability vector p, regardless of its length. The approach used is very similar to that which was used to show that a non-linear weighting function on individual probabilities will generate violations of dominance. The central point is that the evaluation of a prospect, in which two very similar outcomes x_1 and x_2 occur with the probabilities p_1 and p_2, must be 'close' to that of a prospect which is identical except that x_1 replaces x_2, occurring with a total probability $p_1 + p_2$. This imposes constraints on the function h. If it is also assumed, as in previous approaches, that $h_i(p)$ depends only on p_i, then these constraints are satisfied only by the NM expected utility function.

For each $p \in [0,1]$, write $f(p) = h_1(p, 1-p)$. Thus, $f(p)$ defines the behaviour of h on pairs $(p, 1-p)$. The extension of h to triples (p_1, p_2, p_3) will now be described in detail. The approach used can be shown by induction to apply to arbitrary p.

Consider the two prospects $y_1 = \{(x_1, x_2); (p_1, 1-p_1)\}$ and $y_2 = \{(x_1, x_3, x_2); (p_2, p_1 - p_2, 1 - p_1)\}$. As $U(x_3)$ approaches $U(x_1)$, $V(y_2)$ must approach $V(y_1)$. At the limit, $x_1 = x_3$ and $y_1 = y_2$, so that

$$f(p_1)U(x_1) + (1 - f(p_1))U(x_2) = (h_1(p_2, p_1 - p_2, 1 - p_1)$$

$$+ h_2(p_2, p - p_2, 1 - p_1))U(x_1) + h_3(p_2, p_1 - P_2, 1 - p_1)U(x_2).$$

$$(7)$$

Since x_1 and x_2 are chosen arbitrarily and $h(p)$ is independent of x the coefficients on $U(x_2)$ on the right-hand and left-hand sides of (7) must be equal. Hence,

$$h_3(p_2, p_1 - p_2, 1 - p_1) = 1 - f(p_1). \tag{8}$$

Conversely, by setting $U(x_3)$ close to $U(x_2)$ we can show

$$h_1(p_2, p_1 - p_2, 1 - p_1) = f(p_2), \quad \text{and hence} \tag{9}$$

$$h(p_1, p_2, p_3) = (f(p_1), f(p_1 + p_2) - f(p_1), 1 - f(p_1 + p_2)).$$

More generally:

$$h_i(p) = f\left(\sum_{j=1}^{i} p_j\right) - f\left(\sum_{j=1}^{i-1} p_j\right) \tag{10}$$

so that the behaviour of h on arbitrary probability distributions is fully determined by the values of $h(p, 1-p)$ for $0 < p < 1$.

The result shows that $h_i(p)$ depends on all the probabilities $p_1, p_2, \ldots, p_n$ and not merely p_i. Moreover the relationship between the probability of an event x_i and its decision weight depends upon its position in the preference ranking of possible outcomes.

Eq. (10) also offers a natural extension to the case where Y includes continuous probability distributions, a case which cannot be handled at all in the theories of Handa and Kahneman–Tversky.

Let $D(x_0) = P_r\{U(x) < U(x_0)\}$ be the (objective) cumulative distribution function for x. Then D ranges from 0 to 1, and so the function f may be applied to obtain a 'cumulative distribution function' for decision weights, G. Thus

$$G(x_0) = f(D(x_0)). \tag{11}$$

Let the density function associated with G be written g. This function plays the same role for continuous probability distributions as h plays for discrete ones. Thus, anticipated utility is given by

$$V = \int_x^\infty U(x)g(x)\,\mathrm{d}x = \int_x^\infty U(x)\,\mathrm{d}G(x). \tag{12}$$

This result can be proved easily if the integral in (12) is a Riemann integral over a bounded interval $[a, b]$. This is because the integral is formed as a limit (from above and below) of step function integrals which may be related to elements of Y with discrete distributions. In fact we may construct series y_N^* and y_N^{**} such that $y_N^* \, Py \, Py_N^{**}$ for all N and $\lim_{N\to\infty} V(y_N^* = \lim_{N\to\infty} V(y_N^{**}) = V$ so that $V(y) = V$ as required.

Assume without loss of generality that $[a, b] = [0, 1]$ and partition the interval into N sub-intervals, so that

$$I_{iN} = [(i-1)/N, i/N].$$

The probability that y will lie in I_{iN} is given by

$$P_{iN} = \Pr\{y \in I_{iN}\}$$

$$= D(i/N) - D((i-1)/N) \qquad i = 1, 2, \ldots, N. \tag{13}$$

By (11),

$$h_i(\mathbf{p}_N) = f(D(i/N)) - f(D(i-1)/N))$$

$$= g(x_{iN}^*)/N \quad \text{for some } x_{iN}^* \in I_{iN} \tag{14}$$

by the Mean Value Theorem. Define $y_N^{**} = (0, \ldots, N-1/N; p_N)$ and $y_N^* = (i/N, \ldots, 1; p_N)$.

The distributions of y_N^* and y_N^{**} are given by step functions which lie, respectively, above and below D. It is clear that $y_N^* \, Py \, Py_N^{**}$, while

$$V(y_N^{**}) = \sum_{i=1}^{N} h_i(p_N)U(i/N)$$

$$= \frac{1}{N} \sum_{i=1}^{N} g(x_{iN}^*)U(i/N), \quad \text{and} \tag{15}$$

$$V(y_N^{**}) = 1/N \sum_{i=1}^{N} g(x_{iN}^*)U((i-1)/N), \quad \text{so that}$$

$$\lim_{N \to \infty} V(y_N^*) = \lim_{N \to \infty} V(y_N^*) = V.$$

3. Axioms

In order to generate a theory more general than NM expected utility theory, it is necessary to begin with a weaker set of axioms. In particular, it seems appropriate to modify the controversial independence axiom.

The notation adopted here creates some difficulties in comparisons of the two sets of axioms. First, it must be noted that acceptance of the NM complexity axiom (that the value of a compound lottery depends only on the ultimate probability of each outcome) is implicit in the use of this notation. If this axiom did not hold, two prospects, both expressed as (x, p), need not be of equivalent value. Second, the independence and continuity axioms in NM theory are significantly weakened if they apply only to outcomes $x \in X$.

For instance, the independence[3] axiom:

$$y_1 Py_2 \Rightarrow y_1 P\{(y_1, p), (y_2, 1-p)\} \quad \text{for any } p \in [0, 1].$$

becomes a simple statement that preferences preserve dominance if y_1 and y_2 are replaced by elements of X (see Axiom 2).

In addition to the complexity axiom, the usual completeness axiom will be adopted.

Axiom 1. P is complete, reflexive and transitive (completeness).

[3]A widely used version of the independence axiom is: $Y_1(Py_2 \Rightarrow \{(y_1, p), (y_3, 1-p)\}P\{y_2, p), (y_3, 1-p\}$ for any $y_3 \in Y$ and $p \in [0, 1]$. It is this version which is directly contradicted by Allais' results. In combination with the other NM axioms, this version of the independence axiom is equivalent to that given above.

The dominance and continuity axioms will be modified to apply to outcomes only.

Axiom 2. $x_1, x_2 \in X, x_1 P x_2 \Rightarrow x_1 P\{(x_2, x_1); (p, 1-p)\}$ (dominance).

Axiom 3.   If $x_1, x_2, x_3 \in X, x_1 P x_2 P x_3$ there exists p^*, such that

$$x_2 I\{(x_3, x_1); (p^*, 1-p^*)\} \qquad\qquad \text{(continuity).}$$

Finally, a weak independence axiom will be used to ensure that $h(p)$ is independent of x.

Axiom 4.   If $y_1 = \{x, p\}$ and $y_2 = \{x', p\}$ and for each $i, i = 1, 2, \ldots, n$, there exists

$$c_i = CE\{x_i, x_i'); (\tfrac{1}{2}, \tfrac{1}{2})\}, \qquad i = 1, 2, \ldots, n, \quad \text{and}$$

$$x_1^* = CE(y_1), \qquad x_2^* = CE(y_2). \quad \text{Then}$$

$$\{c; p\} I\{(x_1^*, x_2^*); (\tfrac{1}{2}, \tfrac{1}{2})\} \qquad\qquad \text{(independence).}$$

Thus, if each element of c is indifferent to a 50–50 bet consisting of corresponding elements of x and x', $\{c; p\}$ is indifferent to a 50–50 bet consisting of certainty equivalents of $\{x; p\}$ and $\{x'; p\}$.

Thus far, no assumptions have been made about the 'richness' of X and Y. If they have insufficiently many elements, utility functions may be non-unique and the proof of existence theorems is made more complicated. (An existence theorem can be proved in some cases by inventing additional elements of X and Y and extending P to cover them. A utility function which preserves the extended preference ordering will also preserve the original ones.)

The following assumptions will be made:

R.1.   If $x_1, x_2, \ldots, x_n \in X$, $x_n P x_{n-1} P, \ldots, P x_1$, and $\sum_i p_i = 1$, then $\{x; p\} \in Y$.

R.2.   If $y \varepsilon Y$ there exists $x = CE(y) \in X$.

These assumptions are stronger than those required to derive uniqueness results in NM theory because the class of utility functions to be considered is much larger. However, some form of R.1 is required for both theories and R.2 will always be satisfied for the standard situation where X is a connected subset of the real line.

The major result of this paper is:

Proposition 1. Suppose X and Y satisfy R.1 and R.2 and P satisfies Axioms 1–4. Then there exists a function V: Y→R such that

(i) $V(y) \geq V(y')$ *if and only if yPy',*

(ii) $V(x; p) = \sum_i h_i(p) U(x_i)$ *for some functions U and h,*

where $h(1) = 1$ and $h(\frac{1}{2}, \frac{1}{2}) = (\frac{1}{2}, \frac{1}{2})$. If two functions V and V' satisfy (i) and (ii) there exists constants a and b, $a > 0$, such that

(iii) $V'(y) = aV(y) + b$.

The proof, which is not very illuminating, is included in the appendix.

It is clear that Axioms 1–3 are weak forms of the corresponding NM axioms. Axiom 4 can be derived from the NM independence axiom but it is easier to show that any expected utility maximizer must satisfy it, since

$$E[U\{(X_1^*, X_2^*); (\tfrac{1}{2}, \tfrac{1}{2})\}] = \tfrac{1}{2} \sum_i U(x_i) p_i + \tfrac{1}{2} \sum_i U(x_i') p_i$$

$$= \sum_i \tfrac{1}{2}(U(x_i) + U(x_i')) p_i = E[U\{c; p\}]. \tag{16}$$

4. Conditions on the anticipated utility functions

Under the anticipated utility theory, an individual's attitudes to prospects are determined both by their attitudes to the possible outcome and by their attitudes to the probabilities. These are reflected in the utility function, *u*, and the weighting function, *h*, respectively.

With regard to the first, the concepts of risk aversion, risk neutrality and risk preference are still relevant though their interpretation is somewhat different. A risk neutral individual will be indifferent between a 50–50 bet and its expected outcome, while a risk averter will prefer the certain outcome and a risk preferrer the bet. Thus, as in expected utility theory, risk aversion is equivalent to a concave utility function.

The most obvious pattern of probability distortion relates to the treatment of events with small probabilities and extreme outcomes. We may say that an individual overweights extreme events if

(A) $\begin{cases} f(p) \geq p, & p \leq \frac{1}{2}, \\ f(p) \leq p, & p \geq \frac{1}{2}. \end{cases}$

Conversely, an individual underweights extreme events if

(B) $\begin{cases} f(p) \leq p, & p \leq \frac{1}{2}, \\ f(p) \geq p, & p \geq \frac{1}{2}. \end{cases}$

Of course, an individual may conform to neither of these patterns. For example, there may be a number of probabilities for which $f(p) = p$. Even if (A) or (B) is satisfied there may be multiple points of inflexion in addition to that at $(\frac{1}{2}, \frac{1}{2})$.

To avoid the latter possibility the stronger assumptions

(A*) f is concave on $[0, \frac{1}{2}]$ and convex on $[\frac{1}{2}, 1]$, and

(B*) f is convex on $[0, \frac{1}{2}]$ and concave on $[\frac{1}{2}, 1]$

may be used in place of (A) and (B) respectively.

In general, overweighting of extreme events would seem to be the norm. Overweighting of extreme events provides a simple explanation for the Friedman–Savage and Allais paradoxes. On the other hand, it often seems as if events with extremely small probabilities (e.g., less than 10^{-5}) are simply ignored. Kahneman and Tversky discuss this phenomenon, which they describe as 'editing', and suggest it implies that f must be discontinuous near 0 and 1.

I wish to offer a reinterpretation of the 'editing' process which explains both overweighting of extreme events with small probabilities and disregarding those of extremely small ones. It would appear that there is a non-zero-cost of calculation which is incurred if an event is included in our calculations. Hence, events which affect anticipated utility by an amount less than this cost are edited out. Such events either are extremely improbable or have only a miniscule effect on ulity if they do occur.

However, intuitive processes, such as editing, will be refined by trial and error, rather than by deductive reasoning. For 'once in a lifetime' events, such as winning the lottery, this process will not be very effective. There is likely to be a 'conservative' bias against excluding such events from consideration, unless they are very improbable indeed. In the case of lotteries, of course, the editing process will also be counteracting by advertising, which seeks to keep the possibility of winning always in the minds of customers.

Thus, it would appear, the editing process will eliminate some improbable events with extreme outcomes, but, from an objective probability viewpoint, not enough.

The fact that events with extremely low probabilities are ignored does not mean f must be discontinuous. If the range of utility outcomes is bounded, all events with a sufficiently low probability will have a minimal effect on anticipated utility, but it is not necessary to set $f = 0$ to represent this.

A second feature of the transformation f is optimism-pessimism. If, for all p, $f(p) \geq 1 - f(1-p)$ an individual is pessimistic, since the worst outcomes are, on average, overweighted. If $f(p) \leq 1 - f(1-p)$, the individual is optimistic, while if $f(p) = 1 - f(1-p)$ the individual is neutral and h is symmetric.

As mentioned above, pessimism is rather difficult to distinguish empirically from risk aversion. It would thus be possible to require U to be linear, as Handa did. However, this would imply dropping the plausible condition $h(\tfrac{1}{2}, \tfrac{1}{2}) = (\tfrac{1}{2}, \tfrac{1}{2})$ and would also imply constant relative risk aversion for any given odds. The theory presented here is more general and flexible.

5. Stochastic dominance

Most useful applications of the NM theory have been based on the assumption that X is the set of real numbers. (Its elements are generally taken to correspond to levels of real wealth.) The preference ordering P on X is assumed to correspond to the natural ordering, so that individuals always prefer more wealth to less. These preferences may be represented by a monotonic increasing function $U: R \to R$. One of the most important tools of analysis under these conditions is the concept of stochastic dominance [Fishburn (1964)]. Hadar and Russell (1969) have developed stochastic dominance rules for the NM theory. Given random variables y_0 and y_1, with cumulative distribution functions D_0 and D_1 respectively, they define y_1 to first stochastically dominate y_0 (y_1 FSD y_0) if

$$D_0(x) \geq D_1(x) \quad \text{for all } x \tag{17}$$

and to second stochastically dominate y_0 (y_1 SSD y_0) if

$$\int_{-\infty}^{x} D_0(s)\,ds \geq \int_{-\infty}^{x} D_1(s)\,ds \quad \text{for all } x. \tag{18}$$

(The terms first degree and second degree stochastic dominance are also widely used for these conditions.)
They prove[4]

Proposition 2. Let y_1 and y_0 be as above. Then

(i) y_1 FSD y_0 if and only if $E[U(y^1)] \geq E[U(y_0)]$ for all monotonic increasing U.

(ii) y_1 SSD y_0 if and only if $E[U(y_1)] \geq E[U(y_0)]$ for all concave increasing U.

---

[4]Some technical errors in their proof are corrected by Tesfatsion (1976).

Some results of this type can be proved in the AU theory. The FSD result extends simply.[5]

Proposition 3. Let y_0 and y_1 be as above. Then y_1 FSD y_0 if and only if $V(y_1) \geq V(y_0)$ for all anticipated utility functions V.

Proof. 'If'. For any U the function $V(y) = E[U(y)]$ is an anticipated utility function and thus Proposition 2(i) applies.

   'Only if'. Suppose y_1 FSD y_0. Then for any transformation f

$$G_0(x) = f(D_0(x)) \geq f(D_1(x)) = G_1(x) \quad \text{for all } x. \tag{19}$$

Thus by Proposition 2(i) $\int U(x) \, dG_1(x) \geq \int U(x) \, dG_0(x)$ for any monotonic increasing U. Thus by (11), $V(y_1) \geq V(y_0)$ for any anticipated utility function V.

   The SSD case is not so simple. Consider the class V^* of AU functions formed from a concave utility function U and a symmetric transformation h which satisfies condition (A^*). If y_0 is a lottery ticket with a large prize, and y_1 is its actuarial expected value then y_1 SSD y_0, but for some $V \in V^*$, $V(y_0) > V(y_1)$. Thus a complete extension of 2(ii) is not possible (or desirable, since the object of the AU theory is the analysis of phenomena such as this). Some partial extensions may, however, be obtained.

   The basic approach is contained in the following useful special case:

Proposition 4. Let y_0 and y_1 be random variables with equal medians and symmetric distributions and with distribution functions $F_0(s)$ and $F_1(s)$ which intersect finitely often. Then y_1 SSD y_0 if and only if $V(y_1) \geq v(y_0)$ for each $V \in V^*$.

Proof. Since y_0 and y_1 are symmetric,

$$E[y_0] = \text{median } (y_0) = \text{median } (y_1) = E[y_1] = \mu. \tag{20}$$

Let y_1 SSD y_0. For any $x \leq \mu$ we may define a sequence $-\infty = a_0 \leq a_1 \leq \cdots \leq a_n = x$ such that

$$s \in (a_{2i}, a_{2i+1}) \Rightarrow D_0(s) \geq D_1(s)), \qquad i = 1, 2, \ldots,$$
$$s \in (a_{2i+1}, a_{2i+2}) \Rightarrow D_1(s) \geq D_0(s)). \tag{21}$$

---

[5]Analogous definitions and results can be given for discrete probability distributions. Since the proofs are also analogous, only the continuous case will be examined here.

J. Quiggin, *A theory of anticipated utility*   337

It will now be shown that for any f concave on $[0, \frac{1}{2}]$,

$$\int_{a_0}^{a_{2i}} f(D_0(s)) - f(D_1(s)) \, ds \geq f'(D_0(a_{2i-1})) \int_{a_0}^{a_{2i}} (D_0(s) - D_1(s)) \, ds. \tag{22}$$

Let $s \in (a_0, a_1)$. Then by the mean value theorem,

$$f(D_0(s)) - f(D_1(s)) = f'(c)(D_0(s) - D_1(s)) \tag{23}$$

for some c such that $D_1(s) \leq c \leq D_0(s) \leq D_0(a_1)$. By the concavity of f, $f'(c) \geq f'(D_0(a_1))$ and

$$\int_{a_0}^{a_1} f(D_0(s)) - f(D_1(s)) \, ds \geq f'(D_0(a_1)) \int_{a_0}^{a_1} (D_0(s) - D_1(s)) \, ds. \tag{24}$$

By a converse argument, for $s \in (a_1, a_2)$,

$$f(D_1(s)) - f(D_0(s)) \leq f'(D_0(a_1))(D_1(s) - D_0(s)), \quad \text{and} \tag{25}$$

$$\int_{a_1}^{a_2} f(D_0(s)) - f(D_1(s)) \, ds \geq f'(D_0(a_1)) \int_{a_1}^{a_2} D_0(s) - D_1(s) \, ds. \tag{26}$$

Combining (23) and (25) yields the desired result (22) for $i = 1$. Suppose (22) holds for $i = 1, 2, \ldots, k$. Then

$$\int_{a_0}^{a_{2k}} (f(D_0(s)) - f(D_1(s))) \, ds \geq f'(D_0(a_{2k-1})) \int_{a_0}^{a_{2k}} (D_0(s) - {}_1(s)) \, ds. \tag{27}$$

Application of an argument similar to that for $i = 1$ to the interval (a_{2k}, a_{2k+2}) yields

$$\int_{a_{2k}}^{a_{2k+2}} f(D_0(s)) - f(D_1(s)) \, ds \geq f'(D_0(a_{2k+1})) \int_{a_{2k}}^{a_{2k+2}} (D_0(s) - {}_1(s)) \, ds. \tag{28}$$

Since $f'(D_0(a_{2k})) \geq f'(D_0(a_{2k+1}))$ we may combine (27) and (28) to yield the desired result for $i = k + 1$ and hence by induction, for all i.

Now, if n is even, this shows that

$$\int_{-\infty}^{x} f(D_0(s)) - f(D_1(s)) \, ds \geq 0. \tag{29}$$

If n is odd then (22) holds for $2i = a_{n-1}$ and $f(D_0(s)) \geq f(D_1(s))$ for $s \in (a_{n-1}, a_n)$ so that (29) holds in this case also.

338   *J. Quiggin, A theory of anticipated utility*

Now the symmetry of y_0 and y_1 implies that

$$\int_{\mu}^{\mu+d} (1/2 - D_j(s))\, ds = \int_{\mu-a}^{\mu} (D_j(s) - \tfrac{1}{2})\, ds, \qquad j=0,1, \tag{30}$$

$$\int_{\mu}^{\mu+a} (\tfrac{1}{2} - f(D_j(s)))\, ds = \int_{\mu-a}^{\mu} (f(D_j(s)) - \tfrac{1}{2})\, ds, \qquad j=0,1 \tag{31}$$

and hence

$$\int_{\mu}^{\mu+a} (f(D_0(s)) - f(D_1(s)))\, ds = - \int_{\mu-a}^{\mu} (f(D_0(s)) - f(D_1(s)))\, ds, \tag{32}$$

i.e.,

$$\int_{-\infty}^{\mu+a} (f(D_0(s)) - f(D_1(s)))\, ds = - \int_{-\infty}^{\mu-a} (f(D_0(s)) - f(D_1(s)))\, ds \geq 0. \tag{33}$$

The argument of Proposition 3 may now be repeated to yield the desired result.

A useful implication of this result is that, as in the EU theory, mean-variance analysis is valid for comparing normally distributed random variables. For if y_1 has a higher mean and lower variance than y_0 Proposition 3 may be applied to show that $V(y_1) \geq V(y_0)$ for any V. If the means are equal and y_1 has a lower variance, Proposition 4 may be applied for any $V \in V^*$. Thus indifference curves in the $\mu - \sigma$ plane will be correctly shaped for any $V \in V^*$.

The symmetry assumption may be relaxed considerably. Suppose y_0 is symmetric but F_1 satisfies

$$D_1(\mu + a) - \tfrac{1}{2} \leq \tfrac{1}{2} - D_1(\mu - a) \quad \text{for all } a > 0. \tag{34}$$

By the symmetry of f this implies

$$f(D_1(\mu + a)) - \tfrac{1}{2} \leq \tfrac{1}{2} - f(D_1(\mu - a)), \quad \text{and hence} \tag{35}$$

$$\int_{\mu}^{\mu+a} (f(D_1(s)) - \tfrac{1}{2})\, ds \leq \int_{\mu-a}^{\mu} (\tfrac{1}{2} - f(D_1(s)))\, ds. \tag{36}$$

Thus (31) may be replaced by

$$\int_{-\infty}^{\mu+a} (f(D_0(s)) - f(D_1(s)))\, ds \geq \int_{-\infty}^{\mu-a} (f(D_0(s)) - f(D_1(s)))\, ds \geq 0. \tag{37}$$

Condition (34) states that the distribution of y_1 is skewed to the right. [There are distributions with a positive third moment which do not satisfy

(34). However these do not fit the intuitive conception of skewness as well as distributions satisfying (34).] A converse argument can be applied if y_0 is skewed to the left, and y_i is either symmetric or skewed to the right.

6. Concluding comments

Just· as the expected utility theory permits the analysis of behaviour which would be excluded as irrational under a profit-maximization hypothesis, the AU theory permits the analysis of anticipations which are not mathematical expectations.

It may be argued that the adoption of a more general theory makes it harder to obtain useful predictions. The results of section 4 show that much of the dominance analysis which is useful in NM theory can be extended to AU theory. In particular, Proposition 3 shows that no pairwise preference ranking which is inadmissible under NM theory can be admissible under AU theory. Further work is needed in developing conditions under which other results can be extended.

Areas in which AU theory might usefully be applied include the problem of individual's apparent propensity to 'over-insure', and the economic analysis of gambling behavior. The theory is likely to be particularly valuable in the analysis of decisions involving catastrophic (or extremely favourable outcomes) which occur with low probability.

Appendix

The proof of Proposition 1 has two parts. In part (a) an arbitrary choice of values for U for two elements of X is shown to imply that $V(y)$ can have only one possible value of any $y \in Y$. In part (b) it is shown that the function V constructed in this way satisfies conditions (i) and (ii) of the proposition. In both parts of the proof the special status of 50–50 bets is used extensively.

(a) Choose x', $x'' \in X$, $x''Px'$· and set $U(x')=0$, $U(x'')=1$. [In the trivial case when $x''Ix'$ for all x', x'', V must be a constant function and will satisfy conditions (i) and (ii).]

If $x = XE\{(x',x''); (\frac{1}{2},\frac{1}{2})\}$ then by (ii) and Axiom 2, $U(x)=\frac{1}{2}$. More generally, if $U(x_1)=a/2^n$, $U(x_2)=(a+1)/2^n$, $x=CE\{(x_1,x_2); (\frac{1}{2},\frac{1}{2})\}$, $U(x)=(2a+1)/2^{n+1}$. Note that x_2PxPx_1 so that the function U preserves the preference ordering. The set of numbers of the form $a/2^k$ is dense in $[0,1]$ since every real number has a binary expansion. We may thus complete the construction of U on $\{x; x''PxPx'\}$ as follows: Let

$$X_k^* = \{x \in X; U(x)=a/2^k, a=0,1,...,2^k\}, \quad \text{and} \tag{A.1}$$

$$X^* = \bigcup_{k=0}^{\infty} X_k^* \text{ (observe } X_k^* < x_{k+1}^*, \text{ all } k). \quad \text{Then} \tag{A.2}$$

$$U(x) = \sup\{U(x_0): x_0 \in X^*, xPx_0\} = \inf\{U(x_0): x_0 \in X^*, x_0 Px\}.$$

Note once more that U preserves the preference ordering. Now for any x such that $x'' Px Px'$, Axiom 3 requires the existence of $p \in [0, 1]$ such that $x = CE\{(x', x''); (p, 1-p)\}$.

Hence, we can determine $f(p)$ by

$$f(1-p) = 1 - f(p) = U(x). \tag{A.3}$$

By the dominance axiom f is monotone increasing. Hence, letting $U(x)$ range from 0 to 1, $f(p)$ can be determined for all p. As shown above, this is sufficient to determine $h(p)$ for all p.

Construction of U outside the range $[0, 1]$, is done using Axiom 3. If xPx'' [so that $U(x) \geq 1$], there exists p^* such that $x'' = CE\{(x', x; p^*, 1-p^*)\}$. Hence

$$U(x'') = f(p^*)U(x') + (1 - f(p^*))U(x), \quad \text{i.e.,}$$

$$U(x) = 1/(1 - f(p^*)) \quad [\text{since } U(x'') = 1, U(x') = 0]. \tag{A.4}$$

Similarly if $x'Px$, there exists p^* such that

$$x' = CE\{(x, x''); p^*, 1-p^*)\}, \quad \text{and}$$

$$U(x) = -(1 - f(p^*))/f(p^*) = 1 - 1/f(p^*). \tag{A.5}$$

Now U has been determined for all $x \in X$, and h for all $p \in [0, 1]$. Hence, given the initial choices $U(x') = 0$ and $U(x'') = 1$, only one choice is possible for the functions U and h. If, instead, we chose $U(x') = b$, $U(x'') = a + b$ and thus determined a function V', an examination of the construction procedure would show that for all $y \in Y, V'(y) = aV(y) + b$. This completes the proof of uniqueness.

(b) It has already been shown that U preserves the preference ordering for $x_1, x_2 \in X$ such that $x'' Px_2 Px'$, $x'' Px_1 Px'$. But the choice of x'' and x' does not affect the ordering of U [by part (a)] so we can always make this choice to ensure that U preserves the preference ordering for any $x_1, x_2 \in X$.

Similarly for arbitrary $y = \{x, p\}$ it will be shown that a function V based on a selection of x'', x' such that $x'' > x_i > x'$ for all i preserves the ordering P. This result must therefore apply to any V.

By transitivity (Axiom 1) and the fact that U preserves P on X, it is sufficient to prove that for any $x \in X, y \in Y, V(x) = V(y) \Leftrightarrow x = CE(y)$.

Define

$$Y_k^* = \{(x, p) \in Y : x_i \in X_k^*, \text{all } i\}, \quad \text{and} \tag{A.6}$$

$$Y^* = \{\{x, p\} \in Y : x_i \in X^* \text{ all } i\}. \tag{A.7}$$

The density properties of X^* mean that it will be sufficient to prove the desired result for $y \in Y^*$

The result will first be established for the class of 50–50 bets. Suppose x, x_1, $x_2 \in X_k^*$ and $x_2 P x_2$. Then we wish to prove

Lemma 1. $V(x) = V\{(x_1, x_2); (\frac{1}{2}, \frac{1}{2})\}$ *if and only if* $x = CE\{(x_1, x_2); (\frac{1}{2}, \frac{1}{2})\}$.

Proof. We may note that it is sufficient to prove the 'only if' part of the proposition since, for any x_1, $x_2 \in X_k^*$, there exists x_3 such that $U(x_3) = U\{(x_1, x_2); (\frac{1}{2}, \frac{1}{2})\}$. This can be seen by examining the construction procedure. Hence the 'only if' proposition implies that $x_3 = CE\{(x_1, x_2); (\frac{1}{2}, \frac{1}{2})\}$ and that if $x = CE\{(x_1, x_2); (\frac{1}{2}, \frac{1}{2})\}$ then $U(x) = U(x_3)$. Since $x, x_1 \in X_k^*$,

$$U(x) = a/2^k \qquad \text{for some } a, \quad \text{and}$$

$$U(x_1) = (a - b)/2^k \quad \text{for some } b > 0.$$

The proposition holds for $b = 1$ by virtue of the construction procedure. It may be proved inductively for arbitrary b by showing that

(i) if the proposition holds for $b = n$, it holds for $b = 2n$,
(ii) if the proposition holds for $b = b_1$ and $b = b_2$ it holds for $b = (b_1 + b_2)/2$, when this is an integer.

Any positive integer may be formed using (i) and (ii).

(i) Assume the proposition true for $b = n$ and let $U(x_1) = (a - 2n)/2^k$, $U(x_2) = (a + 2n)/2^k$.

Define

$$c_1 = CE\{(x_1, x); \frac{1}{2}, \frac{1}{2})\}, \qquad c_2 = CE\{(x, x_2); (\frac{1}{2}, \frac{1}{2})\}.$$

Then by the inductive hypothesis,

$$V(c_1) = (a - n)/2^k, \qquad V(c_2) = (a + n)/2^k, \text{ and}$$

$$x = CE\{(c_1, c_2); (\frac{1}{2}, \frac{1}{2})\}.$$

Application of Axiom 4 with $y_1 = x = \{(x,x);(\frac{1}{2},\frac{1}{2})\}$, $y_2 = \{(x_1,x_2);(\frac{1}{2},\frac{1}{2})\}$ and $x^* = CE(y_2)$ yields xIx^*, that is

$$x = CE\{(x_1,x_2);(\frac{1}{2},\frac{1}{2})\}, \tag{A.8}$$

which completes part (i),

(ii)   Let $b = (b_1 + b_2)2$ and

$$U(x_1) = (a-b)/2^k, \quad U(x_2) = (a+b)/2^k,$$

$$U(x_3) = (a-b_1)/2^k, \quad U(x_4) = (a+b_1)/2^k,$$

$$U(x_5) = (a-b_2)/2^k, \quad U(x_6) = (a+b_2)/2^k.$$

Define

$$y_1 = \{(x_3,x_5);(\frac{1}{2},\frac{1}{2})\}, \qquad y_2 = \{(x_4,x_6);(\frac{1}{2},\frac{1}{2})\}. \quad \text{Then}$$

$$x_1 = CE(y_1), \qquad x_2 = CE(y_2),$$

$$x = CE\{(x_3,x_4);(\frac{1}{2},\frac{1}{2})\} = CE\{(x_5,x_6);(\frac{1}{2},\frac{1}{2})\}.$$

Application of Axiom 4 to y_1 and y_2 yields

$$x = CE\{(x_1,x_2);(\frac{1}{2},\frac{1}{2})\}. \tag{A.9}$$

and the proof of the Lemma is complete.

For the general result for $y \in Y^*$, we use an inductive argument on the Y_K. For $k = 0$, the construction of h guarantees the result. Assume the result holds for $k = 0, 1, \ldots, n-1$. Let $y = \{x,p\} \in Y_n^*$ and suppose $x_0 = CE(y)$. Define x^* and x^{**} as follows: If $x_i \in X_{n-1}^*$, $x_i^* = x_i = x_i^{**}$. If $x_i \in X_n^* - X_{n-1}^*$, $U(x) = (2a+1)/2^n$ for some a. Choose x_i^*, x_i^{**} such that $U(x_i^*) = a/2^{n-1}$, $U(x_i^{**}) = (a+1)/2^{n-1}$. Then $\{x^*,p\}$ and $\{x^{**},p\}$ are members of Y_{n-1}^*. They also have the properties that

(i) $V\{x,p\} = \frac{1}{2}V\{x^*,p\} + \frac{1}{2}V\{x^{**},p\}$, by construction, and by Lemma 1.
(ii) $x_i^{**} = CE\{(x_i^*,x_i^{**});(\frac{1}{2},\frac{1}{2})\}$ all i.

Hence if $\hat{x}_1^* = CE\{x^*,p\}$, and $\hat{x}_2^* = CE\{x^{**},p\}$,

$$x_0\{Ix,p\}I\{(\hat{x}_1^*,\hat{x}_2^*);(\frac{1}{2},\frac{1}{2})\}, \quad \text{by the inductive hypothesis}$$

$$V(CE\{x,p\})=\tfrac{1}{2}V(x_1^*)+\tfrac{1}{2}V(x_2^*)$$

$$=\tfrac{1}{2}V\{x',p\}+\tfrac{1}{2}V\{x,p\}=V\{x,p\}.$$

References

Allais, Maurice, 1952, Fondemonts d'une theorie positive des choix compartant un risque et critique des postulats et axiomes de l'ecole americaine, Paper presented at Colloque sur les Fondements et applications de la theorie du risque, Davis.

Allais, Maurice, 1953, Le comportement de l'homme rationnel devant le risque: Critique des postulats et axioms de l'ecole Americaine, Econometrica 62, 503–546.

Anderson, Jock, John Dillon and Brian Hardaker, 1977, Agricultural decision analysis (Iowa State University Press, Ames, IA).

Coombs, C.H., 1975, Portfolio theory and the measurement of risk, in: M. Kaplan and S. Schwartz, eds. (Academic Press, New York).

Dugundji, James, 1966, Topology (Allen and Bacon, Boston, MA).

Edwards, W., 1962, Subjective probabilities inferred from decisions, Psychological Review 69, 109–135.

Fellner, W., 1961, Distortion of subjective probabilities as a reaction to uncertainty, Quarterly Journal of Economics 75, 670–699.

Fishburn, Peter, 1964, Decision and value theory (Wiley, New York).

Fishburn, Peter, 1978, On Handa's 'New theory of Cardinal utility' and the maximization of expected return, Journal of Political Economy 86, 321–324.

Friedman, Milton and Leonard J. Savage, 1948, The utility analysis of choices involving risk, Journal of Political Economy 56, 279–304.

Hadar, Joseph and William Russell, 1969, Rules for ordering uncertain prospects, American Economic Review 59, 25–34.

Handa, Jagdish, 1977, Risk, probabilities and a new theory of cardinal utility, Journal of Political Economy 85, 97–122.

Hershey, J. and P. Schoemaker, 1980, Risk taking and problem context in the domain of losses: An expected utility analysis, Journal of Risk and Insurance 47.

Kahneman, Daniel and Amos Tversky, 1979, Prospect theory: An analysis of decision under risk, Econometrica 47, 263–293.

Karmarkar, U., 1978, Subjectively weighted utility: A descriptive extension of the expected utility model, Organisational Behavior and Human Performance 21, 61–72.

Karmarkar, U., 1979, Subjectively weighted utility and the Allais paradox, Organisational Behavior and Human Performance 24, 67–72.

Kunreuther, H., R. Ginsberg, L. Miller, P. Slovic, B. Botkan and N. Katz, 1978, Disaster insurance protection: Public policy lessons (Wiley, New York).

MacCrimmon, K., 1968, Descriptive and normative implications of the decision theory postulates, in: K. Borch and J. Mossin, eds., Risk and uncertainty (MacMillan, London).

Officer, R. and A. Halter, 1968, Utility analysis in a practical setting, American Journal of Agricultural Economics 50, 257–277.

Schoemaker, P. and H. Kunreuther, 1979, An experimental study of insurance decisions, Journal of Risk and Insurance 46, 603–618.

Slovic, P. and A. Tversky, 1974, Who accepts Savages axiom? Behavioral Science 19, 368–373.

Slovic, P., B. Fischhoff, S. Lichtenstein, B. Corrigan and B. Combs, 1977, Preference for insuring against probable small losses: Insurance implications, Journal of Risk and Insurance 44, 237–258.

Tesfatsion, L., 1976, Stochastic dominance and the maximization of expected utility, Review of Economic Studies 43, 301–316.

Tversky, Amos, 1969, Intransitivity of preferences, Psychological Review 76, 31–48.

Von Neumann, John and Oskar Morgenstern, 1944, Theory of games and economic behavior (Princeton University Press, Princeton, NJ).

118-45
[83]
0240-D63, D31
0261-D8
2130-

[5]

Econometrica, Vol. 51, No. 4 (July, 1983)

A GENERALIZATION OF THE QUASILINEAR MEAN WITH APPLICATIONS TO THE MEASUREMENT OF INCOME INEQUALITY AND DECISION THEORY RESOLVING THE ALLAIS PARADOX[1]

By Chew Soo Hong[2]

The main result of this paper is a generalization of the quasilinear mean of Nagumo [29], Kolmogorov [26], and de Finetti [17]. We prove that the most general class of mean values, denoted by $M_{\alpha\phi}$, satisfying *Consistency with Certainty, Betweenness, Substitution-independence, Continuity,* and *Extension,* is characterized by a continuous, nonvanishing weight function α and a continuous, strictly monotone value-like function ϕ. The quasilinear mean M_ϕ results whenever the weight function α is constant. Existence conditions and consistency conditions with first and higher degree stochastic dominance are derived and an extension of a well known inequality among quasilinear means, which is related to Pratt's [31] condition for comparative risk aversion, is obtained.

Under the interpretation of mean value as a certainty equivalent for a lottery, the $M_{\alpha\phi}$ mean gives rise to a generalization of the expected utility hypothesis which has testable implications, one of which is the resolution of the Allais "paradox." The $M_{\alpha\phi}$ mean can also be used to model the equally-distributed-equivalent or representative income corresponding to an income distribution. This generates a family of relative and absolute inequality measures and a related family of weighted utilitarian social welfare functions.

1. INTRODUCTION

On the surface, measures of income inequality, social welfare functions, mean values, and choice under uncertainty appear to be distinct concepts. Specific measures of income inequality include variance, coefficient of variation, relative mean deviation, and the Gini coefficient which is derived from the Lorenz curve. Except for the case of perfect equality, when they would all be zero, different measures tend to produce different rankings of relative inequality among alternative income distributions. This led Dalton [14] to suggest sixty years ago that underlying each measure of income inequality, there is a corresponding social welfare function.

Commonly used examples of mean values such as arithmetic mean, geometric mean, harmonic mean, and root-mean-square (or more generally the rth root of the rth moment of a positive random variable, also known as the general mean of order r) are special cases of a class of mean values called the quasilinear mean. This was first given an axiomatic characterization in 1930 by Nagumo [29] and Kolmogorov [26] independently for a vector of numbers, and extended to

---

[1] Parts of an earlier version of this paper were presented at the Annual Meeting of the Public Choice Society in New Orleans, March, 1981, and at the Third International Conference on Mathematical Modeling in Los Angeles, July/August, 1981.

[2] I would like to thank Richard Auster, David Conn, Angus Deaton, Serge-Christophe Kolm, Fernando Saldanha, two anonymous referees, and especially Shelby Brumelle, Cindy Greenwood, and Ken MacCrimmon for their helpful comments. I am also grateful to the National Science Foundation for research support.

probability distributions in the next year by de Finetti [17].[3] The arithmetic mean was considered, for a long time, to be a good rule-of-thumb for ordering risky prospects until 1738 when Bernoulli [5] published his now famous resolution of the St. Petersburg's paradox. Postulating a logarithmic 'moral' worth or utility function for money, Bernoulli showed that the amount which yields the same utility as the expected moral worth or expected utility of the St. Petersburg lottery is finite. This method, we note, of finding the certainty equivalent of a lottery is the same as calculating its geometric mean. In general, the received expected utility hypothesis is equivalent to adopting the quasilinear mean as a model of certainty equivalence.

The connection between the quasilinear mean and measures of income inequality first appeared in a paper by Atkinson [3] in 1970. Applying Kolm's [25] definition of the representative income—the level of income which if distributed equally would retain the same level of social welfare—to an additively separable (i.e., Utilitarian) and symmetric social welfare function suggested by Dalton, Atkinson obtained a quasilinear-mean model of representative income even though he did not seem to be aware of it.

In this paper, we offer an axiomatic characterization of a generalization of the quasilinear mean, parameterized by an additional weighting function. The motivation for generalizing the quasilinear mean comes from difficulties with its application as a model of certainty equivalence (e.g., the Allais paradox) and as a model of representative income (e.g., the need for a nonuniform, income-specific weighting of individuals). These, together with the ways our generalized mean resolves them, are discussed in Section 5, which describes also a corresponding generalization of the Arrow–Pratt index of local risk aversion. Axioms and related properties of the generalized mean together with some intermediate results are provided in Section 2. Section 3 contains the formal statements of our mean value representation theorems for the case of a compact interval as well as its extension to include noncompact intervals. Additional properties including conditions for consistency with first, second (mean-preserving spread), and higher degree stochastic dominance are derived in Section 4. In the interest of expository clarity, proofs of the formal results of Sections 2, 3, and 4 are collected in the Appendix. In their place, we include discussions of ideas leading to the theoretical results and the intuitive contents of the proofs, or what might be called plausibility arguments.

---

[3]Nagumo [29] and Kolmogorov [26] first characterized the quasilinear mean M_ϕ for a vector of numbers, $(x_1, x_2, \ldots, x_n)$ given by $M_\phi(x) = \phi^{-1}(\sum_{i=1}^{n} \phi(x_i)/n)$, where ϕ is a continuous and strictly monotone function. De Finetti [17] extended their result to the case of simple (finite) probability distributions. The version of the quasilinear mean representation theorem referred to in Section 3 of this paper is due to Hardy, Littlewood, and Polya [19], which followed closely the approach of de Finetti. Aczel [1] provided a characterization of the quasilinear mean using functional equations. Ben-Tal [4] showed that quasilinear means are ordinary arithmetic means under suitably defined addition and scalar multiplication operations. Weerahandi and Zidek [39] obtained a characterization of the more restrictive rth moment mean and Norris [30] did a survey of its applications in Statistics.

QUASILINEAR MEAN   1067

2. AXIOMS AND PROPERTIES OF MEAN VALUE[4]

Let D_J denote the space of probability distributions with all their mass concentrated in some interval J of the real line R (J need not be bounded). We consider a functional M whose domain is D_J. What properties should M possess in order to be a mean value? Remembering the mean-value theorems of elementary calculus, a natural candidate would seem to be the following.

PROPERTY 1 (Intermediate Value Property): $\forall F \in D_J$, $M(F) \in \operatorname{conv} \operatorname{Supp}(F)$.

The support of a distribution F, $\operatorname{supp}(F)$, consists of each point x such that every open set containing x has positive mass. $\operatorname{Conv} \operatorname{supp}(F)$ is the smallest interval containing $\operatorname{supp}(F)$. The Intermediate Value Property requires that the mean of a distribution be neither greater than the maximum attainable value nor less than the minimum attainable value. We adopt the following weaker form of Property 1 as an axiom.

AXIOM 1 (Consistency with Certainty): $\forall x \in J$, $M(\delta_x) = x$.

The distribution δ_x refers to the step function at x which, in terms of probability, indicates obtaining x with probability 1.

Another property that seems reasonable is given by Axiom 2.

AXIOM 2 (Betweenness): $\forall F$, $G \in D_J$, if $M(F) < M(G)$ then $\forall \beta \in (0, 1)$, $M(\beta F + (1 - \beta)G) \in (M(F), M(G))$.

It is straightforward to check that Betweenness is equivalent to Property 2 stated below.

PROPERTY 2 (Mixture-monotonicity): $\forall F$, $G \in D_J$, if $M(F) < M(G)$, then $M(\beta F + (1 - \beta)G) < M(\gamma F + (1 - \gamma)G)$ if $0 < \gamma < \beta < 1$.

LEMMA 1: *Axiom 2 $\Leftrightarrow$ Property 2.*

PROOF: Omitted.

A distribution G is said to stochastically dominate another distribution F in the first degree, denoted by $G \overset{1}{\geq} F$, if G is pointwise always not greater than F. If, in addition, G is strictly less than F at some point, then G stochastically

---

[4] In this paper, the terms axiom and property are used interchangeably. Properties carry the "axiom" label if they appear in the final representation theorem as a characteristic property.

1068   CHEW SOO HONG

dominates F strictly in the first degree, denoted by $G \overset{1}{>} F$. Consistency of mean value with this partial order is stated as Property 3.

PROPERTY 3 (Monotonicity): $\forall F, G \in D_J, g \overset{1}{>} F \Rightarrow M(G) > M(F).$[5]

Despite its normative appeal, the discussion in Section 5B on the measurement of income inequality shows that Monotonicity, as a property of mean value, may not be universally applicable.

The next axiom deals with the effect on mean value of certain changes in the composition of the underlying distribution.

AXIOM 3 (Substitution-independence): *Suppose $\exists F, G, H \in D_J$ and $\beta, \gamma \in (0, 1) \ni M(F) = M(G) \neq M(H)$ and $M(\beta F + (1 - \beta)H) = M(\gamma G + (1 - \gamma)H)$. Then $\forall H' \in D_J, M(\beta F + (1 - \beta)H') = M(\gamma G + (1 - \gamma)H').$*

The following property is an immediate consequence of the Betweenness and the Substitution-independence axioms.

PROPERTY 4 (Weak Substitution): $\forall F, G \in D_J$, if $M(F) = M(G)$ then $\forall \beta \in (0, 1) \exists \gamma \in (0, 1) \ni \forall H \in D_J, M(\beta F + (1 - \beta)H) = M(\gamma G + (1 - \gamma)H).$

LEMMA 2: *Axiom 2 and Axiom 3 $\Rightarrow$ Property 4.*

PROOF: Omitted.

A special case of the Weak Substitution Property, called Quasilinearity by Hardy, Littlewood, and Polya [19] is given by:

PROPERTY 5 (Substitution or Quasilinearity): $\forall F, G, H \in D_J$, if $M(F) = M(G)$, then $\forall \beta \in (0, 1), M(\beta F + (1 - \beta)H) = M(\beta G + (1 - \beta)H).$

Starting with two distributions with the same mean value, Quasilinearity or the Substitution Property requires that mixtures of these distributions with another distribution in the same proportions share the same mean regardless of the distribution that they are mixed with. The Weak Substitution Property allows the above mixture proportions, which give rise to the same mean value, to be different. Note that if we think of mean value as a certainty equivalent, then Quasilinearity is equivalent to Pratt, Raiffa, and Schlaifer's [32] Substitutability Axiom and is similar to Herstein and Milnor's [20] Axiom 3.

---

[5] The Monotonicity property was an axiom in de Finetti's [17] characterization of the quasilinear mean. It is not the case here since Monotonicity is not intrinsic to our generalized mean but can be imposed if needed (cf. Corollary 5).

The following property called Ratio Consistency is a consequence of Axioms 2 and 3

PROPERTY 6 (Ratio Consistency): Suppose $\exists F, G, H \in D_J$ and $\beta_1, \beta_2, \gamma_1, \gamma_2 \in (0, 1) \ni M(F) = M(G) \neq M(H)$ and $M(\beta_i F + (1 - \beta_i)H) = M(\gamma_i G + (1 - \gamma_i)H)$, for $i = 1, 2$. Then

$$\frac{\gamma_1/1 - \gamma_1}{\beta_1/1 - \beta_1} = \frac{\gamma_2/1 - \gamma_2}{\beta_2/1 - \beta_2} .$$

LEMMA 3: *Axioms 2 and 3 $\Rightarrow$ Property 6.*

PROOF: See Appendix A.

The crucial step in the proof of Lemma 3 lies in showing that the function,

$$\tau(\beta) = \frac{\gamma(\beta)/1 - \gamma(\beta)}{\beta/1 - \beta} ,$$

obtained from Lemma 2, satisfies the following functional equation (which is new):

(2.1) $(\beta + \delta)\tau(\beta + \delta) = \beta\tau(\beta) + \delta\tau(\delta/[\beta\tau(\beta) + 1 - \beta])$,

whose only solution is τ being constant. Consequently, γ has to be related to β via the following single parameter family:

(2.2) $\gamma = \beta\tau/(\beta\tau + 1 - \beta); \qquad \tau > 0.$

We may gain some insight about Ratio Consistency via a geometrical interpretation due to Weber [38].[6] Consider a unit simplex formed by three probability distributions F, G, H in Figure 1. Each distribution X within the simplex is specified by its barycentric (areal) coordinates $(\beta_1, \beta_2, \beta_3)$. Suppose F and G have the same mean. Let Z be the mixture, $\gamma G + (1 - \gamma)H$, between G and H having the same mean as the mixture Y, $\beta F + (1 - \beta)H$, between F and H and denote by $\bigcirc$ $(s, 1 - s, 0)$ the point of intersection between YZ and FG produced. Then Ratio Consistency requires $Y'Z'$ produced to originate from the same point O, where the mixtures Y' and Z' between the equal-mean distributions F and G and H also have the same mean. Specifically, it is not difficult to show that the constant τ in expression (2.2) is equal to $1 - s^{-1}$. For expected utility, the point O would be at infinity.

---

[6] Ratio Consistency was originally implied by a stronger version of the Weak Substitution Property which was an axiom in an early version of the paper. The current statement is motivated by Bob Weber's [38] geometrical demonstration which gives rise to an alternative proof of Lemma 2. The reader is referred to Chew [10, 12] for details.

1070   CHEW SOO HONG

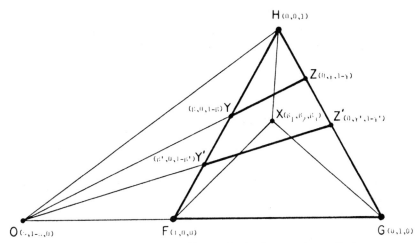

FIGURE 1—Ratio consistency illustrated using barycentric coordinates.

Finally, we require our mean value to be a continuous functional in the sense of Axioms 4 and 5.

AXIOM 4 (Continuity): *If* $\{F_n\}_{n=1}^{\infty} \subset D_J$ *converges in distribution to* $F \in D_J$ *and* F *has a compact support, then* $M(F) = \lim_{n\to\infty} M(F_n)$.

Convergence in distribution has the following characterization which is sometimes used as its definition: F_n converges in distribution to $F \in D_J$ if and only if $\int_J f \, dF_n$ converges to $\int_J f \, dF$, $\forall f \in \bar{C}(J)$, where $\bar{C}(J)$ is the space of all bounded continuous functions on J. The requirement of Continuity is useful because it tells us that the mean of a distribution may be approximated by the mean of a different distribution that is close to it.

When J is a compact interval, it is well known that Axiom 4 is equivalent to continuity of the mean value, M, with respect to the L^1-metric.[7] When J is unbounded the following condition tells us how to estimate the mean value of a distribution F without compact support (if it exists) by its restriction to a compact interval, K, denoted by F_K.

AXIOM 5 (Extension): *Let* $\{K_n\}_{n=1}^{\infty}$ *be an increasing family of compact intervals such that* $\lim_{n\to\infty} K_n = J$; *then* $\forall F \in D_J$, $M(F) = \lim_{n\to\infty} M(F_{K_n})$.

The mean value for a distribution F without compact support, according to Axiom 5, is given by the limit of the mean values of the sequence of truncated distributions, $\{F_{K_n}\}_{n=1}^{\infty}$, for any increasing family of compact intervals, $\{K_n\}_{n=1}^{\infty}$,

---

[7] The L^1-metric between two probability distributions F and G on some compact interval $[A, B]$ is given by $\int_A^B |F(x) - G(x)| \, dx$. This metric does not, however, admit a natural extension to an unbounded interval.

whose limit is J. Since the sequence of mean values, $\{M(F_{K_n})\}_{n=1}^{\infty}$, does not always converge, the mean value for a distribution without compact support need not exist. Consider, for example, the arithmetic mean for a Cauchy distribution.

3. REPRESENTATION THEOREMS

We begin with a statement of the quasilinear mean representation theorem [**19**, page 158]. We denote by $D^0[A, B]$ the restriction of $D[A, B]$ to simple probability distributions (i.e., distributions whose mass is concentrated in a finite set).

THEOREM 1: *Suppose* $\exists M : D^0[A, B] \to R$. *Then M satisfies Axiom 1, Property 4, and Property 5 if and only if there is a continuous, strictly monotone function ϕ on $[A, B]$ such that $\forall F \in D^0[A, B]$,*

$$(3.1) \qquad M(F) = \phi^{-1}\left(\int_A^B \phi\, dF\right).$$

Moreover, $\phi^* : [A, B] \to R$ *satisfies expression (3.1) with ϕ replaced by ϕ^* if and only if* $\exists a, b$ *with* $a \neq 0$ *such that* $\forall x \in [A, B]$,

$$(3.2) \qquad \phi^*(x) = a\phi(x) + b.$$

PROOF: Omitted since it is a special case of Theorem 2.

In other words, the most general *certainty consistent, monotone* and *quasilinear* mean value is given by (3.1). We shall call it the *quasilinear mean*. It is convenient to write the quasilinear mean of a distribution F as $M_\phi(F)$ since it is completely specified by a continuous, strictly monotone function ϕ, up to an affine transformation (3.2).

The following theorem generalizes the quasilinear mean. This is accomplished by introducing an additional weighting function α. For a vector of numbers $(x_1, \ldots, x_n)$, which is written in terms of a uniform simple probability distribution $\sum_{i=1}^n (1/n)\delta_{x_i}$, the generalized mean $M_{\alpha\phi}$ is given by:

$$M_{\alpha\phi}\left(\sum_{i=1}^n \frac{1}{n}\delta_{x_i}\right) = \phi^{-1}\left(\sum_{i=1}^n \left[\alpha(x_i)\Big/\sum_{j=1}^n \alpha(x_j)\right]\phi(x_i)\right).$$

The novelty is in assigning to x_i an $[\alpha(x_i)/\sum_{j=1}^n \alpha(x_j)]$ weight instead of a weight $1/n$. When α is constant, the quasilinear mean results. We are now ready for the statement of our generalized mean value representation theorem. It will be observed that we also extend the analysis in Theorem 1 from $D^0[A, B]$ to $D[A, B]$.

THEOREM 2: *Suppose* $\exists M : D[A, B] \to R$. *Then M satisfies Axiom 1, Axiom 2, Axiom 3, and Axiom 4 if and only if there are continuous functions ϕ (strictly*

CHEW SOO HONG

monotone) and α *(nonvanishing) on* $[A, B]$ *such that* $\forall F \in D[A, B]$,

(3.3) $$M(F) = \phi^{-1}\left(\int_A^B \alpha\phi\, dF \Big/ \int_A^B \alpha\, dF\right).$$

Moreover, $(\alpha^*, \phi^*): [A, B]^2 \to R \times R$ *satisfies expression* (3.3) *with* (α, ϕ) *replaced by* (α^*, ϕ^*) *if and only if* $\exists a, b, c, k$ *with* $a, c \neq 0$ *and* $k > 0$ *such that* $\forall x \in [A, B]$,

(3.4) $$\phi^*(x) = a\frac{k(\phi(x) - \phi(A))}{k(\phi(x) - \phi(A)) + (\phi(B) - \phi(x))} + b, \quad and$$

(3.5) $$\alpha^*(x) = c\alpha(x)\{k(\phi(x) - \phi(A)) + (\phi(B) - \phi(x))\}.$$

PROOF: See Appendix B.

The theorem is proved in stages. Following de Finetti [17], we may explicitly construct ϕ as follows. Denote the mean value $M(S_p)$ of the 2-point probability distribution $S_p \equiv p\delta_B + (1-p)\delta_A$ by $\psi(p)$. Note that it is continuous (from the Betweenness Axiom) and strictly increasing (from Lemma 1 or the Betweenness Axiom) in p. Denoting its inverse by ϕ, we have $M(S_{\phi(x)}) = x$. If we think of $\psi(p)$ as the certainty equivalent corresponding to the extremal lottery $p\delta_B + (1-p)\delta_A$, then ϕ is 'like' a von Neumann–Morgenstern utility function.

We are now ready to construct the weight function $\alpha(x)$. The discussion above shows that the point distribution δ_x and the 2-point distribution $S_{\phi(x)}$ have the same mean values. Lemma 3 in turn tells us that there is a positive number $\alpha(x)$ such that the respective mixtures of δ_x and $S_{\phi(x)}$ with another distribution H, given by $\beta\delta_x + (1-\beta)H$ and

$$\frac{\beta\alpha(x)}{\beta\alpha(x) + 1 - \beta}S_{\phi(x)} + \frac{1-\beta}{\beta\alpha(x) + 1 - \beta}H,$$

also share the same means. In substituting $S_{\phi(x)}$ for δ_x in the mixture $\beta\delta_x + (1-\beta)H$, the amount of change in β in order that the resulting mixture between $S_{\phi(x)}$ and H would still have the same mean is obtained by weighting β by $\alpha(x)$ against a unity weight for $(1 - \beta)$.

Having constructed the ϕ and then the α function, it turns out to be straight-forward to show that mean value of a simple distribution can be written in terms of the functions ϕ and α using expression (3.3). Consider the simple probability distribution $F \equiv \sum_{i=1}^n \theta_i\delta_{x_i}$ consisting of a convex linear combination of point distributions δ_{x_i}. Substituting the 2-point distribution $S_{\phi(x_i)}$ for δ_{x_i} one at a time using the $\alpha(x)$ function without changing the mean value, we arrive at the 2-point distribution, S_q, where q equals $\sum_{i=1}^n [\theta_i\alpha(x_i)/\sum_{j=1}^n \theta_j\alpha(x_j)]\phi(x_i)$. By construction, the mean value for S_q is given by $\phi^{-1}(\sum_{i=1}^n [\theta_i\alpha(x_i)/\sum_{j=1}^n \theta_j\alpha(x_j)]$

$\phi(x_i)$). This is readily recognized to be the summation form of expression (3.3) for the simple probability distribution, $\sum_{i=1}^{n} \theta_i \delta_{x_i}$.

Theorem 2 proves that the most general class of mean values for probability distributions on a compact interval $[A, B]$ satisfying *Consistency with Certainty*, *Betweenness*, *Substitution-independence*, and *Continuity* is characterized by a pair of functions α and ϕ. In keeping with precedent, we denote our generalized mean by $M_{\alpha\phi}$. The restriction to a compact interval in Theorems 1 and 2, however, limits the usefulness of the mean values M_{ϕ} and $M_{\alpha\phi}$ in applications where one cannot specify a priori an upper and a lower bound to the distribution of values or the random variable. This limitation becomes more significant if we want to deal with distributions or random variables which are not bounded. A case in point is the St. Petersburg's lottery. Others include most of the commonly used sampling distributions such as the Normal distribution, the Gamma distribution, as well as the Poisson distribution.

Although we are not aware of any formal attempt to extend the quasilinear mean M_{ϕ} in Theorem 1 to an arbitrary interval J (perhaps unbounded), this problem, similar to the familiar one for von Neumann–Morgenstern utility, is relatively easy to deal with. Consider an increasing sequence of compact intervals $\{[A_i, B_i]\}_{i=0}^{\infty}$ whose limit is J. Beginning with a ϕ_0 defined on $[A_0, B_0]$ we obtain, for each i, the corresponding ϕ_i defined on $[A_i, B_i]$ satisfying $\phi_i(A_0) = \phi_0(A_0)$, and $\phi_i(B_0) = \phi_0(B_0)$. This can be done since the ϕ_i functions are each unique up to an affine transformation (see expression (3.2)). The above procedure leads to the construction of a single ϕ function on J:

$$
\phi(x) = \begin{cases}
\phi_0(x) & \text{if } x \in [A_0, B_0] \\
\quad\vdots & \qquad \vdots \\
\phi_i(x) & \text{if } x \in [A_i, B_i] - [A_{i-1}, B_{i-1}] \\
\quad\vdots & \qquad \vdots
\end{cases}
$$

As long as the support of a distribution F is compact it must be contained in some interval $[A_i, B_i]$ within J. The quasilinear mean value of F would then be given by $M_{\phi_i}(F) = \phi_i^{-1}(\int_{A_i}^{B_i} \phi_i \, dF)$ which is the same as $\phi^{-1}(\int_J \phi \, dF) = M_{\phi}(F)$. What happens if a distribution does not have compact support? The Extension Axiom (Axiom 5) tells us that its mean value $M_{\phi}(F)$ is given by $\lim_{n\to\infty} M_{\phi}(F_{K_n})$, for any increasing family of compact intervals $\{K_n\}_{n=0}^{\infty}$ whose limit is J. Of course, this limit may not always exist. Consider again the nonexistence of the arithmetic mean for a Cauchy distribution.

As it turns out, the $M_{\alpha\phi}$ mean can also be extended to an unbounded interval. Consider an open and possibly unbounded interval (A, B). Let $\{A_i\}_{i=0}^{\infty}$ and $\{B_i\}_{i=0}^{\infty}$ be strictly monotone sequences in (A, B) such that $\lim_{i\to\infty} A_i \downarrow A$ and $\lim_{i\to\infty} B_i \uparrow B$. By construction, the limit of the strictly increasing family of compact intervals $\{[A_i, B_i]\}_{i=0}^{\infty}$ is (A, B). Apply Theorem 2 to each interval $[A_i, B_i]$, to obtain a pair of functions (α_i, ϕ_i) that characterize $M_{\alpha_i\phi_i}$ on $D[A_i, B_i]$.

Unlike the case of the quasilinear mean, we are not able at this point to construct a pair (α, ϕ) on (A, B) since we cannot be sure if it is possible to set $(\alpha_i, \phi_i)(A_0) = (\alpha_0, \phi_0)(A_0)$ and $(\alpha_i, \phi_i)(B_0) = (\alpha_0, \phi_0)(B_0)$ for every i. It is shown in [11, Corollary 1] that as we vary the ratio $k_i = \alpha_i(B_i)/\alpha_i(A_i)$ between 0 and ∞, the ratio $\alpha_i(B_0)/\alpha_i(A_0)$ changes within an open interval $(\underline{h}_i, \bar{h}_i)$. Therefore, if we happen to begin with a pair (α_0, ϕ_0) such that $k_0 = \alpha_0(B_0)/\alpha_0(A_0) \notin (\underline{h}_i, \bar{h}_i)$, then there is no consistent extension to the larger interval $[A_i, B_i]$. The question is whether there is any $\hat{k}_0$ such that for each $[A_i, B_i]$, we can find a (α_i, ϕ_i) satisfying $\alpha_i(B_0)/\alpha_i(A_0) = \hat{k}_0$. Such a $\hat{k}_0$ then allows us to satisfy, for each i, the conditions $(\alpha_i, \phi_i)(A_0) = (\alpha_0, \phi_0)(A_0)$ and $(\alpha_i, \phi_i)(B_0) = (\alpha_0, \phi_0)(B_0)$ using the uniqueness transformations (3.4) and (3.5).

The demonstration that $\hat{k}_0$ exists is obtained by observing that the intervals of permissible k_0, $(\underline{h}_i, \bar{h}_i)$, decreases strictly in both end-points as we extend to larger $[A_i, B_i]$ intervals, i.e., as i increases (see [11, Corollary 2]). By squeezing a compact interval between $(\underline{h}_i, \bar{h}_i)$ and $(\underline{h}_{i+1}, \bar{h}_{i+1})$ for each i, we can apply the nested interval theorem to conclude that $\lim_{i \to \infty}(\underline{h}_i, \bar{h}_i)$ is nonempty. The construction of (α, ϕ) on (A, B) then begins with a pair of functions (α_0, ϕ_0) on $[A_0, B_0]$ such that $\alpha_0(B_0)/\alpha_0(A_0) = \hat{k}_0 \in \lim_{i \to \infty}\{(\underline{h}_i, \bar{h}_i)\}$. We define

$$(\alpha, \phi)(x) = \begin{cases} (\alpha_0, \phi_0)(x) & \text{if } x \in [A_0, B_0], \\ (\alpha_1, \phi_1)(x) & \text{if } x \in [A_1, B_1] - [A_0, B_0], \\ \quad \vdots & \qquad \vdots \\ (\alpha_i, \phi_i)(x) & \text{if } x \in [A_i, B_i] - [A_{i-1}, B_{i-1}], \\ \quad \vdots & \qquad \vdots, \end{cases}$$

such that

$$\alpha_i(B_0)/\alpha_i(A_0) = k_0,$$

$$\alpha_i(A_0) = \alpha_0(A_0),$$

$$\phi_i(B_0) = \phi_0(B_0),$$

and

$$\phi_i(A_0) = \phi_0(A_0) \qquad\qquad (i = 1, 2, 3, \ldots).$$

As is true of the quasilinear mean, the $M_{\alpha\phi}$ mean of a distribution with compact support, given by expression (3.7) below using the (α, ϕ) just constructed, always exists. For a distribution F without compact support, the $M_{\alpha\phi}$ mean according to Axiom 5 would be given by $\lim_{n \to \infty} M_{\alpha\phi}(F_{K_n})$ which, if it exists, is written as $\phi^{-1}(\int_J \alpha\phi \, dF / \int_J \alpha \, dF)$ for an increasing family of compact intervals $\{K_n\}_{n=0}^{\infty}$ whose limit is J. This motivates the following definition of the ratio of integrals, which may exist even if both the numerator and the denominator are unbounded:

$$(3.6) \qquad \int_J \alpha \phi \, dF \Big/ \int_J \alpha \, dF = \lim_{n \to \infty} \left(\int_J \alpha \phi \, dF_{K_n} \Big/ \int_J \alpha \, dF_{K_n} \right),$$

where $\{ K_n \}_{n=0}^{\infty}$ is an increasing sequence of compact intervals whose limit is J, and F_{K_n} denotes the restriction of F to K_n.

It remains to consider the case of a half-open interval J with say the lower end-point $[A, B)$. (The reader is referred to [12] for details in terms of a mixture set.) The possibility of α being unbounded as x tends to A is ruled out because it would otherwise violate Betweenness (Axiom 2). The continuity axiom (Axiom 4) implies that $\lim_{x \to A} \alpha(x) = \alpha(A)$ is well-defined. In order to satisfy Betweenness, it is easy to verify that the remaining permissible cases are given by (i) $\lim_{x \to A} \phi(x)$ is bounded if $\alpha(A)$ is nonzero and (ii) $\lim_{x \to A} \alpha(x)\phi(x)$ is bounded and nonzero if α vanishes at A. The latter would imply that $\lim_{x \to A} \phi(x)$ is infinite.

Hence, we have the following theorem.

THEOREM 3: *Suppose $\exists M : D_J \to R$. Then M satisfies Axiom 1, Axiom 2, Axiom 3, Axiom 4, and Axiom 5 if and only if there are continuous functions ϕ (strictly monotone) and α (nonvanishing except possibly at one endpoint in which case the product $\alpha \cdot \phi$ is nonzero) on J such that $\forall F \in D_J$,*

$$(3.7) \qquad M(F) = \phi^{-1} \left(\int_J \alpha \phi \, dF \Big/ \int_J \alpha \, dF \right).$$

PROOF: Sufficiency follows from the preceding arguments. Necessity is straightforward.   *Q.E.D.*

In order to determine the class of mean-value-preserving transformations on (α, ϕ) in expression (3.7), suppose (α^*, ϕ^*) is one such pair of functions on J. Then, according to Theorem 2, (α^*, ϕ^*) is related to (α, ϕ) on any compact interval $[A, B] \subset \operatorname{Int} J$ via expressions (3.4) and (3.5) which can be rewritten in the manner below:

$$(3.8) \qquad \phi^* \equiv [q\phi + r]/[s\phi + t] \quad \text{and}$$

$$(3.9) \qquad \alpha^* \equiv [s\phi + t]\alpha.$$

It is clear that the transformation in expression (3.8) is strictly monotone since $(rs - qt) = [\phi^*(B) - \phi^*(A)]/[\phi(B) - \phi(A)]$ is nonzero. It is also clear from expression (3.5) that α^* is nonvanishing since this is true of the $[s\phi + t]$ term in expression (3.9).

1076   CHEW SOO HONG

For any other interval $[A', B']$ containing $[A, B]$, we know that (α^*, ϕ^*) would also be related to (α, ϕ) via expressions (3.8) and (3.9) for some $p', q', r',$ and t' on the larger interval $[A', B']$:

(3.10) $\phi^* \equiv [q'\phi + r']/[s'\phi + t']$ and

(3.11) $\alpha^* \equiv [s'\phi + t']\alpha.$

As before, the uniqueness part of Theorem 2 requires ϕ^* to be strictly monotone and α^* to be nonvanishing (since $[s'\phi + t']$ is nonvanishing) on $[A', B']$.

Comparing the expressions for α^* (expressions (3.9) and (3.15)) on the common smaller interval $[A, B]$, we conclude that $s = s'$ and $t = t'$. A similar comparison applied to the ϕ^* function then yields $q = q'$ and $r = r'$. This gives us the uniqueness result for Theorem 3 which is stated as Corollary 1 below:

COROLLARY 1: *Under the hypothesis of Theorem 3, a pair of functions* (α^*, ϕ^*) *satisfies expression (3.7) with* (α, ϕ) *replaced by* (α^*, ϕ^*) *if and only if* $\exists q, r, s,$ *and* t *with* $rs \neq qt$ *and* $s\phi + t$ *nonvanishing on* $\mathrm{Int}\,J$ *such that* (α^*, ϕ^*) *is related to* (α, ϕ) *via expressions (3.8) and (3.9).*

PROOF: Sufficiency follows from the preceding discussion. Necessity is easy to verify. $Q.E.D.$

When the parameter s is zero, ϕ^* is an affine transformation of ϕ and α^* is a ratio transformation of α. A nonzero s 'tilts' α^* relative to α by bringing ϕ into the multiplication coefficient of α. It is, in a sense, an interaction parameter, confounding the influence of the value-like ϕ function with α's in yielding α^*. This may be labeled a "value-weighted" ratio transformation. At the same time, expression (3.8) becomes the ratio of two affine transformations or what one may call a 'rational-affine' transformation.

The rational-affine transformation is really characterized by three rather than four parameters since we can divide the numerator and the denominator by s or t (they cannot both vanish). If t is zero, then:

(3.12) $\phi^* \equiv [r/\phi] + \hat{q}, \quad (\hat{q} = q/s)$ and

(3.13) $\alpha^* \equiv s\phi\alpha.$

Expression (3.12) is like an 'inverse-affine' transformation while α^* in (3.13) is essentially the product (or geometric mean) of ϕ and α. Note that the nonvanishingness condition on α^* can hold only if ϕ is also nonvanishing on $\mathrm{Int}\,J$.

Finally, it is clear, if ϕ is unbounded in both directions, that any nonzero s cannot ensure the nonvanishingness of the $[s\phi + t]$ term in (3.9). Hence, we have the following corollary.

COROLLARY 2: *Under the hypothesis of Theorem 3, if ϕ is unbounded in both directions, then (α, ϕ) is unique up to an affine transformation for ϕ and a ratio transformation for α.*

4. PROPERTIES OF THE $M_{\alpha\phi}$ MEAN

The Intermediate Value Property (Property 1) enjoys a rather special status, somewhat like a defining property, among natural properties of mean values. Even measures such as the median and mode (both are noncontinuous),[8] which are rejects of our generalized mean, exhibit this property. The conclusion that $M_{\alpha\phi}$ has the intermediate value property follows from the observation that

$$M_{\alpha\phi}(F) = c \Leftrightarrow \frac{\int \alpha(x)(\phi(x) - \phi(c))\, dF(x)}{\int \alpha(x)\, dF(x)} = 0.$$

For this expression to hold, clearly, c must lie within the support of F. Hence, we have the following Corollary.

COROLLARY 3: *$M_{\alpha\phi}$ has the Intermediate Value Property.*

In applying mean value as a model of certainty equivalence in the next section, we need to know conditions under which the $M_{\alpha\phi}$ mean of a distribution always exists (cf. the super St. Petersburg paradox [28]).

COROLLARY 4: *$M_{\alpha\phi}$ always exists on D_J if and only if α and $\alpha \cdot \phi$ are bounded on J.*

PROOF: See Appendix C.

For the quasilinear mean (i.e., α is constant) the necessary and sufficient condition for existence is simply that ϕ be bounded. This is well known in the context of expected utility where ϕ can be interpreted as a utility function. The corresponding condition for the generalized mean turns out to be the boundedness of $\alpha \cdot \phi$ as well as α, allowing for the possible unboundedness of ϕ.

Consistency with strict stochastic dominance " $\overset{1}{>}$ " (Property 3: Monotonicity) is also thought to be desirable for many applications of mean value. It is, in addition, a characteristic property of the quasilinear mean. The corollary below gives conditions under which $M_{\alpha\phi}$ is consistent with (non-strict) stochastic dominance " $\overset{1}{\geq}$."

---

[8] Consider the distribution $p\delta_A + (1 - p)\delta_B$, $A < B$. The median of the distribution is A when $p > \frac{1}{2}$, B when $p < \frac{1}{2}$, and in the interval $[A, B)$ when $p = \frac{1}{2}$.

             CHEW SOO HONG

COROLLARY 5: *Suppose* α *and* $\alpha \cdot \phi$ *are both bounded on* J. *Then* $\forall F, G \in D_J$,

$F \overset{1}{\geq} G \Rightarrow M_{\alpha\phi}(F) \geqq M_{\alpha\phi}(G)$ *if and only if* $\forall s \in J$, $\alpha(x)(\phi(x) - \phi(s))$ *is monotone in* x.

PROOF: See Appendix C.

To motivate our discussion of the method of proof of Corollary 5, consider the case of an increasing real-valued function f with continuous partial derivatives. We know that if $y \geq x$, then $0 \leq df(x_\theta)/d\theta = \nabla f|_{x_\theta}.(y - x)$, where ∇f is the gradient of f and x_θ refers to $x + \theta(y - x)$ for $\theta \in (0, 1)$. In our case, we are dealing with a functional $\Omega \equiv \phi \circ M_{\alpha\phi} \equiv \int_J \alpha\phi \, dF / \int_J \alpha \, dF$, which is increasing in the sense of stochastic dominance "$\overset{1}{\geq}$." If $G \overset{1}{\geq} F$, then $G \overset{1}{\geq} F_\theta \overset{1}{\geq} F$ with F_θ referring to the mixture $(1 - \theta)F + \theta G$ or $F + \theta(G - F)$ for $\theta \in (0, 1)$. The requirement that $\Omega(F_\theta)$ increases in θ then becomes

$$(4.1) \qquad \frac{d}{d\theta} \Omega(F_\theta) = \int_J \zeta(x; F_\theta) \, d(G(x) - F(x))$$

$$= \int_J (F(x) - G(x)) \, d\zeta(x; F_\theta) \geqq 0, \qquad \text{where}$$

$$(4.2) \qquad \zeta(x; F) \equiv \left\{ \alpha(x) \Big/ \int_J \alpha \, dF \right\} \{ \phi(x) - \Omega(F) \}.$$

In order that expression (4.1) remains valid for any other distribution H that dominates F, the function $\zeta(x; F)$ (4.2) has to be increasing in x regardless of F. This is analogous to the requirement that the gradient ∇f be positive in order for f to be increasing. The directional derivative (4.1) is also known as the Gâteaux differential and the gradient-like, distribution-specific function, $\zeta(\cdot; F)$, is referred to as the Gâteaux derivative evaluated at the distribution F. Hence, the condition for consistency with stochastic dominance may be alternately stated as:[9] The Gâteaux derivative of Ω at F, $\zeta(\cdot; F)$, is nondecreasing for every F in D_J. This generalizes the corresponding condition for quasilinear mean M_ϕ if we observe that the Gâteaux derivative of $\phi \circ M_\phi$ at F is simply ϕ which is strictly increasing irrespective of F. If we think of ϕ as a von Neumann–Morgenstern utility, then $\zeta(\cdot; F)$ has the interpretation as a distribution (lottery)-specific utility function.

---

[9] In a recent paper, Machina [27] studied, using the L^1-metric, certain properties of a twice-Fréchet differentiable functional for probability distributions on a compact interval. Fréchet differentiability is a stronger requirement than Gâteaux differentiability. Therefore, the method of proofs of Corollaries 5 and 6 can be applied to the functional considered by Machina to obtain consistency conditions for first and second degree stochastic dominance. This approach has the advantage of not needing a metric and therefore avoids the problem of the nonextendability of the L^1-metric to an unbounded interval. Another advantage is its extendability to general probability measures on an arbitrary consequence set.

QUASILINEAR MEAN   1079

Another useful partial order is second degree stochastic dominance "$\overset{2}{\geq}$," defined by:

$$G \overset{2}{\geq} F \quad \text{if} \quad \int_{J^x}(G(y) - F(y))\,dy \leqq 0, \quad \forall x \in J \quad \text{and}$$

(4.3) $$\int_{J}(G(y) - F(y))\,dy = 0$$

where $J^x = \{y \in J : y \leqq x\}$.

The above says that G dominates F in the second degree if they have the same arithmetic mean (when they exist) and the arithmetic mean of G truncated by J^x is not less than that of F truncated by J^x for every x in J. This is equivalent to the notion of *mean-preserving-spread* [24, 33] in uncertainty economics, and the *principle of transfer* [14] which states that a society's welfare is not diminished by a transfer of wealth from the rich to the poor. The quasilinear mean M_ϕ, which, as a model of certainty equivalence, is equivalent to expected utility theory, is consistent with second degree stochastic dominance when ϕ is increasing (decreasing) and concave (convex). Having noted the similarity between ϕ and $\zeta(\cdot; F)$ in deriving consistency conditions for first degree stochastic dominance, we suspect that the corresponding second degree condition for $M_{\alpha\phi}$ is that $\zeta(\cdot; F)$ is concave (convex) if ϕ is increasing (decreasing) for every F in D_J. This is verified as a special case of a more general result developed in the next paragraph.

We begin with the following definition of kth *degree stochastic dominance*,

$$G \overset{k}{\geq} F \quad \text{if} \quad \int_J \left\{ \int_{J^{z_{n-1}}} \left\{ \cdots \left\{ \int_{J^{z_3}} \left\{ \int_{J^{z_2}} (G(z_1) - F(z_1))\,dz_1 \right\} dz_2 \right\} \right. \right.$$

$$\left. \left. \cdots \right\} dz_{n-2} \right\} dz_{n-1} = 0,$$

(4.4)

for $n = 2, \ldots, k$, and

$$\int_{J^{z_k}} \left\{ \int_{J^{z_{k-1}}} \left\{ \cdots \{\text{as above}\} \ldots \right\} dz_{k-2} \right\} dz_{k-1} \leqq 0, \qquad \forall z_k \in J.$$

When the nth moment about the origin exists for distributions F and G for $n = 1, \ldots, k$, then G dominates F in the kth degree if their nth moments agree for $n = 1, \ldots, k$, and the kth moment about the origin of G truncated by J^{z_k} is not less (greater) than that of F truncated at J^{z_k} if k is odd (even) for every z_k in J. The following corollary gives conditions on α and ϕ for consistency of $M_{\alpha\phi}$ with kth degree stochastic dominance.

COROLLARY 6: *Suppose α and $\alpha \cdot \phi$ and their first $(k-1)$ derivatives are continuous and bounded on J. Then $\forall F, G \in D_J$, $G \overset{k}{\geq} F \Rightarrow M_{\alpha\phi}(G) \geq M_{\alpha\phi}(F)$ if* *and only if $\forall F \in D_J$, $\zeta^{(k-1)}(\cdot; F)$ is monotone and in the same (opposite) direction as ϕ when k is odd (even).*

PROOF: See Appendix C.

We end this section by offering a link between $M_{\alpha\phi}$ and M_ϕ extending a well known class of inequalities, called *comparability* by Hardy, Littlewood, and Polya [19]. They proved, for simple probability distributions on a compact interval, that M_ϕ is always less than M_χ if and only if ϕ is more concave than χ, i.e., $\phi \circ \chi^{-1}$ is concave. This result was rediscovered in the context of comparative risk aversion by Pratt [31].

Given a distribution F, we obtain below another distribution F^α via the function α when $\int_J \alpha \, dF$ exists:

(4.5) $\qquad F^\alpha(x) = \int_{J^x} \alpha \, dF \Big/ \int_J \alpha \, dF, \qquad$ for every $\quad x \in J$.

By construction, $M_{\alpha\phi}(F)$ always equals $M_\phi(F^\alpha)$. The function $\alpha / \int_J \alpha \, dF$ has the standard measure-theoretic interpretation as a Radon–Nikodym derivative of F^α with respect to F. Can we define F^α even when $\int_J \alpha \, dF$ does not exist? Our definition of $M_{\alpha\phi}(F)$ when F does not have compact support (expression (3.6)) suggests the following:

(4.6) $\qquad$ Let $\{K_n\}_{n=1}^\infty$ be an increasing family of compact intervals whose

limit is J. Then $\int_J f \, dF^\alpha = \lim_{n \to \infty} \int_{K_n} \alpha f \, dF \Big/ \int_{K_n} \alpha \, dF$, for every

$f \in C(J)$, the space of continuous functions on J.

We have defined F^α so that $M_{\alpha\phi}(F)$ equals $M_\phi(F^\alpha)$ even when $\int_J \alpha \, dF$ does not exist (in this case, F^α is no longer a distribution). Applying Hardy, Littlewood and Polya's comparability to $M_\phi(F^\alpha)$ and $M_\chi(F^\alpha)$, we have the following corollary.

COROLLARY 7: $M_{\alpha\phi}(F) < M_{\alpha\chi}(F) \ \forall F \in D_J$ *if and only if $\phi \circ \chi^{-1}$ is concave.*

The extension of Corollary 7 to the case of nonidentical α's remains an open question. (A partial answer is given in Footnote 14.)

5. APPLICATIONS

We conclude by demonstrating the usefulness of the generalized mean in the areas of decision theory and the measurement of income inequality. Discussions of other potential applications, including the definition of a generalized moment mean in Statistics,[10] will be deferred to subsequent papers.

5A. *Decision Theory*

If we make the standard assumption that a decision maker has von Neumann–Morgenstern utility, u, his certainty equivalent corresponding to a monetary lottery represented by a probability distribution, F, would be given by $u^{-1}(\int_R u\, dF)$, which is simply the expression for a quasilinear mean. The intuition that certainty equivalence is a kind of mean value is an appealing one. We would expect, for instance, that the Intermediate Value Property (Property 1) holds. In order that certainty equivalence may assume the specific quasilinear-mean functional form, it needs to satisfy Consistency with Certainty, Monotonicity, and Quasilinearity. The first two axioms seem normatively appealing and descriptive of actual preferences. When combined with the quasilinearity axiom however, the resulting quasilinear certainty equivalent is not compatible with certain choice behavior first reported by Allais [2]:

EXAMPLE 1: Consider the following lotteries.

$$F_1 \equiv \delta_{\$1,000,000}, \qquad G_1 \equiv 0.80\delta_{\$5,000,000} + 0.20\delta_{\$0},$$

$$F_2 \equiv 0.05\delta_{\$1,000,000} + 0.95\delta_{\$0}, \qquad G_2 \equiv 0.04\delta_{\$5,000,000} + 0.96\delta_{\$0}.$$

People tend to pass up the 0.8 chance at \$5,000,000 in G_1 in favor of receiving \$1,000,000 for sure. Between F_2 and G_2, however, G_2 tends to be preferred to F_2 since the probability of winning \$5,000,000 is close to that of winning \$1,000,000 with \$0 as the common outcome otherwise.

Interpreting M as the certainty equivalent, the above preference pattern implies that $M(F_1) > M(G_1)$ and $M(F_2) < M(G_2)$. We shall show, however, that $M(F_1) > M(G_1)$ implies that $M(F_2) > M(G_2)$. Observe that $G_2 \equiv 0.05G_1 + 0.95\delta_{\$0}$. Quasilinearity implies

$$(5.1) \qquad M(G_2) = M(0.05\delta_{M(G_1)} + 0.95\delta_{\$0}),$$

which is less than $M(F_2) = M(0.05\delta_{\$1,000,000} + 0.95\delta_{\$0})$ by Monotonicity, since $M(G_1)$ is less than \$1,000,000 $= M(F_1)$.

---

[10]For a positive distribution F, we may define the generalized moment mean $M_{s,t}(F)$ to be $M_{x',x^t}(F) \equiv (\int_0^\infty x^{s+t}\, dF / \int_0^\infty x^s\, dF)^{1/t}$. Potential uses of the $M_{s,t}$ mean include: $M_{2,1}$ = standard deviation · coefficient of skewness, and $M_{2,2}$ = standard deviation · (coefficient of Kurtosis + 3)$^{1/2}$. An equality that generalizes the well known result—the product of the arithmetic mean and harmonic mean is equal to the square of the geometric mean for two positive numbers—may be stated in terms of $M_{-1,2}$ ($\equiv$ arithmetic mean · harmonic mean) as: $M_{-1,2}(F) = M_{\log x}(F)$ (the geometric mean), for $F \equiv \sum(1/N)\delta x_i$, with $x_i > 0$, when the frequency polygon of $\log x_i$ is symmetrical about the axis of ordinate at $(1/N)\sum \log x_i$. This motivated Canning's [9] proposal to use $\{M_{-1,2}(F)/M_{\log x}(F)\}^{1/2}$ as a descriptive measure of asymmetry.

Of the above implications, the one due to Quasilinearity (5.1) is most suspect. It requires that a 0.05 chance of getting $M(G_1)$, an amount less than \$1,000,000, be indifferent to a 0.04 chance of getting \$5,000,000 when the latter is preferred to a 0.05 chance of getting \$1,000,000.

Another difficulty with expected utility stems from the observation that some people who persistently stay away from even-chance symmetric bets *at the same time* purchase lottery tickets. A function cannot be both strictly concave and convex within the same interval. In the preference context, this means that expected utility rules out any concurrence of risk aversion and risk proneness within the same interval. The Friedman–Savage hypothesis would not help here since the convex region of their utility function is incompatible with the supposed aversion to even-chance symmetric bets. The reader is referred to [10, Chapter 3] for a more thorough discussion of evidence against the empirical validity of the expected utility hypothesis.

Several alternative theories have appeared in the literature to deal with the Allais paradox. Most of these, including Handa's Theory [18], Karmarkar's theory [23], and prospect theory [21], involve changing the p probability weights in the expected utility representation to some nonlinear $\pi(p_i)$ weights. Theories based on this approach however violate some of the desirable properties of expected utility such as consistency with stochastic dominance, transitivity, betweenness, continuity of preference, and extendability to general distributions including, for example, the St. Petersburg Lottery.

Two other alternatives, Allais' theory [2] and Machina's theory [27], both begin with a preference functional over distributions. At this level of generality, there are few testable implications. Attempting to be more precise, Allais restricted the preference functional to those that depend on the first few moments of a distribution of psychological values. This, however, led to violations of stochastic dominance [10, Chapter 4]. Machina imposed the requirement of Fréchet differentiability on his preference functional and obtained conditions for consistency with stochastic dominance and global risk aversion in terms of the monotonicity and concavity of the distribution-specific Fréchet derivatives, which he called local utility functions. The only specific forms offered by Machina of such a preference functional turn out to violate the Betweenness Property.[11]

The preceding discussion suggests the need for a new alternative that resolves the Allais paradox and at the same time is transitive, consistent with Betweenness and stochastic dominance, permits risk aversion and risk proneness to coexist within the same interval of monetary values, contains expected utility as a limiting case, extendable to general distributions and always gives rise to finite certainty equivalents. This seemingly long list of requirements turns out to be satisfied, simultaneously, by the adoption of the $M_{\alpha\phi}$ mean as a more general

---

[11] It is easy to verify, for equations (6) and (12) in Machina [27], that $V(\beta F + (1 - \beta)G)$ is generally not equal to $V(F)$ or $V(G)$ even when $V(F) = V(G)$.

QUASILINEAR MEAN   1083

model of certainty equivalence.[12] It is an arithmetic exercise to check that if, in Example 1, we apply Theorem 1 to $D[0; 5,000,000]$, and set $\alpha(0) = \alpha(5,000,000) = 1$, $\phi(0) = 0$ and $\phi(5,000,000) = 1$, then F_1 is preferred to G_1 if $\phi(1,000,000) > 0.8$ and G_2 is preferred to F_2 if $\alpha(1,000,000) < 3.8/(5\phi(1,000,000) - 0.2)$ which is less than 1.

Transitivity, Betweenness, and Extendability are generic properties of the $M_{\alpha\phi}$ certainty equivalence. The condition for consistency with stochastic dominance is provided by Corollary 5. The possibility of concurrent risk aversion and risk proneness is demonstrated in [10, Chapter 4].[13] The requirement of global risk aversion may be imposed, if needed, via Corollary 6. The comfort of knowing that the $M_{\alpha\phi}$ certainty equivalence always exists is provided by Corollary 4. The reader is referred to [10, 13] for further details on the development of testable implications of the $M_{\alpha\phi}$ theory. The graphs of a pair of functions (α, ϕ) (taken from [10]) having all the above properties including local risk aversion, defined below (but excluding global risk aversion) are displayed in Figure 2.

We make two additional observations before ending this subsection. Pratt's condition for comparative risk aversion is carried over, via Corollary 7 (see (5.2) below), for the case of individuals with identical α's; i.e., the decision maker whose ϕ is a concavification of the other's will have a lower certainty equivalent for every conceivable lottery. We still do not have a complete characterization of comparative risk aversion when the α's are distinct. Secondly, the Arrow–Pratt index of local risk aversion r has a natural counterpart in the $M_{\alpha\phi}$ certainty equivalence [10, p. 105]:

$$(5.2) \qquad r = -\left(\frac{\phi''}{\phi'} + \frac{2\alpha'}{\alpha} \right) \quad \text{or} \quad -(\log \alpha^2 \phi')',$$

with the usual property that the risk premium $\pi(x; z)$ for a random variable z with mean x and a small variance σ^2 is approximated locally by $\frac{1}{2}\sigma^2 r(x)$. Note that when α is constant, expression (5.2) reduces to the standard Arrow–Pratt index $r = -\phi''/\phi'$ or $(\log \phi')'$.[14]

---

[12] Alternative axiomatizations of the $M_{\alpha\phi}$ theory are given in Chew [12] in terms of a mixture set and in Chew and MacCrimmon [13] in terms of simple probability measures. In addition, the latter paper shows that all known versions of the Allais paradox, together with some new ones, can be derived from a simple structure of lotteries based on three distinct outcomes. It also contains empirically testable implications of the $M_{\alpha\phi}$ theory based on this lottery structure.

[13] This is demonstrated in [10, Chapter 4] by the observation that different methods of assessment of a von Neumann–Morgenstern utility function applied to a $M_{\alpha\phi}$ decision maker with the α and ϕ functions displayed in Figure 2 yield different utility functions with distinct risk characteristics. Specifically, the chaining method produces a concave utility function reflecting the general aversion to symmetric lotteries whereas the probability equivalent method leads to an "S" shape utility function exhibiting risk proneness (favors a small probability of a large gain) near the lower end point. Thus, the $M_{\alpha\phi}$ theory provides a rational explanation for an otherwise "puzzling" phenomena.

[14] An anonymous referee has demonstrated the sufficiency of Pratt's condition for comparative risk aversion for the case of two decision makers with the same ϕ function but different α functions, and provided a perceptive label—the pessimism index—for the α'/α component of the Arrow–Pratt index. We shall refrain from further details here except to note that Pratt's condition can also be shown to be necessary for comparative risk aversion in this case.

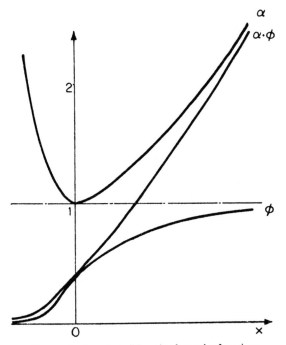

FIGURE 2—An admissible pair of α and ϕ functions.

5B. *Measurement of Income Inequality and Poverty*

The quasilinear mean was given an interpretation by Atkinson [3] as Kolm's [25] 'equally-distributed-equivalent' or representative level of income corresponding to an income distribution. This motivates the use of our $M_{\alpha\phi}$ mean as a more general model of the equally-distributed-equivalent income. Is there any need for a more general measure? Consider two societies with income distributions F and G given by:

$$F \equiv 0.50\delta_{\$1,000} + 0.50\delta_{\$2,000}, \quad \text{and}$$

$$G \equiv 0.50\delta_{\$1,000} + 0.49\delta_{\$2,000} + 0.01\delta_{\$1,000,000}.$$

To some individuals, society F fares better than society G in the sense that, behind the veil of ignorance, a rational individual may choose society F over society G fearing the high likelihood of having to envy the millionaires in society G in case they are not borne among them. Since distribution G stochastically dominates distribution F, $M_{\phi}(F)$ is necessarily less than $M_{\phi}(G)$. Consequently, the Atkinson representative income M_{ϕ} fails to reflect the relative welfare of the two societies for those who believe that society F is better off. Interestingly, since consistency with stochastic dominance is not an intrinsic property of the $M_{\alpha\phi}$ model, $M_{\alpha\phi}(F)$ may be greater than $M_{\alpha\phi}(G)$ without introducing *ad hocisms* such as envy.

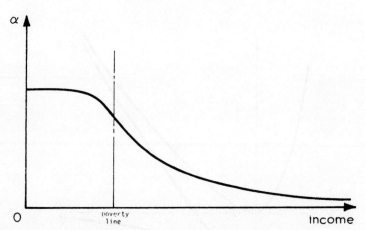

FIGURE 3—An α function that discriminates against the rich.

The departure of $M_{\alpha\phi}$ from M_ϕ can be made clearer if we consider a society of N individuals with incomes, $\{x_i\}_{i=1}^N$. The corresponding equally-distributed-equivalent is given by:

$$(5.3) \qquad M_{\alpha\phi}(F) = \phi^{-1}\left(\sum_{i=1}^N \alpha(x_i)\phi(x_i) \Big/ \sum_{j=1}^N \alpha(x_j) \right).$$

A noteworthy feature of (5.3) is the presence of complementarity across incomes of different individuals. That this is desirable is reinforced by the fact that an individual perceives concurrently the incomes of other individuals in an income distribution whereas only one of a set of mutually exclusive outcomes will obtain in a lottery. We can think of the role of α as assigning discriminatory weights on individuals based on their attained incomes. The egalitarian preference for society F may then be explained in terms of a decreasing discrimination function α that treats wealthy individuals less 'equally' than the poorer people.

In a recent paper on the measurement of poverty, Blackorby and Donaldson [8] applied the notion of equally-distributed-equivalent to the "censored" distribution, i.e., the income distribution truncated at some exogeneously established poverty line. This amounts to having a $M_{\alpha\phi}$ measure with an α that is constant up to the poverty line and zero beyond. It is natural to suggest that a decreasing α with an inflexion point at the poverty line (see Figure 3) would integrate the contribution due to the whole distribution and at the same time be particularly sensitive to the poorer people with incomes below the poverty line.

The $M_{\alpha\phi}$ mean can also be used to generate measures of income inequality as follows:[15] Relative Inequality Index $= 1 - M_{\alpha\phi}/\mu$, and Absolute Inequality Index $= \mu - M_{\alpha\phi}$, where μ denotes the arithmetic mean. If we designate μ_α ($\equiv M_{\alpha,x}$) as a poverty-adjusted arithmetic mean, then we can also use $M_{\alpha\phi}$ to

---

[15] The definitions of the relative and absolute indices are due to Atkinson [3], Blackorby and Donaldson [6, 7], and Kolm [25].

generate the following poverty-adjusted inequality measures: Relative Index
$= 1 - M_{\alpha\phi}(F)/\mu_\alpha(F)$, and Absolute Index $= \mu_\alpha(F) - M_{\alpha\phi}(F)$.

Detailed discussion of the properties of these measures is deferred to a
subsequent paper.[16] We end this subsection with a few brief comments. $M_{\alpha\phi}$
evaluated on a vector of incomes (5.3) is clearly symmetric and so satisfies the
Principle of Impartiality. Corollary 6 provides conditions on α and ϕ such that
$M_{\alpha\phi}$ satisfies the *Principle of Transfer* which is equivalent to the notion of
Mean-Preserving-Spread or second degree stochastic dominance. Finally, we note
that the approach taken here differs from other works in the literature in that the
assumptions are stated directly in terms of properties of a more primitive notion
—equally-distributed-equivalent. This is contrasted with the assertion that a
social welfare function exists (see [3, 6, 25, and 34]) or that an inequality or
poverty index exists (see [8, 16, 22, 35, 36, and 37]).

University of Arizona

Manuscript received March, 1981; final revision received November, 1982.

APPENDIX

A. PROOF OF LEMMA 3

Suppose that $M(H) < M(F) = M(G)$ without loss of generality. Axiom $3 \Rightarrow \exists f: (0, 1) \to (0, 1)$
$\ni \forall \beta \in (0, 1)$.

$$M(\beta F + (1 - \beta)H) = M(f(\beta)G + (1 - f(\beta))H).$$

Lemma $1 \Rightarrow f$ is a strictly increasing function. This together with Lemma 2 implies that f^{-1} exists
and is strictly increasing. Therefore, both f and f^{-1} are continuous functions and differentiable a.e..
Define $\tau: (0, 1) \to R^+$ by $\tau(\beta) = (f(\beta)/1 - f(\beta))/(\beta/1 - \beta)$. It follows that τ is continuous and
differentiable a.e.. We show below that τ is a constant to complete the proof.
Consider $0 < \beta < \beta + \delta < 1$. It follows after substituting G for F using Lemma 2:

(A.1) $M((\beta + \delta)F + (1 - (\beta + \delta))H)$

$$= M\left(\frac{(\beta + \delta)\tau(\beta + \delta)}{(\beta + \delta)\tau(\beta + \delta) + 1 - (\beta + \delta)} G + \frac{1 - (\beta + \delta)}{(\beta + \delta)\tau(\beta + \delta) + 1 - (\beta + \delta)} H \right).$$

Note that

$$(\beta + \delta)F + (1 - (\beta + \delta))H \equiv \beta F + (1 - \beta)\left[\frac{\delta}{1 - \beta} F + \frac{1 - \beta - \delta}{1 - \beta} H \right].$$

[16] Sen [34] and Donaldson and Weymark [15] have shown that the Gini index $I_G(F)$, correspond-
ing to a uniform distribution $F \equiv (1/N)\sum_{i=1}^{N} \delta_{x_i}$, can be written as $I_G(F) = 1 - M_G(F)/\mu_F$, with
$M_G((1/N)\sum_{i=1}^{N} \delta_{x_i}) = \sum_{i=1}^{N} (2i - 1)x_i/\sum_{j=1}^{N} (2j - 1)$, where the x_i's are arranged in descending order.
The integral form of the Gini mean value (representative income) M_G can be shown to be:
$M_G(F) = \int_R [2 - F(z) - F(z^-)]z \, dF(z)$. The Gini mean M_G is not an example of the generalized
mean $M_{\alpha\phi}$ since the weighting function $[2 - F(z) - F(z^-)]$ depends on F. Properties of the Gini
mean in relation to the generalized mean will be treated in a subsequent paper.

Therefore

(A.2)   L.H.S. of (A.1) $= M\left(\beta F + (1 - \beta)\left[\dfrac{\delta}{1 - \beta} F + \dfrac{1 - \beta - \delta}{1 - \beta} H \right] \right)$

$= M\left(\dfrac{\beta \tau(\beta)}{\beta \tau(\beta) + 1 - \beta} G + \dfrac{1 - \beta}{\beta \tau(\beta) + 1 - \beta}\left[\dfrac{\delta}{1 - \beta} F + \dfrac{1 - \beta - \delta}{1 - \beta} H \right] \right),$

after substituting G for F again using Lemma 2.

Applying the same argument for the remaining F-component in expression (A.2), we obtain:

(A.3)   R.H.S. $= M\left(\dfrac{\delta \tau(\delta / \beta \tau(\beta) + 1 - \beta) + \beta \tau(\beta)}{\delta \tau(\delta / \beta \tau(\beta) + 1 - \beta) + \beta \tau(\beta) + 1 - (\beta + \delta)} G \right.$

$\left. + \dfrac{1 - (\beta + \delta)}{\delta \tau(\delta / \beta \tau(\beta) + 1 - \beta) + \beta \tau(\beta) + 1 - (\beta + \delta)} H \right).$

Comparing expressions (A.1) and expression (A.3), it follows that

(A.4) $(\beta + \delta)\tau(\beta + \delta) = \beta \tau(\beta) + \delta \tau(\delta / [\beta \tau(\beta) + 1 - \beta]),$

which can be written as

(A.5) $\dfrac{(\beta + \delta)\tau(\beta + \delta) - \beta \tau(\beta)}{\delta} = \tau(\delta / [\beta \tau(\beta) + 1 - \beta]),$

and equivalently as (replacing $(\beta + \delta)$ and β above by β and $(\beta - \delta)$, respectively),

(A.6) $\dfrac{\beta \tau(\beta) - (\beta - \delta)\tau(\beta - \delta)}{\delta} = \tau(\delta / [(\beta - \delta)\tau(\beta - \delta) + 1 - (\beta - \delta)]).$

The *a.e.* differentiability of the function τ implies that the limit as $\delta \downarrow 0$ of the L.H.S.'s in the above expressions exist and are both equal to $(\beta \tau(\beta))'$ for some β'. Therefore, the corresponding limits at β' for the R.H.S.'s also exist, i.e.,

(A.7) $\lim_{\delta \downarrow 0} \tau(\delta / [\beta' \tau(\beta') + 1 - \beta']) = \lim_{\delta \downarrow 0} \tau(\delta / [(\beta' - \delta)\tau(\beta' - \delta) + 1 - (\beta' - \delta)]) = \tau(0^+).$

Since the existence and equality of the above limits do not depend on the choice of β', it follows that the right-hand as well as left-hand derivatives of the function $(\beta \tau(\beta))'$ exist and are both equal to $\tau(0^+)$ for every $\beta \in (0, 1)$, so that $(\beta \tau(\beta))' \equiv \tau(0^+)$. Hence, $\tau(\beta) \equiv \tau(0^+)$.   *Q.E.D.*

B. PROOF OF THEOREM 2

The Necessity part of the proof is straightforward. To prove Sufficiency, define $\psi : [0, 1] \to [A, B]$ as follows.

(B.1) $\psi(p) = M(S_p), \quad \forall p \in [0, 1], \quad \text{where} \quad S_p \equiv p \delta_B + (1 - p)\delta_A .$

Axiom 1 implies that $\psi(0) = A$ and $\psi(1) = B$. Axiom 2 implies that ψ is strictly increasing. Let $\{p_n\}_{n=1}^{\infty}$ converge to p. Then S_{p_n} converges in distribution to S_p. Axiom 4 implies that $\psi(p) = M(S_p) = \lim_{n \to \infty} M(S_{p_n}) = \lim_{n \to \infty} \psi(p_n)$. It follows that ψ is continuous and strictly increasing and therefore has an inverse $\phi : [A, B] \to [0, 1]$ which is continuous and strictly increasing. If $x = \psi(p)$, then $p = \phi(x)$ and

(B.2) $M(\delta_x) = x = \psi(p) = M(S_p) = M(S_{\tilde{\phi}(x)}).$

For every $x \in [A, B]$, expression (B.2) tells us that δ_x and $S_{\tilde{\phi}(x)}$ have the same means, so that according to Lemma 3 there exists a positive number $\tilde{\alpha}(x)$ such that $\forall H \in D[A, B]$ and $\forall \beta \in [0, 1]$,

(B.3) $\qquad M(\beta \delta_x + (1 - \beta)H) = M\left(\dfrac{\beta \tilde{\alpha}(x)}{\beta \tilde{\alpha}(x) + (1 - \beta)} S_{\tilde{\phi}(x)} + \dfrac{1 - \beta}{\beta \tilde{\alpha}(x) + (1 - \beta)} H\right).$

Hence, we have constructed a positive valued function $\tilde{\alpha} : (A, B) \to R^+$. The following argument establishes the continuity of $\tilde{\alpha}$ on (A, B) and then extends its domain to include the end-points.
Consider

$$g(x) = M\left(\frac{1}{2} \delta_x + \frac{1}{2} \delta_A\right) = M\left(\frac{\tilde{\alpha}(x)}{\tilde{\alpha}(x) + 1} S_{\tilde{\phi}(x)} + \frac{1}{\tilde{\alpha}(x) + 1} \delta_A\right)$$

$$= M(S_{\{\tilde{\alpha}(x)\tilde{\phi}(x)/\tilde{\phi}(x) + 1\}}) = \psi(\tilde{\alpha}(x)\tilde{\phi}(x)/[\tilde{\alpha}(x) + 1]).$$

Let $\{x_n\}_{n=1}^\infty$ converge to $x \in (A, B)$. Then $\frac{1}{2} \delta_{x_n} + \frac{1}{2} \delta_A$ converges in distribution to $\frac{1}{2} \delta_x + \frac{1}{2} \delta_A$. Axiom 4 implies that

$$g(x) = M\left(\frac{1}{2} \delta_x + \frac{1}{2} \delta_A\right) = \lim_{n \to \infty} M\left(\frac{1}{2} \delta_{x_n} + \frac{1}{2} \delta_A\right) = \lim_{n \to \infty} g(x_n).$$

Therefore, g is continuous in (A, B). It follows that $\tilde{\alpha}$ is continuous in (A, B). Let $\{x_n\}_{n=1}^\infty$ converge to B from below; then,

$$\psi\left(\frac{1}{2}\right) = M(S_{(1/2)}) = \lim_{n \to \infty} M\left(\frac{1}{2} \delta_{x_n} + \frac{1}{2} \delta_A\right)$$

$$= \lim_{n \to \infty} g(x_n) = \lim_{n \to \infty} \psi(\tilde{\phi}(x_n)/(1 + 1/\tilde{\alpha}(x_n))).$$

This implies that $\lim_{n \to \infty} \tilde{\alpha}(x_n) = 1$, since $\tilde{\phi}(B) = 1$.
Similarly, we can show that $\lim_{n \to \infty} \tilde{\alpha}(x_n) = 1$ as x_n converges to A from above. We extend $\tilde{\alpha}$ to $[A, B]$ continuously by assigning 1 to $\tilde{\alpha}$ at the end-points.
Now, we are ready to show that, $\forall F \in D^0[A, B]$, the functions $\tilde{\alpha}$ and $\tilde{\phi}$ satisfy condition (3.3). Let $\{x_i\}_{i=1}^n$ be the support of a distribution F in $D^0[A, B]$, and represent F in the form, $F \equiv \sum_{i=1}^n \theta_i \delta_{x_i}$, where $\theta_i = F(x_i) - F(x_i^-)$. It follows that

$$M(F) = M\left(\sum_{i=1}^n \theta_i \delta_{x_i}\right)$$

$$= M\left(\frac{\theta_1 \tilde{\alpha}(x_1)}{\theta_1 \tilde{\alpha}(x_1) + \sum \theta_j} S_{\tilde{\phi}(x_1)} + \sum_{i=2}^n \frac{\theta_i}{\theta_1 \tilde{\alpha}(x_1) + \sum \theta_j} \delta_{x_i}\right),$$

after substituting $S_{\tilde{\phi}(x_1)}$ for δ_{x_1} using expression (B.3). Repeating $(n - 1)$ times on the remaining δ_{x_i} $(i = 2, \ldots, n)$ yields,

$$M(F) = M\left(\sum_{i=1}^n \left\{\frac{\theta_i \tilde{\alpha}(x_i)}{\sum \theta_j \tilde{\alpha}(x_j)}\right\} S_{\tilde{\phi}(x_i)}\right) = M(S_{\{\sum \theta_i \tilde{\alpha}(x_i)\tilde{\phi}(x_i)/\sum \theta_j \tilde{\alpha}(x_j)\}})$$

$$= \psi\left(\sum \theta_i \tilde{\alpha}(x_i)\tilde{\phi}(x_i)/\sum \theta_j \tilde{\alpha}(x_j)\right) = \tilde{\phi}^{-1}\left(\int_A^B \tilde{\alpha}\tilde{\phi} \, dF \Big/ \int_A^B \tilde{\alpha} \, dF\right).$$

Finally, we extend our analysis to $D[A, B]$. Suppose $F \in D[A, B] - D^0[A, B]$. Construct the following sequence $\{F_n\}_{n=1}^\infty$ in $D^0[A, B]$:

$$F_n \equiv F(A)\delta_A + \sum_{i=1}^{2^n} \left\{F\left(A + \frac{i(B - A)}{2^n}\right) - F\left(A + \frac{(i - 1)(B - A)}{2^n}\right)\right\} \delta_{A + i(B - A)/2^n}.$$

By construction, $F_n(x) \to F(x)$, $\forall x \in \{A + i(B - A)/2^n : i, n \in I^+, i \leq 2^n\}$, which is dense in $[A, B]$. Therefore, $\{F_n\}_{n=1}^{\infty}$ converges to F. Axiom 4 implies that

$$M(F) = \lim_{n \to \infty} M(F_n) = \lim_{n \to \infty} \tilde{\phi}^{-1}\left(\int_A^B \tilde{\alpha}\tilde{\phi}\, dF_n \Big/ \int_A^B \tilde{\alpha}\, dF_n\right) = \tilde{\phi}^{-1}\left(\int_A^B \tilde{\alpha}\tilde{\phi}\, dF \Big/ \int_A^B \tilde{\alpha}\, dF\right),$$

since $\tilde{\phi}$, $\tilde{\phi}^{-1}$ and $\tilde{\alpha}$ are continuous on $[A, B]$.

The necessity part of the uniqueness proof is straightforward. For sufficiency, suppose, without losing generality, that the pair of functions (α, ϕ) in expression (3.3) satisfies $\alpha(A) = 1$, $\phi(A) = 0$, and $\phi(B) = 1$. Let (α^*, ϕ^*) be another pair of functions satisfying expression (3.3). Define $(\hat{\alpha}, \hat{\phi})$ by:

(B.4) $\hat{\phi}(x) = [\phi^*(x) - \phi^*(A)]/[\phi^*(B) - \phi^*(A)]$,   and

(B.5) $\hat{\alpha}(x) = \alpha^*(x)/\alpha^*(A)$.

By construction, $(\hat{\alpha}, \hat{\phi})$ has the same mean as (α^*, ϕ^*) and $\hat{\phi}$ equals ϕ at both endpoints and $\hat{\alpha}$ equals α at A. Denote by S_p the 2-point distribution $p\delta_B + (1 - p)\delta_A$. Then $\forall p \in [0, 1]$,

(B.6) $M(S_p) = \phi^{-1}(p\alpha(B)/[p\alpha(B) + 1 - p]) = \hat{\phi}^{-1}(p\hat{\alpha}(B)/[p\hat{\alpha}(B) + 1 - p])$.

It follows that $\forall q \in [0, 1]$,

(B.7) $(\hat{\phi} \circ \phi^{-1})(q) = kq/[kq - 1 - q]$, $k = \hat{\alpha}(B)/\alpha(B) > 0$.

Substituting $q = \phi(x)$ into (B.7) above, we obtain:

(B.8) $\hat{\phi}(x) = k\phi(x)/[k\phi(x) + 1 - \phi(x)]$.

Consider the distribution $T_x \equiv \frac{1}{2}\delta_x + \frac{1}{2}\delta_A$. We have that

(B.9) $M(T_x) = \phi^{-1}(\alpha(x)\phi(x)/[\alpha(x) + 1]) = \hat{\phi}^{-1}(\hat{\alpha}(x)\hat{\phi}(x)/[\hat{\alpha}(x) + 1])$.

Using expression (B.7) and taking $\hat{\phi}$ on both sides, expression (B.9) becomes:

(B.10) $\hat{\alpha}(x)\hat{\phi}(x)/[\hat{\alpha}(x) + 1] = (\hat{\phi} \circ \phi^{-1})(\alpha(x)\phi(x)/[\alpha(x) + 1])$

$$= k\alpha(x)\phi(x)/\{\alpha(x)[k\phi(x) + 1 - \phi(x)] + 1\}.$$

Substituting expression (B.8) into (B.10), we have

(B.11) $\hat{\alpha}(x)/[\hat{\alpha}(x) + 1] = \alpha(x)[k\phi(x) + 1 - \phi(x)]/\{\alpha(x)[k\phi(x) + 1 - \phi(x)] + 1\}$.

Hence,

(B.12) $\hat{\alpha}(x) = \alpha(x)[k\phi(x) + 1 - \phi(x)]$.   *Q.E.D.*

C. PROOF OF COROLLARIES

PROOF OF COROLLARY 4: To prove α is bounded, suppose the contrary that it is unbounded from above. Since α is continuous, J must be noncompact. Let B denote the endpoint (which may be $\pm\infty$) of J towards which α is unbounded (from above). Consider $\{x_i\}_{i=1}^{\infty} \subset J$ such that $\alpha(x_i) = 2^i$. Then

(C.1) $M_{\alpha\phi}\left(\sum_{i=1}^{\infty} 2^{-i}\delta_{x_i}\right) = \lim_{m \to \infty} \phi^{-1}\left(\sum_{i=1}^{m} \phi(x_i)/m\right)$.

But $\lim_{m \to \infty} \sum_{i=1}^{m} \phi(x_i)/m = \lim_{x \to B} \phi(x)$, so that the above limit (C.1) does not exist.

1090 CHEW SOO HONG

To prove that $\alpha \cdot \phi$ is bounded, suppose that it is unbounded from above. Let $\{x_i\}_{i=1}^{\infty} \subset J$ such that $(\alpha \cdot \phi)(x_i) = 2^i$. Then

$$M_{\alpha\phi}\left(\sum_{i=1}^{\infty} 2^{-i}\delta_{x_i} \right) = \lim_{m\to\infty} \phi^{-1}\left(m \bigg/ \sum_{i=1}^{m} 2^{-i}\alpha(x_i) \right),$$

which does not converge. A similar argument establishes the result for the cases of unboundedness from below. $\qquad$ Q.E.D.

PROOF OF COROLLARY 5: We shall assume without loss of generality that ϕ is strictly increasing. To prove sufficiency, suppose $G \overset{1}{\geq} F$. Then $F_{\theta'} \overset{1}{\geq} F_{\theta}$ whenever $\theta' > \theta$, where $F_{\theta} \equiv (1 - \theta)F + \theta G$, $\forall \theta \in (0, 1)$. It is straightforward to check that

(C.2) $\qquad \dfrac{d}{d\theta} \Omega(F_\theta) = \int_J \zeta(x; F_\theta) \, d(G(x) - F(x))$

$$= \int_J (F(x) - G(x)) \, d\zeta(x; F_\theta) \geqq 0,$$

where $\Omega(F) = \int_J \alpha\phi \, dF / \int_J \alpha \, dF$, and

(C.3) $\qquad \zeta(x; F) \equiv \left\{ \alpha(x) \bigg/ \int_J \alpha \, dF \right\} \{\phi(x) - \Omega(F)\},$

which is, by hypothesis, a nondecreasing function for every F. Consider

$$\Omega(G) - \Omega(F) = \int_0^1 \left\{ \int_J (F(x) - G(x)) \, d\zeta(x; F_\theta) \right\} \, d\theta \geqq 0.$$

This implies that $M_{\alpha\phi}(G) \geqq M_{\alpha\phi}(F)$.

To prove necessity, suppose $\alpha(x)(\phi(x) - \phi(s^*))$ is strictly decreasing at some x^* and $s^* \in \text{int } J$. Since $\alpha(x)(\phi(x) - \phi(s))$ is a continuous function, it is strictly decreasing for some open neighborhood $(x^* - \xi, x^* + \xi)$. Assume without loss of generality that $s^* \geqq x^*$. Pick any $y^* > s^*$ and compute p^* such that

$$s^* = M_{\alpha\phi}(p^*\delta_y^* + (1 - p^*)\delta_x'') = M_{\alpha\phi}(F^*), \qquad \text{where} \quad x'' = x^* - \tfrac{1}{2}\xi.$$

Consider $G^* \equiv p^*\delta_{y^*} + (1 - p^*)\delta_{x'}$ for some $x' \in [x^*, x^* + \xi)$. Compute,

$$\int_J (F^*(x) - G^*(x)) \, d\zeta(x; F^*) = (1 - p^*)(\zeta(x'; F^*) - \zeta(x''; F^*)) < 0.$$

But $M_{\alpha\phi}((1 - \theta)F^* + \theta G^*) = M_{\alpha\phi}(F_\theta^*)$ is nondecreasing in θ. This implies that

$$\frac{d}{d\theta} \Omega(F_\theta^*) = \int_J (F^*(x) - G^*(x)) \, d\zeta(x; F_\theta^*) \geqq 0.$$

Since the right-hand side is continuous, its limit as θ approaches 0 from above is nonnegative, which is a contradiction. The extension to the case of possible end-points of J is straightforward. $\qquad$ Q.E.D.

PROOF OF COROLLARY 6: Assume without loss of generality that ϕ is increasing and k is even. To prove sufficiency, suppose $G \overset{k}{\geq} F$. Then $F_{\theta'} \overset{k}{\geq} F_{\theta}$ whenever $\theta' > \theta$, where $F_{\theta} \equiv (1 - \theta)F + \theta G$, for $\theta \in (0, 1)$. Consider

$$\frac{d}{d\theta} \Omega(F_\theta) = \int_J \zeta(x; F_\theta) \, d(G(x) - F(x))$$

$$= (-1)^k \int_J I_k(x) \, d\zeta^{(k-1)}(x; F_\theta) \geq 0,$$

QUASILINEAR MEAN   1091

where $I_k(x)$ is the k-time iterated integral of $(G(x) - F(x))$ on the interval J^x (see expression (4.4)). Since $I_k(x)$ is nonpositive and $\zeta^{(k-1)}$ is nondecreasing (nonincreasing) for k odd (even) $\forall F \in D_J$, it follows that $\Omega(G) - \Omega(F) = \int_0^1 \{\int_J I_k(x) d\zeta(x; F_\theta)\} d\theta \geqq 0$. This implies that $M_{\alpha\phi}(G) \geqq M_{\alpha\phi}(F)$.

The necessity part of the proof follows from an argument that is essentially the same as the one used in the proof of Corollary 5.   *Q.E.D.*

REFERENCES

[1] ACZEL, J. *Lectures on Functional Equations and Their Application.* New York and London: Academic Press, 1966.

[2] ALLAIS, M.: "Le Comportement de l'homme Rationnel Devant le Risque," *Econometrica*, 21(1953), 503–546.

[3] ATKINSON, A. B.: "On the Measurement of Inequality," *Journal of Economic Theory*, 2(1970), 244–63.

[4] BEN-TAL, A.: "On Generalized Means and Generalized Convex Functions," *Journal of Optimization Theory and Applications*, 21(1977), 1–13.

[5] BERNOULLI, D.: "Specimen Theoriae Novae de Mensura Sortis," *Commentarii Academiae Scientiatum Imperalas Petropolitanae*, 5(1738), pp. 175–192; translated as "Exposition of a New Theory on the Measurement of Risk," *Econometrica*, 22(1954), 23–26.

[6] BLACKORBY, C., AND D. DONALDSON: "Measures of Relative Equality and Their Meaning in Terms of Social Welfare," *Journal of Economic Theory*, 18(1978), 59–80.

[7] ———: "A Theoretical Treatment of Ethical Indices of Absolute Inequality," *International Economic Review*, 21(1980), 107.

[8] ———: "Ethical Indices for the Measurement of Poverty," *Econometrica*, 48(1980), 1053–1060.

[9] CANNING, J. B.: "A Theorem Concerning a Certain Family of Averages of a Certain Type of Frequency Distribution," *Econometrica*, 2(1934), 442. The abstract is a reporter's summary of an unpublished paper.

[10] CHEW, S. H.: "Two Representation Theorems and Their Application to Decision Theory," Ph.D dissertation, University of British Columbia, 1980.

[11] ———: "A Generalization of the Quasilinear Mean of Hardy, Littlewood and Polya and Applications," University of Arizona Working Paper, 1980; second revision of a University of Arizona Working Paper, 1979.

[12] ———: "A Mixture Set Axiomatization of Weighted Utility Theory," University of Arizona Working Paper, 1982; revision of a 1981 Working Paper.

[13] CHEW, S. H., AND K. R. MACCRIMMON: "Alpha Utility Theory: A Generalization of Expected Utility Theory," in preparation; revision of two University of British Columbia Working Papers, "Alpha-Nu Choice Theory: A Generalization of Expected Utility Theory" and "Alpha Utility Theory, Lottery Compositions and the Allais Paradox," 1979.

[14] DALTON, H.: "The Measurement of Inequality of Incomes," *Economic Journal*, 20(1920), 348–361.

[15] DONALDSON, D., AND J. A. WEYMARK: "A Single-Paremeter Generalization of the Gini Indices of Inequality," *Journal of Economic Theory*, 22(1980), 67–86.

[16] FIELDS, G. S., AND J. C. H. FEI: "On Inequality Comparisons," *Econometrica*, 46(1978), 303–316.

[17] DE FINETTI, B.: "Sul Concetto di Media" *Giornale dell' Instituto Italiano degli Attuari*, 2(1931), 369–396.

[18] HANDA, JAGDISH: "Risk, Probabilities, and a New Theory of Cardinal Theory," *Journal of Political Economy*, 85(1977), 97–122.

[19] HARDY, G. H., J. E. LITTLEWOOD, AND G. POLYA: *Inequalities.* Cambridge: Cambridge University Press, 1934.

[20] HERSTEIN, I. N., AND J. MILNOR: "An Axiomatic Approach to Measurable Utility," *Econometrica*, 21(1953), 291–297.

[21] KAHNEMAN, D., AND A. TVERSKY: "Prospect Theory: An Analysis of Decision Under Risk," *Econometrica*, 47(1979), 263–291.

[22] KAKWANI, N.: "On a Class of Poverty Measures," *Econometrica*, 48(1980), 437–446.

[23] KARMARKAR, UDAY S.: "Subjectively Weighted Utility: A Discriptive Extension of the Expected Utility Model," *Organizational Behavior and Human Performance*, 21(1978), 61–72.

[24] KOLM, S. CH.: *Le Choix Financiers et Monetaires.* Paris: Dunod, 1966.

1092   CHEW SOO HONG

[25] ———: "The Optimal Production of Social Justice," in *Public Economics*, ed. by J. Margolis and H. Guitton. London/New York: Macmillan, 1969.

[26] KOLMOGOROV, A.: "Sur la Notion de la Moyenne," *Rendiconti Accademia dei Lincei* (6), 12(1930), 388–391.

[27] MACHINA, MARK J.: "Expected Utility Analysis Without the Independence Axiom," *Econometrica*, 50(1982), 277–323.

[28] MENGER, K.: "The Role of Uncertainty in Economics," in *Essays in Mathematical Economics in Honor of Oskar Morgenstern*, ed. by M. Shubik. Princeton: Princeton University Press, 1967. Translated from *Zeitschrift fur Nationaloekonomie*, Band V, Heft 4, 1934, 459–485.

[29] NAGUMO, M.: "Uber eine Klasse der Mittelwerte" *Japan Journal of Mathematics*, 7(1930), 71–79.

[30] NORRIS, N.: "General Means and Statistical Theory," *The American Statistician*, 30(1976), 1–12.

[31] PRATT, JOHN W.: "Risk Aversion in the Small and in the Large," *Econometrica*, 32(1964), 122–136.

[32] PRATT, J. W., H. RAIFFA, AND R. SCHLAIFER: "The Foundations of Decisions Under Uncertainty: An Elementary Exposition," *Journal of the American Statistical Association*, 5a(1964), 353–375.

[33] ROTHSCHILD, M., AND J. E. STIGLITZ: "Increasing Risk: I. A Definition," *Journal of Economic Theory*, 2(1970), 225–243.

[34] SEN, A.: *On Economic Inequality*. Oxford: Oxford University Press, 1973.

[35] ———: "Poverty: An Ordinal Approach to Measurement," *Econometrica*, 44(1976), 219–232.

[36] TAKAYAMA, N.: "Poverty, Income Inequality, and Their Measures: Professor Sen's Axiomatic Approach Reconsidered," *Econometrica*, 47(1979), 747–759.

[37] THEIL, H.: *Economics and Information Theory*. Amsterdam: North-Holland, 1967.

[38] WEBER, R.: Personal Communication, 1980.

[39] WEERAHANDI, S., AND J. ZIDEK: "A Characterization of the General Mean," *Canadian Journal of Statistics*, 7(1979), 83–90.

[6]

KYKLOS Vol. 37 – 1984 – Fasc. 2, 181–205

The Economics of Optimism and Pessimism

A Definition and Some Applications

JOHN D. HEY*

'The optimist proclaims that we live in the best of all possible worlds; and the pessimist fears this is true.'
BRANCH CABELL, *The Silver Stallion*

'Twixt optimist and pessimist
 The difference is droll:
The optimist sees the doughnut,
 The pessimist, the hole.'
McLANDBURGH WILSON, *Optimist and Pessimist*

I. INTRODUCTION

The real world, the world of the economic commentator, is replete with references to optimism and pessimism. The imaginary world of the economic theorist accords them scarcely a mention. Hence this paper: in which we try to bring the two worlds closer together.

We could, of course, solve our problem at the outset by asserting that optimism and pessimism are irrational emotions – unfit to be incorporated into any theory of rational behaviour. Indeed, this is what the conventional wisdom would have us do. But optimism and pessimism do appear to exist in the real world. Indeed, they might offer a partial explanation of why the conventional wisdom is not particularly good at explaining observed behaviour. But we anticipate ourselves: let us first consider some basic notions.

Intuition about optimism and pessimism is rather neatly captured by the two quotations above. The *Shorter Oxford English Dictionary* tells us that the optimist is '... one disposed, under all circumstances, to hope for the best...' while the pessimist is '... one who habitually takes the worst view of things...' This captures the idea that the optimist is more hopeful about the good things than the pessimist, and less fearful about the bad.

*University of York, England.

181

JOHN D. HEY

In an objectively certain world, there is clearly no scope for optimism and pessimism – since everyone knows precisely what is going to happen. Thus subjective uncertainty is a *sine qua non* for the existence of optimism and pessimism. The essential feature of an uncertain world is that one does not know the future that nature (or one's fellow-man) will bring; in such a world, the optimist is one who is more hopeful than the pessimist that nature will prove benevolent, while the pessimist is more fearful than the optimist that nature will prove malevolent. This discussion suggests that optimists may be distinguished from pessimists by the relative likelihood they attach to the possibility that the future will turn out favourable or unfavourable.

If we are prepared to admit the existence of subjective probability attached by individuals to future events, then we can begin to approach a definition of optimism and pessimism. The above discussion suggests that optimists attach a greater probability to favourable events than do pessimists, and a lesser probability to unfavourable events. But this approach to a definition is deficient in that it might simply reflect different subjective assessments, rather than different stances on optimism and pessimism. Thus we would hesitate to class individual A as more pessimistic than individual B simply because $P_A(E) < P_B(E)$, where E is some uncertain event and where $P_I(E)$ denotes individual I's assessment of the probability of event E. Rather, the crucial feature is the *relationship* between the individual's assessment of the probability of the event and the consequence to the individual if that event occurs. For example, it would seem sensible to call someone an optimist if the probability he or she attaches to some event E is greater when E implies a relatively favourable consequence for the individual than when E implies a relatively unfavourable consequence. More specifically, an optimist is someone, for instance, who thinks that E is more likely when faced with the prospect

$$\begin{cases} \text{£100 if E happens} \\ \text{£0 \quad if E does not happen} \end{cases}$$

than when faced with the prospect

$$\begin{cases} \text{£100 if E does not happen} \\ \text{£0 \quad if E happens.} \end{cases}$$

182

THE ECONOMICS OF OPTIMISM AND PESSIMISM

Such a 'bending of the probabilities' is, of course, disallowed by the conventional wisdom which insists that probabilities attached to events are independent of the consequences of those events. But this would seem to be an appropriate characterisation of optimism.

Let us be more specific. The conventional wisdom's insistence on the independence of probabilities and consequences seems only to apply to *realists* or in situations where *objective probabilities* are agreed to exist by the participating individuals. Definitionally, realists are people who do not 'bend probabilities' or allow them to be influenced by consequences; similarly, it appears definitional that so-called objective probabilities cannot be 'bent' or otherwise distorted by those who regard them as objective. However, in situations where objective probabilities do not exist, then the implied subjective probabilities are necessarily bent by optimists and pessimists. Most crucially, the optimist revises *up* the probability of favourable events and revises *down* the probability of unfavourable events, while the pessimist does the opposite. This leads us to our definition.

II. DEFINITION

An *optimist*   revises up the probabilities of favourable events and revises down the probabilities of unfavourable events; the degree of revision depending *inter alia* upon the person's degree of optimism, and the subjectivity of the events (the revision being zero, definitionally, if the person attaches objective probabilities to the events).

A *realist*   keeps the same probabilities irrespective of the consequences.

A *pessimist*   revises down the probabilities of favourable events and revises up the probabilities of unfavourable events; the degree of revision depending *inter alia* upon the person's degree of pessimism, and the subjectivity of the events (the revision being zero, definitionally, if the person attaches objective probabilities to the events).

183

JOHN D. HEY

III. FORMALISATION

We now formalise this definition. But first we require some assumptions and some notation.

We deliberately adopt the familiar framework used in the conventional model of decision-making under uncertainty. Imagine our individual faced with a choice of one from a set of risky choices denoted by $C_1, \ldots, C_I$. Suppose that the consequence A_{ij} to the individual of choosing C_i depends on which state S_j of a set of possible 'states of the world' $S_1, \ldots, S_J$ occurs. We assume that the elements of the sets $\{C_i; i = 1, \ldots, I\}$, $\{S_j; j = 1, \ldots, J\}$ and $\{A_{ij}; i = 1, \ldots, I; j = 1, \ldots, J\}$ are all certain and known; the only uncertainty being that connected with not knowing which state of the world (event) will occur.

Let us first describe how the conventional wisdom, Subjective Expected Utility theory, characterizes individual choice in this framework. We will then show how our definition of optimism and pessimism can be formalised.

Subjective Expected Utility (*SEU*) theory has two components: a utility function u(.) with the consequences A_{ij} as argument; and a probability function p(.) with the states of the world S_j as argument. Choice amongst the C_i is determined by the largest of the $U(C_i)$ as given by

$$U(C_i) = \sum_{j=1}^{J} p(S_j)u(A_{ij}). \tag{1}$$

In the conventional wisdom, both functions p(.) and u(.) are determined by asking the individual about his or her preferences amongst risky choices. We describe this process, beginning first with the utility function.

To save notational complexity, let

$$\{O_k; k = 1, \ldots, K\} \equiv \{A_{ij}; i = 1, \ldots, I; j = 1, \ldots, J\},$$

and suppose that the O's have been appropriately subscripted so that

$$O_1 \succeq O_2 \succeq O_3 \succeq \ldots \succeq O_{K-1} \succeq O_K$$

where ' $\succeq$ ' denotes 'is at least as preferred as'. We assume that

$$O_1 \succ O_K$$

184

THE ECONOMICS OF OPTIMISM AND PESSIMISM

where ' > ' denotes 'is strictly preferred to'; this ensures that the choice problem is non-trivial. Now let us suppose that there exists some randomizing device (such as a roulette wheel) which can be adjusted so that certain events are simulated with some agreed-one 'objective' probabilities. For example, tossing an agreed-fair coin simulates the occurrence of two events, each with 'objective' probability one-half. Using this randomizing device, we can simulate risky choices which yield $O_1, \ldots, O_K$ each with some pre-specified 'objective' probability. Let us denote the typical risky choice by

$$[(O_1, p_1), (O_2, p_2), \ldots, (O_K, p_K)];$$

by this, we mean a risky choice which yields O_1 with probability p_1, O_2 with probability p_2, ..., O_K with probability p_K. We assume that the various possibilities are mutually exclusive and exhaustive, so that

$$\sum_{k=1}^{K} p_k = 1.$$

Now we ask the individual to determine (for each $k = 1, \ldots, K$) the value of the probability u_k for which

$$O_k \sim [(O_1, u_k), (O_K, 1-u_k)], \tag{2}$$

where ' ~ ' denotes 'is indifferent to'. We presume that such a u_k exists and is unique (for each $k = 1, \ldots, K$). We then define u(.) by

$$u(O_k) = \begin{cases} 1 & k = 1 \\ u_k & 1 < k < K, \\ 0 & k = K \end{cases} \tag{3}$$

where u_k ($k = 1, \ldots, K$) is given by (2). This defines the utility function u(.) to be used in formula (1). We note that any function v(.) which satisfies

$$v(O_k) = a + bu(O_k) \qquad (k = 1, \ldots, K)$$

for $b > 0$ can also be used in (1); but no other function can be so used. Thus the utility function is unique only up to a linear transformation.

185

JOHN D. HEY

However, the function must be context-free; that is, its values must be independent of the particular risky choice pairs used in its derivation. Thus, if instead of determining the value of u_k where (2) holds, the individual had been asked to determine the value of p at which

$$O_k \sim [(O_2, p), (O_{K-1}, 1\text{-}p)]$$

(where $2 \leq k \leq K\text{-}1$), then it must follow that the relevant value of p is related to the u(.) values by

$$u_k = pu_2 + (1\text{-}p)u_{K-1}.$$

This context-free utility function is at the very heart of the conventional wisdom. (Later we shall mention context-dependent utility functions, such as those in MACHINA [1982].)

Having determined the utility function, we can now turn to the conventional method of determining the probability function. To do this, we ask the individual to determine (for each $j = 1, \ldots, J$) the consequence O^j for which

$$O^j \sim [(O_1, S_j), (O_K, \bar{S}_j)] \qquad (4)$$

where the risky choice on the right-hand side of (4) yields consequence O_1 if state of the world S_j occurs and consequence O_K otherwise. We then define p(.) by

$$p(S_j) = u(O^j) \qquad (j = 1, \ldots, J) \qquad (5)$$

where O^j is given by (4). This defines the probability function p(.) to be used in formula (1).

Now note crucially that this probability function must also, according to the conventional wisdom, be context-free; that is, its values must be independent of the particular risky choice pairs used in its derivation. Thus, if instead of determining the value of O^j where (4) holds, the individual had been asked to determine the value of O at which

$$O \sim [(O_2, S_j), (O_{K-1}, \bar{S}_j)],$$

THE ECONOMICS OF OPTIMISM AND PESSIMISM

then it must follow that the relevant value of O is related to the p(.) values by

$$u(O) = p(S_j)u_2 + [1-p(S_j)]u_{K-1}.$$

This context-free probability function is at the very heart of the conventional wisdom. Taken in conjunction with the context-free utility function, it implies that both functions can be determined independently, and then combined in formula (1) to predict and explain choice.

Clearly, a context-free probability function rules out the existence of optimism and pessimism, at least as defined by us above. Being context-free, the probabilities are independent of the consequences; this implies realism as defined by us above.

Our view is that the implicit probabilities for optimists and pessimists do indeed depend upon the consequences, and hence are not context-free. Consider, for example, some state of the world S (such as 'President Reagan being re-elected U.S. president' or 'the discovery before 2000 AD of life elsewhere in the galaxy'), and imagine being asked to determine O^1 and O^2 such that

$$O^1 \sim [(O_1, S), (O_K, \bar{S})] \tag{6}$$

and

$$O^2 \sim [(O_1, \bar{S}), (O_K, S)] \tag{7}$$

'Context-freeness' requires that

$$u(O^1) + u(O^2) = 1$$

since (6) implies that $u(O^1) = 1.p(S) + O.[1-p(S)] = p(S)$ whereas (7) implies that $u(O^2) = 1.[1-p(S)] + O.p(S) = 1-p(S)$.

On our definition, an optimist is someone for whom

$$u(O^1) + u(O^2) > 1 \tag{8}$$

whereas a pessimist is someone for whom

$$u(O^1) + u(O^2) < 1 \tag{9}$$

JOHN D. HEY

This follows since an optimist (pessimist) revises up (down) the probabilities of favourable outcomes, and revises down (up) the probabilities of unfavourable outcomes. Thus, we have

$$u(O^1) = 1.[p(S) + \varepsilon^1] + O.[1-p(S)-\varepsilon^1] = p(S) + \varepsilon^1$$

and

$$u(O^2) = 1.[1-p(S) + \varepsilon^2] + O.[p(S)-\varepsilon^2] = 1-p(S) + \varepsilon^2$$

where ε^1 and ε^2 are positive for an optimist and negative for a pressimist. Thus

$$u(O^1) + u(O^2) = 1 + \varepsilon^1 + \varepsilon^2$$

from which we get (8) and (9) above.

Thus, the crucial point of our definition is that, for optimists and pessimists, the probability function is *not* context-free. Hence, to incorporate optimism and pessimism into the conventional wisdom, we need to replace (1), repeated here,

$$U(C_i) = \sum_{j=1}^{J} p(S_j)u(A_{ij}) \qquad\qquad (1) \text{ repeated}$$

by the following

$$U(C_i) = \sum_{j=1}^{J} p(S_j; \underline{A}_i)u(A_{ij}), \qquad\qquad (10)$$

where the vector $\underline{A}_i = (A_{i1}, A_{i2}, ..., A_{iJ})$ denotes the vector of consequences under choice C_i. Further, and most importantly, the function $p(.; \underline{A}_i)$ depends upon the vector $\underline{A}_i$ in the manner specified in section II.

Individuals can now be characterized in two dimensions: first, their attitude to risk; second, their attitude to 'fate' (that is, their optimism/pessimism stance). The first is characterized by the shape of their utility function; the second by the dependence of their probability function on the consequence vector. So we may have risk-averse optimists or risk-loving pessimists or risk-neutral realists, or indeed any combination of risk-loving, risk-neutrality or risk-aversion with optimism, realism or pessimism. We give more details in Section V.

188

THE ECONOMICS OF OPTIMISM AND PESSIMISM

IV. IMPLICATION

We present in this section some illustrations of how the incorporation of optimism and pessimism may explain some well-known apparent violations of *SEU* theory.

1. The Allais paradox

One of the simplest versions of the ALLAIS paradox involves two pairwise choices. The first pair are

$$C_1 = [(3000, 1)] \text{ and } C_2 = [(4000, 0.8), (0, 0.2)]$$

where the amounts are specified in some appropriate currency (pounds sterling, for example). The second pair are

$$C_3 = [(3000, 0.25), (0, 0.75)] \text{ and } C_4 = [(4000, 0.2), (0, 0.8)],$$

the same units of currency being used. The conventional wisdom requires that $C_1 \gtrless C_2$ according as $C_3 \gtrless C_4$. However, numerous laboratory experiments have revealed that the modal preference is for C_1 over C_2 and C_4 over C_3. This pattern violates the conventional wisdom. (Note that $C_1 >$ C_2 if and only if $u(3000) > 0.8u(4000) + 0.2u(0)$ whereas $C_3 > C_4$ if and only if $0.25u(3000) + 0.75u(0) > 0.2u(4000) + 0.8u(0)$. These are algebraically equivalent conditions, irrespective of the values of the u(.) function).

However, consider now a *risk-neutral pessimist*, as defined by us above. Such an individual will revise down the probability of receiving the 4000 in C_2 from 0.8 to 0.8α, where $0 < \alpha < 1$ and where the magnitude of α is a decreasing function of the individual's degree of pessimism. The probability of receiving 0 under C_2 will correspondingly be revised up to $1-0.8\alpha$. Similarly, the probabilities of receiving 3000 under C_3 and 4000 under C_4 will be revised down to $.25\alpha$ and $.2\alpha$ respectively (where we have supposed the same α applies in each case), with corresponding upward revisions of the probability of 0 under C_3 and C_4 to $1-0.25\alpha$ and $1-0.2\alpha$ respectively. Note crucially that no revision can take place with respect to C_1, since this is a situation of certainty. (Note also that we presume that the individual does not perceive the given proba-

189

JOHN D. HEY

bilities as objective, for in such a case no revisions would be appropriate.)

Being risk-neutral, the individual's utility function is

$$u(x) \propto x$$

where x denotes the amount received. Thus, our risk-neutral pessimist will show the following preferences:

$$C_1 \underset{<}{\overset{\geq}{\sim}} C_2 \leftrightarrow 3000 \underset{<}{\overset{\geq}{=}} 0.8\alpha \times 4000 \leftrightarrow \alpha \underset{<}{\overset{\geq}{=}} 0.9375$$

and

$$C_4 \succ C_3 \text{ since } 0.2\alpha \times 4000 > 0.25\alpha \times 3200 \text{ for all } \alpha > 0$$

Thus, if the individual is not *too* pessimistic ($\alpha > 0.9375$), he or she will display one of the pairs of preferences predicted by *SEU* theory (namely $C_2 \succ C_1$ and $C_4 \succ C_3$), while if the individual is more pessimistic ($\alpha < 0.9375$), he or she will display the modal pair or preferences shown in laboratory experiments, namely $C_1 \succ C_2$ and $C_4 \succ C_3$ (see, for example, KAHNEMAN and TVERSKY [1979]). Thus, the incorporation of optimism and pessimism into the conventional wisdom can explain one of the more well-known observed violations of that wisdom.

2. The observations of Krzysztofowicz, Allais et al.

In the early 1950s ALLAIS [1952], and more recently KRZYSZTOFOWICZ [1982], amongst others, noted, in laboratory experiments, discrepancies between two independently-derived cardinal utility functions. The first method of derivation was that described in section III above, which we shall refer to as the *Neuman-Morgenstern method*. The second, which we shall refer to as the *Ordered Utility Differences method*, can be described as follows.

Suppose, for simplicity, that all outcomes are denominated in terms of a common unit, money; so that the argument of the utility function is money. Suppose further, again for expositional simplicity, that we wish to determine the values of the utility function for values of the argument in the range (say) 0 to 100. We can arbitrarily set

190

THE ECONOMICS OF OPTIMISM AND PESSIMISM

$$u(0) = 0 \text{ and } u(100) = 1. \tag{11}$$

Now, to find the value of x such that u(x) = 0.5, we ask each individual the following question:

'What is the value of x such that your preference for 100 rather than x is the same as your preference for x rather than 0?'

The idea behind this question is to determine the value of x such that the *increase* in utility going from 0 to x is the same as the *increase* in utility going from x to 100. Thus

$$u(x) - u(0) = u(100) - u(x)$$

and, using (11) above, this implies

$$u(x) = 0.5.$$

In a similar fashion, x values such that u(x) = 0.25, u(x) = 0.75, and hence u(x) = 0.125, u(x) = 0.375, u(x) = 0.625 and u(x) = 0.875, and so on, can be determined. In this way, the whole of the u(.) function can be calibrated.

ALLAIS and KRZYSZTOFOWICZ both noted that, for most individuals studied, the utility function derived using the *Neuman-Morgenstern method* differed from that derived using the *Ordered Utility Differences method*. From this, they concluded that the conventional wisdom was deficient. As ALLAIS [1952] remarked, '... these results totally invalidate the neo-Bernoullian doctrine which is currently accepted by so many economists and statisticians ...'.

However, as with the ALLAIS paradox, the incorporation of optimism and pessimism can explain this apparent violation of the conventional wisdom. Denote the 'utility function' derived using the *Neuman-Morgenstern method* by v(.), and that using the *Ordered Utility Differences method* by u(.). Suppose that for a particular individual u(a) = v(b) = 0.5, and that a ≠ b so an apparent violation of the accepted wisdom exists. Now recall that b was determined as that value at which the individual was indifferent between

$$[(b, 1)] \text{ and } [(100, 0.5), (0, 0.5)].$$

191

JOHN D. HEY

Figure 1
Two differently derived cardinal utility functions

optimist   realist   pessimist

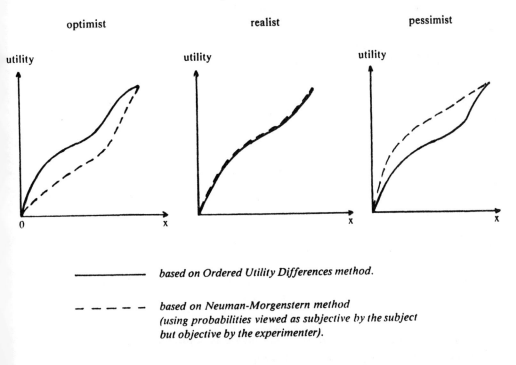

—————————— *based on Ordered Utility Differences method.*

— — — — — *based on Neuman-Morgenstern method*
(using probabilities viewed as subjective by the subject
but objective by the experimenter).

Suppose, however, that the individual is not a realist and therefore revises the probabilities in accordance with his or her optimism/pessimism stance. Then the value of b satisfies

$$u(b) = (0.5 + \varepsilon)u(100) + (0.5 - \varepsilon)u(0) = 0.5 + \varepsilon$$

where ε is positive or negative according as the individual is an optimist or a pessimist. Thus we have

$$u(a) = 0.5 \text{ and } u(b) = 0.5 + \varepsilon$$

and so

$$a \underset{>}{\overset{<}{}} b \text{ according as } \varepsilon \underset{<}{\overset{>}{}} 0.$$

192

THE ECONOMICS OF OPTIMISM AND PESSIMISM

That is, a is less or greater than b depending on whether the individual is an optimist or a pessimist. (For a realist, a and b are equal.) This is illustrated in *Figure 1*. Furthermore the difference between a and b is greater the larger is the individual's degree of optimism or pessimism. (Of course, this argument presumes that the probabilities used in the NEUMAN-MORGENSTERN method are viewed as subjective, and hence subject to revision, by the individual, but as objective by the experimenter.)

Thus, a second apparent violation of the conventional wisdom can be explained by the incorporation of optimism and pessimism.

3. Strength of preference and risky choice

A closely-related phenomenon has been noted by SARIN [1982] amongst others. Consider the following pairs:

$$C_1 = [(+10, S), (+10, \bar{S})] \qquad C_2 = [(-10, S), (+10, \bar{S})]$$

and

$$C_3 = [(+10, S), (-10, \bar{S})] \qquad C_4 = [(-10, S), (-10, \bar{S})]$$

where S denotes some uncertain event and $\bar{S}$ its complement. Now suppose we ask our individual the question:

'Do you prefer the exchange of C_1 for C_2 over the exchange of C_3 for C_4? Or *Vice Versa*? Or are you indifferent?'

According to the conventional wisdom the individual should respond that he or she is indifferent. [If $u(+10) = 1$, $u(-10) = 0$ and $P(S) = p$, then the exchange of C_1 for C_2 changes utility from 1 to 1-p, that is a drop of p; while the exchange of C_3 for C_4 changes utility from p to 0, that is a drop of p.] However, as SARIN [1982] and others have noted, this is not always the case.

Consider the following argument. We have (using an obvious notation)

$$(C_1 - C_2) \gtrless (C_3 - C_4) \text{ according as } 1 - (1 - p + \varepsilon) \gtrless (p + \varepsilon),$$

193

JOHN D. HEY

where p is the 'objective probability' of S and ε is the optimism/pessimism adjustment, being positive or negative depending on whether the individual is an optimist or pessimist (and which, for simplicity, we have taken to be the same in both C_2 and C_3). Then, we have that

$$(C_1 - C_2) \gtreqless (C_3 - C_4) \text{ according as the individual is } \begin{array}{ll} \text{a pessimist} & (\varepsilon < 0) \\ \text{a realist} & (\varepsilon = 0) \\ \text{an optimist} & (\varepsilon > 0) \end{array}$$

Thus, once again, the observed apparent violation of the accepted wisdom can be explained by the incorporation of optimism and pessimism.

4. Other violations of SEU theory

Other apparent violations can be explained in this fashion. These include the phenomenon of 'preference reversals' (see GRETHER and PLOTT [1979], the 'isolation effect' (see KAHNEMAN and TVERSKY [1979] and various other effects described by KAHNEMAN and TVERSKY [1979], MACHINA [1982] and LOOMES and SUGDEN [1982]. However, not all such violations can be so explained.

V. ILLUSTRATION

Suppose an individual is confronted with some random variable Y which is 'objectively' normally distributed with mean μ and variance σ^2. (The interpretation of the word 'objectively' will become clear shortly.) Thus,

$$Y \text{ is 'objectively' } N(\mu, \sigma^2). \tag{12}$$

Now suppose that the reward (or payoff) to the individual is the value of X, this being related to Y by:

$$X = aY + b \tag{13}$$

Clearly, if a is zero then the value of Y is irrelevant, whereas if a is positive (negative) then the return X is positively (negatively) dependent on

194

THE ECONOMICS OF OPTIMISM AND PESSIMISM

Y. If a is positive, then an optimist (pessimist) will revise the probability of Y achieving high values upwards (downwards) and revise the probability of Y achieving low values downwards (upwards). This is equivalent to shifting the distribution function of Y rightwards (leftwards). Thus, the individual perceives the distribution of Y shifted to the right or the left according as to whether he or she is an optimist or pessimist. Similar arguments apply *mutatis mutandis* if a is negative. This discussion can be summarised in the following:

$$\text{Y is subjectively viewed as } N(\mu - ap\sigma, \sigma^2). \tag{14}$$

where p denotes the individual's *pessimism index*, being positive for a pessimist and negative for an optimist, and with its *magnitude* depending on the individual's *degree* of optimism/pessimism. Note from (14) that there is no shift if a is zero (that is, if the reward is unrelated to Y); if p = 0 (that is, if the individual is a realist); or if $\sigma = 0$ (that is, if the reward is certain). These show how the 'objectively' in (12) should be interpreted. Note also that we have assumed in (14) that the magnitude of the shift is greater the larger is the variance of the distribution, but that the perceived variance itself is unchanged. We should, of course, note that the particular formulation specified in (14) is simply an illustrative example; a general characterization is discussed in section VII.

From (13) and (14) it follows that the individual's perception of the reward X is given by:

$$\text{X is subjectively viewed as } N[a(\mu - ap\sigma) + b, a^2\sigma^2]. \tag{15}$$

Now suppose that the individual's utility function displays constant absolute risk aversion, and hence is given by

$$u(x) \; \alpha - \exp(-rx), \tag{16}$$

where r is the (ARROW-PRATT) index of absolute risk aversion (see HEY [1981] section 3.3). It follows from (15) and (16) that the individual's perceived expected utility is

$$\text{(subjective) } EU(X) \propto -\exp\{-r[a(\mu - ap\sigma) + b] + \tfrac{1}{2}r^2a^2\sigma^2\}. \tag{17}$$

195

JOHN D. HEY

Figure 2
(Objective) Risk premia in the illustrative example

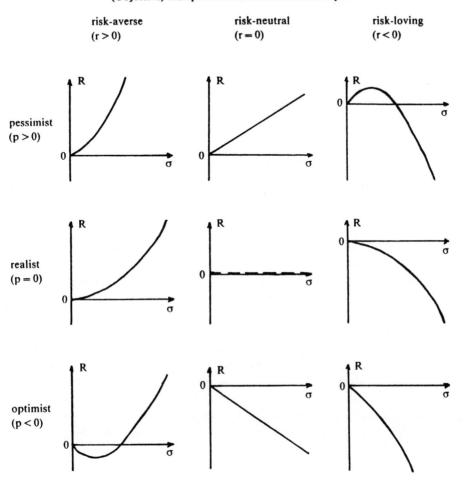

| risk-averse
(r > 0) | risk-neutral
(r = 0) | risk-loving
(r < 0) |

pessimist
(p > 0)

realist
(p = 0)

optimist
(p < 0)

Now the *objective* expected value of X is just $a\mu + b$; thus, the utility of the objective expected value of X is

$$\text{(objective)} \quad U(EX) \propto -\exp[-r(a\mu + b)], \tag{18}$$

where the factor of proportionality is the same as that in (17). Now consider the *objective risk premium* – that is, the risk premium as perceived

196

THE ECONOMICS OF OPTIMISM AND PESSIMISM

by an objective outside observer. This is defined as the R such that (see HEY [1981], section 3.3)

$$\text{(subjective) } EU(X) = \text{(objective) } U(EX - R). \tag{19}$$

Examination of (17), (18) and (19) reveals that this objective risk premium is

$$R = a^2(p\sigma + \tfrac{1}{2}r\sigma^2). \tag{20}$$

Clearly this depends on both the attitude to risk of the individual – as represented by r, the index of absolute risk aversion – and the optimism/pessimism stance of the individual – as represented by p, the index of pessimism. Both p and r can be positive zero or negative; thus we get 9 different possible combinations. These are illustrated in *Figure 2*.

The particularly interesting cases are those of the risk-averse optimist and the risk-loving pessimist. In the former the risk premium is initially negative before becoming positive; this indicates that the optimism outweighs the risk-aversion for small risks, while the opposite is the case for large risks. The reverse situation applies for the risk-loving pessimist. For the risk-averse pessimist and the risk-loving optimist, the effects work in the same direction. Of course, risk-neutrality or realism contribute nothing to the risk premium.

This illustration demonstrates the important point that attitude to risk and attitude to 'fate' do indeed constitute different dimensions of an individual's personality. This reinforces the point already made that the incorporation of optimism and pessimism does add something to the conventional wisdom.

VI. APPLICATION

1. The perfectly competitive firm under (spot) price uncertainty

The seminal article on this topic is that by SANDMO [1971]; a particular example, with a normally distributed price and a constant absolute risk-aversion utility function is presented in BARON [1970]. Let us incorporate optimism and pessimism into this particular example.

JOHN D. HEY

We envisage a one-period model, in which the firm must choose output Q, before knowing what the spot price P is. We assume that P is objectively normally distributed with mean μ and variance σ^2. We further assume that the cost function C(.) is certain and known, and that the firm displays constant absolute risk aversion with respect to profits. Using the specific optimism/pessimism formulation presented in Section V above, we find that the objective of the firm is to choose Q so as to maximise (subjective) expected utility

$$EU(\pi) \propto -\exp\{-r[Q(\mu - Qp\sigma) - C(Q)] + \tfrac{1}{2}r^2Q^2\sigma^2\}.$$

Clearly the solution to this maximisation problem is such that

$$\mu = C'(Q) + Q\sigma(2p + r\sigma). \tag{21}$$

This, of course, reduces to that given by BARON [1970] in the special case when p = 0, that is when the firm is a realist. More generally, the attitude to 'fate' combines with the attitude to risk in much the same way as in section V. More precisely, Q is greater than, equal to, or less than the output that the firm would produce in a certain world (with the price equal to μ) according as 2p + rσ is less than, equal to, or greater than zero. So, once again, optimism can outweigh risk-aversion, and pessimism outweigh risk-loving, for small risks.

The effect of the introduction of a forward market has been analysed by HOLTHAUSEN [1979]. For the specific distribution and utility function adopted above, the solution can be shown to be

$$\left.\begin{aligned} b &= C'(Q) \\ (b - \mu) &= (Q - H)\sigma(2p + r\sigma) \end{aligned}\right\} \tag{22}$$

where b is the (certain) forward price and H is the amount hedged (that is, sold in the forward market). Clearly, the amount produced is determined solely by the forward price, and is therefore independent of the spot price distribution, the attitude to risk and the attitude to 'fate' of the firm. However, the amount hedged does depend on these factors. Once again, the attitude to 'fate' combines with the attitude to risk. We leave it to the reader to explore the implications of different (p, r) combinations.

198

THE ECONOMICS OF OPTIMISM AND PESSIMISM

2. Consumption under income uncertainty

In HEY [1980] we examined the determination of the optimal consumption strategy of an individual in an infinite horizon world with uncertain income. In particular, we examine the by-now-familiar case of (identically but independently) normally distributed incomes (with mean μ and variance σ^2 in each period) combined with a constant absolute risk aversion utility function. We found that the optimal consumption strategy is linear in wealth, viz.

$$C^*(W) = a + bW, \qquad (23)$$

where a and b are related to the parameters of the model.

The incorporation of optimism and pessimism in the manner specified in Section V implies that a and b are now given by

$$\left. \begin{array}{l} a = (\mu - p\sigma) - \tfrac{1}{2}r(R-1)\sigma^2 - \log(R_\varrho)/[r(R-1)] \\ \text{and} \\ (1-b)R = 1. \end{array} \right\} \qquad (24)$$

Here the effect of the pessimism index is simply to shift the intercept of the consumption function – upwards if the individual is an optimist and downwards if the individual is a pessimist. This is precisely the equivalent of a change in the mean μ, which, of course, is effectively what is happening.

VII. GENERALISATION

The particular formulations adopted above are simply illustrative examples. In general, the way that the probabilities are revised, and hence the distributions shifted, depend upon the particular individual and the particular problem.

However, a general characterisation is possible, at least for the case when the utility function has just a single argument. Let us call this argument Y, and let us suppose it is related to some random variable X by

$$Y = W(X). \qquad (25)$$

JOHN D. HEY

Figure 3
Objective and subjective distribution functions (for an optimist with W' > 0)

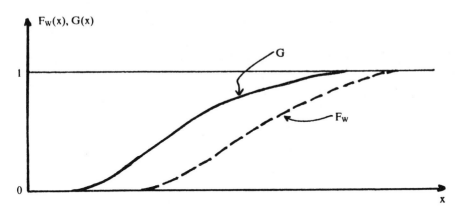

Now the essence of our argument is that optimists and pessimists systematically revise their perception of the distribution of X in a manner that depends upon the relationship of Y to X. For example, consider an optimist and suppose that Y is positively related to X. Then the individual will revise upwards the probabilities attached to high values of X, and revise downwards the probabilities attached to low values. The most general way to characterise this is to note that it implies a rightwards shifting of the distribution function. To be precise, let G(.) denote the 'objective' distribution function of X, and let $F_W(.)$ denote the subjective (or perceived) distribution function of X; the subscript W emphasises the fact that $F_W(.).$ depends crucially on the reward structure W(.). Then, if W' > 0 and the individual is an optimist $F_W(.)$ is G(.) shifted rightwards. *Figure 3* illustrates.

A glance at this *Figure* reveals that this can be simply characterised by noting that F_W first degree stochastically dominates G. (That is, $F_W(x) \leq$ G(x) for all x. See HADAR and RUSSELL [1969].) Let us denote this by $F_W \succ$ G. Then we have, for an optimist, with W' > 0, that $F_W \succ$ G; that is, the subjectively perceived distribution of X first degree stochastically dominates the objective distribution. Generalising, we get *Table 1*.

Note that the middle row and middle column illustrate the meaning of the adjective 'objective' as applied to G.

200

THE ECONOMICS OF OPTIMISM AND PESSIMISM

Furthermore, an increase in pessimism can be characterised by an increase in the parameter p, where

$$\partial F_W(x)/ \ \partial p \gtreqless 0 \ \text{according as} \ W' \gtreqless 0 \qquad (26)$$

Note, of course, that the objective function is given by

$$EU(X) = \int U[W(x)]dF_W(x). \qquad (27)$$

Table 1
A general characterisation

	Optimist	Realist	Pessimist
$W' > 0$	$F_W \succ G$	$G \equiv F_W$	$G \succ F_W$
$W' = 0$	$G \equiv F_W$	$G \equiv F_W$	$G \equiv F_W$
$W' < 0$	$G \succ F_W$	$G \equiv F_W$	$F_W \succ G$

$G \succ F$ denotes that G first-degree stochastically dominates F (that is, $G(x) \le F(x)$ for all x, with strict inequality for at least one x).

Thus (26) is likely to be a particularly useful characterisation, enabling us in general to explore the effects of a change in optimism/pessimism on the relevant optimal strategy.

VIII. CONCLUSION

In this paper, we have provided a general definition of optimism and pessimism, have shown how its incorporation into the accepted wisdom can explain several apparent violations of that wisdom, have given several applications of the definition and have provided a general characterisation. Clearly, its implications need to be explored further, but a start has been made.

This paper represents one of a number of recent contributions adding to, or otherwise amending, the conventional wisdom (*SEU* theory). As we have shown, our formalisation of optimism/pessimism requires that

201

JOHN D. HEY

the objective function for decision-making under uncertainty be modified from

$$U(C_i) = \sum_{j=1}^{J} p(S_j)u(A_{ij}) \qquad (1) \text{ repeated}$$

to

$$U(C_i) = \sum_{j=1}^{J} p(S_j; \underline{A}_i)u(A_{ij}). \qquad (10) \text{ repeated}$$

In this $\underline{A}_i$ denotes the vector of consequences under choice C_i [viz. $(A_{i1}, A_{i2}, \ldots, A_{iJ})$]. Furthermore, the function $p(.; \underline{A}_i)$ depends upon the vector $\underline{A}_i$ in the manner specified in section 2.

Readers familiar with MACHINA [1982] will note that this revision is similar in spirit though different in detail to that proposed by MACHINA. He suggests replacing (1) by

$$U(C_i) = \sum_{j=1}^{J} p(S_j)\dot{u}(A_{ij}; \underline{p}). \qquad (28)$$

where $\underline{p} = [p(S_1), p(S_2), \ldots, p(S_J)]$ is the vector of probabilities.

Indeed, in some ways, (10) can be interpreted as a natural conjugate of (28). Of course, MACHINA takes the probabilities as given, that is, as objective, and operates through the utility function. In (28) $u(.; \underline{p})$ is a *local utility function*, depending specifically on the particular probability distribution. In this light, the $p(.; \underline{A}_i)$ in (10) can be interpreted as a *local probability function*, depending specifically on the particular consequence distribution.

Both our formulation and that of MACHINA are holistic; thus, transitivity over choices is retained. However, there is some evidence to suggest that preferences over risky choices are *not* transitive. This could be incorporated within our approach by further generalising (10) as follows:

$$U(C_i) = \sum_{j=1}^{J} p(S_j; \underline{A}_1, \underline{A}_2, \ldots, \underline{A}_I)u(A_{ij}) \qquad (29)$$

In this, utility is crucially dependent on the *set* of choices $(i = 1, \ldots, I)$ available. This, generally, implies intransitivity. The 'natural conjugate'

202

THE ECONOMICS OF OPTIMISM AND PESSIMISM

to (29) appears to be that suggested by LOOMES and SUGDEN [1982] which replaces (1) by

$$U(C_i) = \sum_{j=1}^{J} p(S_j) u(A_{ij}, A_{2j}, \ldots, A_{1j}).$$ (30)

Here again, as with MACHINA, LOOMES and SUGDEN take the probabilities as given.

SEU theory (1), our theory of optimism and pessimism (10), MACHINA's 'expected utility theory without the independence axiom' (28), our nonholistic generalisation (29) and LOOMES and SUGDEN's regret theory (30) are all special cases of the most general formulation which states that preference is represented by

$$U(C_i) = U(S_1, \ldots, S_J; \underset{\sim}{A}_1, \underset{\sim}{A}_2, \ldots, \underset{\sim}{A}_1).$$ (31)

The restrictions which reduce (31) to (1), (10), (28), (29) or (30) endow the individual theories with predictive power and with testability. The most important step would now appear to be to devise appropriate tests, and subject the various theories to such tests, in order to ascertain their relative validity. I would hope that such tests would provide further support for my theory of optimism and pessimism.

But then, I am an optimist!

REFERENCES

ALLAIS ,M.:'Fondements d'une Theorie Positive des Choix Comportant un Risque et Critique des Postulats et Axiomes de l'ecole Americaine', Memoir III annexed to *Econometrie*, Colloques Internationaux du Centre National de la Recherche Scientifique, vol. XL, Paris, 1952, 257–332; reprinted in English in: ALLAIS, M. and HAGEN, O. (eds.): *Expected Utility Hypotheses and the Allais Paradox*, Reidel, Dordrecht, 1979, 27–145.

BARON, D.P.: 'Price Uncertainty, Utility, and Industry Equilibrium in Pure Competition', *International Economic Review*, 11 (1970), 463–480.

GRETHER, D.M. and PLOTT, C.R.: 'Economic Theory of Choice and the Preference Reversal Phenomenon', *American Economic Review*, 69 (1979), 623–638.

HADAR, J. and RUSSELL, W.R.: 'Rules for Ordering Uncertain Prospects', *American Economic Review*, 59 (1969), 25–34.

HEY, J.D.: 'Optimal Consumption under Income Uncertainty', *Economics Letters*, 5 (1980), 129–133.

JOHN D. HEY

HEY, J. D.: *Economics in Disequilibrium*, Martin Robertson, Oxford, 1981.

HOLTHAUSEN, D. M.: 'Hedging and the Competitive Firm under Price Uncertainty', *American Economic Review*, 69 (1979), 989–995.

KAHNEMAN, D. and TVERSKY, A.: 'Prospect Theory: An Analysis of Decision under Risk', *Econometrica*, 47 (1979), 263–291.

KRZYSZTOFOWICZ, R.: *Risk Attitude Hypotheses of Utility Theory*, paper presented at the First International Conference on the Foundations of Utility and Risk Theory, Oslo, Norway, 1982.

LOOMES, G. and SUGDEN, R.: 'Regret Theory: An Alternative Theory of Rational Choice under Uncertainty', *Economic Journal*, 92 (1982), 805–824.

MACHINA, M. J.: '"Expected Utility" Analysis without the Independence Axiom', *Econometrica*, 50 (1982), 277–323.

SANDMO, A.: 'On the Theory of the Competitive Firm under Price Uncertainty', *American Economic Review*, 61 (1971), 65–73.

SARIN, R. K.: 'Strength of Preference and Risky Choice', *Operations Research*, 30 (1982), 982–997.

SUMMARY

This paper suggests a way of incorporating the important concepts of optimism and pessimism into the accepted model of decision-making under uncertainty. We exploit the primitive notion that an optimist is someone who over-estimates (under-estimates) the likelihood of favourable (unfavourable) outcomes. We show that this incorporation enables us to explain several commonly observed apparent violations of Subjective Expected Utility Theory. Several illustrations and economic applications are presented, and we show that attitude to 'fate' (as evidenced in optimism and pessimism) is a different dimension of personality than attitude to risk. We conclude by relating our extension of *SEU* theory to other recent extensions.

ZUSAMMENFASSUNG

Dieser Artikel schlägt eine Methode vor, die wichtigen Begriffe Optimismus und Pessimismus in das anerkannte Modell der Entscheidung unter Unsicherheit zu integrieren. Wir nützen die primitive Idee aus, ein Optimist sei jemand, der die Wahrscheinlichkeit von günstigen (beziehungsweise ungünstigen) Ergebnissen überschätzt (beziehungsweise unterschätzt). Wir zeigen, daß diese Integrierung uns ermöglicht, mehrere allgemein beobachtete scheinbare Verstösse gegen die *Subjective Expected Utility Theory* zu erklären. Mehrere Beispiele und wirtschaftliche Anwendungen werden vorgelegt, und wir zeigen, daß die Einstellung zum «Schicksal» (durch Optimismus und Pessimismus bewiesen) eine andere Dimension der Persönlichkeit als die Einstellung zum Risiko ist. Zum Abschluß vergleichen wir unsere mit anderen Erweiterungen der *SEU*-Theorie.

204

THE ECONOMICS OF OPTIMISM AND PESSIMISM

RÉSUMÉ

Cet article suggère un moyen d'intégrer les concepts importants d'optimisme et de pessimisme d'une façon couramment acceptée de prendre une décision dans l'incertitude. Nous exploitons la notion primitive qu'un optimiste est quelqu'un qui sur-estime (sous-estime) la possibilité de résultats favorables (défavorables). Nous démontrons que cette intégration nous permet d'expliquer plusieurs apparentes infractions de *Subjective Expected Utility Theory*, qui ont été souvent observées, plusieurs illustrations et applications économiques sont presentées, et nous démontrons que cette attitude vis-à-vis du «destin» (comme prouvée dans l'optimisme et le pessimisme) est une autre dimension de la personnalité que l'attitude vis-à-vis du risque. Nous concluons en appliquant cette théorie étendue à d'autres développements récemment découverts de *SEU* théorie.

THE ECONOMIC JOURNAL

SEPTEMBER 1985

The Economic Journal, **95** *(September 1985),* 575–594
Printed in Great Britain

STOCHASTIC CHOICE FUNCTIONS GENERATED FROM DETERMINISTIC PREFERENCES OVER LOTTERIES*

Mark J. Machina

The fact that neither experimental nor real world choice behaviour is completely deterministic has led several researchers to study the properties of 'stochastic' or 'randomised' choice functions, i.e. choice functions which specify not a single choice but rather the probabilities or frequencies of choosing each of the available alternatives. In the psychological literature, such models of probabilistic choice have been proposed and studied by (among others) Coombs (1969, 1975), Luce (1958, 1959, 1977), Marley (1968, 1981, 1982), Thurstone (1927), and Tversky (1972 *a, b*). Economists who have analysed and/or applied these and similar models include Debreu (1958), Fishburn (1973, 1976), Georgescu-Roegen (1958, 1969), Luce and Raiffa (1957, App. 1), Marschak (1960), McFadden (1974, 1981), Mossin (1968), and Quandt (1956).

When such choice functions are explicitly modelled as the outcome of maximisation behaviour based on some concept of underlying preferences, they are typically represented as being derived from a stochastic preference relation or 'random utility function' over the set of pure alternatives (e.g. Barberá and Pattanaik (1983), Becker *et al.* (1963 *a, b*), Block and Marschak (1960), Chipman (1960), Marley (1982), Marschak (1960), McClennan (1983), and Quandt (1956)). The motivation for such an approach is clear: if when confronted with a choice over two objects the individual chooses each alternative a positive proportion of the time, it seems natural to suppose that this is because he or she 'prefers' each one to the other those same proportions of the time. Justified on either an individual or an aggregative basis (see below), the random preferences model has been applied to the empirical analysis of urban travel demand (e.g. Hausman and Wise (1978), McFadden (1974, 1981)), occupational choice (Boskin (1974, n. 4)), choice of college (Kohn *et al.* 1976)), luncheon menu choice (Bock and Jones (1968, pp. 255–9)), location analysis (Coelho and Wilson (1976), Leonardi (1983)), and other areas of research.

While the random preferences approach seems a very natural explanation of

* I would like to thank Vincent Crawford, Daniel Graham, Vijay Krishna, Michael Rothschild, participants at the Conference on Stochastic Models of Choice, San Sebastian, Spain, June 1983 and the Econometric Society North American Winter Meetings, San Francisco, California, December 1983, and especially an anonymous referee for helpful comments on this material, and the National Science Foundation (Grant No. SES 83–08165) for financial support. All errors and opinions, however, are my own.

individual variability, it nevertheless still possesses several troubling aspects. Does each choice situation induce a new realisation of the random preference ranking or do such realisations occur independently of the frequency of choice situations? Are successive realisations of the preference ranking independent of past realisations? of past choices? Is the realisation of the preference ranking at the time of a given choice situation stochastically independent of the particular set of alternatives available at the time, or if not, what is the nature of the dependence? Finally, is attributing stochastic choice to stochastic preferences in any sense an 'explanation' of such behaviour, or is it merely moving the unexplained source of randomness back a step?

As alluded to above, the random preferences model has also been applied to the analysis of *aggregate* economic data on the basis of an argument which does not rely upon the assumption of individual randomness at all, but rather upon the existence of unobserved characteristics which affect preferences and which vary across individuals. Specifically, if each individual is assumed to have a determinate but unobservable preference ranking, aggregate choice behaviour will correspond to that predicted by the random preferences model, with the distribution of preference rankings over the population corresponding to the random preference ranking and the proportions of individuals choosing each alternative corresponding to the choice probabilities. In fact, it is clear that this will also be true even if individual choice is not determinate, provided it is stochastic in the manner implied by the random preferences model. However, if individual choice is stochastic (and the preponderance of evidence suggests that it is) but *not* in accordance with the random preferences model, this argument breaks down, and the model will not be valid at the aggregate level either.

The purpose of this paper is to provide an alternative model of stochastic choice at the individual level which is not based on unstable (i.e. stochastic) preferences over pure outcomes, but rather on stable (i.e. deterministic) preferences over lotteries. Thus, we shall assume that when the choice function assigns the respective probabilities $(p_1, ..., p_n)$ to the alternatives $\{a_1, ..., a_n\}$ it is not because of an unstable preference ranking which prefers alternative a_i p_i proportion of time, but rather because the individual in fact prefers the lottery yielding $a_1, ..., a_n$ with probabilities $p_1, ..., p_n$ to any of these sure alternatives, or indeed, to any other lottery over the set $\{a_1, ..., a_n\}$. Besides treating choice probabilities as being generated from an explicit maximisation problem as opposed to being inherited from an inexplicably stochastic preference relation, this approach allows us to obtain a better understanding of the nature of transitivity and path independence in stochastic choice, as well as the derivation of other analytical results and predictions. Of course, since the theoretical advantages of one model over another must take second billing to their comparative abilities to stand up to the data, we shall also consider the observationally distinguishable aspects of these as well as some other alternative models of randomised choice.

Section I of the paper offers a formal statement of this 'deterministic preferences' model of stochastic choice, including a simple diagram which will be helpful in illustrating many of our subsequent results, and some refutable implications of the model are derived in Section II. Sections III and IV treat the issues of stochastic intransitivity and path independence. Section V presents some applications of 'generalised expected utility analysis' (Machina, 1982 a, 1983) to the analysis of behaviour in this model. The behavioural implications of this model are contrasted with those of the random preferences model and some other models of stochastic choice in Section VI. Section VII considers the somewhat different implications of the model when preferences over lotteries are quasiconvex in the probabilities, and the paper concludes with some brief remarks concerning possible future directions for research.

I. THE DETERMINISTIC PREFERENCES MODEL OF STOCHASTIC CHOICE

In adopting this approach we therefore assume that the individual possesses a preference function $V(p_1, ..., p_n)$ defined over the set

$$D(A) = \{(p_1, ..., p_n) \mid p_i \in [0, 1], \Sigma p_i = 1\}$$

of lotteries over a set $A = \{a_1, ..., a_n\}$ of (pure) outcomes, and that the individual's choice probabilities over any subset of A correspond to that lottery over the subset which maximises $V(\cdot, ..., \cdot)$.[1] In addition, since there is no reason why the set of available alternatives need not themselves be lotteries (i.e. some alternatives might have random consequences), we also include in the domain of the choice function all (ordered) subsets B of $D(A)$, and accordingly define the (vector-valued) stochastic choice function $C(B)$ as that vector of probabilities over the elements of B which generates the most preferred distribution over A. In terms of our later discussion, it will also be useful to define $C_A(B)$ as the element of $D(A)$ generated by this choice, i.e. as the vector of probabilities over $\{a_1, ..., a_n\}$ induced by the optimal choice probabilities over the elements of B, so that we have

$$C_A(B) = \underset{(p_1, ..., p_n) \in D_A(B)}{\mathrm{argmax}} V(p_1, ..., p_n) \qquad (1)$$

where $D_A(B)$ is the set of all distributions in $D(A)$ generated by randomisations over the elements of B. Thus, for example, if

$$A = \{a_1, a_2, a_3\}, \quad V(p_1, p_2, p_3) \equiv p_1 \cdot p_2 \cdot p_3, \quad \text{and} \quad B = \{0 \cdot 5 a_1 + 0 \cdot 5 a_2, a_3\}$$

(i.e. if B contains the 50:50 gamble over a_1 and a_2 as well as the pure alternative a_3), we would have

$$C(B) = (\tfrac{2}{3}, \tfrac{1}{3}), \quad D_A(B) = \{(p, p, 1 - 2p) \mid p \in [0, \tfrac{1}{2}]\}, \quad \text{and} \quad C_A(B) = (\tfrac{1}{3}, \tfrac{1}{3}, \tfrac{1}{3}).$$

In the case when $A = \{a_1, a_2, a_3\}$ it is useful to represent the lotteries in $D(A)$ by the points in the two-dimensional unit simplex using the standard barycentric coordinate system, as in Fig. 1. Thus if $B = \{a_1, a_2\}$, the individual could attain any probability distribution along the bottom edge of the triangle, and if $B = \{b_1, b_2, b_3, b_4\}$, the individual could attain any distribution in the convex hull

---

[1] As usual, the theoretical and empirical properties of this model will be independent of whether we assume that the individual consciously randomises using the calculated optimal probabilities or merely behaves 'as if' maximising an underlying preference function.

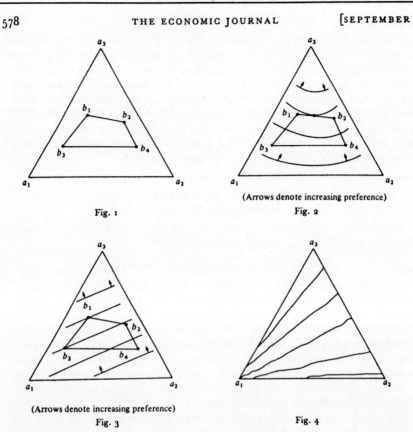

Fig. 1

(Arrows denote increasing preference)

Fig. 2

(Arrows denote increasing preference)

Fig. 3

Fig. 4

of these points. In the case of a general set of the form $A = \{a_1, ..., a_n\}$, $D(A)$ may be thought of as the $n-1$ dimensional unit simplex, and for any set $B \subseteq D(A)$, the set $D_A(B)$ consists of the convex hull of B in $D(A)$.

Since the set $D_A(B)$ will always be a convex polytope in $D(A)$, it follows that the individual will only choose to randomise if his or her preferences are at least somewhere 'quasiconcave in the probabilities', as in Fig. 2.[1] In particular, if the individual were an expected utility maximiser, i.e. if the preference function took the linear form $V(p_1, ..., p_n) \equiv \Sigma u_i\, p_i$ where u_i is the von Neumann–Morgenstern utility of a_i, then indifference curves will be parallel straight lines in the triangle (or more generally, parallel hyperplanes in $D(A)$), and it is clear from Fig. 3 that the individual would never wish to randomise except in the knife-edge case when two (random or pure) alternatives yielded exactly equal levels of expected utility. While this might be taken as ruling out the present approach as a normative basis for individual randomised choice, the *positive* evidence on this issue indicates that

[1] Although the indifference curves in this diagram imply randomisation over the lotteries b_1 and b_2, they do not imply randomisation over the set of *pure* alternatives $\{a_1, a_2, a_3\}$ (rather, a_3 would always be chosen). Fig. 7 below gives an indifference map which *would* lead to randomisation over (two elements of) this choice set, and Fig. 8 gives an example where the individual would choose all three alternatives with positive probability.

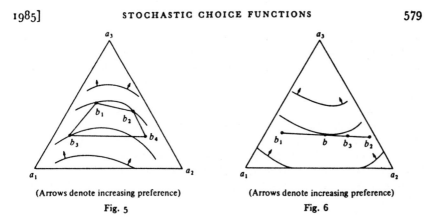

(Arrows denote increasing preference)   (Arrows denote increasing preference)

Fig. 5   Fig. 6

individuals' indifference curves in probability space are typically *not* parallel straight lines.

The most compelling body of evidence on this point consists of those studies by Allais (1979), Hagen (1979), Kahneman and Tversky (1979), Karmarkar (1974), MacCrimmon and Larsson (1979), McCord and de Neufville (1983), Morrison (1967), Moskowitz (1974), Slovic and Tversky (1974), Tversky (1975) and others who have found that indifference curves *systematically* deviate from parallelness in the direction of 'fanning out', as illustrated in Fig. 4. For further discussions and surveys of this evidence, the reader is referred to MacCrimmon and Larsson (1979) and Machina (1982 a, 1983).

Although the above evidence fairly convincingly refutes the expected utility property of parallelness, it has no implications regarding the more immediately relevant issue of curvature, since indifference curves which 'fan out' could be either quasiconcave or quasiconvex, or for that matter, even straight. Regarding this issue, Coombs and Huang (1976, Exp. 1) found a significant proportion (45 %) of violations of the hypothesis of straight line indifference curves, with the majority of violations in the direction of quasiconcavity as opposed to quasiconvexity.[1] Becker *et al.* (1963 b) were similarly able to reject the hypothesis of straight line indifference curves, even though their experimental design was only able to detect violations in the direction of quasiconcavity (see also the remarks of Alchian (1953, pp. 47–8), Coombs (1975) and Markowitz (1959, pp. 219–20) on this issue). Further evidence against the 'straight line' implication that individuals will only randomise in knife-edge cases has been provided by Luce and Shipley (1962), Mosteller and Nogee (1951), and others who found both that randomisation was prevalent and that the choice probabilities typically varied continuously in the makeup of the alternatives.

The final type of curvature, namely strict quasiconvexity, is seen from Fig. 5 never to imply randomisation, even over indifferent alternatives such as b_1 and b_2, and, as in standard consumer theory, implies that choice will vary

---

[1] Although the proportion of violations in their Experiment 2 was much smaller (14 %), it was still over three times the level expected on the basis of chance alone, and once again the majority of violations were in the direction of quasiconcavity.

discontinuously with the elements of the choice set. In light of the very distinct behavioural implications of quasiconvexity and quasiconcavity and the fact that only the latter case admits of regular optima, we shall henceforth assume that the individual's preferences are strictly quasiconcave in the probabilities, deferring consideration of the quasiconvex case until Section VII below.

Finally, we note that if some elements of the choice set B were to lie in the convex hull of other elements, the individual's most preferred lottery might be obtainable by more than one assignment of choice probabilities to the elements of B. In such a situation there is no reason to expect that the choice frequencies over these elements (i.e. the vector $C(B)$) will be stable in the sense of converging to definite long run values. However, as long as preferences are strictly quasiconcave, the most preferred lottery in $D_A(B)$ (i.e. $C_A(B)$) *will* be unique, so that the actual consumption probabilities over $\{a_1, ..., a_n\}$ (and hence their long run frequencies) will be well defined and unique.

II. REFUTABLE IMPLICATIONS ON CHOICE BEHAVIOUR

It is straightforward to show that the above model places several refutable restrictions on the randomised choice functions $C(\cdot)$ and $C_A(\cdot)$. Since they are generated from an underlying transitive preference ranking over lotteries, one immediate implication is that they will satisfy the analogue of Sen's 'Alpha property' (Sen (1970, p. 17)) in this setting, namely

$$\text{if} \quad D_A(B) \subseteq D_A(B^*) \quad \text{and} \quad C_A(B^*) \in D_A(B) \quad \text{then} \quad C_A(B) = C_A(B^*). \quad \text{(I)}$$

(Note that $D_A(B)$ will be a subset of $D_A(B^*)$ if each element of B is either an element of B^* or else a lottery over elements of B^*.) Two special cases of this condition are worth noting. The first, which is not only obvious but is also an implication of the stochastic preferences model, is that if an alternative is never chosen, then eliminating it from the choice set will not alter the individual's choice probabilities over the remaining alternatives, i.e.

$$\text{if} \quad C(\{b_1, b_2, ..., b_m\}) = (0, p_2, ..., p_m) \quad \text{then} \ C(\{b_2, ..., b_m\}) = (p_2, ..., p_m). \quad \text{(II)}$$

(In such a case it is also clear that if b_1 is not collinear with $b_2, ..., b_m$, then small *changes* in b_1 will also have no effect on the choice probabilities.)

The second implication involves the case when $D_A(B)$ and $D_A(B^*)$ are of the same dimensionality, as in Fig. 6. Here the optimal choice over the set $\{b_1, b_2\}$ consists of a $\frac{1}{2}:\frac{1}{2}$ randomisation, i.e. the lottery b. It is clear that when the alternative set is $\{b_1, b_3\}$ where $b_3 = (\frac{1}{4})b_1 + (\frac{3}{4})b_2$, b will still be preferred to any other lottery in the convex hull of $\{b_1, b_3\}$, so that the individual will choose a $\frac{1}{3}:\frac{2}{3}$ randomisation over b_1 and b_3 (i.e. $C_A(\{b_1, b_2\})$ and $C_A(\{b_1, b_3\})$ will be the same element of $D(A)$. More generally, we have

$$\text{if} \qquad C(\{b_1, b_2\}) = (p, 1-p) \quad \text{and} \quad b_3 = qb_1 + (1-q)b_2,$$

where $q \leqslant p$ (resp. $q \geqslant p$), then

$$C(\{b_1, b_3\}) = [(p-q)/(1-q), (1-p)/(1-q)] \ (\text{resp.} \ C(\{b_3, b_2\})$$
$$= [p/q, (q-p)/q)], \quad \text{(III)}$$

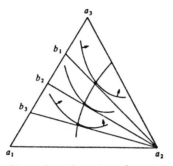

(Arrows denote increasing preference)

Fig. 7

with similar conditions applying for choice sets with three or more elements. We shall see in Section VI that this implication is *not* shared by the random preferences model.

Another class of predictions comes from exploiting the analogy between this model and the standard theory of demand.[1] Consider Fig. 7, where

$$b = (1 - q)\,a_1 + q a_3.$$

In the case where the indifference curves are quasiconcave with more preferred ones lying to the northeast, an increase in q will, by rotating the segment a_2–b clockwise about a_2, trace out a locus of optimal distributions which is precisely analogous to the 'price-consumption locus' of standard demand theory. Thus, by properly transforming the variables of this problem to obtain the analogues of 'income', 'prices', and 'quantities demanded', we may obtain all of the standard behavioural restrictions of demand theory (e.g. the Slutsky equation, symmetry of cross substitution effects, etc.) as refutable implications of the present model. Since the issues of sufficient conditions for a randomised choice function to have been generated by an underlying preference ranking over lotteries and the recoverability of such rankings are also exactly analogous, we shall not explicitly consider them here.

Thus, under the assumption that preferences are quasiconcave in the probabilities, the deterministic preferences model of stochastic choice possesses behavioural implications which are exactly analogous in both their strength and nature to the behavioural implications of standard consumer choice and demand theory. In Sections VI and VII we shall contrast these results with the implications of the random preferences model and the deterministic preferences model in the case of quasiconvex preferences over lotteries.

III. STOCHASTIC INTRANSITIVITY

This approach may also be used to shed some light on the nature of transitivity and intransitivity in stochastic choice. In the literature (e.g. Block and Marschak

---

[1] This observation is due to Vince Crawford. For further applications, see Crawford (n.d.).

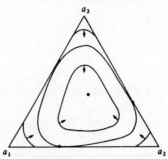

(Arrows denote increasing preference)

Fig. 8

(1960), Coombs (1958), Davidson and Marschak (1959), Fishburn (1973), Luce (1959), Luce and Suppes (1965), Marschak (1955, 1960, 1968)) a randomised choice function is said to exhibit 'weak stochastic transitivity' if it satisfies

$$\text{if} \quad C(\{b_1, b_2\}) = (p, 1-p),\ C(\{b_2, b_3\}) = (q, 1-q)$$
$$\text{and} \quad p, q \geqslant \tfrac{1}{2} \quad \text{then} \quad C(\{b_1, b_3\}) \geqslant \tfrac{1}{2}, \quad \text{(IV)}$$

and to exhibit 'strong stochastic transitivity' if it satisfies

$$\text{if} \quad C(\{b_1, b_2\}) = (p, 1-p),\ C(\{b_2, b_3\}) = (q, 1-q)$$
$$\text{and} \quad p, q \geqslant \tfrac{1}{2} \quad \text{then} \quad C(\{b_1, b_3\}) \geqslant \max\{p, q\}, \quad \text{(IV*)}$$

and we will refer to a choice function as 'stochastically intransitive' if it violates (IV) (and hence (IV*)) for any triple $\{b_1, b_2, b_3\}$. While few if any authors have termed such violations outright 'irrational' (perhaps because we are less confident of our moral certitudes in a world of stochastic behaviour), they are nevertheless thought of as reflecting at least some form of inconsistency, and conditions such as (IV) and (IV*) have typically been regarded as normatively desirable properties of choice.

However, if we view stochastic choice as the maximising behaviour of an individual with deterministic but nonlinear preferences over lotteries, then it turns out that not only is the above notion of 'stochastic intransitivity' in fact completely compatible with a transitive (i.e. 'consistent' or 'rational') underlying preference ranking, but virtually every choice function which displays any randomisation at all will exhibit it!

This first point is illustrated in Fig. 8, which shows a case where the individual would randomise over each of the pairs $\{a_1, a_2\}$, $\{a_2, a_3\}$ and $\{a_3, a_1\}$ with respective probabilities $(\tfrac{2}{3}, \tfrac{1}{3})$, and thus exhibit 'stochastically intransitive' preferences over $\{a_1, a_2, a_3\}$, even though he or she possesses stable transitive preferences over lotteries.[1]

---

[1] As mentioned above, such an indifference map also implies that the individual would choose each of the alternatives a_1, a_2, and a_3 with positive probability, so that we would only expect preferences possibly to take this form if the alternatives were nonmonetary outcomes (e.g. alternative transportation modes) or lotteries, and not, for example, distinct nonstochastic wealth levels. The following point, however, applies to *all* quasiconcave indifference maps.

To see the second point, choose any indifference curve I–I in a region of the simplex where the individual will randomise, i.e. where indifference curves are quasiconcave, as in Fig. 9. Picking a point such as b_1, construct points b_2 and b_3 so that the line segments b_1–b_2 and b_1–b_3 are tangent to I–I at the points b_4 and b_5 which bisect these respective segments, and let b_6 be the most preferred distribution on the segment b_2–b_3. In general, b_6 will *not* bisect b_2–b_3, and without loss of generality, we may assume that b_6 lies to the left of the midpoint. Then, if we consider the three points b_1, b_2' and b_3', it is clear that (*i*) by continuity the most preferred point on the segment b_2'–b_3' will lie to the left of the midpoint (i.e. closer to b_2' than to b_3'); (*ii*) the most preferred point on b_1–b_2' (i.e. b_4) will lie closer to b_1 than to b_2', and (*iii*) the most preferred point on b_1–b_3' (i.e. b_5) will lie closer to b_3' than to b_1. Thus, as in Fig. 8, we have that the individual's preferences over b_1, b_2' and b_3' will be 'stochastically intransitive' in the above defined sense.

These two points suggest that we view the above notion of 'stochastic intransitivity' (i.e. violation of property (IV)) as neither a normatively disturbing nor a descriptively rare phenomenon. Rather, the 'proper' notion of intransitivity in this context ought to be the phenomenon of intransitive underlying preferences over the lotteries themselves, as would be evidenced, for example, by any violation of properties (I), (II) or (III) above. It is *this* phenomenon which is both truly normatively disturbing (it would prevent us from drawing indifference curves in the simplex) and we would expect to observe it rarely, or at least if it were observed, it would contradict the present model.

IV. PATH INDEPENDENCE[1]

The present approach may also be used to clear up a confusion in the literature concerning the 'proper' application of the notion of 'path independence' (e.g. Plott (1973), Parks (1976)) to randomised choice functions. Recall that the intuitive notion of path independence is that, when we consider choosing over a large set of alternatives by breaking up the set, choosing over the subsets and then choosing over these choices, the ultimate choice will 'be independent of the way the alternatives were initially divided up [if at all] for consideration' (Plott (1973, p. 1080)).

In an interesting paper, Kalai and Megiddo (1980) showed that if we define the notion of 'path independence' for randomised choice by the property

$$C_A(B \cup B^*) = C_A[C_A(B) \cup C_A(B^*)]$$

$$\text{for all disjoint subsets } B \text{ and } B^* \text{ of } D(A), \quad (V)$$

then if A contains at least three elements, no unique-valued 'path independent' choice function $C_A(B)$ can ever be a continuous function of the elements of B.

Since randomised choice functions have been proposed as a plausible social decision mechanism (e.g. Barberá and Sonnenschein (1978), Fishburn (1972), Intriligator (1973), Zeckhauser (1969)) and path independence has also been proposed as a normatively desirable condition on social choice (e.g. Arrow (1963, p. 120), Plott (1973)), this result might seem disturbing. However, if we view preferences as deterministically defined over lotteries rather than randomly

[1] The material in this section is based on Machina and Parks (1981).

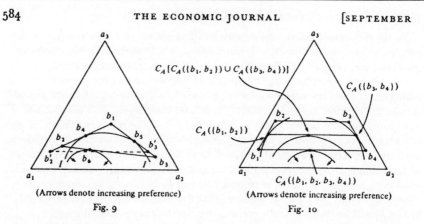

(Arrows denote increasing preference)   (Arrows denote increasing preference)

Fig. 9   Fig. 10

defined over pure alternatives it is straightforward to show (*a*) that condition (V) above is even more restrictive than supposed, in that no unique-valued 'path independent' choice function can be generated by a preference ranking which is *anywhere* continuous on $D(A)$, and (*b*) that even apart from this severe restrictiveness, condition (V) is not the most appropriate definition of the concept of 'path independence' in the context of stochastic choice.

To see the first point, note that if preferences were continuous in any open neighbourhood of $D(A)$ and $C_A(\cdot)$ were unique-valued, indifference curves in $D(A)$ must be strictly quasiconcave and not thick, as in Fig. 10. However, in this case we could always find a set $\{b_1, b_2, b_3, b_4\}$ for which $C_A(\{b_1, b_2, b_3, b_4\})$ did not equal $C_A[C_A(\{b_1, b_2\}) \cup C_A(\{b_3, b_4\})]$, which violates condition (V).

Fig. 10 also illustrates why condition (V) is not a very appealing definition of the notion of path independence in the context of randomised choice, since choosing first over the convex hull of the set $\{b_1, b_2\}$, then over the convex hull of $\{b_3, b_4\}$, and finally over the convex hull of $C_A(\{b_1, b_2\}) \cup C_A(\{b_3, b_4\})$ leaves almost all of the originally feasible choices, i.e. almost all of the convex hull of $\{b_1, b_2, b_3, b_4\}$ completely unconsidered.

From the figure it is also clear that the more appropriate notion of 'path independence' in this context is to restrict ourselves to the case where the convex hull of $B \cup B^*$ is equal to (as opposed to strictly greater than) the union of the convex hulls of B and B^*, or in other words, adopt the definition

$$C_A(B \cup B^*) = C_A[C_A(B) \cup C_A(B^*)] \quad \text{whenever the convex hull of}$$

$$B \cup B^* \text{ equals the union of the convex hulls of } B \text{ and } B^*. \quad (VI)$$

Of course, as in the deterministic case of Plott (1973), this reformulated notion of path independence will automatically be satisfied by any choice function generated by a transitive underlying preference ranking over lotteries.

V. ANALYSIS

Although it is clear that preferences which generate randomised choice in non-knife-edge cases must be nonlinear in the probabilities and hence not expected utility maximising, this does not mean that 'expected utility' analysis may not usefully be applied in such situations. This approach, termed 'generalised expected utility analysis', was developed in Machina (1982a, 1983), where it was shown that the 'linear' analysis of expected utility theory may be applied to the local and global analysis of nonlinear preferences over distributions in precisely the same manner in which multivariate calculus uses linear algebra to analyse the local and global properties of nonlinear functions. To adapt this approach to our current context (see the above papers for a more general and formal treatment), we note that an expected utility maximiser with a preference function $V(p_1, ..., p_n) \equiv \Sigma u_i p_i$ will prefer the distribution $P' = (p'_1, ..., p'_n)$ to the distribution $P = (p_1, ..., p_n)$ if and only if the sign of

$$V(P') - V(P) = \Sigma u_i [p'_i - p_i] \qquad (2)$$

is positive, i.e. if and only if the difference in the expectations of the von Neumann–Morgenstern index $\{u_i, ..., u_n\}$ with respect to the distributions P' and P is positive. In the case where the preference function $V(\cdot, ..., \cdot)$ is *not* expected utility maximising (i.e. is nonlinear) but is at least 'smooth' in the sense of being differentiable in the probabilities, we may take its first order Taylor expansion about P to obtain

$$V(P') - V(P) = \Sigma V_i(P)[p'_i - p_i] + o(|P' - P|), \qquad (3)$$

where $V_i(P) = dV(P)/dp_i$, $o(\cdot)$ is a function which is zero at zero and of higher order than its argument, and $|\cdot|$ is the Euclidian norm, so that we may represent $V(P') - V(P)$ as the sum of a first order or 'linear' term in $(P' - P)$ plus a higher order term, where in this case the linear term may be represented as the difference in the expectation of the index $\{V_1(P), ..., V_n(P)\}$ with respect to the distributions P' and P. In other words, in ranking alternative differential shifts from the distribution P, the individual acts *precisely as would an expected utility maximiser* with the von Neumann–Morgenstern utility index $\{u_i\}$ in equation (2) replaced by the 'local utility index' $\{V_i(P)\}$ evaluated at P.

In Machina (1982a, 1983) this approach was used to show how the 'expected utility' concepts of characterising risk aversion by concavity of the utility function and comparative risk aversion by the Arrow–Pratt ratio in fact possess immediate local and global generalisations to the case of non-expected utility maximising (i.e. nonlinear) preferences over probability distributions (for applications of this analysis, see Epstein (1984) and Machina (1982b, 1984)). We shall not repeat these results here, but rather show how this approach may also contribute to the analysis of stochastic choice functions.

Continuing to consider the case of $A = \{a_1, a_2, a_3\}$, we recall that the indifference curves of an expected utility maximiser will be parallel straight lines and note that the positive normal to these indifference curves (i.e. the normal in the direction of increasing preference) may point in one of six possible directions, corresponding to each of the six possible orderings of the alternatives a_1, a_2 and a_3 (for example, the positive normal in Fig. 11b is seen from Fig. 11a to correspond to the ordering $a_2 \succ a_3 \succ a_1$). By the linearity of preferences in this case we therefore know that the individual would always prefer shifting probability mass from one alternative to another provided the preference ordering indicated by the direction of the normal ranks the latter alternative as preferred to the former.

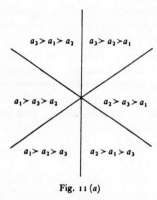

Fig. 11 (a)

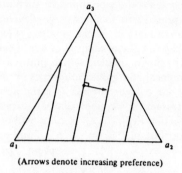

(Arrows denote increasing preference)

Fig. 11 (b)

In the non-expected utility case where the indifference curves are nonlinear but at least smooth, there will exist a linear (i.e. expected utility) approximation to preferences at each distribution in $D(A)$, as illustrated by the parallel straight lines tangent to the individual's indifference curve at P in Fig. 12. It is clear that, by analogy with the expected utility case of Fig. 11 b, the direction of the positive normal to the indifference curve at a distribution P will correspond to the ranking of the *local* utility indices $\{V_1(P), V_2(P), V_3(P)\}$, or in other words to the 'local ordering' of $\{a_1, a_2, a_3\}$, and that all *differential* shifts of probability mass from less to more preferred alternatives in this ordering will be preferred. By a path integration argument similar to those used in Machina (1982a), we can obtain the global result that all (small or large) shifts of probability mass from one alternative to another will always be preferred if and only if the latter alternative is preferred to the former in all of the local orderings (i.e. in the local ordering at every distribution P in the simplex). This, of course, is equivalent to the geometric condition that the positive normals to the indifference curves always lie in one of the directions which orders the latter alternative above the former. Thus, since the normals in Fig. 12 always indicate a ranking where a_2 is preferred to a_3 (either $a_2 \succ a_3 \succ a_1$, $a_2 \succ a_1 \succ a_3$, or $a_1 \succ a_2 \succ a_3$) so that $V_2(P) > V_3(P)$ for all P, it follows that large or small shifts of probability mass from a_3 to a_2 will always be preferred, so that neither the pure alternative a_3 nor a $p:(1-p)$ gamble over a_2 and a_3 will ever be assigned any positive probability in a choice situation which also includes a_2 as an alternative. Another implication of this condition, noted by a referee, is that provided the elements of the choice set are noncollinear, at most two of them will be chosen with positive probability, with the obvious extension to the case of $A = \{a_1, ..., a_n\}$. Additional results linking the properties of the normals to properties of the randomised choice function can similarly be derived.

As a final application, we turn back to the traditional notion of 'stochastic intransitivity' as defined in the literature (see Section III). Defining a situation where the local ordering of two alternatives reverses when we vary P as a 'local preference reversal', it is clear from Fig. 8 that a necessary condition for

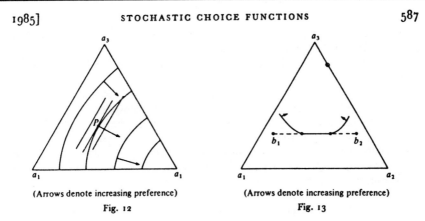

(Arrows denote increasing preference)   (Arrows denote increasing preference)

Fig. 12   Fig. 13

'stochastic intransitivity' in this sense is that there indeed be such a local preference reversal between at least one pair of the alternatives a_1, a_2, or a_3.[1]

VI. COMPARISON WITH OTHER MODELS

In this section we contrast the behavioural implications of the deterministic preferences model with those of the random preferences model and, although a full scale description and comparison would be beyond the scope of this paper, offer a brief overview of some other models of stochastic choice which have appeared in the literature.

The first point to note is that except for property (II) of Section II, the deterministic preferences model places no restrictions on choice probabilities over sets of pure alternatives unless additional restrictions are placed on the functional form of $V(\cdot, ..., \cdot)$. The reason for this is that each set of pure alternatives in A is associated with a different face (or subface) of the simplex $D(A)$, and with no assumptions on $V(\cdot, ..., \cdot)$, we can construct indifference hypersurfaces so as to achieve independently any set of optimal randomisation probabilities over these respective faces. The only restriction is that if the optimal point on a face lies on one of its subfaces this point must also be the optimal point on that subface, which is precisely condition (II) above.

Since it is clear that the random preferences model will also satisfy condition (II), in order to compare the two models it is necessary to extend the latter to the case of choice over lotteries. We adopt the standard approach (e.g. Becker *et al.* 1963*a*, *b*), Block and Marschak (1960), Luce and Suppes (1965)) of assuming that the individual has a stochastic von Neumann–Morgenstern utility index $\{\tilde{u}_i\}$ over the set of pure alternatives and in each choice situation acts so as to maximise the expectation of that utility index which happens to be realised, and shall refer to this extension of the random preferences model as the 'stochastic expected utility model' (the reason it would be inappropriate to consider the more general case of stochastic *nonlinear* preferences over lotteries is that this

---

[1] The locations of the tangencies, on each of the three sides of the triangle implies that at some point each pair of alternatives is ranked as indifferent in the local ranking, which by continuity of the local rankings implies that there must be a local preference reversal between at least one pair of them.

model would contain *both* the stochastic expected utility model and the deterministic preferences model as special cases).

Perhaps the most striking differences in the implications of the two models concern how the choice probabilities vary with the elements of the choice set. One example concerns condition (III) of Section II. Say for example that $C(\{a_1, a_2\}) = (\frac{1}{2}, \frac{1}{2})$, and consider the alternative set $\{a_1, b\}$ where $b = (\frac{1}{3}) a_1 + (\frac{2}{3}) a_2$. Under the deterministic preferences model it is clear that the individual will choose a_1 and b with respective probabilities $\frac{1}{4}$ and $\frac{3}{4}$. However, under the stochastic expected utility model the 50:50 probabilities assigned to $\{a_1, a_2\}$ imply that $\text{prob}(\tilde{u}_1 > \tilde{u}_2) = \text{prob}(\tilde{u}_2 > \tilde{u}_1) = \frac{1}{2}$.[1] Thus, when confronted with the choice set $\{a_1, b\}$, such an individual will choose a_1 half of the time (i.e. whenever $\tilde{u}_1 > \tilde{u}_2$) and b the other half of the time (whenever $\tilde{u}_2 > \tilde{u}_1$). Furthermore, it is clear that unlike the deterministic preferences model, in this situation the random preferences model would assign 50:50 choice probabilities to a_1 and the lottery $qa_1 + (1-q) a_2$ for *any* value of q, and it is straightforward to construct other examples where the choice probabilities are similarly invariant to changes in the components of the alternatives.

Besides these 'flats' in the choice function of a stochastic expected utility individual, another method of discriminating empirically between the two models involves discontinuities in the choice probabilities. From Fig. 7, it is clear that when a deterministic preferences individual is randomising over the alternatives a_2 and $b = (1-q) a_1 + qa_3$, a small increase in the value of q, even though it leads to a more preferred alternative, will lead to a continuous revision in the choice probabilities. However, if the von Neumann–Morgenstern utility indices $\{\tilde{u}_1, \tilde{u}_2, \tilde{u}_3\}$ of a stochastic expected utility maximiser were to take on the values $(3, 2, 1)$, $(1, 3, 2)$, and $(2, 1, 3)$ with equal probability, then his or her choice probabilities over the set $\{(1-q) a_1 + qa_3, a_2\}$ would jump discontinuously from $(\frac{2}{3}, \frac{1}{3})$ to $(\frac{1}{3}, \frac{2}{3})$ as q crossed $\frac{1}{2}$.

It might seem that since each one of the possible realised preference orderings is transitive, the stochastic expected utility model would allow us to avoid the phenomenon of 'stochastic intransitivity' (in the traditional' sense of the first paragraph of Section III). However, while such a phenomenon might not be as ubiquitous as we have seen it to be in the deterministic preferences model, it is nevertheless still perfectly possible in the stochastic expected utility model. In the stochastic expected utility example of the previous paragraph, for example, it is straightforward to show that we will have

$$C(\{a_1, a_2\}) = C(\{a_2, a_3\}) = C(\{a_3, a_1\}) = (\frac{2}{3}, \frac{1}{3}).[2]$$

The stochastic expected utility model will also violate our 'appropriate' notion of path independence, i.e. condition (VI) of Section IV. In the previous example, we see that the individual choosing over $\{a_1, a_2\}$ will end up consuming $a_1 \frac{2}{3}$ of the time and $a_2 \frac{1}{3}$ of the time. If we now strictly reduce the individual's

---

[1] In this example we assume that the distributions of $\tilde{u}_1$ and $\tilde{u}_2$ are continuous. This argument will also carry over to the discrete case under the standard assumption that when the utilities of the two alternatives are equal the individual chooses them with equal probability.

[2] See Quandt (1956, Sect. IV) for a more detailed example of this phenomenon as well as Blyth (1972) for additional examples of such 'probability paradoxes'.

opportunities by defining b as a 50:50 chance of a_1 and a_2 and offering the alternative set $\{a_1, b\}$, we see that the individual will choose these alternatives with respective probabilities $(\frac{2}{3}, \frac{1}{3})$, implying that he or she will now be electing to receive a_1 $\frac{2}{3}$ of the time and a_2 $\frac{1}{3}$ of the time *even though the original option of receiving a_1 $\frac{2}{3}$ of the time and a_2 $\frac{1}{3}$ of the time is still available* (by choosing a_1 and b with the respective probabilities $(\frac{1}{3}, \frac{2}{3})$). Of course, it is important to note that this implication is useful only as a positive test and not as a normative test of the two models, since this path independence violating behaviour is indeed the appropriate thing for such a (stochastic expected utility) individual to do.

Although the above examples offer several ways of discriminating between these two models, perhaps the most important empirical point to make regarding the stochastic expected utility model is that it follows immediately from a result of Becker *et al.* (1963*a*, eq. 29) that the evidence cited in Section I concerning violations of the assumption of parallel indifference curves (e.g. the evidence of Allais (1979), Hagen (1979), Kahneman and Tversky (1979), Karmarkar (1974), MacCrimmon and Larsson (1979), McCord and de Neufville (1983), Morrison (1967), Moskowitz (1974), Slovic and Tversky (1974) and Tversky (1975)) in fact violates the *stochastic* expected utility model as well.[1]

Finally, in addition to the explicit comparison with the deterministic preferences model provided here, the reader is referred to Barberá and Pattanaik (1983), Becker *et al.* (1963*a*), Block and Marschak (1960), Luce and Suppes (1965), Marschak (1960) and McClennan (1983) for additional specific implications of the random preferences model.

Besides the random preferences model, several other models of stochastic choice behaviour have appeared in the literature. The 'Luce' or 'strict utility' model implies the existence of a (nonstochastic) utility index defined over alternatives such that the choice probabilities over any set are proportional to the respective utility indices of its members (see Luce (1959, 1977) and the references cited there, as well as the remarks of Debreu (1960)). The 'Fechner' or 'strong utility' model of choice over pairs of alternatives posits a similar nonstochastic index but assumes that the choice probabilities are a deterministic function of the difference between the utility indices of the pair (see Luce (1958), Luce and Raiffa (1957, App. 1) and the references cited there, as well as the related analyses of Davidson and Marschak (1959), Debreu (1958), Fishburn (1976, 1978) and Tversky and Russo (1969)). Although neither was explicitly formulated as such, Becker *et al.* (1963*a*) have shown that under certain circumstances each is a special case of the random preferences model. Besides the above references, the reader is referred to the excellent surveys and theoretical analyses of these models presented in Becker *et al.* (1963*a*), Block and Marschak (1960), Fishburn (1977), Luce and Suppes (1965) and McFadden (1981), as well as the (mixed) experimental results of Becker *et al.* (1963*b*, *c*, 1964), Edgell *et al.* (1973), Morgan (1974), Rumelhart and Greeno (1971), and the references cited there.

A third class of stochastic choice models are those that generate choice or

---

[1] Specifically, Becker *et al.* showed that the random expected utility model implied that

$$C(\{b_1, b_2\}) = C(\{pb_1 + (1-p) b_3, pb_2 + (1-p) b_3\})$$

for all b_1, b_2, b_3 and $p \in (0, 1)$, which is violated by the evidence in the above studies.

preference rankings via a sequence of random steps. In the 'elimination by aspects' model of Tversky (1972*a*, *b*) (see also Sattath and Tversky (1976)), each alternative is assumed to possess a set of 'aspects', and the individual proceeds by randomly (though not necessarily equiprobably) considering each of the aspects and eliminating all alternatives which do not possess that aspect, proceeding in this manner until only a single alternative remains. Tversky (1972*b*) has shown that this model is both a generalisation of the Luce model as well as a special case of the random preferences model. In addition to the above references, the reader is referred to the generalisation of Corbin and Marley (1974) as well as the related analyses of Marley (1965, 1968).

However, the approach which bears the closest resemblance to the current model, at least in one respect, is the 'portfolio theory' model of Coombs (1969, 1975) (see also Coombs and Meyer (1969) and Coombs and Huang (1970*a*, *b*)). Strictly speaking, it is not actually a model of stochastic choice at all, rather, the individual is assumed to maximise a nonstochastic preference function over lotteries defined in terms of expected value and some (univariate) measure of 'risk', where the individual has a most preferred level of risk for any given level of expected value. While their model is therefore quite close to the standard 'mean–variance' approach of Markowitz (1959) and others, these authors have explicitly considered the case of an individual making a prespecified number of *repeated* choices out of a given set of lotteries, and have shown that the most preferred distribution of total wealth might involve choosing the various lotteries in certain proportions (which will typically depend on the number of pre-specified choices), so that it is 'a deterministic theory that implies a distribution of choices over alternatives' (Coombs and Huang (1970*a*, p. 29)). Thus, although this model implies deterministic choice in one-time choice situations and a deterministic proportion of choices in repeated choice situations, it is nevertheless similar to the present model in that in the latter case the distribution is at least obtained via an explicit maximisation.

VII. THE CASE OF QUASICONVEX PREFERENCES IN THE PROBABILITIES

As a final topic, we consider the implications of the present model when preferences are quasi*convex* in the probabilities, i.e. where the individual is (weakly or strictly) averse to randomisation over indifferent alternatives.

In addition to the instances of strictly quasiconvex preferences rankings observed by Coombs and Huang (1976), there is an additional, theoretical source of quasiconvex preferences over lotteries, namely the existence of delayed resolution or 'temporal' risk. Researchers such as Markowitz (1969, ch. 11), Mossin (1969), Dreze and Modigliani (1972), Spence and Zeckhauser (1972) and Kreps and Porteus (1979) have argued that most economically relevant risks are of this nature and have shown that in such cases the existence of intermediate decisions implies that even expected utility maximisers will possess nonlinear, and in fact quasiconvex, 'induced preferences' over such lotteries. Thus, while not as convenient to analyse as quasiconcave or expected utility preferences, quasiconvex preference rankings should probably not be treated as rare.

Dropping first the assumption of *strict* quasiconcavity, we note that the behavioural implications of 'flats' in indifference curves are straightforward – an individual with preferences as in Fig. 13 who faces the alternative set $\{b_1, b_2\}$ would be indifferent between any randomisation between $\frac{1}{3}:\frac{2}{3}$ and $\frac{2}{3}:\frac{1}{3}$. Thus if $(Q_T, 1 - Q_T)$ were the respective choice frequencies out of T trials, we would not expect Q_T necessarily to converge to any number, however, it will be the case that $\mathrm{prob}[Q_T \epsilon (\frac{1}{3} - \epsilon, \frac{2}{3} + \epsilon)]$ will converge to unity for any positive ϵ. Thus, if we reinterpret the randomised choice function $C(\cdot)$ as giving the range of possible asymptotic choice frequencies, $C(\cdot)$ will no longer necessarily be continuous or unique-valued, however, by analogy with standard consumer theory, it will be an upper semi-continuous correspondence (an extreme example of such preferences is of course the (nonstochastic) expected utility model).

The case of strict quasiconvexity is less straightforward. Here, as seen in Fig. 5, the individual is strictly averse to randomisation even over indifferent alternatives. While the distinction between the individual choosing both alternatives in repeated situations because of indifference or because of a strict preference for randomisation may seem of little operational significance, note that in the strictly quasiconvex case the slightest alteration in either gamble will send the choice probabilities to either zero or unity. Further implications of both quasiconvex as well as quasiconcave preferences over lotteries, including some game–theoretic implications, are discussed in Crawford (n.d.).

VIII. CONCLUSION

The present paper cannot claim to have come close to exhausting the theoretical or empirical aspects of the present model. On the theoretical side, there is clearly room for more work linking the properties of the local utility indices $\{V_i(P)\}$ (in particular, how they vary with P) with the properties of indifference curves in the simplex and the choice functions $C(\cdot)$ and $C_A(\cdot)$. In addition, it would seem appropriate to extend the analysis from the case of a finite alternative set $A = \{a_1, ..., a_n\}$ to the more general case of $A \subseteq R^N$ (e.g. choice over continuously divisible commodity bundles), which would allow for a corresponding 'deterministic preferences' theory of stochastic demand functions.[1]

On the empirical side, we know little about the nature of the indifference curves of individuals exhibiting randomised choice other than that they are at least somewhere quasiconcave, and the 'Slutsky equation' analogy in Section II suggests some intriguing corresponding empirical questions (e.g. are some types of alternatives 'stochastically inferior' or even 'stochastic Giffen goods'?). Finally, it would presumably be worthwhile examining the aggregation properties of this type of model, as well as which functional forms for $V(\cdot)$ lead to the standard 'logit' or 'probit' functional forms, to determine the role that econometric analysis of field data might play in its testing and estimation.

University of California, San Diego

Date of receipt of final typescript, December 1984

[1] See Quandt (1956, Sect. V) and Hildenbrand (1971) for corresponding analyses of the random preferences model and Mossin (1968) for a similar analysis of the Luce model.

REFERENCES

Alchian, A. A. (1953). 'The meaning of utility measurement.' *American Economic Review*, vol. 43, no. 1 (January), pp. 26–50.

Allais, M. (1979). 'The so-called Allais paradox and rational decisions under uncertainty.' In Allais and Hagen (1979).

—— and Hagen, O. (1979). *Expected Utility Hypotheses and the Allais Paradox*. Dordrecht, Holland: D. Reidel.

Arrow, K. J. (1963). *Social Choice and Individual Values*, 2nd ed. New York: John Wiley & Sons.

Barberá, S. and Pattanaik, P. K. (1983). 'Rationalizability of stochastic choices in terms of random orderings.' Manuscript, University of Birmingham.

—— and Sonnenschein, H. (1978). 'Preference aggregation with randomized social orderings.' *Journal of Economic Theory*, vol. 18, no. 2 (August), pp. 244–54.

Becker, G. M., DeGroot, M. H. and Marschak, J. (1963*a*). 'Stochastic models of choice behavior.' *Behavioral Science*, vol. 8, no. 1 (January), pp. 41–55.

—— —— and —— (1963*b*). 'An experimental study of some stochastic models of wagers.' *Behavioral Science*, vol. 8, no. 3 (July), pp. 199–202.

—— —— and —— (1963*c*). 'Probabilities of choices among very similar objects: an experiment to decide between two models.' *Behavioral Science*, vol. 8, no. 4 (October), pp. 306–11.

—— —— and —— (1964). 'Measuring utility by a single-response sequential method.' *Behavioral Science*, vol. 9, no. 3 (July), pp. 226–32.

Block, H. D. and Marschak, J. (1960). 'Random orderings and stochastic theories of response" In *Contributions to Probability and Statistics: Essays in Honor of Harold Hotelling* (ed. I. Olkin *et al.*). Stanford, Calif.: Stanford University Press, 1960. Reprinted in Marschak (1974, vol. 1).

Bock, R. and Jones, L. (1968). *The Measurement and Prediction of Judgement and Choice*. San Francisco: Holden Day.

Boskin, M. (1974). 'A conditional logit model of occupational choice.' *Journal of Political Economy*, vol. 82, no. 2, pt 1 (March/April), pp. 389–98.

Blyth, C. R. (1972). 'Some probability paradoxes in choice among random alternatives.' *Journal of the American Statistical Association*, vol. 67, no. 388 (June), pp. 366–73.

Chipman, J. (1960). 'Stochastic choice and subjective probability.' In *Decisions, Values and Groups*, vol. 1 (ed. D. Willner). New York: Pergamon Press.

Coelho, J. and Wilson, A. (1976). 'The optimum location and size of shopping centres.' *Regional Studies*, vol. 4, no. 4, pp. 413–21.

Coombs, C. H. (1958). 'On the use of inconsistency of preferences in psychological measurement.' *Journal of Experimental Psychology*, vol. 55, no. 1 (January), pp. 1–7.

—— (1969). 'Portfolio theory: a theory of risky decision making.' *La Décision*. Paris: Centre National de la Recherche Scientifique.

—— (1975). 'Portfolio theory and the measurement of risk.' In *Human Judgement and Decision Processes* (ed. M. Kaplan and S. Schwartz). New York: Academic Press.

—— and Huang, L. C. (1970*a*). 'Tests of a portfolio theory of risk preference.' *Journal of Experimental Psychology*, vol. 85, no. 1 (July), pp. 23–9.

—— and —— (1970*b*). 'Polynomial psychophysics of risk.' *Journal of Mathematical Psychology*, vol. 7, no. 2 (June), pp. 317–38.

—— and —— (1976). 'Tests of the betweenness property of expected utility.' *Journal of Mathematical Psychology*, vol. 13, no. 3 (June), pp. 323–37.

—— and Meyer, D. E. (1969). 'Risk-preference in coin-toss games.' *Journal of Mathematical Psychology*, vol. 6, no. 3 (October), pp. 514–27.

Corbin, R. and Marley, A. (1974). 'Random utility models with equality: an apparent, but not actual, generalization of random utility models.' *Journal of Mathematical Psychology*, vol. 11, no. 3 (August), pp. 274–93.

Crawford, V. (n.d.). 'Games and decisions without the independence axiom.' In preparation, University of California, San Diego.

Davidson, D. and Marschak, J. (1959). 'Experimental tests of a stochastic decision theory.' In *Measurement: Definitions and Theories* (ed. C. W. Churchman and P. Ratoosh). New York: Wiley. Reprinted in Marschak (1974, vol. 1).

Debreu, G. (1958). 'Stochastic choice and cardinal utility.' *Econometrica*, vol. 26, no. 3 (July), pp. 440–4.

—— (1960). 'Review of R. D. Luce, *Individual Choice Behavior*.' *American Economic Review*, vol. 50, no. 1 (March), pp. 186–8.

Dreze, J. and Modigliani, F. (1972). 'Consumption decisions under uncertainty.' *Journal of Economic Theory*, vol. 5, no. 3 (December), pp. 308–35.

Edgell, S. E., Geisler, W. S. and Zinnes, J. L. (1973). 'A note on a paper by Rumelhart and Greeno.' *Journal of Mathematical Psychology*, vol. 10, no. 1 (February), pp. 86–90.

Epstein, L. (1984). 'Decreasing risk aversion and mean-variance analysis.' Manuscript, University of Toronto.

Fishburn, P. (1972). 'Lotteries and social choices.' *Journal of Economic Theory*, vol. 5, no. 2 (October), pp. 189–207.

—— (1973). 'Binary choice probabilities: on the varieties of stochastic transitivity.' *Journal of Mathematical Psychology*, vol. 10, no. 4 (November), pp. 327–52.

—— (1976). 'Binary choice probabilities between gambles: interlocking expected utility models.' *Journal of Mathematical Psychology*, vol. 14, no. 2 (October), pp. 99–122.

—— (1977). 'Models of individual preference and choice.' *Synthese*, vol. 36, no. 3 (November), pp. 287–314.

—— (1978). 'A probabilistic expected utility model of binary choice.' *International Economic Review*, vol. 19, no. 3 (October), pp. 633–46.

Georgescu-Roegen, N. (1958). 'Threshold in choice and the theory of demand.' *Econometrica*, vol. 26, no. 1 (January), pp. 157–68.

—— (1969). 'The relation between binary and multiple choice probabilities: some comments and further results.' *Econometrica*, vol. 37, no. 4 (October), pp. 728–30.

Hagen, O. (1979). 'Towards a positive theory of preferences under risk.' In Allais and Hagen (1979)

Hausman, J. and Wise, D. (1978). 'A conditional probit model for qualitative choice: discrete decisions recognising interdependence and heterogeneous preferences.' *Econometrica*, vol. 46, no. 2 (March), pp. 403–26.

Hildenbrand, W. (1971). 'Random preferences and equilibrium analysis.' *Journal of Economic Theory*, vol. 3, no. 4 (December), pp. 414–29.

Intriligator, M. (1973). 'A probabilistic model of social choice.' *Review of Economic Studies*, vol. 40, no. 4 (October), pp. 553–60.

Kahneman, D. and Tversky, A. (1979). 'Prospect theory: an analysis of decision under risk.' *Econometrica*, vol. 47, no. 2 (March), pp. 263–91.

Kalai, E. and Megiddo, N. (1980). 'Path independent choices.' *Econometrica*, vol. 48, no. 3 (April), pp. 781–4.

Karmarkar, U. (1974). 'The effect of probabilities on the subjective evaluation of lotteries.' Sloan School of Business Working Paper No. 698–74, Massachusetts Institute of Technology.

Kohn, M., Manski, C. and Mundel, D. (1976). 'An empirical investigation of factors which influence college-going behavior.' *Annals of Economic and Social Measurement*, vol. 4, no. 4 (Fall), pp. 391–419.

Kreps, D. and Porteus, E. (1979). 'Temporal von Neumann–Morgenstern and induced preferences.' *Journal of Economic Theory*, vol. 20, no. 1 (February), pp. 81–109.

Leonardi, G. (1983). 'The use of random-utility theory in building location-allocation models.' In *Locational Analysis of Public Facilities* (ed. J.-F. Thisse and H. G. Zoller). Amsterdam: North-Holland.

Luce, R. D. (1958). 'A probabilistic theory of utility.' *Econometrica*, vol. 26, no. 2 (April), pp. 193–224.

—— (1959). *Individual Choice Behavior: A Theoretical Analysis*. New York: John Wiley.

—— (1977). 'The choice axiom after twenty years.' *Journal of Mathematical Psychology*, vol. 15, no. 3 (June), pp. 215–33.

—— and Raiffa, H. (1957). *Games and Decisions*. New York: John Wiley.

—— and Shipley, E. F. (1962). 'Preference probability between gambles as a step function of event probability.' *Journal of Experimental Psychology*, vol. 63, no. 1 (January), pp. 42–9.

—— and Suppes, P. (1965). 'Preferences, utility, and subjective probability.' In *Handbook of Mathematical Psychology*, vol. III (ed. R. D. Luce, R. Bush and E. Galanter). New York: Wiley.

MacCrimmon, K. and Larsson, S. (1979). 'Utility theory: axioms versus "paradoxes".' In Allais and Hagen (1979).

Machina, M. (1982a). '"Expected utility" analysis without the independence axiom.' *Econometrica*, vol. 50, no. 2 (March), pp. 277–323.

—— (1982b). 'A stronger characterization of declining risk aversion.' *Econometrica*, vol. 50, no. 4 (July), pp. 1069–79.

—— (1983). 'Generalized expected utility analysis and the nature of observed violations of the independence axiom.' In Stigum and Wenstøp (1983).

—— (1984). 'Temporal risk and the nature of induced preferences.' *Journal of Economic Theory*, vol. 33, no. 2 (August), pp. 199–231.

—— and Parks, R. (1981). 'On path independent randomized choice.' *Econometrica*, vol. 49, no. 5 (September), pp. 1345–7.

Markowitz, H. (1959). *Portfolio Selection: Efficient Diversification of Investments*. New Haven, Conn.: Yale University Press.

Marley, A. (1965). 'The relation between the discard and regularity conditions for choice probabilities.' *Journal of Mathematical Psychology*, vol. 2, no. 2 (July), pp. 242–53.

—— (1968). 'Some probabilistic models of simple choice and ranking.' *Journal of Mathematical Psychology*, vol. 5, no. 2 (June), pp. 311–32.

—— (1981). 'Joint independent random utility models where one of the choice structures satisfies the strict utility model.' *Journal of Mathematical Psychology*, vol. 23, no. 3 (June), pp. 257–72.

—— (1982). 'Random utility models with all choice probabilities expressible as "functions" of the binary choice probabilities.' *Mathematical Social Sciences*, vol. 3, no. 1 (February), pp. 39–56.

Marschak, J. (1955). 'Norms and habits of decision making under uncertainty.' In *Mathematical Models of Human Behavior – Proceedings of a Symposium*. Stamford, Conn.: Dunlap and Associates. Reprinted in Marschak (1974, vol. 1).

—— (1960). 'Binary-choice constraints and random utility indicators.' In *Mathematical Methods in the Social Sciences* (ed. K. J. Arrow *et al.*). Stanford, Calif.: Stanford University Press. Reprinted in Marschak (1974, vol. 1).

—— (1968). 'Decision making: economic aspects.' In *International Encyclopedia of the Social Sciences*, vol. 4 (ed. D. Sills). New York: Macmillan. Reprinted in Marschak (1974, vol. 1).

—— (1974). *Economic Information, Decision, and Prediction* (three volumes). Dordrecht, Holland: D. Reidel.

McCord, M. and de Neufville, R. (1983). 'Empirical demonstration that expected utility decision analysis is not operational.' In Stigum and Wenstøp (1983).

McClennan, A. (1983). 'Binary stochastic choice.' Manuscript, University of Minnesota.

McFadden, D. (1974). 'The measurement of urban travel demand.' *Journal of Public Economics*, vol. 3, no. 4 (November), pp. 303–28.

—— (1981). 'Econometric models of probabilistic choice.' In *Structural Analysis of Discrete Data* (ed. C. Manski and D. McFadden). Cambridge, Mass.: MIT Press.

Morgan, B. (1974). 'On Luce's choice axiom.' *Journal of Mathematical Psychology*, vol. 11, no. 2 (May), pp. 107–23.

Morrison, D. (1967). 'On the consistency of preferences in Allais' paradox.' *Behavioral Science*, vol. 12, no. 5 (September), pp. 373–83.

Moskowitz, H. (1974). 'Effects of problem representation and feedback on rational behavior in Allais and Morlat-type problems.' *Decision Sciences*, vol. 5, no. 2, pp. 225–42.

Mossin, A. (1968). 'Elements of a stochastic theory of consumption.' *Swedish Journal of Economics*, vol. 70, no. 4 (December), pp. 200–20.

Mossin, J. (1969). 'A note on uncertainty and preferences in a temporal context.' *American Economic Review*, vol. 59, no. 1 (March), pp. 172–4.

Mosteller, F. and Nogee, P. (1951). 'An experimental measurement of utility.' *Journal of Political Economy*, vol. 59, no. 5 (October), pp. 371–404.

Parks, R. P. (1976). 'Further results on path independence, quasitransitivity, and social choice.' *Public Choice*, vol. 26 (Summer), pp. 75–87.

Plott, C. R. (1973). 'Path independence, rationality, and social choice.' *Econometrica*, vol. 41, no. 6 (November), pp. 1075–91.

Quandt, R. (1956). 'A probabilistic theory of consumer behavior.' *Quarterly Journal of Economics*, vol. 70, no. 4 (November), pp. 507–36.

Rumelhart, D. and Greeno, J. (1971). 'Similarity between stimuli: an experimental test of the Luce and Restle choice models.' *Journal of Mathematical Psychology*, vol. 8, no. 3 (August), pp. 370–81.

Sattath, S. and Tversky, A. (1976). 'Unite and conquer: a multiplicative inequality for choice probabilities.' *Econometrica*, vol. 44, no. 1 (January), pp. 79–89.

Sen, A. (1970). *Collective Choice and Social Welfare*. San Francisco: Holden Day.

Slovic, P. and Tversky, A. (1974). 'Who accepts Savage's axiom?' *Behavioral Science*, vol. 19, no. 6 (November), pp. 368–73.

Spence, M. and Zeckhauser, R. (1972). 'The effect of the timing of consumption decisions and the resolution of lotteries on the choice of lotteries.' *Econometrica*, vol. 40, no. 2 (March), pp. 401–3.

Stigum, B. and Wenstøp, F. (eds) (1983). *Foundations of Utility and Risk Theory with Applications*. Dordrecht, Holland: D. Reidel.

Thurstone, L. (1927). 'A law of comparative judgement.' *Psychological Review*, vol. 34, no. 4 (July), pp. 273–86.

Tversky, A. (1972a). 'Elimination by aspects: a theory of choice.' *Psychological Review*, vol. 79, no. 4 (July), pp. 281–99.

—— (1972b). 'Choice by elimination.' *Journal of Mathematical Psychology*, vol. 9, no. 4 (November), pp. 341–67.

—— (1975). 'A critique of expected utility theory: descriptive and normative considerations.' *Erkenntnis*, vol. 9, pp. 163–73.

—— and Russo, J. E. (1969). 'Substitutability and similarity in binary choice.' *Journal of Mathematical Psychology*, vol. 6, no. 1 (February), pp. 1–12.

Zeckhauser, R. (1969). 'Majority rule with lotteries on alternatives.' *Quarterly Journal of Economics*, vol. 83, no. 4 (November), pp. 696–703.

An Axiomatic Characterization of Preferences under Uncertainty: Weakening the Independence Axiom*

EDDIE DEKEL

Harvard University, Cambridge, Massachusetts 02138

Received March 6, 1985; revised November 15, 1985

The independence axiom used to derive the expected utility representation of preferences over lotteries is replaced by requiring only convexity, in terms of probability mixtures, of indifference sets. Two axiomatic characterizations are proven, one for simple measures and the other continuous and for all probability measures. The representations are structurally similar to expected utility, and are unique up to a generalization of affine transformations. First-order stochastic dominance and risk aversion are discussed using a method which finds an expected utility approximation to these preferences without requiring differentiability of the preference functional. *Journal of Economic Literature* Classification Numbers: 022, 026. © 1986 Academic Press, Inc.

1. INTRODUCTION

This paper provides an implicit representation for an axiomatic characterization of preferences under uncertainty. Essentially only the controversial independence axiom is changed to the substantially weaker betweenness axiom (Chew [2]), keeping ordering, monotonicity, and continuity type axioms. The betweenness axiom only requires that indifference sets be convex, i.e., if an individual is indifferent between two lotteries, then any probability mixture of these two is equally good. This characterization is of interest for a number of reasons. The betweenness axiom is appealing from a normative viewpoint but is compatible with behavior which is not permitted in expected utility, such as the Allais paradox. It also provides a useful behavioral approach since it is the weakest form under which preferences are both quasiconcave and quasiconvex. Quasiconcavity is

---

* I would like to thank Adam Brandenburger, Jerry Green, Mark Machina, Andreu Mas-Colell, and Roger Myerson for many helpful discussions and comments. I am grateful to Chew Soo Hong for pointing out an error in an earlier version of this paper. Support from NSF Grant IST-8310118 is also gratefully acknowledged.

304

necessary for the proof of existence of a Nash equilibrium, since if preferences are strictly quasiconvex anywhere then a mixed strategy is worse than
one of the pure strategies used with positive probability in that mixed
strategy. Furthermore, quasiconcavity together with risk aversion are sufficient conditions for continuity of asset demands (while risk aversion alone
is not sufficient (Dekel [4])). Quasiconvexity on the other hand is
necessary and sufficient for dynamic consistency of choices under uncertainty (see Green [10]). In general, when temporal decisions are
made—given underlying expected utility preferences—the induced preferences will be quasiconvex (see Kreps and Porteus [11], and Machina [13]).
Thus, in order to guarantee the existence of a Nash equilibrium, dynamic
consistency, and continuous asset demands, we may want to impose
quasiconcavity and quasiconvexity of preferences, giving betweenness—without making the additional restrictions necessary for expected
utility.

The paper begins by presenting the axioms and characterization, discussing recent literature, and proving the representation. Two approaches are
taken, one with a weak continuity axiom provides a representation for all
simple probability measures (those whose support is a finite subset of the
outcome set), and the second imposes a stronger form of continuity which
suffices both to extend the results to the set of all distributions and also
implies that the functional representation is continuous. Then an example
is constructed to show that preferences may satisfy the axioms yet not have
any differentiable preference functional, even when preferences are over the
simplex (hence trivially continuous). This implies that the generalization of
local monotonicity and risk aversion to global conclusions as proven in
Machina [12] might not hold for all preferences of the type discussed here.
However, an alternative and intuitive extension of local properties is
demonstrated by examining the slopes of the indifference hyperplanes.

2. Axiomatic Characterization

There is an underlying compact metric space W which is the space of
outcomes of lotteries, representing, for example, monetary outcomes or
commodity bundles. Preferences, $\succsim$, are defined on the space of all
probability measures (D) or simple probability measures (D_0) on the Borel
field of W. Convex subsets of D and D_0 could also be dealt with; the details
are not presented. From these preferences define the induced strict
preference, $\succ$, and indifference, $\sim$, relations. Preferences over D and D_0
also induce preferences over W, where for any w, $w' \in W$, w is preferred to
w' if the measure assigning probability 1 to w is preferred to the measure
assigning probability 1 to w'. These measures will be denoted w, w' and this

preference relation is written as $\succ$ where no confusion should result, and the context will clarify whether $w \in W$ (the outcome) or $w \in D$ (the degenerate measure) is implied. For any w, w' in W the measure which assigns probability α to w and $1 - \alpha$ to w' is denoted $(\alpha, w; (1 - \alpha), w')$.

The following axioms will be used (where P, Q, R are measures in D and $\bar{w}$, **w**, w', and w'' are outcomes in W).

A1. (a) $\succ$ is a weak order ($\succsim$ is complete, $\succ$ is asymmetric, and both $\succ$ and $\sim$ are transitive).

(b) There exist best and worst elements in D_0 which are the sure outcomes denoted by $\bar{w}$ and **w**. (These are not necessarily unique.)

A2. Solvability: If $P \succ Q \succ R$, then there exists an $\alpha \in (0, 1)$ such that $\alpha P + (1 - \alpha) R \sim Q$.

A3. Monotonicity: If $w = $ **w** or $w = \bar{w}$ and $w' \succ w''$ (resp. $w' \sim w''$), then $(\alpha, w'; (1 - \alpha), w) \succ (\alpha, w''; (1 - \alpha), w)$ for every $\alpha \in (0, 1)$ (resp. $(\alpha, w'; (1 - \alpha), w) \sim (\alpha, w''; (1 - \alpha, w)$ for every $\alpha \in [0, 1]$).

A4. Betweenness: If $P \succ Q$ (resp. $P \sim Q$), then $P \succ \alpha P + (1 - \alpha) Q \succ Q$ for every $\alpha \in (0, 1)$ (resp. $P \sim \alpha P + (1 - \alpha) Q$ for every $\alpha \in [0, 1]$).

PROPOSITION 1. *Preferences over D_0 satisfy A1–A4 if and only if there exists a function $u(\cdot, \cdot)$: $W \times [0, 1] \to \mathbb{R}$ increasing in the preference ordering on W, and continuous in the second argument such that $P \succ Q$ (resp. $P \sim Q$) $\Leftrightarrow V[P] > V[Q]$ (resp. $V[P] = V[Q]$), where $V[F]$ is defined implicitly as the unique $v \in [0, 1]$ that solves*

$$\int u(w, v)\, dF(w) = vu(\bar{w}, v) + (1 - v)\, u(\mathbf{w}, v). \qquad (*)$$

Furthermore $u(w, v)$ is unique up to positive affine transformations which are continuous functions of v. A particular transformation exists setting $u(\mathbf{w}, v) = 0$ and $u(\bar{w}, v) = 1$ for every v, giving the simpler representation (similar to expected utility)

$$\int u(w, V[F])\, dF(w) = V[F]. \qquad (**)$$

The uniqueness characterization of $u(\cdot, \cdot)$ in Proposition 1 is a natural extension of the result in expected utility theory that the Bernoulli utility function is unique up to affine transformations to the framework developed in this paper. To clarify this generalization let $V[F]$ be uniquely defined from $u(\cdot, \cdot)$ by $(*)$ and let $\hat{V}[F]$ be uniquely defined by $(*)$, where $\hat{u}(\cdot, \cdot)$ replaces $u(\cdot, \cdot)$. I say that $u(\cdot, \cdot)$ is unique up to positive affine transformations which are continuous functions of v when $V[F]$ and $\hat{V}[F]$ represent the same preferences if and only if $\hat{u}(w, v) = a(v) u(w, v) + b(v)$ for some $a(v)$ positive continuous and $b(v)$ continuous.

Monotonicity (A3) is a weaker axiom than the standard first-order stochastic dominance axioms (cf. [2, Property 3]). However, as will be seen in Section 4, A1–A4 are sufficient to prove that the preferences are first order stochastic dominance preserving. In the appendix I provide a characterization which does not assume A3. This characterization is similar to Proposition 1, except that $u(w, v)$ is not necessarily increasing in w (see Sect. 3.A).

The characterization in Proposition 1 is an implicit expected utility representation, and the similarity of equation (**) to an expected utility calculation suggests that results from the theory of expected utility can be extended to the framework of this paper. A general result along these lines, based on Epstein's observation [15] that many properties of an optimal choice depend on the indifference curve through that choice and not on the whole indifference map, can be derived. Let U be the set of real valued functions on W, $\bar{U}$ a subset of U and $\bar{D}$ a subset of D. Consider any proposition in expected utility theory of the following form: if $u(\cdot) \in \bar{U}$ then the distribution $F \in D$ which maximizes $\int u(w) \, dF(w)$ is in $\bar{D}$. For example, if u is concave then F is not second order stochastically dominated, and if u also has positive third derivative then the optimal F isn't third order stochastically dominated. This proposition can be extended to implicit expected utility preferences as follows: if $u(\cdot, v) \in \bar{U}$ for every v then the F which maximizes (**) is in $\bar{D}$. This claim follows from corollary 1 in [15]. So if $u(\cdot, v)$ has negative second derivative and positive third derivative with respect to the first argument for every v, then the optimal F is not third order stochastically dominated.

Proposition 1 is related to recent axiomatic work in non-linear utility theory, in particular Chew [2], and Fishburn [6, 7, 8]. There are two distinct approaches in this research, depending on whether transitivity of preferences is assumed [2, 7] or not [6, 8]. It is common in both cases to use a type of symmetry axiom which imposes restrictions on how indifference sets relate to one another, while the betweenness axiom imposes convexity on each indifference set (see the indifference sets in the probability simplices in Fig. 1). Of course, the additional restriction provides stronger results, essentially guaranteeing the skew-symmetry of a bilinear function $\phi: D \times D \to \mathbb{R}$, which represents preferences by $\phi(p, q) > 0$ if and only if $p \succ q$ [6]. With transitivity $\phi(\cdot, \cdot)$ can be decomposed [7] and a weighted expected utility decomposition has been analyzed [2].

The results closest to my work are those of Chew [3] and Fishburn [7]. In [3] Chew has independently provided an implicit weighted utility characterization of preferences satisfying weak order, continuity and sub-

308   EDDIE DEKEL

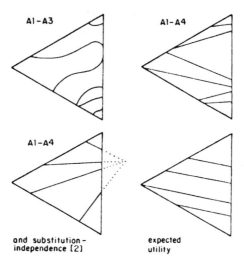

FIGURE 1

stitution axioms which, taken together, are equivalent to A1(a), A2 and A4. Preferences are represented by the solution of an implicit equation which has the form of a weighted utility function (cf. [2]) rather than the implicit expected utility structure in Proposition 1. Fishburn also does not require A1(b) and compactness of W, assuming instead countable boundedness (there exists a countable subset $\bar{D}$ of D such that for every $P \in D$ there is Q, $Q' \in \bar{D}$ with $Q \gtrsim P \gtrsim Q'$). Other than this his axioms are equivalent to A1, A2, and A4 (Continuity in [7] is A2 and Dominance is A4) giving [7, Theorem 1]: Countable boundedness, A1(a), A2, and A4 hold iff there exists a function $f: D \to R$ s.t. $P, Q \in D$, $P \succ Q$ iff $f(P) > f(Q)$ and $f(\alpha P + (1 - \alpha)Q)$ is continuous and increasing (constant) in α if $P \succ Q (P \sim Q)$.

The representation in this paper is a more refined functional form, closer in structure to expected utility, admits a simple analysis of risk aversion and dominance, and has a simple uniqueness characterization.

Proposition 1 bears a formal resemblance to Fishburn's implicit characterization of a certainty equivalent functional $m: D \to \mathbb{R}$ [8]. $m(\cdot)$ is defined from $\int \phi(x, m(P)) \, dP(x) = 0$, where ϕ is a skew symmetric, monotone function and W is an interval of the real line. However, the cancellation axiom in [8] is of the symmetry class, thus ϕ is skew symmetric while $u(\cdot, \cdot)$ may not be. Note that when W is restricted to a compact interval of $\mathbb{R}$, I can use Proposition 1 to provide a mean value representation. Given $u(w, v)$, normalized so that $u(\bar{w}, \cdot) = 1$, $u(\mathbf{w}, \cdot) = 0$, define $p(w)$ as the unique p which satisfies $w \sim (p, \bar{w}; (1 - p), \mathbf{w})$ and define $c(w, w') =$

$u(w, p(w')) - p(w')$. The certainty equivalent $M[F] \equiv \{w \in D \mid w \sim F\}$ satisfies $u(M[F], V[F]) = V[F]$ by (*) so we have $\int c(w, M[F]) \, dF(w) = \int \{u(w, V[F]) - V[F]\} \, dF(w) = 0$. This shows how a generalized mean value without symmetry axioms can be derived using the approach of this paper. (Note that $c(\cdot, \cdot)$ may or may not be skew symmetric depending on whether or not the cancellation axiom is satisfied.)

Before going through the constructive proof, it is worthwhile to consider the intuition of the representation. A4 implies that indifference sets are convex. Since thick indifference sets are ruled out (by A4), we are left with indifference sets as hyperplanes. Recall that preferences of the expected utility type have parallel hyperplanes for indifference sets. Imagine now that given the indifference hyperplane, say $H(v)$, through the lottery $(v, \bar{w}; (1 - v), \mathbf{w})$ we ignore all the other indifference sets and construct instead a collection of parallel hyperplanes. These can be taken to represent preferences satisfying the expected utility hypothesis and therefore there exists a function u_v (the subscript indicating the original hyperplane $H(v)$) which satisfies $\int u_v(\cdot) \, dF(\cdot) =$ the expected utility evaluation of F. If we set, as we are free to do with expected utility preferences, $u_v(\bar{w}) = 1$ and $u_v(\mathbf{w}) = 0$ then for $F = (v, \bar{w}; (1 - v)\mathbf{w})$ we have $u_v(\bar{w})v + u_v(\mathbf{w})(1 - v) = v$. Thus for any $F' \in H(v)$, which is an indifference set both for the original preferences and these artificial expected utility preferences, we know that $\int u_v(\cdot) \, dF'(\cdot) = v$. Doing this for indifference hyperplanes through points $(v, \bar{w}; (1 - v), \mathbf{w})$ for every $v \in (0, 1)$ we get a collection of functions $u_v(w)$ which is exactly $u(w, v)$. The intuition of examining the expected utility extension of a given indifference hyperplane lies behind most of the subsequent results. A number of the proofs are done using the characterization (**). This is not restrictive and is only a choice of normalization.

Proof of Proposition 1. I will choose a normalization and prove the existence of a representation such as (**), and the uniqueness result will extend this to representations of the form (*). For any (p, w) with $w \neq \mathbf{w}$, $w \neq \bar{w}$, and $p \in (0, 1)$ the lottery $(p, \bar{w}; (1 - p), \mathbf{w})$ is either: (i) strictly preferred to w; (ii) strictly worse than w, or (iii) indifferent to w. By solvability find (i) a $\beta \in (0, 1)$ s.t. $(\beta, \bar{w}; (1 - \beta), w) \sim (p, \bar{w}; (1 - p), \mathbf{w})$; or (ii) a $\gamma \in (0, 1)$ s.t. $(\gamma, \mathbf{w}; (1 - \gamma), w) \sim (p, \bar{w}; (1 - p), \mathbf{w})$. In case (i) set $u(w, p) = (p - \beta)/(1 - \beta)$, in case (ii) $u(w, p) = p/(1 - \gamma)$, and in case (iii) $u(w, p) = p$. For $w = \bar{w}$ set $u(\bar{w}, p) = 1$, $\forall p$; and for $w = \mathbf{w}$ set $u(\mathbf{w}, p) = 0$. Since $u(w, v)$ will be shown to be continuous on the open interval $(0, 1)$, extend the definition of $u(w, v)$ to the closed interval by continuity. Diagramatically (see Fig. 2) what has been done is: (a) construct the intersection of the indifference set through $(p, \bar{w}; (1 - p), \mathbf{w})$ with the 2-dimensional simplex with vertices $(\mathbf{w}, w, \bar{w})$; (b) find the line parallel to this intersection going through the w vertex; this is the dashed line in the diagram;

(c) define the point at which that parallel line meets the $(\mathbf{w}, \bar{w})$ edge of the simplex as $u(w, p)$. This is exactly the value that expected utility preferences parallel to the hyperplane through $(p, \bar{w}; (1 - p), \mathbf{w})$ would have assigned to the sure outcome w (if the values of $\bar{w}$ and $\mathbf{w}$ were normalized to 1 and 0).

The proof that (**) actually represents the preferences when using the constructed $u(\cdot, \cdot)$ will proceed in five steps:

   (1)   assigning a value to lotteries $(p, \bar{w}; (1 - p), \mathbf{w})$,

   (2)   considering lotteries on the edges of $(\mathbf{w}, w, \bar{w})$ simplices,

   (3)   considering other two-outcome lotteries,

   (4)   lotteries in a $(\mathbf{w}, w, \bar{w})$ simplex,

   (5)   general simple lotteries.

   (1)   Let $V[p, \bar{w}; (1 - p), \mathbf{w}] = p$, which obviously retains the preference ordering of such lotteries. Substituting in (**) gives $pu(\bar{w}, p) + (1 - p) u(\mathbf{w}, p) = p$ as required.

   (2)   Consider $(\beta, \mathbf{w}; (1 - \beta), w) \sim (p, \bar{w}; (1 - p), \mathbf{w})$. By the previous step it is sufficient to show that $(1 - \beta) u(w, p) + \beta u(\mathbf{w}, p) = p$. By construction $u(w, p) = p/(1 - \beta)$ so $(1 - \beta) p/(1 - \beta) + \beta \cdot 0 = p$ as desired. A similar proof holds for lotteries on the $(w, \bar{w})$ edge.

   (3)   This stage in the proof shows that for lotteries of the type $(\alpha, w'; (1 - \alpha), w'')$ with $w', w'' \in W$, if they are indifferent to, say $(p, \bar{w}; (1 - p), \mathbf{w})$, then $\alpha u(w', p) + (1 - \alpha) u(w'', p) = p$. Since the proof is a simple but lengthy geometric analysis it is provided in Appendix B.

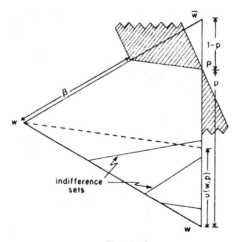

FIGURE 2

(4)   Given $Q = (\mathbf{q}, \mathbf{w}; q, w; \bar{q}, \bar{w}) \sim (p, \bar{w}; (1-p), \mathbf{w})$ with $\mathbf{q} + q + \bar{q} = 1$, examine Fig. 3 to see how Q is viewed as a mixture of the two lotteries on the edge of the simplex, which are indifferent to Q:

$$Q = \alpha(p, \bar{w}; (1-p), \mathbf{w}) + (1-\alpha)(t, \bar{w}; (1-t) w)$$

and

$$Q \sim (p, \bar{w}; (1-p), \mathbf{w}) \sim (t, \bar{w}; (1-t), w).$$

I need to show that $u(\mathbf{w}, p)\mathbf{q} + u(w, p)q + u(\bar{w}, p)\bar{q} = p$. By the decomposition of Q, $\mathbf{q} = \alpha(1-p)$, $q = (1-\alpha)(1-t)$, and $\bar{q} = \alpha p + (1-\alpha)t$. Thus, $u(\mathbf{w}, p)q + u(w, p)q + u(\bar{w}, p)\bar{q} = \alpha[(1-p)u(\mathbf{w}, p) + pu(\bar{w}, p)] + (1-\alpha)[(1-t)u(w, p) + tu(\bar{w}, p)] = \alpha p + (1-\alpha)p = p$, since the first square brackets equal p by step (1) and the latter square brackets equal p by step (2).

(5)   Given a simple measure P which assigns positive weights $p_1,..., p_n$ to $w_1,..., w_n$ and is indifferent to $(p_0, \bar{w}; (1-p_0), \mathbf{w})$ it is necessary to prove that $\sum_{i=1}^{n} p_i u(w_i, p_0) = p_0$. Consider the simplex $\Delta \subset D$ which includes all measures over $w_1,..., w_n$. The intersection of the indifference hyperplane through P with Δ (this intersection is denoted by H) is a compact convex subset of Δ, thus any point $h \in H$ can be written as a finite convex combination of extreme points of H. Therefore, $P = \sum_{i=1}^{m} \lambda_i Q_i$, where $Q_j \in H$ is a lottery assigning probability q_j to w' and $(1-q_j)$ to w'' (these are extreme points of H, where w', $w'' \in \Delta$). By step (3) above $\int u(w, p_0) dQ_j = p_0$. Therefore, $\int u(w, p_0) dP = \int u(w, p_0) d(\sum \lambda_j Q_j) = \sum \lambda_j \int u(w, p_0) dQ_j = \sum \lambda_j p_0 = p_0$. ∎

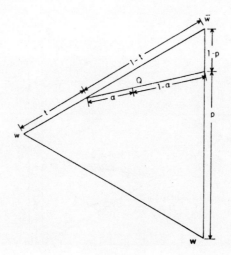

FIGURE 3

312   EDDIE DEKEL

I now present the continuous representation theorem (Proposition 2), since the proofs of the properties and uniqueness results are identical for both representations and are provided in Section 3. Proposition 1 showed that there is a characterization similar to expected utility even when the independence axiom is weakened, for all simple measures on a compact consequence space. In order to get an integral representation theorem for more general measures we need more assumptions (just as in expected utility theory—see Fishburn [5, Chap. 3]). Rather than attempt to provide equivalent theorems for all possible extension results, only one approach of special interest is considered. It allows for a continuous "local utility" function $u(w, v)$ by assuming that preferences are continuous. This is in the spirit of Grandmont [9], adapted to the more general approach of this paper.

A2′. Continuity: The sets $\{P \in D: P \succsim P^*\}$ and $\{P \in D: P^* \succsim P\}$ for all $P^* \in D$ are closed (in the topology of weak convergence).

PROPOSITION 2. *Preferences over D satisfy* A1(a), A2′, A3, A4 *if and only if there exists* $u(\cdot, \cdot)$: $W \times [0, 1] \to \mathbb{R}$ *increasing in the preference ordering of W, continuous in both its arguments, such that* $P \succ Q$ *(resp.* $P \sim Q$*)* $\Leftrightarrow V[P] > V[Q]$ *(resp.* $V[P] = V[Q]$*), where* $V[F]$ *is defined implicitly as the unique* $v \in [0, 1]$ *that solves*

$$\int u(w, v)\, dF(w) = vu(\bar{w}, v) + (1 - v)\, u(\mathbf{w}, v). \qquad (*)$$

Furthermore, $u(w, v)$ is unique up to positive affine transformations which are continuous functions of v.

Proof. A1(b) is implied by compactness of D and A2′. Parts (1)–(4) of the proof are as before and only part (5) changes as below, where $\int u(\cdot, p)\, dQ(\cdot)$ is a continuous linear function of $Q \in D$ since the constructed $u(w, p)$ is continuous by A2′.

(5′) Given a lottery $F(\cdot) \sim (p, \bar{w}; (1 - p)\mathbf{w})$ show that $\int u(w, p)\, dF(w) = p$.

By Choquet's theorem ([14], pp. 19, 20) there exists a probability measure, say v, on the indifference hyperplane H which includes $F(\cdot)$, s.t. v represents F and is supported by the extreme points of H. An extreme point, say x, of H is one which can be represented only by the measure which assigns 1 to all Borel sets of H which include x, zero elsewhere. In this case the extreme points are those on simplex edges, i.e., of the type $(p, w'; (1 - p), w'')$. Thus the continuous linear function $U(Q) \equiv \int u(\cdot, p)\, dQ(\cdot)$ for $Q \in D$ satisfies $U(F) = \int_H U(\cdot)\, dv$, where $v(H \backslash S) = 0$ and

S is the set of all distributions on the indifference hyperplane which are also on simplex edges. Since for each s in S, $U(s) = p$ (by (2) and (3) above); this shows that $U(F) = p$. ∎

3. Properties of the Characterization

A. $u(w, v)$ *Is Increasing in* w

The proof that $u(w, v)$ is increasing in w relies on monotonicity. For any $v \in [0, 1]$ and $w > w'$ consider $P \equiv (v, \bar{w}; (1-v), \mathbf{w})$. If $w > P > w'$ then $u(w, v) > v > u(w', v)$ *by the construction of* $u(\cdot, \cdot)$. If $w > w' > P$ then by A2 find β and β' such that $(\beta, w; (1-\beta), \mathbf{w}) \sim P$ and $(\beta', w'; (1-\beta'), \mathbf{w}) \sim P$. Now, $\beta' > \beta$, since otherwise $P \sim (\beta, w; (1-\beta), \mathbf{w}) > (\beta, w'; (1-\beta), \mathbf{w}) \gtrsim (\beta', w'; (1-\beta'), \mathbf{w}) \sim P$ (where the strict preference follows from A3 and the weak preference can be derived using A4). Thus $u(w, v) = v/\beta$ is greater than $u(w', v) = v/\beta'$. The proof for the case when $P > w > w'$ is similar.

B. *Uniqueness of* $u(w, v)$ *Up to Continuous Positive Affine Transformations*

The proof of uniqueness up to affine trasformations includes two steps. First I show that for any function $g(w, v)$ increasing in w, no preference functional other than those assigning value p to lotteries $F_p \equiv (p, \bar{w}; (1-p), \mathbf{w})$ are represented by (*). Consider these distributions F_p and a possible preferrence functional $H[F_p]$. By substituting into (*), $g(\bar{w}, H[F_p]) p + g(\mathbf{w}, H[F_p])(1-p) = g(\bar{w}, H[F_p]) H[F_p] + g(\mathbf{w}, H[F_p])(1 - H[F_p])$. This implies that $p = H[F_p]$, since $g(\bar{w}, H[F_p]) \neq g(\mathbf{w}, H[F_p])$ by assumption.

The next stage asks whether, for a fixed preference function $V[\cdot]$, there exist transformations of $u(\cdot, \cdot)$ for which $V[F]$ is the solution to (*). Obviously $V[F]$ still solves (*) if we take a positive continuous affine transformation of $u(\cdot, \cdot)$. These are now shown to be the only acceptable transformations. Assume $\int h(w, p) \, dF(w) = h(\mathbf{w}, p)(1-p) + h(\bar{w}, p) p$ and $\int u(w, p) \, dF(w) = p$ so that $h(\cdot, \cdot)$ correctly solves $V[F] = p$. Define $b(p) = h(\mathbf{w}, p)$, $a(p) = [h(\bar{w}, p) - h(\mathbf{w}, p)]$, and $g(w, p) = a(p) u(w, p) + b(p)$. I now show that $g(w, p) = h(w, p)$, so any solution $h(w, p)$ which solves (**) is a generalized affine transformation of $u(w, p)$. For any $F \sim (p, \bar{w}; (1-p), \mathbf{w})$, $\int g(w, p) \, dF(w) = \int [a(p) u(w, p) + b(p)] \, dF(w) = [h(\bar{w}, p) - h(\mathbf{w}, p)] \int u(w, p) \, dF(w) + h(\mathbf{w}, p) = [h(\bar{w}, p) - h(\mathbf{w}, p] p + h(\mathbf{w}, p) = \int h(w, p) \, dF(w)$. Now consider $F_w = (\beta, w; (1-\beta), \mathbf{w})$ or $F_w = (\gamma, w; (1-\gamma)\bar{w})$ such that $F_w \sim F$, one of which exists by solvability. Then either $h(w, p)\beta + h(\mathbf{w}, p)(1 - \beta) = g(w, p)\beta + g(\mathbf{w}, p)(1 - \beta)$ or $h(w, p)\gamma + h(\bar{w}, p)(1 - \gamma) = g(w, p)\gamma + g(\bar{w}, p)(1 - \gamma)$, but since by construction $h(\bar{w}, p) = g(\bar{w}, p)$ and $h(\mathbf{w}, p) = g(\mathbf{w}, p)$ this implies $h(w, p) = g(w, p)$.

C. *Uniqueness of the Implicit Solution*

Since $V[F]$ is defined implicitly, it is necessary to show that the solution to the implicit function is unique. This is done by considering the expected utility extension of these preferences. Assume the solution to (**) is not unique, i.e., in addition to the correct solution v, there exists $\hat{r} \in [0, 1]$, $\hat{v} \neq v$ such that $\int u(w, v)\, dF(w) = v$, $\int u(w, \hat{r})\, dF(w) = \hat{r}$, and $\int u(w, \hat{v})\, dF(w) = \hat{v}$, where $\hat{v}$ is the correct solution for $\hat{F}$. (Solutions where $\hat{v} \notin [0, 1]$ can be ignored since, even if they solve equation (**) they lie outside the range of permissible values — recall that $v \in [0, 1]$.) Holding $\hat{v}$ constant consider $\hat{u}(w) = u(w, \hat{v})$ as a Bernoulli utility function which defines expected utility preferences through $\hat{F}$ and $(\hat{v}, w; (1 - \hat{v}), \mathbf{w})$ but not through F (the latter by assumption that $\hat{v}$ is not the correct solution for F). However, by assumption also $\int \hat{u}(\cdot)\, d\hat{F}(\cdot) = \hat{r} = \int \hat{u}(\cdot)\, dF(\cdot)$, implying that F and $\hat{F}$ do lie in the same indifference hyperplane.

D. *For Every* $w \in W$, $u(w, v)$ *Is Continuous in* v *on the Open Interval* $(0, 1)$

First fix w not indifferent to $\bar{w}$, and consider the simplex with vertices $\mathbf{w}$, w, and $\bar{w}$. Let $B(w) = \{v \mid (v, \bar{w}; (1 - v), \mathbf{w}) \gtrsim w\}$ and note that $B(w)$ is a closed interval from some $\bar{v}$ to 1. The function $\beta(r)$ (which was used in the construction of $u(w, v)$) is defined as the solution of $(\beta, \bar{w}; (1 - \beta), w) \sim (v, \bar{w}; (1 - v), \mathbf{w})$ for any $v \in B(w)$. Clearly $\beta(\bar{v}) = 0$, $\beta(1) = 1$, and $\beta(\cdot)$ is an increasing function (otherwise two indifference lines in the simplex will cross). I now show that $\beta(\cdot)$ is continuous. If not then there exists $v_n \uparrow v$ with $\beta(v) > \lim \beta(v_n)$. So for $\hat{\beta}$ satisfying $\beta(v) > \hat{\beta} > \lim \beta(v_n)$ it is clear that $(v, \bar{w}; (1 - v), \mathbf{w}) \succ (\hat{\beta}, \bar{w}; (1 - \hat{\beta}), w) \succ (v_n, \bar{w}; (1 - v_n), \mathbf{w})$ for every n. Hence there exists a (unique) $\hat{v}$ such that $(\hat{\beta}, \bar{w}; (1 - \hat{\beta}), w) \sim (\hat{v}, \bar{w}; (1 - \hat{v}), \mathbf{w})$ and $\hat{v} \in (v_n, v)$ for every n. But this cannot be satisfied since $v_n \uparrow v$. So the assumption that $\beta(\cdot)$ is not continuous leads to a contradiction. Recall that by construction $u(w, v)$ is equal to $u(w, v) = (v - \beta(v))/(1 - \beta(v))$ for $v \in (\bar{r}, 1)$ and equal to $\bar{r}$ when $v = \bar{r}$, so $u(w, v)$ is continuous for $v \in [\bar{r}, 1)$. A similar proof shows that $u(w, v)$ is continuous for $v \in (0, \bar{v}]$. For $w \sim \bar{w}$ (resp. $w \sim \mathbf{w}$) monotonicity implies that $u(w, v) = u(\bar{w}, v) = 1$ (resp. $u(w, v) = u(\mathbf{w}, v) = 0$).

Continuity is necessary to avoid indifference sets which do not separate the simplex into two disconnected sets. For example, in the simplex with vertices $\mathbf{w}$, w and $\bar{w}$, if $u(w, v) = \frac{1}{4}$ for $v < \frac{1}{2}$ and $u(w, v) = \frac{1}{2}$ for $v \geq \frac{1}{2}$, there would be indifference lines which end inside of the simplex.

4. EXTENDING LOCAL PROPERTIES

This section relates this representation of preferences to Machina's [12] work on non-expected utility preferences. If all preferences satisfying

A1–A4 had a preference functional $U[F]$ which was everywhere Frechet differentiable, then Machina's extension results (that local monotonicity and risk aversion everywhere in D imply global monotonicity and risk aversion) would go through. It is shown below that this is not true, in particular it is shown how to construct a set of indifference lines in the simplex which have no differentiable preference functional representation. However, an alternative approach to extending local results is presented. Rather than examine the first-order approximation to the preference functional (which may not be smooth), if the indifference sets are smooth manifolds then the first order approximation to an indifference curve can be taken and extended to parallel hyperplanes, giving an expected utility approximation. For preferences considered in this paper such an extension is simple. It is shown that for $W \subset \mathbb{R}$ if $u(w, \cdot)$ is increasing in w, then P first order stochastically dominates Q, if and only if $V[P] > V[Q]$. (Note that the property shown in the previous section is that $u(w, v)$ is increasing in w with respect to the preference order on W. Any conclusion on stochastic dominance requires that this induced order is the natural order on the reals, i.e., $w > w'$ if and only if $w > w'$.) Furthermore it is proven that if $u(w, v)$ is concave in w for every v then the individual is averse to mean preserving increases in risk.

Let $f: [0, \frac{1}{2}] \to [0, a]$ for some $a \in (\frac{1}{2}, 1)$ be continuous, strictly increasing with derivative zero a.e. (see Billingsley [1, Ex. 31.1]). Define the indifference sets in a simplex as in Fig. 4. Let $V(\cdot)$ be a functional representing these preferences, so that $V(1, f(y)) = V(0, y)$ for $y \in [0, \frac{1}{2}]$, where the second argument indicates the distance along the simple edge from the lower vertex, and the first argument indicates which edge (1 for the lower sloped edge, and 0 for the vertical edge). If $V(\cdot)$ is differentiable then $V_2(0, y) = V_2(1, f(y)) f'(y)$ wherever $f(\cdot)$ is differentiable. Hence $V_2(0, y) = 0$ a.e., implying that $V(0, y)$ is constant for $y \in [0, \frac{1}{2}]$ (note that

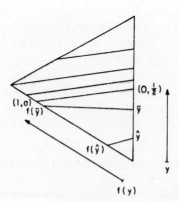

FIGURE 4

$V(0, \cdot)$ is absolutely continuous since it is everywhere differentiable and monotone). However, since these preferences are by assumption strictly increasing along the vertical edge of the simplex, we have a contradiction. Therefore V cannot be differentiable.

PROPERTY 1. *The following statements are equivalent:*

(a) *For any* P, $Q \in D$ *if* P *stochastically dominates* Q *then* P *is preferred to* Q.

(b) $u(w, v)$ *is increasing in* w.

Proof. Assume that P first order stochastically dominates Q, while p and q which solve $\int u(w, p) \, dP(w) = p$ and $\int u(w, q) \, dQ(w) = q$ satisfy $p < q$. The indifference hyperplane through Q separates D into two convex sets:

$$\mu \in U \Rightarrow \int u(w, q) \, d\mu(w) \geqslant \int u(w, q) \, dQ(w) = q$$

$$v \in L \Rightarrow \int u(w, q) \, dv(w) \leqslant \int u(w, q) \, dQ(w) = q.$$

Since P stochastically dominates Q, $P \in U$. If $p < q$ then $(p, \bar{w};$ $(1 - p), \mathbf{w}) \in L$, since $pu(\bar{w}, q) + (1 - p) u(\mathbf{w}, q) = p < q$. So the convex indifference surface through P and $(p, \bar{w}; (1 - p), \mathbf{w})$ lies both above and below the separating hyperplane, thus two indifference sets intersect, obviously leading to a contradiction. The converse is straightforward. ∎

PROPERTY 2. *Concavity of* $u(w, v)$ *in* w *implies risk aversion (in the sense that the individual is weakly averse to mean preserving increases in risk).*

Proof. Assume that $u(w, v)$ is concave in w for every v, and that G differs from F by a mean preserving increase in risk. Hence $\int u(w, v) \, d[G(w) - F(w)] < 0$. Let p and q solve $\int u(w, p) \, dF(w) = p$ and $\int u(w, q) \, dG(w) = q$. Then $q = \int u(w,q) \, d[F(w) + (G(w) - F(w))] < \int u(w, q) \, dF(w)$, so F lies above the indifference hyperplane through q. If $q > p$ then $(p, \bar{w}; (1 - p), \mathbf{w})$ lies below the indifference hyperplane through q. But by betweenness the indifference set which includes $F \sim (p, \bar{w};$ $(1 - p), \mathbf{w})$ is convex, intersecting the separating indifference hyperplane through q, leading to a contradiction; hence $q < p$. ∎

APPENDIX

A. *The Representation Theorem without Monotonicity*

PROPOSITION A.1. *Preferences over D_0 (resp. D) satisfy A1, A2, and A4 (resp. A1(a), A2', and A4) if and only if there exists $u(\cdot, \cdot)$: $W \times [0, 1] \to \mathbb{R}$, continuous in the second argument (resp. continuous in both arguments), such that $P > Q \Leftrightarrow V[P] > V[Q]$ and $P \sim Q \Leftrightarrow V[P] = V[Q]$, where $V[F]$ is defined implicitly as the unique $v \in [0, 1]$ that solves*

$$\int u(w, v)\, dF(w) = vu(\bar{w}, v) + (1 - v)\, u(\mathbf{w}, v). \tag{*}$$

Furthermore, $u(w, v)$ is unique up to positive affine transformations which are continuous in v.

The proof follows essentially the same lines as the proofs of Propositions 1 and 2. However, monotonicity of $u(w, v)$ in w cannot be proven without A3 (see Sect. 3A).

B. *Step 3 in Proving the Representation Theorem*

For any distribution $R = (0, w'; (1 - 0), w'')$ consider the 3-dimensional simplex with vertices $(\mathbf{w}, \bar{w}, w', w'')$, where without loss of generality assume $w'' > w'$. By A2 find p such that $R \sim (p, \bar{w}; (1 - p), \mathbf{w})$, where this last lottery is the point B in the 3-dimensional simplex.

Construct the indifference hyperplane through R (see Fig. 5). I want to show that $\theta u(w', p) + (1 - \theta)\, u(w'', p) = p$. Define C as the lottery $(\gamma, \mathbf{w};$

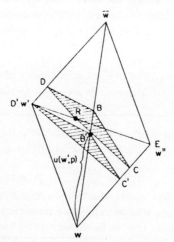

FIGURE 5

318   EDDIE DEKEL

$(1-\gamma)$, w'') $\sim B$, and E as the degenerate lottery w''. Thus, $CE = \gamma$ and $u(w'', p) = p/(1-\gamma)$ by case (ii) on p. 9, with w replaced by w''. Using trigonometric identities based on equilateral triangles with edges of length normalized to 1, using also the lengths γ, θ, and $1 - \theta$ it will be shown that $u(w', p) = ((\theta - \gamma)/\theta) \cdot p/(1-\gamma)$ giving the desired result. Take a parallel shift of the indifference plane through R, D, and C such that the new plane intersects w'. This new plane intersects the (w, w'') edge at point C' and the (w, $\bar{w}$) edge at B'. Recall that by definition $u(w', p)$ is the length of the segment between B' and w. Therefore $u(w', p)$ can be found from the length of RC in triangle REC, where $RE = \theta$, $CE = \gamma$ and $\sphericalangle REC = 60°$, giving $RC = (\theta^2 + \gamma^2 - \gamma\theta)^{1/2}$. Then $\cos \sphericalangle CRE = (2\gamma - \theta)/2(\theta^2 + \gamma^2 - \gamma\theta)^{1/2}$, and $\cos \sphericalangle CR = 2(\theta - \gamma)/2(\theta^2 + \gamma^2 - \gamma\theta)^{1/2}$. By examining the trapezoid with corners (w', R, C, C') one can see that length $CC' = (1 - \theta)\gamma/\theta$ and thus length $wC' = (\theta - \gamma)/\theta$. Looking now at the ($\bar{w}$, w, w'') simplex, $\sin \sphericalangle wBC = \sin 60(1-\gamma)/BC$ and $\sin \sphericalangle BCw = p(\sin 60)/BC$. Thus, since $u(w', p) = B'w = wC'(\sin BCw)/(\sin wBC)$, it has been shown that $u(w', p) = (\theta - \gamma) p/\theta(1-\gamma)$ as desired. ∎

REFERENCES

1. P. BILLINGSLEY, "Probability and Measure," Wiley, New York, 1979.
2. S. H. CHEW, A generalization of the quasi-linear mean with applications to the measurement of income inequality and decision theory resolving the Allais paradox, *Econometrica* 57 (1983), 1065–1092.
3. S. H. CHEW, "Weighted and Semi Weighted Utility Theories, *M*-Estimators and Non-Demand Revelation of Second Price Auctions for an Uncertain Auctioned Object," Mimeograph, Johns Hopkins University, June 1985.
4. E. DEKEL, Asset demands without the independence axiom, mimeograph, Harvard University, 1984.
5. P. C. FISHBURN, "The Foundations of Expected Utility," Reidel, Dordrecht, 1982.
6. P. C. FISHBURN, Nontransitive measurable utility, *J. Math. Psych.* 26 (1982), 31–67.
7. P. C. FISHBURN, Transitive measurable utility, *J. Econ. Theory* 31 (1983), 293–317.
8. P. C. FISHBURN, Implicit mean value and certainty equivalence, mimeograph, AT&T Bell Laboratories, 1984.
9. J. M. GRANDMONT, Continuity properties of a von Neumann–Morgenstern utility, *J. Econ. Theory* 4 (1972), 45–57.
10. J. GREEN, "Dynamic Consistency and Non-linear Utility Theory," H.I.E.R. Discussion Paper No. 1053, april 1984.
11. D. KREPS, AND E. L. PORTEUS, Temporal von Neumann–Morgenstern and induced preferences, *J. Econ. Theory* 20 (1979), 81–109.
12. M. J. MACHINA, "Expected utility" analysis without the independence axiom, *Econometrica* 50 (1982), 277–323.
13. M. J. MACHINA, Temporal risk and the nature of induced preferences, *J. Econ. Theory* 33 (1984), 199–231.
14. R. R. PHELPS, "Lectures on Choquet's Theorem," Van Nostrand, Princeton, N.J., 1966.
15. L. G. EPSTEIN, "Imlicitly Additive Utility and the Nature of Optimal Economic Growth," Mimeograph, University of Toronto, Jan. 1986.

[9]

Economics and Philosophy, 2, 1986. 23-53. Printed in the United States of America.

THE PARADOXES OF ALLAIS AND ELLSBERG

ISAAC LEVI
Columbia University

PRESCRIPTIVE AND DESCRIPTIVE ADEQUACY

In *The Enterprise of Knowledge* (Levi, 1980a), I proposed a general theory of rational choice which I intended as a characterization of a prescriptive theory of ideal rationality. A cardinal tenet of this theory is that assessments of expected value or expected utility in the Bayesian sense may not be representable by a numerical indicator or indeed induce an ordering of feasible options in a context of deliberation. My reasons for taking this position are related to my commitment to the inquiry-oriented approach to human knowledge and valuation favored by the American pragmatists, Charles Peirce and John Dewey. A feature of any acceptable view of inquiry ought to be that during an inquiry points under dispute ought to be kept in suspense pending resolution through inquiry. I contend that this sensible attitude ought to be applied to judgments of probability and value or utility. This consideration ought to lead to a form of indeterminacy in probability judgment, utility judgment and assessments of expected utility.

In Levi, 1980a, I did not examine the extent to which the proposals I made accommodate or fail to accommodate the results of empirical investigations exploring the rationality of probability judgment, utility judgment and decision making which have mushroomed in recent decades.

In this paper, I shall partially remedy this defect by examining the way the proposals under consideration address the so-called "paradoxes" of Allais and Ellsberg, the "preference reversal" phenomena uncovered by Grether and Plott, and responses to the Newcomb problem. I shall show that the theory of rational choice found in (Levi,

1980a) can give accounts of responses of experimental subjects in a systematic manner.

The relation between prescriptions regulating rational belief, rational preference and valuation, and rational decision making, on the one hand, and what empirical studies reveal about the judgments and conduct of deliberating agents, on the other, is a troubling one. It is always open to someone defending a conception of ideal rationality to insist that empirical evidence indicating deviation from the prescriptions favored by his or her recommendations proves only the urgency of educating stiff-necked humanity to think and deliberate better. Determined empiricists, by way of contrast, may contend that prescriptions which are systematically and pervasively violated by human agents are useless even in their capacity as norms and ought to be abandoned or tailored to the empirical data.

I think the truth lies somewhere between these extremes. It is quixotic to seek to construct a system of prescriptions for coherent and rational decision making which human agents can always and automatically obey. No matter how attractive a system of norms may be and no matter how easy it is relative to rival systems to make the computations requisite for its application, it is to be expected that situations will arise where the calculations needed for applying the system will be sufficiently complex to outstrip the capacity of human agents unaided by assorted technologies such as books, pencil and paper, computers, and mathematical approximations. And even with such crutches, problems may arise where the resources of the computational technology will be stretched beyond their limits. This general consideration ought to suggest that the extreme empiricist attitude is excessive in its demands. We ought to be prepared to settle for less than a system of norms which are applicable by human beings on all occasions and which they may be expected to apply with a high degree of regularity.

On the other hand, it would be a mistake for students of norms of ideal rationality to ignore data on actual decision making altogether. It is one thing to point out that human beings have limited computational capacity, limited memory, tend to ignore subtle differences, and are often distracted by emotional upset of one sort or another, and that such limitations can and do lead to deviations from ideal rationality. It is quite another to suppose that all deviations from some system of norms can be attributed to failures of these kinds. It will, indeed, often be difficult to decide whether failures of computational capacity or emotional upset adequately account for failures of rationality. Still on occasions where the agent insists on going his or her own way in spite of apparently successsful efforts having been made to explain to the agent that he or she is deviating from the norms of rationality under consideration, we should conclude that the agent, at any rate, refuses to subscribe to the norms. If such refusal is sufficiently widespread, the adequacy of the norms as universal ideals should be open to question. Rather than looking for methods to encourage delinquent individuals to change their ways, it may be worth asking whether the ideals of rationality ought to be modified to render the wayward agent respectable. Even here, theoretical arguments in favor of retaining the ideals should sometimes win the day; but the pressure to revise the ideals ought to be greater when deviations from them cannot be attributed to lack of memory, computational capacity, inattention, emotional instability and the like than when such explanations seem more readily available.

I acknowledge at the outset that the considerations I have mentioned, which excuse those who study prescriptive ideals of rationality from accommodating data concerning deviation from their norms, are vague. I cannot myself make them more precise. One may hope that as investigations of these matters in psychology, economics, and the other social sciences proceed, we may improve upon these vaguely specified excuses in a fruitful way. For the present, I shall remain content to assume that this vaguely drawn distinction can be made between deviations from norms of ideal rationality which call for behavior modification (rather than revision of the ideals) and deviations which call for modification of the norms themselves.

In addition to offering my own analysis of the various "paradoxes" of rational choice, I shall also consider other approaches to the puzzling phenomena noticed by Allais and Ellsberg. It will be argued that none of these approaches can accommodate all these cases in the way the scheme I shall present can and, moreover, that these proposals have unfortunate consequences which even their own advocates ought to find disquieting.

None of this proves that the proposals I favor are superior to their competitors. Efforts at proof are, I fear, futile. But if these proposals do better than rival schemes in accommodating the puzzling cases, that should surely be considered an argument in their favor.

Along the way, I shall point out one variant of the puzzles generated by Allais which the theory under examination cannot digest. My own suspicion is that this particular type of case is an example of a deviation from rationality which may be attributed to inattention and failure to calculate and, hence, ought to be counted as human failure rather than a failure of the ideals of rationality being proposed.

This claim will no doubt be disputed. Given the fact that the proposals offered here accommodate a much wider variety of the phenomena canvassed than the available alternatives (at least those with which I am familiar), the balance of reasons remains in their favor – pending the construction of a more comprehensive approach or a strong argument showing that my explanation of the indigestibility of the case in question is untenable on empirical or theoretical grounds.

Several features of the proposals advanced here may provoke strong dissent. I shall take note in passing of deviations from conditions on consistency of choice and from conceptions of the relation between choice and preference which lie at the core of much thinking in economics and decision theory. Where I suspect others will see vice, I often see virtue or, if not virtue, nothing vicious. Given the systematic generality of the theory, its range of applicability, and its attractiveness from the vantage point of the inquiry-oriented approach to knowledge and value I borrow from Peirce and Dewey, my dissent from orthodoxy on these matters represents something more than wilful perversity. My hope is that others whose antecedent commitments differ from mine will recognize the generality of the theory as sufficient grounds for giving it a serious hearing in spite of its alleged warts and blemishes.

RISK AND UNCERTAINTY

In chapter 2 of their justly celebrated *Games and Decisions*, R.D. Luce and H. Raiffa classify decision problems into three categories: decision making under certainty, under risk, and under uncertainty (p.15). Decision making under certainty obtains if "each action is known to lead invariably to a specific outcome." Risk obtains "if each action leads to one of a set of possible specific outcomes, each outcome occurring with a known probability," and uncertainty obtains "if either action or both has as its consequence a set of possible specific outcomes, but where the probabilities of these outcomes are completely unknown or are not even meaningful."

When Luce and Raiffa speak of known or unknown probabilities, they intend objective or statistical probabilities. According to their taxonomy, if an agent does not know the objective probabilities of outcomes of a given action but, nonetheless, assigns definite numerical probabilities to the possible outcomes of an action given that it is implemented, which represent his or her degrees of belief or confidence, the decision problem remains an instance of decision making under uncertainty. Thus, they discuss the proposal of L.J. Savage to rely on numerical personal probabilities in these circumstances under the rubric of decision making under uncertainty rather than under risk (p.300).

Luce and Raiffa themselves acknowledge that Savage's personalism "reduces the decision problem from one of uncertainty to one of risk" (p.300) confessing thereby to a certain confusion in their taxonomy. Savage favored maximizing expected utility where the expectations are calculated using the decision maker's personal or credal probabilities. In decision making under risk, as construed by Luce and Raiffa, one should also maximize expected utility. But here the expectation-determining probabilities are alleged to be objective, statistical probabilities or chances or, more accurately, the statistical probabilities the decision maker assumes, takes for granted, or is certain obtain. Luce and Raiffa cannot quite make up their mind as to whether to stick to this characterization or to regard decision making under risk as present whenever it is appropriate to maximize expected utility, regardless of the status of the expectation-determining probabilities.

When an agent is certain that a coin is fair and is about to be tossed and knows nothing else relevant to the outcome of the toss, his personal degree of belief that the coin will land heads on that occasion ought to be 0.5. That is the noncontroversial core of principles of direct inference (Levi, 1980a, ch.12). If offered a gamble where he wins S utiles on heads and wins nothing otherwise, the agent ought to be willing to pay up to 0.5S utiles for the privilege (assuming neither taste nor aversion for gambling). Thus, the probabilities used to compute expected value are equal to the statistical probabilities the agent is certain obtain; but we can with justice regard these expectations determining probabilities as personal or credal probabilities, as per Savage. The only difference is that these personal probabilities are grounded in knowledge or certain conviction in the truth of assertions about statistical probabilities.

Savage, of course, followed de Finetti in rejecting statistical probabilities (when not reduced to personal probabilities) as metaphysical moonshine, although he was more polite than de Finetti in saying so (Savage, 1954, p.54). According to Charles Peirce, however, it is metaphysically preposterous to suppose that worlds are as plentiful as blackberries. He is best understood as asserting that we are entitled to judgments of numerically definite credal probability usable in computing expected value only when these can be justified by direct inference from knowledge of statistical probabilities (Levi, 1980b). So are the modern founders of statistical theory, R.A. Fisher, J. Neyman, and E.S. Pearson. (See Fisher, 1959, pp. 31–35, and Pearson, 1962, p. 277.) In spite of their opposition to Bayesianism these authors agreed with Savage that if one is in a situation where there is a warrant for making numerically definite credal probability judgments, one should regard these probability judgments as appropriate to use in computing expected value or utility and, in assessing policy, should maximize expected utility relative to such credal probabilities.

To be sure, Savage differed from Fisher and Neyman with respect to the scope of applicability of the principle that expected utility to be maximized. But according to the reconstruction I have just briefly outlined, that scope coincided, for all of them, with the range of legitimate judgments of numerically definite credal probability. Their disagreements boiled down to differences in their views as to the conditions under which numerically definite credal probability judgments are legitimate. Peirce, Fisher, Neyman and Pearson thought these conditions are far more circumscribed than Savage did.

Luce and Raiffa restrict the category of decision making under risk to cases where numerically definite credal probabilities can be derived from knowledge of simple statistical hypotheses specifying definite objective probability distributions.

But since the very intelligibility of objective probability is a matter of controversy and, even among those who agree that it is intelligible, the conditions under which it is legitimate to make numerically definite credal probability judgments remain problematic, it does not seem sensible to characterize decision making under risk in a manner which makes the importance of the category stand or fall with the cogency of a controversial outlook in probabilistic epistemology.

For this reason, I have tended to think of decision making under risk as arising in any context where an agent legitimately assigns numerically definite credal probabilities to hypotheses about the outcomes of feasible options. In other words, decision making under risk is any context in which maximizing expected utility is the appropriate criterion for identifying admissible options.

On this view, decision making under uncertainty arises when it is illegitimate to make numerically definite credal probability judgments. On Savage's theory, it is always legitimate to make such judgments. There is no such thing as decision making under uncertainty.

More important, this way of presenting things emphasizes the correct insight of the Luce and Raiffa approach that when we are entitled to make numerically definite credal probability judgments legitimately, appraisals of feasible options with respect to expected utility or value ought to take precedence over alternative valuations of the feasible options. I do not pretend to have a proof of this claim. Any alleged proof will seem to the determined skeptic like question begging.

Fortunately there is a broad consensus among both Bayesians and many non-Bayesians that when it is legitimate for an agent to make numerically definite credal probability judgments about the outcomes of the options available to him, he should evaluate those options with respect to expected utility. The existence of this consensus indicates that defending the priority of considerations of expected utility is not a pivotal issue in much of the criticism of Bayesian decision theory.

The chief bone of contention between Bayesians and many anti-

Bayesians concerning both statistical theory and decision making has been the conditions under which it is legitimate for agents to assign numerically definite credal probabilities appropriate for computing expected utilities to hypotheses.

No doubt there is another anti-Bayesian tradition, primarily spawned by economists rather than statisticians, who have been skeptical of the explanatory power of the expected utility hypothesis even when probability judgments may be made with numerical definiteness. Thus, Alfred Marshall, who assumed that the marginal utility of income diminished as income increased, regarded willingness to accept even money bets as the product of "pleasure derived from the excitement of gambling – a pleasure likely to engender a restless, feverish character unsuited for steady work as well as for the higher and more solid pleasures of life" (Marshall, 1920, n.9, p.694). Marshall's view has often been understood as an acknowledgement that agents fail to maximize expected utility even when probabilities are numerically definite and, indeed, was so construed by M. Friedman and L.J. Savage (1948, pp.280–81). I have not myself understood why an agent who accepts even money bets because of a taste for gambling even though the marginal utility of income decreases fails to be an expected-utility maximizer;[1] but, for better or worse, interest in phenomena of risk aversion and risk attraction, among other things, has persuaded some authors that even when probabilities are numerically definite, expected utility may fail to be maximized.

In recent years, the injunction that expected utility be maximized has also been criticized by advocates of some form of causal decision theory which favors invoking a new version of the principle that expected causal utility be maximized (Gibbard and Harper, 1978).

In my judgment, those cases where people appear to be deviating from the injunction to maximize expected utility, and where it takes a heavy dose of Bayesian dogmatism to insist that the agents are behaving unreasonably, can by and large be understood as situations where either credal probability judgments which are numerically definite cannot legitimately be made, or utility assignments unique up to a positive affine transformation are inappropriate. It is indeterminacy, and not

---

1. Having either a taste or an aversion for gambling is consistent with being an expected-utility maximizer. However, there is then no well defined utility of money function. An extra dollar received for sure and an extra dollar received as the outcome of gambling increase utility by different amounts. Hence, strictly speaking the principle of diminishing marginal utility of money is meaningless. But if we restrict its scope to the utility of money received other than by gambling, perhaps its intelligibility can be saved. When so restricted, the principle of diminishing marginal utility of money and the expected utility principle may both be satisfied by someone who accepts even money odds on 50-50 gambles. Some theorists may prefer to retain the idea of a utility of money function and sacrifice the expected utility hypothesis.

risk aversion or causal structure, which is the salient feature of those contexts where the applicability of Bayesian decision theory breaks down.

When situations arise where the principle of maximizing expected utility cannot render a verdict as to what is optimal or admissible because numerically definite credal probability judgments cannot be acceptably made, we may look to some principle of decision making under uncertainty as a secondary criterion to use. This much I have adopted from the outlook of Luce and Raiffa as just amended.

However, the vision Luce and Raiffa offer us suggests that the difference between decision making under risk and under uncertainty is an all-or-nothing affair. Either we are entitled to assign numerically definite credal and expectation-determining probabilities and to maximize expected utility relative to them or we are not entitled to make any credal probability judgments at all.

The tendency to see matters in this way spills over to discussions of risk management and public policy where disputes arise as to whether one should take into account expected costs and benefits or whether one should fixate on worst possible cases. (For a discussion of this polarization in connection with assessing the safety of nuclear power plants, see Levi, 1980a, appendix.)

Abraham Wald is one of the many who insisted that if a probability distribution "existed," the option bearing maximum expected utility (or, since Wald spoke in terms of "risk," the option bearing minimum expected risk) is an "optimum" (Wald, 1950, p.16). On the other hand, if a probability distribution does not "exist" or "is unknown to the experimenter," Wald regarded "minimax solutions" recommending minimizing the maximum possible risk as "reasonable" (Wald, 1950, p.18).

Wald sought to determine the conditions which a decision problem should satisfy under which minimax solutions are also "Bayes solutions"–i.e., maximize utility or minimize expected risk relative to some definable probability distribution regardless of whether such a distribution "exists" (characterizes some stochastic process). (See especially Wald, 1950, ch.3.) This seems to suggest that, for Wald, under the "general conditions" he describes for decision making under uncertainty, all probability distributions over the given space of consequences or states are permissible to use in computing expected utility. That is to say, we should recognize as admissible with respect to expected utility any option which comes out best in expected utility relative to some such distribution. Rather than say that the agent makes no probability judgment, I prefer to say that the agent makes no numerically definite credal probability judgment. But he does make credal probability judgments. In decision making under uncertainty, he refuses to rule out any consistent distribution from being permissible to use in computing expectations, whereas in numerically definite probability judgments, he rules out all but one distribution.

When matters are put this way, the dichotomy between decision making under risk .and under uncertainty gives way to a more finely grained set of distinctions. There can be intermediate credal states between numerically definite credal probability judgments and the maximally indeterminate ones that characterize decision making under uncertainty. A credal state for propositions belonging to some suitably specified space of possibilities may be represented by a single credal probability distribution (the uniquely permissible one), the set of all distributions over that space (the maximally indeterminate credal state) or by any convex subset of that maximally indeterminate set (Levi, 1980a, chapters 4.1,5 and 9).

IMPRECISION AND INDETERMINACY: THE ELLSBERG PROBLEM

There is a widespread tendency to confuse indeterminate credal probability judgments of the sort I am describing with forms of self-ignorance – i.e., the ignorance of one's own numerically definite credal probability judgments. This tendency is especially prevalent among Bayesians, who tend to the view that at least ideally rational agents ought always to have numerically definite credal states. In the face of the apparent fact that perfectly sensible agents refuse to make numerically definite judgments, such strict Bayesians tend to see the lack of numerical definiteness as the product of a measurement problem. They are prepared to acknowledge such indefiniteness in much the same spirit that they will acknowledge that length may be measured by a certain measuring stick to the nearest thirty-sixth of an inch. To report that the width of a table as measured by such a stick is three feet ought more carefully to be a report that the width is three feet plus or minus one seventy-second of an inch. In this way, we express our ignorance as to the true unknown precise value of the width if we think there be such. So too, indefiniteness in credal probability is supposed to represent our ignorance as to our unknown strictly Bayesian credal state.

According to the view I am proposing, credal states may be genuinely indeterminate. An agent who is fully in touch with his views may insist that he regards all distributions in a given set as permissible to use in computing expectations rather than that he is ignorant as to which of the distributions in a given set is the uniquely permissible one to use in computing expectations. The failure to single out a unique distribution cannot be remedied by more precise techniques of measurement.

The difference to which I am pointing may be approached from a

somewhat different angle – namely, the ramifications of indeterminacy
for decision making.

Consider the following problem posed by Daniel Ellsberg (Ellsberg,
1961). We are given an urn containing 30 red balls and 60 balls which
are white or blue in unknown proportions. The decision maker is
offered the following hypothetical choice with the reward contingent
on the color of a ball drawn from the urn.

	Red	White	Blue
A	100	0	0
B	0	100	0

Here the decision maker knows that the objective probability of
obtaining a red ball is ⅓ and that the objective probability of obtaining a
white is anywhere from 0 to ⅔ in increments of sixtieths. If the agent's
credal state concerning the hypotheses as to the precise contents of the
urn (there are 61 hypotheses as to the precise proportions of white
balls in the urn) is maximally indeterminate, there are some permissible distributions according to which the expected value of choosing A
is greater than that of choosing B and some according to which the
ranking is the other way around. (There is, of course, one according to
which they are equal in value.) Both options are admissible with respect to expected utility (**E-admissible**). We have a decision problem
under uncertainty and may invoke a secondary criterion.

The criterion I favor using is a maximin criterion or rather a lexicographical maximin. If one speaks of losses rather than benefits or utilities, the criterion is a minimax or lexicographical minimax criterion.

Ellsberg had alleged that using maximin would be of no help in
this particular example. The "worst possible case" is 0 for both options
A and B and the second worse case is 100. Maximin cannot decide – or
so it seems.

But there are many ways to compute worst possible cases. The
method favored by Abraham Wald considered a case to be distinguished according to which hypothesis concerning the precise contents
of the urn is true. In this sense, there are 61 possible cases in the
Ellsberg problem corresponding to each of the 61 hypotheses specifying how many of the sixty non-red balls are white and how many are
blue. One can compute, for each such case, the expected value of an
option conditional on the truth of that case and then assess security
levels. (Indeed, when the payoffs are represented as losses, these expectations are precisely what Wald called "risks" (Wald, 1950, p.12).
No matter which of these 61 hypotheses is true, the expected value of
A is 100/3. This value and not 0 is now regarded as the security level
for A because it is the conditional expected utility payoff for each of the

61 cases and hence is the worst possible payoff among these 61 cases. Turning to option B, the conditional expected utility payoff when 60 balls are white and none blue is 200/3. The payoff declines as the number of white balls is reduced and becomes 0 when all 60 balls are blue. The security level for B is therefore 0. Whereas the way we calculated security levels originally assigned equal 0 security levels to both A and B, according to the Wald approach the security level associated with option A is 100/3 and the security level associated with option B is 0. Option A becomes uniquely admissible.

I do not think there is any way of deciding which method of determining security levels is preferable or rational. That question ought to be left up to the decision maker and is to be regarded as a value commitment on the agent's part. Still it is rationally acceptable for a decision maker to follow Wald's method and to choose A because it is the maximin solution. Although Ellsberg was right in observing that the first way to use maximin cannot decide between A and B, Wald's way of doing so does. Hence, if we find a decision maker who chooses A over B, and if we assume that his credal probability judgments are indeterminate in the manner indicated, we may infer, according to the model I am proposing, that he is fixing security levels after the fashion of Wald. Someone else who regards both A and B as admissible should be judged to be assessing security in another way – perhaps as Ellsberg suggests. Neither agent is irrational. They differ in their concern for security.

But now consider the following decision problem:

	Red	White	Blue
C	100	0	100
D	0	100	100

As before, both options are E-admissible. If we follow Wald's method, the security level for C is 100/3 as before; but the security level for D is now 200/3 so that D should be chosen. Again one does not have to fix security levels in this fashion. One could fix them so that both options remain admissible; but it is rationally acceptable to regard D as uniquely admissible. And, indeed, the agent who regards A as uniquely admissible in the first problem should regard D as uniquely admissible in the second problem.

Now the strict Bayesian thinks of the lack of definiteness in the representation of the agent's credal state as due to imprecision in measurement, and insists that the ideally rational agent is committed or ought to be committed to a uniquely permissible distribution even if the agent cannot tell precisely what that distribution is. Such a strict Bayesian will insist that the choice of A over B and D over C is rationally untenable. It is acceptable to regard A as uniquely admissible in the first problem and C in the second or B uniquely admissible in the first and D in the second. And one might regard both as admissible in each problem. But what the Wald theory recommends here is utterly forbidden. It violates the "sure-thing principle."

The sure-thing principle states that if an agent were to consider two distinct decision problems which had identical pay-off structures, except that relative to one column in the first all payoffs were given the value *a*, whereas in the corresponding column in the second problem all payoffs were given the value *b*, then, if A is strictly preferred to B in the first, it is in the second as well (Savage, 1954, pp.20–22).

The strict Bayesian thinks that the recommendations I have allowed to be reasonable violate the sure-thing principle; for the strict Bayesian supposes that the decision maker is committed to behaving as if he had a numerically definite credal state whether he can tell what it is or not, and hence that the agent is committed to ranking the options in a manner which yields a weak ordering.

But on the view I favor, considerations of expected utility fail to yield an ordering of the options. The options are noncomparable with respect to expected utility. Since A is not preferred to B in the first problem (nor, for that matter, is it indifferent to B), there is no violation of the sure-thing principle.

What is true is that the use of the Wald criterion leads to choosing an option which is best according to one subclass of permissible distributions in problem 1 (those for which the probability of blue is no less than ⅓) and another subclass in problem 2 (those for which it is less than ⅓).

The strict Bayesian thinks this is incoherent or wishful thinking. One cannot modify one's credal probability judgment simply because the payoff matrix has changed.

But on the view I favor, there has been no modification of the credal state. It is indeterminate in both problems and in the same way. The same set of distributions is permissible to use in computing expectations. And in both problems considerations of expected value fail to render a verdict. The use of the Wald version of the maximin criterion is not designed to single out a more determinate credal state relative to which one will maximize expected utility. Rather considerations of expected utility having failed to render a verdict, considerations of security are brought into play. To do this is not to endorse a pessimistic or paranoid credal state in lieu of the one with which one initially began. It is not to modify the credal state from its pristine indeterminacy at all.[2]

2. Theorem 3.9 of Wald, 1950 asserts that under certain conditions any minimax solution of a decision problem is a Bayes solution relative to a "least favorable" probability distribution. This rhetoric has tended to foster the view that advocacy of minimax or maximin is a species of pessimism or paranoia.

Care must be taken in understanding the force of this account of the Ellsberg problem. It is supposed here that the agent is offered the first choice in a context where he takes for granted that he is not being offered the second and is offered the second in a context where he takes for granted that he is not being offered the first. Of course, no real-life decision maker with a minimal amount of consciousness and memory can be placed in both contexts. The responses we have been considering are hypothetical reactions to hypothetical scenarios.

If the decision maker were offered both pairs of options simultaneously or in some temporal order and recognized this to be the case, he should address both problems together. He may then be taken to have four options: choose A and C, A and D, B and C and B and D. Each of the four options turns out to be E-admissible. But only the joint choices of A and D and B and C are admissible when considerations of security are brought into play. Yet, when the two problems are considered separately, one cannot regard B as uniquely admissible in the first problem and C as uniquely admissible in the second.

Suppose one is offered a 50-50 mixture of A and D and a 50-50 mixture of B and C. The two "compound" lotteries reduce to the same simple lottery and, hence, should be regarded as indifferent to one another. This allegedly violates an "independence" postulate because A is preferred to B and D to C yet a mixture of A and D is indifferent to a mixture of B and C (Raiffa, 1961, p.694). Once more the charge is false. There is no such violation; for A is not preferred to B and D is not preferred to C. There is no *preference* one way or the other in either case.

Thus, the account I have given using the Wald version of the maximin principle as a secondary criterion of admissibility when considerations of expected utility fail to render a verdict manage to yield the verdicts in the Ellsberg problem which Ellsberg reports to be prevalent among those who address it. At the same time, counter to the arguments of staunch defenders of the Bayesian faith, like Raiffa, endorsement of these recommendations does not lead to absurd recommendations when we confront a choice between a mixture of A and D and a mixture of B and C. There is no violation of the sure-thing principle. The so-called independence postulate remains intact. Every admissible option is a Bayes solution according to the credal state.

Recently Peter Gärdenfors and Nils-Eric Sahlin have suggested another approach to the Ellsberg problem (Gärdenfors and Sahlin, 1982, pp. 374–377; Levi, 1982b, pp.401–408). They too begin with a set of probability distributions to represent the state of probability judgment. They compute for each option its lowest expectation value and recommend maximizing the lowest expectation value. Elsewhere in the statistical literature this has been called "gamma minimax." (See

36   ISAAC LEVI

Berger, 1980, pp.134–135, who credits Robbins, 1964 with the first explicit formulation of the idea.)

Gamma minimax seems to me to be objectionable for two reasons:

(1) It fails to require every admissible option to be a Bayes solution – i.e., to be best in expected utility according to some permissible probability. This objection may not appear decisive to those who
mean to challenge the primacy of E-admissibility as a test of admissibility. But as noted earlier, many critics of strict Bayesian doctrine do not
appear to object to the primacy of E-admissibility. They ask rather
where the numbers come from. Wald, who was no Bayesian, was quite
anxious to identify the conditions under which minimax solutions are
Bayes solutions. The objection is serious even if it is not decisive.

(2) One of the advantages of insisting on the primacy of E-admissibility is that it provides insurance against recognizing as admissible an
option which is dominated by another option in the admissible set.
Gamma minimax lacks the virtue. Teddy Seidenfeld has constructed an
argument which shows that gamma minimaxers can be inveigled into
choosing options dominated by other feasible options.[3]

The failure of gamma minimix to yield a Bayes' solution does not
emerge in the Ellsberg problem. It can be seen in the following
example:

Suppose an urn contains black and white balls in an unknown

3. Imagine a shell game with two shells, the left and the right. According to option L, the
   agent wins 100 dollars if there is a peanut under the left shell and wins $10 if the peanut is
   under the right shell. According to option R, the agent wins $100 if the peanut is under
   the right shell and $10 if the peanut is under the left shell. The largest price a gamma
   minimaxer would be prepared to pay for either gamble is $10. Consider now a lottery
   where there is a 50-50 chance of receiving gamble L or gamble R. The gamma minimax
   value in utiles for this gamble is equal to the expected utility of a 50-50 gamble for $100 or
   $10 and this will have a dollar gamble greater than $10. Let this value be $25. Consider
   now a choice between the following pair of lotteries: According to lottery I, if a fair coin
   lands heads up, the agent has a choice between gamble L and $9 and if the coin lands tails
   up, the agent has a choice between R and $9. Because, according to gamma minimax, L is
   preferred to $9 and R to $9, lottery I is equivalent to the 50-50 chance of receiving L or R
   and this has a value of $25. According to lottery II, if the coin lands heads up, the agent
   has a choice between L and $11 and if the coin lands tails up, he has a choice between R
   and $11. If lottery II is taken, the agent will choose the money according to gamma
   minimax regardless of what happens. Hence, the gamble is worth $11. Hence, the
   gamma minimizer will choose lottery I over lottery II. Consider, however, that if the coin
   lands head up, the dollar value of I is $10 while that of II is $11. The same obtains if the
   coin lands tails up. Option II dominates option I while gamma minimaxers such as
   Gärdenfors and Sahlin favor option I. According to the proposal I made, by way of
   contrast, both options are as admissible in a choice between $10 and gamble L. But that
   does not mean that they are of equal value or utility. The same holds for a choice between
   R and $10. Indeed, in a choice between L and $11 for sure, both options are E-admissible.
   The same holds for a choice between R and $11. Hence, option II does not dominate
   option I. It is possible to recommend I without recommending a dominated option.

proportion ranging from 40% black to 60% black. Three decision problems are then considered:

Case 1. The agent is offered a gamble where the agent wins 55 utiles if a black is drawn and loses 45 utiles if a white is drawn. He can either accept the gamble or refuse it and neither win or lose.

Case 2. The agent is offered a gamble where the agent wins 55 utiles if a white is drawn and loses 46 utiles if a black is drawn. He can either accept the gamble or refuse it and neither win nor lose.

Case 3. The agent can accept the gamble from case 1, the gamble from case 2 or refuse both. He must choose one and only one of these options.

In case 1, both options are E-admissible, but refusing to gamble brings greater security so that refusal is uniquely admissible.

In case 2, both options are E-admissible, but refusal brings greater security and is uniquely admissible.

In case 3, refusal is not E-admissible, but the other two options are. Since of the two gambles, the security level in case 1 is higher, that option is uniquely admissible.

According to the Gärdenfors-Sahlin approach, refusal is uniquely admissible in all three cases. But in case 3, refusal is not a Bayes solution.

It is, to be sure, possible to object to the criteria of admissibility advanced here as rival to gamma minimax that the choices in the three cases which I have just described violate property α (Sen,1970, p.17) otherwise known as independence of irrelevant alternatives in one of its many senses (Levi, 1974, 1980a).

(Let T be a set of options containing x and let S be a subset of T also containing x. A criterion of admissibility defines a "choice function" over subsets of some large set U of options (which we take to include the sets T and S) which takes as values sets of feasible options. Such a choice function has property α if and only if given that $x \in C(T)$, $x \in C(S)$. That is to say, x is admissible in S if it is admissible in T.

In my judgment, failure to satisfy property α is merely one symptom of the fact that there is no ordering of the options with respect to expected utility due to the indeterminacy of probability judgment. We have to decide whether we are going to abandon the requirement that admissible options be Bayes solutions or abandon property α and with it the demand that the feasible options can be ordered with respect to whether they are better or worse. I favor the latter course. In either case, we have deviated from the path of true Bayesianism – even when Bayesians allow for imprecision in the measurement of probability. The difference between my approach and the approach of advocates of gamma minimax is that they seek an ordering of the options as better or worse alternatives to the Bayesian one. I reject that alternative and insist, instead, that when credal indeterminacy is present, there often is no ranking of the options as better or worse. But no matter how one views the matter, the insistence on the presence of credal indeterminacy represents a position substantially different from the strict Bayesian point of view according to which, owing to the frailty of human nature, we are not in a position to recognize numerically definite credal probabilities but we should, nonetheless, proceed as if we were committed to such probabilities as best we can.

Perhaps it will be helpful to those who resist the idea of allowing violations of property α to consider an example where the indeterminacy which leads to violation of property α does not derive from indeterminacy in probability judgment. Consider a choice between three job candidates where the demand is for a good stenographer-typist. Each candidate is given a typing test and a stenography test. The test scores for candidates J, D, and L are 100, 91 and 90 for typing and 90, 91 and 100 for stenography. Under these circumstances, the manager may not be able to average the scores into a single score but may be in suspense between different ways to weight the scores. So even though he faces a decision problem under certainty, he is conflicted in his utility judgments and regards many different utility functions as permissible. According to some permissible utility functions J beats D beats L. According to others L beats D beats J. And there are other weak orderings as well. (For example, L beats D which ranks together with J.) Still no matter what permissible function is used, D is never optimal. So D is not E-admissible. But J and L are.

The manager may take the view that when professional considerations cannot decide, he will choose on the basis of the extent to which the candidate belongs to an underprivileged minority. Here D is most underprivileged, J is next and L is least underprivileged.

Thus, the manager chooses J in the threeway choice. Before he can implement the choice, L withdraws. The manager reconsiders and now finds both J and D to be E-admissible. That is because J beats D according to some permissible utility functions, D beats J according to others and they are ranked together according to one. This leads him to choose D because D is more underprivileged than J. Property α has been violated.

The breakdown of α in this instance appears in the context of decision making under certainty. The appeal to the gamma minimax criterion utilized by Gärdenfors and Sahlin does not suffice to prevent it. Nor should we want an account of rational choice to prevent it. The office manager's valuations are perfectly sensible. Any theory of rationality which says otherwise displays its own inadequacy.

In this case, the office manager orders the candidates with respect to their competence as typists and as stenographers. In addition, he ranks them with respect to their level of disadvantage. But he cannot legitimately, according to his own lights, aggregate these different valuations into a single "all things considered" valuation which ranks the options he faces as better or worse. The office manager is not obliged as a rational agent to fix on a definite ranking, all things considered. Indeed, sometimes it may be illegitimate for him to do so.

If this is right, we have a precedent for recognizing the occasional legitimacy of similar verdicts in the context of decision making under uncertainty. Counter the the approach of Gärdenfors and Sahlin, it may be rational, all things considered, not to rank the options as better or worse due, perhaps, to indeterminacy in probability judgment. We should resist the lust for order when there is no warrant for it.

INDETERMINACY IN UTILITY AND THE ALLAIS PROBLEM

The approach of Gärdenfors and Sahlin is an excellent example of how authors sensitive to the deficiencies in Bayesian dogma are driven to an unjustifiably severe rejection of Bayesianism because of the yearning for order. There are other critics of Bayesianism who, by appealing to other kinds of violations of the sure-thing principle, end up doing essentially the same. The best known criticism of this sort appeals to predicaments which are variants of the problems introduced into discussion by M. Allais in the 1950s (Allais, 1952,1953). These problems are interesting because they are not examples of decision making under uncertainty. At the same time, they are not exactly examples of decision making under risk. Although numerically definite credal probability judgments can be derived from knowledge of chances, as in decision making under risk, expected utility calculations remain indeterminate due to problems with the utility function.

Suppose a decision maker faces an urn containing 1 red, 89 white and 10 blue balls from which one is to be selected at random. Two options are offered given as follows:

	Red	White	Blue
E	$1,000,000	$1,000,000	$1,000,000
F	$0	$1,000,000	$5,000,000

Compare the decision the agent would make in this case with the choice he would make were the option as follows:

	Red	White	Blue
G	$1,000,000	$0	$1,000,000
H	$0	$0	$5,000,000

Observe that in this case the agent can ground his judgments of credal probability in knowledge of objective or statistical probability via direct inference. If there is any indeterminacy in credal probability judgment, it will presumably be due to distrust, on the part of those who are presented with these problems, of the data given them. Still these are explicitly hypothetical problems where the agents are invited to contemplate taking the decisions on the assumption that the objective probabilities are as specified. There should be no excuse for distrust here, and charity suggests that we should not interpret the responses to these problems in this light.

Yet, many authors have confirmed the observation of Allais that the predominant response choice in the first problem is E whereas H is the choice in the second problem (Hagen, 1979; Kahneman and Tversky, 1979; and MacCrimmon and Larsson, 1979). If choice reveals preference, E is preferred over F and H over G. And this system of preference violates the sure-thing principle.

But in this case, unlike the Ellsberg problem, we cannot deny that options are ordered with respect to expected utility because of indeterminacy in the probabilities used to calculate expected utility.

If there is any indeterminacy in expected utility here, it will have to be in the utilities assigned to the payoffs – which have been specified in money. And, in the Allais problem, it should not be surprising that there is indeterminacy in these utilities. Even if we agree that the marginal utility of money diminishes with income received and, indeed, that the difference between a million dollars and nothing is greater than the difference between five million and a million, we would still have to determine whether the first difference was more than, less than, or exactly equal to 10 times the second difference. It is doubtful whether any one of us is committed to a utility of money function so precise as to allow a univocal answer to this question. But if not, then we may find ourselves in a situation where several distinct utility functions are permissible to use together with our numerically determinate credal state to compute expected utility and where, as a result, both E and F are E-admissible in the first problem while G and H are E-admissible in the second. Of course, if we withdraw the assumption that marginal utility of income decreases and allow indeterminacy on this point as well, the same result will emerge.

If one evaluates security levels by means of Wald's risk functions, it turns out that assessments of security levels go indeterminate due to the indeterminacy in the utility function. Recall, however, that there is no principle of reason which requires assessing security in Wald's way. That depends on the decision maker's values. And it is entertainable that some agents who do conform to Wald's view of security will revert to an appeal to security levels fixed according to ultimate monetary payoffs when the Wald method fails to yield a verdict.

This attitude towards fixing security levels conforms well to the puzzling behavior in the Allais problem. Since the security level of E is better than that of F, it is chosen in the first problem. In the second problem, the security level is the same for both options; but the second worst outcome is better according to H than according to G, so that H may be chosen. Still E is not preferred to F (i.e., it does not have greater expected utility). And H is not preferred to G. There is no violation of the sure-thing principle.

To avoid misunderstanding, it should be made clear that the suggested analysis of the Allais problem does not recommend that the agent change his utility-of-money function when shifting from the first decision problem to the second as Cyert and Degroot (1974) suggest. In both problems, the same set of utility-of-money functions is permissible and that set of permissible utility functions represents the agent's values in both contexts.

This analysis of the Allais problem is based on the same criteria for admissibility as were invoked in connection with the Ellsberg problem. First a test for E-admissibility was deployed. That test identifies the set of feasible options which are E-admissible – i.e., which are ranked optimal according to some permissible expected utility function defined over the feasible set. Then lexicographical maximin solutions are determined relative to the agent's assessments of security levels from among the E-admissible options. (In some cases, assessments of security levels could go indeterminate. I shall not discuss such cases here; but they are allowed by the proposal.)

The only novelty in the Allais case derives from the fact that the multiplicity of permissible expected utility functions arises from indeterminacy in the utility functions defined over the space of consequences of the feasible options and not from indeterminacy in the probability functions. (Needless to say, indeterminacy in expected utility can be a product of indeterminacy both in utility of consequences and probability.)

We already encountered indeterminacy in utility when discussing the example of the office manager hiring a secretary. In that case, the source of the indeterminacy derived from a conflict in the decision maker's values. The office manager sought a good typist and a good stenographer and when the job applicants available did not combine the desiderata in a smooth way, the office manager faced a conflict in values that could not be resolved prior to making a decision.

When faced with the challenge of "aggregating" several utility indicators representing rival desiderata, the view I am proposing holds that any aggregation representing a potential resolution of the conflict ought to be a weighted average of the utility indicators characterizing the desiderata. I do not pretend to be able to demonstrate the propriety of this approach any more than I can demonstrate the propriety of taking E-admissibility as the first criterion of admissibility. But assumptions found in Blackwell and Girshick (1954, pp. 116–119), Fleming (1952, pp. 366–384) and Harsanyi (1955, pp. 309–321) can be adapted to provide a foundation for this view. I hope to elaborate on this in a forthcoming book.

Another way in which indeterminacy in utility arises in cases where agents are paid off in risky prospects and where the expected values of these prospects are indeterminate because of indeterminacy in the credal probabilities. Money might be just such a prospect for most individuals, at least to some extent. Granted that most agents will prefer more money to less, so that all permissible utility-of-money functions will be positive monotonic transformations of cash value, and granted, for the sake of the argument, that the marginal utility of money is decreasing, it is at least entertainable that enough indeterminacy in the utility-of-money function obtains to yield the results widely reported concerning the Allais problem. Indeed, these results can be interpreted as furnishing some indication of indeterminacy in utility-of-money functions.

One could test the conjecture about indeterminacy in another way, thereby obtaining an independent check concerning the extent to which experimental subjects responding to Allais-type problems conform to the model I am suggesting. Offer experimental subjects a lottery with 10 chances out of 11 of winning $5,000,000 and another lottery where the agent wins a million for sure. If my conjecture about the Allais problem is correct, the agent should take the second lottery, because both options are E-admissible and considerations of security favor a million for sure. One might in addition seek to ascertain the greatest lower bound on chances for the $5,000,000 which would induce the agent to choose the first lottery. If this bound is less than certainty (as the approach offered here suggests it should be), then compare the lottery with odds for $5,000,000 slightly less than this greatest lower bound with receiving an amount smaller than a million for sure. If there is indeterminacy in utility, it is to be expected that for smaller amounts close to a million, the agent will choose the sure thing and if the indeterminacy is considerable, the amount subtracted from a million could be substantial. I take it that the obstacles to testing this prediction are no greater than in other experiments concerned with assessments of risk and uncertainty.

Beginning with Allais himself, those who have studied problems like the ones he raised have presupposed that ideally rational agents satisfy certain minimal conditions of consistency which entail, so Allais himself maintained, that the ideally rational agents evaluate lotteries or

other such "random prospects" in a manner which induces a weak
ordering of these prospects as better or worse. In addition, if an agent
faces a choice between two lotteries or "random prospects" (Allais,
1952, p.38) where the probability of the value of the payoff being less
than m according to prospect P is no greater than according to prospect
P' for all m and smaller for at least one m, P is to be strictly preferred to
P'. (Allais, 1952, pp.39–41 and p.78. Allais calls this the "axiom of
absolute preference.") P is said to "stochastically dominate" P' (Borch,
1979, pp. 194–195).[4]

It is clear from his discussion that Allais is concerned not merely
with the question of describing the risk-taking behavior of humans, but
with formulating a conception of the ideals of rational decision making
which takes uncertainty and risk into account. Allais quite rightly seeks
to put principles of rationality into a framework which avoids ruling
out as irrational modes of decision-making conduct which manifest
predilections for one sort of goals and values rather than another. He
focuses on a thin conception of rationality which addresses issues of
consistency alone.

4. Suppose the lotteries P and P' utilize the same stochastic process. If, for any given
outcome o, of the process, lottery P pays at least as much as P' and for at least one
such outcome pays more, P not only stochastically dominates P' but dominates P' in
the ultimate payoff. If P dominates P' in the ultimate payoff, it stochastically dominates P'; but the converse need not hold. If we are given a fixed stochastic process
and lottery P yields lottery Q, for outcome o, while P' yields Q,' for oucome o,, it is
possible for P to dominate P' with respect to payoffs in lotteries (so that for every i, Q,
is at least as great as Q,' and for some i is greater) without dominating P' with respect
to the ultimate payoff. We may, therefore, distinguish three senses in which someone
can prohibit a lottery from being preferred by another which dominates it:
  (1) One can prohibit a lottery from being preferred by another which dominates
it with respect to some way of specifying payoffs.
  (2) One can prohibit a lottery from being preferred by another which dominates
it with respect to some privileged way of specifying ultimate or "sure" payoffs.
  (3) Given the specification of ultimate or sure payoffs, one can prohibit a lottery
from being preferred by another which stochastically dominates it.
  Prohibition (1) is the demand insisted upon by Bayesians. It is satisfied by the
proposals I have made as well. It can be satisfied even if one refuses to recognize a
system of ultimate or "sure" payoffs. Allais and those who have taken his approach
seriously begin by identifying a system of ultimate or sure payoffs (often monetary
prizes) and regard lotteries or random prospects to be assignments of probabilities to
these prizes. Allais is prepared to abandon prohibition (1) and insist on prohibition (3)
which, in turn, entails prohibition (2). Prohibition (3) is, in effect, the axiom of absolute preference.
  Anyone, who like myself, is sceptical of grounding decision theory on some fundamental system of ultimate payoffs will be dissatisfied with the idea of imposing
requirements on preference which presuppose such a system. Although the von Neumann-Morgenstern approach is also concerned with evaluating lotteries in a context
where ultimate payoffs are recognized, the requirements imposed can remain satisfied
even if the erstwhile ultimate payoffs are replaced by lotteries.

Although Allais' approach to rationality does seem to me eminently sensible in these respects, he betrays his own ambition by insisting that a rational agent should be in a position to order his options. Since Allais insisted that the choice of E over F and H over G are eminently rational choices (rightly in my opinion), he concluded that, given this rationality, the choice must reveal preference for E over F and H over G. Consequently, he concluded that rational agents may violate Savage's sure-thing principle or, alternatively, the so-called independence axiom.

But the thesis that rational agents should have valuations of options which induce a weak ordering of the alternatives he appraises is an instance of that dogma which, in my judgment, forms the soft underbelly of Bayesian dogma. Just as Ellsberg and Gärdenfors and Sahlin respond to the Ellsberg problem in a manner which retains the weak-ordering assumption while abandoning the sure-thing principle, so too Allais and, following him, writers like E.F. McClennen (1983), misdiagnose the trouble with Bayesianism. They tamper with the sure-thing principle or the independence axiom in order to save the demand that rational agents have valuations satisfying the requirements of a weak ordering.

Those who have attended to Allais' work have often been more interested in exploring the extent to which humans deviate from Bayesian norms of rationality in order to criticize the descriptive, predictive, and explanatory value of Bayesian theory. This seems to be true, for example, of Kahneman and Tversky (1979), MacCrimmon and Larsson (1979), Ole Hagen (1979), Mark Machina (1982), and Chew Soo Hong (1981). However, they all take for granted that the agents' choices in situations like the Allais problem "reveal" preferences which are embeddable in a weak ordering, and seek to devise models for choice behavior which cover the sort of behavior manifested in Allais-type problems while preserving weak ordering. As has become apparent, however, there are several proposals available for achieving this end. More to the point, the debate over the merits of various models often turns on questions like whether behavior according to the models satisfies other conditions like the so-called condition of stochastic dominance. Kahneman and Tversky (1979, pp. 283–284) are prepared to abandon not only the independence postulate, but stochastic dominance.[5] Machina (1982, p.292), however, objects to their prospect the-

---

5. Prospect theory allows for violations of dominance in ultimate payoffs and not merely violations of stochastic dominance. Kahneman and Tversky seek to mitigate the difficulty by postulating that dominated alternatives are recognized and eliminated by decision makers prior to evaluating random prospects. This leads to the use of a choice function violating property α as Kahneman and Tversky, in effect, point out utilizing an example from Raiffa, 1968, pp.75–76. Since Kahneman and Tversky seem to take for granted that pairwise choice reveals preference, the implication is that transitivity of preference is violated.

ory precisely because it violates stochastic dominance. If the only motivation were descriptive adequacy, there appears to be no basis one
way or the other for requiring satisfaction of stochastic dominance. Nor
are considerations of explanatory adequacy, simplicity, and the like
obviously on Machina's side. Machina's insistence on stochastic dominance looks like prescriptive lawgiving, whether he says so or not.

I do not mean to suggest that there is anything wrong with Machina's insistence on stochastic dominance. I am, however, somewhat
puzzled by his devotion to this requirement given that he is willing to
abandon the substitution postulate which implies such dominance.

In any case, Machina's efforts to show that one can satisfy stochastic dominance while deviating from the substitution principle, accommodating the Allais phenomena, and preserving ordering can be
shown to fail thanks to an argument of Teddy Seidenfeld.[6]

But even if we ignore these substantial troubles plaguing the efforts
of those who would follow Allais and MacClennen in seeking a system
of norms which demand that agents order their options but allow
violation of the independence axiom or the sure thing principle, there
is another consideration which argues against such approaches. None
of the schemes for accommodating the responses to Allais' problem
which undermine sure thing principles accommodate the Ellsberg
problem as well.[7] However, if one is prepared to abandon the requirement that all alternatives are weakly ordered, one can not only recognize that no violation of sure thing reasoning is displayed, but analyze
both the Ellsberg and Allais problems according to the principles of a
single decision theory. When it comes to descriptive adequacy as well
as normative attractiveness, the proposals I have been making are superior to any of those which have been advanced up until now – provided one is prepared to abandon the dogma that alternatives ought to
be ordered with respect to value.

There is at least one type of example discussed by Allais (1952,

6. Consider two lotteries L_1 and L_2 which are both valued at $10. Machina allows for the
   violation of the substitution principle through a violation of "mixture dominance"
   (Chew, 1981, p.4). In particular a 50-50 mixture of these two lotteries could be valued
   more than $10 – say $25. Substitute the two lotteries for the options L and R in the
   argument of footnote 3, and the result will be that an option will be recommended
   which is not only stochastically dominated, but dominated in the ultimate payoffs. As
   in the argument in footnote 3, the reasoning works only on the assumption that all
   lotteries are weakly ordered.
7. Chew prohibits violations of the substitution principle through mixture dominance
   (Chew, 1981, p.4). The violation of substitution according to Allais can be construed
   as a case where mixture dominance is satisfied. But the Ellsberg phenomenon is a
   clear case of violation of mixture dominance. Hence, Chew's proposal cannot, even in
   principle, rationalize the Ellsberg phenomenon. Whether some variant of approaches
   like Machina's, which allow for violations of mixture dominance, can rationalize the
   Ellsberg phenomenon remains an open question; but, as we have seen, such approaches must violate stochastic dominance.

pp. 90–92) and studied by Hagen (1979, pp. 283–297), MacCrimmon and Larsson (1979, pp. 350–359) and by Kahneman and Tversky (1979, p. 267) which does not seem to be accounted for by this approach. These examples exemplify the "common ratio effect."

Suppose, for example, that an agent is offered two options with the following payoffs:

I $1,000,000 with probability .75 $0 otherwise.
II $5,000,000 with probability .60 $0 otherwise.

In addition, he is invited to choose between the following pair

III $1,000,000 with probability .05 $0 otherwise.
IV $5,000,000 with probability .04 $0 otherwise.

Observe that the ratio of the probabilities of a million and of five million are the same in both problems and should, according to an expected utility calculation, yield the same ordering of the options as the substitution axiom requires.

Yet MacCrimmon and Larsson report that out of 17 subjects 6 switched from choosing I to choosing IV, in violation of the independence assumption (1979, fig.3(i), p. 357). Similar results are reported by Kahneman and Tversky (1979, problems 7 and 8).

This result cannot be rationalized by the approach I have used before. If there is sufficient indeterminacy in the utility function to render options I and II E-admissible in the first problem and III and IV E-admissible in the second, the security levels are the same for I and II and the secondary security level for II is superior. This suggests that in the first pair, II ought to be chosen over I – counter to the practice of the experimental subjects.

Of course, it is far from obvious that both options I and II are E-admissible in the first problem. When discussing the first Allais problem (the so-called "common consequence" problem), we concluded that the utility function for the range of monetary values for $0 to $5,000,000 rendered it indeterminate as to whether a gamble where one has a chance of 10/11 of winning 5 million is better, worse, or indifferent to a million for sure – at least for many experimental subjects. However, those same subjects could very well prefer a million for sure to an 80% chance of winning $5,000,000. This shows only that the utility of money function is partially indeterminate. And that would account for the choice of I over II.

But then, if the independence postulate is observed, III should be chosen over IV. The experimental data suggest, under this interpretation, that the independence postulate is, indeed, violated.

Observe, however, that the violation can be explained as due to a

tendency on the part of experimental subjects not to distinguish probability .04 from probability .05, and to treat them as equal. If they do
so, the choice of IV over III becomes the optimal option in expected
utility.

Thus, even if it is conceded that in this type of common probability-
ratio problem the independence postulate is violated, the violation can
be attributed to a tendency on the part of experimental subjects to neglect small differences in probability assignments. In the MacCrimmon
and Larsson examples, the differences neglected are in the second decimal place, whereas in the Kahneman and Tversky example (which
yielded a more striking shift) the probability differences are in the third
decimal place.

It is not my purpose to deny that individuals make errors of this
sort and violate widely advocated principles of decision making or that
they violate the principles which I myself favor.

But the interest which developed in the Allais common-consequence
problem and in the Ellsberg problems derives from a sense that the
responses which appear to violate the independence and sure-thing
principles are not foolish and cannot be attributed to neglect of the
importance of small differences in numerical magnitudes or other errors
likely to crop up in rough computation.

It does not seem to be the case that the violation of the independence postulate exhibited in the common ratio of probabilites cases of
the sort studied by MacCrimmon and Larsson or by Kahneman and
Tversky impose pressure to reconsider norms of rational choice in quite
the way the Ellsberg problem or the common-consequence problem of
Allais can do. There is a readily available explanation of the failure in
terms of the short cuts individuals use in making computations. We
may easily concede that the norms of rationality in general and the
strong independence principle in particular are violated, and perhaps
even that no amount of effort will prevent anyone from failing to
observe them on at least some occasions, as long as we can attribute
the failures to limitations on computational capacity, the errors we
make in our efforts to simplify our computational tasks, or our vulnerability to emotional disturbance. We can, so it seems, admit the existence of violations of the strong independence condition arising in
common ratio problems without pressure to modify commitment to the
sure-thing principle or strong independence axiom. The experiments
done on the common ratio problem exemplify deviations from norms
of rationality which point in the direction of educating the experimental subjects rather than modifying the norms.

If this claim is right, then I think we are in a position to say that
insofar as the violations of the strong independence axiom identified
by Allais cannot be attributed to failures of computation, they are not
violations at all but are due to indeterminacy in the agent's utility

48   Isaac Levi

assessments comparable to the indeterminacy in probability assessments present in the Ellsberg problem and having a parallel impact on the proper analysis of decision problems.

PREFERENCE REVERSAL

This conclusion may be reinforced by considering the following pair of gambles:
1. A million dollars with probability .9.
2. 5 million with probability .8.

Suppose the utility function for money is such that U ($x) is any function in the convex hull of $\log(x + 1)$ and $\log(0.1x + 1)$.

The expected utilities of the two gambles are 12.44 and 12.34 respectively according to the first function with corresponding dollar values of $252,000 and $239,000. According to the second utility function the expected utilities are 10.35 and 10.49 with corresponding dollar values of $11,000 and $12,300.

Both options are E-admissible because they come out optimal according to some permissible utility function in the set. Leximin favors the gamble on the 5 million (gamble 2). Suppose, however, we modify the gambles slightly. We charge a small amount – say $10 for the 5 million dollar gamble. Both options should remain E-admissible. But now leximin favors gamble 1. Observe, however, that the range of dollar values for the pair of gambles will be altered only negligibly. It will still remain the case that the smallest dollar value for gamble 2 will be higher than the smallest dollar value for gamble 1. Hence, if asked for the smallest price at which he would sell gamble 1, the answer should be $11,100 and for gamble 2 it should be $12,300. For lower prices, retaining the gamble would be uniquely E-admissible. For prices of $11,100 and $12,300 both retaining and selling become E-admissible and selling is the maximin solution.

The upshot is that in the modified version of the solution, gamble 1 should be chosen over gamble 2, yet the lowest price at which the agent ought to sell gamble 2 ought to be higher than the lowest price at which he ought to sell gamble 1. As far as I can see, the situation I have just described reproduces the phenomenon reported by Grether and Plott (1979) and others (Reilly, 1982) on so-called "preference reversal."[8] On my account, of course, there is no preference reversal – only indeterminacy in preferences.

8. I cannot cite decisive evidence that my scheme models the Grether-Plott phenomenon because the reports of the experimental design and results provided by Grether and Plott do not furnish information relevant to this matter. They invite experimental subjects to compare pairs of bets of types 1 and 2 (so-called "P-bets and $-bets"). Counter to the impression given on p.623 of (Grether and Plott, 1979), each bet in a given pair always incurs a risk of loss. However, in some pairs, the losses are greater

NEWCOMB'S PROBLEM

Finally and very briefly, I should mention that the tendency on the part of some respondents to the Newcomb problem to choose the so-called two-box solution is itself explainable as due to indeterminacy in the probability judgments of the agent.

An agent is told that he has a choice between receiving the contents of a transparent box containing $1,000 together with the contents of an opaque box or the contents of the opaque box alone.

The agent is told that a demon is an extremely reliable predictor of his choices. Moreover, the demon places a million dollars in the opaque box if he predicts the agent will choose the opaque box alone. Otherwise he places nothing in the opaque box.

When asked how they would choose, it is alleged that people divide between those favoring one box and those favoring two.

One can make sense out of these responses if one keeps in mind that the assumption that the demon is a reliable predictor of the agent's choices would normally be taken to mean that conditional on the demon predicting his choice of one (two) boxes, the probability of his choosing one (two) boxes is high. But, in the standard formulation of the problem, the probabilties of the demon predicting his choice correctly given his choosing one (two) boxes are not stated. To obtain these conditional probabilities from the conditional probabilities given in the assumption of the demon's reliability as a predictor, assumptions need to be made concerning the unconditional probabilities of the demon predicting one way or the other. If the agent's judgments of unconditional probability are indeterminate, the conditional expected utility functions for the two options may go indeterminate. Hence, both options could be E-admissable. Maximin recommends the two-box solution (Levi, 1975). This result rationalizes the choice of two boxes without introducing any new principle of causal decision theory but merely by acknowledging the presence of indeterminacy in probability and, perhaps, utility judgment.

CONCLUSION

On the view I favor, the Bayesians are right in giving pride of place to considerations of expected utility. Their critics are right, however, in

---

for P-bets and in some pairs, the losses are greater for $-bets. Grether and Plott do not report, however, the percentages of experimental subjects who choose members of pairs in a way which minimizes such losses (and, hence, maximizes security). Hence, although their results and those of Reilly appear compatible with my model, there is an unsettled empirical question about their experiments which is relevant to the empirical adequacy of the model I have proposed.

complaining that some of the ways in which agents appear to deviate from Bayesian ideals of rationality cannot be explained away as due to failures of computational capacity, memory, attention, discrimination and the like, or to emotional upset.

Unfortunately most of the critics of expected utility have failed to come up with prescriptive accounts of rational choice having the generality of Bayesian decision theory. The proposals made to accommodate the Allais problem fail to handle the Ellsberg problem and vice-versa. And none seem to handle the preference reversal phenomenon. From the Bayesian point of view, these proposals look like ad hoc repairs. And in my judgment, the Bayesians are right.

This view is reinforced by the fact that all of the proposals made have implications which even their advocates ought to find embarrassing. As we have seen, they tend to recommend the choice of options dominated by other options in a sense in which such choice seems clearly to be avoided.

In this essay, I have argued that the Bayesians are wrong in insisting that probabilities and utilities should be so definite that expected utility can always provide a verdict. Not only does such a view entail the conclusion that the experimental results we have mentioned establish a far more deep-running irrationality in human decision makers than seems necessary to suppose, but it condemns those who are anxious about catastrophic possibilities of various energy policies, of the dissemination of various kinds of drugs, of weapons development policies, etc., to the status of irrational fools.

By admitting that we are in doubt much of the time in our judgments of probability and our evaluations of states and options, we are in a position to make systematic sense of the tension between considerations of expected value and security. The insights of Bayesians and maximiners can be preserved in a principled fashion free from the charge of ad hoc eclecticism which may with some justice be brought against those who attack the priority of the expected utility principle. We have seen that allegedly deviant responses to Ellsberg's problem, the standard Allais problem, the Grether-Plott preference reversal problem and the Newcomb problem can all be rationalized within the framework of a single system of norms for rational choice. The proposals made are more general than the Bayesian theory. Indeed, Bayesian theory becomes a limited special case. The proposals allow a wider variety of behaviors to be non-deviant than either the Bayesian theory or the views of those who attack the priority of the expected utility principle. They do not make fools of us unnecessarily.

As indicated, the scheme advanced here cannot accommodate one kind of deviant behavior connected with problems posed by Allais – to wit, the common ratio problem. But as I have argued, an examination of the cases reported suggests that these deviations may be of the sort which a prescriptive account of rational choice need not be expected to rationalize.

To obtain the benefits claimed for these proposals, the requirement that rational agents be in a position to opt for the best, all things considered, according to some weak ordering of their options as better or worse, has had to be abandoned and in a rather severe manner. The indeterminacies in probabilities, utilities and expected utilities allowed together with the criteria of admissibility proposed undermine widely shared assumptions concerning rationality.

In my view, the benefits clearly outweigh the costs. Even so, more can be done. Extensive experimentation may be undertaken to ascertain the extent to which the prescriptions of the theory proposed here are satisfied by decision makers. And those devoted to order can take up the challenge to construct a theory as general as the one advanced here while still meeting their own requirements. Pending such developments, a system of prescriptions preserving the insights of Bayesians and maximiners ought to be taken very seriously by students of rational choice, especially when it seems to avoid making fools of us all unnecessarily.[9]

REFERENCES

Allais, M. 1952. "The Foundations of a Positive Theory of Choice involving Risk and a Criticism of the Postulates and Axioms of the American School," translation of "Fondements d'une Théorie Positive des Choix Comportant un Risque et Critique des Postulats et Axiomes de L'École Américaine." In *Expected Utility Hypotheses and the Allais Paradox*, by M. Allais and O. Hagen, pp. 27–145. Reidel.

Allais, M. 1953. "Le comportement de l'Homme Rationnel Devant le Risque: Critique des Postulats et Axiomes de l'Ecole Americaine," *Econometrica* 21:503–46.

Allais, M., and Hagen, O. 1979. *Expected Utility Hypotheses and the Allais Paradox*. Reidel.

Berger, J.O. 1980. *Statistical Decision Theory*. Springer-Verlag.

Borch, K. 1979. "Utility and Stochastic Dominance." In *Expected Utility Hypotheses and the Allais Paradox*, by M. Allais and O. Hagen, pp.193–201. Reidel.

Blackwell, D., and Girshick, M.A. 1954. *Theory of Games and Statistical Decisions*. New York: Wiley.

9. My first published account of the Allais problem is in Levi, 1982. In Levi, 1982b, I introduced the analysis of the Ellsberg problem. Two other authors have subsequently offered analyses along similar lines. G.W. Bassett has an unpublished manuscript on the subject. F. Schick (1984, pp.47–51) blames indeterminacy of probability for the Ellsberg phenomenon and indeterminacy of utility for the Allais problem. He asserts that we "might look for extra-rational grounds" on which to decide between what I would call "E-admissible" options. Schick does not seem to think that the use of maximin or leximin is regulated by considerations of rationality. It seems to me, however, that given the agent's assessment of security, one can regard the injunction to maximize security relative to that assessment among the E-admissible options a thin principle of rationality. The assessment of security itself, of course, is "extra rational."

Chew, Soo Hong. 1981. "A Mixture Set of Axiomatization of Weighted Utility Theory." Fourth revision of a 1981 working paper.

Cyert, R.M., and Degroot, M. 1974. "Adaptive Utility." In *Adaptive Economic Models*, edited by R.H. Day and T. Grove. Academic Press. Reprinted in *Expected Utility Hypotheses and the Allais Paradox*, by M. Allais and O. Hagen, pp.223–41. Reidel.

Ellsberg, D. 1961. "Risk, Ambiguity, and the Savage Axioms." *Quarterly Journal of Economics* 75, 643–69.

Fisher, R.A. 1959. *Statistical Methods and Scientific Inference*, 2nd ed. Hafner.

Fleming, M. 1952. "A Cardinal Concept of Welfare." *Quarterly Journal of Economics* 66: 366–84.

Friedman, M., and Savage, L.J. 1948. "The Utility Analysis of Choices Involving Risk." *Journal of Political Economy* 56: 279–304.

Gärdenfors, P., and Sahlin, N.-E. 1982. "Unreliable Probabilities, Risk Taking and Decision Making." *Synthese* 53: 361–86.

Gibbard, A., and Harper, W. 1978. "Counterfactuals and Two Kinds of Expected Utility." In *Foundations and Applications of Decision Theory, v.1*, edited by C.A. Hooker, J.J. Leach and E.F. McClennen, pp.125–62. Reidel.

Grether, D.M., and Plott, C.R. 1979. "Economic Theory of Choice and the Preference Reversal Phenomenon," *The American Economic Review* 69: 623–38.

Hagen, O. 1979. "Towards a Positive Theory of Preferences Under Risk." In *Expected Utility Hypotheses and the Allais Paradox*, by M. Allais and O. Hagen, pp.271–302. Reidel.

Harsanyi, J.C. 1955. "Cardinal Welfare, Individualistic Ethics, and Interpersonal Comparisons of Utility." *Journal of Political Economy* 63: 309–21.

Kahneman, D., and Tversky, A. 1979. "Prospect Theory: An Analysis of Decision Making under Risk." *Econometrica* 47: 263–91.

Levi, I. 1974. "On Indeterminate Probabilities." *Journal of Philosophy* 71: 391–418.

———. 1975. "Newcomb's Many Problems." *Theory and Decision* 6: 161–75. Reprinted in *Decisions and Revisions*, by I. Levi, pp.245–56. Cambridge.

———. 1980a. *The Enterprise of Knowledge*. MIT.

———. 1980b. "Induction and Self Correcting According to Peirce." In *Science, Belief and Behaviour: Essays in Honour of R.B. Braithwaite*, edited by D.H. Mellor, pp. 127–40. Cambridge.

———. 1982. "Conflict and Social Agency." *Journal of Philosophy* 79: 231–47. Reprinted in *Decisions and Revisions*, by I. Levi, pp.257–70. Cambridge.

———. 1982b. "Ignorance, Probability and Rational Choice." *Synthese* 53: 387–417.

———. 1984. *Decisions and Revisions*. Cambridge.

Luce, R.D., and Raiffa, H. 1958. *Games and Decisions*. Wiley.

Marshall, A. 1920. *Principles of Economics*, 8th edition. MacMillan.

Machina, M. 1982. "Expected Utility Analysis without the Independence Axiom," *Econometrica* 50: 277–323.

MacCrimmon, K.R., and Larsson, S. 1979. "Utility Theory: Axioms versus 'Paradoxes.' " In *Expected Utility Hypotheses and the Allais Paradox*, by M. Allais and O. Hagen, pp. 333–409. Reidel.

McClennen, E.F. 1983. "Sure-Thing Doubts." Draft of paper prepared for the First International Conference on Foundations of Utility and Risk Theory.

Pearson, E.S. 1962. "Some Thoughts on Statistical Inference." Reprinted in *Selected Papers of E.S. Pearson*, pp. 276–83. University of California Press.

Raiffa, H. 1961. "Risk, Ambiguity, and the Savage Axioms: Comment." *Quarterly Journal of Economics* 75: 690–95.

Raiffa, H. 1968. *Decision Analysis: Introductory Lectures on Choices Under Certainty*. Addison Wesley.

THE PARADOXES OF ALLAIS AND ELLSBERG   53

Reilly, R.J. 1982. "Preference Reversal: Further Evidence and Some Suggested Modifica-
    tions in Experimental Design." *American Economic Review* 72: 576–84.
Robbins, H. 1964. "The Empirical Bayes Approach to Statistical Decision Problems."
    Annals of Mathematical Statistics 35: 1–20.
Savage, L.J. 1954. *The Foundations of Statistics*. Wiley.
Schick, F. 1984. *Having Reasons*. Princeton.
Sen, A.K. 1970. *Collective Choice and Social Welfare*. Holden-Day.
Wald, A. 1950. *Statistical Decision Functions*. Wiley.

[10]

Review of Economic Studies (1986) LIII, 271–282
© 1986 The Society for Economic Analysis Limited

0034-6527/86/00170271$02.00

Disappointment and Dynamic Consistency in Choice under Uncertainty

GRAHAM LOOMES
University of York

and

ROBERT SUGDEN
University of East Anglia

The central proposition of disappointment theory is that an individual forms expectations about uncertain prospects, and that if the actual consequence turns out to be worse than (or better than) that expectation, the individual experiences a sensation of disappointment (or elation) generating a decrement (or increment) of utility which modifies the basic utility derived from the consequence. By incorporating a simple disappointment-elation function into a model of individual choice, many observed violations of conventional expected utility axioms—including violations of Savage's sure-thing principle and the "isolation effect"—can be predicted and defended as rational and dynamically consistent behaviour.

1. INTRODUCTION

A theory of rational choice under uncertainty called "regret theory" was presented simultaneously by ourselves (1982) and by David Bell (1982).[1] We showed that a number of frequently replicated violations of conventional expected utility can be predicted by a regret-rejoice model and can be defended as rational behaviour.

However, not all violations of conventional theory can be explained by regret alone. Nor does regret seem to be the only psychological experience that enters into choice behaviour. In this paper we try to show how "disappointment"—and its counterpart, "elation"—may also have an important part to play. We shall argue that although our disappointment model may explain violations which our regret model does not, and vice-versa, they have a number of features and predictions in common, and are complementary rather than competing elements in a developing alternative theory of rational choice.

2. THE MODEL

The basic propositions underlying our model are as follows. It is suggested that, when considering any uncertain prospect, an individual forms some *prior expectation* about that prospect. After the uncertainty is resolved, the individual experiences one particular consequence of the prospect: if that consequence falls short of the prior expectation, then in addition to the utility derived from the consequence itself, the individual also experiences some degree of disappointment; whereas if the consequence is better than the prior expectation, the individual also feels some measure of elation.

This general intuition, and the terms disappointment and elation, were first suggested by Bell (1985). However, as we shall later show, our formulation of disappointment-elation, and some implications of our model, are rather different from Bell's.

To maintain compatibility with the basic framework of regret theory, we propose that the ith prospect be represented as an *action*, A_i, which is an n-tuple of state-contingent consequences. The probability that the jth state will occur is p_j where $0 < p_j \leqq 1$ and $\sum_{j=1}^{n} p_j = 1$. The consequence of the ith action under the jth state is denoted x_{ij}, and we assume that for any individual there exists a *basic utility*[2] function, $C(\cdot)$, unique up to an increasing linear transformation, which assigns a real-valued utility index to every conceivable consequence. For convenience, we write $C(x_{ij})$ as c_{ij}. This index is a classical cardinal measure of the ex post utility derived from any consequence in any circumstances where regret, rejoicing, disappointment or elation do not arise.

For the purposes of this paper, we shall suspend all consideration of regret and rejoicing in order to concentrate on the impact of disappointment and elation. To ease the exposition, we *initially* consider only *one-stage* gambles, although later we shall extend the analysis to include multi-stage gambles.

As a measure of the *prior expectation* of A_i, we take the value of expected basic utility, $\sum_{j=1}^{n} p_j c_{ij}$ which we denote $\bar{c}_i$. We represent disappointment and elation by a single differentiable real-valued function $D(\cdot)$ which assigns a decrement or increment of utility to every possible value of $c_{ij} - \bar{c}_i$, the difference between the basic utility of the consequence if the jth state occurs, and the prior expectation.

This increment or decrement of utility modifies the basic utility of any consequence in an action, so that the overall, or *modified* utility experienced under the jth state is $c_{ij} + D(c_{ij} - \bar{c}_i)$. We then denote the *expected modified utility* of the ith action as E_i where

$$E_i = \sum_{j=1}^{n} p_j [c_{ij} + D(c_{ij} - \bar{c}_i)]. \tag{1}$$

Our theory is that an individual tries to anticipate any disappointment or elation, and chooses so as to maximise expected modified utility. Denoting the relations of strict preference, weak preference and indifference as $>$, $\geqslant$ and $\sim$, our theory is that for all $A_i, A_k : A_i \gtrless A_k \Leftrightarrow E_i \gtreqless E_k$.

Notice that since equation (1) assigns a real-valued index E_i to every action A_i, the relation $\geqslant$ of weak preference must be complete, reflexive and transitive. It is clear, therefore, that this model of choice under uncertainty—unlike regret theory—cannot explain observations of non-transitive choices.

To make predictions about choice behaviour, we need to impose some restrictions on the shape of $D(\cdot)$. Our fundamental intuition, that disappointment is painful and elation pleasurable, requires that $D(c_{ij} - \bar{c}_i) \gtreqless 0 \Leftrightarrow c_{ij} - \bar{c}_i \gtreqless 0$. Notice that with $D(0) = 0$, an individual choosing under certainty behaves as though maximising basic utility.

Our intuition also suggests that the degree of disappointment (elation) is a non-decreasing function of the magnitude of the negative (positive) gap between outcome and prior expectation: that is, $D'(c_{ij} - \bar{c}_i) \geqq 0$.

Individuals for whom $D(\cdot)$ is linear will behave as though maximising expected basic utility, so that their behaviour will be consistent with conventional expected utility theory. However, individuals whose $D(\cdot)$ functions take any other form are liable to violate the conventional theory. In our model we assume a particular kind of non-linearity: that $D(c_{ij} - \bar{c}_i)$ is convex for all positive values of $c_{ij} - \bar{c}_i$ and concave for all negative values. The intuition here is that the intensity of disappointment and elation both increase at the margin. To preserve first order stochastic dominance preference[3] we also assume that $D'(c_{ij} - \bar{c}_i) < 1$ for all $c_{ij} - \bar{c}_i$.

We shall make two more assumptions about the functions $D(\cdot)$ and $C(\cdot)$ mainly to simplify the exposition. Neither are *necessary* for our general results, but both are convenient.

First, we have no strong a priori argument for supposing that disappointment is in general a more intense sensation than elation, or vice versa, and so we provisionally adopt the neutral assumption that for all c_{ij}, $\bar{c}_i$: $D(c_{ij} - \bar{c}_i) = -D(\bar{c}_i - c_{ij})$.

Second, although it may be widely believed that, when consequences are increments or decrements of wealth, for many individuals $C(\cdot)$ is concave (i.e. diminishing marginal utility of wealth) we shall assume initially that $C(\cdot)$ is linear. The reason is simply to highlight the work being done in the model by the anticipation of disappointment and elation.

We shall now show how this small number of fairly weak assumptions can explain and/or predict a range of violations of conventional theory.

3. VIOLATIONS OF THE INDEPENDENCE AXIOM

Although some violations of the independence axiom, such as the common consequence and common ratio effects in the case of statistically independent actions, can be explained by regret theory, violations of the independence axiom in the form of Savage's (1954) "sure-thing principle" cannot (see Loomes and Sugden (1982 p. 813 and p. 819)). Nevertheless, such violations have been observed by Moskowitz (1974) and Slovic and Tversky (1974), among others.

To see how disappointment-elation may explain *this* evidence, consider the pair of actions depicted in Table I. All consequences are given in the form of basic utilities; $c > 0$, $0 < \lambda < 1$, $0 < p \leq 1$. To analyse violations of the sure-thing principle, we shall hold all probabilities and consequences constant, *except the common consequence* c^*.

TABLE I

	States of the world and probabilities		
Action	S_1 λp	S_2 $(1-\lambda)p$	S_3 $1-p$
A_1	λc	λc	c^*
A_2	c	0	c^*

In Table I both actions have the same prior expectation, which we shall denote $\bar{c}$. This condition will later be dropped, but it is a convenient starting point. Applying equation (1) and simplifying, we get:

$$A_1 \gtreqless A_2 \Leftrightarrow D(\lambda c - \bar{c}) \gtreqless \lambda D(c - \bar{c}) + (1 - \lambda)D(-\bar{c}). \tag{2}$$

Notice that c^* influences expression (2) only through $\bar{c}$. To see the significance of this, consider Figure 1, which portrays a disappointment-elation function that corresponds to our assumptions.[4]

A_1 is preferred to, indifferent to, or less preferred than A_2 according to whether the broken line $P_1 P_3$ passes below, through, or above the point P_2. Figure 1 shows the case where $A_1 \sim A_2$.

It is clear that if all three points lie on the convex segment of the function—which is assured if $c^* \leq -\lambda cp/(1-p)$ so that $-\bar{c} \geq 0$—then $A_1 < A_2$; likewise if all three points lie on the concave segment—i.e. if $c^* \geq c(1-\lambda p)/(1-p)$ so that $c - \bar{c} \leq 0$—then $A_1 > A_2$.

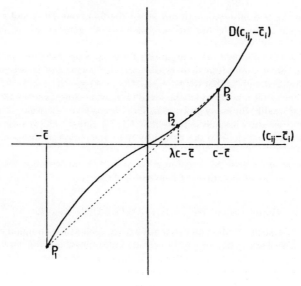

FIGURE 1

Thus we see that there exists some value θ in the range $-\lambda cp/(1-p) < \theta < c(1-\lambda p)/(1-p)$ such that $A_1 \gtrless A_2 \Leftrightarrow c^* \gtrless \theta$: in other words, as c^* falls through this range, there will at some point be a switch from $A_1 > A_2$ to $A_1 < A_2$, which is the violation of Savage's sure-thing principle that has been so frequently observed.

Note that this result holds even if $D(\xi)$ is not equal to $-D(-\xi)$ for all ξ, so long as the other assumptions hold. However, if we do assume that $D(\xi) = -D(-\xi)$ for all ξ, we can be more precise about θ and its relationship with λ and p. If $c^* = \lambda c$, $\lambda > 0.5$ is sufficient to ensure $A_1 > A_2$; and if $c^* = 0$, $p < 0.5$ is sufficient to ensure $A_1 < A_2$. Thus if $0 < p < 0.5 < \lambda < 1$, θ will be in the range $0 < \theta < \lambda c$, so that reducing c^* from λc to 0 will generate a reversal from $A_1 > A_2$ to $A_1 < A_2$.

This result is based on the case where the expected basic utility is the same for both actions and where our assumptions about $D(\cdot)$ all hold. However if we concentrate on cases where $0 < p < 0.5 < \lambda < 1$, we may relax some of the other conditions without undermining our explanation of the empirical evidence.

In particular, we can consider cases where $\bar{c}_1 \neq \bar{c}_2$. Given $p < 0.5$ we can construct an action A_3 differing from A_2 only by offering a less valuable consequence under S_1 with a basic utility of $c - d$. Now $\bar{c}_3 < \bar{c}_1$, but for sufficiently small d it will still be the case that $A_1 < A_3$ when $c^* = 0$; but since A_3 is dominated by A_2, it must still be the case that $A_1 > A_3$ when $c^* = \lambda c$. Hence the reversal will still occur as c^* is reduced from λc to 0.

By a similar argument, given $\lambda > 0.5$ we can construct an action A_4 offering a consequence under S_1 with a basic utility $c + e$. For sufficiently small e it will still be the case that $A_1 > A_4$ when $c^* = \lambda c$; but since A_4 dominates A_2 it must also be the case that $A_1 < A_4$ when $c^* = 0$, again entailing a reversal as c^* is reduced from λc to 0.

So we can envisage a range of cases where we observe reversals even though the expected basic utilities, and hence the expected money values, of the actions may differ.

If we also relax the assumption that $C(\cdot)$ is linear, and instead take that function to be concave, the disparities between expected money values may be even wider. And indeed it appears that the pattern of violation is observable across quite wide disparities in expected value: Kahneman and Tversky (1979, Problems 1 and 2) observed substantial reversals in a case where the expected value of the gamble was very close to the value of the certain prospect—2409 Israeli pounds compared with 2400; but similarly substantial numbers of reversals have been observed with the Allais (1953) problem where the expected value of the gamble—Fr. 1·39 million—is considerably greater than the value of the certainty—Fr. 1 million. Perhaps more significant is that in both cases λ and p lie within the ranges discussed above: in the Kahneman and Tversky experiment, $\lambda = 0·97$ and $p = 0·34$, while in the Allais problem $\lambda = 0·91$ and $p = 0·11$.

We do not claim that reversals will *not* occur under other conditions, such as $\lambda < 0·5$ and $p > 0·5$.[5] The purpose of this section has been simply to illustrate how the disappointment-elation model works, and how, under conditions where $\lambda > 0·5$ and $p < 0·5$, it generates fairly strong predictions about violations of the sure-thing principle which appear to be consistent with a substantial body of observed behaviour.

Essentially the same argument can be used to show that the common ratio effect is consistent with our theory. As before, A_1 and A_2 are the actions described in Table I, but we set $c^* = 0$ and let p become the variable. The empirical evidence (see, for example, Kahneman and Tversky 1979, 1981) shows a systematic tendency for individuals to switch from $A_1 > A_2$ to $A_1 < A_2$ as p decreases. Bearing in mind that much of the empirical evidence involves choices where the expected values of the alternatives are the same or similar, that it is often the case in these experiments that $\lambda > 0·5$, and that changes in p, like the changes in c^* in the common consequence effect, influence expression (2) through their impact on $\bar{c}$, it is not difficult to see that the common ratio effect is predicted by disappointment theory in essentially the same way as the violation of the sure-thing principle in the form of the common consequence effect.

4. OTHER MODELS

If regret and rejoicing are set aside, our theory makes the expected modified utility of any single-stage action depend only on the nature of the consequences of that action and their respective probabilities. In this respect, our theory is one of a class of theories in which individuals have preference orderings over probability distributions of consequences but in which these orderings do not necessarily satisfy the independence axiom. Models with such properties were suggested by Samuelson (1950, p. 170) and Allais (1953), and later variants were proposed by (among others) Hagen (1979), Chew and MacCrimmon (1979), Fishburn (1983), Machina (1982) and Bell (1985).

We shall not discuss all those other theories here, but concentrate on two: Bell's (1985) model of disappointment and elation; and Machina's (1982) Generalized Expected Utility analysis.

Bell presents a theory of preference orderings over two-outcome lotteries, which offer the consequences x, y with probabilities p, $1-p$; consequences are increments or decrements of wealth such that $x > y$. Such a lottery is written (x, p, y). Bell assumes that the marginal (basic) utility of wealth is constant, which allows us to measure utility on the same scale as wealth.

Bell defines two functions $c_1(\cdot, \cdot, \cdot)$ and $c_2(\cdot, \cdot, \cdot)$ so that $c_1(x, p, y)$ represents the certainty-equivalent value of the experience of winning x in the lottery (x, p, y) and $c_2(x, p, y)$ represents the certainty-equivalent value of the experience of winning y in the same lottery. These values may, of course, also be interpreted as utility indices. Bell then assumes that the certainty-equivalent value of the lottery itself is equal to $pc_1(x, p, y) + (1-p)c_2(x, p, y)$.

Applying our own theory to the same two-outcome lottery, and making the same assumption of linearity in the basic utility function, the certainty-equivalent value of the lottery is $p[x + D(x - \bar{c})] + (1-p)[y + D(y - \bar{c})]$ where $\bar{c} = px + (1-p)y$. The two theories would be equivalent, as far as this case is concerned, if $c_1(x, p, y) = x + D(x - \bar{c})$ and $c_2(x, p, y) = y + D(y - \bar{c})$.

Bell then imposes a restriction that he calls "linear expectations". This says that for all x, p and y, and for any constants a and b (where $b > 0$), $c_1(a + bx, p, a + by) = a + bc_1(x, p, y)$ and $c_2(a + bx, p, a + by) = a + bc_2(x, p, y)$. Given that $C(\cdot)$ is linear, it is easy to check that our model would satisfy this condition only if $D(\xi)$ was linear for all $\xi > 0$ *and* linear for all $\xi < 0$.

Retaining *our* assumption that $D(\cdot)$ is differentiable, Bell's restriction would require $D(\xi)$ to be linear for all ξ so that the theory would yield the same predictions as expected utility theory. However, if it is assumed only that $D(\cdot)$ is continuous, Bell's restriction would allow the function to be kinked at the origin.

Bell considers this case explicitly, assuming (to use our terminology) that $D'(\xi)$ is greater for $\xi < 0$ than for $\xi > 0$. This formulation is consistent with *some* observations of the common consequence and common ratio effects, but it cannot explain these effects when individuals are choosing between actions with the same expected money value; whereas our non-linear $D(\cdot)$ function is consistent with such observations, as we showed in the previous section.

Bell extends his model beyond the simple kinked-linear formulation by making disappointment and elation depend on more than the difference between the individual's prior expectation and the consequence subsequently experienced.

In effect, Bell assumes that for given values of x and $\bar{c}$, $c_1(x, p, y)$ is also a function of p, decreasing as p increases; likewise, for given values of y and $\bar{c}$, $c_2(x, p, y)$ decreases as p increases. Thus in Bell's extended model, unlike ours, there is no unique index of elation or disappointment associated with particular values of $(x - \bar{c})$ or $(y - \bar{c})$. In this respect, our formulation is both simpler than Bell's and more easily able to encompass lotteries with more than two outcomes.

So it is clear that although we share Bell's basic intuition about disappointment and elation, we model them rather differently. To bring out the differences between our theory and a number of other models in the same class, we now turn to the work of Machina.

Machina (1983) has shown that the models of Chew and MacCrimmon (1979) and Fishburn (1983) both imply a "fanning out" of indifference curves over probability distributions (for an earlier example of this functional form, see Samuelson (1950)). Consider the case where there are three consequences with basic utilities $c_3 > c_2 > c_1$ occurring with probabilities p_3, $1 - p_1 - p_3$, and p_1 respectively. For any set $\{c_3, c_2, c_1\}$ a triangle diagram such as in Figure 2 can be constructed. Conventional expected utility axioms require that an individual's preferences correspond to a set of indifference curves all of which have the same slope, so that the individual's preference between any two prospects f_1 and f_2 depends on whether the slope of the line connecting them is less than, equal to, or greater than the slope of the indifference curves. Hence conventional expected utility theory entails that if we construct any other pairs of prospects, such as f_3 and f_4, or f_5 and f_6, which lie on lines with the same slope as the one connecting f_1 and f_2, then the preferences between those pairs will be the same as the preference between f_1 and f_2.

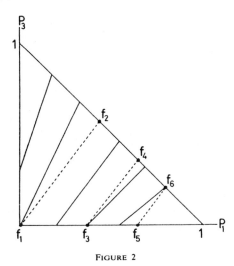

FIGURE 2

However if the indifference curves fan out, as in Figure 2, an individual may both prefer f_1 to f_2 and prefer f_4 to f_3, which is consistent with the common ratio effect. Other violations, such as the common consequence effect, can likewise be shown to be consistent with indifference maps of this kind.

Machina (1982) has offered a general non-parametric characterisation of the "fanning out" of the indifference curves, in the form of his Hypothesis II. He defines a "local utility function" $U(x; F)$ where x is any consequence and F is any probability distribution of consequences. When ranking differential shifts from F, the individual behaves as if his local utility function was a von Neumann–Morgenstern function. Hypothesis II is that for any x, and for any F, F^* where F^* stochastically dominates F, the local utility function is at least as concave at F^* as at F.

Since our theory predicts the common consequence and common ratio effects, it is natural to ask whether it is simply a special case of Machina's general characterisation. Clearly, our model fits into Machina's framework to the extent that it proposes a preference functional over (single-stage) probability distributions. The corresponding local utility function is:

$$U(x_{ij}; F) = c_{ij}[1 - \textstyle\sum_{j=1}^{n} p_j D'(c_{ij} - \bar{c}_i)] + D(c_{ij} - \bar{c}_i). \qquad (3)$$

(To derive this function, notice that $U(x; F)$ measures the rate at which utility changes as the probability associated with x changes. Thus $U(x_{ij}, F) = \partial E_i / \partial p_j$.)

Equation (3) shows that our assumptions that $C(\cdot)$ is an increasing function and that $0 \leqq D'(c_{ij} - \bar{c}_i) < 1$ for all $c_{ij} - \bar{c}_i$ are sufficient for $U'(x_{ij}; F) > 0$ and hence for first-order stochastic dominance preference. Our assumptions about $D(\cdot)$ suggest that the local utility function may be concave over low values of x_{ij} and convex over high values. (It will certainly have these properties if $C(\cdot)$ is linear.) This would be consistent with the phenomenon of simultaneous insurance and gambling.

However, our formulation does not in general satisfy Hypothesis II. Consider again Figure 2. The implication of "fanning out" is that if a reversal of preference occurs, there will be no "re-reversal": that is to say, the reduction in the slope of the indifference curves which tends to occur as we move rightwards from $\{f_1, f_2\}$ to $\{f_3, f_4\}$, continues as we move further to the right so that if $f_1 > f_2$ and $f_3 < f_4$ it cannot be the case that $f_5 > f_6$.

However, this is not a necessary implication of our disappointment model. It *does* hold if f_1 and f_2 have the same expected basic utilities; but if we relax that assumption, it is possible to construct examples where $f_1 > f_2$, $f_3 < f_4$ and $f_5 > f_6$.[6]

We should stress that our theory does not predict that such re-reversals *must* occur; they are no more than *possibilities*. We know of no evidence of systematic re-reversals. (Most experimenters investigating the common consequence and common ratio effects have confronted their subjects with a *couple* of pairwise choice problems; but to observe re-reversals, it would be necessary to give subjects at least a *triple*.) So we do not claim that in this respect our theory is *superior* to the class of theories encompassed by Hypothesis II—merely that it is *different*.

A second respect in which our model differs from Machina's concerns the analysis of multi-stage gambles. Machina's approach is based on general propositions about *all* probability distributions over final consequences, and therefore invokes the compound probability axiom—the principle of reducing complex prospects to simple ones by applying the calculus of probabilities. Until now, we have framed our theory in terms of simple single-stage gambles. However, as we show in the next section, when we extend our theory to include multi-stage gambles, we draw a distinction between single- and multi-stage gambles and predict the violation of the compound probability axiom known as the "isolation effect" which lies outside the scope of Machina's model.

5. MULTI-STAGE GAMBLES AND THE "ISOLATION EFFECT"

As part of an experiment reported by Tversky and Kahneman (1981, p. 455 and footnote 15), subjects were presented with three choice problems as follows:

Problem 1
  A: The certainty of $30.
  B: 0·8 chance of $45; 0·2 chance of 0.

Problem 2
  C: A first stage, in common with D, giving a 0·75 chance of dropping out and receiving 0, and a 0·25 chance of going through to the second stage; the second stage gives the certainty of $30.
  D: A first stage, in common with C, giving a 0·75 chance of dropping out and receiving 0, and a 0·25 chance of going through to the second stage; the second stage gives a further lottery, with a 0·8 chance of $45 and a 0·2 chance of 0.

Problem 3
  E: 0·25 chance of $30; 0·75 chance of 0.
  F: 0·2 chance of $45; 0·8 chance of 0.

Consider Problems 1 and 3. This couple of problems is one in which the common ratio effect can be observed. Tversky and Kahneman found this effect at work: 85 of their 205 subjects exhibited the conjunction of preferences A > B and E < F.

Now consider Problems 2 and 3. C and D have, respectively, the same probability distribution of final consequences as E and F. Any theory of choice under uncertainty that incorporates the compound probability axiom—that complex prospects can be expressed as simple ones by applying the calculus of probabilities—entails $C \gtrless D \Leftrightarrow E \gtrless F$.

Many theories are based on the fundamental assumption that individuals have preference orderings over probability distributions of final consequences, and thus incorporate the compound probability axiom. Some such theories—including Chew and MacCrimmon (1979), Machina (1982) and Fishburn (1983)—are compatible with the common ratio effect. Theories of this kind would predict that the common ratio effect would be observed just as frequently between Problem 1 and Problem 2 as between Problem 1 and Problem 3.

Tversky and Kahneman, however, found that subjects tended to reverse their preferences much more frequently between Problems 1 and 3 than between Problems 1 and 2. (See also Kahneman and Tversky (1979).) They called this "the isolation effect", which they interpret as a case of the more general phenomenon of "framing effects".

Framing effects occur when a choice problem with a given logical structure elicits different responses according to the way it is presented; and there seems little doubt that such effects *do* occur.[7] However, we are reluctant to classify the isolation effect in this way since it seems to be connected with a principle of rational choice that has considerable intuitive appeal: dynamic consistency.

Consider Problems 1 and 2. In Problem 2, C and D offer the same 0·25 chance of reaching the second stage and receiving, respectively, prospects A and B as in Problem 1. Since choosing (say) C rather than D amounts to committing oneself to receiving A rather than B in the event that one is successful in the first stage, dynamic consistency requires that for any individual $A \gtrless B \Leftrightarrow C \gtrless D$.

Clearly, any theory that accommodates the common ratio effect must dispense either with dynamic consistency or with the compound probability axiom. If the compound probability axiom is retained, the isolation effect is left unexplained (except as a framing effect); but if dynamic consistency is retained, the isolation effect is a logical corollary of the common ratio effect.

Tversky and Kahneman's results suggest that dynamic consistency is violated much less frequently than the compound probability axiom; of the 85 subjects who exhibited the common ratio effect, 20 violated the former and 65 the latter.

To explain why people may respond sufficiently differently to one-stage and two-stage gambles that they violate the compound probability axiom, we develop another insight of Bell's (1985), namely, that the sum total of disappointment and elation may be affected by the way in which uncertainty is resolved through time.

The point may be illustrated concretely by reference to Tversky and Kahneman's prospects D and F. With F, there is a single moment when the uncertainty is resolved, whereupon an individual may expect to feel some degree of disappointment (probability 0·8) or elation (probability 0·2). However, with D the uncertainty is resolved in two stages: at the end of the first stage there may be disappointment (probability 0·75) or elation (probability 0·25)—but not necessarily the same *intensities* of disappointment and elation as with *F*; and for those who experience elation from winning a valuable lottery ticket in the first round, there is the possibility of subsequent disappointment or further elation depending on the outcome of the second stage. Clearly, then, although both D and F involve the same probability distribution over final consequences, the logic of our theory allows individuals to anticipate quite different patterns of disappointment and elation, and therefore provides no justification for an axiom which reduces any multi-stage gamble to an equivalent single-stage gamble simply by applying the probability calculus.

On the other hand, the principle of dynamic consistency *does* seem compatible with our theory, and we can incorporate it quite straightforwardly into a treatment of two-stage gambles—a treatment which can be applied to any two consecutive stages, and therefore generalises quite naturally to gambles involving any number of stages.

In our earlier formulation, there were n states of the world and all uncertainty was resolved simultaneously. Let us now interpret those states as the possible outcomes of the *first* stage of a two-stage problem, and let at least one consequence x_{ij} be able to take the form of an uncertain action defined in relation to a subsequent set of states conditional upon the occurrence of state j at the end of the first stage. Let A_i' be that consequent action, and E_i' its expected modified utility. We can then incorporate dynamic consistency by assuming $C(x_{ij}) = E_i'$ which, together with the other central assumptions of our theory, entails that $C \gtrless D \Leftrightarrow A \gtrless B$, but entails no such implication between $\{C, D\}$ and $\{E, F\}$. Thus to the extent that our model predicts the common ratio effect, it also predicts the isolation effect.

6. CONCLUSION

In this paper we have tried to combine intuitive appeal and functional simplicity to produce a model of choice under uncertainty that generates a wide range of predictions which are consistent with observed behaviour. And although there are other models which share some of the same predictions, we have shown that the implications of our theory differ in important respects from these.

However, our theory claims to do more than predict a range of violations of the sure-thing principle and the compound probability axiom: it provides an explanation for them within a framework of rational choice.

In contrast, many writers who have recognised the limitations of expected utility theory for predictive purposes have been reluctant to abandon the idea that violations of that theory are in some way irrational or normatively unacceptable (cf. Savage (1954, pp. 102–103), Morgenstern (1979, p. 180), Kahneman and Tversky (1979, p. 277), Bell (1985, p. 26–27)).

We are not, of course, the only theorists to doubt the normative appeal of the standard axioms of expected utility theory. But merely to construct a rival system of axioms, however elegant and however compatible with experimental evidence, is not to answer the question: "*Why* can it be rational to violate the sure-thing principle or the compound probability axiom?"

We believe that our analysis *does* provide an answer to that question. In our theory, people seek consistently to maximise expected satisfaction, where that expectation includes the anticipation of possible disappointment and elation. We cannot see any reason for regarding such a maximand as irrational; nor do we think that any simple experience of satisfaction, whatever its source, can be designated either rational or irrational.

This conclusion is in some degree supported by the evidence of an experiment conducted by Slovic and Tversky (1974). They found that a number of people who violated the sure-thing principle continued to wish to do so even after being exposed to the argument—due to Savage—that such behaviour is inconsistent. MacCrimmon (1968, p. 21) reported rather larger shifts towards conformity with conventional postulates during interviews with his repondents, but noted that "most of the persistent violations that did occur involved Postulate 2" (Savage's sure-thing principle). In a more recent experiment, MacCrimmon and Larsson (1979, pp. 366–369) recorded a greater preference for an

Allais-type counter-axiom argument than for either of two Savage-type arguments, even among respondents whose observed choices were consistent with the sure-thing principle. Thus it would appear that a number of people do not subscribe to all the principles of rationality that have appealed to conventional theorists. Our theory may explain why this is so.

By basing a theory of choice on psychological assumptions rather than behavioural axioms it is sometimes possible to provide a unified explanation for patterns of behaviour that would otherwise appear to be quite unrelated. Our analysis of the isolation effect provides an example. Since this effect is a violation of the compound probability axiom rather than of the independence axiom, it appears at first sight to be unconnected with the common consequence and common ratio effects. We have been able to show that violations of the compound probability axiom and violations of the independence axiom may have a common rationale.

In a more fundamental sense, all of these violations may have the same underlying rationale as violations of the transitivity axiom. This can be seen by comparing the present theory with regret theory. Both theories assume that the individual seeks to maximise the mathematical expectation of satisfaction. In the present theory, the satisfaction derived from any consequence depends in part on a comparison between that consequence and the other consequences of the same action in different states of the world. In regret theory, the satisfaction derived from a consequence depends in part on a comparison between that consequence and the consequences of other actions in the same state of the world. These two kinds of comparison are not mutually exclusive, and at the psychological level they have much in common. Disappointment and regret are different kinds of pain that one may experience when one reflects on "what might have been". Both, we suggest, are natural human emotions, and ones that can be recognised through introspection. We can see no reason for supposing either emotion to be more natural—still less, more rational—than the other.

Because regret theory makes comparisons *across actions* but *within states of the world*, it can predict violations of the transitivity axiom but not violations of the sure-thing principle; whereas disappointment theory, which makes comparisons *across states of the world* but *within actions* can predict violations of the sure-thing principle, but not violations of transitivity. However, both theories generate many of the same predictions such as the common consequence and common ratio effects in the case of statistically independent prospects, simultaneous gambling and insurance, and the isolation effect. Given the similarity of the fundamental structure of both theories, there may be grounds for thinking that a more general theory of rational choice under uncertainty may encompass both regret and disappointment.

First version received March 1984; final version accepted June 1985 (Eds.)

An earlier version of this paper was presented at the Second International Conference on Utility and Risk Theory. We are grateful to the participants at that Conference, and in particular Mark Machina and David Bell for their comments and suggestions.

NOTES

1. Peter Fishburn's SSB utility theory was also being developed at that time (see Fishburn (1982)). For further details of the relationship between regret theory and SSB utility, see Loomes and Sugden (1983) and Machina (1983).

2. The corresponding concept in regret theory was called "choiceless utility". We now believe that the more general term "basic utility" is more appropriate.

3. See Section 4 for a proof that this condition entails first-order stochastic dominance preference.

282   REVIEW OF ECONOMIC STUDIES

4. For the sake of clarity, Figure 1 has been drawn with the scale of the vertical axis double the scale of the horizontal axis.

5. It is not difficult to construct numerical examples in which such reversals will occur.

6. Consider this example. As in Table I, the probabilities of states S_1, S_2 and S_3 are λp, $(1-\lambda)p$ and $1-p$ respectively, and λ is fixed at 0·8. However, c_{11}, $c_{12} \neq \lambda c_{21}$. Instead, $c_{11} = c_{12} = 250$ while $c_{21} = 300$; $c_{22} = c_{23} = c_{13} = 0$. $D(\xi) = \xi^2/(\xi + 50)$ for all $\xi \geq 0$ and $-\xi^2/(50 - \xi)$ for all $\xi < 0$. Readers may check that when $p = 1$, $A_1 > A_2$; when $p = 0·5$, $A_1 < A_2$; and when $p = 0·2$, $A_1 > A_2$ again.

7. See, for instance, the striking example in Tversky and Kahneman (1981) where subjects respond very differently according to whether a particular problem is presented in terms of "lives saved" or "lives lost".

REFERENCES

ALLAIS, M. (1953), "Le Comportement de l'Homme Rationnel devant le Risque; Critique des Postulats et Axiomes de l'Ecole Americaine", *Econometrica*, **21**, 503-546.

BELL, D. E. (1982), "Regret in Decision Making Under Uncertainy", *Operations Research*, **30**, 961-981.

BELL, D. E. (1985), "Disappointment in Decision Making Under Uncertainty", *Operations Research*, **33**, 1-27.

CHEW, S. and MacCRIMMON, K. (1979), "Alpha-Nu Choice Theory: A Generalization of Expected Utility Theory" (Working Paper No. 669, University of British Columbia Faculty of Commerce).

FISHBURN, P. (1982), "Nontransitive Measurable Utility", *Journal of Mathematical Psychology*, **25**, 31-67.

FISHBURN, P. (1983), "Transitive Measurable Utility", *Journal of Economic Theory*, **31**, 293-317.

HAGEN, O. (1979), "Towards a Positive Theory of Preferences under Risk", in Allais, M. and Hagen, O. (eds.) *Expected Utility Hypotheses and the Allais Paradox* (Dordrecht: Reidel) 271-302.

KAHNEMAN, D. and TVERSKY, A. (1979). "Prospect Theory: An Analysis of Decision under Risk", *Econometrica*, **47**, 263-291.

LOOMES, G. and SUGDEN, R. (1982), "Regret Theory: An Alternative Theory of Rational Choice Under Uncertainty", *Economic Journal*, **92**, 805-824.

LOOMES, G. and SUGDEN, R. (1983), "Regret Theory and Measurable Utility", *Economics Letters*, **12**, 19-21.

MacCRIMMON, K. R. (1968), "Descriptive and Normative Implications of the Decision Theory Postulates", in Borch, K. and Mossin, J. (eds.) *Risk and Uncertainty*. (I.E.A.) 3-23.

MacCRIMMON, K. R. and LARSSON, S. (1979), "Utility Theory: Axioms versus 'Paradoxes'", in Allais, M. and Hagen, O. (eds.) *Expected Utility Hypotheses and the Allais Paradox* (Dordrecht: Reidel) 333-409.

MACHINA, M. J. (1982), "'Expected Utility' Analysis Without the Independence Axiom", *Econometrica*, **50**, 277-323.

MACHINA, M. J. (1983), "The Economic Theory of Behavior Towards Risk: Theory, Evidence and New Directions" (Technical Report No. 433 of the Center for Research on Organizational Efficiency, Stanford University).

MORGENSTERN, O. (1979), "Some Reflections on Utility", in Allais M. and Hagen, O. (eds.) *Expected Utility Hypotheses and the Allais Paradox* (Dordrecht: Reidel) 175-183.

MOSKOWITZ, H. (1974), "Effects of Problem Presentation and Feedback on Rational Behavior in Allais and Morlat Type Problems", *Decision Sciences*, **5**, 225-242.

SAMUELSON, P. (1950), "Probability and the Attempts to Measure Utility", *Economic Review*, **1**, 167-173.

SAVAGE, L. J. (1954) *The Foundtions of Statistics* (New York: Wiley).

SLOVIC, P. and TVERSKY, A. (1974), "Who Accepts Savage's Axiom?", *Behavioral Science*, **19**, 368-373.

TVERSKY, A. and KAHNEMAN, D. (1981), "The Framing of Decisions and the Psychology of Choice", *Science*, **211**, 453-458.

[11]

MANAGEMENT SCIENCE
Vol. 33, No. 11, November 1987
Printed in U.S.A.

LOTTERY DEPENDENT UTILITY*

JOAO L. BECKER AND RAKESH K. SARIN

Programa de Pos-Graduacao em Administracao, Universidade Federal Do Rio Grande Do Sul, 90000-Porto Alegre-RS, Brazil

Fuqua School of Business, Duke University, Durham, North Carolina 27706

In this paper we propose a model for decision making under risk that is capable of predicting empirically observed preference patterns that have been found to be incompatible with the expected utility model. The model departs from the classical expected utility model by allowing utilities to depend on the lottery. The dependence of utilities on the lottery being evaluated is achieved by restricting the utility measure to a convenient parametric family of functions. The idea then is to use each lottery to determine a specific parameter value thus characterizing the utility function for each particular lottery. The expected value of this lottery dependent utility function provides the overall measure of preference. The model retains the properties of transitivity, stochastic dominance, and continuity. It also permits types of analyses, such as exploitation of basic attitudes toward risk through risk aversion properties, that have been found useful in decision theory.

The primary use of our model is in descriptive or predictive research and applications. For some decision makers who wish to retain the preference patterns that are incompatible with the substitution principle, even after the implications of their choices are made transparent, our model could be of prescriptive use as well.

(UTILITY THEORY; PREFERENCE THEORY)

1. Introduction

Suppose you are offered a choice between receiving a sure outcome $500 or a lottery in which you have a 0.5 chance of receiving $1,000 and a 0.5 chance of receiving $0. If you are risk averse you will choose the sure outcome $500. Now, suppose you are offered a choice between two lotteries. In the first lottery you have a 0.04 chance of receiving $500 and a 0.96 chance of receiving $0. In the second lottery you have a 0.02 chance of receiving $1,000 and a 0.98 chance of receiving $0. Suppose, in this situation you prefer the second lottery. If you are an expected utility maximizer, your choices in the two situations above are inconsistent. That is, there exists no *fixed* utility function defined over dollar outcomes that will provide simultaneously a higher expected utility for the options you chose. If, however, we allow the utility function to vary with the lottery then the expected value of this *lottery dependent utility* could indeed produce the preference pattern that you exhibited. This simple observation provides the motivation for the model developed in this paper.

Of course, we cannot permit utility to depend on lotteries in an unconstrained, arbitrary manner. We will require the transitivity property to be satisfied. In addition, the property of monotonicity or the preference for first order stochastically dominating lotteries will be maintained.

The model developed here may be useful in predicting choices, for example, in consumer decision research. In addition, the proposed model provides flexibility in those prescriptive situations where the decision maker's choices do not satisfy the substitution principle (assumption needed for fixed utility function) even when the implications of such choices are made transparent. This would be the case if, loosely speaking, the decision maker behaves in a risk averse manner when the chance of a gain is high but insists on risk prone behavior when the chance of the same gain is small.

* Accepted by Robert L. Winkler; received September 19, 1986. This paper has been with the authors 1 month for 1 revision.

In the next section some notation and an overview of the lottery dependent expected utility model are provided. In §3, the assumptions and the development of the model are presented. Risk aversion properties that are useful in further specializing the model are discussed in §4. In §5, it is shown that the model is capable of explaining some of the paradoxes discussed in the literature. The assessment procedure for the model is discussed in §6. Finally, in §7, some concluding remarks and suggestions for further research are presented. The proofs are contained in the appendix.

2. Notation and an Overview of the Model

Let $x_0, x^* \in R, x_0 < x^*$. Let $D[x_0, x^*]$ denote the set of all cumulative probability distribution functions F (also called lotteries, gambles, or prospects) over the interval $[x_0, x^*]$. A lottery resulting in $x \in [x_0, x^*]$ with probability one is denoted by F_x. Note that $D[x_0, x^*]$ is closed under convex combination, i.e., if $F, G \in D[x_0, x^*]$ and $\alpha \in [0, 1]$, then $\alpha F + (1 - \alpha)G \in D[x_0, x^*]$. It should be emphasized that although we talk about combination of cumulative probability distributions, we will work only with single stage lotteries. That is, $\alpha F + (1 - \alpha)G$ does not represent a two-stage gamble in which one gets F with probability α and G with probability $1 - \alpha$. Instead, it just represents a single stage gamble whose cumulative probability distribution is the function $\alpha F + (1 - \alpha)G$. Let $\succ$ denote an asymmetric binary relation assumed to exist on $D[x_0, x^*]$. Let $\sim$ denote the symmetric complement of $\succ$ (i.e., $F \sim G$ if and only if neither $F \succ G$ nor $G \succ F$) and $\succsim$ denote the union of $\succ$ and $\sim$ (i.e., $F \succsim G$ if and only if $F \succ G$ or $F \sim G$). We say F is preferred to G if $F \succ G$, and the decision maker is indifferent between F and G if $F \sim G$. For convenience we assume that the preference relation is increasing, i.e., for $x, y \in [x_0, x^*]$, if $x > y$ then $F_x \succ F_y$. In this context x_0 and x^* will be interpreted as the worst and best outcomes respectively. If $G(x) - F(x) \geq 0$ for all $x \in [x_0, x^*]$, we write $F \succ_{st} G$ and say that F stochastically dominates G. It can be shown that $F \succ_{st} G$ if and only if $E_F[f(x)] \geq E_G[f(x)]$ for all increasing real functions f defined on $[x_0, x^*]$, where E_F denotes expectation with respect to F (see Quirk and Saposnick 1962).

We will present axioms that imply the existence of an order preserving real valued function U defined on $D[x_0, x^*]$. For any $F, G \in D[x_0, x^*]$, $F \succsim G$ if and only if $U(F) \geq U(G)$. In this paper we examine a specific functional form for $u_F(x)$ such that:

$$U(F) = \int_{x_0}^{x^*} u_F(x)dF(x) = E_F[u_F(x)]. \tag{1}$$

We will call U *lottery dependent expected utility*. In (1), u_F is a real valued function that is interpreted, because of its dependence on F, as a lottery dependent utility function. Observe that (1) does not impose any restriction on the functional form of U. This can be easily seen by the identity $U(F) \equiv E_F[U(F)]$, defining $u_F(x) = U(F)$. However, to be useful and testable, a model should specify a particular form of $u_F(x)$. As shown in Table 1, a large number of models that have appeared in the literature can be framed as (1) by appropriately defining u_F. The list presented in the table is not exhaustive and the models are presented in their original notation. For an explanation of their many elements, the reader is referred to the original work.

We will be able to show that preference patterns (ranking of lotteries) implied by any chosen U can be obtained from some appropriately defined lottery dependent utility functions that belong to a parametric family of functions. Thus we will use

$$u_F(x) = u(x, c_F), \tag{2}$$

where c_F is a constant that depends on F. Specifically, (1) and (2) imply that for a given F, knowing the value of $U(F)$, we can always determine a c_F such that:

$$U(F) = E_F[u(x, c_F)]. \tag{3}$$

TABLE I

Lottery Dependent Utility Functions for Several Models of Decisions under Risk
(Presented in their Original Notation)

Model	Lottery Dependent Utility (u_F)
Classic (1944)	$u_F = u$
Preston and Baratta (1948)	$u_F(x_i) = \dfrac{P_i^*}{p_i} x_i$
Allais (1952)	$u_F = u - \lambda(u - E_F[u])^2$
Edwards (1955)	$u_F(x_i) = \dfrac{P_i^*}{p_i} u_i$
Pruitt (1962)	$u_F(x_i) = \dfrac{p_i^*}{p_i} |x_i| + g(\Sigma_i p_i x_i^-)$
Krelle (1968)	$u_F = \varphi_F(u)$
Hagen (1969)	$u_F = u + u \dfrac{G(E_F[(u - E_F[u])^2])}{E_F[u]} + h \dfrac{(u - E_F[u])^3}{E_F[(u - E_F[u])^2]}$
Bernard (1974)	$u_F(x_i) = x_i^a p_i^{c-1}$
Handa (1977)	$u_F(x_i) = \dfrac{x_i h(p_i)}{p_i}$
Karmarkar (1978)	$u_F(x_i) = \dfrac{w_i}{p_i \Sigma_i w_i} u(x_i)$
Kahneman and Tversky (1979)	$u_F(x_i) = \dfrac{\pi(p_i)}{p_i} v(x_i)$
Chew and MacCrimmon (1979a)	$u_F = \dfrac{\alpha v}{E_F[\alpha]}$
Machina (1982)	$u_F = R + \frac{1}{2} E_F[S]S$
Quiggin (1982)	$u_F(x_i) = \dfrac{h_i(p)}{p_i} U(x_i)$
Fishburn (1983)	$u_F = \dfrac{u}{w}$
Bell (1985)	$u_F(x) = \begin{cases} x + e(x - \bar{x}) & \text{if } \quad x \geq \bar{x}, \\ x + d(x - \bar{x}) & \text{if } \quad x < \bar{x} \end{cases}$

To operationalize the model given by (3), we must be able to determine c_F from the knowledge of F and then use it to determine $U(F)$. If c_F does not depend on probabilities, that is if it is a constant for all F then we obtain the classical expected utility model (EU). As a first simple generalization we will assume c_F to be linear in probabilities. This assumption implies that for the composite lottery $H = \alpha F + (1 - \alpha)G$, $c_H = \alpha c_F + (1 - \alpha)c_G$. Further, there exists a real function $h(x)$ such that

$$c_F = \int_{x_0}^{x^*} h(x)dF(x) = E_F[h(x)]. \tag{4}$$

The function $h(x)$ in (4) is specific to a decision maker. While there is no simple intuitive interpretation for $h(x)$, we will show how $h(x)$ can be assessed and how in a specific model it provides insights into a decision maker's attitude toward risk. By substituting (4) in (3) we obtain our model that we will call *lottery dependent expected utility model* (LDEU):

$$U(F) = E_F[u(x, E_F[h(x)])]. \tag{5}$$

Most of the results in this paper are derived for the general model given by (5). We also examine the properties of an exponential model which is a specific case of (5).

We should stress that in spite of some similarity in notation, our lottery dependent utility $u(x, c_F)$ and the local utility $u(x; F)$ of Machina (1982a) are two distinct concepts. Machina's local utility function defined for a given F is, loosely speaking, the slope of the tangent to $U(F)$ at F. This local utility function, $u(x; F)$ can be used to rank differential shifts from F and thus provides an *approximation* to $U(G) - U(F)$ for G sufficiently close to F. Thus,

$$U(G) - U(F) \simeq \int u(x; F)(dG(x) - dF(x)).$$

The lottery dependent utility functions $u(x, c_F)$ and $u(x, c_G)$ are used to *exactly* compute $U(F)$ and $U(G)$ regardless of closeness of F and G. Thus,

$$U(G) - U(F) = \int u(x, c_G)dG(x) - \int u(x, c_F)dF(x).$$

Of course, there exists a tangent approximation to our model and for that matter to *any* "smooth" $U(F)$. In this sense Machina's local utility function is not a model of preference per se but it is rather an elegant analytical tool applicable in a wide variety of situations. In fact, we will employ it to derive some results for our model.

We should qualify that we do not propose a theory for prescriptive decision making. Instead, we develop a model that possesses flexibility in predicting a wide variety of preference patterns and yet may be interpreted as a simple extension of the EU model.

3. Development of the Lottery Dependent Expected Utility Model (LDEU)

We first present three axioms that imply the existence of an order preserving real valued function U defined on $D[x_0, x^*]$.

Axiom 1. $D[x_0, x^*]$ is completely ordered by $\succsim$.

Axiom 2. For $F, G, H \in D[x_0, x^*]$, if $F \succsim G \succsim H$ then there exists an $\alpha \in [0, 1]$ such that $G \sim \alpha F + (1 - \alpha)H$.

Axiom 3. For $F, G \in D[x_0, x^*]$, if $F \succ_{st} G$, $F \ddagger G$, then $F \succ G$.

Axiom 1 requires that any two distributions F and G be comparable ($F \succsim G$ or $G \succsim F$) through the preference relation $\succsim$ and that this relation be transitive (if $F \succsim G$ and $G \succsim H$, then $F \succsim H$). Axiom 2 is a continuity axiom that has been used in many developments, e.g. see Herstein and Milnor (1953), Chew and MacCrimmon (1979a), and Fishburn (1983). Axiom 3 requires that stochastically dominating lotteries be preferred. This axiom, we believe, will be satisfied by everyone if the lotteries are presented in an orderly manner (for example, as cumulative graphs).

THEOREM 1. *If Axioms 1–3 are satisfied, then there exists a real valued function U defined on $D[x_0, x^*]$ such that for any $F, G \in D[x_0, x^*]$, $F \succsim G$ if and only if $U(F) \geqslant U(G)$.*

We now have a function U which could be interpreted as an ordinal preference function defined on the space of lotteries. We assign to the best lottery (x^* with probability 1) $U(F_{x^*}) = 1$ and to the worst lottery (x_0 with probability 1) $U(F_{x_0}) = 0$. If $F = \alpha F_{x^*} + (1 - \alpha)F_{x_0}$ for some α, then $U(F) = \alpha$.

We will now show that U can be represented as a lottery dependent expected utility model in which the lottery dependent utility functions belong to a parametric family of functions. We will work with a class of functions $u(x, c)$ for $x \in [x_0, x^*]$, and $c \in (\underline{c}, \bar{c})$, satisfying Properties 1 and 2 below. Specifically, we will assume that u is monotonic to preserve the preference for stochastically dominating lotteries and differentiable to obtain continuous and smooth representation for U. Further, we require that for any x, we are able to assign utility as close to both zero or one as desired.

Property 1. For every c_F, $u(x, c_F)$ is increasing and differentiable in x, $u(x_0, c_F) = 0$, and $u(x^*, c_F) = 1$, where c_F is a constant particular to an F.

Property 2. For every $x \in (x_0, x^*)$, $u(x, c)$ is increasing and differentiable in c, $\lim_{c \to \bar{c}} u(x, c) = 1$, and $\lim_{c \to \underline{c}} u(x, c) = 0$.

Several functions $u(x, c)$ satisfy Properties 1 and 2. A specific example will be presented later.

THEOREM 2. *For any $u(x, c)$ satisfying Properties 1 and 2 and for any given $F \in D[x_0, x^*]$, there exists a number c_F such that*

$$U(F) = \int_{x_0}^{x^*} u(x, c_F)dF(x) = E_F[u(x, c_F)].$$

An immediate implication of Theorem 2 is that the preference patterns implied by any underlying $U(F)$ can also be obtained from $E_F[u(x, c_F)]$ by appropriately choosing c_F.

As we discussed in the previous section, we *assume* that as a first simple approximation c_F is linear in probabilities. This assumption implies that there exists a real function h such that $c_F = E_F[h(x)]$. Therefore, our LDEU model (5) is obtained by simply substituting $c_F = E_F[h(x)]$ in the result of Theorem 2. This assumption about c_F allows us to operationalize the model and provide testable hypotheses on behavior. We are aware that it may restrict the set of preference patterns permitted by the model. Our analysis reported later, however, shows that the LDEU model (5) possesses a great deal of flexibility in permitting a wide variety of attitude toward risk, violation of substitution principle, and in predicting preference patterns that are plausible but cannot be predicted by some existing models e.g. prospect theory and Chew and MacCrimmon's weighted utility theory.

We now examine some properties of the function h. The following two lemmas establish the continuity of h and U.

LEMMA 1. *$h(x)$ is continuous in $[x_0, x^*]$.*

This lemma permits us to fit a smooth function through few assessed $h(x)$ points. To show the continuity of U, we say that $F^{(n)}$ *converges weakly* to F if $F^{(n)}$ is a sequence of lotteries in $D[x_0, x^*]$ and $F^{(n)}(x) \to F(x)$ at each continuity point of $F \in D[x_0, x^*]$. It is well known that $F^{(n)}$ converges weakly to F if and only if $E_{F^{(n)}}[f(x)] \to E_F[f(x)]$ for all continuous real functions f defined on $[x_0, x^*]$.

LEMMA 2. *Let $F^{(n)} \in D[x_0, x^*]$ converging weakly to $F \in D[x_0, x^*]$. Then $U(F^{(n)}) \to U(F)$.*

Continuity is a desirable condition for mathematical models; in addition, this lemma allows us to use the results developed by Machina (1982).

The function h, however, cannot be arbitrary as the model should preserve stochastic dominance. A sufficient condition to satisfy Axiom 3 (stochastic dominance) is that $h(x)$ be increasing. To see this, suppose $F \succ_{st} G$ then $c_F > c_G$ if $h(x)$ is increasing. Thus $u(x, c_F) > u(x, c_G)$ for every x by Property 2. By stochastic dominance and Property 1, $E_F[u(x, c_F)] > E_G[u(x, c_F)] > E_G[u(x, c_G)]$. The necessary and sufficient condition satisfying Axiom 3 is somewhat complicated.

THEOREM 3. *Axiom 3 is satisfied if and only if for every $F \in D[x_0, x^*]$, $u(x, c_F) + E_F[u_2(x, c_F)]h(x)$ is increasing, where $u_2(x, c)$ denotes $du(x, c)/dc$.*

As one special case of our model (5), we will examine the properties of an exponential model:

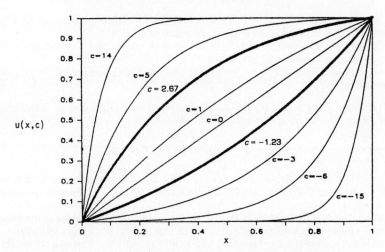

u(x,c)

FIGURE 1.   Lottery Dependent Utility Functions for the Exponential Model.

$$u(x, c_F) = \frac{1 - e^{-c_F((x-x_0)/(x^*-x_0))}}{1 - e^{-c_F}} \qquad \text{if} \qquad c_F \neq 0,$$

$$= \frac{x - x_0}{x^* - x_0} \qquad \text{if} \qquad c_F = 0, \qquad (6)$$

where $c_F = E_F[h(x)]$. Various $u(x, c_F)$ obtained by (6) are shown in Figure 1. Most of our results do not require the assumption of the exponential form (6). However, significant computational simplicity is achieved if this form is assumed. We will refer to the exponential form as LDEU(exp) whenever we require it. The exponential form has been widely used in analysis and applications of EU model. We believe that in practical application LDEU model with exponential form will be attractive. It may be worthwhile to examine the properties of alternative forms such as power, logarithm, polynomial etc. An example of one alternative form for $u(x, c_F)$ is $(f(x))^{1/c_F}$, where f is increasing with $f(x_0) = 0, f(x^*) = 1$, and $c_F \in (0, \infty)$.

4.   Risk Aversion Properties

In the EU model, risk aversion properties are exploited to restrict the class of applicable utility functions and to reduce the assessment effort (see Keeney and Raiffa 1976). In our model, we will show that risk aversion properties impose restrictions on h which simplify assessment and ensure that the calibrated model is consistent with some behavioral properties that the decision maker may wish to satisfy. Since in our model the utility function varies with the lottery we will define a concept of *lottery specific risk aversion*. Let us first review some definitions.

DEFINITION 1.   The *certainty equivalent* of a lottery F is the amount x_F such that the decision maker is indifferent between receiving F and the degenerate lottery F_{x_F}.

DEFINITION 2.   Two lottery dependent utility functions $u^1(x, c)$ and $u^2(x, c)$ are *strategically equivalent* if and only if they imply the same preference ranking for any two lotteries.

THEOREM 4. $u^1(x, c_F)$ and $u^2(x, c_F)$ are strategically equivalent if and only if $u^1(x, c) = k_1 + k_2 u^2(x, c)$, for all x and c, where k_1 and $k_2 > 0$ are two constants.

Clearly, certainty equivalents of a lottery using two strategically equivalent utility functions will be identical. We require that risk aversion properties remain invariant with respect to strategically equivalent utility functions.

DEFINITION 3.   A decision maker is *risk averse with respect to a lottery F* if he or she prefers the expected consequence of the lottery F, $\bar{x}_F$, to the lottery itself, *risk prone* if prefers the lottery to the expected consequence, and *risk neutral* if is indifferent between the two.

A simple example for LDEU(exp) will demonstrate the lottery specific risk aversion. Suppose $x_0 = -5$, $x^* = 5$, and $h(x) = x$. Let F be a lottery in which 2 is received with probability 0.5, and -2 is received with probability 0.5, denoted $0.5F_2 + 0.5F_{-2}$. By (4) $c_F = 0.5 \times 2 + 0.5 \times -2 = 0$. By (6), $u(x, c_F) = (x + 5)/10$. Thus, $U(F) = 0.5$. The utility of the expected consequence of the lottery is also 0.5 and hence the decision maker is risk neutral with respect to F. Now, consider $G = 0.9F_2 + 0.1F_{-2}$. In this case $c_G = 1.6$. By (6),

$$u(x, c_G) = \frac{1 - e^{-1.6((x+5)/10)}}{1 - e^{-1.6}} .$$

Thus, $u(G) = 0.9u(2, 1.6) + 0.1u(-2, 1.6) = 0.807$. The utility of the expected consequence of the lottery is 0.817 and hence the decision maker is risk averse with respect to G. Similarly, if we define $H = 0.1F_2 + 0.9F_{-2}$, we find that the decision maker is risk prone with respect to H. In fact, in this example, for a lottery $\alpha F_x + (1 - \alpha)F_{-x}$, the decision maker is risk neutral if $\alpha = 0.5$, risk averse if $\alpha > 0.5$, and risk prone if $\alpha < 0.5$, for all $x_0 < x < x^*$.

DEFINITION 4.   A decision maker is *globally risk averse* if $U(F_{\bar{x}_F}) > U(F)$, *globally risk prone* if $U(F_{\bar{x}_F}) < U(F)$, and *globally risk neutral* if $U(F_{\bar{x}_F}) = U(F)$, for all lotteries F.

DEFINITION 5.   The *risk premium* for a lottery F, RP_F, is the difference between the expected consequence of the lottery and its certainty equivalent, $RP_F = \bar{x}_F - x_F$.

The relationship between certainty equivalent, risk premium, and risk aversion is obtained in a straightforward manner.

THEOREM 5.   *A decision maker is globally risk averse if and only if $x_F < \bar{x}_F$ for any nondegenerate $F \in D[x_0, x^*]$.*

As a corollary of Theorem 5, it is immediately seen that a decision maker is globally risk averse if and only if $RP_F > 0$ for any nondegenerate $F \in D[x_0, x^*]$.

It should be noted that in spite of a close analogy with the EU model several results may not be valid for our LDEU model. For example, in the EU model a decision maker who prefers the expected consequence of a lottery with 0.5 chance of x_1 and 0.5 chance of x_2, for any $x_1, x_2 \in [x_0, x^*]$, $x_1 \neq x_2$, to the lottery itself is globally risk averse. In our model, this condition is not sufficient to obtain global risk aversion. Further, in LDEU(exp), if $c_F = c$ for all F (EU model holds) then the sign of c determines global risk aversion. Unfortunately, in LDEU(exp), the sign of c_F alone does not permit us to draw conclusions on risk aversion. Before we discuss conditions that establish relationship between h and risk aversion, we state a specific situation where the information on the sign of c_F indeed is sufficient for risk aversion.

LEMMA 3.   *Suppose $h(x) = ax + b$. In* LDEU(exp), $c_F > 0$ *implies risk averse*, $c_F < 0$ *implies risk prone, and* $c_F = 0$ *implies risk neutral behavior with respect to F.*

Clearly, using Lemma 3, if $h(x) = ax + b$ and $c_F > 0$ for all F then the decision maker is globally risk averse. The following theorem shows that, more generally, so long as the function h is concave and positive the global risk aversion will be ensured.

THEOREM 6.   *In* LDEU(exp), *if* $h > 0$ *and concave then the decision maker is globally risk averse and if* $h < 0$ *and convex then the decision maker is globally risk prone.*

Finally, a sufficient condition on h that satisfies Axiom 3 (stochastic dominance) and ensures that a mean preserving increase in risk is less preferred is given by **Lemma 4** below. A lottery $G = F + l$, $E_l[x] = 0$, is said to yield a mean preserving increase in risk for lottery F because it has a higher spread but the same mean (see Rothschild and Stiglitz (1970)). We denote $F \succ_2 G$ and say that F is *less risky* than G.

LEMMA 4.   *In* LDEU(exp), *if* h *is positive, concave, and increasing then* $U(F) \geq U(G)$ *whenever* $F \succ_2 G$, *for all* F, $G \in D[x_0, x^*]$.

The necessary and sufficient condition for maintaining the preference for less risky lotteries, where "less risky" is as defined above, is obtained analogous to Theorem 3.

THEOREM 7.   *For* F, $G \in D[x_0, x^*]$, $U(F) \geq U(G)$ *whenever* $F \succ_2 G$ *if and only if for every* $F \in D[x_0, x^*]$, $u(x, c_F) + E_F[u_2(x, c_F)]h(x)$ *is increasing and concave.*

Lemma 4 or Theorem 7 can be used to restrict h for a decision maker who dislikes a mean preserving increase in risk. We now investigate the measure of risk aversion analogous to the Arrow-Pratt measure (Arrow 1971, Pratt 1964) for our model. Using Machina's (1982a) results, we can obtain the measure of risk aversion with respect to F denoted $R(x, F)$.

DEFINITION 6.   A measure of risk aversion with respect to a lottery $F \in D[x_0, x^*]$ and $x \in [x_0, x^*]$ is given by

$$R(x, F) = -\frac{u''(x, c_F) + E_F[u_2(x, c_F)]h''(x)}{u'(x, c_F) + E_F[u_2(x, c_F)]h'(x)} \tag{7}$$

where u' and u'' are respectively the first and the second derivative of $u(x, c)$ with respect to x.

For a specified lottery F, the term $-u''(x, c_F)/u'(x, c_F)$ is the constant c_F in LDEU(exp) and the term $E_F[u_2(x, c_F)]$ is a positive constant. If $R(x, F)$ is positive (negative) for all F and x then the decision maker will be globally risk averse (risk prone). Similarly, if $R^1(x, F)$ for individual 1 is higher than $R^2(x, F)$ for individual 2 for all x, then individual 1 is more risk averse than individual 2 with respect to F. Individual 1 is globally more risk averse if this condition holds for all F. The following results are easily obtained.

THEOREM 8.   *Two utility functions are strategically equivalent if and only if they have the same risk aversion function.*

THEOREM 9.   *If* $R(x, F)$ *is positive (negative) for all* x *and* F, *then the decision maker is globally risk averse (risk prone).*

THEOREM 10.   *If* $R^1(x, F) > R^2(x, F)$ *for all* x *and* F *then* $RP_F^1 > RP_F^2$ *for all* F, *where* RP_F^i *denotes the risk premium for lottery* F *obtained with the utility function* $u^i(x, c_F)$.

So far we have derived some results that establish relationships between h and risk averse behavior. Now we discuss a further specialization of risk averse behavior.

DEFINITION 6.   A decision maker is *decreasingly risk averse* if the risk premium for a lottery $F + \Delta$ that is obtained by adding a constant Δ to all outcomes of F is smaller than the risk premium for F, for all F and Δ such that F, $F + \Delta \in D[x_0, x^*]$. To obtain decreasing risk aversion, we use Machina (1982b, Theorem 1).

THEOREM 11.   *If* $-(u''(x, c_F) + E_F[u_2(x, c_F)]h''(x)/\int [u'(x, c_F) + E_F[u_2(x, c_F)] \times h'(x)dF(x))$ *is everywhere nonincreasing in* x *and* F *then the utility function* $u(x, c)$ *is decreasingly risk averse.*

Thus, we can incorporate appropriate risk aversion properties in the LDEU model. These properties are useful in analysis and in calibration of the model.

5. Explanation of Some Paradoxes

There has been an accumulating body of empirical evidence that in some well-defined situations the predictions of the EU model are inconsistent with the actual responses for a large number of subjects (see Kahneman and Tversky 1979). These inconsistencies frequently occur because of the violation of the substitution principle of the classical utility theory; though, violations of both transitivity and stochastic dominance have also been noted. In this section we show that the LDEU model is capable of predicting preference patterns that will be deemed "paradoxical" if an EU model is employed. It is important to recognize that the LDEU model merely provides an additional flexibility in allowing the prediction of some preference patterns that are incompatible with the EU model; it does not require that such preference patterns must be observed for the model to be applicable.

The Common Ratio Effect

It has been observed that a majority of the subjects prefer lottery A_1 to B_1 and a majority prefer lottery B_2 to A_2 in the following two choice situations:

Situation 1.

A_1: win \$3,000 for sure	versus	B_1: 0.8 chance to win \$4,000
		0.2 chance to win \$0

Situation 2.

A_2: 0.25 chance to win \$3,000	versus	B_2: 0.20 chance to win \$4,000
0.75 chance to win \$0		0.80 chance to win \$0

Such a choice pattern is inconsistent with the expected utility model. In the LDEU(exp) model, if we let $x^* = 4,000$ and $x_0 = 0$, then

$$U(A_1) = u(3000, c_{A_1}), \qquad U(B_1) = 0.8,$$

$$U(A_2) = 0.25u(3000, c_{A_2}), \qquad U(B_2) = 0.2, \qquad \text{where}$$

$$c_{A_1} = h(3000) \qquad \text{and} \qquad c_{A_2} = 0.25h(3000) + 0.75h(0).$$

Suppose $h(0) = 0.2$ and $h(3000) = 1.5$. Then using (6) we get $U(A_1) = 0.869$ and $U(A_2) = 0.199$, which implies preference of A_1 over B_1 and B_2 over A_2. More generally, for $0 < x < y$, let

A_1: win \$x,
B_1: q chance of \$y and $(1 - q)$ chance of \$0,
A_2: p chance of \$x and $(1 - p)$ chance of \$0,
B_2: pq chance of \$y and $(1 - pq)$ chance of \$0.

The preference for A_1 over B_1 and B_2 over A_2 is implied by LDEU so long as

$$h(x) > k, \qquad \text{and} \qquad ph(x) + (1 - p)h(0) < k,$$

where k is a constant given by the equation $u(x, k) = q$. In the numerical example above using LDEU(exp) $k = 0.5622$. Our model can, in fact, predict the "switch point," $p = p^*$, below which the preference pattern switches and becomes incompatible with the expected utility model. In our numerical example, this switch point is 0.278 which is obtained by solving:

$$h(0) = 0.2 = \frac{k - p^*h(x)}{1 - p^*} = \frac{0.5662 - 1.5p^*}{1 - p^*}.$$

We can use the switch point to test the predictive validity of the model. Alternatively, we can use the choices between successive pairs of gambles A_2 and B_2 obtained from A_1 and B_1 by varying p, to identify the switch point which in turn can be used to determine h values.

Allais Paradox (The Common Consequence Effect)

The most well known example of the violation of the expected utility model is the "Allais Paradox" (Allais 1953) based on the following gambles:

A'_1:	win 1 million for sure	B'_1:	10% chance of 5 million
			89% chance of 1 million
			1% chance of 0 million
A'_2:	11% chance of 1 million	B'_2:	10% chance of 5 million
	89% chance of 0 million		90% chance of 0 million.

Many experiments (see Morrison 1967 and MacCrimmon and Larsson 1979) have confirmed that in a large number of settings (some include moderate payoffs and moderate probabilities) the pattern of preference of A'_1 over B'_1 and B'_2 over A'_2 is exhibited by a large number of subjects. This preference pattern is inconsistent with the expected utility model. In the EU model utility of 1 million is constant and that leads to the paradox. In the LDEU model the choice of $h(0)$, $h(1)$, and $h(5)$ allows the flexibility that A'_1 over B'_1 and B'_2 over A'_2 can be simultaneously preferred.

Becker (1986) has examined the preference patterns for LDEU, Chew and Mac-Crimmon's weighted utility theory (1979a) and prospect theory using the general HILO structure proposed by Chew and MacCrimmon (1979b). This analysis is useful in providing insights into how our assumption, $c_F = E_F[h(x)]$, restricts the preference patterns that can be predicted by the LDEU model. In this structure there are 16 possible preference patterns. Of these 16 only 2 are consistent with the EU model, at most 4 with the prospect model, 6 with Chew and MacCrimmon's model, and 14 with the LDEU model. In fact, the six preference patterns that are consistent with Chew and MacCrimmon's model are also consistent with the LDEU(exp) with $h(x) = ax + b$ (a simple model that can be completely specified by merely two indifference judgments). An implication of this observation is that in the empirical study reported by Chew and Waller (1986, Table 2), the LDEU model is consistent with 98% of responses in experiment 1 and with 97% of responses in experiment 2. In contrast, Chew and MacCrimmon's model is consistent with 62% of responses in experiment 1 and 71% in experiment 2. A thorough comparison of the alternative models is beyond the scope of this paper; however, this analysis suggests that the LDEU model does possess a great deal of flexibility in predicting empirically observed preference patterns in spite of the restrictive assumption on c_F.

Utility Assessor's Dilemma

There are several methods for assessing the classical utility function. These methods should yield, with proper allowance for assessment errors, the same utility function. However, the results from alternative methods often yield utility functions that differ in systematic ways. McCord and de Neufville (1984), Hershey, Kunreuther, and Schoemaker (1982), Karmarkar (1978), and others have found that higher the probability level used in assessment, more risk averse the recovered utility function looks like. Our LDEU model permits these apparent inconsistencies.

Suppose an individual's certainty equivalent for a lottery with a 0.5 chance of x^* and a 0.5 chance of x_0 is determined. Let us denote, for simplicity in notation, this certainty equivalent $x_{0.5}$. Next, the certainty equivalent $x_{0.25}$ for a lottery with a 0.5 chance of $x_{0.5}$

and a 0.5 chance of x_0 is determined. Similarly, the certainty equivalent $x_{0.75}$ for a lottery with a 0.5 chance of x^* and a 0.5 chance of $x_{0.5}$ is also determined. We now have five points on the utility curve. Additional points, if desired, can be assessed using this strategy of successive subdivisions. Now, suppose we independently fix p at some chosen level and determine the certainty equivalent $y_p \in [x_0, x^*]$ for the lottery with p chance of x^* and $(1 - p)$ chance of x_0. The utility of both x_p obtained in the first assessment and y_p obtained in the second assessment should equal p in the EU model. Therefore, we should obtain, for example, $x_{0.25} = y_{0.25}$ and $x_{0.75} = y_{0.75}$. The finding of the studies cited earlier imply that often $x_{0.75} > y_{0.75}$ and $x_{0.25} < y_{0.25}$. An application of the LDEU model yields:

$$u(x_{0.5}, h(x_{0.5})) = 0.5,$$

$$u(x_{0.25}, h(x_{0.25})) = 0.5u(x_{0.5}, 0.5h(x_{0.5}) + 0.5h(x_0))$$

$$u(x_{0.75}, h(x_{0.75})) = 0.5 + 0.5u(x_{0.5}, 0.5h(x_{0.5}) + 0.5h(x^*)).$$

If we assume $h(x)$ increasing and since $u(x, c)$ is increasing in each argument, we obtain:

$$u(x_{0.25}, h(x_{0.25})) < 0.25 \quad \text{and} \quad u(x_{0.75}, h(x_{0.75})) > 0.75.$$

Using the p-value method, we elicit

$$u(y_{0.25}, h(y_{0.25})) = 0.25 \quad \text{and} \quad u(y_{0.75}, h(y_{0.75})) = 0.75.$$

Thus, $x_{0.25} < y_{0.25}$ and $x_{0.75} > y_{0.75}$ conforming with the observed empirical data.

Lottery Dependent Gambling and Insurance Behavior

The expected utility model permits insurance and gambling behavior if the utility function contains both concave and convex segments as shown by Friedman and Savage (1948). For a given interval $[a, b]$, $a < b$, if a decision maker prefers the expected consequence of any lottery with 0.5 chance of x and 0.5 chance of y to the lottery for x, $y \in [a, b]$, $x \ddagger y$, then the utility function will be concave in this interval. Suppose a decision maker prefers the lottery with p chance of b and $(1 - p)$ chance of a to the expected consequence $(pb + (1 - p)a)$ when p is small and prefers the expected consequence to the lottery when p is large. Such a gambling behavior (preference for lottery) and insurance behavior (preference for the sure expected consequence) based on the level of p are incompatible with the EU model. We conjecture that for every interval $[a, b]$, $a < b$, a person will exhibit both the insurance and gambling behavior. This conjecture is formalized in the following behavioral hypothesis.

Behavioral Hypothesis. For any $a, b \in [x_0, x^*]$, $a < b$, there exists an $\alpha^* \in (0, 1)$, $\alpha F_b + (1 - \alpha)F_a \succ F_{ab+(1-\alpha)a}$ if $\alpha < \alpha^*$, and $F_{ab+(1-\alpha)a} \succ \alpha F_b + (1 - \alpha)F_a$ if $\alpha > \alpha^*$.

Intuitively, this behavioral hypothesis requires a switch in behavior from risk seeking to risk averse. While no classical utility function can satisfy this hypothesis, even the LDEU model needs to be constrained to be consistent with it. Specifically, in LDEU(exp), h must be increasing and concave between x_0 and x and convex between x and x^* where x is such that $h(x) = 0$. We note that in several nonexpected utility theories the probability weight function does not depend on the consequence associated with the probability (Handa 1977, Kahneman and Tversky 1979, Luce and Narens 1985, etc.) Our hypothesis can be used to test these theories. More generally, if α^* varies with a and b then utility must depend on the entire lottery. For example, an implication of regret theory (Bell (1982)) is that $\alpha^* = 0.5$ for all a and b (assuming a linear value function).

Several other empirical observations, such as the reflection effect and probabilistic insurance (Kahneman and Tversky 1979), can be explained using the LDEU model.

However, the observations of violations of transitivity, stochastic dominance, and framing effects cannot be explained by our model.

6. Assessment of the LDEU Model

Assessment of the LDEU(exp) model is surprisingly simple. We require certainty equivalents x_p of lotteries with a p chance of x^* and a $(1 - p)$ chance of x_0 for some chosen p values. The function $h(x)$ can be estimated from these responses by fitting a curve through the estimated $h(x_p)$ values. To obtain $h(x_p)$ we solve for c in

$$p = \frac{1 - e^{-c((x_p - x_0)/(x^* - x_0))}}{1 - e^{-c}},$$

which yields $h(x_p) = c$. A hypothetical example with $x_0 = 0$ and $x^* = \$100$ is shown below:

p	0.01	0.05	0.10	0.30	0.50	0.70	0.90	0.95	0.99
x_p	\$4	\$8	\$12	\$27	\$45	\$62	\$80	\$84	\$87
$h(x_p)$	−2.41	−0.942	−0.399	0.298	0.403	0.706	1.51	2.29	4.34

We can fair a curve through these assessed points and use this as h in computing $U(F)$ for any arbitrary F.

A more rigorous approach for assessing h can be developed by exploiting the qualitatively stated behavioral requirements of the decision maker. Risk aversion properties can be employed to restrict h. Conditions that imply a particular analytical form for h will also simplify the assessment. One such condition is stated below.

THEOREM 12.   *In the* LDEU(exp) *model,* $h(x) = ax + b$, $x \in [x_0, x^*]$ *if and only if for any* $F, G, H \in D[x_0, x^*]$ *such that* $E_F[x] = E_G[x]$ *and* $E_H[x] = 0$, $F \sim G$, *then* $F + H \sim G + H$.

This theorem requires that if two lotteries with equal means are indifferent then the lotteries obtained by a mean preserving spread should also be indifferent. A violation of this property for any given pair of lotteries F and G and some H clearly rules out the LDEU(exp) model with linear h. However, if this property is satisfied and yet h is not found to be linear in actual assessment then two possibilities exist. One is that there is response error. The second is that $u(x, c_F)$ is not exponential to begin with. It will be a useful future research endeavor to investigate necessary and sufficient conditions that imply simultaneously the exponential model as well as some analytical form for h.

It is possible to directly assess $u(x, c_F)$ without assuming the functional form for u (e.g. exponential) if we make an assumption about the functional form for h. An interactive scheme will be needed if both u and h are assumed to be unknown. However, the number of judgments required will be large. For predictive purposes we believe that it is advisable to start out with a simple model (e.g. LDEU(exp)) and then add complexity if required. Empirical data will be needed to make further progress in designing and evaluating alternative assessment schemes.

7. Conclusions and Suggestions for Further Research

In this paper we have proposed a model for decision making under uncertainty that is capable of predicting patterns of empirically observed preferences that are incompatible with the expected utility model. In the expected utility model the utilities associated with alternative outcomes remain invariant with the lottery in which these outcomes appear. In our model the utility measure itself depends on the lottery being evaluated. The idea is to restrict the utility measure to a convenient parametric family of functions and then to use each lottery to determine a specific parameter value thus characterizing the utility function for each particular lottery. The expected value of this lottery specific utility function with respect to the lottery provides the overall measure of preference that is used for ranking alternative lotteries. The model thus represents a natural extension of the EU model. Because of its close resemblance with the EU model, our model permits the types of analyses that have been found useful in decision theory, for example, stochastic dominance and exploitation of various basic attitudes toward risk through risk aversion properties. The model preserves transitivity, first order stochastic dominance, and continuity but permits violation of the substitution principle.

We see that our model is primarily useful for descriptive or predictive research and applications. For the decision makers who wish to maintain the pattern of preferences that violate the substitution principle, even after the implications of such preferences are made transparent, our model could be employed in a prescriptive setting as well. We note that implications of our model do not lead to any violation of external rationality in the sense that a money pump can be made out of a person who behaves according to the predictions of our model. Persuasion or self-introspection are the only means by which a person is convinced to follow the EU preference pattern in situations such as the one described in the introduction of the paper.

There are several directions for future research and some have been noted in the previous sections. An open problem is the conditions that imply the parameter $c_F = E_F[h(x)]$. The model requires empirical testing and comparisons with other models.

A promising direction of research that will enhance the application of the model is to define behaviorally appealing conditions that imply various functional forms of the model. Further research on assessment of the model will also be useful.

In our continuing research we are exploring how the LDEU model can be employed in decision analysis to break the complex decision problem down to simple components and then integrate these components for recommending a preferred course of action. Specifically, we wish to preserve the "principle of optimality" that allows roll-back in a decision tree while permitting a relaxation of the substitution principle. We will have to forego the equivalence of the extensive and the normal forms of decision trees but many other properties that simplify computation and permit a "divide and conquer" strategy can be retained.[1]

---

[1] This research was partially supported by the Office of Naval Research, The National Science Foundation and CAPES—Brazil. We gratefully acknowledge their support. We are also thankful to the Departmental Editor and two reviewers for several helpful suggestions on an earlier draft of this paper.

Appendix

PROOF OF THEOREM 1. Let $F \in D[x_0, x^*]$. Axioms 1 and 3 imply $F_{x^*} \succsim F \succsim F_{x_0}$. Define $U(F) \in [0, 1]$ such that $F \sim U(F)F_{x^*} + (1 - U(F))F_{x_0}$. By Axiom 2, $U(F)$ exists. It is unique to avoid violation of Axiom 3. Now, for F, $G \in D[x_0, x^*]$, $F \succsim G \leftrightarrow U(F)F_{x^*} + (1 - U(F))F_{x_0} \succsim U(G)F_{x^*} + (1 - U(G))F_{x_0} \leftrightarrow U(F) \geq U(G)$. ∎

PROOF OF THEOREM 2. If $F \in D[x_0, x^*]$, let the φ^u-*transform* of F be the function defined for $\lambda \in (\underline{c}, \bar{c})$ by

$$\varphi_F^u(\lambda) = \int_{x_0}^{x^*} u(x, \lambda)dF(x) = E_F[u(x, \lambda)],$$

where the function u satisfies Properties 1 and 2. Now, φ_F^u possesses the following properties:
(i) $\lim_{\lambda \to \bar{c}} \varphi_F^u(\lambda) = 1 - F(x_0)$;
(ii) $\lim_{\lambda \to \underline{c}} \varphi_F^u(\lambda) = 1 - \lim_{x \to x^{*-}} F(x)$;
(iii) if $F = \alpha F_{x^*} + (1 - \alpha)F_{x_0}$ for some $\alpha \in [0, 1]$, $\varphi_F^u = \alpha$; and
(iv) if $F \neq \alpha F_{x^*} + (1 - \alpha)F_{x_0}$ for any $\alpha \in [0, 1]$, φ_F^u is increasing and continuous.

Let α and β be the value of the jump of F at x_0 and x^* respectively. If $\alpha + \beta < 1$, let $G \in D[x_0, x^*]$, G not jumping at x_0 or x^*, such that $F = \alpha F_{x_0} + (1 - \alpha - \beta)G + \beta F_{x^*}$. Since

1380   JOAO L. BECKER AND RAKESH K. SARIN

$$\alpha F_{x_0} + (1 - \alpha)F_{x^*} \succ_{st} \alpha F_{x_0} + (1 - \alpha - \beta)G + \beta F_{x^*} \succ_{st} (1 - \beta)F_{x_0} + \beta F_{x^*},$$

Axiom 3 implies $1 - \alpha > U(F) - \beta$.

The φ^u-transform associated with F is continuous and increasing from β to $1 - \alpha$. Therefore, there exists a (unique) c_F such that

$$U(F) = \varphi_F^u(c_F) = \int_{x_0}^{x^*} u(x, c_F)dF(x).$$

If $\alpha + \beta = 1$ then $F = \beta F_{x^*} + (1 - \beta)F_{x_0}$, and $U(F) = \beta$. In this case property (iii) of the φ^u-*transform* of F states that $\varphi_F^u(\lambda) = \beta$ for all λ, trivially implying the existence of c_F such that

$$U(F) = \varphi_F^u(c_F) = \int_{x_0}^{x^*} u(x, c_F)dF(x). \quad \blacksquare$$

PROOF OF LEMMAS 1 AND 2.   See Becker (1986).

PROOF OF THEOREM 3.   It follows directly from Machina (1982a, Theorem 1) by noting that if, as our model states,

$$U(F) = \int_{x_0}^{x^*} u\left(x, \int_{x_0}^{x^*} h(x)dF(x)\right)dF(x),$$

then its local utility function is given by

$$U(x, F) = u\left(x, \int_{x_0}^{x^*} h(x)dF(x)\right) + \left[\int_{x_0}^{x^*} u_2\left(x, \int_{x_0}^{x^*} h(x)dF(x)\right)\right]h(x)$$

$$= u(x, c_F) + E_F[u_2(x, c_F)]h(x). \quad \blacksquare$$

PROOF OF THEOREM 4.   Suppose the certainty equivalent for a lottery F using $u^2(x, c)$ is x_F^2. If $u^1(x, c) = k_1 + k_2 u^2(x, c)$ then the certainty equivalent x_F using $u^1(x, c)$ is obtained by solving

$$k_1 + k_2 u^2(x_F, c_{x_F}) = E_F[k_1 + k_2 u^2(x, c_F)],$$

which yields $x_F = x_F^2$; thus u^1 and u^2 will produce the same preference ranking for lotteries.

To show the converse, let $F_x \sim \alpha F_{x^*} + (1 - \alpha)F_{x_0}$ so that

$$u^i(x, c_{F_x}) = \alpha u^i(x^*, c_{F_{x^*}}) + (1 - \alpha)u^i(x_0, c_{F_{x_0}}), \qquad \text{for} \quad i = 1, 2.$$

Letting $i = 2$, solving for α, and substituting this value of α in the expression with $i = 1$, we get the desired result. $\blacksquare$

PROOF OF THEOREM 5.   Since preferences are increasing in x, global risk aversion is equivalent to

$$U(F_{\bar{x}_F}) > U(F) = U(F_{x_F}) \leftrightarrow \bar{x}_F > x_F. \quad \blacksquare$$

PROOF OF LEMMA 3.   If $c_F > 0$ then

$$U(F) = E_F[u(x, c_F)] \leq u(\bar{x}_F, c_F)$$

$$= u(\bar{x}_F, E_F[h(x)])$$

$$= u(\bar{x}_F, h(\bar{x}_F)) \qquad \text{(by linearity of } h)$$

$$= U(F_{\bar{x}_F}).$$

Thus risk aversion is implied. Similarly, for $c_F < 0$ risk prone behavior is implied. $\blacksquare$

PROOF OF THEOREM 6.   Suppose $h > 0$ and concave. Then $c_F > 0$ for all F, which yields

$$U(F) = E_F[u(x, c_F)] \leq u(\bar{x}_F, c_F)$$

$$= u(\bar{x}_F, E_F[h(x)])$$

$$\leq u(\bar{x}_F, h(\bar{x}_F)) \qquad \text{(by concavity of } h)$$

$$= U(F_{\bar{x}_F}).$$

Similarly global risk proneness is obtained if $h < 0$ and convex. $\blacksquare$

PROOF OF LEMMA 4.   If $F \succ_2 G$ and $c_F > 0$ (h positive), then u is concave and $E_F[u(x, c_F)] \geq E_G[u(x, c_F)] \geq E_G[u(x, c_G)]$ since $c_F > c_G$ (h increasing and concave) and Property 2 holds. $\blacksquare$

PROOF OF THEOREM 7.   It follows directly from Machina (1982a, Theorem 2) by noting, as showed in the proof of Theorem 3, that the local utility function of our model is given by $U(x, F) = u(x, c_F) + E_F[u_2(x, c_F)]h(x)$. $\blacksquare$

PROOF OF THEOREM 8. Let $u^1(x, c) = k_1 + k_2 u^2(x, c)$, $k_2 > 0$. Clearly $u^{1'} = k_2 u^{2'}$, $u^{1''} = k_2 u^{2''}$, and $u_2^1(x, c)$ = $k_2 u_2^2(x, c)$. By Definition 6, $R^1(x, F) = R^2(x, F)$.

To prove the converse, define $u_m(x, c_F) = u(x, c_F) + E_F[u_2(x, c_F)]h(x)$. Now, follow Pratt (1964) by noting that

$$-R(x, F) = \frac{d}{dx}[\log u'_m(x, c_F)],$$

and by integrating both sides, exponentiating and finally integrating again, the desired result is obtained. ∎

PROOF OF THEOREM 9. If $R(x, F) > 0$, then $u''_m < 0$ because $u'_m > 0$ by Theorem 3. This implies u_m is increasing and concave, which in its turn implies that $\bar{x}_F \succ F$ for all F and hence global risk aversion. Similarly, $R(x, F) < 0$ for all F implies global risk proneness. ∎

PROOF OF THEOREM 10. Let $u_m(x, c_F) = u^1(x, c_F) + E_F[u_2^1(x, c_F)]h^1(x)$, and $v_m(x, c_F) = u^2(x, c_F) + E_F[u_2^2(x, c_F)]h^2(x)$. Since $R^1(x, F) > R^2(x, F)$ for all x and F, following Pratt (1964) we can obtain, for a given F,

$$R^2(x, F) - R^1(x, F) = \frac{d}{dx}\left[\log \frac{u'_m}{v'_m}\right] < 0.$$

Now,

$$\frac{d}{dt} u_m(v_m^{-1}(t)) = \frac{u'_m(v_m^{-1}(t))}{v'_m(v_m^{-1}(t))},$$

which is decreasing in t for any given F because $\log(u'_m/v'_m)$ is decreasing. Therefore, $u_m(v_m^{-1}(t))$ is a concave function of t for any given F. Define $U(F) = E_F[u^1(x, c_F)]$ and $V(F) = E_F[u^2(x, c_F)]$. Machina (1982, Theorem 4) shows that if u_m is a concave transformation of v_m and if F^* differs from F by a simple compensated spread from the point of view of V, then $U(F^*) \le U(F)$. Since F differs from x_F^1 by a simple compensated spread with respect to $V(\cdot)$, $U(F) \le U(F_{x_F^1})$. Since $U(F) = U(F_{x_F^1})$, then $x_F^2 \ge x_F^1$. Further, $RP_F^i = \bar{x}_F^i - \bar{x}_F^i$, $RP_F^1 \ge RP_F^2$ for all F as desired. ∎

PROOF OF THEOREM 11. It follows directly from Machina (1982b, Theorem 1) by noting, as showed in the proof of Theorem 3, that the local utility function of our model is given by $U(x, F) = u(x, c_F) + E_F[u_2(x, c_F)]h(x)$. ∎

PROOF OF THEOREM 12. We have that $c_F = c_G = c_{F+H} = c_{G+H} = c$. We are given

$$E_F\left[\frac{1 - e^{-cx}}{1 - e^{-c}}\right] = E_G\left[\frac{1 - e^{-cx}}{1 - e^{-c}}\right].$$

To show that $F + H \sim G + H$, note that

$$E_{F+H}\left[\frac{1 - e^{-c(x+y)}}{1 - e^{-c}}\right] = \frac{1}{1 - e^{-c}} - \frac{1}{1 - e^{-c}} E_{F+H}[e^{-cx}e^{-cy}]$$

$$= \frac{1}{1 - e^{-c}} - \frac{1}{1 - e^{-c}} E_F[e^{-cx}]E_H[e^{-cy}].$$

Similarly, expand

$$E_{G+H}\left[\frac{1 - e^{-c(x+y)}}{1 - e^{-c}}\right],$$

and since $E_F[e^{-cx}] = E_G[e^{-cx}]$, we obtain the desired result.

To see that a nonlinear function h cannot satisfy the condition for all F, G and H, we note that for some H, $c_{F+H} \neq c_F$ and $c_{G+H} \neq c_G$ if h is not linear. Now, $E_{F+H}[\cdot] \neq E_{G+H}[\cdot]$. ∎

References

ALLAIS, M., "Le comportement de l'homme rationnel devant le risque: critique des postulats et axiomes de l'ecole americaine," *Econometrica*, 21 (1953), 503–546.
———, "The So Called Allais Paradox and Rational Decisions under Uncertainty," in M. Allais and O. Hagen (Eds.), *Expected Utility Hypothesis and the Allais Paradox*. D. Reidel Publishing Company, Dordrecht, Holland, 1979a.
———, "The Foundations of a Positive Theory of Choice Involving Risk and a Criticism of the Postulates and Axioms of the American School," in M. Allais and O. Hagen (Eds.), *Expected Utility Hypothesis and the Allais Paradox*. D. Reidel Publishing Company, Dordrecht, Holland, 1979b.
ARROW, K. J., *Essays in the Theory of Risk Bearing*, Markham, Chicago, 1971.
BECKER, J. L., "A New Model of Decisions under Risk Using the Concept of Lottery Dependent Utility," doctoral dissertation, University of California, Los Angeles, 1986.
BELL, D. E., "Regret in Decision Making under Uncertainty," *Oper. Res.*, 30 (1982), 961–982.
———, "Disappointment in Decision Making under Uncertainty," *Oper. Res.*, 33, 1 (January–February 1985), 1–27.

1382   JOAO L. BECKER AND RAKESH K. SARIN

BERNARD, G., "On Utility Functions," *Theory and Decisions,* 5 (1974), 205–242.
CHEW, S. H. AND K. R. MACCRIMMON, "Alpha-Nu Choice Theory: A Generalization of Expected Utility Theory," Working paper No. 669, University of British Columbia Faculty of Commerce and Business Administration, Vancouver, 1979a.
——— AND ———, "Alpha Utility Theory, Lottery Composition and the Allais Paradox," Working paper No. 686, University of British Columbia Faculty of Commerce and Business Administration, Vancouver, 1979b.
——— AND W. S. WALLER, "Empirical Tests of Weighted Utility Theory," *J. Math. Psychology,* 30 (1986), 55–72.
EDWARDS, W., "The Prediction of Decisions among Bets," *J. Experimental Psychology,* 50 (1955), 201–214.
FISHBURN, P. C., "Transitive Measurable Utility," *J. Economic Theory,* 31 (1983), 293–317.
FRIEDMAN, M. AND L. SAVAGE, "The Utility Analysis of Choices Involving Risks," *J. Political Economy,* 56 (1948), 279–304.
HAGEN, O., "Separation of Cardinal Utility and Specific Utility of Risk in Theory of Choice under Uncertainty," *Stats. Tidsskrift,* 3 (1969), 81–107.
HANDA, J., "Risk, Probabilities, and a New Theory of Cardinal Utility," *J. of Political Economy,* 85 (1977), 97–122.
HERSTEIN, I. N. AND J. MILNOR, "An Axiomatic Approach to Measurable Utility," *Econometrica,* 21 (1953), 291–297.
HERSHEY, J. C., H. C. KUNREUTHER AND P. H. J. SCHOEMAKER, "Sources of Bias in Assessment Procedures for Utility Functions," *Management Sci.,* 28, 8 (August 1982), 936–954.
KAHNEMAN, D. AND A. TVERSKY, "Prospect Theory: An Analysis of Decision under Risk," *Econometrica,* 47 (1979), 263–291.
KARMARKAR, U. S., "Subjectively Weighted Utility: A Descriptive Extension of the Expected Utility Model," *Organizational Behavior and Human Performance,* 21 (1978), 61–72.
KEENEY, R. L. AND H. RAIFFA, *Decisions with Multiple Objectives: Preferences and Value Tradeoffs,* John Wiley and Sons, New York, 1976.
KRELLE, W., *Präferenz und entschleidungstheorie,* Mohr, Tübingen, 1968.
LUCE, R. D. AND L. NARENS, "Classification of Concatenation Measurement Structures According to Scale Type," *J. Math. Psychology,* 29 (1985), 1–72.
MACCRIMMON, K. R. AND S. LARSSON, "Utility Theory: Axiom versus paradoxes," in M. Allais and O. Hagen (Eds.), *Expected Utility Hypothesis and the Allais Paradox.* D. Reidel Publishing Company, Dordrecht, 1979.
MACHINA, M. J., "Expected Utility Analysis without the Independence Axiom," *Econometrica,* 50 (1982a), 277–323.
———, "A Stronger Characterization of Declining Risk Aversion," *Econometrica,* 50, 4 (July 1982b), 1069–1079.
MCCORD, M. R. AND R. DE NEUFVILLE, "Utility Dependence on Probability: An Empirical Demonstration," *J. Large Scale Systems,* 6 (1984), 91–103.
MORRISON, D. G., "On the Consistency of Preferences in Allais' Paradox," *Behavioral Sci.,* 12 (1967), 373–383.
PRATT, J. W., "Risk Aversion in the Small and in the Large," *Econometrica,* 32 (1964), 122–136.
PRESTON, M. G. AND P. BARATTA, "An Experimental Study of the Auction-Value of an Uncertain Outcome," *Amer. J. Psychology,* 61 (1948), 183–193.
PRUITT, D. G., "Pattern and Level of Risk in Gambling Decisions," *Psychological Rev.,* 69 (1962), 187–201.
QUIGGIN, J., "A Theory of Anticipated Utility," *J. Economic Behavior and Organization,* 3 (1982), 323–343.
QUIRK, J. P. AND R. SAPOSNIK, "Admissibility and Measurable Utility Functions," *Rev. Economic Studies,* 29, 2 (1962), 140–146.
ROTHSCHILD, M. AND J. E. STIGLITZ, "Increasing Risk. I. A Definition," *J. Economic Theory,* 2 (1970), 225–243.
SAVAGE, L. J., *The Foundations of Statistics,* John Wiley & Sons, New York, 1954.
VON NEUMANN, J. AND O. MORGENSTERN, *Theory of Games and Economic Behavior,* Princeton University Press, Princeton, NJ, 1944, 2nd ed., 1947, 3rd ed., 1953, John Wiley & Sons, New York.

[12]

JOURNAL OF ECONOMIC THEORY **41**, 270–287 (1987)

265-82

[87]

0222

DOP

Some Implications of
a More General Form of Regret Theory*

GRAHAM LOOMES

*Department of Economics and Related Studies,
University of York, York YO1 5DD, England*

AND

ROBERT SUGDEN

*School of Economic and Social Studies,
University of East Anglia, Norwich NR4 7TJ, England*

Received March 6, 1984; revised March 19, 1986

Regret theory entails the possibility of non-transitive pairwise choices. It therefore raises questions about how individuals choose from sets of more than two actions, especially when there exists a subset of pairs of actions over which preferences cycle. A generalization of regret theory is suggested and is compared and contrasted with Fishburn's generalization of SSB utility theory. It is also shown that under this generalization an individual with non-transitive pairwise preferences will not be caught in a never-ending cycle and is not vulnerable to being "money-pumped" into bankruptcy. *Journal of Economic Literature* Classification Numbers: 022, 026.   © 1987 Academic Press, Inc.

1. INTRODUCTION

This paper examines the relationship between two new theories of choice under uncertainty, *regret theory*, which was developed independently by us [9, 11] and by Bell [1], and *skew-symmetric bilinear utility theory* (or *SSB theory*), which was developed by Fishburn [3, 5]. Although the two theories have very different starting points—regret theory starts from psychological intuitions while SSB theory is axiomatically based—they are known to have a good deal in common [10, 13]. We shall explore these common features in the context of a formulation of regret theory that is more general than previous versions. Developing an insight of Machina's

* We should like to acknowledge the helpful comments of Mark Machina, an anonymous referee, and an Associate Editor.

270

[13] we shall show how in an important special case—choice over pairs of statistically independent prospects defined in terms of three "pure" consequences—particular restrictions on our general theory generate transitive preferences that are consistent with the otherwise very different theories of Chew and MacCrimmon [2] and Machina [12].

In general, however, both regret theory and SSB theory can allow non-transitive preferences over pairs of alternatives (actions or prospects). To date neither theory has been generalized to apply to all feasible sets of alternatives, although Fishburn [5] has offered a method by which SSB theory could generate choices over a special class of non-finite feasible sets. However, the rationale of regret theory leads us to propose an alternative approach to this problem.

2. SSB Theory and Regret Theory

Let $X = \{x_1, ..., x_m\}$ be a set of *consequences*. A *prospect* is a probability distribution of consequences; a typical prospect is denoted $p = (p_1, ..., p_m)$, where $\sum p_g = 1$. Let $\Psi(\cdot, \cdot)$ be a real-valued function defined on $X \times X$, satisfying the property of skew-symmetry (i.e., for all x_g, x_h: $\Psi(x_g, x_h) = -\Psi(x_h, x_g)$) and unique up to a similarity transformation. We may now define a function $\phi(\cdot, \cdot)$ on the set of ordered pairs of prospects:

$$\phi(p, q) = \sum_{g=1}^{m} \sum_{h=1}^{m} p_g q_h \Psi(x_g, x_h). \tag{1}$$

This is Fishburn's *skew-symmetric bilinear (SSB) function*. (Its skew-symmetry is ensured by the skew-symmetry of $\Psi(\cdot, \cdot)$.[1]) Letting $\succ$, $\succeq$ and $\sim$ denote strict preference, weak preference and indifference, respectively, Fishburn's theory is that for all prospects p, q:

$$p \gtrless q \Leftrightarrow \phi(p, q) \gtrless 0. \tag{2}$$

Fishburn [3] shows that if an individual's preferences over prospects satisfy three axioms ("continuity," "dominance" and "symmetry") they can be represented by an SSB function.

Regret theory differs from SSB utility theory in that preferences are defined over *actions* rather than prospects. Let $S = \{S_1, ..., S_n\}$ be a set of *states of the world*. For each state S_j there is a probability π_j, where $\sum \pi_j = 1$. An action is an n-tuple of state-contingent consequences; a typical

---

[1] Note that $\phi(p, q) = \Psi(x_g, x_h)$ if $p_g = q_h = 1$. Thus it is possible to present SSB theory—as Fishburn does—solely in terms of $\phi(\cdot, \cdot)$. Our presentation helps to highlight the links between SSB theory and regret theory.

action is denoted $A_i = (x_{i1}, ..., x_{in})$. To allow comparability with SSB theory, let every consequence x_{ij} be an element of the set X. Consider an individual who has to choose one of two actions, A_i or A_k. Suppose he chooses A_i and then state S_j occurs. He receives the consequence x_{ij}; he also knows that, had he chosen A_k rather than A_i, he would have received x_{kj}. The fundamental intuition behind regret theory is that "having x_{ij} and missing out on x_{kj}" is a composite experience; the utility the individual derives from this experience depends on x_{kj} as well as on x_{ij}. Here "utility" is to be interpreted in the classical Benthamite or Bernouillian sense, as a sensation or mental state. Let $M(x_{ij}, x_{kj})$ represent the level of satisfaction[2] derived from this experience; $M(\cdot, \cdot)$ is a real-valued function, unique up to a positive linear transformation, defined on $X \times X$.

Regret theory postulates that an individual chooses so as to maximize the expectation of utility, defined in terms of $M(\cdot, \cdot)$. Thus

$$A_i \gtreqless A_k \Leftrightarrow \sum_{j=1}^{n} \pi_j M(x_{ij}, x_{kj}) \gtreqless \sum_{j=1}^{n} \pi_j M(x_{kj}, x_{ij}). \tag{3}$$

We may now define a function $\Psi(\cdot, \cdot)$ such that for all $x_i, x_j \in X$: $\Psi(x_i, x_j) \equiv M(x_i, x_j) - M(x_j, x_i)$. Note that this definition makes $\Psi(\cdot, \cdot)$ a skew-symmetric function on $X \times X$ which is unique up to a similarity transformation. Thus the $\Psi(\cdot, \cdot)$ function of regret theory has all the properties of the $\Psi(\cdot, \cdot)$ function of SSB utility theory. Expression (3) may now be rewritten as

$$A_i \gtreqless A_k \Leftrightarrow \sum_{j=1}^{n} \pi_j \Psi(x_{ij}, x_{kj}) \gtreqless 0. \tag{4}$$

Now consider a choice between two *prospects*, p and q. This choice problem cannot be analysed in terms of regret theory unless the matrix of state-contingent consequences is defined: a given pair of prospects may be consistent with many different matrices. But let us consider the special case in which p and q are statistically independent. Then we may define m^2 states of the world; the typical state in which prospect p yields x_g and prospect q yields x_h has the probability $p_g q_h$. Making use of (4),

$$p \gtreqless q \Leftrightarrow \sum_{g=1}^{m} \sum_{h=1}^{m} p_g q_h \Psi(x_g, x_h) \gtreqless 0. \tag{5}$$

This result corresponds exactly with (1) and (2) of SSB theory. To this extent, then, SSB theory is a special case of regret theory: it is regret theory applied to statistically independent prospects.

---

[2] In previous presentations of regret theory we have referred to this "level of satisfaction" as "modified utility."

We shall now consider three additional conditions that might be imposed on $\Psi(\cdot, \cdot)$.

OPC: *ordering of pure consequences.* There is a complete, reflexive and transitive preference relation $\geqslant$ on the set X, such that for all $x_g, x_h \in X$: $x_g \geqslant x_h \Leftrightarrow \Psi(x_g, x_h) \geqslant 0$.

I: *increasingness.* For all $x_f, x_g, x_h \in X$: $\Psi(x_f, x_g) \gtreqless 0 \Leftrightarrow \Psi(x_f, x_h) \gtreqless \Psi(x_g, x_h)$.

C: *convexity.* For all x_f, x_g, $x_h \in X$: $[\Psi(x_f, x_g) > 0$ and $\Psi(x_g, x_h) > 0$ and $\Psi(x_f, x_h) > 0] \Rightarrow \Psi(x_f, x_h) > \Psi(x_f, x_g) + \Psi(x_g, x_h)$.

OPC is an entirely conventional condition which seems particularly unexceptionable in the case in which consequences are increments of wealth.

If OPC holds, I may be interpreted as requiring that Ψ is "increasing" in its first argument—that is, $\Psi(x_g, x_h)$ increases whenever a more-preferred consequence x_g is substituted for a less-preferred one. For this to be true in regret theory, it is sufficient that $M(\cdot, \cdot)$ is "increasing" in its first argument and "non-increasing" in its second. In other words, the experience of "having x_g and missing out on x_h" is strictly more pleasurable, the more preferred is x_g, and weakly less pleasurable, the more preferred is x_h. This, we suggest, accords with most people's intuitions about regret.

OPC entails the existence of a "basic utility function" $C(\cdot)$ defined on X, unique up to a positive monotonic transformation and representing the preference relation $\geqslant$ on the set of pure consequences. If I is assumed, too, $\Psi(x_g, x_h)$ can be written as a function of $C(x_g)$ and $C(x_h)$, increasing in $C(x_g)$.

In previous presentations of regret theory we have gone beyond this by assuming a particular functional form for $\Psi(x_g, x_h)$. We have assumed that $\Psi(x_g, x_h)$ can be written as the function $Q(C(x_g) - C(x_h))$, where $C(\cdot)$ is unique only up to an increasing linear transformation. If it is further assumed that $Q(\cdot)$ is convex for positive values of $C(x_g) - C(x_h)$, regret theory predicts a wide range of observed violations of expected utility theory [9, 11]. Our present condition C defines this concept of convexity more directly, without requiring a specific functional form for $\Psi(x_g, x_h)$. We shall show that this is sufficient to generate the main predictions of regret theory.

3. REGRET THEORY WITH INDEPENDENT PROSPECTS

Throughout this section of this paper we shall consider only prospects that are statistically independent. In this special case, regret theory and SSB theory are equivalent.

It is convenient to begin by defining a function $\Phi(\cdot,\cdot)$ on the set of ordered pairs (x_g, q), where x_g is a consequence and q is a prospect. The function is defined by

$$\Phi(x_g, q) \equiv \sum_h q_h \Psi(x_g, x_h). \tag{6}$$

Thus $\Phi(x_g, q) = \phi(p, q)$ if $p_g = 1$; in effect, $\Phi(x_g, q)$ is an evaluation of the consequence x_g in relation to the prospect q. Since $\phi(q, q) = 0$, it follows that

$$\sum_g q_g \Phi(x_g, q) = 0. \tag{7}$$

Expressions (5), (6) and (7) can be combined to yield

$$p \gtreqless q \Leftrightarrow \sum_g (p_g - q_g) \, \Phi(x_g, q) \gtreqless 0. \tag{8}$$

In conventional expected utility theory, the corresponding implication is

$$p \gtreqless q \Leftrightarrow \sum_g (p_g - q_g) \, U(x_g) \gtreqless 0, \tag{9}$$

where $U(x_g)$ is a von Neumann–Morgenstern utility function. Thus for any given prospect q, the preference ranking of each prospect p *in relation to q* implied by regret theory is identical to the ranking that would be implied by conventional expected utility theory if $U(x_g) = \Phi(x_g, q)$. In this sense $\Phi(x_g, q)$ might be interpreted as a von Neumann–Morgenstern utility function that is relevant for all pairwise choices that involve q.[3]

If OPC is assumed, it is possible to define a concept of (first-order) stochastic dominance: for any prospects p, q, p stochastically dominates q iff (a) for all $x_g \in X$, the probability that p will generate a consequence at least as preferred as x_g is at least as great as the corresponding probability for q and (b) for some $x_g \in X$, the probability for p exceeds the probability for q. There is *first order stochastic dominance preference* if $p \succ q$ is true whenever p stochastically dominates q.

It is not difficult to show that regret theory entails first-order stochastic dominance preference over independent prospects if OPC and I hold. OPC and I entail that $\Phi(x_g, q)$, is "increasing" in x_g (i.e., $\Phi(x_g, q) \gtreqless \Phi(x_h, q) \Leftrightarrow x_g \gtreqless x_h$). Thus for any given q, $\Phi(x_g, q)$ has the same properties as a von Neumann–Morgenstern utility function. Since stochastic dominance preference is a property of conventional expected utility theory, it must be

[3] The argument contained in this paragraph is due to Mark Machina. Fishburn [3, Lemmas 1–3] shows that a similar result can be derived from SSB theory even in the absence of the symmetry axiom.

a property of regret theory, too. In generating this result, I is critical; OPC alone is insufficient, as Fishburn [5, Theorem 7] has shown.

Some insights can be gained by considering the following special case. Let p, q, r be any three independent prospects. Let s be the prospect that gives p, q, r with probabilities ρ_p, $1 - \rho_p - \rho_r$, ρ_r. Let Z be the set of all such prospects s; each prospect is to be understood as being statistically independent of every other one. Z can be represented in (ρ_p, ρ_r) space as the set of points for which $0 \leqslant \rho_p + \rho_r \leqslant 1$: this is a *triangle diagram* of the kind used by Machina [12]. The corners of the triangle, $(1, 0)$, $(0, 0)$ and $(0, 1)$, represent the prospects p, q and r, respectively. If preferences satisfy the axioms of conventional expected utility theory, indifference classes are parallel lines in the triangle diagram (see [12]). (There is one exceptional case: if $p \sim q \sim r$, then all points in Z belong to the same indifference class.)

Now consider the implications of regret theory; for the present, none of the conditions OPC, I or C will be imposed. Take any s in Z. The ranking of prospects *relative to s* can be represented by a partition of Z into three subsets $M(s) = \{t \in Z \mid t \succ s\}$, $I(s) = \{t \in Z \mid t \sim s\}$, $L(s) = \{t \in Z \mid t \prec s\}$: these are the sets of prospects that are respectively more preferred than, indifferent to, and less preferred than s. In regret theory $\succ$ is an asymmetric relation and $\sim$ is a symmetric one; thus for all s, $t \in Z$: $t \in M(s) \Leftrightarrow s \in L(t)$ and $t \in I(s) \Leftrightarrow s \in I(t)$.

For any given s, the ranking of prospects in relation to s is determined by the sign of the expectation of $\Phi(x_g, s)$; this ranking must have the same properties as a ranking in conventional expected utility theory. There are therefore only two possibilities: *either* (i) $I(s) = Z$ or (ii) there is a line $I^*(s)$ in (ρ_p, ρ_r) space such that $I(s) = I^*(s) \cap Z$ and such that all points in Z to one side of this line belong to $M(s)$ and all points to the other side belong to $L(s)$.

In case (ii), but not necessarily in case (i), $I(s)$ is an *indifference class*, i.e., a set of prospects each of which is indifferent to every other. In other words, in case (ii), for any prospects t and u that lie on $I(s)$, $t \sim u$. (There are two possibilities for $I(t)$: either $I(t) = Z$ or $I(t) = I(s)$. In either case $u \in I(t)$, i.e., $t \sim u$.)

Now first suppose that for the three basic prospects in the triangle diagram we have $p \sim q$, $q \sim r$ and $p \sim r$. Since p, q and r do not lie on a common line, possibility (ii) cannot be true for them. From this it is easy to deduce that possibility (i) must be true for all $s \in Z$: every prospect in Z is indifferent to every other, i.e., Z is an indifference class. However, from now on we shall assume that there is a strict preference over at least one pair of prospects, say $r \succ p$. This entails the existence of a family of $I^*(s)$ lines.

It can be proved that all these $I^*(s)$ lines pass through a single point in (ρ_p, ρ_r) space; a limiting case is that these lines are parallel, as in conventional expected utility theory. (For a proof that this result follows from the axioms of SSB theory, see Fishburn [3]. Alternatively, for any s in the interior of Z, the equation for $I^*(s)$ can be constructed from (5). Because of the skew-symmetry of Ψ, no three such equations can be linearly independent of one another.)

Now consider any two prospects s, t such that $s > t$. Then s and t must lie on separate indifference lines $I^*(s)$, $I^*(t)$. Let v be the point at which all indifference lines intersect. Consider the line through s at right angles to sv. The *direction of preference* along this line (i.e., from prospects over which s is preferred to prospects that are preferred over s) may be defined as clockwise or counter-clockwise in relation to v. It is easy to prove that if the direction of preference at s is clockwise (counter-clockwise), so also is the direction of preference at t. Thus at all points in Z (other than v itself) the direction of preference is the same.

Two cases may now be distinguished. The first case is where v, the point at which indifference lines intersect, is *not* an element of Z. This case is illustrated in Fig. 1; the arrows show the direction of preference (counter-clockwise). It is clear that the preference relation $\geqslant$ is transitive on Z. The second case, illustrated in Fig. 2, is where v is an element of Z. This generates a cycle of preference over the three basic prospects. (Figure 2 shows a counter-clockwise cycle: $q > r$, $r > p$, $p > q$.) For every prospect s in Z where $s \neq v$, there is another prospect t such that $s < t$; for all s in Z, $s \sim v$. (In Fig. 2, v is in the interior of Z. If v is on the boundary of Z there is a preference/indifference cycle over the basic prospects. For example, if $v = q$, a counter-clockwise direction of preference gives $q \sim r$, $r > p$, $p \sim q$.)

One implication of all this is that if $\geqslant$ is transitive over three prospects p, q, r it is also transitive over all probability mixes of these prospects. This result is of particular interest in the case in which p, q, r are pure consequences. Let p, q, r correspond with consequences x_1, x_2, x_3 (i.e.,

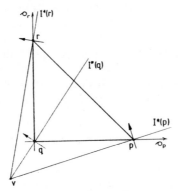

FIG. 1. Transitive preferences.

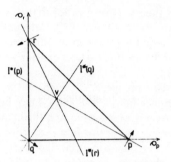

FIG. 2.   Non-transitive preferences.

$p_1 = q_2 = r_3 = 1$). Then if OPC holds there is a preference ordering over $\{p, q, r\}$; thus regret theory will generate a preference ordering over all independent prospects defined for the set of consequences $\{x_1, x_2, x_3\}$.

This result is significant because a number of experimentally observed violations of conventional expected utility theory can be represented in terms of a particular kind of preference ordering over three-consequence prospects. Let x_1, x_2, x_3 be consequences such that $x_1 \prec x_2 \prec x_3$; thus $p \prec r$, $q \prec r$ and $p \prec q$. If Z, the set of all probability mixes of p, q, r, is represented in a diagram like Fig. 1, expected utility theory would generate a family of upward-sloping parallel indifference lines. If instead the indifference lines "fan out" from a point south-west of q, as in Fig. 1, the individual's preferences will be consistent with the common consequence, common ratio and utility evaluation effects (Machina [12, 13]). These "effects" are all systematic violations of conventional expected utility theory which have been observed in replicated experiments. Chew and MacCrimmon [2] and Fishburn [4] have presented a theory of preference orderings over prospects which produces "fanning out" indifference lines, as in Fig. 1, for the three-consequence case. Machina [12] has presented a more general form of the same kind of theory. In his "generalized expected utility analysis" there is a preference ordering over all prospects; in the three-consequence case the indifference curves "fan out" but need not be straight lines.

If OPC holds, regret theory generates a family of upward-sloping indifference lines which intersect at a single point. The equations[4] for $I^*(p)$ and $I^*(r)$ are respectively

$$(1 - \rho_p - \rho_r)\, \Psi(x_2, x_1) + \rho_r \Psi(x_3, x_1) = 0 \tag{10}$$

---

[4] Strictly, $I^*(p)$ and $I^*(r)$ are undefined because the sets $I(p)$ and $I(r)$ are singletons. Equations (10) and (11) may be interpreted as the limits of $I^*(s)$ as s tends to p and as s tends to r.

and

$$p_p \Psi(x_3, x_1) + (1 - p_p - p_r) \Psi(x_3, x_2) = 0. \tag{11}$$

These indifference lines intersect to the south-west of q, and thus the preference map has Machina's "fanning out" property, if and only if the gradient of $I^*(p)$ is less than the gradient of $I^*(r)$, that is, if and only if

$$\frac{\Psi(x_2, x_1)}{\Psi(x_3, x_1) - \Psi(x_2, x_1)} < \frac{\Psi(x_3, x_1) - \Psi(x_3, x_2)}{\Psi(x_3, x_2)}. \tag{12}$$

This inequality is entailed by the convexity condition C. Thus if OPC and C both hold, regret theory generates preferences over three-consequence gambles that have the same characteristics as those generated by Chew and MacCrimmon's theory—which in turn is a special case of Machina's. This accounts for many of the similarities between the predictions of the three theories.

The theories of Chew and MacCrimmon and Machina both generate transitive preference orderings over *all* sets of prospects. However, if there are four or more consequences, regret theory can generate non-transitive preferences over statistically independent prospects even though preferences over the pure consequences may be transitive. Here is an example. Let consequences be measured in dollars and let there be four consequences, $x_1 = 0, x_2 = 20, x_3 = 27, x_4 = 49$. Let

$$\Psi(x_g, x_h) = x_g - x_h + \frac{(x_g - x_h)^2}{x_g - x_h + 10} \qquad \text{for all } x_g \geqslant x_h. \tag{13}$$

This function satisfies OPC, I and C. Then over the prospects $p = (0, 1, 0, 0)$, $q = (0.25, 0, 0.75, 0)$, $r = (0.6, 0, 0, 0.4)$ regret theory generates the cycle $p \succ q$, $q \succ r$, $r \succ p$.

Why are non-transitive preferences compatible with OPC when there are four pure consequences but not when there are only three? Part of the answer seems to be as follows.

Consider again the case in which preferences are defined on Z, where Z is the set of all probability mixes of three distinct prospects (which are not necessarily pure consequences). Then Z can be represented in a triangle diagram; either Z is an indifference class or there is a *single* family of indifference lines, all of which intersect at a single point. If preferences over the three basic prospects are transitive, this point of intersection must lie outside Z, and so preferences over *all* prospects in Z must be transitive.

Now consider how these conclusions are affected if Z is defined as the set of all probability mixes of four distinct prospects (again, not necessarily pure consequences). Now Z can be represented in three-dimensional probability space; instead of a "triangle diagram" there is a "pyramid diagram." As in the three-prospect case, if any two distinct prospects s, t are indifferent to one another, then the set of prospects on the line through s and t constitutes an indifference class.[5]

In the three-consequence case there is (at most) only one family of indifference lines; but in the four-consequence case any plane section through Z may have its own family of indifference lines. On any such plane these lines may intersect at a point *outside* Z, in which case preferences over prospects on this plane are transitive; but it may be that these lines intersect at a point *inside* Z, in which case preferences over prospects on this plane are non-transitive. In the special case in which the four basic prospects are pure consequences, OPC entails that preferences are transitive over each of the four faces of the pyramid, since each of these is a set of probability mixes of three pure consequences; however, as the counter-example shows, this does *not* entail that preferences are transitive over all other planes.

4. Regret Theory without Independent Prospects

We shall now relax the assumption of independent prospects and discuss the general case in which preferences are defined over actions. Consider the three actions described in Table I. Suppose that there is a preference ordering $x_1 \prec x_2 \prec x_3$ over the three consequences. Then regret theory yields the implication

$$A_1 \gtreqless A_2 \Leftrightarrow A_2 \gtreqless A_3 \Leftrightarrow A_3 \gtreqless A_1$$
$$\Leftrightarrow \Psi(x_1, x_3) + \Psi(x_2, x_1) + \Psi(x_3, x_2) \gtreqless 0. \tag{14}$$

If C holds, there is a preference cycle over the three actions

$$A_1 \prec A_2, \qquad A_2 \prec A_3, \qquad A_3 \prec A_1.$$

Cycles not dissimilar to this have been observed experimentally. Consider the actions described in Table II; consequences are measured in dollars. The $\Psi(\cdot, \cdot)$ function defined in (13) yields $A_1 \prec A_2$, $A_2 \prec A_3$, $A_3 \prec A_1$. (Note that (13) makes $\Psi(x_g, x_h)$ a convex function of $x_g - x_h$ for all x_g, x_h, where $x_g \geq x_h$; any function with this property would generate the same cycle.) This cycle may be interpreted as an instance of "preference reversal" [6-8]. Let $y = w + u$, where w is the individual's datum level of wealth and u takes some value in the range $0 < u < 1$. Then A_2, seen in

---

[5] If there happen to be three distinct prospects s, t, u, not on a common line but where $s \sim t$, $s \sim u$, and $t \sim u$, then the set of prospects on the plane through s, t and u is an indifference class. It is not clear, however, that such triples are *necessarily* to be found.

TABLE I

State of the World and Probability

Action	1/3	1/3	1/3
A_1	x_1	x_2	x_3
A_2	x_3	x_1	x_2
A_3	x_2	x_3	x_1

relation to the datum level of wealth, is a gamble with a positive actuarial value, offering a one-third probability of a gain and a two-thirds probability of a loss. In the preference reversal literature this is called a "$-bet": the *dollar value* of winning is relatively high. A_3 is a gamble with the same actuarial value as A_2, offering a two-thirds probability of a gain and a one-third probability of a loss. This is a "P-bet": the *probability* of winning is relatively high. $A_2 \prec A_3$ entails that the P-bet is preferred to the $-bet. However, $A_1 \prec A_2$ and $A_3 \prec A_1$ entail that the $-bet is preferred to an actuarially equivalent certainly, while the converse is true for the P-bet; thus the certainly equivalent value of the $-bet must be higher than that of the P-bet.

The case described in Table I establishes that preferences over *actions* are not necessarily transitive, even if there are only three consequences. Note also that all three actions in Table I can be represented by the same prospect $p = (1/3, 1/3, 1/3)$: A_1, A_2 and A_3 are stochastically equivalent to one another. Since regret theory can generate strict preferences between stochastically equivalent actions, it cannot be formulated in terms of preferences over prospects.

In the light of this, it is not surprising that regret theory does not in general satisfy the condition of stochastic dominance preference. Let the consequences in Table I be measured in dollars. Let a fourth action A_4 be defined by $A_4 = (x_3 - \delta, \ x_1 - \delta, \ x_2 - \delta)$, where $\delta > 0$; note that A_4 is stochastically dominated by A_1. Nevertheless, given appropriate continuity conditions, any $\Psi(\cdot, \cdot)$ function satisfying C will yield $A_1 \prec A_4$ for a sufficiently small δ. (For example, let $x_1 = 0$, $x_2 = 10$, $x_3 = 20$ and $\delta = 0.01$. Then the function defined in (13) yields $A_1 \prec A_4$.)

TABLE II

State of the World and Probability

Action	1/3	1/3	1/3
A_1	y	y	y
A_2	$y+2$	$y-1$	$y-1$
A_3	$y+1$	$y+1$	$y-2$

If OPC holds, it is possible to define a different concept of dominance. One action A_i *statewise dominates* another action A_k iff $x_{ij} \geqslant x_{kj}$ is true for all states S_j and $x_{ij} > x_{kj}$ is true for some state S_j. Note that statewise dominance entails stochastic dominance but not vice versa. It is clear from (4) that regret theory has the property of *statewise dominance preference*: $A_i > A_k$ is true whenever A_i statewise dominates A_k.

5. NON-PAIRWISE CHOICE

In regret theory and SSB theory the relation $\geqslant$, whether defined over actions or over statistically independent prospects, is not necessarily transitive. This raises an obvious problem: how are choices made when there are more than two actions or prospects to choose among?

Clearly there are many different ways of generalizing regret theory so that it applies to non-pairwise choices. In this section we shall suggest one possible generalization, which seems to us to remain faithful both to the formal structure of the original theory and to the psychological intuitions that lay behind it.

As in our presentation of regret theory in Section 2, let $S_1, ..., S_n$ be states of the world with probabilities $\pi_1, ..., \pi_n$, where $\sum \pi_j = 1$. Let Z be any feasible set of two or more actions defined in terms of these states of the world. Now consider an individual who confronts this feasible set and chooses one particular action A_i. Then state S_j occurs. The individual receives the consequence x_{ij}; he also knows that for every action $A_k \in Z$ (where $k \neq i$) there is a consequence x_{kj} that he might have had, had he chosen differently. Generalizing the argument in Section 2, what the individual experiences is "having x_{ij} and missing out on all of the consequences x_{kj}." If we let $Z_j = \{x_{ij} \mid A_i \in Z\}$, the individual's experience can be described as "having x_{ij} and missing out on the set of consequences $Z_j - \{x_{ij}\}$." Then we may define a real-valued function $M^*(\cdot, \cdot)$, unique up to a positive linear transformation, such that $M^*(x_{ij}, Z_j - \{x_{ij}\})$ represents the level of satisfaction derived from this composite experience. The original function $M(\cdot, \cdot)$ then corresponds with the special case of pairwise choice: if $Z = \{A_i, A_k\}$, $M^*(x_{ij}, Z_j - \{x_{ij}\}) = M(x_{ij}, x_{kj})$.

One implication of this formulation is the following. Suppose that two actions A_i, A_k have identical consequences under some state S_j, that is, $x_{ij} = x_{kj}$. Consider any two feasible sets Y, Z, where $Y = Z - \{A_k\}$. Then $Y_j = Z_j$, and so $M^*(x_{ij}, Z_j - \{x_{ij}\}) = M^*(x_{ij}, Y_j - \{x_{ij}\})$. In other words, the level of satisfaction derived from choosing A_i in the event that state S_j occurs is unaffected by whether or not A_k is in the feasible set. This seems to be in accord with psychological intuition: if the individual is actually experiencing the consequence x_{ij}, there is no reason for regret or rejoicing over the fact that a different choice might have brought about *the same* consequence.

A more important implication is that the weak preference relation $\succcurlyeq$ defined in (3) is set-specific. A proposition of the form $A_i \succcurlyeq A_k$ states that the expected utility of "choosing A_i and rejecting A_k" is at least as great as that of "choosing A_k and rejecting A_i"; in other words, choosing A_i *from the set* $\{A_i, A_k\}$ is at least as preferred as choosing A_k *from the same set.* So $A_i \succcurlyeq A_k$ cannot be interpreted as an *unconditional* proposition about the preference ranking of A_i and A_k; it is a preference ranking *conditional on the feasible set being* $\{A_i, A_k\}$. The logic of regret theory can be made more transparent by defining a separate *set-specific* preference relation $\succcurlyeq_Z$ for each two-action feasible set Z. Then $A_i \succcurlyeq A_k$ is shorthand for "$A_i \succcurlyeq_Z A_k$, where $Z = \{A_i, A_k\}$."

The fundamental hypothesis behind (3) is that an individual chooses so as to maximize the mathematical expectation of satisfaction, defined in terms of $M(\cdot, \cdot)$. This hypothesis can be generalized quite naturally as follows. For compactness, we shall define a function $E(A_i, Z)$ such that

$$E(A_i, Z) \equiv \sum_{j=1}^{n} \pi_j M(x_{ij}, Z_j - \{x_{ij}\}). \tag{15}$$

Thus $E(A_i, Z)$ stands for the expected value of satisfaction to be derived by choosing the action A_i from the set Z. Then we make the following hypothesis about set-specific preferences:

$$A_i \gtrless_Z A_k \Leftrightarrow E(A_i, Z) \gtrless E(A_k, Z). \tag{16}$$

Note that this implies that, for any given feasible set Z, $\succcurlyeq_Z$ is a transitive relation. We hypothesize that from any set Z, an individual will choose an action that is maximally preferred *in terms of* $\succcurlyeq_Z$.

To complete the generalization of Section 2, we should need to reformulate the conditions OPC, I and C so that they applied to the function $M^*(\cdot, \cdot)$. In this paper, however, we shall concentrate on two implications of our generalization that do not require any restrictions on $M^*(\cdot, \cdot)$.

6. RANDOMIZING CHOICE: FISHBURN'S PROPOSAL

We shall now examine how our suggested generalization of regret theory compares with Fishburn's [5] proposal for generalizing SSB theory. Fishburn proves the following theorem. Let Q be any finite set of independent prospects, and let $H(Q)$ be its convex hull—that is, the set of all probability mixes of the prospects in Q. Then there must exist some measure $p^* \in H(Q)$ such that $p^* \succcurlyeq p$ for all $p \in H(Q)$. Fishburn suggests that this result offers a solution to the problem of choosing from a set of prospects over which pairwise preferences cycle. He considers a case where an individual faces the feasible set $Q = \{p, q, r\}$ and has the pairwise preferences $p \succ q$, $q \succ r$ and $r \succ p$. He argues that the individual could expand her feasible set to $H(Q)$ by randomizing her choices. Then there must exist a measure p^* that is maximally preferred in this set *in terms of the pairwise-choice preference relation* $\succcurlyeq$. Fishburn suggests that "if she decides to decide the issue by lottery, it seems reasonable to use p^* since it is at least as preferred as every other measure" [5, p. 138].

By contrast, our generalization of regret theory does not offer such a solution. To see why, consider the nature of $H(Q)$. In effect, Fishburn's proposal for expanding the feasible set involves the creation of a set of two-stage lotteries, each of these lotteries being a vector of probabilities, one probability for each prospect in Q. In this context, each prospect in Q may be regarded as a two-stage lottery which assigns a probability of unity to one prospect.

Let L be the set of all such two-stage lotteries, and let R be any set of lotteries such that $Q \subseteq R \subseteq L$. Then the following result can be proved: if some prospect p is maximally preferred in Q in terms of $\succcurlyeq_Q$, it is also maximally preferred in R in terms of $\succcurlyeq_R$. Thus if p is chosen from Q, there is no reason not to choose p if two-stage lotteries are added to the feasible set.

We shall prove this for the simple case in which $Q = \{p, q, r\}$ and $R = \{p, q, r, p^*\}$, where p^* is the lottery that assigns the probabilities $\lambda_1, \lambda_2, 1 - \lambda_1 - \lambda_2$ to p, q, r; but this proof can easily be generalized.

The central idea behind the proof is that, although the prospects p, q, r are, by assumption, statistically independent of one another, the lottery p^* is *not statistically independent of p, q, r*. An individual who initially faces the feasible set $\{p, q, r\}$ and who has access to a random device is able to generate additional options in the form of two-stage lotteries; but she is not able to generate *statistically independent* probability-mixes of p, q, r.

Table III describes p, q, r and p^* as *actions*, that is, as n-tuples of state-

TABLE III

Event and Probability

Action	E_1 λ_1	E_2 λ_2	E_3 $1 - \lambda_1 - \lambda_2$
p	p	p	p
q	q	q	q
r	r	r	r
p^*	p	q	r

contingent consequences. In each event E_1, E_2, E_3 (i.e., each outcome of the first stage of the lottery) the consequence of each action is itself a prospect, and so for the purposes of regret theory each event should be subdivided into states of the world. But note that in every state belonging to E_1, the actions p and p^* have identical consequences; in every state belonging to E_2, q and p^* have identical consequences; and in every state belonging to E_3, r and p^* have identical consequences. Hence p^* is not statistically independent of the other three actions. (Compare the discussion of the "isolation effect" in [9].)

First suppose that the feasible set is $Q = \{p, q, r\}$. According to our generalization of regret theory there must be a set-specific preference ordering $\succcurlyeq_Q$; and so one or more of p, q, r must be maximally preferred in Q in terms of this ordering. Suppose that p is maximally preferred in this sense. Then

$$E(p, Q) = \max_{s \in Q} [E(s, Q)]. \tag{17}$$

Now suppose that the feasible set is expanded to R by addition of p^*. Notice that, for every state S_j, the addition of p^* does not expand Z_j, the set of consequences that are feasible for that state. (If $S_j \in E_1$, the consequence associated with p^* is identical with the consequence associated with p; and so on.) Thus: $E(p, Q) = E(p, R)$; $E(q, Q) = E(q, R)$; $E(r, Q) = E(r, R)$; and

$$E(p^*, R) = \lambda_1 E(p, Q) + \lambda_2 E(q, Q) + (1 - \lambda_1 - \lambda_2) E(r, Q). \tag{18}$$

Hence (17) entails

$$E(p, R) = \max_{s \in R} [E(s, R)] \tag{19}$$

or, equivalently: p is maximally preferred in R in terms of $\succcurlyeq_R$.

This is an implication of our generalization of regret theory that is quite distinct from the implication of Fishburn's generalization of SSB utility theory, and which, in principle at least, offers the possibility of discriminating between the two on the basis of empirical evidence.

Take any case in which an individual has a cycle of pairwise preference over three independent prospects, say $p \succ q$, $q \succ r$, $r \succ p$. SSB theory and regret theory both predict the existence of some two-stage lottery p^* such that the individual has the *pairwise* preferences $p^* \succcurlyeq p$, $p^* \succcurlyeq q$, $p^* \succcurlyeq r$. Fishburn's generalization implies that p^* will be chosen from the set $\{p, q, r, p^*\}$. Leaving aside the possibility of indifference, our generalization implies the opposite: at least one of p, q, r will be maximally preferred in $\{p, q, r, p^*\}$ in terms of the relevant set-specific ordering, and so p^* will *not* be chosen.

7. THE MONEY PUMP ARGUMENT

It is often suggested than an individual with cyclical preferences can become locked into an endless chain of trades. For example, suppose that over three actions A_1, A_2, A_3 an individual has the preferences $A_1 \prec A_2$, $A_2 \prec A_3$, $A_3 \prec A_1$, and that he starts out with A_1. If he is offered the opportunity to exchange A_1 for A_2, it is argued he will accept it; then if he is offered the opportunity to exchange A_2 for A_3, he will accept this too; and so on indefinitely. At each stage (it is said) the individual has a *strict* preference for the next action in the chain, and so there seems to be scope for a broker to operate a money pump whereby the individual is induced to pay a small sum of money for the privilege of making each exchange. This argument is often used to support the claim that cyclical preferences are inconsistent (see, e.g., [14, p. 78–80]). We shall now show that this argument does not apply to our generalization of regret theory.

First consider the case of an individual who can foresee all the trading opportunities that he will confront. He starts out with A_1. He knows that he will be offered the opportunity to exchange A_1 for A_2; he knows that if he accepts this exchange, he will be offered the opportunity to exchange A_2 for A_3; if he accepts *this* exchange, he will be able to exchange A_3 for A_1, and so on. Then it will be clear to him at the outset that his feasible set is $\{A_1, A_2, A_3\} = Z$; he will choose the action (or in the case of indifference, *an* action) that is maximally preferred in Z in terms of $\succeq_Z$. Since $\succeq_Z$ is an ordering, a maximally preferred action must exist. There will never be any reason for the individual to make more than two trades (the number of trades required to reach A_3). After each trade his feasible set remains $\{A_1, A_2, A_3\}$, so there is no reason for him to revise his original decision about which action to take. This argument does not seem to be peculiar to regret theory; it would apply to any theory in which preferences were set-specific.

Now consider the case of a naive individual who is always unable to foresee any trading opportunities beyond the one he currently faces. In this case the *first* trading opportunity will undoubtedly be perceived as a straightforward pairwise choice. Since $A_1 \prec A_2$ by assumption, the individual will consent to the first trade. Then, having accepted A_2, he is offered the opportunity to exchange it for A_3. We shall argue that, even if no further trading opportunities are foreseen, this opportunity will *not* be perceived as a simple pairwise choice.

Regret and rejoicing are *ex post* experiences; they occur not at the moment of choice but only after the relevant uncertainty has been resolved. At the moment of choice these experiences are merely anticipated. What the invidividual anticipates is his psychological response, in each state of the world, to his having chosen one action and rejected others. Viewed *ex*

286 LOOMES AND SUGDEN

post, the set of rejected actions contains all actions rejected during the period before the uncertainty was resolved; the *order* in which the actions were rejected seems to have no particular significance.

Consider the naive individual who has exchanged A_1 for A_2 and is then confronted with a choice between A_2 and A_3. Because he cannot foresee future trading opportunities, he believes (wrongly) that A_1 is no longer feasible for him. However, nothing that he does now can nullify the fact that he has already rejected A_1. Thus he knows that when, *ex post,* he looks back on his choices, the set of actions he might have chosen—the *retrospective feasible set*—will be $\{A_1, A_2, A_3\} = Z$. He must choose whether he will ultimately experience "having chosen A_2 and having rejected A_3 *and* A_1," or "having chosen A_3 and having rejected A_2 *and* A_1." Thus whether or not he accepts the second trading opportunity will depend on the ranking of A_2 and A_3 *in terms of* $\succcurlyeq_Z$. Only if $A_2 \prec_Z A_3$ will he have a strict preference for trade. By the same argument, if he does make the second exchange, he will have a strict preference for making the third exchange (taking him back to A_1) only if $A_3 \prec_Z A_1$. But here the chain of trades must come to an end. To suppose that the individual also has a strict preference for making the fourth exchange is to suppose that $A_1 \prec_Z A_2$, but the transitivity of the relation $\succcurlyeq_Z$ makes this a logical impossibility. So even the most naive individual cannot be induced to go round the cycle more than once. Since this result depends on the retrospective nature of regret and rejoicing, it may not apply to other theories of choice in which preferences are set-specific.

REFERENCES

1. D. BELL, Regret in decision making under uncertainty, *Oper. Res.* **20** (1982), 961–981.
2. S. CHEW AND K. MACCRIMMON, "Alpha-Nu Choice Theory: A Generalization of Expected Utility Theory," Working Paper No. 669, University of British Columbia, 1979.
3. P. FISHBURN, Nontransitive measurable utility, *J. Math. Psych.* **26** (1982), 31–67.
4. P. FISHBURN, Transitive measurable utility, *J. Econ. Theory* **31** (1983), 293–317.
5. P. FISHBURN, Dominance in SSB utility theory, *J. Econ. Theory* **34** (1984), 130–148.
6. D. GRETHER AND C. PLOTT, Economic theory of choice and the preference reversal phenomenon, *Amer. Econ. Rev.* **69** (1979), 623–638.
7. S. LICHTENSTEIN AND P. SLOVIC, Reversals of preference between bids and choices in gambling decisions, *J. Exper. Psych.* **89** (1971), 46–55.
8. H. LINDMAN, Inconsistent preferences among gambles, *J. Exper. Psych.* **89** (1971), 390–397.
9. G. LOOMES AND R. SUGDEN, Regret theory: An alternative theory of rational choice under uncertainty, *Econ. J.* **92** (1982), 805–824.
10. G. LOOMES AND R. SUGDEN, Regret theory and measurable utility, *Econ. Lett.* **12** (1983), 19–22.
11. G. LOOMES AND R. SUGDEN, A rationale for preference reversal, *Amer. Econ. Rev.* **73** (1983), 428–432.

12. M. MACHINA, "Expected utility" analysis without the independence axiom, *Econometrica* **50** (1982), 277–323.
13. M. MACHINA, "The Economic Theory of Individual Behavior towards Risk: Theory, Evidence and New Directions," Technical Report No. 433, Institute for Mathematical Studies in the Social Sciences, Stanford University, California, 1983.
14. H. RAIFFA, "Decision Analysis," Addison–Wesley, Reading, Mass., 1968.

[13]

Economic Perspectives— Volume 1, Number 1 — Summer 1987 — Pages 121–154

Choice Under Uncertainty:
Problems Solved and Unsolved

Mark J. Machina

Fifteen years ago, the theory of choice under uncertainty could be considered one of the "success stories" of economic analysis: it rested on solid axiomatic foundations, it had seen important breakthroughs in the analytics of risk, risk aversion and their applications to economic issues, and it stood ready to provide the theoretical underpinnings for the newly emerging "information revolution" in economics.[1] Today choice under uncertainty is a field in flux: the standard theory is being challenged on several grounds from both within and outside economics. The nature of these challenges, and of our profession's responses to them, is the topic of this paper.

The following section provides a brief description of the economist's canonical model of choice under uncertainty, the expected utility model of preferences over random prospects. I shall present this model from two different perspectives. The first perspective is the most familiar, and has traditionally been the most useful for addressing standard economic questions. However the second, more modern perspective will be the most useful for illustrating some of the problems which have beset the model, as well as some of the proposed responses.

Each of the subsequent sections is devoted to one of these problems. All are important, some are more completely "solved" than others. In each case I shall begin with an example or description of the phenomenon in question. I shall then review the empirical evidence regarding the uniformity and extent of the phenomenon. Finally, I shall report on how these findings have changed, or are likely to change, or ought to

---

[1] E.g. von Neumann and Morgenstern (1947) and Savage (1954) (axiomatics); Arrow (1965), Pratt (1964) and Rothschild and Stiglitz (1970) (analytics); Akerlof (1970) and Spence and Zeckhauser (1971) (information).

■ *Mark J. Machina is Associate Professor of Economics, University of California, San Diego, La Jolla, California.*

change, the way we view and model economic behavior under uncertainty. On this last topic, the disclaimer that "my opinions are my own" has more than the usual significance.[2]

The Expected Utility Model

The Classical Perspective: Cardinal Utility and Attitudes Toward Risk

In light of current trends toward generalizing this model, it is useful to note that the expected utility hypothesis was itself first proposed as an alternative to an earlier, more restrictive theory of risk-bearing. During the development of modern probability theory in the 17th century, mathematicians such as Blaise Pascal and Pierre de Fermat assumed that the attractiveness of a gamble offering the payoffs $(x_1, \ldots, x_n)$ with probabilities $(p_1, \ldots, p_n)$ was given by its expected value $\bar{x} = \sum x_i p_i$. The fact that individuals consider more than just expected value, however, was dramatically illustrated by an example posed by Nicholas Bernoulli in 1728 and now known as the *St. Petersburg Paradox*:

> Suppose someone offers to toss a fair coin repeatedly until it comes up heads, and to pay you \$1 if this happens on the first toss, \$2 if it takes two tosses to land a head, \$4 if it takes three tosses, \$8 if it takes four tosses, etc. What is the largest sure gain you would be willing to forgo in order to undertake a single play of this game?

Since this gamble offers a $1/2$ chance of winning \$1, a $1/4$ chance of winning \$2, etc., its expected value is $(1/2) \cdot \$1 + (1/4) \cdot \$2 + (1/8) \cdot \$4 + \cdots = \$1/2 + \$1/2 + \$1/2 + \cdots = \$\infty$, so it should be preferred to any finite sure gain. However, it is clear that few individuals would forgo more than a moderate amount for a one-shot play. Although the unlimited financial backing needed to actually make this offer is somewhat unrealistic, it is not essential for making the point: agreeing to limit the game to at most one million tosses will still lead to a striking discrepancy between most individuals' valuations of the modified gamble and its expected value of \$500,000.

The resolution of this paradox was proposed independently by Gabriel Cramer and Nicholas's cousin Daniel Bernoulli (Bernoulli, 1738/1954). Arguing that a gain of \$200 was not necessarily "worth" twice as much as a gain of \$100, they hypothesized that the individual possesses what is now termed a *von Neumann-Morgenstern utility function* $U(\cdot)$, and rather than using expected value $\bar{x} = \sum x_i p_i$, will evaluate gambles on the basis of expected utility $\bar{u} = \sum U(x_i) p_i$. Thus the sure gain ξ which would yield the same utility as the Petersburg gamble, i.e. the certainty equivalent of this gamble,

---

[2]In keeping with the spirit of this journal, references have been limited to the most significant examples of and/or most useful introductions to the literature in each area. For further discussions of these issues see Arrow (1982), Machina (1983a, 1983b), Sugden (1986) and Tversky and Kahneman (1986).

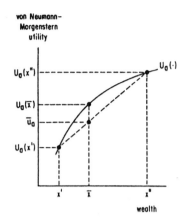

Fig. 1a. Concave utility function of a risk averter

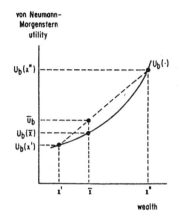

Fig. 1b. Convex utility function of a risk lover

is determined by the equation

(1) $$U(W + \xi) = (1/2) \cdot U(W + 1) + (1/4) \cdot U(W + 2)$$

$$+ (1/8) \cdot U(W + 4) + \cdots$$

where W is the individual's current wealth. If utility took the logarithmic form $U(x) \equiv \ln(x)$ and $W = \$50{,}000$, for example, the individual's certainty equivalent ξ would only be about $9, even though the gamble has an infinite expected value.

Although it shares the name "utility," $U(\cdot)$ is quite distinct from the ordinal utility function of standard consumer theory. While the latter can be subjected to any monotonic transformation, a von Neumann-Morgenstern utility function is cardinal in that it can only be subjected to transformations of the form $a \cdot U(x) + b$ ($a > 0$), i.e. transformations which change the origin and/or scale of the vertical axis, but do not affect the "shape" of the function.[3]

To see how this shape determines risk attitudes, consider Figures 1a and 1b. The monotonicity of $U_a(\cdot)$ and $U_b(\cdot)$ in the figures reflects the property of stochastic dominance preference, where one lottery is said to stochastically dominate another one if it can be obtained from it by shifting probability from lower to higher outcome levels.[4] Stochastic dominance preference is thus the probabilistic analogue of the attitude that "more is better."

Consider a gamble offering a $2/3 : 1/3$ chance of the outcomes x' or x''. The points $\bar{x} = (2/3) \cdot x' + (1/3) \cdot x''$ in the figures give the expected value of this

[3]Such transformations are often used to normalize the utility function, for example to set $U(0) = 0$ and $U(M) = 1$ for some large value M.
[4]Thus, for example, a $2/3 : 1/3$ chance of $100 or $20 and a $1/2 : 1/2$ chance of $100 or $30 both stochastically dominate a $1/2 : 1/2$ chance of $100 or $20.

gamble, and $\bar{u}_a = (2/3) \cdot U_a(x') + (1/3) \cdot U_a(x'')$ and $\bar{u}_b = (2/3) \cdot U_b(x') + (1/3) \cdot U_b(x'')$ give its expected utilities for $U_a(\cdot)$ and $U_b(\cdot)$. For the concave utility function $U_a(\cdot)$ we have $U_a(\bar{x}) > \bar{u}_a$, which implies that this individual would prefer a sure gain of $\bar{x}$ (which would yield utility $U_a(\bar{x})$) to the gamble. Since someone with a concave utility function will in fact always prefer receiving the expected value of a gamble to the gamble itself, concave utility functions are termed risk averse. For the convex utility function $U_b(\cdot)$ we have $\bar{u}_b > U_b(\bar{x})$, and since this preference for bearing the risk rather than receiving the expected value will also extend to all gambles, $U_b(\cdot)$ is termed risk loving. In their famous article, Friedman and Savage (1948) showed how a utility function which was concave at low wealth levels and convex at high wealth levels could explain the behavior of individuals who both incur risk by purchasing lottery tickets as well as avoid risk by purchasing insurance. Algebraically, Arrow (1965) and Pratt (1964) have shown how the degree of concavity of a utility function, as measured by the curvature index $-U''(x)/U'(x)$, determines how risk attitudes, and hence behavior, will vary with wealth or across individuals in a variety of situations. If $U_c(\cdot)$ is at least as risk averse as $U_d(\cdot)$ in the sense that $-U_c''(x)/U_c'(x) \geq -U_d''(x)/U_d'(x)$ for all x, then an individual with utility function $U_c(\cdot)$ would be willing to pay at least as much for insurance against any risk as would someone with utility function $U_d(\cdot)$.

Since a knowledge of $U(\cdot)$ would allow us to predict preferences (and hence behavior) in any risky situation, experimenters and applied decision analysts are frequently interested in eliciting or recovering their subjects' (or clients') von Neumann-Morgenstern utility functions. One method of doing so is termed the fractile method. This approach begins by adopting the normalization $U(0) = 0$ and $U(M) = 1$ (see Note 3) and fixing a "mixture probability" $\bar{p}$, say $\bar{p} = 1/2$. The next step involves finding the individual's certainty equivalent ξ_1 of a $1/2 : 1/2$ chance of M or 0, which implies that $U(\xi_1) = (1/2) \cdot U(M) + (1/2) \cdot U(0) = 1/2$. Finding the certainty equivalents of the $1/2 : 1/2$ chances of ξ_1 or 0 and of M or ξ_1 yields the values ξ_2 and ξ_3 which solve $U(\xi_2) = 1/4$ and $U(\xi_3) = 3/4$. By repeating this procedure (i.e. $1/8$, $3/8$, $5/8$, $7/8$, $1/16$, $3/16$, etc.), the utility function can (in the limit) be completely assessed.

Our discussion so far has paralleled the economic literature of the 1960s and 1970s by emphasizing the flexibility of the expected utility model compared to the Pascal-Fermat expected value approach. However, the need to analyze and respond to growing empirical challenges has led economists in the 1980's to concentrate on the behavioral restrictions implied by the expected utility hypothesis. It is to these restrictions that we now turn.

A Modern Perspective: Linearity in the Probabilities as a Testable Hypothesis

As a theory of individual behavior, the expected utility model shares many of the underlying assumptions of standard consumer theory. In each case we assume that the objects of choice, either commodity bundles or lotteries, can be unambiguously and objectively described, and that situations which ultimately imply the same set of availabilities (e.g. the same budget set) will lead to the same choice. In each case we

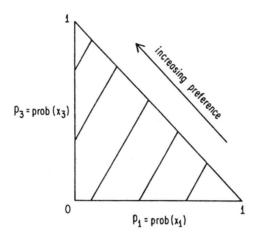

Fig. 2. Expected utility indifference curves in the triangle diagram

also assume that the individual is able to perform the mathematical operations necessary to actually determine the set of availabilities, e.g. to add up the quantities in different sized containers or calculate the probabilities of compound or conditional events. Finally, in each case we assume that preferences are transitive, so that if an individual prefers one object (either a commodity bundle or a risky prospect) to a second, and prefers this second object to a third, he or she will prefer the first object to the third. We shall examine the validity of these assumptions for choice under uncertainty in some of the following sections.

However, the strongest implication of the expected utility hypothesis stems from the form of the expected utility maximand or preference function $\Sigma U(x_i)p_i$. Although this preference function generalizes the expected value form $\Sigma x_i p_i$ by dropping the property of linearity in the payoffs (the x_i's), it retains the other key property of this form, namely linearity in the probabilities.

Graphically, we may illustrate the property of linearity in the probabilities by considering the set of all lotteries or prospects over the fixed outcome levels $x_1 < x_2 < x_3$, which can be represented by the set of all probability triples of the form $P = (p_1, p_2, p_3)$ where $p_i = \text{prob}(x_i)$ and $\Sigma p_i = 1$. Since $p_2 = 1 - p_1 - p_3$, we can represent these lotteries by the points in the unit triangle in the (p_1, p_3) plane, as in Figure 2.[5] Since upward movements in the triangle increase p_3 at the expense of p_2 (i.e. shift probability from the outcome x_2 up to x_3) and leftward movements reduce p_1 to the benefit of p_2 (shift probability from x_1 up to x_2), these movements (and more generally, all northwest movements) lead to stochastically dominating lotteries

---

[5] Thus if $x_1 = \$20$, $x_2 = \$30$ and $x_3 = \$100$, the prospects in Note 4 would be represented by the points $(p_1, p_3) = (1/3, 2/3)$, $(p_1, p_3) = (0, 1/2)$ and $(p_1, p_3) = (1/2, 1/2)$ respectively. Although it is fair to describe the renewal of interest in this approach as "modern," versions of this diagram go back at least to Marschak (1950).

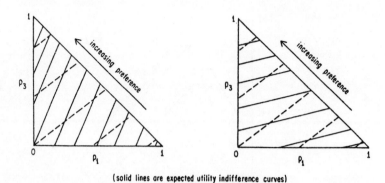

(solid lines are expected utility indifference curves)
(dashed lines are iso-expected value lines)

Fig. 3a. Relatively steep indifference curves of a   Fig. 3b. Relatively flat indifference curves of a risk
              risk averter   lover

and would accordingly be preferred. Finally, since the individual's indifference curves in the (p_1, p_3) diagram are given by the solutions to the linear equation

$$(2) \quad \bar{u} = \sum_{i=1}^{3} U(x_i)p_i = U(x_1)p_1 + U(x_2)(1 - p_1 - p_3) + U(x_3)p_3 = \text{constant}$$

they will consist of parallel straight lines of slope $[U(x_2) - U(x_1)]/[U(x_3) - U(x_2)]$, with more preferred indifference curves lying to the northwest. This implies that in order to know an expected utility maximizer's preferences over the entire triangle, it suffices to know the slope of a single indifference curve.

To see how this diagram can be used to illustrate attitudes toward risk, consider Figures 3a and 3b. The dashed lines in the figures are not indifference curves but rather *iso-expected value lines*, i.e. solutions to

$$(3) \quad \bar{x} = \sum_{i=1}^{3} x_i p_i = x_1 p_1 + x_2(1 - p_1 - p_3) + x_3 p_3 = \text{constant}$$

Since northeast movements along these lines do not change the expected value of the prospect but do increase the probabilities of the tail outcomes x_1 and x_3 at the expense of the middle outcome x_2, they are examples of *mean preserving spreads* or "pure" increases in risk (Rothschild and Stiglitz, 1970). When the utility function $U(\cdot)$ is concave (i.e. risk averse), its indifference curves can be shown to be steeper than the iso-expected value lines as in Figure 3a,[6] and such increases in risk will lead to lower indifference curves. When $U(\cdot)$ is convex (risk loving), its indifference curves will be flatter than the iso-expected value lines (as in Figure 3b) and increases in risk will lead

---

[6]This follows since the slope of the indifference curves is $[U(x_2) - U(x_1)]/[U(x_3) - U(x_2)]$, the slope of the iso-expected value lines is $[x_2 - x_1]/[x_3 - x_2]$, and concavity of $U(\cdot)$ implies $[U(x_2) - U(x_1)]/[x_2 - x_1] > [U(x_3) - U(x_2)]/[x_3 - x_2]$ whenever $x_1 < x_2 < x_3$.

to higher indifference curves. If we compare two different utility functions, the one which is more risk averse (in the above Arrow-Pratt sense) will possess the steeper indifference curves.

Behaviorally, we can view the property of linearity in the probabilities as a restriction on the individual's preferences over probability mixtures of lotteries. If $P^* = (p_1^*, \ldots, p_n^*)$ and $P = (p_1, \ldots, p_n)$ are two lotteries over a common outcome set $\{x_1, \ldots, x_n\}$, the $\alpha : (1 - \alpha)$ probability mixture of P^* and P is the lottery $\alpha P^* + (1 - \alpha)P = (\alpha p_1^* + (1 - \alpha)p_1, \ldots, \alpha p_n^* + (1 - \alpha)p_n)$. This may be thought of as that prospect which yields the same ultimate probabilities over $\{x_1, \ldots, x_n\}$ as the two-stage lottery which offers an $\alpha : (1 - \alpha)$ chance of winning either P^* or P. Since linearity in the probabilities implies that $\Sigma U(x_i)(\alpha p_i^* + (1 - \alpha)p_i) = \alpha \cdot \Sigma U(x_i)p_i^* + (1 - \alpha) \cdot \Sigma U(x_i)p_i$, expected utility maximizers will exhibit the following property, known as the *Independence Axiom* (Samuelson, 1952):

> If the lottery P^* is preferred (resp. indifferent) to the lottery P, then the mixture $\alpha P^* + (1 - \alpha)P^{**}$ will be preferred (resp. indifferent) to the mixture $\alpha P + (1 - \alpha)P^{**}$ for all $\alpha > 0$ and P^{**}.

This property, which is in fact equivalent to linearity in the probabilities, can be interpreted as follows:

> In terms of the ultimate probabilities over the outcomes $\{x_1, \ldots, x_n\}$, choosing between the mixtures $\alpha P^* + (1 - \alpha)P^{**}$ and $\alpha P + (1 - \alpha)P^{**}$ is the same as being offered a coin with a probability of $1 - \alpha$ of landing tails, in which case you will obtain the lottery P^{**}, and being asked before the flip whether you would rather have P^* or P in the event of a head. Now either the coin will land tails, in which case your choice won't have mattered, or else it will land heads, in which case you are 'in effect' back to a choice between P^* or P, and it is only 'rational' to make the same choice as you would before.

Although this is a prescriptive argument, it has played a key role in economists' adoption of expected utility as a descriptive theory of choice under uncertainty. As the evidence against the model mounts, this has lead to a growing tension between those who view economic analysis as the description and prediction of what they consider to be rational behavior and those who view it as the description and prediction of observed behavior. We turn now to this evidence.

Violations of Linearity in the Probabilities

The Allais Paradox and "Fanning Out"

One of the earliest and best known examples of systematic violation of linearity in the probabilities (or equivalently, of the independence axiom) is the well-known *Allais Paradox* (Allais, 1953, 1979). This problem involves obtaining the individual's

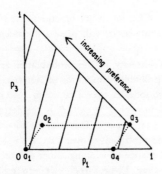
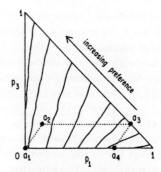

Fig. 4a. Expected utility indifference curves and the   Fig. 4b. Indifference curves which 'fan out' and the
               Allais Paradox   Allais Paradox

preferred option from each of the following two pairs of gambles (readers who have never seen this problem may want to circle their own choice from each pair before proceeding):

$$a_1: \begin{cases} 1.00 \text{ chance of } \$1,000,000 \end{cases} \text{ versus } a_2: \begin{cases} .10 \text{ chance of } \$5,000,000 \\ .89 \text{ chance of } \$1,000,000 \\ .01 \text{ chance of } \$0 \end{cases}$$

and

$$a_3: \begin{cases} .10 \text{ chance of } \$5,000,000 \\ .90 \text{ chance of } \$0 \end{cases} \text{ versus } a_4: \begin{cases} .11 \text{ chance of } \$1,000,000 \\ .89 \text{ chance of } \$0 \end{cases}$$

Defining $\{x_1, x_2, x_3\} = \{\$0; \$1,000,000; \$5,000,000\}$, these four gambles are seen form a parallelogram in the (p_1, p_3) triangle, as in Figures 4a and 4b. Under the expected utility hypothesis, therefore, a preference for a_1 in the first pair would indicate that the individual's indifference curves were relatively steep (as in Figure 4a), and hence a preference for a_4 in the second pair. In the alternative case of relatively flat indifference curves, the gambles a_2 and a_3 would be preferred.[7] However, researchers such as Allais (1953), Morrison (1967), Raiffa (1968) and Slovic and Tversky (1974) have found that the modal if not majority preferences of subjects has been for a_1 in the first pair and a_3 in the second, which implies that indifference curves are not parallel but rather fan out, as in Figure 4b.

    One of the criticisms of this evidence has been that individuals whose choices violated the independence axiom would "correct" themselves once the nature of their violation was revealed by an application of the above coin-flip argument. Thus, while even Savage chose a_1 and a_3 when first presented with this example, he concluded upon reflection that these preferences were in error (Savage, 1954, pp. 101–103).

[7]Algebraically, these cases are equivalent to the expression $[.10 \cdot U(5,000,000) - .11 \cdot U(1,000,000) + .01 \cdot U(0)]$ being negative or positive, respectively.

Although his own reaction was undoubtedly sincere, the hypothesis that individuals would invariably react in such a manner has not been sustained in direct empirical testing. In experiments where subjects were asked to respond to Allais-type problems and then presented with arguments both for and against the expected utility position, neither MacCrimmon (1968), Moskowitz (1974) nor Slovic and Tversky (1974) found predominant net swings toward the expected utility choices.

Additional Evidence of Fanning Out

Although the Allais Paradox was originally dismissed as an isolated example, it is now known to be a special case of a general empirical pattern termed the *common consequence effect*. This effect involves pairs of probability mixtures of the form:

$$b_1: \alpha\delta_x + (1 - \alpha)P^{**} \quad \text{versus} \quad b_2: \alpha P + (1 - \alpha)P^{**}$$

and

$$b_3: \alpha\delta_x + (1 - \alpha)P^* \quad \text{versus} \quad b_4: \alpha P + (1 - \alpha)P^*$$

where δ_x denotes the prospect which yields x with certainty, P involves outcomes both greater and less than x, and P^{**} stochastically dominates P^*.[8] Although the independence axiom clearly implies choices of either b_1 and b_3 (if δ_x is preferred to P) or else b_2 and b_4 (if P is preferred to δ_x), researchers have found a tendency for subjects to choose b_1 in the first pair and b_4 in the second (MacCrimmon, 1968; MacCrimmon and Larsson, 1979; Kahneman and Tversky, 1979; Chew and Waller, 1986). When the distributions δ_x, P, P^* and P^{**} are each over a common outcome set $\{x_1, x_2, x_3\}$, the prospects b_1, b_2, b_3 and b_4 will again form a parallelogram in the (p_1, p_3) triangle, and a choice of b_1 and b_4 again implies indifference curves which fan out, as in Figure 4b.

The intuition behind this phenomenon can be described in terms of the above "coin-flip" scenario. According to the independence axiom, preferences over what would occur in the event of a head should not depend upon what would occur in the event of a tail. In fact, however, they may well depend upon what would otherwise happen.[9] The common consequence effect states that the better off individuals would be in the event of a tail (in the sense of stochastic dominance), the more risk averse they become over what they would receive in the event of a head. Intuitively, if the distribution P^{**} in the pair $\{b_1, b_2\}$ involves very high outcomes, I may prefer not to bear further risk in the unlucky event that I don't receive it, and prefer the sure outcome x over the distribution P in this event (i.e. choose b_1 over b_2). But if P^* in $\{b_3, b_4\}$ involves very low outcomes, I may be more willing to bear risk in the (lucky)

---

[8]The Allais Paradox choices a_1, a_2, a_3, and a_4 correspond to b_1, b_2, b_4 and b_3, where $\alpha = .11$, $x = \$1,000,000$, P is a 10/11 : 1/11 chance of $5,000,000 or $0, P^* is a sure chance of $0, and P^{**} is a sure chance of $1,000,000. The name of this phenomenon comes from the "common consequence" P^{**} in $\{b_1, b_2\}$ and P^* in $\{b_3, b_4\}$.

[9]As Bell (1985) notes, "winning the top prize of $10,000 in a lottery may leave one much happier than receiving $10,000 as the lowest prize in a lottery."

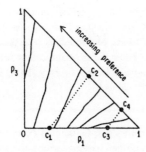

Fig. 5a. Indifference curves which fan out and the common ratio effect

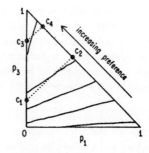

Fig. 5b. Indifference curves which fan out and the common ratio effect with negative payoffs

event that I don't receive it, and prefer the lottery P to the outcome x in this case (i.e. choose b_4 over b_3). Note that it is not my beliefs regarding the probabilities in P which are affected here, merely my willingness to bear them.[10]

A second class of systematic violations, stemming from another early example of Allais (1953), is known as the *common ratio effect*. This phenomenon involves pairs of prospects of the form:

$$c_1: \left\{ \begin{array}{l} p \text{ chance of } \$X \\ 1 - p \text{ chance of } \$0 \end{array} \right. \quad \text{versus} \quad c_2: \left\{ \begin{array}{l} q \text{ chance of } \$Y \\ 1 - q \text{ chance of } \$0, \end{array} \right.$$

and

$$c_3: \left\{ \begin{array}{l} rp \text{ chance of } \$X \\ 1 - rp \text{ chance of } \$0 \end{array} \right. \quad \text{versus} \quad c_4: \left\{ \begin{array}{l} rq \text{ chance of } \$Y \\ 1 - rq \text{ chance of } \$0, \end{array} \right.$$

where $p > q$, $0 < X < Y$ and $r \in (0, 1)$, and includes the "certainty effect" of Kahneman and Tversky (1979) and the ingenious "Bergen Paradox" of Hagen (1979) as special cases.[11] Setting $\{x_1, x_2, x_3\} = \{0, X, Y\}$ and plotting these prospects in the (p_1, p_3) triangle, the segments $\overline{c_1 c_2}$ and $\overline{c_3 c_4}$ are seen to be parallel (as in Figure 5a), so that the expected utility model again predicts choices of c_1 and c_3 (if the individual's indifference curves are steep) or else c_2 and c_4 (if they are flat). However, experimental studies have found a systematic tendency for choices to depart from these predictions

[10] In a conversation with the author, Kenneth Arrow has offered an alternative phrasing of this argument: The widely maintained hypothesis of decreasing absolute risk aversion asserts that individuals will display more risk aversion in the event of a loss, and less risk aversion in the event of a gain. In the common consequence effect, individuals display more risk aversion in the event of an opportunity loss, and less risk aversion in the event of an opportunity gain.

[11] The former involves setting $p = 1$, and the latter consists of a two-step choice problem where individuals exhibit the effect with $Y = 2X$ and $p = 2q$. The name "common ratio effect" comes from the common value of $\text{prob}(X)/\text{prob}(Y)$ in the pairs $\{c_1, c_2\}$ and $\{c_3, c_4\}$.

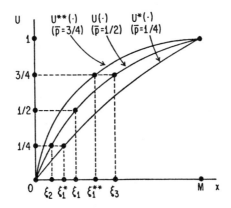

Fig. 6a. 'Recovered' utility functions for mixture probabilities 1/4, 1/2 and 3/4

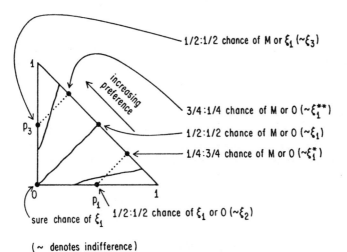

(~ denotes indifference)

Fig. 6b. Fanning out indifference curves which generate the responses of Figure 6a

and de Neufville (1983, 1984) have found a tendency for higher values of $\bar{p}$ to lead to the "recovery" of higher valued utility functions, as in Figure 6a. By illustrating the gambles used to obtain the values ξ_1, ξ_2 and ξ_3 for $\bar{p} = 1/2$, ξ_1^* for $\bar{p} = 1/4$ and ξ_1^{**} for $\bar{p} = 3/4$, Figure 6b shows that, as with the common consequence and common ratio effects, this *utility evaluation effect* is precisely what would be expected

---

[12] Kahneman and Tversky (1979), for example, found that 80 percent of their subjects preferred a sure gain of 3,000 Israeli pounds to a .80 chance of winning 4,000, but 65 percent preferred a .20 chance of winning 4,000 to a .25 chance of winning 3,000.

in the direction of preferring c_1 and c_4,[12] which again suggests that indifference curves fan out, as in the figure (Tversky, 1975; MacCrimmon and Larsson, 1979; Chew and Waller, 1986). In a variation on this approach, Kahneman and Tversky (1979) replaced the gains of $\$X$ and $\$Y$ in the above gambles with losses of these magnitudes, and found a tendency to depart from expected utility in the direction of c_2 and c_3. Defining $\{x_1, x_2, x_3\}$ as $\{-Y, -X, 0\}$ (to maintain the condition $x_1 < x_2 < x_3$) and plotting these gambles in Figure 5b, a choice of c_2 and c_3 is again seen to imply that indifference curves fan out. Finally, Battalio, Kagel and MacDonald (1985) found that laboratory rats choosing among gambles which involved substantial variations in their actual daily food intake also exhibited this pattern of choices.

A third class of evidence stems from the elicitation method described in the previous section. In particular, note that there is no reason why the mixture probability $\bar{p}$ must be $1/2$ in this procedure. Picking any other $\bar{p}$ and defining ξ_1^*, ξ_2^* and ξ_3^* as the certainty equivalents of the $\bar{p}: (1 - \bar{p})$ chances of M or 0, ξ_1^* or 0, and M or ξ_1^* yields the equations $U(\xi_1^*) = \bar{p}$, $U(\xi_2^*) = \bar{p}^2$, $U(\xi_3^*) = \bar{p} + (1 - \bar{p})\bar{p}$, etc., and such a procedure can also be used to recover $U(\cdot)$.

Although this procedure should recover the same (normalized) utility function for any mixture probability $\bar{p}$, researchers such as Karmarkar (1974, 1978) and McCord from an individual whose indifference curves departed from expected utility by fanning out.[13]

Non-Expected Utility Models of Preferences

The systematic nature of these departures from linearity in the probabilities have led several researchers to generalize the expected utility model by positing nonlinear functional forms for the individual preference function. Examples of such forms and researchers who have studied them include:

(4) $\qquad \sum \nu(x_i)\pi(p_i)$ $\qquad$ Edwards (1955)
$\qquad\qquad\qquad\qquad\qquad\qquad\qquad\qquad$ Kahneman and Tversky (1979)

(5) $\qquad \dfrac{\sum \nu(x_i)\pi(p_i)}{\sum \pi(p_i)}$ $\qquad$ Karmarkar (1978)

(6) $\qquad \dfrac{\sum \nu(x_i)p_i}{\sum \tau(x_i)p_i}$ $\qquad$ Chew (1983)
$\qquad\qquad\qquad\qquad\qquad\qquad\qquad\qquad$ Fishburn (1983)

(7) $\sum \nu(x_i)[g(p_1 + \cdots + p_i) - g(p_1 + \cdots + p_{i-1})]$ Quiggin (1982)

(8) $\qquad \sum \nu(x_i)p_i + [\sum \tau(x_i)p_i]^2$ $\qquad$ Machina (1982)

[13] Having found that ξ_1 which solves $U(\xi_1) = (1/2) \cdot U(M) + (1/2) \cdot U(0)$, choose $\{x_1, x_2, x_3\} = \{0, \xi_1, M\}$, so that the indifference curve through $(0,0)$ (i.e. a sure gain of ξ_1) also passes through $(1/2, 1/2)$ (a $1/2 : 1/2$ chance of M or 0). The order of $\xi_1, \xi_2, \xi_3, \xi_1^*$ and ξ_1^{**} in Figure 6a is derived from the individual's preference ordering over the five distributions in Figure 6b for which they are the respective certainty equivalents.

Many (though not all) of these forms are flexible enough to exhibit the properties of stochastic dominance preference, risk aversion/risk preference and fanning out, and (6) and (7) have proven to be particularly useful both theoretically and empirically. Additional analyses of these forms can be found in Chew, Karni and Safra (1987), Fishburn (1964), Segal (1984) and Yaari (1987).

Although such forms allow for the modelling of preferences which are more general than those allowed by the expected utility hypothesis, each requires a different set of conditions on its component functions $\nu(\cdot)$, $\pi(\cdot)$, $\tau(\cdot)$ or $g(\cdot)$ for the properties of stochastic dominance preference, risk aversion/risk preference, comparative risk aversion, etc. In particular, the standard expected utility results linking properties of the function $U(\cdot)$ to such aspects of behavior will generally not extend to the corresponding properties of the function $\nu(\cdot)$ in the above forms. Does this mean that the study of non-expected utility preferences requires us to abandon the vast body of theoretical results and intuition we have developed within the expected utility framework?

Fortunately, the answer is no. An alternative approach to the analysis of non-expected utility preferences proceeds not by adopting a specific nonlinear function, but rather by considering nonlinear functions in general, and using calculus to extend the results from expected utility theory in the same manner in which it is typically used to extend results involving linear functions.[14]

Specifically, consider the set of all probability distributions $P = (p_1, \ldots, p_n)$ over a fixed outcome set $\{x_1, \ldots, x_n\}$, so that the expected utility preference function can be written as $V(P) = V(p_1, \ldots, p_n) \equiv \Sigma U(x_i)p_i$, and think of $U(x_i)$ not as a "utility level" but rather as the coefficient of $p_i = \text{prob}(x_i)$ in this linear function. If we plot these coefficients against x_i as in Figure 7, the expected utility results of the previous section can be stated as:

Stochastic Dominance Preference: $V(\cdot)$ will exhibit global stochastic dominance preference if and only if the coefficients $\{U(x_i)\}$ are increasing in x_i, as in the figure.

Risk Aversion: $V(\cdot)$ will exhibit global risk aversion if and only if the coefficients $\{U(x_i)\}$ are concave in x_i,[15] as in the figure.

Comparative Risk Aversion: The expected utility preference function $V^*(P) \equiv \Sigma U^*(x_i)p_i$ will be at least as risk averse as $V(\cdot)$ if and only if the coefficients $\{U^*(x_i)\}$ are at least as concave in x_i as $\{U(x_i)\}$.[16]

Now take the case where the individual's preference function $\mathscr{V}(P) = \mathscr{V}(p_1, \ldots, p_n)$ is not linear (i.e. not expected utility) but at least differentiable, and consider its partial derivatives $\mathscr{U}(x_i; P) \equiv \partial \mathscr{V}(P)/\partial p_i = \partial \mathscr{V}(P)/\partial \text{ prob}(x_i)$. Pick some probability distribution P_0 and plot these $\mathscr{U}(x_i; P_0)$ values against x_i. If they

---

[14] Readers who wish to skip the details of this approach may proceed to the next section.

[15] As in Note 6, this is equivalent to the condition that $[U(x_{i+1}) - U(x_i)]/[x_{i+1} - x_i] < [U(x_i) - U(x_{i-1})]/[x_i - x_{i-1}]$ for all i.

[16] This is equivalent to the condition that $U^*(x_i) \equiv \rho(U(x_i))$ for some increasing concave function $\rho(\cdot)$.

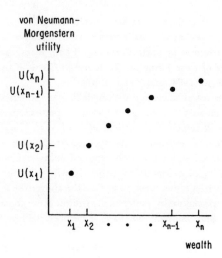

Fig. 7. von Neumann-Morgenstern utilities as coefficients of the expected utility preference function $V(p_1, \ldots, p_n) \equiv \Sigma U(x_i)p_i$

are again increasing in x_i, it is clear that any infinitesimal stochastically dominating shift from P_0, such as a decrease in some p_i and matching increase in p_{i+1}, will be preferred. If they are again concave in x_i, any infinitesimal mean preserving spread, such as a drop in p_i and (mean preserving) rise in p_{i-1} and p_{i+1}, will make the individual worse off. In light of this correspondence between the coefficients $\{U(x_i)\}$ of an expected utility preference function $V(\cdot)$ and the partial derivatives $\{\mathscr{U}(x_i; P_0)\}$ of the non-expected utility preference function $\mathscr{V}(\cdot)$, we refer to $\{\mathscr{U}(x_i; P_0)\}$ as the individual's local utility indices at P_0.

   Of course, the above results will only hold precisely for infinitesimal shifts from the distribution P_0. However, we can exploit another result from standard calculus to show how "expected utility" results may be applied to the exact global analysis of non-expected utility preferences. Recall that in many cases, a differentiable function will exhibit a specific global property if and only if that property is exhibited by its linear approximations at each point. For example, a differentiable function will be globally nondecreasing if and only if its linear approximations are non-decreasing at each point. In fact, most of the fundamental properties of risk attitudes and their expected utility characterizations are precisely of this type. In particular, it can be shown that:

Stochastic Dominance Preference: A non-expected utility preference function $\mathscr{V}(\cdot)$ will exhibit global stochastic dominance preference if and only if its local utility indices $\{\mathscr{U}(x_i; P)\}$ are increasing in x_i at each distribution P.

Risk Aversion: $\mathscr{V}(\cdot)$ will exhibit global risk aversion if and only if its local utility indices $\{\mathscr{U}(x_i; P)\}$ are concave in x_i at each distribution P.

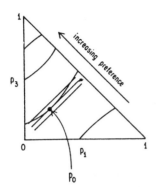

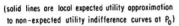

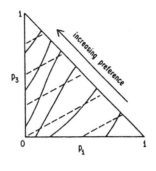

(solid lines are local expected utility approximation   (dashed lines are iso-expected value lines)
to non-expected utility indifference curves at P_0)

Fig. 8a. Tangent 'expected utility' approximation   Fig. 8b. Risk aversion of every local expected
to non-expected utility indifference curves   utility approximation is equivalent to global risk
aversion

Comparative Risk Aversion: The preference function $\mathcal{V}^*(\cdot)$ will be globally at least as risk averse as $\mathcal{V}(\cdot)$[17] if and only if its local utility indices $\{\mathcal{U}^*(x_i; P)\}$ are at least as concave in x_i as $\{\mathcal{U}(x_i; P)\}$ at each P.

Figures 8a and 8b give a graphical illustration of this approach for the outcome set $\{x_1, x_2, x_3\}$. Here the solid curves denote the indifference curves of the non-expected utility preference function $\mathcal{V}(P)$. The parallel lines near the lottery P_0 denote the tangent "expected utility" indifference curves that correspond to the local utility indices $\{\mathcal{U}(x_i; P_0)\}$ at P_0. As always with differentiable functions, an infinitesimal change in the probabilities at P_0 will be preferred if and only if they would be preferred by this tangent linear (i.e. expected utility) approximation. Figure 8b illustrates the above "risk aversion" result: It is clear that these indifference curves will be globally risk averse (averse to mean preserving spreads) if and only if they are everywhere steeper than the dashed iso-expected value lines. However, this is equivalent to all of their *tangents* being steeper than these lines, which is in turn equivalent to all of their local expected utility approximations being risk averse, or in other words, to the local utility indices $\{\mathcal{U}(x_i; P)\}$ being concave in x_i at each distribution P.

My fellow researchers and I have shown how this and similar techniques can be applied to further extend the results of expected utility theory to the case of non-expected utility preferences, to characterize and explore the implications of preferences which "fan out," and to conduct new and more general analyses of economic behavior under uncertainty (Machina, 1982; Chew, 1983; Fishburn, 1984; Epstein, 1985; Allen, 1987; Chew, Karni and Safra, 1987). However, while I feel that

---

[17]For the appropriate generalizations of the expected utility concepts of "at least as risk averse" in this context, see Machina (1982, 1984).

they constitute a useful and promising response to the phenomenon of non-linearities in the probabilities, these models do not provide solutions to the more problematic empirical phenomena of the following sections.

The Preference Reversal Phenomenon

The Evidence

The finding now known as the preference reversal phenomenon was first reported by psychologists Lichtenstein and Slovic (1971). In this study, subjects were first presented with a number of pairs of bets and asked to choose one bet out of each pair. Each of these pairs took the following form:

$$P\text{-bet:}\begin{cases} p \text{ chance of } \$X \\ 1-p \text{ chance of } \$x \end{cases} \text{ versus } \$\text{-bet:}\begin{cases} q \text{ chance of } \$Y \\ 1-q \text{ chance of } \$y, \end{cases}$$

where X and Y are respectively greater than x and y, p is greater than q, and Y is greater than X (the names "P-bet" and "$\$$-bet" come from the greater probability of winning in the first bet and greater possible gain in the second). In some cases, x and y took on small negative values. The subjects were next asked to "value" (state certainty equivalents for) each of these bets. The different valuation methods used consisted of (1) asking subjects to state their minimum selling price for each bet if they were to own it, (2) asking them to state their maximum bid price for each bet if they were to buy it, and (3) the elicitation procedure of Becker, DeGroot and Marschak (1964), in which it is in a subject's best interest to reveal his or her true certainty equivalents.[18] In the latter case, real money was used.

The expected utility model, as well as each of the non-expected utility models of the previous section, clearly implies that the bet which is actually chosen out of each pair will also be the one which is assigned the higher certainty equivalent.[19] However, Lichtenstein and Slovic found a systematic tendency for subjects to violate this prediction by choosing the P-bet in a direct choice but assigning a higher value to the $\$$-bet. In one experiment, for example, 127 out of 173 subjects assigned a higher sell price to the $\$$-bet in every pair in which the P-bet was chosen. Similar findings were obtained by Lindman (1971), and in an interesting variation on the usual experimental setting, by Lichtenstein and Slovic (1973) in a Las Vegas casino where customers actually staked (and hence sometimes lost) their own money. In another real-money

---

[18] Roughly speaking, the subject states a value for the item, and then the experimenter draws a random price. If the price is above the stated value, the subject forgoes the item and receives the price. If the drawn price is below the state value, the subject keeps the item. The reader can verify that under such a scheme it can never be in a subject's best interest to report anything other than his or her true value.

[19] Economic theory tells us that income effects could cause an individual to assign a lower bid price to the object which, if both were free, would actually be preferred. However, this reversal should not occur for either selling prices or the Becker, DeGroot and Marschak elicitations. For evidence on sell price/bid price disparities, see Knetsch and Sinden (1984) and the references cited there.

experiment, Mowen and Gentry (1980) found that groups who could discuss their (joint) decisions were, if anything, more likely than individuals to exhibit the phenomenon.

Although the above studies involved deliberate variations in design in order to check for the robustness of this phenomenon, they were nevertheless received skeptically by economists, who perhaps not unnaturally felt they had more at stake than psychologists in this type of finding. In an admitted attempt to "discredit" this work, economists Grether and Plott (1979) designed a pair of experiments which, by correcting for issues of incentives, income effects, strategic considerations, ability to indicate indifference and other items, would presumably not generate this phenomenon. They nonetheless found it in both experiments. Further design modifications by Pommerehne, Schneider and Zweifel (1982) and Reilly (1982) yielded the same results. Finally, the phenomenon has been found to persist (although in mitigated form) even when subjects are allowed to engage in experimental market transactions involving the gambles (Knez and Smith, 1986), or when the experimenter is able to act as an arbitrageur and make money off of such reversals (Berg, Dickhaut and O'Brien, 1983).

Two Interpretations of this Phenomenon

How you interpret these findings depends on whether you adopt the worldview of an economist or a psychologist. An economist would reason as follows: Each individual possesses a well-defined preference relation over objects (in this case lotteries), and information about this relation can be gleaned from either direct choice questions or (properly designed) valuation questions. Someone exhibiting the preference reversal phenomenon is therefore telling us that he or she (1) is indifferent between the P-bet and some sure amount ξ_P, (2) strictly prefers the P-bet to the $-bet, and (3) is indifferent between the $-bet and an amount ξ_s greater than ξ_P. Assuming they prefer ξ_s to the lesser amount ξ_P, this implies that their preferences over these four objects are cyclic or intransitive.

Psychologists on the other hand would deny the premise of a common underlying mechanism generating both choice and valuation behavior. Rather, they view choice and valuation (even different forms of valuation) as distinct processes, subject to possibly different influences. In other words, individuals exhibit what are termed *response mode effects*. Excellent discussions and empirical examinations of this phenomenon and its implications for the elicitation of probabilistic beliefs and utility functions can be found in Hogarth (1975), Slovic, Fischhoff and Lichtenstein (1982), Hershey and Schoemaker (1985) and MacCrimmon and Wehrung (1986). In reporting how the response mode study of Slovic and Lichtenstein (1968) led them to actually predict the preference reversal phenomenon, I can do no better than quote the authors themselves:

"The impetus for this study [Lichtenstein and Slovic (1971)] was our observation in our earlier 1968 article that choices among pairs of gambles appeared to be influenced primarily by probabilities of winning and losing, whereas buying and selling prices were primarily determined by the dollar amounts that could be won or lost. ... In our 1971 article, we argued that, if the information in a gamble is processed differently when making choices and setting prices, it should be possible to construct pairs of gambles such that people would choose one member of the pair but set a higher price on the other."

Slovic and Lichtenstein (1983)

Implications of the Economic Worldview

The issue of intransitivity is new neither to economics nor to choice under uncertainty. May (1954), for example, observed intransitivities in pairwise rankings of three alternative marriage partners, where each candidate was rated highly in two of three attributes (intelligence, looks, wealth) and low in the third. In an uncertain context, Blyth (1972) has adapted this approach to construct a set of random variables $(\tilde{x}, \tilde{y}, \tilde{z})$ such that $\mathrm{prob}(\tilde{x} > \tilde{y}) = \mathrm{prob}(\tilde{y} > \tilde{z}) = \mathrm{prob}(\tilde{z} > \tilde{x}) = 2/3$, so that individuals making pairwise choices on the basis of these probabilities would also be intransitive. In addition to the preference reversal phenomenon, Edwards (1954, pp. 404–405) and Tversky (1969) have also observed intransitivities in preferences over risky prospects. On the other hand, researchers have shown that many aspects of economic theory, in particular the existence of demand functions and of general equilibrium, are surprisingly robust to dropping the assumption of transitivity (Sonnenschein, 1971; Mas-Colell, 1974; Shafer, 1974).

In any event, economists have begun to develop and analyze models of nontransitive preferences over lotteries. The leading example of this is the "expected regret" model developed independently by Bell (1982), Fishburn (1982) and Loomes and Sugden (1982). In this model of pairwise choice, the von Neumann-Morgenstern utility function $U(x)$ is replaced by a *regret/rejoice function* $r(x, y)$ which represents the level of satisfaction (or if negative, dissatisfaction) the individual would experience if he or she were to receive the outcome x when the alternative choice would have yielded the outcome y (this function is assumed to satisfy $r(x, y) \equiv -r(y, x)$). In choosing between statistically independent gambles $P^* = (p_1^*, \ldots, p_n^*)$ and $P = (p_1, \ldots, p_n)$ over a common outcome set $\{x_1, \ldots, x_n\}$, the individual will choose P^* if the expectation $\sum_i \sum_j r(x_i, x_j) p_i^* p_j$ is positive, and P if it is negative.

Note that when the regret/rejoice function takes the special form $r(x, y) \equiv U(x) - U(y)$ this model reduces to the expected utility model, since we have

$$(9) \qquad \sum_i \sum_j r(x_i, x_j) p_i^* p_j$$

$$\equiv \sum_i \sum_j \left[U(x_i) - U(x_j) \right] p_i^* p_j \equiv \sum_i U(x_i) p_i^* - \sum_j U(x_j) p_j$$

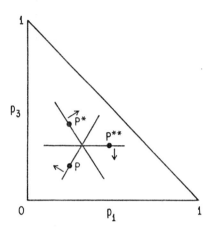

Fig. 9. 'Indifference curves' for the expected regret model

so that the individual will prefer P^* to P if and only if $\Sigma_i U(x_i) p_i^* > \Sigma_j U(x_j) p_j.$ [20] However, in general such an individual will neither be an expected utility maximizer nor have transitive preferences.

However, this intransitivity does not prevent us from graphing such preferences, or even applying "expected utility" analysis to them. To see the former, consider the case when the individual is facing alternative independent lotteries over a common outcome set $\{x_1, x_2, x_3\}$, so that we may again use the triangle diagram to illustrate their "indifference curves," which will appear as in Figure 9. In such a case it is important to understand what is and is not still true of these indifference curves. The curve through P will still correspond to the set of lotteries that are indifferent to P, and it will still divide the set of lotteries that are strictly preferred to P (the points in the direction of the arrow) from the ones to which P is strictly preferred. Furthermore, if (as in the figure) P^* lies above the indifference curve through P, then P will lie below the indifference curve through P^* (i.e. the individual's ranking of P and P^* will be unambiguous). However, unlike indifference curves for transitive preferences, these curves will cross,[21] and preferences over the lotteries P, P^* and P^{**} are seen to form an intransitive cycle. But in regions where the indifference curves do not cross (such as near the origin) the individual will be indistinguishable from someone with transitive (albeit non-expected utility) preferences.

To see how expected utility results can be extended to this nontransitive framework, fix a lottery $P = (p_1, \ldots, p_n)$ and consider the question of when an (independent) lottery $P^* = (p_1^*, \ldots, p_n^*)$ will be preferred or not preferred to P. Since

[20] When $r(x, y)$ takes the form $r(x, y) \equiv \nu(x)\tau(y) - \nu(y)\tau(x)$, this model will reduce to the (transitive) model of equation (6). This is the most general form of the model which is compatible with transitivity.
[21] In this model the indifference curves will all cross at the same point. This point will thus be indifferent to all lotteries in the triangle.

$r(x, y) \equiv -r(y, x)$ implies $\sum_i \sum_j r(x_i, x_j) p_i p_j \equiv 0$, we have that P^* will be preferred to P if and only if

$$(10) \quad 0 < \sum_i \sum_j r(x_i, x_j) p_i^* p_j = \sum_i \sum_j r(x_i, x_j) p_i^* p_j - \sum_i \sum_j r(x_i, x_j) p_i p_j$$

$$= \sum_i \left[\sum_j r(x_i, x_j) p_j \right] p_i^* - \sum_i \left[\sum_j r(x_i, x_j) p_j \right] p_i$$

$$= \sum_i \phi(x_i; P) p_i^* - \sum_i \phi(x_i; P) p_i$$

In other words, P^* will be preferred to P if and only if it implies a higher expectation of the "utility function" $\phi(x_i; P) \equiv \sum_j r(x_i, x_j) p_j$ than P. Thus if $\phi(x_i; P)$ is increasing in x_i for all lotteries P the individual will exhibit global stochastic dominance preference, and if $\phi(x_i; P)$ is concave in x_i for all P the individual will exhibit global risk aversion, even though he or she is not necessarily transitive (these conditions will clearly be satisfied if $r(x, y)$ is increasing and concave in x). The analytics of expected utility theory are robust indeed.

The developers of this model have shown how specific assumptions on the form of the regret/rejoice function will generate the common consequence effect, the common ratio effect, the preference reversal phenomenon, and other observed properties of choice over lotteries. The theoretical and empirical prospects for this approach accordingly seem quite impressive.

Implications of the Psychological Worldview

On the other hand, how should economists respond if it turns out that the psychologists are right, and the preference reversal phenomenon really is generated by some form of response mode effect (or effects)? In that case, the first thing to do would be to try to determine if there were analogues of such effects in real-world economic situations.[22] Will individuals behave differently when determining their valuation of an object (e.g. reservation bid on a used car) than when reacting to a fixed and non-negotiable price for the same object? Since a proper test of this would require correcting for any possible strategic and/or information-theoretic (e.g. signalling) issues, it would not be a simple undertaking. However, in light of the experimental evidence, I feel it is crucial that we attempt it.

Say we found that response mode effects did not occur outside of the laboratory. In that case we could rest more easily, although we could not forget about such issues completely: experimenters testing other economic theories and models (e.g. auctions) would have to be forever mindful of the possible influence of the particular response mode used in their experimental design.

[22] It is important to note that neither the evidence of response mode effects (e.g. Slovic, 1975) nor their implications for economic analysis are confined to the case of choice under uncertainty.

On the other hand, what if we did find response mode effects out in the field? In that case we would want to determine, perhaps by going back to the laboratory, whether the rest of economic theory remained valid provided the response mode is held constant. If this were true, then with further evidence on exactly how the response mode mattered, we could presumably incorporate it as a new independent variable into existing theories. Since response modes tend to be constant within a given economic model, e.g. quantity responses to fixed prices in competitive markets, valuation announcements (truthful or otherwise) in auctions, etc., we should expect most of the testable implications of this approach to appear as cross-institutional predictions, such as systematic violations of the various equivalency results involving prices versus quantities or second price-sealed bid versus oral English auctions. In such a case, the new results and insights regarding our theories of institutions and mechanisms could be exciting indeed.[23]

Framing Effects

Evidence

In addition to response mode effects, psychologists have uncovered an even more disturbing phenomenon, namely that alternative means of representing or "framing" probabilistically equivalent choice problems will lead to systematic differences in choice. An early example of this phenomenon was reported by Slovic (1969), who found that offering a gain or loss contingent on the joint occurrence of four independent events with probability p elicited different responses than offering it on the occurrence of a single event with probability p^4 (all probabilities were stated explicitly). In comparison with the single-event case, making a gain contingent on the joint occurrence of events was found to make it more attractive, and making a loss contingent on the joint occurrence of events made it more unattractive.

In another study, Payne and Braunstein (1971) used pairs of gambles of the type illustrated in Figure 10. Each of the gambles in the figure, known as a *duplex gamble*, involves spinning the pointers on both its "gain wheel" (on the left) and its "loss wheel" (on the right), with the individual receiving the sum of the resulting amounts. Thus an individual choosing Gamble A would win $.40 with probability .3 (i.e. if the pointer in the gain wheel landed up and the pointer in the loss wheel landed down), would lose $.40 with probability .2 (if the pointers landed in the opposite positions), and would break even with probability .5 (if the pointers landed either both up or both down). An examination of Gamble B reveals that it has an identical underlying distribution, so that subjects should be indifferent between the two gambles regardless

---

[23]A final "twist" on the preference reversal phenomenon: Holt (1986) and Karni and Safra (1987) have shown how the procedures used in most of these studies will only lead to truthful revelation of preferences under the added assumption that the individual satisfies the independence axiom, and has given examples of transitive non-expected utility preference rankings which lead to the typical "preference reversal" choices. How (and whether) experimenters will be able to address this issue remains to be seen.

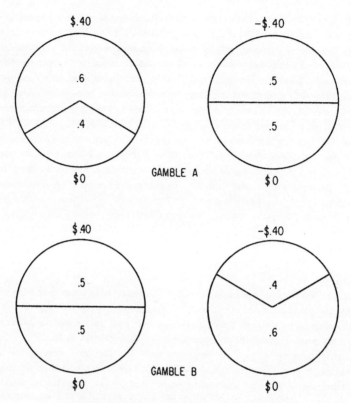

Fig. 10. Duplex gambles with identical underlying distributions

of their risk preferences. However, Payne and Braunstein found that individuals in fact chose between such gambles (and indicated nontrivial strengths of preference) in manners which were systematically affected by the attributes of the component wheels. When the probability of winning in the gain wheel was greater than the probability of losing in the loss wheel for each gamble (as in the figure), subjects tended to choose the gamble whose gain wheel yielded the greater probability of a gain (Gamble A). In cases where the probabilities of losing in the loss wheels were respectively greater than the probabilities of winning in the gain wheels, subjects tended toward the gamble with the lower probability of losing in the loss wheel.

Finally, although the gambles in Figure 10 possess identical underlying distributions, continuity suggests that a slight worsening of the terms of the preferred gamble could result in a pair of non-equivalent duplex gambles in which the individual will actually choose the one with the stochastically dominated underlying distribution. In an experiment where the subjects were allowed to construct their own duplex gambles by choosing one from a pair of prospects involving gains and one from a pair of prospects involving losses, stochastically dominated prospects were indeed chosen (Tversky and Kahneman, 1981).[24]

A second class of framing effects involves the phenomenon of a *reference point*. Theoretically, the variable which enters an individual's von Neumann-Morgenstern utility function should be total (i.e. final) wealth, and gambles phrased in terms of gains and losses should be combined with current wealth and re-expressed as distributions over final wealth levels before being evaluated. However, economists since Markowitz (1952) have observed that risk attitudes over gains and losses are more stable than can be explained by a fixed utility function over final wealth, and have suggested that the utility function might be best defined in terms of changes from the "reference point" of current wealth. This stability of risk attitudes in the face of wealth variations has also been observed in several experimental studies.[25]

Markowitz (p. 155) also suggested that certain circumstances may cause the individual's reference point to temporarily deviate from current wealth. If these circumstances include the manner in which a given problem is verbally described, then differing risk attitudes over gains and losses can lead to different choices depending upon the exact description. A simple example of this, from Kahneman and Tversky (1979), involves the following two questions:

In addition to whatever you own, you have been given 1,000 (Israeli pounds). You are now asked to choose between a $1/2 : 1/2$ chance of a gain of 1,000 or 0 or a sure gain of 500.

and

In addition to whatever you own, you have been given 2,000. You are now asked to choose between a $1/2 : 1/2$ chance of loss of 1,000 or 0 or a sure loss of 500.

These two problems involve identical distributions over final wealth. However, when put to two different groups of subjects, 84 percent chose the sure gain in the first problem but 69 percent chose the $1/2 : 1/2$ gamble in the second. A nonmonetary version of this type of example, from Tversky and Kahneman (1981, 1986), posits the following scenario:

Imagine that the U.S. is preparing for the outbreak of an unusual Asian disease, which is expected to kill 600 people. Two alternative programs to combat the disease have been proposed. Assume that the exact scientific estimate of the

[24] Subjects were asked to choose either (A) a sure gain of $240 or (B) a $1/4 : 3/4$ chance of $1,000 or $0, and to choose either (C) a sure loss of $750 or (D) a $3/4 : 1/4$ chance of $-$1,000 or 0. 84 percent chose A over B and 87 percent chose D over C, even though B + C dominates A + D, and choices over the combined distributions were unanimous when they were presented explicitly.
[25] See the discussion and references in Machina (1982, pp. 285–86).

consequences of the programs are as follows:

If program A is adopted, 200 people will be saved.

If Program B is adopted, there is 1/3 probability that 600 people will be saved, and 2/3 probability that no people will be saved.

Seventy-two percent of the subjects who were presented with this form of the question chose Program A. A second group was given the same initial information, but the descriptions of the programs were changed to read:

If Program C is adopted 400 people will die.

If Program D is adopted there is 1/3 probability that nobody will die, and 2/3 probability that 600 people will die.

Although this statement of the problem is once again identical to the former one, 78 percent of the respondents chose Program D.

In other studies, Schoemaker and Kunreuther (1979), Hershey and Schoemaker (1980), McNeil, Pauker, Sox and Tversky (1982) and Slovic, Fischhoff and Lichtenstein (1982) have found that subjects' choices in otherwise identical problems will depend upon whether they are phrased as decisions whether or not to gamble or whether or not to insure, whether the statistical information for different therapies is presented in terms of cumulative survival probabilities or cumulative mortality probabilities, etc. For similar examples of this phenomenon in non-stochastic situations, see Thaler (1980).

In a final class of examples, not based on reference point effects, Moskowitz (1974) and Keller (1982) found that the proportion of subjects choosing in conformance with or in violation of the independence axiom in examples like the Allais Paradox was significantly affected by whether the problems were described in the standard matrix form (e.g. Raiffa, 1968, p. 7), decision tree form, or as minimally structured written statements. Interestingly enough, the form which was judged the "clearest representation" by the majority of Moskowitz's subjects (the tree form) led to the lowest degree of consistency with the independence axiom, the highest proportion of fanning out choices, and the highest persistency rate of these choices (pp. 234, 237–38).

Two Issues Regarding Framing

The replicability and pervasiveness of the above types of examples is indisputable. However, before being able to assess their implications for economic modelling we need to resolve two issues.

The first issue is whether these experimental observations possess any analogue outside of the laboratory. Since real-world decision problems do not present themselves as neatly packaged as the ones on experimental questionnaires, monitoring such effects would not be as straightforward. However this does not mean that they do not exist, or that they cannot be objectively observed or quantitatively measured. The real-world example which comes most quickly to mind, and is presumably of no small importance to the involved parties, is whether gasoline price differentials should be represented as "cash discounts" or "credit surcharges." Similarly, Russo, Krieser and Miyashita (1975) and Russo (1977) found that the practice, and even method, of displaying unit price information in supermarkets (information which consumers could calculate for themselves) affected both the level and distribution of consumer expenditures. The empirical marketing literature is no doubt replete with findings that we could legitimately interpret as real-world framing effects.

The second, more difficult issue is that of the independent observability of the particular frame that an individual will adopt in a given problem. In the duplex gamble and matrix/decision tree/written statement examples of the previous section, the different frames seem unambiguously determined by the form of presentation. However, in instances where framing involves the choice of a reference point, which presumably include the majority of real-world cases, this point might not be objectively determined by the form of presentation, and might be chosen differently, and what is worse, unobservably, by each individual.[26] In a particularly thorough and insightful study, Fischhoff (1983) presented subjects with a written decision problem which allowed for different choices of a reference point, and explored different ways of predicting which frame individuals would adopt, in order to be able to predict their actual choices. While the majority choice of subjects was consistent with what would appear to be the most appropriate frame, Fischhoff noted "the absence of any relation within those studies between [separately elicited] frame preference and option preference." Indeed to the extent that frame preferences varied across his experiments, they did so inversely to the incidence of the predicted choice.[27] If such problems can occur in predicting responses to specific written questions in the laboratory, imagine how they could plague the modelling of real world choice behavior.

Framing Effects and Economic Analysis: Have We Already Solved this Problem?

How should we respond if it turns out that framing actually is a real-world phenomenon of economic relevance, and in particular, if individuals' frames cannot always be observed? I would argue that the means of responding to this issue can already be found in the "tool box" of existing economic analysis.

Consider first the case where the frame of a given economic decision problem, even though it should not matter from the point of view of standard theory, can at least be independently and objectively observed. I believe that economists have in fact already solved such a problem in their treatment of the phenomenon of "uninformative advertising." Although it is hard to give a formal definition of this term, it is widely felt that economic theory is hard put to explain a large proportion of current advertising in terms of traditional informational considerations.[28] However, this has

---

[26] This is not to say that well-defined reference points never exist. The reference points involved in credit surcharges vs. cash discounts, for example, seem unambiguous.

[27] Fischhoff (1983, pp. 115–16). Fischhoff notes that "If one can only infer frames from preferences after assuming the truth of the theory, one runs the risk of making the theory itself untestable."

[28] A wonderful example, offered by my colleague Joel Sobel, are milk ads which make no reference to either price or a specific dairy. What could be a more well-known commodity than milk?

hardly led economists to abandon classical consumer theory. Rather, models of uninformative advertising proceed by quantifying this variable (e.g. air time) and treating it as an additional independent variable in the utility and/or demand function. Standard results like the Slutsky equation need not be abandoned, but rather simply reinterpreted as properties of demand functions holding this new variable constant. The amount of advertising itself is determined as a maximizing variable on the part of the firm (given some cost curve), and can be subjected to standard comparative static analysis.

In the case when decision frames can be observed, framing effects can presumably be modelled in an analogous manner. To do so, we would begin by adopting a method of quantifying, or at least categorizing, frames. The second step, some of which has of course already been done, is to study both the effect of this new independent variable holding the standard economic variables constant, and conversely, to retest our standard economic theories in conditions where we carefully held the frame fixed. With any luck we would find that, holding the frame constant, the Slutsky equation still held.

The next step in any given modelling situation would be to ask "who determines the frame?" If (as with advertising) it is the firm, then the effect of the frame upon consumer demand, and hence upon firm profits, can be incorporated into the firm's maximization problem, and the choice of the frame as well as the other relevant variables (e.g. prices and quantities) can be simultaneously determined and subjected to comparative static analysis, just as in the case of uninformative advertising.

A seemingly more difficult case is when the individual chooses the frame (for example, a reference point) and this choice cannot be observed. Although we should not forget the findings of Fischhoff (1983), assume that this choice is at least systematic in the sense that the consumer will jointly choose the frame and make the subsequent decision in a manner which maximizes a "utility function" which depends both on the decision and the choice of frame. In other words, individuals make their choices as part of a joint maximization problem, the other component of which (the choice of frame or reference point) cannot be observed.

Such models are hardly new to economic analysis. Indeed, most economic models presume that the agent is simultaneously maximizing with respect to variables other than the ones being studied. When assumptions are made on the individual's joint preferences over the observed and unobserved variables, the well-developed *theory of induced preferences*[29] can be used to derive testable implications on choice behavior over the observables. With a little more knowledge on exactly how frames are chosen, such an approach could presumably be applied here as well.

The above remarks should not be taken as implying that we have already solved the problem of framing in economic analysis or that there is no need to adapt, and if necessary abandon, our standard models in light of this phenomenon. Rather, they

---

[29] E.g. Milne (1981). For an application of the theory of induced preferences to choice under uncertainty, see Machina (1984).

reflect the view that when psychologists are able to hand us enough systematic evidence on how these effects operate, economists will be able to respond accordingly.

Other Issues: Is Probability Theory Relevant?

The Manipulation of Subjective Probabilities

The evidence discussed so far has primarily consisted of cases where subjects have been presented with explicit (i.e. "objective") probabilities as part of their decision problems, and the models which have addressed these phenomena possess the corresponding property of being defined over objective probability distributions. However, there is extensive evidence that when individuals have to estimate or revise probabilities for themselves they will make systematic mistakes in doing so.

The psychological literature on the processing of probabilistic information is much too large even to summarize here. However, it is worth noting that experimenters have uncovered several "heuristics" used by subjects which can lead to predictable errors in the formation and manipulation of subjective probabilities. Kahneman and Tversky (1973), Bar-Hillel (1974) and Grether (1980), for example, have found that probability updating systematically departs from Bayes Law in the direction of underweighting prior information and overweighting the "representativeness" of the current sample. In a related phenomenon termed the "law of small numbers," Tversky and Kahneman (1971) found that individuals overestimated the probability of drawing a perfectly representative sample out of a heterogeneous population. Finally, Bar-Hillel (1973), Tversky and Kahneman (1983) and others have found systematic biases in the formation of the probabilities of conjunctions of both independent and non-independent events. For surveys, discussions and examples of the psychological literature on the formation and handling of probabilities see Edwards, Lindman and Savage (1963), Slovic and Lichtenstein (1971), Tversky and Kahneman (1974) and the collections in *Acta Psychologica* (December 1970), Kahneman, Slovic and Tversky (1982) and Arkes and Hammond (1986). For examples of how economists have responded to some of these issues see Arrow (1982), Viscusi (1985) and the references cited there.

The Existence of Subjective Probabilities

The evidence referred to above indicates that when individuals are asked to formulate probabilities they do not do it correctly. However, these findings may be rendered moot by evidence which suggests that when individuals making decisions under uncertainty are not explicitly asked to form subjective probabilities, they might not do it (or even act as if doing it) at all.

In one of a class of examples due to Ellsberg (1961), subjects were presented with a pair of urns, the first containing 50 red balls and 50 black balls and the second also containing 100 red and black balls but in an unknown proportion. When faced with the choice of staking a prize on: (R_1) drawing a red ball from the first urn, (R_2)

drawing a red ball from the second urn, (B_1) drawing a black ball from the first urn, or (B_2) drawing a black ball from the second urn, a majority of subjects strictly preferred (R_1) over (R_2) and strictly preferred (B_1) over (B_2). It is clear that there can exist no subjectively assigned probabilities p: $(1 - p)$ of drawing a red vs. black ball from the second urn, even $1/2 : 1/2$, which can simultaneously generate both of these strict preferences. Similar behavior in this and related problems has been observed by Raiffa (1961), Becker and Brownson (1964), Slovic and Tversky (1974) and MacCrimmon and Larsson (1979).

Life (and Economic Analysis) Without Probabilities

One response to this type of phenomenon has been to suppose that individuals "slant" whatever subjective probabilities they might otherwise form in a manner which reflects the amount of confidence/ambiguity associated with them (Fellner, 1961; Becker and Brownson, 1964; Fishburn, 1986; Hogarth and Kunreuther, 1986). In the case of the complete ignorance regarding probabilities, Arrow and Hurwicz (1972), Maskin (1979) and others have presented axioms which imply principles such as ranking options solely on the basis of their worst and/or best outcomes (e.g. maximin, maximax), the unweighted average of their outcomes ("principle of insufficient reason"), or similar criteria.[30] Finally, generalizations of expected utility theory which drop the standard additivity and/or compounding laws of probability theory have been developed by Schmeidler (1986) and Segal (1987).

Although the above models may well capture aspects of actual decision processes, the analytically most useful approach to choice in the presence of uncertainty but the absence of probabilities is the so-called *state-preference* model of Arrow (1953/1964), Debreu (1959) and Hirshleifer (1966). In this model uncertainty is represented by a set of mutually exclusive and exhaustive *states of nature* $S = \{s_i\}$. This partition of all possible unfoldings of the future could be either very coarse, such as the pair of states {it rains here tomorrow, it doesn't rain here tomorrow} or else very fine, so that the definition of a state might read "it rains here tomorrow and the temperature at Gibraltar is 75° at noon and the price of gold in New York is below $700.00/ounce." Note that it is neither feasible nor desirable to capture all conceivable sources of uncertainty when specifying the set of states for a given problem: it is not feasible since no matter how finely the states are defined there will always be some other random criterion on which to further divide them, and not desirable since such criteria may affect neither individuals' preferences nor their opportunities. Rather, the key requirements are that the states be mutually exclusive and exhaustive so that exactly one will be realized, and (for purposes of the present discussion) that the individual cannot influence which state will actually occur.

Given a fixed (and say finite) set of states, the objects of choice in this framework consist of alternative *state-payoff bundles*, each of which specifies the outcome the individual will receive in every possible state. When the outcomes are monetary payoffs, for example, state-payoff bundles take the form $(c_1, \ldots, c_n)$, where c_i denotes

[30]For an excellent discussion of the history, nature and limitations of such approaches, see Arrow (1951).

the payoff the individual would receive should state s_i occur. In the case of exactly two states of nature we could represent this set by the points in the (c_1, c_2) plane. Since bundles of the form (c, c) represent prospects which yield the same payoff in each state of nature, the 45° line in this plane is known as the *certainty line*.

Now if the individual did happen to assign probabilities $\{p_i\}$ to the states $\{s_i\}$, each bundle $(c_1, \ldots, c_n)$ would imply a specific probability distribution over wealth, and we could infer his or her preferences (i.e. indifference curves) over state-payoff bundles. However, since these bundles are defined directly over the respective states and without reference to any probabilities, it is also possible to speak of preferences over these bundles without making any assumptions regarding the coherency, or even existence, of such probabilistic beliefs. Researchers such as the ones cited above as well as Yaari (1969), Diamond and Yaari (1972) and Mishan (1976) have shown how this indifference curve-based approach can be used to derive results from individual demand behavior through general equilibrium in a context which requires neither the expected utility hypothesis nor the existence or commonality of subjective probabilities. In other words, life without probabilities does not imply life without economic analysis.

Final Thoughts

Welfare Implications. Although the theme of this paper has been the descriptive theory of choice under uncertainty, another important issue is the implications of these developments for normative economics. Can welfare analysis be conducted in the type of world implied by the above models?

The answer to this question depends upon the model. Fanning-out behavior and the non-expected utility models used to characterize it, as well as the state-payoff approach of the previous section, are completely consistent with the assumption of well-defined, transitive individual preference orderings, and hence with traditional welfare analysis along the lines of Pareto, Bergson and Samuelson (e.g. Samuelson, 1947/1983, Ch. VIII). For example, the proof of Pareto-efficiency of a system of complete contingent-commodity markets (Arrow, 1953/1964; Debreu, 1959, Ch. 7) requires neither the expected utility hypothesis nor the assumption of well-defined probabilistic beliefs. On the other hand, it is clear that the preference reversal phenomenon and framing effects, and at least some of the non-transitive and/or non-economic models used to address them, will prove much more difficult to reconcile with welfare analysis, at least as currently practiced.

A Unified Model? Another issue is the lack of a unified model capable of simultaneously handling all of the phenomena described in this paper: fanning-out, the preference reversal phenomenon, framing effects, probability biases and the Ellsberg paradox. After all, it is presumably the same ("typical") individuals who are exhibiting each of these phenomena—shouldn't there be a single model out there capable of generating them all?

Although I am doubtful of our present ability to do this, I am also doubtful about the need to establish a unified model as a prerequisite for continued progress. The aspects of behavior considered in this paper are very diverse, and if (like the wave versus particle properties of light) they cannot be currently unified, this does not mean that we cannot continue to learn by studying and modelling them separately.

An Essential Criterion.   The evidence and theories reported in this paper have taken us a long way from the classical expected utility approach presented at the outset. To what extent will these new models be incorporated into mainstream economic thought and practice? I believe the answer will depend upon a single factor: the extent to which they can address the important issues in the economics of uncertainty, such as search, investment, bargaining or auctions, to which the expected utility model has been so usefully applied.

■ *I am grateful to Brian Binger, John Conlisk, Jim Cox, Vincent Crawford, Gong Jin Dong, Elizabeth Hoffman, Michael Rothschild, Carl Shapiro, Vernon Smith, Joseph Stiglitz, Timothy Taylor and especially Joel Sobel for helpful discussions on this material, and the Alfred P. Sloan Foundation for financial support.*

References

Akerlof, George A., "The Market for 'Lemons': Quality Uncertainty and the Market Mechanism," *Quarterly Journal of Economics*, August 1970, *84*, 488–500.

Allais, Maurice, "Le Comportement de l'Homme Rationel devant le Risque, Critique des Postulates et Axiomes de l'École Americaine," *Econometrica*, October 1953, *21*, 503–46.

Allais, Maurice, "The Foundations of a Positive Theory of Choice Involving Risk and a Criticism of the Postulates and Axioms of the American School," in Allais and Hagen (1979).

Allais, Maurice and Ole Hagen, eds., *Expected Utility Hypotheses and the Allais Paradox.* Dordrecht, Holland: D. Reidel, 1979.

Allen, Beth, "Smooth Preferences and the Local Expected Utility Hypothesis," *Journal of Economic Theory*, 1987, forthcoming.

Arkes, Hal R. and Kenneth R. Hammond, eds., *Judgement and Decision Making: An Interdisciplinary Reader.* Cambridge: Cambridge University Press, 1986.

Arrow, Kenneth J., "Alternative Approaches to the Theory of Choice in Risk-Taking Situations," *Econometrica*, October 1951, *19*, 404–37. Reprinted in Arrow (1965).

Arrow, Kenneth J., "Le Role des Valeurs Boursières pour la Répartition le meilleure des

risques," *Économetrie*, Colloques Internationaux du Centre National de la Recherche Scientifique, Paris, 1953, *40*, 41–47. English translation: *Review of Economic Studies*, April 1964, *31*, 91–96.

Arrow, Kenneth J., *Aspects of the Theory of Risk-Bearing*, Helsinki: Yrjo Jahnsson Saatio, 1965.

Arrow, Kenneth J., "Risk Perception in Psychology and Economics," *Economic Inquiry*, January 1982, *20*, 1–9.

Arrow, Kenneth J. and Leonid Hurwicz, "An Optimality Criterion for Decision-Making under Ignorance." In Carter, C. F. and J. L. Ford, eds., *Uncertainty and Expectations in Economics.* Oxford: Basil Blackwell, 1972.

Bar-Hillel, Maya, "On the Subjective Probability of Compound Events," *Organizational Behavior and Human Performance*, June 1973, *9*, 396–406.

Bar-Hillel, Maya, "Similarity and Probability," *Organizational Behavior and Human Performance*, April 1974, *11*, 277–82.

Battalio, Raymond C., John H. Kagel and Don N. MacDonald, "Animals' Choices over Uncertain Outcomes," *American Economic Review*, September 1985, *75*, 597–613.

Becker, Selwyn W. and Fred O. Brownson, "What Price Ambiguity? Or the Role of Ambiguity in Decision-Making," *Journal of Political Economy*, February 1964, *72*, 62–73.

Becker, Gordon M., Morris H. DeGroot and Jacob Marschak, "Measuring Utility by a Single-Response Sequential Method," *Behavioral Science*, July 1964, 9, 226–32.

Bell, David E., "Regret in Decision Making Under Uncertainty," *Operations Research*, September–October 1982, 30, 961–81.

Bell, David E., "Disappointment in Decision Making Under Uncertainty," *Operations Research*, January–February 1985, 33, 1–27.

Berg, Joyce E., John W. Dickhaut and John R. O'Brien, "Preference Reversal and Arbitrage," manuscript, University of Minnesota, September 1983.

Bernoulli, Daniel, "Specimen Theoriae Novae de Mensura Sortis," *Commentarii Academiae Scientiarum Imperialis Petropolitanae*, 1738, 5, 175–92. English translation: *Econometrica*, January 1954, 22, 23–36.

Blyth, Colin R., "Some Probability Paradoxes in Choice from Among Random Alternatives," *Journal of the American Statistical Association*, June 1972, 67, 366–73.

Chew Soo Hong, "A Generalization of the Quasilinear Mean With Applications to the Measurement of Income Inequality and Decision Theory Resolving The Allais Paradox," *Econometrica*, July 1983, 51, 1065–92.

Chew Soo Hong, Edi Karni and Zvi Safra, "Risk Aversion in the Theory of Expected Utility with Rank Dependent Probabilities," *Journal of Economic Theory*, 1987, forthcoming.

Chew Soo Hong and William Waller, "Empirical Tests of Weighted Utility Theory," *Journal of Mathematical Psychology*, March 1986, 30, 55–72.

Debreu, Gerard, *Theory of Value: An Axiomatic Analysis of General Equilibrium*. New Haven: Yale University Press, 1959.

Diamond, Peter A. and Menahem Yaari, "Implications of the, Theory of Rationing for Consumer Choice Under Uncertainty," *American Economic Review*, June 1972, 62, 333–43.

Edwards, Ward, "The Theory of Decision Making," *Psychological Bulletin*, July 1954, 51, 380–417.

Edwards, Ward, "The Prediction of Decisions Among Bets," *Journal of Experimental Psychology*, September 1955, 50, 201–14.

Edwards, Ward, Harold Lindman and Leonard J. Savage, "Bayesian Statistical Inference for Psychological Research," *Psychological Review*, May 1963, 70, 193–242.

Ellsberg, Daniel, "Risk, Ambiguity and the Savage Axioms," *Quarterly Journal of Economics*, November 1961, 75, 643–69.

Epstein, Larry, "Decreasing Risk Aversion and Mean-Variance Analysis," *Econometrica*, 1985, 53, 945–61.

Fellner, William, "Distortion of Subjective Probabilities as a Reaction to Uncertainty," *Quarterly Journal of Economics*, November 1961, 75, 670–89.

Fischhoff, Baruch, "Predicting Frames," *Journal of Experimental Psychology: Learning, Memory and Cognition*, January 1983, 9, 103–16.

Fishburn, Peter C., "Nontransitive Measurable Utility," *Journal of Mathematical Psychology*, August 1982, 26, 31–67.

Fishburn, Peter C., "Transitive Measurable Utility," *Journal of Economic Theory*, December 1983, 31, 293–317.

Fishburn, Peter C., "SSB Utility Theory: An Economic Perspective," *Mathematical Social Sciences*, 1984, 8, 63–94.

Fishburn, Peter C., "A New Model for Decisions Under Uncertainty," *Economics Letters*, 1986, 21, 127–30.

Friedman, Milton and Leonard J. Savage, "The Utility Analysis of Choices Involving Risk," *Journal of Political Economy*, August 1948, 56, 279–304.

Grether, David M., "Bayes Rule as a Descriptive Model: The Representativeness Heuristic," *Quarterly Journal of Economics*, November 1980, 95, 537–57.

Grether, David M. and Charles R. Plott, "Economic Theory of Choice and the Preference Reversal Phenomenon," *American Economic Review*, September 1979, 69, 623–38.

Hagen, Ole, "Towards a Positive Theory of Preferences Under Risk," in Allais and Hagen (1979).

Hershey, John C. and Paul J. H. Schoemaker, "Risk-Taking and Problem Context in the Domain of Losses—An Expected Utility Analysis," *Journal of Risk and Insurance*, March 1980 47, 111–32.

Hershey, John C. and Paul J. H. Schoemaker, "Probability Versus Certainty Equivalence Methods in Utility Measurement: Are They Equivalent?," *Management Science*, October 1985, 31, 1213–31.

Hirshleifer, Jack, "Investment Decision Under Uncertainty: Applications of the State-Preference Approach," *Quarterly Journal of Economics*, May 1966, 80, 252–77.

Hogarth, Robin, "Cognitive Processes and the Assessment of Subjective Probability Distributions," *Journal of the American Statistical Association*, June 1975, 70, 271–89.

Hogarth, Robin and Howard Kunreuther, "Decision Making Under Ambiguity," *Journal of Business*, October 1986, Prt. 2, 4, 225–50.

Holt, Charles A., "Preference Reversals and the Independence Axiom," *American Economic Review*, June 1986, 76, 508–15.

Kahneman, Daniel, Paul Slovic and Amos Tversky, eds., *Judgement Under Uncertainty: Heuristics and Biases*, Cambridge: Cambridge University Press, 1982.

Kahneman, Daniel and Amos Tversky, "On the Psychology of Prediction," *Psychological Review*, July 1973, *80* 237–51.

Kahneman, Daniel and Amos Tversky, "Prospect Theory: An Analysis of Decision Under Risk," *Econometrica*, March 1979, *47*, 263–91.

Karmarkar, Uday S., "The Effect of Probabilities on the Subjective Evaluation of Lotteries," Massachusetts Institute of Technology Sloan School of Business Working Paper, 1974.

Karmarkar, Uday S., "Subjectively Weighted Utility: A Descriptive Extension of the Expected Utility Model," *Organizational Behavior and Human Performance*, February 1978, *21*, 61–72.

Karni, Edi and Zvi Safra, " 'Preference Reversal' and the Observability of Preferences by Experimental Methods," *Econometrica*, 1987, forthcoming.

Keller, L. Robin, "The Effects of Decision Problem Representation on Utility Conformance," manuscript, University of California, Irvine, 1982.

Knetsch, Jack L. and J. A. Sinden. "Willingness to Pay and Compensation Demanded: Experimental Evidence of an Unexpected Disparity in Measures of Value," *Quarterly Journal of Economics*, August 1984, *99*, 507–21.

Knez, Marc and Vernon L. Smith, "Hypothetical Valuations and Preference Reversals in the Context of Asset Trading," manuscript, University of Arizona, 1986.

Lichtenstein, Sarah and Paul Slovic, "Reversals of Preferences Between Bids and Choices in Gambling Decisions," *Journal of Experimental Psychology*, July 1971, *89*, 46–55.

Lichtenstein, Sarah and Paul Slovic, "Response-Induced Reversals of Preference in Gambling: An Extended Replication in Las Vegas," *Journal of Experimental Psychology*, November 1973, *101*, 16–20.

Lindman, Harold, "Inconsistent Preferences Among Gambles," *Journal of Experimental Psychology*, May 1971, *89*, 390–97.

Loomes, Graham and Robert Sugden, "Regret Theory: An Alternative Theory of Rational Choice Under Uncertainty," *Economic Journal*, December 1982, *92*, 805–24.

MacCrimmon, Kenneth R., "Descriptive and Normative Implications of the Decision-Theory Postulates." In Borch Karl H., and Jan Mossin, eds., *Risk and Uncertainty: Proceedings of a Conference Held by the International Economic Association*. London: Macmillan, 1968.

MacCrimmon, Kenneth R. and Stig Larsson, "Utility Theory: Axioms Versus 'Paradoxes,' " in

Allais and Hagen (1979).

MacCrimmon, Kenneth R. and Donald A. Wehrung, *Taking Risks: The Management of Uncertainty*, New York: The Free Press, 1986.

Machina, Mark J., " 'Expected Utility' Analysis Without the Independence Axiom," *Econometrica*, March 1982, *50*, 277–323.

Machina, Mark J., "The Economic Theory of Individual Behavior Toward Risk: Theory, Evidence and New Directions," Stanford University Institute for Mathematical Studies in the Social Sciences Technical Report, 1983a.

Machina, Mark J., "Generalized Expected Utility Analysis and the Nature of Observed Violations of the Independence Axiom," 1983b, in Stigum and Wenstøp (1983).

Machina, Mark J., "Temporal Risk and the Nature of Induced Preferences," *Journal of Economic Theory*, August 1984, *33*, 199–231.

Markowitz, Harry "The Utility of Wealth," *Journal of Political Economy*, April 1952, *60*, 151–58.

Marschak, Jacob, "Rational Behavior, Uncertain Prospects, and Measurable Utility," *Econometrica*, April 1950, *18*, 111–41. "Errata," *Econometrica*, July 1950, *18*, 312.

Mas-Colell, Andreu, "An Equilibrium Existence Theorem Without Complete or Transitive Preferences," *Journal of Mathematical Economics*, December 1974, *3*, 237–46.

Maskin, Eric, "Decision Making Under Ignorance with Implications for Social Choice," *Theory and Decision*, September 1979, *11*, 319–37.

May, Kenneth O., "Intransitivity, Utility, and the Aggregation of Preference Patterns," *Econometrica*, January 1954, *22*, 1–13.

McCord, Marc and Richard de Neufville, "Empirical Demonstration that Expected Utility Analysis Is Not Operational." In Stigum and Wenstøp (1983).

McCord, Marc and Richard de Neufville, "Utility Dependence on Probability: An Empirical Demonstration," *Large Scale Systems*, February 1984, *6*, 91–103.

McNeil, Barbara J., Stephen G. Pauker, Harold C. Sox, Jr. and Amos Tversky, "On the Elicitation of Preferences for Alternative Therapies," *New England Journal of Medicine*, May 1982, *306*, 1259–62.

Milne, Frank, "Induced Preferences and the Theory of the Consumer," *Journal of Economic Theory*, April 1981, *24*, 205–17.

Mishan, E. J., "Choices Involving Risk: Simple Steps Toward an Ordinalist Analysis," *Economic Journal*, December 1976, *86*, 759–77.

Morrison, Donald G., "On the Consistency of Preferences in Allais' Paradox," *Behavioral Science*, September 1967, *12*, 373–83.

Moskowitz, Herbert, "Effects of Problem Representation and Feedback on Rational Behavior in Allais and Morlat-Type Problems," *Decision Sciences*, 1974, *5*, 225–42.

Mowen, John C. and James W. Gentry, "Investigation of the Preference-Reversal Phenomenon in a New Product Introduction Task," *Journal of Applied Psychology*, December 1980, *65*, 715–22.

Payne, John W. and Myron L. Braunstein, "Preferences Among Gambles with Equal Underlying Distributions," *Journal of Experimental Psychology*, January 1971, *87*, 13–18.

Pommerehne, Werner W., Friedrich Schneider and Peter Zweifel, "Economic Theory of Choice and the Preference Reversal Phenomenon: A Reexaminaton," *American Economic Review*, June 1982, *72*, 569–74.

Pratt, John W., "Risk Aversion in the Small and in the Large," *Econometrica*, January/April 1964, *32*, 122–36.

Quiggin, John, "A Theory of Anticipated Utility," *Journal of Economic Behavior and Organization*, December 1982, *3*, 323–43.

Raiffa, Howard, "Risk, Ambiguity, and the Savage Axioms," *Quarterly Journal of Economics*, November 1961, *75*, 690–94.

Raiffa, Howard, *Decision Analysis: Introductory Lectures on Choice Under Uncertainty*. Reading, Mass.: Addison-Wesley, 1968.

Reilly, Robert J., "Preference Reversal: Further Evidence and Some Suggested Modifications of Experimental Design," *American Economic Review*, June 1982, *72*, 576–84.

Rothschild, Michael and Joseph E. Stiglitz, "Increasing Risk: I. A Definition," *Journal of Economic Theory*, September 1970, *2*, 225–43.

Russo, J. Edward, "The Value of Unit Price Information," *Journal of Marketing Research*, May 1977, *14*, 193–201.

Russo, J. Edward, Gene Krieser and Sally Miyashita, "An Effective Display of Unit Price Information," *Journal of Marketing*, April 1975, *39*, 11–19.

Samuelson, Paul A., *Foundations of Economic Analysis*, Cambridge, Mass.: Harvard University Press, 1947. Enlarged Edition, 1983.

Samuelson, Paul A., *Foundations of Economic Analysis*, Cambridge, Mass.: Harvard University Press, 1947. Enlarged Edition, 1983.

Savage, Leonard J., *The Foundations of Statistics*, New York: Wiley, 1954. Revised and Enlarged Edition, New York: Dover, 1972.

Schmeidler, David, "Subjective Probability and Expected Utility Without Additivity," manuscript, Tel-Aviv University, 1986.

Schoemaker, Paul J. H. and Howard Kunreuther, "An Experimental Study of Insurance Decisions," *Journal of Risk and Insurance*,

December 1979, *46*, 603–18.

Segal, Uzi, "Nonlinear Decision Weights with the Independence Axiom," manuscript, University of California, Los Angeles, November 1984.

Segal, Uzi, "The Ellsberg Paradox and Risk Aversion: An Anticipated Utility Approach," *International Economic Review*, 1987, forthcoming.

Shafer, Wayne J., "The Nontransitive Consumer," *Econometrica*, September 1974, *42*, 913–19.

Slovic, Paul, "Manipulating the Attractiveness of a Gamble Without Changing its Expected Value," *Journal of Experimental Psychology*, January 1969, *79*, 139–45.

Slovic, Paul, "Choice Between Equally Valued Alternatives," *Journal of Experimental Psychology: Human Perception and Performance*, August 1975, *1*, 280–87.

Slovic, Paul, Baruch Fischhoff and Sarah Lichtenstein, "Response Mode, Framing, and Information Processing Effects in Risk Assessment." In Hogarth, Robin ed., *New Directions for Methodology of Social and Behavioral Science: Question Framing and Response Consistency*. San Francisco: Jossey-Bass, 1982.

Slovic, Paul, Baruch Fischhoff and Sarah Lichtenstein, "Relative Importance of Probabilities and Payoffs in Risk Taking," *Journal of Experimental Psychology*, November 1968, Prt. 2, *78*, 1–18.

Slovic, Paul, Baruch Fischhoff and Sarah Lichtenstein, "Comparison of Bayesian and Regression Approaches to the Study of Information Processing in Judgment," *Organizational Behavior and Human Performance*, November 1971, *6*, 649–744.

Slovic, Paul, Baruch Fischhoff and Sarah Lichtenstein, "Preference Reversals: A Broader Perspective," *American Economic Review*, September 1983, *73*, 596–605.

Slovic, Paul and Amos Tversky, "Who Accepts Savage's Axiom?," *Behavioral Science*, November 1974, *19*, 368–73.

Sonnenschein, Hugo F., "Demand Theory Without Transitive Preferences, With Applications to the Theory of Competitive Equilibrium," In Chipman, John S., Leonid Hurwicz, Marcel K. Richter, and Hugo F. Sonnenschein, eds., *Preferences, Utility and Demand*. New York: Harcourt Brace Jovanovich, 1971.

Spence, A. Michael and Richard J. Zeckhauser, "Insurance, Information and Individual Action," *American Economic Review Papers and Proceedings*, May 1971, *61*, 380–87.

Stigum, Bernt and Fred Wenstøp, *Foundations of Utility and Risk Theory with Applications*, Dordrecht, Holland: D. Reidel, 1983.

Sugden, Robert, "New Developments in the Theory of Choice Under Uncertainty," *Bulletin of*

Economic Research, January 1986, *38*, 1–24.

Thaler, Richard, "Toward a Positive Theory of Consumer Choice," *Journal of Economic Behavior and Organization*, March 1980, *1*, 39–60.

Tversky, Amos, "Intransitivity of Preferences," *Psychological Review*, January 1969, *76*, 31–48.

Tversky, Amos, "A Critique of Expected Utility Theory: Descriptive and Normative Considerations," *Erkenntnis*, 1975, *9*, 163–73.

Tversky, Amos and Daniel Kahneman, "Belief in the Law of Small Numbers," *Psychological Bulletin*, July 1971, *2*, 105–10.

Tversky, Amos and Daniel Kahneman, "Judgement under Uncertainty: Heuristics and Biases," *Science*, September 1974, *1*, *185*, 1124–31.

Tversky, Amos and Daniel Kahneman, "The Framing of Decisions and the Psychology of Choice," *Science*, January 1981, *211*, 453–58.

Tversky, Amos and Daniel Kahneman, "Ex-

tensional vs. Intuitive Reasoning: The Conjunction Fallacy in Probability Judgment," *Psychological Review*, October 1983, *90*, 293–315.

Tversky, Amos and Daniel Kahneman, "Rational Choice and the Framing of Decisions," *Journal of Business*, October 1986, Prt. 2, *4*, 251–78.

Viscusi, W. Kip, "Are Individuals Bayesian Decision Makers?" *American Economic Review Papers and Proceedings*, May 1985, *75*, 381–85.

von Neumann, John and Oskar Morgenstern, *Theory of Games and Economic Behavior*. Princeton: Princeton University Press, 1944. 2nd Ed., 1947. 3rd Ed., 1953.

Yaari, Menahem, "Some Remarks on Measures of Risk Aversion and On their Uses," *Journal of Economic Theory*, October 1969, *1*, 315–29.

Yaari, Menahem, "The Dual Theory of Choice Under Risk," *Econometrica*, January 1987, *55*, 95–115.

[14]

OR Spektrum (1987) 9:129–151

OR Spektrum
© Springer-Verlag 1987

Recent Developments in Modelling Preferences under Risk

M. Weber* and C. Camerer**

* Lehr- und Forschungsgebiet Allg. Betriebswirtschaftslehre, RWTH Aachen, Templergraben 64, D-5100 Aachen
** Department of Decision Sciences, The Wharton School, University of Pennsylvania, Philadelphia, PA 19104, USA

Received June 5, 1987; Accepted in revised form July 27, 1987

Summary. Ever since von Neumann and Morgenstern presented their expected utility theory, the axioms (assumptions) underlying their theory have been intensely debated and tested. Recently, a variety of theories have been presented which model preferences by weakening some of the assumptions of expected utility theory. We describe some of these theories, examine their properties, and provide insights into how they work. Implications for different areas of business research are discussed.

Zusammenfassung. Seit von Neumann und Morgenstern die Erwartungsnutzentheorie vorgestellt haben, werden die dieser Theorie zugrunde liegenden Axiome (Annahmen) intensiv diskutiert. Während man in der Vergangenheit entweder für oder gegen die Theorie war, wurden in letzter Zeit eine Reihe von neuen Ansätzen vorgestellt, die die Erwartungsnutzentheorie durch Abschwächung der ursprünglichen Annahmen erweitern. Nach einer Darstellung der neuen Modelle der erweiterten Erwartungsnutzentheorie werden diese verglichen und bezüglich ihrer Anwendbarkeit in verschiedenen Gebieten der Betriebswirtschaftslehre untersucht.

1. Introduction

It is clear that people do not maximize expected monetary value when making choices in risky decision situations. For instance, they sometimes engage in gambling and buy insurance. This behavior is clearly demonstrated by the Petersburg paradox, in which people refuse to pay a modest amount of money for a lottery with an infinite expected value. To account for this behavior Bernoulli [8] proposed that people maximize the expected value of a cardinal utility function which represents the strength of preference for certain outcomes. Bernoulli assumed this utility function was logarithmic, but his choice of a log function – and even maximization of an expected utility function – was somewhat arbitrary. It was not until two centuries later that von Neumann and Morgenstern [78] provided a sound theoretical foundation for using expected utility (EU) as a guide to decision making under risk. They showed that if a decision maker's preferences obey certain intuitively appealing axioms, that person should choose among risky options as if he or she is maximizing expected utility. The basic EU paradigm has remained unchanged for 40 years. For the areas within management and economics that need a theory which either predicts or prescribes human behavior in risky decision situations, expected utility theory has become fundamental.

Since the axioms underlying expected utility theory were first presented, several empirical studies have shown that decision makers' preferences do not always obey these axioms. This fact alone is not especially disturbing. After all, people routinely make errors in judgement tasks and therefore use tools like a meter or a calculator to avoid errors. But violations of the EU axioms are not necessarily errors, because people often do not change their choices even after it is made clear to them that their choices are violating the axioms. Thus, there are two reasons to reconsider expected utility theory: *(1)* If people intuitively violate the axioms, the EU model may not accurately describe their behavior; and *(2)* since some people willingly violate the axioms in some situations, the validity of the axioms as prescriptive rules must be questioned.

The problems associated with expected utility (EU) theory have been known for a long time, and discussed widely. Recently a fast-growing body of literature has evolved in which *models* of the patterns of preferences which are inconsistent with EU are proposed. Most of these alternative theories relax some of the axioms underlying the expected utility model, and include EU as a special case, so they are often called "generalized utility theories". *The objective of this paper is to review these recently developed generalized utility theories.*

We should first mention some topics we will *not* review. We will only discuss situations in which probabilities are objectively known, thus avoiding situations with "ambiguity", (Ellsberg [26]), e.g., where probabilities are not known, but lie somewhere between 0 and 1. For recent empirical and theoretical research on this topic see Curley and Yates [19], Curley, Yates and Abrams [20], Einhorn and Hogarth [25], Fishburn [34], [35], Gärdenfors and Sahlin [40], [41], Hazen [45], Kahn and Sarin [48], Morris [75], Nau [77], Schmeidler [83], and Segal [88].

We will not discuss research on preference reversals, which points out fundamental problems with almost all choice theories (e.g., Grether and Plott [42] and Lichtenstein and Slovic [61]). We also do not discuss most of the research which applies utility theory in natural contexts (e.g., Kunreuther et al. [58]).

There are other reviews of generalized utility theories. (See Bell and Farquhar [7], Fishburn [37], [38], Machina [72], [73], and Sugden [95]). In contrast to these reviews, we will describe most of the known generalizations of EU, with less emphasis on technical detail and more emphasis on intuitive meaning. Our intended reader is somewhat familiar with EU, but unfamiliar with generalized utility theories. Our goal is to lower the cost of understanding and applying these exciting new developments in modelling preferences under risk.

We proceed as follows. In Sect. 2 a review of the foundations of EU is given. We will also discuss empirical evidence of violations of the axioms of EU. An overview of the different approaches to generalize EU is given in Sect. 3. In Sect. 4 we will show how the new theories account for some of the observed behavior and show relations between theories. Section 5 is a discussion of the implications of these theories for practical applications and theoretical applications in fields of business research. An outlook on future research possibilities concludes the paper in Sect. 6.

2. Expected Utility Theory and Empirical Evidence

We begin this section by describing the EU model and its underlying assumptions. Then some of the major properties of EU theory which are relevant for the rest of the paper are described. Empirical evidence which shows the need to generalize EU is reviewed at the end of the section. See Schoemaker [84] for a good review of EU theory.

2.1 The Axioms of Expected Utility Theory

First we will introduce our notation. We denote outcomes by lowercase letters, e.g., x or x_i, which are assumed to be final wealth positions unless otherwise noted. Lotteries among outcomes are denoted by uppercase letters, e.g., X. We assume for the sake of simplicity that the number of possible outcomes of lotteries is finite. Therefore, we can describe a lottery X by the vector $(x_1, p_1; \ldots; x_n, p_n)$ (x_1 occurs with probability p_1, x_2 with probability p_2, etc.). A certain outcome x can be considered a lottery $(x, 1)$. We will denote a lottery among lotteries (a "compound lottery", or "mixture"), in which X occurs with probability p and Y occurs with probability $1-p$, by $pX + (1-p)Y$.

Preferences between a pair of lotteries X and Y will be denoted $X \sim Y$ (X is different to Y), $X \gtrsim Y$ (X is preferred to or indifferent to Y), and $X \lesssim Y$ (Y is preferred to or indifferent to X).

The goal of a theory of preference is to represent preferences by a numerical utility index, such that one lottery X is preferred to another lottery Y if and only if the numerical utility of X is greater than the numerical utility of Y. Assumptions about preferences (which are called axioms) determine the specific way in which the utility of a lottery is calculated. Note that in the theories we discuss, decision makers have preferences over lotteries which can be represented by probability distributions of outcomes. In other theories of "subjective expected utility" (e.g., Savage [82]), decision makers choose *acts* which yield different *consequences* depending upon the *state of nature* (or state, for short). In subjective EU, the states do not have objective probabilities. Instead, preferences over acts reveal both a utility function over acts and a set of "personal" or subjective probabilities over states. We will refer to the differences between expected utility and subjective expected utility when it is necessary for the explanation of new theories.

There are several systems of EU axioms for preference over lotteries which lead, for all practical purposes, to the same von Neumann-Morgenstern expected utility model (see Fishburn [28], [30] and MacCrimmon and Larsson [69] for thorough discussions). Most systems are variations of the following set of axioms (see e.g. Herstein and Milnor [46]):

a) Completeness and Transitivity (Complete Ordering)
b) Continuity
c) Independence

The expected utility axioms imply that a lottery X is preferred to a lottery Y if and only if the expected utility of X, called $EU(X)$, is larger than $EU(Y)$. The expected utility of a lottery is

$$EU(X) = \sum_{i=1}^{n} p_i u(x_i). \tag{1}$$

Obviously this is a very special way to measure the utility of a lottery X. But this summation form is the only correct way to calculate a utility index which represents preferences if those preferences obey the three axioms. We now consider the three axioms in turn.

Complete Ordering:

Completeness: For any X and Y, either $X \gtrsim Y$ or $X \lesssim Y$.

Transitivity: If $X \gtrsim Y$, and $Y \gtrsim Z$, then $X \gtrsim Z$.

These axioms require that the decision maker be able to make up his mind about preferences for *any* pair of lotteries, and his preferences over pairs must be transitive. (Actually, there are several definitions of transitivity. See Fishburn [33], e.g., for a more thorough discussion.)

Continuity: Given X, Y, Z such that $X \gtrsim Y \gtrsim Z$, there exists a probability p in $[0,1]$ such that $Y \sim pX + (1-p)Z$.

Continuity implies that all lotteries of intermediate preference are indifferent to *some* mixture between a pair of better and worse lotteries.

The complete ordering and continuity axioms are basically the same as in similar theories for decision making under certainty (e.g. Debreu [22] and Krantz, Luce, Suppes and Tversky [59]). These axioms are sufficient to imply the existence of a real-valued utility function which represents the decision maker's ranking of the lotteries (e.g., Machina [72, p. 7]). The important difference between decision making under certainty and decision making under risk is that we would like to have a utility function on lotteries which enables us to derive the utility of a lottery from its components, i.e. the outcomes and their probabilities in a simple way. EU and the various generalized EU models differ in how this decomposition of the utility function on lotteries is done. The EU decomposition is implied by the EU independence axiom.

EU *Independence:* If $X \gtrsim Y$, then for any p in $[0, 1]$ and any Z, $pX + (1-p)Z \gtrsim pY + (1-p)Z$.

The independence axiom states that a preference between two lotteries should be independent of any common (or "irrelevant") components, as if those common components are cancelled out. In Savage's subjective EU, the equivalent axiom is called the "sure-thing principle": If two acts have the same consequence in a particular state, then that state should be ignored in determining preferences between the acts.

The utility function in expected utility theory is only unique up to a positive linear transformation: Any $u' = au + b$ (where a is positive) will represent preferences exactly the same way as u does. Put differently, we can arbitrarily choose numbers for the origin and the scale of our utility function.

2.2 Properties and Implications of EU

The axioms take preferences over lotteries as the primitive that a utility function is meant to represent. These axioms do not offer any clue about the "riskiness" of a lottery or the "value" of its outcomes. Indeed, the psychological value of a lottery's outcomes and the utility of those outcomes need not be the same, because value can be measured in a riskless context while utility is only inferred from risky choices (see Dyer and Sarin [24], Keeney and Raiffa [53], Sarin [81] and Wilhelm [102]). For an overview on how to measure the psychological value in a riskless context see Keller and Farquhar [56]. Other approaches which take the riskiness of a lottery as the primitive (e.g., Keller, Sarin and Weber [57], Luce [66] and Pollatsek and Tversky [79]) or attempt to develop risk-value models of choice (e.g., Coombs [18]) are therefore quite different from EU.

The expected utility form (1) has several implications which result directly from the independence axiom. First, the expected utility of a two-stage lottery (i.e., a lottery with outcomes which are lotteries) is the same as the expected utility of a single-stage lottery with the same probability distribution of final outcomes. This property is essential for the "unfolding" or backward induction of decision trees.

Second, the expected utility of a lottery is "linear in probabilities" since $\mathrm{EU}(pX + (1-p)Y) = p\mathrm{EU}(X) + (1-p)\mathrm{EU}(Y)$. Linearity in probabilities directly implies the "common consequence" and "common ratio" properties. The common consequence property states that adding or subtracting a common outcome (with the same probability) to two lotteries does not change the preference between those lotteries. The common ratio property states that the preference between a pair of lotteries does not change when probabilities in both lotteries are multiplied by the same positive number (and the remaining probability is attached to a common consequence). For example, if you prefer $(100, .5; 0, .5)$ to $(200, .3; 0, .7)$ then you must prefer $(100, .5\alpha; 0, 1-.5\alpha)$ to $(200, .3\alpha; 0, 1-.3\alpha)$ for any α which yields probabilities between 0 and 1, i.e. $\alpha \in (0,2]$.

Third, by requiring preferences among lotteries to depend only on the components of those lotteries that differ, the independence axiom forces the expected utility of a lottery to be a combination of utilities of different outcomes $u(x_i)$ which are determined *independently* of other outcomes and probabilities in the lottery.

The strong implications of the independence axiom can be illustrated by graphing three-outcome lotteries in a two-dimensional triangle diagram, first used by Mar-

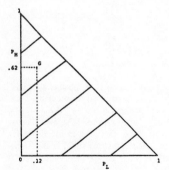

Fig. 1. Representing 3-outcome lotteries

schak [74] and revived by Machina [70]. Define three arbitrary outcomes x_L, x_M, x_H (low, medium, high) with $X_H \gtrsim X_M \gtrsim X_L$. In our discussion, these x will be Deutsch Mark amounts (DM), but they could easily be lotteries over non-monetary outcomes. Consider the set of lotteries over these three outcomes, where the outcomes occur with probabilities p_L, p_M, and p_H. Since $p_M = 1 - p_H - p_L$, we can graph these lotteries in two dimensions, p_H and p_L. For example, in Figure 1 the arbitrary lottery $(x_H, .62; x_M, .26; x_L, .12)$ is point G.

Rankings over lotteries imply indifference curves connecting equally preferred lotteries in the triangle diagram. The shape of the indifference curves depends on the specific independence axiom used. In EU, the set of lotteries with a specific expected utility level u^* satisfies

$$u^* = p_H u(x_H) + (1 - p_H - p_L)u(x_M) + p_L u(x_L) \qquad (2)$$

or, rearranging,

$$p_H = p_L \frac{u(x_M) - u(x_L)}{u(x_H) - u(x_M)} + \frac{u^* - u(x_M)}{u(x_H) - u(x_M)} \qquad (3)$$

Notice that (3) is a linear equation of the form $p_H = p_L b + a$. Since all the utilities in (3) are constants (for a fixed u^*), the indifference curves connecting points of equal expected utility are straight lines with the same slope and with intercepts that depend upon u^*, as in Fig. 1.

One can interpret the slope of the curves as a "marginal rate of substitution" of p_H for p_L, or the "price" of probabilistic units of the high outcome x_H in terms of probabilistic units of the low outcome x_L. The independence axiom, which implies that the curves are parallel, therefore implies that the marginal rate of substitution is constant throughout the diagram.

The slope of the indifference curves is also a reflection of the degree of "risk-aversion". The degree of risk-

aversion a person exhibits is reflected in the shape of his or her utility function. A person who is averse to risks always prefers a certain payment c to a lottery with expected value c. A risk-seeker prefers the lottery to the certain payment c. Risk-aversion implies that the utility function is concave (i.e., the second derivative of $u(x)$ is negative, or utility is marginally declining). The standard assumption in applications of EU to theories in economics and finance is that people are risk-averse.

The more risk-averse a person is, the higher is the value of $u(x_M)$ (holding $u(x_L)$ and $u(x_H)$ constant), and the steeper is the slope of the curves (by (3)). More risk-averse people essentially demand a higher price to take on unit of low probability p_L. As the degree of risk-aversion is defined by the utility function independent of the probabilities and the utilities are the same in the whole diagram (i.e. $u(x_L)$, $u(x_M)$ and $u(x_H)$) the degree of risk-aversion is constant and independent of the location of lotteries in the diagram.

It is useful to know under what conditions a lottery X should be preferred to a lottery Y for *any* function. In choice under certainty, a numerical outcome x should be preferred to an outcome y if $x > y$ (assuming utility is monotonically increasing). If x and y have several attributes, x is preferred to y if it is preferred on each attribute. In these certain cases, we say that x "dominates" y. The analogous concept in choice under risk is "stochastic dominance". First note that the cumulative distribution function of a lottery X is defined as $F(x \leqslant t)$, the probability that a numerical outcome x is less than or equal to some specific outcome t, for all possible specific outcomes. A lottery X "first-order" stochastically dominates a lottery Y if the cumulative probability of every possible outcome x is always greater or equal for Y than for X. (There are higher orders of stochastic dominance, defined analogously, but we will take "stochastic dominance" to mean first-order dominance.) Graphically, stochastic dominance implies that the cumulative distribution function of X is never above that of Y. The expected utility of a stochastically dominant lottery will be greater than the expected utility of a dominated lottery for *any* utility function that is nondecreasing. In the triangle diagram, the lotteries which stochastically dominate a lottery G are the lotteries to the northwest of G. Stochastically dominant lotteries should be preferred to G because they have a lower p_1 (less chance of the worst outcome) and a higher p_3 (more chance of the best outcome) than G.

2.3 Empirical Evidence of the Validity of the Axioms

So what evidence is there that the axioms of EU need to be changed in order to generalize expected utility theory?

Most people find the axioms an appealing foundation for rational decision making. However, people will often violate the axioms in certain decision situations, and when the violation is pointed out to them, people are often unwilling to change their preferences. Violations are often referred to as paradoxes. We will present some paradoxes involving the independence axiom, then discuss the intuition behind them. Violations of the complete ordering and continuity axioms are discussed by MacCrimmon and Larsson [69]. For convenience all examples are denoted in Deutsch Marks.

The most well-known paradox is due to Allais [1], [3]. The decision maker is presented with two pairs of choices: X vs. Y and X' vs. Y'.

X: 1 million DM with probability 1

Y: 5 million DM with probability 0.10
     1 million DM with probability 0.89
     0   DM with probability 0.01

and

X': 1 million DM with probability 0.11
      0   DM with probability 0.89

Y': 5 million DM with probability 0.10
      0   DM with probability 0.90

Many people prefer X to Y and Y' to X' (see, e.g., Kahneman and Tversky [49], and MacCrimmon and Larsson [69]). Suppose we set $u(0) = 0$ and $u(5$ mill DM$) = 1$ (which we have the freedom to do). Then expected utility theory implies that X is preferrred to Y if and only if

$$u(1 \text{ million DM}) > 0.10 + 0.89 \, u(1 \text{ million DM}). \quad (4)$$

The common consequence property implies that we can substract the lottery 0.89 chance of winning 1 million DM, i.e. $0.89 \, u(1$ million DM$)$, from both sides of (4), which yields

$$0.11 \, u(1 \text{ million DM}) > 0.10 \quad (5)$$

But Y' preferred to X' implies $0.11 \, u(1$ million DM$) > 0.10$, a direct contradiction of (5).

The independence axiom requires that the only difference between the pairs of lotteries (their "common consequence" of a 0.89 chance of winning 1 million DM in the pair X and Y, or a 0.89 chance of winning 0 in the pair X' and Y') be ignored. There are several psychological reasons why a decision maker may *not* ignore the

common consequence. These explanations are the starting point for some of the generalized theories described below.

The first paradox is sometimes called the "common consequence effect". A second paradox, also due originally to Allais, is called the "common ratio" effect. People are asked to choose one lottery from each of two pairs of lotteries:

X: 3000 DM with probability 1

Y: 4000 DM with probability 0.80
     0 DM with probability 0.20

and

X': 3000 DM with probability 0.25
      0 DM with probability 0.75

Y': 4000 DM with probability 0.20
      0 DM with probability 0.80.

Most people choose X over Y and Y' over X'. The first choice implies $u(3000) > 0.8 \, u(4000)$, while the second choice implies $0.25 \, u(3000) < 0.20 \, u(4000)$, an obvious violation because the probabilities in the second choice are simply a multiple of the probabilities in the first choice. The evaluation of one outcome of a lottery seems to depend on the other parameters of the lottery, as if the utility of 3000 DM is different when attached to a 0.20 probability or a probability of 1.

Savage, a famous proponent of subjective expected utility, first exhibited the common consequence effect when he chose X over Y and Y' and X' during lunch with Allais. After seeing that his choices implied a violation of independence, Savage quickly changed his choices to be consistent with the axiom. Savage also proposed a way of illustrating the lotteries which would make the violation of independence clear to other people. Imagine the probabilities of winning as chances of drawing tickets from a box of 100 tickets, then divide tickets into groups by their consequences. The choice between X and Y from above would then look like

	outcome if X	outcome if Y
tickets 1–10	1 million DM	5 million DM
ticket 11	1 million DM	0
tickets 12–100	1 million DM	1 million DM

and the choice between X' and Y' would look like

	outcome if X'	outcome if Y'
tickets 1–10	1 million DM	5 million DM
ticket 11	1 million DM	0
tickets 12–100	0	0

Savage's diagram makes the existence of a (different) common consequence in both pairs of choices quite obvious. MacCrimmon [68] found that when the violation was made clear subjects often did change their preferences to conform with the axiom. However, Slovic and Tversky [92] found as many subjects switching *toward* violations as were switching away. Moskowitz [76] and Keller [55] found that presenting the lotteries using three different representations made a small difference in the fraction of people violating independence.

3. Generalized Utility Theories: Presentation of Models

In this section we present several theories which generalize EU, typically by assuming a weaker independence condition. Our brief descriptions will emphasize how the models differ from EU. Models will be compared with each other in the next section.

3.1 Approaches to Generalizing Expected Utility Theory

All the approaches we describe follow the path of Bernoulli and von Neumann and Morgenstern by introducing more general assumptions about preferences in order to model a wider variety of behavior. These general assumptions can come from three directions: Empirical data, axiomatic generalizations, and intuition about choices. Each route by itself could lead to a more general theory. Data can inspire more general functional forms, axioms can be weakened, and additional constructs can be added to capture intuition about choices. Most theories actually incorporate some of all three elements.

For instance, prospect theory (Kahneman and Tversky [49], Sect. 3.2 below) is clearly built from data and intuition. SSB theory (skew-symmetric bilinear utility, see Fishburn [31] and Sect. 3.8) was originally developed by weakening axioms. However, some theories which start with an intuitive approach lead to results very much like SSB (see regret theory, Sect. 3.8).

In the descriptions below, we emphasize the results of the search for new theories, i.e., the different functional forms of the theories. However, in evaluating the theories it is useful to remember their original motivations. It is also useful to search for the intuition and testable implications in axiomatically-derived theories, and to search for formal properties of intuitive theories.

3.2 Models with a General Separable Utility Function

EU and expected monetary value are both special cases of a general preference function V which is separable in its components,

$$V(X) = \sum_{i=1}^{n} f(x_i, p_i). \qquad (6)$$

This classification is useful because it is a direct generalization of expected value and EU. Expected monetary value corresponds to $f(x_i, p_i) = p_i x_i$, and EU corresponds to $f(x_i, p_i) = p_i u(x_i)$. Other forms for f have been investigated too:

i) $f(x_i, p_i) = w(p_i) x_i$ \qquad Handa [44]

ii) $f(x_i, p_i) = w(p_i) u(x_i)$ \quad Kahneman and Tversky [49]

The distinctive feature of these models is the function $w(p_i)$, which derives psychological "decision weights" from probabilities (although Kahneman and Tversky's prospect theory has other unusual properties discussed below). Note also that decision weights $w(p_i)$ do not depend on the outcome x_i.

A related form in which $f(x_i, p_i)$ is not separable, because weights are normalized, was proposed by Karmarkar [50]:

iii) $f(x_i, p_i) = w(p_i) u(x_i) / \sum_{i=1}^{n} w(p_i).$

He suggested $w(p_i) = p_i^{\alpha} / (p_i^{\alpha} + (1 - p_i)^{\alpha})$, with the parameter α measuring the degree of transformation of probabilities into weights.

Models with decision weights are more general than EU (which is a special case, with $w(p_i) = p_i$), so they can explain some behavior that EU cannot. However, these theories have one unattractive quality: The preference function for each component need not be linear in probabilities (i.e. $f(x_i, p_i + q_i)$ need not equal $f(x_i, p_i) + f(x_i, q_i)$), but nonlinearity necessarily leads to violations of stochastic dominance. Excluding violations of dominance implies $w(p_i) = p_i$, as in EU (Fishburn [29], Quiggin [80]).

To see why nonlinearity implies dominance violations, suppose $f(x_i, p_i + q_i)$ is larger than $f(x_i, p_i) + f(x_i, q_i)$. (If it is smaller, take δ to be negative in what follows.) Consider the lotteries $G = (x_i, p_i + q_i; 0, 1 - p_i - q_i)$ and $G' = (x_i + \delta, p_i; x_i, q_i; 0, 1 - p_i - q_i)$, which is derived from G by adding a small positive payoff δ with probability p_i. Note that G' stochastically dominates G. Then there is an δ sufficiently small that

$$f(x_i, p_i + q_i) + f(0, 1 - p_i - q_i) > f(x_i + \delta, p_i) + f(x_i, q_i)$$
$$+ f(0, 1 - p_i - q_i) \qquad (7)$$

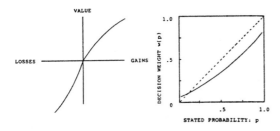

Fig. 2. Hypothetical value function (*left*) and decision weight function (*right*) (from Kahneman and Tversky [49])

or

$$V(G) > V(G')$$

Thus, G will have a higher utility number than G', even though G is stochastically dominated by G'.

Violations of stochastic dominance preference are certainly undesirable from a prescriptive viewpoint. Since violations of dominance have been observed (Tversky and Kahneman [99]), a good descriptive theory should account for such violations, but it should not predict them in a wide variety of situations (see Machina [72, pp. 95–99]).

The prospect theory of Kahneman and Tversky [49] is special because it only applies to a restricted domain of lotteries and it differs from EU in three ways. First, it assumes that people "edit" lotteries "to organize and reformulate the options so as to simplify subsequent evaluation and choice" (Kahneman and Tversky, [49, p. 274]). Examples of editing operations are: "coding", setting a reference point to which outcomes will be compared; "segregation", separating a riskless outcome from a risky lottery; and "combination", simplifying a lottery by combining probabilities with identical outcomes. Prospect theory avoids the problem of choosing dominated lotteries by assuming that people check for dominance within the editing procedure. However, indirect violations of dominance caused by intransitivities cannot be edited out (Machina [72, p. 97], Segal [87]). As a psychological description of how people behave, prospect theory's editing operations are appealing, but they are not always well defined so they are hard to test and apply. However, disregarding the economic paradigm of using choice data, the test of editing operations would become much easier.

Second, the utility function is replaced by a "value function" $v(x_i)$ which represents the psychological value of *changes* in wealth from some *reference* point. The idea that people value changes from a reference point is essential to prospect theory because it assumes that losses are psychologically different from gains. Specifically, losses are worse than gains, and the loss part of the value

function is convex (implying risk-seeking for losses) while the gain part is concave (implying risk-aversion).

Third, prospect theory postulates the existence of a decision weight function which we will, for consistency, denote as $w(p)$ (Kahneman and Tversky refer to the function $\pi(p)$). Decision weights "measure the impact of events on the desirability of prospects, and not merely the perceived likelihood of these two events" (Kahneman and Tversky [49, p. 280]). Based on empirical data, they propose a specific form of $w(p)$ which is: Increasing in p; discontinuous at the endpoints 0 and 1 (with $w(0) = 0$ and $w(1) = 1$); greater than p for small p (i.e. $w(p) > p$); subadditive for small p (i.e. $w(rp) > rw(p)$); subcertain (i.e. $w(p) + w(1-p) < 1$); and subproportional (i.e. $w(pq)/w(p) < w(prq)/w(pr)$, $r \in (0, 1)$. A hypothetical decision weight function with these properties, and a typical value function, are shown in Fig. 2.

We should add that the function *ii)* only applies to "regular prospects" with one zero outcome and two non-zero outcomes, or two non-zero outcomes on different sides of the reference point. A related form is proposed for other prospects.

The selection of a reference point is important because preferences might depend on arbitrary decisions about how to choose a reference point (or "frame" a problem). Consider two decision problems in Kahneman and Tversky [49, p. 273].

I. In addition to whatever you own, you have been given 1000.
You are now asked to choose between
A: (1000, .50; 0, .50) and *B:* (500, 1)

II. In addition to whatever you own, you have been given 2000.
You are now asked to choose between
C: (−1000, .50; 0, .50) and *D:* (−500, 1)

Both problems are identical in terms of final wealth position, so if utility depends only on final wealth position decisions should be identical (i.e., either prefer A and C, or B and D). However, 84% of their subjects preferred B over A but only 31% preferred D over C. (For further discussion of framing see Tversky and Kahneman [98], [99]).

Even though prospect theory was designed to explain empirical data in an intuitive way, Kahneman and Tversky [49, p. 289] have given a set of axioms for prospect theory. The independence axiom of EU is replaced by a weaker independence axiom.

Prospect Theory Independence

$(x_1,p_1;x_2,p_2;0,1-p_1-p_2) \succsim$
$(x_1,p_1;x_3,p_3;0,1-p_1-p_3)$

if and only if

$(x_4,p_4;x_2,p_2;0,1-p_4-p_2) \succsim$
$(x_4,p_4;x_3,p_3;0,1-p_4-p_3)$.

Intuitively the axiom states that preferences between the components (x_2,p_2) and (x_3,p_3) should be independent of the other components with which they are combined. This axiom, together with other axioms, implies the general separable form but does *not* imply linearity in the probabilities. To separate the weighting and value functions requires another axiom, "distributivity": $(x_1,p_1;x_2,p_1;1-2p_1) \sim (x_3,p_1;1-p_1)$ if and only if $(x_1,p_2;x_2,p_2;1-2p_2) \sim (x_3,p_2;1-p_2)$ (for $p_i < .5$).

These axioms and most of the properties of prospect theory have not been thoroughly tested, and the way people choose frames and edit is not fully resolved. Kahneman and Tversky's position is that framing and editing are rather arbitrary and may be impossible to describe parsimoniously. Our view is that prospect theory is such a radical departure from EU that it will take much further research to put it to the test and refine it. Especially framing effects seem to be so genuine that they might be included in other generalizations of EU.

Luce and Narens [67] developed a very general representation to model preferences. We only want to briefly mention a special case of the theory, named dual bilinear utility representation (DBUR). Their formulation is based on acts of the form (x_1, A, x_2), which means one receives x_1 if A occurs and x_2 otherwise.

A preference of one act being preferred to another can be modelled by a dual bilinear utility if and only if the utility is larger for the preferred act, and if the utility of an act can be written as

$$DBUR(x_1,A,x_2) = u(x_1)w^+(A)+u(x_2)(1-w^+(A))$$
$$\text{if } x_1 \succ x_2$$
$$= u(x_1) \quad \text{if } x_1 \sim x_2$$
$$= u(x_1)w^-(A)+u(x_2)(1-w^+(A))$$
$$\text{if } x_1 \prec x_2$$

The main new idea of this theory lies in the weighting functions w^+ and w^- whose application depends on the preference between the two outcomes x_1 and x_2. Thus DBUR is not general separable. However, it was presented here because its functional form strongly resembles prospect theory. If $w^+ = w^-$ and some further more technical assumptions hold, DBUR is equal to subjective expected utility theory.

3.3 Rank-Dependent Expected Utility

We show above that models based on a general separable utility function sometimes predict that dominated lotteries have higher utilities than dominating lotteries, which is an undesirable result. One way to remedy this shortcoming is to let the weighting function transform the entire probability distribution of outcomes. An important class of theories of this sort are expected utility theories with "rank-dependent probabilities", or rank-dependent expected utility theories (RDEU).

In RDEU, the decision weight of a probability p_i depends on the other p_i and on the rank of outcome x_i compared to other outcomes. Consider n outcomes x_i which are ordered in preference, $x_1 \precsim ..x_i \precsim .. x_n$. If the preference relation on lotteries obeys certain axioms (described below) it can be represented by an expected utility function of the form

$$RDEU(X) = \sum_{i=1}^{n} u(x_i)w(p_1, ...,p_i) \qquad (8)$$

with $w(p_i, ...,p_i) = g(\sum_{j=1}^{i} p_j) - g(\sum_{j=1}^{i-1} p_j)$.

It is also assumed that $g(1) = 1, g(0) = 0$, and $g(p_0) = 0$. Note that if $g(x) = x$, and $w(p_1, ...,p_i) = p_i$ RDEU reduces to EU. If $g(p)$ is concave it overweights the worst outcomes, and if $g(p)$ is convex it underweights these outcomes with respect to the best outcomes.

A special case of RDEU was first proposed by Quiggin [80], to remedy the problem of stochastic dominance violations in models with general separable utility functions. To see how RDEU avoids dominance violations, first recall the definition of stochastic dominance: a lottery A stochastically dominates B if the cumulative distribution of A lies below the distribution of B. As long as $g(x)$ is monotonic, the transformed cumulative distribution of A will still lie below the transformed cumulative distributon of B, so RDEU will always predict preference for stochastically dominating lotteries (i.e., $\text{RDEU}(A) > \text{RDEU}(B)$).

Quiggin's "anticipated utility theory" was extended by Segal [86], Chew [12], and Chew, Karni and Safra [14]. Quiggin's axioms require $g(0.5) = 0.5$, which is empirically undesirable because then $g(x)$ cannot be convex or concave for all values of x, as seems necessary to explain empirical paradoxes (Segal [89]). Quiggin's formulation also implies possible violations of the reduction of compound lotteries axiom. Chew, Karni, and Safra [14] show that people are always risk-averse if and only if the utility function $u(x)$ and the probability transformation function $g(x)$ are both concave.

Yaari [100] proposed a special case of RDEU (called "dual EU") in which $u(x) = x$. It is "dual" to EU because decision weights are nonlinear but utility is a linear function of money, exactly the opposite as in EU. In general, $\text{RDEU}(X)$ can be calculated by first plotting the cumulative probability distribution of the lottery X, $F(X)$. In EU, after the horizontal axis is transformed from x to $u(x)$ the area under the cumulative distribution gives $\text{EU}(X)$. Yaari's dual theory transforms the vertical axis from $F(x)$ to $g(F(x))$, and the area under the curve is then $\text{RDEU}(X)$.

The motivation for Yaari's dual theory is the simple idea that the value function for certain wealth might be different from the utility function that is recovered from preferences among lotteries. By allowing probabilities to be transformed, he is able to locate attitudes toward risk in probability weights and therefore separate risk attitude from the shape of the utility function for wealth (the two are combined in EU).

Suppose $g(x)$ is concave. Then $u(x_1)$ gets weighted by $w(p_1)$, which in this case is greater than p_1, so the worst (lowest-ranked) outcome gets overweighted compared to its untransformed probability. Similarly, the best (highest-ranked) outcomes get underweighted for concave $g(x)$. Since $u(x) = x$ in Yaari's version of RDEU, risk-aversion is captured purely by curvature in $g(p)$ rather than by curvature in $u(x)$. A concave $g(p)$ weights low-rank outcomes most highly, much as a concave utility function in EU weights low-rank outcomes more highly by attaching higher per monetary unit utility to them.

Yaari uses five axioms to prove that a rank-dependent expected utility function as in (8) represents preferences with linear utility ($u(x_i) = a + bx_i$). His axioms ensure existence of $\text{RDEU}(X)$ and stochastic dominance. Yaari's independence axiom can be expressed several ways. One version is the "comonotonic cancellation condition".

Let X, Y, and Z be random variables with outcomes that depend on the existence of events (as in Savage's subjective EU, which uses acts that yield consequences in different states). For example, X is the profit of a ski-resort operator, Y is the number of hours ski lifts are used, and Z is the number of beers drunk during the daytime, all of which depend on the state of the weather. Two random variables are *comonotonic* if a change in the event implies a change in the outcomes of the random variables in the same direction. In the example, if the weather changes from good skiing conditions to bad skiing conditions, X and Y will both decrease, whereas Z will probably increase. Therefore, X and Y are comonotonic, but X and Z (and Y and Z) are not.

Combining two random variables X and Z, written $X + Z$, means adding their outcomes. In our example, good skiing weather will yield high profits and not much beer drunk. Intuitively, a lack of comonotonicity means that combining two random variables hedges risk. Now we are able to state the comonotonic cancellation conditon.

Comonotonic Cancellation (Dual EU Independence)

If X and Z, and Y and Z, are comonotonic then

$$X \succsim Y \text{ if and only if } X + Z \succsim Y + Z.$$

Intuitively, if Z is a random variable which does not provide a hedge against either X or Y, then preferences between X and Y should be the same after adding Z. This axiom requires that adding the *outcomes* of Z does not change the preference between X and Y, while Savage's sure-thing principle requires that adding a *state* (with identical consequences) does not change the preference. It is therefore reasonable that the sure-thing principle causes utility to be linear in probabilities (which are derived from states) while comonotonic cancellation causes utility to be linear in outcomes.

3.4 Weighted Utility Theory

Weighted utility theory (WEU) has appeared in several forms. It was first discovered by Chew and MacCrimmon [15] and called "alpha-nu choice theory", but it is known as the "ratio form" (Bolker [9], Fishburn [32]), or the "quasilinear mean" applied to choice (Chew [11]).

Since EU is linear in probabilities, the utility of a compound lottery is simply $U(pX + (1-p)Y) = pU(X) + (1-p)U(Y)$. In WEU the utility function u is not linear but "*weighted linear*". That is, there exists a positive weight function $w(x_i)$, a function of lotteries or outcomes, such that

$$\text{WEU}(X) = \sum_{i=1}^{n} p_i w(x_i) u(x_i) / \sum_{i=1}^{n} p_i w(x_i). \qquad (9)$$

Note that if $w(x_i)$ is constant, the weights cancel out and WEU collapses to EU. Both functions $w(x_i)$ and $u(x_i)$ are linear in probabilities. Furthermore, if preferences are represented by the functions (u, w), then there exist constants a, b, c, d (with $ad > bc$) so that $u' = (au + b)/(cu + d)$ and $w' = w(cu + d)$ order lotteries in the same way.

A psychological interpretation of the weighting function was offered by Weber [101]. He argued that the weight $w(x_i)$ can be thought of as the "conceivability", or vividity or salience, of the outcome x_i. In a lottery which offers 1 million DM we might say "winning that much money is hard to imagine", as if the perceived likelihood of winning depends on the size of the outcome. We can model this with a small value of $w(1$ million DM), which reduces the product of the probability and utility of 1 million DM according to (9). The conceivability interpretation suggests a plausible shape for the weighting function: for small outcomes near the status quo, $w(x_i)$ might be fairly large, while extremely good or bad outcomes have low $w(x_i)$.

Chew and MacCrimmon [15], Chew [10], [11], Weber [101], and Fishburn [32] discuss axiomatizations for WEU. In Chew [10], [11] WEU has four axioms: transitivity, continuity, dominance and a weakened version of the EU independence axiom. The WEU independence axiom states:

WEU *Independence.* Assume two lotteries X and Y such that $X \sim Y$. Then for any p in $(0, 1)$, there exists a q in $(0, 1)$ such that $pX + (1 - p)Z \sim pY + (1 - q)Z$ for any lottery Z.

WEU independence requires that once p is specified, the decision-maker can choose a value of q to make the two compound lotteries indifferent, independent of the lottery Z chosen. The independence axiom of EU demands that q equal p, which is a much stronger requirement.

Others have derived a "ratio form" representation which is equivalent to weighted utility (Weber [101], Fishburn [32], and originally, Bolker [9]). They show that $X \succ Y$ if and only if $V(X)/W(X) > V(Y)/W(Y)$, where V and W are expectations defined by $V(X) = \sum_{i=1}^{n} p_i v(x_i)$ and $W(X) = \sum_{i=1}^{n} p_i w(x_i)$. In this form, preferences are represented by the ratio of two functions on lotteries (which are linear in probabilities). If we define $v(x_i) = u(x_i)w(x_i)$, then the ratio form and weighted utility are equivalent: Dividing the expectation of $u(x_i)w(x_i)$ by the expectation of $w(x_i)$ yields the WEU in expression (9).

Chew [13] derived a more general form of weighted utility, called "implicit weighted utility", abbreviated IWEU, (see also Fishburn [32, theorem 1], and Dekkel [23]), by using a weaker independence axiom:

Implicit WEU *Independence.* Assume two lotteries X and Y such that $X \sim Y$, and any lottery Z. Then for any p in $(0, 1)$, there exists a q in $(0, 1)$ such that

$$pX + (1 - p)Z \sim qY + (1 - q)Z.$$

Implicit WEU independence allows the choice of q to depend upon p (as in WEU independence) and on Z. One might question characterizing this condition as "independence". In WEU independence, q can depend on p but the same q must hold for *all* Z. Implicit WEU independence leads to weighted utility of the form

$$IWEU(X) = \sum_{i=1}^{n} p_i w(x_i, IWEU(X))u(x_i)/$$

$$\sum_{i=1}^{n} p_i w(x_i, IWEU(X)). \qquad (10)$$

That is, the weighting function $w(x_i, IWEU(X))$ can depend on the outcome x_i *and* the implicit weighted utility of the lottery being considered. IWEU is extremely general. It is purely a product of weakening independence, with little basis in intuition or empirical observation.

3.5 Disappointment and Related Theories

Consider two lotteries, a 0.99 chance of winning 50,000 DM with a 0.01 chance of winning nothing, and a 0.99 chance of losing 50,000 DM with a 0.01 chance of winning nothing. If you win nothing in both lotteries, do you feel the same satisfaction (as utility theory requires)? Perhaps not, because winning nothing in the first lottery may cause "disappointment", a feeling of dissatisfaction with the outcome relative to your expectation. Winning nothing in the second lottery may produce "elation", the opposite feeling.

Disappointment-elation theory (DET) allows transitive preferences to include anticipation of disappointment or elation (see Bell [6], Loomes and Sudgen [65]). Though we used two lotteries in our example, DET states that the utility of a *single* lottery depends on the utility of outcomes and on disappointment or elation. DET is an example of a theory that modifies EU by including a psychological attribute which is intuitively meaningful. DET incorporates feelings resulting from comparison of outcomes within one lottery, while intuitively-based regret theories (Sect. 3.8) incorporate feelings of regret that result from comparison of outcomes between two lotteries.

We first describe Loomes and Sudgen's approach, then show the relation to Bell's model.

DET assumes there is a real-valued function v which measures the value $v(x_i)$ of a certain outcome x_i, up to a positive linear transformation. Loomes and Sugden call this "basic utility" (or earlier, "choiceless" or "riskless" utility). In a lottery, decision makers are assumed to get diminishing or additional value from an outcome, beyond its basic utility, if the outcome falls short of or exceeds some expectation. Loomes and Sugden suggest the expectation that outcomes are compared to, denoted v^*, is the expectation of the basic utilities of the outcomes, i.e. $v^* = \sum_{i=1}^{n} p_i\, v(x_i)$. If utility of an outcome is the outcome's basic utility plus any disappointment or elation, then $u(x_i) = v(x_i) + D(v(x_i) - v^*)$ where $D(v(x_i) - v^*)$ is the disappointment or elation attached to the outcome x_i. The utility of a lottery is then

$$\text{DET}(X) = \sum_{i=1}^{n} p_i(v(x_i) + D(v(x_i) - v^*)) \qquad (11)$$

If $D(v(x_i) - v^*)$ is linear, the summed $D(v(x_i) - v^*)$ terms equal zero and DET reduces to maximizing expected basic utility. The preference relation represented by (11) is transitive (Loomes and Sugden [65, p. 281]) because each lottery X is represented by the numerical value of $\text{DET}(X)$ and numbers are transitive. To ensure that stochastically dominating lotteries have larger values of $\text{DET}(X)$ they assume that the derivative of $D(.)$ with respect to $v(x_i)$ exists and is between 0 and 1 (Loomes and Sudgen [65, p. 272], Sudgen [95, p. 13]). In addition they assume on intuitive grounds that $D(x)$ is convex for positive x (elation) and concave for negative x (disappointment).

Note that the utility of a specific outcome in a lottery depends on v^*, which is a characteristic of the entire lottery. Therefore, utilities of outcomes cannot be calculated independently of other outcomes and their probabilities. It can also be shown that DET does not necessarily predict the same preference for a two-stage lottery and a statistically equivalent one-stage lottery (i.e., the reduction of compound lotteries assumption can be violated).

We can rewrite $\text{DET}(X)$ as $v^* + \sum_{i=1}^{n} p_i D(v(x_i) - v^*)$. This form is very similar to the utility function suggested by Allais [2] and Hagen [43]. Allais assumes $D(v(x_i) - v^*)$ is equal to $-a(v(x_i) - v^*)^2$, i.e., the expected value of $D(.)$ is the variance of basic utility times a constant. In Hagen's model D is a function of the variance and the skewness (the third moment) of the distribution of basic utilities. Violations of dominance in Hagen's model can therefore be investigated by knowing some general properties of the function $D(.)$ (see Sudgen [95, p. 13]).

Bell [6] proposes a simple model and proves the existence of a more generalized form. In his simple model $D(.)$ is linear but kinked at the origin, so $\text{DET}(x_i) = v(x_i) + e(v(x_i) - v^*)$ if $v(x_i) - v^* > 0$ and $\text{DET}(x_i) = v(x_i) + d(v(x_i) - v^*)$ if $v(x_i) - v^* < 0$ (where d and e are constants measuring the degrees of disappointment and elation.) Note that if $e = d$, DET collapses to maximizing expected basic utility. His more general model deals only with lotteries with two outcomes x and y (with $x > y$), where x occurs with probability p. In that model, disappointment and elation can depend upon the probabilities of the outcomes. Bell's general form is $\text{DET}(X) = y + (x - y)w(p)$. The weighting function $w(p)$ derived from disappointment and elation may closely resemble the decision weighting function in prospect theory under some conditions.

DET models have two parts: v^* and $\sum_{i=1}^{n} p_i D(x_i - v^*)$. The first part can be interpreted as the value of a lottery, and the second part as a measure of its riskiness. $D(.)$ could be compared with general risk measures, e.g. those proposed by Stone [94]. To pursue this approach further it would be helpful to first derive general axioms for DET, to compare them with axioms for risk measures or to lay the axiomatic foundation for a general risk-value model.

3.6 Lottery Dependent Expected Utility

Lottery dependent expected utility (LDEU) was recently introduced by Becker and Sarin [4]. They model explicitly what is implicit in several other generalized utility models: the utility function used to evaluate an outcome x_i is allowed to depend on the lottery the outcome is part of. (In EU the utility function is independent of the lottery). In LDEU it is possible to be risk prone over the interval [0,3000] for one lottery and risk averse over the same interval [0,3000] for another lottery.

LDEU assumes completeness, transitivity, continuity, and stochastic dominance. Other technical conditions ensure that there exists a number c_X so that lotteries are ranked by their LDEU, given by

$$\text{LDEU}(X) = \sum_{i=1}^{n} p_i u(x_i, c_X) \qquad (12)$$

To operationalize the LDEU model, one has to find a sample way to define c_X and a simple functional form for $u(x, c_X)$. Suppose c_X is linear in probabilities (i.e., if $X \sim aY + (1-a)Z$ then $c_X \sim a c_Y + (1-a)c_Z$). Then there exists a real valued function h, so that $c_X = \sum_{i=1}^{n}$

$p_i h(x_i)$. A sufficient condition for LDEU to satisfy stochastic dominance is that h is increasing. If h is constant then c_X is constant for all X and LDEU collapses to EU.

As a special form for $u(x, c)$, Becker and Sarin suggest $u(x, c_X) = 1 - \exp(-c_X x')/(1 - \exp(-c_X))$ (with $u(x, c_X) = x'$ for $c_X = 0$), where $x' = (x - x_L)/(x - x_H)$ and x_L resp. x_H are the lowest resp. highest possible outcomes. As Becker and Sarin show, it is relatively easy to assess utility functions based on these two assumptions.

LDEU has no independence axiom. However, assumptions about c_X or h do imply some type of independence. For instance, if u is the exponential model described in the previous paragraph and h is linear in x, then it can be shown that if decision makers are indifferent between two lotteries X and Y, they should also be indifferent between lotteries X' and Y' obtained from X and Y by mean-preserving spreads (Becker and Sarin [4, p. 24]. More general statements may emerge from future research.

3.7 Machina's Generalized Expected Utility Analysis

The approach of Machina [70–72], is quite different from the other generalized utility theories. Machina has not tried primarily to generalize EU to explain patterns of preferences. Instead, he asked whether properties of EU, which are used when EU is applied in economic theory, hold under assumptions about preferences which are weaker than EU.

Machina works with preference "functionals", real-valued functions of cumulative probability distributions of outcomes denoted by F, G, etc.. He assumes completeness, transitivity, and continuity, which are sufficient to prove the existence of a preference functional $V(F)$. He also assumes the preference functional is smooth, or differentiable, in a specific sense.

Machina does *not* use an independence axiom to put further mathematical restrictions on the form of the preference functional $V(F)$. Instead, he asks what general properties an unrestricted form of $V(F)$ might have.

Using an approximation which satisfies his differentiability restriction, he shows that for every smooth V there exists a local utility function $u(x; F)$ at each F. Thus, the local utility of x can depend on the lottery F, while the independence axiom of EU requires that these local utility functions all equal $u(x)$. This $u(x; F)$ can be used to rank differential shifts from F in the neighborhood of F. As in standard differential calculus, the linear approximation of V, i.e. the tangent represented by the local utility function $u(x; F)$, is a good local approximation for V (cf. Dekkel [23]). For lotteries near F, the decision-maker will therefore prefer the lotteries with the highest expected utility, even if he or she does not maximize expected utility for all lotteries. By

analogy, an EU maximizer choosing between nearly equal lotteries will prefer the one with a higher expected value even if he or she has a nonlinear utility function for money (because a small portion of the utility curve is well approximated by a straight line). Machina also shows that the preference function $V(F)$ can be obtained by path integral if we know $u(x; F)$ at all points of F.

More important, Machina proved that certain properties of the local utility functions carry over to properties of the preference functional $V(F)$, i.e. global statements about the utility functional can be derived from properties of the local utility functions, *without* any independence axiom. If all local utility functions exhibit risk-aversion or stochastic dominance, then the preference functional $V(F)$ will have those properties too. Therefore, economic theories which rely on assumptions of risk-aversion and EU maximization by agents are still valid if the agents' local utility functions exist and are all risk-averse, even if agents are not EU maximizers (e.g., even if they violate the EU independence condition).

3.8 Regret Theory and Skew-Symmetric Bilinear Utility Theory

In the Allais paradox described in Sect. 2, people often choose 1 million DM over a lottery with a 0.10 chance of 5 million DM, a 0.89 chance of 1 million DM, and a 0.01 chance of nothing. If they choose the lottery, disaster strikes, and they get nothing then they may feel "regret" from having chosen the "wrong" alternative, as if their utility depends on the difference between money received and money foregone. If they choose the lottery and win 5 million DM they might feel "rejoicing" (in addition to the utility of winning 5 million DM) because they won more than the certain 1 million DM foregone.

The theories described in this section try to model feelings of regret and rejoicing in pairwise decisions. Loomes and Sudgen [64] and Bell [5] developed models to capture their intuitions about the sensation of regret, as in the lottery example. By weakening the axioms of EU, Fishburn [31] developed a theory called "SSB", for skew-symmetric bilinear utility, which is closely related to regret. Most remarkably, Chew and MacCrimmon's weighted utility (section 3.3 above), turns out to be equivalent to SSB when transitivity is assumed!

Regret theories and SSB are different from all the other approaches presented so far in that regret and SSB model preferences on pairwise choices of lotteries. Their preference functions have two lotteries as an argument (e.g., $S(X, Y)$) rather than one lottery as in EU and related forms. Regret and SSB are not necessarily transitive.

We will follow Sudgen [95] and first present a general form of regret theory and discuss its relation to SSB.

We then show the axiomatic foundation of SSB, and discuss its connection to weighted utility.

Suppose you have to choose between lotteries $X = (x_1, p_1; \ldots; x_n, p_n)$ and $Y = (x_1, q_1; \ldots; x_n, q_n)$ which have the same outcomes with different probabilities. Assume that both lotteries are resolved independently (which is not necessary, but makes comparison of regret and SSB easier). If we choose X and get x_i, we get some basic utility $v(x_i)$ from x_i along with the regret or rejoicing from having *not* received the outcome x_j from Y. This led to the original regret model, where M is the utility of getting x_i and not getting x_j:

$$M(x_i, x_j) = v(x_i) + R(v(x_i) - v(x_j)), \qquad (13)$$

(Loomes and Sudgen [64, p. 809] and Bell [5, p. 969]). Analogously to disappointment theory $v(x_i)$ is basic utility and $R(.)$ represents regret or rejoicing. $R(.)$ is assumed to be strictly increasing, with $R(0) = 0$. In regret theory it is assumed that a decision maker wants to maximize the expected value of $M(.,.)$. If the two lotteries are assumed to be independent, the chance of receiving x_i and foregoing x_j is $p_i q_j$. We can therefore define the expected regret $ER(X, Y)$ as

$$ER(X, Y) = \sum_{i=1}^{n} \sum_{j=1}^{n} p_i q_j M(x_i, x_j). \qquad (14)$$

An alternative X is preferred to an alternative y if and only if $ER(X, Y)$ is greater than $ER(Y, X)$. Define the function $S(x_i, x_j)$ to be $M(x_i, x_j) - M(x_j, x_i)$. Then $X \succ Y$ if and only if $\sum_{i=1}^{n} \sum_{j=1}^{n} S(x_i, x_j) > 0$. $S(X, Y)$ ($= ER(X, Y) - ER(Y, X)$) is simply the preference function for X over Y in Fishburn's SSB theory.

SSB utility theory gets its name from the function $S(X, Y)$, which is skew-symmetric ($S(X, Y) = -S(Y, X)$) and bilinear (S is linear in probabilities in both arguments, i.e. $S(aX + 1 - a)X', Y) = aS(X, Y) + (1 - a)S(X', Y)$ and $S(X, aY + (1 - a)Y') = aS(X, Y) + (1 - a)S(X, Y')$). Fishburn [31] assumes that preferences obey completeness (*without* transitivity), continuity, and dominance (also called convexity, or betweenness). (Dominance states that if $A \succ B$ and $A \succsim C$, then A is preferred to any lottery between B and C, and if $A \sim B$, then A and B are indifferent to any lottery between them.) The essential axiom in SSB is symmetry, which is a straightforward weakening of EU independence (and less obviously, is equivalent to WEU independence):

SSB *Symmetry Axiom.* Suppose $X \succsim Y \succsim Z$ and $Y \sim 0.5X + 0.5Z$. Then

$pX + (1 - p)Z \sim 0.5X + 0.5Y$ if and only if
$pZ + (1 - p)X \sim 0.5Z + 0.5Y.$

(Note that EU requires $p = 0.75$.) Symmetry and the other axioms imply the existence of an SSB function $S(X, Y)$ with $S(X, Y) \geqslant 0$ if and only if $X \succsim Y$.

While symmetry is the driving force behind SSB, its intuitive meaning is unclear. Graphically, it implies that if one indifference curve in a two dimensional triangle diagram is a 45-degree line, other indifference curves will be symmetric around that line (but they need not be parallel as in EU). It is straightforward to show that an SSB function $S(X, Y)$ will satisfy this axiom, but there is no intuitive reason why this axiom necessarily implies the form $S(X, Y)$. SSB does not assume transitivity (Fishburn [31]). When transitivity is assumed (Fishburn [32]), SSB reduces to weighted utility theory. The kinship of SSB and WEU can be seen graphically in Sect. 4, because both theories require that indifference curves intersect in a point.

Up to now, we have ignored an important difference between SSB and regret theory by assuming preferences for (statistically independent) probability distributions of outcomes. But regret theory can also be used for state-contingent outcomes, as in Savage's subjective EU, though SSB cannot. Fishburn has axiomatized a variant of SSB for state-contingent outcomes which he calls SSA, for skew-symmetric additive theory (Fishburn [33], [36]). SSA accepts the sure-thing principle and therefore cannot explain all the paradoxes; but it allows intransitive preferences, and adding transitivity to SSA yields EU (Fishburn [36, p. 13]).

When outcomes are state-contingent, regret and SSA can account for unusual patterns of preferences. Consider the choice between acts X and Y, where X and Y yield differing consequences depending upon which state (a roll of a die) occurs:

state (number on die)						
act	1	2	3	4	5	6
X	500	600	700	800	900	1000
Y	600	700	800	900	1000	500

If the states are all equally likely (as with rolls of a die), then the lotteries X and Y have exactly the same probability distribution of outcomes. In all theories that represent preferences on single lotteries (including EU, SSB, et al.), one must be indifferent between X and Y. But in regret theory and SSA one can prefer Y to X, for instance, if a 5/6 chance of regretting an opportunity loss of 100 outweighs a 1/6 chance of rejoicing over an opportunity gain of 500.

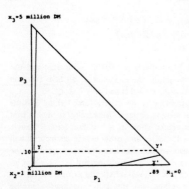

Fig. 3. The common consequence effect

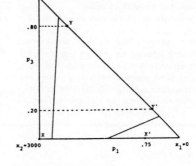

Fig. 4. The common ratio effect

4. Comparison of Generalized Expected Utility Models

Up to now we have presented several models that generalize EU. In this section we will compare the models, using the triangle diagrams to show how indifference curves differ across theories and to show how theories explain the common consequence and common ratio paradoxes. We also review the few empirical studies of generalized expected utility models.

4.1 Explanation of Paradoxes in a Triangle Diagram

Recall the triangle diagram we used to explain expected utility theory (Fig. 1). We can also use this diagram to show how the paradoxes violate EU, and how generalized theories explain them.

Consider the set of lotteries with three possible outcomes, $x_3 = 5$ million DM, $x_2 = 1$ million DM, and $x_1 = 0$. The lotteries used in section 2 to illustrate the common consequence effect are plotted in Fig. 3. The two lotteries $X = (x_1, 0; x_2, 1; x_3, 0)$ and $Y = (x_1, .01; x_2, .89; x_3, .10)$ are plotted in the lower left-hand corner of the triangle. $X' = (x_1, .89; x_2, .11; x_3, 0)$ and $Y' = (x_1, .90; x_2, 0; x_3, .10)$ are in the lower right-hand corner. In both cases, the Y lottery is obtained by shifting the X lottery to the right by 0.01 (i.e., increasing p_1 by 0.01) and upward by 0.10 (i.e., increasing p_3 by 0.10). The pair X', Y' is simply the pair X, Y slid along the bottom of the diagram, to the right. Moving the pair X, Y around the diagram changes their common consequence x_2 and its probability p_2. If indifference curves are parallel straight lines, as EU predicts, then either X is on a higher indifference curve than Y, which implies X' is on a higher indifference curve than Y', or Y is on a higher indifference curve than X (and Y' on a higher curve than

X'). The pattern $X \succsim Y$, $Y, \succ X'$ is paradoxical. It suggests indifference curves are non-parallel, like the hypothetical curves shown in Fig. 3.

The common ratio effect can be shown similarly. Take $x_1 = 0$, $x_2 = 3000$ DM, and $x_3 = 4000$ DM, as in our example from Sect. 2. Then the pairs X, Y and X', Y' shown in Fig. 4 have a common ratio of p_3 to p_2 (1.0 to 0.8 and 0.25 to 0.20, respectively). Parallel indifference curves again dictate a choice of X and X', or Y and Y', but the typical choice of subjects is $X \succ Y$ and $Y' \succ X'$. Hypothetical indifference curves of the sort drawn in Fig. 4, which are *not* parallel, can explain these choices.

The common consequence and the common ratio effects can both be explained by indifference curves that "fan out", as if curves in the lower right-hand corner are flatter, and curves in the left-hand corners are steeper. Recall that the slope of curves reflects the degree of risk-aversion (flat curves reflect risk-seeking, steep curves reflect risk-aversion). Therefore, fanning out is consistent with the notion that people are more risk-seeking in the lower right-hand corner and more risk-averse in the left-hand corners.

The fanning out property was formalized by Machina [70]. He showed what fanning out implies about "local utility functions" in his hypothesis II: Whenever a distribution G is first-order stochastically dominated by a distribution F, then $-u''(x_F)/u'(x_F) \geqslant -u''(x_G)/u'(x_G)$ for all x (where u' and u'' are the first and second derivatives of u with respect to x). Since $-u''/u'$ is a measure of the degree of risk-aversion (the well-known Arrow-Pratt measure), Machina's hypothesis amounts to saying that local utility functions are less risk-averse for stochastically dominated lotteries, see Fig. 5.

It is rather easy to compare generalized utility theories by the shape of the indifference curves they predict.

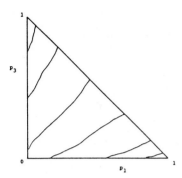

Fig. 5. Indifference curves predicted by Machina's "fanning out" hypothesis

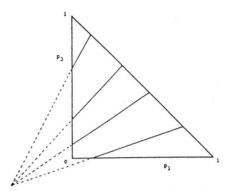

Fig. 8. Indifference curves predicted by weighted utility theory (WEU)

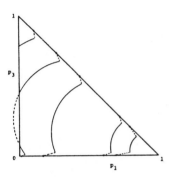

Fig. 6. Indifference curves predicted by prospect theory (PT) (without editing)

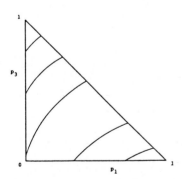

Fig. 7. Indifference curves predicted by rank-dependent utility theory (RDEU)

Prospect theory is the hardest. Suppose we ignore framing and editing rules, take the lotteries to be regular lotteries with $u(x_2) = .5$, take the value of lotteries to be the values of outcomes weighted by decision weights, and estimate the weighting function by a quadratic approximation. The resulting curves are shown in Fig. 6. They are extremely bowed (reflecting nonlinearity in decision weights) and discontinuous near the edges where p_2 or p_3 are zero or one. Of course, these are *not* a complete depiction of how prospect theory explains choices, but they give us a benchmark to compare other theories. Note that prospect theory can explain the common consequence and common ratio effects because curves are steepest in the lower left-hand corner and flat in the right-hand corner.

The general shape of indifference curves in rank-dependent expected utility theory can be deduced with some simple calculus. Typical curves for a risk-averse person (concave $g(x)$) are shown in Fig. 7. They do *not* fan out throughout the diagram, but the curves are very steep around the lower left-hand corner. This captures the idea that people demand a high price (a high ratio of increments in p_3 and p_1) to move away from the certain 1 million DM in the common consequence paradox, because they weight the possibility of getting 0 very highly.

In weighted utility theory, indifference curves have a simple shape: They are straight lines, intersecting at a point outside the diagram. (If the point is infinitely far away, the curves are parallel, so WEU reduces to EU.) If the point of intersection is to the lower left, as in Fig. 8, then the indifference curves fan out; but if the point is in the upper right, the curves fan *in*. Notice that in WEU, unlike prospect theory and RDEU, the curves fan out *throughout* the diagram. As one moves in a northwest direction, toward the upper left-hand corner, the curves

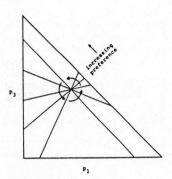

Fig. 9. Indifference curves predicted by regret and SSB

are constantly getting steeper. In implicit weighted utility theory curves are straight lines but they are not parallel and they do not intersect inside the diagram. Indeed, the only testable quality of those curves is that they are straight.

In EU, indifference curves never intersect; in WEU, they intersect at a point outside the diagram; but in regret and SSB, the curves may intersect *inside* the diagram because of intransitivity, as in Fig. 9.

4.2 Formal Comparison of the Models

Figure 10 is a tree diagram relating the axiomatic structure of all the theories we have described. There are other similarities between theories that are not based on resemblance of axioms (see Sect. 3.1). For instance, regret and disappointment theories can be thought of as including additional attributes in an EU framework. And prospect theory is driven by psychological intuition which is not entirely captured by axioms (e.g., the editing and reference point ideas).

The goal of this section is to explain Fig. 10. Numbers attached to names and theories correspond to the sections of our paper where particular models were first described.

Completeness, transitivity and continuity together allow us to establish some well-behaved preference function to rank-order lotteries (Machina 3.7). An independence condition gives us the general separable utility models, as in prospect theory for instance (3.2). These models are characterized by transformation of probabilities p_i which depend only on p_i. The models can violate dominance. If we add the stochastic dominance condition we can either get rank-dependent utility theory (RDEU, 3.3), disappointment theory (DET, 3.5) or lottery dependent utility theory (LDEU, 3.6). RDEU

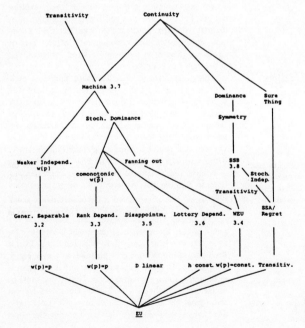

Fig. 10. Relations between generalized preference theories and EU

requires the comonotonic cancellation axiom and derives a representation where each probability p_i is transformed in a way that depends on the whole probability distribution. DET is derived by intuition about how decision makers incorporate disappointment in their decisions. Analogously LDEU is also derived by some specific assumptions. The only theories which necessarily agree with Machina's fanning out hypothesis are some special cases of LDEU (3.6) and weighted expected utility theory (WEU, 3.4), which is derived by the additional assumption of weak independence.

Assuming dominance and symmetry, but not transitivity, gives skew-symmetric bilinear expected utility theory (SSB, 3.8). Taking a different route and assuming all of Savage's axioms except for transitivity gives SSA, which contains regret models as a special case. SSA reduces to SSB for statistically independent acts (lotteries). SSB plus transitivity yields WEU, while SSA plus transitivity yields EU.

The conditions under which different theories collapse to EU will not be repeated here. They can easily be derived from Fig. 10, where symbols correspond to the specific symbols used above.

4.3 Empirical Evidence for Generalized Utility Models

All the models try to predict behavior (and some also claim to be useful for prescription, see Sect. 5.1). The ultimate test of their value is to see how well they predict. There are different ways to test these models. First we can observe behavior in very specific decision situations, e.g. those which build on common ratio and common consequence effects. We could check whether the models can in principle explain the observed behavior in these so-called paradoxical situations. This was how Allais demonstrated the problems underlying EU. However, new specific decision situations must be designed because all the new theories were developed to explain the original paradoxes. Second, we could assess the parameters of generalized utility models to see which model predicts actual behavior more precisely. In case a new theory is in principle able to explain some paradoxical behavior it does not necessarily follow that after assessing the parameters the model will predict the actual behavior.

There are some obstacles to testing new theories. Since generalized theories all have more parameters than EU, they are always better able to explain observed choices. The question is whether the additional parameters can be assessed reliably, so that a generalized theory fit to one set of data can predict better than EU on another set of data from the same subjects. It is possible that new theories developed to explain paradoxes might predict more poorly than EU for "normal" lotteries,

e.g. a 50–50 chance of getting 0 DM and 100 DM. Therefore, it is useful to assess the whole preference function (or some parts of it in widely differing domains).

Most of these theories are so new that very little empirical testing has been conducted. We will briefly describe tests of prospect theory (for an attempt at predicting frames in prospect theory see Fischhoff [27]), WEU, regret, and several competing theories. Methods for assessing the different preference functions are described separately in Sect. 5.2.

Currim and Sarin [21] conducted two experiments to test prospect theory. In both they assessed each subject's riskless value function ($= u$) and decision weight function ($= w$) as well as his or her EU utility function. In both experiments the decision maker had to choose between pairs of lotteries. These holistic, intuitive preference statements were used as a validation sample. Experiment 1 was characterized by "normal" decision situations and experiment 2 contained paradoxical types of choices. Currim and Sarin found that the properties of the u and w functions postulated in prospect theory (PT) held in both experiments, but there was some indication that the decision weight function is different for positive and negative outcomes. Overall, EU and PT predicted choices about equally well, but the authors concluded that more work needs to be done.

Chew and Waller [17] tested WEU by presenting subjects with four pairwise choices, called the HILO structure (see Chew and MacCrimmon [16]). These choices are a straightforward generalization of the choices used to demonstrate common ratio and common consequence effects. In a series of four pairwise choices by a single subject, there are 16 possible patterns. Six of the patterns are consistent with WEU and 2 are consistent with EU. Chew and Waller conducted two experiments, 1 and 2 respectively, 22% and 31% of the choice patterns within subjects were compatible with EU, 62% (71%) were compatible with all forms of WEU, and 33% (31%) could be explained by the fanning-out version of WEU shown in Fig. 8 (which Chew and Waller call the "light hypothesis"). It would be interesting to know what fraction of the 62% of the patterns explained by WEU, or the 38% unexplained by WEU, could be accounted for by other theories.

Loomes [63] constructed a set of lotteries X and Y in which the probability distributions of the outcomes in X and Y were identical, but the statistical dependence between X and Y outcomes varied. Only regret theory and SSA can account for switches in preferences between X and Y, or vice versa, as the degree of dependence changed. He found a highly significant number of reversals in several different choice problems, as predicted by regret theory.

Starmer and Sugden [93] constructed several choice problems to distinguish between EU, the fanning-out hypothesis, RDEU, and prospect theory. They found that the fraction of non-EU choice patterns by subjects, around a third, was only slightly higher than the fraction of unreliable choices (i.e., choices of different lotteries when the same question is posed twice), which was around 26%. The non-EU choices did not systematically follow either fanning-out or fanning-in, so choices did not uniformly support any of the generalized theories they considered. However, their results are tentative.

In general, the most powerful tests might come from behavioral hypotheses which separate theories. For example, not all theories predict fanning out; so if fanning out is observed, several theories can be rejected. Some theories predict that indifference curves are straight lines, while others do not. Straight line indifference curves are caused by the "betweeness" property, i.e., if one is indifferent between A and B, one is also indifferent between any compound lottery (i.e. lottery between them) and A and B.

5. Implications for Applications and Practice

5.1 Are Generalized Utility Theories Descriptive or Prescriptive?

Roughly speaking, utility theories are applied in two ways: To *describe* choices people actually make; and to *prescribe* choices people should make. All the generalized utility theories we have reviewed were created to describe actual patterns of choice that could not be accounted for by EU. Do these theories also yield good normative prescriptions? The answer depends largely on the logical appeal of each theory's axioms and implications, and its psychological appeal as a faithful representation of preferences. To our knowledge, generalized theories have *not* yet been used for prescription in actual decision making.

The theories in which probabilities are each weighted nonlinearly (Handa [44], Kahneman and Tversky [49], Karmarkar [50]) yield violations of stochastic dominance, a sufficiently undesirable property so that we would probably not want to use these theories to tell people what to do. Regret theories and some variants of SSB utility violate transitivity, an axiom that most people also hesitate to abandon (see MacCrimmon and Larsson [69]). However, if regret has genuine psychological effects, it seems wrong to ignore it. At the very least, researchers and decision analysts can point out to a decision maker how much he or she is paying for psychological regret. After all, the tradeoff between the logic of transitivity and the psychology of regret is left

to the people they study or advise. There is little evidence of how people do resolve that trade-off.

Rank-dependent probability EU and weighted utility have appealing axioms, since they weaken independence in natural ways with no undesirable consequences. However, even those theories are not without controversy as prescriptions. For example, in a situation of repeated choices one would not advise a decision maker with a linear utility function to violate the expected value principle. Should we advise people to apply a theory (weighted utility) which makes them act as if some outcomes are more or less conceivable than others, even though the outcome probabilities are known? This also seems like a flimsy basis for advice.

A familiar line of reasoning in economics is that adherence to certain axioms is enforced by the threat of market discipline, whether the axioms are logically appealing or not. If people violate transitivity they can be subjected to a "money pump" or "Dutch book" — — a sequence of exchanges, which are each willingly accepted, such that they are left strictly worse off than when they began. If a person violates transitivity by preferring A to B, B to C, and C to A, we can get him to exchange A for B, B for C, and C for A, charging a small sum each time. He begins with A and ends with A, losing money each time through the cycle. Even if people dislike the logic of transitivity, the argument goes, they *must* like it or go broke. (Of course, people may anticipate the cycle and refuse to accept each individual change.) However, we know of no money pump argument which enforces the EU independence axiom or preferences for stochastically dominating lotteries.

It may be that the best descriptive theories of choice will never be prescriptively appealing (Tversky and Kahneman [99]). After all, descriptive theories of the intuitive statistical inferences people draw, or complex repeated judgments they make, are different from normative theories. In prospect theory, violations of stochastic dominance and dependence of choices on arbitrary framing give the theory descriptive power but ruin its prescriptive appeal. Kahneman and Tversky argue that people *like* the EU axioms, so EU is perfectly adequate for prescription but another theory (such as prospect theory) is needed to describe actual behavior.

We feel it is too soon to abandon hope that a good theory could both describe and prescribe (at least until framing and dominance violations are better established empirically). It is certainly conceivable that a theory which weakens the independence axiom could replace EU as a prescriptive theory. But there is a deeper matter here: If one is guided only by probability distributions over final wealth in a multistage setting (a decision tree) then EU seems to be the only applicable theory (LaValle and Wapman [60]). Sad, uninteresting, but true. Or as one colleague said, good, interesting, and true.

5.2 Assessment of Parameters of Utility Functions

In general, assessment of utility and weighting functions in the generalized utility theories we have reviewed is much like assessing an EU utility function, but typically more tedious.

Depending on how and why different generalized theories were developed, the actual assessment of the preference function is of varying importance. We want to *briefly* discuss the assessment procedure for prospect theory, Yaari's rank dependent utility, Chew's weighted utility, and lottery dependent utility. Note that Machina's analysis does not aim at assessing a preference function.

In prospect theory one has to assess the decision weight function w and the value function v (with respect to some reference point). Currim and Sarin [21] suggest assessing the riskless value function first and basing the assessment of the probability weight function on the value function. There may be other ways to assess the functions simultaneously using conjoint measurement.

For the value function we first have to define a specific gain as a benchmark and assign a certain amount of points to it. Some other gain amounts are then compared to this benchmark. The points attached to these gains should correspond to the satisfaction derived from them relative to the satisfaction derived from the benchmark. The responses can then be used to fit some functional form for the value function. In addition one could also use an indifference method. (See von Winterfeldt and Edwards [103] for an overview). To assess the w function, a decision maker is asked to determine certainty equivalents x^* for a series of lotteries $(x, p; 0, 1 - p)$, with p varying. Since $w(p) = u(x^*)/u(x)$ the decision weight function is easy to determine, once we know the value function u. Assessing Yaari's $g(x)$ function is straightforward, because he assumes the utility of money is linear. The RDEU of the lottery $(1, p; 0, 1 - p)$ is simply $1 g(p)$. Therefore, $g(p)$ "is the *amount of money which, when received with certainty, is regarded by the decision maker as equivalent to the prospect of receiving* $1 *with probability* p *and* $0 *with probability* 1 - p" (Yaari [100]). (It seems unlikely that $g(p)$ would appear very non-linear in such an assessment.) In the generalizations of RDEU in which utility may be non-linear, the utility function $u(x)$ and $g(p)$ must be assessed simultaneously, which requires a more elaborate procedure.

Weighted utility is relatively easy to assess. Since there is some freedom in picking endpoints for the weighting function $w(x)$, choose $w(x_1) = w(x_n) = 1$, where x_1 and x_n are minimal and maximal outcomes. Since the weighted utility of lotteries $(x_n, p; x_1, 1 - p)$ is just p (because the weights cancel out), the utility function $u(x)$ can be elicited by getting certainty-equivalents x_i for all p between 0 and 1. Suppose x_j is the certainty-equivalent for the lottery $(x_n, p; x_1, 1 - p)$. Then

$u(x_j) = p$. The weight $w(x_j)$ is $r(1 - q)/q(p - r)$, where q is the probability that makes $(x_j, q; x_1, 1 - q)$ indifferent to $(x_n, r; x_1, 1 - r)$ for a particular r. (The robustness of the procedure can be checked by eliciting values of q for many different values of r, and seeing if $r(1 - q)/q(p - r)$ is constant as the theory predicts.)

In lottery dependent expected utility the complexity of the assessment procedure depends heavily on the assumptions made about u, c_X, and h. Suppose u is given by the exponential model, c_X is linear in probabilities (i.e. h exists), and h is linear. Then we need to elicit certainty-equivalents for two simple lotteries to assess the function LDEU. If we assume no specific functional form for h, LDEU can be easily assessed by asking the decision maker for a series of certainty equivalents for simple $(x_H, p; x_L, 1 - p)$ lotteries.

5.3 Applications to Business Research

Applications of generalized utility theories to business disciplines are understandably rare, because the theories are new and more difficult to apply than EU. But generalized theories can potentially explain much puzzling behavior and open wide new areas of research. Roughly speaking, generalized utility theories might be used to explain behavior of individuals acting alone, in games, or in markets.

For instance, imagine fitting functional forms from generalized theories to data from individual choices or judgments of value. In marketing, generalized theories might be useful for predicting risky choices by consumers, e.g., warranty purchase or responses to new products.

EU was originally axiomatized by von Neumann and Morgenstern to serve as a basis for the theory of games. Therefore, it is appropriate to ask what happens to basic results in game theory if players do not follow EU. If games have Nash equilibrium outcomes in which players use "pure strategies" (single choices), then there is no risk in choices and EU is not needed: Ordinal preferences which satisfy completeness and transitivity are sufficient to establish an equilibrium. However, some model of preferences under risk in needed if players use "mixed strategies" (random combinations of simple "pure" strategies). Under EU, a Nash equilibrium involving mixed strategies always exists. Fishburn and Rosenthal [39] proved that a Nash equilibrium also exists under SSB. Since most of game theory consists of identifying equilibria and studying their properties, the fact that equilibrium always exist under SSB means that most results derived by assuming EU also hold true for SSB.

Weber [101] applied weighted utility theory to the study of auctions. Under EU, prices should be identical in sealed-bid auctions and "Dutch" auctions (in which prices descend from above until a bidder buys the object, as in a typical German Gemüsegroßmarkt). However, in experiments Dutch auction prices are usually *lower* than prices in sealed-bid auctions. Weber showed that this finding is consistent with weighted utility maximization, if the weighting function $w(x_i)$ is decreasing and concave in potential payoffs. (Weber also noted that in negotiations between a buyer and seller, a seller naming a sequence of prices is like a Dutch auction, while a seller making a take-it-or-leave-it offer is like a sealed-bid auction, so the study of formal auctions may apply to informal negotiations as well.) Bell [6, p. 23] showed that Dutch auction prices could be either lower or higher than sealed-bid auction prices, depending upon assumptions about disappointment. Karni and Safra [51], [52] studied the impact of non-EU preferences on bidding in English (ascending-bid) auctions and second-price or "Vickrey" auctions (in which the high bidder wins the auctioned object at the second-highest price). They proved that bidders must obey EU for English and second-price auction bids to be the same. Second-price auction bids will not generally be value-revealing (i.e., bidders will not bid their true valuations) unless preferences obey EU (cf. Chew [13]), but English auctions will be value-revealing as long as preferences obey "betweenness", as in EU, WEU, or SSB.

Markets for insurance are one setting in which generalized utility theories might help explain market behavior. Schulze, McCelland, and Coursey [74a] found that prices paid for insurance in sealed-bid auction experiments were better explained by prospect theory than by EU. People sometimes argue that insurance markets do not function well (i.e., firms charge more than people will pay) because of ambiguity about the probabilities of losses (Hogarth and Kunreuther [47]). However, most of the generalized theories designed specifically to explain ambiguity-aversion (which we have *not* reviewed) can explain this failure of insurance markets.

Yaari [100] has applied rank-dependent probability utility theory to the problem of optimal portfolio diversification. Application of more general theories to this fundamental problem might prove even more useful. Indeed, financial economics is now awash with evidence of puzzling market inefficiencies (e.g., Keim [54]), which might be explained by new models of preferences underlying market equilibrium.

The prospect theory idea that people value gains and losses relative to a reference point, and the hypothesized shape of the value function, have been useful in explaining behavior in financial markets and in marketing applications. Applying the reference point idea requires a theory of "mental accounting" (Thaler [96]), the rules people use to decide whether to change their reference point after experiencing gains and losses.

For instance, since a dividend of amount D paid on a share of stock actually reduces the stock price by roughly the same amount D, investors should not care whether dividends are paid or not. (Depending on tax laws, they may even dislike them.) But investors *love* dividends. One explanation of their preference is that a dividend is put into a separate mental account from a change in stock price (or capital gain C). If the accounts are perceived separately the combination of a dividend D and a capital loss or gain C may be preferrable to the larger capital gain $C + D$ which would result if no dividend was paid (Shefrin and Statman [90]). Another example from finance is that investors sometimes sell successful stocks too early, and unsuccessful stocks too late, to reap tax benefits from the reduction in long-term (six months) capital gains (Shefrin and Statman [91]). Loewenstein [62] showed that changes in reference points can explain differences in time preference of individuals which are inconsistent with EU.

The idea of mental accounting has been applied to marketing problems by Thaler [97]. He argued that several losses will be accounted for together, because the marginal pain of a loss on top of other losses is less than the pain of a single loss. Gains will be accounted for separately, by the opposite logic. Marketing decisions about packaging of products and transactions may therefore affect consumer behavior in ways that cannot be predicted by EU. For example, one should package products with several features or parts so that each feature (gain) is packaged separately, while the total cost (loss) is a single lump sum.

6. Conclusion and Future Research

Several new theories have been developed to explain observed behavior which is paradoxical for expected utility theory. In reviewing them we have attempted to balance understanding of their axiomatic foundations with an appreciation of their underlying intuition.

Much research remains to be done to truly understand decision making under risk, and new research is indeed emerging rapidly. We expect this review will have to be extended soon. It seems especially clear that new empirical efforts are needed to distinguish between theories, since all these theories can explain most of the original paradoxes.

Applications of generalized utility theories to areas which currently rely on EU will show the true value of these theories. The handful of examples presented above barely scratch the surface of the work that might be done.

Acknowledgement. We would like to thank Professors Jon Baron, Franz Eisenführ, Robin Keller, Karl Mosler, and two anonymous referees. We especially thank Professor Rakesh Sarin for helpful comments, and all the girls in the UCLA sculpture garden for inspiring us to think about preferences.

References

1. Allais M (1953) Le comportement de l'homme rationel devant le risque: Critique des postulats et axiomes de l'école americaine. Econometrica 21:503–546
2. Allais M (1979) The foundation of a positive theory of choice involving risk and a criticism of the postulates and axioms of the American school. In: Allais M, Hagen O (eds) Expected utility hypotheses and the Allais paradox. Reidel, Dordrecht, pp 27–145
3. Allais M (1979) The so-called Allais paradox and rational decisions under uncertainty. In: Allais M, Hagen O (eds) Expected utility hypotheses and the Allais paradox. Reidel, Dordrecht, pp 437–699
4. Becker JL, Sarin RK (1986) Lottery dependent utility. Working Paper, Graduate School of Management, UCLA, Los Angeles
5. Bell DE (1982) Regret in decision making under uncertainty. Oper Res 30:961–981
6. Bell DE (1985) Disappointment in decision making under uncertainty. Oper Res 33:1–27
7. Bell DE, Farquhar PH (1986) Perspectives on utility theory. Oper Res 34:179–183
8. Bernoulli D (1738, 1954) Specimen theoriae novae de mensura sortis. Comments Acad Sci Imper Petropolitanae 5:175–192, translated by Sommer L (1954) Econometrica 22:23–36
9. Bolker ED (1966) A simultaneous axiomatization of utility and subjective probability. Philos Sci 34:292–312
10. Chew SH (1982) A mixture set axiomatization of weighted utility theory. Discussion Paper No 82–4, College of Business and Public Administration, University of Arizona, Tuscon
11. Chew SH (1983) A generalization of the quasilinear mean with applications to the measurement of income inequality and decision theory resolving the Allais paradox. Econometrica 51:1065–1092
12. Chew SH (1984) An axiomatization of the rank dependent quasilinear mean generalizing the gini mean and the quasilinear mean. Manuscript, Department of Political Economy, Johns Hopkins University, Baltimore
13. Chew SH (1985) Implicit-weighted and semi-weighted utility theories, M-estimators, and non-demand revelation of second-price auctions for an uncertain auctioned object. Working Paper No 155, Department of Political Economy, Johns Hopkins University, Baltimore
14. Chew SH, Karni E, Safra Z (1987) Risk aversion in the theory of expected utility with rank dependent probabilities. J Econ Theory 42:370–381
15. Chew SH, MacCrimmon KR (1979) Alpha-nu choice theory: A generalization of expected utility theory. Working Paper No. 669, Faculty of Commerce and Business Administration, University of British Columbia, Vancouver
16. Chew SH, MacCrimmon KR (1979) Alpha utility theory, lottery composition and the Allais paradox. Working Paper No. 686, Faculty of Commerce and Business Administration, University of British Columbia, Vancouver
17. Chew SH, Waller WS (1986) Empirical tests of weighted utility theory. J Math Psychol 30:55–72
18. Coombs CH (1975) Portfolio theory and the measurement of risk. In: Kaplan MF, Schwartz SC (eds) Human judgement and decision making processes, Academic Press, New York, pp. 63–85

19. Curley SP, Yates JF (1985) The center and range of the probability interval as factors affecting ambiguity preferences. Organ Behav Human Dec Proc 36:273–287
20. Curley SP, Yates JF, Abrams RA (1986) Psychological sources of ambiguity avoidance. Organ Behav Human Dec Proc 38:230–256
21. Currim IS, Sarin RK (1986) Empirical evaluation of properties and predictive power of prospect theory. Working Paper, Graduate School of Management, UCLA, Los Angeles
22. Debreu G (1959) Theory of value: An axiomatic analysis of general equilibrium. Yale University Press, New Haven
23. Dekkel E (1986) An axiomatic characterization of preferences under uncertainty: Weakening the independence axiom. J Econ Theory 40:304–318
24. Dyer JS, Sarin RK (1982) Relative risk aversion. Manag Sci 28:875–886
25. Einhorn HJ, Hogarth RM (1985) Ambiguity and uncertainty in probabilistic inference. Psychol Rev 92:433–461
26. Ellsberg D (1961) Risk, ambiguity and the Savage axioms. Q J Econ 75:643–669
27. Fischhoff B (1983) Predicting frames. J Exp Psychol: Learning, Memory and Cognition 9:103–116
28. Fishburn PC (1970) Utility theory for decision making. Wiley, New York
29. Fishburn PC (1978) On Handa's new theory of cardinal utility and the maximization of expected return. J Polit Econ 86:321–324
30. Fishburn PC (1982) The foundation of expected utility. Reidel, Dordrecht
31 Fishburn PC (1982) Nontransitive measurable utility. J Math Psychol 26:31–67
32. Fishburn PC (1983) Transitive measurable utility. J Econ Theory 31:293–317
33. Fishburn PC (1984) SSB utility theory: An economic perspective. Math Soc Sci 8:63–94
34. Fishburn PC (1985) Uncertainty aversion and separated effects in decision making under uncertainty. Working Paper, AT & T Bell Laboratories, Murray Hill
35. Fishburn PC (1986) A new model for decisions under uncertainty. Econ Lett 21:127–130
36. Fishburn PC (1986) Reconsiderations of decision under uncertainty. Working Paper, AT & T Bell Laboratories, Murray Hill
37. Fishburn PC (1987) Nonlinear preference and utility theory. John Hopkins University Press, Baltimore
38. Fishburn PC (1987) Generalizations of expected utility theory: A survey of recent proposals. Working Paper, AT & T Bell Laboratories, Murray Hill
39. Fishburn PC, Rosenthal RW (1986) Non-cooperative games and nontransitive preferences. Math Soc Sci 12:1–7
40. Gärdenfors P, Sahlin N-E (1982) Unreliable probabilities, risk taking, and decision making. Synthese 53:361–386
41. Gärdenfors P, Sahlin N-E (1983) Decision making with unreliable probabilities. Br J Math Stat Psychol 36:240–251
42. Grether DM, Plott CR (1979) Economic theory of choice and the preference reversal phenomenon. Am Econ Rev 69:623–638
43. Hagen O (1979) Towards a positive theory of preference under risk. In: Allais M, Hagen O (eds) Expected utility and the Allais paradox. Reidel, Dordrecht, pp 271–302
44. Handa J (1977) Risk, probabilities and a new theory of cardinal utilities. J Polit Econ 85:97–122
45. Hazen GB (1986) Subjectively weighted utility. Working Paper No. 86–08, Department of Industrial Engineering and Management Science, Northwestern University, Evanston

46. Herstein IN, Milnor J (1953) An axiomatic approach to measurable utility. Econometrica 21:291–297

47. Hogarth RM, Kunreuther H (1985) Ambiguity and insurance decisions. Am Econ Rev 75:386–390

48. Kahn BE, Sarin RK (1987) Modelling ambiguity in decisions under uncertainty. Working Paper, Graduate School of Management, UCLA, Los Angeles

49. Kahneman D, Tversky A (1979) Prospect theory: An analysis of decision under risk. Econometrica 47:263–291

50. Karmarkar US (1978) Subjectively weighted utility: A descriptive extension of the expected utility model. Organ Behav Human Perform 21:61–72

51. Karni E, Safra Z (1987) Dynamic consistency in English auctions and expected utility theory. Working Paper, Department of Political Economy, Johns Hopkins University, Baltimore

52. Karni E, Safra Z (1987) Revelations in auctions and the structure of preferences. Working Paper, Department of Political Economy, Johns Hopkins University, Baltimore

53. Keeney RL, Raiffa H (1976) Decisions with multiple objectives. Wiley, New York

54. Keim D (1983) Size related anomalies and stock return seasonality. J Fin Econ 14:13–32

55. Keller LR (1985) Effects of problem representation on the sure-thing and substitution principle. Manag Sci 31:738–751

56. Keller LR, Farquhar PH (1987) The measurement of value functions. Working Paper, Graduate School of Management, UC Irvine, Irvine

57. Keller LR, Sarin RK, Weber M (1986) Empirical investigation of some properties of the perceived riskiness of gambles. Organ Behav Human Dec Proc 38:114–130

58. Kunreuther H, Ginsberg R, Miller L, Slovic P, Botkan B, Katz N (1978) Disaster insurance protection: Public policy lessons. Wiley, New York

59. Krantz DH, Luce RD, Suppes P, Tversky A (1971) Foundations of measurement. Academic Press, New York

60. LaValle IH, Wapman KR (1986) Rolling back decision trees requires the independence axiom. Manag Sci 32:382–385

61. Lichtenstein S, Slovic P (1971) Reversals of preference between bids and choices in gambling decisions. J Exp Psychol 89:46–55

62. Loewenstein G (1986) Frames of mind in intertemporal choice. Working Paper, Center for Decision Research, University of Chicago, Chicago

63. Loomes G (1987) Predicted violations of the invariance principle in choice under uncertainty. Working Paper, Center for Experimental Economics, University of York, York

64. Loomes G, Sudgen R (1982) Regret theory: An alternative theory of rational choice under uncertainty. Econ J 92:805–824

65. Loomes G, Sudgen R (1986) Disappointment and dynamic consistency in choice under uncertainty. Rev Econ Stud LIII:271–282

66. Luce RD (1981, 1982) Several possible measures of risk. Theory Dec 12:217–228, correction 13:381

67. Luce RD, Narens L (1985) Classification of concatenation measurement structures according to scale type. J Math Psychol 29:1–72

68. MacCrimmon KR (1968) Descriptive and normative implications of the decision theory postulate. In: Borch K, Mossin J (eds) Risk and uncertainty. MacMillian, New York, pp 3–23

69. MacCrimmon KR, Larsson S (1979) Utility theory: Axioms versus 'paradoxes'. In: Allais M, Hagen O (eds) Expected utility and the Allais paradox. Reidel, Dordrecht, pp 333–409

70. Machina MJ (1982) 'Expected utility' analysis without the independence axion. Econometrica 50:277–323

71. Machina MJ (1982) A stronger characterization of declining risk aversion. Econometrica 50:1069–1079

72. Machina MJ (1983) The economic theory of individual behavior toward risk: Theory, evidence and new directions. Technical report No. 433, Center for Research on Organizational Efficiency, Stanford University, Stanford

73. Machina MJ (1987) Decision making in the presence of risk. Science 236:537–543

74. Marschak J (1950) Rational behavior, uncertain prospects, and measurable utility. Econometrica 18:111–141

74a. McClelland G, Schulze WH, Coursey D (1987) Valuing risk: A comparison of expected utility theory with models from cognitive psychology. Working Paper, University of Colorado, Boulder

75. Morris PA (1986) The credibility of probabilities. Paper presented at the ORSA/TIMS meeting. October 1986, Miami Beach

76. Moskowitz H (1974) Effects of problem representation and feedback on rational behavior in Allais and Morlat-type problems. Dec Sci 5:225–242

77. Nau RF (1986) A new theory of indeterminate probabilities and utilities. Working Paper No. 8609, Fuqua School of Business, Duke University, Durham

78. von Neumann J, Morgenstern O (1947) Theory of games and economic behavior. 2nd edn. University Press, Princeton

79. Pollatsek A, Tversky A (1970) A theory of risk. J Math Psychol 7:540–553

80. Quiggin J (1982) A theory of anticipated utility. J Econ Behav Organ 3:323–343

81. Sarin RK (1982) Strength of preference and risky choice. Oper Res 30:982–997

82. Savage LJ (1954) The foundations of statistics. Wiley, New York

83. Schmeidler D (1984) Subjective probability and expected utility without additivity. Preprint 84, Institute for Mathematics and Its Applications, University of Minnesota, Minneapolis

84. Schoemaker PJH (1982) The expected utility model: Its variants, purposes, evidence and limitations. J Econ Lit 30:529–563

86. Segal U (1984) Non-linear decision weights with the independence axiom. Working Paper, Department of Economics, UCLA, Los Angeles

87. Segal U (1985) On the axiomatic foundation of prospect theory. Working Paper, Economics Department, University of Pennsylvania, Philadelphia

88. Segal U (1986) The Ellsberg paradox and risk aversion: An anticipated utility approach. Working Paper No. 362, Department of Economics, UCLA, Los Angeles

89. Segal U (1986) Some remarks on Quiggin's anticipated utility. Working Paper No. 392, Department of Economics, UCLA, Los Angeles

90. Shefrin HM, Statman M (1984) Explaining investor preference for cash dividends. J Fin Econ 13:253–282

91. Shefrin HM, Statman M (1985) The disposition to sell winners too early and ride losers too long: Theory and evidence. J Fin 40:777–790

92. Slovic P, Tversky A (1974) Who accepts Savage's axiom? Behav Sci 19:368–373

93. Starmer C, Sugden R (1987) Violations of the sure-thing principle: An experimental test of some competing hypo-

theses. Working Paper, School of Economic and Social Studies, University of East Anglia, Norwich

94. Stone BK (1973) A general class of three-parameter risk measures. J Fin 28:657–685

95. Sudgen R (1986) New developments in the theory of choice under uncertainty. Bull Econ Res 38:1–24

96. Thaler R (1980) Toward a positive theory of consumer choice. J Econ Behav Organ 1:39–60

97. Thaler R (1985) Using mental accounting in a theory of consumer choices. Mark Sci 4:199–214

98. Tversky A, Kahneman D (1981) The framing of decisions and the psychology of choice. Science 211:453–458

99. Tversky A, Kahneman D (1986) Rational choice and the framing of decisions. J Business 59:S251–S278

100. Yaari ME (1987) The dual theory of choice under risk. Econometrica 55:95–115

101. Weber RJ (1982) The Allais paradox Dutch auctions, and alpha-utility theory. Working Paper No. 536, J. L. Kellog Graduate School of Management, Northwestern University, Evanston

102. Wilhelm J (1986) Zum Verhältnis von Höhenpräferenz und Risikopräferenz. Z betriebswirt Forsch 38:467–492

103. von Winterfeldt D, Edwards W (1986) Decision analysis and behavioral research. Cambridge University Press, Cambridge

[15]

Econometrica, Vol. 55, No. 1 (January, 1987), 95–115

THE DUAL THEORY OF CHOICE UNDER RISK

By Menahem E. Yaari[1]

This paper investigates the consequences of the following modification of expected utility theory: Instead of requiring independence with respect to probability mixtures of risky prospects, require independence with respect to direct mixing of payments of risky prospects. A new theory of choice under risk—a so-called dual theory—is obtained. Within this new theory, the following questions are considered: (i) numerical representation of preferences; (ii) properties of the utility function; (iii) the possibility for resolving the "paradoxes" of expected utility theory; (iv) the characterization of risk aversion; (v) comparative statics. The paper ends with a discussion of other non-expected-utility theories proposed recently.

KEYWORDS: Risk, uncertainty, utility, duality.

1. INTRODUCTION

IN THIS ESSAY, a new theory of choice under risk is being proposed. It is a theory which, in a sense that will become clear, is *dual* to expected utility theory, hence the title "dual theory." Risky prospects are evaluated in this theory by a cardinal numerical scale which resembles an expected utility, except that the roles of payments and probabilities are reversed. This theme—the reversal of the roles of probabilities and payments—will recur throughout the paper. I should emphasize that playing games, with probabilities masquerading as payments and payments masquerading as probabilities, is not my object. Rather, I hope to convince the reader that the dual theory has intrinsic economic significance and that, in some areas, its predictions are superior to those of expected utility theory (while in other areas the reverse will be the case).

Two reasons have prompted me to look for an alternative to expected utility theory. The first reason is methodological: In expected utility theory, the agent's attitude towards risk and the agent's attitude towards wealth are forever bonded together. At the level of fundamental principles, risk aversion and diminishing marginal utility of wealth, which are synonymous under expected utility theory, are horses of different colors. The former expresses an attitude towards risk (increased uncertainty hurts) while the latter expresses an attitude towards wealth (the loss of a sheep hurts more when the agent is poor than when the agent is rich). A question arises, therefore, as to whether these two notions can be kept separate from each other in a full-fledged theory of cardinal utility. The dual theory will have this property.

The second reason that leads me to look for an alternative to expected utility theory is empirical: Behavior patterns which are systematic, yet inconsistent with expected utility theory, have often been observed. (Two prominent references, among many others, are Allais (1953) and Kahneman–Tversky (1979).) So deeply

[1] Two earlier versions of this paper have been circulated as research reports (in October, 1984, under the title "Risk Aversion Without Diminishing Marginal Utility," and in February, 1985, under the title "Risk Aversion Without Diminishing Marginal Utility and the Dual Theory of Choice under Risk"). If there has been improvement in the course of these revisions, it is due, in large measure, to many comments and suggestions received from friends and colleagues. I wish to thank them all. Special thanks go to the Co-Editor and Associate Editor of *Econometrica*.

rooted is our commitment to expected utility, that we tend to regard such behavior patterns as "paradoxical", perhaps even as "irrational." The dual theory, it turns out, rationalizes many of the "paradoxes" of expected utility theory. Obviously, the dual theory will have its own "paradoxes", many of which turn out to become rationalized under expected utility. Roughly speaking, we find each theory resolving "paradoxes" in the other theory.

The dual theory has the property that utility is linear in wealth, in the sense that applying an affine transformation to the payment levels of two gambles always leaves the direction of preference between them unchanged. (Under expected utility, this is true only when the agent is risk neutral.) In order to forestall needless arguments, let me come clean right away and say that I do not consider linearity in payments an empirically viable proposition. Behavior which is inconsistent with such linearity is probably often observed. However, such evidence should be viewed in proper perspective: Behavior which is inconsistent with linearity in *probabilities*—a vital component of expected utility theory—is also often observed. I shall return to this matter in Section 4, below.

In studying the behavior of *firms*, linearity in payments may in fact be an appealing feature. Under the dual theory, maximization of a linear function of profits can be entertained simultaneously with risk aversion. How often has the desire to retain profit maximization led to contrived arguments about firms' risk neutrality?

The most general way of using cardinal utility to treat choice under risk is one where preferences are represented by a measure which is defined on appropriate subsets of the payment-probability plane. Both expected utility and the dual theory are special cases of this approach, with the measure representing preferences being a *product* measure, factorizable into two marginal measures. In expected utility, the marginal measure along the probability axis is Lebesgue measure, and in the dual theory, the marginal measure along the payment axis is Lebesgue measure. Dropping the condition that one of the marginal measures be Lebesgue produces a theory which generalizes both expected utility and dual theory. A special version of this generalized theory has been proposed recently by Quiggin (1982), in a paper which studies the perception of risk from a cognitive point of view. The case of preferences being represented by a nonfactorizable measure has, to the best of my knowledge, not yet been studied.

An extension of the dual theory to the multivariate case exists, and is explored in a separate paper (Yaari (1986)). It is interesting to note that, in the multivariate version of the dual theory, linearity in payments ceases to be an issue.

2. A REPRESENTATION THEOREM

Let V be the set of all random variables defined on some given probability space, with values in the unit interval. I shall assume that the underlying probability space is "rich", in the sense that all distributions with supports contained in the unit interval can be generated from elements of V. For each $v \in V$, define the *decumulative distribution function* (DDF for short) of v, to be denoted G_v, by

$$G_v(t) = \Pr\{v > t\}, \quad 0 \leq t \leq 1.$$

G_v is always nonincreasing, right-continuous, and satisfies $G_v(1) = 0$. For all $v \in V$, the following convenient relationship holds:

(1) $$\int_0^1 G_v(t)\, dt = Ev,$$

where Ev stands for the expected value of v.

The values of the random variables in V will be interpreted as payments, denominated in some monetary unit. This makes each $v \in V$ interpretable as a gamble or a lottery which a decision maker might consider holding. Restricting the values of random variables in V to the unit interval can be interpreted, via the choice of a suitable measurement scale, to mean that (i) no gambles can be considered which involve a possible loss exceeding the decision maker's total wealth, and (ii) no gambles exist which offer prizes exceeding some predetermined large number.

A preference relation $\succsim$ is assumed to be defined on V. Let the symbols $\succ$ and $\sim$ stand for strict preference and indifference, respectively. The following axiom suggests itself:

AXIOM A1—*Neutrality: Let u and v belong to V, with respective DDF's G_u and G_v. If $G_u = G_v$, then $u \sim v$.*

This axiom restricts attention to preferences which are not state-dependent. It implies, in particular, that preference among DDF's can be defined in an unambiguous manner. Specifically, we may construct a preference relation $(\succsim)$ among DDF's by writing $G(\succsim)H$ if, and only if, there exist two elements, u and v, of V such that $G_u = G$, $G_v = H$, and $u \succsim v$. Under Axiom A1, the assertions $u \succsim v$ and $G_u(\succsim)G_v$ are equivalent. Our assumptions on V imply that the domain of the relation $(\succsim)$ is the set of all DDF's with supports contained in the unit interval. More precisely, let a family of functions Γ be defined by

$$\Gamma = \{G:[0,1] \to [0,1] \mid G \text{ is nonincreasing, right-continuous and}$$
$$\text{satisfies } G(1) = 0\}.$$

Then, the assertion $G(\succsim)H$ is meaningful for every pair of functions, G and H, in Γ.

In order to reduce cumbersome notation, and with the reader's indulgence, I shall henceforth use the symbol $\succsim$ both for preference among random variables and for preference among DDF's. (In other words, the parentheses in $(\succsim)$ will henceforth be dropped.)

We can now proceed to the remaining axioms:

AXIOM A2—*Complete weak order: $\succsim$ is reflexive, transitive, and connected.*

AXIOM A3—*Continuity* (with respect to L_1-convergence): *Let G, G', H, H', belong to Γ; assume that $G \succ G'$. Then, there exists an $\varepsilon > 0$ such that $\|G - H\| < \varepsilon$ and $\|G' - H'\| < \varepsilon$ imply $H \succ H'$, where $\| \ \|$ is the L_1-norm, i.e., $\|m\| = \int |m(t)|\, dt$.*

It should be noted that the continuity assumed in A3 is stronger than that required for the development of standard expected utility theory. (The reason for this will become apparent shortly.)

AXIOM A4—*Monotonicity* (with respect to first-order stochastic dominance): *If* $G_u(t) \geqslant G_v(t)$ *for, all* t, $0 \leqslant t \leqslant 1$, *then* $G_u \gtrsim G_v$.

With Axioms A1–A4 in hand, one can proceed to write down an appropriate independence axiom and obtain the result that preferences are representable by expected utility comparisons. Specifically consider:

AXIOM A5EU—*Independence*: *If* G, G', *and* H *belong to* Γ *and* α *is a real number satisfying* $0 \leqslant \alpha \leqslant 1$, *then* $G \gtrsim G'$ *implies* $\alpha G + (1 - \alpha)H \gtrsim \alpha G' + (1 - \alpha)H$.

For the record, I shall now state the expected utility theorem. Before doing so, let me introduce the following notation: If x and p both lie in the unit interval, then $[x; p]$ will stand for a random variable that takes the values x and 0 with probabilities p and $1 - p$, respectively.

THEOREM 0: *A preference relation* $\gtrsim$ *satisfies Axioms A1–A4 and A5EU if, and only if, there exists a continuous and nondecreasing real function* ϕ, *defined on the unit interval, such that, for all* u *and* v *belonging to* V,

(2) $u \gtrsim v \Leftrightarrow E\phi(u) \geqslant E\phi(v)$.

Moreover, the function ϕ, *which is unique up to a positive affine transformation, can be selected in such a way that, for all* t *satisfying* $0 \leqslant t \leqslant 1$, $\phi(t)$ *solves the preference equation*

(3) $[1; \phi(t)] \sim [t; 1]$.

PROOF: See, e.g., Fishburn (1982, Theorem 3, p. 28). It follows readily from Axioms A2–A4 and A5EU that the premises of Fishburn's theorem hold, with the unit interval acting as the set of consequences and with distributions representing probability measures. The conclusion, therefore, is that a function ϕ satisfying (2) exists, uniquely up to a positive affine transformation and, moreover, that equation (3) provides the construction of ϕ. That ϕ is continuous and nondecreasing follows directly from A3 and A4, respectively, in conjunction with (3). Finally, the fact that the converse also holds is established by straightforward verification.
                                                                    Q.E.D.

The dual theory of choice under risk is obtained when the independence axiom of expected utility theory (Axiom A5EU) is taken and, so to speak, "laid on its side." Instead of independence being postulated for convex combinations which are formed along the probability axis, it will now be postulated for convex combinations which are formed along the payment axis. The best way to do this is to consider appropriately defined *inverses* of distribution functions.

DUAL THEORY OF CHOICE   99

Let $G \in \Gamma$, so that G is the DDF of some $v \in V$. Now define a set-valued function, $\hat{G}$, by writing, for $0 \le t \le 1$,

$$\hat{G}(t) = \{x \mid G(t) \le x \le G(t-)\}$$

where $G(t-) = \lim_{s \to t, s < t} G(s)$ for $t > 0$, and $G(0-) = 1$. $\hat{G}$ is simply the set-valued function which "fills up" the range of G, to make it coincide with the unit interval. The values of $\hat{G}$ are closed and for each p, $0 \le p \le 1$, there exists some t such that $p \in \hat{G}(t)$. Using $\hat{G}$, we may now proceed to define the (generalized) *inverse* of G, to be denoted G^{-1}, by writing

(4) $G^{-1}(p) = \min \{t \mid p \in \hat{G}(t)\}$.

Note that G^{-1}, like G, belongs to Γ and that, for all $G \in \Gamma$, $(G^{-1})^{-1} = G$. Furthermore, if G and H belong to Γ and $\| \ \|$ stands for L_1-norm, then $\|G - H\| = \|G^{-1} - H^{-1}\|$. Of course, if G is invertible, then G^{-1} is just the usual inverse function of G.

A mixture operation for DDF's may now be defined as follows: If G and H belong to Γ and if $0 \le \alpha \le 1$, then $\alpha G \boxplus (1 - \alpha)H$ is the member of Γ given by

(5) $\alpha G \boxplus (1 - \alpha)H = (\alpha G^{-1} + (1 - \alpha)H^{-1})^{-1}$.

If $J = \alpha G \boxplus (1 - \alpha)H$, for some $0 \le \alpha \le 1$, then I shall say that J is a *harmonic convex combination* of G and H. With the operation $\boxplus$, the set Γ of all DDF's becomes a *mixture space*, in the sense of Herstein and Milnor (1953).

Returning to the preference relation $\succsim$, we are now in a position to state the axiom that gives rise to the dual theory of choice under risk:

AXIOM A5—*Dual Independence*: *If G, G' and H belong to Γ and α is a real number satisfying $0 \le \alpha \le 1$, then $G \succsim G'$ implies $\alpha G \boxplus (1-\alpha)H \succsim \alpha G' \boxplus (1-\alpha)H$.*

The economic significance of this axiom will be discussed in Section 3, below. The following representation theorem is now available:

THEOREM 1: *A preference relation $\succsim$ satisfies Axioms A1–A5 if, and only if, there exists a continuous and nondecreasing real function f, defined on the unit interval, such that, for all u and v belonging to V,*

(6) $u \succsim v \iff \displaystyle\int_0^1 f(G_u(t)) \, dt \ge \int_0^1 f(G_v(t)) \, dt$.

Moreover, the function f, which is unique up to a positive affine transformation, can be selected in such a way that, for all p satisfying $0 \le p \le 1$, $f(p)$ solves the preference equation

(7) $[1; p] \sim [f(p); 1]$.

PROOF: Define a binary relation $\succsim^*$ on the family Γ of DDF's, as follows:

$$G \succsim^* H \quad \text{if, and only if,} \quad G^{-1} \succsim H^{-1},$$

for all G and H in Γ. Clearly, if u and v are random variables in V, then

$$u \succsim v \quad \Leftrightarrow \quad G_u^{-1} \succsim^* G_v^{-1}.$$

Checking Axioms A2–A4, we find that they hold for $\succsim$ if, and only if, they hold for $\succsim^*$. Furthermore, $\succsim$ satisfies A5 if, and only if, $\succsim^*$ satisfies A5EU. Hence, from Theorem 0, it follows that $\succsim$ satisfies A1–A5 if, and only if, $\succsim^*$ has the appropriate expected utility representation. In other words, $\succsim$ satisfies A1–A5 if, and only if, there exists a continuous and nondecreasing function f, defined on the unit interval, such that

$$u \succsim v \quad \Leftrightarrow \quad -\int_0^1 f(p) \, dG_u^{-1}(p) \geq -\int_0^1 f(p) \, dG_v^{-1}(p)$$

is true for all u and v in V. Let G be any member of Γ. Then, the equation

$$-\int_0^1 f(p) \, dG^{-1}(p) = \int_0^1 f(G(t)) \, dt$$

holds, by introducing the change of variable $p = G(t)$, and this proves the first part of the theorem. Now, applying the second part of Theorem 0 to $\succsim^*$, we find that f can be selected so as to satisfy the preference equation

$$(8) \qquad G_{[1;f(p)]} \sim^* G_{[p;1]}$$

for $0 \leq p \leq 1$. Note, however, that if G is the DDF of $[x; p]$ then G^{-1} is the DDF of $[p, x]$. Therefore, a rewriting of (8) in terms of the original preference relation, $\succsim$, produces (7). This completes the proof of the theorem.   *Q.E.D.*

Let v belong to V, with DDF G_v, and let $U(v)$ be defined by

$$(9) \qquad U(v) = \int f(G_v(t)) \, dt,$$

with f defined in (7). Theorem 1 tells us that the function U is a *utility* on V, when preferences satisfy A1–A5. The hypothesis of the Dual Theory is that agents will choose among random variables so as to maximize U. This is in analogy (and in contrast) with the hypothesis of expected utility theory, which is that agents choose among random variables so as to maximize the function W, given by

$$(10) \qquad W(v) = E\phi(v) = -\int_0^1 \phi(t) \, dG_v(t),$$

with ϕ defined in (3). Note, incidentally, that (10) can be rewritten in a manner that makes the analogy with (9) stand out more clearly. Specifically we have

$$W(v) = \int_0^1 \phi(G_v^{-1}(p)) \, dp.$$

Let $\succeq$ satisfy A1–A5, and let f be defined by (7). The phrase "*f represents* $\succeq$" will be used as convenient shorthand for the much longer phrase "the function U, derived from f in (9), is a utility representing $\succeq$."

The utility U of the dual theory has two noteworthy properties: First, U assigns to each random variable its *certainty equivalent*. In other words, if v belongs to V, then $U(v)$ is equal to that sum of money which, when received with certainty, is considered by the agent equally as good as v. The second important property of U is *linearity in payments*: When the values of a random variable are subjected to some fixed positive affine transformation, the corresponding value of U undergoes the same transformation. The following propositions provide a precise statement of these properties.

PROPOSITION 1: *Under Axioms A1–A5, the relationship*

(11) $v \sim [U(v); 1]$

holds for every $v \in V$.

PROOF: It follows from (9) that $U([x; 1]) = x$ for all x, $0 \leq x \leq 1$. In particular, $U([U(v); 1]) = U(v)$ and, by Theorem 1, $[U(v); 1] \sim v$, as was to be shown.
                                                                                Q.E.D.

REMARK: In expected utility theory, the following *dual* to Proposition 1 exists: Let $\succeq$ satisfy A1–A4 and A5EU, and let ϕ and W be defined by (3) and (10), respectively. Then, $v \sim [1; W(v)]$ is true for every $v \in V$.

PROPOSITION 2: *Let v belong to V and let a and b be two real numbers, with $a > 0$. Define a function $av + b$ by writing $(av + b)(s) = av(s) + b$ for each state-of-nature s, and assume that $0 \leq av(s) + b \leq 1$ for all s. Then, $U(av + b) = aU(v) + b$.*

PROOF: Let G_v and G_{av+b} be the DDF's of v and $av + b$, respectively. Note that, for every t, $0 \leq t \leq 1$, we have

$$G_{av+b}(t) = \begin{cases} 1 & \text{for } 0 \leq t < av_0 + b, \\ G_v\left(\dfrac{t-b}{a}\right) & \text{for } t \geq av_0 + b, \end{cases}$$

where v_0 is the infimum of the range of v. Hence,

$$U(av + b) = av_0 + b + \int_{av_0 + b}^{1} f(G_{av+b})(t)) \, dt$$

$$= av_0 + b + \int_{av_0 + b}^{1} f\left(G_v\left(\frac{t-b}{a}\right)\right) dt.$$

Introducing the change of variable $s = (t - b)/a$, we get

$$U(av + b) = a\left[v_0 + \int_{v_0}^{1} f(G_v(s)) \, ds \right] + b$$

$$= aU(v) + b,$$

as was to be shown.   *Q.E.D.*

COROLLARY: *If the preference relation $\gtrsim$ satisfies A1–A5, then, for all u and v belonging to V, we have*

$$u \gtrsim v \quad \Leftrightarrow \quad au + b \gtrsim av + b,$$

provided $a > 0$ and provided $au + b$ and $av + b$ both belong to V. In words, under A1–A5, agents always display constant absolute risk aversion as well as constant relative risk aversion.

PROOF: Apply Proposition 2.   *Q.E.D.*

Note that under expected utility theory, an agent with constant absolute risk aversion as well as constant relative risk aversion must be *risk-neutral,* i.e., this agent's preferences always rank random variables by comparing their means. Under the dual theory, we have linearity (in the sense of Proposition 2 and its Corollary) without risk neutrality being implied in any way. Indeed, let us see how risk neutrality is characterized under the dual theory. It follows from (6), in conjunction with (1), that under Axioms A1–A5, the agent's preference relation $\gtrsim$ ranks random variables by comparing their means if, and only if, the function f representing $\gtrsim$ coincides with the identity, i.e., $f(p) = p$ for $0 \leq p \leq 1$. In other words, risk neutrality is characterized in the dual theory by the function f in (7) being the identity. But there is nothing in Theorem 1 to *force* f to coincide with the identity: Any continuous and nondecreasing function f, satisfying $f(0) = 0$ and $f(1) = 1$ can be obtained in (7), for some preference relation $\gtrsim$ satisfying A1–A5. In the dual theory, the agent's attitude towards wealth—restricted as it is—does not prejudice the agent's attitude towards risk.

It is interesting to compare the construction of the function f in the dual theory with the construction of the von Neumann–Morgenstern utility ϕ in expected utility theory. Consider the preference equation

(11) $[1; p] \sim [t; 1]$.

We know, from (7) and (3), that $f(p)$ is the value of t that solves (11), while $\phi(t)$ is the value of p that solves (11). It follows, therefore, that $f = \phi^{-1}$. Of course, when writing $f = \phi^{-1}$, we should not lose sight of the fact that only *one* of the two functions, ϕ and f, can be relevant to the characterization of the agent's overall behavior in risky situations.

DUAL THEORY OF CHOICE   103

3. THE MEANING OF DUAL INDEPENDENCE

In the foregoing section, dual independence (Axiom A5) appeared without an economic interpretation. My aim now is to re-state A5 in a way that will make its economic content clear.

Consider once again the set V of random variables, on which preferences are defined, and let (S, Σ, P) be the underlying probability space. (V, then, is the set of all Σ-measurable functions on S, with values in the unit interval.)

DEFINITION: Let u and v belong to V. We say that u and v are *comonotonic* if, and only if, for every s and s' in S, the inequality

$$(u(s) - u(s'))(v(s) - v(s')) \geq 0$$

is true.

This definition makes it possible to state the following axiom, directly on preference among random variables (without going to distributions):

AXIOM A5*—*Direct Dual Independence*: *Let* u, v, *and* w *belong to* V *and assume that* u, v, *and* w *are pairwise comonotonic. Then, for every real number* α *satisfying* $0 \leq \alpha \leq 1$, $u \gtrsim v$ *implies* $\alpha u + (1 - \alpha)w \gtrsim \alpha v + (1 - \alpha)w$.

Note that here we are dealing with ordinary convex combinations of real functions and that $\alpha u + (1 - \alpha)w$ is *not* a probability mixture of u and w.

It turns out that A5 and A5* are, in fact, equivalent:

PROPOSITION 3: *Let* $\gtrsim$ *be a preference relation on* V, *satisfying Axiom A1. Then,* $\gtrsim$ *satisfies Axiom A5* *if, and only if, the corresponding preference relation among DDF's (also denoted* $\gtrsim$*) satisfies Axiom A5.*

PROOF: Under Axiom A1, the underlying probability space can be chosen to suit our convenience, as long as all DDF's in Γ can be generated. Accordingly, let (S, Σ, P) consist of the unit interval, the Borel sets, and Lebesgue measure. Now let u, v, and w be pairwise comonotonic and suppose that A5 holds. We must show that $u \gtrsim v$ implies $\alpha u + (1 - \alpha)w \gtrsim \alpha v + (1 - \alpha)w$, where $0 \leq \alpha \leq 1$. By comonotonicity, there exists a measure-preserving transformation, mapping the unit interval onto itself which, when composed with any of the random variables u, v, and w, rearranges it in nonincreasing order, without affecting its distribution. Thus, without loss of generality, we may assume not only that u, v, and w are pairwise comonotonic, but that each one of them is a nonincreasing function on the unit interval. Moreover, having selected Lebesgue measure for the underlying probability measure, we find that the right-continuous *inverse* of u, u^{-1}, is precisely the DDF G_u of u, and similarly for v and w. Therefore, the assertion that $G_u \gtrsim G_v$ implies $\alpha G_v \boxplus (1 - \alpha)G_w \gtrsim \alpha G_v \boxplus (1 - \alpha)G_w$ in A5 reduces precisely to $u \gtrsim v$

implying $\alpha u + (1-\alpha)w \gtrsim \alpha v + (1-\alpha)w$. Conversely, let G, G', and H belong to Γ and assume that A5* holds. We must show that

$$G \gtrsim G' \quad \text{implies} \quad \alpha G \boxplus (1-\alpha)H \gtrsim \alpha G' \boxplus (1-\alpha)H, \quad \text{for} \quad 0 \leq \alpha \leq 1.$$

Defining u, v, and w to be the inverses of G, G', and H, respectively, we find that u, v, and w are pairwise comonotonic so, by A5*, $u \gtrsim v$ implies $\alpha u + (1-\alpha)w \gtrsim \alpha v + (1-\alpha)w$. This assertion, when written in terms of preference among DDF's, gives the desired result, and the proof is complete.   Q.E.D.

The foregoing proposition makes it clear that the economic interpretation of dual independence lies in the intuitive meaning of comonotonicity. Recall that comonotonicity is a distribution-free property, in the sense that it is invariant under changes in the underlying probability measure. It is, in fact, an analogue of perfect correlation for this distribution-free setting. When two random variables are comonotonic, then it can be said that neither of them is a *hedge* against the other. The variability of one is never tempered by counter-variability of the other. (A discussion of this no-hedge condition appeared in Yaari (1969), where comonotonic random variables were referred to as "bets on the same event.") Suppose, for example, that u and v are random variables such that $u \gtrsim v$. Would this preference be retained when both u and v are mixed, half and half, with some third random variable, say w? (Recall that we are not dealing here with a probability mixture, but rather with a pointwise averaging of the values of the two random variables.) If the agent whose preferences are being discussed is risk averse, and w is a hedge against v but not against u, then this agent might well have reason to reverse the direction of preference: i.e., the assertions $u \gtrsim v$ and $\frac{1}{2}v + \frac{1}{2}w > \frac{1}{2}u + \frac{1}{2}w$ will both be true. Similarly, if the agent for whom $u \gtrsim v$ is true is risk seeking, and w is a hedge against u but not against v, then, once again, there will be reason for the agent to reverse the direction of preference as above. Thus, the demand that $u \gtrsim v$ should imply $\alpha u + (1-\alpha)w \gtrsim \alpha v + (1-\alpha)w$ seems to be justified only in the case where w is neither a hedge against u nor a hedge against v. This is precisely what dual independence says. Actually, dual independence is *weaker*, in that the conclusion is only required to hold when u and v themselves are not a hedge against each other. This further weakening becomes important when the agent's initial wealth is allowed to vary. In this paper, however, variations in initial wealth will not be considered.

We see, in summary, that dual independence requires the direction of preference to be retained under mixing of payments, provided hedging is not involved. Two comments are in order at this point.

(a) Comonotonicity, i.e. the no-hedge condition, is sensitive to random variables being changed on sets of probability zero. In a recent paper, Röell (1985) has adopted a weaker notion of comonotonicity, defined with joint distributions, which is invariant under changes occurring on sets of probability zero. Röell then uses this alternative definition in an axiom like A5*.

(b) Axiom A5* is, of course, quite strong, and one could think of weakening it in the following way: Suppose that u, v, and w are pairwise comonotonic and that $u \gtrsim v$. Then, $\alpha u + (1 - \alpha)w \gtrsim \alpha v + (1 - \alpha)w$ should be required to hold only if w is *relatively* a better hedge against u than against v. (Presumably, one could try to define the relation "relatively a better hedge..." using correlation coefficients.) This condition would weaken the notion of independence, in comparison with A5*, while simultaneously restricting the analysis to the case of a risk averse agent. Exploring the resulting theory would be, it seems to me, an interesting task. Here, A5* will be maintained, with risk aversion to be treated separately (see Section 5, below).

4. PARADOXES AND DUAL PARADOXES

Behavior which is inconsistent with expected utility theory has been observed systematically, and often such behavior has been branded "paradoxical." As it turns out, behavior which is "paradoxical" under expected utility theory is, in many cases, entirely consistent with the dual theory. This does not mean, however, that the dual theory is "paradox-free." We find, on the contrary, that for each "paradox" of expected utility theory, one can usually construct a "dual paradox" of the dual theory, by interchanging the roles of payments and probabilities. Under these "dual paradoxes," reasonable behavior—and probably easily observable behavior—is found to be inconsistent with the dual theory and to be entirely in keeping with expected utility theory. I would like to illustrate this, using a couple of prominent examples.

A famous "paradox" of expected utility theory is the so-called *common ratio effect*: Dividing all the probabilities by some common divisor reverses the direction of preference. Kahnemen and Tversky (1979), for example, have found that a great majority of subjects prefer $[0.3; 1]$ over $[0.4; 0.8]$ but that an equally large majority prefer $[0.4; 0.2]$ over $[0.3; 0.25]$. (The symbol $[x; p]$, it will be recalled, stands for a random variable which takes the values x and 0 with probabilities p and $1 - p$, respectively. Here, payments are measured in units of \$10,000, so that $[0.3; 1]$ is the gamble that yields \$3000 with certainty, etc.) This pattern, which is obviously inconsistent with expected utility theory, is entirely in keeping with the dual theory. Specifically, with the utility U defined in (9), we find that $U([0.3; 1]) = 0.3$, $U([0.4; 0.8]) = (0.4)f(0.8)$, $U([0.3; 0.25]) = (0.3)f(0.25)$ and $U([0.4; 0.2]) = (0.4)f(0.2)$, and these numbers will support the preference pattern $[0.3; 1] > [0.4; 0.8]$ and $[0.4; 0.2] > [0.3; 0.25]$ if

$$f(0.8) < \frac{3}{4} < \frac{f(0.2)}{f(0.25)}.$$

This inequality is satisfied, for example, when f is of the form $f(p) = p/(2 - p)$, for $0 \le p \le 1$. (This f is in fact *risk averse*, as we shall see in Section 5.)

Now, to get a "dual paradox" for the common ratio effect, we must look for a case where dividing all the *payments* by some common factor would lead to preference reversal. In order to obtain such behavior, which would clearly be inimical to the dual theory, we would have to gather a group of subjects, pay each one of them \$5 per hour for "Participating in an Interesting Experiment on

Decision Making" and proceed to elicit from these subjects a pattern of responses which is inconsistent with constant relative risk aversion. Alas, I cannot claim to have done this. But happily I join the critics of the dual theory in saying that such "deviant" behavior is, no doubt, quite common.

A similar state of affairs exists with Allais' celebrated paradox (Allais (1953)). On the one hand, the non-expected-utility preference pattern, which Allais had found prevalent, turns out to be consistent with the dual theory. On the other hand, examples can be found which resemble Allais' gambles—with the roles of payments and probabilities reversed—where one would expect to observe behavior which is inconsistent with the dual theory while being consistent with expected utility theory. I shall omit the details.

Proceeding now to the theory of *income distribution*, we find yet another "paradox": Newbery (1979) has shown that there does *not* exist a von Neumann–Morgenstern utility whose expected value ranks distributions (with a fixed mean) in the same order as their Gini coefficients of equality. (The Gini coefficient of equality is defined as twice the area under the Lorenz Curve.) Under expected utility theory, it is "irrational" to evaluate income distributions according to the Gini coefficient. Given the frequency with which the Gini has actually been used for comparing income distributions, Newbery's finding is surely as much a paradox of expected utility theory as the common ratio effect or Allais' gambles. Under the dual theory, the paradox disappears. In fact, if we let the function f of Theorem 1 be given by $f(p) = p^2$ for $0 \le p \le 1$, we find that, for DDF's with a fixed integral, the ordering induced by the integral $\int f(G(t))\, dt$ is precisely the Gini equality ordering. Indeed, for mean-normalized distributions, the quantity $\int (G(t))^2\, dt$ is precisely the Gini equality coefficient for G. This result is due to Dorfman (1979). Now, as might be expected, it is easy to think of a "paradox" that would be the *dual* of the foregoing: Just as Gini-type measures of equality (or of inequality) are not rationalizable under expected utility theory, so Atkinson's (1970) measures of equality (or of inequality) are not rationalizable under the dual theory.

5. RISK AVERSION

How would risk aversion be characterized under the dual theory? The following heuristic argument is meant to sound suggestive: Under expected utility theory, preferences are represented by a von Neumann–Morgenstern utility, ϕ. Under the dual theory, preferences are represented by a function f, as per Theorem 1. The construction of ϕ and f in the two theories (equations (3) and (7)) implies that $f = \phi^{-1}$. Since the concavity of ϕ is equivalent to the convexity of ϕ^{-1} and since, under expected utility, the concavity of ϕ characterizes risk aversion, we should expect the *convexity* of f to characterize risk aversion under the dual theory. Showing that this conclusion is indeed correct—even though f and ϕ belong to different theories—is my task in the present section.

Letting $\gtrsim$ be a preference relation on V, as before, we say that $\gtrsim$ is risk averse if $v = u + \text{noise}$ implies $u \gtrsim v$: Adding noise can never be $\gtrsim$-improving. Drawing on the work of Blackwell (1950) and Rothschild–Stiglitz (1970), we obtain the following definition:

DEFINITION: Let u and v belong to V, with DDF's G_u and G_v, respectively, and consider the inequality

$$(12) \qquad \int_0^T G_u(t)\, dt \ge \int_0^T G_v(t)\, dt.$$

A preference relation $\succsim$ on V is said to be *risk averse* if $u \succsim v$ whenever (12) holds for all T satisfying $0 \le T \le 1$, with equality for $T = 1$.

The following theorem is now available:

THEOREM 2: *Consider the class of preference relations on V satisfying Axioms A1–A5. A preference relation $\succsim$ in this class is risk averse if, and only if, the function f representing $\succsim$ (see Theorem 1) is convex.*

PROOF: Let $\succsim$ satisfy A1–A5, and assume that $\succsim$ is risk averse. Take five real numbers, x, y, p, q, r, such that $0 \le y \le x \le 1$ and $0 \le q \le p \le r \le 1$, and construct two random variables, u and v, in the following manner: u takes the values x, y, and 0 with probabilities q, $r - q$, and $1 - r$, respectively, and v takes the values x and 0 with probabilities p and $1 - p$, respectively. Assume that $(p - q)x = (r - q)y$. Then, by direct calculation, (12) holds for $0 \le T \le 1$, with equality for $T = 1$. Hence, $u \succsim v$. By Theorem 1, $u \succsim v \iff U(u) \ge U(v)$, where U is defined in (9). Computing, one finds that $U(u) = yf(r) + (x - y)f(q)$ and $U(v) = xf(p)$. The following implication

$$(13) \qquad (p - q)x = (r - q)y \implies yf(r) + (x - y)f(q) \ge xf(p)$$

has therefore been derived, for any five numbers, x, y, p, q, r satisfying $0 \le y \le x \le 1$ and $0 \le q \le p \le r \le 1$. Note that (13) is trivial when $r = q$, so assume $r > q$. Define λ, $0 \le \lambda \le 1$, by writing $\lambda = (p - q)/(r - q)$ and note that $p = \lambda r + (1 + \lambda)q$. Now (13) reduces to the condition that

$$y = \lambda x \implies yf(r) + (x - y)f(q) \ge xf(\lambda r + (1 - \lambda)q)$$

must hold for all λ and x in the unit interval. For $x > 0$, this is precisely the statement that f is convex. Conversely, let $\succsim$ satisfy A1–A5 and suppose that u and v satisfy (12) for $0 \le T \le 1$, with equality for $T = 1$. Then, by a theorem of Hardy, Littlewood, and Polya (1929, Theorem 10), the inequality

$$\int_0^1 f(G_u(t))\, dt \ge \int_0^1 f(G_v(t))\, dt$$

holds for every convex and continuous f. Checking (9), we conclude that $U(u) \ge U(v)$—or $u \succsim v$—holds whenever f is continuous and convex. Thus, if the function f of Theorem 1 is convex, then $\succsim$ is risk averse, as was to be shown.   Q.E.D.

The fact that risk aversion is characterized in the dual theory by the convexity of f has a useful interpretation when f happens to be differentiable. Let v belong to V, with DDF G_v, and let $U(v)$ be the utility number assigned to v under the dual theory, i.e., $U(v) = \int f(G_v(t))\, dt$. If f is differentiable, then the expression for $U(v)$ can be integrated by parts to obtain

$$U(v) = \int_0^1 tf'(G_v(t))\, dF_v(t),$$

where F_v is the *cumulative* distribution of v. Note that $\int f'(G_v(t))\, dF_v(t) = 1$, i.e., $\{f'(G_v(t))\}$ is a system of nonnegative weights summing to 1, and recall that $\int t\, dF_v(t)$ is the mean of v. In $U(v)$, a similar integral is being calculated, but each t is given a weight $f'(G_v(t))$. In other words, $U(v)$ is a corrected mean of v, in which the payment level t receives a weight of size $f'(G_v(t))$. If f is convex, then f' is nondecreasing; i.e., those values of t for which $G_v(t)$ is small receive relatively low weights and those values of t for which $G_v(t)$ is large receive relatively high weights. Thus, $U(v)$ is a corrected mean of v, in which low payments (bad outcomes) receive relatively high weights while high payments (good outcomes) receive relatively low weights. The agent behaves pessimistically, as though bad outcomes are more likely than they really are and good outcomes are less likely than they really are. It should be emphasized however, that this is *not* a case where probabilities are being distorted in the agent's perception. For the analysis undertaken in this essay deals with how perceived risk is processed into choice, and not with how actual risk is processed into perceived risk. This is necessarily true in any theory that subscribes to the neutrality axiom, A1. Let (S, Σ, P) be the probability space underlying the set V, over which preferences are defined. Then, the measure P must be interpreted as the agent's *perceived* probability measure, whether it coincides with some "objective" probability measure or not. If P were a measure that was liable to be modified (or "distorted") before entering the agent's choice process, then assuming neutrality with respect to P would have been completely unwarranted.

Having seen how risk aversion is characterized under the dual theory, one is led to ask about how the *degree* of risk aversion might be assessed, and to seek tools for carrying out *comparisons* of risk aversion. These topics are taken up in a separate paper (Yaari (1986)).

6. LIQUIDITY PREFERENCE AND COMPARATIVE STATICS

One of the hallmarks of expected utility theory is its treatment of portfolio selection. It is therefore interesting to see how the dual theory would cope with this classical topic. We begin by considering Tobin's (1958) basic liquidity preference problem.

There are two assets: A safe asset (cash) and a risky security. The rate of return on cash is 0 and the rate of return on the risky security is θ, where θ is a random variable distributed on the interval $[-1, a]$, for some $a > 0$. One must assume, of course, that $E\theta > 0$. A decision maker wishes to invest a fixed amount K,

DUAL THEORY OF CHOICE   109

satisfying $0 \leqslant K \leqslant 1/(1 + a)$, and faces the problem of dividing this amount between cash and the risky security. Let x be the amount invested in the risky security, $0 \leqslant x \leqslant K$. Then, the decision maker's gross return from his/her portfolio is given by the random variable $K + \theta x$, which belongs to the class V of the previous sections.

Let $\succsim$ be the decision maker's preference order on V, and assume that $\succsim$ satisfies Axioms A1–A5 of Section 2. Then, by Theorem 1, there exists a continuous and nondecreasing real function f, satisfying the preference equation (7), such that picking the best portfolio is equivalent to selecting an x in the interval $[0, K]$ so as to maximize the quantity

(14) $$\Psi(x) = \int_0^1 f(G_{K + \theta x}(t))\, dt,$$

where $G_{K + \theta x}$ is the DDF of $K + \theta x$.

PROPOSITION 4: *The function $\Psi(\cdot)$, defined in (14), is of the form*

$$\Psi(x) = K + cx, \quad 0 \leqslant x \leqslant K,$$

where the constant c, is given by

(15) $$c = \int_{-1}^{a} f(G_\theta(t))\, dt - 1,$$

with G_θ being the DDF of θ.

PROOF: Essentially the same as the proof of Proposition 2, in Section 2.
                                                                     Q.E.D.

With $\Psi(x)$ being linear in x, we find the dual theory predicting plunging, rather than diversification. Specifically, letting x^* be the maximizer of $\Psi(x)$ under $0 \leqslant x \leqslant K$, we find, from Proposition 4, that

$$x^* = \begin{cases} 0 & \text{if } \int_{-1}^{\infty} f(G_\theta(t))\, dt < 1, \\[2ex] \text{any value in } [0, K] & \text{if } \int_{-1}^{\infty} f(G_\theta(t))\, dt = 1, \\[2ex] K & \text{if } \int_{-1}^{\infty} f(G_\theta(t))\, dt > 1. \end{cases}$$

The term "plunging" must not be confused with risk seeking. Indeed, consider a risk averse investor. Under the dual theory, the behavior of such an agent can be described, so to speak, as waiting in the wings until the rate of return is high enough, and then going whole hog. Under expected utility theory, on the other hand, diversification is universal, in the sense that the amount invested in the risky security is always positive, sometimes reaching the total available for investment. This point deserves to be emphasized: Under expected utility, a risk averse investor will always put *some* resources into a risky security, provided its expected rate of return is positive. I am prepared to argue that both positions— "never stay put" in expected utility theory and "stay put until plunging becomes justified" in the dual theory— are extreme. Real investment behavior probably lies somewhere in between.

The dual theory, because of its linearity property, tends to produce corner solutions in optimization problems. This is why we get plunging behavior in the foregoing liquidity preference problem. However, it is easy to think of more complex portfolio problems, where diversification and corner solutions can coexist. Let us consider, for example, a three asset portfolio selection problem, with a safe asset (cash) earning no return and two risky securities whose rates of return are independent, identically distributed random variables. Under the dual theory, a risk averse investor facing this situation will either hold his/her assets in cash or in a diversified portfolio consisting of the two risky securities in equal amounts. Letting θ be the random variable describing the rate of return on this mixed asset and letting x be the amount invested in it, we find that Proposition 4 is applicable as it stands for the analysis of the investor's decision in this situation. An analysis of the general portfolio selection problem, in a dual theory setting, appears in Röell (1985).

We come now to the question of comparative statics. I shall claim that, despite the awkwardness brought about by corner solutions, the dual theory possesses desirable comparative statics properties. The framework, once again, will be that of the basic, two asset, liquidity preference problem. Recall that, under the dual theory, optimal behavior in this setting is determined by the constant c, given in (15). Plunging is optimal if $c > 0$, and holding back is optimal if $c < 0$. The constant c, therefore, acts like a measure of the agent's propensity to invest (i.e., to plunge), with environmental changes that reduce c tending to inhibit plunging and environmental changes that raise c tending to encourage plunging. Thus, it would be of interest to see how changes in various parameters affect this constant. Looking at equation (15), we note that c depends, on the one hand, on the function f representing the preference relation $\succsim$ and, on the other hand, on the DDF G, describing the rate of return on the risky security. To study the effect of a change in f, consider two functions, f_1 and f_2, representing two preference relations, $\succsim_1$ and $\succsim_2$, respectively. Intuitively, if $\succsim_1$ is more risk averse than $\succsim_2$, then f_1 will lie uniformly below f_2. (For a more rigorous discussion, see Yaari (1986).) Thus, if $\succsim_1$ is more risk averse than $\succsim_2$, then the corresponding respective values of c in (15), call them c_1 and c_2, will satisfy $c_1 \leq c_2$: Increased risk aversion inhibits plunging, and, as we might expect, the more risk averse the population the fewer the plungers.

Also of interest is the effect of a change in the distribution of returns on optimal behavior. In particular, one would like to know what the effect would be of an increase in the *riskiness* of the rate of return on the constant c. Consider two random variables, θ_1 and θ_2, taking values in the interval $[-1, a]$ and satisfying $E\theta_1 = E\theta_2 > 0$. Suppose that θ_1 is riskier than θ_2 (i.e., $\theta_1 = \theta_2 + \text{noise}$) and let c_1

and c_2 be the values of the constant c in (15), for $\theta = \theta_1$ and $\theta = \theta_2$, respectively. Assume that the investor is risk averse. Then, it is easy to see that the inequality $c_1 \leq c_2$ must hold. (This can be seen either directly in (15), or by looking at the equation $c = (\Psi(K) - K)/K$ and noting that $\Psi(K)$ is the utility which is assigned, under the dual theory, to the random variable $(1 + \theta)K$. For a risk averse agent, this utility decreases as riskiness increases.) Thus, we find that increased riskiness inhibits plunging, when investors are risk averse. With risk averse investors, the more risky the rate of return, the fewer the plungers. Compare this observation with the corresponding result in expected utility theory: Under expected utility, a risk averse investor may actually *increase* his/her security holding, in response to a rise in the riskiness of the security. Increased riskiness only inhibits investment under suitable assumptions on the *third* derivative of the utility function, assumptions that govern the relationship between the degree of risk aversion and the level of wealth. Under the dual theory, the only property needed is risk aversion itself.

Comparative statics without third derivative conditions is a general feature of the dual theory. This feature comes into its own in the multivariate version of the theory, where corner solutions no longer prevail. (See Yaari (1986) for details.)

7. MACHINA, QUIGGIN, SCHMEIDLER

The dual theory of choice under risk needs to be viewed in the light of other non-expected-utility theories that have been proposed recently. For want of space, I shall restrict my attention to three prominent and representative contributions, namely those of Mark Machina, John Quiggin, and David Schmeidler. I wish to emphasize that restricting myself in this way should by no means be construed as belittling the various other contributions to non-expected-utility theory that have appeared recently. I apologize also for imposing my own notation upon the work that I am about to cite.

In a paper well on its way to becoming a milestone, Machina (1982) studies preference among random variables in a spirit not unlike that of Section 2, above. In particular, conditions closely resembling Axioms A1–A4 are imposed. Like expected utility theory and the dual theory, Machina also needs a fifth axiom, but he rejects independence, whether "primal" or "dual". Instead, Machina's fifth condition is one that ensures existence of a Frechet-differentiable functional, call it "the Machina functional" and let it be denoted M, such that $u \succsim v \Leftrightarrow M(G_u) \geq M(G_v)$ holds for all random variables u and v, with respective DDF's G_u and G_v. Machina's fifth axiom is not stated directly on the preference relation and, to the best of my knowledge, a general axiom on preferences guaranteeing the existence of a suitable Machina functional has not yet been discovered. (However, see Allen (1986).) Of course, Axiom A5EU will do it, because of the linearity of M under expected utility. Axiom A5, on the other hand, fails to produce a suitable Machina functional. An example of this is easily obtained, by taking the function f that represents preferences under the dual theory to be nondifferentiable. Recently, Chew, Karni, and Safra (1985) have shown, in fact, that even when f is differentiable, the functional M given by $M(G) = \int f(G(t))\,dt$ need not be Frechet differentiable. Strictly speaking, the dual theory falls outside Machina's framework. However, there does exist an extension of Machina's work, in which Frechet differentiability is replaced by the weaker Gateaux differentiability. (See Chew, Karni, and Safra, op. cit.) The dual theory does fall into this extended Machina framework, in those cases where the function f representing preferences happens to be differentiable. Indeed, the extended Machina framework can be used to prove a special case of our Theorem 2, namely that if preferences satisfy A1–A5 and the resulting function f is differentiable, then risk aversion is equivalent to f being convex. The main difference between Machina's work and the work being presented here is, in my opinion, a difference of *intent*. Machina's aim is to construct a general tool for analyzing *all* non-expected-utility theories. The aim of the dual theory, on the other hand, is to concentrate on a specific alternative.

Now let me try, as best I can, briefly to summarize Quiggin's proposal (Quiggin (1982)) in a way that will facilitate comparison with the dual theory. The basic approach is perceptional: Probabilities are liable to be adjusted (or distorted) in the decision maker's perception, before becoming an input in the decision process. We could think of a real function h such that, if p is a probability, then $h(p)$ stands for how p is perceived. A modified expected utility theory can now be constructed using what the agent perceives when facing a random variable. Specifically, if the agent faces a random variable taking the values $x_1, \ldots, x_n$ with probabilities $p_1, \ldots, p_n$, respectively, then, under such a modified theory, the utility number assigned to the random variable would be of the form $\sum h(p_i)\phi(x_i)$, with ϕ being a von Neumann–Morgernstern utility. Quiggin looks at this representation and notes, as several others have, that under continuity and mononicity (Axioms A3 and A4) the function h in the foregoing representation must coincide with the identity. He therefore offers the following more general representation: The utility number to be assigned to a random variable taking the values $x_1, \ldots, x_n$ with probabilities $p_1, \ldots, p_n$, respectively, shall be of the form $\sum h_i(p_1, \ldots, p_n)\phi(x_i)$, where $h = (h_1, \ldots, h_n)$ is now an n-component vector function, defined on the $(n-1)$-dimensional unit simplex. (Such a vector function is required to exist for every positive integer n.) The decision weight being applied to the ith value of the random variable now depends not only on p_i but on the entire vector $(p_1, \ldots, p_n)$. Quiggin now finds that, in order for this new representation to be consistent with A3 and A4, there must exist a real function f, defined on the unit interval, such that

$$h_i(p_1, \ldots, p_n) = f\left(\sum_{j=i}^{n} p_j\right) - f\left(\sum_{j=i+1}^{n} p_j\right).$$

He is therefore led to seek axioms which imply that preferences can be represented by a utility of the form

$$(16) \qquad Q(x_1, \ldots, x_n, p_1, \ldots, p_n) = \sum_{i=1}^{n} \phi(x_i)\left[f\left(\sum_{j=i}^{n} p_j\right) - f\left(\sum_{j=i+1}^{n} p_j\right)\right],$$

and he finds that a suitably weakened version of A5EU, together with suitable versions of A2, A3, and A4 will do the trick. (The neutrality axiom, A1, whose appropriateness in a theory of risk perception is questionable, is assumed implicitly.) Rewriting (16) for any random variable v belonging to V, we find preferences being represented by a utility Q of the form

$$(17) \qquad Q(v) = \int_0^1 \phi(t) \, d(f \circ G_v)(t) = \int_0^1 f(G_v(t)) \, d\phi(t),$$

where G_v is the DDF of v and ϕ is a von Neumann–Morgenstern utility. Now, when ϕ is the identity, (17) reduces to (9) and when f is the identity, (17) reduces to (10). Quiggin's representation theorem generalizes the representation theorems of both expected utility theory and the dual theory.

Since Quiggin's approach is perceptional, there is an empirical observation that he can use. This is the observation, often noted by students of risk perception, that a 50–50 proposition is in fact perceived by decision makers as a 50–50 proposition. The implication of this, under Quiggin's theory, is that, when facing 50–50 propositions, agents always act like expected utility maximizers, and this property is relied upon heavily in Quiggin's arguments. It follows, however, from this property that the function f in (17) must satisfy $f(\tfrac{1}{2}) = \tfrac{1}{2}$. This fact, in conjunction with the recent work of Chew, Karni, and Safra (1985), implies that all risk averse agents in Quiggin's framework must be expected utility maximizers, because the only convex f satisfying $f(0) = 0$, $f(\tfrac{1}{2}) = \tfrac{1}{2}$, and $f(1) = 1$ is the identity. (Perhaps I should mention also that Quiggin's representation theorem is incorrect as it stands. Utility representations of the form $\sum x_i w(p_i)$, with w continuous and satisfying $w(p) + w(1 - p) \leqslant 1$ for all p, satisfy Quiggin's axioms but they do not agree with (17), unless $w(p) = p$. To fix things up, Quiggin's Dominance Axiom must certainly be modified, and possibly also his Independence Axiom.)

It is interesting to note that the dual theory can serve as a building block in an alternative axiomatization of (17). The idea is related to a recent paper by Shubik (1985). Suppose that an agent who faces a random variable v, belonging to V, acts in the following way: First, the agent considers the payment levels $v(s)$, for all states-of-nature s. Each payment level, $v(s)$, is processed by the agent into a utility level, $\phi(v(s))$, where ϕ is a cardinal utility generated from some *riskless* intensity-of-preference framework. (See, e.g., Shapley (1975).) Now the agent faces the random variable $\phi(v)$ which belongs to V, under a suitable normalization of a bounded ϕ. The axioms of the dual theory (i.e., Axioms A1–A5 above) may now be postulated for preferences among these utility-valued random variables. The result is a theory in which preferences among the original, money-valued, random variables are represented by a utility of the form $U(\phi \circ v)$, where U is defined in (9). But now we find that $U(\phi \circ v) = \int f(G_v(t)) \, d\phi(t)$ for some appropriate real function f, so (17) is obtained as a utility representation for preferences among the money-valued random variables.

Finally, an interesting relationship between utility representations of the form (17) and the notion of comonotonicity (see Section 3) can be seen in a recent paper by Schmeidler (1984). Schmeidler's concern is to show that preference

114 MENAHEM E. YAARI

among *acts* (not among random variables) can be represented, under suitable assumptions, by an expected utility, in which expectation is taken with respect to some *nonadditive* measure. (An act is a measurable real function on some measurable space without a probability.) Following Anscombe and Aumann (1963), Schmeidler assumes that agents can always toss coins, if they wish, thereby obtaining "objective" probability mixtures of acts. What Anscombe and Aumann had done was to write down an independence axiom for such mixtures which, together with other suitable axioms, implies that preference among acts has an expected utility representation. Schmeidler's idea is to require this kind of independence only for pairwise comonotonic acts. From this, together with other standard axioms, he obtains the result that there exists a von Neumann-Morgenstern utility ϕ and a nonadditive measure μ such that $u \succsim v \Leftrightarrow \int \phi(u) \, d\mu \geq \int \phi(v) \, d\mu$ holds for every pair of acts, u and v. (This result has recently been extended by Gilboa (1985) to the case where uncertainty is totally subjective; i.e., "objectively" mixed acts are not necessarily available.) Now let us return to (17) and recall that the preference relation being treated there is over *random variables*, with some underlying probability measure, P. Defining a nonadditive measure μ by $\mu = f \circ P$, we find preferences being represented precisely by Schmeidler's utility, $\int \phi(v) \, d\mu$. Note that Schmeidler's independence axiom deals with *probability* mixtures of comonotonic functions, whereas the independence axiom of the dual theory (Axiom A5*) deals with pointwise mixtures of the *values* of comonotonic functions.

Institute for Advanced Studies, Hebrew University, Givat Ram, Jerusalem, Israel

Manuscript received March, 1985; revision received May, 1986.

REFERENCES

ALLAIS, M. (1953): "Le Comportement de l'Homme Rationnel devant le Risque," *Econometrica*, 21, 503-546.
ALLEN, B. (1986): "Smooth Preferences and the Local Expected Utility Hypothesis," *Journal of Economic Theory*, forthcoming.
ANSCOMBE, F. J., AND R. J. AUMANN (1963): "A Definition of Subjective Probability," *Annals of Mathematical Statistics*, 34, 199-205.
ATKINSON, A. B. (1970): "On the Measurement of Inequality," *Journal of Economic Theory*, 2, 244-263.
BLACKWELL, D. (1950): "Comparison of Experiments," *Proceedings of the 2nd Berkeley Symposium on Mathematical Statistics*. Berkeley: University of California Press, 93-102.
CHEW, S. H., E. KARNI, AND Z. SAFRA (1985): "Risk Aversion in the Theory of Expected Utility with Rank Dependent Probabilities," Working Paper No. 16-85, Foerder Institute, Tel-Aviv University.
DORFMAN, R. (1979): "A Formula for the Gini Coefficient," *Review of Economics and Statistics*, 61, 146-149.
FISHBURN, P. C. (1982): *The Foundations of Expected Utility*. Dordrecht: Reidel Publishing Co.
GILBOA, I. (1985): "Expected Utility with Purely Subjective Non-Additive Probabilities," Working Paper No. 6-85, Foerder Institute, Tel-Aviv University.
HARDY, G. H., J. E. LITTLEWOOD, AND G. POLYA (1929): "Some Simple Inequalities Satisfied by Convex Functions," *Messenger of Mathematics*, 58, 145-152.
HERSTEIN, I. N., AND J. MILNOR (1953): "An Axiomatic Approach to Measurable Utility," *Econometrica*, 21, 291-297.

KAHNEMAN, D., AND A. TVERSKY (1979): "Prospect Theory: An Analysis of Decision under Risk," *Econometrica*, 47, 263–291.

MACHINA, M. J. (1982): "Expected Utility Analysis without the Independence Axiom," *Econometrica*, 50, 277–323.

NEWBERY, D. (1979): "A Theorem on the Measurement of Inequality," *Journal of Economic Theory*, 2, 264–266.

QUIGGIN, J. (1982): "A Theory of Anticipated Utility," *Journal of Economic Behavior and Organization*, 3, 225–243.

RÖELL, A. (1985): "Risk Aversion in Yaari's Rank-Order Model of Choice under Uncertainty," mimeo., London School of Economics.

ROTHSCHILD, M., AND J. E. STIGLITZ (1970): "Increasing Risk: A Definition," *Journal of Economic Theory*, 2, 225–243.

SCHMEIDLER, D. (1984): "Subjective Probability and Expected Utility without Additivity," IMA Preprint Series, University of Minnesota.

SHAPLEY, L. S. (1975): "Cardinal Utility from Intensity Comparisons," RAND Publication R-1683-PR.

SHUBIK, M. (1985): "A Note on Cardinal Utility with Probability Mixtures and Intensity Comparisons," Cowles Foundation Preliminary Paper No. 850423, Yale University.

TOBIN, J. (1958): "Liquidity Preference as Behavior Toward Risk," *Review of Economic Studies*, 25, 65–86.

YAARI, M. E. (1969): "Some Remarks on Measures of Risk Aversion and on Their Uses," *Journal of Economic Theory*, 1, 315–329.

———— (1986): "Univariate and Multivariate Comparisons of Risk Aversion: A New Approach," forthcoming in *Essays in Honor of Kenneth J. Arrow*, ed. by W. P. Heller, R. Starr, and D. Starrett. Cambridge: Cambridge University Press.

[16]

JOURNAL OF ECONOMIC THEORY **49**, 207–240 (1989)

A Unifying Approach to
Axiomatic Non-expected Utility Theories*

S. H. CHEW

*Department of Political Economy, Johns Hopkins University,
Baltimore, Maryland 21218*

AND

L. G. EPSTEIN

*Department of Economics, University of Toronto,
Toronto, Ontario, Canada M5S 1A1*

Received July 1, 1987; revised December 9, 1988

This paper unifies the two principal thrusts in the literature on axiomatic theories of transitive preferences which generalize expected utility theory; namely, the betweenness conforming theories and the rank-dependent theories. The unification is achieved in two respects. First, new axiomatizations are provided for the existing theories based on separability restrictions in outcome space. These axiomatizations bring into clear focus both the similarities and the differences between the existing theories. Second, an axiomatization is provided for a new class of preferences which includes existing classes as special cases. *Journal of Economic Literature* Classification Numbers: 022, 026. © 1989 Academic Press, Inc.

1. INTRODUCTION

There is a recent and growing literature on preferences beyond the received expected utility theory. The bulk of these works maintain a continuity requirement. In addition to continuity, one may impose a smoothness requirement to examine whether "expected utility analysis" may be applicable in a "local" sense (Machina [21]). Another direction is to specifically weaken certain properties of expected utility to axiomatically characterize more general preference functionals.

If transitivity is maintained, then there are two discernible approaches within the axiomatic direction.[1] One maintains the betweenness property —a probability mixture of two lotteries is intermediate in preference

---

* This research was supported by NSF Grant SES 8607232. We are also indebted to Mark Machina, Uzi Segal, Peter Wakker, and a referee for numerous suggestions and comments.
[1] For examples of axiomatic nontransitive theories, see Fishburn [14].

between the individual lotteries—of expected utility. Recent works in this approach include Chew and MacCrimmon [7], Chew [3, 4], Fishburn [15], Nakamura [22], and Dekel [12]. We refer to these theories as *implicit linear utility* (ILU) theories.

The other may be labeled the rank-dependent or rank-linear utility (RLU) approach. It is distinguished by the rank ordering of outcomes prior to the applying of the representation. Rank-linear theories have been proposed by Quiggin [23], Yaari [26], Segal [25], Chew [5], and Green and Jullien [18]. There is no intersection between the two approaches other than expected utility theory.

Our paper is concerned with the unification of the two approaches. This is accomplished in two respects. First, new axiomatizations are provided for the ILU and RLU theories. The axiomatizations are based principally on separability restrictions in outcome space and on (a variation of) a well known result from demand theory regarding additive utilities [10] and [17].[2] Both ILU and RLU satisfy separability conditions, but on different domains. Thus both the similarities and the differences between the two theories are put into clear focus. In contrast, such a focus is not provided by the existing disparate axiomatizations.

A second contribution of the paper is the axiomatization of a class of continuous preferences called implicit rank-linear utility (IRLU). Since this class includes both ILU and RLU as special cases, it provides a unifying framework for these existing theories. (See Fig. 3, which will be explained further below.) Moreover, IRLU contains several interesting new classes of preferences which are discussed in varying degrees of detail below.

It is worth emphasizing the "practical" importance of the generality of IRLU. As things stand now, a modeler who wishes to specify a transitive non-expected utility preference ordering (possibly to explain behavioral paradoxes or for some other reason) must choose between the two alternatives of ILU and RLU. Even if he finds some appeal in the axiomatic bases for each, the modeller must make the discrete choice between the two. On the other hand, the IRLU class retains elements of both theories. Thus it provides opportunities for adoption of "intermediate" specifications.

In Section 2, we present some notation, a representation theorem for a continuous utility function on probability distributions, and several examples of non-expected utility theories which have appeared in the literature. Section 3 presents some new utility functionals and corresponding separability axioms. Section 4 presents and discusses the main representation theorem as well as further results on uniqueness and risk aversion. Some new specializations of the implicit rank-linear utility representation are provided in Section 5. Concluding remarks are offered in Section 6.

---

[2] For a corresponding axiomatization of expected utility theory, see [2].

2. PRELIMINARIES

We adopt the following notation. X is an interval in $\mathbb{R}$. $D(X) = \{F, G, H, ...\}$ denotes the space of c.d.f.'s on X, endowed with the weak convergence topology. A distribution function that is concentrated at a single point $s \in X$ is denoted by δ_s, where

$$\delta_s(t) = \begin{cases} 1 & t \geq s \\ 0 & t < s. \end{cases} \tag{2.1}$$

We denote by $D^0(X)$ the set of c.d.f.'s having finite supports. Elements of $D^0(X)$ can be written as

$$F \equiv \sum_{i=1}^{n} p_i \delta_{x_i}, \quad (p_i > 0), \tag{2.2}$$

where $\text{supp}(F) = \{x_1, ..., x_n\}$.

The following axioms apply to a binary relation $\preccurlyeq$ on $D(X)$.

Axiom O (Ordering). $\preccurlyeq$ is complete and transitive.

Axiom C (Continuity). $\forall F \in D(X)$, $\{G \in D(X): G \preccurlyeq F\}$ and $\{G \in D(X): F \preccurlyeq G\}$ are closed.

The existence of a numerical representation for $\preccurlyeq$ follows from Debreu [11].

THEOREM 1. *There is a continuous utility function* $V: D(X) \to \mathbb{R}$ *iff* $\preccurlyeq$ *satisfies Axioms* O *and* C.

Axiom M (Monotonicity). $\forall H \in D(X)$, $p \in (0, 1]$ and $s, t \in X, s < t$ implies

$$p\delta_s + (1 - p) H \prec p\delta_t + (1 - p) H.$$

It is known that, on $D^0(X)$, Axiom M is equivalent to monotonicity in the sense of first order stochastic dominance. Therefore, any continuous utility V on $D(X)$ satisfying Axiom M is monotone in the sense of first order stochastic dominance on $D(X)$. In particular, $V(\sum_{i=1}^{N} (1/N) \delta_{x_i})$ is continuous and increasing on X^N. (Note that "monotonicity" and "increasingness" are intended in the strict sense.)

The bulk of the literature in the economics of uncertainty restricts the utility function V further and requires that it have the form

$$V\left(\sum_{i=1}^{N} p_i \delta_{x_i} \right) = \sum_{i=1}^{N} p_i v(x_i) \tag{2.3}$$

for some v that is increasing and continuous on X. (For the remainder of this section, we restrict ourselves to simple c.d.f.'s. The formulations for

general c.d.f.'s are defined in the natural fashion and will appear below.)
Such *expected utility* (EU) or *linear utility* (LU) functionals imply parallel
and linear indifference curves in the probability simplex corresponding to
gambles with three possible outcomes (Fig. 1). It is convenient to work
throughout with the certainty equivalent functional $m(\cdot)$, defined by
$V(\delta_m) = V(F)$, that is ordinally equivalent to $V(\cdot)$. Thus (2.3) takes the
form

$$v\left(m\left(\sum_{i=1}^{n} p_i \delta_{x_i} \right) \right) = \sum_{i=1}^{n} p_i v(x_i). \tag{2.4}$$

A more general specification, called *weighted utility* (WU), has the form
(Chew [3])

$$v\left(m\left(\sum_{i=1}^{n} p_i \delta_{x_i} \right) \right) = \sum_{i=1}^{n} p_i w(x_i) v(x_i) \Big/ \sum_{i=1}^{n} p_i w(x_i), \tag{2.5}$$

where on X, w is positive valued and v is increasing and both are continuous. Its indifference curves in the simplex are also linear but they are
all rays projected from a point O on the extension of the indifference ray
through the intermediate outcome. If $w \equiv$ constant, EU is obtained and the
projection point O is at infinity.

Finally, in order to provide further perspective for the analysis to follow,
we define *rank-dependent expected utility* (RDEU), which takes the form

$$v\left(m\left(\sum_{i=1}^{n} p_i \delta_{x_i} \right) \right) = \sum_{i=1}^{n} v(x_i) \left[g\left(\sum_{j=1}^{i} p_j \right) - g\left(\sum_{j=1}^{i-1} p_j \right) \right], \tag{2.6}$$

where the outcomes have been arranged so that $x_1 \leqslant \cdots \leqslant x_n$, v is increasing and continuous on X, and $g: [0, 1] \to [0, 1]$ is increasing, continuous,
and onto. (See Quiggin [23], Yaari [26], Segal [25], and Chew [5].)
When $g(p) \equiv p$, EU is obtained. In general, however, m (or V) can be
viewed as an expected utility function only with respect to the c.d.f. $g(F)$
derived from F via the transformation function g. The consequences of the
latter for indifference curves in the simplex are demonstrated in Fig. 1. The
curves are generally nonlinear but they retain a form of parallelism—the
tangents of the indifference curves along the $x - \bar{x}$ edge are parallel.

The unifying perspective for these and other utility functionals which we
propose in this paper is via separability properties in the space of state-
contingent outcomes. The EU functional (2.4) has the well-known strong
or additive separability structure. The WU and RDEU functionals also
involve summation in fundamental ways which suggests that their essential
nature may, at least in part, correspond to appropriate separability properties. We will identify the latter in the next section where some more general
classes of functionals will be introduced.

AXIOMATIC NON-EXPECTED UTILITY   211

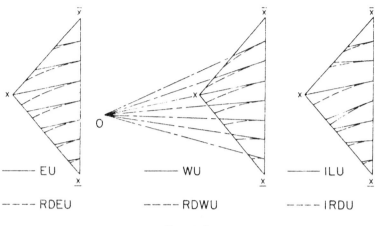

FIGURE 1.

3. UTILITY FUNCTIONALS AND SEPARABILITY AXIOMS

Three classes of utility functionals and their corresponding separability axioms are described here. In each case, the utility functional V as well as the corresponding certainty equivalent functional m is continuous and monotone. Functional forms are specified first for simple distributions. The formulations for general c.d.f.'s are given at the end of the section.

We refer to m as an *implicit linear utility* (ILU) certainty equivalent if $\exists \tau: X \times X \to \mathbb{R}$ with $\tau(\cdot, y)$ continuous and increasing $\forall y \in X$ and $\tau(x, x) \equiv 0$ such that $m(F)$ is given by the unique implicit solution y to

$$\sum_{i=1}^{n} p_i \tau(x_i, y) = 0. \tag{3.1}$$

(See Dekel [12], for example.) If $\tau(x, y) = w(x)[r(x) - v(y)]$, then (3.1) admits an explicit solution $y = m(F)$ which coincides with weighted utility (2.6).[3] ILU implies straight line indifference curves within the simplex (Fig. 1) which need not all emanate from a single point as in WU.

In order to formulate the separability axiom corresponding to ILU we need some further notation. For any partition $I_N^s \cup I_N^r$ of $I_N = \{1, ..., N\}$, let $X^N = X^{(s)} \times X^{(r)}$ be the corresponding decomposition of X^N. Let $k = \|I_N^s\|$ and $N - k = \|I_N^r\|$. Let $T = (T^1, ..., T^N)$, where T^k is a correspondence from X^N into X^k. All separability axioms in the paper have the form:

---

[3] Fishburn [16] axiomatized a different subclass of ILU for which τ is skew-symmetric.

212   CHEW AND EPSTEIN

Axiom TS (*T*-Separability).   For all $x = (x_1, ..., x_N) \in X^N$ and all decompositions $X^{(c)} \times X^{(r)}$ of X^N,

$$\sum_{i=1}^{N} \left(\frac{1}{N}\right) \delta_{x_i} \sim \frac{k}{N} \delta_{c^*} + \sum_{i \in I'} \left(\frac{1}{N}\right) \delta_{x_i}$$

$$\Rightarrow \sum_{i \in I^c} \left(\frac{1}{N}\right) \delta_{x_i} + \sum_{i \in I'} \left(\frac{1}{N}\right) \delta_{y_i} \sim \frac{k}{N} \delta_{c^*} + \sum_{i \in I'} \left(\frac{1}{N}\right) \delta_{y_i}, \qquad \forall y' \in T^k(x).$$

The interpretation of the axioms is as follows: The quantity c^* is a *certainty equivalent* for x^c, *contingent* on x^r. The above condition is met if c^* is invariant with respect to the change from x^r to any y^r in $T^k(x)$. Clearly, the specification of T determines the nature of the restriction imposed by the invariance requirement. Thus, we refer to the latter as *T-Separability*.

Some examples will help to clarify this notion. First, if each T^k is defined so that $T^k(x) = X^k$, then c^* is invariant with respect to any substitution of y^r for x^r that is consistent with the domain restriction that lottery outcomes lie in X. This yields the usual additive separability to which we refer simply as separability.

Axiom S (Separability).   *T*-Separatility where $T^k(x) \equiv X^k$.

Axiom S is satisfied by linear utility functionals. The more general utility functions considered in this paper satisfy weaker axioms. Thus, for example, for ILU the invariance of the contingent certainty equivalent c^* holds only if changes from x^r to y^r are required to preserve indifference as in the following axiom.

Axiom IS (Indifference Separability).   *T*-separability where

$$T^k(x) = \left\{ y' \in X^k : \sum_{i=1}^{N} \left(\frac{1}{N}\right) \delta_{x_i} \sim \sum_{i \in I^c} \left(\frac{1}{N}\right) \delta_{x_i} + \sum_{i \in I'} \left(\frac{1}{N}\right) \delta_{y_i} \right\}.$$

To see the motivation for the latter axiom and those that follow, consider the choices represented in Fig. 2. There are 100 equally likely states. The outcomes L, I, and H are in ascending order of preference. The contingent certainty equivalent $c_s^*(A)$ of A for states 1 to q, contingent on outcome s for states $q + 1$ to 100, is always I. Axiom M implies that the contingent certainty equivalent $c_s^*(B)$ lies between L and H. Savage's sure-thing principle (STP) or Axiom S requires that $c_s^*(B)$ be invariant to changes in s. However, the standard Allais paradox corresponds to $c_s^*(B) < I$ when $s = I$ and $c_s^*(B) > I$ when $s = L$. The original parameters

AXIOMATIC NON-EXPECTED UTILITY   213

		States		
		$1\cdots p$ $p+1$	$\cdots$	q $q+1\cdots 100$
Acts	A	I	I	s
	B	L	H	s

FIG. 2. The standard Allais parodox.

were $(L, I, H; p, q) = (0, 1$ million Fr, 5 million Fr; 1, 11$).^4$ Since comparisons of the state-contingent form in Fig. 2 do not involve timing or multiple stage considerations, the standard Allais paradox directly tests the invariance of $c_s^*(B)$ with respect to changes in s.

There have been several replications of the standard Allais paradox with different outcome and probability parameters (see, e.g., MacCrimmon and Larsson [20], Kahneman and Tversky [19], Chew and Waller [9]). The consistent finding from the empirical studies is that $c_s^*(B)$ is higher when $s = L$ than when $s = I$, thus violating the invariance implication of STP. This provides the motivation for our weakening of the STP by restricting the domain of invariance of c^*. The empirical evidence is however consistent with IS (and each of the weaker axioms specified below), since changing from $s = L$ to $s = I$ violates the indifference restriction in IS (and the corresponding rank restrictions in the other axioms).

The next class of utility functionals generalizes RDEU. Its representation is based on a function $\varphi: X \times [0, 1] \to \mathbb{R}$ which is continuous in each argument, $\varphi(\cdot, 0) \equiv 0$, and φ satisfies

$$\varphi(x, p) - \varphi(x, q) - \varphi(y, p) + \varphi(y, q) > 0, \qquad \forall x > y \text{ and } p > q. \quad (3.2)$$

(For example, in the differentiable case, (3.2) is equivalent to the positivity of the cross partial derivative φ_{12}.) The *rank-linear utility* (RLU) certainty equivalent m for $F \equiv \sum_{i=1}^n p_i \delta_{x_i}$ is given by the solution to

$$\varphi(m(F), 1) = \sum_{i=1}^n \left[\varphi\left(x_i, \sum_{j=1}^i p_j\right) - \varphi\left(x_i, \sum_{j=1}^{i-1} p_j\right) \right], \quad (3.3)$$

where the x_i's are arranged in ascending order. (See Segal [25] and Green and Jullien [18] for closely related functional forms.) Since $\varphi(\cdot, 1)$ is continuous and increasing, (3.3) provides an explicit representation. The LHS of (3.2) represents an increase in utility of (3.3) from $F \equiv (q - p)\delta_x + (1 - q + p)G$ to $F' \equiv (q - p)\delta_y + (1 - q + p)G$ where

---

[4] Our exposition of the Allais paradox is due to Savage [24, p. 103] who considered the validity of STP self-evident once alternatives are represented in terms of state-contingent outcome vectors.

$[x, y] \cap \operatorname{supp} G = \varnothing$. In this way, Condition (3.2) guarantees that the RLU certainty equivalent satisfies Axiom M on $D^0(X)$. The subclass RDEU corresponds to the case where φ has the multiplicatively separable form $\varphi(x, p) = v(x) g(p)$. The behavior of the indifference curves for RLU generalizes those of RDEU in that the parallelism noted earlier for the latter case is absent.

To formulate the separability requirement for RLU, we introduce the notation $X_\uparrow^N = \{x \in X^N : x_1 \leqslant \cdots \leqslant x_N\}$ and for any x, we denote by $x_\uparrow = (x_{[1]}, ..., x_{[N]})$ its increasing rearrangement. We say that x and $y \in X^N$ are *rank preserving* if $x_{[i]} \in [y_{[i-1]}, y_{[i+1]}]$ and $y_{[i]} \in [x_{[i-1]}, x_{[i+1]}]$ $\forall i$, where $x_0 = y_0 \equiv -\infty$ and $x_{N+1} = y_{N+1} \equiv \infty$. The next separability axiom, called rank separability, imposes the invariance of the contingent certainty equivalent only when the substitution of y' for x' does not change the rank ordering of the outcomes.[5]

Axiom RS (Rank Separability). *T*-separability where $\forall x \in X^N$, $\forall k$, $T^k(x) = \{y' \in X^k : x$ and (x^c, y') are rank-preserving$\}$.

This axiom is consistent with the evidence cited earlier regarding the Allais paradox since changing from $s = L$ to $s = I$ violates rank-preservation in RS.

The final class of utility functionals, called *implicit rank linear utility* (IRLU), generalizes all of the above. The functional form is based on a function $\psi: X \times [0, 1] \times X \to \mathbb{R}$ that is continuous in each of the first two arguments; $\forall (x, p, y) \in X \times [0, 1] \times X$, $\psi(x, 0, y) = \psi(y, p, y) = 0$; and $\psi(\cdot, \cdot, y)$ satisfies (3.2) $\forall y \in X$. For each $F \equiv \sum_{i=1}^n p_i \delta_{x_i}$, $m(F)$ is the unique solution y to

$$\sum_{i=1}^n \left[\psi\left(x_i, \sum_{j=1}^i p_j, y\right) - \psi\left(x_i, \sum_{j=1}^{i-1} p_j, y\right)\right] = 0, \qquad (3.4)$$

where $x_1 \leqslant \cdots \leqslant x_n$. ILU is the special case corresponding to

$$\psi(x, p, y) = p\tau(x, y), \qquad (3.5)$$

and RLU corresponds to

$$\psi(x, p, y) = \alpha(y)[\varphi(x, p) - \varphi(y, p)] \qquad (3.6)$$

for some $\alpha: X \to \mathbb{R}^+$. Indifference curves in the simplex for general IRLU have no discernible special properties.

The special structure of IRLU can be characterized by the following separability axiom which, naturally, weakens both IS and RS.

[5] In a income inequality context, Ebert [13] uses the same axiom to characterize the counterpart of RLU.

Axiom IRS (Indifference Rank-Separability). *T*-separability where $\forall k$
$\forall x \in X^N$, $T^k(x) = \{ y^r \in X^k : \sum_{i=1}^N (1/N)\, \delta_{x_i} \sim \sum_{i \in r} (1/N)\, \delta_{x_i} + \sum_{i \in r} (1/N)\, \delta_{y_i}$
and x and (x^c, y^r) are rank-preserving}.

Thus, IRS requires that contingent certainty equivalents be invariant only
when substitutions preserve both indifference and rank ordering.

These classes of utility functionals and their interrelationships are
represented in Fig. 3. The most general class is IRLU. Its representation is
based on the function ψ of the three variables x, p, and y. The specializations of this ψ indicated in the figure lead to the other classes listed above,
as well as to other theories which have appeared in the literature.

We now extend the definition of IRLU utility functionals from $D^0(X)$ to

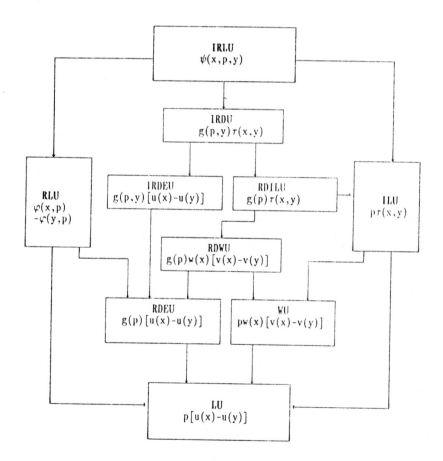

Fig. 3. Specializations of IRLU.

$D(X)$. For the ILU subclass, the extension is straightforward; simply replace (3.1) by

$$\int_X \tau(x, y)\, dF(x) = 0. \tag{3.1'}$$

That is, $m(F)$ is the unique solution y to the above equation. The LU representation is, of course,

$$v(m(F)) = \int_X v(x)\, dF(x). \tag{3.7}$$

The extension is more complicated in cases where there is sensitivity to rank. We require the following construction: For any function $\varphi: X \times [0, 1] \to \mathbb{R}$ which satisfies (3.2) and the conditions immediately preceding it, we define the *partial expectation* $E_2(\varphi, F)$ first on $D^0(X)$. Given a simple distribution $F \equiv \sum_{i=1}^N p_i \delta_{x_i}, x \in X_1^N$,

$$E_2(\varphi, F) \equiv \int_X d_2\varphi(x, F(x)) \equiv \sum_{i=1}^N [\varphi(x_i, h_i) - \varphi(x_i, h_{i-1})],$$

where

$$h_i = \sum_{j=1}^i p_j \qquad \text{for } i \geq 1 \text{ and } h_0 = 0.$$

Given a sequence $\{F_n\} \subset D^0(X)$ which converges weakly to F, we prove via Lemma A in Appendix 1 that $\mathrm{Lim}_{n \to \infty} E_2(\varphi, F_n)$ exists and is independent of the choice of the sequence. Thus, for $F \in D(X) \backslash D^0(X)$, we define $E_2(\varphi, F) = \mathrm{Lim}_{n \to \infty} E_2(\varphi, F_n)$ for any sequence $\{F_n\}$ in $D^0(X)$ which converges weakly to F. Condition (3.2) ensures that $E_2(\varphi, \cdot)$ is monotone on $D(X)$ in the sense of first degree stochastic dominance.

To define RLU, for any $F \in D(X)$, replace (3.3) by

$$\varphi(m(F), 1) = \int_X d_2\varphi(x, F(x)). \tag{3.3'}$$

If $\varphi(x, p) = v(x) g(p)$, then we obtain

$$v(m(F)) = \int_X v(x)\, dg(F(x)), \tag{2.6'}$$

which defines the general RDEU corresponding to (2.6).

Finally, for IRLU, if ψ is a function satisfying the conditions surrounding (3.4), then for each y, $E_2(\psi(\cdot, \cdot, y), F)$ is well defined. Thus we can define IRLU on $D(X)$ by requiring that $m(F)$ uniquely solve

$$\int_X d_2\psi(x, F(x), y) = 0. \tag{3.4'}$$

4. Representation Theorem

The relation between the separability axioms and the classes of utility functionals defined above is summarized in Theorem 2, which is the central result in this paper. The proof, found in Appendix 4, makes use of Theorem A in Appendix 3 dealing with the existence of additive utilities. Henceforth, with the exception of the end of this section, we assume that X is the compact interval $[\underline{x}, \bar{x}]$.

THEOREM 2. *Let X be a compact interval. A binary relation $\precsim$ on $D(X)$ satisfies Axioms O, C, M, and $\mathcal{B}$ iff it can be represented by a utility function satisfying $\mathcal{A}$, where*

$\mathcal{A}$	LU	ILU	RLU	IRLU
$\mathcal{B}$	S	IS	RS	IRS

The necessity of the axioms given the appropriate functional forms is readily verified using the definitions of the latter on the set of simple distributions. But their sufficiency is nontrivial and is the principal contribution of the theorem.

The theorem falls short of a complete description of the implications of the stated axioms in that we have not spelled out conditions for ψ that correspond to the continuity and monotonicity of $\succsim$ Similarly, the definition of IRLU asserts that $m(F)$ is uniquely defined by the solution to (3.4) or (3.4'); but we have not provided an explicit condition on ψ which is equivalent to uniqueness. (These deficiencies apply only to the ILU and IRLU classes. For LU and RLU, $m(F)$ is explicitly defined as in (3.5) and (3.3') so that uniqueness holds trivially. The continuity and monotonicity of LU are well known. The continuity and monotonicity properties of RLU follow from the corresponding properties for $E_2(\varphi, \cdot)$ given the assumptions made for φ.)

But we do provide, in Appendix 2, two sets of simple conditions on ψ that are sufficient for the IRLU functional m to satisfy the desired continuity, monotonicity, and uniqueness of solution. They guarantee that $\int_X d_2\psi(x, F(x), y)$ is decreasing in y, which is the key to proving uniqueness and monotonicity. Both sets of conditions reduce in the ILU case to

$$\forall x \in X, \ \tau(x, \cdot) \text{ is continuous and decreasing.} \tag{4.1}$$

A class of IRLU functionals is described in Section 5. Another example is provided by taking

$$\psi(x, p, y) = p\tau(x, y) + g(p)[v(x) - v(y)], \tag{4.2}$$

where $g: [0, 1] \to [0, 1]$ is continuous, increasing, and onto, and where τ satisfies (4.1), $\tau(x, x) = 0$, $\tau(\cdot, y)$ continuous and increasing on X. (It is readily verified that ψ in (4.2) satisfies the conditions in Lemma B of Appendix 2.) Note that ψ is the sum of ψ_1 and ψ_2, where ψ_1 corresponds to an ILU functional and ψ_2 corresponds to an RLU functional, but the utility function corresponding to ψ does not belong to any of the subclasses of IRLU described in Fig. 4.

Given IRLU represented by ψ, it is clear, for any positive valued function α on X and $\hat{\psi}$ defined by

$$\hat{\psi}(x, p, y) = \alpha(y)\, \psi(x, p, y), \qquad\qquad (4.3)$$

that $\hat{\psi}$ represents the same ordering. In fact (4.3) defines the uniqueness class of ψ.

COROLLARY 1. *The functions ψ and $\hat{\psi}$ represent the same IRLU ordering if and only if there exists a positive valued function α on X such that* $\forall(x, p, y) \in X \times [0, 1] \times X$, $\hat{\psi}(x, p, y) \equiv \alpha(y)\, \psi(x, p, y)$.

Proof. See Appendix 4.

Since risk aversion is a basic hypothesis in uncertainty theory, we turn now to a characterization of risk aversion for IRLU in terms of ψ. A number of definitions of risk aversion have appeared in the literature. Machina [21] provided a Fréchet based characterization of the equivalence among the three definitions of risk aversion—mean-preserving-spread, conditional risk premium, and conditional asset demand—based on the concavity of the Fréchet derivative referred to as the local utility function. This result cannot be directly applied here because IRLU is not generally Fréchet differentiable (see Chew, Karni, and Safra [6] for a demonstration in terms of RDEU).

We apply the characterization of risk aversion for continuous utility functionals in Chew and Mao [8]. Given an elementary lottery $\sum_{i=1}^{N} (1/N)\,\delta_{x_i}$ and a continuous utility functional V, V is risk averse (as defined in Machina [21]) if and only if, for each N, $V(\sum_{i=1}^{N} (1/N)\,\delta_{x_i})$ is *Schur-concave* on X^N, i.e., for $(x_1,\ldots, x_N) \in X_1^N$,

$$V\left(\frac{1}{N}\delta_{x_k - \varepsilon} + \frac{1}{N}\delta_{x_{k+1}+\varepsilon} + \sum_{i \neq k, k+1} \frac{1}{N}\delta_{x_i}\right)$$

is nonincreasing in ε for values of ε that do not alter the ranks of $x_k - \varepsilon$ and $x_{k+1} + \varepsilon$.

The following is proved in Appendix 4.

THEOREM 3. *Given an* IRLU *preference* ψ, ψ *is risk averse if and only if* $\forall x, x', y \in X$, $p, p' \in [0, 1)$, *with* $x > x'$, $p > p'$,

$$\psi(x, p, y) - \psi(x, p', y) \text{ is concave in } x, \qquad (4.4)$$

and

$$\psi(x, p, y) - \psi(x', p, z) \text{ is concave in } p. \qquad (4.5)$$

Note that (4.4) and (4.5) can be equivalently stated as

$$\psi(x, p, y) - \psi(x, p', y) - \psi(x', p, y) + \psi(x', p', y) \qquad (4.6)$$

is concave in x and in p separately. Suppose ψ is differentiable in the first two arguments. Then the latter risk aversion condition is

$$\psi_{12}(\cdot, \cdot, y) \text{ is nonincreasing.} \qquad (4.7)$$

Recall that the monotonicity condition (3.2) when applied to ψ is equivalent to $\psi_{12} > 0$ a.e. The above conditions are the counterpart for IRLU of the familiar restrictions for LU theories that marginal utility is positive (for monotonicity) and nonincreasing (for risk aversion).

In the case of ILU, (4.6) specializes to the concavity of $\tau(\cdot, y)$. If we specialize further to LU, we obtain the familiar result that concavity of the von Neumann–Morgenstern utility index characterizes risk aversion. For RDEU, (4.6) is equivalent to the concavity of v and g, which is consistent with Yaari [26] and Chew, Karni, and Safra [6].

We devote the remainder of this section to the case when X is not restricted to being a compact interval. First we observe that the separability proof of Theorem 2 does not depend on the compactness of X. Consequently, the construction of ψ can be accomplished on a noncompact X and the resulting utility functional represents the preference ordering on $D^0(X)$. Consider the following continuity requirement.

Axiom CC (Compact Continuity). For every compact interval $K \subset X$, $\preccurlyeq$ is continuous on $D(K)$.

When X is unbounded, the above is weaker than the continuity defined by Axiom C. By adopting CC, we can immediately obtain the extension below of Theorem 2 to $D^c(X)$, the set of c.d.f.'s in $D(X)$ having compact supports.

COROLLARY 2. *Theorem 2 holds on* $D^c(X)$ *if Axiom C is replaced by Axiom CC.*

In this case, we may define the certainty equivalent of $F \in D(X) \backslash D^c(X)$ by

$$m(F) = \lim_{n \to \infty} m(F_{K_n}),$$

220   CHEW AND EPSTEIN

where $\{K_n\}$ is an arbitrary increasing sequence of compact intervals which converges to X. Of course, as in the case of risk neutrality, the domain of $m(\cdot)$ may not be all of $D(X)$. This means that the corresponding preference ordering is complete on $D^c(X)$ but not necessarily complete on $D(X)$.

5. RANK–DEPENDENT SPECIALIZATIONS

Theorem 2 provides axiomatizations for the classes of utility functionals contained in the larger boxes in Fig. 3. Some of the remaining boxes are considered here.

In Sections 2 and 3, we referred to rank-dependent expected utility (RDEU). Here, we consider an implicit form for RDEU, called *implicit rank-dependent utility* (IRDU), which has not appeared in the literature. The relation between IRLU and IRDU parallels that between RLU and RDEU. This parallel is clear from the point of view of functional representation since both specializations correspond to ψ's being multiplicatively separable in x and p. In other words, for IRLU,

$$\psi(x, p, y) \equiv g(p, y)\, \tau(x, y) \tag{5.1}$$

and for RLU,

$$\varphi(x, p) - \varphi(y, p) \equiv g(p)[u(x) - u(y)], \tag{5.2}$$

where $\forall y \in X,\ g(\cdot, y)\colon [0, 1] \to [0, 1]$ is continuous, increasing and onto. In the former case, the mean value functional $m(\cdot)$ satisfies

$$\int_X \tau(x, m(F))\, dg(F(x), m(F)) = 0, \tag{5.3}$$

while the latter case, of course, leads to (3.6).

For IRDU, the condition (4.6) for risk aversion specializes to

$$g(\cdot, y) \text{ and } \tau(\cdot, y) \text{ are both concave}, \qquad \forall z \in X. \tag{5.4}$$

This condition reduces easily to the risk aversion conditions for all other boxes in Fig. 3 with the exception of RLU.

In the case of IRDU, we can also obtain an appealing condition for the unique existence of the implicit solution to (3.4′). IRDU is given by the solution to

$$\int_X \tau(x, y)\, dg(F(x), y) = 0. \tag{5.5}$$

Suppose that τ satisfies (4.1) and

$$g(p, y) \leqslant g(p, y') \qquad \text{whenever } y < y'. \tag{5.6}$$

Then unique existence as well as continuity and monotonicity of the solution to (5.5) follows from Lemma C in Appendix 2.

When $\tau(x, y) = v(x) - v(y)$ (we label the corresponding utility functional as *implicit rank-dependent expected utility* (IRDEU)), the certainty equivalent functional m solves

$$v(m(F)) = \int_X v(x) \, dg(F(x), m(F)). \tag{5.7}$$

This functional generalizes RDEU by permitting the transformation function g to depend on the level of utility. Viewed in these terms, Condition (5.6) may be interpreted as the decision maker's displaying a greater degree of 'pessimism' in transforming the given probability distribution F by $g(\cdot, y)$ when comparing gambles to which he assigns higher levels of utility. This interpretation is compatible with the Allais type behavior discussed in Section 3 and also below.

The following is a simple class of g functions for IRDEU. Given continuous, increasing, and onto functions $a: [0, 1] \to [0, A]$ and $b: [0, 1] \to [0, B]$, define for $y \in [0, \infty)$

$$g(p, y) = [a(p) + yb(p)]/[A + yB].$$

It is clear that (5.6) is satisfied as long as $a(p)/A \leqslant b(p)/B$. As y increases from 0 to ∞, the probability transformation function changes from $a(\cdot)/A$ asymptotically towards $b(\cdot)/B$.

A different subclass of IRDU, which is in a sense polar to (5.7), is called *rank-dependent implicit linear utility* (RDILU). In it, the function τ, but not the transformation function g, may depend on the utility level. Thus $m(F)$ satisfies

$$\int_X \tau(x, m(F)) \, dg(F(x)) = 0. \tag{5.8}$$

If g is the identity function, ILU is obtained. Since WU is the only explicit theory within ILU, it is of interest to consider the weighted utility specialization of RDILU class given by $\tau(x, y) = w(x)[v(x) - v(y)]$ which yields an explicit theory that integrates elements of RDEU and ILU. We term this *rank-dependent weighted utility* (RDWU); $m(F)$ satisfies

$$v(m(F)) = \int_X v(x) w(x) \, dg(F(x)) \bigg/ \int_X w(x) \, dg(F(x)). \tag{5.9}$$

222   CHEW AND EPSTEIN

The behavior of the specializations of IRLU on a three-outcome probability simplex is presented in Fig. 1. The three outcomes $\underline{x}$, x, and $\bar{x}$ are arranged in ascending order of preference. We have already observed that the ILU specializations have straight indifference curves. The indifference curves for WU are projected from a point O on the indifference curve through x extended, and those of EU are parallel in alignment.

The rank-dependent specializations have nonstraight indifference curves except when they coincide with ILU. (We sketch the indifference curves corresponding to a risk averse agent.) We can identify a property which is shared by the ILU and IRLU theories. The tangents of the indifference curves along the $\underline{x} - \bar{x}$ edge behave exactly as their ILU counterparts. For IRDU, the only restriction is that these initial tangents do not intersect even though they are not themselves indifference curves. In general, IRLU does not satisfy such a restriction.

It is known that Allais type choice behavior corresponds to indifference curves in the simplex becoming steeper as one moves along a direction of increasing preference. (This is often called the "fanning" property.) In Fig. 1, the natural classes of preferences displaying this property consist of WU and RDWU depending on whether having straight indifference curves is desirable. While RDEU has been shown to be compatible with the Allais paradox, the parallelism of the initial tangents makes fanning a possibility only if g is concave, which is compatible with risk aversion.

The preceding discussion suggests that there is enough information based on the behavior on simplexes to characterize further specializations of IRLU. We do not pursue the possibility here. But we do provide an axiomatization, in a different vein, of the IRDU class. The axiom also serves to axiomatize RDEU in a parallel fashion, thus supporting the parallelism drawn at the beginning of this section.

Axiom MS (Multiplicative Separability). $\forall p, q, r, s \in (0, 1)$ and $m \in X$, $\exists \alpha \in (0, 1)$ such that $\forall F \in D(X)$, $x, x', y, y' \in J$, an open interval of X with $F(J) = 0$, $F (\inf J) = r$, $x < x'$, $y < y'$,

$$\delta_m \sim \frac{p}{2} \delta_x + \frac{p}{2} \delta_{x'} + (1-p) F \sim \frac{p}{2} \delta_y + \frac{p}{2} \delta_{y'} + (1-p) F,$$

and $\forall G \in D(X)$ with $G(J) = 0$, $G(\inf J) = s$, if

$$\delta_m \sim \alpha q \delta_x + (1 - \alpha) q \delta_{x'} + (1 - q) G,$$

then

$$\delta_m \sim \alpha q \delta_y + (1 - \alpha) q \delta_{y'} + (1 - q) G$$

THEOREM 4. *Under Theorem* 2, IRLU (RLU) *is of the form* (6.2) ((6.3)) *if and only if* $\prec$ *satisfies additionally Axiom* MS.

Proof. See Appendix 5.

6. CONCLUDING REMARKS

The major contribution of this paper is the unification it provides, as illustrated in Fig. 3, of a number of generalizations of expected utility. The paper suggests several promising directions for future research, First, we have introduced a number of new classes of utility functions whose properties and usefulness need to be explored further. For a number of specifications of IRLU, axiomatizations need to be provided. In a different vein, we may investigate the possibility of other generalizations of LU based on different variations of the separability axioms than those considered in this paper.

There is a well-known link between mean values and indices of income inequality via the notion of the representative income. For example, the special case of RDEU with $\psi(x, p, y) \equiv [1 - (1 - p)^2][x - y]$ corresponds to the Gini index, while Chew [3] applied WU to income inequality measurement. Our separability axioms have clear interpretations in this context. We intend to explore further the usefulness of IRLU and its various subclasses for inequality measurement.

APPENDIX 1: PARTIAL EXPECTATION ON $D(X)$

LEMMA 1. *Let* φ *be as in Section 3 and* $X = [\underline{x}, \bar{x}]$. *Suppose* $\{F_n\}$ *in* $D^0(X)$ *converges weakly to* $F \in D(X)$. *Then* $E_2(\varphi, F) = \text{Lim}_{n \to \infty} E_2(\varphi, F_n)$ *exists and is independent of the choice of* $\{F_n\}$. *Moreover,* $E_2(\varphi, \cdot)$ *is monotone in the sense of first-degree stochastic dominance if* φ *satisfies* (3.2).

Proof. Define a finite signed measure λ on the Borel sets of $X \times [0, 1]$ by $\lambda((y, x] \times (q, p]) = \varphi(x, p) - \varphi(x, q) + \varphi(y, p) - \varphi(y, q)$. Define $*F = \{(a, b) \in X \times [0, 1]: b \geq F(a)\}$. Observe that $E_2(\varphi, F) = \lambda(*F) + \varphi(x, 1)$ on $D^0(X)$. Consider a sequence $\{F_n\}$ in $D^0(X)$ which converges weakly (in distribution) to $F \in D(X) \backslash D^0(X)$. Let 1_A denote the indicator function for $A \subset X \times [0, 1]$. Then $\lambda(*F \backslash *F_n) = \int_{X \times [0, 1]}[1_{*F} - 1_{*F_n}] d\lambda \to 0$ since 1_{*F_n} converges to 1_{*F} a.e. with respect to λ and $1_{X \times [0, 1]}$ is integrable. We define $E_2(\varphi, F) = \text{Lim}_{n \to \infty} E_2(\varphi, F_n) = \lambda(*F) + \varphi(\underline{x}, 1)$. This limit is clearly not dependent on the choice of the convergent sequence. Thus, we have extended $E_2(\varphi, \cdot)$ continuously from $D^0(X)$ to $D(X)$.[6]

[6] The observation that RLU can be viewed as a measure on epigraphs of distribution functions is due to Segal [25].

224   CHEW AND EPSTEIN

If φ satisfies (3.2), then λ is a positive measure. Thus, monotonicity of $E_2(\varphi, \cdot)$ follows from the observation that $^*F \subset {}^*G$ if G dominates F in the first degree.   Q.E.D.

It is clear that Lemma A can be extended to an unbounded X by requiring $\varphi(\cdot, p)$ to be bounded for each $p \in [0, 1]$.

APPENDIX 2:   *Sufficient Conditions for* IRLU

We provide two lemmas which describe sufficient conditions for ψ to define an IRLU functional. The first lemma is applicable to Example (4.2). Numerous other such examples can be constructed, since if ψ_1 and ψ_2 each satisfies the conditions of Lemma B, then so does any positive linear combination. Lemma C is applicable to the IRDU class discussed in Section 5.

LEMMA B. ψ *defines an* IRLU *functional if*

(S1) $\psi: X \times [0, 1] \times X \rightarrow \mathbb{R}$ *is continuous in each of the first two arguments, and* $\forall$ $(x, p, y) \in X \times [0, 1] \times X$, $\psi(x, 0, y) = \psi(y, p, y) = 0$, *and* $\psi(\cdot, \cdot, y)$ *satisfies* (3.2);

(S2) $\forall x \in X$ *and* $p, q \in [0, 1], p > q$, $\psi(x, p, \cdot) - \psi(x, q, \cdot)$ *is continuous and decreasing.*

Proof.   Note that for $F \equiv \sum_{i=1}^{N} (1/N) \delta_{x_i}$ in $D^0(X)$, $\int_X d_2\psi(x, F(x), y)$ is given by

$$\sum_{i=1}^{N} \{\psi(x_i, h_i, y) - \psi(x_i, h_{i-1}, y)\}, \qquad (A.2.1)$$

where $h_i = \sum_{j=1}^{i} p_j$. Existence of a solution on $D^0(X)$ follows from the continuity of $\int_X d_2\psi(x, F(x), y)$ in y and its assuming opposite signs at the extreme points of the support of F. Uniqueness of the solution to (3.4) on $D^0(X)$ follows from the decreasingness in y of (A.2.1).

To prove monotonicity on $D^0(X)$, note that a small increase in x_i increases the ith term within the summation (A.2.1). In order to restore equality with 0, y has to be increased since each term in the summation is decreasing in y.

Now, consider distributions in $D(X)$. For $y \in X$, define as in Lemma A a finite measure $\lambda(\cdot, y)$ on Borel subsets of $X \times [0, 1]$ by using Expression (3.2) for $\psi(\cdot, \cdot, y)$. Denote $\mathscr{L}(y) = \{(a, b) \in X \times [0, 1]: a \leqslant y\}$. Observe from Lemma A that

$$\int_X d_2\psi(x, F, y) = \lambda(1_{*F}, y) - \lambda(1_{\mathscr{L}(y)}, y). \qquad (A.2.2)$$

call this the Chatterjee–Samuelson equilibrium and we use it to define equilibrium behavior whenever possible. There are, however, many other equilibria in a double auction in the absence of cheap talk (including the "no-trade" equilibrium above), only some of which satisfy the conditions that Chatterjee and Samuelson assumed. Leininger *et al.* [9] and Satterthwaite and Williams [14] explore some of these alternative equilibria, and we use one in our model when it is not possible to use the Chatterjee–Samuelson equilibrium.

In our game, as in every cheap-talk game, there is an uncommunicative (or "babbling") equilibrium: if cheap talk is taken to be meaningless, then parties are willing to randomize uninformatively over the possible messages. But there are also two more interesting equilibria in which cheap talk is meaningful. In one, serious bargaining takes place only if both parties claim to be "keen"; in the other, a single such claim suffices. In both of these equilibria, serious bargaining does not occur if neither party claims to be "keen".

In the first of these equilibria with meaningful cheap talk, the Chatterjee–Samuelson equilibrium reappears: everyone claims to be "keen" except those types who are sure not to trade.[3] In this equilibrium, cheap talk is credible, but does not affect the equilibrium outcome: the mapping from type-pairs to bids and probability of trade is the same as in the Chatterjee–Samuelson equilibrium, which has no cheap talk.

In the other equilibrium, however, cheap talk matters in an important way: low-value buyers and high-value sellers are willing to jeopardize continued negotiation so as to improve their bargaining position; those who have more at stake cannot afford this risk. We focus on this equilibrium because it involves second-stage bidding strategies that could not be equilibrium strategies in the absence of talk.

We analyze our equilibrium in the standard case in which v_s and v_b are independently and uniformly distributed on $[0, 1]$. We show in the Appendix that the following strategies for the cheap-talk stage are part of a perfect Bayesian equilibrium. Buyers above the critical type

$$y = \frac{22 + 12\sqrt{2}}{49} = 0.795$$

say "keen" while those below say "not keen." Sellers below $(1 - y)$ say "keen," while those above say "not keen."

If both parties say "not keen" then the negotiation effectively ends, as

---

[3] In the standard case in which v_b and v_s are independently and uniformly distributed on $[0, 1]$, all buyers with $v_b > \frac{1}{4}$ and all sellers with $v_s < \frac{3}{4}$ claim to be "keen." Strictly, the other types of buyers and sellers, who will not trade, may say anything. But if there are any costs of serious bargaining, then they must say "not keen."

Proof. We will prove that $\int_X d_2\psi(x, F(x), \cdot)$ decreases. The remaining arguments are similar to those in the preceding proof.

First, let $F \in D^0(X)$ and let $y < y'$. Then

$$\int_X d_2\psi(x, F(x), y) - \int_X d_2\psi(x, F(x), y')$$

$$= \sum_{i=1}^{N} [\psi(x_i, h_i, y)) - \psi(x_i, h_{i-1}, y) - \psi(x_i, h_i, y') + \psi(x_i, h_{i-1}, y')]$$

$$= \sum_{i=1}^{N} \{\psi(x_i, 1, y)[\bar{\psi}(x_i, h_i, y) - \bar{\psi}(x_i, h_{i-1}, y)]$$

$$\quad - \psi(x_i, 1, y')[\bar{\psi}(x_i, h_i, y') - \bar{\psi}(x_i, h_{i-1}, y')]\}$$

$$= I_1 + I_2, \tag{A.2.3}$$

where

$$I_1 = \sum_{i=1}^{N} [\psi(x_i, 1, y) - \psi(x_i, 1, y')][\bar{\psi}(x_i, h_i, y) - \bar{\psi}(x_i, h_{i-1}, y)]$$

and

$$I_2 = \sum_{i=1}^{N} \psi(x_i, 1, y') \cdot [\bar{\psi}(x_i, h_i, y) - \bar{\psi}(x_i, h_{i-1}, y)$$

$$\quad - \bar{\psi}(x_i, h_i, y') + \bar{\psi}(x_i, h_{i-1}, y')].$$

We know that $I_1 \geqslant 0$ by (S3) and (S5). By applying $\bar{\psi}(x, 1, z) \equiv 1$, $\bar{\psi}(x, 0, z) \equiv 0$, and summation by parts, we can rewrite

$$I_2 = \sum_{i=2}^{N} [\psi(x_{i-1}, 1, y') - \psi(x_i, 1, y')]$$

$$\quad \times [\bar{\psi}(x_{i-1}, h_{i-1}, y) - \bar{\psi}(x_{i-1}, h_{i-1}, y')].$$

Set $p = 1$ and $q = 0$ in (2.6) to deduce that $\psi(\cdot, 1, y')$ is increasing. Then $I_2 \geqslant 0$ by (S3). Moreover, $I_1 + I_2 > 0$.

For $F \in D(X)$, we can pass to the limit in the above argument and conclude that the difference in (A.2.3) is given by

$$\int_X d_2\theta(x, F(x)) + \int_X [\bar{\psi}(x, F(x), y') - \bar{\psi}(x, F(x), y)] \, d\psi(x, 1, y'),$$

where $\theta(x, p) \equiv \bar{\psi}(x, p, y)[\psi(x, 1, y) - \psi(x, 1, y')]$ and the second term is a Stieltjes integral with respect to $\psi(\cdot, 1, y')$. Since $\theta(x, \cdot)$ is nondecreasing,

AXIOMATIC NON-EXPECTED UTILITY 227

the first term is nonnegative. The second term is nonnegative by (S3) and the increasingness of $\psi(\cdot, 1, y')$. Moreover, the sum of the two terms is strictly positive by (S3). Q.E.D.

APPENDIX 3: ADDITIVE UTILITY ON A SUBSET OF X^N

The additive utility theorem of Debreu [10] and Gorman [17] is usually stated in the setting of a product of arc-connected topological spaces. Here, we establish a variant for Euclidian domains that are not Cartesian products. The terminology—complete strict separability—is adopted from Gorman. For each $i = 1, ..., N$, π_i denotes the ith coordinate projection map.

THEOREM A. *Let $\Omega \subset X^N$ ($N > 2$) have a nonempty and connected interior and let V be a continuous and increasing utility function on Ω. Suppose that for each $\bar{x} \in \Omega$, the corresponding indifference surface $\{x \in \Omega: V(x) = V(\bar{x})\}$ is connected. Then V is completely strictly separable if and only if there exist continuous, increasing functions*

$$u^i: \pi_i(\Omega) \to \mathbb{R}$$

and an increasing function

$$\zeta: \sum_{i=1}^{N} \text{Rng}(u^i) \to \mathbb{R}$$

such that

$$V(x) = \zeta\left(\sum_{i=1}^{N} u^i(x_i) \right).$$

Proof. Necessity is obvious. We observe that the validity of the theorem for the case when $\Omega = \prod_{i=1}^{N} J_i$ is an interval in X) is well known. Therefore, for an open rectangle $O = \prod_{i=1}^{N} (a_i, b_i) \subset \Omega$, there are

$$u^i(\cdot, O): (a_i, b_i) \to \mathbb{R}$$

such that $V(\cdot, 0) = \sum_{i=1}^{N} u^i(\cdot, O)$ is a utility function on O.

Suppose $O \cap O' \neq \phi$, where O' is another open rectangle in Ω. We can extend $V(\cdot, O)$ to $O \cup O'$ by selecting those $u^i(\cdot, O')$'s such that $u^i(\cdot O) \equiv u^i(\cdot, O')$ on $O \cap O'$. This can be done because the u^i's are unique up to similar affine transformations (i.e., u^i's and $\hat{u}^i$'s are equivalent if there are $c > 0$ and d_i's such that $\hat{u}^i \equiv cu^i + d_i$). We have

$$u^i(x, O \cup O') = \begin{cases} u^i(x, O) & x \in O \\ u^i(x, O') & x \in O' - O. \end{cases}$$

Hence, $V(x, O \cup O') = \sum u^i(x_i, O \cup O')$ is a utility function on $O \cup O'$.

By repeated applications of the above 'piecing together' of locally defined additive utility functions, we can construct, for each $\bar{x} \in \Omega$, an additive representation on a strip of minimum thickness $\eta > 0$ centered on the indifference surface containing $\bar{x}$. We can further piece together these additive functions to obtain an additive function U, $U(x) = \sum_{i=1}^{N} u^i(x_i)$, defined on all of Ω.

By the nature of the above construction, V and U are ordinally equivalent locally, i.e., on a sufficiently small neighborhood of any point in Ω. Since indifference surfaces of V are connected, it follows that U is constant on each such indifference surface. Thus, U and V are ordinally equivalent on Ω.   Q.E.D.

APPENDIX 4: REPRESENTATION, UNIQUENESS, AND RISK AVERSION

Denote by $D^r(X)$ the set of c.d.f.'s in $D^0(X)$ for which the probability of each outcome is rational. Each such c.d.f. can be expressed in the form $F = \sum_{i=1}^{N} (1/N)\, \delta_{x_i}$ for some N.

Proof of Theorem 2. First, we make the following observation. For $x \in X^N$, if $y \in X^N$ is obtained from x by a permutation of the components of x, then

$$\sum_{i=1}^{N} \left(\frac{1}{N}\right) \delta_{y_i} \equiv \sum_{i=1}^{N} \left(\frac{1}{N}\right) \delta_{x_i}$$

so that $V_N(x) \equiv V(\sum_{i=1}^{N} (1/N)\, \delta_{x_i})$ is symmetric on X^N.

(Sufficiency) First, we establish the result for IRLU. Observe that $m(\sum_{i=1}^{N} \delta_{x_i})$, $x \in X_\uparrow^N$, is given by the unique solution to

$$\sum_{i=1}^{N} \{\psi(x_i, i/N, y) - \psi(x_i, [i-1]/N, y)\} = 0.$$

It follows that m is completely separable on the intersection of $X_\uparrow^N$ and the indifference surface in X^N corresponding to $m(\sum_{i=1}^{N} (1/N)\, \delta_{x_i})$. Thus, IRS is satisfied.

The verification of sufficiency for LU, RLU, and ILU is similar.

(Necessity) *Case* i ($\mathscr{A}, \mathscr{B}$) = (LU, S). For $x \in X^N$ ($N > 2$), Axiom S and monotonicity imply that V_N is completely strictly separable in the sense of [17]. By Gorman [17, pp. 388–389], there exist continuous and increasing functions

$$u_N^i : X \to \mathbb{R}, \qquad i = 1, ..., N$$

and an increasing function

$$\zeta_N: \sum_{i=1}^{N} \mathrm{Rng}(u_N^i) \to \mathbb{R}$$

such that

$$V_N(x) = \zeta_N \left(\sum_{i=1}^{N} u_N^i(x_i) \right).$$

Symmetry of V_N implies that $u_N^i \equiv u_N^j \equiv u_N$.
  Define the certainty equivalence functional m by

$$V(\delta_{m(F)}) = V(F).$$

Then, for $x \in X^N$,

$$V(\delta_{m(\Sigma(1/N)\delta_{x_i})}) = V_N(m1) = V_N(x)$$

yields

$$N u_N(m) = \sum_{i=1}^{N} u_N(x_i).$$

Observe that each u_N is unique up to affine transformations and any two different u_N and u_K are equivalent to each other since they are each equivalent to u_{NK}. Therefore, we can pick $u \equiv u_3$ and define

$$u \left(m \left(\sum_{i-1}^{N} \left(\frac{1}{N} \right) \delta_{x_i} \right) \right) = \sum_{i=1}^{N} \left(\frac{1}{N} \right) u(x_i)$$

for any $x \in X^N$, and for $N = 3, 4, 5, \ldots$.
  The extension of m from $D^c(X)$ to $D(X)$ is standard under continuity.

Case ii $(\mathscr{A}, \mathscr{B}) = (\mathrm{ILU}, \mathrm{IS})$: For $\bar{x} \in X^N$ $(N > 3)$, define

$$\mathscr{I}(\bar{x}) = \left\{ x \in X^N: \sum_{i=1}^{N} \left(\frac{1}{N} \right) \delta_{x_i} \sim \sum_{i=1}^{N} \left(\frac{1}{N} \right) \delta_{\bar{x}_i} \right\}.$$

Let

$$\mathscr{I}(\bar{x})_{-1} = \{ x \in X^{N-1}: (x, z) \in \mathscr{I}(\bar{x}) \text{ for some } z \in X \}$$

be the projection of $\mathscr{I}(\bar{x})$ on X^{N-1}. Since V is symmetric, the $\mathbb{R}^{N-1}$ projection of $\mathscr{I}(\bar{x})$ is not dependent on the location of the component deleted. This is why we denote the projection by $\mathscr{I}(\bar{x})_{-1}$ rather than $\mathscr{I}(\bar{x})_{-i}$.

Define an ordering $\leqslant_x^{N-1}$ on $\mathscr{I}(\bar{x})_{-1}$ by

$$x \leqslant_x^{N-1} y \Leftrightarrow c_x(x) \leqslant c_x(y),$$

where $c_x(x)$ is defined by

$$\sum_{i=1}^{N-1} \left(\frac{1}{N}\right) \delta_{x_i} + \frac{1}{N}\delta_z \sim \frac{N-1}{N}\delta_{c_x(x)} + \frac{1}{N}\delta_z \sim \sum_{i=1}^{N}\left(\frac{1}{N}\right)\delta_{x_i}.$$

Axiom IS implies that $\leqslant_x^{N-1}$ is completely strictly separable on $\mathscr{I}(\bar{x})_{-1}$ and satisfies the other hypotheses in Theorem A in Appendix 3. Therefore, there are continuous, increasing functions

$$u_{N-1}^i(\cdot;\bar{x}): \pi_i(\mathscr{I}(\bar{x})_{-1}) \to \mathbb{R}$$

(where π_i is the ith-coordinate projection operator) and an increasing function

$$\zeta_N: \sum_{i=1}^{N-1} \operatorname{Rng}(u_{N-1}^i) \to \mathbb{R}$$

such that $\leqslant_x^{N-1}$ is represented by $V_{N-1}(\cdot;\bar{x})$, where

$$V_{N-1}(x;\bar{x}) \equiv \zeta_N\left(\sum_{i=1}^{N} u_{N-1}^i(x_i;\bar{x})\right).$$

Since $V_{N-1}(\cdot;\bar{x})$ must be symmetric, $u_{N-1}^i(\cdot;\bar{x}) \equiv u_{N-1}^j(\cdot;\bar{x}) \equiv u_{N-1}(\cdot;\bar{x})$.

It remains to show that the ordering represented by $\sum_{i=1}^{N} u_{N-1}(x_i;\bar{x})$ has $\mathscr{I}(\bar{x})$ as an indifference set. Suppose there exists $x \in X^N$ with $x \sim \bar{x}$ such that

$$\sum_{i=1}^{N} u_{N-1}(x_i,\bar{x}) > \sum_{i=1}^{N} u_{N-1}(\bar{x}_i,\bar{x}).$$

(The reverse inequality may be handled similarly.) This is only possible if x and $\bar{x}$ have no common component (since if they have a common component, say the Nth, then $x \sim \bar{x} \Rightarrow x_{-N} \sim_x^{N-1} \bar{x}_{-N} \Rightarrow$

$$\sum_{i=1}^{N} u_{N-1}(x_i,\bar{x}) = \sum_{i=1}^{N} u_{N-1}(\bar{x}_i,\bar{x})).$$

Pick (x_k, x_j) such that $x_k > \bar{x}_k$ and $x_j < \bar{x}_j$. Replace x_k by $x_k^1 > \bar{x}_k$ such that $\sum_{i \neq k} u_{N-1}(x_i,\bar{x}) + u_{N-1}(x_k^1,\bar{x}) = \sum_{i=1}^{N} u_{N-1}(\bar{x}_i,\bar{x})$. We can rule out $x_k^1 \leqslant \bar{x}_k$. Otherwise, even if $x_k^1 = \bar{x}_k$,

$$\sum_{i \neq k} u_{N-1}(x_i,\bar{x}) + u_{N-1}(x_k^1,\bar{x}) < \sum_{i=1}^{N} u_{N-1}(\bar{x}_i,\bar{x}) \qquad (A.4.1)$$

since $(x_1, ..., x_k^1, ..., x_N) \prec \bar{x}$.

Next we replace x_j by $x_j^2 < \bar{x}_j$ such that

$$\sum_{i \neq k,j} \frac{1}{N} \delta_{x_i} + \frac{1}{N} \delta_{x_k^1} + \frac{1}{N} \delta_{x_j^2} \sim \sum_{i=1}^{N} \left(\frac{i}{N}\right) \delta_{x_i}. \qquad (A.4.2)$$

Again, we rule out the possibility that $x_j^2 \geqslant \bar{x}_j$. Otherwise, at $x_j^2 = \bar{x}_j$, LHS of (A.4.2) > RHS of (A.4.2) since $\sum_{i \neq k,j} u_{N-1}(x_i, \bar{x}) + u_{N-1}(x_k^1, \bar{x}) + u_{N-1}(x_j^2, \bar{x}) > \sum_{i=1}^{N} u_{N-1}(\bar{x}_i, \bar{x})$.

We continue this process in order to construct a sequence $\{y^k\} \subset X^N$ with the property that, when m is odd, $y^m \prec \bar{x}$ and $\sum_{i=1}^{N} u_{N-1}(y_i^m, \bar{x}) = \sum_{i=1}^{N} u_{N-1}(\bar{x}_i, \bar{x})$; when m is even, $y^m \sim \bar{x}$ and $\sum_{i=1}^{N} u_{N-1}(y_i^m, \bar{x}) > \sum_{i=1}^{N} u_{N-1}(\bar{x}_i, \bar{x})$. Both x_k^m (m odd) and x_j^m (m even) converge since they are monotone bounded sequences. Moreover, $x_k^m \downarrow \bar{x}_k$ and $x_j^m \uparrow \bar{x}_j$. Therefore, $\lim_{m \to \infty} y^m = y \sim \bar{x} \sim x$. Since y shares two common components with $\bar{x}$ and $N-2$ common components with x, we have $\sum_{i=1}^{N} u_{N-1}(x_i, \bar{x}) = \sum_{i=1}^{N} u_{N-1}(y_i, \bar{x}) = \sum_{i=1}^{N} u_{N-1}(\bar{x}_i, \bar{x})$, which is a contradiction.

Moreover, we can conclude that (A.4.1) holds if and only if $x \succ \bar{x}$ since we can decrease the components of x until it is indifferent to $\bar{x}$, at which point we have equality.

As in the proof of Case (i), all the u_{N-1} ($N > 3$) are equivalent. We can choose $u \equiv u_3$ to generate the implicit equality

$$u\left(m\left(\sum \frac{1}{N} \delta_{x_i}\right), m'\right) = \frac{1}{N} \sum u(x_i, m'),$$

where $\sum (1/N) \delta_{x_i} \sim \sum (1/N) \delta_{x_i} \sim \delta_{m'}$. A standard extension argument again yields $\forall F \in D(X)$, $m(F)$ as an implicit solution of

$$u(m, m) = \int_X u(x, m) \, dF(x). \qquad (A.4.3)$$

The above becomes

$$\int_X \tau(x, m) \, dF(x) = 0 \qquad (A.4.4)$$

if we define

$$\tau(x, y) \equiv u(x, y) - u(y, y). \qquad (A.4.5)$$

The uniqueness of the solution $m(F)$ follows as in Case (iv) below.

Case iii $(\mathscr{A}, \mathscr{B}) = $ (RLU, RS). Axiom RS implies that V_N is completely strictly separable on $X_\uparrow^N$. Theorem A in Appendix 3 is applicable and implies the existence of continuous increasing functions

$$u_N^i : X \to \mathbb{R}, \qquad i = 1, ..., N$$

consider the one-step equilirium in which trade occurs with certainty at price $\frac{1}{2}$.

Substituting all this into (5) yields

$$(1-y)(y-\tfrac{1}{2})+\tfrac{1}{3}y(\tfrac{7}{4}y-1)^2=(1-y)(\tfrac{5}{4}y-\tfrac{1}{2}),$$

which has solutions

$$y=\{22\pm12\sqrt{2}\}/49 = 0.103 \text{ or } 0.795.$$

Since the analysis of the second term of (5) proved that $y>\frac{4}{7}$, the solution is $y=0.795$, which exceeds $\frac{5}{8}$, confirming that the Chatterjee–Samuelson equilibrium indeed breaks down when both parties say "keen."

This completes our derivation of the equilibrium value of y. We next state and prove Lemma 1, which describes our equilibrium. Finally, we prove Propositions 1 and 2.

LEMMA 1. *The following behavior defines the equilibrium path of a perfect Bayesian equilibrium in our two-stage bargaining game.* (Our proof does not require explicit descriptions of the optimal bids following deviations in the cheap-talk phase, so we omit these bids from the description of equilibrium.)

Buyer. (A) If $v_b < y$ then

(i) say "not keen" in the first stage, and

(ii) if the seller says "not keen" in the first stage then bid $p_b=0$ in the second stage, but if the seller says "keen" in the first stage then bid

$$p_b=\min\{\tfrac{2}{3}v_b+\tfrac{1}{12}y, \tfrac{2}{3}-\tfrac{5}{12}y\}$$

in the second stage.

(B) If $v_b \geqslant y$ then

(i) say "keen" in the first stage, and

(ii) if the seller says "keen" in the first stage then bid $p_b=\frac{1}{2}$ in the second stage, but if the seller says "not keen" in the first stage then bid

$$p_b=\tfrac{2}{3}v_b+\tfrac{1}{4}(1-y)+\tfrac{1}{12}$$

in the second stage.

Seller. (A) If $v_s > 1-y$ then

(i) say "not keen" in the first stage, and

Define $c(\cdot, \bar{x})_i : \mathscr{I}_1(\bar{x})_{-i} \to \mathbb{R}$ by

$$\sum_{i=1}^{N-1} \left(\frac{1}{N}\right) \delta_{x_i} + \frac{1}{N}\delta_z \sim \frac{N-1}{N} \delta_{c(x,x)_i} + \frac{1}{N}\delta_z \sim \sum_{i=1}^{N} \left(\frac{1}{N}\right) \delta_{\bar{x}_i}.$$

Axiom IRS implies that the $\preccurlyeq_{(x,i)}^{N-1}$ ordering defined by $c(\cdot, \bar{x})_i$ is completely strictly separable on $\mathscr{I}_1(\bar{x})_{-i}$ for each i. By applying Theorem A in Appendix 3, we have that, for each i, there are continuous, increasing functions $u^i_{N-1,i} : \pi_j(.\mathscr{I}_1(\bar{x})_{-i}) \to \mathbb{R}$ such that

$$\sum_{j \neq i} u^i_{N-1,i}(c(x, \bar{x})_i) = \sum_{j \neq i} u^i_{N-1,i}(x_i, \bar{x}). \tag{A.4.8}$$

Extend the $\preccurlyeq_{(x,i)}^{N-1}$ ordering trivially to comparisons of x and y in X_1^N, where $x_{-i}, y_{-i} \in \mathscr{I}_1(\bar{x})_{-i}$ and $x_i = y_i$, by requiring $x \preccurlyeq y$ if and only if $c(x_{-i}, \bar{x})_i \leqslant c(y_{-i}, \bar{x})_i$. In the above extended sense, we observe that $\preccurlyeq_{(x,i)}^{N-1}$ and $\preccurlyeq_{(x,j)}^{N-1}$ coincide over comparisons of $x, y \in X_1^N$, where $x_{-i}, y_{-i} \in \mathscr{I}_1(\bar{x})_{-i}, x_{-j}, y_{-j} \in \mathscr{I}_1(\bar{x})_{-j}$, and $(x_i, x_j) = (y_i, y_j)$. We have

$$u^k_{N-1,i}(\cdot, \bar{x}) = u^{k'}_{N-1,j}(\cdot, \bar{x}),$$

where k and k' refer to the same rank relative to $\bar{x}$ (i.e., $k = k'$ if $i \leqslant (\geqslant)$ $k, j \leqslant (\geqslant) k; k = k' + 1$ if $i \leqslant k, j \geqslant k'; k = k' - 1$ if $i \geqslant k, j \leqslant k'$). In other words, the $u^k_{N-1,i}(\cdot, \bar{x}) \equiv u^k_{N-1}(\cdot, \bar{x})$ functions do not depend on i. Construct

$$u^j_N(\cdot, \bar{x}) = \begin{cases} u^j_{N-1,N}(\cdot, \bar{x}), & j = 1, ..., N-1 \\ u^{N-1}_{N-1,1}(\cdot, \bar{x}), & j = N. \end{cases} \tag{A.4.9}$$

Then $\sum u^j_N(\cdot, \bar{x})$ represents the conditional ordering $\preccurlyeq_{(x,i)}^{N-1}$ for each i.

We need to show that the above representation coincides with $\mathscr{I}_1(\bar{x})$ whenever $\sum_{i=1}^N (1/N) \delta_{x_i} \sim \sum_N^N) \delta_{x_i}$. Suppose there exists $x \in X_1^N$ with $x \sim \bar{x}$ such that

$$\sum_{i=1}^N u^i_N(x_i, \bar{x}) > \sum_{i=1}^N u^i_N(\bar{x}_i, \bar{x}). \tag{A.4.10}$$

(The reverse inequality may be treated similarly.) This is only possible if $x_i \neq \bar{x}_i$ for each i. Pick $x_k > \bar{x}_k$ and $x_j < \bar{x}_j$ such that $k = 1$ or $x_{k-1} < \bar{x}_k$ and $j = N$ or $x_{j+1} > \bar{x}_j$. Replace x_k by $x^1_k > \bar{x}_k$ such that $\sum_{i \neq k} u^i_N(x_i, \bar{x}) + u^i_N(x^1_k, \bar{x}) = \sum_{i=1}^N (\bar{x}_i, \bar{x})$. Next, replace x_j by $x^2_j < \bar{x}_j$ such that $\sum_{i \neq k,j} (1/N) \delta_{x_i} + (1/N) \delta_{x^1_k} + (1/N) \delta_{x^2_j} \sim \sum_{i=1}^N (1/N)) \delta_{\bar{x}_i}$. Continuing the process, we obtain a sequence $\{y^k\} \subset X_1^N$ with the property that, when m is odd, $y''' \prec \bar{x}$ and $\sum_{i=1}^N u_N^i(y_i''', \bar{x}) = \sum_{i=1}^N u_N^i(\bar{x}_i, \bar{x})$; when m is even, $y''' \sim \bar{x}$ and $\sum_{i=1}^N u_N^i(y_i''', \bar{x}) > \sum_{i=1}^N u_N^i(\bar{x}_i, \bar{x})$. Observe that $x_k^{2m-1} \downarrow \bar{x}_k$ and $x_j^{2m} \uparrow \bar{x}_j$, so that $\text{Lim}_{m \to \infty} y''' = y \sim \bar{x} \sim x$. This yields a contradiction. Note as in the proof of Case (ii) that (A.4.10) holds if and only if $x \succ \bar{x}$.

For each $m \in X$, we define $\mathscr{I}(m) = \{F \in D(X): F \sim \delta_m\}$. For each N, we can go through the preceding construction to obtain the $u_N^i(\cdot, m)$'s which represent the ordering on $\mathscr{I}(m) \cap X_1^N$. Construct $\psi: X \times [0, 1]^* \times X \to \mathbb{R}$ by

$$\psi\left(x, \frac{i}{N}, m\right) = \sum_{j=1}^i u_N^j(x, m) - \sum_{j=1}^N u_N^j(m, m) \qquad (A.4.11)$$

and extend its domain for the second argument continuously to $[0, 1)$. It follows that, $\forall F \in D^c(X)$, the certainty equivalent $m(F)$ is given by an implicit solution of

$$\int_X d_2 \psi(x, F(x), y) = 0. \qquad (A.4.12)$$

To see that $m(F)$ is the unique implicit solution, suppose there exists $y' \in X$ satisfying $\int_X d_2 \psi(x, F, y') = 0$ but $y' \neq m(F)$. Let $F' \in D^c(X)$ be such that $y' = m(F')$ and $\int_X d_2 \psi(x, F', y') = 0$. We conclude that $\int_X d_2 \psi(x, F', y')) = \int_X d_2 \psi(x, F, y'))$. This implies $F \sim F'$ which is a contradiction.

We have shown that ψ represents $m(\cdot)$ on $D^c(X)$ in the sense that, $\forall F \in D^c(X)$, $m(F)$ is the unique solution to the equation $\int_X d_2 \psi(x, F, y) = 0$. We now show that in the same sense ψ represents $m(\cdot)$ on all of $D(X)$. Let $\{F^n\}$ be an increasing sequence in $D^c(X)$ which converges to $F \in D(X)$ so that $y^n = m(F^n)$ converges to y. Suppose

$$\int_X d_2 \psi(x, F(x), y) < 0.$$

Then the above would hold under a small lateral shift η in F denoted by $F_{+\eta}$; i.e., $\int_X d_2 \psi(x, F_{+\eta}(x), y) < 0$. This implies that for n sufficiently large, $\int_X d_2 \psi(x, F_{+\eta}^n(x), y) < 0$, i.e., $F_{+\eta}^n \prec \delta_y$ since $\{F_{+\eta}^n\} \subset D^c(X)$. This in turn implies that $F_{+\eta} \preccurlyeq F$ which is a contradiction.

Finally, we observe that the following properties of ψ, which appear in the definition of IRLU, hold. The continuity of ψ in x and in p holds by construction. Condition (2.7) for $\psi(\cdot, \cdot, y)$ is equivalent to the increasingness of the branch utility functions $u_N^i(x, y)$.   Q.E.D.

Proof of Corollary 1. Sufficiency of (4.3) is obvious. To prove necessity, suppose ψ and $\hat{\psi}$ both represent the same IRLU ordering. For each N, we construct $u^j_N, \hat{u}^j_N : X \times X \to \mathbb{R}$ via

$$u^j_N(x, y) = \psi\left(x, \frac{j}{N}, y\right) - \psi\left(x, \frac{j-1}{N}, y\right),$$

$$\hat{u}^j_N(x, y) = \hat{\psi}\left(x, \frac{j}{N}, y\right) - \hat{\psi}\left(x, \frac{j-1}{N}, y\right).$$

Since u^j_N's and $\hat{u}^j_N$'s provide additive utility representations of the same ordering over X^N, they are related by the similar positive affine transformation

$$\hat{u}^j_N(\cdot, y) = \alpha_N(y) u^j_N(\cdot, y) + \beta^j_N(y), \tag{A.4.13}$$

so that

$$\hat{\psi}\left(x, \frac{i}{N}, y\right) = \sum_{j=1}^{i} [\hat{u}^j_N(x, y) - \hat{u}^j_N(y, y)]$$

$$= \alpha_N(y) \sum_{j=1}^{N} [u^j_N(x, y) - u^j_N(y, y)] = \alpha_N(y) \psi\left(x, \frac{i}{N}, y\right).$$

Clearly, α_N cannot depend on N in the above expression. Hence, the conclusion follows by continuous extension of ψ in the second argument from the rationals to $[0, 1]$.   Q.E.D.

Proof of Theorem 3. It is easier to proceed using the following statement of Condition (4.6): Given $\varepsilon, \gamma > 0, y \in X$.

$$\Delta(x, p, \varepsilon, \gamma, y) = \psi(x + \varepsilon, p + \gamma, y) - \psi(x + \varepsilon, p, y)$$

$$- \psi(x, p + \gamma, y) + \psi(x, p, y) \tag{4.6'}$$

is nonincreasing in (x, p), for $[x, x + \varepsilon] \times [p, p + \gamma] \subset X \times [0, 1]$. In view of the equivalence between MRA and Schur-concavity on $D^c(X)$ for a continuous, monotone utility functional on $D(X)$ [8, Corollary 2], it suffices to prove

(i): (4.6') implies that IRLU is Schur-concave on $D^c(X)$, and

(ii): MRA implies that (4.6') holds.

Case (i). To prove the necessity of (4.6') for MRA, suppose $\exists p, \varepsilon, \gamma \in (0, 1)$ and $x, x', y \in X$ $(x' > x)$ such that $\Delta(x', p, \varepsilon, \gamma, y) > \Delta(x, p, \varepsilon, \gamma, y)$. Let $\kappa = mi$,

$$f\left(\frac{i}{N}\right) = \Delta\left(x, p, \kappa, \frac{i}{N}\gamma, y\right),$$

and

$$f'\left(\frac{i}{N}\right) = A\left(x', p, \kappa, \frac{i}{K}\gamma, y\right).$$

Note that $f(0) = f'(0) = 0$ and $f(1) < f'(1)$.

For each N, we will show that

$$f\left(\frac{i}{N}\right) - f\left(\frac{i-1}{N}\right) \geqslant f'\left(\frac{i+1}{N}\right) - f'\left(\frac{i}{N}\right) \qquad (i = 1, ..., N-1). \quad (A.4.14)$$

Pick any N and $1 < i < N$. Consider

$$\frac{\gamma}{N}\delta_{x+\kappa} + \frac{\gamma}{N}\delta_{x'} + \left(1 - \frac{2}{N}\gamma\right)F \sim \delta_y, \qquad (A.4.15)$$

where $F(x + \kappa) = p + ((i - 1/N)\gamma$, $F(x') = p + (i/N)\gamma$, and $[x, x' + \kappa] \cap$ supp $F = \phi$. Then the IRLU of (A.4.15) is given by an expression having the form

$$A + \theta\left(x + \kappa, p + \frac{i-1}{N}\gamma, \frac{\gamma}{N}, y\right) + \theta\left(x', p + \frac{i}{N}\gamma, \frac{\gamma}{N}, y\right) + B = 0, \quad (A.4.16)$$

where

$$\theta(x, p, \gamma, y) \equiv \psi(x, p + \gamma, y) - \psi(x, p, y). \qquad (A.4.17)$$

Since $\preccurlyeq$ satisfies MRA,

$$\frac{\gamma}{N}\delta_x + \frac{\gamma}{N}\delta_{x'+\kappa} + \left(1 - \frac{2}{N}\gamma\right)F \preccurlyeq \frac{\gamma}{N}\delta_{x+\kappa} + \frac{\gamma}{N}\delta_{x'} + \left(1 - \frac{2}{N}\gamma\right)F \sim \delta_y.$$

In terms of IRLU, the above yields

$$A + \theta\left(x, p + \frac{i-1}{N}\gamma, \frac{\gamma}{N}, y\right) + \theta\left(x', p + \frac{i}{N}\gamma, \frac{\gamma}{N}, y\right) + B \leqslant 0. \quad (A.4.18)$$

Subtracting (A.4.16) from (A.4.18) yields

$$f\left(\frac{i}{N}\right) - f\left(\frac{i-1}{N}\right) \geqslant f'\left(\frac{i+1}{N}\right) - f'\left(\frac{i}{N}\right).$$

It follows that $\forall N$,

$$f\left(\frac{N-1}{N}\right) \leqslant f'(1) - f'\left(\frac{1}{N}\right).$$

Taking the limit as N tends to ∞ and by continuity of Δ in γ, $f(1) \leqslant f'(1)$ which is a contradiction. (The other case where Δ is strictly increasing in p is essentially the same.)

Case (ii). Now we prove the sufficiency of (4.6′) for the Schur-concavity of V on $D''(X)$. For $(x_1, ..., x_N) \in X_1^N$, consider $m(\sum_{i=1}^{N} (1/N)\, \delta_{x_i}) = y$. Let $\varepsilon > 0$ be such that $x_{k-1} \leqslant x_k - \varepsilon$, $x_{k+1} + \varepsilon \leqslant x_{k+2}$. Then (4.6′) implies that

$$\Delta\left(x_k, \frac{k}{N}, \varepsilon, \frac{1}{N}, y\right) - \Delta\left(x_k - \varepsilon, \frac{k}{N}, \varepsilon, \frac{1}{N}, y\right) + \Delta\left(x_k - \varepsilon, \frac{k}{N}, \varepsilon, \frac{1}{N}, y\right)$$

$$- \Delta\left(x_k - \varepsilon, \frac{k-1}{N}, \varepsilon, \frac{1}{N}, y\right) \geqslant 0.$$

Rewriting the above yields

$$\psi\left(x_{k+1} + \varepsilon, \frac{k+1}{N}, y\right) - \psi\left(x_{k+1} + \varepsilon, \frac{k}{N}, y\right)$$

$$+ \psi\left(x_k - \varepsilon, \frac{k}{N}, y\right) - \psi\left(x_k - \varepsilon, \frac{k-1}{N}, y\right)$$

$$\leqslant \psi\left(x_{k+1}, \frac{k+1}{N}, y\right) - \psi\left(x_{k+1}, \frac{k}{N}, y\right)$$

$$+ \psi\left(x_k, \frac{k}{N}, y\right) - \psi\left(x_k, \frac{k-1}{N}, y\right), \tag{A.4.19}$$

which is equivalent to

$$m\left(\frac{1}{N}\delta_{x_k - \varepsilon} + \frac{1}{N}\delta_{x_{k+1} + \varepsilon} + \sum_{i \neq k, k+1} \frac{1}{N}\delta_{x_i}\right) \leqslant y. \qquad \text{Q.E.D.}$$

Appendix 5: Multiplicative Separability

Proof of Theorem 4. We provide the proof for the IRLU case. The result for the RLU case follows. Necessity of the RLU case is implied by the existing proof. For sufficiency, observe that iff ψ is RLU and satisfies (5.1), then $\tau(x, y) = \varphi(x, 1) - \varphi(y, 1)$. Thus (5.2) is implied.

To prove the necessity of the IRLU case, suppose $\psi(x, p, y) \equiv g(p, y)\, \tau(x, y)$. Define

$$v(x, p, r, y) = \psi(x, r+p, y) - \psi(x, r, y). \tag{A.5.1}$$

Then $v(x, r, y) \equiv [g(r+p, y) - g(r, y)]\, \tau(x, y)$. Note that $v(\cdot, p, r, y)$ is proportional to $v(\cdot, q, s, y)$ for $(q, s) \neq (p, r)$.

Given (p, q, r, s, y), the α in the hypothesis of Axiom MS will be given by the unique solution of $b_2/a_2 = b_1/a_1$, where

$$b_2 = g(s+q, m) - g(s+\alpha q, m), \qquad a_2 = g(s+\alpha q, m) - g(s, m),$$
$$b_1 = g(r+p, m) - g(r+p/2, m), \qquad a_1 = g(r+p/2, m) - g(r, m).$$

Consider $v(x, p/2, r+p/2, m)$, $v(x, p/2, r, m)$, $v(x, (1-\alpha)q, s+\alpha q, m)$ and $v(x, \alpha q, s, m)$. The result follows from the observation that the certainty equivalent m given by

$$\frac{p}{2}\delta_x + \frac{p}{2}\delta_{x'} + (1-p) F \sim \delta_m \sim \alpha q \delta_x + (1-\alpha) q \delta_{x'} + (1+q) G, \quad (A.5.2)$$

where $F(x) = r$, $G(x) = s$, and $x, x' \notin \operatorname{supp} F \cup \operatorname{supp} G$, is respectively of the form

$$A_1 + a_1 \tau(x, m) + b_1 \tau(x', m) + B_1 = 0$$

and

$$A_2 + a_2 \tau(x, m) + b_2 \tau(x', m) + B_2 = 0.$$

To prove sufficiency, define

$$v(x, p, r, m) = \psi(x, r+p, m) - \psi(x, r, m).$$

Note that multiplicative separability of ψ is equivalent to $v(\cdot, p, r, m)$'s being proportional to $v(\cdot, q, s, m)$ for $(p, r) \neq (q, s)$. Given $x \in J$, $p \in (0, 1]$, $r \in [0, 1)$, define the function c by

$$v(x-\varepsilon, p, r+p/2, m) + v(x+c(\varepsilon, x, p, r), p/2, r, m) = v(x, p, r, m).$$

Axiom MS implies that for any $q \in (0, 1]$, $s \in [0, 1)$, $\exists \alpha \in (0, 1)$ such that

$$v(x-\varepsilon, q, s+\alpha q, m) + v(x+c(\varepsilon, x, p, r), \alpha q, s, m) = v(x, q, s, m),$$

i.e., c is not dependent on (q, s). Thus

$$v(\cdot, q, s+\alpha q, m) + v(\cdot, \alpha q, s, m) \qquad (A.5.3)$$

and

$$v(\cdot, p, r+p/2, m) + v(\cdot, p/2, r, m) \qquad (A.5.4)$$

define the 'same' indifference curve through $(x, x) \in J^2$. By varying the choice of $x \in J$ and $F, G \in D(X)$ while maintaining the constancy of m,

AXIOMATIC NON-EXPECTED UTILITY   239

we conclude that (A.5.3) and (A.5.4) are equivalent additive utility representations for the orderings induced on $(x, x') \in J^2$ via (A.5.2). Since additive utility is unique up to a positive affine transformation and $v(m, p, m) = 0 \; \forall m$, it follows that

$$v(\cdot, q, s + \alpha q, m)/v(\cdot, p, r + p/2, m) \equiv v(\cdot, \alpha q, s, m)/v(\cdot, p/2, r, m)$$

$$\equiv \text{constant.} \qquad\qquad \text{Q.E.D.}$$

REFERENCES

1. P. Billingsley, "Convergence of Probability Measures," Wiley, New York, 1968.
2. C. Blackorby, R. Davidson, and D. Donaldson, A homiletic exposition of the expected utility hypothesis, *Economica* **44** (1977), 351–358.
3. S. H. Chew, A generalization of the quasilinear mean with applications to the measurement of income inequality and decision theory resolving the Allais paradox, *Econometrica* **51** (1983), 1065–1092.
4. S. H. Chew, Axiomatic utility theories with the betweenness property, *Ann. Oper. Res.*, in press.
5. S. H. Chew, "An Axiomatization of the Rank-Dependent Quasilinear Mean Generalizing the Gini Mean and the Quasilinear Mean," Economics Working Paper #156, Johns Hopkins University, 1985.
6. S. H. Chew, E. Karni, and Z. Safra, Risk aversion in the theory of expected utility with rank-dependent probabilities, *J. Econ. Theory* **42** (1987), 370–381.
7. S. H. Chew and K. R. MacCrimmon, "Alpha Utility Theory: A Generalization of Expected Utility Theory," Faculty of Commerce and Business Administration Working Paper #669, University of British Columbia, 1979.
8. S. H. Chew and M. H. Mao, A Schur-Concave Characterization of Risk Aversion for Nonlinear, Nonsmooth Continuous Preferences," Working Paper 157, Johns Hopkins University, 1985.
9. S. H. Chew and W. S. Waller, Empirical tests of weighted utility theory, *J. Math. Psych.* **30** 1986), 55–72.
10. G. Debreu, Topological methods in cardinal utility theory, *in* "Mathematical Methods in the Social Sciences" (K. Arrow, S. Karlin, and P. Suppes, Eds), Stanford Univ. Press, Stanford, 1959.
11. G. Debreu, Continuity properties of Paretian utility, *Int. Econ. Rev.* **5** (1964), 285–293.
12. E. Dekel, An axiomatic characterization of preferences under uncertainty, *J. Econ. Theory* **40** (1986), 304–318.
13. U. Ebert, Measurement of inequality: an attempt at unification and generalization, *Soc. Choice Welfare* **5** (1988), 147–169.
14. P. C. Fishburn, Nontransitive measurable utility, *J. Math. Psych.* **26** (1982), 31–67.
15. P. C. Fishburn, Transitive measurable utility, *J. Econ. Theory* **31** (1983), 293–317.
16. P. C. Fishburn, Implicit mean value and certainty equivalence, *Econometrica* **54** (1986), 1197–1205.
17. W. M. Gorman, The structure of utility functions, *Rev. Econ. Stud.* **35** (1968), 367–390.
18. J. Green and B. Jullien, Ordinal independence in nonlinear utility theory, *J. Risk Uncert.*, in press.
19. D. Kahneman and A. Tversky, Prospect theory: an analysis of decision under risk, *Econometrica* **47** (1979), 263–291.

20. K. R. MacCRIMMON AND S. LARSSON, Utility theory: axioms versus paradoxes, *in* "The Expected Utility Hypothesis and the Allais Paradox" (M. Allais and O. Hagen, Eds.), Reidel, Dordrecht, 1979.

21. M. J. MACHINA, 'Expected utility' analysis without the independence axiom, *Econometrica* **50** (1982), 277–323.

22. Y. NAKAMURA, "Nonlinear Utility Analysis," Ph.D. thesis, University of California, Davis, 1984.

23. J. QUIGGIN, Anticipated utility theory, *J. Econ. Behav. Organ.* **3** (1982), 323–343.

24. J. SAVAGE, "The Foundations of Statistics," Wiley, New York, 1954.

25. U. SEGAL, Axiomatic representation of expected utility with rank-dependent probabilities, *Ann. Oper. Res.*, in press.

26. M. E. YAARI, The dual theory of choice under risk: risk aversion without diminishing marginal utility, *Econometrica* **55** (1987), 95–115.

[17]

Journal of Risk and Uncertainty, 2: 235–264 (1989)
© 1989 Kluwer Academic Publishers

Prospective Reference Theory:
Toward an Explanation of the Paradoxes

W. KIP VISCUSI
Department of Economics, Duke University, Durham, North Carolina 27706

Key words: risk, expected utility, irrationality, prospect theory

Abstract

This article develops a variant of the expected utility model termed *prospective reference theory*. Although the standard model occurs as a limiting case, the general approach is that individuals treat stated experimental probabilities as imperfect information. This model is applied to a wide variety of aberrant phenomena, including the Allais paradox, the overweighting of low-probability events, the existence of premiums for certain elimination of risks, and the representativeness heuristic. The prospective reference theory model predicts most of the observed behavioral patterns rather than being potentially reconcilable with such phenomena.

Since World War II, expected utility theory has become the dominant economic paradigm for analyzing choices under uncertainty. This prominence in the economics literature has been coupled with an expanding body of research providing empirical tests of different components of the theory. A major theme of the work, much of which has consisted of experimental studies by psychologists, has been that expected utility theory does not provide a reliable predictive guide to behavior. These studies observe that individual choices are often inconsistent, violating one or more of the von Neumann–Morgenstern (1953) axioms. In addition, the Bayesian formulations of the model such as those of Savage (1972) and Raiffa (1968) have been challenged because individuals' probabilistic beliefs often do not conform with those hypothesized in the model.[1]

There are two possible responses to this wave of research. First, one could reject the evidence contradicting the conventional expected utility theory as not being representative of economic behavior. The deviations from rationality typically pertain to experimental contexts rather than market contexts, and if there is a market imperfection, there is still no evidence that the deviation from full

Kenneth Arrow and Robert Viscusi provided helpful comments. A preliminary version of this article was presented at the 1987 AEA meetings.

rationality is large. Moreover, there is much empirical evidence regarding risk taking and insurance behavior that is consistent with the expected utility model. This defense of the conventional analysis is often pertinent, particularly with respect to some of the more speculative experimental results, but as a general response it is inadequate. As economists such as Arrow (1982) have observed, the mounting evidence contradicting the expected utility model does present a legitimate challenge to the theory that cannot be dismissed out of hand.

The second approach to this research is to accept its implications and abandon or amend the conventional model. A widely discussed alternative framework is that of prospect theory developed by Kahneman and Tversky (1979). Their innovative analysis alters the expected utility framework by adopting a utility function with a distinctive shape and abandoning the linear probability weights on the payoffs. Tversky and Kahneman (1985) have cast this framework as an alternative to the expected utility model rather than as an amendment of it, since they claim that "deviations of actual behavior from the normative model are . . . too fundamental to be accommodated by relaxing the normative system." A less sweeping modification of the expected utility model is that of Machina (1982), who drops the independence axiom but still preserves many of the essential features and predictions of the expected utility framework.[2] The amendments to the standard model by Kahneman and Tversky, Machina, and others make it possible to reconcile some aberrant phenomena such as the Allasi paradox with rational behavior.

When judging the performance of the expected utility model in comparison to alternative approaches, it is essential to place comparable demands on the competing theories. The expected utility model has quite specific empirical predictions and, as a result, can be potentially invalidated in an empirical test. In contrast, alternatives such as prospect theory have much less formal structures that can be used to establish unambiguous predictions and as a consequence are better able to avoid paradoxes and empirical inconsistencies. Under the prospect theory approach, the framing and editing processes do not have an associated theory that is sufficiently precise to generate unambiguous predictions, and the preference and valuation functions have unspecified nonlinear shapes that allow great leeway in terms of behavior that is potentially consistent with the model. This flexibility greatly diminishes the predictive power of the theory so that in many instances one is limited to post hoc ergo propter hoc explanations of behavior.

The framework to be developed here, termed *prospective reference theory (PRT)*, stems from the standard expected utility model, but rather than amending or dropping any of its basic assumptions regarding choice, the manner in which probabilities enter the analysis is altered. The concern here with perceptional elements shares many concerns with the approach taken in prospect theory, but unlike that analysis this formulation will be consistent with a quasi-Bayesian learning process. Depending on one's orientation, one can view this model as being a modified prospect theory model with a Bayesian structure imposed on the risk perceptions, or an expected utility model in which stated probabilities are treated as imperfect information and are then processed in Bayesian fashion. This approach shares with the prospect theory model an emphasis on empirical regularities in the nature of the risk perceptions, which may contribute to apparent inconsistencies in decisions. Thus, it is the nature of risk perceptions rather than inadequacies in the way that choices are made that accounts for the observed anomalies in behavior.

The genesis of this research is a series of three empirical analyses of risk perceptions and individual behavior. In Viscusi and O'Connor (1984), the risk perception function that will be used in this article to explain the experimental paradoxes was found to provide an excellent characterization of workers' risk perceptions when these workers were presented with chemical labels. In particular, the beta distribution parameters that were estimated had the predicted effect when included in a wage equation, as workers demanded compensating differentials for higher risk levels and for more precisely understood risks. In Viscusi (1985), the same risk perception function was applied to data gathered by psychologists with respect to perceptions of fatality risks, and this approach provided an alternative and a "more rational" explanation of the observed patterns. As will be discussed below, the observed variation in the bias in risk perceptions with respect to differences in the level of the risk is exactly what one would predict based on a Bayesian learning model. Most recently, the analysis of consumers' responses to risk presented in Viscusi, Magat, and Huber (1987) provides additional support for the economic importance of these phenomena. Consumer valuations of risk changes follow the same general types of patterns that the risk perception studies suggest should be evidenced in market outcomes. The relationship of these empirical studies to the analysis of economic paradoxes will be articulated further below.

The basic assumption driving the analysis is that individuals' attitudes toward uncertain prospects are influenced by a reference risk level. These reference risks may involve an assumption that each lottery outcome is equally likely or, in the case of lottery outcomes with which the individual has some related experience, the probability assessment could differ across payoffs. The reference risk in effect serves as the individual's prior probability. When presented with a new lottery, the probabilistic belief is updated in standard Bayesian fashion from this reference point. Even in the case of the experimental lotteries, the individual may not place absolute confidence in stated probabilities but instead may act as if he has received imperfect information that he uses to update his probabilistic beliefs from the reference risk level.

The resulting formulation is well behaved in that the perceived probabilities have the same mathematical properties as a standard probability measure. This attractive property arises because the assessed probabilities involve no more than ascertaining the posterior probability assessment using a standard Bayesian framework. Since the PRT model does not alter any of the basic principles of rational choice, it is also consistent with empirical evidence supporting the expected utility model. Moreover, unlike the standard framework, it explains the Allais paradox and a wide variety of other phenomena cited as contradicting the standard expected utility model.

The PRT model also has considerable power, since it predicts many of the empirical regularities that have been adopted as assumptions within the prospect theory framework. What is perhaps most stroking is that most of the deviant phenomena identified as paradoxes in the literlature are *predicted* by the theory. This feature is a stronger property than having a model with theoretical predictions that are ambiguous and as a consequence can be potentially reconciled with any pattern of observed behavior under special circumstances. Under the prospect theory approach, the main emphasis is on summarizing the various forms of irrational behavior that have been observed and to identify the broad character of systematic empirical regularities. The approach taken here will be the opposite in that a theoretical framework will be developed that predicts the empirical regularities rather than using the observed regularities as the essential components of a descriptive theory.

The importance of this distinction lies at the heart of what economic models can contribute. The ultimate purpose of such models is to predict behavior in circumstances for which we have not yet observed behavior. If the predictive power of a theory is limited to situations that have been observed previously, then the power of the theory will be severely limited. Moreover, a theory based solely on empirical regularities can never be invalidated and as a result can never serve as a true theory of decisions in any fundamental sense.

Section 1 of this article will discuss the nature of the formation of probabilistic perceptions for the symmetric reference point situation in which all lottery outcomes are assessed initially as being equally probable. This reformulation of the preceptional concerns leads to modification of the standard axioms of expected utility, but does not require a modification of any of the choice-related properties. As is indicated in section 2, lotteries continue to be valued by a linear function of the utility of the payoffs, but the specific functional form need not be equivalent to the traditional expected utility value. The nature of these differences and some of the general properties of expected utility within prospective reference theory are also discussed in section 2. Section 3 indicates how the PRT model can be used to reconcile a wide variety of divergent phenomena with rational behavior. These aberrations include different variants of the Allais paradox, the overweighting of low-probability events, the existence of certainty premiums for complete elimination of a risk, and several other phenomena that have played a prominent role in challenges to the rational model. The PRT approach consequently predicts a wide range of empirical phenomena that have played a dominant role in the literature on the rationality of choice under uncertainty. As observed in the concluding section 4, the PRT approach by no means exhausts all forms of irrational behavior that have been observed. Nevertheless, it does provide a logically consistent framework that retains the key elements of the standard expected utility model while also recognizing the role of cognitive processes within a rational information processing framework.

1. Prospective reference theory

1.1. The formation of perceptions

Before discussing the role of reference risk in perception formation, it is instructive to review the elements of the Bayesian approach that will be adopted in this article. Individual risk perceptions will be characterized using a beta probability distribution. For lotteries involving two possible outcomes, the standard beta distribution will be used to characterize risk perceptions. With more than two outcomes, the multivariate generalization of the beta distribution—the Dirichlet distribution— will be employed.[3] The beta family of distributions is highly flexible and can assume a wide variety of skewed or symmetric shapes. Moreover, it is ideally suited to analyzing independent and identically distributed Bernoulli traials. To the extent that one can view probabilities in a lottery as equivalent to some mixture in a hypothetical urn from which one makes a random draw, as in Raiffa (1968), the stochastic process assumed here corresponds to the thought experiment that is utilized by the advocates of a Bayesian expected utility framework.

The particular parameterization of the distribution developed here is useful in empirical tests of the bivariate version of the model. Consider a multivariate outcome situation where there are n possible outcomes. Let the prior probability of outcome i be q_i, and let the individual observe ξ trials of which a fraction p_i are outcome i. Let γ be a parameter of the prior distribution corresponding to the informational content of the individual's prior beliefs. Then the posterior probability p_i^* outcome i is given by

$$p_i^* = \frac{\gamma q_i + \xi p_i}{\gamma + \xi}. \tag{1}$$

The individual acts as if he has observed γ trials in forming his prior q_i. He then observes ξ trials, and his posterior probability is a simple weighted average of q_i and p_i where the weights correspond to the fraction of his total information associated with his prior probability and with the experiment he has observed. In contexts using data on individual behavior, it is often feasible to estimate ξ/γ—the relative informational content of the experiment.[4] For example, hazard warning labels with very strong informational content were found to have very high values of ξ/γ (see Viscusi and O'Connor, 1984).

The perceptional structure of prospective reference theory utilizes this basic framework but introduces an additional stage in the preference formation process. Suppose that an individual faces a lottery on some prize, and he is told that p is the chance that he will win the prize. He will not treat this probabilistic information as fully informative, but will view it as providing incomplete information that he uses in standard Bayesian fashion to update his prior probability of success—which is here termed his *reference risk*.

The framework is consistent with two possible scenarios. First, the individual may be legitimately suspicious of supposedly "hard" probabilities, particularly if he does not have full confidence in the experiment being performed. The second possibility is that this behavior may reflect an inherent aspect of individuals' information processing whereby individuals act as if risk information is imperfect. Thus, the functioning of individuals' cognitive processes may lead to this partial learning phenomenon. Even under this second interpretation, however, the processing of the information and subsequent decisions will be assumed to occur in a rational, Bayesian manner that is augmented by the role of reference risks. Although the discussion in this section focuses on the situation in which there are symmetric reference points for all lottery outcomes, each of the above interpretations of reference points is consistent with multiple reference points that depend on the lottery outcome, the decision context, and the nature of the risk.

Consider a lottery with possible payoffs $(A_1, A_2, \ldots A_n)$ where each payoff A_i has a stated probability $p_i(0 \leqslant p_i \leqslant 1)$ that satisfies

$$\sum_{i=1}^{n} p_i = 1. \tag{2}$$

In the symmetric-reference-point case, the individual views each possible outcome as being equally likely, so the reference point is $1/n$. (See the appendix for an extension of the model to asymmetric reference points.) The informational content γ of the prior probability and the lottery information ξ are assumed to be the same for all payoffs, although this assumption could easily be relaxed in situations where there is a rationale for doing so. The perceived probability function P modifies the stated probability in a Bayesian manner, where

$$P(p_i) = \frac{\gamma(1/n) + \xi p_i}{\gamma + \xi}. \tag{3}$$

In situations in which informational content ξ varies by payoff, the notation $P(p_i, \xi_i)$ will be used.

The two extreme informational cases lead to dominance of one component of the perception function. If γ equals zero or if ξ/γ is arbitrarily large, then the perceptions equal the stated probabilities p_i, and the results are the same as in conventional decision models in which the probabilities are taken at face value. Similarly, if ξ/γ equals zero the individual places no weight on the lottery information and is guided solely by the reference risk.

The two p_i values that merit special treatment are the two cases of certainty, where $p_i = 0$ or 1. The certainty situation is easier to process, so to the extent that reference points play a role because of cognitive limitations, they will be less prominent in this case. Similarly, if it is individuals' underlying distrust of the accuracy of probabilistic information that is the driving force behind reference effects, the introduction of certainty should eliminate these concerns. Both of these factors lead credible lottery descriptions of certain events to be treated at face value, so that

$$P(0) = 0 \text{ and } P(1) = 1. \tag{4}$$

There may, however, be exceptional cases in which the lottery descriptions are not fully credible, and therefore the respondent may have a reason to believe that the stated certainty is only a rough approximation. For the n-payoff case, where the payoff for the certain events are included among the n payoffs, we will then have the value

$$P(0) = \frac{\gamma(1/n)}{\gamma + \xi},$$

and

$$P(1) = \frac{\gamma(1/n) + \xi}{\gamma + \xi}.$$

The discussion below will focus on the usual situation in which equation 4 holds, on the assumption that the certain events will be treated differently for the reasons stated above.

Thus, the role of reference effects is to convert a stated probability into a perceived probability following equations 3 and 4. In effect, reference effects introduce an earlier stage into a Bayesian learning process in situations that are normally considered to be simple situations in which lottery descriptions provide full information. The introduction of the reference-risk stage into the learning process by no means precludes subsequent stages of experimentation. Consider a situation in which an individual can acquire information regarding some lottery with probability p_i of outcome A. In the usual case, the p_i value serves as the prior probability, whereas within the prospective reference theory model the $P(p_i)$ value serves this function. Having made this modification, analysis of any situation of information acquisition proceeds in the usual fashion.

1.1.1. Properties of perceptions with reference points. Except for the two certainty cases, perceived probabilities can be characterized by a linear function of the stated probabilities, as is illustrated in figure 1 for the symmetric reference point case. For some value p_f, stated and perceived values are equal. For the symmetric rewards case, p_f equals $1/n$ so that, for example, p_i equals .5 for the binary outcome case. Low probabilities below p_f are perceived as being larger than their stated

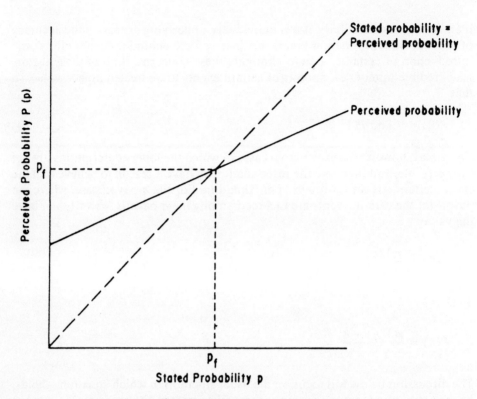

Fig. 1. Relation between perceived and stated probabilities.

values, and high probabilities above p_f are perceived as being smaller than their stated values. Changes in the reference point due, for example, to an increase in the number of lottery outcomes alter the vertical intercept and result in parallel shifts of the perceived probability line. Increases in the informational content ξ of the lottery rotate the perception function counterclockwise until in the limiting case of $\xi \to \infty$ it coincides with the 45° line. Similarly, boosting γ raises the weight on the prior probability so that as γ/ξ rises the perception line becomes horizontal, and the stated probability p plays no role.

The reference perception function is well behaved. Each perceived probability is in the appropriate range, where $0 < P(p_i) < 1$ for all p_i. In addition, perceived probabilities are additive. Suppose that there are n possible outcomes, where none of these has a p_i value of 0 or 1. Then

$$\sum_{i=1}^{n} P(p_i) = \sum_{i=1}^{n} \frac{\gamma(1/n) + \xi p_i}{\gamma + \xi} = 1,$$

from equation 2. Suppose there is some outcome A_{n+1} for which the stated p_i equals 0. In that situation in which the certain information is credible, outcome A_{n+1} is simply ignored and each of the remaining outcomes has an associated probability $1/n$. If outcome A_{n+1} has a p_i value of 1, all other outcomes drop out of the analysis. It matters little whether one assigns a reference probability $1/(n + 1)$ to events A_1 through A_n coupled with an arbitrarily large value of ξ/γ, or alternatively one views the decision maker as pruning his analysis to consider only outcomes with a finite probability of occurrence.[5]

The reference probability function accords generally with observed patterns of risk perception, as will be discussed in section 3.2. It follows the form analyzed with respect to worker risk perceptions by Viscusi and O'Connor (1984) and with respect to fatality risk perceptions by Viscusi (1985). In the latter case, the patterns of risk perception of different fatality risks found by researchers in psychology (Lichtenstein et al., 1978) were analyzed. That study found that people overestimate small risks such as botulism and underestimate large risks such as diabetes. Equation 3 was the functional form used to investigate these perceptions, as will be discussed further in section 3.

There is an additional parallel with Kahneman and Tversky's prospect theory model (1979) in which their decision weight function $\pi(p_i)$ serves an analogous role to the reference risk perception function $P(p_i)$. Their approach is similarly based on the widely observed empirical phenomenon that individuals tend to overestimate low-probability events and underestimate high probabilities. As in their formulation, the perception of certain events is not altered here (equation 4), and the perception of intermediate risks is transformed through a risk perception function.

Several differences with the prospect theory approach are noteworthy.[6] First, the reference risk perception function is generated by a rational Bayesian updating process from a reference risk level that is specified precisely, whereas decision weights reflect empirical patterns for which there is presently no well-defined theory for predicting their precise shape. Prospect theory does not impose any restrictions or make any predictions with respect to the location of the cross-over point p_f, the steepness of the curvature of the $\pi(p)$ function, or the exact behavior of this function as one approaches the extreme probability values 0 and 1. Second, decision weights are a nonlinear function rather than a linear function, which will lead to inherent inconsistency with the expected utility model. Third, whereas reference risk perceptions are additive, decision weights need not be. Indeed, Kahneman and Tversky (1979) stress that "decision weights are not probabilities: they do not obey the probability axioms and they should not be interpreted as measures of degree of belief . . . π is not a probability measure and it will be shown later that $\pi(p) + \pi(1 - p)$ is typically less than unity." They term this subadditivity *subcertainty*.

A second line of related research is the psychology literature on anchoring. Experimental studies suggest that probability assessments may be anchored in some initial value that usually stems from the wording of the questionnaire. Individuals then adjust their perceptions partially from the anchor toward the true probability.[7] These anchors are analogous in spirit to reference risk levels, except that they are not as well behaved. For example, whereas reference probability levels sum to 1 across all states, anchors need not. Moreover, the existence of anchors is typically treated as evidence of irrationality. To the extent that anchoring models have been estimated empirically, it has been with nonlinear functions that are usually subadditive.[8] Thus, anchoring models are viewed as alternatives to a Bayesian framework. Discussions of anchoring touch on some of the same phenomena as does the reference risk perception analysis, so that each approach addresses a similar class of concerns. However, the methodological approach is non-Bayesian, the choices usually violate the principles of rationality, and the empirical properties are quite different.

1.2. Implications for expected utility theory: the symmetric reference risk case

The modifications required to incorporate reference risk perceptions in the standard axioms of expected utility theory do not disturb its basis structure. In effect, one need only introduce a previous informational stage before the evaluation of any lottery. One's assessment of the lottery is then governed by the posterior probability of each outcome obtained using the reference perception as the prior probability, which is a quasi-Bayesian procedure.

One has considerable leeway in choosing the set of axioms for expected utility, including, for example, those of Arrow (1971) and Savage (1972). The specific formulation affects the degree of generality of the theory, but there are many strong parallels in the structure of assumptions. Here the assumptions employed by Luce and Raiffa (1957), which sacrifice some generality but are pertinent to the discrete lottery outcome situation adopted here, will be utilized. The set of assumptions adopted closely parallels the Luce and Raiffa (1957) framework. The fundamental changes that drive the distinctive aspects of this article's approach pertain to how individuals form their risk assessments (assumption 2) and how they process probability information presented in a compound lottery (assumption 3).

The first assumption, which is identical to that in the Luce and Raiffa (1957) formulation, is that individuals can order alternative lottery outcomes and do so in a transitive manner:

Assumption 1 (ordering of alternatives). The *preference or indifference* ordering, $\geqslant$, holds between any two prizes, and it is transitive. Formally, for any A_i and A_j, either $A_i \geqslant A_j$, or $A_j \geqslant A_i$, and if $A_i \geqslant A_j$ and $A_j \geqslant A_k$ then $A_i \geqslant A_k$.

The second assumption, concerning lottery perceptions, is a new and pivotal addition to the axiom set, since it presents a departure from the normal situation in which stated lottery probabilities are treated at face value. In effect, probabilities are processed through a Bayesian cognitive filter. In the symmetric reference point case with n prizes, individuals will employ their posterior assessment of the risk as their perceived probability, using $1/n$ as their prior probability and the stated value

$(p_1, A_1; p_2, A_2)$ will be used to denote a lottery that offers a chance p_1 of prize A_1 and a chance p_2 of prize A_2. More specifically, we have the following:

Assumption 2 (lottery perceptions). A stated lottery L defined by $L = p_1, A_1; p_2, A_2; \ldots; p_n, A_n)$ is perceived by the decision maker as $L^* = (P(p_1), A_1; P(p_2), A_2; \ldots; P(p_n), A_n)$, where

$$P(p_i) = \frac{\gamma(1/n) + \xi p_i}{\gamma + \xi}.$$

Since γ and ξ are nonnegative constants and the p_i values sum to 1, the perceived probabilities $P(p_i)$ also sum to 1. The reference perception formulation here assumes that reference points are symmetric. Both the informational content γ and the prior probability $1/n$ of each outcome are assumed to be identical. This assumption can be relaxed, but there is little basis for doing so for the types of lotteries considered in much of the experimental literature on decision making. Similarly, ξ could vary according to different payoffs if the new information about different components of the lottery differed, but this is not likely to be the case for abstract experimental lotteries. The assumptions made about the symmetry of reference perceptions make the predictions of the model less ambiguous than if γ, ξ, and the perceived prior probability all varied across payoffs. In this instance, the informational requirements needed by an external observer wishing to make behavioral predictions would be far greater.

The next assumption concerning the reduction of compound lotteries parallels more traditional formulations, except that individuals convert each component probability into a perceived probability.

Assumption 3 (reduction of compound lotteries). One is indifferent between a compound lottery and a simple lottery on the A_i's computed using the ordinary probability calculus, where all stated probabilities p_i are viewed as $P(p_i)$. If stated lottery $L(i)$ is defined as $L(i) = (p_1(i), A_1; p_2(i), A_2; \ldots; p_n(i), A_n)$, for $i = 1, 2, \ldots, m$, and the associated perceived lottery is defined as $L^*(i) = (P(p_1(i)), A_1; P(p_2(i)), A_2; \ldots; P(p_n(i)), A_n)$, then the compound lottery $(s_1, L(1); s_2, L(2); \ldots; s_m, L(m))$ will be equivalent to some simple full information (i.e., $P(r_i) = r_i$) lottery $(r_1, A_1; r_2, A_2; \ldots; r_n, A_n)$, where $r_j = P(s_1)P(p_j(1)) + P(s_2)P(p_j(2)) + \ldots + P(s_m)P(p_j(m))$.

Although this assumption represents a direct generalization of the standard approach to the reference perception situation, its implications are by no means innocuous. Suppose, for example, the individual faces a lottery with the compound probabilities s and p. The assumption here is that he will first process these probabilities through the reference perception function and then multiply them rather than performing these operations in the opposite order. Thus, $P(s)P(p) \neq P(sp)$, so the result will be different than if the compounding operation were done first. The validity of this assumption is an empirical issue that will be discussed below. A principal implication is that the framing of compound lotteries will be consequential—a result that has often been stressed in the psychology literature.[9] Presenting a reduced compound lottery will be perceived differently than the series of individual lotteries.

The next assumption pertaining to the continuity of lottery outcomes is a direct analogue of the standard formulation.

Assumption 4 (continuity). Each prize A_i is indifferent to some lottery on A_1 (highest ranked outcome) and A_n (lowest ranked outcome). One can construct a full information lottery with a probability of u_i of A_1 such that A_i is indifferent to $[u_i, A_1; (1 - u_i), A_n] = \hat{A}_i$ for some u_i, where $A_1 > A_i > A_n$.

This assumption that a full information reference lottery exists is somewhat stronger than what is required, since there will be an infinity of partial information lotteries with finite ξ_i that will also suffice as the reference lottery. If, however, γ/ξ_i were very large, it might not be possible to vary the perceived reference probability sufficiently to establish an equivalent reference lottery. Since this reference lottery procedure is only a hypothetical thought experiment for establishing a utility metric, it suffices to assume that we can construct a lottery so that individuals will perceive the probability of A_i as being u_i. Rather than index the preference payoffs according to both a stated probability and some precision parameter, they will be stated in terms of the full information lottery counterparts or, equivalently, in terms of their perceived probabilities.

Assumption 5 (substitutability). In any lottery $L, \hat{A}_i$ is substitutable for A_i, that is, $(p_1, A_1; \ldots; p_i, A_i; \ldots; p_n, A_n)$ is indifferent to $(p_1, A_1; \ldots; p_i, \hat{A}_i; \ldots; p_n, A_n)$.

Clearly, this substitutability hinges on individuals perceiving compound lotteries in the manner described in assumption 4. Otherwise, the value of the lottery might change upon substitution, leading to potential inconsistencies.

The next assumptions are also identical to the Luce and Raiffa (1957) formulation, except that assumption 7 has been modified to take into account the formulation of risk perceptions.

Assumption 6 (transitivity). Preference and indifference among lottery tickets are transitive relations.

Assumption 7 (monotonicity). A lottery $(p, A_1; (1 - p)A_n)$ is preferred or indifferent to $(p', A_1; 1 - p', A_n)$ if and only if $P(p) \geqslant P(p')$.

It should be noted that if the lotteries share a common value of ξ, the requirement in assumption 7 is simly that $p \geqslant p'$, as in the traditional formulation.

These assumptions ensure that each payoff can be replaced by a lottery on the highest and lowest valued payoffs, which establishes the utility metric. Through the reduction of compound lotteries we can reduce any lottery into a simple lottery on the highest- and lowest-valued payoffs, which, by assumption 7, can be ranked according to the probability of receiving payoff A_1. Thus, following the standard reasoning, we are led to a variant on the basic result.

Expected utility theorem. If the preference or indifference relation satisfies assumptions 1 through 7, there are numbers u_i associated with basic prizes A_i such that for two lotteries L and L' the magnitudes of the expected values $P(p_1)u_1 + P(p_2)u_2 + \ldots + P(p_n)u_n$ and $P(p_1')u_1 + P(p_2')u_2 + \ldots + P(p_n')u_n$ reflect the preference between lotteries.

2. Properties of individual decisions

2.1. General implications for expected utility theory

If we let $EU^*(L)$ denote the expected utility of lottery L within PRT and $U(A_i)$ denote the value u_i, then the value of a lottery will be determined by

$$EU^*(L) = \sum_{i=1}^{n} P(p_i)U(A_i),$$

which is analogous to the standard expected utility value

$$EU(L) = \sum_{i=1}^{n} p_i U(A_i).$$

Thus, the principal amendments to the expected utility model are the replacement of actual probabilities by perceived probabilities (assumption 2) and the specification of how these perceptions are formed when facing compound lotteries (assumption 3).

Since the reference perception function $P(p_i)$ is a linear transformation of p_i, expected utility remains a linear function of the utilities. More specifically, using equation 3 we can express $EU^*(L)$ as

$$EU^*(L) = \frac{\gamma}{\gamma + \xi} \left[\sum_{i=1}^{n} (1/n)U(A_i) \right] + \frac{\xi}{\gamma + \xi} \left[\sum_{i=1}^{n} p_i U(A_i) \right].$$

If we define $EU_0(L)$ as the utility of a random lottery on the payoffs in lottery L, or

$$EU_0(L) = \sum_{i=1}^{n} (1/n)U(A_i),$$

then we can write

$$EU^*(L) = \frac{\gamma}{\gamma + \xi} [EU_0(L)] + \frac{\xi}{\gamma + \xi} [EU(L)]. \tag{5}$$

Thus, expected utility is a weighted average of the rewards one would obtain from a random lottery on the payoffs and the conventional expected utility value. The weights are the relative information content $\gamma/(\gamma + \xi)$ associated with the reference probability and the relative informational content $\xi/(\gamma + \xi)$ of the stated lottery.

Whether the individual's expected utility is higher or lower within the PRT approach hinges on whether the random lottery offers higher or lower expected rewards than with the expected utility model. After some algebraic manipulation, the difference is given by

$$EU^*(L) - EU(L) = \frac{\gamma}{\gamma + \xi} [EU_0(L) - EU(L)].$$

Thus, the difference is the gap between $EU_0(L)$ and $EU(L)$, weighted by the fraction of the informational content associated with the reference point. For γ equal to zero, there is no difference in the approaches, since the role of the reference point drops out. If ξ equals zero, the reference risk perceptions dominate and the change in expected utility equals the difference between EU_0 and $EU(L)$.

A slight modification of this relationship can also be used to compare two different lotteries. Suppose that lottery A is of the form $(p_1,A_1; \ldots ;p_n,A_n)$ and lottery B is of the form $(q_1,B_1; \ldots ;q_m,B_m)$, where m need not equal n. Upon taking differences, one obtains the result that

$$EU^*(A) - EU^*(B) = \frac{\gamma}{\gamma + \xi} [EU_0(A) - EU_0(B)] + \frac{\xi}{\gamma + \xi} [EU(A) - EU(B)].$$

The difference in expected values equals the difference in the expected utility from a random lottery weighted by the fraction of the informational content associated with the reference probability plus the conventional expected utility difference weighted by the fraction of the informational content associated with the lottery.

Because reference risk perceptions dampen the influence of the stated terms of a lottery, changes in lottery probabilities have less effect than they otherwise would. Consider a binary lottery with a top prize A_1 and a bottom prize A_2, so that we can set $U(A_1)$ equal to 1 and $U(A_2)$ equal to 0. In a standard expected utility framework, boosting the chance of receiving A_1 from $.5p$ to p will increase the expected utility of the lottery by $.5p$. In contrast, with reference probabilities playing a role, the change in the perceived probability of success will only be

$$P(p) - P(.5p) = \frac{.5\gamma + \xi p}{\gamma + \xi} - \frac{.5\gamma + .5\xi p}{\gamma + \xi} = \frac{.5\xi p}{\gamma + \xi} < .5p.$$

As ξ/γ rises, the relative informational content of the lottery increases so that in the limiting case the change in expected utility equals $.5p$.

The PRT formulation also highlights the importance of lottery framing—an issue that has been a major theme in the psychology literature. Consider the two lotteries $L_1 = (\frac{1}{2}, 0; \frac{1}{2}, 1)$ and $L_2 = (\frac{1}{2}, 0; \frac{1}{4}, 1; \frac{1}{4}, 1 - \varepsilon)$. Lottery L_1 stochastically dominates L_2 in terms of the stated lottery terms, and in the limiting case $(\xi/\gamma \rightarrow \infty)$ individuals will prefer L_1. This dominance does not hold in terms of the perceived lottery attractiveness, and for sufficiently small ε lottery L_2 will be preferred. The source of the preference is that by creating a new state with a positive reward, individuals will tend to assign a lower prior probability (⅓ rather than ½) to the chance of no positive payoff. This change in the prior will be reflected at least in part in individuals' perceived probabilities of lottery outcomes.

Such behavior is by no means unreasonable, nor does it represent a logical inconsistency. Consider the limiting case of imperfectly informative lottery information. If one were given no probability information but was simply told that there is a lottery with payoffs [0,1] and another lottery with three possible payoffs [0,1,1 − ε], then if one treated each state as being equally likely, the second lottery would be preferred, since it offers a ⅔ chance of a payoff of roughly 1, whereas the first option offers a ½ chance of such a reward. Within the realm of the perceived properties of lotteries, stochastic dominance is not violated. Discussions of rationality and consistency must take place given the manner in which lottery information is processed by the decision maker, which may differ from how the lottery terms are stated. A noteworthy aspect of the role of framing is that within the context of prospective reference theory, the influence of lottery framing is linked to quite precise empirical predictions. In contrast, psychological models of behavioral choice have noted the importance of framing effects, but thus far have offered no systematic basis for predicting their influence.

2.2. Relative odds and compound lotteries

Several of the principal predictions of the prospective reference approach hinge on the effect on ratios and products of probabilities. In the usual case, altering the scale of relative probabilities is not consequential. Thus, the ratio of probabilities .6/.3 is associated with the same relative odds as .8/.4. The perceived probabilities may not, however, be the same, since $P(.6)/P(.3)$ may not equal $P(.8)/P(.4)$.

Consider the general issue of how altering the probability ratio p/q by some scale fraction α will alter the probability ratio, where α is not so large that either αp or αq exceeds 1. In the symmetric n-outcome case, we have the result that

$$\frac{\partial}{\partial \alpha} \frac{P(\alpha p)}{P(\alpha q)} = \frac{\gamma \xi (1/n)(p - q)}{[\gamma(1/n) + \xi q \alpha]^2}. \tag{6}$$

For values of $p = q$, the odds ratio is unaffected by α and always equals 1; for $p > q$, increasing α raises the discrepancy in the relative odds by increasing the weight on the lottery probability p, which exceeds q, compared with the reference risk $1/n$, which is the same in both cases. The opposite result occurs for $p < q$, since raising α in this case reduces the odds ratio.

These results consequently include as a special case the prediction that

$$\frac{P(p)}{P(q)} \leqslant \frac{P(\alpha p)}{P(\alpha q)} \cdot \tag{7}$$

for $p < q$ and $\alpha < 1$. Reducing the influence on the stated probability through the factor α and thus increasing the weight on the reference probabilities, which are equal, will tend to equalize the odds ratio in this case. Thus, as we make the component probabilities in a ratio of probabilities smaller, the probabilities are viewed as more similar. For example, the value of .002/.004 is viewed as being closer to 1 that is .2/.4.

Equation 7 is a rewritten form of Kahneman and Tversky's (1979) "general principle underlying substitution axiom violations." In their analysis, they have observed that as an empirical regularity individuals behave in accordance with equation 7. Thus, many prominent experimental phemomena such as the Allais paradox, which will be addressed in section 3, can be traced to their relationship. The PRT approach can be viewed as providing a theoretical basis for the prospect theory analysis. Equation 7 is a prediction of the PRT model, whereas within prospect theory it is an empirical regularity incorporated as an assumption.[10]

As we noted with respect to assumption 3, the compounding of lotteries is also affected by the role of reference probabilities. Lottery 1 and lottery 2 in figure 2, which are equivalent under expected utility theory, will consequently be perceived differently.

A variant on this compounding issue is whether it is desirable to introduce additional compounding on the lottery on some prize. Suppose that there is a probability pq that the prize will be rewarded. Should the lottery be framed in a manner so that pq is the announced probability of winning, or should the lottery be staged in a sequence in which there will be some probability p that one will enter round 2 of the lottery with a subsequent chance q of success? In effect, one would win a lottery ticket on a lottery ticket. Thus the two alternative choices are the lotteries sketched in figure 3. If lottery 2 is preferred to lottery 1, one could continue to enhance its attractiveness by introducing an arbitrarily large number of stages.

Unlike the more symmetric compounding case in figure 2, compounding a lottery on the chance to win a prize is always undesirable. In particular, the condition $P(pq) > P(p)P(q)$ can be rewritten as

$$\frac{.5\gamma + \xi pq}{\gamma + \xi} > \frac{(.5\gamma + \xi p)}{(\gamma + \xi)} \frac{(.5\gamma + \xi q)}{(\gamma + \xi)} \cdot$$

which reduces to

$$1 + 2pq > p + q,$$

which always holds for permissible values of p and q.

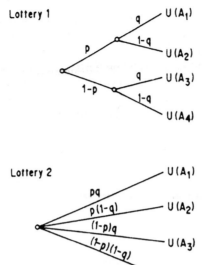

Fig. 2. Compound versus simple lotteries.

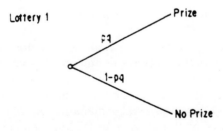

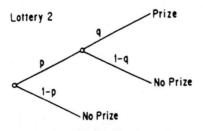

Fig. 3. Compounding a lottery on a prize.

Although it will be shown below that individuals will tend to overestimate low-probability events, the introduction of additional compounding that in effect subdivides a probability into the product of successively smaller probabilities will lower the perceived chance of success. This property accords with typical lottery structures, which award prizes rather than lottery tickets for a subsequent stage. To the extent that such phenomena of compound lottery tickets are observed, one must appeal to other economic factors such as the utility associated with anticipation for lotteries resolved over time.

3. Applications to empirical and experimental phenomena

Before examining the application of the model to various aberrant phenomena that have been observed, it should be emphasized that the PRT framework is consistent with the wide body of empirical evidence supporting the subjective expected utility framework. Since the prospective reference theory model includes expected utility theory as a special case for which ξ/γ is arbitrarily large, as one might expect for frequently repeated market transactions, there is no need to reconcile the theory with existing evidence in support of the expected utility model. As a result, the emphasis here will be on highlighting how the model explains phenomena that contradict the expected utility model.

3.1. Overweighting of low probabilities and certainty premiums

The influential study by Lichtenstein et al. (1978) demonstrated that individuals tend to overassess low-probability events and underassess high-probability events. This risk-related bias is a central theme in the psychology of risk literature, and it has been incorporated as an assumption in Kahneman and Tversky's (1979) prospect theory model. Whereas the usual explanation offered for this phenomenon is that it reflects a form of irrationality, in the PRT approach it is viewed as the consequence of a conventional Bayesian learning process.

A bias of this type is exactly what one would predict from the prospective reference theory framework. From equation 3,

$$P(p) > p \qquad \text{if } p < 1/n$$

and

$$P(p) < p \qquad \text{if } p > 1/n,$$

which is the observed pattern. In Viscusi (1985), the functional form in equation 3 is fitted to the original Lichtenstein et al. (1978) data, and observed behavior is shown to be consistent with a rational Bayesian updating process from an initial reference risk. The apparent bias in risk perceptions is exactly what oen would expect with a rational Bayesian learning process in which only partial information has been acquired. The critical test of rationality is whether there is a risk-related bias in the degree of learning. In particular, is there a probability-related difference in the degree of updating ξ/γ from the reference risk toward the actual probabilities? For the Lichtenstein et al. (1978) sample, it is shown in Viscusi (1985) that there is no statistically significant bias of this sort, which is the risk-related bias issue that is more pertinent for any test of individual rationality.

One manifestation of this overestimation of low probabilities is that individuals will be willing to pay a certainty premium for reductions of risk that completely eliminate the risk. Thus, any given incremental risk reduction Δp will be more highly valued if this reduction leads to zero risk than if it achieves only partial risk reduction, whereas standard economic models predict that the last incremental risk reduction should be less highly valued.

There are two types of experimental evidence in support of this phenomenon. The first consists of studies such as Kahneman and Tversky (1979).[11] Experimental subjects prefer hypothetical insurance policies that reduce the risk from $p/2$ to 0 to policies that reduce the risk from p to $p/2$. This result is a direct consequence of the nature of risk perceptions. Since $P(0)$ is assumed to be a full information probability equal to 0, we have $P(p) - P(p/2) < P(p/2) - P(0)$, since

$$\frac{.5\gamma + p\xi}{\gamma + \xi} - \frac{.5\gamma + .5p\xi}{\gamma + \xi} < \frac{.5\gamma + .5p\xi}{\gamma + \xi} - 0,$$

as one can readily verify. The driving force behind this effect in the present analysis and in prospect theory is that a zero probability is treated at face value, and hence there is a jump in the perceived probability. If 0 were treated as imperfect information with the same reference risk probability .5 and the same weight ξ as the other outcome, no certainty effect would be observed. Thus, the existence of certainty premiums is consistent with the PRT formulation in which certain events with probability 0 or 1 are viewed as being fully informative.

Similarly, an analysis of consumer valuations of product risk reductions in a quasi-market experiment with over 1500 consumers also reveals the existence of certainty premiums. The results in table 1 present consumers' willingeness to pay for incremental risk reductions of 5/10,000, where these results are give for four injury pairs and three different starting risk values. Consumers initially display diminishing marginal valuations of risk reduction for the reduction in the product risk rate from 15/10,000 to 10/10,000 and then to 5/10,000. However, the valuation of the last incremental risk reduction that eliminates the risk completely is valued by a greater amount than the preceding increment. This result contradicts a standard expected utility model but accords with PRT and with approaches such as prospect theory. More generally, one would predict that individuals will tend to overreact to small risks such as the chance of a Tylenol poisoning due to product tampering or the risk of being a victim of a terrorist act while vacationing in Europe.

Table 1. Consumers' marginal valuations of reducing both risks by a probability of 5 injuries per 10,000

Starting risk (injuries/10,000 bottles)	Marginal willingness to pay (dollars/bottle) (standard errors of mean)			
	Inhalation— skin poisoning	Inhalation— child poisoning	Gassing— eye burn	Child poisoning— gassing
15	1.04	1.84	0.65	0.99
	(0.10)	(0.35)	(0.04)	(0.15)
10	0.34	0.54	0.19	0.24
	(0.05)	(0.12)	(0.03)	(0.11)
5	2.41	5.71	0.83	0.99
	(0.14)	(1.05)	(0.10)	(0.12)

Source: Mean values are from Viscusi, Magat, and Huber (1987). The standard errors were generated for this article.

3.2. The representativeness heuristic

Since the PRT approach is a quasi-Bayesian approach, psychological evidence that contradicts the validity of the Bayesian updating process poses a potentially critical challenge to the framework. Chief among these difficulties is evidence in support of the representativeness heuristic, whereby respondents assessing the chance that an event belonging to class A or class B tend to place less weight on the base-rate conditions than Bayes' theorem requires.

Consider the following example from Tversky and Kahneman (1982). Under scenario 1, subjects are given a personal description of a worker that is intended to be worthless information, and are told that the group from which the description was drawn consisted of 70 lawyers and 30 engineers. In effect, individuals tended to ignore the prior probabilities regarding the mix of engineers and lawyers, treating this ratio as closer to 50–50 than the 70–30 and 30–70 splits.[12]

This apparent dampening of the difference in the assessed probabilities is what PRT predicts. If the occupational mix information were equivalent to 100 draws from an urn, ξ would equal 100. Using this value of ξ,

$$P(\text{engineer}|70 \text{ engineers}, 30 \text{ lawyers}) = \frac{.5\gamma + .7(100)}{\gamma + 100}.$$

and

$$P(\text{engineer}|30 \text{ engineers}, 70 \text{ lawyers}) = \frac{.5\gamma + .3(100)}{\gamma + 100}.$$

The ratio of the assessed probabilities in the two situations satisfies the condition

$$1 \leqslant \frac{P(\text{engineer}|70 \text{ engineers, 30 lawyers})}{P(\text{engineer}|30 \text{ engineers, 70 lawyers})} = \frac{.5\gamma + 70}{.5\gamma + 30} \leqslant \frac{.7}{.3}.$$

For high values of γ for which there is relatively low weight placed on the occupational mix information, the probability ratio approaches 1, which is what has
been observed experimentally.

In a variant of this study undertaken by Grether (1980), subjects placed greater
reliance on the mix information as the experiment was repeated. The PRT approach predicts such behavior, since as subjects have more experience with the experimental information and are given feedback that indicates that the information
is accurate, then the relative weight ξ/γ placed on the base occupational mix information will rise. Under this interpretation, the information presented becomes
more credible with repetition. The alternative explanation that individuals learn
how to play with repetition is not required. Experimental subjects may be fully
rational from the outset.

3.3. The Allais paradox

The most prevalent class of experimental phenomena contradicting the expected
utility model consists of various violations of the substitution axiom. When a particular lottery L is substituted into another lottery context, the apparent valuation
of lottery L often changes. The well-known Allais paradox epitomizes this
phenomenon, which has been replicated in a variety of experimental contexts with
different lottery structures. Since all of these phenomena involve the same principle of substitution axiom violations in equation 7, the original version of the Allais
paradox will be discussed here.[13]

In the original Allais paradox, subjects exhibited the following preferences:

$$P(1) \ U(100) > P(.10) \ U(500) + P(.89) \ U(100) + P(.01) \ U(0), \tag{8}$$

and

$$P(.11) \ U(100) + P(.89) \ U(0) < P(.10) \ U(500) + P(.90) \ U(0). \tag{9}$$

Within the standard expected utility framework in which $P(p) = p$, the only difference between these two sets of lottery pairs is that $.89 \ U(10)$ has been subtracted
from both sides of equation 8 to produce equation 9. Yet the preferences have been
reversed. If, however, we substitute the PRT values for the perceived probabilities,
equations 8 and 9 become

$$U(100) > \frac{(.33\gamma + .1\xi)}{\gamma + \xi} \ U(500) + \frac{(.33\gamma + .89\xi)}{\gamma + \xi} \ U(100) + \frac{(.33\gamma + .01\xi)}{\gamma + \xi} \ U(0),$$

$$\tag{10}$$

and

$$\frac{(.5\gamma + .11\xi)}{\gamma + \xi} U(100) + \frac{(.5\gamma + .89\xi)}{\gamma + \xi} U(0) <$$

$$\frac{(.5\gamma + .1\xi)}{\gamma + \xi} U(500)$$

$$+ \frac{(.5\gamma + .9\xi)}{\gamma + \xi} U(0). \tag{11}$$

If we set $U(0) = 0$, then we can rewrite equation 10 as

$$U(100) > \frac{.33\gamma + .1\xi}{.67\gamma + .11\xi} U(500), \tag{12}$$

and equation 11 becomes

$$U(100) < \frac{.5\gamma + .1\xi}{.5\gamma + .11\xi} U(500). \tag{13}$$

Conditions 12 and 13 are not contradictory, provided that

$$\frac{.5\gamma + .1\xi}{.5\gamma + .11\xi} > \frac{.33\gamma + .1\xi}{.67\gamma + .11\xi},$$

which is *always* true except in the full information case where ξ is infinite, in which case a strict equality prevails.

Thus, the PRT approach is a framework that is more than possibly consistent with the Allais paradox. It predicts that such a phenomenon will always occur except for fully informative probabilities. The underlying rationale for this version of the Allais paradox is that $P(1)$ equals 1, whereas the other probabilities are governed by equation 4. Although a certainty effect is dominant in this case, other substitution axiom violations without a certainty effect can be reconciled using equation 7. The PRT explanation for the Allais paradox stems from the manner in which information is perceived and processed. This paradoxical behavior is predicted by the theory rather than being potentially consistent with the theory.[14]

3.4. Compound lotteries and the isolation effect

Another class of phenomena that are prominent in the psychology literature that can be addressed with the symmetric PRT model are inconsistencies that arise with compound lotteries.[15] Under the first scenario, an individual is told that he has a .75 chance of 0 and a .25 probability of facing a second lottery in which he will have a choice between (.8, 4000; .2, 0) and (1.0, 3000). Respondents prefer the certain reward of 3000 in round 2. Under the expected utility framework, this lottery sequence can be expressed as a choice between (.2, 4000; .8, 0) and (.25, 3000; .75, 0), where the second lottery is preferred when the lotteries are described sequentially. When offered this lottery choice directly, however, individuals reverse their preferences, since they now prefer to take the chance to win the prize of 4000. The manner in which the different lotteries are decomposed and edited in these two cases is termed the *isolation effect* in prospect theory.[16]

The PRT formulation of preference formation and assumption 3 concerning perceptions of compound lotteries reflect an approach similar to that of prospect theory. More specifically, setting $U(0) = 0$, under the first scenario respondents exhibit the preferences

$$U(3000) > \frac{.5\gamma + .8\xi}{\gamma + \xi} U(4000),$$

and under the second scenario

$$\frac{.5\gamma + .2\xi}{\gamma + \xi} U(4000) > \frac{.5\gamma + .25\xi}{\gamma + \xi} U(3000).$$

One can verify that these inequalities will hold for all nonzero values of γ. This class of phenomena contradicts the expected utility framework but will always occur in the PRT model. The driving force of the effect is the assumption that, when confronting compound lotteries, each individual probability will be processed separately using the reference probability function. Thus, the editing and perceptual explanations that have been offered in the literature are incorporated in the PRT model in an explicit manner that yield unambiguous predictions regarding how individuals will process complex lottery information.

4. Conclusions

The recent literature in economics and psychology, particularly that dealing with what has been termed *prospect theory,* has identified a wide variety of systematic violations of the expected utility model. These violations were first observed with respect to hypothetical experiments, but recent evidence suggests that they are of consequence for economic behavior as well.

If our objective is to develop a model with descriptive as well as prescriptive validity, then some modification of expected utility theory is required. The issue is which alternative framework we should adopt and how big a departure from the full rationality case we wish to make. Perhaps the major drawback of abandoning a well-defined theory is that the alternative may have less predictive validity. To take the extreme case, one might simply summarize recent evidence as indicating that people are irrational. Such a judgment may be correct as far as it goes, but it does not indicate the nature of the departure from rationality or enable us to predict the patterns of behavior in new situations.

By introducing the role of a reference risk from which individuals revise their probability assessments when presented probabilistic information, one can generalize the expected utility model to address these phenomena without altering its fundamental character. This modification incorporates many of the concerns raised in the literature, such as those treated by prospect theory, but it also embodies a quasi-Bayesian structure that is consistent with empirical evidence in support of expected utility theory. Since the expected utility framework is a special case of the PRT model, there is no need to reconcile the two frameworks.

The PRT model with symmetric reference points has substantial predictive power, since the value of the reference point is specified. This framework is particularly applicable to phenomena that have been observed in experimental contexts. Among phenomena that are *predicted* by the PRT symmetric reference risk model are the following: overweighting of low probabilities, premiums for certain eliminations of a risk, the representativeness heuristic, and the Allais paradox and related violations of the substitution axiom. This substantial power to predict these aberrant phenomena distinguishes the PRT approach from many alternative models designed to explain apparently irrational behavior.

Researchers in psychology, and the developers of prospect theory in particular, have played a valuable role in highlighting systematic behavioral deviations from the standard expected utility model. The PRT model does not address all of the challenges that have been advanced against the expected utility model. Nevertheless, it does resolve a wide range of difficulties that have played a prominent role in the literature, while at the same time retaining the attractive features of a rational model of economic choice uncertainty. If we let individuals' risk perceptions reflect the perceptual problems and informational inadequacies that affect decisions, then the subsequent behavior accords quite closely with rational economic behavior.

Appendix. Extension to multiple reference points

A.1. Modifying the model for multiple reference risks

The symmetric reference risk model provides a framework for analysis of individuals confronting abstract lotteries and situations in which we have no basis for determining how individuals' prior beliefs differ from a random chance at a particular outcome. In most decision contexts, however, the individual has some prior experience regarding a particular event, so that his assessed prior probability of outcome i will not be $1/n$, but some other value π_i. This value π_i may be influenced by past observations of such events, inferences based on similar events, and related factors.[17] This appendix will describe how the analysis can be modified to incorporate such phenomena.

If we abstract from differences in informational content across events, the assessed probability of event i will be

$$P(p_i) = \frac{\gamma \pi_i + \xi p_i}{\gamma + \xi}.$$

The values of γ and ξ can also be permited to vary by events, but doing so complicates the analysis and is not needed for any of the specific examples considered. Generalizing the analysis to permit differing degrees of informational content across events is also possible.

The nature of the formation of probability assessments is, however, not completely straightforward. Consider the following three lotteries. In lottery 1, there is a 50–50 chance that the individual will win a car, or (.5, car; .5, 0). For concreteness, suppose that the individual's past experience with such lotteries has been unfavorable, so that the π(car) value is below .5, resulting in $P(.5, car) < .5$. In lottery 2, the top prize is a boat, or (.5, boat; .5, 0). For analogous reasons, suppose that π(boat) value is below .5, so that $P(.5, boat) < .5$. In lottery 3, the individual will win either a car or a boat, or (.5, car; .5, boat).

There are three possible solutions. First, if the π values are consistent across lotteries, then $P(.5, car) + P(.5, boat) < 1$, violating additivity. One method for resolving the inconsistency across lotteries 1–3 is to assume that individuals have common prior probabilities, not multiple prior probabilities, so that both π(car) and π(boat) equal .5. Such an assumption excludes any meaningful role for individuals' prior information, however. A second solution to the inconsistency involves the perception of a different lottery than is stated. If the individual believed that there was a nonzero chance that those offering the lottery would renege on either prize, giving him perhaps 0 payoff, then in effect the lottery has been misrepresented. Once the payoff 0 is included, the assessed probabilities can sum to 1. One could develop the analysis below based on this assumption, but there would be an indeterminacy regarding the value of the omitted payoff.

An approach to resolving potential inconsistencies that will be adopted here is to assume that the π values depend not only on the individual prize but also on the other prizes in the particular lottery. Thus, the chance that the individual will receive a boat hinges on what alternative prizes he might also receive. The role of individual learning pertains to the entire lottery structure, not just one payoff. In this instance, the set of possible payoffs is taken at face value, but the assessed probability of any particular prize depends on the entire set of prizes in that lottery.

Consider a standard lottery of the form $(p_1, A_1; p_2, A_2; \ldots; p_n, A_n)$. In this case, the individual acts as if he has the prior probability $\pi(A_i; A_1, \ldots, A_{i-1}, A_{i+1}, \ldots, A_n)$, which will be denoted by π_i in situations where the set of pertinent payoffs is unambiguous. These prior probabilities are assumed to be nonnegative and to sum to 1.

The perceived probability $P(p_i, A_i; A_1, \ldots, A_{i-1}, A_{i+1}, \ldots, A_n)$ will be denoted by P_i, where

$$P_i = \frac{\gamma \pi_i + \xi p_i}{\gamma + \xi}.\tag{14}$$

It follows from the assumed properties of π_i that

$$\sum_{i=1}^{n} P_i = 1.$$

In the multiple reference point case, the reference points π_i satisfy all of the usual properties of a probability measure, as do the P_i values.

The change in the perceptional formulation of the reference points leaves the basic assumptions largely unchanged. Assumption 3 for lottery perceptions is modified by replacing the $P(p_i)$ equation by equation 14. Two additional assumptions are also critically involved—in particular, those pertaining to the reduction of compound lotteries and sub-stitutability. In each case, the role of contextual factors could potentially cause intract-able difficulties.

One can resolve such problems by making π_i depend only on the particular lottery im-bedded within a larger decision tree. For example, suppose there is a compound lottery in which there is a chance s of facing the lottery $(p_1, A_1; 1 - p_1, A_2)$ and a chance $1 - s$ of receiv-ing A_3. Then the reference points for A_1 and A_2 are assumed to be independent of A_3, making it possible to substitute equivalent lotteries and to reduce a compound lottery in which the influence of the reference point is retained. This assumption is in the same spirit as the earlier assumption regarding the perception of compound lotteries in accordance with the isolation effect.

Thus, in reducing compound lotteries under assumption 3, one continues to assume that the compound probabilities consist of the product of two probabilities, each of which has been transformed using the reference probability formulation, except that $P(p_j(i))$ is calculated using the multiple reference point equation 14.

Similarly, the substitutability assumption can be generalized directly, since a shift in the context of a particular lottery is irrelevant because the other branches of the decision tree are assumed to be irrelevant. One must, however, impose the additional assumption that the substitution of equivalent utility items does not alter the reference point. Consider two lotteries—$(p, A_1; 1 - p, A_2)$ and $(p, A_1; 1 - p, A_3)$. If the individual is indifferent between A_2 and A_3, then $\pi(A_1; A_2)$ must equal $\pi(A_1; A_3)$.

A.2. The Ellsberg paradox

The multiple reference point model can be used to explain one of the most basic and well-known violations of rational behavior—the Ellsberg paradox.[18] Consider the following basic version of the Ellsberg paradox. Urn 1 has 100 red and black balls, but the mix is not known. Urn 2 has 100 balls, 50 of which are red and 50 of which are black. You can win a $100 prize if you correctly pick the ball color for the urn you choose. The observed behavior is that people are indifferent between drawing a red ball or black ball from urn 1. They would rather draw a red ball from urn 2 than from urn 1 and would rather draw a black ball from urn 2 than from urn 1. These patterns of preferences are inconsistent unless the assessed probabilities for the uncertain urn are subadditive.

Rather than defining events in terms of colors of balls, define them in terms of drawing the color ball associated with the awarding of a $100. Thus, the individual has some prior probability $\pi(\$100; 0) < .5$ of winning the prize when there are two ball colors involved. Moreover, to achieve additivity, $\pi(\$100; 0)$ and $\pi(0; \$100)$ must sum to 1. There are two possi-ble interpretations of this prior probability. First, the individual may believe that the experi-ment is being manipulated against him in some manner, thus leading to a below-average chance of success. Thus, even converting his chance of success to a "hard" probability by choosing the ball color based on the tossing of a fair coin, as suggested by Raiffa (1961), may not be effective if he believes that the presence of ambiguity creates greater opportunities for manipulation of the experiment. Second, based on past experience with lotteries he may be pessimistic of the chance of winning regardless of the ball color he picks. This belief may be a quite rational reflection of his past experiences, since almost all available lotteries are at actuarially unfair odds.

The perceived probability of drawing a winning ball will be given by

$$P(.5) = \frac{\gamma\pi(\$100; 0) + .5\xi}{\gamma + \xi}.$$

For urn 1, the value of ξ is 100, and $P(.5) < .5$, as is observed. For urn 2, the value of ξ exceeds 100, and if the individual takes the experiment at face value, then $\xi \to \infty$, and the resulting value of $P(.5)$ will exceed that for urn 1 and will equal .5 in the full information case. Thus, the precision of the information associated with urn 2 eliminates the role of the pessimistic reference risk $\pi(\$100; 0)$.

The traditional explanation for the Ellsberg paradox is that individuals slant ambiguous probabilities downward, leading to subadditivity. No such subadditivity is required, however. In a multiple reference point model in which individuals' reference point reflects a chance of winning the prize below what would occur with a random lottery, the observed behavior will occur. One would expect $\pi(\$100; 0)$ to be below .5, given the actuarially unfair nature of available lotteries with which the individual has had experience.

Notes

1. It should be noted, however, that claims regarding the predictive validity of the theory vary. For example, Raiffa (1968) emphasizes the normative purposes of the model as a guide to decision making, whereas Savage (1972) notes that even though "the behavior of people does often flagrantly depart from the theory," the framework may nevertheless be useful as a predictive guide since "a theory is not to be altogether rejected because it is not absolutely true."

2. Other discussions of violations of the expected utility model and alternatives to it appear in Allais (1953), Bell (1982), Einhorn and Hogarth (1985, 1986), Ellsberg (1961), Fischhoff et al. (1981), Fischhoff and Beyth-Marom (1983), Grether (1980), Hogarth and Kunreuther (1985), Kahneman and Tversky (1982), Raiffa (1961), Viscusi (1985), Viscusi, Magat, and Huber (1987), Viscusi and O'Connor (1984) and Zeckhauser (1986).

3. The Dirichlet distribution reduces to a standard beta distribution in the bivariate case. For further discussion of the Dirichlet distribution, see Johnson and Kotz (1972), pp. 231–235.

4. The value of ξ/γ has been estimated in Viscusi (1985) and in Viscuis and O'Connor (1984), whereas ξ and γ could not be estimated.

5. In the unusual cases in which outcomes with stated certainty p_i values of 0 and 1 are really viewed as being subject to a stochastic process, one simply incorporates the expanded set of possible outcomes into the reference probabilities. With both such events included, for example, the reference probability becomes $1/(n + 2)$, where n is the number of lottery outcomes with associated p_i values between 0 and 1. As before, the perceived probabilities sum to 1.

6. In addition to the differences cited below, decision weights also may not be well defined near 0 or 1, since Kahneman and Tversky (1979) omit any decision weight values near 0 or 1 from their graph of the decision weight function (1979, figure 4, p. 283).

7. For a discussion of anchoring phenomena, see Tversky and Kahneman (1982), pp. 14–18, Slovic, Fischhoff, and Lichtenstein (1982), pp. 481–482, and Einhorn and Hogarth (1985, 1986).

8. See, for example, Einhorn and Hogarth (1985).

9. See, for example, the studies by Tversky and Kahneman (1982) and Kahneman and Tversky (1979).

10. Kahneman and Tversky (1979) describe this property as the "empirical generalization concerning the manner in which the substitution axiom is violated. . . . This property is incorporated into an alternative theory. . . ."

11. In addition to the example here, their problems 14 and 14' involve a similar principle and can also be explained with the PRT framework.

12. This neglect was context-dependent, since it was greater when a description of the worker was provided than when it was not. This pattern suggests that the informational content ξ that respondents associate with the information provided concerning the mix of workers may be reduced by the provision of other information provided in the experiments that may lead respondents to, in effect, ignore or discount the veracity of the occupational mix information.

13. One can readily verify that these other cases can be reconciled with the PRT approach. See, in particular, problems 1–8 in Kahneman and Tversky (1979), which exemplify this phenomenon, as does the certainty effect considered in section 3.1 of this article.

14. The prospect theory explanation is similar in spirit, except that the paradox is not a prediction of the theory. Other possible explanations following different approaches appear in Machina (1982), Luce and Raiffa (1957), and Bell (1982).

15. See Kahneman and Tversky (1979), pp. 271–273. The particular phenomenon was observed by Tversky in earlier work.

16. *Ibid*, p. 271.

17. For a discussion of these influences, see Slovic, Fischhoff, and Lichtenstein (1982).

18. See both the original article by Ellsberg (1961), the illuminating discussion by Raiffa (1961), and the modern revivals of this phenomenon by Einhorn and Hogarth (1985, 1986) and Hogarth and Kunreuther (1985).

References

Allais, Maurice. (1953). "Le Comportement de l' Homme Rationnel Devant le Risque: Critique des Postulats et Axioms de l' Ecole Americaine," *Econometrica* 21, 503–546.

Arrow, Kenneth. (1971). *Essays in the Theory of Risk-Bearing*. Chicago: Markham Publishing Co.

Arrow, Kenneth. (1982). "Risk Perception in Psychology and Economics," *Economic Inquiry* 20, 1–9.

Bell, David. (1982). "Regret in Decision Making under Uncertainty," *Operations Research* 30, 961–981.

Einhorn, Hillel, and Robin Hogarth. (1985). "Ambiguity and Uncertainty in Probabilistic Inference," *Psychological Review* 92, 433–461.

Einhorn, Hillel, and Robin Hogarth. (1986). "Decision Making under Ambiguity," *Journal of Business* 59, S225–S250.

Ellsberg, Daniel. (1961). "Risk, Ambiguity, and the Savage Axioms," *Quarterly Journal of Economics* LXXV, 643–669.

Fischhoff, Baruch, et. al. (1981). *Acceptable Risk*. Cambridge: Cambridge University Press.

Fischhoff, Baruch, and R. Beyth-Marom. (1983). "Hypothesis Evaluation from a Bayesian Perspective," *Psychological Review* 70, 239–260.

Grether, David. (1980). "Bayes Rule as a Descriptive Model: The Representativeness Heuristic," *Quarterly Journal of Economics* XCV, 537–557.

Hogarth, Robin, and Howard Kunreuther. (1985). "Ambiguity and Insurance Decisions," *American Economic Review Papers and Proceedings* 75, 386–390.

Johnson, Norman L., and Samuel Kotz. (1972). *Distributions in Statistics: Continuous Multivariate Distributions*. New York: Wiley.

Kahneman, Daniel, and Amos Tversky. (1979). "Prospect Theory: An Analysis of Decision under Risk," *Econometrica* 47, 263–291.

Kahneman, Daniel, and Amos Tversky. (1982). "The Psychology of Preferences," *Scientific American* 246, 160–173.

Kunreuther, Howard, et. al. (1978). *Disaster Insurance Protection*. New York: Wiley-Interscience.

Lichtenstein, Sara, et. al. (1978). "Judged Frequency of Lethal Events," *Journal of Experimental Psychology: Human Learning and Memory* 4, 551–578.

Luce, R. Duncan, and Howard Raiffa. (1957). *Games and Decisions*. New York: John Wiley and Sons.

Machina, Mark. (1982). "Expected Utility Analysis without the Independence Axiom," *Econometrica* 50, 277–323.

Raiffa, Howard. (1968). *Decision Analysis*. Reading: Addison-Wesley.

Raiffa, Howard. (1961). "Risk, Ambiguity, and the Savage Axioms: Comment," *Quarterly Journal of Economics* LXXV, 690–694.

Savage, Leonard J. (1972). *The Foundations of Statistics*. (Second revised edition.) New York: Dover Publications.

Tversky, Amos, and Daniel Kahneman. (1986). "Rational Choice and the Framing of Decisions," *Journal of Business* 59, S251–S278.

Cambridge: Cambridge University Press.

Tversky, Amos, and Daniel Kuhneman. (1986). "Rational Choice and the Framing of Decisions," *Journal of Business* 59, S251–S278.

Viscusi, W. Kip. (1985). "A Bayesian Perspective on Biases in Risk Perception," *Economic Letters* 17, 59–62.

Viscusi, W. Kip. (1985). "Are Individuals Bayesian Decision Makers?" *American Economic Review* 75, 381–385.

Viscusi, W. Kip, and Wesley A. Magat. (1987). *Learning about Risk: Consumer and Worker Responses to Hazard Warnings*. Cambridge: Harvard University Press.

Viscusi, W. Kip, Wesley A. Magat, and Joel Huber. (1987). "An Investigation of the Rationality of Consumer Valuations of Multiple Health Risks," *Rand Journal of Economics* 18, 465–479.

Viscusi, W. Kip, and Charles O'Connor. (1984). "Adaptive Responses to Chemical Labeling: Are Workers Bayesian Decision Makers?" *American Economic Review* 74, 942–956.

von Neumann, John, and Oskar Morgenstern. (1953). *Theory of Games and Economic Behavior*. (Third edition.) New York: John Wiley and Sons.

Zeckhauser, Richard. (1986). "Behavioral Versus Rational Economics: What You See Is What You Conquer," *Journal of Business* 59, S435–S449.

[18]

PETER WAKKER

UNDER STOCHASTIC DOMINANCE CHOQUET-EXPECTED UTILITY AND ANTICIPATED UTILITY ARE IDENTICAL

ABSTRACT. The aim of this paper is to convince the reader that Choquet-expected utility, as initiated by Schmeidler (1982, 1989) for decision making under uncertainty, when formulated for decision making under risk naturally leads to anticipated utility, as initiated by Quiggin/Yaari. Thus the two generalizations of expected utility in fact are one.

Keywords: Nonadditive probabilities, decision making under risk, decision making under uncertainty, prospect theory, Choquet-expected utility, anticipated utility, rank-dependent utility, cumulative utility, comonotonicity.

1. HISTORY, MOTIVATION AND PREVIEW

In the beginning of the eighties Schmeidler (1982; published 1989) and Quiggin/Yaari (published 1982/1987) devised new generalizations of expected utility. The new idea of both of these generalizations was to deal with probabilities in a nonadditive way. Many previous trials to use nonadditive probabilities (e.g. in Edwards, 1954, and in Kahneman and Tversky, 1979; these authors themselves did not use an interpretation of nonadditive probabilities) adopted a way to integrate with respect to nonadditive probabilities, seemingly dual to expected utility, but at closer study unsound. Kahneman and Tversky themselves already pointed out the major problem in their way of integration; further comments are given in Quiggin (1982), and illustrations are given in Wakker (1989c). The problem had already been known to L. J. Savage. The main contribution of Schmeidler and Quiggin/Yaari was to find a sound way to integrate with respect to nonadditive probabilities, a way which turned out to have been found already by the mathematician Choquet (1953/4).

It was immediately understood that the ways of integration of Schmeidler and Quiggin/Yaari were related, see for instance Yaari (1987, p. 114). Nevertheless the data equivalence of the two approaches for decision making under risk (DMUR), as pointed out in

Theory and Decision **29**: 119–132, 1990.
© 1990 *Kluwer Academic Publishers. Printed in the Netherlands.*

120   PETER WAKKER

this paper, has not been observed before, to the best of our knowledge. A possible explanation may be the following. In Schmeidler's approach, which we propose to call the *Choquet-expected utility* (*CEU*) approach, the 'subjective' probabilities (not given *a priori*) are dealt with in a new, nonadditive, way. Also there occur objective ('known') probabilities, but it is essential for Schmeidler's proof, and also in accordance with his interpretations, that these be dealt with in the (traditional) additive way. The crucial new idea in Quiggin/Yaari's set-up, to the contrary, is that objective ('known') probabilities be dealt with in a nonadditive way.

Nevertheless the approach of Quiggin/Yaari, the *anticipated utility* (*AU*) approach, is the natural version of the CEU approach when adapted to DMUR, as we shall argue. To do this, *firstly* an alternative derivation of the CEU approach must be established, one which does not need the auxiliary tool of objective probabilities to be dealt with in an additive way. Such an alternative derivation has been obtained in Gilboa (1987), Wakker (1989a, b), and Nakamura (1990). Once the possibility of such an alternative derivation has been accepted, knowledge of its details is not needed for the identification of CEU and AU. Hence this paper does not repeat those details.

Secondly (see Section 3), we have to show that DMUR, the context to which AU applies, can be considered a special case of decision making under uncertainty (DMUU), the context to which CEU applies. We shall only show the formal relatedness, and not enter conceptual discussions. The work of Section 3 has use on its own, in elucidating the risk/uncertainty dichotomy as introduced by Knight (1921), and in giving an 'algorithm' to translate results from DMUR to DMUU and vice versa. Section 3 can be read independently of Subsections 2.2 and 2.3.

Now CEU can directly be applied to DMUR. Then, *thirdly* (see Section 4) and finally, we show equivalence of the following two approaches to DMUR:

- AU with stochastic dominance.
- CEU with stochastic dominance.

The obtained identification enables the application of techniques, developed before for CEU, to AU. Thus results for AU can be generalized; this will be elaborated in Wakker (1990). We derive the present result in full generality, without imposing restrictions upon the state space, probabilities, probability transformations, consequences, utilities, or whatever. To do this, in Definition 5 the natural version of stochastic dominance for general consequence spaces will be given, generalizing the traditional stochastic dominance that has been formulated for monetary consequences and increasing utility.

Proofs are given in the Appendix. Let us finally refer to Fishburn (1988), giving a survey of CEU, AU, and many other deviations from expected utility.

2. CEU FOR DMUU

In this section we sketch the CEU approach to DMUU, as initiated by Schmeidler (1982, 1989). For easy accessibility we shall not introduce measure-theoretic structure; the latter can be introduced exactly as in Schmeidler (1982, 1989) (supplemented in Wakker, 1989e).

2.1. Elementary Definitions of Decision Making Under Uncertainty

In decision making under uncertainty (DMUU) the lack of information of the decision maker is modeled through a set S, the set of *states* (*of nature*). Exactly one state is the 'true state', the other states are not true. Subsets of S are *events*. A decision maker is uncertain about which state of nature is true, and has not any influence on the truth of the states. As an example one may think of a horse race that will take place. Every horse is identified with a state; $s \in S$ designates the 'state' that horse s will win.

$\mathscr{C}$ denotes the set of *consequences*. The set $\mathscr{F}$ is the set of all *acts*, i.e., functions from S to $\mathscr{C}$. If a decision maker chooses an act f, this results in consequence $f(s)$ for (him or) her, where s is the true state of nature. For instance, acts may designate bets for money on horses. Since the decision maker is uncertain about which horse will win, (he or) she is uncertain which amount of money will result from a bet.

By $\geq$ we denote the preference relation of the decision maker on $\mathscr{F}$. As usual, we write $f > g$ if $f \geq g$ and not $g \geq f$, $f \leq g$ if $g \geq f$, $f < g$ if

122   PETER WAKKER

$g > f$, and $f \simeq g$ if $f \geq g$ and $g \geq f$. We call $\geq$ a *weak order* if it is complete ($f \geq g$ or $g \geq f$ for all f, g) and transitive. Further $\geq$ is *trivial* if $f \geq g$ for all f, g. A function $V: \mathcal{F} \rightarrow \Re$ *represents* $\geq$ if $[f \geq g] \Leftrightarrow [V(f) \geq V(g)]$. (The term utility function is reserved in this paper for the function U in the sequel; the expectation of U will represent $\geq$.) We shall often identify consequences with the associated constant acts. Thus, for α, $\beta \in \mathscr{C}$, we may write $\alpha \geq \beta$, etc.

2.2. The Choquet-Integral and CEU

A function $v: 2^S \rightarrow [0, 1]$ is a *capacity* ('nonadditive probability') if $v(\emptyset) = 0$, $v(S) = 1$, and v is *monotonic w.r.t. set-inclusion*, i.e., $A \supset B \Rightarrow v(A) \geq v(B)$. Further v is a *probability measure* if it is a capacity that is *additive*, i.e., $v(A \cup B) = v(A) + v(B)$ for all disjoint A, B. In literature often a continuity condition is imposed on capacities, requiring for any sequence of events $(A_1, A_2, \ldots)$:

$$[\forall j: A_{j+1} \subset A_j, \bigcap_{j=1}^{\infty} A_j = A] \Rightarrow [\lim_{j \to \infty} v(A_j) = v(A)],$$

and requiring the same with $\supset$, $\cup$ instead of $\subset$, $\cap$. In this paper the continuity restriction is not imposed. For probability measures the continuity condition is known to be equivalent to *countable additivity*, i.e., for any countable disjoint sequence of events the probability of the union of these events is the sum of the probabilities. Whenever we require countable additivity of a probability measure we will make it explicit.

For a capacity v, and a function $\phi: S \rightarrow \Re$, the *Choquet-integral* of ϕ (with respect to v), denoted $\int_S \phi \, dv$, or $\int \phi \, dv$, is

$$\int_0^{\infty} v(\{s \in S: \phi(s) \geq \tau\}) \, d\tau$$

$$+ \int_{-\infty}^{0} [v(\{s \in S: \phi(s) \geq \tau\}) - 1] \, d\tau. \tag{1}$$

For probability measures the Choquet-integral is identical to the usual integral. Elucidations and illustrations for the Choquet-integral are given in Wakker (1989b, Section VI.2).

DEFINITION 1. We say that *Choquet-expected utility (CEU)* applies if there exist a *utility function* $U : \mathscr{C} \to \Re$ and a capacity v on S, so that $f \mapsto \int_S (U \circ f) \, dv$ represents $\geq$. The integral is the *Choquet-expected utility (CEU)* of f.

2.3. Transforming Additive Probabilities

One way to obtain a capacity is to take an additive probability measure P on S, a nondecreasing function $\varphi : [0,1] \to [0,1]$ with $\varphi(0) = 0$, $\varphi(1) = 1$, and then take as capacity the 'distorted probability' $v := \varphi \circ P$. Obviously the probability measure P may simply be a mathematical device, without any interpretation associated with it. Two other extreme cases are, firstly, the case of DMUU, where P is not given and must be derived from other sources, and secondly, the case of DMUR, where P is a 'given objective' probability measure, known in advance. This second case will be considered in Section 4. Let us now comment shortly on the first case.

Under CEU one may wonder whether *there exists* a probability measure P so that $v = \varphi \circ P$, with φ nondecreasing. This is the case if and only if there exists a probability measure P so that, for $\geq '$ on S defined by $A \geq 'B \Leftrightarrow v(A) \geq v(B)$, we have $P(A) \geq P(B) \Rightarrow A \geq 'B$. Questions about the existence of such a probability measure P are studied in 'comparative probability theory', see Wakker (1981, supplementing Savage, 1954), Gilboa (1985, explicitly indicating the significance for AU), or Fishburn (1986, giving a survey). See also Luce (1988, Section 6). The five-point example in Kraft, Pratt, and Seidenberg (1959) can be used to show that there exist, even for a finite state space, capacities which cannot be obtained as nondecreasing transforms of an additive probability, even so when the capacities satisfy a kind of 'ordinal additivity'.

Section 4 will introduce AU, and will show that it is a special case of CEU, so that it is not more general. The above observation shows, in addition, that CEU is *strictly* more general.

3. FROM DMUU TO DMUR AND VICE VERSA

In Subsection 2.1 we sketched the approach of DMUU. In the usual approach to DMUR, which we shall also call *DMUR without states,* one takes as point of departure a consequence set $\mathscr{C}$, a collection of countably additive probability distributions over $\mathscr{C}$, and a preference relation over these probability distributions.

As a preparation for showing the relatedness of AU and CEU, this elementary section shows the way to consider DMUR as a special case of DMUU, in the sense that DMUU requires less structure so can be applied more generally. The main step is carried out in Subsection 3.2, showing that in DMUR it is no restriction to assume an 'underlying' state space. In Subsection 3.1 we start from the general model of DMUU, and show which restrictive assumptions must be added to end up in a case of DMUR. Subsection 3.2 then shows that all cases of DMUR can be thought to have been obtained like that.

3.1. From DMUU to DMUR

(*DMUU*) *Firstly*, we start from the general set-up of DMUU as described in Subsection 2.1, with as primitives the state space S, the consequence set $\mathscr{C}$, the acts, and the preference relation $\geq$ over the acts.

(*Intermediate set-up*) *Secondly*, we add the assumption that at the outset an *objective* probability measure P on S is given; it is custom to assume, and so shall we do, that this objective probability measure is countably additive. The set-up now obtained will be called the *intermediate set-up*. Any act $f: S \to \mathscr{C}$ induces a countably additive probability distribution over the consequences, assigning to every subset of the consequence set the probability of its inverse under the act. In the intermediate set-up the probability distribution can be without any relevance to the decision maker.

(*DMUR with states*) *Thirdly*, we add the restrictive assumption characteristic for DMUR. It states that all relevant information of an act is contained in the probability distribution which the act induces on the consequences. Its formal statement is as follows:

ASSUMPTION 2 [DMUR]. *If two acts induce the same probability distribution over consequence, then they are ($\approx$-)equivalent.*

Yaari (1987) called this assumption 'neutrality', Fishburn (1988) called it the 'reduction principle'. It will be implied by the stronger and natural condition of stochastic dominance as we shall formulate it in the sequel. We call the set-up now obtained *DMUR with states*. In it, (preferences on) acts and probability distributions are equivalent; they will often be identified and interchanged.

(*DMUR without states*) *Fourthly* and finally, if all acts which induce the same probability distribution over consequences are equivalent, then we may describe any act by the induced probability distribution, *forget about the state space, the acts, and P*, and use the naturally induced preference relation on the probability distributions over consequences. This is in accord with a tradition in mathematical statistics and probability theory. There one often works with probability distributions, having in mind that these are probability distributions of random variables (= acts) defined on a probability space, but leaving the probability space and the random variables unmentioned, simply because these are needed nowhere in the analysis. What has resulted is the usual approach of DMUR, without states. In literature there is usually the further restrictive assumption that all probability distributions over (a σ-field over) $\mathscr{C}$ must be available. To achieve that, we must add the assumption that (S, P) is 'rich enough' to generate all these. The next subsection will give further comments.

3.2. From DMUR to DMUU

To claim that DMUR is truly a special case of DMUU, we must show that each case of DMUR can be the result of the procedure sketched in the previous subsection. I.e., starting from the usual set-up of DMUR (without states), with a consequence set $\mathscr{C}$ and countably additive probability distributions over $\mathscr{C}$, we must show that we can always construct a state space S with a probability distribution P on S, generating all the considered probability distributions. This is shown in the next paragraph, is somewhat technical, and may be taken for granted.

One can for instance assume that all considered probability distributions are independent, and take as probability space a Cartesian product of dimension as large as the cardinality of the set of considered probability distributions, with all coordinate sets equal to $\mathscr{C}$. This procedure can also be adopted if the probability measures are not countably additive, and $\mathscr{C}$ is general. In DMUR, where choices between probability distributions are to be made by a decision maker, joint distributions of different probability distributions over $\mathscr{C}$ are not considered, they are irrelevant. Hence the above procedure can be considered a trivial application of a theorem of Kolmogorov, see Feller (1966, Theorem IV.6.1). Usually simpler spaces will suffice. For instance, for the case $\mathscr{C} \subset \mathfrak{R}$, the state space $[0, 1]$ endowed with the uniform distribution will suffice to generate all countably additive probability distributions over $\mathfrak{R}$, through generalized 'inverses' of distribution functions.

It has now also been established that there is no essential difference between DMUR with or without states. We may always assume the states to be given, and so we shall do.

4. AU AS SPECIAL CASE OF CEU

In this section we introduce AU, and show how to derive it from CEU.

4.1. AU

We consider the context of DMUR with states. The integral below is a Choquet-integral, with respect to the capacity $\varphi \circ P$.

DEFINITION 3. *Anticipated utility* (AU) *applies when there exist a utility function* $U : \mathscr{C} \to \mathfrak{R}$ *and a nondecreasing transformation* $\varphi : [0, 1] \to [0, 1]$ *with* $\varphi(0) = 0$, $\varphi(1) = 1$, *so that (with* P_f *the probability distribution over* $\mathscr{C}$ *induced by an act* f) $\geq$ *is represented by*

$$P_f \mapsto \int_S (U \circ f) \, \mathrm{d}\varphi \circ P . \tag{2}$$

The integral is the *anticipated utility* (AU) of the act f, or of the distribution P_f.

As the essential new idea of AU we take the fact that first the probability measure P is transformed nondecreasingly before expectation is calculated. Other conditions met in literature, such as continuity of φ and linearity of U as in Yaari (1987), or continuity of φ and the equality $\varphi(\frac{1}{2}) = \frac{1}{2}$ (and possibly some unmentioned continuity of U) as in Quiggin (1982), or boundedness of U and convex-rangedness of $\varphi \circ P$ as in Gilboa (1987), or continuity of U as in the author's papers, or continuity and strict increasingness of U and φ as in Chew (1989), or 'solvability' as in Nakamura (1990), to our view are not crucial aspects of AU, and are only used to simplify analyses.

Several alternative terms for AU are used in literature. Chew, Karni and Safra (1987) use the term 'expected utility with rank dependent probabilities'. Yaari (1987) uses the term 'dual theory'; this seems most suited for the special case of linear utility, as considered in his paper. AU theory in full generality is a generalization of expected utility, rather than a dual. Also the appealing term 'cumulative utility' has occurred.

The following equivalent formulation is suited for DMUR without states, because no states or acts are used. For simplicity we assume that U is nonnegative. Let $G_{U \circ f}$ be the *decumulative distribution function* of $U \circ f$, i.e., $G_{U \circ f} : \tau \mapsto P([U \circ f \geq \tau])$. The representing function in (2) can be seen to be equal to:

$$P_f \mapsto \int_{[0, \infty[} \tau \, d(-\varphi \circ G_{U \circ f}(\tau)) \,. \tag{3}$$

This formulation shows that different acts which induce the same probability distribution over $\mathscr{C}$ are valued the same, as should be for DMUR. One can consider the above integral to be a usual (expected-utility-)integral, not of the distribution given by $G_{U \circ f}$, but of the 'transformed distribution' given by $\varphi \circ G_{U \circ f}$. Right-continuity of φ will guarantee that $\varphi \circ G_{U \circ f}$ indeed is the decumulative distribution function of a countably additive distribution; continuity of φ will be characterized in Wakker (1990). We prefer not to require continuity of φ in the general definition of AU, because we want to be able to include for instance maxmin behavior, and other kinds of discontinuities at probabilities 0 or 1.

We could write (3) alternatively by deleting the minus sign and replacing $\varphi \circ G_{U \circ f}$ by $\psi \circ F_{U \circ f}$, with $\psi : \tau \mapsto 1 - \varphi(1 - \tau)$, and $F_{U \circ f}$ the usual cumulative distribution function of $U \circ f$, i.e., $F_{U \circ f} : \tau \mapsto P([U \circ f \leq \tau])$.

4.2. Applying CEU to DMUR

Let us start from the 'intermediate set-up' described in Subsection 3.1, with given P but without Assumption 2. This is a special case of DMUU, and nothing prevents us from applying CEU. The objective probability measure P, while present, simply does not have to be used. The following lemma shows when it is used after all.

LEMMA 4. *Let $\geq$ be nontrivial, let the intermediate set-up apply, and let CEU apply. Then there exists a transformation $\varphi: [0, 1] \to [0, 1]$ so that $v = \varphi \circ P$ if and only if Assumption 2 applies, i.e., if and only if DMUR with states applies.*   □

The above lemma does not yet give AU because the transformation φ does not have to be nondecreasing. For example, with $\mathscr{C}$ a nondegenerate interval, U identity, $S = \{s_1, s_2\}$, and $P(s_1) > P(s_2) > 0$, we are still free to choose $\varphi(P(s_1)) < \varphi(P(s_2))$. However, if the state space S is so rich that for every $P(A) > P(B)$ we can find a B' so that $P(B') = P(B)$ and $B' \subset A$, then because of monotonicity of capacities $\varphi(P(A)) \geq \varphi(P(B')) = \varphi(P(B))$ follows. The mentioned richness holds, under countable additivity of P, if and only if either the state space is atomless, or it consists of a finite number of equally-probable atoms. We will not derive AU from the richness-condition in the way as just suggested, but rather from the natural condition of stochastic dominance. Stochastic dominance is usually formulated for the case where consequences are real numbers and (utility/)preferences are increasing. The condition below is the natural generalization to general consequences. Also it is the natural generalization to acts instead of distributions.

DEFINITION 5. We say for acts f, g that f *(weakly, first-order) stochastically dominates g* if

$$[\forall \alpha \in \mathscr{C}: P(f(s) \geq \alpha) \geq P(g(s) \geq \alpha)].$$

We say $\geq$ satisfies *(monotonicity w.r.t. weak first-order) stochastic dominance* if $f \geq g$ whenever f stochastically dominates g.

IDENTIFYING CEU AND AU   129

Obviously, if f and g induce the same probability distribution over the consequences, then they stochastically dominate each other. By stochastic dominance of $\geq$, f and g then must be equivalent. So we have:

$$\text{Stochastic dominance of } \geq \text{ implies Assumption 2}. \qquad (4)$$

I.e., under stochastic dominance DMUR applies. It may be argued that our version of stochastic dominance for acts contains two separate ideas, firstly, the idea of Assumption 2, secondly, the idea of stochastic dominance for distributions over consequences.

LEMMA 6. *Let* $\geq$ *be nontrivial. Let the intermediate set-up apply, and let CEU apply. Then there exists a nondecreasing transformation* $\varphi : [0, 1] \rightarrow [0, 1]$ *so that* $\upsilon = \varphi \circ P$, *if and only if stochastic dominance is satisfied.* $\square$

The existence of φ in the above lemma is exactly what defines AU. Since by definition AU is a special case of CEU, the following theorem results:

THEOREM 7. *Let* $\geq$ *be nontrivial. Let the intermediate set-up apply, and let stochastic dominance hold. Then CEU applies if and only if AU applies.*

5. CONCLUSION

We have given a general procedure for 'translating' results from decision making under uncertainty into results for decision making under risk. This suggests that decision making under uncertainty is the more basic of the two set-ups. By means of the procedure we have shown that two generalizations of expected utility, introduced independently for different contexts, at closer study in fact are one. We rephrase, taking the noncontroversial stochastic dominance for granted,

Choquet-expected utility,
when applied to DMUR, is identical to
Anticipated utility.

130   PETER WAKKER

ACKNOWLEDGEMENT

The research has been made possible by a fellowship of the Royal Netherlands Academy of Arts and Sciences, and a fellowship of the Netherlands Organization for Scientific Research.

APPENDIX; PROOFS

PROOF of Lemma 4. First suppose Assumption 2 holds. We prove that $v = \varphi \circ P$ for some transformation φ. It suffices to show that for any events A, B, $P(A) = P(B) \Rightarrow v(A) = v(B)$. So let $P(A) = P(B)$. Since $\geq$ is nontrivial, the utility function U used in CEU is not constant. So let $U(\alpha) > U(\beta)$. According to Assumption 2 we have, with $\alpha 1_A + \beta 1_{A^c}$ denoting the act assigning α to A and β to A^c, $\alpha 1_A + \beta 1_{A^c} \approx \alpha 1_B + \beta 1_{B^c}$. Substituting CEU's gives $v(A)U(\alpha) + (1 - v(A))U(\beta) = v(B)U(\alpha) + (1 - v(B))U(\beta)$. This implies $v(A) = v(B)$.

Conversely, suppose a φ as in the lemma exists. We derive Assumption 2. Let acts f and g induce the same probability distribution over consequences. Then each of these acts has the same CEU since in the Choquet-integrals of $f \circ U$ respectively $g \circ U$ we find the same integrands.   □

PROOF of Lemma 6. First suppose φ exists and is nondecreasing. To derive stochastic dominance, let f stochastically dominate g. By nondecreasingness of φ, $\varphi(P(U \circ f \geq \tau)) \geq \varphi(P(U \circ g \geq \tau))$. Substituting this in the Choquet-integrals of $U \circ f$ and $U \circ g$ shows that $f \geq g$.

Next we assume stochastic dominance holds, and derive (existence, which could also be derived from Formula 4 and Lemma 4 and) nondecreasingness of φ. It can be seen that it is sufficient to show that for any events A, B, $P(A) \geq P(B) \Rightarrow v(A) \geq v(B)$. So let $P(A) \geq P(B)$. Since $\geq$ is nontrivial, the utility function U used in CEU is not constant. So let $U(\alpha) > U(\beta)$. By stochastic dominance we have $\alpha 1_A + \beta 1_{A^c} \geq \alpha 1_B + \beta 1_{B^c}$. Substituting CEU's gives $v(A)U(\alpha) + (1 - v(A))U(\beta) \geq v(B)U(\alpha) + (1 - v(B))U(\beta)$. This implies $v(A) \geq v(B)$.   □

IDENTIFYING CEU AND AU   131

REFERENCES

Chew, S. H.: 1989, 'An Axiomatic Generalization of the Quasilinear Mean and Gini Mean with Application to Decision Theory', Johns Hopkins University and Tulane University; rewritten version of Chew, S. H. (1985), 'An Axiomatization of the Rank-Dependent Quasilinear Mean Generalizing the Gini Mean and the Quasilinear Mean', Economics Working Paper #156, Johns Hopkins University.

Chew, S. H., Karni, E., and Safra, Z.: 1987, 'Risk Aversion in the Theory of Expected Utility with Rank Dependent Probabilities', *Journal of Economic Theory* **42**, 370–381.

Choquet, G.: 1953–4, 'Theory of Capacities', *Annales de l'Institut Fourier* (Grenoble), 131–295.

Edwards, W.: 1954, 'The Theory of Decision Making', *Psychological Bulletin* **51**, 380–417.

Feller, W.: 1966, *An Introduction to Probability Theory*, Vol. II, Wiley, New York.

Fishburn, P. C.: 1986, 'The Axioms of Subjective Probability', *Statistical Science* **1**, 335–358.

Fishburn, P. C.: 1988, *Nonlinear Preference and Utility Theory*, Johns Hopkins University Press, Baltimore.

Gilboa, I.: 1985, 'Subjective Distortions of Probabilities and Non-Additive Probabilities', Working paper 18–85, Foerder Institute for Economic Research, Tel-Aviv University, Ramat Aviv, Israel.

Gilboa, I.: 1987, 'Expected Utility with Purely Subjective Non-Additive Probabilities', *Journal of Mathematical Economics* **16**, 65–88.

Kahneman, D. and Tversky, A.: 1979, 'Prospect Theory: An Analysis of Decision under Risk', *Econometrica* **47**, 263–291.

Knight, F. H.: 1921, *Risk, Uncertainty, and Profit*, Houghton Mifflin, New York.

Kraft, C. H., Pratt, J. W., and Seidenberg, A.: 1959, 'Intuitive Probability on Finite Sets', *Annals of Mathematical Statistics* **30**, 408–419.

Luce, R. D.: 1988, 'Rank-Dependent, Subjective Expected-Utility Representations', *Journal of Risk and Uncertainty* **1**, 305–332.

Nakamura, Y.: 1990, 'Subjective Expected Utility with Non-Additive Probabilities on Finite State Space', University of Tsukuba, Tsukuba, Ibaraki, Japan.

Quiggin, J.: 1982, 'A Theory of Anticipated Utility', *Journal of Economic Behaviour and Organization* **3**, 323–343.

Savage, L. J.: 1954, *The Foundations of Statistics*, Wiley, New York. (Second edition 1972, Dover, New York.)

Schmeidler, D.: 1982, 1989, 'Subjective Probability and Expected Utility without Additivity', *Econometrica* **57** (1989), 571–587; first version 1982.

Wakker, P. P.: 1981, 'Agreeing Probability Measures for Comparative Probability Structures', *The Annals of Statistics* **9**, 658–662.

Wakker, P. P.: 1989a, 'Continuous Subjective Expected Utility with Nonadditive Probabilities', *Journal of Mathematical Economics* **18**, 1–27.

Wakker, P. P.: 1989b, *Additive Representations of Preferences*, A New Foundation of Decision Analysis, Kluwer (Academic Publishers), Dordrecht.

Wakker, P. P.: 1989c, 'Transforming Probabilities without Violating Stochastic Dominance', in E. E. Ch. I. Roskam (ed.), *Mathematical Psychology in Progress*, Springer, Berlin, 29–48.

132   PETER WAKKER

Wakker, P. P.: 1989d, 'A Behavioral Foundation for Fuzzy Measures', *Fuzzy Sets and Systems*, forthcoming.

Wakker, P. P.: 1989e, 'From Finite- to Infinite-Dimensional Integral Representations; Unbounded Utility for Savage (1954) and Others', Duke University, Fuqua School of Business, working paper 8928.

Wakker, P. P.: 1990, In preparation.

Yaari, M. E.: 1987, 'The Dual Theory of Choice under Risk', *Econometrica* **55**, 95–115.

University of Nijmegen,
Nijmegen Institute for Cognition research and
* Information technology (NICI),*
Nijmegen, The Netherlands.

[19]

Econometrica, Vol. 59, No. 1 (January, 1991), 139–163

MIXTURE SYMMETRY AND QUADRATIC UTILITY[1]

By S. H. Chew, L. G. Epstein, and U. Segal

The independence axiom of expected utility theory has recently been weakened to the betweenness axiom. In this paper an even weaker axiom, called mixture symmetry, is presented. The corresponding functional structure is such that utility is a betweenness functional on part of its domain and quadratic in probabilities elsewhere. The experimental evidence against betweenness provides one motivation for the more general theory presented here. Another advantage of the mixture symmetric class of utility functions is that it is sufficiently flexible to permit the disentangling of attitudes towards risk and towards randomization.

Keywords: Uncertainty, betweenness, quadratic utility, mixture symmetry.

1. INTRODUCTION

EXPERIMENTAL STUDIES have revealed widespread and systematic violations of expected utility theory and more particularly of its cornerstone, the independence axiom (Machina (1982)). Consequently, several recent studies have proposed weaker axioms which define theories of choice under uncertainty that are compatible with the experimental evidence. One such axiom, called betweenness, is the basis for the theories described in Chew (1983, 1989), Fishburn (1983), Nakamura (1983), and Dekel (1986). The betweenness axiom—if two probability distributions are indifferent, then any probability mixture of them is equally as good—implies that indifference curves in the probability simplex are straight lines in the three-outcome probability simplex (and more generally, are hyperplanes in higher dimensional simplices). But there also exists evidence which contradicts betweenness. Thus in this paper we present a weaker axiom, called mixture symmetry, which is both simple and tractable. Mixture symmetry permits indifference curves in the simplex to be nonlinear; moreover, the deviations from linearity which it admits accord well with the available empirical evidence. In addition, the corresponding utility functions have a convenient functional structure.

Consider two indifferent lotteries represented by their cumulative distribution functions F and G. Mixture symmetry requires that any probability mixture $\alpha F + (1 - \alpha)G$, with $0 < \alpha < \frac{1}{2}$, be indifferent to a mixture $\beta F + (1 - \beta)G$ for some $\beta \in (\frac{1}{2}, 1)$ (though not necessarily indifferent to F and G). In the remainder of this introduction we explain the structure of the implied utility functions and elaborate on the motivation for the paper.

Since mixture symmetry is weaker than betweenness, the betweenness-conforming utility functionals described in the papers cited in the opening para-

[1] We are grateful to J. Aczèl for discussion of the functional equation aspects of the problem solved in the paper and to Mark Machina, the editor, and two referees for helpful suggestions. A referee pointed out an error in an earlier version. Chew and Epstein received financial support from the National Science Foundation and Segal wishes to acknowledge the financial support of the Social Sciences and Humanities Research Council of Canada.

graph satisfy mixture symmetry. The latter is also satisfied by all utility functionals that are "quadratic in probabilities." In fact, these two examples exhaust the utility functionals satisfying mixture symmetry (and some auxiliary hypotheses) in the sense that every such functional is betweenness-conforming on part of its domain and quadratic elsewhere. This representation, described in Theorems 4 and 6, is the major result of the paper. Note that the use of quadratic utility functionals as (part of) a generalization of expected utility is intuitive (apart from the appeal of the mixture symmetry axiom) when viewed from the perspective of standard calculus, since expected utility is linear in probabilities.

While the betweenness based theories can explain much of the experimental evidence against expected utility theory such as the Allais paradox, there exists some evidence, surveyed in Machina (1985, p. 579), contradicting betweenness. Given betweenness, utility is both quasiconcave and quasiconvex in the space of cumulative distribution functions. Assuming the axiom of reduction of compound lotteries, quasiconcavity (quasiconvexity) implies an affinity for (aversion to) randomization between indifferent lotteries. Thus evidence of randomized choice, which has been found by some studies, implies quasiconcavity and, except for knife-edge cases, rules out linearity. By an alternative approach, Becker et al. (1963) are able to reject linearity, even though their experimental design is only capable of detecting violations in the direction of quasiconcavity. Coombs and Huang (1976) find a significant proportion (45%) of violations of betweenness, with 59% of the violations being in the direction of strict quasiconcavity and 41% consistent with strict quasiconvexity. Chew and Waller (1986) embed a test of betweenness along with the standard Allais paradox and the common ratio effect within a single design. They also find some evidence against betweenness (see Section 5 below). Overall, the evidence shows significant violations of betweenness but does not provide justification for ruling out either quasiconcavity or quasiconvexity.[2] In Section 5 we describe some evidence, taken from the Chew and Waller study, which suggests a systematic nature to violations of betweenness.

Our objective is to develop an axiomatic theory of preference which can account for the prevalent empirical evidence against the independence axiom as well as the more limited evidence against betweenness. In addition, the axiomatic theory described below is sufficiently flexible so that either quasiconcavity or quasiconvexity can be accommodated, in conjunction with the usual hypothesis of risk aversion. Such flexibility is also appealing on theoretical grounds since attitudes towards risk and attitudes towards randomization between indifferent probability distributions represent two conceptually distinct aspects of preference. The ability to separate attitudes towards risk from attitudes towards randomization is particularly important in game theory where attitudes towards randomization are critical. Thus, for example, the quasiconcavity of utility is needed for the proof of existence of a Nash equilibrium, since

------

[2] For theoretical arguments in support of quasiconvexity, see Machina (1984) and Green (1987). We consider the latter in Section 5.

if preferences are strictly quasiconvex the agent will be averse to the randomization of strategies which an equilibrium may require. (Recently, however,
Crawford (1990) has proposed an alternative notion of equilibrium which exists
even if utility is strictly quasiconvex.)

Of course, one can also achieve a separation between risk aversion and
attitudes towards randomization by positing a general preference functional that
is Fréchet differentiable (Machina (1982)). We adopt the view, implicit in the
literature on axiomatic generalizations of expected utility, that good theory
development involves guarded departures from expected utility. Moreover, the
existence of an axiomatic basis contributes to such a development, both in
judging the extent of the deviation of the model from expected utility and in
elucidating the empirical implications of the adopted utility specification, thereby
facilitating the efficient explanation of empirical evidence.

There exists an alternative axiomatic generalization of expected utility theory,
called rank-dependent or anticipated utility theory, which has been proposed in
order to explain Allais-type behavior (see Quiggin (1982), Yaari (1987), Segal
(1989), and Chew (1985)). However, in the latter paper it is shown that
rank-dependent utility exhibits risk aversion if and only if it is quasiconvex. Thus
strict quasiconcavity and risk aversion cannot be jointly accommodated within
this theory. Generalizations of rank-dependent theory which retain a central
role for the rank ordering of outcomes are described in Segal (1989), Green and
Jullien (1988), and Chew and Epstein (1990). It is straightforward to show that
these generalizations suffer from similar inflexibility.

The next section presents our axioms. Functional forms are described in
Section 3 and representation theorems are presented in Section 4. Section 5
concludes with a comparison of the systematic violations of betweenness admitted by our framework and some empirical and theoretical evidence regarding
the nature of such violations. Most proofs are relegated to appendices.

2. AXIOMS

We consider a complete and transitive preference ordering $\geq$ on $D(X)$, the
set of cumulative distribution functions (c.d.f.'s) on the compact set $X \subset R^1$.
Endow $D(X)$ with the topology of weak convergence. The following axioms are
imposed on $\geq$:

CONTINUITY: *For each* $F \in D(X)$, $\{G \in D(X): G \geq F\}$ *and* $\{G \in D(X): F \geq G\}$ *are closed.*

MONOTONICITY: $\geq$ *is increasing in the sense of first degree stochastic dominance.*[3]

By Debreu (1964), there is no loss of generality in assuming that $\geq$ can be
represented by a utility functional $V: D(X) \to R^1$.

---

[3] Throughout the paper, "increasing" is intended in the strict sense.

For completeness, we write the independence axiom.[4]

INDEPENDENCE: *For every F, G and H $\in D(X)$ and $\alpha \in [0, 1]$,*

$$F \sim G \Rightarrow \alpha F + (1 - \alpha)H \sim \alpha G + (1 - \alpha)H.$$

The nature of independence can be understood by reference to the probability simplex in the case of lotteries having three possible outcomes. The axiom implies that indifference curves in the simplex are straight and parallel. The bulk of the empirical evidence discussed by Machina (1982) is inconsistent with parallelism. This evidence motivated the development of betweenness-conforming theories which have straight but nonparallel indifference curves in the simplex. The betweenness axiom is stated below.

BETWEENNESS: *For every F and G $\in D(X)$ and $\alpha \in [0, 1]$,*

$$F \sim G \Rightarrow \alpha F + (1 - \alpha)G \sim F.$$

Given continuity and monotonicity (see footnote 4), betweenness is the conjunction of quasiconcavity and quasiconvexity, which we state below.

QUASICONCAVITY: *For each F and G $\in D(X)$ and $\alpha \in (0, 1)$,*

$$F \sim G \Rightarrow \alpha F + (1 - \alpha)G \gtrsim F.$$

QUASICONVEXITY: *For each F and G $\in D(X)$ and $\alpha \in (0, 1)$,*

$$F \sim G \Rightarrow F \gtrsim \alpha F + (1 - \alpha)G.$$

The strict forms of these axioms are defined in the obvious way.

It will be useful to define a notion which is intermediate between quasiconcavity and strict quasiconcavity. First, say that an indifference set $I(F) = \{G \in D(X): G \sim F\}$ is planar if it is convex and is not equal to the singleton $\{F\}$. Say that $\gtrsim$ satisfies proper quasiconcavity if it is quasiconcave and if it contains no planar indifference sets. Proper quasiconvexity is defined similarly.

In the introduction we cited evidence contradicting betweenness. Thus we propose a further weakening of independence, which is compatible with either quasiconcavity or quasiconvexity but does not imply either. Our central axiom is as follows:

MIXTURE SYMMETRY: *For every F and G in $D(X)$, $F \sim G \Rightarrow \forall \alpha \in (0, \frac{1}{2})$ $\exists \beta \in (\frac{1}{2}, 1)$ such that $\alpha F + (1 - \alpha)G \sim \beta F + (1 - \beta)G$.*

---

[4] Given continuity and monotonicity, this form of independence is equivalent to the more common formulation involving weak preference rather than indifference. Similarly, the betweenness axiom below is equivalent, given continuity and monotonicity, to the form of betweenness that appears in Chew (1983) and Dekel (1986). They assume that the "better than" and "worse than" sets are both convex in the mixture sense.

The axiom requires that given $F \sim G$, any probability mixture which places strictly less weight on F, be indifferent to some other mixture in which F receives more weight than G. Clearly, mixture symmetry is implied by betweenness since given the latter all probability mixtures are indifferent to F; however, the converse is false as demonstrated amply below.

Our objective is to formulate a positive theory of preference which can be consistent with empirical evidence, but the normative case for mixture symmetry is still worth noting. Since the latter is weaker than the independence axiom, the well known normative argument for the latter applies also to mixture symmetry. Mixture symmetry might, however, be acceptable even if independence and betweenness are rejected. To see this, interpret probability mixtures in the usual way (e.g., Raiffa (1970, p. 82)) as two-stage lotteries. The additional uncertainty introduced through the first stage experiment may render the probability mixture $\alpha F + (1 - \alpha)G$ sufficiently distinct from the component single-stage lotteries F and G that, contrary to the prescriptions of independence and betweenness, $\alpha F + (1 - \alpha)G$ may not be indifferent to F. (Such a distinction between two-stage and single-stage lotteries is emphasized by Segal (1990).) On the other hand, if α and β are both in the open interval $(0, 1)$, then $\alpha F + (1 - \alpha)G$ and $\beta F + (1 - \beta)G$ both involve some uncertainty at the first stage and they could plausibly be indifferent for suitable choices of α and β. For example, it might be the case that $\beta = 1 - \alpha$ satisfies the requirement of mixture symmetry. As a concrete illustration of this latter case, consider an experiment in which a ball is drawn from an urn containing red and blue balls in proportions α and $(1 - \alpha)$. The color drawn determines whether F or G is received in the second stage. One might be indifferent as to whether red leads to F or to G, while at the same time not being indifferent between F and this two-stage lottery.

The above discussion draws attention to a stronger form of mixture symmetry in which the requisite indifference is necessarily satisfied by the choice $\beta = 1 - \alpha$, as illustrated in Figure 1. We make the following formal definition:

STRONG MIXTURE SYMMETRY: *For every F and $G \in D(X)$ and $\alpha \in [0, 1]$,*

$$F \sim G \Rightarrow \alpha F + (1 - \alpha)G \sim (1 - \alpha)F + \alpha G.$$

In fact, given continuity and monotonicity, strong mixture symmetry is equivalent to mixture symmetry, as described in the following theorem (proven in Appendix 1).

THEOREM 1: *Let $\geq$ satisfy continuity and monotonicity on $D(X)$. Then $\geq$ satisfies mixture symmetry if and only if it satisfies strong mixture symmetry.*

3. FUNCTIONAL FORMS

Now turn to functional forms for utility functionals. First we will be interested in functionals W which satisfy betweenness. As shown by Chew (1989) and

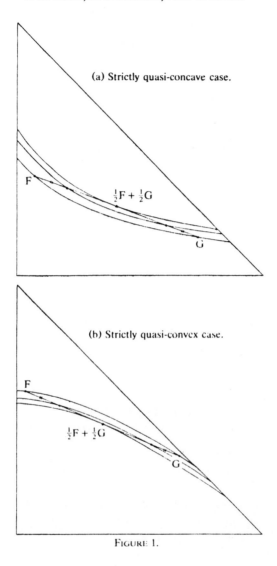

(a) Strictly quasi-concave case.

$\frac{1}{2}F + \frac{1}{2}G$

F

G

(b) Strictly quasi-convex case.

F

$\frac{1}{2}F + \frac{1}{2}G$

G

FIGURE 1.

Dekel (1986), they are defined implicitly by an equation of the form

(1) $\int h(x, W(F))\, dF(x) = 0$

for some function h with suitable properties. If $h(x, s)$ is of the form $h(x, s) = w(x)[v(x) - s]$, then W is a weighted utility function (Chew (1983)) which reduces to expected utility if w is constant. If h is continuous, if $h(x, \cdot)$ is decreasing, and if $h(\cdot, z)$ is increasing and concave for all z, then W satisfies continuity, monotonicity, and risk aversion in the sense of aversion to mean preserving spreads. For details, the reader is referred to the cited papers.

Of primary interest here is the class of quadratic functions. A utility functional V is said to be quadratic in probabilities if it can be expressed in the form

$$(2) \qquad V(F) = \iint \phi(x, y) \, dF(x) \, dF(y), \qquad F \in D(X),$$

for some symmetric function $\phi \colon X \times X \to R^1$. There is no loss of generality in restricting ϕ to be symmetric, since an arbitrary $\phi(x, y)$ can always be replaced by $(\phi(x, y) + \phi(y, x))/2$. For c.d.f.'s F having finite support $\{x_1, \ldots, x_n\}$ and corresponding probabilities $p_1, \ldots, p_n$, $V(F)$ takes the form

$$(3) \qquad V(F) = \sum_{i=1}^{n} \sum_{j=1}^{n} \phi(x_i, x_j) p_i p_j.$$

The general quadratic functional form in (2) appears in a footnote in Machina (1982, p. 295). In the text of his paper, Machina discusses the special case corresponding to

$$\phi(x, y) = v(x)v(y) + (w(x) + w(y))/2,$$

which leads to

$$(4) \qquad V(F) = \left(\int v(x) \, dF(x) \right)^2 + \int w(x) \, dF(x).$$

A similar example has $\phi(x, y) = [v(x)w(y) + v(y)w(x)]/2$, and

$$(5) \qquad V(F)\left(\int v(x) \, dF(x) \right)\left(\int w(x) \, dF(x) \right),$$

i.e., the product of two expected utility functionals.

Two additional examples will clarify the scope of the structure in (2). First, if $\phi(x, y) = (v(x) + v(y))/2$, then

$$(6) \qquad V(F) = \int v(x) \, dF(x).$$

Thus, expected utility (linearity in probabilities) is a special case of (2). Finally, let

$$(7) \qquad \phi(x, y) = \max(v(x), v(y)).$$

Then[5]

$$(8) \qquad V(F) = \int v(x) \, d[F^2(x)],$$

---

[5] To establish (8), verify it first for c.d.f.'s which have finite support and in which all outcomes are equally likely. If the possible outcomes are $x_1 < x_2 < \cdots < x_n$, then

$$\iint \phi \, dF \, dF = \sum \frac{(2i - 1)}{n^2} v(x_i) = \int v(x) \, dF^2(x).$$

The above class of c.d.f.'s is dense in $D(X)$ and thus (8) may be extended to all of $D(X)$. Similarly if $\phi(x, y) = \min(v(x), v(y))$, then $\iint \phi \, dF \, dF = \int v(x) \, d[1 - (1 - F(x))^2]$, which is the special case of rank dependent utility theory for which $g(p) = 1 - (1 - p)^2$.

146   S. H. CHEW, L. G. EPSTEIN, AND U. SEGAL

which is the special case of rank dependent utility theory ($V(F = \int v(x) d[g(F(x))]$, where $g: [0,1] \to [0,1]$ is increasing and onto) in which the probability transformation function g is quadratic, $g(p) = p^2$.

In the remainder of this section we explore some properties of the quadratic functional form. First it is natural to wonder about the uniqueness class of ϕ. One might conjecture that ϕ^i, $i = a, b$, represent the same preference ordering if and only if they are related by a positive linear transformation. But that is readily disproven since $\phi^a(x, y) \equiv v(x)v(y)$ and $\phi^b(x, y) \equiv (v(x) + v(y))/2$ define the same expected utility ordering if $v > 0$. The conjecture is true, however, if the expected utility, or linear in probabilities, case is excluded. It is convenient, therefore, to introduce the following terminology: say that a quadratic function V on $D(X)$ is proper if it is not ordinally equivalent to an expected utility function. The uniqueness class of ϕ can now be described as follows.

THEOREM 2: *Let V^a and V^b be quadratic functionals of the form in* (2) *and corresponding to ϕ^a and ϕ^b respectively. Then V^a and V^b are ordinally equivalent if and only if either of the following conditions is satisfied*:

(i) *V^a and V^b are ordinally equivalent to expected utility functions in which case $\exists u: X \to R$ and constants A^i, B^i, and C^i such that*

(9) $\phi^i(x, y) = A^i u(x) u(y) + B^i(u(x) + u(y)) + C^i$, $i = a, b$,

where the functions $A^i x^2 + 2 B^i x + C^i$, $i = a, b$, are increasing on the range of u;

or

(ii) *V^a and V^b are proper quadratic in which case $\exists \alpha$ and β, $\beta > 0$, such that*

$$\phi^a(x, y) = \alpha + \beta \phi^b(x, y) \qquad \forall(x, y) \in X^2.$$

PROOF: (ii) Assume ordinal equivalence of V^a and V^b. Evaluate the utility of the gamble with outcomes $x < y < z$ and the corresponding probabilities $1 - p - q$, p, and q. If ϕ^i is used, the utility is

$$V^i = \phi^i(x, x)(1 - p - q)^2 + \phi^i(y, y)p^2 + \phi^i(z, z)q^2 + 2\phi^i(y, z)pq$$
$$+ 2\phi^i(x, y)p(1 - p - q) + 2\phi^i(x, z)q(1 - p - q).$$

Fix x, y, and z and view V^i as a (quadratic) function of p and q. By hypothesis, V^a and V^b are ordinally equivalent. The desired conclusion now follows from Lemma A3.1 in the Appendix which shows that V^a and V^b must be cardinally equivalent. The converse is trivial.

(i) The sufficiency of (9) is clear, since it implies that

$$V^i(F) = h^i\left(\int u(z)\, dF(z)\right), \qquad \text{where} \qquad h^i(x) = A^i x^2 + 2B^i x + C^i.$$

To prove its necessity we may assume that for each i,

$$\int\int \phi^i(x, y)\, dF(x)\, dF(y) = h^i\left(\int u(x)\, dF(x)\right),$$

for some u and increasing h^i. When F is the c.d.f. for the binary gamble $(x, p; y, 1 - p)$, we obtain

$$(10) \quad p^2\phi^i(x, x) + (1 - p)^2\phi^i(y, y) + 2p(1 - p)\phi^i(x, y)$$
$$= h^i(pu(x) + (1 - p)u(y)).$$

Then h^i must be quadratic as in the statement of the proposition.

For the degenerate gamble which yields x with certainty, (10) implies $\phi^i(x, x) = h^i(u(x))$. Substitution into (10) yields (9).   *Q.E.D.*

Frequently we wish V (or the underlying preference order) to satisfy properties such as continuity, monotonicity, and risk aversion, the latter in the sense of aversion to mean preserving spreads. The restrictions on ϕ corresponding to these properties for V are described below.

THEOREM 3: *Let $\geq$ be represented by the function V in (2). Then $\geq$ is continuous if and only if ϕ is jointly continuous on X^2. Moreover, given continuity, the ordering is (i) monotonic if and only if (i') $\phi(\cdot, y)$ is nondecreasing and $\phi(x, x) > \phi(y, y)$ whenever $y < x, (x, y) \in X^2$; and the ordering is (ii) risk averse if and only if (ii') $\phi(\cdot, y)$ is concave $\forall y \in X$.*

These conditions on ϕ are readily imposed in the context of the above examples, with the single exception that (7) cannot satisfy the concavity requirement. Thus the rank dependent functional (8) is not always averse to mean preserving spreads, an observation which is consistent with Chew, Karni, and Safra (1987). Note that V defined in (4) is both quasiconvex (indeed convex) and risk averse if $v > 0$ and v and w are both concave. Also, the functional defined in (5) is both quasiconcave (since $\log V(\cdot)$ is concave) and risk averse if both v and w are concave and positive. This substantiates the claim in the introduction regarding the flexibility of the theory developed here with respect to the separation of risk aversion and attitudes towards randomization.[6]

The proof of Theorem 3 is facilitated by consideration of the differentiability properties of quadratic functionals. Since these properties are also of independent interest we examine them briefly. First, it can be shown as in Chew, Karni, and Safra (1987) that the rank dependent functional (8) is not Fréchet differentiable. Thus the quadratic is generally not differentiable in that sense.[7] But that paper also shows that much of the machinery developed by Machina (1982) under the assumption of Fréchet differentiability can be adapted to the more general framework of Gateaux differentiability. In particular, one can define local utility functions which play a similar role to that in Machina's work.

---

[6] A sufficient condition on ϕ for the quasiconcavity or quasiconvexity of utility can be derived as follows: For c.d.f.'s with finite support, $V(F)$ is a quadratic form in the probabilities with coefficient matrix $(\phi(x_i, x_j))_{i,j}$. Thus V is quasiconcave on $D(X)$ if $(\phi(x_i, x_j))_{i,j}$ is negative semi-definite for all $x_1, \ldots, x_n$ and n. But this property is not readily verified given a specification for ϕ.

[7] The existence and continuity of the cross partial derivative $\phi_{12}(x, y)$ is sufficient for V to be Fréchet differentiable. The sufficiency of more general conditions is established in Appendix 5.

148   S. H. CHEW, L. G. EPSTEIN, AND U. SEGAL

Moreover, quadratic functionals are always Gateaux differentiable since

(11) $\quad \dfrac{d}{dt}V((1-t)F+tG)\Big|_{t=0^+} = \int u(x;F)\,d(G(x)-F(x)),$ where

$$u(x;F) = 2\int \phi(x,y)\,dF(y).$$

The function $u(\cdot;F)$ is the local utility function at F.

By the above noted extension of Machina's analysis, risk aversion of V is equivalent to the concavity of $u(\cdot;F)$ $\forall F$. Take F to be the degenerate distribution concentrated at y and conclude that the concavity of $\phi(\cdot,y)$ $\forall y \in X$ is necessary for risk aversion. Since it is clearly sufficient for the concavity of $u(\cdot;F)$ and hence also for risk aversion, we have proven that (ii) $\Leftrightarrow$ (ii') in Theorem 3. The remainder of the proof is provided below.

PROOF OF THEOREM 3: Assume V is continuous and let $(x_n,y_n)\to(x,y)$. Denote by δ_z the degenerate c.d.f. which assigns unit mass to z. Then

$$\delta_{x_n}\to\delta_x \Rightarrow V(\delta_{x_n})\to V(\delta_x) \Rightarrow \phi(x_n,x_n)\to\phi(x,x).$$

Similarly, $\phi(y_n,y_n)$ converges to $\phi(y,y)$. Also, $\forall p\in(0,1)$,

$$V\big(p\delta_{x_n}+(1-p)\delta_{y_n}\big)$$
$$\to V\big(p\delta_x+(1-p)\delta_y\big)$$
$$\Rightarrow \{p^2\phi(x_n,x_n)+2p(1-p)\phi(x_n,y_n)+(1-p)^2\phi(y_n,y_n)\}$$
$$\to \{p^2\phi(x,x)+2p(1-p)\phi(x,y)+(1-p)^2\phi(y,y)\},$$

which implies $\phi(x_n,y_n)\to\phi(x,y)$. Thus ϕ is continuous. The converse is immediate since ϕ is continuous and bounded on $X\times X$.

(i) $\Leftrightarrow$ (i'): The monotonicity of $\geq$ implies that $u(\cdot;F)$ is nondecreasing and $\phi(x,x)=V(\delta_x)>V(\delta_y)=\phi(y,y)$ if $x>y$. (Recall that the monotonicity axiom is strict.) For the converse, assume (i'). It is enough to show that $V(\sum_{i=1}^n p_i\delta_{x_i})$ is increasing in each x_j for which $p_j>0$, which is true since

$$V\left(\sum_1^n p_i\delta_{x_i}\right) = \sum_{i\neq j}\sum_{k\neq j}\phi(x_i,x_k)p_ip_k + p_j^2\phi(x_j,x_j) + 2\sum_{i\neq j}\phi(x_i,x_j)p_ip_j.$$

The equivalence of (ii) and (ii') was proven above.   *Q.E.D.*

Finally, note that the proper quadratic functional form can "explain" the behavioral evidence against expected utility theory. In particular it can satisfy Machina's Hypothesis II (Machina (1982, pp. 310–311)) and thus can explain the Allais paradox, the common consequence effect, the common ratio effect, and other behavioral evidence. Of course, betweenness functionals can also resolve these behavioral paradoxes (Chew (1983)). Moreover, it is readily shown that proper quadratic functionals and betweenness functionals define disjoint classes.

4. REPRESENTATION THEOREMS

In this section the preceding axioms and functional forms are related. In particular, the consequences of mixture symmetry are derived.

It is readily verified that the quadratic functional form satisfies mixture symmetry. Indeed, it satisfies strong mixture symmetry since

$$(12) \qquad V(\alpha F + (1 - \alpha)G) - V((1 - \alpha)F + \alpha G)$$
$$= [\alpha - (1 - \alpha)][V(F) - V(G)].$$

On the other hand, since betweenness-conforming functionals satisfy mixture symmetry but are not necessarily quadratic, it is clear that mixture symmetry does not characterize quadratic functionals. However, it does (in conjunction with some of the other axioms) imply that the utility functional is quadratic on part of its domain and betweenness-conforming on the complementary region. This characterization is described precisely in the theorems to follow.

THEOREM 4: *Let the preference ordering* $\geq$ *on* $D(X)$ *satisfy continuity, monotonicity, and quasiconcavity (quasiconvexity). Then* $\geq$ *satisfies mixture symmetry if and only if it can be represented numerically by a utility function* V *which has the following form: there exists* $F_0 \in D(X)$ *such that*

$$(13) \qquad V(F) = \begin{cases} Q(F), & \forall F \geq (\leq)F_0, \\ W(F), & \forall F \leq (\geq)F_0, \end{cases}$$

where W *satisfies betweenness and where* Q *is a proper quadratic function.*

The betweenness functional W has the structure described in (1) and Q is a proper quadratic specialization of (2). Thus (13) provides a complete description of the functional structure of V, which structure is illustrated in the 3-outcome probability simplex in Figure 2. In that figure, region III (I) is void if the ordering is quasiconvex (quasiconcave). It is evident that any V which combines a quadratic and betweenness functional as in (13) satisfies mixture symmetry. The necessity of (13) is nontrivial, however, and is proven in Appendices 2-4. Appendix 2 treats the case of c.d.f.'s corresponding to three outcome gambles. This proof is accomplished by establishing a link between mixture symmetry and a characteristic property of conics called the projection property. The extension to finite outcome gambles is considered in Appendix 3 and the proof is completed in Appendix 4.

Consider the consequence for Theorem 4 of strengthening quasiconcavity or quasiconvexity to their proper forms (see Section 2). Clearly, the betweenness region is thereby eliminated and a globally quadratic utility function is implied. Thus we immediately obtain the following result.

THEOREM 5: *Let* $\geq$ *satisfy continuity, monotonicity, and proper quasiconcavity (quasiconvexity). Then* $\geq$ *satisfies mixture symmetry if and only if it can be represented numerically by a proper quadratic utility function of the form* (2).

     S. H. CHEW, L. G. EPSTEIN, AND U. SEGAL

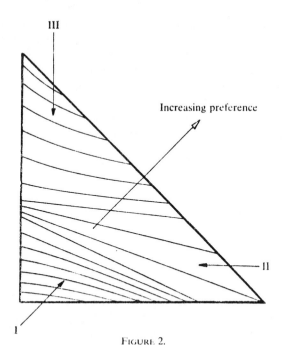

FIGURE 2.

The consequences for functional structure if the quasiconcavity and quasiconvexity axioms are deleted are unspecified above. In the 3-outcome probability simplex, it follows from Appendix 2 that V must be defined by three regions as in Figure 2: it is proper quadratic and quasiconcave (quasiconvex) in the upper (lower) region and betweenness-conforming in the intermediate region. But more complicated structures are possible on higher dimensional simplices. For example, consider the quadratic utility function given by

$$V(F) = \left(\int u(x)\, dF(x) \right)^2 + \left(\int v(x)\, dF(x) \right)\left(\int w(x)\, dF(x) \right),$$

where u, v, and w are continuous, positive, increasing, and concave functions on X. On the hyperplane $\{F: \int u(x)\, dF(x) = K\}$, V resembles the example in (5) and can be shown to be quasiconcave. On the other hand, on the hyperplane $\{F: \int w(x)\, dF(x) = K'\}$, V resembles the example in (4) and can be shown to be quasiconvex. It follows that V is neither quasiconcave nor quasiconvex on any open convex subset of $D(X)$. Indeed, even in the 4-outcome probability simplex there exist regions where V is neither quasiconcave nor quasiconvex.

We can establish the general structure portrayed in Figure 2, i.e., where both regions I and III may be nonempty, under the following circumstances. Recall that an indifference set $I(F) = \{G \in D(X): G \sim F\}$ is planar if it is convex and is not equal to the singleton $\{F\}$. Two possibilities exist—either $\exists F^0 \in D(X)$ such that the corresponding indifference set $I(F^0)$ is planar, or there does not. The latter case is illustrated by the example given above. In the former case, the desired structure may be established in the following way.

THEOREM 6: *Let* $\geq$ *satisfy continuity and monotonicity on* $D(X)$. *Suppose further that* $\exists F^0 \in D(X)$ *such that the indifference set* $I(F^0)$ *is planar. Then* $\geq$ *satisfies mixture symmetry if and only if it can be represented by a utility function* V *which has the following form*:

$$(14) \qquad V(F) = \begin{cases} Q_2(F), & F^2 \leq F, \\ W(F), & F^1 \leq F \leq F^2, \\ Q_1(F), & F \leq F^1, \end{cases}$$

for some F^1 *and* $F^2 \in D(X)$, $F^1 \leq F^0 \leq F^2$, *where* W *satisfies betweenness and where* Q_1 *and* Q_2 *are proper quadratic functionals.*

PROOF: Since $I(F^0)$ is not a singleton by assumption, F^0 cannot be the worst or best element in $D(X)$. Let $x_{\min} = \min\{x : x \in X\}$. Choose $F \sim G > F^0$ and $H_1 = \delta_{x_{\min}}$, H_2, and H_3 in $D(X)$ such that (i) F and G lie in the interior of the simplex $\Delta(H_1, H_2, H_3)$ consisting of all probability mixtures of H_1, H_2, and H_3; and (ii) the portion $\mathcal{T}$ of the indifference curve containing F and G which lies between them is connected in the interior of $\Delta(H_1, H_2, H_3)$. The ranking of $(1 - p - q)\delta_{x_{\min}} + pH_2 + qH_3$ is increasing in p and q. Therefore, Appendix 2 and the structure portrayed in Figure 1 apply to a neighborhood of $\mathcal{T}$ in $\Delta(H_1, H_2, H_3)$. It follows, using Lemma A1.2, that $\geq$ is quasiconcave on that part of $D(X)$ which lies above $I(F^0)$, i.e., on $\{F \in D(X): F \geq F^0\}$. Similarly, it must be quasiconvex on the region below F^0, $\{F \in D(X): F \leq F^0\}$. Moreover, if there are two distinct planar indifference sets in $D(X)$, then all indifference sets between them must be planar.

Let $B = \cup\{I(F): F \in D(X), I(F) \text{ is planar}\}$. Let $F^1(F^2)$ be a worst (best) element in the closure of B. Clearly, $I(F^1)$ and $I(F^2)$ are planar. Moreover, the ordering $\geq$ satisfies proper quasiconcavity on the region strictly above F^2 and thus Theorem 5, restricted to this subdomain of $D(X)$, may be applied to yield the desired quadratic utility representation there. Similarly for the region strictly below F^1. The desired utility representation on the betweenness region follows from Chew (1989) and Dekel (1986).   *Q.E.D.*

In Section 3 we provided examples of utility functionals satisfying our axioms. To conclude this section we describe an example of a continuous and monotonic functional which is betweenness-conforming on part of its domain and quadratic on the remainder. Thus the "schizophrenic" functional structure (13) or (14) cannot be improved upon given the axioms in Theorems 4 and 6.

EXAMPLE: Let $X = [0, 1]$,

$$\phi(x, y) \equiv 4xy - 2x^2y - 2xy^2 + x^2 + y^2 - \tfrac{1}{2} \qquad \text{and}$$

$$V(F) = \begin{cases} \iint \phi(x, y) \, dF(x) \, dF(y), & \mu(F) \geq \tfrac{1}{2}, \\ \mu(F), & \mu(F) \leq \tfrac{1}{2}, \end{cases}$$

where $\mu(F)$ denotes the mean of F. Then ϕ is increasing and continuous. Moreover, V is well-defined and continuous, since

$$\iint \phi(x, y) \, dF(x) \, dF(y) = 4\mu^2(F) - 2\mu(F) \int x^2 \, dF(x)$$

$$- 2\mu(F) \int y^2 \, dF(y)$$

$$+ \int x^2 \, dF(x) + \int y^2 \, dF(y) - \tfrac{1}{2}$$

$$= \tfrac{1}{2} \qquad \text{if} \qquad \mu(F) = \tfrac{1}{2}.$$

Finally, V clearly satisfies betweenness on the region where $\mu(F) \leq \tfrac{1}{2}$, but not elsewhere. For example, $V(F) = V(G) = 9/8 \neq V(\tfrac{1}{2}F + \tfrac{1}{2}G)$, where F corresponds to the gamble with equiprobable payoffs $\tfrac{1}{2}$ and 1 while G yields payoffs 0 and 1 with probabilities $3/16$ and $13/16$ respectively.

5. DISCUSSION

In the introduction we cited some evidence against betweenness. Here we describe some preliminary evidence, taken from Chew and Waller (1986), regarding the nature of observed violations of betweenness. Then we comment upon our representation results in light of this evidence. We also relate our discussion to Green's (1987) theoretical argument against quasiconcavity.

Chew and Waller investigated the nature of indifference curves in the three-outcome probability simplex. The outcome parameters used, as well as the resulting frequencies of nonbetweenness observations, are described in Table I. While the overall frequencies of betweenness violations (32% for Experiment 1 and 22% for Experiment 2) are not significantly greater than the chance hit rate of $1/2$, it is noteworthy that the nature of the betweenness violations displays a systematic dependence on the outcome parameters. Quasiconcave (quasiconvex) behavior is most pronounced when the outcomes are all positive (negative).

Such behavior accords well with the result in Theorem 6, whereby quasiconcavity prevails in the "upper" part of the domain and quasiconvexity in the lower "portion." In fact, we can apply Theorem 6 to each of the outcome sets $X = \{-100, -40, 0, 40, 60, 100\}$ and $X = \{-5,000, 0, 10,000, 15,000, 20,000, 27,000, 30,000\}$, and deduce that preference is more likely to be quasiconcave for the more attractive comparisons (e.g., contexts 1a, 2a, 2b) and quasiconvex for the less attractive comparisons (e.g., contexts 1c, 2c).

TABLE I[a]

		Experiment 1			Experiment 2		
		a	b	c	a	b	c
Outcomes	x_1	0	−40	−100	10,000	0	−5,000
	x_2	40	0	−40	27,000	10,000	0
	x_3	100	60	0	30,000	20,000	15,000
% quasiconvexity patterns		0	11	21	4	3	11
% quasiconcavity patterns		32	21	11	19	22	5
% nonbetweenness patterns		32	32	32	23	25	16

[a]Total number of observations = 56.

Green (1987) argues in support of quasiconvexity by demonstrating that a quasiconcave agent may be manipulated into making a series of choices that leave him stochastically dominated by his initial position. One possible "explanation" of quasiconcavity is that it reflects the "utility of gambling," or the "consumption" benefits of randomization. Viewed in this light, Theorem 6 is appealing. It suggests that a preference for randomization can be satiated in a losing streak. In particular the potential losses that can be traced to quasiconcavity are bounded and represent a "price" paid for the enjoyment of gambling.

Department of Economics and A. B. Freeman School of Business, Tulane University, New Orleans, LA 70118, and Department of Economics, University of California, Irvine, CA 92717, U.S.A.,
Department of Economics, University of Toronto, Toronto, Canada M5S 1A1
and
Department of Economics, University of Toronto, Toronto, Canada M5S 1A1

Manuscript received August, 1988; final revision received November, 1989.

APPENDIX 1: PROOF OF THEOREM 1

The proof is accomplished via a sequence of lemmas. Continuity, monotonicity, and mixture symmetry are assumed throughout. Also, $F\alpha G$ denotes $\alpha F + (1-\alpha)G$. The set of mixtures of F_1, F_2, and F_3 is denoted $\Delta(F_1, F_2, F_3)$, or simply Δ with the F_i's suppressed. The set of mixtures of F_1 and F_2 is denoted $[F_1, F_2]$.

LEMMA A1.1: *Let $F \sim G$ where F and G lie in the interior of $D(X)$. If there exists $\alpha \in (0,1)$ such that $F \sim F\alpha G$, then for every $\alpha \in (0,1), F \sim F\alpha G$.*

PROOF: There exist F' and G' in $D(X)$ and $x_{min} \equiv \min\{x : x \in X\}$ such that F and G lie in the interior of $\Delta(\delta_{x_{min}}, F', G')$. Moreover, the preference relation is monotonic on this set in the sense that the ranking of $pF' + qG' + (1-p-q)\delta_{x_{min}}$ is increasing in p and q. This monotonicity, which is weaker than consistency with first degree stochastic dominance, is used below.

154   S. H. CHEW, L. G. EPSTEIN, AND U. SEGAL

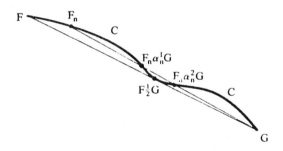

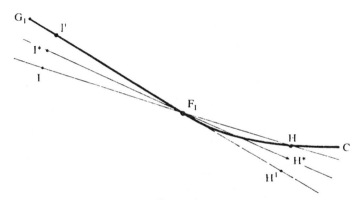

FIGURE 3a.

If the set $\{\alpha: F\alpha G \sim F\}$ is dense in $[0,1]$, the lemma follows by continuity. Otherwise, there is a segment $[\beta_1, \beta_2]$ such that for $\alpha \in (\beta_1, \beta_2)$, $F\alpha G \nsim F$, but for $\alpha \in \{\beta_1, \beta_2\}$, $F\alpha G \sim F$. By hypothesis, it is impossible that $\beta_1 = 0$ and $\beta_2 = 1$. Suppose $\beta_2 < 1$. (The argument for $\beta_1 > 0$ is similar.) For $\beta_3 > \beta_2$ such that $\beta_3 - \beta_2 < \beta_2 - \beta_1$ it follows that $F\beta_3 G \nsim F$, otherwise $F\beta_2 G$, $F\beta_1 G$ and $F\beta_3 G$ imply a violation of mixture symmetry. Since $F1G = F$, it follows that $2\beta_2 - \beta_1 \leq 1$. Now let $\beta_3 = \min\{\beta \in [2\beta_2 - \beta_1, 1]: F\beta G \sim F\}$. By continuity, the minimum exists and $F\beta_3 G \sim F$. If $\beta_3 - \beta_2 > \beta_2 - \beta_1$, then $F\beta_2 G$, $F\beta_1 G$ and $F\beta_3 G$ violate mixture symmetry. Thus $\beta_3 - \beta_2 = \beta_2 - \beta_1$.

By repeating the above arguments we obtain scalars $0 = \gamma_0 < \cdots < \gamma_i < \gamma_{i+1} < \cdots < \gamma_{n+1} = 1$ such that $n \geq 1$ and for $i = 1, \ldots, n$,

$$F\gamma_i G \sim F, \quad \gamma_i = (\gamma_{i+1} + \gamma_{i-1})/2,$$

and $F\alpha G \nsim F$, $\forall \alpha \in \cup_0^n (\gamma_i, \gamma_{i+1})$. Refer to $\{F\gamma_i G: i = 0, \ldots, n+1\}$ as a uniform partition of $[F, G]$ with partition length $\gamma_{i+1} - \gamma_i$. We show that such a partition is impossible. It suffices to consider the case $n = 1$ above and to rule out the following: $F \sim G$, $F\frac{1}{2}G \sim F$, and for every other $\alpha \in (0,1)$, $F\alpha G \nsim F$. By mixture symmetry this implies

(i) $F\alpha G \geq F$, $\quad \forall \alpha \in (0,1)$, or

(ii) $F\alpha G \leq F$, $\quad \forall \alpha \in (0,1)$,

with strict preference in either case when $\alpha \notin \{0, 1/2, 1\}$.

Suppose (ii) applies. (The argument for (i) is similar.) Let C be the indifference curve through F and G. Let $F_n \to F$, $F_n \sim F$, and $\forall n F_n$ is between F and G (see Figure 3a). Since $F > F\alpha G$, for sufficiently large n the chord joining F_n and G intersects C at least once between F_n and $F\frac{1}{2}G$ and at least once between $F_2^1 G$ and G. Thus $\exists \alpha_n^1 > \alpha_n^2$ such that $F_n \alpha_n^1 G \sim F_n \alpha_n^2 G \sim F$, $\alpha_n^1 \to 1/2$ and $\alpha_n^2 \to 1/2$. By the above discussion applied to $[F_n, G]$ rather than $[F, G]$, we deduce the existence of a uniform partition of $[F_n, G]$ of length no greater than $\alpha_n^1 - \alpha_n^2$, which approaches 0 as $n \to \infty$. By continuity, therefore, $F \alpha G \sim F$, $\forall \alpha \in (0, 1)$, which yields the desired contradiction.   Q.E.D.

CONCLUSION 1: *If $F \sim G$, then $\geq$ is either quasiconcave or quasiconvex on $[F, G]$.*

Say that $[F_1, F_2]$ is an isopreference if all of its elements are indifferent to one another and if $F_1 \neq F_2$.

LEMMA A1.2: *Let F and $G \in \text{int}(D(X))$.*
(a) *If $[F_1, G_1] \subset [F, G]$ is an isopreference, then so is $[F, G]$.*
(b) *If $F \sim G$, then $F_2^1 G$ is a best or worst element in $[F, G]$. Moreover, if $F \alpha^* G \sim F_2^1 G$ for some $\alpha^* \neq \frac{1}{2}$, then $[F, G]$ is an isopreference.*

PROOF: As in the proof of the previous lemma $\exists \Delta < D(X)$, containing F and G, where the ordering is monotonic.
(a) Refer to Figure 3b, where it is assumed that the indifference curve C containing $[F_1, G_1]$ is not linear. There is no loss of generality in supposing that $[F_1, G_1]$ is a maximal isopreference in $[F, G]$. Suppose also that the quasiconcave case applies. (The other case may be treated similarly.) Choose H, I, H' and I' such that $F_1 = H \alpha I = H' \alpha' I'$ with $\alpha > \frac{1}{2}$, $H > I$, and $I' > H'$. By continuity, there exists H^* and I^* such that $F_1 = H^* \alpha I^*$, $H^* \sim I^*$, and for $\beta < \alpha$, $F_1 > H^* \beta I^*$, a violation of mixture symmetry.
(b) Suppose that $F_2^1 G \geq F$. Let $F \alpha^* G > F_2^1 G$ for some $\alpha^* \neq \frac{1}{2}$, say $\alpha^* < \frac{1}{2}$. By mixture symmetry $\exists \beta^* > \frac{1}{2}$ for which $F \alpha^* G \sim F \beta^* G$. By continuity $\exists \alpha_0 \in (0, \alpha^*)$, $F_2^1 G < F \alpha_0 G < F \alpha^* G$. Let $\beta_0 > \frac{1}{2}$ be a corresponding probability weight provided by mixture symmetry. Then $F_0 \equiv F \alpha_0 G$ and $G_0 \equiv F \beta_0 G$ violate Conclusion 1. Thus $F_2^1 G \geq F \alpha G$, $\forall \alpha \in [0, 1]$.
If $F_2^1 G \sim F$, then $[F, G]$ is an isopreference by Lemma A1.1. Thus it remains only to consider the case $F^* G \sim F_2^1 G > F$ for some $\alpha^* \neq \frac{1}{2}$. Let

$$\underline{\alpha} \equiv \min \{\alpha \in [0, 1]: F \alpha G \sim F_2^1 G\} \qquad \text{and}$$

$$\bar{\alpha} \equiv \max \{\alpha \in [0, 1]: F \alpha G \sim F_2^1 G\}.$$

Then $\underline{\alpha} < \frac{1}{2} < \bar{\alpha}$ by mixture symmetry. By Lemma A1.1, $[F \underline{\alpha} G, F \bar{\alpha} G]$ is an isopreference. By part (a) the same is true of $[F, G]$.   Q.E.D.

PROOF OF THEOREM 1: Let F and G lie in the interior of $D(X)$. Suppose $F \alpha G \sim F \beta G$ and $\beta \neq 1 - \alpha$. Then $F_2^1 G$ is a best or worst point in $[F \alpha G, F \beta G]$ but yet is not a midpoint. By Lemma A1.2, therefore, $[F, G]$ is an isopreference and so $F \alpha G \sim F(1 - \alpha)G$ trivially.
If F and G are on the boundary, take $F_n \to F$, $G_n \to G$, $F_n \sim G_n$, F_n and $G_n \in \text{int}(D(X))$. Then

$$F_n \alpha G_n \sim F_n(1 - \alpha)G_n \ \forall n \Rightarrow F \alpha G \sim F(1 - \alpha)G.$$ Q.E.D.

APPENDIX 2: PROOF OF THEOREM 4 IN THE 3-OUTCOME CASE

This appendix deals exclusively with c.d.f.'s for three outcome gambles. Thus we consider $S^2 = \{(p, q) \in R_+^2: p + q \leq 1\}$, where p and q are the probabilities associated with the intermediate and largest outcomes respectively, and we write $V(p, q)$. The continuity and monotonicity axioms imply that V is continuous and increasing on S^2. Note that indifference curves in S^2 are connected. (Otherwise, there would be distinct indifferent points along the edge joining $(1, 0)$ and $(0, 1)$ which would violate first degree stochastic dominance.) Of course, mixture symmetry (or equivalently, strong mixture symmetry) is maintained. Neither quasiconcavity nor quasiconvexity is assumed in this appendix.

LEMMA A2.1: *Each indifference curve lying in the interior of S^2 is either strictly convex, strictly concave, or a straight line.*

156   S. H. CHEW, L. G. EPSTEIN, AND U. SEGAL

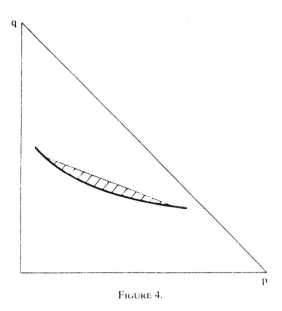

FIGURE 4.

PROOF: Follows from Lemmas A1.1 and A1.2.   Q.E.D.

We show below that S^2 is divided into regions I, II, and III (some of which may be empty) such that indifference curves are strictly concave, linear, and strictly convex in regions I, II, and III respectively (see Figure 2). Region I is below and to the left of II, the latter is below and to the left of III, and the boundaries between I and II and between III are linear indifference curves.

We will show that the preference ordering can be represented by a proper quadratic function on III. (A similar argument applies to I while the desired representation on II follows from Chew (1989) and Dekel (1986).) This is done by establishing the representation on each small open rectangle in III. Such open rectangles exist if III is nonempty, since given a strictly convex indifference curve as in Figure 4, all indifference curves in the shaded region above it must also be strictly convex. We can write region III $= \cup_1^+ O_i$, where each O_i is an open rectangle having a quadratic representation V_i and where $O_i \cap O_{i+1} \neq \emptyset \ \forall i \geqslant 1$. V_i and V_{i+1} are ordinally equivalent on $O_i \cap O_{i+1}$ and thus also cardinally equivalent there by Lemma A3.1. We can redefine V_{i+1} if necessary to guarantee that $V_{i+1} = V_i$ on $O_i \cap O_{i+1}$. By starting this argument at $i = 1$ we can construct a quadratic function V on region III which represents $\succeq$ on each O_i. Indifference curves are connected subsets of region III. Thus it is straightforward to show that V is constant along indifference curves and subsequently that it represents $\succeq$ on region III.

The arguments to follow should be understood to apply to a rectangle which lies wholly in III. The (income) expansion paths (e.p.) of the indifference map play a central role. Two points a and b lie on the same expansion path if there is a common subgradient to the indifference curves at a and b.

The proof presented below may be outlined as follows: we show that (i) all e.p.'s are linear, and (ii) they are perspective, i.e., they have a common point of intersection, which could be at infinity if they are parallel lines (Lemmas A2.3–5). By strong mixture symmetry and the quasiconcavity which prevails in the subdomain upon which we focus, the optimal mix between two indifferent bundles is the midpoint between them. Thus each e.p. bisects the chords of an indifference curve which have absolute slope equal to the price ratio underlying the e.p. We conclude that indifference curves in S^2 possess the following projection property: the loci of midpoints of parallel chords are perspective. It is known (Coxeter (1974)) that conics have the projection property. We prove the converse (Theorem A2.1) to establish that indifference curves are conics, from which the desired representation for V follows.

LEMMA A2.2: *All expansion paths are straight lines. Moreover, each expansion path is a locus of midpoints of parallel chords of an indifference curve.*

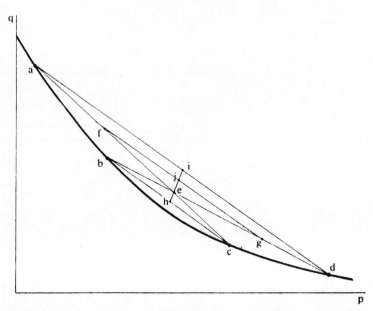

FIGURE 5.

PROOF: Refer to Figure 5. Start with h and i, points on an e.p. Draw the chord through h with absolute slope equal to a price ratio underlying the e.p. In this way points b and c are defined. By drawing a parallel chord through i, the points a and d may be constructed. Next draw the lines ac and bd with intersection point e.

Strong mixture symmetry and quasiconcavity $\Rightarrow h$ and i are the midpoints of bc and ad respectively. It follows by plane geometry that e is on the line hi. By construction it is not the midpoint of ac or bd. (Otherwise ad and bc would have the same length.) Let f be the point on ac that is symmetric to e, in the sense of being the mirror image of e in a reflection through the midpoint of ac. Construct g similarly on bd. By strong mixture symmetry, $f \sim e \sim g$. Let j be the midpoint of fg. Then by plane geometry j is on hi and, by strong mixture symmetry and quasiconcavity, it is on the given e.p.

This proves that given any two points h and i on the e.p., there exists a third point on the e.p. that is also on the line segment hi. Thus the e.p. must be linear. Note that h, i, and j are midpoints of the respective parallel chords.   Q.E.D.

LEMMA A2.3: *If two e.p.'s intersect, then there is another e.p. lying between them such that the three paths have a common intersection point.*

PROOF: Refer to Figure 6. Start with the indifference curve and with the two e.p.'s A and B, with the slopes of bd and ce for A and B respectively. The points c and e can be chosen so that $cd \parallel be$. By strong mixture symmetry, $bh = hd$ and $ci = ie$. Construct $ae \parallel bd$ with midpoint g and $bf \parallel ce$ with midpoint j. Let l and m be the midpoints of be and cd respectively. Then these points are on the same straight line C, C is an e.p., and it intersects A and B at their common intersection point.   Q.E.D.

We assert, without proof, that the limit of a sequence of *e.p.*'s is itself an *e.p.* More precisely, the following is true:

LEMMA A2.4: *Let* $(p^n, q^n) \to (p^0, q^0)$ *where all points lie on a given indifference curve. Let* $q = r_n p + s_n$ *be corresponding e.p.'s going through these points,* $n = 0, 1, \ldots$ *. Then* $r_n \to r_0$ *and* $s_n \to s_0$.

LEMMA A2.5: *Either all e.p.'s are parallel straight lines or they have a common intersection point.*

158   S. H. CHEW, L. G. EPSTEIN, AND U. SEGAL

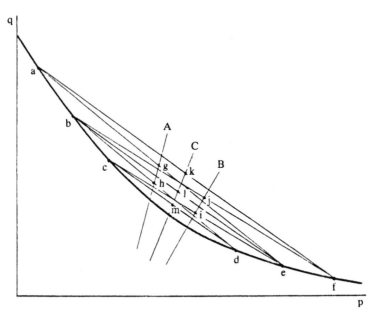

FIGURE 6.

PROOF: Suppose there exist intersecting e.p.'s A and B as in Figure 6. Denote by z their common intersection point and by λ_A and λ_B their intersections with the indifference curve shown. Use the preceding two lemmas to argue that $\exists$ a dense subset of the segment of the indifference curve lying between λ_A and λ_B, such that through each point in the set there is an e.p. which contains z. By Lemma A2.4, all e.p.'s that lie between A and B contain z. We can apply Lemma A2.3 repeatedly to prove that the qualifier "between A and B" may be dropped.   Q.E.D.

We have now established the projection property described at the beginning of this appendix. The next step is to prove that this property implies that indifference curves are conics. A conic is uniquely determined by five distinct arbitrary points. (Note that there are five free coefficients in $ap^2 + bq^2 + cpq + dp + eq$.) When the center of projection O is given, or (in the case of a parabola) when the center is at infinity, if the common slope of expansion paths is also given, then the conic is uniquely determined by three distinct arbitrary points. We can use any two of the three points to define a chord and then generate a fourth point by drawing a parallel chord from the third point such that the straight line from O (or the line parallel to expansion paths when O is at infinity), which bisects the first chord, also bisects the second chord. One additional step, with a similar construction, leads to a fifth point.

THEOREM A2.1: *A curve in R^2 is a conic if and only if it has the projection property, i.e. if and only if the loci of midpoints of parallel chords are perspective.*

PROOF: For the necessity of the projection property see Coxeter (1974). We prove sufficiency in the case where the center of projection O is finite. The argument for the case where O is at infinity is similar.

Refer to Figure 7. Given any two parallel chords a_0a_0' and a_1a_1', let Q_1 be the unique conic through a_0, a_0' and a_1 with center O. Let OM_0 bisect a_0a_0'. By the projection property, it must also bisect a_1a_1'. Moreover, since the conic Q_1 satisfies the projection property, $a_1' \in Q_1$. We will prove that C coincides with Q_1 for points along Q_1 between a_0 and a_1, and between a_0' and a_1'.

Construct another parallel chord a_2a_2' between a_0a_0' and a_1a_1' such that $a_0a_2'\|a_2a_1'$. Let Q_2 be the unique conic through a_0, a_0' and a_2 with center 0. As before, $a_2' \in Q_2$. Let ON_0 bisect a_0a_2' and consequently also a_2a_1'. It follows from the noted projection property of conics that a_1' and $a_1 \in Q_2$. Thus $\{a_0, a_0', a_1\} \subset Q_1 \cap Q_2 \Rightarrow Q_1 = Q_2 \Rightarrow a_2' \in Q_1$.

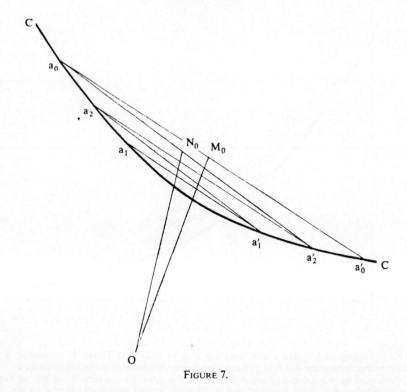

FIGURE 7.

Let $C[a_0, a_1]$ denote that portion of C lying between a_0 and a_1 and define $D \equiv C[a_0, a_1] \cap Q_1$. As above we can show that if a and b belong to D, then $\exists c \in D$ lying between a and b. Since D is a closed subset of $C[a_0, a_1]$, it follows that D is dense in $C[a_0, a_1]$ and hence that $D = C[a_0, a_1]$. Evidently, $C = Q_1$ between a_0 and a_1 and also between a_0' and a_1'. We finally conclude that $C = Q_1$ since the choice of $a_1 a_1'$ is arbitrary.   Q.E.D.

The Theorem and Lemma A2.5 imply that each indifference curve is the graph of a quadratic function. Since e.p.'s are linear and have a common point of intersection, we can translate the coordinate system to a new origin such that the utility function V is homothetic in the new system. It follows that the same quadratic function applies to all indifference curves. Therefore, each one may be represented in the form

$$f(p, q) = K,$$

where f is a quadratic function (i.e., a second order polynomial function), and where K, but not f, varies across indifference curves. Thus the preference ordering may be represented by a proper quadratic utility function.

This establishes the desired representation on the shaded region in Figure 4. By working with overlapping regions, the representation can be extended to the entire region lying above any strictly convex indifference curve. That is because it is impossible, given the quadratic representation, to have indifference curves in Figure 2 flattening out and eventually becoming linear as one moves in the northeast direction.

APPENDIX 3: Proof of Theorem 4 for CDF's With Finite Support

For 3-outcome gambles the desired representation follows from Appendix 2. Here we extend the representation result to the class of c.d.f.'s with finite support. For fixed outcomes $x_0 < \cdots < x_n$ in $X, n \geqslant 3$, utility depends on the corresponding probability vector. Thus the domain of V is taken to be $S^n \equiv \{(p_1, \ldots, p_n) \in R_+^n : \Sigma_1^n p_i \leq 1\}$, where V is increasing, continuous, and satisfies quasiconcavity and mixture symmetry. The case of quasiconvexity can be treated similarly.

We will make use of the following lemma (used also in the proof of Theorem 2), which describes conditions under which the ordinal equivalence of two proper quadratic functions implies that they are cardinally equivalent.

LEMMA A.3.1: *Let f and g be proper quadratic functions defined on a convex subset of R^n such that*

(A3.1) $f(\cdot) = \Theta(g(\cdot))$

for some increasing Θ. Then Θ is linear on Rng g.

The proof follows readily by computing the Hessians of both sides of (A3.1). Details are omitted.

Say that $H \subset S^n$ is a plane of dimension k if $H = H' \cap S^n$, where H' is a k-dimensional plane in R^n. Denote by $V|H$ the restriction to H of V.

To show that V has the desired representation on S^n, we show by induction on k that $\forall k \leq n$, the following obtains:

$P(k)$: For each k-dimensional plane $H \subset S^n$, if C is an indifference set of $V|H$ which is not a singleton, then either
   (i) C is a plane of dimension $(k-1)$ or k, or
   (ii) for each $p^0 \in \text{int } (S^n) \cap C$ there exists an open neighborhood N of p^0 in H and a proper quadratic function $f: N \to R^1$ such that for every indifference set C'

$$C' \cap N = \{p \in N : f(p) = K\}, \quad \text{for some } K.$$

From $P(n)$ it then follows that each indifference set of V is planar or has local quadratic representations. As in the case of S^2 (Appendix 2), quadratic representations can be constructed so that they coincide on overlapping regions. Therefore, we deduce the existence of regions in S^n analogous to the (proper quasiconcave) quadratic and betweenness regions in Figure 2. That the latter must lie below the former follows from the corresponding fact for S^2, e.g., consider restrictions of V to 2-dimensional subspaces of S^n.

Turn to the proof of $P(k)$ and let $k = 2$. Appendix 2 proves $P(2)$ restricted to 2-dimensional planes H such that for some i_1 and i_2, $p \in H \Rightarrow p_i = 0 \ \forall i \neq i_1, i_2$. We now show that $P(2)$ is true, i.e., the desired property holds for all two-dimensional planes in S^n, provided the preference relation is quasiconcave.

Let H be a plane in S^n, and let p^0 lie in the relative interior of H. Assume first that p^0 is a minimum point of $\succeq$. Let $p^1, p^2 \in H$ such that $p^0 \in (p^1, p^2)$ the open line segment between p^1 and p^2 (the corresponding closed segment is denoted $[p^1, p^2]$). By quasiconcavity at least one of these two points, say p^1, satisfies $p^1 \sim p^0$. If $p^2 \sim p^0$, then by Lemmas A1.1 and A1.2 the entire line in H containing $[p^1, p^2]$ is an indifference set. If $p^2 \succ p^0$, then by quasiconcavity, the set $[p^1, p^0]$ is an indifference set, and so is the line containing this chord in H. This line separates H into two parts. By quasiconcavity, not both of them can contain points strictly preferred to p^0; hence by Lemma A1.2, H is an indifference set.

If p^0 is a maximum point, then by quasiconcavity and Appendix 1 either the indifference set containing it in H is linear, or p^0 is a unique maximum point. In the latter case, it is sufficient by continuity to prove $P(2)$ for all other points in the interior of H.

We proceed assuming that p^0 is neither a minimum nor a maximum point of $\succeq$ in H. Let p^* be a maximum point of $\succeq$ in H. By continuity, there are neighborhoods B^0 of p^0 and B^* of p^* such that $\forall p^2 \in B^0$ and $\forall p^3 \in B^*$, $p^3 > p^2$. Let $L(p^2, p^3)$ be the line containing p^2 and p^3. For $p^2 \in B^0$ and $p^3 \in B^*$ it follows by quasiconcavity that on $L(p^2, p^3) \cap B^0$, the order $\succeq$ is monotonic in the direction from p^2 to p^3.

Let $p, p' \in B^*$ such that $p' \notin L(p^0, p)$. Let $T: H \to R^2$ be a linear transformation such that $T(p^0) = (0,0)$, $T(p) = (1,0)$, and $T(p') = (0,1)$. For $x, y \in T(H)$, define $x \succeq_T y \Leftrightarrow T^{-1}(x) \succeq T^{-1}(y)$. Around $T(p^0) = (0,0)$ the order $\succeq_T$ is monotonic. (To see this, let $x \succ y$, $x \neq y$ be close enough to $(0,0)$. By the nature of T, the slope of $L(T^{-1}(x), T^{-1}(y))$ is between that of $L(p^0, p)$ and $L(p^0, p')$. Therefore, if y is close enough to $(0,0)$, then $B^* \cap L(T^{-1}(x), T^{-1}(y)) \neq \varnothing$.) By Appendix 2, $\succeq_T$ is quadratic around $(0,0)$. Hence $\succeq$ is quadratic around p^0.

Assume $P(k-1)$ and prove $P(k)$. Let $k = n$; the argument for general k is similar but notationally more cumbersome. Suppose C, an indifference set of V, is neither a singleton nor a plane. Let $p^0 \in C$ lie in the interior of S^n. By Lemma A1.2 $\exists p^1 \in C$ such that $(p^0, p^1) \cap C = \varnothing$.

Next we can find $p^2 \in C$ sufficiently close to p^1 such that $(p^0, p^2) \cap C = \emptyset$ and $p^2 - p^0$ is not a scalar multiple of $p^1 - p^0$. Proceeding inductively, we find $p^1, \ldots, p^n$ such that $(p^0, p^i) \cap C = \emptyset$ $\forall i$ and $R^n = \text{span}\{p^i - p^0: i = 1, \ldots, n\}$. Let H^i be the unique $(n-1)$-dimensional plane through p^0 spanned by $\{p^j - p^0: j = 1, \ldots, n, j \neq i\}$. Then $C \cap H^i$ is not a plane since $\{p^0, p^j\} \subset C \cap H^i$ for $j \neq i$ but $[p^0, p^i]$ does not lie in C. Therefore, condition (ii) of $P(n-1)$ applies to $C \cap H^i$ and this is true for each i. Let $\{N^i\}$ be the open sets provided by (ii).

Without loss of generality (choose a suitable linear transformation), suppose that $p^i - p^0$ is e^i, the unit vector in the ith coordinate direction in R^n. Then $H^i = \{p \in S^n: p_i = p_i^0\}$ is the ith coordinate hyperplane through p^0. By above, V is ordinally equivalent to a proper quadratic function f^i on the open region $N^i \subset H^i$, for $i = 1, 2, \ldots, n$. Redefine V so that it is proper quadratic on N^1 ($V \equiv f^1$). Then on $N^1 \cap N^2$, V and f^2 are ordinally equivalent and proper quadratic. (They are clearly quadratic on $N^1 \cap N^2$. They are also proper quadratic functions there since $\{p^0, p^n\} \subset C \cap N^1 \cap N^2$, but $(p^0, p^n) \cap C = \emptyset$.) By Lemma A3.1, the transformation relating V and f^2 is linear and hence V is a proper quadratic on N^2. Similarly, V is a proper quadratic on each N^i.

By continuity, there exists an open neighborhood M of p^0 in S^n, such that V is proper quadratic on the intersection of each coordinate hyperplane with M. (To see this, let $\bar{H}^i$ be parallel to H^i and sufficiently close to it and let $\bar{N}^i \subset H^i$ be the image of $N^i \subset H^i$ under this parallel translation. By continuity, we can assume that V does not satisfy betweenness on $\bar{N}^i$ and so it is ordinally quadratic there by the induction hypothesis. Since V is proper quadratic on $N^i \cap N^j$, $j \neq i$, we can assume that it is proper quadratic also on $N^i \cap N^j$. As before, we can conclude that V is proper quadratic on each $\bar{N}^i$.)

It now follows that V is proper quadratic on an open region in S^n. To see this, consider the hyperplanes which fix the 1st and nth coordinates of p where the quadratic nature of V implies that (locally)

$$
V(p_1, \ldots, p_n) = \sum_{i=1}^{n-1} \sum_{j=i}^{n-1} \phi_{ij}(p_n)(p_i - p_i^0)(p_j - p_j^0) + \sum_{i=1}^{n-1} \gamma_i(p_n)(p_i - p_i^0)
$$

$$
= \sum_{i=2}^{n} \sum_{j=i}^{n} \Psi_{ij}(p_1)(p_i - p_i^0)(p_j - p_j^0) + \sum_{i=2}^{n} \delta_i(p_1)(p_i - p_i^0).
$$

(The normalization $V(p^0) = 0$ has been adopted.) From these two equations, V must be twice differentiable. Also, from the first equation for V, for each $i < n$, $V_{p_i p_i}$ is independent of $p_1, \ldots, p_{n-1}$. Thus, from the second equation for V it follows that $\delta_i(\cdot)$ is linear for $i < n$ and $\Psi_{ij}(\cdot)$ is constant for $i, j < n$. If we replace the nth coordinate hyperplane above by the kth, $k = 2, \ldots, n-1$, we can conclude that $\delta_n(\cdot)$ is linear and that $\Psi_{ij}(\cdot)$ is constant even if i or $j = n$. Thus V is quadratic. It is proper quadratic because each of its coordinate hyperplane restrictions is.

APPENDIX 4: COMPLETION OF THE PROOF OF THEOREM 4

The proof of Theorem 4 is completed here. Two steps remain.

STEP 1: We showed above that when restricted to gambles with $n + 1$ outcomes, V is ordinally equivalent to a quadratic function in the probabilities $p_1, \ldots, p_n$ of the largest n outcomes. We would like a "symmetric" representation that is quadratic in all the probabilities $p_0, p_1, \ldots, p_n$. That is, given that

(A4.1)　　$V(p_1, \ldots, p_n) = \sum_{i,j=1}^{n} \alpha_{ij} p_i p_j + \sum_{i=1}^{n} \beta_i p_i + \gamma$,

we want to rewrite V in the form

(A4.2)　　$V = \sum_{i=0}^{n} \sum_{j=0}^{n} \phi_{ij} p_i p_j$, where $\sum_{i=0}^{n} p_i = 1$.

The desired symmetric coefficients ϕ_{ij} are readily found by equating the expressions in (A4.1) and (A4.2) and exploiting $\sum_0^n p_i = 1$.

S. H. CHEW, L. G. EPSTEIN, AND U. SEGAL

STEP 2: We need to extend the representation (A4.2) to all c.d.f.'s in $D(X)$. Let $Y = \{x_0, x_1, \ldots\}$ be a countable dense subset of X. Denote by $\phi''(x_i, x_j)$, $i, j = 0, \ldots, n$, the coefficients corresponding to (A4.2) of the quadratic representation for $D'' \equiv \{$c.d.f.'s having support in $\{x_0, x_1, \ldots, x_n\}\}$ and let V^n be the quadratic utility function defined on D''. Then V^n and V^{n+1} are ordinally equivalent on their common domain D''. By the proof of Theorem 2(ii), therefore, $\exists \alpha, \beta$ such that

$$\phi^{n+1}(x_i, x_j) = \alpha + \beta \phi''(x_i, x_j), \qquad 0 \leqslant i, j \leqslant n.$$

Thus we can continually redefine the ϕ'''s so that

$$\phi^{n+1}(x_i, x_j) = \phi''(x_i, x_j), \qquad 0 \leqslant i, j \leqslant n.$$

Define ϕ on $Y \times Y$ as $\lim_{n \to \infty} \phi^n$ and extend ϕ to $X \times X$ by

$$\phi(x, x') \equiv \sup \{\phi(x_i, x_j) : (x_i, x_j) \in Y \times Y, x_i \leqslant x, x_j \leqslant x'\}.$$

This ϕ will do for the quadratic functional in (13).

APPENDIX 5: FRÉCHET DIFFERENTIABILITY OF QUADRATIC UTILITY

We describe sufficient conditions, expressed in terms of ϕ, for the quadratic functional (3) to be Fréchet differentiable. Let ϕ be continuous on X^2.

The sufficient condition is that $\exists K > 0$ such that

$$(A5.1) \qquad |\phi(x', y') - \phi(x', y) - \phi(x, y') + \phi(x, y)| \leqslant K |x' - x| |y' - y|$$

$\forall x, y, x'$ and y' in X. Note that (A5.1) is satisfied if $\phi_{12}(\cdot, \cdot)$ exists and is continuous (and hence bounded) on X^2. Then

$$\phi(x', y') - \phi(x', y) - \phi(x, y') + \phi(x, y) = \int_y^{y'} \int_x^{x'} \phi_{12}(s, t) \, ds \, dt \Rightarrow (A5.1) \quad \text{with}$$

$$K \equiv \max |\phi_{12}(\cdot)|.$$

We show that (A5.1) implies that V is Fréchet differentiable and in particular, that $|R|/\|G - F\|_1 \to 0$ as $\|G - F\|_1 \to 0$, where

$$R \equiv V(G) - V(F) - \int u(\cdot; F) \, d(G - F),$$

$\|\cdot\|_1$ denotes the L^1 norm, and $u(\cdot; F)$ is the local utility function defined in (11). It suffices to prove that

$$(A5.2) \qquad |R| \leqslant K \cdot (\|G - F\|_1)^2, \qquad \forall F, G \in D(X).$$

Moreover, (A5.2) is implied if the inequality there is proven for all c.d.f.'s corresponding to gambles with finitely many equally likely outcomes. So let

$$F = n^{-1} \sum_{i=1}^n \delta_{s_i} \qquad \text{and} \qquad G = n^{-1} \sum_{i=1}^n \delta_{t_i}.$$

Then

$$R = V(G) - V(F) - \int u(\cdot; F) \, d(G - F)$$

$$= \iint \phi(x, y) \, d(G(x) - F(x)) \, d(G(y) - F(y))$$

$$= n^{-2} \sum_i \sum_j \left[\phi(s_i, s_j) + \phi(t_i, t_j) - \phi(s_i, t_j) - \phi(s_j, t_i) \right]$$

$$\Rightarrow |R| \leqslant n^{-2} K \sum_i \sum_j |s_i - t_i| |s_j - t_j|$$

$$= K \left(n^{-1} \sum |s_i - t_i| \right)^2 = K (\|G - F\|_1)^2.$$

MIXTURE SYMMETRY   163

REFERENCES

BECKER, G. M., M. E. DEGROOT, AND J. MARSCHAK (1963): "An Experimental Study on Some Stochastic Models for Wagers," *Behavioral Science*, 8, 199–202.

CHEW, S. H. (1963): "A Generalization of the Quasilinear Mean with Applications to the Measurement of Income Inequality and Decision Theory Resolving the Allais Paradox," *Econometrica*, 51, 1065–1092.

——— (1989): "Axiomatic Utility Theories with the Betweenness Property," *Annals of Operations Research*, 19, 273–298.

——— (1985): "An Axiomatization of the Rank-Dependent Quasilinear Mean Generalizing the Gini Mean and the Quasilinear Mean," Economics Working Paper #156, Johns Hopkins University.

CHEW, S. H., AND L. G. EPSTEIN (1990): "A Unifying Approach to Axiomatic Non-Expected Utility Theories," *Journal of Economic Theory*, 49, 207–240.

CHEW, S. H., E. KARNI, AND Z. SAFRA (1987): "Risk Aversion in the Theory of Expected Utility with Rank-Dependent Probabilities," *Journal of Economic Theory*, 42, 370–381.

CHEW, S. H., AND W. S. WALLER (1986): "Empirical Tests of Weighted Utility Theory," *Journal of Mathematical Psychology*, 30, 55–72.

COOMBS, C. R., AND L. C. HUANG (1976): "Tests of the Betweenness Property of Expected Utility Theory," *Journal of Mathematical Psychology*, 13, 323–337.

COXETER, H. S. M. (1974): *Projective Geometry*. Toronto: University of Toronto Press.

CRAWFORD, V. P. (1990): "Equilibrium Without Independence," *Journal of Economic Theory*, 50, 127–154.

DEBREU, G. (1964): "Continuity Properties of Paretian Utility," *International Economic Review*, 5, 285–293.

DEKEL, E. (1986): "An Axiomatic Characterization of Preferences under Uncertainty," *Journal of Economic Theory*, 40, 304–318.

FISHBURN, P. C. (1983): "Transitive Measurable Utility," *Journal of Economic Theory*, 31, 293–317.

GREEN, J. R. (1987): "'Making Book Against Onself', the Independence Axiom, and Nonlinear Utility Theory," *Quarterly Journal of Economics*, 102, 785–796.

GREEN, J. R., AND B. JULLIEN (1988): "Ordinal Independence in Nonlinear Utility Theory," *Journal of Risk and Uncertainty*, 1, 355–387.

KREPS, D. M. AND E. L. PORTEUS (1979): "Temporal von Neumann-Morgenstern and Induced Preferences," *Journal of Economic Theory*, 20, 81–109.

MACHINA, M. J. (1982): "Expected Utility Analysis Without the Independence Axiom," *Econometrica*, 50, 277–323.

——— (1984): "Temporal Risk and the Nature of Induced Preferences," *Journal of Economic Theory*, 33, 199–231.

——— (1985): "Stochastic Choice Functions Generated from Deterministic Preferences over Lotteries," *Economic Journal*, 95, 575–594.

NAKAMURA, Y. (1984): "Nonlinear Utility Analysis," Ph.D. Thesis, University of California Davis.

QUIGGIN, J. (1982): "A Theory of Anticipated Utility," *Journal of Economic Behavior and Organization*, 3, 323–343.

RAIFFA, H. (1970): *Decision Analysis*. Reading, Mass.: Addison-Wesley.

SEGAL, U. (1989): "Anticipated Utility: A Measure Representation Approach," *Annals of Operations Research*, 19, 359–373.

——— (1990): "Two-Stage Lotteries Without the Reduction Axiom," *Econometrica*, 58, 349–377.

YAARI, M. E. (1987): "The Dual Theory of Choice under Risk," *Econometrica*, 55, 95–115.

[20]

Econometrica, Vol. 59, No. 3 (May, 1991), 667–686

A THEORY OF DISAPPOINTMENT AVERSION

By Faruk Gul[1]

An axiomatic model of preferences over lotteries is developed. It is shown that this model is consistent with the Allais Paradox, includes expected utility theory as a special case, and is only one parameter (β) richer than the expected utility model. Allais Paradox type behavior is identified with positive values of β. Preferences with positive β are said to be disappointment averse. It is shown that risk aversion implies disappointment aversion and that the Arrow-Pratt measures of risk aversion can be generalized in a straight-forward manner, to the current framework.

Keywords: Preferences over lotteries, expected utility theory, independence axiom, risk aversion, Arrow-Pratt measures of risk aversion.

INTRODUCTION

The purpose of this paper is to develop an axiomatic model of decision making under uncertainty that (i) includes expected utility theory as a special case, (ii) is consistent with the Allais Paradox, and (iii) is the most restrictive possible model that satisfies (i) and (ii) above.

The difficulty is in providing a precise sense in which (iii) can be satisfied. We propose to do this as follows: We will present an intuitive explanation of the Allais Paradox. Then we will replace the independence axiom of expected utility theory with an alternative axiom which explicitly incorporates our intuitive explanation. An additional axiom which does not conflict with the intuitive explanation or with expected utility maximization will also be imposed. Analysis of the resulting model will reveal that it does indeed satisfy (i) and (ii) above and that no further qualitative restriction can be imposed without violating either (i) or (ii). Our aim is to show that the type of behavior exhibited by a large number of subjects in Allais' original experiment can be interpreted intuitively and justified within the framework of a reasonable model.

With this in mind, in what follows we characterize preferences that are described completely by a real-valued function u on the set of prizes and a real number $\beta > -1$ (Theorem 1). We show that u is unique up to an affine transformation and β is unique. Hence we isolate a class of preferences that is one parameter richer than von Neumann-Morgenstern preferences. We further show that $\beta = 0$ corresponds to the case of expected utility theory (where u is the von Neumann-Morgenstern utility function). We describe preferences with $\beta \geqslant 0$ as disappointment[2] averse and establish the equivalence of strict disap-

[1] I am indebted to Elchanan Ben-Porath, Eddie Dekel, Darrell Duffie, David Kreps, Mark Machina, Dilip Mookherjee, Ariel Rubinstein, Hugo Sonnenschein, Robert Wilson, two anonymous referees, and especially Outi Lantto for their help and criticism.
[2] The term *disappointment* was first used by Bell (1985) and Loomes and Sugden (1986). While we have borrowed the word from them, our motivation and the class of preferences that we consider are different.

668   FARUK GUL

pointment aversion (i.e. $\beta > 0$) and Allais Paradox type behavior (Theorem 2). Finally we show the relationship between risk aversion and disappointment aversion (Theorems 3–5). In particular we show that in this model risk aversion implies disappointment aversion.

THE ALLAIS PARADOX[3]

Consider an individual who is faced with the following two choice problems:

PROBLEM 1: Choose either p_1 or p_2 where p_1 is a degenerate lottery which yields 200 dollars for sure and p_2 is a lottery that yields 300 dollars with probability .8 and 0 dollars with probability .2.

PROBLEM 2: Choose either $\bar{p}_1$ or $\bar{p}_2$ where $\bar{p}_1$ is a lottery which yields 200 dollars with probability .5 and 0 dollars with probability .5 and $\bar{p}_2$ is a lottery which yields 300 dollars with probability .4 and 0 dollars with probability .6.

The propensity of decision makers to choose p_1 if confronted with the first problem and $\bar{p}_2$ if confronted with the second, is a phenomenon that is now widely known as the Allais Paradox. The term *paradox* is due to the fact that such preferences are not consistent with expected utility maximization.[4] In particular, this pair of choices is inconsistent with the independence axiom, which is a necessary condition for expected utility maximization. The independence axiom states that given any three lotteries p_1, p_2, and r and a number $\alpha \in (0,1]$, p_1 is preferred to p_2 implies $\alpha p_1 + (1 - \alpha)r$ is preferred to $\alpha p_2 + (1 - \alpha)r$ (where $\alpha p_1 + (1 - \alpha)r$ denotes the lottery which yields any prize x with probability $\alpha p_1(x) + (1 - \alpha)r(x)$).

Letting r be the lottery which yields 0 dollars for sure, α equal $\frac{1}{2}$, and observing that $\bar{p}_1 = \alpha p_1 + (1 - \alpha)r$, $\bar{p}_2 = \alpha p_2 + (1 - \alpha)r$ establishes that the Allais Paradox above constitutes a violation of the independence axiom. Observe that in Problem 1, lottery p_1 has no chance of yielding a disappointing outcome whereas lottery p_2 has a .2 chance of yielding a disappointing outcome. One possible explanation of why the independence axiom fails in this particular example is that the lottery with a lower probability of disappointment suffers more when it is mixed with an inferior lottery (i.e., $r = 0$ dollars for sure); that is, if the lotteries were nearly indifferent initially, the lottery with the higher probability of disappointment becomes preferred after being mixed with the inferior lottery.

---

[3] This is not Allais' (1979) most famous example. This particular version is sometimes called the "Allais Ratio Paradox." It is also referred to as the common ratio effect or common consequence effect by Kahnemann and Tversky (1979). We use it here because the intuitive explanation of the type we wish to isolate is easier to express in terms of this slightly simpler example. However, the same intuitive argument applies to both this and the original version of the Allais Paradox and the notion of disappointment aversion resolves both versions.

[4] To check this note that $p_1 \succ p_2$ implies $u(200) > .8u(300) + .2u(0)$ and $\bar{p}_1 \prec \bar{p}_2$ implies $.5u(200) + .5u(0) < .4u(300) + .6u(0)$; i.e. $u(200) < .8u(300) + .2u(0)$, a contradiction.

In the words of Savage (1972, page 102), "Many people prefer Gamble 1 (p_1) to Gamble 2 (p_2) because, speaking qualitatively, they do not find the chance of winning a very large fortune in place of receiving a large fortune outright adequate compensation for even a small risk of being left in the status quo. Many of the same people prefer Gamble 4 ($\bar{p}_2$) to Gamble 3 ($\bar{p}_1$); because, speaking qualitatively, the chance of winning is nearly the same in both gambles, so the one with the much larger prize seems preferable." While 300 and 200 dollars hardly qualify as very large and large fortunes, it is clear that Savage's interpretation of the original version is closely related to our intuitive explanation here. What Savage calls the chance of winning is one minus what we have called the probability of disappointment which we will define formally in our model.

Before we begin our formal analysis two basic questions need to be addressed. First, why concentrate on the Allais Paradox as opposed to other systematic violations for the expected utility hypothesis? Second, what distinguishes our approach from other axiomatic models of choice under uncertainty that allow for Allais Paradox type behavior?

There is a large body of work on observed violations of the expected utility model. Historically the Allais Paradox has played a very significant role in the development of this literature. This is no doubt in part due to the intuitive appeal of the Allais Paradox choices. Hence it would appear that the Allais Paradox is a natural starting point for any attempt at reconciling the normative theory of choice under uncertainty with the existing empirical evidence.

One can identify at least three distinct ways that the non-expected utility literature has dealt with observed violations of the expected utility theory:

(a) By emphasizing the need for a purely descriptive theory. Such work has either attempted to describe the actual decision making process that is used by the subjects (see Kahneman and Tversky (1979) and Rubinstein (1988)) or to identify useful (i.e., consistent with the existing empirical evidence) functional forms. Regret theory (Bell (1982), Loomes and Sugden (1982)), the disappointment theory of Bell (1985) and Loomes and Sugden (1982), the subjective expected value models used in the psychology literature (see Edwards (1953) and Tversky (1967) among others) are some of the many examples that can be included under this category. What is common to this particular body of work is the emphasis on descriptive aspects and skepticism regarding relevance of a normative theory. Hence the models mentioned above often violate even the most basic desiderata of choice under uncertainty (transitivity, stochastic dominance, etc.).

(b) By rejecting the normative appeal of the independence axiom. Allais (1979) and Machina (1982) belong in this category. Allais argues for a cardinal measure of utility over sure prospects and postulates that individuals' utility for uncertain prospects will depend on the distribution of the cardinal measure, typically its first three moments. Machina (1982) considers preferences that can be represented by a "smooth" preference functional and develops the machinery for analyzing the local properties of a preference functional. He offers two empirical hypotheses which he states in terms of these local properties. The first is risk aversion. The second which is called Hypothesis II is shown to imply behavior consistent with the Allais Paradox and a number of other observed violations of the expected utility theory. A more detailed comparison between the model of this paper and Machina's generation of expected utility theory will be provided after the formal analysis of the next section.

(c) By modifying the independence axiom. This class of papers starts by offering similar (typically weaker) alternatives to the independence axiom. The resulting model is defended by pointing out that it is consistent with observed violations of expected utility theory and by arguing that the alternative assumption is more compelling than the independence axiom. Some examples of this type of work are: Chew and MacCrimmon (1979), Dekel (1986), Fishburn (1983), and Yaari (1987).

This paper belongs among the work cited under (c) above. What distinguishes the model of this paper is our emphasis on the Allais Paradox and the direct role it plays in our axiomatization. Hence we provide a narrow interpretation of the Allais Paradox and search for a generalization of expected utility theory which is consistent with this interpretation and yet allows us to retain as much of the insight offered by expected utility theory as possible.

The Model

For some b, w such that $b > w$, let $X = [w, b]$ be the set of all prizes. Let $\mathscr{L}$ be the set of all simple lotteries over these prizes. That is, $p \in \mathscr{L}$ implies that supp(p), the support of p is finite. For any $p, q \in \mathscr{L}$ and $\alpha \in [0, 1]$, $\alpha p + (1 - \alpha)q$ denotes the lottery $r \in \mathscr{L}$ such that for all $x \in X$, $r(x) = \alpha p(x) + (1 - \alpha)q(x)$. When there is no risk of confusion we use $x \in X$ to denote the lottery p such that $p(x) = 1$. $\succsim$ is a binary relation on $\mathscr{L}$. We use $p \succ q$, "p is strictly preferred to q", to denote $p \succsim q$ and not $q \succsim p$. We use $p \sim q$, "p is indifferent to q", to denote $p \succsim q$ and $q \succsim p$.

Since, typically, we want to interpret $x \in X$ as a quantity of money, $x > y$ iff $x \succ y$, will be a maintained assumption throughout this paper.

DEFINITION 1: For any $\succsim$ and p, let

$$B(p, \succsim) = \{q \in \mathscr{L} \mid x \in \text{supp}(q) \text{ implies } x \succsim p\};$$

$$W(p, \succsim) = \{q \in \mathscr{L} \mid x \in \text{supp}(q) \text{ implies } p \succsim x\}.$$

We sometimes use $B(p), W(p)$ instead of $B(p, \succsim)$ and $W(p, \succsim)$.

Thus $B(p)$ and $W(p)$ denote the set of lotteries with supports consisting of prizes respectively, better than and worse than p.

DEFINITION 2: (α, q, r) is an *elation/disappointment decomposition* (EDD) of p iff $q \in B(p)$, $r \in W(p)$ and $\alpha q + (1 - \alpha)r = p$.

Thus an EDD of p is constructed as follows: The lottery is divided into two parts, those prizes which are preferred to the certainty equivalent of p (called elation prizes) and those prizes which are less preferred to the certainty equivalent of p (called disappointment prizes). Then we normalize by dividing the probability of all elation prizes by α, the sum of all elation prize probabilities and obtain q. Similarly we divide all disappointment prize probability by $1 - \alpha$ and obtain r. Hence $\alpha q + (1 - \alpha)r = p$ (note that $\alpha q + (1 - \alpha)r$ is p, not just indifferent to p). Obviously if the certainty equivalent of p is not in the support of p there is a unique EDD for p. Otherwise there will be an infinity of EDD's for p. To see this note that $(.2, x. x)$, $(.7, x, x)$ and $(0, b, x)$ are all EDD's of x.

Next we define elation, $e(p)$, and disappointment, $d(p)$, probabilities for a lottery p. Note that if p does not yield its certainty equivalent with positive probability, then $e(p) + d(p) = 1$ and $D(p) = \{(e(p), q, r)\}$ for some $q, r \in \mathscr{L}$.

DEFINITION 3: $e(p) \equiv \sum_{x > p} p(x)$ and $d(p) \equiv \sum_{p > x} p(x)$.

We use $D(p)$ to denote the set of all EDD's of p. Instead of $(\alpha, q, r) \in D(\alpha q + (1 - \alpha)r)$ or equivalently $(\alpha, q, r) \in D((\alpha, q, r))$ we simply write $(\alpha, q, r) \in D$ where $D = \bigcup_{p \in \mathscr{L}} D(p)$. (Note that by definition if (α, q, r) is an EDD it must be an EDD of $\alpha q + (1 - \alpha)r$.)

AXIOM 1—Preference Relation: $\succeq$ *is complete and transitive.*

AXIOM 2—Continuity: *For all $p \in \mathscr{L}$ the sets $\{q \in \mathscr{L} \mid q \succeq p\}$ and $\{q \in \mathscr{L} \mid p \succeq q\}$ are closed (under the topology generated by the L^1 metric).*[5]

Axiom 2 implies that the function CE: $\mathscr{L} \rightarrow [w, b]$ such that $CE(p) \sim p$ (i.e. CE is the certainty equivalent of p) is well-defined.

Next we will present a restriction of the independence axiom to the case in which the disappointment probabilities of the lotteries p_1 and p_2 are the same and no elation (disappointment) prize of p_i switches over to being a disappointment (elation) prize of $ap_i + (1 - a)x$. The motivation for this is the intuitive explanation of the Allais Paradox that was presented earlier. Consider the lotteries $p'_i = tp_i + (1 - t)x$ as t decreases from 1 to a. If $p_1 \succeq p_2$ and no elation (disappointment) prize of p'_i switches to being a disappointment (elation) prize, then the disappointment probabilities of p'_1 and p'_2 are always the same; hence our intuitive explanation of the Allais Paradox is not applicable so we would expect the conclusion of the independence axiom to be valid.

---

[5] To be more precise, let f: $\mathscr{L} \rightarrow \mathscr{L}^1$ where $f(p)$ is the cdf associate with p. Then, Axiom 2 requires that $f(\{q \in \mathscr{L} \mid q \succeq p\})$ and $f(\{q \in \mathscr{L} \mid p \succeq q\})$ are closed (for every $q \in \mathscr{L}$) in the relative topology on $f(\mathscr{L})$ generated by the L^1 metric.

AXIOM 3—Weak Independence: $p_1 \succsim p_2$, $a \in [0,1]$, $z \in X$ implies $ap_1 + (1-a)z \succsim ap_2 + (1-a)z$ whenever there exists $(\lambda, q_i, r_i) \in D(p_i)$ such that $q_i \in B(ap_i + (1-a)z)$ and $r_i \in W(ap_i + (1-a)z)$ for $i = 1, 2$.

It can be seen from the proof of Theorem 1, that Axioms 1–3 imply betweenness. That is if $\succsim$ satisfies Axioms 1–3 and $p \succ q(p \sim q)$, then $p \succ \alpha p + (1-\alpha)q \succ q(p \sim \alpha p + (1-\alpha)q)$ for all $\alpha \in (0,1)$. Hence preferences which satisfy Axioms 1–3 belong to the class studied by Dekel (1986).

Axiom 3 captures our intuitive explanation of the Allais Paradox by enabling the independence axiom to fail when disappointment effects are present. However, in order to verify the "minimality" criterion (iii) discussed in the introduction, we need to determine if the class of preferences which are characterized by Axioms 1–3 can be restricted further without excluding expected utility preferences of our intuitive explanation. To put it differently, are there situations in which the independence axiom would be applicable but our intuitive explanation would not? Consider the following example:

Let $\alpha x + (1-\alpha)w \succsim \alpha p + (1-\alpha)w$ and $p \in B(\alpha p + (1-\alpha)w)$. Thus the decision-maker prefers substituting x in place of p in $\alpha p + (1-\alpha)w$ when p consists of elation prizes of $\alpha p + (1-\alpha)w$. Now assume that $p \in W(\alpha b + (1-\alpha)p)$. Hence p consists of disappointment prizes of $\alpha b + (1-\alpha)p$. Note that the independence axiom would imply that $\alpha b + (1-\alpha)x \succsim \alpha b + (1-\alpha)p$ whenever $\alpha x + (1-\alpha)w \succsim \alpha p + (1-\alpha)w$. Furthermore observe that $\alpha b + (1-\alpha)x$, $\alpha b + (1-\alpha)p$, $\alpha x + (1-\alpha)w$, and $\alpha p + (1-\alpha)w$ all have the same disappointment probability $(1-\alpha)$. Thus substituting x in place of p does not result in the type of effect discussed in our intuitive explanation of the Allais Paradox. Hence we would again expect the independence axiom to hold (i.e., $\alpha b + (1-\alpha)x \succsim \alpha b + (1-\alpha)p$). This will be Axiom 4. To see why this particular application of the independence axiom is not covered by Axiom 3, note that by requiring that no elation prize switches to being a disappointment prize, Axiom 3 severs the connection between the individual's evaluation of elation prizes and his evaluation of disappointment prizes.

AXIOM 4—Symmetry: For $i = 1, 2$, $(\alpha, p_i, w), (\alpha, b, p_i) \in D$ implies

$$\alpha p_1 + (1-\alpha)w \succsim \alpha p_2 + (1-\alpha)w \qquad \text{iff}$$

$$\alpha b + (1-\alpha)p_1 \succsim \alpha b + (1-\alpha)p_2.$$

THEOREM 1: $\succsim$ satisfies Axioms 1–4 if and only if there exist functions u: $X \to \Re$ and γ: $[0,1] \to [0,1]$ such that: (i) $(\alpha_i, q_i, r_i) \in D(p_i)$ for $i = 1, 2$ implies $p_1 \succsim p_2$ iff $\gamma(\alpha_1)\Sigma_x u(x)q_1(x) + (1 - \gamma(\alpha_1))\Sigma_x u(x)r_1(x) \geq \gamma(\alpha_2)\Sigma_x u(x)q_2(x) + (1 - \gamma(\alpha_2))\Sigma_x u(x)r_2(x)$; (ii) γ', u' satisfy (i) above implies $u' = au + b$ for some $a > 0$, $b \in \Re$ and $\gamma' = \gamma$; (iii) u is continuous and there exists $\beta \in (-1, \infty)$ such

DISAPPOINTMENT AVERSION   673

that

$$\gamma(\alpha) = \frac{\alpha}{1 + (1 - \alpha)\beta} \qquad \text{for all} \qquad \alpha \in [0, 1].$$

PROOF: See Appendix.

Theorem 1 establishes that if Axioms 1–4 hold, then there exists a utility function $V: \mathscr{P} \to \mathfrak{R}$ which represents $\succsim$ and furthermore $V(p)$ can be calculated by taking an EDD (α, q, r) of p, computing the expected utilities of the elation and disappointment parts (q and r respectively) with respect to the utility index u, and taking a $\gamma(\alpha)$ weighted average of these utilities. Hence u and β are parameters of the individual's preferences and $V(p)$ is defined implicitly by the procedure above. To see that $V(p)$ is not explicitly defined note that the certainty equivalent of p needs to be known in order to determine an EDD of p.

However, a simple and finite algorithm (see Appendix) will enable us to construct all EDD's of p and commute $V(p)$ for arbitrary u and β.

The fact that $V(p)$ is well defined for any $\succsim$ which satisfies Axioms 1–4 is guaranteed by Theorem 1. However, this does not preclude the possibility that there might be no non-expected utility preference which satisfies Axioms 1–4. Defining $V(u, \beta, p)$ implicitly by $V(u, \beta, p) = \gamma(\alpha)Eu(q) + (1 - \gamma(\alpha))Eu(r)$ for some α, q, r such that $\alpha q + (1 - \alpha)r = p$ and $x \in \text{supp}(q)$ implies $u(x) \geqslant V(u, \beta, p)$ and $x \in \text{supp}(r)$ implies $u(x) \leqslant V(u, \beta, p)$ and showing that $V(u, \beta, \cdot)$ is a well defined function for arbitrary strictly increasing, continuous u and $\beta \in (-1, \infty)$ would establish that Axioms 1–4 characterize a rich class of preferences. This can be done using simple manipulations of the definition of $V(u, \beta, p)$.

Observe that expected utility theory corresponds to the special case $\gamma(\alpha) = \alpha$; that is, $\beta = 0$. Furthermore, if $\beta > 0$, then $\gamma(\alpha) < \alpha$ for all $\alpha \in (0, 1)$ and $\gamma(\alpha)$ is convex. If $-1 < \beta < 0$ then $\gamma(\alpha) > \alpha$ for all $\alpha \in (0, 1)$ and $\gamma(\alpha)$ is concave. We say that $\succsim$ is disappointment averse if $\beta \geqslant 0$ and $\succsim$ is elation loving if $\beta \in (-1, 0]$. Note that unlike risk aversion, disappointment aversion is, by definition, a global property. Theorem 2 below (and its proof) reveals that β is a measure of the extent to which $\succsim$ is prone to Allais Paradox type behavior. Since the preferences which satisfy Axioms 1–4 are only one-parameter (β) richer than expected utility preferences, it would appear that no additional qualitative restrictions can be imposed without excluding either our intuitive explanation of the Allais Paradox or certain expected utility preferences.

THEOREM 2: *Let $\succsim$ satisfy Axioms 1–4 and $p \sim q$. Then if $\beta > 0$ ($\beta < 0$) there exists $\bar{a} > 0$ such that (i) $a < \bar{a}$, $c(p) > c(q)$ implies $ax + (1 - a)p \succ (\prec)ax + (1 - a)q$ for $x \succ p$; (ii) $a < \bar{a}$, $d(p) > d(q)$ implies $ax + (1 - a)p \succ (\prec)ax + (1 - a)q$ for $p \succ x$.*

674   FARUK GUL

PROOF: See Appendix.

Let (u, β) denote the generic preference satisfying Axioms 1–4.
Define

$$\phi(x,v) = \begin{cases} u(x) & \text{for } x \text{ such that } u(x) \leq v, \\ \dfrac{u(x) + \beta v}{1 + \beta} & \text{for } x \text{ such that } u(x) > v. \end{cases}$$

Observe that by using the definition of $v(p)$ provided in Theorem 1 we obtain that $\sum_x \phi(x,v)p(x) = v$ iff $V = v(p)$, hence ϕ is the local utility function for the preference (u, β) (see Dekel (1986) for the definition and analysis of local utility functions of this form).

Roughly speaking, given Axioms 1, 2, Axiom 3 guarantees that the local utility function has the following property: All elation prizes are evaluated with respect to one utility function and all disappointment prizes are evaluated with respect to another utility function. Symmetry (Axiom 4) guarantees that these utility functions represent the same preferences. That is, the utility function for elation prizes $(u(x) + \beta v)/(1 + \beta)$ is a (positive) affine transformation of the utility function for disappointment prizes, $u(x)$.

Abandoning the symmetry (Axiom 4) assumption would lead to the following local utility function:[6]

$$\phi(x,v) = \begin{cases} u_d(x) & \text{for } x \text{ such that } u_d(x) \leq v, \\ u_e(x) - u_e(u_d^{-1}(v)) + v & \text{for } x \text{ such that } u_d(x) > v, \end{cases}$$

where u_d, u_e are two distinct functions from $[w, b]$ to $\Re$. Note that Axiom 4 implies $u_e - u_e(u_d^{-1}(v)) + v$ and hence u_e, is an affine transformation of u_d and expected utility implies $u_e = u_d$.

It can be shown that for preferences which satisfy Axioms 1–4, $\beta \geq 0$ iff $d(\sum \phi(x,v)p(x))/dv$ is an increasing function of $d(p)$, the probability of disappointment (among p such that $V(p) = v$). This observation can be used to extend the notion of disappointment aversion to preferences which satisfy Axioms 1–3. For such preferences $d(\sum \phi(x,v)p(x))/dv$ is a decreasing function of $d(p)$ iff $(u_e'(y)/u_d'(y)) < 1$ for y such that $u_d(y) = v$. But now disappointment aversion has become a local property and global disappointment aversion can be imposed by requiring disappointment aversion at every point y. With this extended definition of disappointment aversion the results that Allais Paradox implies disappointment aversion (Theorem 2) and that risk aversion implies disappointment aversion (Theorem 3) can be generalized to preferences which satisfy Axioms 1–3.

We end this section by noting that imposing Axiom 4 is consistent with our objective of seeking a model in which any deviation from expected utility theory can be ascribed to disappointment aversion. Furthermore adding Axiom 4

---

[6] The existence of some local utility function is guaranteed by Dekel's (1986) Proposition 1 and the fact that Axioms 1–3 imply betweenness. Furthermore Axiom 3 implies that (local) preferences over disappointment outcomes and elation outcomes (but not combinations of disappointment and elation outcomes) are independent of v. Then a suitable normalization yields the representation provided above.

enables us to analyze a particular simple subclass of the preferences that satisfy Axioms 1–3 for which we can obtain a nearly closed form representation.

DISAPPOINTMENT AVERSION AND RISK AVERSION

In this section we analyze the relationship between disappointment aversion and risk aversion and develop measures of risk aversion for preferences satisfying Axioms 1–4. Hence, in what follows we will concentrate only on preferences satisfying Axioms 1–4 and sometimes use (u, β) to denote such preferences.

THEOREM 3: (u, β) *is risk averse* (*in the sense of weakly not preferring mean-preserving spreads*) *iff* $\beta \geq 0$ *and* u *is concave.*

PROOF: Dekel (1986) establishes that $\succeq$ is risk averse iff the local utility function is concave. Note that $\phi(x, v)$ is concave if $\beta \geq 0$ and u is concave.
$$Q.E.D.$$

There are two main implications of Theorem 3. The first one is that risk aversion implies disappointment aversion. The second is that disappointment aversion and the concavity/convexity of u determine the individual's attitude towards risk.

The possibility of having concave u and $\beta < 0$ or convex u and $\beta > 0$ enables us to obtain preferences that display risk aversion with respect to certain types of gambles and risk loving with respect to others. For example, if $\beta = 4$ and $u(x) = x$ for $x \leq 0$ and $u(x) = 5x$ when $x > 0$ (hence x is convex), then the individual will be risk averse with respect to even chance gambles and gambles which yield a large loss with small probability but will be risk loving with respect to gambles that involve winning a large prize with small probability if his initial income is low. Hence, there are preferences consistent with Axioms 1–4 such that at all income levels, the individual would not accept fair even chance gambles, yet would still be willing to buy less than fair insurance. Furthermore such an individual would be willing to buy, at certain income levels, tickets to the state lottery.

It is possible to develop measures of absolute, relative, and comparative risk aversion for preferences satisfying Axioms 1–4, similar to those developed by Arrow and Pratt for expected utility theory. Of course, these measures coincide with the corresponding Arrow-Pratt measures when $\beta = 0$. However, it is interesting that essentially the same Arrow-Pratt measures are appropriate even when $\beta \neq 0$. More specifically, let $R_u^a(x) = -u''(x)/u'(x)$ and $R_u^r(x) = -xu''(x)/u'(x)$; then by noting that β does not depend on x and essentially replicating the corresponding proofs of expected utility theory we obtain the following theorem.

THEOREM 4: (u, β) *is increasingly* (*decreasingly, constant*) *absolute* (*relative*) *risk averse iff* $R^a(R^r)$ *is increasing* (*decreasing, constant*).

DEFINITION 4: $\succeq_1$ *is more risk averse than* $\succeq_2$ *iff* $p \succeq_1 x$ *implies* $p \succeq_2 x$ *for all* $p \in \mathcal{S}$, $x \in X$.

676   FARUK GUL

THEOREM 5: (u_1, β_1) *is more risk averse than* (u_2, β_2) *if* $\beta_1 \geqslant \beta_2$ *and* $R_{u_1}^a(x) \geqslant R_{u_2}^a(x)$ *for all* $x \in (w, b)$. *Furthermore if* (u_1, β_1) *is more risk averse than* (u_2, β_2), *then* $\beta_1 \geqslant \beta_2$.

PROOF: See Appendix.

Machina (1984) provides the following stronger notion of comparative risk aversion: $\succsim_1$ is more risk averse than $\succsim_2$ iff for all $\lambda \in [0, 1]$, $p, p' \in \mathscr{L}$; $\lambda p' + (1 - \lambda)p \sim_2 \lambda p' + (1 - \lambda)\bar{x}$ and $\lambda p' + (1 - \lambda)p \sim_1 \lambda p' + (1 - \lambda)x$ implies $x \leqslant \bar{x}$.

Given Theorem 3 and the observation that β and the curvature of u determines the curvature of the local utility function, we would expect that being more risk averse corresponds to having a higher β and a more concave u. This is almost correct in the sense that (u_1, β_1) is more risk averse (in the stronger sense) than (u_2, β_2) iff $R_{u_1}^a(x) \geqslant R_{u_2}^a(x)$ for all $x \in (w, b)$ and $\beta_1 \geqslant 0 \geqslant \beta_2$. To see why $\beta_1 \geqslant 0 \geqslant \beta_2$ cannot be replaced by $\beta_1 \geqslant \beta_2$, note that if $\beta_1 \geqslant \beta_2 > 0$,[7] then both (u_1, β_1) and (u_2, β_2) are risk averse (Theorem 3). Furthermore the certainty equivalent y_2, of $\lambda p + (1 - \lambda)p'$ for (u_2, β_2) is greater than its certainty equivalent y_1, for (u_1, β_1) (Theorem 5). Then, at y_2, the local utility function ϕ_1 is smooth whereas the local utility function ϕ_2 has a concave kink. This means that ϕ_1 is less concave than ϕ_2 at y_2. Machina (1982), however, shows that more risk aversion is equivalent to the greater concavity of the local utility function.[8] Thus the comparison fails. Intuitively the fact that $y_2 > y_1$ makes it possible for (u_2, β_2) to view p' as increasing the probability of disappointment while (u_1, β_1) views p' as decreasing the probability of disappointment and therefore is less reluctant to accept it.

OTHER MODELS ON DECISION MAKING UNDER UNCERTAINTY AND EXPERIMENTAL EVIDENCE

It should be noted that although we have so far concentrated on the case where X is a compact interval, it is clear that the type of preference that we have been considering can just as well be defined on $\mathscr{L}$ when X is either finite or an unbounded interval and $\mathscr{L}$ includes nonsimple lotteries. All of the qualitative conclusions of this paper (Theorems 2–5) would still hold. If X is finite, however, Axioms 1–4 are not sufficient to characterize (u, β) preferences. This is due to the fact that our proof necessitates that certainty equivalents be well defined. The case of unbounded X and/or nonsimple lotteries can be dealt with as is done in expected utility theory. For nonsimple lotteries a finite algorithm for explicitly computing $V(p)$ would no longer exist. Instead an algorithm which converges to $V(p)$ can be constructed.

The most striking feature of these preferences is that by adding only one new variable, β, to the expected utility model, we are able to construct a class of

---

[7] A symmetric argument applies to the case $0 > \beta_1 \geqslant \beta_2$.
[8] Theorem 4 of Machina (1982) assumes the global differentiability of local utility functions. However, similar arguments can be used for the preferences considered here.

preferences which include the *EU* model as a special case, are compatible with many of the observed violations of this model, and enable us to explain these violations in terms of the notion of disappointment aversion. Observe that when we are comparing binary lotteries with each other or binary lotteries with sure things, then the functional form we have considered can be expressed as

$$V(ax + (1-a)z) = \pi_1(a)u(x) + \pi_2(1-a)u(z)$$

$$= \frac{a}{1+(1-a)\beta}u(x) + \frac{(1-a)(1+\beta)}{1+(1-a)\beta}u(z)$$

where $x \geqslant z$ and obviously $\pi_2(1-a) = 1 - \pi_1(a)$.

But this is very similar to the subjective expected utility models that have been used extensively in the psychology and economics literature (see, for example, Kahneman and Tversky (1979)) and is a special case (for binary lotteries) of Quiggin (1982).

Note also that for the case of $\beta > 0$, the weight function of the good prize is convex. Hence, a small increase in the probability of the good prize increases utility much more, when the chance of getting the good prize is already high. This is very suggestive of what Kahneman and Tversky (1979) refer to as the tendency for "people [to] overweight outcomes that are considered certain, relative to outcomes that are merely probable," i.e., the so-called certainty effect. The class of (u, β) preferences also have the following feature: If X is finite and $|X| = n$, then the preferences of any individual can be determined uniquely by asking him $n - 1$ simple questions and solving a quadratic equation. This is only one more than the number of questions one would need to ask under the assumptions of expected utility theory.

Consider a person, with preferences (u, β), who will receive income x in state 1 and income y in state 2. Let α and $(1 - \alpha)$ denote the probabilities of states 1 and 2 respectively (see Figure 1). An indifference curve for such a person will be described by the equation

$$\frac{\alpha}{1+(1-\alpha)\beta}u(x) + \frac{(1-\alpha)(1+\beta)}{1+(1-\alpha)\beta}u(y) = v \qquad \text{for } x \geqslant y$$

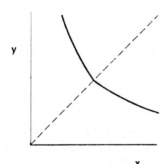

FIGURE 1

and

$$\frac{1-\alpha}{1+\alpha\beta}u(y) + \frac{\alpha(1+\beta)}{1+\alpha\beta}u(x) = v \qquad \text{for } y > x.$$

Hence

$$\frac{dy}{dx} = -\frac{\alpha u'(x)}{(1-\alpha)u'(y)(1+\beta)} \qquad \text{if } y < x,$$

$$\frac{dy}{dx} = -\frac{\alpha u'(x)(1+\beta)}{(1-\alpha)u'(y)} \qquad \text{if } y > x.$$

Thus if u is concave and $\beta > 0$, then these preferences would look as in Figure 1 above. Note that the shape of the indifference curve on either side of the 45° line is determined by the curvature of u and the nature of the kink is determined by β. In particular there will be a kink so long as $\beta \neq 0$. Figure 1 shows why $\beta > 0$ is necessary for risk aversion (see Theorem 3). This particular shape of the indifference curve has two important implications. The first is that risk averse individuals will purchase full insurance at less than fair odds; the second is that these preferences are not "differentiable" when $\beta \neq 0$ and hence do not belong to the class of preferences considered by Machina (1982).

Figure 2 illustrates the indifference map of (u, β) for lotteries over three prizes x, y, z where $x < y < z$. Hence any point (p_x, p_z) in Figure 2 corresponds to the lottery p such that $p(x) = p_x$, $p(y) = 1 - p_x - p_z$, and $p(z) = p_z$. After normalizing u so that $u(z) = 1$ and $u(x) = 0$, the indifference curve through any lottery p such that $p \succ y$ is defined by equation (1) and the indifference curve through any p such that $p \precsim y$ is defined by equation (2):

$$(1) \qquad p_z = \frac{(1+\beta)[u(y)p_x + v - u(y)]}{1 + \beta v - (1+\beta)u(y)} \qquad \text{for } v > u(y),$$

$$(2) \qquad p_z = \frac{(u(y) + \beta v)p_x + v - u(y)}{1 - u(y)} \qquad \text{for } v \leqslant u(y).$$

Both 1 and 2 can be derived from the definition of $V(p)$ provided in Theorem 1.

Equations 1 and 2 imply that the indifference curves on the top half of Figure 2 all intersect at the point $((1 - u(y))/u(y)\beta, (1+\beta)/\beta)$ and indifference curves on the bottom half of Figure 2 all intersect at the point $(-1/\beta, -(1+\beta)u(y)/\beta(1-u(y)))$. Hence for $\beta > 0$ all indifference curves in the bottom half are "fanning out" and all indifference curves in the top half are coming together from left to right (as depicted in Figure 2). For $\beta < 0$ the opposite is true. Hence for the case of lotteries over three prizes, taking the preference (u, β) and "flipping" half of its indifference map, we obtain the type of preference considered by Chew and MacCrimmon (1979) and Fishburn

DISAPPOINTMENT AVERSION 679

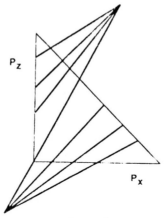

P_z

P_x

FIGURE 2

(1985) which are defined by the property that all indifference curves originate from the same point.

Machina (1982, 1987) considers a large class of systematic violations of the expected utility model and shows that these violations, which are frequently encountered in experiments, all imply that indifference curves in Figure 2 are fanning out. Since any individuals with preferences (u, β) will have indifference curves that fan out either in the top half or the bottom half (but not both) of Figure 2, no such individual can exhibit all of the violations considered by Machina.

It is undeniably true that fanning out over some range is necessary for Allais Paradox type behavior. The preference (u, β) will display the fanning out properly over the range concerning the Allais Paradox if and only if $\beta > 0$. Hence there is no conflict between Machina's observation regarding fanning out and Theorem 2. There are however substantial differences in the two interpretations of the Allais Paradox and the underlying approaches to violations of expected utility theory. Whereas Machina views the Allais Paradox as a special case of (global) fanning out, we have emphasized our narrower intuitive explanation and sought to provide a model which incorporates this intuitive explanation while retaining many of the features of expected utility theory. In the case of lotteries over three outcomes no two distinct lotteries can be indifferent and have the same disappointment probability. Thus Figure 2 understates the similarity between (u, β) preferences and expected utility theory. To see this, consider the following example: Suppose $\succeq$ satisfies

(3) $\frac{1}{2} \times \left(\frac{1}{2} \times 1000 + \frac{1}{2} \times 800 \right) + \frac{1}{2} \times 100 \sim \frac{1}{2} \times 880 + \frac{1}{2} \times 100 \sim 400;$

then Axioms 1–4 imply that $\succeq$ satisfies

(4) $\frac{1}{2} \times \left(\frac{1}{2} + 1000 + \frac{1}{2} \times 800 \right) + \frac{1}{2} \times 50 \sim \frac{1}{2} \times 880 + \frac{1}{2} \times 50.$

Under Axioms 1–4 the necessity of satisfying (4) whenever (3) is satisfied does not conflict in the displaying Allais Paradox type behavior at every income level. Under Machina's interpretation any individual who displays Allais type behavior at every income level and satisfies (3) must violate (4). This follows immediately from fanning out.

Not surprisingly there is some empirical and experimental evidence conflicting with Axioms 1–4 and Hypothesis II. In particular for $\beta > 0$ (which we consider to be the more important case), (u, β) will be consistent with the common ratio effect, partly consistent with the common sequence effect (including the Allais Paradox), and inconsistent with the common ratio effect with negative numbers (see Machina (1987)). Conversely for $\beta < 0$, (u, β) will be consistent with the common ratio effect with negative numbers, partly consistent with the common consequence effect (excluding the Allais Paradox), and inconsistent with the common ratio effect.

Neilson (1989) considered lotteries over three prizes and concludes that existing empirical evidence suggests the need for preferences which fan in on the top part and fan out on the bottom part of the probability triangle (i.e., exactly the situation depicted by Figure 2). The model of this paper (for $\beta > 0$) always has this property. To put it another way, we have identified Allais Paradox with precisely this mixed-fanning property.

CONCLUSION

We have taken what is considered to be the most compelling argument against the independence axiom and attempted to find an alternative to expected utility theory which is immune to this particular argument and yet retains as much of the expected utility theory as possible. The notion of disappointment aversion offers good intuition as to why the independence axiom is so often violated. Axioms 1–4 aim to capture the notion of disappointment aversion that lead to a rather restricted class of preferences with acceptable normative properties capable of accommodating many of the experimental results. The simple characterization of these preferences suggest that they might constitute a useful step in better understanding the failure of the independence axiom.

Graduate School of Business, Stanford University, Stanford, CA 94305, U.S.A.

Manuscript received April, 1988; final revision received April, 1990.

APPENDIX

PROOF OF THEOREM 1: The proof will make use of the following two lemmas.

LEMMA 1: (I) $x > y$, $\lambda \in (0, 1)$ implies $x > \lambda x + (1 - \lambda)y > y$.
(II) $\lambda, a \in (0,1)$, $y > z$, $p = ay + (1 - a)z$ imply (1) $\lambda x + (1 - \lambda)p > p$ whenever $x > p$; (2) $p > \lambda x + (1 - \lambda)p$ whenever $p > x$; (3) $x \sim \lambda x + (1 - \lambda)p$ whenever $x \sim p$; (4) $x > \lambda x + (1 - \lambda)p$ whenever $x > p$; (5) $\lambda x + (1 - \lambda)p > x$ whenever $p > x$.
(III) II above holds for arbitrary p.

PROOF: (I) Assume the contrary; then there exists λ such that $\lambda x + (1 - \lambda)y \succsim x$ or $y \succsim \lambda x + (1 - \lambda)y$. Take the first case and let $\alpha = \inf\{\lambda \in [0, 1] | \lambda x + (1 - \lambda)y \succsim x\}$. By Axiom 2 $\alpha \in (0, 1)$ and $\alpha x + (1 - \alpha)y \sim x$. Then Axiom 3 implies that $\alpha^2 x + (1 - \alpha^2)y \sim \alpha x + (1 - \alpha)y$ if $x \succsim \alpha^2 x + (1 - \alpha^2)y \succsim y$. But this follows immediately from Axiom 3. Hence $\alpha^2 x + (1 - \alpha^2)y \succsim \alpha x + (1 - \alpha)y \succsim x$. But $\alpha^2 < \alpha$ which contradicts the fact that α is the infimum. A similar argument establishes a contradiction for the $y \succsim \alpha x + (1 - \alpha)y$ case.

(II) (1) Assume the contrary; hence there exists $\lambda, a \in (0, 1)$, $p = ay + (1 - a)z$, and $x \in X$ such that $x \succ p$ and $p \succsim \lambda x + (1 - \lambda)p$. Then by Axiom 2 there exists $\lambda^* \in (0, 1)$ such that $\lambda^* x + (1 - \lambda^*)p \sim p$. Let $T = \{(y, z) | ay + (1 - a)z \sim p\}$ and $\Delta = \{y^* - z^* > 0 | y^* \succsim \lambda^* x + (1 - \lambda^*)(ay^* + (1 - a)z^*) \succsim z^*$ for $(y^*, z^*) \in T\}$. By assumption Δ is nonempty. Let $\delta = \inf \Delta$. Then by Axiom 2 there exist y^* such that $ay^* + (1 - a)(y^* - \delta) \sim p$ and then, by Axiom 3, $\lambda^* x + (1 - \lambda^*)(ay^* + (1 - a)(y^* - \delta)) \sim p$. Therefore, by Axiom 2, $\delta = 0$; otherwise we can find $\bar{y}$ such that $\bar{y} \succsim \lambda^* x + (1 - \lambda^*)(a\bar{y} + (1 - a)(\bar{y} - \delta)) \succsim \bar{y} - \delta$, $a\bar{y} + (1 - a)(\bar{y} - \delta) \sim p$, and $0 < \bar{\delta} < \delta$, which contradicts the fact that $\delta = \inf \Delta$. But if $\delta = 0$, by Axiom 2, $\lambda^* x + (1 - \lambda^*)y^* \sim p$ and $y^* \sim p$ which contradicts (I) above.

(2) follows from a symmetric argument.

(3) follows from (1) above and Axiom 2.

(4) If $x \succ y$, then set

$$\hat{p} = \frac{\lambda}{\lambda + (1 - \lambda)a}x + \frac{(1 - \lambda)a}{\lambda + (1 - \lambda)a}y.$$

Then by (I) and (II) (2) above we have $\hat{p} \succ tz + (1 - t)\hat{p}$ whenever $t \in (0, 1)$. Set $t = (1 - \lambda)(1 - a)$ to obtain $\hat{p} \succ tz + (1 - t)\hat{p} = \lambda x + (1 - \lambda)p$. But $x \succ \hat{p}$ by (I), so $x \succ \lambda x + (1 - \lambda)p$.

If $y \succsim x$ then let $\alpha^* x + (1 - \alpha^*)p \sim x$ and $T = \{(y^*, z^*) | y^* \succsim \alpha^* x + (1 - \alpha^*)(ay^* + (1 - a)z^*) \succsim z^*$ and $ay^* + (1 - a)z^* \sim p\}$. Define $\bar{y} = \inf\{y | (y, z) \in T$ for some $z \in X\}$. Observe that $\bar{y} = x$. Otherwise by Axiom 3 (and Axiom 2) $\alpha^* x + (1 - \alpha^*)(a\bar{y} + (1 - a)\bar{z}) \sim p$ for some $\bar{z}$. This would imply that there exists $y' < \bar{y}$ and z' such that $(y', z') \in T$, a contradiction to the fact that $\bar{y}$ is the infimum. But if $\bar{y} = x$ we have $\alpha^* x + (1 - \alpha^*)(ax + (1 - a)\bar{z}) \sim x$ and $\bar{z} < x$ which contradicts (I) above.

(5) follows from a symmetric argument to the one provided in (4) above.

(III) The results of (II) can be generalized to p with arbitrary supports as follows: assume that (1)-(5) hold for all p such that $|\text{supp}(p)| \leqslant n$. Then for p such that $|\text{supp}(p)| = n + 1$ we can conclude by Axiom 2 that there exists $v \in (w, b)$ such that $v \sim p$. Let $\Delta = \{\lambda \in (0, 1) | p \succsim \lambda x + (1 - \lambda)p\}$ for some $x \succ p$. If (I) is false, then Δ is nonempty. If $\inf \Delta = 0$, then choose $(a, q, r) \in D(p)$ such that $x' \sim p$ implies $x' \in \text{supp}(r)$. Next let $(a, y, z) \sim p$ for some $y > z$. By Axiom 2 such y and z exist. Finally choose $\lambda^* \in \Delta \cap \{\lambda > 0 | y \succsim \lambda x + (1 - \lambda)(ay + (1 - a)z) \succsim z, r \in W(\lambda x + (1 - \lambda)p)\}$. By Axiom 2 such λ^* exist. Then Axiom 3 implies $\lambda^* x + (1 - \lambda^*)p \sim \lambda^* x + (1 - \lambda^*)(ay + (1 - a)z)$. But by (II) $\lambda^* x + (1 - \lambda^*)(ay + (1 - a)z) \succ p$, hence a contradiction.

If $\inf \Delta \neq 0$ there exists some $\hat{r} \in (w, x)$ such that $\hat{r} = CE(\alpha x + (1 - \alpha)p)$ for some $\alpha \in (0, \lambda)$ and for all $\varepsilon > 0$ there exists $\alpha' \in (\alpha, \alpha + \varepsilon)$ such that $CE(\alpha' x + (1 - \alpha')p) < CE(\alpha x + (1 - \alpha)p)$. Set $\hat{p} = \alpha x + (1 - \alpha)p$ and observe that $\inf \hat{\Delta} = 0$ where $\hat{\Delta} = \{\hat{\lambda} \in (0, 1) | \hat{p} \succsim \hat{\lambda} x + (1 - \hat{\lambda})p\}$. Hence we can use the argument above to establish the desired conclusion.

(2) follows from a symmetric argument.

(3) follows from Axiom 2 and (1) above.

(4) Assume the contrary; then choose α such that $0 < \alpha < \lambda^*$, $a \in (0, 1)$, $q, r \in \mathscr{S}$ and $z < x$ such that $(a, q, r) \in D(\alpha x + (1 - \alpha)p)$, $\lambda^* = \inf\{\lambda | \lambda x + (1 - \lambda)p \succsim x\}$ and $x' \in \text{supp}(p)$ and $x' < x$ implies $x' < V$. By Axiom 2 all of this is possible. Then set $c = (\lambda^* - \alpha)/(1 - \alpha)$ and observe that

$$cx + (1 - c)(\alpha x + (1 - \alpha)p) = \lambda^* x + (1 - \lambda^*)p \sim x, \qquad \text{by Axiom 2,}$$

$$cx + (1 - c)(\alpha x + (1 - \alpha)p) \sim cx + (1 - c)(ax + (1 - a)z), \qquad \text{by Axiom 3.}$$

Hence $x \sim (cx + (1 - c)ax + (1 - c)(1 - a)z)$, contradicting (I) above.

(5) follows from a symmetric argument.   Q.E.D.

Next we will define a binary relation R on $\mathscr{S}^0 = \{p \in \mathscr{S} | w \in \text{supp}(p)$ implies $b \notin \text{supp}(p)\}$. sRs' iff $(a, s, r) \in D, (a, s', r) \in D$ implies $as + (1 - \alpha)r \succsim as' + (1 - \alpha)r$. We write $s|s'$ to denote sRs' and $s'Rs$.

It is easy to see that Axiom 2, Axiom 3, and Lemma 1 (III) imply the following, stronger version of A3:

AXIOM 3: For $i = 1, 2$ $(\alpha, q_i, r_i) \in D(p_i)$, $q_i \in B(\lambda x + (1 - \lambda)p_i)$ and $r_i \in W(\lambda x + (1 - \lambda)p_i)$, $\lambda \in [0, 1]$ implies $p_1 \succsim p_2$ iff $\lambda x + (1 - \lambda)p_1 \succsim \lambda x + (1 - \lambda)p_2$.

But Axiom 1, Axiom 3*, and Lemma 1 (III) imply that R is preference relation on $\mathscr{L}^0$.

LEMMA 2: *sIy implies for all* $\lambda \in [0,1]$, $\lambda s + (1-\lambda)p \sim \lambda y + (1-\lambda)p$ *whenever*

$$s \in B(\lambda s + (1-\lambda)p) \cup W(\lambda s + (1-\lambda)p).$$

PROOF: It follows from Axiom 3* and Lemma 1 (II) that $s \in B(\lambda s + (1-\lambda)p)$ implies sIy iff $\lambda s + (1-\lambda)p \sim \lambda y + (1-\lambda)p$. Assume that $s \in W(\lambda s + (1-\lambda)p)$. Then by Axiom 3* and Lemma 1 (III) we have $\lambda s + (1-\lambda)p \sim \lambda y + (1-\lambda)p$ iff $\alpha s + (1-\alpha)b \sim \alpha y + (1-\alpha)b$ for all α sufficiently small. But then Axiom 4 implies that $\lambda s + (1-\lambda)p \sim \lambda y + (1-\lambda)p$ iff $\alpha s + (1-\alpha)w \sim \alpha y + (1-\alpha)w$ for all α such that $s \in B(\alpha s + (1-\alpha)w)$; that is, $\lambda s = (1-\lambda)p \sim \lambda y + (1-\lambda)p$ iff sIy. Q.E.D.

PROOF OF THEOREM 1: Define w_0 such that $w < w_0 < b$ and a function $\alpha_0: [w_0, b] \to (0,1]$ such that $\alpha_0(x)x + (1-\alpha_0(x))w \sim w_0$ for all $x \in [w_0, b]$. Axiom 2 and Lemma 1 establish that α_0 is well-defined and continuous. It is easy to show, using Lemma 1, that α_0 is strictly decreasing. Next define $u_0: [w_0, b] \to [0,1]$ by

$$u_0(x) = \frac{\alpha_0(b)(1-\alpha_0(x))}{(1-\alpha_0(b))\alpha_0(x)}.$$

If follows from the continuity and strict decreasingness of α_0 that u_0 is continuous and strictly increasing. We will now show that (*) sRr iff $\sum_x u_0(x)s(x) \geq \sum_x u_0(x)r(x)$ for all $s, r \in \mathscr{L}(w_0)$ where $\mathscr{L}(w_0) = \{p \in \mathscr{L} \mid x \in \text{supp}(p) \text{ implies } x \geq w_0\}$. To do this first we will show that $\alpha_0(x)[u(x)b + (1-u(x))w_0] + (1-\alpha_0(x))w \sim \alpha_0(x)x + (1-\alpha_0(x))w$. By Lemma 1 (III), part (3), $t\alpha_0(b) + (1-t)w_0 + t(1-\alpha_0(b))w \sim w_0$. Set

$$t = \frac{1-\alpha_0(x)}{1-\alpha_0(b)}.$$

So,

$$\frac{\alpha_0(b)(1-\alpha_0(x))}{1-\alpha_0(b)} \cdot b + \frac{\alpha_0(x)-\alpha_0(b)}{1-\alpha_0(b)} w_0 + (1-\alpha_0(x))w \sim w_0;$$

hence,

$$\alpha_0(x)\left[\frac{\alpha_0(b)(1-\alpha_0(x))}{(1-\alpha_0(b))\alpha_0(x)}b + \left(1 - \frac{\alpha_0(b)(1-\alpha_0(x))}{(1-\alpha_0(b))\alpha_0(x)}\right)w_0\right] + (1-\alpha_0(x))w \sim w_0;$$

i.e.,

$$\alpha_0(x)[u_0(b)b + (1-u_0(x))w_0] + (1-\alpha_0(x))w \sim w_0.$$

Therefore

$$\alpha_0(x)[u_0(x)b + (1-u_0(x))w_0] + (1-\alpha_0(x))w \sim \alpha_0(x)x + (1-\alpha_0(x))w.$$

Then, applying Lemma 2 yields that for all s such that $\text{supp}(s) = 2$,

$$\genfrac{(}{)}{0pt}{}{*}{*} \qquad s \in B(\alpha s + (1-\alpha)p) \cup W(\alpha s + (1-\alpha)p)$$

implies $\alpha s + (1-\alpha)p \sim \alpha y + (1-\alpha)p$ iff $\sum_x u(x)s(x) = u(y)$. Hence, applying ($\overset{*}{*}$) repeatedly establishes that ($\overset{*}{*}$) holds for arbitrary s. A3 and Lemma 1 imply that $\alpha y + (1-\alpha)p \succsim \alpha y' + (1-\alpha)p$. Therefore ($\overset{*}{*}$) establishes the desired conclusion.

Choose some sequence $\{w_i\}_{i=1,2,\dots}$ such that $w < w_{i+1} < w_i$ for $i = 1,2\dots$ and $\lim_{i \to \infty}\{w_i\} = w$. Define $\alpha_i: [w_i, b] \to [0,1]$ by substituting w_i in place of w_0 in the definition of α_0. Furthermore let

$$u_i(x) = \frac{\alpha_i(b)}{1-\alpha_i(b)}\frac{(1-\alpha(x))}{\alpha(x)}.$$

By the argument above, u_i satisfies (*). Note that on the interval $[w_i, b]$ both u_i and u_{i+1} satisfy (*); hence $u_{i+1} = au_i + c$ by a familiar argument from expected utility theory. $u_{i+1}(b) = u_i(b) = 1$, so $a = 1 - c$. Furthermore $u_i(w_i) = 0$; hence $0 \leqslant c$ and therefore $0 < c < 1$ and $u_{i+1} = (1 - c)u_i + c \geqslant u_i$. Hence $u_i(x)$ is an increasing sequence. Let $j^*(x) = \inf\{j | w_j \leqslant x\}$ for all $x \in (w, b]$. Define $u(x)$ by $u(x) = \lim_{i > j^*(x)} u_i(x)$. Clearly $u(x)$ is well-defined for all $x \in (w, b]$; furthermore for all i, u_i satisfies strict monotonicity, (*), and continuity, and hence u satisfies those properties also. Note that since $\lim_{x \to w} u(x) = 0$, u can be extended to $[w, b]$ with all of those properties by setting $u(w) = 0$.

Next define $\gamma: [0, 1] \to [0, 1]$ by $\gamma(\alpha) = u(x)$ where $\alpha b + (1 - \alpha)w \sim x$. It follows from Axiom 2 that γ is well-defined and continuous. From Lemma 1 it follows that γ is strictly increasing. Furthermore $\gamma(1) = 1$, $\gamma(0) = 0$. We will show that $\gamma(\alpha) = \alpha/(1 + (1 - \alpha)\beta)$ for some $\beta \in (-1, \infty)$. Let $\alpha > \hat{\alpha}$ and $\gamma(\alpha) = u(x)$, $\gamma(\hat{\alpha}) = u(y)$. By definition $\alpha b + (1 - \alpha)w \sim x$. By Lemma 1 (II) part (3) $\lambda \alpha b + (1 - \lambda)x + \lambda(1 - \alpha)w \sim x$. Choose λ such that $(1 - \lambda)u(x) = u(y)$. Then $\alpha b + (1 - \alpha)w \sim \alpha[\lambda b + (1 - \lambda)x] + (1 - \alpha)[(1 - \lambda)x + \lambda w]$. From (*) and Axiom 3 we have

$$\alpha b + (1 - \alpha)w \sim \alpha[\lambda b + (1 - \lambda)x] + (1 - \alpha)y.$$

By taking a $\hat{\alpha}/\alpha$ convex combination of both sides with w and applying Axiom 3 we get

$$\hat{\alpha}b + (1 - \hat{\alpha})w \sim \hat{\alpha}[\lambda b + (1 - \lambda)x] + \hat{\alpha}\frac{(1 - \alpha)}{\alpha}y + \frac{\alpha - \hat{\alpha}}{\alpha}w.$$

Let a satisfy $a + (1 - a)u(y) = u(x)$; then Axiom 3 and (*) yields

$$\hat{\alpha}b + (1 - \hat{\alpha})w \sim \hat{\alpha}(\lambda + (1 - \lambda)a)b + \left[\hat{\alpha}(1 - \lambda)(1 - a) + \frac{\hat{\alpha}(1 - \alpha)}{\alpha}\right]y + \frac{\alpha - \hat{\alpha}}{\alpha}w.$$

Then by Axiom 3

$$\hat{\alpha}b + (1 - \hat{\alpha})w \sim \frac{\hat{\alpha}(\lambda + (1 - \lambda)a)}{D}b + \left[1 - \frac{\hat{\alpha}(\lambda + (1 - \lambda)a)}{D}\right]w,$$

where $D = 1 - \hat{\alpha}(1 - \lambda)(1 - a) - (\hat{\alpha}(1 - \alpha)/\alpha)$. But this implies that

$$\hat{\alpha} = \frac{\hat{\alpha}(\lambda + (1 - \lambda)a)}{D}.$$

Substituting the value for λ and a, and some simplifying, yields:

$$u(y) = \frac{u(x)\hat{\alpha}(1 - \alpha)}{\alpha(1 - u(x)) - \hat{\alpha}(\alpha - u(x))}.$$

Substituting $\gamma(\alpha)$ for $u(x)$ and $\gamma(\hat{\alpha})$ for $u(y)$, we obtain

$$\gamma(\hat{\alpha}) = \frac{\gamma(\alpha)\hat{\alpha}(1 - \alpha)}{\alpha(1 - \gamma(\alpha)) - \hat{\alpha}(\alpha - \gamma(\alpha))};$$

that is,

$$\gamma(\hat{\alpha}) = \frac{\hat{\alpha}}{\dfrac{\gamma(\alpha)(1 - \alpha) + \alpha - \gamma(\alpha)}{\gamma(\alpha)(1 - \alpha)} - \hat{\alpha}\dfrac{\alpha - \gamma(\alpha)}{\gamma(\alpha)(1 - \alpha)}}.$$

Define

$$\beta(\alpha) = \frac{\alpha - \gamma(\alpha)}{\gamma(\alpha)(1 - \alpha)};$$

then,

$$\gamma(\hat{\alpha}) = \frac{\hat{\alpha}}{1 + (1 - \hat{\alpha})\beta(\alpha)}.$$

684   FARUK GUL

If we can show that $\beta(\alpha)$ is a constant, we are done. For $0 < \hat{\alpha} < \alpha < 1$,

$$\beta(\hat{\alpha}) = \frac{\hat{\alpha} - \gamma(\hat{\alpha})}{\gamma(\hat{\alpha})(1 - \hat{\alpha})}.$$

Substituting

$$\gamma(\hat{\alpha}) = \frac{\hat{\alpha}}{1 + (1 - \hat{\alpha})\beta(\alpha)}$$

into the above equation yields $\beta(\hat{\alpha}) = \beta(\alpha)$. Hence β is constant. $\beta > -1$ follows from the fact that $b > \alpha b + (1 - \alpha)w$ for all $\alpha \in (0,1)$ (by Lemma 1). Next we will show that the function

$$V(p) = \gamma(\alpha)\sum_x u(x)q(x) + (1 - \gamma(\alpha))\sum_x u(x)r(x)$$

represents $\succeq$ for $(\alpha, q, r) \in D(p)$. To show this we will prove that $(\alpha, x, z) \in D$ implies $(\alpha, x, z) \sim y$ iff $\gamma(\alpha)u(x) + (1 - \gamma(\alpha))u(z) \sim u(y)$. Then, the fact that V represents $\succeq$ will follow from Lemma 2 and the observation that $\alpha x^* + (1 - \alpha)y^* > \alpha x^* + (1 - \alpha)z^*$ iff $y^* > z^*$.

$$(\alpha, x, z) \sim y \quad \text{iff} \quad \alpha(cb + (1 - c)y) + (1 - \alpha)(dy + (1 - d)w) \sim y$$

for $c = (u(x) - u(y))/(1 - u(y))$ and $d = u(z)/u(y)$ (by Lemma 2).
Hence $(\alpha, x, z) \sim y$ iff $\alpha cb + [\alpha(1 - c) + (1 - \alpha)d]y + (1 - \alpha)(1 - d)w \sim y$. Hence $(\alpha, x, z) \sim y$ iff $tb + (1 - t)w \sim y$ where

$$t = \frac{\alpha c}{1 - \alpha(1 - c) - (1 - \alpha)d}.$$

But by construction

$$tb + (1 - t)w \sim y \quad \text{iff}$$

$$\gamma(t) = u(y), \quad \text{i.e. iff}$$

$$\frac{t}{1 + (1 - t)\beta} = u(y), \quad \text{i.e. iff}$$

$$t = \frac{u(y)(1 + \beta)}{1 + u(y)\beta}.$$

Substituting for t, c, and d yields

$$(\alpha, x, z) \sim y \quad \text{iff}$$

$$\alpha = \frac{(1 + \beta)(u(y) - u(z))}{u(x) - u(z) + \beta[u(y) - u(z)]} \quad \text{which holds iff}$$

$$\gamma(\alpha)u(x) + (1 - \gamma(\alpha))u(z) = u(y).$$

Hence we have proven part (i) and (iii) of the theorem. That u is unique up to an affine transformation follows from the familiar argument of expected utility theory. The uniqueness of γ is obvious.   Q.E.D.

An Algorithm for Computing V(p)

Let $\{x_1, x_2, \ldots x_k\}$ be the support for some lottery p. Without loss of generality assume $x_j > x_{j-1}$ for all $j = 2, 3, \ldots k$. If $CE(p) \notin \{x_1, x_2, \ldots x_k\}$, then there exists a unique j^* such that $\{x_1, x_2, \ldots x_{j^*}\}$ constitute all the disappointment prizes of p and $\{x_{j+1}, x_{j+2}\ldots x_k\}$ constitute all the elation prizes of p. Hence there are $k - 1$ candidates for an EDD of p. These are (α_j, q_j, r_j) (for $j = 1, 2, \ldots, k - 1$) where $\alpha_j = \sum_{i=j+1}^{k} p(x_i)$, $q_j(x) = 0$ for $x \notin \{x_{j+1}, x_{j+1}, \ldots x_k\}$, $q_j(x) = p_j(x)/\alpha_j$ for $x \in \{x_{j+1}, x_{j+2}\ldots x_k\}$, $r_j(x) = 0$ for $x \notin \{x_1, x_2\ldots x_j\}$, and $r_j(x) = p(x)/(1 - \alpha_j)$ for $x \in \{x_1, x_2\ldots x_j\}$. Let $\hat{V}(\alpha_j, q_j, r_j) = \gamma(\alpha_j)Eu(q_j) + (1 - \gamma(\alpha_j))Eu(r_j)$ where $\gamma(\alpha) = \alpha/(1 + (1 - \alpha)\beta)$. The condition $u(x_j) < \hat{V}(\alpha_j, q_j, r_j) < u(x_{j+1})$ will be satisfied if and only if $j = j^*$. For j^*, $\hat{V}(\alpha_{j^*}, q_{j^*}, r_{j^*}) = V(p)$ and $\{(\alpha_{j^*}, q_{j^*}, r_{j^*})\} = D(p)$. Hence in at most $k - 1$ steps we can isolate the unique EDD of p and determine $V(p)$. If $CE(p) \in \text{supp}(p)$ then there will exist a unique j^* such that $\hat{V}(\alpha_{j^*-1}, q_{j^*-1}, r_{j^*-1}) = \hat{V}(\alpha_{j^*}, q_{j^*}, r_{j^*}) = u(x_{j^*})$. For $j < j^* - 1$, $\hat{V}(\alpha_j, q_j, r_j)$ and for $j > j^*$, $\hat{V}(\alpha_j, q_j, r_j) < u(x_{j^*})$. Thus $D(p) = \{(\alpha, q, r) | \alpha q + (1 - \alpha)r = p$ and $q(x) = 0$ if $x \notin \{x_{j^*}, x_{j^*-1}, \dots x_k\}$, $r(x) = 0$ if $x \notin \{x_1, x_2, \dots x_j\}\}$. Furthermore for all $(\alpha, q, r) \in D(p)$, $\hat{V}(\alpha, q, r) = u(x_{j^*}) = V(p)$. So again in at most $k - 1$ steps, $V(p)$ and $D(p)$ can be determined.

PROOF OF THEOREM 2: Let $e(p) > e(q)$, $x \succ p$, and $\beta > 0$. Then there exists $(\alpha, s, r) \in D(p)$ such that $\alpha = e(p)$. Furthermore, by Axiom 2, there exists $\bar{a} > 0$ such that $s \in B(ax + (1 - a)p)$ and $r \in W(ax + (1 - a)p)$ for all $a < \bar{a}$. Then for $a < \bar{a}$,

$$V(ax + (1 - a)p) = \gamma(a + (1 - a)\alpha) \cdot \frac{au(x) + (1 - a)\alpha c}{a + (1 - a)\alpha} + (1 - \gamma(a + (1 - a)\alpha))d$$

where $c = \sum_y u(y)s(y)$ and $d = \sum_y u(y)r(y)$. Hence,

$$\frac{dV(ax + (1 - a)p)}{da}\bigg|_{a=0} = \gamma'(\alpha)(1 - \alpha)c + \gamma(\alpha)\frac{u(x) - c}{\alpha} - \gamma'(\alpha)(1 - \alpha)d.$$

Substituting $\gamma'(\alpha) = 1 + \beta/(1 + (1 - \alpha)\beta)^2$ and $\gamma(\alpha) = \alpha/1 + (1 - \alpha)\beta$ and rearranging terms yields

$$\frac{dV(ax + (1 - a)p)}{da}\bigg|_{a=0} = \frac{u(x)}{1 + (1 - \alpha)\beta} - \frac{\alpha c + (1 - \alpha)(1 + \beta)d}{(1 + (1 - \alpha)\beta)^2}$$

$$= \frac{u(x) - V(p)}{1 + (1 - \alpha)\beta} = \frac{u(x) - V(p)}{1 + (1 - e(p))\beta}.$$

Repeating the same argument for q yields

$$\frac{dV(ax + (1 - a)q)}{da}\bigg|_{a=0} = \frac{u(x) - V(q)}{1 + (1 - e(q))\beta}.$$

By assumption $V(p) = V(q)$ and $u(x) - V(p) > 0$. Hence $e(p) > e(q)$ implies

$$\frac{dV(ax + (1 - a)p)}{da}\bigg|_{a=0} > \frac{dV(ax + (1 - a)q)}{da}\bigg|_{a=0},$$

which establishes that $ax + (1 - a)p \succ ax + (1 - a)q$ for sufficiently small a. All remaining cases follow from symmetric arguments.

Q.E.D.

PROOF OF THEOREM 5: First we will prove that $\beta_2 > \beta_1$ implies $\succeq_1$ is not more risk averse than $\succeq_2$. Choose $x \in (w, b)$ and $\varepsilon > 0$. Let α solve

$$u_1(x) = \frac{\alpha u_1(x + \varepsilon) + (1 - \alpha)(1 + \beta_1)u_1(x - \varepsilon)}{1 + (1 - \alpha)\beta_1}.$$

Then obviously $x \sim p$ where $p(x + \varepsilon) = \alpha$ and $p(x - \varepsilon) = 1 - \alpha$. Using Taylor series expansion of u_1 around x we obtain

$$(1 + (1 - \alpha)\beta_1)u_1(x) = \alpha[u_1(x) + \varepsilon u_1'(x)]$$
$$+ (1 - \alpha)(1 + \beta_1)[u_1(x) - \varepsilon u_1'(x)] + o(\varepsilon);$$

hence

$$\alpha = \frac{1 + \beta_1}{2 + \beta_1} + o(\varepsilon).$$

Similar argument establishes that if $a'(x + \varepsilon) + (1 - a')(x - \varepsilon) \sim_2 x$, then

$$\alpha' = \frac{1 + \beta_2}{2 + \beta_2} + o(\varepsilon).$$

Hence for ε sufficiently small $\alpha' > \alpha$. That is $x \succ_2 \alpha(x + \varepsilon) + (1 - \alpha)(x - \varepsilon) = p$.

Next assume that $R_1^a(x) \geq R_2^a(x)$ for all $x \in (w, b)$, $\beta_1 \geq \beta_2$ and $p \succeq_1 \bar{x}$. Then, in particular $p \sim_1 x$ for some $x > \bar{x}$. Since u_1 and u_2 are unique only up to affine transformations we can, without

686   FARUK GUL

loss of generality, assume that $u_1(x) = u_2(x)$ and $u_1'(x) = u_2'(x)$. Then note that $u_1(y) < u_2(y)$ for all $y \in [w, b]$. Let $(\alpha, q, r) \in D(p, \succeq_1)$. Then we have

$$\gamma_1(\alpha) \sum_y u_1(y)q(y) + (1 - \gamma_1(\alpha)) \sum_y u_1(y)r(y) = u_1(x).$$

But $u_1(x) = u_2(x)$, $\gamma_1(\alpha) \leqslant \gamma_2(\alpha)$ and $u_1(y) \leqslant u_2(y)$; hence

$$\gamma_2(\alpha) \sum_y u_2(y)q(y) + (1 - \gamma_2(\alpha)) \sum_y u_2(y)r(y) \geqslant u_2(x).$$

Therefore

$$u_2(x) \leqslant \sum_y u_2(y)p(y) + \beta_2 \sum_{y \leqslant x} (u_2(y) - u_2(x))p(y).$$

Since $V_2(p) = \sum_y u_2(y)p(y) + \beta_2 \sum_{y < p}(u_2(y) - V_2(p))p(y)$, $V_2(p) \geqslant u_2(x)$, which establishes that $p \succeq_2 x \succeq_2 \bar{x}$ and proves that $\succeq_1$ is more averse than $\succeq_2$.   *Q.E.D.*

REFERENCES

ALLAIS, M. (1979): "The Foundations of a Positive Theory of Choice Involving Risk and a Criticism of the Postulates and Axioms of the American School," in *Expected Utility Hypothesis and the Allais Paradox*, ed. by M. Allais and O. Hagen. Dordrecht, Holland: D. Reidel Publishing Co.
BELL, D. (1982): "Regret in Decision Making Under Uncertainty," *Operations Research*, 30, 961–981.
——— (1985): "Disappointment in Decision Making Under Uncertainty," *Operations Research*, 33, 1–27.
CHEW, S. H., AND K. MACCRIMMON (1979): "Alpha-Nu Choice Theory: A Generalization of Expected Utility Theory," University of British Columbia, Faculty of Commerce and Business Administration, Working Paper No. 686.
DEKEL, E. (1986): "An Axiomatic Characterization of Preferences Under Uncertainty: Weakening the Independence Axiom," *Journal of Economic Theory*, 40, 309–318.
EDWARDS, W. (1953): "Probability-Preferences in Gambling," *American Journal of Psychology*, 66, 56–67.
FISHBURN, P. C. (1983): "Transitive Measurable Utility," *Journal of Economic Theory*, 31, 293–317.
KAHNEMAN, D., AND A. TVERSKY (1979): "Prospect Theory: An Analysis of Decision Under Risk," *Econometrica*, 47, 263–291.
LOOMES, G., AND R. SUGDEN (1982): "Regret Theory: An Alternative Theory Rational Choice Under Uncertainty," *Economic Journal*, 92, 805–824.
——— (1986): "Disappointment and Dynamic Consistency in Choice Under Uncertainty," *Review of Economic Studies*, 53, 271–282.
MACHINA, M. J. (1982): "Expected Utility Without the Independence Axiom," *Econometrica*, 50, 273–323.
——— (1984): "Temporal Risk and the Nature of Induced Preferences," *Journal of Economic Theory*, 33, 199–231.
——— (1987): "Choice Under Uncertainty: Problems Solved and Unsolved," *Journal of Economic Perspectives*, 1, 121–154.
NEILSON, W. S. (1989): "Behavior in the Probability Triangle," mimeo.
QUIGGIN, J. (1982): "A Theory of Anticipated Utility," *Journal of Economic Behavior and Organization*, 3, 225–243.
RUBINSTEIN, A. (1988): "Similarity and Decision-Making Under Risk," *Journal of Economic Theory*, 46, 145–153.
SAVAGE, L. J. (1972): *Foundations of Statistics*. New York: Dover Publications.
TVERSKY, A. (1967): "Utility Theory and Additivity Analysis of Risky Choices," *Journal of Experimental Psychology*, 75, 27–36.
YAARI, M. E. (1987): "The Dual Theory of Choice Under Risk," *Econometrica*, 55, 95–115.

[21]

Journal of Risk and Uncertainty, 5:297–323 (1992)
© 1992 Kluwer Academic Publishers

Advances in Prospect Theory:
Cumulative Representation of Uncertainty

AMOS TVERSKY
Stanford University, Department of Psychology, Stanford, CA 94305-2130

DANIEL KAHNEMAN*
University of California at Berkeley, Department of Psychology, Berkeley, CA 94720

Key words: cumulative prospect theory

Abstract

We develop a new version of prospect theory that employs cumulative rather than separable decision weights and extends the theory in several respects. This version, called cumulative prospect theory, applies to uncertain as well as to risky prospects with any number of outcomes, and it allows different weighting functions for gains and for losses. Two principles, diminishing sensitivity and loss aversion, are invoked to explain the characteristic curvature of the value function and the weighting functions. A review of the experimental evidence and the results of a new experiment confirm a distinctive fourfold pattern of risk attitudes: risk aversion for gains and risk seeking for losses of high probability; risk seeking for gains and risk aversion for losses of low probability.

Expected utility theory reigned for several decades as the dominant normative and descriptive model of decision making under uncertainty, but it has come under serious question in recent years. There is now general agreement that the theory does not provide an adequate description of individual choice: a substantial body of evidence shows that decision makers systematically violate its basic tenets. Many alternative models have been proposed in response to this empirical challenge (for reviews, see Camerer, 1989; Fishburn, 1988; Machina, 1987). Some time ago we presented a model of choice, called prospect theory, which explained the major violations of expected utility theory in choices between risky prospects with a small number of outcomes (Kahneman and Tversky, 1979; Tversky and Kahneman, 1986). The key elements of this theory are 1) a value function that is concave for gains, convex for losses, and steeper for losses than for gains,

*An earlier version of this article was entitled "Cumulative Prospect Theory: An Analysis of Decision under Uncertainty."

This article has benefited from discussions with Colin Camerer, Chew Soo-Hong, David Freedman, and David H. Krantz. We are especially grateful to Peter P. Wakker for his invaluable input and contribution to the axiomatic analysis. We are indebted to Richard Gonzalez and Amy Hayes for running the experiment and analyzing the data. This work was supported by Grants 89-0064 and 88-0206 from the Air Force Office of Scientific Research, by Grant SES-9109535 from the National Science Foundation, and by the Sloan Foundation.

and 2) a nonlinear transformation of the probability scale, which overweights small probabilities and underweights moderate and high probabilities. In an important later development, several authors (Quiggin, 1982; Schmeidler, 1989; Yaari, 1987; Weymark, 1981) have advanced a new representation, called the rank-dependent or the cumulative functional, that transforms cumulative rather than individual probabilities. This article presents a new version of prospect theory that incorporates the cumulative functional and extends the theory to uncertain as well to risky prospects with any number of outcomes. The resulting model, called cumulative prospect theory, combines some of the attractive features of both developments (see also Luce and Fishburn, 1991). It gives rise to different evaluations of gains and losses, which are not distinguished in the standard cumulative model, and it provides a unified treatment of both risk and uncertainty.

To set the stage for the present development, we first list five major phenomena of choice, which violate the standard model and set a minimal challenge that must be met by any adequate descriptive theory of choice. All these findings have been confirmed in a number of experiments, with both real and hypothetical payoffs.

Framing effects. The rational theory of choice assumes description invariance: equivalent formulations of a choice problem should give rise to the same preference order (Arrow, 1982). Contrary to this assumption, there is much evidence that variations in the framing of options (e.g., in terms of gains or losses) yield systematically different preferences (Tversky and Kahneman, 1986).

Nonlinear preferences. According to the expectation principle, the utility of a risky prospect is linear in outcome probabilities. Allais's (1953) famous example challenged this principle by showing that the difference between probabilities of .99 and 1.00 has more impact on preferences than the difference between 0.10 and 0.11. More recent studies observed nonlinear preferences in choices that do not involve sure things (Camerer and Ho, 1991).

Source dependence. People's willingness to bet on an uncertain event depends not only on the degree of uncertainty but also on its source. Ellsberg (1961) observed that people prefer to bet on an urn containing equal numbers of red and green balls, rather than on an urn that contains red and green balls in unknown proportions. More recent evidence indicates that people often prefer a bet on an event in their area of competence over a bet on a matched chance event, although the former probability is vague and the latter is clear (Heath and Tversky, 1991).

Risk seeking. Risk aversion is generally assumed in economic analyses of decision under uncertainty. However, risk-seeking choices are consistently observed in two classes of decision problems. First, people often prefer a small probability of winning a large prize over the expected value of that prospect. Second, risk seeking is prevalent when people must choose between a sure loss and a substantial probability of a larger loss.

Loss aversion. One of the basic phenomena of choice under both risk and uncertainty is that losses loom larger than gains (Kahneman and Tversky, 1984; Tversky and Kahneman, 1991). The observed asymmetry between gains and losses is far too extreme to be explained by income effects or by decreasing risk aversion.

The present development explains loss aversion, risk seeking, and nonlinear preferences in terms of the value and the weighting functions. It incorporates a framing process, and it can accommodate source preferences. Additional phenomena that lie beyond the scope of the theory—and of its alternatives—are discussed later.

The present article is organized as follows. Section 1.1 introduces the (two-part) cumulative functional; section 1.2 discusses relations to previous work; and section 1.3 describes the qualitative properties of the value and the weighting functions. These properties are tested in an extensive study of individual choice, described in section 2, which also addresses the question of monetary incentives. Implications and limitations of the theory are discussed in section 3. An axiomatic analysis of cumulative prospect theory is presented in the appendix.

1. Theory

Prospect theory distinguishes two phases in the choice process: framing and valuation. In the framing phase, the decision maker constructs a representation of the acts, contingencies, and outcomes that are relevant to the decision. In the valuation phase, the decision maker assesses the value of each prospect and chooses accordingly. Although no formal theory of framing is available, we have learned a fair amount about the rules that govern the representation of acts, outcomes, and contingencies (Tversky and Kahneman, 1986). The valuation process discussed in subsequent sections is applied to framed prospects.

1.1. Cumulative prospect theory

In the classical theory, the utility of an uncertain prospect is the sum of the utilities of the outcomes, each weighted by its probability. The empirical evidence reviewed above suggests two major modifications of this theory: 1) the carriers of value are gains and losses, not final assets; and 2) the value of each outcome is multiplied by a decision weight, not by an additive probability. The weighting scheme used in the original version of prospect theory and in other models is a monotonic transformation of outcome probabilities. This scheme encounters two problems. First, it does not always satisfy stochastic dominance, an assumption that many theorists are reluctant to give up. Second, it is not readily extended to prospects with a large number of outcomes. These problems can be handled by assuming that transparently dominated prospects are eliminated in the editing phase, and by normalizing the weights so that they add to unity. Alternatively, both problems can be solved by the rank-dependent or cumulative functional, first proposed by Quiggin (1982) for decision under risk and by Schmeidler (1989) for decision under uncertainty. Instead of transforming each probability separately, this model transforms the entire cumulative distribution function. The present theory applies the cumulative functional separately to gains and to losses. This development extends prospect theory to uncertain as well as to risky prospects with any number of outcomes while preserving most of its essential features. The differences between the cumulative and the original versions of the theory are discussed in section 1.2.

Let S be a finite set of states of nature; subsets of S are called events. It is assumed that exactly one state obtains, which is unknown to the decision maker. Let X be a set of consequences, also called outcomes. For simplicity, we confine the present discussion to monetary outcomes. We assume that X includes a neutral outcome, denoted 0, and we interpret all other elements of X as gains or losses, denoted by positive or negative numbers, respectively.

An uncertain prospect f is a function from S into X that assigns to each state $s \ \varepsilon \ S$ a consequence $f(s) = x$ in X. To define the cumulative functional, we arrange the outcomes of each prospect in increasing order. A prospect f is then represented as a sequence of pairs (x_i, A_i), which yields x_i if A_i occurs, where $x_i > x_j$ iff $i > j$, and (A_i) is a partition of S. We use positive subscripts to denote positive outcomes, negative subscripts to denote negative outcomes, and the zero subscript to index the neutral outcome. A prospect is called strictly positive or positive, respectively, if its outcomes are all positive or nonnegative. Strictly negative and negative prospects are defined similarly; all other prospects are called mixed. The positive part of f, denoted f^+, is obtained by letting $f^+(s) = f(s)$ if $f(s) > 0$, and $f^+(s) = 0$ if $f(s) \le 0$. The negative part of f, denoted f^-, is defined similarly.

As in expected utility theory, we assign to each prospect f a number $V(f)$ such that f is preferred to or indifferent to g iff $V(f) \ge V(g)$. The following representation is defined in terms of the concept of *capacity* (Choquet, 1955), a nonadditive set function that generalizes the standard notion of probability. A capacity W is a function that assigns to each $A \subset S$ a number $W(A)$ satisfying $W(\phi) = 0$, $W(S) = 1$, and $W(A) \ge W(B)$ whenever $A \supset B$.

Cumulative prospect theory asserts that there exist a strictly increasing value function $v: X \to \mathrm{Re}$, satisfying $v(x_0) = v(0) = 0$, and capacities W^+ and W^-, such that for $f = (x_i, A_i)$, $-m \le i \le n$,

$$V(f) = V(f^+) + V(f^-),$$

$$V(f^+) = \sum_{i=0}^{n} \pi_i^+ v(x_i), \quad V(f^-) = \sum_{i=-m}^{0} \pi_i^- v(x_i), \tag{1}$$

where the decision weights $\pi^+(f^+) = (\pi_0^+, \ldots, \pi_n^+)$ and $\pi^-(f^-) = (\pi_{-m}^-, \ldots, \pi_0^-)$ are defined by:

$$\pi_n^+ = W^+(A_n), \pi_{-m}^- = W^-(A_{-m}),$$
$$\pi_i^+ = W^+(A_i \cup \ldots \cup A_n) - W^+(A_{i+1} \cup \ldots \cup A_n), 0 \le i \le n - 1,$$
$$\pi_i^- = W^-(A_{-m} \cup \ldots \cup A_i) - W^-(A_{-m} \cup \ldots \cup A_{i-1}), 1 - m \le i \le 0.$$

Letting $\pi_i = \pi_i^+$ if $i \ge 0$ and $\pi_i = \pi_i^-$ if $i < 0$, equation (1) reduces to

$$V(f) = \sum_{i=-m}^{n} \pi_i v(x_i). \tag{2}$$

The decision weight π_i^+, associated with a positive outcome, is the difference between the capacities of the events "the outcome is at least as good as x_i" and "the outcome is strictly better than x_i." The decision weight π_i^-, associated with a negative outcome, is the difference between the capacities of the events "the outcome is at least as bad as x_i" and "the outcome is strictly worse than x_i." Thus, the decision weight associated with an outcome can be interpreted as the marginal contribution of the respective event,[1] defined in terms of the capacities W^+ and W^-. If each W is additive, and hence a probability measure, then π_i is simply the probability of A_i. It follows readily from the definitions of π and W that for both positive and negative prospects, the decision weights add to 1. For mixed prospects, however, the sum can be either smaller or greater than 1, because the decision weights for gains and for losses are defined by separate capacities.

If the prospect $f = (x_i, A_i)$ is given by a probability distribution $p(A_i) = p_i$, it can be viewed as a probabilistic or risky prospect (x_i, p_i). In this case, decision weights are defined by:

$$\pi_n^+ = w^+(p_n), \pi_{-m}^- = w^-(p_{-m}),$$
$$\pi_i^+ = w^+(p_i + \ldots + p_n) - w^+(p_{i+1} + \ldots + p_n), 0 \leq i \leq n - 1,$$
$$\pi_i^- = w^-(p_{-m} + \ldots + p_i) - w^-(p_{-m} + \ldots + p_{i-1}), 1 - m \leq i \leq 0.$$

where w^+ and w^- are strictly increasing functions from the unit interval into itself satisfying $w^+(0) = w^-(0) = 0$, and $w^+(1) = w^-(1) = 1$.

To illustrate the model, consider the following game of chance. You roll a die once and observe the result $x = 1, \ldots, 6$. If x is even, you receive $\$x$; if x is odd, you pay $\$x$. Viewed as a probabilistic prospect with equiprobable outcomes, f yields the consequences $(-5, -3, -1, 2, 4, 6)$, each with probability 1/6. Thus, $f^+ = (0, 1/2; 2, 1/6; 4, 1/6; 6, 1/6)$, and $f^- = (-5, 1/6; -3, 1/6; -1, 1/6; 0, 1/2)$. By equation (1), therefore,

$$V(f) = V(f^+) + V(f^-)$$
$$= v(2)[w^+(1/2) - w^+(1/3)] + v(4)[w^+(1/3) - w^+(1/6)]$$
$$+ v(6)[w^+(1/6) - w^+(0)]$$
$$+ v(-5)[w^-(1/6) - w^-(0)] + v(-3)[w^-(1/3) - w^-(1/6)]$$
$$+ v(-1)[w^-(1/2) - w^-(1/3)].$$

1.2. Relation to previous work

Luce and Fishburn (1991) derived essentially the same representation from a more elaborate theory involving an operation $\bigcirc$ of joint receipt or multiple play. Thus, $f \bigcirc g$ is the composite prospect obtained by playing both f and g, separately. The key feature of their theory is that the utility function U is additive with respect to $\bigcirc$, that is, $U(f \bigcirc g) = U(f) + U(g)$ provided one prospect is acceptable (i.e., preferred to the status quo) and the other is not. This condition seems too restrictive both normatively and descriptively. As noted by the authors, it implies that the utility of money is a linear function of money if for all sums of money x, y, $U(x \bigcirc y) = U(x + y)$. This assumption appears to us inescapable because the joint receipt of x and y is tantamount to receiving their sum. Thus, we expect the decision maker to be indifferent between receiving a $10 bill or receiving a $20 bill and returning $10 in change. The Luce–Fishburn theory, therefore, differs from ours in two essential respects. First, it extends to composite prospects that are not treated in the present theory. Second, it practically forces utility to be proportional to money.

The present representation encompasses several previous theories that employ the same decision weights for all outcomes. Starmer and Sugden (1989) considered a model in which $w^-(p) = w^+(p)$, as in the original version of prospect theory. In contrast, the rank-dependent models assume $w^-(p) = 1 - w^+(1 - p)$ or $W^-(A) = 1 - W^+(S - A)$. If we apply the latter condition to choice between uncertain assets, we obtain the choice model established by Schmeidler (1989), which is based on the Choquet integral.[2] Other axiomatizations of this model were developed by Gilboa (1987), Nakamura (1990), and Wakker (1989a, 1989b). For probabilistic (rather than uncertain) prospects, this model was first established by Quiggin (1982) and Yaari (1987), and was further analyzed by Chew (1989), Segal (1989), and Wakker (1990). An earlier axiomatization of this model in the context of income inequality was presented by Weymark (1981). Note that in the present theory, the overall value $V(f)$ of a mixed prospect is not a Choquet integral but rather a sum $V(f^+) + V(f^-)$ of two such integrals.

The present treatment extends the original version of prospect theory in several respects. First, it applies to any finite prospect and it can be extended to continuous distributions. Second, it applies to both probabilistic and uncertain prospects and can, therefore, accommodate some form of source dependence. Third, the present theory allows different decision weights for gains and losses, thereby generalizing the original version that assumes $w^+ = w^-$. Under this assumption, the present theory coincides with the original version for all two-outcome prospects and for all mixed three-outcome prospects. It is noteworthy that for prospects of the form $(x,p;y, 1 - p)$, where either $x > y > 0$ or $x < y < 0$, the original theory is in fact rank dependent. Although the two models yield similar predictions in general, the cumulative version—unlike the original one—satisfies stochastic dominance. Thus, it is no longer necessary to assume that transparently dominated prospects are eliminated in the editing phase—an assumption that was criticized by some authors. On the other hand, the present version can no longer explain violations of stochastic dominance in nontransparent contexts (e.g., Tversky and Kahneman, 1986). An axiomatic analysis of the present theory and its relation to cumulative utility theory and to expected utility theory are discussed in the appendix; a more comprehensive treatment is presented in Wakker and Tversky (1991).

1.3. Values and weights

In expected utility theory, risk aversion and risk seeking are determined solely by the utility function. In the present theory, as in other cumulative models, risk aversion and risk seeking are determined jointly by the value function and by the capacities, which in the present context are called cumulative weighting functions, or weighting functions for short. As in the original version of prospect theory, we assume that v is concave above the reference point ($v''(x) \leq 0, x \geq 0$) and convex below the reference point ($v''(x) \geq 0, x \leq 0$). We also assume that v is steeper for losses than for gains $v'(x) < v'(-x)$ for $x \geq 0$. The first two conditions reflect the principle of diminishing sensitivity: the impact of a change diminishes with the distance from the reference point. The last condition is implied by the principle of loss aversion according to which losses loom larger than corresponding gains (Tversky and Kahneman, 1991).

The principle of diminishing sensitivity applies to the weighting functions as well. In the evaluation of outcomes, the reference point serves as a boundary that distinguishes gains from losses. In the evaluation of uncertainty, there are two natural boundaries— certainty and impossibility—that correspond to the endpoints of the certainty scale. Diminishing sensitivity entails that the impact of a given change in probability diminishes with its distance from the boundary. For example, an increase of .1 in the probability of winning a given prize has more impact when it changes the probability of winning from .9 to 1.0 or from 0 to .1, than when it changes the probability of winning from .3 to .4 or from .6 to .7. Diminishing sensitivity, therefore, gives rise to a weighting function that is concave near 0 and convex near 1. For uncertain prospects, this principle yields subadditivity for very unlikely events and superadditivity near certainty. However, the function is not well-behaved near the endpoints, and very small probabilities can be either greatly over-weighted or neglected altogether.

Before we turn to the main experiment, we wish to relate the observed nonlinearity of preferences to the shape of the weighting function. For this purpose, we devised a new demonstration of the common consequence effect in decisions involving uncertainty rather than risk. Table 1 displays a pair of decision problems (I and II) presented in that order to a group of 156 money managers during a workshop. The participants chose between prospects whose outcomes were contingent on the difference d between the closing values of the Dow-Jones today and tomorrow. For example, f' pays $25,000 if d exceeds 30 and nothing otherwise. The percentage of respondents who chose each prospect is given in brackets. The independence axiom of expected utility theory implies that f is preferred to g iff f' is preferred to g'. Table 1 shows that the modal choice was f in problem I and g' in problem II. This pattern, which violates independence, was chosen by 53% of the respondents.

Table 1. A test of independence (Dow-Jones)

		A	B	C	
		if $d < 30$	if $30 \leq d \leq 35$	if $35 < d$	
Problem I:	f	$25,000	$25,000	$25,000	[68]
	g	$25,000	0	$75,000	[32]
Problem II:	f'	0	$25,000	$25,000	[23]
	g'	0	0	$75,000	[77]

Note: Outcomes are contingent on the difference d between the closing values of the Dow-Jones today and tomorrow. The percentage of respondents ($N = 156$) who selected each prospect is given in brackets.

Essentially the same pattern was observed in a second study following the same design. A group of 98 Stanford students chose between prospects whose outcomes were contingent on the point-spread d in the forthcoming Stanford–Berkeley football game. Table 2 presents the prospects in question. For example, g pays \$10 if Stanford does not win, \$30 if it wins by 10 points or less, and nothing if it wins by more than 10 points. Ten percent of the participants, selected at random, were actually paid according to one of their choices. The modal choice, selected by 46% of the subjects, was f and g', again in direct violation of the independence axiom.

To explore the constraints imposed by this pattern, let us apply the present theory to the modal choices in table 1, using \$1,000 as a unit. Since f is preferred to g in problem I,

$$v(25) > v(75)W^+(C) + v(25)[W^+(A \cup C) - W^+(C)]$$

or

$$v(25)[1 - W^+(A \cup C) + W^+(C)] > v(75)W^+(C).$$

The preference for g' over f' in problem II, however, implies

$$v(75)W^+(C) > v(25)W^+(C \cup B);$$

hence,

$$W^+(S) - W^+(S - B) > W^+(C \cup B) - W^+(C). \qquad (3)$$

Thus, "subtracting" B from certainty has more impact than "subtracting" B from $C \cup B$. Let $W_+(D) = 1 - W^+(S - D)$, and $w_+(p) = 1 - w^+(1 - p)$. It follows readily that equation (3) is equivalent to the subadditivity of W_+, that is, $W_+(B) + W_+(D) \geq W_+(B \cup D)$. For probabilistic prospects, equation (3) reduces to

$$1 - w^+(1 - q) > w^+(p + q) - w^+(p),$$

or

$$w_+(q) + w_+(r) \geq w_+(q + r), q + r < 1.$$

Table 2. A test of independence (Stanford–Berkeley football game)

		A if $d < 0$	B if $0 \leq d \leq 10$	C if $10 < d$	
Problem I:	f	\$10	\$10	\$10	[64]
	g	\$10	\$30	0	[36]
Problem II:	f'	0	\$10	\$10	[34]
	g'	0	\$30	0	[66]

Note: Outcomes are contingent on the point-spread d in a Stanford–Berkeley football game. The percentage of respondents ($N = 98$) who selected each prospect is given in brackets.

Allais's example corresponds to the case where $p(C) = .10, p(B) = .89$, and $p(A) = .01$.

It is noteworthy that the violations of independence reported in tables 1 and 2 are also inconsistent with regret theory, advanced by Loomes and Sugden (1982, 1987), and with Fishburn's (1988) SSA model. Regret theory explains Allais's example by assuming that the decision maker evaluates the consequences as if the two prospects in each choice are statistically independent. When the prospects in question are defined by the same set of events, as in tables 1 and 2, regret theory (like Fishburn's SSA model) implies independence, since it is additive over states. The finding that the common consequence effect is very much in evidence in the present problems undermines the interpretation of Allais's example in terms of regret theory.

The common consequence effect implies the subadditivity of W_+ and of w_+. Other violations of expected utility theory imply the subadditivity of W^+ and of w^+ for small and moderate probabilities. For example, Prelec (1990) observed that most respondents prefer 2% to win $20,000 over 1% to win $30,000; they also prefer 1% to win $30,000 and 32% to win $20,000 over 34% to win $20,000. In terms of the present theory, these data imply that $w^+(.02) - w^+(.01) \geq w^+(.34) - w^+(.33)$. More generally, we hypothesize

$$w^+(p + q) - w^+(q) \geq w^+(p + q + r) - w^+(q + r), \qquad (4)$$

provided $p + q + r$ is sufficiently small. Equation (4) states that w^+ is concave near the origin; and the conjunction of the above inequalities implies that, in accord with diminishing sensitivity, w^+ has an inverted S-shape: it is steepest near the endpoints and shallower in the middle of the range. For other treatments of decision weights, see Hogarth and Einhorn (1990), Prelec (1989), Viscusi (1989), and Wakker (1990). Experimental evidence is presented in the next section.

2. Experiment

An experiment was carried out to obtain detailed information about the value and weighting functions. We made a special effort to obtain high-quality data. To this end, we recruited 25 graduate students from Berkeley and Stanford (12 men and 13 women) with no special training in decision theory. Each subject participated in three separate one-hour sessions that were several days apart. Each subject was paid $25 for participation.

2.1. Procedure

The experiment was conducted on a computer. On a typical trial, the computer displayed a prospect (e.g., 25% chance to win $150 and 75% chance to win $50) and its expected value. The display also included a descending series of seven sure outcomes (gains or losses) logarithmically spaced between the extreme outcomes of the prospect. The subject indicated a preference between each of the seven sure outcomes and the risky prospect. To obtain a more refined estimate of the certainty equivalent, a new set of seven sure outcomes was then shown, linearly spaced between a value 25% higher than the lowest amount accepted in the first set and a value 25% lower than the highest amount rejected. The certainty equivalent of a prospect was estimated by the midpoint between the lowest accepted value and the highest rejected value in the second set of choices. We wish to emphasize that although the analysis is based on certainty equivalents, the data consisted of a series of choices between a given prospect and several sure outcomes. Thus, the cash equivalent of a prospect was derived from observed choices, rather than assessed by the subject. The computer monitored the internal consistency of the responses to each prospect and rejected errors, such as the acceptance of a cash amount lower than one previously rejected. Errors caused the original statement of the problem to reappear on the screen.[3]

The present analysis focuses on a set of two-outcome prospects with monetary outcomes and numerical probabilities. Other data involving more complicated prospects, including prospects defined by uncertain events, will be reported elsewhere. There were 28 positive and 28 negative prospects. Six of the prospects (three nonnegative and three nonpositive) were repeated on different sessions to obtain the estimate of the consistency of choice. Table 3 displays the prospects and the median cash equivalents of the 25 subjects.

A modified procedure was used in eight additional problems. In four of these problems, the subjects made choices regarding the acceptability of a set of mixed prospects (e.g., 50% chance to lose $100 and 50% chance to win x) in which x was systematically varied. In four other problems, the subjects compared a fixed prospect (e.g., 50% chance to lose $20 and 50% chance to win $50) to a set of prospects (e.g., 50% chance to lose $50 and 50% chance to win x) in which x was systematically varied. (These prospects are presented in table 6.)

2.2. Results

The most distinctive implication of prospect theory is the fourfold pattern of risk attitudes. For the nonmixed prospects used in the present study, the shapes of the value and the weighting functions imply risk-averse and risk-seeking preferences, respectively, for gains and for losses of moderate or high probability. Furthermore, the shape of the weighting functions favors risk seeking for small probabilities of gains and risk aversion for small probabilities of loss, provided the outcomes are not extreme. Note, however, that prospect theory does not imply perfect reflection in the sense that the preference between any two positive prospects is reversed when gains are replaced by losses. Table 4 presents, for each subject, the percentage of risk-seeking choices (where the certainty equivalent exceeded expected value) for gains and for losses with low ($p \leq .1$) and with high ($p \geq .5$) probabilities. Table 4 shows that for $p \geq .5$, all 25 subjects are predominantly risk averse for positive prospects and risk seeking for negative ones. Moreover, the entire fourfold pattern is observed for 22 of the 25 subjects, with some variability at the level of individual choices.

Although the overall pattern of preferences is clear, the individual data, of course, reveal both noise and individual differences. The correlations, across subjects, between

Table 3. Median cash equivalents (in dollars) for all nonmixed prospects

Outcomes	Probability								
	.01	.05	.10	.25	.50	.75	.90	.95	.99
(0, 50)			9		21		37		
(0, −50)			−8		−21		−39		
(0, 100)		14		25	36	52		78	
(0, −100)		−8		−23.5	−42	−63		−84	
(0, 200)	10		20		76		131		188
(0, −200)	−3		−23		−89		−155		−190
(0, 400)	12								377
(0, −400)	−14								−380
(50, 100)			59		71		83		
(−50, −100)			−59		−71		−85		
(50, 150)		64		72.5	86	102		128	
(−50, −150)		−60		−71	−92	−113		−132	
(100, 200)		118		130	141	162		178	
(−100, −200)		−112		−121	−142	−158		−179	

Note: The two outcomes of each prospect are given in the left-hand side of each row; the probability of the second (i.e., more extreme) outcome is given by the corresponding column. For example, the value of $9 in the upper left corner is the median cash equivalent of the prospect (0, .9; $50, .1).

the cash equivalents for the same prospects on successive sessions averaged .55 over six different prospects. Table 5 presents means (after transformation to Fisher's *z*) of the correlations between the different types of prospects. For example, there were 19 and 17 prospects, respectively, with high probability of gain and high probability of loss. The value of .06 in table 5 is the mean of the $17 \times 19 = 323$ correlations between the cash equivalents of these prospects.

The correlations between responses within each of the four types of prospects average .41, slightly lower than the correlations between separate responses to the same problems. The two negative values in table 5 indicate that those subjects who were more risk averse in one domain tended to be more risk seeking in the other. Although the individual correlations are fairly low, the trend is consistent: 78% of the 403 correlations in these two cells are negative. There is also a tendency for subjects who are more risk averse for high-probability gains to be less risk seeking for gains of low probability. This trend, which is absent in the negative domain, could reflect individual differences either in the elevation of the weighting function or in the curvature of the value function for gains. The very low correlations in the two remaining cells of table 5, averaging .05, indicate that there is no general trait of risk aversion or risk seeking. Because individual choices are quite noisy, aggregation of problems is necessary for the analysis of individual differences.

The fourfold pattern of risk attitudes emerges as a major empirical generalization about choice under risk. It has been observed in several experiments (see, e.g., Cohen,

Table 4. Percentage of risk-seeking choices

Subject	Gain		Loss	
	$p \leq .1$	$p \geq .5$	$p \leq .1$	$p \geq .5$
1	100	38	30	100
2	85	33	20	75
3	100	10	0	93
4	71	0	30	58
5	83	0	20	100
6	100	5	0	100
7	100	10	30	86
8	87	0	10	100
9	16	0	80	100
10	83	0	0	93
11	100	26	0	100
12	100	16	10	100
13	87	0	10	94
14	100	21	30	100
15	66	0	30	100
16	60	5	10	100
17	100	15	20	100
18	100	22	10	93
19	60	10	60	63
20	100	5	0	81
21	100	0	0	100
22	100	0	0	92
23	100	31	0	100
24	71	0	80	100
25	100	0	10	87
Risk seeking	78[a]	10	20	87[a]
Risk neutral	12	2	0	7
Risk averse	10	88[a]	80[a]	6

[a]Values that correspond to the fourfold pattern.
Note: The percentage of risk-seeking choices is given for low ($p \leq .1$) and high ($p \geq .5$) probabilities of gain and loss for each subject (risk-neutral choices were excluded). The overall percentage of risk-seeking, risk-neutral, and risk-averse choices for each type of prospect appear at the bottom of the table.

Jaffray, and Said, 1987), including a study of experienced oil executives involving significant, albeit hypothetical, gains and losses (Wehrung, 1989). It should be noted that prospect theory implies the pattern demonstrated in table 4 within the data of individual subjects, but it does not imply high correlations across subjects because the values of gains and of losses can vary independently. The failure to appreciate this point and the limited reliability of individual responses has led some previous authors (e.g., Hershey and Schoemaker, 1980) to underestimate the robustness of the fourfold pattern.

Table 5. Average correlations between certainty equivalents in four types of prospects

	L⁺	H⁺	L⁻	H⁻
L⁺	.41	.17	−.23	.05
H⁺		.39	.05	−.18
L⁻			.40	.06
H⁻				.44

Note: Low probability of gain = L⁺; high probability of gain = H⁺; low probability of loss = L⁻; high probability of loss = H⁻.

2.3. Scaling

Having established the fourfold pattern in ordinal and correlational analyses, we now turn to a quantitative description of the data. For each prospect of the form $(x, p; 0, 1 - p)$, let c/x be the ratio of the certainty equivalent of the prospect to the nonzero outcome x. Figures 1 and 2 plot the median value of c/x as a function of p, for positive and for negative prospects, respectively. We denote c/x by a circle if $|x| < 200$, and by a triangle if $|x| \geq 200$. The only exceptions are the two extreme probabilities (.01 and .99) where a circle is used for $|x| = 200$. To interpret figures 1 and 2, note that if subjects are risk neutral, the points will lie on the diagonal; if subjects are risk averse, all points will lie below the diagonal in figure 1 and above the diagonal in figure 2. Finally, the triangles and the circles will lie on top of each other if preferences are homogeneous, so that multiplying the outcomes of a prospect f by a constant $k > 0$ multiplies its cash equivalent $c(kf)$ by the same constant, that is, $c(kf) = kc(f)$. In expected utility theory, preference homogeneity gives rise to constant relative risk aversion. Under the present theory, assuming $X = \text{Re}$, preference homogeneity is both necessary and sufficient to represent v as a two-part power function of the form

$$v(x) = \begin{cases} x^\alpha & \text{if } x \geq 0 \\ -\lambda(-x)^\beta & \text{if } x < 0. \end{cases} \tag{5}$$

Figures 1 and 2 exhibit the characteristic pattern of risk aversion and risk seeking observed in table 4. They also indicate that preference homogeneity holds as a good approximation. The slight departures from homogeneity in figure 1 suggest that the cash equivalents of positive prospects increase more slowly than the stakes (triangles tend to lie below the circles), but no such tendency is evident in figure 2. Overall, it appears that the present data can be approximated by a two-part power function. The smooth curves in figures 1 and 2 can be interpreted as weighting functions, assuming a linear value function. They were fitted using the following functional form:

$$w^+(p) = \frac{p^\gamma}{(p^\gamma + (1-p)^\gamma)^{1/\gamma}}, \quad w^-(p) = \frac{p^\delta}{(p^\delta + (1-p)^\delta)^{1/\delta}}. \tag{6}$$

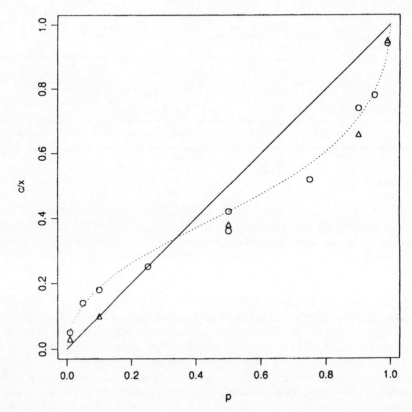

Figure 1. Median c/x for all positive prospects of the form $(x, p; 0, 1 - p)$. Triangles and circles, respectively, correspond to values of x that lie above or below 200.

This form has several useful features: it has only one parameter; it encompasses weighting functions with both concave and convex regions; it does not require $w(.5) = .5$; and most important, it provides a reasonably good approximation to both the aggregate and the individual data for probabilities in the range between .05 and .95.

Further information about the properties of the value function can be derived from the data presented in table 6. The adjustments of mixed prospects to acceptability (problems 1–4) indicate that, for even chances to win and lose, a prospect will only be acceptable if the gain is at least twice as large as the loss. This observation is compatible with a value function that changes slope abruptly at zero, with a loss-aversion coefficient of about 2 (Tversky and Kahneman, 1991). The median matches in problems 5 and 6 are also consistent with this estimate: when the possible loss is increased by k the compensating gain must be increased by about $2k$. Problems 7 and 8 are obtained from problems 5 and 6, respectively, by positive translations that turn mixed prospects into strictly positive ones. In contrast to the large values of θ observed in problems 1–6, the responses in problems 7 and 8 indicate that the curvature of the value function for gains is slight. A

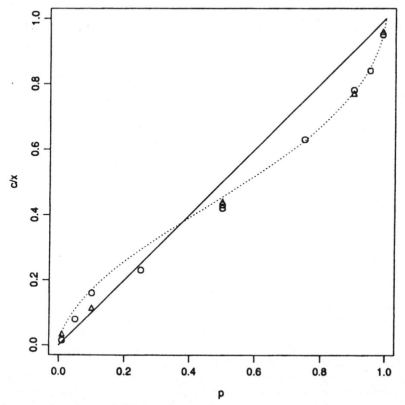

Figure 2. Median c/x for all negative prospects of the form $(x, p; 0, 1 - p)$. Triangles and circles, respectively, correspond to values of x that lie below or above − 200.

decrease in the smallest gain of a strictly positive prospect is fully compensated by a slightly larger increase in the largest gain. The standard rank-dependent model, which lacks the notion of a reference point, cannot account for the dramatic effects of small translations of prospects illustrated in table 6.

The estimation of a complex choice model, such as cumulative prospect theory, is problematic. If the functions associated with the theory are not constrained, the number of estimated parameters for each subject is too large. To reduce this number, it is common to assume a parametric form (e.g., a power utility function), but this approach confounds the general test of the theory with that of the specific parametric form. For this reason, we focused here on the qualitative properties of the data rather than on parameter estimates and measures of fit. However, in order to obtain a parsimonious description of the present data, we used a nonlinear regression procedure to estimate the parameters of equations (5) and (6), separately for each subject. The median exponent of the value function was 0.88 for both gains and losses, in accord with diminishing sensitivity. The median λ was 2.25, indicating pronounced loss aversion, and the median

Table 6. A test of loss aversion

Problem	a	b	c	x	θ
1	0	0	−25	61	2.44
2	0	0	−50	101	2.02
3	0	0	−100	202	2.02
4	0	0	−150	280	1.87
5	−20	50	−50	112	2.07
6	−50	150	−125	301	2.01
7	50	120	20	149	0.97
8	100	300	25	401	1.35

Note: In each problem, subjects determined the value of x that makes the prospect (a, ½; b, ½) as attractive as (c, ½; x, ½). The median values of x are presented for all problems along with the fixed values a,b,c. The statistic $\theta = (x - b)/(c - a)$ is the ratio of the "slopes" at a higher and a lower region of the value function.

values of γ and δ, respectively, were 0.61 and 0.69, in agreement with equations (3) and (4) above.[4] The parameters estimated from the median data were essentially the same. Figure 3 plots w^+ and w^- using the median estimates of γ and δ.

Figure 3 shows that, for both positive and negative prospects, people overweight low probabilities and underweight moderate and high probabilities. As a consequence, people are relatively insensitive to probability difference in the middle of the range. Figure 3 also shows that the weighting functions for gains and for losses are quite close, although the former is slightly more curved than the latter (i.e., $\gamma < \delta$). Accordingly, risk aversion for gains is more pronounced than risk seeking for losses, for moderate and high probabilities (see table 3). It is noteworthy that the condition $w^+(p) = w^-(p)$, assumed in the original version of prospect theory, accounts for the present data better than the assumption $w^+(p) = 1 - w^-(1 - p)$, implied by the standard rank-dependent or cumulative functional. For example, our estimates of w^+ and w^- show that all 25 subjects satisfied the conditions $w^+(.5) < .5$ and $w^-(.5) < .5$, implied by the former model, and no one satisfied the condition $w^+(.5) < .5$ iff $w^-(.5) > .5$, implied by the latter model.

Much research on choice between risky prospects has utilized the triangle diagram (Marschak, 1950; Machina, 1987) that represents the set of all prospects of the form (x_1, p_1;x_2,p_2;x_3,p_3), with fixed outcomes $x_1 < x_2 < x_3$. Each point in the triangle represents a prospect that yields the lowest outcome (x_1) with probability p_1, the highest outcome (x_3) with probability p_3, and the intermediate outcome (x_2) with probability $p_2 = 1 - p_1 - p_3$. An indifference curve is a set of prospects (i.e., points) that the decision maker finds equally attractive. Alternative choice theories are characterized by the shapes of their indifference curves. In particular, the indifference curves of expected utility theory are parallel straight lines. Figures 4a and 4b illustrate the indifference curves of cumulative prospect theory for nonnegative and nonpositive prospects, respectively. The shapes of the curves are determined by the weighting functions of figure 3; the values of the outcomes (x_1,x_2,x_3) merely control the slope.

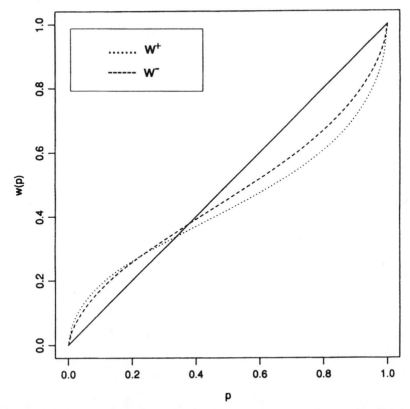

Figure 3. Weighting functions for gains (w^+) and for losses (w^-) based on median estimates of γ and δ in equation (12).

Figures 4a and 4b are in general agreement with the main empirical generalizations that have emerged from the studies of the triangle diagram; see Camerer (1992), and Camerer and Ho (1991) for reviews. First, departures from linearity, which violate expected utility theory, are most pronounced near the edges of the triangle. Second, the indifference curves exhibit both fanning in and fanning out. Third, the curves are concave in the upper part of the triangle and convex in the lower right. Finally, the indifference curves for nonpositive prospects resemble the curves for nonnegative prospects reflected around the 45° line, which represents risk neutrality. For example, a sure gain of $100 is equally as attractive as a 71% chance to win $200 or nothing (see figure 4a), and a sure loss of $100 is equally as aversive as a 64% chance to lose $200 or nothing (see figure 4b). The approximate reflection of the curves is of special interest because it distinguishes the present theory from the standard rank-dependent model in which the two sets of curves are essentially the same.

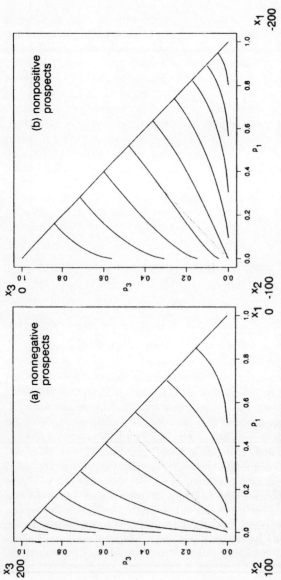

Figure 4. Indifference curves of cumulative prospect theory (a) for nonnegative prospects ($x_1 = 0, x_2 = 100, x_3 = 200$), and (b) for nonpositive prospects ($x_1 = -200, x_2 = -100, x_3 = 0$). The curves are based on the respective weighting functions of figure 3. ($\gamma = .61$, $\delta = .69$) and on the median estimates of the exponents of the value function ($\alpha = \beta = .88$). The broken line through the origin represents the prospects whose expected value is x_2.

2.4. Incentives

We conclude this section with a brief discussion of the role of monetary incentives. In the present study we did not pay subjects on the basis of their choices because in our experience with choice between prospects of the type used in the present study, we did not find much difference between subjects who were paid a flat fee and subjects whose payoffs were contingent on their decisions. The same conclusion was obtained by Camerer (1989), who investigated the effects of incentives using several hundred subjects. He found that subjects who actually played the gamble gave essentially the same responses as subjects who did not play; he also found no differences in reliability and roughly the same decision time. Although some studies found differences between paid and unpaid subjects in choice between simple prospects, these differences were not large enough to change any significant qualitative conclusions. Indeed, all major violations of expected utility theory (e.g. the common consequence effect, the common ratio effect, source dependence, loss aversion, and preference reversals) were obtained both with and without monetary incentives.

As noted by several authors, however, the financial incentives provided in choice experiments are generally small relative to people's incomes. What happens when the stakes correspond to three- or four-digit rather than one- or two-digit figures? To answer this question, Kachelmeier and Shehata (1991) conducted a series of experiments using Masters students at Beijing University, most of whom had taken at least one course in economics or business. Due to the economic conditions in China, the investigators were able to offer subjects very large rewards. In the high payoff condition, subjects earned about three times their normal monthly income in the course of one experimental session! On each trial, subjects were presented with a simple bet that offered a specified probability to win a given prize, and nothing otherwise. Subjects were instructed to state their cash equivalent for each bet. An incentive compatible procedure (the BDM scheme) was used to determine, on each trial, whether the subject would play the bet or receive the "official" selling price. If departures from the standard theory are due to the mental cost associated with decision making and the absence of proper incentives, as suggested by Smith and Walker (1992), then the highly paid Chinese subjects should not exhibit the characteristic nonlinearity observed in hypothetical choices, or in choices with small payoffs.

However, the main finding of Kachelmeier and Shehata (1991) is massive risk seeking for small probabilities. Risk seeking was slightly more pronounced for lower payoffs, but even in the highest payoff condition, the cash equivalent for a 5% bet (their lowest probability level) was, on average, three times larger than its expected value. Note that in the present study the median cash equivalent of a 5% chance to win $100 (see table 3) was $14, almost three times the expected value of the bet. In general, the cash equivalents obtained by Kachelmeier and Shehata were higher than those observed in the present study. This is consistent with the finding that minimal selling prices are generally higher than certainty equivalents derived from choice (see, e.g., Tversky, Slovic, and Kahneman, 1990). As a consequence, they found little risk aversion for moderate and high probability of winning. This was true for the Chinese subjects, at both high and low payoffs, as well as for Canadian subjects, who either played for low stakes or did not receive any payoff. The most striking result in all groups was the marked overweighting of small probabilities, in accord with the present analysis.

Evidently, high incentives do not always dominate noneconomic considerations, and the observed departures from expected utility theory cannot be rationalized in terms of the cost of thinking. We agree with Smith and Walker (1992) that monetary incentives could improve performance under certain conditions by eliminating careless errors. However, we maintain that monetary incentives are neither necessary nor sufficient to ensure subjects' cooperativeness, thoughtfulness, or truthfulness. The similarity between the results obtained with and without monetary incentives in choice between simple prospects provides no special reason for skepticism about experiments without contingent payment.

3. Discussion

Theories of choice under uncertainty commonly specify 1) the objects of choice, 2) a valuation rule, and 3) the characteristics of the functions that map uncertain events and possible outcomes into their subjective counterparts. In standard applications of expected utility theory, the objects of choice are probability distributions over wealth, the valuation rule is expected utility, and utility is a concave function of wealth. The empirical evidence reported here and elsewhere requires major revisions of all three elements. We have proposed an alternative descriptive theory in which 1) the objects of choice are prospects framed in terms of gains and losses, 2) the valuation rule is a two-part cumulative functional, and 3) the value function is S-shaped and the weighting functions are inverse S-shaped. The experimental findings confirmed the qualitative properties of these scales, which can be approximated by a (two-part) power value function and by identical weighting functions for gains and losses.

The curvature of the weighting function explains the characteristic reflection pattern of attitudes to risky prospects. Overweighting of small probabilities contributes to the popularity of both lotteries and insurance. Underweighting of high probabilities contributes both to the prevalence of risk aversion in choices between probable gains and sure things, and to the prevalence of risk seeking in choices between probable and sure losses. Risk aversion for gains and risk seeking for losses are further enhanced by the curvature of the value function in the two domains. The pronounced asymmetry of the value function, which we have labeled loss aversion, explains the extreme reluctance to accept mixed prospects. The shape of the weighting function explains the certainty effect and violations of quasi-convexity. It also explains why these phenomena are most readily observed at the two ends of the probability scale, where the curvature of the weighting function is most pronounced (Camerer, 1992).

The new demonstrations of the common consequence effect, described in tables 1 and 2, show that choice under uncertainty exhibits some of the main characteristics observed in choice under risk. On the other hand, there are indications that the decision weights associated with uncertain and with risky prospects differ in important ways. First, there is abundant evidence that subjective judgments of probability do not conform to the rules of probability theory (Kahneman, Slovic and Tversky, 1982). Second, Ellsberg's example and more recent studies of choice under uncertainty indicate that people prefer some sources of uncertainty over others. For example, Heath and Tversky (1991) found that individuals consistently preferred bets on uncertain events in their area of expertise over matched bets on chance devices, although the former are ambiguous and the latter are not. The presence of systematic preferences for some sources of uncertainty calls for different weighting functions for different domains, and suggests that some of these functions lie entirely above others. The investigation of decision weights for uncertain events emerges as a promising domain for future research.

The present theory retains the major features of the original version of prospect theory and introduces a (two-part) cumulative functional, which provides a convenient mathematical representation of decision weights. It also relaxes some descriptively inappropriate constraints of expected utility theory. Despite its greater generality, the cumulative functional is unlikely to be accurate in detail. We suspect that decision weights may be sensitive to the formulation of the prospects, as well as to the number, the spacing and the level of outcomes. In particular, there is some evidence to suggest that the curvature of the weighting function is more pronounced when the outcomes are widely spaced (Camerer, 1992). The present theory can be generalized to accommodate such effects, but it is questionable whether the gain in descriptive validity, achieved by giving up the separability of values and weights, would justify the loss of predictive power and the cost of increased complexity.

Theories of choice are at best approximate and incomplete. One reason for this pessimistic assessment is that choice is a constructive and contingent process. When faced with a complex problem, people employ a variety of heuristic procedures in order to simplify the representation and the evaluation of prospects. These procedures include computational shortcuts and editing operations, such as eliminating common components and discarding nonessential differences (Tversky, 1969). The heuristics of choice do not readily lend themselves to formal analysis because their application depends on the formulation of the problem, the method of elicitation, and the context of choice.

Prospect theory departs from the tradition that assumes the rationality of economic agents; it is proposed as a descriptive, not a normative, theory. The idealized assumption of rationality in economic theory is commonly justified on two grounds: the conviction that only rational behavior can survive in a competitive environment, and the fear that any treatment that abandons rationality will be chaotic and intractable. Both arguments are questionable. First, the evidence indicates that people can spend a lifetime in a competitive environment without acquiring a general ability to avoid framing effects or to apply linear decision weights. Second, and perhaps more important, the evidence indicates that human choices are orderly, although not always rational in the traditional sense of this word.

Appendix: Axiomatic Analysis

Let $F = \{f : S \to X\}$ be the set of all prospects under study, and let F^+ and F^- denote the positive and the negative prospects, respectively. Let $\geq$ be a binary preference relation on F, and let $\approx$ and $>$ denote its symmetric and asymmetric parts, respectively. We assume that $\geq$ is complete, transitive, and strictly monotonic, that is, if $f \neq g$ and $f(s) \geq g(s)$ for all $s \in S$, then $f > g$.

For any $f, g \in F$ and $A \subset S$, define $h = fAg$ by: $h(s) = f(s)$ if $s \in A$, and $h(s) = g(s)$ if $s \in S - A$. Thus, fAg coincides with f on A and with g on $S - A$. A preference relation $\geq$ on F satisfies *independence* if for all $f, g, f', g' \in F$ and $A \subset S, fAg \geq fAg'$ iff $f'Ag \geq f'Ag'$. This axiom, also called the sure thing principle (Savage, 1954), is one of the basic qualitative properties underlying expected utility theory, and it is violated by Allais's common consequence effect. Indeed, the attempt to accommodate Allais's example has motivated the development of numerous models, including cumulative utility theory. The key concept in the axiomatic analysis of that theory is the relation of comonotonicity, due to Schmeidler (1989). A pair of prospects $f, g \in F$ are *comonotonic* if there are no $s, t \in S$ such that $f(s) > f(t)$ and $g(t) > g(s)$. Note that a constant prospect that yields the same outcome in every state is comonotonic with all prospects. Obviously, comonotonicity is symmetric but not transitive.

Cumulative utility theory does not satisfy independence in general, but it implies independence whenever the prospects fAg, fAg', $f'Ag$, and $f'Ag'$ above are pairwise comonotonic. This property is called *comonotonic independence*.[5] It also holds in cumulative prospect theory, and it plays an important role in the characterization of this theory, as will be shown below. Cumulative prospect theory satisfies an additional property, called *double matching*: for all $f, g \in F$, if $f^+ \approx g^+$ and $f^- \approx g^-$, then $f \approx g$.

To characterize the present theory, we assume the following structural conditions: S is finite and includes at least three states; $X = \text{Re}$; and the preference order is continuous in the product topology on Re^k, that is, $\{f \in F : f \geq g\}$ and $\{f \in F : g \geq f\}$ are closed for any $g \in F$. The latter assumptions can be replaced by restricted solvability and a comonotonic Archimedean axiom (Wakker, 1991).

Theorem 1. Suppose $(F^+, \geq)$ and $(F^-, \geq)$ can each be represented by a cumulative functional. Then $(F, \geq)$ satisfies cumulative prospect theory iff it satisfies double matching and comonotonic independence.

The proof of the theorem is given at the end of the appendix. It is based on a theorem of Wakker (1992) regarding the additive representation of lower-diagonal structures. Theorem 1 provides a generic procedure for characterizing cumulative prospect theory. Take any axiom system that is sufficient to establish an essentially unique cumulative (i.e., rank-dependent) representation. Apply it separately to the preferences between positive prospects and to the preferences between negative prospects, and construct the value function and the decision weights separately for F^+ and for F^-. Theorem 1 shows that comonotonic independence and double matching ensure that, under the proper rescaling, the sum $V(f^+) + V(f^-)$ preserves the preference order between mixed prospects. In order to distinguish more sharply between the conditions that give rise to a one-part or a two-part representation, we need to focus on a particular axiomatization of the Choquet functional. We chose Wakker's (1989a, 1989b) because of its generality and compactness.

For $x \in X, f \in F$, and $r \in S$, let $x\{r\}f$ be the prospect that yields x in state r and coincides with f in all other states. Following Wakker (1989a), we say that a preference relation satisfies *tradeoff consistency*[6] (TC) if for all $x, x', y, y' \in X, f, f', g, g' \in F$, and $s, t \in S$.

$$x\{s\}f \preceq y\{s\}g, x'\{s\}f \succeq y'\{s\}g \text{ and } x\{t\}f' \succeq y\{t\}g' \text{ imply } x'\{t\}f' \succeq y'\{t\}g'.$$

To appreciate the import of this condition, suppose its premises hold but the conclusion is reversed, that is, $y'\{t\}g' > x'\{t\}f'$. It is easy to verify that under expected utility theory, the first two inequalities, involving $\{s\}$, imply $u(y) - u(y') \geq u(x) - u(x')$, whereas the other two inequalities, involving $\{t\}$, imply the opposite conclusion. Tradeoff consistency, therefore, is needed to ensure that "utility intervals" can be consistently ordered. Essentially the same condition was used by Tversky, Sattath, and Slovic (1988) in the analysis of preference reversal, and by Tversky and Kahneman (1991) in the characterization of constant loss aversion.

A preference relation satisfies *comonotonic tradeoff consistency* (CTC) if TC holds whenever the prospects $x\{s\}f, y\{s\}g, x'\{s\}f$, and $y'\{s\}g$ are pairwise comonotonic, as are the prospects $x\{t\}f', y\{t\}g', x'\{t\}f'$, and $y'\{t\}g'$ (Wakker, 1989a). Finally, a preference relation satisfies *sign-comonotonic tradeoff consistency* (SCTC) if CTC holds whenever the consequences x, x', y, y' are either all nonnegative or all nonpositive. Clearly, TC is stronger than CTC, which is stronger than SCTC. Indeed, it is not difficult to show that 1) expected utility theory implies TC, 2) cumulative utility theory implies CTC but not TC, and 3) cumulative prospect theory implies SCTC but not CTC. The following theorem shows that, given our other assumptions, these properties are not only necessary but also sufficient to characterize the respective theories.

Theorem 2. Assume the structural conditions described above.

    a. (Wakker, 1989a) Expected utility theory holds iff $\succeq$ satisfies TC.
    b. (Wakker, 1989b) Cumulative utility theory holds iff $\succeq$ satisfies CTC.
    c. Cumulative prospect theory holds iff $\succeq$ satisfies double matching and SCTC.

A proof of part c of the theorem is given at the end of this section. It shows that, in the presence of our structural assumptions and double matching, the restriction of tradeoff consistency to sign-comonotonic prospects yields a representation with a reference-dependent value function and different decision weights for gains and for losses.

Proof of theorem 1. The necessity of comonotonic independence and double matching is straightforward. To establish sufficiency, recall that, by assumption, there exist functions π^+, π^-, v^+, v^-, such that $V^+ = \Sigma \pi^+ v^+$ and $V^- = \Sigma \pi^- v^-$ preserve $\succeq$ on F^+ and on F^-, respectively. Furthermore, by the structural assumptions, π^+ and π^- are unique, whereas v^+ and v^- are continuous ratio scales. Hence, we can set $v^+(1) = 1$ and $v^-(-1) = 0 < 0$, independently of each other.

Let Q be the set of prospects such that for any $q \in Q, q(s) \neq q(t)$ for any distinct $s, t \in S$. Let F_g denote the set of all prospects in F that are comonotonic with G. By comonotonic independence and our structural conditions, it follows readily from a theorem of Wakker

(1992) on additive representations for lower-triangular subsets of Re^k that, given any $q \ \varepsilon$ Q, there exist intervals scales $\{U_{qi}\}$, with a common unit, such that $U_q = \sum_i U_{qi}$ preserves $\geq$ on F_q. With no loss of generality we can set $U_{qi}(0) = 0$ for all i and $U_q(1) = 1$. Since V^+ and V^- above are additive representations of $\geq$ on F_q^+ and F_q^-, respectively, it follows by uniqueness that there exist $a_q, b_q > 0$ such that for all i, U_{qi} equals $a_q \pi_i^+ v^+$ on Re^+, and U_{qi} equals $b_q \pi_i^- v^-$ on Re^-.

So far the representations were required to preserve the order only within each F_q. Thus, we can choose scales so that $b_q = 1$ for all q. To relate the different representations, select a prospect $h \neq q$. Since V^+ should preserve the order on F^+, and U_q should preserve the order within each F_q, we can multiply V^+ by a_h, and replace each a_q by a_q/a_h. In other words, we may set $a_h = 1$. For any $q \ \varepsilon \ Q$, select $f \ \varepsilon \ F_q, g \ \varepsilon \ F_h$ such that $f^+ \approx g^+ > 0, f^- \approx g^- > 0$, and $g \approx 0$. By double matching, then, $f \approx g \approx 0$. Thus, $a_q V^+(f^+) + V^-(f^-) = 0$, since this form preserves the order on F_q. But $V^+(f^+) = V^+(g^+)$ and $V^-(f^-) = V^-(g^-)$, so $V^+(g^+) + V^-(g^-) = 0$ implies $V^+(f^+) + V^-(f^-) = 0$. Hence, $a_q = 1$, and $V(f) = V^+(f^+) + V^-(f^-)$ preserves the order within each F_q.

To show that V preserves the order on the entire set, consider any $f, g \ \varepsilon \ F$ and suppose $f \geq g$. By transitivity, $c(f) \geq c(g)$ where $c(f)$ is the certainty equivalent of f. Because $c(f)$ and $c(g)$ are comonotonic, $V(f) = V(c(f)) \geq V(c(g)) = V(g)$. Analogously, $f > g$ implies $V(f) > V(g)$, which complete the proof of theorem 1.

Proof of theorem 2 (part c). To establish the necessity of SCTC, apply cumulative prospect theory to the hypotheses of SCTC to obtain the following inequalities:

$$V(x\{s\}f) = \pi_s v(x) + \sum_{r \varepsilon S - s} \pi_r v(f(r))$$

$$\leq \pi_s' v(y) + \sum_{r \varepsilon S - s} \pi_r' v(g(r)) = V(y\{s\}g)$$

$$V(x'\{s\}f) = \pi_s v(x') + \sum_{r \varepsilon S - s} \pi_r v(f(r))$$

$$\geq \pi_s' v(y') + \sum_{r \varepsilon S - s} \pi_r' v(g(r)) = V(y'\{s\}g).$$

The decision weights above are derived, assuming SCTC, in accord with equations (1) and (2). We use primes to distinguish the decision weights associated with g from those associated with f. However, all the above prospects belong to the same comonotonic set. Hence, two outcomes that have the same sign and are associated with the same state have the same decision weight. In particular, the weights associated with $x\{s\}f$ and $x'\{s\}f$ are identical, as are the weights associated with $y\{s\}g$ and with $y'\{s\}g$. These assumptions are implicit in the present notation. It follows that

$$\pi_s v(x) - \pi_s' v(y) \leq \pi_s v(x') - \pi_s' v(y').$$

Because x, y, x', y' have the same sign, all the decision weights associated with state s are identical, that is, $\pi_s = \pi_s'$. Cancelling this common factor and rearranging terms yields $v(y) - v(y') \geq v(x) - v(x')$.

Suppose SCTC is not valid, that is, $x\{t\}f \geq y\{t\}g'$ but $x'\{t\}f' < y'\{t\}g'$. Applying cumulative prospect theory, we obtain

$$V(x\{t\}f') = \pi_t v(x) + \sum_{r \in S-t} \pi_r v(f'(r))$$

$$\geq \pi_t v(y) + \sum_{r \in S-t} \pi_r v(g'(r)) = V(y\{t\}g')$$

$$V(x'\{t\}f') = \pi_t v(x') + \sum_{r \in S-t} \pi_r v(f'(r))$$

$$< \pi_t v(y') + \sum_{r \in S-t} \pi_r v(g'(r)) = V(y'\{t\}g').$$

Adding these inequalities yields $v(x) - v(x') > v(y) - v(y')$ contrary to the previous conclusion, which establishes the necessity of SCTC. The necessity of double matching is immediate.

To prove sufficiency, note that SCTC implies comonotonic independence. Letting $x = y$, $x' = y'$, and $f = g$ in TC yields $x\{t\}f' \geq x\{t\}g'$ implies $x'\{t\}f' \geq x'\{t\}g'$, provided all the above prospects are pairwise comonotonic. This condition readily entails comonotonic independence (see Wakker, 1989b).

To complete the proof, note that SCTC coincides with CTC on $(F^+, \geq)$ and on $(F^-, \geq)$. By part b of this theorem, the cumulative functional holds, separately, in the nonnegative and in the nonpositive domains. Hence, by double matching and comonotonic independence, cumulative prospect theory follows from theorem 1.

Notes

1. In keeping with the spirit of prospect theory, we use the decumulative form for gains and the cumulative form for losses. This notation is vindicated by the experimental findings described in section 2.
2. This model appears under different names. We use *cumulative utility theory* to describe the application of a Choquet integral to a standard utility function, and *cumulative prospect theory* to describe the application of two separate Choquet integrals to the value of gains and losses.
3. An IBM disk containing the exact instructions, the format, and the complete experimental procedure can be obtained from the authors.
4. Camerer and Ho (1991) applied equation (6) to several studies of risky choice and estimated γ from aggregate choice probabilities using a logistic distribution function. Their mean estimate (.56) was quite close to ours.
5. Wakker (1989b) called this axiom *comonotonic coordinate independence*. Schmeidler (1989) used *comonotonic independence* for the mixture space version of this axiom: $f \geq g$ iff $\alpha f + (1 - \alpha)h \geq \alpha g + (1 - \alpha)h$.
6. Wakker (1989a, 1989b) called this property *cardinal coordinate independence*. He also introduced an equivalent condition, called the absence of *contradictory tradeoffs*.

References

Allais, Maurice. (1953). "Le comportement de l'homme rationel devant le risque, critique des postulates et axiomes de l'ecole americaine," *Econometrica* 21, 503–546.

Arrow, Kenneth J. (1982). "Risk Perception in Psychology and Economics," *Economic Inquiry* 20, 1–9.

Camerer, Colin F. (1989). "An Experimental Test of Several Generalized Utility Theories," *Journal of Risk and Uncertainty* 2, 61-104.

Camerer, Colin F. (1992). "Recent Tests of Generalizations of Expected Utility Theory." In W. Edwards (ed.), *Utility: Theories, Measurement and Applications*, Boston, MA: Kluwer Academic Publishers.

Camerer, Colin F. and Teck-Hua Ho. (1991). "Nonlinear Weighting of Probabilities and Violations of the Betweenness Axiom." Unpublished manuscript, The Wharton School, University of Pennsylvania.

Chew, Soo-Hong. (1989). "An Axiomatic Generalization of the Quasilinear Mean and the Gini Mean with Application to Decision Theory," Unpublished manuscript, Department of Economics, University of California at Irvine.

Choquet, Gustave. (1955). "Theory of Capacities," *Annales de L'Institut Fourier* 5, 131-295.

Cohen, Michele, Jean-Yves Jaffray, and Tanios Said. (1987). "Experimental Comparison of Individual Behavior Under Risk and Under Uncertainty for Gains and for Losses," *Organizational Behavior and Human Decision Processes* 39, 1-22.

Ellsberg, Daniel. (1961). "Risk, Ambiguity, and the Savage Axioms," *Quarterly Journal of Economics* 75, 643-669.

Fishburn, Peter C. (1988). *Nonlinear Preference and Utility Theory*. Baltimore, MD: The Johns Hopkins University Press.

Gilboa, Itzhak. (1987). "Expected Utility with Purely Subjective Non-additive Probabilities," *Journal of Mathematical Economics* 16, 65-88.

Heath, Chip and Amos Tversky. (1991). "Preference and Belief: Ambiguity and Competence in Choice Under Uncertainty," *Journal of Risk and Uncertainty* 4, 5-28.

Hershey, John C. and Paul J. H. Schoemaker. (1980). "Prospect Theory's Reflection Hypothesis: A Critical Examination," *Organizational Behavior and Human Performance* 25, 395-418.

Hogarth, Robin and Hillel Einhorn. (1990). "Venture Theory: A Model of Decision Weights," *Management Science* 36, 780-803.

Kachelmeier, Steven J. and Mohamed Shehata. (1991). "Examining Risk Preferences Under High Monetary Incentives: Experimental Evidence from The People's Republic of China," *American Economic Review*, forthcoming.

Kahneman, Daniel, Paul Slovic, and Amos Tversky (eds.). (1982). *Judgment Under Uncertainty: Heuristics and Biases*. New York: Cambridge University Press.

Kahneman, Daniel and Amos Tversky. (1979). "Prospect Theory: An Analysis of Decision Under Risk," *Econometrica* 47, 263-291.

Kahneman, Daniel and Amos Tversky. (1984). "Choices, Values and Frames," *American Psychologist* 39, 341-350.

Loomes, Graham and Robert Sugden. (1987). "Regret Theory: An Alternative Theory of Rational Choice Under Uncertainty," *The Economic Journal* 92, 805-824.

Loomes, Graham and Robert Sugden. (1987). "Some Implications of a More General Form of Regret Theory," *Journal of Economic Theory* 41, 270-287.

Luce, R. Duncan and Peter C. Fishburn. (1991). "Rank- and Sign-dependent Linear Utility Models for Finite First-order Gambles," *Journal of Risk and Uncertainty* 4, 29-59.

Machina, Mark J. (1987). "Choice Under Uncertainty: Problems Solved and Unsolved," *Economic Perspectives* 1(1), 121-154.

Marschak, Jacob. (1950). "Rational Behavior, Uncertain Prospects, and Measurable Utility," *Econometrica* 18, 111-114.

Nakamura, Yutaka. (1990). "Subjective Expected Utility with Non-additive Probabilities on Finite State Space," *Journal of Economic Theory* 51, 346-366.

Prelec, Drazen. (1989). "On the Shape of the Decision Weight Function." Unpublished manuscript, Harvard Graduate School of Business Administration.

Prelec, Drazen. (1990). "A 'Pseudo-endowment' Effect, and its Implications for Some Recent Non-expected Utility Models," *Journal of Risk and Uncertainty* 3, 247-259.

Quiggin, John. (1982). "A Theory of Anticipated Utility," *Journal of Economic Behavior and Organization* 3, 323-343.

Savage, Leonard J. (1954). *The Foundations of Statistics*. New York: Wiley.

Schmeidler, David. (1989). "Subjective Probability and Expected Utility without Additivity," *Econometrica* 57, 571–587.

Segal, Uzi. (1989). "Axiomatic Representation of Expected Utility with Rank-dependent Probabilities," *Annals of Operations Research* 19, 359–373.

Smith, Vernon L. and James M. Walker. (1992). "Monetary Rewards and Decision Cost in Experimental Economics." Unpublished manuscript, Economic Science Lab, University of Arizona.

Starmer, Chris and Robert Sugden. (1989). "Violations of the Independence Axiom in Common Ratio Problems: An Experimental Test of Some Competing Hypotheses," *Annals of Operations Research* 19, 79–102.

Tversky, Amos. (1969). "The Intransitivity of Preferences," *Psychology Review* 76, 31–48.

Tversky, Amos and Daniel Kahneman. (1986). "Rational Choice and the Framing of Decisions," *The Journal of Business* 59(4), part 2, S251–S278.

Tversky, Amos and Daniel Kahneman. (1991). "Loss Aversion in Riskless Choice: A Reference Dependent Model," *Quarterly Journal of Economics* 107(4), 1039–1061.

Tversky, Amos, Shmuel Sattath, and Paul Slovic. (1988). "Contingent Weighting in Judgment and Choice," *Psychological Review* 95(3), 371–384.

Tversky, Amos, Paul Slovic, and Daniel Kahneman. (1990). "The Causes of Preference Reversal," *The American Economic Review* 80(1), 204–217.

Viscusi, Kip W. (1989). "Prospective Reference Theory: Toward an Explanation of the Paradoxes," *Journal of Risk and Uncertainty* 2, 235–264.

Wakker, Peter P. (1989a). *Additive Representations of Preferences: A New Foundation in Decision Analysis.* Dordrecht, The Netherlands: Kluwer Academic Publishers.

Wakker, Peter P. (1989b). "Continuous Subjective Expected Utility with Nonadditive Probabilities," *Journal of Mathematical Economics* 18, 1–27.

Wakker, Peter P. (1990). "Separating Marginal Utility and Risk Aversion." Unpublished manuscript, University of Nijmegen, The Netherlands.

Wakker, Peter P. (1991). "Additive Representations of Preferences, a New Foundation of Decision Analysis; the Algebraic Approach." In J. D. Doignon and J. C. Falmagne (eds.), *Mathematical Psychology: Current Developments.* Berlin: Springer, pp. 71–87.

Wakker, Peter P. (1992). "Additive Representations on Rank-ordered Sets; Part II: The Topological Approach," *Journal of Mathematical Economics,* forthcoming.

Wakker, Peter P. and Amos Tversky. (1991). "An Axiomatization of Cumulative Prospect Theory." Unpublished manuscript, University of Nijmegen, the Netherlands.

Wehrung, Donald A. (1989). "Risk Taking over Gains and Losses: A Study of Oil Executives," *Annals of Operations Research* 19, 115–139.

Weymark, J. A. (1981). "Generalized Gini Inequality Indices," *Mathematical Social Sciences* 1, 409–430.

Yaari, Menahem E. (1987). "The Dual Theory of Choice Under Risk," *Econometrica* 55, 95–115.

[22]

Econometrica, Vol. 62, No. 6 (November, 1994), 1251–1289

THE PREDICTIVE UTILITY OF GENERALIZED EXPECTED UTILITY THEORIES

By David W. Harless and Colin F. Camerer[1]

Many alternative theories have been proposed to explain violations of expected utility (EU) theory observed in experiments. Several recent studies test some of these alternative theories against each other. Formal tests used to judge the theories usually count the number of responses consistent with the theory, ignoring systematic variation in responses that are inconsistent. We develop a maximum-likelihood estimation method which uses all the information in the data, creates test statistics that can be aggregated across studies, and enables one to judge the predictive utility—the fit and parsimony—of utility theories. Analyses of 23 data sets, using several thousand choices, suggest a menu of theories which sacrifice the least parsimony for the biggest improvement in fit. The menu is: mixed fanning, prospect theory, EU, and expected value. Which theories are best is highly sensitive to whether gambles in a pair have the same support (EU fits better) or not (EU fits poorly). Our method may have application to other domains in which various theories predict different subsets of choices (e.g., refinements of Nash equilibrium in noncooperative games).

KEYWORDS: Expected utility theory, non-expected utility theory, prospect theory, model selection, Allais paradox.

DISSATISFACTION WITH THE EMPIRICAL ACCURACY of expected utility (EU) theory has led many theorists to develop generalizations of EU. The development of alternatives to EU, in turn, has led to a vigorous new round of experiments testing the empirical validity of the new theories against each other and against EU (Battalio, Kagel, and Jiranyakul (1990), Camerer (1989, 1992), Chew and Waller (1986), Conlisk (1989), Harless (1992), Prelec (1990), Sopher and Gigliotti (1990), Starmer and Sugden (1989)). The experiments test robustness of previously observed EU violations (Allais (1953), Kahneman and Tversky (1979)) and test the accuracy of predictions in new domains.

The recent studies are informative and useful—for example, recent results have already guided development of some new theories[2]—but there is still substantial confusion about what the new studies say. For example, the Chew and Waller (1986) data have been cited as supporting weighted EU theory (by Chew and Waller), as supporting the "fanning out" hypothesis (by Machina (1987)), and as supporting a mixture of fanning out and "fanning in" (by Conlisk (1989)).

In this paper we show that confusion about the results of the new studies can be largely resolved by more powerful statistical tests. Our paper makes three contributions: We present new tests, which gain power by using all the information available in patterns of observed choices (most earlier tests threw away

---

[1] Thanks to John Conlisk, Dave Grether, Bill Neilson, Nat Wilcox, and a co-editor and two anonymous referees for helpful comments, to Drazen Prelec and John Kagel for supplying their data, and especially to Teck-Hua Ho for collaboration in the project's early stages. Camerer's work was supported by NSF Grant SES-90-23531 and by the Russell Sage Foundation, where he visited during the 1991–1992 academic year.
[2] See Neilson (1992a, 1992b), Chew, Epstein, and Segal (1991).

some important information); the test statistics we derive can be added across studies, enabling us to aggregate data (nearly 8,000 choices) and increasing power further; and we give a method for trading off fit and parsimony of various theories. Hence, our work explores the predictive utility—fit and parsimony—of various utility theories.

The result is a menu of theories. Researchers can pick a theory from the menu, depending on the price they are willing to pay (in poorer fit) for added parsimony. Aggregating across all studies, the menu is: mixed fanning, prospect theory, EU, and expected value (EV); but the results are sensitive to the domain of gambles.

The paper proceeds as follows. The next section illustrates our method, and predictions of several generalized EU theories, with one study. Section 2 reviews the results from several choice studies. Section 3 aggregates the results from 23 data sets and 2,000 choice patterns, and describes a method for trading off fit and parsimony. In Section 4 we draw conclusions.

1. ILLUSTRATION OF OUR MAXIMUM-LIKELIHOOD ANALYSIS

The study by Battalio, Kagel and Jiranyakul (1990), one of several we include in our analyses, will illustrate our method and the predictions of several generalized utility theories. In one part of their study, subjects chose one lottery (or expressed indifference) out of each of three pairs. Each pair consisted of one lottery, denoted S for "safer," and a mean-preserving spread of S, denoted R for "riskier." The pairs were:

Pair 1: $S1 = (-\$20, .6; -\$12, .4)$ $R1 = (-\$20, .84; \$0, .16)$

Pair 2: $S2 = (-\$12)$ $R2 = (-\$20, .6; \$0, .4)$

Pair 3: $S3 = (-\$12, .2; \$0, .8)$ $R3 = (-\$20, .12; \$0, .88)$

Figure 1 shows the three pairs in a unit triangle diagram (Marschak (1950), Machina (1982)). In the diagram, each lottery is plotted as a point along the

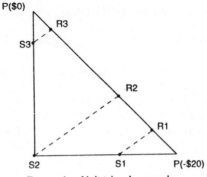

FIGURE 1.—Unit triangle example.

GENERALIZED EXPECTED UTILITY   1253

TABLE I

CONSISTENT PATTERNS FOR BATTALIO, KAGEL, AND JIRANYAKUL REAL LOSSES

Pattern 123	Observed Frequency	EU	Fan Out	Fan In	MF	RD-cave gIE	RD-cave fDE	RD-vex gDE	RD-vex fIE	PT
SSS	7	X	X	X	X	X	X	X	X	
SSR	1			X	X	X	X	X		
SRS	1							X	X	
SRR	1			X	X		X	X	X	
RSS	3		X		X	X	X		X	
RSR	0			X	X	X	X			
RRS	8		X		X	X		X	X	X
RRR	7	X	X	X	X	X	X	X	X	X

$p(-\$20)$ and $p(0)$ axes. Notice that the pairs are related in a particular geometric way: The lines connecting the lotteries in each pair are parallel. Furthermore, two of the pairs have a common ratio of outcome probabilities—for example, $p(-\$12)/p(-\$20)$ equals $1/.6 = 5/3$ in pair 2, and $.2/.12 = 5/3$ in pair 3. The two pairs form a "common ratio" problem. (In pair 1, the ratio of the differences in outcome probabilities between lotteries, $(.4-0)/(.84-.6)$, has the ratio $5/3$ too.)

Most choice theories do not predict precisely whether people will pick S or R in each pair. Instead, theories restrict patterns of choices across pairs. For example, a person who obeys EU judges gambles by the expectation of the utilities of their outcomes. Thus, a person who obeys EU and prefers $S2$ to $R2$ (denoted $S2 \succ R2$) reveals that $u(-\$12) > .6u(-\$20)$ (setting $u(\$0) = 0$ for simplicity). But $u(-\$12) > .6u(-\$20)$ implies $.2u(-\$12) > .12u(-\$20)$, which predicts $S3 \succ R3$. By a similar calculation, $S1 \succ R1$. EU therefore predicts that people who choose S in one pair will choose S in the other pairs too, so EU allows the pattern denoted SSS—the choice of $S1$, $S2$, and $S3$. Alternatively, an EU-maximizer with $R2 \succ S2$ must prefer $R1$ and $R3$ to $S1$ and $S3$, so EU allows the pattern RRR, but not the other six possible patterns.

The patterns allowed by each theory in the BKJ study are shown in Table I (marked by X's). We review the predictions of each theory briefly. Much more detail is available in Machina (1982, 1987), Fishburn (1988), and Camerer (1989, 1992).

EU: As described above, EU predicts patterns SSS or RRR in Table I. Graphically, EU requires the indifference curves that connect sets of equally-preferred gambles to be parallel straight lines. That implies preference for the S lottery in each pair, or the R lottery in each pair.

Fanning out: Machina (1982) proposed a generalization of EU in which Frechet differentiability of a preference functional guaranteed that similar lotteries could be approximately ranked by the EU of a "local" utility function. (In EU, the local utility functions are all the same.) He also suggested that many violations of EU could be explained by the hypothesis that as the lotteries being ranked become better (in the sense of stochastically-dominating improvements), local utility functions become more concave (reflecting greater local risk-aversion). Graphically, Machina's hypothesis implies that indifference curves "fan out:" curves become steeper as one moves in the direction of increasing preference, from the lower right hand corner to the upper left hand corner. Besides the EU-conforming patterns *SSS* and *RRR*, fanning out allows any patterns in which preferences switch from *R* to *S* from pairs 1 to 3, viz., patterns *RSS* and *RRS*.

Fanning in: The opposite of fanning out is "fanning in," the tendency of indifference curves to become flatter, not steeper, in the direction of increasing preference. There is little *a priori* evidence suggesting fanning in, but we consider it for completeness. Fanning in allows patterns *SSR* and *SRR* (along with the EU patterns).

Mixed fan (MF): There is some evidence that indifference curves fan out for less favorable lotteries (like pair 1) and fan in for more favorable ones (like pair 3), suggesting a hybrid "mixed fan" hypothesis (cf. Neilson (1992a)) in which the direction of fanning switches within a triangle diagram. The point at which fanning switches from out to in (moving to the northwest) might lie outside the space of choices, so both fanning out patterns and fanning in patterns are consistent with MF. Mixed fanning also allows a pattern that neither fanning out nor fanning in allows, viz., fanning out between pairs 1 and 2, and fanning in between pairs 2 and 3, the pattern *RSR*. The only pattern which is excluded is *SRS*.

EU with rank-dependent weights (RD): There are several generalizations of EU in which outcome utilities are weighted "rank-dependently" or "cumulatively" (Quiggin (1982), Yaari (1987), Chew, Karni, and Safra (1987), Green and Jullien (1988), Segal (1987, 1989), Tversky and Kahneman (1992)). In most of these theories, a decumulative distribution function (one minus the cumulative distribution function) is transformed by a continuous, monotonic function $g(p)$, with $g(0) = 0$ and $g(1) = 1$; outcomes are weighted by differences or differentials of the transformed decumulative. If $g(p)$ is *convex* then high-ranked outcomes are underweighted and unit triangle indifference curves are *concave* (denoted RD-cave); curves also fan out along the base of the triangle, and fan in along the left side. If $g(p)$ is *concave* then high-ranked outcomes are overweighted and indifference curves are *convex* (denoted RD-vex); curves fan in along the base of the triangle, and fan out along the left side. If $g(p) = p$ then each outcome is simply weighted by its probability, as in EU.

RD theories do not make precise predictions about choices in the BKJ study unless further restrictions are placed on the shape of $g(p)$. Segal (1987) showed that if $g(p)$ is convex (indifference curves are concave) and has increasing elasticity (i.e., $pg'(p)/g(p)$ is increasing in p) then indifference curves will exhibit a common ratio effect: fanning out in the southeast portion of the triangle (*SSx, RRx, RSx* allowed; *SRx* not allowed). We denote predictions when indifference curves are concave (and $g(p)$ is convex with *i*ncreasing *e*lasticity) as RD-cave *g*IE. The theory makes different predictions when indifference curves are convex and $g(p)$ is concave (denoted RD-vex) and when cumulative probabilities are weighted instead of decumulatives (denoted by labeling the weighting function f rather than g). The predictions of four variants of RD with elasticity conditions are shown in Table I. Quiggin's (1982) original form of rank-dependent expected utility, called "anticipated utility," presumed $f(.5) = .5$ with $f(p)$ concave below $.5(f(p) > p)$ and convex above $.5(f(p) < p)$ (see also Quiggin (1993)). This form excludes no patterns in 8 of the 23 studies we consider later, so we say nothing more about it except in footnote 23.

Prospect theory (PT): Kahneman and Tversky (1979) proposed a descriptive theory embodying several empirical departures from EU. We test an extremely simplified form of prospect theory which incorporates several of its key features: The value function, or utility function over riskless amounts, is assumed to have a reference point of \$0 (i.e., $v(\$0) = 0$) and to be strictly concave for gains and strictly convex for losses (exhibiting a "reflection effect"); probabilities are assumed to be transformed by a decision weight function $\pi(p)$;[3] and lotteries are ranked by the sum of their weighted outcome values.[4]

All the predictions we derive based on prospect theory require only reflection of the value function and certain general properties of decision weights as hypothesized in Kahneman and Tversky (1979). The properties of the probability transformation function $\pi(p)$ we use in making predictions are subcertainty $(\pi(p) + \pi(1 - p) < 1)$, subproportionality $(\pi(rp)/\pi(rq) > \pi(p)/\pi(q)$, for $p < q$ and $0 < r < 1)$, and convexity of π for probabilities above .01, which allows for overweighting small probabilities and underweighting larger probabilities (but we assume only that the crossover point occurs somewhere between .1 and .3). In the BKJ study prospect theory predicts $v(S2) = v(-12)$ and $v(R2) = \pi(.6)v(-20)$. Convexity of $v(x)$ for losses implies $v(-12) < .6v(-20)$; underweighting of high probabilities implies $\pi(.6) < .6$. Together they imply $v(-12) < \pi(.6)v(-20)$, predicting a preference for R2 over S2. Prospect theory also predicts a preference for R1 over S1, but makes no prediction about choices in pair 3.[5] Here, the theory as we have characterized it allows only the two patterns RRS and RRR, so it is just as parsimonious as EU.

Additional theories: There are many other choice theories besides those whose predictions are shown in Table I. We consider some and neglect others. The historical predecessor to EU, expected value maximization (EV), predicted that people would choose lotteries according to expected value. In some studies,

---

[3] Tversky and Kahneman (1992) show how to extend prospect theory in several ways, including cumulative weighting as in the rank-dependent theories.

[4] In addition, "irregular lotteries," which have only positive or only negative outcomes, are valued by segregating the certain outcome from the uncertain part.

[5] S1 chosen over R1 implies $(1 - \pi(.6))v(-12) + \pi(.6)v(-20) > \pi(.84)v(-20)$; the convexity of the value function implies $1 - \pi(.6) > (1/.6)(\pi(.84) - \pi(.6))$ which contradicts the assumption that π is convex. Prospect theory makes no prediction about choices in pair 3 because $S3 \gtrless R3$ as $\pi(.12) \gtrless .6\pi(.2)$. Convexity of the value function for losses means PT predicts preference for the riskier lottery when lotteries are mean-preserving risk spreads except when the decision weight function overweights small probabilities (such as the .12 probability of $-\$20$ in R3).

including the BKJ study illustrated by Table I, lotteries in a pair had the same expected value. Then we took EV to be identical to EU.[6]

If the local utility function in generalized utility is constant along an indifference curve, then "implicit EU" (IEU) results (Dekel (1986), Chew (1989)). IEU predicts linear indifference curves, thus satisfying the betweenness axiom, a weakened form of independence. (Betweenness requires that a reduced-form probability mixture of any two lotteries should not be worse or better than both; the mixture should lie between them in preference.) IEU is only tested in studies which ask subjects to choose between lotteries in two or more pairs which lie on the same line in the triangle diagram. In the BKJ study IEU allows any pattern (since no two pairs lie on the same line).

In "weighted utility" theory (WEU), a special case of IEU, lottery utilities are computed by multiplying an outcome's utility by its probability and by a normalized weighting function which depends on the outcome (Chew and MacCrimmon (1979), Chew (1983), Fishburn (1982, 1983)). In all the studies we consider, WEU is the same as combining either fanning out and fanning in (depending on the shape of the weighting function) with linearity of indifference curves; we denote these brands of WEU as WEU-out and WEU-in. In some studies, like BKJ, the predictions of WEU-out (WEU-in) are the same as those of fanning out (in).

Combining mixed fanning with linear indifference curves yields a hybrid we call "linear mixed fan" (LMF). This theory was suggested by Neilson (1992a). Gul's (1991) disappointment-based theory is slightly more restrictive but observationally equivalent to LMF in all the studies we review. (However, a special study could be designed to separate LMF and Gul's theory.)

Theories *not* included in the tables below include lottery-dependent utility (Becker and Sarin (1987)), ordinal utility (Green and Jullien (1988)), prospective reference theory[7] (Viscusi (1989)), combinations of rank-dependent and weighted utility (Chew and Epstein (1990)), and the cumulative extension of prospect theory proposed recently (Tversky and Kahneman (1992)). We address some of these theories in the footnotes and Section 3. Others may be easily tested using our method after the hard work of determining which choice patterns the theories allow is finished.

---

[6] Alternatively, when one gamble is a mean-preserving spread of another, one could interpret EV to imply that subjects are indifferent between the gambles in each pair. Under that interpretation, each pattern is equally likely (the EV maximizer chooses by flipping a fair coin). Tests of that restriction are reported in footnote 27. Another approach allows each indifferent pair to have a different choice proportion, then estimate the likelihood-maximizing proportions from the data. (The coin-flip approach restricts the proportions to be .5.) But this approach allows EV to fit too well: if the choice-proportion parameters are allowed to differ across pairs, EV, so interpreted, may "explain" fanning out or fanning in. We could allow other theories (which have EV as a special case) the same luxury of extra choice-proportion parameters, but then we quickly run out of degrees of freedom in many data sets.

[7] We have not included prospective reference theory in the main analysis because we only study experiments with three, four, and five pairwise choices (see footnote 21), and none of these experiments adequately tests the predictions of prospective reference theory. For tests of the specific predictions of prospective reference theory with two pairwise choices, see Harless (1993).

GENERALIZED EXPECTED UTILITY   1257

Graphical Comparison of Theories

A simple, appealing way to judge a theory is to calculate the fraction of observed patterns that are consistent with the theory. EU allows the patterns *SSS* and *RRR*. Table I shows that seven people picked *SSS* and seven picked *RRR*, so 14 of 28 (50%) chose as predicted by EU. The four patterns allowed by fanning out were picked by 25 of 28 subjects (89%).

An obvious drawback of this method is that theories which allow more patterns will always have a higher proportion of consistent choices. A simple test which puts theories on more equal footing compares the proportion of consistent choices with the proportion of patterns allowed (i.e., the proportion of choices that would be consistent if choices were actually made randomly). For example, EU patterns capture 50% of the choices, but allow just 2 of 8 possible patterns (25%). A *z* test measures the likelihood of such accurate prediction if

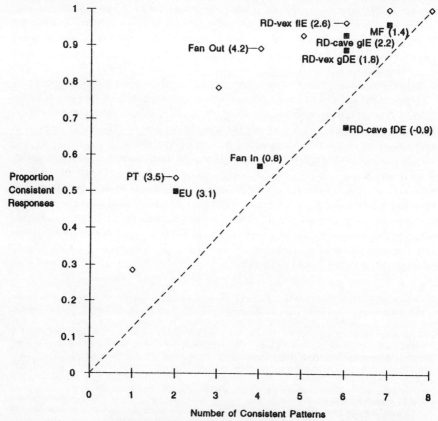

Z statistics (in parentheses) test each theory against the random choice null hypothesis.

FIGURE 2.—Battalio, Kagel, and Jinanyakul: Real losses, Series 1.

choices were made randomly (e.g., Chew and Waller (1986)). For EU, the z statistic is $(.50 - .25)/[(.25)(.75)/28)]^{1/2}$, or $z = 3.1$ ($p = .001$). For fanning out, which allows four of eight possible patterns (50%) and explains 89% of the choices, $z = 4.2$($p = 1.3E - 05$).

There are many plausible ways to compare the accuracy of theories (e.g., comparing their z statistics). We developed a graphical method of displaying accuracy which permits easy ranking of theories by several criteria. Figure 2 gives an example using the BKJ data.

Figure 2 shows the proportion of consistent responses (y axis) and the number of patterns allowed (x axis), for several theories. The open diamonds represent the "data frontier:" the highest possible consistent proportions for each number of consistent patterns. For example, the three most common patterns, RRS, RRR, and SSS were chosen by 29%, 25%, and 25% of the subjects, respectively. The best one-pattern theory would have only 29% consistent. The best two-pattern theory would have 54% consistent, and so on. (Note that the data frontier is always (weakly) concave.) The data frontier therefore shows the best a theory can possibly do. Points representing different theories must always lie below the data frontier or lie right on it (as prospect theory, fanning out, and RD-vex-f IE do, in Figure 2). The hatched "random choice line" represents the proportions consistent that would result if people chose randomly.

A look at Figure 2 suggests some visual ways to judge theories. Good theories should be close to the data frontier, and far from the random choice line. The z statistic (shown in parentheses in Figure 2) gives a formal measure of how far each point is from the random choice line; fanning out does best by that criterion ($z = 4.2$). The difference between the proportion consistent and the proportion of patterns allowed, a measure advocated by Selten (1991), is the vertical (or horizontal) distance from the random choice line; fanning out does best by that criterion also.[8] The ratio measure, the proportion of consistent choices *per pattern*, is measured by the slope of the line connecting each theory point to the origin; prospect theory is best by that measure (27% per pattern). An opposite measure is the proportion of *in*consistent choices per *in*consistent pattern (sometimes called the "outside ratio"), measured by the slope of the line connecting each theory point to the upper right corner. A good theory makes the outside ratio low; RD-vex-f IE is best by that measure.

The various criteria reward theories for different kinds of predictive accuracy. The ratio statistic (slope from origin) rewards more parsimonious theories which capture the most common pattern(s). The outside ratio (slope from upper right corner) rewards broader theories which exclude uncommon patterns.

---

[8] The z statistic and the difference measure are closely related because the z statistic is simply the difference measure divided by $(p(1-p)/n)^{1/2}$. Since the number of observed pattern choices n is the same for all the theories, compared to the difference measure the z statistic favors theories with low and high values of p (i.e., theories that predict very few or very many patterns).

Figure 2 shows that many of the generalizations of EU are surprisingly parsimonious and accurate. For example, in this study prospect theory predicts the same number of patterns as EU (two) but it explains more choices and beats EU by all the measures given above. Fanning out permits twice as many patterns as EU, but it accounts for nearly twice as many choices (and beats EU by the measures except ratio). The graph is useful for screening out dominated theories—those which allow the same number of patterns (or more) but have fewer consistent responses than other theories. Dominated theories lie to the lower right of theories which dominate them. In Figure 2, prospect theory dominates EU, fanning out dominates fanning in, RD-vex-g DE and RD-cave-f DE, and RD-vex-f IE dominates mixed fan and the other rank-dependent theories.

Note that we use the terms parsimonious in a very specific sense, to denote the number of patterns a theory allows. However, the number of patterns a theory allows does not necessarily correspond to the number of free parameters or free functions it uses. Theories which appear unparsimonious because they have many additional free parameters or free functions might, with minimal restrictions on those functions, predict relatively few patterns (prospect theory is an example). Contrarily, a theory which has only one free parameter more than EU may allow a wide range of patterns and hence be unparsimonious by our standard (Gul's (1991) one-parameter disappointment-based theory is an example).

Comparing Theories with Maximum-Likelihood Error Rate Analysis

The analyses expressed visually in Figure 2 have two severe shortcomings: First, there is no single compelling measure by which to compare theories. Second, all the criteria throw away information by collapsing the entire distribution of responses into a single number—the proportion of choices consistent with a theory.

Our test overcomes these problems. We characterize a theory as a restriction on the proportions of subjects that have true preferences corresponding to each of the eight patterns. For example, EU permits two types of subjects, a proportion p_1 of consistent risk-averters who prefer SSS, and a proportion $1 - p_1$ of consistent risk-preferrers who prefer RRR. In previous work (including the studies we reanalyze in this paper, some of which are our own), if a subject were to choose, say, RRS or SRR, the response was simply counted as inconsistent with EU. The premise of our test is that systematic variation in unpredicted patterns should count against a theory: if many people choose RRS and few choose SRR, a theory which predicts nobody will choose either should be penalized more heavily.

Penalizing theories for systematic variation in unpredicted patterns requires some allowance for error; otherwise, a single observation of an unpredicted pattern would immediately invalidate a theory. Therefore, we allow the possibility of erroneous deviations from underlying preferences so we can judge the *degree* of inconsistency of an observation.[9] For example, suppose EU is true—people prefer either *RRR* or *SSS*—but subjects make random errors which are independent and equally likely across the three choices. For those subjects with true preference pattern *RRR*, the patterns which occur because of one error (*SRR*, *RSR*, and *RRS*) should be equally likely, and should be more likely than the two-error patterns (*SSR*, *SRS*, and *RSS*). For those subjects with true preference pattern *SSS*, the patterns which occur because of one error (*RSS*, *SRS*, and *SSR*) should be equally likely and should be more likely than the two error patterns (*SRR*, *RSR*, and *RRS*). Thus, EU can be characterized as a restriction on allowed patterns (*SSS* and *RRR* patterns only), which implies—when error is assumed—that some inconsistent patterns are more likely than others. By assuming a range of true underlying preferences (restricted by the theory) and an error rate, each theory makes interconnected predictions about the relative frequency of *each* consistent and inconsistent pattern. We can then use the entire distribution of choices to judge a theory, rather than simply counting totals of consistent or inconsistent choices, or restricting attention to two choices as previous studies have.[10]

The BKJ data illustrate how our method works. Fanning out allows four types of subjects: Those who choose *SSS*, *RSS*, *RRS*, and *RRR*. Call the proportions of people with each preference $p(SSS)$, $p(RSS)$, $p(RRS)$, and $p(RRR)$. The theory predicts that there are no subjects with true preference for *SSR*, *SRS*, *SRR*, and *RSR*, but those patterns can result if people make errors in expressing true preferences. Errors occur with probability ε, and are independent for each choice. For fanning out, Table II shows the patterns which can result for each of the true preferences for various numbers of errors, and the resulting likelihood function. For example, a *RSS*-type who makes exactly two errors—which happens with probability $p(RSS)\varepsilon^2(1 - \varepsilon)$—could choose, *SRS*, *SSR*, or *RRR*. The total probability of choice *RRR* is $p(SSS)\varepsilon^3 + p(RSS)\varepsilon^2(1 - \varepsilon) + p(RRS)\varepsilon(1 - \varepsilon)^2 + p(RRR)(1 - \varepsilon)^3$. For each theory we find values of the true pattern proportions and the error rate (restricted to lie between 0 and 0.5) which maximize the likelihood of the distribution of responses under each theory's restrictions on consistent patterns.

We assume a single error rate for all three choices for several reasons. First, it is a parsimonious and conservative approach to explaining the distribution of choice responses. Many researchers have implicitly adopted independent and equal errors in statistical tests of choice theories with two pairwise choices. We take that underlying model of errors and apply it to data sets with three or more

---

[9] When indifference curves are convex (i.e., preferences are quasi-concave), what we call "errors" might be expressions of strict preference for randomization (Machina (1985), Crawford (1988)). We show in an unpublished Appendix (available on request) that our tests are equivalent to the proper test when indifference curves are convex.

[10] Conlisk (1989) used a similar error rate with two pairs, but didn't make use of the error rate in his statistical test. Starmer and Sugden (1989) and Lichtenstein and Slovic (1971) incorporated error rates too.

GENERALIZED EXPECTED UTILITY

TABLE II

EXAMPLE OF OCCUPATION OF PATTERNS WHEN SUBJECTS MAKE ERRORS:
FANNING OUT IN BATTALIO, KAGEL, AND JIRANYAKUL

Consistent Pattern	Zero Errors	One Error	Two Errors	Three Errors
SSS	SSS	RSS, SRS, SSR	RRS, RSR, SRR	RRR
RSS	RSS	SSS, RRS, RSR	SRS, SSR, RRR	SRR
RRS	RRS	SRS, RSS, RRR	SSS, SRR, RSR	SSR
RRR	RRR	SRR, RSR, SRR	SSR, SRS, RSS	SSS

Fanning out likelihood function

$$[\,p(SSS)(1-\varepsilon)^3 \;+ p(RSS)\varepsilon(1-\varepsilon)^2 + p(RRS)\varepsilon^2(1-\varepsilon) \;+ p(RRR)\varepsilon^3\,]^{(\text{frequency }SSS)} \times$$

$$[\,p(SSS)\varepsilon(1-\varepsilon)^2 + p(RSS)\varepsilon^2(1-\varepsilon) + p(RRS)\varepsilon^3 \quad\;\; + p(RRR)\varepsilon^2(1-\varepsilon)\,]^{(\text{frequency }SSR)} \times$$

$$[\,p(SSS)\varepsilon(1-\varepsilon)^2 + p(RSS)\varepsilon^2(1-\varepsilon) + p(RRS)\varepsilon(1-\varepsilon)^2 + p(RRR)\varepsilon^2(1-\varepsilon)\,]^{(\text{frequency }SRS)} \times$$

$$[\,p(SSS)\varepsilon^2(1-\varepsilon) + p(RSS)\varepsilon^3 \quad\;\; + p(RRS)\varepsilon^2(1-\varepsilon) + p(RRR)\varepsilon(1-\varepsilon)^2\,]^{(\text{frequency }SRR)} \times$$

$$[\,p(SSS)\varepsilon(1-\varepsilon)^2 + p(RSS)(1-\varepsilon)^3 \;+ p(RRS)\varepsilon(1-\varepsilon)^2 + p(RRR)\varepsilon^2(1-\varepsilon)\,]^{(\text{frequency }RSS)} \times$$

$$[\,p(SSS)\varepsilon^2(1-\varepsilon) + p(RSS)\varepsilon(1-\varepsilon)^2 + p(RRS)\varepsilon^2(1-\varepsilon) + p(RRR)\varepsilon(1-\varepsilon)^2\,]^{(\text{frequency }RSR)} \times$$

$$[\,p(SSS)\varepsilon^2(1-\varepsilon) + p(RSS)\varepsilon(1-\varepsilon)^2 + p(RRS)(1-\varepsilon)^3 \;+ p(RRR)\varepsilon(1-\varepsilon)^2\,]^{(\text{frequency }RRS)} \times$$

$$[\,p(SSS)\varepsilon^3 \quad\;\; + p(RSS)\varepsilon^2(1-\varepsilon) + p(RRS)\varepsilon(1-\varepsilon)^2 + p(RRR)(1-\varepsilon)^3\,]^{(\text{frequency }RRR)}$$

pairwise choices where the same model of errors generates more powerful tests of the choice theories.

Second, allowing error rates to be choice-dependent can lead to nonsensical results. For example, having two independent error rates in the two-pair case allows EU to explain any observed pattern proportions (leaving zero degrees of freedom), and results in negative degrees of freedom for more general theories. A middle ground is to make error rates depend on some feature of the choice—e.g., how "close" the gambles are (in expected value or in a Euclidean metric applied to the triangle diagram), or how costly an error is. The main obstacle to doing this well is to develop a theory of decision cost. It is inappropriate to assume that an error is less likely in a pair of choices with high EV, say, unless EV is the theory being tested. Then the problem of determining decision cost becomes recursive: The cost of an error in a particular choice pair depends on the theory being tested. We don't think that more complex theories (beyond EU, say) will generate strong restrictions on error rates across choices, but it would be useful to try.

Third, theorists have developed alternatives to EU emphasizing structural explanations: EU axioms are weakened to encompass a broader set of behaviors (additional patterns in this case). Our approach reflects this emphasis by testing pattern-based explanations of choice with the simple, restrictive assumption of independent and equal errors. Again, another approach is to combine a theory of decision cost with less expansive structural explanations.[11] Yet another path

---

[11] Nat Wilcox commented that more sophisticated error explanations may generate related error rates that differ for each pairwise choice. Having two independent error rates in the two-pair case does generate nonsensical results, but two dependent error rates may be sensible if justified by a more sophisticated theory of errors. The hard work of constructing such a theory remains.

is to test specific parametric forms of theories and allow choices to be stochastic. We think parametric estimation of this sort, with associated error theories, is an important direction for further research; Camerer and Ho (in press) and Hey and Orme (1993) are a start. Our approach, and the more sharply focused parametric approach, are complementary. We test theories in their fullest generality; if a theory is rejected using our method, we can safely abandon it. The parametric approach, on the other hand, could show that a theory which passes our tests is still difficult to specify parsimoniously. For example, we test a very general form of prospect theory, which fits reasonably well. Further tests are needed to establish whether there is a simple family of probability weighting functions—which are central in prospect theory—that also fit well (there appears to be; see Tversky and Kahneman (1992), Camerer and Ho (in press)).

Fourth, we assume errors are independent because we find no form of dependence persuasive. If we truly interpret the errors as "error"—like trembles in noncooperative games—then dependence seems illogical. One can imagine alternative assumptions. For example, a thoughtful referee suggested an example in which one theory predicts a pattern RR and another predicts RS, and the data consist of $1/3$ choices of each SS, RR, and RS. Under our approach the RS theory predicts best, since it can explain the SS and RR choices as only one error away from RS. RR theory predicts poorly because RS patterns are one error away but SS patterns are two errors away. We think RS *should* be considered better. To rank the RR and RS theories as equally good is to assume that RS and SS deviations from the RR pattern are equally likely, which forces us to think of an error as the choice of an *entire pattern* against true preference (rather than a particular choice against preference). This route takes us back where many studies started—by simply adding up the fraction of unpredicted patterns. Another argument against this route is *reductio ad absurdum*: This path requires us to think that a person who actually prefers $RR \ldots RR$ (n times) is equally likely to err by choosing $RR \ldots RS$ as by choosing $SS \ldots SS$. That seems to invoke an unnatural theory of errors.

Table III shows maximum-likelihood estimates for several theories. For example, the estimated fanning out proportions are .320, .072, .327, and .281; the estimated error rate is .073. Comparing these estimates with unrestricted proportion estimates gives a log likelihood chi-squared statistic (X^2) testing the goodness-of-fit of the fanning out hypothesis.[12] For fanning out, $X^2 = 1.9$ with 3 degrees of freedom[13] ($p = .588$), so we cannot reject the restriction on true pattern proportions imposed by fanning out.

The maximum-likelihood test is more powerful than the z test described above; theories which survive the z test may not survive the maximum-likeli-

---

[12] That is, the chi-squared statistic tests the hypothesis that the underlying proportions of people with preferences for SSR, SRS, SRR, and RSR are zero. Of course, the predicted proportions of people exhibiting these four patterns of preference will still be positive because of the error rate.

[13] The number of degrees of freedom for a theory is the number of patterns minus the number of linearly independent parameters minus one (so that expected frequencies under the maximum likelihood estimates add to the total sample size).

GENERALIZED EXPECTED UTILITY   1263

TABLE III
Battalio, Kagel, and Jiranyakul: Real Losses, Series 1

Pattern 123[a]	Observed Frequency	EU	Fan Out	Fan In	MF	RD-cave gIE	RD-cave fDE	RD-vex gDE	RD-vex fIE	PT
SSS	7	.435	.320	.435	.283	.295	.339	.349	.309	
SSR	1			0	.026	.023	0	.003		
SRS	1							0	.003	
SRR	1			0	.029		0	.012	.027	
RSS	3		.072		.092	.081	.164		.082	
RSR	0				0	0	0			
RRS	8		.327		.315	.322		.372	.319	1
RRR	7	.565	.281	.565	.255	.279	.497	.264	.260	0
	$n = 28$									
Error Rate		.209	.073	.209	.038	.059	.183	.095	.056	.357
Chi-squared Statistic	15.8	1.9	15.8	1.0	1.6	14.4	2.8	1.5	17.2	
Degrees of Freedom	5	3	3	0	1	1	1	1	5	
P Value		.007	.588	.001	0	.200	$1.5E-4$	.093	.220	.004
Posterior Odds for EU[b]			0.03	28.0	2.47	0.65	380	1.17	0.61	2.02

[a] Outcomes: $-\$20, -\$12, \$0$. Probabilities: $S1(.6, .4, 0)$, $R1(.84, 0, .16)$; $S2(0, 1, 0)$, $R2(.6, 0, .4)$; $S3(0, .2, .8)$, $R3(.12, 0, .88)$.
[b] Posterior odds for EU against each model under minimal prior information.

hood test. For example, EU performs well compared to a random-choice benchmark: It allows 25% of the possible patterns, and accounts for 50% of actual patterns chosen for a z statistic of 3.1. Table III shows, however, that EU cannot explain the systematic variation in its inconsistent patterns. EU predicts that *SRR*, *RSR*, and *RRS* will all be chosen equally often (the maximum likelihood estimates give an expected frequency for each of three patterns of 2.49), but the observed frequencies for the three patterns are 1, 0, and 8. While EU does well by the z test, the chi-squared test shows that EU is unable to account for the variation in the inconsistent patterns ($p = .007$).

The maximum-likelihood test gives two indications of predictive adequacy that aid in diagnosing why some theories fit the data poorly. First, a poor theory must invoke a high error rate to explain frequent choice of patterns it did not allow. For example, prospect theory allows true patterns of *RRS* and *RRR* but many subjects chose *SSS*. A high error rate (.357) is needed to explain why so many subjects chose *SSS* (since the theory interprets the *SSS* choices as two errors by people who truly prefer *RRS*, or three errors by those who prefer *RRR*). Direct estimates of error rates, derived by having subjects make the same choice twice without realizing it, suggest a natural rate of 15–25% (Starmer and Sugden (1989), Camerer (1989), and unpublished data collected by Harless; cf. Battalio, Kagel and Jiranyakul (1990, fn. 13)). Error rates much higher than the natural rates, like the .357 estimated for prospect theory, indicate a poor fit. Error rates which are much lower, like the .038 estimated from mixed fanning, indicate overfitting (i.e., using too many allowed patterns, rather than natural error, to explain the distribution of choices).

1264 D. W. HARLESS AND C. F. CAMERER

Second, poorly fitting theories have patterns for which the maximum-likelihood estimate of the true proportion is zero. Such a theory sacrifices parsimony with no increase in accuracy. For example, the mixed fan hypothesis allows seven of eight patterns in Table III. Coupled with an error rate, that should be enough free proportion parameters to exactly fit the observed choices ($X^2 = 0$). But it isn't: One pattern probability, $p(RSR)$, is estimated to be zero (its unconstrained maximum-likelihood value was negative); the chi-squared statistic for mixed-fan is therefore 1.0 and, with no degrees of freedom, its p-value is zero.

The chi-squared test makes the fit-parsimony tradeoff explicit, but does not resolve the problem of picking the best theory. Theories with more patterns obviously ought to fit better, but how much better must the fit be to justify additional proportion parameters? A formal way to evaluate theories with different numbers of parameters is the "minimal prior information" posterior odds criterion. Klein and Brown (1984) show that when prior information in an experiment is minimized (the expected gain in information from the experiment is made much larger than the information in the prior) the Bayesian posterior odds criterion for Model 1 against Model 2 is $[n^{-(K_1-K_2)/2}]$ [Maximized Likelihood under Model 1/Maximized Likelihood under Model 2], where n is the sample size and K_1 and K_2 are the number of free parameters in the two models. The second term measures the comparative fit of the two models, while the first term adjusts the fit for the difference in dimension of the two models and the sample size.[14]

The posterior odds for EU against each other theory are shown at the bottom of Table III. Fanning out generates the smallest posterior odds (0.03) for EU, providing strong evidence against EU.

Posterior odds is one of several criteria for selecting between models of different parsimony. In Section 3 we discuss some other criteria for model selection; most of them treat unparsimonious theories less harshly than posterior odds do. Posterior odds and other model selection criteria also neglect the estimated error rate, which could (in principle) be traded off against fit and parsimony. We include posterior odds simply as a suggestion for how fit and parsimony might be weighed and to impose consistency on those tradeoffs.

Table III showed data in which subjects actually suffered a loss (from a stake of money given to them initially). Figure 3 and Table IV show results from hypothetical choices over the same set of gambles. (In experiments with hypo-

---

[14] Another formal way to evaluate some of the theories uses nested hypothesis tests. For example, the EU restriction on pattern proportions is nested within the fanning out restriction. Where hypotheses are nested, the reader can easily undertake such an hypothesis test by subtracting the goodness-of-fit chi-squared statistics in the tables. For example, in Table III the chi-squared statistic testing the EU restrictions on pattern proportions against the fanning out restrictions is $(15.8 - 1.9) = 13.9$ with $(5 - 3) = 2$ degrees of freedom; the nested hypothesis test rejects the EU restrictions ($p = 0.001$). We do not report the nested hypothesis tests because they add little information beyond the goodness-of-fit statistics and because there are many cases where PT and EU are nonnested so the test cannot be applied.

GENERALIZED EXPECTED UTILITY   1265

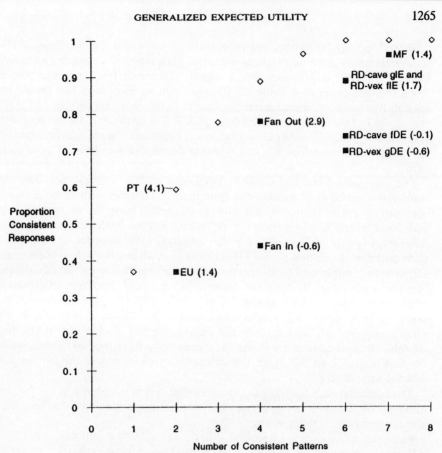

Z statistics (in parentheses) test each theory against the random choice null hypothesis.

FIGURE 3.—Battalio, Kagel, and Jiranyakul: Hypothetical losses, Series 1.

thetical choices subjects were instructed to choose as if one of their choices would be played out for real payoffs.) Comparing the figures provides a glimpse of how motivating subjects, by playing one of the gambles they chose, affects their choices. Figure 2 (real) and Figure 3 (hypothetical) look similar. Prospect theory, fanning out, and RD-vex-f IE are undominated in Figure 2; prospect theory, fanning out, RD-vex-f IE, and mixed fanning are undominated in Figure 3.

The maximum-likelihood error rate analyses reported in Tables III and IV show some subtle differences which are hidden by the figures. Compared to data with hypothetical losses (Table IV), the data for real losses (in Table III) have lower error rates (except for PT). It appears that paying subjects reduces variance (Smith and Walker (1993)). But paying subjects does not increase their adherence to EU. Instead, the lower variance in the real-loss data implies that EU is rejected with real data ($p = .007$), but fits better with hypothetical data

1266   D. W. HARLESS AND C. F. CAMERER

TABLE IV
BATTALIO, KAGEL, AND JIRANYAKUL: HYPOTHETICAL LOSSES, SERIES 1

Pattern 123[a]	Observed Frequency	EU	Fan Out	Fan In	MF	RD-cave gIE	RD-cave fDE	RD-vex gDE	RD-vex fIE	PT
SSS	0	0	0	0	0	0	0	0	0	
SSR	0			0	0	0	0	0		
SRS	1							0	0	
SRR	2			0	.063		0	0	.014	
RSS	5		.207		.186	.190	.273		.209	
RSR	3				.088	.048	0			
RRS	6		.225		.247	.238		.406	.226	.406
RRR	10	1	.568	1	.416	.524	:727	.594	.551	.594
	$n = 27$									
Error Rate		.284	.130	.284	.055	.111	.180	.204	.123	.204
Chi-squared Statistic		11.7	2.5	11.7	1.6	2.3	5.6	6.7	2.5	6.7
Degrees of Freedom		5	3	3	0	1	1	1	1	5
P Value		.039	.476	.009	0	.131	.018	.010	.116	.243
Posterior Odds for EU			0.27	27.0	24.3	6.6	34.9	60.6	7.3	0.08

[a] Outcomes: $-\$20, -\$12, \$0$. Probabilities: $S1(.6, .4, 0), R1(.84, 0, .16); S2(0, 1, 0), R2(.6, 0, .4); S3(0, .2, .8), R3(.12, 0, .88)$.

($p = .039$). (The z statistics paint the opposite, misleading, picture: EU does better with real losses, $z = 3.1$, then hypotheticals, $z = 1.4$.)

In Figures 2 and 3 prospect theory dominates EU; both theories allow two patterns but prospect theory picks out the two most highly occupied patterns for both real losses and hypothetical losses. The error rate analyses show that prospect theory generates an excellent fit for the hypothetical losses (Table IV), but generates a poor fit—marginally worse than EU—for real losses (Table III). Risk preference for losses makes PT as parsimonious as EU, but that parsimony comes at too high a price for real losses: the highly occupied SSS pattern is excluded.

2. OTHER CHOICE STUDIES

In this section we review the results of three other studies. We highlight the distinctive features of each study and draw some conclusions. The results of these and several other studies are formally aggregated in Section 3.

Harless

Harless (1992) examined choices over real gain and real loss lotteries (one lottery was played with real payoffs) in common consequence lottery pairs just inside the triangle boundary. Some people have suggested that systematic deviations from EU disappear in the triangle interior (Conlisk (1989), Camerer (1992)). If it is true, this fact is important. A gamble on the boundary has some outcomes which have zero probability. Moving off the boundary into the interior means that an outcome which had zero probability now has positive probability. Therefore, the disappearance of deviations as one moves from the boundary to

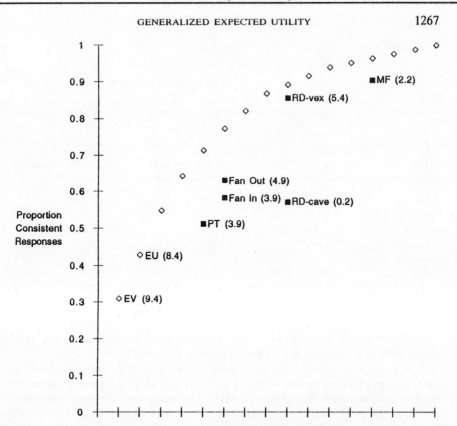

Z statistics (in parentheses) test each theory against the random choice null hypothesis.
FIGURE 4.—Harless: Real gains from unit triangle interior.

the interior suggests the source of the deviations may be nonlinear weighting of low probabilities (cf. Neilson (1992b)).

The conclusion appears to be overstated, at least for gains. The results are shown in Figure 4 and Table V for gains, and in Figure 5 and Table VI for losses. The tables and figures show the responses of Harless's original subjects plus the responses of 38 more subjects.[15]

Figure 4 shows the data frontier for gains. The figure is useful for screening out RD-cave ($z = 0.2$) and fanning in (which is dominated by fanning out), but does not help distinguish among the other theories. The chi-squared error rate analysis in Table V rules out several theories which pass the z test—for

[15] We recruited undergraduates from Wharton as additional subjects (using exactly the same procedures as in the original study) to bring the sample size to a level appropriate for the chi-squared test. We also gathered additional responses to augment the Chew and Waller (1986) data set. The test for the explanatory power of the models over the entire distribution of responses requires a larger sample size than the test of models' performance compared to random choice.

1268

D. W. HARLESS AND C. F. CAMERER

TABLE V
HARLESS: REAL GAINS FROM UNIT TRIANGLE INTERIOR

Pattern 1357[a]	Observed Frequency	EV	EU	Fan Out	Fan In	MF	RD-cave	RD-vex	PT
SSSS	10		.256	.213	.252	.174	.252	.187	.252
SSSR	2				0	.009	0		0
SSRS	2						0		
SSRR	4				.010	.053	.010		.010
SRSS	2							0	
SRSR	1				0	0		0	
SRRS	4							.050	
SRRR	6				0	.083		.094	
RSSS	1			0		0	0		
RSSR	1					0	0		
RSRS	1			0		.002	0		
RSRR	1					0	0		0
RRSS	10			.173		.147		.150	
RRSR	8					.080		.071	
RRRS	5			0		.057		.019	
RRRR	26	1	.744	.614	.738	.395	.738	.429	.738
	$n = 84$								
Error Rate		.366	.219	.166	.216	.092	.216	.107	.216
Chi-squared Statistic		59.9	29.2	15.8	29.2	7.1	29.2	8.8	29.2
Degrees of Freedom		14	13	9	9	2	6	6	10
P Value		$1.2E-7$	.006	.071	.001	.029	$5.7E-5$	.186	.001
Posterior Odds for EU		$5.1E+5$		8.6	6,902	$5.9E+5$	$5.3E+6$	200	753

[a] Outcomes: $0, $3, $6. Probabilities: $S1(.84, .14, .02)$, $R1(.89, .01, .10)$; $S3(.04, .94, .02)$, $R3(.09, .81, .10)$; $S5(.44, .14, .42)$, $R5(.49, .01, .5)$; $S7(.04, .14, .82)$, $R7(.09, .01, .9)$.

example, EV has the highest z statistic but has the lowest chi-squared p value. The conjecture that EU violations disappear in the interior appears to be false, since the chi-squared test gives a p value of .006. Nevertheless, no other theory accounts for the distribution of non-EU choices parsimoniously. Fanning out, mixed fan, and RD-vex have higher p values than EU, but they waste degrees of freedom on sparsely occupied patterns.

The posterior odds ratios favor EU over all competitors, showing that while EU *is* systematically violated, its competitors are no more accurate (adjusting for the number of patterns they allow). However, EU has a larger error rate than more general theories; if we could trade off error rates with fit and parsimony, other theories might look better. For example, RD-vex has a higher p value than EU (.186 versus .006) and a lower error rate (.107 versus .219), but the posterior odds of EU against RD-vex are 200-to-1. Forcing EU to have a lower error rate would shift the odds toward RD-vex.[16] Furthermore, the poor

---

[16] The error rate is always at least as large for EU than for more general theories which include EU, but the posterior odds criterion does not penalize EU for its high error rate. Dave Grether suggested a way to correct this bias, by computing posterior odds after restricting the error rate to be the same for all theories. However, there is no obviously correct way to choose a single rate, or estimate one from the data. The reader should keep in mind that the posterior odds we report put EU in the best possible light.

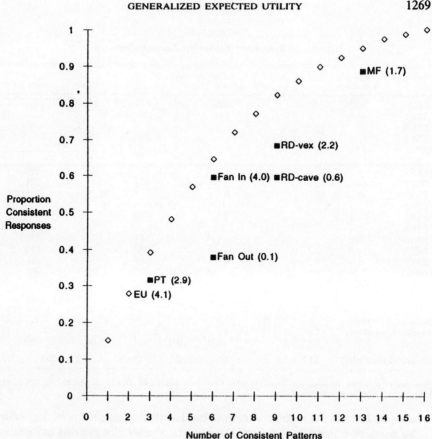

Z statistics (in parentheses) test each theory against the random choice null hypothesis.

FIGURE 5.—Harless: Real losses from unit triangle interior.

absolute fit of EU ($p = .006$) means there is room for improvement: A theory which restricts fanning out, allowing pattern *RRSS* but ruling out the other non-EU patterns, would lead to strong evidence against EU (posterior odds of 0.01 for EU).

Figure 5 and Table VI give results for gambles over small losses. Again the z statistic can mislead: EU has a higher z statistic for gains ($z = 8.4$) than losses ($z = 4.1$), but the chi-squared p values are reversed ($p = .006$ for gains, $p = .133$ for losses). In both cases, EU beats all competitors by the posterior odds ratio.

In the BKJ study prospect theory poorly fit the real loss data from the triangle boundary. Here prospect theory poorly fits loss data from the triangle interior (Table VI). In both loss studies the R gambles are mean-preserving spreads of the S gambles. For border gambles in BKJ, risk preference for losses makes PT as parsimonious as EU. For interior gambles in the Harless study, risk preference for losses makes PT nearly as parsimonious as EU. In both cases prospect

1270   D. W. HARLESS AND C. F. CAMERER

TABLE VI
HARLESS: REAL LOSSES FROM UNIT TRIANGLE INTERIOR

Pattern 1357[a]	Observed Frequency	EU	Fan Out	Fan In	Mixed Fan	RD-cave	RD-vex	PT
SSSS	10	.430	.430	.229	.201	.232	.297	
SSSR	9			.154	.138	.268		
SSRS	2					0		
SSRR	3			0	0	0		
SRSS	4						0	
SRSR	7			.167	.111		.251	.650
SRRS	3						0	
SRRR	6			.025	.103		.017	0
RSSS	1		0		0	0		
RSSR	2				0	0		
RSRS	1		0		0	0		
RSRR	7				.101	0		
RRSS	4		0		.063		.007	
RRSR	6				.057		.004	
RRRS	2		0		0		0	
RRRR	12	.570	.570	.425	.226	.500	.424	.350
	$n = 79$							
Error Rate		.281	.281	.222	.141	.248	.236	.362
Chi-squared Statistic		18.7	18.7	7.4	3.2	11.3	10.2	22.8
Degrees of Freedom		13	9	9	2	6	6	12
P Value		.133	.028	.592	.204	.080	.117	.030
Posterior Odds for EU			6,241	22.5	$1.2E + 7$	$1.1E + 5$	$6.2E + 4$	68.2

[a] Outcomes: $-\$4, -\$2, \$0$. Probabilities: $S1(.8, .18, .02)$, $R1(.88, .02, .1)$; $S3(.02, .96, .02)$, $R3(.1, .8, .1)$; $S5(.41, .18, .41)$, $R5(.49, .02, .49)$; $S7(.02, .18, .80)$, $R7(.10, .02, .88)$.

theory's fit is worse than that of EU because the common pattern SSSS is excluded.

For losses, note that fanning in is the only challenger to EU as a parsimonious theory that also achieves reasonable fit—in sharp contrast to the fanning out for gains in the triangle interior (Table V). Fanning in for losses inside the triangle is also prevalent in our reanalysis of data from Camerer (1992). Mixed fan can account for both fanning out for gains and fanning in for losses inside the triangle, but it fits poorly because it uses too many free parameters to explain patterns that are occupied only because of random error.[17]

---

[17] In the Harless and BKJ experiments subjects were allowed to respond that they were indifferent between two lotteries. For example, in Harless's study using real gain lotteries, in addition to the 84 subjects in Table V, there were two subjects that indicated they were indifferent between lotteries S1 and R1. Letting I represent indifference, their responses were IRSR and ISRR. We exclude such responses from our main analysis, but in footnote 26 we summarize how little the results change when indifference responses are included. We assume that the indifference response may belong to one of several patterns and assign indifference responses to maximize the likelihood function for each theory. For example, for each theory an IRSR response may be assigned to the SRSR or RRSR pattern, whichever yields a higher likelihood for the theory.

Chew and Waller

The Chew and Waller (1986) study combines three common consequence choices with a common ratio lottery choice, allowing a test of whether indifference curves are linear. Figure 6 and Table VII contain the responses to the Chew and Waller hypothetical small gain choices on the triangle boundary (their context 1A) for the 56 subjects in their study and 43 new subjects we recruited. Figure 6 suggests that violations of EU appear to be due to fanning out or convex indifference curves (RD-vex): theories which lack these features are generally dominated by theories which have them.

The figure does not show whether the assumption of parallel indifference curves (EU) should be sacrificed for linear indifference curves that fan out (WEU-out), general fanning out, or RD-vex, since all those theories have high z statistics. The chi-squared test in Table VII provides a definite answer. Fanning out fits quite well ($p = .087$), with fewer patterns than other theories with

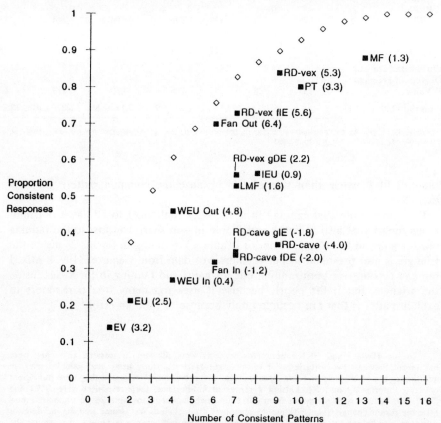

Z statistics (in parentheses) test each theory against the random choice null hypothesis.

FIGURE 6.—Chew and Waller: Hypothetical moderate gains, Context 1A.

TABLE VII
CHEW AND WALLER: HYPOTHETICAL MODERATE GAINS, CONTEXT 1A

Patterns OILH[a]	Observed Frequency	EV	EU	WEU Out	WEU In	LMF	IEU	Fan Out	Fan In	MF	RD-cave	RD-cave gIE	RD-cave fDE	RD-vex	RD-vex gDE	RD-vex fIE	PT
SSSS	7		.358	.173	.358	.173	.173	.152	.358	.111	.090	.090	.090	.130	.127	.134	.119
SSSR	3			0	0	0	0	0	0	.018	0	0	0				.033
SSRS	9			.146		.146	.146			.056	.415	.415	.415				.025
SSRR	0			0		0	0			0	0	0	0				0
SRSS	8													.039	.246	.067	
SRSR	4									.057				.054	.009		.434
SRRS	21							.480		.363				.403		.418	.018
SRRR	7				0				0	.016				0			
RSSS	1									.002	0	0	0				
RSSR	1									0	0	0	0	0	0	0	0
RSRR	2					0	0		0	0	0	0	0	.011	0	.025	0
RRSS	0					0	0	0	0	.016				.182		.171	
RRSR	3									.192					.452		
RRRS	16			.494		.494	.494	.161		.169			.495	.181	.166	.185	.176
RRRR	14	1	.642	.187	.642	.187	.187	.207	.642		.495	.495					.195
n = 99																	
Error Rate	.452		.339	.243	.339	.243	.243	.178	.344	.121	.301	.301	.301	.143	.234	.157	.157
Chi-square Statistic	86.9		82.0	49.9	82.0	49.9	49.9	15.2	82.0	10.3	71.1	71.1	71.1	11.2	44.5	13.4	14.2
Degrees of Freedom	14		13	11	11	8	7	9	9	2	6	8	8	6	8	8	5
P Value	$1E-12$		$5E-12$	$6.4E-7$	$6.1E-13$	$4.2E-8$	$1.5E-8$	.087	$6E-14$	.006	$2E-13$	$3E-12$	$3E-12$	.084	$5E-7$	.098	.015
Posterior Odds for EU	1.2		$1.1E-5$	$6.4E-7$	99.0	0.01	0.11	$3.0E-11$	9,801	$2.6E-5$	$4.1E+4$	$3E-12$	$3E-12$	$4.0E-9$	$7.2E-4$	$1.3E-10$	$1.8E-7$

[a] Outcomes: $0, $40, $100. Probabilities: SO(0,1,0), RO(.5,0,.5); SI(0,1,0), RI(.05,.9,.05); RL(.95,0,.05); SL(.9,.1,0); SH(0,.1,.9), RH(.05,0,.95).

comparably good fits, and has the lowest posterior odds ratio ($3.0E - 11$, the strongest evidence against EU).[18]

All the theories that assume linear indifference curves—EV, EU, WEU, linear mixed fan (LMF), and implicit EU—fit poorly by the chi-squared test.[19] Chew and Waller (1986) concluded that WEU-out was superior to EU because its z statistic was higher. In our analysis (including 43 new subjects), WEU-out does provide a much better fit than EU using the chi-squared test and posterior odds ratio, but those tests also show that several theories with nonlinear indifference curves are even better than WEU-out.

Table VII shows another way in which the maximum-likelihood error-rate analysis is more informative than simply counting pattern frequencies. Nine subjects chose pattern *SSRS*, many more than expected under random choice. Fanning out allows that pattern, but its maximum likelihood estimate for the proportion of subjects who truly prefer *SSRS* is zero. Introducing the parameter $p(SSRS)$ to the model that already had consistent patterns *SSSS*, *SRRS*, *RRRS*, and *RRRR* did not improve the fit even though *SSRS* choices were common. The estimated proportion of subjects with true *SSRS* pattern preference is low because raising the estimate increases the expected frequencies of neighboring patterns (*RSRS*, *SRRS*, *SSSS*, and *SSRR*), but those expected frequencies already exceed observed frequencies. Fanning out could afford to exclude *SSRS*, even though it is chosen often, because it is fed by errors from the *SSSS* and *SRRS* patterns and therefore has a high expected frequency (6.6) even if *SSRS* is excluded.

Sopher and Gigliotti

Sopher and Gigliotti (1990) gathered responses to the Allais Paradox common consequence pairs and three other common consequence pairs from the triangle boundary (Table VIII). They also gathered responses to comparable choices in the triangle interior (Table IX). When lotteries lie in the interior, the EV pattern (*RRRRR*) is chosen much more often. The chi-squared test in Table VIII shows that EU has a terrible fit for lotteries on the boundary of the triangle ($p = 1.5E - 25$). EU fits substantially better for interior lotteries, but the p value is still low ($3.7E - 10$). By the posterior odds ratios EU is worse than many theories for boundary lotteries (Table VIII) but better than every alternative except prospect theory for interior lotteries (Table IX). (In Harless's data using interior lotteries, Tables V and VI, EU is better than every other theory by the posterior odds ratio.) The success of prospect theory stems from increased precision for interior gambles (allowing only 7 of 32 patterns) com-

---

[18] Becker and Sarin (1987) note that their lottery dependent utility theory accounts for 98–99% of the choices by allowing 14 of the 16 possible patterns. But one can account for the distribution of responses with far fewer patterns; the posterior odds for fanning out against lottery dependent EU are $2.27E + 06$.

[19] Camerer and Ho (in press) reach a similar conclusion from a review of ten studies testing the betweenness axiom (which creates linear indifference curves).

TABLE VIII

SOPHER AND GIGLIOTTI: COMMON CONSEQUENCE HYPOTHETICAL LARGE GAINS ON UNIT TRIANGLE BOUNDARY

Pattern 12345[a]	Observed Frequency	EV	EU	WEU Out	WEU In	LMF	IEU	Fan Out	Fan In	MF	RD-cave	RD-vex	PT
SSSSS	4		.114	0	.114	0	0	0	.114	.023	.016	.088	.024
SSSSR	2					0	0		0	.001	0		0
SSSRS	0								0	0	0		0
SSSRR	1				0	0	0						
SSRSS	1												
SSRSR	1							.191					
SSRRS	1			.218		.116	.116			0	0		0
SSRRR	8			.116		.111	.111	0		.053	.104		.064
SRSSS	6					.150	.150	.334		.022	.002		.004
SRSSR	6					.002	.002			.176	.221		.206
SRSRS	25									.043	.095		.099
SRSRR	8									.125			
SRRSS	18									.038			
SRRSR	7						0		0	.141	0	0	0
SRRRS	25								0		.251	0	.256
SRRRR	0												
RSSSS	1												
RSSSR	0												
RSSRS	1					0	0	0		.011		0	
RSSRR	2					0	0	0		.007		0	.028
RSRSS	1												
RSRSR	0							0		0		.043	
RSRRS	1									.027		0	.013
RSRRR	5			.029		.095	.095	0		.018		.135	.023
RRSSS	0					0	0	0		.051		0	0
RRSSR	4				0	0	0		0	.007		0	
RRSRS	11				0				0	.009			
RRSRR	2									0			
RRRSS	5									.248	.311	.734	.283
RRRSR	2												
RRRRS	2												
RRRRR	37	1	.886	.637	.886	.526	.526	.475	.886				.129
	n = 186												
Error Rate		.343	.299	.237	.299	.212	.212	.198	.299	.060	.147	.280	.129
Chi-Square Statistic		200.2	189.9	144.8	189.9	135.5	135.5	97.4	189.9	15.4	53.9	186.1	49.1
Degrees of Freedom		30	29	26	26	20	15	23	23	10	18	18	13
P Value		4.6E − 27	1.5E − 25	1.9E − 18	7.4E − 27	3.6E − 19	1.8E − 21	4.0E − 11	3.2E − 28	4.6E − 17	1.9E − 05	5.9E − 30	4.3E − 06
Posterior Odds for EU		12.5		4.1E − 7	2.537	0.02	1.2E + 4	5.3E − 14	6.4E + 6	4.6E − 17	9.1E − 18	5E + 11	3.8E − 13

[a] Outcomes: S0, S1M, S5M. Probabilities: S1(0, 1, 0), R1(.01, .89, .1); S2(.89, .11, 0); R2(.9, 0, .1); S3(0, .11, .89), R3(.01, 0, .99); S4(.79, .11, .1), R4(.8, 0, .2); S5(.01, .89, .1), R5(.02, .78, .2).

TABLE IX

SOPHER AND GIGLIOTTI: COMMON CONSEQUENCE HYPOTHETICAL LARGE GAINS FROM UNIT TRIANGLE INTERIOR

Pattern 12345[a]	Observed Frequency	EV	EU	WEU Out	WEU In	LMF	IEU	Fan Out	Fan In	MF	RD-cave	RD-vex	PT
SSSSS	17		.235	.231	.235	.189	.175	.231	.179	.152	.175	.195	.175
SSSSR	1												
SSSRS	0						0				0		
SSSRR	2				0	0	0		0	0	.006		.016
SSRSS	1										0		
SSRSR	0								0	0	.072		.064
SSRRS	9						.084	0	0		.019		.023
SSRRR	6								.102	.056	0		
SRSSS	2												
SRSSR	0			.010	.010	0	0	0		0	.002		
SRSRS	2									0	0		
SRSRR	2									.019	.028		
SRRSS	4					.012	.024			0			
SRRSR	3									.084	.039		.058
SRRRS	8					.136	.066			.113	.122		.122
SRRRR	21											.012	
RSSSS	8						0					0	
RSSSR	0				0		0						
RSSRS	0				0	.011	.014		.055	.059		.050	
RSSRR	1					.016	0		0	0		0	
RSRSS	5							0		.004			
RSRSR	2						.006		0	0		0	
RSRRS	3				0	0	0			0		0	
RSRRR	7				0			0		0		0	
RRSSS	0									0		0	
RRSSR	3			0				0		0		0	
RRSRS	0									.004		0	
RRSRR	5									0		0	
RRRSS	2												
RRRSR	5												
RRRRS	4												
RRRRR	61	1	.752	.746	.752	.637	.615	.746	.651	.508	.533	.729	.542
	n = 184												
Error Rate		.327	.186	.184	.186	.148	.130	.184	.151	.104	.112	.173	.118
Chi-Square Statistic		231.5	102.6	102.3	102.6	77.0	64.1	102.3	81.7	43.8	49.6	95.9	52.6
Degrees of Freedom		30	29	26	26	20	15	23	23	18	18	18	24
P Value		5.4E−33	3.7E−10	5.2E−11	4.7E−11	1.3E−08	4.9E−08	5.5E−12	1.7E−08	3.6E−06	8.6E−05	1.3E−12	6.6E−04
Posterior Odds for EU		7E+26		2.189	2.496	4.3E+4	3.1E+7	5.5E+6	184	5.5E+8	9.04	1E+11	6.2E−6

[a] Outcomes: $0, $1M, $5M. Probabilities: S1(.01, .98, .01), R1(.02, .87, .11), S2(.80, .19, .01), R2(.81, .08, .11); S3(.01, .19, .80), R3(.02, .08, .90); S4(.70, .19, .11), R4(.71, .08, .21); S5(.02, .87, .11), R5(.03, .76, .21).

pared to boundary gambles (allowing 18 of 32), which serves it well since there are fewer systematic patterns with interior gambles.[20]

There is another interesting difference between interior and boundary results. Fanning out fits better than fanning in for boundary lotteries (Table VIII) and the opposite is true for interior lotteries (Table IX). Neither theory fits well for both sets of gambles.

The data provide little reason to replace the independence assumption in EU with the weaker assumption of betweenness. The theories which assume betweenness have high posterior odds supporting EU. The only exception is WEU-out on the boundary, but in that case several other theories have even better posterior odds than WEU-out.

Perhaps the most striking feature of Tables VIII and IX is the large number of maximum likelihood estimates which equal zero. All the generalizations of EU are guilty. Under the error rate approach, the distribution of responses may be explained with relatively few consistent patterns. EU is too lean (it allows too few patterns to explain the distribution); generalizations of EU are too fat (they predict too many useless patterns or the wrong ones).

3. AGGREGATION OF RESULTS ACROSS STUDIES

Sections 1 and 2 demonstrate that the error rate analysis of choice data is more powerful than statistical tests employed previously. In general, some conclusions drawn from earlier studies are reversed by our analyses—e.g., in some cases a theory with a high z statistic, which predicts much better than a random choice benchmark, cannot account for variation in unpredicted patterns and hence is rejected by the chi-squared test while a theory with a lower z statistic is not rejected by the chi-squared test. And while EU performs relatively better with gambles in the triangle interior (compared to generalizations), by our tests it is easily rejected there too. Some new conclusions appear too—e.g., paying subjects appears to lower the error rate, *increasing* rejection of EU and many other theories rather than inducing conformity to them. Many theories have been proposed to explain violations of EU such as the common consequence and common ratio effect. Our method uses the distribution of responses across combinations of common consequence and common ratio choice problems generating tests with more power showing that some of the

---

[20] There are some instances, such as the Sopher and Gigliotti data sets, where we do not impose restrictions on a theory's parameters across data sets. We take each set of pairwise choices from a unit triangle as a separate data set. Since subjects were randomly assigned to either the boundary or interior treatment in the Sopher and Gigliotti study, the risk preferences between the two groups should be identical. Hence, one could consider adding the restriction for EU that the proportion of subjects prefering *SSSSS* must be the same for lotteries on the boundary and the interior. The other instance where cross-data set restrictions could be considered involves gain and loss triangles with choice pairs having mean-preserving risk spreads to test prospect theory's reflection effect (Battalio, Kagel, and Jiranyakul (1990), Camerer (1989, 1992)). Since reflection is confirmed in these studies, we suspect that imposing the restrictions might make prospect theory fare better and theories not incorporating reflection, such as EU, fare worse. We do not impose cross-data set restrictions because there is no precise prediction for many of the generalizations of EU.

candidate theories *cannot* explain the distribution of responses while others can. Our method clearly demonstrates that some theories are losers as they are less parsimonious and have a poorer fit than other theories. The posterior odds ratios also provide an unequivocal method for trading off fit and parsimony in comparing EV, EU, and the generalizations. (In contrast, analysis based on the proportion of consistent responses yields conflicting conclusions for each of three measures, difference, inside ratio, and outside ratio.) And the analysis has another important advantage: Since the sum of several independent random variables with chi-squared distributions also has a chi-squared distribution, chi-squared statistics from different experiments may be added to gauge each theory's performance across a variety of subjects, investigators, experimental methods, and so on, as long as the experiments are independent. Aggregation tells us whether deviations from EU are robust across studies.

The independence of studies is hard to evaluate. For our purposes, independence means that conditional on the truth of a particular theory, a sample of results from one experiment did not influence the results from another. Nonindependence could arise because the same subjects are represented by choices in multiple data sets, or because some investigators designed their experiments based on earlier results. The amount of design dependence is difficult to measure empirically. It is surely substantial because virtually all the studies we aggregate used some variation on familiar common consequence, common ratio, betweenness-testing, and framing problems introduced by Allais (1953) and Kahneman and Tversky (1979) and many used a design adapted from Chew and Waller (1986) (proposed initially by Chew and MacCrimmon (1979)). Since we cannot measure the degree of dependence between studies reliably, we offer two caveats to our aggregation analyses (which assume independence): First, violations of independence imply that the p values we compute by adding chi-squared statistics are too low; skeptical readers might adjust them upward to reflect the degree of dependence they think exists. Second, in many cases a single study generates p values low enough to cast severe doubt on one or more theories, so even if studies are perfectly dependent (i.e., are pure replications which differ only by sampling error) the data are sufficient to reject some theories.

With the caveat about our heavy-handed independence assumption in mind, we discuss the result of aggregating different studies. Included in our chi-squared aggregation are the results from the seven data sets presented in Sections 2 and 3 and the results from sixteen more data sets from Battalio, Kagel, and Jiranyakul (1990), Camerer (1989, 1992), Chew and Waller (1986), and Sopher and Gigliotti (1990) presented in an unpublished Appendix (available upon request).[21]

---

[21] We excluded studies with two-pair patterns. Tests like ours are correct but severely limited when applied in a two-choice case (e.g., Conlisk (1989), Battalio, Kagel, and Jiranyakul (1990), Prelec (1990)). Two pairs (four patterns) do not span a broad range of gambles, and hence are too few to distinguish all the theories we consider. For example, in a two-pair test weighted and implicit EU cannot be distinguished, and mixed fanning allows all four patterns.

1278   D. W. HARLESS AND C. F. CAMERER

TABLE X
PERFORMANCE OF THEORIES USING MEASURES BASED ON PERCENTAGE CONSISTENT RESPONSES

	Sum of Squared Z Statistics	Degrees of Freedom	P Value	Ratio Measure	Difference Measure	Outside Ratio
EV	1,432	23	$9E-289$	4.14	.17	.81
EU	1,183	23	$2E-235$	3.03	.20	.76
WEU-Out	599	23	$8E-112$	1.89	.22	.66
WEU-In	383	23	$6E-67$	1.61	.14	.78
LMF	279	23	$9E-46$	1.31	.15	.53
IEU	36	6	$3E-06$	1.16	.08	.84
Fan Out	547	23	$5E-101$	1.75	.23	.64
Fan In	308	23	$1E-51$	1.45	.13	.80
MF	291	21	$2E-49$	1.25	.16	.41
RD-cave	155	14	$6E-26$	1.27	.12	.78
RD-cave g IE	247	19	$1E-41$	1.33	.16	.67
RD-cave f DE	242	19	$2E-40$	1.31	.14	.72
RD-vex	118	14	$2E-18$	1.22	.12	.73
RD-vex g DE	79	19	$3E-09$	1.13	.06	.86
RD-vex f IE	129	19	$3E-18$	1.21	.10	.77
PT	627	23	$1E-117$	1.73	.24	.57

Consider first the measures of theory performance based on percentage of consistent responses aggregated over all 23 studies (Table X).[22] The z statistics (comparing each theory's percentage of consistent responses to a random choice null hypothesis) are squared (so that they become chi-squared statistics) and summed (keeping the sign when theories generate negative z statistics). The extreme p values show that each model does much better than would be expected if choices were random. This is an important conclusion, but does not tell us whether theories fail to account for variation in excluded patterns and gives no clear way to choose among theories. Also given in Table X for each theory are the ratio measure (the proportion consistent divided by the proportion of consistent patterns), difference measure (proportion consistent minus proportion consistent patterns), and outside ratio (the proportion of inconsistent responses divided by the proportion of inconsistent patterns) weighted by sample size and aggregated over the 23 studies. None of the measures selects EU. The difference measure selects PT. The ratio measure selects the most parsimonious theory (EV). The outside ratio selects the broadest theory which excludes uncommon patterns (mixed fan). Besides having no good reason to choose one measure over the others, the measures of theory performance in Table X are incomplete because they throw away information about the distribution of responses in consistent and inconsistent patterns.

The sum of chi-squared statistics from the maximum likelihood error analysis over all 23 data sets are given in Table XI. All the theories have extremely low p

[22] Even in studies without specific tests of betweenness, WEU-out is tested whenever fanning out is tested; hence, the sum of squared z statistics for WEU-out includes squared z statistics for fanning out from studies that do not test for betweenness. A similar statement holds for WEU-in, rank-dependent theories with elasticity conditions, and LMF.

GENERALIZED EXPECTED UTILITY   1279

TABLE XI

SUM OF CHI-SQUARED STATISTICS OVER ALL STUDIES

	Sum of Chi-squared Statistics	Degrees of Freedom	P Value
EV	1,289.0	253	$3E - 138$
EU	902.5	243	$1E - 76$
WEU-Out	611.6	189	$5E - 46$
WEU-In*	869.0	189	$1E - 87$
LMF*	386.4	96	$2E - 36$
IEU*	294.0	50	$3E - 36$
Fan Out	520.3	175	$6E - 36$
Fan In*	837.7	175	$4E - 87$
MF	153.0	58	$2E - 10$
RD-cave	289.4	74	$3E - 27$
RD-cave g IE	327.3	97	$1E - 26$
RD-cave f DE*	340.9	97	$7E - 29$
RD-vex*	428.7	74	$2E - 51$
RD-vex g DE*	679.1	97	$4E - 88$
RD-vex f IE*	548.2	97	$4E - 64$
PT	400.9	167	$3E - 21$

*Theory is dominated by another with a lower chi-squared statistic and at least as many degrees of freedom.

values. Tables X and XI together tell the whole story: each theory performs much better than would be expected if choices were random (Table X), but there is systematic variation in the patterns they don't predict too (Table XI). In Table XI asterisks indicate dominated theories, which fit worse (higher chi-squared statistics) *and* are less parsimonious (fewer degrees of freedom) than some other theory. Half of the theories—all variations of RD-vex, RD-cave f DE, fanning in, and all the theories incorporating betweenness except WEU out—are dominated.[23]

Since the results from individual studies in Sections 1 and 2 indicate that theories perform quite differently under different conditions (boundary versus interior, for example), Table XII decomposes the sum of chi-squared statistics by location in the triangle (boundary, interior) and outcomes (large gain, small gain, small loss) of gambles used in the studies. (A decomposition of hypotheti-

[23] We also tested the Quiggin (1982, 1993) anticipated utility (AU) proposal for rank-dependent expected utility, in which $f(.5) = .5$ and $f(p)$ is concave (convex) below (above) .5. This restriction excludes some patterns in the studies reviewed, but even then AU allows many more patterns than other theories do. AU cannot be tested in 8 of the 23 studies because it excludes no patterns at all. (MF excludes some patterns in 21 of 23 studies. EV, EU, PT, and fanning exclude patterns in all 23 studies.) Aggregating over the studies that do test AU, AU generates a log likelihood chi-squared statistic of 147.7 (df = 55, $p = 2.0E - 10$). In the menu of best theories in Table XIII, AU would be chosen for $m < 1.8$ and MF would be chosen for $1.8 \leqslant m < 2.3$ (but this is not surprising because AU makes fewer predictions, and hence has fewer degrees of freedom, than MF). Further restrictions on the AU $f(p)$ function would make the theory more parsimonious. For example, one could restrict the function to be symmetric around .5 ($f(p) = 1 - f(1 - p)$) or require the concave and convex portions to satisfy an elasticity condition. The studies described herein are not efficiently designed to test AU in the Quiggin form; more sharply-designed studies would be useful.

TABLE XII

DECOMPOSITION OF SUM OF CHI-SQUARED STATISTICS

Boundary of Unit Triangle

	Large Gains Chi-squared Statistic	Large Gains Degrees of Freedom	Large Gains P Value	Large Gains Minimum m Value	Small Gains Chi-squared Statistic	Small Gains Degrees of Freedom	Small Gains P Value	Small Gains Minimum m Value	Small Losses Chi-squared Statistic	Small Losses Degrees of Freedom	Small Losses P Value	Small Losses Minimum m Value
EV	515.8	80	$6E-65$	[7.4]	125.9	34	$2E-12$	[4.9]	49.2	20	$3E-4$	3.3
EU	486.0	76	$5E-61$		121.0	33	$6E-12$		26.1	13	.016	0.9
WEU-Out	295.8	65	$4E-31$	17.3	66.2*	24	$8E-6$	6.1	43.1*	13	$4E-5$	1.8
WEU-In	482.9*	65	$4E-65$	0.3	121.0*	24	$6E-15$	0.0	17.8*	3	$5E-4$	2.0
LMF	184.5*	43	$2E-19$	9.1	60.9*	11	$6E-9$	2.7	15.2*	3	.002	2.8
IEU	160.2*	22	$6E-23$	6.0	54.5*	10	$4E-8$	2.9	24.4	3	.011	1.8
Fan Out	243.7	60	$5E-24$	15.1	28.7	20	.094	7.1	33.2*	11	$5E-4$	1.8
Fan In	482.4*	60	$3E-67$	0.2	121.0*	20	$2E-16$	0.0	2.6	0	0	2.3
MF	43.7	27	.022	9.0	16.7	2	$2E-4$	3.4	17.1*	3	.001	1.9
RD-cave	89.3*	26	$7E-9$	7.9	85.2*	9	$1E-14$	1.5	21.0*	5	.001	1.9
RD-cave g IE	119.8*	43	$4E-9$	11.1	88.7*	13	$2E-13$	1.6	37.1*	5	$6E-7$	0.8
RD-cave f DE	113.2	43	$3E-8$	11.3	92.8*	13	$4E-14$	1.4	5.0	3	.172	2.6
RD-vex	270.5*	26	$2E-42$	4.3	20.3	9	.016	4.2	14.5*	5	.013	2.3
RD-vex g DE	463.8*	43	$6E-72$	0.7	67.9*	13	$2E-9$	2.7	9.0	5	.109	2.7
RD-vex f IE	376.0*	43	$1E-54$	3.3	30.3*	13	.004	4.5				
PT	100.5	34	$2E-8$	9.2	41.5	24	.015	8.8	35.7	19	.011	13.5

Interior of Unit Triangle

	Large Gains Chi-squared Statistic	Large Gains Degrees of Freedom	Large Gains P Value	Large Gains Minimum m Value	Small Gains Chi-squared Statistic	Small Gains Degrees of Freedom	Small Gains P Value	Small Gains Minimum m Value	Small Losses Chi-squared Statistic	Small Losses Degrees of Freedom	Small Losses P Value	Small Losses Minimum m Value
EV	503.4	72	$6E-66$	[80.3]	64.4	24	$1E-5$	[30.7]	30.3	23	.141	
EU	182.3	68	$2E-12$		33.7	23	.070					
WEU-Out	174.1	57	$9E-14$	0.7								
WEU-In	175.4*	57	$6E-14$	0.6								
LMF	111.9*	35	$6E-10$	2.1								
IEU	64.1*	15	$5E-8$	2.2								
Fan Out	174.1*	54	$1E-14$	0.6	19.3	15	.200	1.8	30.1*	15	.012	0.0
Fan In	154.5	54	$1E-11$	2.0	33.6*	15	.004	0.0	13.0	15	.602	2.2
MF	78.7	25	$2E-7$	2.4	7.1	2	.029	1.3	4.2	2	.122	1.2
RD-cave	52.8	20	$9E-5$	2.7	30.9*	8	$1E-4$	0.2	14.1*	8	.079	1.1
RD-vex	104.0*	20	$2E-13$	1.6	11.6	8	.170	1.5	17.3*	8	.027	0.9
PT	110.6	51	$3E-6$	4.2	50.8*	19	$1E-4$	-4.3	61.8*	20	$4E-6$	-10.5

cal vs. real-payoff results showed no interesting, reliable differences other than those noted in Section 1.) For small losses all the studies used mean-preserving risk spreads so the predictions of EV and EU are identical (but see footnote 27).

Some theories are dominated in nearly every category in Table XII (WEU-in, LMF, and IEU). For other theories the decomposition in Table XII reveals areas of strength and weakness of theories. As the individual studies suggested, whether lotteries lie on the boundary (where lottery supports are different) or the interior (where supports are the same) makes a tremendous difference for the performance of EU. On the boundary of the triangle the p values for EU are all quite low, and EU fits only slightly better than EV. In the triangle interior, however, EU manages a miraculous recovery.

The boundary-interior distinction also reveals differences in the performance of the alternative theories. Fanning out dominates fanning in on the boundary, but in the interior fanning in does better for large gains and small losses. Further, since violations of EU are less systematic in the triangle interior, theories which allow the same number of patterns in the triangle interior as on the boundary (all the theories except PT) have a substantial handicap. Nevertheless, there are indications that systematic deviations from EU occur even in the triangle interior (for example, in the Harless and Sopher and Gigliotti data sets) so there may be room for leaner generalizations to improve upon EU even in the triangle interior.

The boundary and interior classification proves quite useful as a diagnostic tool for prospect theory. For small gains and small losses on the boundary of the triangle PT achieves a good fit (except for BKJ real losses in Table III); because the riskier lotteries are (usually) mean preserving risk spreads of the safer lotteries, PT's property of risk aversion for gains and risk preference for losses (except for small probabilities) makes it quite parsimonious. (For small losses PT has just one fewer degree of freedom than EU.) For small gains and small losses in the triangle interior lotteries are again (usually) mean preserving, but PT has an awful fit. The data therefore provide evidence against reflection—risk aversion for gains and risk preference for losses—when lottery supports are the same.[24] Large gains lotteries are not mean preserving, so PT is not very parsimonious; it wastes degrees of freedom on useless patterns and its fit is undistinguished. However, for large gains in the interior PT allows fewer patterns than on the boundary, making it almost as parsimonious as fanning out or WEU; there it fits relatively well.

Table XII also suggests the possibility that curvature of indifference curves may depend on the size of outcomes: RD-cave dominates RD-vex for large gains but is dominated by RD-vex for small gains and small losses. Although the chi-squared statistics differ by orders of magnitude, the effect may be due to

[24] Note that all the experiments which used real-loss payoffs actually deducted losses from an initial stake subjects had been given. If subjects frame these lotteries as choices over net gain outcomes, the reflection effect predicted by prospect theory is diluted. However, reflection is apparent in boundary lotteries with different support.

differences in the locations of the lottery pairs. The possibility that curvature depends on the size of outcomes deserves further investigation.

The decomposition in Table XII is informative, but the central question of the paper remains: Which alternative to EU competes with EU as the best, parsimonious model?

A large statistical literature on model selection criteria gives guidance on trading off fit (chi-squared) and parsimony (degrees of freedom). Many of these criteria are described by the rule "pick the model for which $X^2 - m$(degrees of freedom) is smallest," where the multiplier m penalizes the use of free parameters. The number m is a marginal rate of substitution between chi-squared and degrees of freedom, or the price of precision.

Various authors have proposed values for m. The Klein and Brown minimal information posterior odds criterion corresponds to the Schwarz criterion (1978) $m = \log n$, where n is the sample size. Others have proposed model selection criteria with smaller multipliers, such as the Akaike criterion, $m = 2$ (Akaike (1973)), the local Bayes factor, $m = 3/2$ (Smith and Spiegelhalter (1980)), $m = 1$ (Nelder and Wedderburn (1972)), the posterior Bayes factor, $m = \log(2) = .69$ (Aitkin (1991)), and the simple maximum likelihood criterion, $m = 0$.

The range of values for m indicates substantial controversy over how to trade off fit and parsimony. We are reluctant to recommend a value of m, but we can impose consistency on the reader's selection of m. Return to Table XII. For each generalization of EU we give the minimum value of m that would lead to the selection of EU over that generalization. For example, for large gains on the boundary of the triangle, the minimum m value to select EU over PT is 9.2; if the reward for degrees of freedom is less than 9.2 then PT should be selected over EU. The reader is invited to reflect on his or her preferences for parsimony, ponder the statisticians' advice on appropriate m values, and choose an m.[25]

The reader selecting an m value high enough to choose EU over all the generalizations faces a dilemma, however. In Table XII we also give [in brackets] the value of m that leads to selection of EV over EU. For large gains on the boundary of the triangle, for example, EV is selected over EU for an m value of 7.4 or higher. The EV-EU fit-parsimony comparison provides the most damning evidence against EU: on the triangle boundary a value of m high enough to lead to the selection of EU over all the generalizations necessarily implies the selection of EV over EU. The reader who highly prizes parsimony must choose EV over EU when the supports of the lotteries are different. However, in the triangle interior (where supports are the same) there are reasonable m values for which EU should be selected over the generalizations and also over EV.

Table XIII provides a compact summary of the results of all the studies. For each of the classifications in Table XII, we show the menu of best, parsimonious

---

[25] On the boundary of the triangle the Schwarz criterion multiplier values are 6.3 for large gains, small gains 5.4, and small losses 4.8. In the triangle interior the Schwarz criterion multiplier values are 6.3 for large gains, small gains 5.5, and small losses 5.5.

TABLE XIII

THE BEST THEORIES FOR VALUES OF THE MULTIPLIER ASSIGNED
TO DEGREES OF FREEDOM (m)

Boundary of Unit Triangle (Lotteries with Different Support)					
Large Gains		Small Gains		Small Losses	
m Value	Best Theory	m Value	Best Theory	m Value	Best Theory
$m < 4.3$	MF	$m < 0.5$	MF	$m < 0.8$	MF
$4.3 \leqslant m < 7.7$	RD-cave f DE	$0.5 \leqslant m < 0.8$	RD-vex	$0.8 \leqslant m < 1.9$	RD-vex
$7.7 \leqslant m < 10.4$	Fan Out	$0.8 \leqslant m < 3.2$	Fan Out	$1.9 \leqslant m < 13.5$	PT
$10.4 \leqslant m < 14.7$	WEU Out	$3.2 \leqslant m < 6.1$	PT	$13.5 \leqslant m$	EU/EV
$14.7 \leqslant m$	EV	$6.1 \leqslant m$	EV		

Interior of Unit Triangle (Lotteries with Same Support)					
Large Gains		Small Gains		Small Losses	
m Value	Best Theory	m Value	Best Theory	m Value	Best Theory
$m < 1.2$	RD-cave	$m < 0.8$	MF	$m < 0.7$	MF
$1.2 \leqslant m < 4.2$	PT	$0.8 \leqslant m < 1.1$	RD-vex	$0.7 \leqslant m < 2.2$	Fan In
$4.2 \leqslant m < 80.3$	EU	$1.1 \leqslant m < 1.8$	Fan Out	$2.2 \leqslant m$	EU/EV
$80.3 \leqslant m$	EV	$1.8 \leqslant m < 30.7$	EU		
		$30.7 \leqslant m$	EV		

All Studies	
m Value	Best Theory
$m < 2.3$	MF
$2.3 \leqslant m < 6.6$	PT
$6.6 \leqslant m < 38.6$	EU
$38.6 \leqslant m$	EV

theories depending on the multiplier m attached to degrees of freedom. For all the studies combined the menu is (in order of increasing taste for parsimony): Mixed fanning, prospect theory, EU, and EV.[26,27]

A theory on one of the Table XIII menus has passed a more rigorous test than simply being undominated. For example, EU is never dominated, but it is never selected as the best model when lottery supports are different. EU is selected for a broad range of m values for lotteries in the interior of the triangle (where lottery supports are the same); the Schwarz criterion selects EU in every case in the interior. Nevertheless, even in the triangle interior EU's performance is not beyond reproach; EU's p value for large gains is small, and in some cases EU is only the best theory when the multiplier values are large. A

[26] The results are changed very little if indifference responses from the BKJ and Harless studies are included (see footnote 17). If each indifference response is assigned to maximize the likelihood function for each individual theory, then the menu of best theories over all studies is: MF for $m \leq 2.4$, PT for $2.4 \leqslant m < 6.6$, EU for $6.6 \leqslant m < 38.7$, and EV for $38.7 \leqslant m$.

[27] EV may also be interpreted as predicting equal pattern proportions for studies with mean-preserving spread choices (see footnote 6). Aggregated over all studies, this interpretation of EV generates a chi-squared statistic of 1502.7 with 129 degrees of freedom for a p value of $1E - 166$. In Table XIII the values of m at which EV becomes best are: 14.7, 5.6, 8.0 (boundary), 80.3, 15.0, 15.7 (interior), and 16.7 instead of 38.6 (all studies).

refinement of prospect theory or a new theory which captured the boundary-interior differences could come within striking distance of EU even in the triangle interior.[28] The m value menu provides no support for betweenness as a middle ground between independence and nonlinear indifference curves: stick by independence (EV on the boundary, EU in the interior) or abandon independence and its weaker cousin betweenness for, say, prospect theory.

4. CONCLUSION

Daniel Bernoulli resolved the St. Petersburg Paradox by replacing mathematical expectation with moral expectation. But Nicholas Bernoulli, who formulated the St. Petersburg paradox, never accepted his cousin's solution, believing that there should be a single fair price for the game. As Stigler (1950) writes, economists may find it surprising that Nicholas Bernoulli and eighteenth century mathematicians believed that the St. Petersburg Paradox could only be "solved" by finding a single price for the game. Might future economists find it peculiar that twentieth century economists held firmly to EU in the face of the Allais paradox and other violations? Stigler's analysis of the development of utility theory through the beginning of this century leads him to three criteria for successful theories: generality, congruence with reality (or fit, in our terms), and manageability. We mention each of these criteria in summarizing the main points of this paper.

There have been many experimental studies comparing EU with competing theories of decision making under risk. Many of these studies use a similar format: Subjects are given several pairwise choices between choices (for example, picking the riskier gamble from one pair implies picking the riskier gamble in another pair). Various theories can then be cast as predictions about patterns of choices that should be observed. We note two important features of our approach: First, our goal is to discriminate among theories which attempt to *describe* actual choices; we have nothing to say about the normative appeal of EU or its generalizations. Second, the generalizability of our results is limited to the extent that naturally-occurring choices are different from lotteries with well-specified probabilities of monetary outcomes.

We conducted analyses of 23 data sets containing nearly 8,000 choices and 2,000 choice patterns, and aggregated the results. We draw several specific conclusions.

(1) All the theories are rejected by a chi-squared test. For every theory there is systematic variation in excluded patterns which could, in principle, be explained by a more refined theory.

---

[28] As explained in footnote 7, we do not include prospective reference theory (PRT) in the main analysis because none of the studies included here adequately test the predictions of the theory. It is notable that PRT coincides with EU for choices between gambles in the triangle interior, where EU predicts most accurately, but not for boundary gambles for which EU predicts poorly. PRT illustrates how capturing the boundary-interior distinction can improve the predictive utility of a theory. If we were to include PRT in the menus in Table XIII, PRT would not appear on any of the menus for gambles on the boundary of the triangle (PRT is dominated for large gains and for small gains). But since PRT is identical to EU in the interior, over all studies PRT would be selected over PT for $m \geqslant 4.4$ and EU would be selected over PRT for $m \geqslant 9.3$.

(2) There is room for improvement in two directions. Some theories, like EU and WEU, are too lean: They could explain the data better by allowing a few more common patterns. Other theories, such as mixed fanning and rank-dependent EU, are too fat: They allow a lot of patterns which are rarely observed. Our analyses provide theorists with a way to diagnose empirical shortcomings of current theories, and perhaps inspiration for new theorizing.

(3) There are dramatic differences between theory accuracy when the gambles in a pair have different support (they lie on the triangle boundary) and when they have the same support (they lie in the triangle interior). EU predicts poorly when support is different, and predicts well when support is the same. The transition from the boundary to the interior implies adding support, typically a small probability of an outcome. Therefore, the accuracy of EU in the interior and its inaccuracy on the boundary suggests that nonlinear weighting of small probabilities is empirically important in explaining choice behavior. This conclusion has been suggested before, but is confirmed dramatically by our analysis. Indeed, Morgenstern (1979) himself accepted that EU had limited applicability when probabilities were low:

> "Now the von Neumann-Morgenstern utility theory, as any theory, is only an approximation to an undoubtedly much richer and far more complicated reality than that which the theory describes in a simple manner.
> ...one should now point out that the domain of our axioms on utility theory is also restricted. Perhaps we should have pointed that out, instead of assuming that this would be understood *ab ovo*. For example, the probabilities used must be within certain plausible ranges and not go to 0.01 or even less to 0.001, then to be compared with other equally tiny numbers such as 0.02, etc. Rather, one imagines that a normal individual would have some intuition of what 50:50 or 25:75 means, etc." (Morgenstern (1979, p. 178).)

(4) The broadest conclusion of our analysis is that there are some losers among competing theories, and some winners. Losers include general theories which rely on betweenness rather than independence, and theories which assume fanning in throughout the triangle; those theories are dominated by other theories which use fewer free parameters and are more accurate. There is some irony here: Some of the theories we test were developed after theorists had seen some of the data sets—these include mixed fan (which we concocted), linear mixed fan or disappointment-aversion theory, lottery dependent utility, etc. It is clear that the development of linear mixed fanning, say, was influenced by data we use to test linear mixed fan. Instead of presenting a problem, the results testify to the power of our approach: We are able to reject some theories using the same data which were taken as inspiration, or support, for developing the theory in the first place.

We cannot declare a single winner among theories—much as we cannot declare a best ice cream or university—because the best theory depends on one's tradeoff between parsimony and fit. But suppose a researcher can specify a single parameter expressing the price of precision, or the reduction in goodness-of-fit (measured by a chi-squared statistic) necessary to justify allowing an extra free parameter. (Some statistical criteria suggest what this price should be.) We construct a menu of theories which are best at each price-of-precision; researchers can then use the menu to decide which theory to adopt, depending on the price they are willing to pay.

When lotteries have different support, there is *never* a price-of-precision which justifies using EU; anyone who values parsimony enough to use EU over all the generalizations should use EV instead of EU. Combining all the studies (see the bottom of Table XIII), the menu of best theories is: mixed fanning, prospect theory, EU, and EV. Statistical criteria suggest various prices of precision which favor either mixed fanning or EU; the middle ground between high and low prices favors prospect theory.

We cannot give a more definitive answer to the question of which theory is best because people use theories for different purposes. A researcher interested in a broad theory, to explain choices by as many people as possible, cares less for parsimony and more for accuracy; she might choose mixed fanning or prospect theory. A decision analyst who wants to help people make more coherent decisions, by adhering to axioms they respect but sometimes wander from, might stick with EU or EV. A mathematical economist who uses the theory as a brick to build theories of aggregate behavior may value parsimony more highly; she might choose EU or EV (though she should never use EU when choices involve gambles with different support).

However, an historical parallel described by Stigler (1950) may be instructive for those who cling to EU:

> "Economists long delayed in accepting the generalized utility function because of the complications in its mathematical analysis, although no one (except Marshall) questioned its realism...Manageability should mean the ability to bring the theory to bear on specific economic problems, not ease of manipulation. The economist has no right to expect of the universe he explores that its laws are discoverable by the indolent and the unlearned. The faithful adherence for so long to the additive utility function strikes one as showing at least a lack of enterprise" (Stigler (1950, pp. 393–394).)

The pairwise-choice studies suggest that violations of EU are robust enough that modeling of aggregate economic behavior based on alternatives to EU is well worth exploring. So far there have been relatively few such efforts.[29] Ultimately, most of the payoff for economics will come from replacing EU in models of individual behavior with more accurate descriptive principles or a single formal theory. Our results suggest which replacements are most promising, and which modifications of the currently available theories are most productive.

We see our paper as summarizing a chapter in the history of empirical studies of risky choice. We think the weight of evidence from recent studies with multiple pairwise choices, when aggregated across those studies, is sufficiently great that new pairwise-choice studies are unlikely to budge many basic conclusions—the statistical value-added of more such studies is low (compared to the

---

[29] Epstein (1990) reviews some recent efforts by economists.

value-added of new approaches). However, this sweeping conclusion leans heavily on the assumption that different studies are completely independent (which they likely are not). If studies are highly dependent then our results are overstated, and there may still be substantial value in using the pairwise-choice paradigm to exploring new domains of gambles (e.g., gambles over losses, gambles with many possible outcomes, gambles with very low probabilities); more data *could* change the way at least some theories are ranked.

If our analysis closes the chapter on pairwise-choice empirics (or summarizes the much that we know so far), then it opens new chapters as well—particularly, a chapter devoted to combining structural explanations of choice problems with more sophisticated theories of errors. Empirical studies fitting individual non-EU functions and parameters to subjects are useful and relatively rare (see Daniels and Keller (in press), Hey and Di Cagno (1990), Tversky and Kahneman (1992)). Studies that test axioms directly—e.g., Wakker, Erev, and Weber (1993) test comonotonic independence, the crucial ingredient in rank-dependent approaches—are useful too. Function-fitting, and our approach, both allow heterogeneous preferences. (The fact that estimated pattern proportions are fairly even across patterns suggest there *is* substantial heterogeneity.) For analytical tractability, it is often useful to assume homogeneity (in representative-agent models); then the sensible empirical question is which single theory, and which precise parameter values, fits everyone's choices best (see Camerer and Ho (in press)).

Finally, our general method could be applied in other domains. For example, various noncooperative solution concepts permit different sets of choices in games. Theories could be characterized as restrictions on allowable patterns of choices, and the distribution of patterns could be explicitly connected through an error rate. For example, McKelvey and Palfrey (1992) apply a similar error theory to fit various equilibrium concepts to experimental data on the "centipede" game, and to test restrictions imposed by different concepts; El-Gamal and Grether (1993) apply a similar analysis to experimental data on probability judgments. Most importantly, our method would allow one to judge which concepts, like Nash equilibrium or its various refinements (and coarsenings), best trade off parsimony and accuracy. A similar method could be applied to compare solution concepts in cooperative games. The discussion above shows how our method uses more information and hence is more powerful than methods which judge theories only by the percentage of consistent responses (e.g., Selten (1987)).

Dept. of Economics, Virginia Commonwealth University, Richmond, VA 23284, U.S.A.

and

Graduate School of Business, University of Chicago, 1101 E. 58th St., Chicago, IL 60637, U.S.A.

Manuscript received February , 1992; final revision received February, 1994.

REFERENCES

AITKIN, M. (1991): "Posterior Bayes Factors," *Journal of the Royal Statistical Society*, Series B, 53, 111–142.

AKAIKE, H. (1973): "Information Theory and an Extension of the Maximum Likelihood Principle," in *Proceedings of the 2nd International Symposium on Information Theory*, ed. by N. Petrov and F. Csadki. Budapest: Akademiai Kiado.

ALLAIS, M. (1953): "'Le Comportement de l'Homme Rationnel devant le Risque, Critique des Postulates et Axiomes de l'Ecole Americaine," *Econometrica*, 21, 503–546.

BATTALIO, R. C., J. H. KAGEL, AND K. JIRANYAKUL (1990): "Testing Between Alternative Models of Choice Under Uncertainty: Some Initial Results," *Journal of Risk and Uncertainty*, 3, 25–50.

BECKER, J. L., AND R. SARIN (1987): "Lottery Dependent Utility," *Management Science*, 33, 1367–1382.

CAMERER, C. F. (1989): "An Experimental Test of Several Generalized Utility Theories," *Journal of Risk and Uncertainty*, 2, 61–104.

––––––– (1992): "Recent Tests of Generalizations of EU Theories," in *Utility: Theories, Measurement, and Applications*, ed. by W. Edwards. Dordrecht: Kluwer.

CAMERER, C. F., AND T.-H. Ho (in press): "Violations of the Betweenness Axiom and Nonlinearity in Probability," *Journal of Risk and Uncertainty*, forthcoming.

CHEW, S. H. (1983): "A Generalization of the Quasilinear Mean with Applications to the Measurement of Income Inequality and Decision Theory Resolving the Allais Paradox," *Econometrica*, 51, 1065–1092.

––––––– (1989): "Axiomatic Utility Theories with the Betweenness Property," *Annals of Operations Research*, 19, 273–298.

CHEW, S. H., AND L. G. EPSTEIN (1990): "A Unifying Approach to Axiomatic Non-Expected Utility Theories," *Journal of Economic Theory*, 49, 207–240.

CHEW, S. H., L. G. EPSTEIN, AND U. SEGAL (1991): "Mixture Symmetry and Quadratic Utility," *Econometrica*, 59, 139–163.

CHEW, S. H., E. KARNI, AND Z. SAFRA (1987): "Risk Aversion in the Theory of Expected Utility with Rank Dependent Probabilities," *Journal of Economic Theory*, 42, 370–381.

CHEW, S. H., AND K. R. MacCRIMMON (1979): "The HILO Structure and the Allais Paradox," University of British Columbia Working Paper.

CHEW, S. H., AND W. WALLER (1986): "Empirical Tests of Weighted Utility Theory," *Journal of Mathematical Psychology*, 30, 55–62.

CONLISK, J. (1989): "Three Variants on the Allais Example," *American Economic Review*, 79, 392–407.

CRAWFORD, V. P. (1988): "Stochastic Choice with Quasiconcave Preference Functions," Department of Economics 88-28, University of California, San Diego.

DANIELS, R. L., AND L. R. KELLER (in press): "An Experimental Evaluation of the Descriptive Validity of Gamble Dependent Utility," *Journal of Risk and Uncertainty*, forthcoming.

DEKEL, E. (1986): "An Axiomatic Characterization of Preferences Under Uncertainty: Weakening the Independence Axiom," *Journal of Economic Theory*, 40, 304–318.

EL-GAMAL, M., AND D. GRETHER (1993): "Uncovering Behavioral Strategies: Likelihood-based Experimental Data-mining," Caltech Division of Social Sciences and Humanities Working Paper.

EPSTEIN, L. G. (1990): "Behavior Under Risk: Recent Developments in Theory and Applications," University of Toronto Department of Economics Working Paper.

FISHBURN, P. C. (1982): "Nontransitive Measurable Utility," *Journal of Mathematical Psychology*, 26, 31–67.

––––––– (1983): "Transitive Measurable Utility," *Journal of Economic Theory*, 31, 293–317.

––––––– (1988): *Nonlinear Preference and Utility Theory*. Baltimore, MD: Johns Hopkins Press.

GREEN, J. R., AND B. JULLIEN (1988): "Ordinal Independence in Nonlinear Utility Theory," *Journal of Risk and Uncertainty*, 1, 355–387. (Erratum, vol. 2, p. 119.)

GUL, F. (1991): "A Theory of Disappointment Aversion," *Econometrica*, 59, 667–686.

HARLESS, D. W. (1992): "Predictions About Indifference Curves Inside the Unit Triangle: A Test of Variants of Expected Utility Theory," *Journal of Economic Behavior and Organization*, 18, 391–414.

––––––– (1993): "Experimental Tests of Prospective Reference Theory," *Economic Letters*, 43, 71–76.

HEY, J. D., AND D. DiCAGNO (1990): "Circles and Triangles: An Experimental Estimation of Indifference Lines in the Marschak-Machina Triangle," *Journal of Behavioral Decision Making*, 3, 279–306.

GENERALIZED EXPECTED UTILITY   1289

HEY, J., AND C. ORME (1993): "Investigating Parsimonious Generalizations of Expected Utility Theory using Experimental Data," University of York Centre for Experimental Economics Working Paper.

KAHNEMAN, D., AND A. TVERSKY (1979): "Prospect Theory: An Analysis of Decision Under Risk," *Econometrica*, 47, 263–291.

KLEIN, R. W., AND S. J. BROWN (1984): "Model Selection When There is 'Minimal' Prior Information," *Econometrica*, 52, 1291–1312.

LICHTENSTEIN, S., AND P. SLOVIC (1971): "Reversal of Preferences Between Bids and Choices in Gambling Decisions," *Journal of Experimental Psychology*, 89, 46–55.

MACHINA, M. J. (1982): "'Expected Utility' Analysis Without the Independence Axiom," *Econometrica*, 50, 277–323.

—— (1985): "Stochastic Choice Functions Generated from Deterministic Preferences over Lotteries," *Economic Journal*, 95, 575–594.

—— (1987): "Choice Under Uncertainty: Problems Solved and Unsolved," *Journal of Economic Perspectives*, 1, 121–154.

MARSCHAK, J. (1950): "Rational Behavior, Uncertain Prospects, and Measurable Utility," *Econometrica*, 18, 111–141.

McKELVEY, R., AND T. PALFREY (1992): "An Experimental Investigation of the Centipede Game," *Econometrica*, 60, 803–836.

MORGENSTERN, O. (1979): "Some Reflections on Utility Theory," in *EU Hypotheses and the Allais Paradox*, ed. by M. Allais and O. Hagen. Dordrecht: D. Reidel.

NEILSON, W. S. (1992a): "A Mixed Fan Hypothesis and its Implications for Behavior Towards Risk," *Journal of Economic Behavior and Organization*, 19, 197–212.

—— (1992b): "Some Mixed Results on Boundary Effects," *Economics Letters*, 39, 275–278.

NELDER, J. A., AND R. W. M. WEDDERBURN (1972): "Generalized Linear Models," *Journal of the Royal Statistical Society*, Series A, 135, 370–384.

PRELEC, D. (1990): "A 'Pseudo-Endowment' Effect and its Implications for Some Recent Non-EU Models," *Journal of Risk and Uncertainty*, 3, 247–259.

QUIGGIN, J. (1982): "A Theory of Anticipated Utility," *Journal of Economic Behavior and Organization*, 3, 323–343.

—— (1993): "Testing Between Alternative Models of Choice Under Uncertainty: Comment," *Journal of Risk and Uncertainty*, 6, 161–164.

SCHWARZ, G. (1978): "Estimating the Dimension of a Model," *Annals of Statistics*, 6, 461–464.

SEGAL, U. (1987): "Some Remarks on Quiggin's Theory of Anticipated Utility," *Journal of Economic Behavior and Organization*, 8, 145–154.

—— (1989): "Anticipated Utility: A Measure Representation Approach," *Annals of Operations Research*, 19, 359–373.

SELTEN, R. (1987): "Equity and Coalition Bargaining in Experimental Three Person Games," in *Laboratory Experiments in Economics: Six Points of View*, ed. by A. Roth. Cambridge: Cambridge University Press.

—— (1991): "Properties of a Measure of Predictive Success," *Mathematical Social Sciences*, 21, 153–200.

SMITH, A. F. M., AND D. J. SPIEGELHALTER (1980): "Bayes Factors and Choice Criteria for Linear Models," *Journal of the Royal Statistical Society*, Series B, 42, 213–220.

SMITH, V., AND J. WALKER (1993): "Monetary Rewards and Decision Cost in Experimental Economics," *Economic Inquiry*, 31, 245–261.

SOPHER, B., AND G. GIGLIOTTI (1990): "A Test of Generalized Expected Utility," Department of Economics, Rutgers University.

STARMER, C., AND R. SUGDEN (1989): "Probability and Juxtaposition Effects: An Experimental Investigation of the Common Ratio Effect," *Journal of Risk and Uncertainty*, 2, 159–178.

STIGLER, G. J. (1950): "The Development of Utility Theory. II," *Journal of Political Economy*, 58, 373–396.

TVERSKY, A., AND D. KAHNEMAN (1992): "Advances in Prospect Theory: Cumulative Representation of Uncertainty," *Journal of Risk and Uncertainty*, 5, 297–323.

VISCUSI, K. W. (1989): "Prospective Reference Theory: Toward An Explanation of the Paradoxes," *Journal of Risk and Uncertainty*, 2, 235–264.

WAKKER, P., I. EREV, AND E. WEBER (1993): "Comonotonic Independence: The Critical Test Between Classical and Rank-Dependent Utility Theories," University of Chicago Center for Decision Research Working Paper.

YAARI, M. E. (1987): "The Dual Theory of Choice Under Risk," *Econometrica*, 55, 95–115.

[23]

Econometrica, Vol. 62, No. 6 (November, 1994), 1291–1326

INVESTIGATING GENERALIZATIONS OF EXPECTED UTILITY THEORY USING EXPERIMENTAL DATA

By John D. Hey and Chris Orme[1]

A number of generalizations of the expected utility preference functional are estimated using experimentally generated data involving 100 pairwise choice questions repeated on two separate occasions. Likelihood ratio tests are conducted to investigate the statistical superiority of the various generalizations, and the Akaike information criterion is used to distinguish between them. The economic superiority of the various generalizations is also explored and the paper concludes that, for many subjects, the superiority of several of the generalizations is not established.

Keywords: Expected utility, non-expected utility, risk, preference functionals, pairwise choice, experiments.

1. INTRODUCTION

Experimentally observed violations of expected utility theory (EUT) have stimulated a deluge of generalized preference functionals, almost all containing EUT as a special case. Rather obviously, such generalizations "explain" observed preferences better than EUT, at the expense, equally obviously, of predictive power. This paper reports the outcome of an experimental investigation designed to discover whether (a subset of) these generalizations explain observed data *significantly* better (in a statistical sense) and whether the implied behavior (in an economic sense) is significantly different.

We use experimentally-generated data on preferences to estimate a number of preference functionals. Within the constraints imposed by our data, we tried to estimate as many of the alternative preference functionals as possible. The simplest, of course, is the risk neutral preference functional; an individual with such a functional simply chooses on the basis of *expected value*. The most popular preference functional in use in economics is the expected utility functional; if an individual has such a functional then he or she chooses on the basis of *expected utility*. In this case, estimation of the preference functional is equivalent to estimation of the (Neumann-Morgenstern) utility function. This can be done either without restriction (that is, by estimating the utility associated with each possible outcome) or with some restriction on the functional form (for example, by assuming constant absolute risk aversion). Here we report results using the former approach. Given that our experiment involved just four

[1] We are grateful to the ESRC for financing the experiments reported in this paper and EXEC, the Centre for Experimental Economics at the University of York. Our thanks also to Norman Spivey for writing the software for this experiment and to Michele Bernasconi and Giacomo Pignataro, Research Fellows at the Centre. Our thanks to Graham Loomes for numerous comments, and also to participants at the FUR-VI conference in Paris in June 1992, particularly Colin Camerer, Paul Schoemaker, and Barry Sopher, and to participants at numerous other seminars and conferences, particularly Glenn Harrison. Finally, our grateful thanks to two extremely helpful and constructive referees whose comments improved the paper enormously, as did the comments of a co-editor.

outcomes, this implies that estimation of the expected utility preference functional involves the estimation of four utility values.[2]

The various generalizations of expected utility theory (EUT) estimated in this paper can be classified in a number of ways. For our present purposes the most convenient way is related to the number of *extra* parameters involved in the respective theories: some theories have relatively few extra parameters; some have relatively many—though the numbers may be reduced by the adoption of particular functional forms. The most parsimonious generalizations are disappointment aversion theory (Gul (1991)) and prospective reference theory (Viscusi (1989)); both these involve just *one* extra parameter—irrespective of the number of outcomes and the values of the probabilities. Somewhat less parsimonious is weighted utility theory (Chew (1983)) which requires $(n - 2)$ extra parameters—where n is the number of outcomes in the decision problem; these are the *weights* referred to in the theory's name.

The class of models which come under the title of rank dependent expected utility (see, inter alia, Quiggin (1982), Yaari (1987), and Chew, Karni, and Safra (1987)) involve a second function which operates on the cumulative probabilities. The same considerations apply to this function as to the utility function discussed earlier: it can either be estimated without any restrictions or some specific functional form can be assumed. The problem with the first approach is that a relatively large number of parameters have to be estimated. In the context of this experiment, where the cumulative probabilities take the values $i/8$, for $i = 0, \ldots, 8$, this would involve the estimation of 7 additional parameters.[3] Given the nature of our data we felt that this was too many parameters to estimate. We therefore adopted the following strategy: first, we took two specific functional forms for this probability function—one the power function, and the other a form recommended in Quiggin (1982)—each of these involved just one parameter, so estimation of the rank dependent preference functional under either of these specific functional forms involved just one extra parameter relative to expected utility theory; second, we imposed no functional form on the probability function, but, in order to cut down the number of estimated parameters, we imposed linearity on the utility function; that is, we assumed risk neutrality (in the context of the rank dependent story)—this is Yaari's dual theory (Yaari (1987)). This theory, unlike the other theories which *are* generalizations of expected utility theory, is not such a generalization—though it *is* a generalization of the risk neutral theory.

A preference functional which approaches the pairwise decision problem from a totally different (nonholistic) perspective is that of regret theory. This involves the comparison of each outcome with every other possible outcome, and, in the absence of any restriction on the functional form of these relative "preferences," it involves the estimation of $(n - 1)(n/2 - 1)$ extra parameters relative to expected utility theory. A theory with a rather similar perspective is

---

[2] Though, because of normalization, one of these can be fixed arbitrarily—see later.
[3] The values for $i = 0$ and $i = 8$ are fixed at 0 and 1 respectively.

that of quadratic utility theory (Chew et al. (1991)); this involves $n(n-1)/2$ extra parameters.

For each of our subjects, we estimate each of these preference functionals. These estimations enable us to begin to answer the question as to whether (any of) these generalizations is significantly better than EUT (and, indeed, whether EUT and Yaari's dual theory are in turn significantly better than risk neutrality).

The plan of the paper is as follows: Section 2 describes the experimental design and Section 3 the preference functionals under investigation; Section 4 discusses the estimation procedure and Section 5 the results of the estimation; Section 6 then looks at the economic significance of the results, while Section 7 concludes. Appendices contain technical material. The invitation and instructions for the experiment can be obtained from the authors, as well as the computer program and the data generated by the experiment.

2. THE EXPERIMENTAL DATA

The results reported in this paper are part of the findings of a four-part experiment conducted with 80 subjects over a period of a week to 10 days. Each of the 80 subjects performed on separate days (separated by at least one day in every case) a total of four experiments: *Circles* 1, *Dynamics* 1, *Circles* 2, and *Dynamics* 2, in that order. The experiments which concern this paper are the two *Circles* experiments; the two *Dynamics* experiments consisted of a fairly complicated dynamic decision problem under risk. For the analysis of these latter experiments some indication of the subjects' preference functionals was required; this was part of the reason for running the *Circles* experiments, but the analysis of these experiments is self-contained. The average payment made to the 80 subjects over these four experiments was £46.86, with a standard deviation of £15.65; the maximum payment to any one subject was £83.35 and the minimum £7.41. The time taken to complete the experiments varied from subject to subject (we allowed them, and indeed encouraged them, to proceed at their own pace), but the average time was about 45 minutes for each of the *Dynamics* experiments and about 35 minutes for each of the *Circles* experiments. Thus, ignoring any time taken outside the experimental laboratory, the average payment was around £17.50 per hour spent doing the experiments. This is considerably above the marginal wage rate of the subjects performing the experiment, who were all students at the University of York on EXEC's computerized register and who were recruited by mail-shot. Details of the invitation posted to those on the register and the instructions given to those who volunteered are available on request. It was repeatedly emphasized that payment for each experiment was independent of the other experiments, but that no payment would be made until all four experiments had been completed by the subject. Accordingly, we paid subjects for all four experiments after they had performed the final one. Precise details of the payment mechanism are given below.

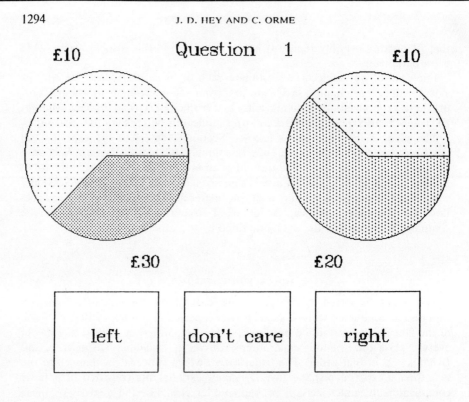

FIGURE 1.—A screen dump from the circles experiment.

Each of the *Circles* experiments consisted of 100 pairwise choice questions presented on a computer screen. In each of the 100 questions, subjects were presented with a choice between two risky prospects, portrayed in the form of segmented circles. An example is illustrated in Figure 1; in this, the left-hand circle represents a risky prospect in which there is a five-eighths chance of getting £10 and a three-eighths chance of getting £30; the right-hand circle represents a risky prospect in which there is a three-eighths chance of getting £10 and a five-eighths chance of getting £20. By pressing "*l*" (respectively "*d*" or "*r*") subjects could indicate a preference for the left-hand prospect (respectively indifference or a preference for the right hand prospect). Once they were satisfied with the indicated preference they pressed "Enter" to confirm their choice and moved on to the next question. The incentive mechanism was straightforward: subjects were told that when they had answered all 100 questions, then one of the questions would be chosen at random (using a "roulette wheel" the circumference of which was calibrated from 1 to 100) and their answer to that particular question recalled. Their preferred choice on that particular question was then noted for playing out on completion of all four

TABLE I

THE TWENTY-FIVE PAIRS OF QUESTIONS[a]

p_1	p_2	p_3	q_1	q_2	q_3
.625	.000	.375	.375	.625	.000
.375	.625	.000	.500	.250	.250
.000	1.000	.000	.125	.500	.375
.125	.750	.125	.250	.500	.250
.500	.375	.125	.625	.125	.250
.250	.750	.000	.375	.000	.625
.250	.625	.125	.375	.250	.375
.250	.250	.500	.125	.625	.250
.125	.375	.500	.000	1.000	.000
.125	.250	.625	.000	.500	.500
.125	.875	.000	.250	.625	.125
.250	.750	.000	.500	.000	.500
.625	.375	.000	.750	.125	.125
.125	.500	.375	.250	.000	.750
.125	.750	.125	.375	.125	.500
.375	.375	.250	.500	.125	.375
.000	.750	.250	.125	.375	.500
.500	.125	.375	.375	.500	.125
.750	.000	.250	.625	.375	.000
.250	.375	.375	.375	.000	.625
.000	.875	.125	.125	.625	.250
.000	.625	.375	.125	.250	.625
.250	.500	.250	.125	.875	.000
.500	.500	.000	.625	.125	.250
.250	.500	.250	.375	.250	.375

[a] The left-hand gamble takes the values y_1, y_2, and y_3 with respective probabilities p_1, p_2, and p_3 and the right-hand side gamble takes the values y_1, y_2, and y_3 with respective probabilities q_1, q_2, and q_3. The y vector takes the values (£0, £10, £20), (£0, £10, £30), (£0, £20, £30), and (£10, £20, £30).

experiments; if on that question they had indicated indifference, then the experimenter decided which prospect was to be played out.[4] The actual mechanism for "playing out" a particular prospect (at the conclusion of all four experiments) was also straightforward: the prospect had previously been noted on a circular template which was then physically put on top of the "roulette wheel" which the subject then spun themselves. The implication for honest reporting of preferences seemed to be abundantly clear to the subjects.[5] This procedure had been used earlier in a pilot experiment reported in Hey and Di Cagno (1990). In this pilot, subjects were asked just 60 questions and we discovered that 60 was fewer than we could reasonably ask within the attention span of the subjects.

[4] The mechanism by which the experimenter would choose was not specified.
[5] We are, of course, aware of the objections raised by Holt (1986) to the effect that, if the subject's preference functional is not EU, then this incentive mechanism may not induce honest reporting of preferences. We are also aware of work by Starmer and Sugden (1991) which suggests that this may not be a problem in practice. Much depends on how subjects reduce multi-stage gambles to single stage gambles, and, in particular, on whether they use the certainty-equivalent mechanism. If they do, then Holt's objection loses much of its force.

The 100 questions were composed of 4 sets of (the same) 25 questions, each set applied to 3 of the 4 amounts £0, £10, £20, and £30. The probabilities were all multiplies of one-eighth—and the subjects were informed of this.[6] Table I gives details of these 25 pairs.[7] The 100 questions were arranged in random order. The same 100 questions were used in *Circles* 1 and *Circles* 2, except insofar as the order was changed randomly and the positions of the two circles in each question reversed (so that if a prospect was on the left in *Circles* 1 it was on the right in *Circles* 2 and *vice versa*). This procedure enabled us to carry out a consistency check on the subjects' answers; this is something which is very rarely done in this type of experiment. The average consistency rate turned out to be around 75%.[8]

3. THE PREFERENCE FUNCTIONALS

First, some notation. Let $x = (x_1, x_2, x_3, x_4)$ denote the four consequences (£0, £10, £20, and £30) used in this experiment; let $p = (p_1, p_2, p_3, p_4)$ denote the respective probabilities in the gamble on the left-hand side of the computer screen and $q = (q_1, q_2, q_3, q_4)$ denote the respective probabilities in the gamble on the right-hand side. All the theories considered imply a valuation of the left-hand gamble relative to the right-hand gamble; and, *except* in the case of regret theory, these valuations are obtained by simply subtracting the valuation of the right-hand gamble from the valuation of the left-hand gamble. Regret theory arrives directly at a relative evaluation. The details are as follows, where $V(p, q)$ denotes the relative evaluation (that is, the subject prefers the left-hand gamble to the right-hand gamble if and only if $V(p, q)$ is greater than zero, and is indifferent between them if $V(p, q)$ is equal to zero). The two letters to the left of the theory's name are the abbreviation that we will be using henceforth to refer to that theory.

RN—Risk *Neutrality*:

$$V(p, q) = W(p) - W(q) \qquad \text{where}$$

$$W(r) = k[r_2 x_2 + r_3 x_3 + r_4 x_4].$$

(Recall that $x_1 = 0$.)

Here the parameter to be estimated is k. (See later concerning the normalization of the error variance to unity.)

---

[6] This avoids possible misperceptions of the probabilities. We decided that any finer division of the probabilities—say into tenths—would be too difficult for the subjects; whilst any cruder division —say into sixths—would be too uninformative for us.

[7] Perhaps we should note that there is a design problem in the choice of these 25 pairs, and, more generally, in the choice of the 100 pairs. Some choices will lead to more accurate estimates than other choices. However, the "best" choice depends on the subject's actual preference functional—which we do not know *ex ante*. A useful discussion of these and related issues can be found in Mueller and Ponce de Leon (1992).

[8] Note that this is a check as to whether subjects give the same answer when confronted with essentially the same question, though with left and right reversed and with the question appearing in a different position in the set of questions. They were never given exactly identical questions so we cannot test the consistency rate under identical conditions.

EU—*Subjective Expected Utility Theory*:

$$V(p,q) = W(p) - W(q) \qquad \text{where}$$

$$W(r) = r_2u(x_2) + r_3u(x_3) + r_4u(x_4).$$

Here the parameters to be estimated are $u(x_i)$, $i = 2,3,4$. Note that we have normalized[9] so that $u(x_1) = 0$. For expected utility theory, as is well known, the utility function is unique only up to a linear transformation, which usually means that one can set *two* utility values arbitrarily. However, as we shall show later, the second normalization is taken care of by our assumption concerning the nature of the error term. Note that **EU** reduces to **RN** when $u(x) = kx$—implying two restrictions in the context of this experiment.

DA—*Disappointment Aversion Theory*:

This is a model introduced by Gul (1991); it models behavior as incorporating ex post disappointment or elation, depending on whether the actual outcome is worse or better than that expected, with the decision-maker anticipating such feelings ex ante. Here our characterization appears different from that in Gul (1991), but it can be shown (see Appendix 1) that they are identical; ours is more useful for our present purposes.

$$V(p,q) = W(p) - W(q) \qquad \text{where}$$

$$W(r) = \min\{W_1, W_2, W_3\} \qquad \text{and where}$$

$$W_1 = \frac{[(1+\beta)r_2u(x_2) + (1+\beta)r_3u(x_3) + r_4u(x_4)]}{(1 + \beta r_1 + \beta r_2 + \beta r_3)},$$

$$W_2 = [(1+\beta)r_2u(x_2) + r_3u(x_3) + r_4u(x_4)]/(1 + \beta r_1 + \beta r_2),$$

$$W_3 = [r_2u(x_2) + r_3u(x_3) + r_4u(x_4)]/(1 + \beta r_1).$$

Again, we have normalized so that $u(x_1) = 0$. Here the parameters to be estimated are $u(x_i)$, $i = 2,3,4$ and β. The parameter β is Gul's additional parameter; if $\beta = 0$, **DA** reduces to **EU**.

PR—*Prospective Reference Theory*:

This is a model introduced by Viscusi (1989); it models behavior as depending upon a preference functional which is a weighted average of the expected utility functional using the correct probability weights and the expected utility functional using equal probability weights for all the non-null outcomes.

$$V(p,q) = W(p) - W(q) \qquad \text{where}$$

$$W(r) = \lambda[r_2u(x_2) + r_3u(x_3) + r_4u(x_4)]$$

$$+ (1-\lambda)[c_2u(x_2) + c_3u(x_3) + c_4u(x_4)]$$

where $c_i = 1/n(r)$ if $r_i > 0$ and 0 otherwise, and where $n(r)$ is the number of nonzero elements in the vector r. Here the normalization is the same as the

---

[9] An alternative interpretation, of course, is that $u(x_i)$ measures the difference between the utility of x_i and the utility of x_1. The difference is inessential.

expected utility normalization: $u(x_1) = 0$. Here the parameters to be estimated are $u(x_i)$, $i = 2, 3, 4$ and λ. Viscusi (1989) refers to λ as the weight of the "relative information content...associated with the stated lottery" and $(1 - \lambda)$ as the weight of the "relative information content...associated with the reference probability." Note that if $\lambda = 1$ then **PR** reduces to **EU**.

   QU—**Q**uadratic *Utility*:

   This is a model introduced by Chew, Epstein, and Segal (1991). Its motivation is the weakening of the independence axiom of EUT to an axiom (even weaker than the betweenness axiom) known as mixture symmetry. This requires that if F and G are the cumulative probability functions of two risky prospects about which an individual feels indifferent, then for any mixture $\alpha F + (1 - \alpha)G$ with $0 < \alpha < 0.5$ there is some β ($0.5 < \beta < 1$) such that this mixture is indifferent for this individual to the mixture $\beta F + (1 - \beta)G$. The implied preference functional:

$$V(p, q) = W(p) - W(q) \qquad \text{where}$$

$$W(r) = \sum_{i=1}^{4} \sum_{j=1}^{4} \psi(x_i, x_j) r_i r_j$$

and where $\psi(x_i, x_j) = \psi(x_j, x_i)$. Here we normalize so that $\psi(x_1, x_1) = 0$. Note that **QU** reduces to **EU** if $\psi(x_i, x_j) = [u(x_i) + u(x_j)]/2$ for all i and j, a total of 6 restrictions in the context of this experiment.

   RD—**R**egret *Theory* (*with* **D**ependence):

   The regret model was effectively introduced simultaneously by Bell (1982) and by Loomes and Sugden (1982); it was later generalized by Loomes and Sugden (1987). It models behavior as incorporating ex post regret or rejoicing depending upon whether the outcome under the actual choice is worse or better than the outcome that would have resulted from the rejected choice, with the decision-maker anticipating such feelings ex ante. We estimate two versions, this first assuming dependence between the two gambles in the manner described below:

$$V(p, q) = z_1 \psi(x_2, x_1) + z_2 \psi(x_3, x_2) + z_3 \psi(x_4, x_3)$$
$$+ z_4 \psi(x_3, x_1) + z_5 \psi(x_4, x_2) + z_6 \psi(x_4, x_1).$$

Here the $z = (z_1, z_2, z_3, z_4, z_5, z_6)$ is a function (which cannot easily be written in analytical form—see Appendix 1) of p and q. This "dependence" characterization assumes that the subject juxtaposes the two gambles in the orientation in which they appear on the screen. So, for example, in Question 1 as it appears in Figure 1, we have $z_1 = 0.0$ (because £0 and £10 are never juxtaposed), $z_2 = 0.250$ (because £20 appears on the right-hand gamble and £10 appears on the left-hand gamble between southwest and northwest (one-quarter of the time)), $z_3 = -0.375$ (because £30 appears on the left-hand gamble and £20 appears on the right-hand gamble between southwest and east (three-eighths of the time)), and $z_4 = z_5 = z_6 = 0.0$ (because £20 and £0, and £30 and £10, and £30 and £0 are never juxtaposed). Here the parameters to be estimated are the $\psi(x_i, x_j)$ for $j = 1, 2, 3$ and $i > j$, though, given the gambles used in this experiment $\psi(x_4, x_1)$

cannot be estimated since x_4 and x_1 are never juxtaposed. Note that **RD** reduces to **EU** if $\psi(x_i, x_j) = u(x_i) - u(x_j)$ for all x_i and x_j; a total of two restrictions in the context of this experiment.

RI—**R**egret Theory (with Independence):

This second version of regret theory assumes independence between the two gambles, as described below.

$$V(p, q) = (p_1 q_2 - p_2 q_1)\psi(x_2, x_1) + (p_2 q_3 - p_3 q_2)\psi(x_3, x_2)$$
$$+ (p_3 q_4 - p_4 q_3)\psi(x_4, x_3) + (p_1 q_3 - p_3 q_1)\psi(x_3, x_1)$$
$$+ (p_2 q_4 - p_4 q_2)\psi(x_4, x_2) + (p_1 q_4 - p_4 q_1)\psi(x_4, x_1).$$

This characterization assumes that the subject views the two gambles as being statistically independent. The parameters to be estimated are the same as in the **RD** model. Note that **RI** reduces to **EU** if $\psi(x_i, x_j) = u(x_i) - u(x_j)$ for all x_i and x_j; a total of three restrictions in the context of this experiment.

RP—**R**ank Dependence with the **P**ower Weighting Function:

The rank dependent expected utility model is the outcome of a number of contributions, including Quiggin (1982), Yaari (1987), and Chew, Karni and Safra (1987). It models behavior as ranking the outcomes in order of preference and then distorting the decumulative probabilities (of getting at least a given outcome) through some "probability weighting function." We estimate two versions, this first assuming that the probability weighting function takes the specific functional form of the *power* function.

$$V(p, q) = u(x_2)[W_1(p) - W_1(q)] + u(x_3)[W_2(p) - W_2(q)]$$
$$+ u(x_4)[W_3(p) - W_3(q)] \qquad \text{where}$$

$$W_1(r) = w(r_2 + r_3 + r_4) - w(r_3 + r_4),$$
$$W_2(r) = w(r_3 + r_4) - w(r_4),$$
$$W_3(r) = w(r_4),$$
$$w(r) = r^\gamma.$$

Here the parameters to be estimated are $u(x_i)$, $i = 2, 3, 4$, and γ. Note that **RP** reduces to **EU** if $\gamma = 1$.

RQ—**R**ank Dependence with the 'Quiggin' Weighting Function:

This second version of rank dependent **EU** assumes that the weighting function $w(\cdot)$ takes the specific functional form recommended by Quiggin (1982). It allows the probability function to be S-shaped:

$$w(r) = r^\gamma / [r^\gamma + (1 - r)^\gamma]^{1/\gamma}.$$

Here the parameters to be estimated are $u(x_i)$, $i = 2, 3, 4$, and γ. Note that **RQ** reduces to **EU** if $\gamma = 1$.

WU—*Weighted Utility Theory*:

This model was proposed by Chew (1983) and Dekel (1986) inter alia. It takes as its raison d'etre the relaxation of the strong independence axiom (of EUT) to a form known as the weak independence axiom (see Chew (1983)). This requires that if F and G are the cumulative probability functions of two risky prospects about which the individual feels indifferent, then for any mixture $\alpha F + (1 - \alpha)H$ there is some β for which this mixture is indifferent for this individual to the mixture $\beta G + (1 - \beta)H$ for all H:

$$V(p, q) = W(p) - W(q) \qquad \text{where}$$

$$W(r) = \left[w_2 r_2 u(x_2) + w_3 r_3 u(x_3) + r_4 u(x_4) \right] / \left[r_1 + r_2 w_2 + r_3 w_3 + r_4 \right].$$

Here w_2 and w_3 are the *weights* attached to x_2 and x_3. Once again, the normalization is that $u(x_1)$ is put equal to zero; in addition, we set the weights attached to x_1 and x_4 equal to unity (see Chew (1983)). Here the parameters to be estimated are $u(x_i)$, $i = 2, 3, 4$, and w_2 and w_3. Note that **WU** reduces to **EU** if w_2 and w_3 (the weights attached to x_2 and x_3 respectively) are additionally both equal to unity.

YD—*Yaari's Dual Model*:

As already discussed, this model proposed by Yaari (1987) is a special case of the rank dependent expected utility model where the probability function is left completely general but the utility function is assumed to be linear:

$$V(p, q) = W(p) - W(q) \qquad \text{where}$$

$$W(r) = k \big[(x_2 - x_1) w(r_2 + r_3 + r_4) + (x_3 - x_2)$$

$$\times w(r_3 + r_4) + (x_4 - x_3) w(r_4) \big] \qquad \text{where}$$

$$w(r) = \beta_i \quad \text{if} \quad r = 0.125i, \quad i = 1, \dots, 7;$$

$$w(0) = 0 \quad \text{and} \quad w(1) = 1.$$

Here the parameters to be estimated are the β_i $(i = 1, \dots, 7)$ and k. Note that **YD** reduces to **RN** if $\beta_i = 0.125i$ (for $i = 1, \dots, 7$), a total of 7 restrictions in the context of this experiment.

4. THE ESTIMATION PROCEDURE

We assume that all subjects are different. We therefore fit each of the 11 preference functionals discussed above to the subject's stated preferences for each of the 80 subjects *individually*. For the purposes of estimation, we need to make some assumption about the *stochastic* structure underlying the observations. The theories themselves are of no help in this respect since they are all theories of *deterministic* choice.[10] This, in turn, implies (if none of the preference functionals discussed above fits any subject's stated preferences exactly and if no other preference functional not considered here is in fact the correct functional) that the subject must be stating his or her preferences *with some error*. Such error may arise from a variety of sources: the subjects could misunderstand the nature of the experiment; they could press the wrong key by

---

[10] There *are* theories of stochastic choice, but these are not the concern of this paper, nor indeed of much of the recent debate concerning preference functionals.

accident; they could be in a hurry to complete the experiment; they could be motivated by something other than maximizing their welfare from participating in the experiment. For rather obvious reasons, we confine attention to what we might term "genuine" error—mistakes, carelessness, slips, inattentiveness, etc. —and we make what is possibly the most natural assumption for an economist to make: namely that the effect of such error is to add a white noise, normally distributed, zero-mean error term to the valuations given by the various preference functionals. The Central Limit Theorem could be invoked to support such an assumption.[11] This would suggest that the stated preferences were based on the value of y^*, given by:

$$y^* = V(p,q) + \varepsilon \qquad \text{where } \varepsilon \text{ is } N(0,1).$$

Note that we have put the error variance equal to unity. This is a further normalization. An alternative procedure, say with the expected utility characterization, would be, in addition to $u(x_1) = 0$, to put (say) $u(x_4) = 1$ and then specify the error variance to be σ^2; in this case we would estimate σ in addition to $u(x_2)$ and $u(x_3)$. We choose instead to put the error variance equal to unity and then estimate $u(x_2)$, $u(x_3)$, and $u(x_4)$. The difference is inessential, though we do have to be careful in interpreting the results: other things being equal, under our procedure, a subject who makes relatively small errors will have relatively large values for $u(x_2)$, $u(x_3)$, and $u(x_4)$, while a subject who makes relatively large errors will have relatively small values for $u(x_2)$, $u(x_3)$, and $u(x_4)$. Under the alternative procedure, the relatively careful subject would have a relatively small value for σ.

We need now to distinguish between two types of subject: (1) a subject who *always* expressed a strict preference for either the left-hand gamble or the right-hand gamble; (2) a subject who *sometimes*[12] expressed indifference between the left- and right-hand gambles. We should emphasize that these distinctions must be made separately for each of the two circles experiments, since there were some subjects who always expressed strict preference in *Circles* 1 but sometimes expressed indifference in *Circles* 2, and vice versa.

These two types of subjects need to be treated differently. The first type is straightforward; our assumptions imply that the data generating mechanism is

---

[11] We are, however, exploring other possibilities: for example, that questions vary in their difficulty, and hence that the error variance varies from question to question. In a sense, this simply removes the problem one stage: we now need to specify what determines the difficulty of a question. However, we do have data, for each subject, on how long it took the subject to answer each question; preliminary estimations suggest that the error variance may be proportional to this time, though one needs to correct for a general speeding up of the time to answer as subjects proceeded through the 100 questions. For some other thoughts in this direction see Wilcox (1993).

[12] It is not clear why they might do this, for even if they are genuinely indifferent between the two gambles, there is nothing for them to gain by saying so. Contrariwise, there is no reason for them not to do so. This *might* have serious consequences for our estimation procedures, if, for example, a subject were to always reply "1" when genuinely indifferent, but it is not clear what might be done to identify or rectify such bias.

1302   J. D. HEY AND C. ORME

given by:

left-hand gamble stated as preferred if $y^* > 0$,

right-hand gamble stated as preferred if $y^* \leq 0$.

For the second type, we need to make an additional assumption about the circumstances under which indifference is stated. The natural assumption is that this occurs whenever y^* is close to zero, and that closeness should be defined in a symmetrical manner. This gives as the data generating mechanism:

left-hand gamble stated as preferred if $y^* > \tau$,

right-hand gamble stated as preferred if $y^* \leq -\tau$,

indifference stated if $-\tau < y^* \leq \tau$.

Here we have an additional parameter to estimate: the *threshold* parameter τ. Note that for the first type of subject, our assumptions effectively constrain τ to be equal to zero; if, on the other hand, we tried to use the second data generating mechanism for type (1) subjects, the maximum likelihood estimate of τ for them would also be zero, since by definition such subjects never reported indifference.

Finally, we assume that the errors are independently distributed across questions. This completes the stochastic specification. Maximum likelihood methods were used to derive the parameter estimates. Technical details are given in Appendix 2 and Orme (1995).

5. THE ESTIMATED PREFERENCE FUNCTIONALS

We refer to the data obtained from *Circles* 1 as *Data Set* 1; that obtained from *Circles* 2 as *Data Set* 2; and these two data sets combined as *Data Set* 3. We estimated each of the 11 preference functions described in Section 3 for each of the 80 subjects for each of these three data sets. This gives a total of 2,640 estimated preference functionals, a grand total of 12,960 behavioral parameters[13] and 1,221 threshold parameters.[14] Clearly there is not space to present all estimates here,[15] but we should draw attention to some of the more interesting features of the estimated models.

Possibly of fairly immediate concern is whether the estimated models "make sense" in terms of their coefficients. There are a number of criteria one might use in judging this. The first is whether the coefficients have the right signs, or more generally are in the right ranges. For all the models which involve some kind of utility valuations, we would expect (on the presumption that some money is preferred to none) that all these utility coefficients would be positive; likewise, in the regret models we would expect all the Ψ coefficients to be

---

[13] RN has just 1 parameter; EU has 3; each of DA, PR, RK, and RP has 4; RD and WU both have 5; RI has 6; YD has 8 parameters; and QU has 9 parameters.
[14] Of the 240 = (3 times 80) subject/data sets, 111 expressed indifference on at least one of the 100 questions.
[15] We can provide a full set of results, and data, on request.

positive, and in the quadratic utility model likewise. In addition, in prospective reference theory, the parameter λ should lie between 0 and 1 for the theory to "make sense;" in the two versions of rank dependent expected utility theory the parameter γ should be positive; and in weighted utility theory, the weights w_2 and w_3 should both be positive. In disappointment aversion theory the parameter β should be greater than -1. Finally, in Yaari's dual model we would expect the parameter k to be positive and all the β values to lie between 0 and 1 (since they are (distorted) probabilities). Table II gives a summary (across subjects for each data set) of how often such restrictions were met. Clearly risk neutrality does not fare particularly well, since, as we shall see, this functional does not fit the data very well for the majority of the subjects. Most of the other theories however perform fairly well on this criterion, though YD understandably falls down rather often—as the criteria are rather strict.

In addition, Figure 2 presents a number of informative histograms: in Figure 2a of the distribution of the β parameter in the disappointment aversion model; in Figure 2b of the λ parameter in the prospective reference model; and in Figures 2c and 2d of the γ parameter in the two versions of the rank dependent model. Additionally, Figure 3a presents a scatter diagram of the w_2 versus the w_3 parameters in the weighted utility model.

There are a number of things to note from these figures. First (from Figure 2a) it can be seen that the β parameter in the disappointment aversion model takes both negative and positive values, which is at odds with the explanation proffered by Gul (1991), where a positive value is suggested. Second (from Figure 2b), the λ parameter in the prospective reference model is occasionally larger than unity—which is disallowed by the theory; this, of course, is reflected in the entries in Table 2.[16] Third (from Figures 2c and 2d) the γ parameter in the two versions of the rank dependent model take values both greater and smaller than unity; this indicates that the weighting function takes a variety of shapes. Fourth (from Figure 3a) it seems to be the case that the estimated w_2 and w_3 values are fairly symmetrically distributed around unity (which is the special case when WU reduces to EU).

A second possible criterion is whether the estimated coefficients satisfy the implied (strict) *monotonicity* conditions. For example, in the various models which imply some kind of utility valuations, we would expect the coefficients to be increasing in the monetary amounts; that is $u(x_4) > u(x_3) > u(x_2) > 0$. In the regret formulations, the theory requires that $\psi(x_i, x_j)$ be increasing in x_i and decreasing in x_j. In the quadratic utility model, the theory requires that $\psi(x_i, x_j)$ be increasing in x_i and that $\psi(x_i, x_i)$ be larger than $\psi(x_j, x_j)$ if x_i is larger than x_j. Finally, in Yaari's dual model, (strict) monotonicity requires that the coefficients β_i be (strictly) increasing in i, and that β_1 be (strictly) positive and β_7 (strictly) less than 1. Table III summarizes how well the various models

---

[16] We did not constrain any of the parameters to lie in their theoretically-approved ranges in the estimation process. If we had, then in those cases such as those in the prospective reference model where the estimated value of λ is outside the range zero to one, with the imposition of the restriction the model would simply have reduced to expected utility.

TABLE II
SUMMARY OF CORRECT SIGNS ON COEFFICIENTS

Model	a	b		
		Data Set 1	Data Set 2	Data Set 3
RN	80	34	26	30
EU	240	240	240	240
DA	320	320	320	320
PR	320	297	298	302
QU	720	693	678	693
RD	400	387	376	391
RI	480	467	457	471
RP	320	319	320	320
RQ	320	320	320	320
WU	400	398	399	400
YD	640	465	423	459

Key: a—total number of estimated coefficients; b—total number
of coefficients with the correct sign.

satisfy these monotonicity requirements. Understandably, those models with
more requirements (particularly **QU**, **RD**, **RI**, and **YD**) do rather worse than
those with less requirements. Nevertheless, it is instructive to see how well **EU**,
DA, **PR**, **RP**, **RQ**, and **WU** do on this test.

A third possible criterion concerns the *concavity/convexity* properties of the
various models. Table IV summarizes these properties for the various estimated
functionals. As far as **EU** and its various near generalizations (**DA**, **PR**, **WU**, **RP**,
and **RQ**) are concerned, it is interesting to note that the dominant pattern is
either concavity everywhere (indicating risk aversion everywhere) or concavity
followed by convexity—indicating risk aversion for small amounts of money and
risk loving for larger amounts. We should note that for the two special cases of
rank dependence where a specific functional form is chosen for the probability
weighting function (**RP** and **RQ**), the table entries refer to the utility function.
This is not the case for **YD**—but here no clear pattern emerges (which is hardly
surprising).

Figure 3 presents a number of scatter diagrams of certain key parameters.
Table III confirms that the regret specifications do not conform particularly well
to the convexity property assumed by Loomes and Sugden (1987); this reflects
the results of Table IV.

A fourth possible criterion is whether the parameter estimates are stable
across data sets. The usual Chow test can be applied in this context: if we
denote by LL_i the log-likelihood of a particular model under Data Set i, then
under the null hypothesis that the coefficients *are* the same in both Data Set 1
and Data Set 2, the statistic

$$2[(LL_1 + LL_2) - LL_3]$$

will have a chi-square distribution with k degrees of freedom where k is the
number of estimated parameters in that particular model. Table V summarizes
the results of carrying out this test for each of the 11 preference functionals at

(a) Histogram for the beta variable in the disappointment aversion model (outlying values for subjects 16, 38, 59, and 64 put equal to zero).

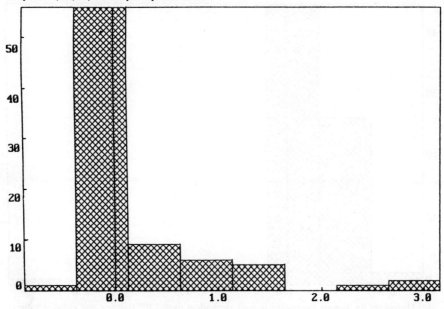

(b) Histogram for lambda parameter in prospective reference model (value of missing estimate for subject 76 put equal to 0.0).

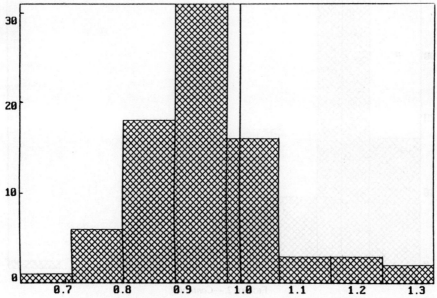

FIGURE 2.—Distributions of certain selected estimated coefficients.

(c) Histogram for gamma parameter in rank dependent model RK.

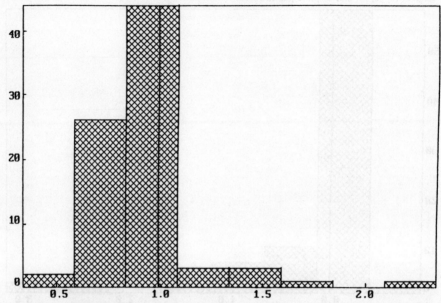

(d) Histogram for gamma parameter in rank dependent model RP (missing and outlying values for subjects 16, 59, and 62 put to 1.0).

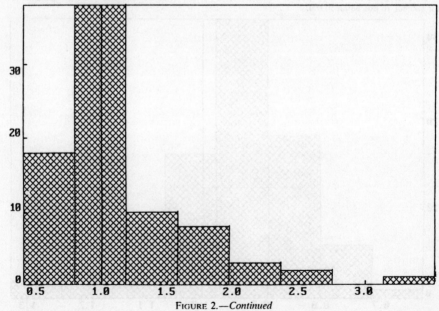

FIGURE 2.—*Continued*

EXPECTED UTILITY THEORY   1307

TABLE III

SUMMARY OF SATISFACTION OF MONOTONICITY CONDITIONS
ON COEFFICIENTS

Model	Data Set 1	Data Set 2	Data Set 3
EU	77	75	75
DA	77	70	77
PR	78	74	79
QU	25	35	40
RD	47	34	53
RI	46	44	52
RP	76	77	74
RQ	79	76	79
WU	74	72	77
YD	26	20	26

both the 5% and the 1% significance level. It will be seen that there is considerable instability between the two data sets, with significantly different estimates (at the 5% level) for more than half the subjects. One might legitimately enquire why this is the case. One possible explanation is that between the first and second repetitions of the experiment the subjects thought about the nature of the experiment rather more deeply than they had before the first repetition, to the effect that the second repetition reflects their "true" preferences, whilst the first contains more "noise." It is not clear that the data supports this interpretation; an alternative explanation is that each repetition is just a smallish sample of observations of the true behavior—with randomness *suggesting* different explanations on the two repetitions. Further repetitions would be needed to distinguish between these two alternatives.

We now turn to one of the key issues: do the more general theories fit the data significantly better than the less general theories? Of our 11 preference functionals, we have three "levels" of functional: at the bottom level is RN; at the middle level are EU and YD; and at the top level are the remaining 8

TABLE IV

SUMMARY OF CONVEXITY / CONCAVITY PROPERTIES

Model	Data Set 1				Data Set 2				Data Set 3			
	a	b	c	d	a	b	c	d	a	b	c	d
EU	40	3	33	4	52	3	24	1	49	2	27	2
DA	35	2	39	3	49	1	29	1	45	2	32	1
PR	46	2	30	2	56	2	21	1	55	0	24	1
QU	25	2	*	*	35	1	*	*	36	2	*	*
RD	11	18	*	*	15	12	*	*	12	19	*	*
RI	9	22	*	*	11	19	*	*	8	23	*	*
RP	40	1	36	3	47	1	31	1	48	1	30	1
RQ	42	3	33	2	50	2	27	1	47	0	32	1
WU	35	4	37	4	54	1	23	2	49	1	26	4
YD	0	5	0	0	0	6	0	0	0	9	0	0

Key: a: strictly concave everywhere; b: strictly convex everywhere; c: s-shaped—first concave then convex; d: s-shaped—first convex then concave; *: not tested (see text).

(a) Scatter plot of $w2$ vs. $w3$ for weighted utility model (missing and outlying values for subjects 10, 51, 53, and 80 put at 1.0).

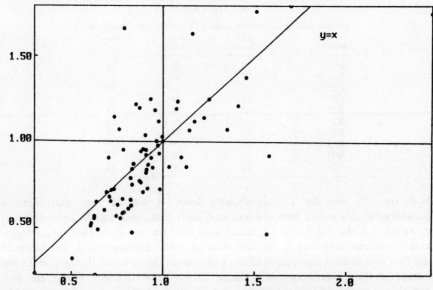

(b) Scatter plot of $\psi(£20, £0)$ vs. $\psi(£20, £10) + \psi(£10, £0)$ for regret RD model.

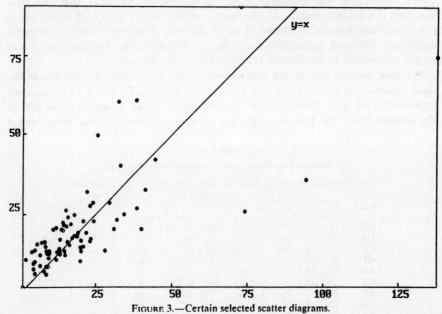

FIGURE 3.—Certain selected scatter diagrams.

(c) Scatter plot of $\psi(\pounds30, \pounds10)$ vs. $\psi(\pounds30, \pounds20) + \psi(\pounds20, \pounds10)$ for regret RD model.

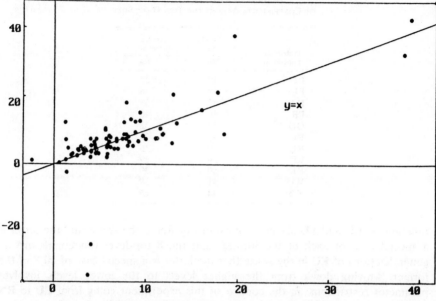

(d) Scatter plot of $\psi(\pounds30, \pounds0)$ vs. $\psi(\pounds30, \pounds10) + \psi(\pounds10, \pounds0)$ for regret RD model.

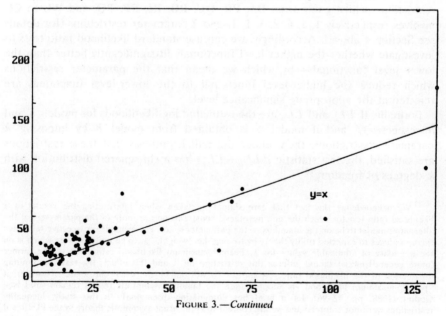

FIGURE 3.—*Continued*

TABLE V

RESULTS OF TESTS OF STABILITY
OF COEFFICIENTS ACROSS THE TWO DATA SETS

Preference Functional	Number of subjects for whom test significant at	
	5%	1%
RN	39	27
EU	48	36
DA	47	35
PR	49	40
QU	50	32
RD	49	35
RI	49	36
RP	50	39
RK	50	39
WU	51	38
YD	34	25

functionals. **EU** and **YD** are generalizations of **RN** in the sense that the latter is a special case of each of the former; and the 8 top-level functionals are all generalizations of **EU** in the sense that the latter is a special case of all 8 of the former. Moving down from the higher levels to the lower levels involves parameter restrictions: in the context of this experiment going from **EU** to **RN** involves 2 parameter restrictions, going from **YD** to **RN** involves 7 parameter restrictions, whilst going from **DA, PR, QU, RD, RI, RP, RQ**, and **WU** to **EU** involves respectively 1, 1, 6, 2, 3, 1, 1, and 2 parameter restrictions (for details see Section 4 above). Accordingly, we can use standard likelihood ratio tests to investigate whether the higher level functionals fit significantly better than the lower level functionals—by which we mean that the parameter restrictions which reduce the higher-level functional to the lower-level functional are rejected at the appropriate significance level.

Formally, if LL_a and LL_b are the estimated log-likelihoods for models a and b respectively, and if model a is obtained from model b by imposing k parameter restrictions, then, under the null hypothesis that these restrictions are satisfied, the test statistic $2(LL_b - LL_a)$ has a chi-squared distribution with k degrees of freedom.[17]

---

[17] We acknowledge the fact that care should be taken when interpreting the results of a likelihood ratio test for which the null hypothesis constrains one or more of the parameters of the alternative model to lie on the boundary of the parameter space. For example, prospective reference theory reduces to expected utility theory by forcing the "weight," λ, to be unity, a value which is on the boundary of admissible values for λ. Formal maximum likelihood estimation of the former (more general) model should enforce this restriction on λ and this effects the resulting limiting distribution of the likelihood ratio test statistic (it will not be the usual chi-square). However, if "pseudo-maximum likelihood" is adopted then the familiar asymptotic results remain valid (see Godrey (1988, pp. 92–96), for a brief but illuminating discussion). In this study, inequality restrictions were not enforced and we are content to apply usual asymptotic theory to the likelihood ratio test statistic. Finally, we should also comment on the fact that, for some parameter sets, the likelihood function in the **DA** model can have a cusp at the value $\beta = 0$ (the **EU** special case); this means that the likelihood functional is not differentiable at the maximum value—which creates problems for the usual test procedures.

TABLE VI

LIKELIHOOD RATIO TESTS OF THE SUPERIORITY
OF THE HIGHER LEVEL MODELS

(1) The Top Level Functionals versus Expected Utility

Number of subjects for whom test significant at

	5%			1%		
Preference Functional	Data Set 1	Data Set 2	Data Set 3	Data Set 1	Data Set 2	Data Set 3
DA	18	26	27	11	13	22
PR	30	41	44	24	27	36
QU	31	38	46	20	23	36
RD	16	15	22	8	7	10
RI	36	36	44	21	19	33
RP	24	22	31	12	13	22
RQ	38	42	46	28	34	39
WU	36	35	43	20	23	28

(2) Expected Utility and Yaari Dual Model versus Risk Neutrality

Number of subjects for whom test significant at

	5%			1%		
Preference Functional	Data Set 1	Data Set 2	Data Set 3	Data Set 1	Data Set 2	Data Set 3
EU	72	73	74	69	72	73
YD	61	74	74	54	68	71

Table VI reports the results of carrying out such tests for each of the three Data Sets. The bottom part of the table shows that risk neutrality is rejected in favor of both **EU** and **YD** for the vast majority of the subjects. The top part of the table contains a number of interesting features, perhaps the most notable of which is the rather obvious fact, particularly at the 1% level, that **EU** is rejected (in favor of one of the top-level functionals) for considerably more subjects on the combined data set (Data Set 3) than on each of the two individual data sets. This lends support to the tentative hypothesis suggested above that behavior actually is more complicated than **EU**, but that in small samples (because of the rather weak nature of our data) **EU** is not rejected (because of the lack of significant evidence against).

Table VI also gives some insight into which of the top level functionals might be better explanations than others.[18] Looking first at the two regret formulations, **RD** and **RI**, it can be seen that the data support the latter. This suggests that subjects perceived the two lotteries as being played out independently, rather than juxtaposed in the fashion that they appear on the screen. We must admit that our original supposition was that subjects would assume independence, and that the idea to estimate regret assuming dependence was suggested by one of the referees, but it is nice to estimate the two and see the independence result emerging (rather than being assumed). Generally, regret does well,

---

[18] Though we must emphasize that we believe that individuals are different and that what might be a good theory for one individual might be a bad theory for another.

TABLE VII

AVERAGE RANKINGS (USING THE AKAIKE INFORMATION CRITERION)

	RN	EU	DA	PR	QU	RD	RI	RP	RQ	WU	YD
Data Set 1	10.1	5.2	6.0	4.0	6.3	6.3	5.3	4.8	3.5	4.7	9.6
Data Set 2	10.5	5.4	5.2	4.0	6.2	6.5	5.4	5.4	3.9	4.9	8.7
Data Set 3	10.5	5.9	5.7	3.9	5.2	6.7	5.1	5.4	3.8	4.9	8.9

as does prospective reference theory and the two versions of the rank dependent model (**RP** and **RQ**), but disappointment aversion does rather badly. Quadratic utility does reasonably well.

The eight top level functionals are *not* nested within each other, so one cannot use nested test statistics to test between them. Nor are **EU** and **YD** nested within each other. However, one can use the Akaike information criterion to provide a ranking of the various functionals. In this context, the Akaike information criterion is given by (see Amemiya (1980))

$$\text{AIC} = -2\log L(\hat{\alpha})/T + 2k/T$$

where $L(\hat{\alpha})$ is the maximized log-likelihood for a particular estimated preference functional, k is the number of estimated parameters in that functional, and T is the number of observations. Akaike suggests the ranking of different models on the basis of this: the smaller is AIC the better the model. Since T is constant across all models, this implies ranking the models according to the magnitude of $CLL = \log L(\hat{\alpha}) - k$. (Here we are using CLL to denote the corrected-log-likelihood.)

The table in Appendix Three gives the details of the rankings which emerge from this exercise. In Table VII are average rankings—averaged over all subjects. We doubt if these have much meaning, given our firm belief that different subjects are different, and have different preference functionals. But, for what it is worth, Table VII suggests that the rank dependent model with the Quiggin weighting function emerges as the overall winner on this criterion, with the prospective reference model a reasonably close second (but recall that for a sizeable number of subjects the λ parameter is in the wrong range). **EU** does reasonably well, though both **RN** and **YD** do very badly. However, this does mask a considerable variation across subjects—as Appendix 3 clearly demonstrates. For example, whilst **YD** does very badly when averaged, it is ranked highest for subjects 10 and 65 on Data Set 3.

In Table VIII we bring together the significance tests and the rankings. It is constructed as follows (ignore for the time being the *small* numbers in the table and the material at the foot of the table). For each subject and for each data set we first see if expected utility, Yaari's dual model, or any of the eight top-level functionals are significantly better at the 1% level than risk neutrality; if none are, we put **RN** in Table VIII. If only one (of **EU**, **YD** and the 8 top level functionals) is, we enter it into Table VIII. If **EU** and at least one of the top level functionals are significantly better than **RN** at the 1% level, we then test to

EXPECTED UTILITY THEORY   1313

TABLE VIII

SUMMARY OF OVERALL VIEW AT 1%; ECONOMIC SIGNIFICANCE OF DEPARTURES
FROM EXPECTED UTILITY

(For explanation of the procedures used see the text.)

Subject	Data Set 1	Data Set 2	Data Set 3	Subject	Data Set 1	Data Set 2	Data Set 3
1	EU 23	8RQ 34	EU 27	41	16QU428	16QU423	12WU625
2	5PR231	7RQ 34	6RQ232	42	EU 32	9RI625	4PR 28
3	31RI7 7	18QU53	23QU72	43	13PR225	13RD 31	11DA433
4	21DA 530	5RQ 26	15DA 527	44	EU 19	7QU315	5QU416
5	12QU 29	EU 29	6RI528	45	8RD 10	9RI 8	8RI29
6	12WU328	18QU629	14QU529	46	7RI 28	7WU 33	EU 31
7	EU 20	EU 28	EU 20	47	8RP 29	EU 32	6RP229
8	10RP 10	14RP219	12RP214	48	18RD 31	22PR232	13PR 28
9	EU 14	EU 13	EU 11	49	RN	RN	RN
10	19QU320	YD 12	YD 10	50	13RQ421	13RQ418	12RQ620
11	EU 23	11QU 23	EU 23	51	EU 24	EU 24	EU 24
12	9PR232	10PR331	11QU632	52	22PR66	EU 28	12PR311
13	EU 16	RN	EU 10	53	EU 28	EU 26	5QU 26
14	EU 27	EU 26	EU 26	54	22PR56	21PR321	21PR63
15	EU 35	EU 31	EU 33	55	EU 30	11RP331	8RP230
16	EU 20	26RQ726	15RQ419	56	16QU319	18QU219	16QU519
17	8RQ231	10RQ327	8RQ529	57	9WU727	5RQ229	6WU727
18	EU 30	EU 26	EU 28	58	16RI219	17RI531	10RI321
19	EU 29	9WU527	13QU528	59	YD 28	27RQ73	19RQ710
20	EU 26	EU 30	EU 28	60	EU 33	23WU738	15QU736
21	13PR223	EU 32	9PR227	61	RN	RN	8QU 2
22	10RI 29	7RQ227	7RI328	62	RN	YD 41	24PR79
23	EU 27	EU 27	EU 27	63	18PR424	EU 29	9PR226
24	23QU36	EU 17	RN	64	10RQ323	7RQ332	9RQ627
25	15RQ429	8WU227	11RQ528	65	EU 14	YD 23	YD 17
26	7PR 32	EU 36	7PR233	66	12RQ327	EU 31	8RQ228
27	EU 15	EU 17	8WU216	67	5DA 26	EU 21	EU 24
28	10RP 22	14QU226	10QU223	68	21PR521	12PR222	16PR521
29	25RI323	EU 30	11RQ225	69	14RI519	13RI517	13PR518
30	15PR240	EU 25	11PR233	70	EU 24	21PR223	14PR 24
31	EU 37	11RQ424	15RQ330	71	13RQ523	YD 26	12RQ720
32	EU 37	EU 27	EU 31	72	RN	RN	RN
33	22RQ315	7RQ 23	15RQ321	73	12RI644	20QU538	16QU840
34	EU 30	EU 32	EU 30	74	17RI226	16DA 24	13RI325
35	9RQ223	22QU521	14PR522	75	13RQ 20	8WU332	EU 23
36	12RP319	YD 33	21QU723	76	10RQ226	9PR229	9RQ428
37	16QU 17	EU 23	14QU319	77	EU 27	10PR233	EU 30
38	16RQ321	16PR410	16PR715	78	EU 30	EU 32	EU 30
39	EU 31	7RP322	4DA226	79	14RI417	10RD 32	9RI323
40	EU 22	EU 33	EU 27	80	13PR542	9WU525	14RI634

Average percentage differences in prediction

	Data Set 1	Data Set 2	Data Set 3
Using EU rather than "best"	8.2%	7.3%	8.2%
Using RN rather than EU or YD	23.1%	24.6%	22.8%

see if any of the 8 top-level preference functionals are significantly better than EU at the 1% level; if none are, we put either **YD** or **EU** in Table VIII—the choice being determined by which of the two has the highest ranking on the Akaike criterion. If only one is we enter that in Table VIII. If more than one is, we then determine a "winner" using the rankings of the Appendix 3 table based on the Akaike information criterion; so, for example, if **PR**, **DA**, and **WU** are all significantly better than **EU** at the 1% level, and if **DA** has the highest corrected log-likelihood of **PR**, **DA**, **WU** (and **YD** if it is itself significantly better than **RN**), we enter **DA** into Table VIII. Where there are several such top-level functionals significantly better than **EU**, we also enter the *number* of such functionals in Table VIII (in *italics* after the "best" functional). Consider, for example, subject 1: on Data Set 1, **EU** is significantly better than **RN** but none of the top level functionals are significantly better than **EU**; the same is true for this subject for Data Set 3; for Data Set 2, **EU** is significantly better than **RN** *and* only **RQ** is significantly better than **EU**. This is a relatively clear-cut case; others are not so clear cut. Consider, for example, Subject 3: on Data Set 1, **EU** is significantly better than **RN**, and *seven* of the eight top level functionals are significantly better than **EU**—of these **RI** emerges as the best on the Akaike information criterion. So even though we conclude that for this subject and this data set, **RI** is the overall "best," this interpretation should be treated with caution. Indeed, a notable feature of Table VIII is the rather large number of top level functionals significantly better than **EU** when at least one is (an average of 3.60 on Data Set 1, of 3.71 on Data Set 2, and 4.27 on Data Set 3). This indicates *either* that our data are insufficiently informative to distinguish between the top level functionals *or* that the top level functionals are observationally very close. If the latter is the case, then the issue of which is the "best" of them loses much of its urgency; the advice would then be to choose the simplest to implement.

In Table IX is a summary of the "winners at 1%" using this procedure. For Data Set 1 (2), 32 (30) of the subjects seem to be best explained by **EU** or its special case (risk neutrality). For the remaining subjects, the two regret formulations "account" for some 7 to 11 of the subjects (with once again, the independence version emerging as the better of the two), while the two rank dependent formulations "account" for 15 or 16. Prospective reference theory again puts up a creditable performance, and quadratic utility does reasonably well, while disappointment aversion and Yaari's dual model come in very clearly at the back. On Data Set 3, **EU** and **RN** now "account" for just 21 of the subjects—for possible reasons that we have already discussed—with **PR**, **QU**, and **RQ** emerging as the strongest rival contenders. Table IX also gives a summary of "winners at 5%" using the same procedure. The previously **EU** and **RN** cases seem to be fairly uniformly distributed across the other models.

The inferences that can be drawn from Table IX about the adequacy or otherwise of **EU** are not, however, clear cut—mainly because of the large number of generalizations of **EU** under consideration. As this research has evolved, and as the number of generalizations under consideration has increased, the number of subjects for whom **EU** emerges as "the winner" has

EXPECTED UTILITY THEORY   1315

TABLE IX

SUMMARY OF "WINNERS" AT 1% AND "WINNERS" AT 5%

Winners at 1%	Model	Data Set 1	Data Set 2	Data Set 3
	RN	4	4	3
	EU	28	26	18
	DA	2	1	3
	PR	11	8	14
	QU	6	9	14
	RD	2	2	0
	RI	9	4	7
	RP	4	3	3
	RQ	11	12	13
	WU	2	6	3
	YD	1	5	2
Winners at 5%	Model	Data Set 1	Data Set 2	Data Set 3
	RN	3	0	1
	EU	18	15	13
	DA	3	4	4
	PR	12	11	15
	QU	7	10	15
	RD	3	3	0
	RI	11	5	7
	RP	5	5	4
	RQ	14	14	15
	WU	3	7	4
	YD	1	6	2

declined. This is inevitable, though it is not clear how one should judge the rate of decline. With just one generalization (of **EU**) under consideration, one would expect to find it emerge "the winner at 5%" *even if* **EU** *was the true model* for approximately 5% of the subjects—that is, for 4 subjects. With 9 generalizations, totally independent in some appropriate sense, one might expect *one* of them to emerge "the winner at 5%" *even if* **EU** *was the true model* for up to a maximum of 9 times 4 (equals 36) subjects (though the precise number depends on the relationships between the various generalizations). On this argument, **EU** does indeed seem to perform rather well—though Monte Carlo work would be needed to shed more accurate light on such issues.

One rather interesting feature of Table VIII is the pattern that emerges from a comparison of the "best fitting" preference functional on Data Set 1 and that on Data Set 2. Table X gives a summary of the transition matrix. This implies that 17 out of the 32 **EU** and **RN** subjects on Data Set 1 stayed loyal to **EU** (and **RN**) on Data Set 2, 5 out of the 15 rank dependent subjects (**RP** and **RQ**) on Data Set 1 stayed loyal to rank dependency on Data Set 2, and that just 4 of the 11 regret subjects (**RD** and **RI**) stayed loyal to regret on Data Set 2. However, one should be a little careful in interpreting this table, since a particular model could be the winner on one data set and a loser on the other—whilst only having "lost" by a very small margin.

1316   J. D. HEY AND C. ORME

TABLE X

TRANSITION MATRIX BETWEEN DATA SET 1 AND DATA SET 2

		RN	EU	DA	PR	QU	RD	RI	RP	RQ	WU	YD	TOTAL
						Data Set 2							
	RN	3	0	0	0	0	0	0	0	0	0	1	4
	EU	1	14	0	2	2	0	1	2	3	2	1	28
	DA	0	1	0	0	0	0	0	0	1	0	0	2
Data	PR	0	5	0	3	0	1	0	0	1	1	0	11
Set	QU	0	3	0	0	2	0	0	0	0	0	1	6
1	RD	0	0	0	1	0	0	1	0	0	0	0	2
	RI	0	1	1	0	2	1	2	0	1	1	0	9
	RP	0	1	0	0	1	0	0	1	0	0	1	4
	RQ	0	1	0	2	1	0	0	0	4	2	1	11
	WU	0	0	0	0	1	0	0	0	1	0	0	2
	YD	0	0	0	0	0	0	0	0	1	0	0	1
	TOTAL	4	26	1	8	9	2	4	3	12	6	5	80

A closer examination of the results for Data Set 3 (Data Sets 1 and 2 combined) and a comparison with the two separate Data Sets (1 and 2) suggests that non-EU behavior is "resulting" as a consequence of EU-behavior on one Data Set and non-EU on the other. This suggests that our earlier tentative hypothesis may indeed be correct: with more data non-EU behavior seems to be apparent, but with relatively little data, its uninformativeness does not allow rejection of the null hypothesis (EU behavior). Lying behind these ideas is, of course, the sizeable *noise* in the data. To this we now turn.

6. THE ECONOMIC SIGNIFICANCE OF THE ESTIMATED FUNCTIONALS

Since, in all the estimated preference functionals, the standard deviation of the error term is normalized to unity, the economic significance (importance) of the error term depends upon the magnitude of the coefficients in the estimated functionals: other things being equal, large coefficients imply that errors are relatively unimportant while small coefficients imply relatively important errors. Rather than report the coefficients (of which there are rather many) we present material in two tables, Tables XI and VIII, which report some relevant summary statistics; Table XI is concerned with an absolute analysis, Table VIII with a comparative analysis.

Consider first Table XI which reports the distribution of a "determination/vacillation index" over all 80 subjects for each data set and for each preference functional. This "determination/vacillation index" is computed as follows (examine Figure 4): each estimated preference functional (for each data set for each subject) gives an estimated value $\hat{V}$ of the valuation of the difference between the left-hand and right-hand gambles for each of the 100 questions. Suppose it is as illustrated in Figure 4. A Preference Subject (that is, one who always reports strict preference) will report that he or she prefers the left-hand to the right-hand gamble if $\hat{V} + \epsilon$ exceeds zero (where ϵ is $N(0, 1)$). This happens a proportion r of the time. Similarly, the subject will report

EXPECTED UTILITY THEORY 1317

TABLE XI

DETERMINATION / VACILLATION INDEX VALUES
Value of 100 indicates complete determination,
value of 0 complete vacillation.
All index values are averages over 100 questions.
Histogram of above index values over all subjects.

Data Set 1 Range	RN	EU	DA	PR	QU	RD	RI	RP	RQ	WU	YD
0–10	15	0	0	0	0	0	0	0	0	0	0
11–20	18	1	0	0	0	0	0	1	0	0	1
21–30	18	4	4	1	0	3	1	1	1	1	4
31–40	16	9	7	8	5	6	6	9	7	8	15
41–50	8	18	20	16	11	17	12	17	15	14	24
51–60	0	15	15	15	20	19	25	15	20	21	18
61–70	2	12	12	16	16	12	13	14	13	12	10
71–80	3	17	15	19	12	15	11	18	17	15	6
81–90	0	3	6	3	15	7	11	4	6	8	1
91–100	0	1	1	2	1	1	1	1	1	1	1

Data Set 2 Range	RN	EU	DA	PR	QU	RD	RI	RP	RQ	WU	YD
0–10	18	1	0	0	0	1	0	0	0	0	0
11–20	12	1	0	0	0	1	0	0	0	0	0
21–30	14	3	5	0	0	2	0	5	1	0	2
31–40	11	7	5	4	3	6	4	6	4	5	6
41–50	17	12	13	13	8	9	13	8	10	14	19
51–60	3	6	7	11	14	11	12	11	13	9	16
61–70	2	14	10	13	8	9	8	9	9	10	18
71–80	3	22	19	20	17	20	20	21	24	22	12
81–90	0	13	19	16	22	18	17	17	17	16	4
91–100	0	1	2	3	8	3	6	3	2	4	3

Data Set 3 Range	RN	EU	DA	PR	QU	RD	RI	RP	RQ	WU	YD
0–10	20	0	0	0	0	0	0	0	0	0	0
11–20	15	0	0	0	0	0	0	1	0	0	1
21–30	15	6	5	1	1	5	2	4	1	3	4
31–40	15	13	13	10	8	12	11	10	12	10	21
41–50	8	12	12	15	14	11	15	15	14	15	19
51–60	3	10	9	14	12	10	9	8	12	10	11
61–70	2	16	19	16	14	18	18	18	16	18	16
71–80	2	20	18	20	18	18	15	20	21	18	6
81–90	0	1	2	2	11	4	8	2	2	4	1
91–100	0	2	2	2	2	2	2	2	2	2	1

preference for the right-hand gamble a proportion p of the time.[19] If either p or r is unity, then the subject is certain which of the two will be reported as preferred; if $p = r = 1/2$ then the subject is completely uncertain as to which will be reported as preferred. Thus the value of $100|p - r|$ indicates the degree of determination or vacillation in the subject's response: if $100|p - r| = 100$ then the subject is completely determined; if $100|p - r| = 0$ then the subject is completely vacillating. Our index (for a preference subject) is the average value

[19] Note: $r = \text{Prob}(\varepsilon > -\hat{V})$, $p = \text{Prob}(\varepsilon \leqslant -\hat{V})$, and $p + r = 1$.

The Economics of Uncertainty I

J. D. HEY AND C. ORME

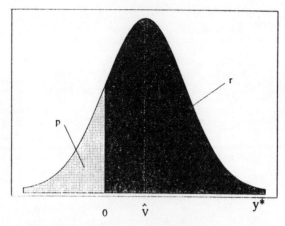

1: A Preference Subject

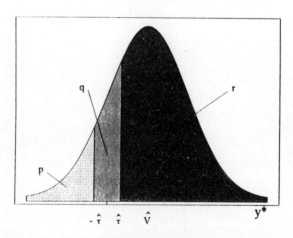

2 An Indifference Subject

FIGURE 4.—Characterization of determination/vacillation index.

of $100|p - r|$ over all 100 questions. For an indifference subject, that is a subject who reports indifference sometimes (in terms of our models when $\hat{V} + \varepsilon$ lies between $-\hat{\tau}$ and $\hat{\tau}$, where $\hat{\tau}$ is the estimated threshold), our index is again calculated as the average value of $100|p - r|$, though here the meaning of p and r are slightly different.[20]

Table XI reflects remarkable differences in subjects' determination. For some subjects, for some data sets, and for some preference functionals the index is as low as 0; figures below 50 occur frequently: such a subject would, on average, choose one of the two gambles 75% of the time and the other 25% of the time.

[20] Note: $r = \text{Prob}(\varepsilon > -\hat{V} + \hat{\tau})$, $p = \text{Prob}(\varepsilon < \hat{V} - \hat{\tau})$, and $p + r < 1$.

This implies sizeable error. Or, of course, it could indicate genuine indifference combined with an infinitesimally small error.

The results of a comparative test are reported in the *small* numbers in Table VIII. Here the *small* number *before* the name of the winning preference functionals represents the average percentage of the time that the best fitting top-level functional comes up with a different prediction from the expected utility functional. (Of course, if there are no top level functionals better than **EU**, then no number is entered.) The argument goes as follows (examine Figure 5): consider first a preference subject. Let $\hat{V}_a$ and $\hat{V}_b$ be the estimated valuation of the difference between the left-hand and right-hand gambles given

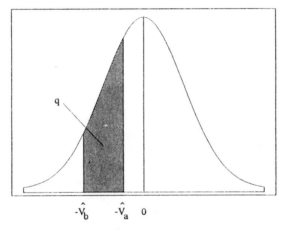

1: A Preference Subject

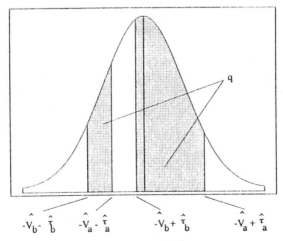

2: An Indifference Subject

FIGURE 5.—Calculation of proportions with different predictions.

1320   J. D. HEY AND C. ORME

by Models a and b respectively. Then left (right) is reported as preferred under Model a if $\varepsilon > (\leqslant) - \hat{V}_a$ and left (right) as preferred under Model b if $\varepsilon > (\leqslant) - \hat{V}_b$. Thus (if $\hat{V}_a < \hat{V}_b$ as illustrated in Figure 5) different predictions will emerge from the two models if ε lies between $-\hat{V}_b$ and $-\hat{V}_a$ which occurs with probability q. The average value of 100 times this is reported as the (small) number before the name of the functional in Table VIII.

For an indifference subject, the calculation is slightly different, and now involves not only $\hat{V}_a$ and $\hat{V}_b$ but also the estimated thresholds $\hat{\tau}_a$ and $\hat{\tau}_b$ under the two models. In Figure 5 we present a particular configuration. Here different predictions would occur from the two models if

$$ - \hat{V}_b - \hat{\tau}_b \leqslant \varepsilon < -\hat{V}_a - \hat{\tau}_a $$

(indifference reported under b and right reported as preferred under a) or if

$$ - \hat{V}_b + \hat{\tau}_b \leqslant \varepsilon < -\hat{V}_a + \hat{\tau}_a $$

(left reported as preferred under b and indifference reported under a). So the percentage of the time that different predictions would result from the two models is 100 times the total of the shaded area. We have similar arguments under different configurations. The number before the name of the preference functional in Table VIII reports the average value of these percentage differences.

The *small* number *after* the name of the best-fitting preference functional in Table VIII reports the average percentage of the time that the **EU** (or **YD** if it is the "best-fitting") functional comes up with a different prediction from the risk neutral functional. (Of course, if **RN** is the best-fitting functional then no number is entered.) So, for example, for Subject 2 on Data Set 1, for whom **PR** is the best-fitting functional, the two numbers 5 and 31 indicate that **PR** and **EU** predict different choices on 5 of the 100 questions, while **EU** and **RN** predict different choice on 31 of the 100 questions. Note that this measure is entirely symmetrical—and does not imply anything about "correctness." So, for Subject 2 on Data Set 1, if **PR** were this subject's correct functional, but instead we used the estimated **EU** functional we would make mistakes in prediction 5% of the time; similarly, if **EU** were this subject's correct functional, but instead we used the estimated **PR** functional, then again we would make mistakes in prediction 5% of the time. Note also that, although this measure is symmetrical, the theories are not—in the sense that the top functionals are more complicated and more difficult to apply than **EU**. So, if one were faced with a choice between using **PR** and getting things wrong 5% of the time, or using **EU** and getting things wrong 5% of the time, then the latter would be preferred since **EU** is a simpler theory to apply.[21]

The foot of Table VIII provides a summary. It is abundantly clear from this that using **RN** rather than **EU** (or **YD**) can lead to sizeable errors, whilst the

---

[21] Apropos of this, it is instructive to observe the almost complete lack of applications of the new theories; contrast this to the enormous number of applications of EU in all areas of economics. Of course, this statement is one of fact, not of opinion concerning the merit of such applications.

magnitude of the errors in using **EU** rather than the "appropriate" top level functional is considerably smaller. But whether "just over 8%" is within acceptable margins of error we leave to others to judge.

7. CONCLUSIONS

Expected utility theory (and its special case, risk neutrality) emerges from this analysis fairly intact. For possibly 39% of the subjects (on the two individual data sets), **EU** appears to fit no worse than any of the other models (though the situation is not so clear when the two individual data sets are combined). For the other 61% of the subjects, one or more of the eight "top-level" functionals (or, occasionally, **YD**) fits significantly better in statistical terms, though often the economic significance is not all that great. Of the eight "top-level" functionals it would appear that the two rank dependent functionals and the quadratic utility model emerge as strongest contenders (with the Quiggin weighting function having a modest lead over its power weighting function rival). Next comes the two regret formulations combined (with the independence version having a decisive advantage in this context over the dependence version), followed by prospective reference theory. Disappointment aversion theory and Yaari's dual model come a rather poor last.

However, we should emphasize once more that this interpretation of our results needs to be taken with caution—since our sample of 80 subjects was in no sense representative. So there is no guarantee that our results are in any sense representative.[22] Perhaps the next step in this line of research is to work with representative samples?

However, possibly the overriding feature of our analysis is the importance of *error*. Table XI (our determination/vacillation indices) shows very clearly how important such errors are. Until now, most authors have been relatively unconcerned about such errors, except insofar as their implication for the appropriate statistical procedures to use when testing between various competing hypotheses is concerned—though there are exceptions to this general rule, in particular, Starmer and Sugden (1991) and Loomes, Starmer, and Sudgen (1991). Some discussion is also contained in Harless and Camerer (1992). There is also a voluminous, though now rather dated and curiously neglected, literature on *stochastic choice* models (see, for an introduction to the literature and one of the few attempts to relate it to the present debate, the paper by Machina (1985)). But the present debate is almost entirely concerned with deterministic choice models. Our results suggest quite strongly that the truth is *not* going to be found along this deterministic choice route, unless some account is taken of errors. There is clearly a problem of identifying the underlying "true" model because of these errors—indeed it could be argued that the lack of significance for some of the top-level functionals for some of the subjects in our study could

---

[22] Yet, at the same time, there is no reason to believe that our results are necessarily *un*representative of the economic population at large, or more unrepresentative than the results from previous experiments which stimulated the various new models to a large degree.

simply result from this noise, combined with rather uninformative data. (Perhaps we should try to find ways of generating more powerful data?[23])

Nevertheless, we are tempted to conclude by saying that our study indicates that behavior can be reasonably well modelled (to what might be termed a "reasonable approximation") as "EU plus noise." Perhaps we should now spend some time on thinking about the noise, rather than about even more alternatives to EU?

Dept. of Economics and Related Studies, University of York, Heslington, York YO1 5DD, United Kingdom.

Manuscript received March, 1992; final revision received January, 1994.

APPENDIX 1

A. THE DERIVATION OF THE DISAPPOINTMENT AVERSION SPECIFICATION

We provide just an outline of the proof. We restrict attention to a gamble involving at most three outcomes, the utilities of which we denote by u_i with respective probabilities p_i ($i = 1, 2, 3$). From Gul (1991, p. 678) it is clear that we can write (where V is the value of the preference functional for the gamble):

$$V = V_1 \quad \text{if} \quad p_3 \geqslant (1 + \beta)(u_2 - u_1)/(u_3 - u_2)p_1.$$

$$V = V_2 \quad \text{if} \quad p_3 < (1 + \beta)(u_2 - u_1)/(u_3 - u_2)p_1.$$

where

$$V_1 = [(1 + \beta)p_1 u_1 + (1 + \beta)p_2 u_2 + p_3 u_3]/[1 + \beta p_1 + \beta p_2],$$

$$V_2 = [(1 + \beta)p_1 u_1 + p_2 u_2 + p_3 u_3]/[1 + \beta p_1].$$

Elementary algebra shows that $V_1 \geqslant V_2$ if and only if $p_3 < (1 + \beta)(u_2 - u_1)/(u_3 - u_2)p_1$, from which it follows that

$$V = \min(V_1, V_2).$$

The formula in Section 3 follows by generalizing this result to four outcomes. A detailed proof is available on request.

B. COMPUTER PROGRAM GENERATING PROBABILITIES FOR RD SPECIFICATION

This program takes as input the vector (p_1, p_2, p_3, p_4) giving the probabilities in the left-hand circle and the vector (q_1, q_2, q_3, q_4) giving the probabilities in the right-hand circle and computes the vector z which is used in the formula for the RD model given in Section 3 above.

```
subroutine regprobs(p,q,z,n)
double precision z(400,50)
integer p(200,4),q(200,4)
dimension ncp(4),ncq(4),npc(6),nop(4,4)
do 100 i = 1,n
ncp(1) = p(i, 1)
ncq(1) = q(i,1)
do 100 j = 2,4
jm1 = j - 1
ncp(j) = ncp(jm1) + p(i,j)
ncq(j) = ncq(jm1) + q(i,j)
```

[23] See, for a start in this direction, Carbone and Hey (1992). See also Mueller and Ponce de Leon (1992).

```
100    continue
       ip = 1
       iq = 1
       do 200 j = 1,4
       do 200 k = 1,4
       nop(j,k) = 0
200    continue
       do 300 j = 1,1000
210    if (j.le.ncp(ip)) go to 250
       ip = ip + 1
       go to 210
250    if (j.le.ncq(iq)) go to 260
       iq = iq + 1
       go to 250
260    nop(ip,iq) = nop(ip,iq) + 1
300    continue
       npc(1) = nop(2,1)-nop(1,2)
       npc(2) = nop(3,2)-nop(2,3)
       npc(3) = nop(4,3)-nop(3,4)
       npc(4) = nop(3,1)-nop(1,3)
       npc(5) = nop(4,2)-nop(2,4)
       npc(6) = nop(4,1)-nop(1,4)
       do 400 j = 1,6
       z(i,j) = dble(npc(j))/1000
400    continue
1000   continue
       return
       end
```

APPENDIX 2

DETAILS OF THE ESTIMATION SOFTWARE

Although available software, such as *LIMDEP 6.0* (Greene (1991)), can be employed to estimate the standard *probit* and *ordered probit* models encountered here, the standard assumption imposed on the deterministic specification would have to be one of linearity in parameters. This, however, can be at odds with the maintained theory, as in the case of the disappointment aversion model. Also, standard software does not necessarily exploit the global concavity property of the log-likelihoods (in the context of probit and ordered probit models) which guarantees the uniqueness of any obtained maximum (if one exists). For these reasons, and because of the large number of model estimations required, a purpose built program was developed in order to find the appropriate maximum likelihood estimates.

The numerical optimization procedure, which proved to be very efficient computationally, was based on the ideas described in Orme (1995). Orme's work focuses on the calculation of efficient test statistics after maximum likelihood estimation of a model which is specified solely in terms of a "regression" function (which, it is emphasized, need not be linear in parameters) and an ancillary parameter. Such models include the familiar *Tobit* or *censored regression model*, the *truncated regression model*, and, in particular, the *ordered probit model* where the ancillary parameter is the threshold, τ. The iteration routine employed to locate the maximum likelihood estimates is developed from Fisher's method of scoring, whereby

$$\hat{\theta}_{s+1} = \hat{\theta}_s + \lambda_s \hat{A}_s^{-1} \hat{g}_s$$

where $\hat{\theta}_s$ is the value of θ (the unknown parameter vector to be estimated) at the sth iterate, $\hat{A}_s$ is the expected information matrix evaluated at $\hat{\theta}_s$ (which is guaranteed positive definite), $\hat{g}_s$ is the gradient vector, and λ_s is a suitably chosen step length. Using this, a standard first order Taylor series expansion of the log-likelihood about $\hat{\theta}_s$ shows that, for λ_s sufficiently small an improvement in the log-likelihood can always be achieved until the maximum is reached. A search procedure, invoked at each iterate, was used to find the appropriate value for λ.

The above is a fairly well known and standard technique. The computational simplicity and efficiency arises from the observation that the *direction* at the sth iterate, $\hat{d}_s = \hat{A}_s^{-1} \hat{g}_s$, can be

1324   J. D. HEY AND C. ORME

constructed as $(W'W)^{-1}W'r$, which is the *ordinary least squares* "slope" estimate obtained from a regression of r on W. Furthermore, one convergence criterion which can be usefully employed is $\hat{d}_s'A_s^{-1}\hat{d}_s = r'W(W'W)^{-1}W'r$, the *uncentered explained sum of squares* from the same regression. Finally at the last iterate asymptotic standard errors can be easily estimated using the square-roots of the diagonal elements of $(W'W)^{-1}$, and this is how they were calculated here; alternatively, the standard errors outputted from the OLS regression of r on W (at the final iterate) would be asymptotically valid.

The regressor matrix, W, and the left hand side vector, r, needed for these regressions are in *double-length form* having dimensions $(2n \times k)$ and $(2n \times 1)$, respectively, where n is the sample size and k is the number of unknown parameters to be estimated by maximum likelihood. These variables require some calculation and the interested reader is referred to Orme (1995) for further details.

Apart from affording a certain amount of computational simplicity, not to mention elegance, this procedure proved to be extremely efficient at locating the maximum of the log-likelihood for most models and subjects with the minimum of intervention. This is quite a remarkable feature given the large number of numerical optimizations required. It should also be noted here that standard likelihood inferential procedures should be treated with caution in the case of the *disappointment aversion* model since it is not continuously differentiable in parameters. (For notational details see Orme (1995).)

APPENDIX 3

DETAILED RANKINGS USING THE AKAIKE CRITERION

S	Data Set 1 R E D P Q R R R R W Y N U A R U D I P Q U D	Data Set 2 R E D P Q R R R R W Y N U A R U D I P Q U D	Data Set 3 R E D P Q R R R R W Y N U A R U D I P Q U D
1	B 3 4 2 9 7 8 5 1 6 A	B 6 5 2 9 8 4 7 1 3 A	B 5 3 2 9 8 7 4 1 6 A
2	B 5 6 1 9 8 7 4 2 3 A	B 7 6 2 4 9 5 8 1 3 A	B 5 7 2 8 9 3 6 1 4 A
3	9 A B 6 2 3 1 8 5 4 7	8 A B 5 1 9 3 7 4 2 6	9 A B 6 1 7 2 8 4 3 5
4	B 9 1 8 2 7 5 3 6 4 A	B 5 2 3 9 8 7 4 1 6 A	B 9 1 8 2 7 5 3 6 4 A
5	B 8 6 5 1 7 2 9 4 3 A	B 7 2 8 6 9 3 1 5 4 A	B 9 4 6 3 8 1 7 5 2 A
6	B 5 9 8 2 7 3 4 6 1 A	B 8 9 6 1 7 4 3 2 5 A	B 7 9 6 1 8 3 5 2 4 A
7	A 3 7 2 9 1 5 6 4 8 B	B 3 6 2 9 5 8 7 1 4 A	B 3 5 1 9 6 8 4 2 7 A
8	9 4 8 7 3 A 5 1 6 2 B	A 4 6 3 2 8 9 1 5 7 B	A 3 7 4 2 9 8 1 6 5 B
9	A 1 5 2 9 7 8 4 3 6 B	B 2 5 1 A 9 8 6 3 4 7	B 1 5 4 9 7 8 2 3 6 A
10	A 5 8 7 1 9 2 4 6 3 B	A 6 4 5 B 2 8 3 7 9 1	7 6 A 8 2 B 3 5 9 4 1
11	B 4 5 6 9 7 1 3 8 2 A	B 3 6 7 1 9 4 2 5 8 A	B 3 6 7 2 9 4 1 5 8 A
12	B 6 8 1 2 9 7 4 3 5 A	B 7 8 1 3 9 6 5 2 4 A	B 7 8 2 1 9 6 5 3 4 A
13	A 6 8 4 3 9 1 7 5 2 B	4 2 5 8 6 3 A 1 7 9 B	B 5 8 6 1 9 2 3 7 4 A
14	B 1 5 2 9 6 8 4 3 7 A	B 1 5 3 9 7 8 2 4 6 A	B 2 3 1 9 4 8 6 5 7 A
15	B 2 3 5 6 8 9 1 4 7 A	B 4 1 2 9 7 8 5 3 6 A	B 3 1 2 8 7 9 5 4 6 A
16	B 5 6 8 9 1 2 3 7 4 A	B 9 2 3 7 A 6 5 1 4 8	B 9 3 4 8 A 6 5 1 7 2
17	B 6 8 2 4 9 5 7 1 3 A	B 8 9 7 2 4 3 5 1 6 A	B 8 9 4 2 6 3 7 1 5 A
18	B 1 5 3 9 6 7 4 2 8 A	B 1 5 2 9 7 8 3 4 6 A	B 1 5 2 9 7 6 4 3 8 A
19	B 7 1 4 6 9 8 2 3 5 A	B 8 6 9 4 3 2 5 7 1 A	B 8 4 6 1 9 7 2 5 3 A
20	B 2 8 6 7 1 9 3 4 5 A	B 1 6 3 9 7 8 2 5 4 A	B 2 5 8 9 3 4 7 6 1 A
21	B 4 5 1 9 7 8 3 2 6 A	B 6 1 2 9 4 3 7 8 5 A	B 3 4 1 9 8 7 5 2 6 A
22	B 8 9 5 2 4 1 6 3 7 A	B 3 5 2 9 8 6 7 1 4 A	B 5 9 3 7 4 1 6 2 8 A
23	B 6 5 8 7 3 2 9 1 4 A	B 2 5 3 9 7 8 1 4 6 A	B 9 6 7 2 3 5 8 1 4 A
24	4 5 A 9 1 6 3 7 8 2 B	B 2 3 1 9 6 8 5 4 7 A	8 1 5 3 2 A 9 7 6 4 B
25	B 7 2 4 8 9 5 6 1 3 A	B 7 2 8 5 9 3 4 6 1 A	B 8 3 5 7 9 4 6 1 2 A
26	B 3 5 1 9 7 8 4 2 6 A	B 6 8 1 4 3 2 9 5 7 A	B 3 5 1 9 7 8 6 2 4 A
27	A 8 6 5 3 4 9 2 7 1 B	B 2 6 5 9 8 1 7 4 3 A	B 9 8 7 2 4 3 6 5 1 A
28	A 4 6 7 3 2 9 1 5 8 B	B 8 9 7 1 3 2 6 5 4 A	B 4 8 5 1 3 9 2 6 7 A
29	B 7 A 4 9 3 1 5 2 6 8	B 2 1 5 9 7 8 4 3 6 A	B 6 7 4 9 3 2 8 1 5 A
30	B 6 5 1 9 7 4 8 2 3 A	B 3 4 2 9 5 8 6 1 7 A	B 5 3 1 9 8 6 7 2 4 A
31	A 5 6 1 7 3 9 4 2 8 B	B 8 7 2 5 6 4 9 1 3 A	B 8 9 2 3 4 5 7 1 6 A
32	B 2 4 3 6 9 8 1 5 7 A	B 5 2 8 9 3 4 6 7 1 A	B 4 2 6 9 5 3 8 7 1 A
33	A 7 3 2 B 9 6 8 1 4 5	B 7 2 3 8 9 5 4 1 6 A	B 8 3 2 9 6 4 7 1 5 A
34	B 1 5 2 9 6 8 4 3 7 A	B 3 1 8 9 2 4 7 6 5 A	B 1 2 3 9 4 8 5 6 7 A
35	B 5 9 2 6 7 4 8 1 3 A	B 7 A 4 1 8 2 9 5 3 6	B 7 A 1 4 8 3 9 2 5 6
36	B 9 3 7 2 8 6 1 5 4 A	B 9 5 8 2 A 7 3 4 6 1	B A 3 8 1 9 7 2 6 5 4

APPENDIX 3 (*Continued*)

S	Data Set 1	Data Set 2	Data Set 3
37	B 7 9 5 1 8 3 2 6 4 A	B 6 8 1 3 7 5 2 4 9 A	B 7 9 3 1 8 5 2 4 6 A
38	B 8 3 2 5 6 7 A 1 4 9	B 8 7 1 9 6 4 A 2 5 3	B 9 4 1 7 8 5 A 2 6 3
39	B 5 2 7 8 9 4 6 1 3 A	B 6 4 7 2 8 9 1 3 5 A	B 7 1 9 3 8 6 2 5 4 A
40	B 1 5 3 9 7 8 2 4 6 A	B 1 5 2 9 6 8 3 4 7 A	B 2 9 6 8 1 3 4 5 7 A
41	B 8 5 6 1 9 3 7 4 2 A	B 8 5 6 1 7 4 9 3 2 A	B 9 5 6 2 7 3 8 4 1 A
42	B 2 5 3 9 7 8 1 4 6 A	B 7 5 4 6 2 1 8 9 3 A	B 6 2 1 9 3 4 8 7 5 A
43	B 7 3 1 9 6 5 8 2 4 A	B 4 2 6 9 1 3 8 7 5 A	B 8 1 5 6 2 4 9 7 3 A
44	B 2 5 4 A 8 9 3 1 7 6	B 7 6 A 1 8 9 2 4 5 3	B 8 5 A 1 7 9 6 3 4 2
45	A 3 9 7 8 1 2 6 5 4 B	A 5 6 3 9 2 1 7 4 8 B	B 7 9 6 3 2 1 8 5 4 A
46	B 5 7 3 9 2 1 8 4 6 A	B 5 4 8 6 2 3 7 9 1 A	B 2 4 1 9 6 7 5 3 8 A
47	A 2 5 3 6 7 9 1 4 8 B	B 4 6 8 2 1 5 3 7 9 A	B 3 7 5 2 4 8 1 6 9 A
48	A 2 8 7 9 1 3 4 6 5 B	B 4 6 1 A 8 5 7 2 3 9	B 4 6 1 8 2 9 5 3 7 A
49	1 2 5 4 9 8 A 6 3 7 B	6 5 3 1 A 8 9 4 2 7 B	1 3 2 6 A 5 9 4 7 8 B
50	B 9 8 4 5 7 2 6 1 3 A	B 9 4 2 7 A 6 8 1 5 3	B 8 5 2 6 A 4 9 1 3 7
51	B 2 5 1 9 7 8 4 3 6 A	B 1 2 3 9 6 8 4 5 7 A	B 3 5 1 9 7 8 4 2 6 A
52	8 B 9 1 5 A 6 7 2 4 3	B 3 7 2 9 1 8 5 6 4 A	B 6 7 1 8 A 5 3 2 4 9
53	B 1 6 4 7 8 9 3 2 5 A	B 5 8 2 4 9 1 7 3 6 A	B 7 9 4 1 6 2 8 3 5 A
54	8 A B 1 6 9 7 5 3 2 4	B 8 7 1 6 9 4 A 2 3 5	B 9 A 1 7 8 4 6 2 5 3
55	B 3 4 2 A 8 9 1 5 7 6	B 8 3 9 2 7 5 1 6 4 A	B 4 2 6 3 8 9 1 7 5 A
56	A 6 9 7 1 5 4 2 8 3 B	A 6 9 7 1 3 4 2 8 5 B	A 6 9 7 1 5 3 2 8 4 B
57	B 9 4 8 3 6 2 5 7 1 A	B 5 3 2 9 8 6 7 1 4 A	B 9 3 8 4 7 2 6 5 1 A
58	A 3 6 7 9 2 1 4 5 8 B	B 6 8 5 4 9 1 7 3 2 A	B 7 9 3 4 8 1 6 2 5 A
59	B 9 6 3 7 A 8 5 2 4 1	9 A 8 3 5 B 7 6 1 4 2	B 9 5 3 7 A 8 4 1 6 2
60	B 4 6 2 7 1 9 8 3 5 A	B 8 4 9 3 6 2 5 7 1 A	B 9 4 8 1 3 2 5 6 7 A
61	2 7 8 9 1 B 3 5 6 4 A	2 3 1 6 9 4 A 5 7 B 8	2 8 3 9 1 B 5 4 7 6 A
62	1 2 4 6 B 8 9 3 5 7 A	9 A 7 3 6 B 5 8 2 4 1	9 A 8 1 7 B 5 6 2 4 3
63	B 7 8 1 5 6 3 9 2 4 A	B 3 4 6 9 1 8 2 5 7 A	B 6 5 1 8 9 4 7 2 3 A
64	B 7 3 2 9 8 6 5 1 4 A	B 8 3 2 7 6 5 9 1 4 A	B 9 3 2 6 7 5 8 1 4 A
65	B 6 8 2 A 9 4 5 1 3 7	B 6 8 3 7 A 5 9 4 2 1	B 4 7 5 6 A 3 8 9 2 1
66	B 6 9 2 3 8 7 4 1 5 A	B 4 1 2 9 8 6 5 3 7 A	B 5 9 2 3 8 4 7 1 6 A
67	B 7 1 6 9 4 3 5 8 2 A	B 1 2 3 9 6 8 5 4 7 A	B 5 1 3 9 8 7 2 6 4 A
68	B 7 9 1 5 8 4 6 2 3 A	B 3 8 1 9 5 7 4 2 6 A	B 8 9 1 5 7 4 6 2 3 A
69	B 7 6 3 5 9 1 8 2 4 A	B 8 9 2 7 5 1 6 3 4 A	B 8 9 1 5 7 3 6 2 4 A
70	B 1 5 2 9 6 8 4 3 7 A	B 3 7 1 A 9 8 5 2 6 4	B 3 5 1 9 6 8 4 2 7 A
71	B 8 6 3 2 A 5 7 1 4 9	B 9 4 3 7 A 8 5 2 6 1	B 9 6 4 3 A 8 7 1 5 2
72	3 2 7 1 B 8 9 5 4 6 A	3 4 8 5 2 7 B 9 6 A 1	6 4 8 2 1 9 A 7 3 5 B
73	B 9 5 7 4 3 1 8 6 2 A	B 8 3 7 1 9 6 2 5 4 A	B 9 2 8 1 7 5 4 6 3 A
74	B 3 7 5 9 2 1 8 6 4 A	B 5 1 6 7 9 3 8 4 2 A	B 6 3 9 5 2 1 7 8 4 A
75	B 6 4 2 9 3 5 7 1 8 A	B 6 9 2 5 8 4 7 3 1 A	B 2 7 5 8 1 4 6 3 9 A
76	B 8 2 7 4 9 5 3 1 6 A	B 7 6 1 5 9 3 8 2 4 A	B 6 7 2 4 9 3 8 1 5 A
77	A 3 7 6 9 1 4 2 5 8 B	B 5 8 1 9 6 4 7 2 3 A	B 3 6 1 9 8 7 2 4 5 A
78	B 1 6 3 9 2 8 5 4 7 A	B 4 6 3 1 7 9 2 5 8 A	B 5 7 1 4 2 9 3 6 8 A
79	B 7 9 3 8 5 1 6 2 4 A	B 4 3 6 9 1 2 5 7 8 A	B 6 7 2 9 4 1 8 3 5 A
80	B 8 9 1 2 7 4 6 3 5 A	B 8 7 2 4 5 3 9 6 1 A	B 8 9 3 2 6 1 7 5 4 A

Key: A: 10th; B: 11th; S: Subject Number.

REFERENCES

AMEMIYA, T. (1980): "Selection of Regressors," *International Economic Review*, 2, 331–354.

BELL, D. (1982): "Regret in Decision Making Under Uncertainty," *Operations Research*, 30, 961–981.

CARBONE, E., AND J. D. HEY (1992): "Estimation of Expected Utility and Non-Expected Utility Preference Functionals Using Complete Ranking Data," in *Models and Experiments on Risk and Rationality*, ed. by B. Munier and M. J. Machina. Dordricht: Kluwer Academic Publishers.

CHEW, C. S. (1983): "A Generalization of the Quasilinear Mean with Applications to the Measurement of Income Inequality and Decision Theory Resolving the Allais Paradox," *Econometrica*, 51, 1065–1092.

1326   J. D. HEY AND C. ORME

CHEW, C. S., L. G. EPSTEIN, AND U. SEGAL (1991): "Mixture Symmetry and Quadratic Utility," *Econometrica*, 59, 139-164.

CHEW, C. S., E. KARNI, AND Z. SAFRA (1987): "Empirical Tests of Weighted Utility Theory," *Journal of Mathematical Psychology*, 30, 55-72.

DEKEL, E. (1986): "An Axiomatic Characterization of Preferences Under Uncertainty—Weakening the Independence Axiom," *Journal of Economic Theory*, 40, 304-318.

GODFREY, L. G. (1988): *Misspecification Tests in Econometrics*, Econometric Society Monograph Number 16. Cambridge: Cambridge University Press.

GREENE, W. H. (1991): *LIMDEP 6.0*. Econometric Software Inc.

GUL, F. (1991): "A Theory of Disappointment Aversion," *Econometrica*, 59, 667-686.

HARLESS, D., AND C. D. F. CAMERER (1992): "The Utility of Generalized Expected Utility Theories," paper presented at the FUR-VI conference at GRID, June, 1992.

HEY, J. D., AND D. DI CAGNO (1990): "Circles and Triangles: An Experimental Estimation of Indifference Lines in the Marschak-Machina Triangle," *Journal of Behavioral Decision Making*, 3, 279-306.

HOLT, C. A. (1986): "Preference Reversals and the Independence Axiom," *American Economic Review*, 76, 508-515.

LOOMES, G. C., C. STARMER, AND R. SUGDEN (1991): "Observing Violations of Transitivity by Experimental Methods," *Econometrica*, 59, 425-439.

LOOMES, G. C., AND R. SUGDEN (1982): "Regret Theory: An Alternative Theory of Rational Choice Under Uncertainty," *Economic Journal*, 92, 805-824.

———— (1987): "Some Implications of a More General Form of Regret Theory," *Journal of Economic Theory*, 41, 270-287.

MACHINA, M. J. (1985): "Stochastic Choice Functions Generated from Deterministic Preferences over Lotteries," *Economic Journal*, 95, 575-594.

MUELLER, W. G., AND A. C. PONCE DE LEON (1992): "Optimal Design of an Experiment in Economics," Research Report No. 31, Department of Statistics, University of Economics, Vienna.

ORME, CHRIS (1995): "On the Use of Artificial Regressions in Certain Microeconometric Models," *Econometric Theory*, 11, forthcoming.

QUIGGIN, J. (1982): "A Theory of Anticipated Utility," *Journal of Economic Behavior and Organization*, 3, 323-343.

STARMER, C., AND R. SUGDEN (1991): "Does the Random-Lottery Incentive System Elicit True Preferences?" *American Economic Review*, 81, 971-978.

VISCUSI, W. K. (1989): "Prospective Reference Theory: Toward an Explanation of the Paradoxes," *Journal of Risk and Uncertainty*, 2, 235-264.

WILCOX, N. T. (1993): "Lottery Choice: Incentives, Complexity and Decision Time," *Economic Journal*, 103 (forthcoming).

YAARI, M. E. (1987): "The Dual Theory of Choice Under Risk," *Econometrica*, 55, 95-115.

Name Index

Kahneman, D. 30–32, 36–7, 41–5, 47, 57,
  59, 61, 63, 77, 81, 86, 97–8, 101, 104,
  108, 155, 159, 175, 185, 223, 227, 229–30,
  241, 244–6, 251, 257, 259, 291–2, 294,
  305, 309, 320–24, 334, 340, 350, 367, 396,
  403, 410, 412–14, 424, 465, 473, 483–5,
  489, 496, 501, 503, 505, 510, 513–15, 521,
  536, 546
Kalai, E. 179
Karmarker, U. 98, 101–2, 135, 175, 185,
  251, 258, 322, 334
Karni, E. 295, 297, 325, 336, 356–8, 372–3,
  432, 446, 513, 550, 557
Keeney, R. 254, 319
Keim, D. 336
Keller, L. 319, 322, 546
Klambauer, G. 67, 87
Klein, R. 523, 541
Knez, M. 299
Knight, F. 425
Kochenberger, G. 6, 18
Kohn, M. 171
Kolm, S. 119, 137
Kolmogorov, A. 118, 431
Kraft, C. 428
Krantz, D. 319
Krelle, W. 251
Kreps, D. 86, 186, 192
Krieser, G. 307
Krzysztofowicz, R. 155–6
Kunreuther, H. 97, 258, 306, 310, 318, 336

Larsson, S. 5, 20, 61, 63, 77, 86, 175, 185,
  223, 227, 229–30, 246, 258, 291, 294, 318,
  321, 332, 367, 474
LaValle, I. 334
Lebesgue 348
Leonardi, G. 171
Levi, I. 206, 210, 213–14, 218, 220, 232
Lichtenstein, S. 22, 44, 298, 299, 300, 306,
  308, 403, 412–13
Lieberman, B. 64
Lindman, H. 44. 309
Littlewood, J. 121, 133, 352
Loewenstein, G. 336
Loomes, G. 44, 159, 168, 239, 300, 326–9,
  333, 465, 491, 556, 562, 579
Lorenz 118, 351
Luce, R. 171, 175, 178, 183, 185–6, 209–11,
  213, 259, 319, 324, 404, 406, 428, 484,
  487

MacCrimmon, K. 5, 20, 61–3, 77, 86, 97–9,
  175, 185, 223, 227, 229–30, 241–2, 245–6,

251–3, 258, 266, 272–3, 291, 294, 299,
  318, 321–2, 325–6, 328, 333–4, 362, 367,
  466, 515, 536
MacDonald, D. 294
Machina, M. 42–3, 45, 73, 135, 151, 159,
  167–8, 173, 181–2, 192, 201–2, 227–8,
  241–5, 251–3, 256, 262–3, 265–6, 272–3,
  294, 297, 318–19, 323, 328, 330–33, 335,
  356–7, 361, 372, 396, 438–41, 444, 446–7,
  465–6, 472, 474–6, 483, 498, 510–13, 579
Mackay, A. 46
Magat, W. 397, 414
Mao, M. 372
Markowitz, H. 6, 7, 14, 17, 19, 50, 52–3, 55,
  57–9, 80, 81, 175, 186, 305
Marley, A. 171, 186
Marschak, J. 171, 177, 183, 185, 298,
  319–20, 498, 511
Marshall, A. 212, 545
Mas-Colell, A. 300
Maskin, E. 310
May, K. 300
McClelland, G. 336
McClennan, A. 171, 185
McClennen, E. 227
McCord, M. 175, 185, 258, 294
McFadden, D. 171, 185
McKelvey, R. 546
McNeil, B. 306
Megiddo, N. 179
Menger, K. 55–6
Meyer, D. 186
Milnor, J. 57, 121, 252, 318, 344
Mishan, E. 311
Miyashita, S. 307
Modigliani, F. 186
Morgan, B. 185
Morgenstern, O. 18, 30, 32, 35, 42, 44, 48,
  50, 53, 76, 79, 83, 97, 125–6, 131, 134,
  155–8, 174, 181, 183–4, 243, 246, 269–70,
  284–6, 300, 305, 317–18, 335, 351, 357–8,
  373, 395, 463, 544, 549
Morris, P. 318
Morrison, D. 60, 175, 185, 258, 290
Moskowitz, H. 44, 175, 239, 291, 306, 322
Mossin, J. 171, 186
Mosteller, F. 55, 57–8, 175
Mowen, J. 299
Mueller, W. 580

Nagumo, M. 118
Nakamura, Y. 362, 425, 432, 438, 488
Narens, L. 259, 324
Nash 192, 335, 439, 510, 546

The International Library of Critical Writings in Economics

Microeconomic Theories of Imperfect Competition
Jacques Thisse and Jean Gabszewicz

The Economics of Increasing Returns
Geoffrey Heal

The Balance of Payments
Michael J. Artis

Cost-Benefit Analysis
Arnold Harberger and Glenn P. Jenkins

The Economics of Unemployment
P.N. Junankar

Mathematical Economics
Graciela Chichilnisky

Economic Growth in the Long Run
Bart van Ark

Gender in Economic and Social History
K.J. Humphries and J. Lewis

The Economics of Local Finance and Fiscal Federalism
Wallace Oates

Privatization in Developing and Transitional Economies
Colin Kirkpatrick and Paul Cook

Input-Output Analysis
Heinz Kurz and Christian Lager

Political Business Cycles
Bruno Frey

The Economics of the Arts
Ruth Towse

The Economics of Energy
Paul Stevens

The Economics of Intellectual Property
Ruth Towse

Ecological Economics
Robert Costanza, Charles Perrings and Cutler Cleveland

The Economics of Tourism
Clem Tisdell

The Economics of Productivity
Edward Wolff

The Economics of Organization and Bureaucracy
Peter Jackson

Independent Central Banks and Economic Performance
Sylvester Eijffinger

The Economics of the Commodity Markets
David Greenaway and Wyn Morgan

Realism and Economics: Studies in Ontology
Tony Lawson

Women in the Labor Market
Marianne A. Ferber

New Developments in Game Theory
Eric S. Maskin

Economic Demography
T. Paul Schultz